THE
EXPOSITOR'S BIBLE COMMENTARY

with the New International Version

VOLUMES AND CONTRIBUTORS

Volume 1
Introductory Articles: General,
Old Testament, New Testament

Volume 2
Genesis: *John H. Sailhamer*
Exodus: *Walter C. Kaiser Jr.*
Leviticus: *R. Laird Harris*
Numbers: *Ronald B. Allen*

Volume 3
Deuteronomy: *Earl S. Kalland*
Joshua: *Donald H. Madvig*
Judges: *Herbert Wolf*
Ruth: *F. B. Huey Jr.*
1, 2 Samuel: *Ronald F. Youngblood*

Volume 4
1, 2 Kings: *Richard D. Patterson
and Hermann J. Austel*
1, 2 Chronicles: *J. Barton Payne*
Ezra, Nehemiah: *Edwin Yamauchi*
Esther: *F. B. Huey Jr.*
Job: *Elmer B. Smick*

Volume 5
Psalms: *Willem A. VanGemeren*
Proverbs: *Allen P. Ross*
Ecclesiastes: *J. Stafford Wright*
Song of Songs: *Dennis F. Kinlaw*

Volume 6
Isaiah: *Geoffrey W. Grogan*
Jeremiah: *Charles L. Feinberg*
Lamentations: *H. L. Ellison*
Ezekiel: *Ralph H. Alexander*

Volume 7
Daniel: *Gleason L. Archer Jr.*
Hosea: *Leon J. Wood*
Joel: *Richard D. Patterson*
Amos: *Thomas E. McComiskey*
Obadiah: *Carl E. Armerding*
Jonah: *H. L. Ellison*
Micah: *Thomas E.
McComiskey*
Nahum, Habakkuk: *Carl E. Armerding*
Zephaniah: *Larry Walker*
Haggai: *Robert L. Alden*
Zechariah: *Kenneth L. Barker*
Malachi: *Robert L. Alden*

Volume 8
Matthew: *D. A. Carson*
Mark: *Walter W. Wessel*
Luke: *Walter L. Liefeld*

Volume 9
John: *Merrill C. Tenney*
Acts: *Richard N. Longenecker*

Volume 10
Romans: *Everett F. Harrison*
1 Corinthians: *W. Harold Mare*
2 Corinthians: *Murray J. Harris*
Galatians: *James Montgomery Boice*

Volume 11
Ephesians: *A. Skevington Wood*
Philippians: *Homer A. Kent Jr.*
Colossians: *Curtis Vaughan*
1, 2 Thessalonians: *Robert L. Thomas*
1, 2 Timothy: *Ralph Earle*
Titus: *D. Edmond Hiebert*
Philemon: *Arthur A. Rupprecht*

Volume 12
Hebrews: *Leon Morris*
James: *Donald W. Burdick*
1, 2 Peter: *Edwin A Blum*
1, 2, 3 John: *Glenn W. Barker*
Jude: *Edwin A. Blum*
Revelation: *Alan F. Johnson*

THE

EXPOSITOR'S BIBLE COMMENTARY

with the New International Version

Introductory Articles

VOLUME 1

General
Old Testament
New Testament

Frank E. Gæbelein general editor

ZONDERVAN®

GRAND RAPIDS, MICHIGAN 49530

ZONDERVAN.COM/
AUTHORTRACKER

ZONDERVAN®

The Expositor's Bible Commentary, Volume 1
Copyright © 1979 by Zondervan

Requests for information should be addressed to:
Zondervan, *Grand Rapids, Michigan 49530*

ISBN-10: 0-310-60891-0
ISBN-13: 978-0-310-60891-2

This edition is printed on acid-free paper.

Printed in the United States of America

08 09 10 11 12 • 10 09 08 07 06 05 04 03 02

CONTENTS

PREFACE

The title of this work defines its purpose. Written primarily by expositors for expositors, it aims to provide preachers, teachers, and students of the Bible with a new and comprehensive commentary on the books of the Old and New Testaments. Its stance is that of a scholarly evangelicalism committed to the divine inspiration, complete trustworthiness, and full authority of the Bible. Its seventy-eight contributors come from the United States, Canada, England, Scotland, Australia, New Zealand, and Switzerland, and from various religious groups, including Anglican, Baptist, Brethren, Free, Independent, Methodist, Nazarene, Presbyterian, and Reformed churches. Most of them teach at colleges, universities, or theological seminaries.

No book has been more closely studied over a longer period of time than the Bible. From the Midrashic commentaries going back to the period of Ezra, through parts of the Dead Sea Scrolls and the Patristic literature, and on to the present, the Scriptures have been expounded. Indeed, there have been times when, as in the Reformation and on occasions since then, exposition has been at the cutting edge of Christian advance. Luther was a powerful exegete, and Calvin is still called "the prince of expositors."

Their successors have been many. And now, when the flood of new translations and their unparalleled circulation have expanded the readership of the Bible, the need for exposition takes on fresh urgency.

Not that God's Word can ever become captive to its expositors. Among all other books, it stands first in its combination of perspicuity and profundity. Though a child can be made "wise for salvation" by believing its witness to Christ, the greatest mind cannot plumb the depths of its truth (2 Tim. 3:15; Rom. 11:33). As Gregory the Great said, "Holy Scripture is a stream of running water, where alike the elephant may swim, and the lamb walk." So, because of the inexhaustible nature of Scripture, the task of opening up its meaning is still a perennial obligation of biblical scholarship.

How that task is done inevitably reflects the outlook of those engaged in it. Every biblical scholar has presuppositions. To this neither the editors of these volumes nor the contributors to them are exceptions. They share a common commitment to the supernatural Christianity set forth in the inspired Word. Their purpose is not to supplant the many valuable commentaries that have preceded this work and from which both the editors and contributors have learned. It is rather to draw on the resources of contemporary evangelical scholarship in producing a new reference work for understanding the Scriptures.

A commentary that will continue to be useful through the years should handle contemporary trends in biblical studies in such a way as to avoid becoming outdated when critical fashions change. Biblical criticism is not in itself inadmissible, as some have mistakenly thought. When scholars investigate the authorship, date, literary characteristics, and purpose of a biblical document, they are practicing biblical criticism. So also when, in order to ascertain as nearly as possible the original form of the text, they deal with variant readings, scribal errors, emendations, and other phenomena in the manuscripts. To do these things is essential to responsible exegesis and exposition. And always there is the need to distinguish hypothesis from fact, conjecture from truth.

The chief principle of interpretation followed in this commentary is the grammatico-historical one—namely, that the primary aim of the exegete is to make clear the meaning of the text at the time and in the circumstances of its writing. This endeavor to understand what in the first instance the inspired writers actually said must not be confused with an inflexible literalism. Scripture makes lavish use of symbols and figures of speech; great portions of it are poetical. Yet when it speaks in this way, it speaks no less truly than it does in its historical and doctrinal portions. To understand its message requires attention to matters of grammar and syntax, word meanings, idioms, and literary forms—all in relation to the historical and cultural setting of the text.

The contributors to this work necessarily reflect varying convictions. In certain controversial matters the policy is that of clear statement of the contributors' own views followed by fair presentation of other ones. The treatment of eschatology, though it reflects differences of interpretation, is consistent with a general premillennial position. (Not all contributors, however, are premillennial.) But prophecy is more than prediction, and so this commentary gives due recognition to the major lode of godly social concern in the prophetic writings.

THE EXPOSITOR'S BIBLE COMMENTARY is presented as a scholarly work, though not primarily one of technical criticism. In its main portion, the Exposition, and in Volume 1 (General and Special Articles), all Semitic and Greek words are transliterated and the English equivalents given. As for the Notes, here Semitic and Greek characters are used but always with transliterations and English meanings, so that this portion of the commentary will be as accessible as possible to readers unacquainted with the original languages.

It is the conviction of the general editor, shared by his colleagues in the Zondervan editorial department, that in writing about the Bible, lucidity is not incompatible with scholarship. They are therefore endeavoring to make this a clear and understandable work.

The translation used in it is the New International Version (North American Edition). To the International Bible Society thanks are due for permission to use this most recent of the major Bible translations. The editors and publisher have chosen it because of the clarity and beauty of its style and its faithfulness to the original texts.

To the associate editor, Dr. J. D. Douglas, and to the contributing editors—Dr. Walter C. Kaiser, Jr. and Dr. Bruce K. Waltke for the Old Testament, and Dr. James Montgomery Boice and Dr. Merrill C. Tenney for the New Testament—the general editor expresses his gratitude for their unfailing cooperation and their generosity in advising him out of their expert scholarship. And to the many other contributors he is indebted for their invaluable part in this work. Finally, he owes a special debt of gratitude to Dr. Robert K. DeVries, executive vice-president of the Zondervan Publishing House; Rev. Gerard Terpstra, manuscript editor; and Miss Elizabeth Brown, secretary to Dr. DeVries, for their continual assistance and encouragement.

Whatever else it is—the greatest and most beautiful of books, the primary source of law and morality, the fountain of wisdom, and the infallible guide to life—the Bible is above all the inspired witness to Jesus Christ. May this work fulfill its function of expounding the Scriptures with grace and clarity, so that its users may find that both Old and New Testaments do indeed lead to our Lord Jesus Christ, who alone could say, "I have come that they may have life, and have it to the full" (John 10:10).

FRANK E. GAEBELEIN

ABBREVIATIONS

A. General Abbreviations

A	Codex Alexandrinus	MT	Masoretic text
Akkad.	Akkadian	n.	note
א	Codex Sinaiticus	n.d.	no date
Ap. Lit.	Apocalyptic Literature	Nestle	Nestle (ed.) *Novum*
Apoc.	Apocrypha		*Testamentum Graece*
Aq.	Aquila's Greek Translation	no.	number
	of the Old Testament	NT	New Testament
Arab.	Arabic	obs.	obsolete
Aram.	Aramaic	OL	Old Latin
b	Babylonian Gemara	OS	Old Syriac
B	Codex Vaticanus	OT	Old Testament
C	Codex Ephraemi Syri	p., pp.	page, pages
c.	*circa*, about	par.	paragraph
cf.	*confer*, compare	‖	parallel passage(s)
ch., chs.	chapter, chapters	Pers.	Persian
cod., codd.	codex, codices	Pesh.	Peshitta
contra	in contrast to	Phoen.	Phoenician
D	Codex Bezae	pl.	plural
DSS	Dead Sea Scrolls (see E.)	Pseudep.	Pseudepigrapha
ed., edd.	edited, edition, editor; editions	Q	Quelle ("Sayings" source
e.g.	*exempli gratia*, for example		in the Gospels)
Egyp.	Egyptian	qt.	quoted by
et. al.	*et alii*, and others	q.v.	*quod vide*, which see
EV	English Versions of the Bible	R	Rabbah
fem.	feminine	rev.	revised, reviser, revision
ff.	following (verses, pages, etc.)	Rom.	Roman
fl.	flourished	RVm	Revised Version margin
ft.	foot, feet	Samar.	Samaritan recension
gen.	genitive	SCM	Student Christian Movement Press
Gr.	Greek	Sem.	Semitic
Heb.	Hebrew	sing.	singular
Hitt.	Hittite	SPCK	Society for the Promotion
ibid.	*ibidem*, in the same place		of Christian Knowledge
id.	*idem*, the same	Sumer.	Sumerian
i.e.	*id est*, that is	s.v.	*sub verbo*, under the word
impf.	imperfect	Syr.	Syriac
infra.	below	Symm.	Symmachus
in loc.	*in loco*, in the place cited	T	Talmud
j	Jerusalem or	Targ.	Targum
	Palestinian Gemara	Theod.	Theodotion
Lat.	Latin	TR	Textus Receptus
LL.	Late Latin	tr.	translation, translator,
LXX	Septuagint		translated
M	Mishnah	UBS	The United Bible Societies'
masc.	masculine		Greek Text
mg.	margin	Ugar.	Ugaritic
Mid	Midrash	u.s.	*ut supra*, as above
MS(S)	Manuscript(s)	viz.	*videlicet*, namely

vol.	volume	Vul.	Vulgate
v., vv.	verse, verses	WH	Westcott and Hort, *The*
vs.	versus		*New Testament in Greek*

B. Abbreviations for Modern Translations and Paraphrases

AmT	Smith and Goodspeed, *The Complete Bible, An American Translation*	LB	The Living Bible
		Mof	J. Moffatt, *A New Translation of the Bible*
ASV	American Standard Version, American Revised Version (1901)	NAB	The New American Bible
		NASB	New American Standard Bible
		NEB	The New English Bible
Beck	Beck, *The New Testament in the Language of Today*	NIV	The New International Version
		Ph	J. B. Phillips *The New Testament in Modern English*
BV	Berkeley Version (The Modern Language Bible)		
		RSV	Revised Standard Version
JB	The Jerusalem Bible	RV	Revised Version — 1881–1885
JPS	*Jewish Publication Society Version of the Old Testament*	TCNT	Twentieth Century New Testament
KJV	King James Version	TEV	Today's English Version
Knox	R.G. Knox, *The Holy Bible: A Translation from the Latin Vulgate in the Light of the Hebrew and Greek Original*	Wey	*Weymouth's New Testament in Modern Speech*
		Wms	C. B. Williams, *The New Testament: A Translation in the Language of the People*

C. Abbreviations for Periodicals and Reference Works

AASOR	*Annual of the American Schools of Oriental Research*	BAG	Bauer, Arndt, and Gingrich: *Greek-English Lexicon of the New Testament*
AB	*Anchor Bible*		
AIs	de Vaux: *Ancient Israel*	BC	Foakes-Jackson and Lake: *The Beginnings of Christianity*
AJA	*American Journal of Archaeology*		
AJSL	*American Journal of Semitic Languages and Literatures*	BDB	Brown, Driver, and Briggs: *Hebrew-English Lexicon of the Old Testament*
AJT	*American Journal of Theology*	BDF	Blass, Debrunner, and Funk: *A Greek Grammar of the New Testament and Other Early Christian Literature*
Alf	Alford: *Greek Testament Commentary*		
ANEA	*Ancient Near Eastern Archaeology*	BDT	Harrison: *Baker's Dictionary of Theology*
ANET	Pritchard: *Ancient Near Eastern Texts*	Beng.	Bengel's *Gnomon*
		BETS	*Bulletin of the Evangelical Theological Society*
ANF	Roberts and Donaldson: *The Ante-Nicene Fathers*	BJRL	*Bulletin of the John Rylands Library*
ANT	M. R. James: *The Apocryphal New Testament*		
		BS	*Bibliotheca Sacra*
A-S	Abbot-Smith: *Manual Greek Lexicon of the New Testament*	BT	*Babylonian Talmud*
		BTh	*Biblical Theology*
AThR	*Anglican Theological Review*	BW	*Biblical World*
BA	*Biblical Archaeologist*	CAH	*Cambridge Ancient History*
BASOR	*Bulletin of the American Schools of Oriental Research*	CanJTh	*Canadian Journal of Theology*
		CBQ	*Catholic Biblical Quarterly*

CBSC	*Cambridge Bible for Schools and Colleges*	HUCA	*Hebrew Union College Annual*
CE	*Catholic Encyclopedia*	IB	*The Interpreter's Bible*
CGT	*Cambridge Greek Testament*	ICC	*International Critical Commentary*
CHS	Lange: *Commentary on the Holy Scriptures*	IDB	*The Interpreter's Dictionary of the Bible*
ChT	*Christianity Today*	IEJ	*Israel Exploration Journal*
Crem	Cremer: *Biblico-Theological Lexicon of the New Testament Greek*	Int	*Interpretation*
		INT	E. Harrison: *Introduction to the New Testament*
DDB	*Davis' Dictionary of the Bible*	IOT	R. K. Harrison: *Introduction to the Old Testament*
Deiss BS	Deissmann: *Bible Studies*		
Deiss LAE	Deissmann: *Light From the Ancient East*	ISBE	*The International Standard Bible Encyclopedia*
DNTT	*Dictionary of New Testament Theology*	ITQ	*Irish Theological Quarterly*
EBC	*The Expositor's Bible Commentary*	JAAR	*Journal of American Academy of Religion*
EBi	*Encyclopaedia Biblica*	JAOS	*Journal of American Oriental Society*
EBr	*Encyclopaedia Britannica*		
EDB	*Encyclopedic Dictionary of the Bible*	JBL	*Journal of Biblical Literature*
EGT	Nicoll: *Expositor's Greek Testament*	JE	*Jewish Encyclopedia*
EQ	*Evangelical Quarterly*	JETS	*Journal of Evangelical Theological Society*
ET	*Evangelische Theologie*	JFB	Jamieson, Fausset, and Brown: *Commentary on the Old and New Testament*
ExB	*The Expositor's Bible*		
Exp	*The Expositor*		
ExpT	*The Expository Times*	JNES	*Journal of Near Eastern Studies*
FLAP	Finegan: *Light From the Ancient Past*	Jos. Antiq.	Josephus: *The Antiquities of the Jews*
GR	*Gordon Review*	Jos. War	Josephus: *The Jewish War*
HBD	*Harper's Bible Dictionary*	JQR	*Jewish Quarterly Review*
HDAC	Hastings: *Dictionary of the Apostolic Church*	JR	*Journal of Religion*
		JSJ	*Journal for the Study of Judaism in the Persian, Hellenistic and Roman Periods*
HDB	Hastings: *Dictionary of the Bible*		
HDBrev.	Hastings: *Dictionary of the Bible*, one-vol. rev. by Grant and Rowley	JSOR	*Journal of the Society of Oriental Research*
		JSS	*Journal of Semitic Studies*
HDCG	Hastings: *Dictionary of Christ and the Gospels*	JT	*Jerusalem Talmud*
		JTS	*Journal of Theological Studies*
HERE	Hastings: *Encyclopedia of Religion and Ethics*	KAHL	Kenyon: *Archaeology in the Holy Land*
HGEOTP	Heidel: *The Gilgamesh Epic and Old Testament Parallels*	KB	Koehler-Baumgartner: *Lexicon in Veteris Testament Libros*
HJP	Schurer: *A History of the Jewish People in the Time of Christ*	KD	Keil and Delitzsch: *Commentary on the Old Testament*
HR	Hatch and Redpath: *Concordance to the Septuagint*	LSJ	Liddell, Scott, Jones: *Greek-English Lexicon*
HTR	*Harvard Theological Review*	LTJM	Edersheim: *The Life and Times of Jesus the Messiah*

MM	Moulton and Milligan: *The Vocabulary of the Greek Testament*		*Testament aus Talmud und Midrash*
MNT	Moffatt: *New Testament Commentary*	SHERK	*The New Schaff-Herzog Encyclopedia of Religious Knowledge*
MST	McClintock and Strong: *Cyclopedia of Biblical, Theological, and Ecclesiastical Literature*	SJT	*Scottish Journal of Theology*
		SOT	Girdlestone: *Synonyms of Old Testament*
NBC	Davidson, Kevan, and Stibbs: *The New Bible Commentary*, 1st ed.	SOTI	Archer: *A Survey of Old Testament Introduction*
NBCrev.	Guthrie and Motyer: *The New Bible Commentary*, rev. ed.	ST	*Studia Theologica*
		TCERK	Loetscher: *The Twentieth Century Encyclopedia of Religious Knowledge*
NBD	J. D. Douglas: *The New Bible Dictionary*	TDNT	Kittel: *Theological Dictionary of the New Testament*
NCB	*New Century Bible*		
NCE	*New Catholic Encyclopedia*	TDOT	*Theological Dictionary of the Old Testament*
NIC	*New International Commentary*	Theol	*Theology*
NIDCC	Douglas: *The New International Dictionary of the Christian Church*	ThT	*Theology Today*
		TNTC	*Tyndale New Testament Commentaries*
NovTest	*Novum Testamentum*		
NSI	Cooke: *Handbook of North Semitic Inscriptions*	Trench	Trench: *Synonyms of the New Testament*
NTS	*New Testament Studies*	UBD	*Unger's Bible Dictionary*
ODCC	*The Oxford Dictionary of the Christian Church*, rev. ed.	UT	Gordon: *Ugaritic Textbook*
		VB	Allmen: *Vocabulary of the Bible*
Peake	Black and Rowley: *Peake's Commentary on the Bible*	VetTest	*Vetus Testamentum*
PEQ	*Palestine Exploration Quarterly*	Vincent	Vincent: *Word-Pictures in the New Testament*
PNFl	P. Schaff: *The Nicene and Post-Nicene Fathers* (1st series)	WBC	*Wycliffe Bible Commentary*
		WBE	*Wycliffe Bible Encyclopedia*
PNF2	P. Schaff and H. Wace: *The Nicene and Post-Nicene Fathers* (2nd series)	WC	*Westminster Commentaries*
		WesBC	*Wesleyan Bible Commentaries*
PTR	*Princeton Theological Review*	WTJ	*Westminster Theological Journal*
RB	*Revue Biblique*	ZAW	*Zeitschrift für die alttestamentliche Wissenschaft*
RHG	Robertson's *Grammar of the Greek New Testament in the Light of Historical Research*	ZNW	*Zeitschrift für die neutestamentliche Wissenschaft*
		ZPBD	*The Zondervan Pictorial Bible Dictionary*
RTWB	Richardson: *A Theological Wordbook of the Bible*	ZPEB	*The Zondervan Pictorial Encyclopedia of the Bible*
SBK	Strack and Billerbeck: *Kommentar zum Neuen*	ZWT	*Zeitschrift für wissenschaftliche Theologie*

D. Abbreviations for Books of the Bible, the Apocrypha, and the Pseudepigrapha

OLD TESTAMENT

Gen	2 Chron	Dan
Exod	Ezra	Hos
Lev	Neh	Joel
Num	Esth	Amos
Deut	Job	Obad
Josh	Ps(Pss)	Jonah
Judg	Prov	Mic
Ruth	Eccl	Nah
1 Sam	S of Songs	Hab
2 Sam	Isa	Zeph
1 Kings	Jer	Hag
2 Kings	Lam	Zech
1 Chron	Ezek	Mal

NEW TESTAMENT

Matt	1 Tim
Mark	2 Tim
Luke	Titus
John	Philem
Acts	Heb
Rom	James
1 Cor	1 Peter
2 Cor	2 Peter
Gal	1 John
Eph	2 John
Phil	3 John
Col	Jude
1 Thess	Rev
2 Thess	

APOCRYPHA

1 Esd	1 Esdras
2 Esd	2 Esdras
Tobit	Tobit
Jud	Judith
Add Esth	Additions to Esther
Wisd Sol	Wisdom of Solomon
Ecclus	Ecclesiasticus (Wisdom of Jesus the Son of Sirach)
Baruch	Baruch

Ep Jer	Epistle of Jeremy
S Th Ch	Song of the Three Children (or Young Men)
Sus	Susanna
Bel	Bel and the Dragon
Pr Man	Prayer of Manasseh
1 Macc	1 Maccabees
2 Macc	2 Maccabees

PSEUDEPIGRAPHA

As Moses	Assumption of Moses
2 Baruch	Syriac Apocalypse of Baruch
3 Baruch	Greek Apocalypse of Baruch
1 Enoch	Ethiopic Book of Enoch
2 Enoch	Slavonic Book of Enoch
3 Enoch	Hebrew Book of Enoch
4 Ezra	4 Ezra
JA	Joseph and Asenath
Jub	Book of Jubilees
L Aristeas	Letter of Aristeas
Life AE	Life of Adam and Eve
Liv Proph	Lives of the Prophets
MA Isa	Martyrdom and Ascension of Isaiah
3 Macc	3 Maccabees
4 Macc	4 Maccabees
Odes Sol	Odes of Solomon
P Jer	Paralipomena of Jeremiah

Pirke Aboth	Pirke Aboth
Ps 151	Psalm 151
Pss Sol	Psalms of Solomon
Sib Oracles	Sibylline Oracles
Story Ah	Story of Ahikar
T Abram	Testament of Abraham
T Adam	Testament of Adam
T Benjamin	Testament of Benjamin
T Dan	Testament of Dan
T Gad	Testament of Gad
T Job	Testament of Job
T Jos	Testament of Joseph
T Levi	Testament of Levi
T Naph	Testament of Naphtali
T 12 Pat	Testaments of the Twelve Patriarchs
Zad Frag	Zadokite Fragments

E. Abbreviations of Names of Dead Sea Scrolls and Related Texts

CD	Cairo (Genizah text of the) Damascus (Document)	1QSa	Appendix A (Rule of the Congregation) to 1QS
DSS	Dead Sea Scrolls	1QSb	Appendix B (Blessings) to 1QS
Hev	Nahal Hever texts	3Q15	Copper Scroll from Qumran Cave 3
Mas	Masada Texts		
Mird	Khirbet mird texts	4QFlor	Florilegium (or Eschatological Midrashim) from Qumran Cave 4
Mur	Wadi Murabba'at texts		
P	Pesher (commentary)		
Q	Qumran	4Qmess ar	Aramaic "Messianic" text from Qumran Cave 4
1Q,2Q,etc.	Numbered caves of Qumran, yielding written material; followed by abbreviation of biblical or apocryphal book.	4QPrNab	Prayer of Nabonidus from Qumran Cave 4
		4QTest	Testimonia text from Qumran Cave 4
QL	Qumran Literature		
1QapGen	Genesis Apocryphon of Qumran Cave 1	4QTLevi	Testament of Levi from Qumran Cave 4
1QH	*Hodayot* (Thanksgiving Hymns) from Qumran Cave 1	4QPhyl	Phylacteries from Qumran Cave 4
1QIsa^{a, b}	First or second copy of Isaiah from Qumran Cave 1	11QMelch	Melchizedek text from Qumran Cave 11
1QpHab	Pesher on Habakkuk from Qumran Cave 1	11QtgJob	Targum of Job from Qumran Cave 11
1QM	*Milhamah* (War Scroll)		
1QS	*Serek Hayyahad* (Rule of the Community, Manual of Discipline)		

TRANSLITERATIONS

Hebrew

א = '	ד = *d*	י = *y*	ס = *s*	ר = *r*
ב = *b*	ה = *h*	כ = *k*	ע = '	שׂ = *ś*
ב = *ḇ*	ו = *w*	כ = *ḵ*	פ = *p*	שׁ = *š*
ג = *g*	ז = *z*	ל = *l*	פ = *p̄*	ת = *t*
ג = *ḡ*	ח = *ḥ*	מ ם = *m*	צ = *ṣ*	ת = *ṯ*
ד = *d*	ט = *ṭ*	נ = *n*	ק = *q*	

(ה)ָ = *â (h)*	ָ = *ā*	ַ = *a*	ֳ = *o*
ִי = *ê*	ֶה = *ě*	ֲ = *e*	ֱ = *e*
ִ = *î*	ֹ = *ō*	ִ = *i*	ֲ = *e (if vocal)*
וֹ = *ô*		ָ = *o*	ֳ = *o*
וּ = *û*		ֻ = *u*	

Aramaic

' *b g d h w z ḥ ṭ y k l m n s* ' *p ṣ q r š ś t*

Arabic

' *b t ṯ ǧ ḥ ḫ d ḏ r z s š ṣ ḍ ṭ ẓ* ' *ġ f q k l m n h w y*

Ugaritic

' *b g d ḏ h w z ḥ ḫ ṭ ẓ y k l m n s ṣ* ' *ġ p ṣ q r š t ṯ*

xv

Greek

α	—	a	π	—	p	αι	—	ai
β	—	b	ρ	—	r	αυ	—	au
γ	—	g	σ,ς	—	s	ει	—	ei
δ	—	d	τ	—	t	ευ	—	eu
ε	—	e	υ	—	y	ηυ	—	ēu
ζ	—	z	φ	—	ph	οι	—	oi
η	—	ē	χ	—	ch	ου	—	ou
θ	—	th	ψ	—	ps	υι	—	hui
ι	—	i	ω	—	ō		
κ	—	k				ῥ	—	rh
λ	—	l	γγ	—	ng	ʿ	—	h
μ	—	m	γκ	—	nk		
ν	—	n	γξ	—	nx	ᾳ	—	ā
ξ	—	x	γχ	—	nch	ῃ	—	ē
ο	—	o				ῳ	—	ō

THE AUTHORITY AND INSPIRATION OF THE BIBLE

Carl F.H. Henry

Carl F.H. Henry

A.B., A.M., Wheaton College; B.D., Th.D., Northern Baptist Theological Seminary; Ph.D., Boston University, Litt.D., Seattle Pacific College; Litt.D., Wheaton College; L.H.D., Houghton College

Lecturer-at-Large, World Vision International

THE AUTHORITY AND INSPIRATION OF THE BIBLE

I. Introduction

The Bible is the sacred Christian book. The fate of Christianity turns on its supernatural origin, the factuality of its redemptive history, and the validity of its teaching.

This essay deals with the divine authority and inspiration of the Judeo-Christian Scriptures. It presents the case for Scripture as a divinely given record of supernatural revelation and as the authentic exposition of the meaning of that revelation. It deals first with the authority of the Bible and then with the fact and nature of its inspiration.

In view of their confidence in the divine inspiration of the scriptural writings, the Greek Christians spoke long ago of *ta biblia*—in effect, "*the books* par excellence"—and appended to Scripture such adjectives as "divine," "canonical," and "holy." When referring to inspired books collectively, the early Christians spoke of "the Scriptures," even as the OT previously had been so designated (Dan 9:2); the singular form "the Scripture" (*hē graphē*) they reserved for a stipulated passage (contrast Matt 21:42, "Have you never read in the Scriptures . . . ?" with Mark 12:10, "Haven't you read this scripture . . . ?"; cf. Luke 4:21; John 20:9; James 2:8). The subsequent use of the singular—"the Bible"—for the whole corpus of writings reflects the Christian conviction that this collection of books is not merely an anthology of assorted writings whose authors speak reliably for God, but one comprehensively unified divine utterance.

The OT and NT together, reflecting in their various parts a common view of the nature and work of the Creator-Redeemer God, constitute the Bible. The writings bear on the theme of the history of God's special dealings with his covenant people, focusing first on the Exodus and then on the Resurrection. The sixty-six books are the religious documents of a particular community of faith, with the unifying motif of divine promise, expectation, and fulfillment. But at an even more profound level their cohesive bond is found in the supernatural inspiration of both the prophetic and the apostolic writings; the Spirit of God was held to be decisively involved in the production of these documents.

The study of comparative religions has for almost a century stimulated interest in the variety of "sacred writings" connected with different world religions. The Bible, however, holds its place through its persuasive claim to the distinctive divine inspiration of its writers and their teachings. Although devotees of other than biblical religions regard as sacred certain literary traditions associated with their faiths, the express claim of religious writers to be vehicles of divine disclosure is not nearly so common as often presupposed.

Spokesmen for non-Christian religions have themselves countered the neo-Protestant ecumenical cliché, nurtured by modernist views of the exaggerated immanence of God in nature, history, and mankind, that there is divine revelation in all religions. Buddhists protest that this theory too generously bestows upon Buddhism what would be unacceptably destructive of Buddhist tenets—i.e., the Christian insistence that God is personal—since Hinayana Buddhism is atheistic. The sacred Chinese books claim no supernatural inspiration or authority, Confucianism being less a religion than a venerable moral tradition. Among the great religions of the world, the living God significantly appears as the speaking God only in Judaism, Christianity, and Islam—and the Koran's considerable borrowing from the Judeo-Christian Scriptures is indisputable. The Koran is really the product of one man, Muhammad, whose fragmented writings were gathered after his death into a single book exasperatingly lacking in arrangement. Since Muslims consider the Koran an earthly copy of a heavenly original and view its every letter as uncreated and eternal, the words of the Koran preempt features that the NT reserves for the personal *Logos* of God (cf. John 1:1–3). The Zoroastrian Zend-Avesta reflects not only a composite character, but a variety of religious conceptions as well. The so-called sacred books of other religions, including the Book of Mormon, assume much less the character of a unified book than does the Bible, and their mythological features, questionable historical particulars, and inconsistencies of religious perspective should put us on guard against speaking of "the Bibles of mankind."

To insist that the Bible has a supernatural basis that sets it apart, one need not deny all value to the literature of other religions. Much of this literature is associated with great past civilizations and historical epochs of grandeur. Nor need one deny that broken fragments of spiritual and moral truth survive outside the biblical heritage, even if they are expressed there in a conceptual context that is highly confusing when tested by the scriptural revelation. The qualities of one kind or another attributed to the literature of various religious traditions hardly justify an indifference to the qualitatively distinct claim made for the Judeo-Christian Scriptures—i.e., that the Bible is the authoritative word of the Creator-Redeemer God who enters into the historical destinies of a fallen race and provides redemption in the incarnate, crucified, and risen Son, Jesus Christ.

II. The Authority of the Bible

The first fact to be affirmed about the Bible is its divine authority. To be sure, other considerations, such as its inspiration and infallibility, are in important respects interwoven with this. But the Bible presents itself, first and foremost, as the Word of the Lord, given to man through chosen recipients and transmitters of divine redemptive revelation.

Along with the OT, Christians have inherited their view of an authoritative Scripture from the Hebrews. This conviction of the divine authority of Scripture was reinforced by Jesus of Nazareth, the prophetically promised Messiah who identified as God's Spirit-breathed Word not only the prophetic writings but also the apostolic witness that was to constitute the NT.

As authoritative, God's Word is rationally intelligible and dynamically vital. As inspired, his Word is intentionally written and inerrantly given.

A. God's Word As Rationally Intelligible

From the outset, the Bible depicts the self-revealing God as articulating his revelation in intelligible propositions. Nothing is more characteristic of Scripture than its insistence that the living God reveals himself in his spoken Word, and that this Word takes the form of rational communication.

Secular religious philosophers have through the centuries jeopardized their case for the reality of God whenever they have ignored the fact of intelligible divine self-disclosure. The weakness of all empirical proofs—arguments that supposedly lead to the infinite on the basis of observation of the non-God (i.e., nature, history, man)—is not that they always "prove" less than the sovereign Creator of biblical revelation. It is that these arguments do not really demonstrably "prove" anything at all. By the empirical evidence they adduce, secular religious philosophers seek to justify a belief in God they already hold on other grounds, albeit often unacknowledged.

The case for the reality of God, however, stands or falls with the fact of divine self-revelation as a basis of religious faith. Neglect of divine self-disclosure obscures a decisively important activity of the living God, so that secular philosophy as a consequence is vexed by a variety of postulated options—many gods, a diminished god, or no god at all.

The theology of the recent past, on the other hand, has emphasized God's self-revelation only to miss the significance of revelation as a mental act. The dialectical theology of Karl Barth and Emil Brunner formulated the Word of God as simply a personal presence sporadically encountering responsive sinners and summoning them to unreserved trust. Here supernatural revelation was held to be not propositional, yet personal. God communicates—so it was said—not truths or information about himself, but solely himself in salvific activity. The Truth and Word of the self-revealing God, as expounded by Barth, are not at all to be identified with truths and words of Scripture, not even with statements ascribed directly to God by the prophets in their oft-repeated formula "Thus saith the Lord." Rather, God's "Truth" and "Word" were said to differ from what truth and word mean in every other realm of human discourse. According to Barth, God's Truth and Word consist of supernatural personal presence experienced in responsive trust, but do not take the form of intelligible propositions and universally valid statements.

While this neo-Protestant emphasis on personal confrontation was intended to protect the reality of God (assertedly known only in believing faith), in contrast with secular arguments for God's existence (based on the non-God), it nonetheless involved a profoundly unbiblical theory of divine disclosure. Its dismissal of the intelligible rational features of divine self-revelation led, contrary to Barth's intentions, to the eclipse of

God's very reality. Barth's theology of paradox, according to which divine revelation involves no communication of information but only redemptive relationships known in faith-response, was wholly vulnerable to Rudolf Bultmann's existential redirection and internalization of revelation.

Bultmann used Barth's own emphasis that revelation communicates no valid truths to demolish Barthian confidence in the triunity of God, the reality of the supernatural, and the external factuality of miracles, such as the resurrection of Jesus of Nazareth from the dead. If Barth imparted a cryptic character to the Truth and Word of God encountered by man, Bultmann went even further. For him the cross and resurrection of Jesus are a semantic or linguistic coding for an internal experience of dying to self and rising to authentic being—an experience made possible through the leap of faith in answer to God's transcendent call. Revelation, argued Bultmann, tells us only about ourselves and not at all about God apart from ourselves. Thus delineations of the supernatural, of the Trinity, of the incarnation and resurrection of the Logos, are mythical.

No student of the history of ideas should have been surprised that the "death of God" mentality should follow from the theology of Bultmann. Leaders of the God-is-dead stir—Thomas J.J. Altizer, William Hamilton, and Paul van Buren—all were directly or indirectly influenced by the "kerygmatic theology." This theology emphasized that Christ meets us only in the preaching of him, in inner confrontation. It misunderstood divine revelation as nonconceptual, contrary to the insistent witness of the prophetic-apostolic heritage. What kind of "god" is it, after all, whose "reality" I can know only by rejecting—as the kerygmatic theologians demanded—all valid information about him even on the basis of revelation, by denying that he is revealed either in the cosmos or history or society, and by rejecting any possibility of conceptual or rational access, and instead relying wholly on an intense inner leap of faith or subjective decision? Such an enormous leap, it became increasingly clear, placed too much logical strain on the intellectual capacities even of American religious activists. From kerygmatic presuppositions, secular atheists insisted, the conclusion to be consistently drawn is that God as a transcendent personal being is a nonentity.

If neo-Protestant theologians unwittingly undermined God's reality and authority through their refusal to connect his self-revelation with the rational-verbal content of Scripture, logical positivist philosophers deliberately rejected the existence and reality of the God of the Bible on the ground that theological claims could not be validated by empirical scientific method. To be sure, it would have surprised neither Moses nor Isaiah nor Paul that the modern methodology of laboratory science cannot confirm claims made for the invisible and immaterial Spirit or self-revealed Yahweh who stands at the heart of the Bible. What would have astonished them is that a group of learned modern scholars would become so infatuated with a single and limited way of knowing as to make it the omnicompetent way to knowledge.

By mid-century, however, logical positivism already stood self-discredited as nonsense through its own insistence that, tautologies of logic and mathematics excepted, only statements verifiable or falsifiable by scientific empiricism can be considered either meaningful (or true) or meaningless (or false). The positivist credo could not itself meet the boldly heralded positivistic test of empirical verifiability.

One lasting fruit of analytic philosophy, even if nurtured by the frustrations of linguistic analysis, is the growing acknowledgment that a sentence or proposition is the minimal unit of meaning or truth. This is especially significant because of kerygmatic theology's unwitting loss of the reality of God through its forfeiture of propositional revelation as distinguished from sporadic personal encounters.

Hence neo-Protestant theology and positivistic philosophy alike attest by their own disintegration that (1) we undermine the reality of revelation if we speak of divine disclosure in terms of anything less than intelligible sentences and meaningful words and (2) nothing less than the communication of ideas and words in propositional or sentence form must be involved if revelation is held to be either meaningful or true. Therefore both the witness of Scripture itself to the nature of God's self-disclosure and the self-destructive consequences implicit in religious and philosophical alternatives serve to revive present-day interest in the historic evangelical insistence on the rational-verbal character of divine disclosure.

If we speak of the Word of God as authoritative, its authority must be that of an intelligible divine Word mediated by the Logos of God. The divine Logos is the mediating agent in all revelation. This mediated Word is conveyed in rational-verbal form and is scripturally given. Even Jesus of Nazareth, as the incarnate Logos, spoke of his very words as the Father's doing: "The words I say to you are not just my own. Rather, it is the Father, living in me, who is doing his work" (John 14:10).

B. God's Word As Dynamically Vital

God, who reveals himself in his intelligible Word, is also personally and powerfully present in his Word, either in creation or preservation, grace or judgment. His Word defines and expresses his sovereign power and the dependence of everything else on his will. All other authority is derivative and contingent, a right or permission conferred by God from the ultimate seat of power ("There is no authority except that which God has established," Rom 13:1). Angels are divinely invested with whatever authority they exercise (Rev 18). Satan's sphere of dominion is a temporary bestowal (Acts 26:18; Col 1:13). As for Antichrist, even his power is granted to him (Rev 13:2, 4).

Civil government derives its authority from divine determination and is God's instrument of justice and order in a fallen society (Rom 13). So Pilate wielded an authority he had not inherently but derivatively (John 19:11). The forces of destruction in fallen nature and history are not inherent but derived (Rev 6:8, 9:3, 10, 19). Even the authorization enabling forgiven sinners to enter God's kingdom comes from Jesus (John 1:12), who is divinely authorized and empowered to act (John 10:18) and endowed with authority to forgive sins (Mark 2:10). God's Word alone has the final say, invariably carrying out his will and fulfilling his intentions: "So is my word that goes out from my mouth: it will not return to me empty, but shall accomplish what I desire and achieve the purpose for which I sent it" (Isa 55:11). God's Word has a transcendent supernatural force. His prophecy carries inner assurance of historical fulfillment. Even nature passes away, but Yahweh's Word endures: "The grass withers, and the flowers fall, but the word of our God stands forever" (Isa 40:8).

The emphasis on God's powerful Word spans the Bible from the creation account to that of the final judgment. In the narrative of beginnings, the fact that God creates by his Word stands in the forefront: "And God said ... and it was so" (Gen 1:3, 11, 14–15, 24). As his Word brings the orderly cosmos out of the formless primal creation, so God's Word in history shapes the emerging Hebrew nation in the midst of wayward humanity, and so too at the ultimate climax of history men and nations will be judged by God's authoritatively powerful Word. Only God has the last word. "He does not take back his words" (Isa 31:2). All humanly grounded words have merely contingent significance: human beings must often take back or "eat" their words. Even when not injurious, our words are often idle and recall Jesus' warning: "Men will have to give account on the day of judgment for every careless word they have spoken. For by your words you will be acquitted, and by your words you will be condemned" (Matt 12:36–37). God's Word sets the precedent for cocreative and coredemptive use of language in interpersonal relationships.

God's Word, in short, shares his very own attributes. It is living, active, powerful, penetrating as a surgeon's scalpel, bringing all man's thoughts and ideas under searching divine scrutiny and criticism: "The word of God is living and active. Sharper than any double-edged sword, it penetrates even to dividing soul and spirit, joints and marrow; it judges the thoughts and attitudes of the heart" (Heb 4:12).

That the scripturally given Word shares these features as the veritable Word of God is clear from the manner in which the Gospels, depicting Jesus of Nazareth in the context of the prophetic word, speak frequently of the absolute necessity of fulfillment of Scripture, quoting Jesus himself: "How then would the Scriptures be fulfilled that say it must happen in this way?" (Matt 26:54). "Yes, what is written about me is reaching its fulfillment" (Luke 22:37). "Everything must be fulfilled that is written about me in the Law of Moses, the Prophets and the Psalms" (Luke 24:44). Here Jesus explicitly connects the necessity for fulfillment of God's Word with the express teaching of Scripture. The impression left on the apostles by this precedent is apparent from the larger NT (cf. Peter: "Brothers, the Scripture had to be fulfilled . . . ," Acts 1:16).

On the surface of it, to speak of the Bible as divinely authoritative may seem—and some modernist critics have formulated this as a theological objection—to elevate a second authority alongside that of God himself, or alongside Jesus Christ as Head of the church, or alongside the Spirit as the Giver of life. But does the Protestant principle *sola scriptura* really elevate a historical phenomenon to the level of divine majesty, ascribing too little to the living God because it ascribes too much to the Bible? Does it confer godlike worth in a subtle or sinister way on a human book with its human phrasing and vocabulary, thus putting it in devilish antithesis to the authentically divine and thereby affirming what must be devoutly resisted in the name of God, Christ, Spirit, revelation, and (some would even say) of the prophets and apostles themselves? Are the modern theological motivations for relativizing the Bible really nourished by a determination to preserve or protect the uncompromised absoluteness of God? Or does not the assault on an absolute Word or Bible and on an absolute God rather go hand in hand? Does not the substitution of exotic theological notions for the authoritative doctrine of Scripture involve the denial to God of one or another of the priorities that are rightfully and biblically his?

How remarkable it is that Scripture itself—not modern religionists—precisely and most forcefully reminds us of the uncompromisable priority and sovereignty and authority of God. How else in fact has the West—or for that matter, mankind anywhere—come to affirm the irreducible absoluteness of God except through the seemingly "absolutized" witness of Holy Scripture?

What is really at issue in the Protestant principle is not the absolutizing or "divinizing" of the relative—whether of human beings, or of holy men, or of human words at their profoundest, or of human thought at its purest. Rather, it is a matter solely of God speaking in his Word, supernaturally to and through chosen men, making his thoughts and message known to those who must otherwise have been strangers to them. The struggle against the authority of the Bible is therefore inseparable from the struggle against divine authority, even as the struggle for the authority of the Bible is a struggle for transcendent authority and against any transcendent authority higher than God. Indeed there would be no special revelation for us at all had not God chosen prophets

and apostles and charged them to transmit his Word in the form not only of oral proclamation but of letter and book. The rejection of the authority of revelation in the concrete
form and content of Scripture therefore works against spirit and life rather than fostering
them, as critics of the evangelical principle contend.

From his insistence that "authority in the absolute sense resides in the truth alone, or,
in religious language, in the mind and will of God," C.H. Dodd proceeds to circumvent
any self-subsistent external authority given in objective form, whether that form is the
Scriptures or the teaching of Jesus. The Bible "becomes" God's Word as man's spirit is
moved to respond subjectively "to the Spirit that utters itself in the Scriptures."[1] But one
can hardly consider Dodd's own declaration "an entirely non-dogmatic statement which
anyone might accept as a starting-point" (words with which he dismisses an alternative
view)[2] when he states that the Spirit exists and sporadically "utters itself." Indeed, Dodd
concedes the circularity of his exposition of divine authority: "We look to the Bible for
guidance toward religious truth; we recognize this truth by reference to our own
religious standards."[3]

Dodd's emphasis that the Spirit's witness centers in "a unity of experience in which
'subjective' and 'objective' are one"[4] is not as far removed as some may think from the
more recent "new morality," which affirms that love possesses a homing instinct for
doing the right thing in the absence of objectively revealed principles. And situation
ethics, in turn, offers no persuasive alternative to the notion of radical secularity that man
himself defines the true and the good and postulates whatever gods or values express
his individual distinctiveness. That is surely not what Dodd intends. But, speak as he will
of biblical authority, his view of Scripture—reverently as he may handle it on many
occasions—compels him finally to bracket the word "authority" when he speaks of the
Bible[5] and to regard Scripture not as "the last word" but only as "the 'seminal word' out
of which fresh apprehension of truth springs in the mind of man."[6] So what began as
a defense of absolute truth in the mind of God alone[7] concludes without any objectively
uttered and authoritatively apprehended Word of God.

There is, to be sure, but one absolute priority: the sovereign Creator and Lord of all.
In principle, the evangelical believer acknowledges no ultimate authority but the authority of the living God—authoritative even above human reasoning, scientific and theological opinion, ecclesiastical tradition, cultural consensus, empirical observation, and all
else. No book emphasizes as does the Bible that God is the true source and seat of
authority. When he speaks of God as supreme authority, the Christian means that he
acknowledges as final only the authority of the living God, who has become incarnate
in Jesus Christ, man's only Savior and Lord. More specifically, the evangelical believer
acknowledges the supreme authority solely of the living God, embodied in Jesus Christ,
whom no man can confess as Lord except by the Holy Spirit, the divine communicator
and superintendent of the prophetic-apostolic writings (John 14:26; 2 Tim 3:16). The
affirmation of the authority of Scripture represents a determination not to seek the Word
of God elsewhere than in the Spirit-inspired, Christ-pledged, and God-intended source

---

[1]C.H. Dodd, *The Authority of the Bible* (London: Nisbet, 1952), pp. 289–90, 296–97.
[2]Ibid., p. 293.
[3]Ibid., p. 297, n. 1.
[4]Ibid.
[5]Ibid., p. 299.
[6]Ibid., p. 300.
[7]Ibid., p. 289.

of the revelational Word. Although he did not apply the principle elsewhere as fully as he might have and ought to have, Barth was quite right when he asserted that "Holy Scripture is the Word of God for the Church, that it is Jesus Christ for us. ..."[8] The primitive NT churches possessed the words of Jesus only as an apostolically given word. Jesus had in fact entrusted to chosen men guided by the Spirit the whole task of interpreting the salient features of his life, teaching, and work (John 14:26). The apostles imposed their inspired writings on the early Christians not as their own word but as God's: "We also thank God continually because, when you received the word of God, which you heard from us, you accepted it not as the word of men, but as it actually is, the word of God ..." (1 Thess 2:13).

Through his revealed Word, reliably conveyed in Holy Scripture, God publishes the fact and direction of his authority over mankind. In the OT era he exercised authority over Israel through prophets, priests, and kings as appointed agents or authorized representatives whose task included proclaiming his messages (Jer 1:7ff.), teaching his laws (Deut 31:11; Mal 3:7), and ruling accordingly (Deut 17:18ff.). The written Scriptures were the statute-book by which God instructed, warned, and judged his ancient people (Ps 119; cf. 2 Kings 22–23).

W.C.G. Proctor does not put the matter too strongly when he writes, "It is through the Bible that Jesus Christ now exercises his divine authority, imparting authoritative truth, issuing authoritative commands, and imposing an authoritative norm by which all the arrangements or statements made by the church must be shaped and corrected."[9] In this sense, it may be insisted that apostolic authority has not been delegated to others—church fathers, bishops, or an authoritative church or hierarchy—but that apostolic authority remains a reality through the authoritative NT writings through which the risen Lord himself holds sway over the church by the Spirit.

We speak meaningfully of the Bible as Holy Scripture only if we recognize it not simply as one of a number of the shaping forces of Christian life and experience, but rather as the one divinely given Word by which God intends to rule the Christian community and in which he presently confronts the church with a norm higher than her own consciousness. In the Bible the church does not merely memorialize a divine Word once given to long-deceased prophets and apostles but no longer God's Word for us—a Word that could again be a living Word of God only if those special servants in generations past could be raised from the dead to speak their message afresh or only if in our own experience we duplicate and parallel the reception of revelation as it came to those chosen prophets and apostles. For the Bible *is* God's Word now. It is his authoritative Word, in and through and by which the Spirit addresses us today. The Spirit indeed alone imparts life. But he does so only in and through and by the Word, and never without the Word. The scriptural revelation is not simply a Word of God that was vital yesterday; it is the Word of God that is currently vigorous and active in grace or judgment. It is the Word of God present and living in the form and content of Scripture, the Word identical with the words received and transmitted by chosen prophets and apostles, the Word God has spoken and still speaks authoritatively. Divine revelation is Scripture's very own pulsebeat, demanding our respectful hearing and the obedient conformity of our minds and ways to its requirements. The authority of the Bible derives from God's speaking in these statements and words. Scripture is indeed what God

---

[8]Karl Barth, *Church Dogmatics* (New York: Scribner, 1956), I/2, p. 544).
[9]*Baker's Dictionary of Theology*, ed. Everett F. Harrison, s.v. "authority."

himself would have us know and would have us obey in the church as Word of God.

C. God's Word As Deliberately Written

That the authoritative Word of God has the written form of Scripture is not a decision left to prophets or apostles, but one inherent in God's intention for special revelation from the very first. There is for us no special revelational access to God that detours around Scripture, no other way open to the sinner that guarantees reliable conclusions about God's plan and purpose. There is no way to another Word in which God speaks differently from the way he speaks in the Bible, no appeal to the Holy Spirit or even to Christ Jesus or to Elohim-Yahweh (the Maker and Lord of all) that will enable us to acquire some special revelation by which we will be able to "pick and choose" in Scripture between what is authentic or inauthentic. Nor is there any private revelation that enables us to establish Scripture as "special revelation" written, nor any revered church tradition or religious consensus that equips us to discern the real sense of Scripture (as if it were obscure!) or to supplement Scripture (as if it were insufficient and incomplete!).

It is the Bible that is God's authoritative Word. Whoever would speak of God as authoritative over human life, yet clouds the authority of the Bible, in effect obscures an authoritative God. Those who appeal, in distinction from the Bible, to some Christ immediately knowable, or to a mystical relationship to the Holy Spirit on the margin of Scripture (even if rationalized as a confrontation the Bible allegedly witnesses to), or who arm themselves with an impressive consensus of contemporary theologians about the dangers of taking the Bible as literally true—these all end up by subordinating the Bible to speculation. They abridge or amend its teaching by authorizing the fallible human self (the critical expert's included) to criticize infallibly the prophetic-apostolic disclosure of the Word of God. Critics who compromise the authority of Scripture almost invariably correlate the authority of God with speculative notions of God's Word and its implications for man's answerability to God and duty to his fellow-men. The church is not determinative of Scripture, but Scripture is authoritative over the church; whatever authority the church has, she has solely on the basis of the revelational prerogative of God.

Were the Bible, as some would have it, only a "relative authority" (What is that but a circuitous denial of its normative character?), then the appeal to a special revelation of God could be readily correlated with the consciousness of the church and the voice of an ecclesiastical hierarchy could be substituted for that of the transcendent Lord or, more modestly, put on a par with God's voice. Or the special revelation of God could be blurred into sporadic personal encounters the objectivity of which could only be highly suspect, however vigorously their supernatural character might be asserted. Or the "relative authority" of the Bible could be assimilated readily to the supposed radical relativity of all religious experience.

Not for nothing, therefore, do the church confessions speak of God's Word as authoritative in the form and content of Holy Scripture. Recovering what the medieval church lost, the Lutheran Formula of Concord (1577) speaks of "the prophetic and apostolic writings of the Old and New Testaments" as "the one judge, rule and guide" and "the only touchstone."

The Bible is not a dead authority just because it is a written book. Because it is a book, it may seem on the surface to lack the vitality of personal confrontation and proclamation. But why, because it is a book, must it be considered incompatible with the speaking

11

God or a diminution of the oral, prophetic-apostolic proclamation? That the prophets and apostles who were God's chosen bearers of special revelation are known to us through the instrumentality of Scripture does not reduce but enhances the force of this revelation. The Bible is, in fact, fully as forceful and definite as the living prophets and apostles were in their time. Indeed, because of its very written nature, their message is guarded against supplementation, abridgement, alteration, and all other contingencies to which a merely oral statement is vulnerable. Even if oral tradition in ancient times displayed a remarkable capacity for accurate transmission, the written testament is less exposed to alteration by chance and self-interest. While sharing with oral communication the risk of misinterpretation, the written record preserves the author's conceptual-verbal intention in a fixed form in the light of which all subtractions, additions, corruptions, and misconceptions can be criticized. That the prophetic-apostolic revelation is addressed in writing to the church challenges every effort by the church to regard herself as the source of revelation, or even of the given revelation's sure meaning. For the church must always come to terms with what stands written. Without the authoritative books, all the ancient traditions transmitted through the church may easily be misconceived as a message that comes from the church, and the church itself is more readily disposed to modify them. But if Holy Scripture is divinely given, the possibility of reformation remains even for a church that has made itself the seat of divine authority. Whatever churchmen may say about the Bible, so far as the modern church is concerned the Book is theonomously and independently "there," objectively voicing the divinely authoritative Word and repeatedly calling the church to reckon with what is written.

The canonical Scriptures are therefore God's providential gift to the church, preserving the community of faith from vulnerability to legend, superstition, unfounded tradition, corruptive invention, and much else. The biblical Word of revelation is the supernaturally given Word central to the prophetic-apostolic witness. Concerning the writing prophets, O. Procksch notes: "The element of revelation is plainly present in the concept of word. For it is as revelation that the books are collected. But this element is present from the very first in the prophetic concept of the word...."[10] The Judeo-Christian comprehension of divine self-revelation issues not in a set of guidelines for cultivating private revelational relationships with Yahweh. It rather requires the preservation and translation of books containing the verbally articulated revelation of the Creator-Redeemer God.

A decision for an authoritative Bible therefore becomes a matter of obedience to the prophetic-apostolic disclosure and to the priority of God's revelational Word. Holy Scripture is the authority of God in the church, the authority of Christ in the church, the authority of the Holy Spirit in the church, the authority of the prophetic-apostolic revelation in the church.

Geldenhuys summarizes as the evidence of the NT and of the early Christian writings this sequence in respect to divine authority: (1) the historical fact of the supreme authority of the Lord Jesus, (2) the fact of the unique authority given to and exercised by the Lord's chosen apostles to lay the foundations of the church once-for-all, (3) the early church's acknowledgment of the foregoing and its acceptance of the apostolic writings as authoritative, and (4) the inevitable consequence of a canonical NT clothed with the authority of the Lord and his apostles.[11]

10TDNT 4:96, s.v. "lego."
11Norval Geldenhuys, *Supreme Authority: The Authority of the Lord, His Apostles and the New Testament* (London: Marshall, Morgan & Scott, 1953), p. 120.

Without an authoritative Scripture, the church is powerless to overcome not only human unregeneracy but also satanic deception. Where the church no longer lives by the Word of God it is left to its own devices and soon is overtaken by the temptations of Satan and the misery of sin and death. In Eden, Satan displayed his readiness to come as an angel of light, raising doubt about God's authoritative Word and twisting that Word to his own advantage (Gen 3:1, 4–5). In the wilderness temptation, the Second Adam confronted Satan with what stands written in Deuteronomy (Matt 4:4). When in turn Satan ventured to quote the written Word in the Psalms in a biased way (4:6), Jesus did not respond by resorting to some higher authority, for no appeal transcends Scripture as the authoritative divine Word; rather, he thwarted Satan by twice more facing him with the unchangeable written Word of God (4:7, 10).

III. The Inspiration of the Bible

If divine authority is the first feature predicated of the Bible, what is next most prominently affirmed is its divine inspiration. To guard against modern misunderstandings, one might preferably speak of the divine "spiration" of the Bible, had not theologians already taken over this term for the activity by which the Holy Spirit proceeds from the Father and the Son. The term *expiration*—but for its modern association with death —would convey the right connotation; its equally proper sense of breathing forth, exhaling, and emitting reflects the emphasis of 2 Timothy 3:16 that "all Scripture is God-breathed" (*theopneustos*). In modern usage the term inspiration, unfortunately, suggests an act of "breathing into." Moreover, it is used in secular society as a synonym for a wide variety of phenomena, ranging from a hunch to artistic genius. The apostolic emphasis is that God "breathed out" what the sacred writers convey in the biblical writings. The emphasis falls on divine initiative and impartation rather than on human creativity; Scripture owes its origin and nature to what God breathed out. In short, the Bible's life-breath as a literary deposit is divine.

The concept of a God who is personally active in the external world of nature and history runs counter to the outlook of scientism now prevalent in the modern Western world. Scientism comprehends the externally real world solely in terms of impersonal processes and events and leaves no scope for explanation in terms of personal agency; the reality of God is considered only internally significant as a subjective stance of faith. That God acts and speaks could, from this point of view, be regarded only as a metaphorical account. As contemporary secularists speak of "acts of God" with tongue in cheek, so they disallow any literal significance to the notion of a speaking God. As for the belief that God communicates with man, they consigned this to the childhood or adolescence of human history.

A. *Does God Speak to Man?*

The Scriptures set the doctrines of revelation and inspiration in the context of the God who speaks, not simply in the context of the God who acts. The biblical writers ground their proclamation of an authoritative Word of God in the prior initiative of the speaking God. And the Christian church in her confessional statements insists that God veritably speaks.

The Bible insists that God not only addresses mankind universally through nature, history, and the reason and conscience of man, but that he also addresses his Word articulately to chosen persons in a special way. Time and again Yahweh is identified as the speaking God who communicates his message to a specific individual in a particular place at a given time. See, for example, many statements such as these: "The words of Jeremiah. . . . The word of the LORD came to him in the thirteenth year of the reign of Josiah" (Jer 1:1, 2). "The word of the Lord came to Hosea . . . during the reigns of Uzziah, Jotham . . ." (Hos 1:1). "The word of the Lord came to Micah . . . in the days of Jotham" (Mic 1:1).

The manner in which God communicated his Word has obvious implications for the doctrines of revelation and inspiration. If representations of God as a speaking God are merely a matter of figurative language, i.e., a literary device by which a human writer ascribes supreme significance to his own exalted religious ideas, that is one thing. But in that event we must disown what the biblical writers themselves say about the necessary relationship of their words to the speaking God. We must also reject the confessional statements of the historic churches about God's verbal revelation and the divine inspiration of the Scriptures.

Among recent evangelical scholars who have probed the way God speaks in Scripture is Nicholas Wolterstorff, Professor of Philosophy at Calvin College. He properly reminds us that the Bible itself precludes any notion that God literally talks the way human beings talk, that is, by forming words with mouth and vocal cords, since God is Spirit and has no body.[12] Although Scripture frequently mentions God's mouth (Num 12:8; Deut 32:1; Isa 55:11; Lam 3:38, et al.) and even his voice (Deut 4:33; Ps 18:13; 95:6; cf. Matt 3:16; Heb 3:6, 15, et al.), the Scripture itself requires us to regard such representations as anthropomorphic rather than literal. God "does not," Wolterstorff says "*utter* words . . . as sounds having meaning in some language."

Nevertheless, God may "in some other fashion *produce* words—sounds having meaning—which are heard by men . . . words from some language of ours." In brief, God does not "literally talk, forming words with mouth and vocal cords," yet if he "uses language to speak to us, it will be one of our interpersonal, human languages."[13]

Wolterstorff's rule for recognizing what is figurative in the biblical account of God's speech is legitimate, viz., scriptural teaching is itself decisive. What do the biblical writers affirm, then, about God's manner of speaking when they assert that the prophetic word is divinely grounded? In contrast with admittedly anthropomorphic representations of words phonetically uttered by God's mouth or voice, no internal biblical evidence supports the notion that the sacred writers resort only to metaphor when they employ such phrases as "God spoke" and refer to "the word of the Lord."

To be sure, God tells us about himself and his purposes by his words and deeds. But, as Wolterstorff emphasizes, that is not a fully adequate representation of God's speaking to man. "Many of the things which God speaks to us are not things which his works and deeds tell us about him. In fact, it does not even make sense to identify what God says with what his works and deeds reveal to us, except in cases in which God makes an assertion"[14]—e.g., when God explicitly asserts that his power and divinity are revealed

---

[12]"On God Speaking," *The Reformed Journal* (July-August, 1969), p. 8.
[13]Ibid., p. 9.
[14]Ibid., p. 10.

in the creation (Rom 1). "The peculiarity of the biblical vision is lost if one allows only that God is revealed, denying that he speaks; or if one mistakenly interprets the claim that God speaks as being the same as the claim that God is revealed."[15]

Wolterstorff contends that God produced sounds having meaning not by uttering words, that is, not by performing a language-act, but by a "speech-act" that need not involve the use of words. When the biblical writers "talked of God's speaking, what they were talking about is God's performing of various speech-acts (not language-acts)" and "when they talked of God's Word, what they were talking of is the speech-objects of God's speech." Such divine speech-acts need not have involved any language-acts at all, though in some cases they may have involved "producing" some verbal sounds.[16]

Wolterstorff's concern is to take seriously the explicit rejection by evangelical Christianity of the notion, often attributed by critics to conservative evangelicals, that God dictated the Bible. Evangelical Christians insist that God did not dictate what the biblical authors spoke and wrote. Yet the Bible is authoritative because God himself has spoken biblically and even today speaks in this way. The words we have from Amos and Isaiah and Paul, though not to be viewed as divine dictation, are nevertheless to be viewed as the very words God spoke. And this claim can be properly made, Wolterstorff adds, for the words contained in any responsible Bible translation, in any language no less than in the original.

This leaves us with the difficult problem of sorting out what God was and is saying from what belongs only to the prophet's or writer's manner of expressing this.

Wolterstorff develops his distinction between the divine speech-act and the human language-act in two ways: (1) Deputized spokesmen often speak authoritatively for those who commission them, though they employ words not actually communicated by their superiors and (2) what really counts in virtually all speech is the speech-act that is the utterance of words. We shall consider these points in order.

Of the deputized spokesman, Wolterstorff says,

> A human being often authorizes or deputizes a designated spokesman "to 'speak for' him, to speak 'in his name,' 'on his behalf.' " . . . In such a case the . . . person need not repeat exactly some words given him by the first [person] in order that he shall speak for the first. On the contrary, the first may not have put his greeting into words at all. . . . All that is required is that the speaker 'be in tune with' the one for whom he is speaking.[17]

In support of God's commissioning, authorizing, or deputizing prophets to speak for him, Wolterstorff appeals to Deuteronomy 18. He emphasizes that God's Word and man's word must not be thought to be in total antithesis, as if the latter could not under certain circumstances also be the former. While in some instances what the prophets say derives from "slow reflection" or "the sudden dawning of conviction," Wolterstorff notes that sometimes God spoke directly to them. Usually they do not tell us "in what configuration of factors or events" God spoke to them. But we are told that to some God spoke in dreams, in visions, in voices, in the casting of lots, "in short . . . by way of various happenings in their experience."[18]

15Ibid.
16Ibid., p. 11.
17"How God Speaks," *The Reformed Journal* (September, 1969), p. 17.
18Ibid., p. 18.

The question remains, however, whether the prophets were left at times merely to intuit or prognosticate what they represented as a divine message and word given in articulate form. Without clarity at this point, the acknowledgment that God sometimes spoke directly to the prophets provides no clear antithesis to their own formulation not simply of the wording but also of the content of the message. Deuteronomy 18 does more than establish the prophet as a divinely deputized spokesman; it correlates his mission with the proclamation of God's divinely given words. Yahweh says, "I will put my words in his mouth, and he will tell them everything I command him. . . . But a prophet who presumes to speak in my name anything I have not commanded him to say . . . must be put to death" (Deut 18:18, 20). While biblical references to "the mouth of God" are clearly anthropomorphic, no such doctrinal necessity exists for interpreting as anthropomorphic the repeated biblical emphasis on words God has legitimated in the mouths of his chosen spokesmen—e.g., "I, even I, will be with your mouth, and teach you what you are to say" (Exod 4:12; cf. 13:9); "The Lord put a word in Balaam's mouth" (Num 23:5, cf. v.16); "And I have put my words in your mouth" (Isa 51:16; cf. Jer 1:9, 5:14). The most emphatic passage is doubtless Ezekiel 3:27: "But when I speak to you, I will open your mouth, and you shall say to them, 'Thus says the Lord God'" (RSV). Those who heard the prophetic proclamation considered that the words of the prophets did have a divine legitimation ("The word of the LORD from your mouth is the truth," 1 Kings 17:24).

Does Wolterstorff assimilate the reception of revelation by prophets and apostles and their vocational calling too much to the way all God's people may be said to be addressed by him in revelation and deputized by him for proclamation? Does he thus do less than justice to the cognitive and verbal precision of God's communication in prophetic-apostolic revelation and inspiration? Certainly Christ's followers are deputized as ambassadors to proclaim God's message, so that by way of this witness God speaks to the world today. But does this adequately establish the dependence of our message on the biblical norm for the intelligible and verbal reliability of the content of revelation?

Why, Wolterstorff asks, cannot God speak to contemporary prophets as he did to ancient prophets by way of dreams, voices, visions, or speak through a race riot, or an act of kindness, or death, or fall of a nation, or collapse of a cause? There is, of course, no evangelical limitation on divine omnipotence that precludes such possibilities; the question can only be whether God actually does speak this way. As for God's general revelation in history and in the mind and conscience of man, a continuing variety of means is possible. Moreover, as for God's special providence in the lives of believers, his personal presence and care may take many forms. But Wolterstorff says more: God speaks to us today "in fundamentally the same ways that he spoke to men in the past"— not solely in our dependence on Scripture but "by way of the happenings of public and private history" and "by way of his contemporary deputies speaking."[19]

The church's criterion, he adds, "is the word of God spoken long ago by way of his ancient prophets and apostles, and preeminently by his Son. If we are to speak for God today, our speaking must be in accord with the word of God spoken in antiquity. That word spoken long ago is criteriological for our contemporary speaking for God."[20] Wolterstorff emphatically affirms that God's Word spoken in Christ by the speaking of the prophets and apostles and of Jesus is still divinely addressed to us by way of the

---

[19]"Canon and Criterion," *The Reformed Journal* (October, 1969), p. 10.
[20]Ibid., p. 11.

biblical writings. "In reading the writings of the biblical writers . . . we discover what is the word of God to us."[21] He adds, "The Church says that God has spoken a word which was meant for and is applicable to us today; and that it comes to us by way of these documents of the community.[22]

The nature of this criterion requires clarification. For Wolterstorff the Scriptures provide "a reliable report of, and with genuine instances of, what it was that God said by way of the speaking of his ancient deputies."[23] But does not Scripture convey a content identifiable as God's express statements to the biblical writers?

By his emphasis on divine speech-acts in distinction from word-acts, Wolterstorff does not intend to imply the noncognitive significance of such speech-acts. What we really care about in all speech, whether human or divine, he says, is the speech-act, except in cases where for aesthetic reasons we care about the very words themselves. Our concern in communication is not with how an assertion is made or a command given, but with what is asserted or commanded. He contends, moreover, that as we can perform speech acts without words (by gestures, works of art, etc.), so God on many occasions may perform speech-acts without any language-act at all.

Such a representation of divine communication, it seems to this writer, may apply less appropriately to the content of the biblical revelation than to the universal divine revelation in nature and history, as a work of cosmic beauty and of the external activity of God, and to the disclosure of God to the mind and conscience of mankind generally.

Yet Wolterstorff does not deny that God, who can produce sounds (though he does not utter them) sometimes expressly conveyed his truth in human concepts and human words. Sometimes, he tells us, the prophets repeated the express words that God "produced."

But, he adds, "not all of the Bible can be viewed as either report or instance of God's speaking by way of ancient man."[24] The Psalms almost entirely, and most of the wisdom literature, are to be viewed not as a record of what God said to ancient Israel, but rather as the words whereby ancient Israel addressed God.

No reader will question that the religious life embraces many elements, including awe and worship, moral obligation, and much else. But the evangelical view of inspiration has viewed the teaching of the biblical writers even on such related matters as being bestowed by the superintendence of the Spirit.

Wolterstorff proposes a second reason for hesitating to identify the biblical words as God's Word. "God spoke . . . by way of the speaking of men who were themselves members of that ancient culture," and who, when speaking for God, "are not lifted out of their cultural condition, thereby saying things which reflect no culturally conditioned frame of beliefs about the world. Their speech on God's behalf reveals the beliefs characteristic of their culture." Furthermore, the biblical writers in their writing reflect not only prevalent cultural beliefs, but "their speech on God's behalf reveals personal as well as cultural idiosyncracies."[25]

How are we to reconcile this with their claim that they were speaking for God? The key, as Wolterstorff sees it, is that "the deputy may . . . speak for his deputizer without

---

21"How God Speaks," p. 19.
22Ibid., p. 20.
23"Canon and Criterion," p. 11.
24Ibid.
25Ibid., p. 12.

ever having been given the exact words he is to say."[26] "Taking the Bible as canonical and the anciently spoken word of God as criteriological" does not oblige us to accept all the beliefs and teachings of the sacred writers.[27] The line between what in Scripture we are obligated to accept and what we are not obligated to accept must nevertheless not be drawn by some criterion external to the Bible, for "to employ external criteria is either to hold that the anciently spoken word is not normative for all our beliefs, or to hold that the biblical record is not a fully canonical report and instance of God's ancient speech. . . . To take the Word of God spoken by ancient man as normative for our entire lives, including our speaking on God's behalf, and to take the Holy Scriptures as canonical report and instance of that anciently spoken Word, demands . . . that we use only internal structural considerations in trying to decide what is the essential Word of God there recorded and there instantiated." Only "by reference to *internal structural* considerations are we permitted to discriminate what is authentically divine," for "God's word spoken by prophets and apostles is normative for our entire lives—for our speaking on his behalf today, but also for our cosmological views."[28] The internal structure of the sacred writings enables us to distinguish "between the message of a book and examples used to convey that message; between the point of a passage and the various things presupposed by the particular manner of making the point; between what is essential in the total discourse and what is not." Internal structural considerations "are relevant in trying to decide in how far and in what respect" the writer was speaking "God's message, God's Word, and in how far and in what respect the beliefs expressed were only cultural and personal idiosyncracies."[29]

This approach of Wolterstorff is commendable for its recognition of Scripture as a distinctive canon of writings, its emphasis on the Word of God spoken by its writers as normative for the entirety of our lives, its rejection of external secular criteria for discriminating the essential content of Scripture, and its insistence that the biblical representations of God speaking his word through chosen messengers must not be dismissed as mere metaphor. In accord with evangelical theology, moreover, he rejects a "dictation" theory of inspiration, recognizing that the sacred writings reflect the stylistic peculiarities and personality traits of the individual writers, and concedes that the biblical writers in many respects shared the limited cultural perspectives of their times even as modern Christians do.

But for all that, Wolterstorff's exposition of the way God specially reveals himself is confusing and unsatisfactory. For one thing, the emphasis on "internal structural considerations" as criteriological is nebulous; no objective principle is adduced for distinguishing where the biblical writers are held not to say what God says. If this means only that the analogy of Scripture is decisive for the meaning of any apparently obscure passage, that is one thing. But why is it not rather suggested that what the biblical writers *teach as doctrine* is to be considered as what, in their view, God says? It is one thing to say that we are not obliged to accept all the beliefs of the biblical writers, not even some beliefs implied in the way they formulate their teaching. It is quite another thing to say that Christians are not obliged to accept "all the . . . teachings of the sacred writers." That the biblical writers shared in many respects the cultural limitations of their day is not surprising, but if they promulgated as the Word of God the theories of men, the

---

[26]Ibid., p. 13.
[27]Ibid., p. 14.
[28]Ibid., pp. 14, 15.
[29]Ibid.

whole notion of intelligible divine revelation is jeopardized. It should be obvious that if one's cultural limitations inherently preclude any communication of permanently valid truths, then not even Wolterstorff could claim that his account of the speaking God tells us what is truly the case.

Nor need we be troubled by the emphasis on the biblical writers' exercising vocabulary choice in their communication of divine disclosure. A variation of words need not invalidate the concept of revelational truth, provided that the choice of words faithfully conveys the meaning of the revelation. A proposition, implicit or explicit, is the minimal unit of meaning and truth. As long as words do not alter the sense, some variety of expression is compatible with intelligible revelation. Yet Wolterstorff curiously makes but one reference, and that in a minimizing way, concerning propositional revelation.[30] The reason for his avoidance of emphasis on divine revelation in propositional form, he explains, is that God's communication includes the issuance of commands, expressions of consolation, etc., and hence presumably consists of much more than asserting propositions. Nevertheless, Wolterstorff concedes that much of God's Word to man is concerned with "truths." But unless such issuances and expressions are implicitly propositional, is their meaning and objective truth fully assured? To this writer it appears that the only way Wolterstorff can persuasively maintain his emphasis that the words the prophets speak do have divine authority and are properly prefaced by "Thus saith the Lord" in view of an underlying divine speech-act, is on the premise of propositional disclosure, so that the words convey what Yahweh thinks and teaches. Commandments like "Thou shalt not kill" are imperatives; yet their grammatical form does not dismantle the claim that revelation is concerned primarily with communicating truth. Imperatives are not true or false propositions, but can be translated into propositions from which a cognitive inference can be drawn (e.g., "To kill is wrong").

On Wolterstorff's approach, the Bible remains a reliable report of what the prophets and apostles—and presumably Jesus, as well—teach, but its readers can no longer confidently appeal to its teaching as true and authoritative. To be sure, "we are not to view each book as having the tacit preface: 'And God spoke to me saying, Write down the following words.' "[31] Yet one must not allow this broad disclaimer to cancel what the writers themselves to whom God's special disclosure came tell us about the nature of divine revelation and inspiration. Does it not do less than justice to what the prophets and apostles say about the content of revelation and inspiration if we imply that they received only God's message in general and that the words they ascribe directly to Yahweh are not *in truth* his words?

Whatever must be said for dreams, visions, and the like, the prophets themselves, and the apostle Paul likewise, find in the intelligibly communicated Word of God the fixed center of revelation. Paul no less than the prophets commends those who "when [they] received the word of God, which [they] heard from us . . . accepted it not as the word of men, but as it actually is, the word of God . . ." (1 Thess 2:13).

Do not some of the writers insistently preface their reports with "Thus saith the Lord"? If they are not trustworthy in representing this broad claim, why should they be thought trustworthy respecting its subordinate particulars, even if one tries to distinguish general message from supportive details? Would not the appeal of the biblical writers to the biblical Word itself as the express Word of Yahweh or of the Spirit, an

---

[30]"On God Speaking," p. 10.
[31]Ibid., p. 14.

appeal made even by Jesus—and in some cases to what might be regarded as supportive detail—otherwise be ill-founded? Then Jesus Christ would at best represent an exception in respect of the communication of divine revelation in verbal form, or else he exaggerated when he spoke of giving the disciples the Father's very words (John 17:8). Did not Jesus himself speak of the language-object, not simply of the speech-object—to borrow Wolterstorff's distinction—as divinely authorized: "These words you hear are not my own; they belong to the Father who sent me" (John 14:24)?

Geoffrey Bromiley tells us that evangelical Christians need not be timid about the doctrine of verbal inspiration. His comments are timely: "The case against verbal inspiration is not as strong as it looks. . . . There is no reason why verbal inspiration should entail an ignoring of the personal characteristics of the authors. Indeed, the more seriously the words are taken, the more significant are the peculiarities of the writers."[32] The fact that exegesis is concerned with the writer's thought does not reduce the significance of his words, for one must study the words, singly and contextually, to get a precise understanding of the thought. "The main point about verbal inspiration," Bromiley writes, "is not that the words are inspired rather than their content, but that there is no such thing as the one without the other. . . . The content is not to be had without this form."[33]

B. *The Witness of the Bible Itself to Divine Inspiration*

It is ironical that, alongside a flourishing biblical scholarship, the doctrine of biblical inspiration is now under more intense fire than ever. This attack comes not only from those who reject the supernatural but in numerous cases from theists who insist that the traditional Christian view inadequately reflects the biblical data. The pressing tasks of Christian theology include, therefore, wrestling with the doctrine of inspiration in the context of contemporary textual problems. Too frequently the discussion of inspiration has been carried on either by scholars who marshal the problems to demolish any consideration of inspiration or by those who concentrate on the doctrine and fail to face some of the problems. The century-old interest in literary analysis of the Bible was usually pursued on the premise of exaggerated divine immanence and evolutionary dependence, a stance that mitigates against both miraculous revelation and divine inspiration. Yet the literary-historical method did not of itself require a rejection of a high view of revelation and inspiration, since its subordination to pantheistic and developmental views was arbitrary. But, as Martin Woudstra notes, the subsequent emphasis of form-critical method on the history of literary genrés, which assumes an oral tradition decisively shaped by communal sociological processes, leaves far less room for an evangelical view of inspiration. "If oral tradition played as large a role as current opinion asserts, and if this tradition already had a great deal of fixity prior to its inscripturation . . . if communal beliefs are as decisive in the shaping of the traditions as form criticism asserts, is there any point where these beliefs begin to assume the form of divine revelation? . . . Can a real doctrine of inspiration emerge from a form-critical method of interpretation?"[34]

Given the contemporary critical viewpoint, the NT verses pertaining to biblical

---

[32]Geoffrey Bromiley, "The Inspiration and Authority of Scripture," *Eternity* (August, 1970), p. 14.
[33]Ibid., p. 15.
[34]Martin H. Woudstra, "The Inspiration of the Old Testament," in *The Bible—The Living Word of God*, ed. Merrill C. Tenney (Grand Rapids: Zondervan, 1968), pp. 126, 127.

inspiration and having in view especially the OT writings (2 Tim 3:16; 2 Peter 1:21, et al.) are regarded as having little more than historical value. Such texts merely reflect the prevailing tradition, so it is said, which is similarly mirrored in the appeal of the Gospel writers, especially Matthew, to OT prophecies alleged to be fulfilled in Jesus of Nazareth. The NT view of Scripture is held to be neither authoritative nor factual, but merely expressive of a devout sentiment current in apostolic times. The critical approach therefore sponsors a dichotomy between faithful exegesis and historical fidelity.

But history cannot be compiled from imagination. The writer of history must consult sources if he wishes to claim that his work gives a reliable report of the past. And the NT view of OT events is not a creation *ex nihilo*. It has deep roots in the OT. Not only do the prophets frequently preface their written proclamation with the explicit identification *debar yahweh* ("the word of the Lord"), but the expression is also used (cf. Hos 1:1, Joel 1:1, Mic 1:1, Zeph 1:1) as a covering phrase for the collection of their communications in book form. Some modern critics exaggerate the dynamic character of the Hebrew *dabar* (word) and consider its application to written prophecy a petrifying of the dynamics of the term. But Barr is surely right in insisting that recent modern theology overstates the dynamic nature of the term.[35] The prophet Jeremiah does full justice to the dynamic vitality of God's *dabar*, yet declares that the words of Yahweh are to be recorded in the "roll of a book" so that the written word may turn Israel and Judah from their wicked ways (Jer 36:2, 3). The written word may therefore be viewed as no less potent than the spoken word.

Some critics attribute the introductory formula "the word of the Lord" in the prophetic books to the hand of a later redactor who allegedly held a more "static" view of *debar yahweh* than the prophets themselves. But the prophetic books contain within them the insistent identification of the written message as the Word of the Lord (cf. Jer 29:4, 8, 14, 16, 17, 20, 30), and if this too is ascribed to redactors, the manuscripts seem so pervasively exposed to unsure revision as to vastly reduce their historical value in support of any view whatever. As Woudstra remarks, "The Biblical evidence . . . indicates that the written words are to be regarded as fully adequate vehicles of God's thoughts, in no way less direct in either power or authority than their oral counterparts."[36]

Assuming that the formula "the word of the Lord which came . . ." does in fact imply a prophetic claim to divine inspiration, some neo-Protestant critics contend that the failure of others of the prophetic books to carry this introductory formula implies that not all the prophets shared this view, that a more "static" or bookish theory of inspiration developed gradually as a corruption of the "dynamic" conception of *debar yahweh*, and that this view was subsequently detached from specific revelations of Yahweh and correlated with the entirety of the sacred writings. Vriezen, for example, argues that the omission of the superscription in the great prophetic works of Isaiah, Jeremiah, and Ezekiel was occasioned by the inclusion in these collections of "many other things besides divine messages."[37] Yet the Book of Jeremiah, while omitting the superscription, nonetheless not only identifies its content on numerous occasions as *debar yahweh*, but, as Woudstra notes, uses the formula to introduce sections which contain material other than what Vriezen would designate as a divine message (cf. Jer 32). Indeed, Jeremiah betrays no reluctance to identify as the divine Word what the prophet himself is

---

[35]James Barr, *Semantics of Biblical Language* (London: Oxford, 1961), pp. 129ff.
[36]Woudstra, "Inspiration of the Old Testament," p. 132.
[37]T.C. Vriezen, *An Outline of Old Testament Theology* (Wageninger: H. Veenman, 1958), p. 95.

asserting. Whether Yahweh or Jeremiah is identified as spokesman (the oscillation between the two is especially apparent in chapters 8 and 9; cf. also 36:6, 10), the written account is adduced as the Word of the Lord. As Beegle puts it, the prophets "have an absolute conviction that their messages come from Yahweh."[38] Yahweh "put a word" in Balaam's mouth (Num 23:5); Yahweh declared of Moses, "With him I speak mouth to mouth, clearly" (Num 12:8 RSV); and in calling Jeremiah, Yahweh affirmed, "I have put my words in your mouth" (Jer 1:9).

The OT claim in behalf of written revelation does not begin with the period of the great prophets but long antedates them. The Pentateuch itself refers frequently to the "ten words," which were originally given orally, as having been written upon tables of stone by God's own finger (Exod 31:18; Deut 4:13; 5:22; 9:10; 10:2, 4). The conception of written revelation is one that prevailed as early as Mosaic times with no intimation that an inscripturation of the word of Yahweh in any way mitigates its dynamic force. The Pentateuch includes the written "law," "the words of the covenant," and much else that is correlated with the Word of the Lord, so that from the beginnings of the history of the Hebrew nation the written perpetuation of the revelation of Yahweh seems to be in view. The teaching and writing of God's revelational truth are frequently coordinated. The written form invests the specific Word of God with historical durability and prevents it from being absorbed by general revelation and assimilated to and submerged by myth and legend. The written documents hold the character of decisive testimony and witness (cf. Deut 31:22) and occupy a definitive place in respect to God's covenant with Israel.

The honor in which Jesus of Nazareth held the OT at once attests the intention of the prophets and presages the attitude of the apostles toward Scripture. He deplored as inadequate the merely formal deference of the scribes and Pharisees. By their traditions they virtually nullified the authoritative Word of God. Marcel tells us that "from the manner in which Christ quotes Scripture we find that he recognizes and accepts the Old Testament in its entirety as possessing a normative authority, as the true Word of God. . . . He seals with his authority numerous facts which are related in Scripture, and the historicity of numerous events: we are therefore instructed to believe them *all*" (Marcel's italics).[39]

The apostolic regard for Scripture does not exceed that of Jesus; all that was "written in the past" by the biblical writers "was written to teach us" (Rom 15:4) and is "useful" (2 Tim 3:16). The prophets were not themselves always aware of the implications of the words they transmitted (1 Peter 1:10, 11), so that they sometimes wrote from beyond their own knowledge and comprehension.

C. *Modern Redefinitions of Inspiration*

Since the mid-nineteenth century the climate of thought in frontier philosophical and theological circles has been hostile to the idea of the formulation of divine revelation in truths and words. Even Hegel, who might seem a notable exception, spoke of revelation only in terms of concepts, not of verbal propositions. The reconstruction of the Christian doctrine of revelation in wholly noncognitive and nonverbal categories has during the past half century centered in the emphasis on divine *self-disclosure* viewed dialectically

---

[38]Dewey M. Beegle, *Scripture, Tradition and Infallibility* (Grand Rapids: Eerdmans, 1973), p. 26.

[39]Pierre Marcel, "Our Lord's Use of Scripture," in *Revelation and the Bible*, ed. C.F.H. Henry, 4th ed. (Grand Rapids: Baker, 1967), p. 133.

or existentially, whereas in the decades before World War I anti-intellectualist emphasis in religion fell rather on the limitations of human reason and the nontheoretical nature of religious experience.

The biblical doctrine of inspiration cannot be maintained in a vacuum. It stands or falls, as does every other premise, as part of a larger constellation of convictions. The reality of God known in divine revelation and the nature of that revelation are foundational Christian concerns. The strength of the evangelical insistence on propositional revelation lies in the fact that in matters of objective truth a judgment or sentence is the logical atom that cannot be split without destroying meaning. A revelation of only isolated names and disparate words would blur meaning. Behind the evangelical insistence on verbal inspiration stands the Christian confidence in God's lucid intelligible disclosure.

The term *propositional revelation* is sometimes thought to be unfortunate because the biblical record obviously includes a variety of literary forms (e.g., poetry, parable, didactic prose, prophecy, letters) and of mediums of revelation (dreams, visions, theophanies, etc.). But as Pinnock has said, "Wordless revelation . . . is mere mysticism," much as contemporary theologians may dignify it as "personal" confrontation. The "overwhelming virtue" of the term *propositional revelation* is its reference "to a body of truth, however transmitted, which originates with God and which provides the subject matter of theology."[40] The denial that divine revelation embraces the communication of revealed information about God and his purposes for man and the world has as its consequence the reduction of theology from a science of the transcendent God to a game of dart-throwing at a nebulous infinity.

Characteristic of modern speculation is its correlation of the discussion of divine disclosure not with intelligible truth but rather with human experience as a much broader and vaguer category. In neo-Protestant circles the impetus for this correlation came from Schleiermacher, who, by seeking in religious experience a basis for asserting the reality of God, hoped to counter Hume's emphasis that experiential considerations do not lead beyond agnosticism in respect to the existence of a Supreme Being. Schleiermacher postulated the feelings, particularly the feeling of absolute dependence on the cosmic whole (which for twentieth-century man has been mollified by an exuberant sense of the scientific conquest of nature), as the locus of religious experience. But he emphasized that such experience gives us no knowledge of God in himself, as he objectively is, but only a sense of God-in-relation-to-us. The definition of God in valid terms remained therefore an open matter, while the reality of God was held to be a universal experience. Twentieth-century neo-Protestant theology correlated the theme of revelation dramatically with God's initiative and emphasized divine self-disclosure. Nevertheless, it set itself as firmly as Schleiermacher had against the traditional Christian insistence on rational revelation conveying objectively valid information about God's inherent nature, or for that matter about his purposes in nature and history and society.

The significance of this theological departure from the Christian heritage can best be gauged when we remember that the conflict between the Reformers and Rome concerned not the existence of revealed truth, on which neither side wavered, but rather the subordinate—though highly important—issues of the source and interpretation of revelation. The neo-Protestant disinterest in the historic view of inspiration and its

---

[40]Clark Pinnock, "The Inspiration of the New Testament," in *The Bible—The Living Word of Revelation*, ed. Merrill C. Tenney (Grand Rapids: Zondervan, 1968), p. 144.

reinterpretation of inspiration (along with other biblical doctrines) in dynamic or subjective terms must be seen as a reflex of its prior rejection—in deference to modern philosophical assumptions—of a theology of rational-verbal disclosure. Behind the revolt against the doctrine of biblical inspiration lies the century-old rejection by neo-Protestant theologians of a theology centering in the intelligible revelation of a sovereign personal God, who enters into verbal covenant with man. All objections to inspiration adduced by an appeal to so-called errors of truth or fact in the biblical writings, all suggestions that the biblical writers would cease to be human were they to tell the truth and nothing but the truth even while inspired by the Holy Spirit, must be pushed back to a prior issue: *Is it assumed, contrary to the prophetic-apostolic witness itself, that the Living God does not speak his word to men in intelligible form?* If we assume the noncognitivity of revelation, all other so-called objections to biblical inspiration are rationalizations of a previous negation that disallows any emphasis that the written Scriptures possess revelational status.

The Bible is alike demoted from direct revelational significance by the salvation-history, dialectical, and new hermeneutical schools. According to the *Heilsgeschichte* theory, revelation is to be found in God's special acts in history; the significance of Scripture lies in its existence as a record that derives from those who were contemporaneous with the events and who interpreted them for the people of God. The documents are not in themselves considered divinely inspired but are rather held to be the human response of devout men to the redemptive events of biblical history. But not even the fact that writers were contemporaneous with the events would establish their interpretation as normative, if God himself is mute concerning the meaning of his acts. Without articulate divine revelation, so-called special events or redemptive acts are readily assimilated wholly into the stream of universal history. In that case, their "saving" significance is limited to the faith-stance of imaginative interpreters. The historic Christian view is that Scripture indeed contains the eyewitness accounts of devout persons who lived contemporaneously with the dramatic redemptive acts of biblical history, and that beyond this, the Bible is an inspired record conveying divinely imparted truth about God and his redemptive activity in behalf of an estranged humanity.

The dialectical view, anticipated by Kierkegaard, developed by Barth, and popularized by Brunner, views Scripture as a fallible witness to a revelational encounter in which Christ manifests his personal reality without any disclosure of objectively valid information. The manner in which this theory distorts the significance of the Bible is a consequence of its notion that revelation is personal and nonpropositional. Revelation is said to be divine *self-disclosure*, not the communication of truths; hence the content of revelation is not to be found by historical-philological exegesis of the words and truth of Scripture. Since the Bible "witnesses" by "pointing" to a transcendent divine confrontation with man, its propositional statements being considered fallible, it follows that even where Scripture is declared to be fallible its role as a witness is not considered impaired. In principle this means that even were the Bible to bear witness to a false god, it must be considered as witnessing to the true God. Kierkegaard in fact wrote that "if . . . one who lives in an idolatrous community prays with the entire passion of the infinite, although his eyes rest upon the image of an idol . . . [he] prays in truth to God though he worships an idol."[41] It is remarkable, though not wholly surprising in view of his

---

[41]Soren Kierkegaard, *Concluding Unscientific Postscript*, tr. by David F. Swenson (Princeton: Princeton University Press, 1941), pp. 179–80.

sympathies for the encounter theology and his defense of the notion of subjective in distinction from objective truth, that Beegle remarks that "there is certainly some truth" in Kierkegaard's emphasis.[42]

This confusion results from a failure to recognize that a god of "noncognitive self-revelation" cannot in any confident sense be the *true* God at all. Despite the dialectical emphasis that Christ is the Truth known in personal encounter, the correlation of revelation with subjective faith in contrast to reason is destructive of God, revelation, and all else as valid intelligible conceptualities. Barth assuredly quoted Scripture with more deference than most recent neo-Protestant theologians. Often in his dogmatic writings he appealed to it decisively. Yet his theory of revelation required him to dismiss the historic Christian insistence on the objective inspiredness of the sacred writings. Instead, Barth promulgated a dynamic theory of inspiration, whereby the Bible is merely an instrumental frame of "witness" within which God personally encounters man on the occasion of responsive obedience. On the contrary, the historic Christian view is that the Bible indeed witnesses to Christ the mediator of revelation and redemption, but that this witness is expressed in the valid propositional truths of a written revelation. While the eternal Christ is ontologically the Logos or Word of God, Scripture is epistemologically the Logos or Word of God. There is no need, on the basis of the biblical witness, to correlate the Word of God solely with the personal in contrast with the propositional (cf. Rev 1:9, where the Logos of God is the message proclaimed by John) or to insist on an absolute antithesis between the Word of God and the Bible.

The new hermeneutic influenced by Martin Heidegger likewise deprives Scripture of revelational value and considers it the framework for a "language-event," an internal encounter in which one experiences authentic being. In this view, the objective truth and historical factuality of the biblical accounts are dispensable; yet contemporary hermeneutical ingenuity is considered able, in Pinnock's words, "to release the existential genie in the text, and to recreate for the reader that original encounter" of a noncognitive sort that the early Christians are alleged to have experienced.[43] To be sure, the transformation of the sinner and the experience of new creaturehood in Christ are indispensable aspects of NT realities. But not even these isolated facets of the biblical revelation can be authentically salvaged apart from valid revelational truth and the historical factuality of the redemptive work of God. The Bible is not the mystical context for an existential language-event, unless one obscures and distorts its enduring significance as a divinely inspired literary deposit in which the nature and content of divine revelation are authoritatively set forth in valid intelligible form.

D. *The Nature and Scope of Inspiration*

Inspiration is *that supernatural influence of the Holy Spirit whereby the sacred writers were divinely supervised in their production of Scripture, being restrained from error and guided in the choice of words they used, consistently with their disparate personalities and stylistic peculiarities.* God is the source of Holy Scripture; Christ Jesus is the central message; and the Holy Spirit, who inspired it and illumines its message to the reader, bears witness by this inscripturated Word to the Word enfleshed, crucified, risen, and returning.

Any survey of the divine plan of redemption must take note of the decisive role of the

---

[42]Beegle, *Scripture, Tradition, and Infallibility,* p. 38; cf. p. 48.
[43]Pinnock, "Inspiration of the New Testament," p. 146.

Scriptures. The Bible is the source of every article of the Christian faith and the sole judge of Christian doctrine and morals, and through its relationship to the Holy Spirit, it serves as a continuing means of grace. The written Word has held an authoritative significance from the earliest periods of the history of redemption. It is no mere addition to the revelation of God and his purposes, but integral to it. The divine saving activity did not consist only of special historical events and orally inspired utterances; it included also the provision of a written record of permanent importance, so that Scripture itself belongs to the pattern of God's revelation. Indeed, the content of divine revelation would itself be rendered intellectually imprecise in its continuing formulation were it not for the Scriptures. Only in view of divine inspiration is the Bible lifted above the relativities of history and entitled to priority over all words that are merely human.

Christianity is in one sense therefore undeniably a book religion. It has cherished from the outset a fixed verbal deposit of revelational truth. Jesus Christ and the apostles viewed written Scripture as divinely given (John 10:35), as produced by the Spirit of God (2 Peter 1:21), and as a provision in the form of a permanent literary record of information necessary to man's salvation (2 Tim 3:15). The prophetically promised Messiah, Jesus Christ, who himself possessed primary authority (Matt 7:27), designated and endowed chosen followers who through the Spirit would specially witness to his person and work (Matt 10:1; John 14:26; 16:13; Heb 2:3, 4). The NT canon, collected after the completion of the period of apostolic revelation, is comprised of Gospels and Epistles written during the apostolic age. (See the article THE CANON OF THE NEW TESTAMENT.) As the prophets were divinely chosen and called to communicate the nature and meaning of God's redemptive promise, so the apostles were moved by the Spirit to convey the sense and scope of its fulfillment in Jesus of Nazareth.

The biblical view that a divine activity accounts for the production of the sacred writings—in short, that Scripture is God-breathed—rules out any derivation of the Bible from a presumptively latent divinity immanent in man. It emphasizes rather a transcendent divine initiative and impulsion. Biblical inspiration is something other than a striking manifestation of artistic or poetic talent, far less an ecstatic or frenzied state or psychic seizure of some kind. In pagan usage the term referred primarily to the psychic state of the writer, concentrating on the notion of psychological possession more than on what was said or written (cf. Plato's dialogue *Ion: or, of the Iliad,* in which he speaks of poetic frenzy, *furor poeticus* in classical criticism). In biblical usage the term does not refer primarily to the person at all, but rather to the verbal end product or literary document. Warfield properly focused the two factors of biblical inspiration as concerned both with an internal activity and an outward result: "The Biblical writers are inspired . . . by the Holy Spirit so that the product of their activities transcends human powers and becomes Divinely authoritative."[44] The result of inspiration is that God's revelation is fully, permanently, and reliably committed to writing, assuring as a consequence the full trustworthiness of the prophetic-apostolic writings. The biblical view, moreover, is that all Scripture is divinely inspired—Scripture as a whole and in all parts looked at as parts of this whole. The notion of degrees of inspiration, a doctrine found in Philo and borrowed from Plato, has no support in the Bible.

Although Scripture is a divinely authoritative Word, it is misleading to speak, as some do, either of the divinity of Scripture or of the humanity of Scripture. That the Bible has

---

[44]B.B. Warfield, *The Inspiration and Authority of the Bible* (Philadelphia: Presbyterian and Reformed, 1948), p. 131.

more than human authority is not here questioned, nor that it also has distinctively human features. In view of this, some have called it a divine-human book, but this too is misleading, implying a *tertium quid* of sorts. No doubt an analogy of some kind prevails between the doctrine of the incarnation and that of inscripturation, involving at once the divine and the human,[45] yet the similarity must not be overdrawn. To argue from the God-man to a God-book does less than justice to the human element in the Bible. For good reason, evangelical Christianity rejects any reduction of the doctrine of scriptural inspiration to divine dictation. The incarnation is the sinless expression of one divine person in a human as well as a divine nature; inscripturation is the act of the divine Spirit as he superintends various fallible and sinful human persons in their inerrant oral and written expression of the truth of God consistently with their diverse personalities and stylistic peculiarities.

It must be kept in mind that the biblical writers do not aim to provide us with a textbook of modern science or history, or even a systematic exposition of moral philosophy or of theology in the usual modern understanding. That is not to say that the Scriptures are incapable of logical systematization, or that modern texts are objectively written, while Scripture is objectionably partisan; far from it. Few modern scholars would think of using a modern text more than a decade old in most fields because of the continuing need of revision, whereas a scholar in theology or religion who never uses the Bible is somewhat less than a scholar. All historical writing is selective and all science subject to change, because revision is a condition of the belief in scientific progress. But the Bible adduces relevant data that historians and scientists must reckon with if their accounts of the course of events and the nature of things are not to be oversimplified. The Bible is by no means a complete history, even of the Hebrews, nor does it aim to provide the details of physics, psychology, and other specialized disciplines. But scholars in these fields disregard what it teaches as doctrine bearing upon such areas only at the risk of developing arbitrarily truncated theories.

The biblical writers give us interpreted history. Indeed, all historical writing is interpreted, because every writer inevitably excludes certain events and includes others, and does so according to some evaluative principle or criterion. The redemptive acts and their meaning, on which the sacred writers concentrate, have objective grounding in God's revelational disclosure. The redemptive history is, to be sure, salvific not solely because of a personal faith-stance; the faith-stance is elicited by redemptive acts in the external world. The divine redemptive events are not self-interpreting, but their meaning is granted in God's special disclosure to chosen prophets and apostles.

That Jesus Christ was crucified is an historical event that some secular textbooks covering the history of that period of world affairs might consider too insignificant even to mention. But the Gospels correlate it, with the Incarnation and the Resurrection, as the most important event bearing on fallen human history. Moreover, that "Christ died for our sins" is not something derivable from sense observation. A casual observer might in fact be disposed to think that the Nazarene died as a moral culprit and culpable sinner. But "according to the Scriptures," the divinely inspired Word, the death of Jesus has an incomparable significance as a propitiation for the sins of the world.

The Bible does not aim to present a complete chronology of events, whether it deals with creation narrative or with salvation history, including incarnation history. But the stated purpose of the biblical writings is to give man all that is necessary and sufficient

---

[45]Cf. ISBE, s.v. "inspiration," an article by Warfield.

for his redemptive rescue and obedient service of his Maker. Though the biblical writers sometimes view the one saving work of God from various angles and for differing purposes, what they tell us is reliable and adequate. Matthew subordinates much of the chronology of the ministry of Jesus to a topical arrangement serviceable for instruction. Luke omits much of the material contained in Mark in what is still an orderly account that bulwarks catechetical indoctrination (cf. 1:4). John openly comments on the radical selectivity that underlies the fourth Gospel (20:30, 31).

Much can be learned from a study of literary forms. But negative form-criticism has no sound basis for its notion that the Gospel narratives are theological fabrications of historic fact designed to promote the apologetic interests of the apostolic community. Even its assumption that a long period intervened between the life and ministry of Jesus and the writing of the Gospels—an assumption that need not in and of itself establish their untrustworthiness in respect to historical data—has had to cope with a contrary tide of competent opinion in respect to dates of composition. Today it is widely conceded that all the NT writings could have been written during the lifetime of the apostles. Albright, for example, believed that all the NT books had been written by A.D. 80, and Robinson thinks all the canonical NT books were written before A.D. 70.[46] Many themes thought by critical scholars a few generations ago to constitute evidence of dependence on second-century religious or philosophical sources, and hence to attest a second-century origin, have been found also in the Dead Sea Scrolls. Some critics now argue for a very early dating for John's Gospel, albeit for the wrong reason of supposed literary dependence on the Essene writings. The lack of a long time span between the Gospel events and the written records argues for the integrity of the Gospels. Moreover, the absence of contrary writings challenging the apostolic accounts is significant. Also, one can hardly overstate the importance of the fact that the chief critic and persecutor of the early Christians, Saul of Tarsus, exchanged costly loyalties and wrote the earliest apostolic letters as a spokesman for Jesus Christ, not to Jewry only but to Gentiles as well.

That the Scriptures are set within the cultural context of their times, a milieu in many respects conspicuously different from our own, is now often made a basis for distrusting the verbal reliability of the Bible. The hermeneutical approach of much biblical exegesis today simply assumes that the present relevance of a text is not to be found in any permanently valid and objective meaning, but rather in an internal personal response whereby one comes existentially to trust God unreservedly. The insistence that all truth is culturally conditioned is, however, self-refuting nonsense. Were the claim true, not even this verdict could be taken as the transcultural truth. To be sure, the Spirit of God inspired the biblical writings over many centuries and in a considerable variety of cultural contexts. But what is precontemporary is not necessarily fallacious or unworthy. In fact, the most sophisticated moderns have shown themselves capable of believing amazing and even incredible myths, such as Nordic superiority, Negro inferiority, evolutionary utopianism, technocratic scientism, the coming Communist kingdom, and so on.

What the Bible teaches, sorted out at times into elements held to be specially ludicrous to a thinking modern—e.g., the virgin birth of Jesus—on the ground that the causal mechanism of the universe known to the contemporary scientist precludes such happenings, gains a very different prospect once it is realized that science in the twentieth

---

46William F. Albright, *From the Stone Age to Christianity*, 2nd ed. (New York: Doubleday, Anchor Books, 1957), p. 23 (cf. Albright interview, "Toward a More Conservative View," *Christianity Today*, January 18, 1963) p. 3; J.A.T. Robinson, *Redating the New Testament* (Philadelphia: Westminster, 1976), p. 10.

century makes no claim to tell us how nature is objectively constituted. On the contrary, it leaves such grandiose pronouncements to speculative gnostics who parade in the garb of science.

Exhibiting toward miracle a dogmatic hostility that many physical scientists now shun, some radically secular historians contend that a scholar violates his historical consciousness if he admits events in the past for which no analogy can be adduced in present-day experience. The covert assumption here is not merely that if God works miracles he must work them for contemporary doubting Thomases specializing in historical positivism under the pretense of scientific objectivity or that no once-for-all miracle can be acknowledged in the past unless it happens once again in the present (that is, happens twice-for-all, or, rather once-for-all-and-again for the secular historian). The assumption is also that the whole of nature and history (past, present, and future) is so pervaded by a comprehensive principle of determinism that no exception to its rigorous uniformity is possible or conceivable under any circumstances whatever. Say what one will about any scholar's right to philosophical presuppositions, one thing at least that cannot be claimed for such an approach as has just been described, however much it may defer to modernity, is the virtue of scientific humility. Nor does it do justice to what a genuine historical consciousness requires in probing the past. For the factuality of the bodily resurrection of Jesus Christ does not ultimately depend at all on historically observable factors in the twentieth century. It depends rather on historically decisive factors in the first century that even twentieth-century speculative biases cannot successfully undo.

Inspiration did not elevate the prophets untouchably above the cultural climate of their age, nor invest them with personal infallibility, any more than it endowed them with moral sinlessness. It requires a remarkable aloofness to objectivity, however, to disdain the ancients simply because they do not share modern prejudices and to assume implicitly that the contemporary critic is free of cultural indebtedness and more immune to limitations of knowledge than the ancients. The matter of inspiration aside, contemporary philosophy is not necessarily an improvement on ancient philosophy; indeed, not a few thinkers consider much of contemporary philosophy notably inferior to it and preoccupied with pseudoproblems. Not even modern science can claim to have the last word, or progress in science would be precluded. Though modern science has achieved striking advances in human comfort and convenience, it has not defined the essential nature and objective structure of the external world, nor can it do so. Moreover, it has placed new possibilities for evil into the hands of wicked men.

Nor did divine inspiration equip the biblical writers with a comprehensive explanation of the nature of things. Neither did it conceal hints of future scientific discoveries that would become apparent to the ingenious expositor of Scripture. It did, however, convey information serviceable in the formulation of a world-and-life view that does full justice to the nature, activity, and purposes of God in the cosmos, history, and life of man in society. What the biblical writers teach as doctrine is not to be dismissed as culture-conditioned speculation.

The language and idiom of people in all ages are culture conditioned, as are the secular conceptualities through which life is thought to hold meaning and worth. But basic thought forms have their ground in the image of God and man and are universal. Furthermore, revelation, instead of being a distillate of contemporary culture at its best, is divinely addressed to the reason of man and is transcultural. So prophetic inspiration did not abandon its recipients to the limitations of their own day, but rather, in superintendence of the biblical writers, preserved them from error and guided them in their choice of vocabulary to express the truth of God.

Pinnock lists some of the traits of human authorship in the Bible that evangelical scholars clearly recognize: a prescientific view of the world; lack of precision, judged by the criteria of a computer age; deliberate inclusion or exclusion of certain details in historical narration to register a special impact on the reader; the arrested time factor in eschatological teaching; citation of the OT from a variety of textual sources; use of rabbinic modes of argument; and differences of detail in some Gospel narratives.[47] Divine inspiration is not incompatible with such phenomena, which sometimes find their justification in the purpose of revelation, in the historical context, or in other factors.

One may agree with Bruce that a "Maginot-line mentality" is hardly an asset when it comes to the doctrine of Scripture, since it is God, not we ourselves, who is the Bible's supreme defense.[48] But neither will the cause of truth be served by a disregard for the laws of logic and a forfeiture of rational consistency in expounding religious knowledge. We must ask why modern critics tend to shrug off the notion of biblical infallibility as naive, and consider the scriptural statements about the authority of the Word to be devout but inaccurate religious sentiment. Embarrassed in the presence of the historic theological standards of their own denominations, they seek to substitute modern confessions of faith. In some cases, attracted by neo-Protestant notions of a "dynamic" rather than scriptural authority, that is, an authority allegedly rooted in the Spirit's direct internal confrontation, even some evangelical scholars have abandoned the effort to reconcile difficult Bible passages as a task requiring more energy than it is worth and have thrown in the sponge in respect to inerrancy. The consequence has often been an unstable view of religious authority, in which Scripture is inconsistently questioned in one paragraph and appealed to decisively in the next, without elaborating any persuasive principle for objectively discriminating what is to be accepted or rejected in its teaching.

Within a single decade Beegle was driven to revise or supplement numerous positions taken in his work on *The Inspiration of Scripture*, and in the later volume *Scripture, Tradition and Infallibility* (1973) he moves to strike a more positive note in behalf of biblically oriented Christians, while yet assimilating his views of Scripture to those of Roman Catholicism. The essential critical contention remains unchanged, however, that evangelicals should compromise their confidence in the inerrancy of the Bible and, with neoorthodox theologians, rely instead only on the Spirit to accomplish God's purpose through Scripture.

In the recent past, evangelical scholars have devoted more attention to textual phenomena with an eye to a reconciliation of apparently discordant or discrepant statements. If the task of evangelical theology is to expound what Scripture itself teaches in a progressive and systematic manner, the task of evangelical biblical studies must surely include a serious concern for reconciling textual phenomena with the textual teaching about inspiration.

Beegle emphasizes that "the best results are obtained when induction precedes deduction. . . . The message is not hidden or esoteric, and there is no need to have the aid of the Holy Spirit in the inductive process."[49] Yet Beegle proceeds immediately to the phenomena of Scripture, rather than to an inductive study of the teaching of Scripture about itself, and particularly to the high view of Scripture that Jesus had—the One of

---

[47]Pinnock, "Inspiration of the New Testament," p. 155.
[48]F.F. Bruce in foreword to Beegle, *Scripture, Tradition and Infallibility*, p. 8.
[49]Beegle, *Scripture, Tradition and Infallibility*, pp. 17, 18.

whom the Spirit witnesses. Jesus' view of Scripture and a limited number of critical phenomena are balanced against each other and, in view of unsolved difficulties, the conclusion is promulgated that the Bible is errant.

One recalls by way of contrast the comment of the renowned exegete Bishop H.C.G. Moule: "He [Christ] absolutely trusted the Bible, and, though there are in it things inexplicable and intricate that have puzzled me so much, I am going, not in a blind sense, but reverently to trust the Book because of *Him*."[50]

On the basis of fewer than a dozen difficulties that he prejudges to have involved autographic errors by the inspired writers, Beegle takes a position alien to that of Jesus and the apostles and of historic evangelical faith by denying the infallibility of Scripture. Gaebelein cautions that "the Christian who in his view of the Bible stands on any lower ground than that on which his Lord stood does so at his spiritual peril."[51] Gaebelein also remarks that "the attitude of suspended judgment toward Bible difficulties ... is constantly being vindicated, as archaeology has solved one Biblical problem after another, and as painstaking re-examination of discrepancies has finally led to answers."[52] On the bearing of archaeology on the Bible, he quotes Nelson Glueck, the distinguished Jewish archaeologist, as follows: "No archaeological discovery has ever been made that contradicts or controverts historical statements in Scripture."[53]

To impute error to the biblical writers is easy, but in the absence of logical contradiction it requires an infallible verdict (or infallible critic) to insist that reconciliation is absolutely impossible. Higher critics have an unenviable record of mistaken judgments hurriedly passed on the biblical narratives, though this is often unknown to contemporary readers because of the continuing revision of their texts and the failure of most contemporary critics to acknowledge the mistakes of the past. For examples of such mistakes, it was insisted that writing was unknown in Moses' day, that the Hittites were a grandiose construction of biblical imagination, and even that Jesus of Nazareth never lived—such verdicts being passed by respected scholars in leading universities, who were not on that account free from philosophical prejudice or immune from premature judgment.

Ramm indicates the factors that could serve to mitigate the apparent contraditions in so complex a matter as the resurrection appearances reported in the Gospels. The interpreter must take into account the meaning of the original language; the fact that the use of approximation, or of different schemes of reckoning, or textual corruption, might explain numerical contradictions; the possibility of the reader's misinterpretation of elements in the narrative; the risk of superficial identification of two similar events; the fact that one account may give the precise wording, and another merely the sense; and the possibility that the fuller account can explain a shorter one.[54]

If Scripture is God-breathed, so that the source of its doctrine and vitality is that same God who breathed into man "the breath of life" (Gen 2:7), the biblical critic has reason for sobriety in whatever verdicts he pronounces on it. By no means is this said in order to forestall the legitimate tasks of scholarly investigation. But in the presence of a divine initiative, man's initial response is properly one of awe, of listening with wonder to a

---

[50] J.B. Harford and F.C. MacDonald, *The Life of Bishop Moule* (London: Hodder & Stoughton, 1922), p. 138.
[51] Frank E. Gaebelein, "The Unity of the Bible," in *Revelation and the Bible*, ed. C.F.H. Henry (Grand Rapids: Baker, 1967), p. 398.
[52] Ibid., p. 397.
[53] The *New York Times* "Book Review," (October 28, 1956).
[54] Bernard Ramm, *Protestant Biblical Interpretation*, 1950 (Grand Rapids: Baker, n.d.).

heartbeat and pulsebeat that would not otherwise have come into being, of hearing what the Spirit would say to and through his amazing production. The theologian or exegete is not to decide in advance, in view of a prevalent historical consciousness or cultural conceptuality, what the Spirit may say or must have said. For what the Spirit of God says may deliberately crisscross the presuppositions of the modern age, however pridefully held. The critic's inescapable duty is to comprehend God's Word as given in the biblical revelation, not to garner the enthusiasm of contemporary man.

The proper beginning of responsible exegesis is therefore the free subordination of all human thought and conviction to the biblical revelation. The biblical disclosure, given in verbal form, is to challenge and criticize all our conceptions. Not that we are asked to measure our own views by the thoughts and ideas of ancient prophets and apostles. Instead, we are summoned to know the teaching of chosen and inspired witnesses who had similarly to bring their own prejudices to a halt and whom God has authorized and empowers to express his very own Word. Barth remarks, "Scriptural exegesis rests on the assumption that the message which scripture has to give us, even in its apparently most debatable and least assimilable parts, is in all circumstances truer and more important than the best and most necessary things that we ourselves have said or can say."[55] One may go even further. Biblical exegesis rests on the assumption that here alone divine inspiration has given us the veritable Word of God by which all that a person says and does will stand or fall in the judgment. Hence the exhortation in one of Jesus' parables: "They have Moses and the Prophets; let them listen to them" (Luke 16:29), anticipated by the prophet Isaiah: "To the law and to the testimony! If they do not speak according to this word, they have no light of dawn" (Isa 8:20).

This writer believes that nobody has successfully answered Warfield's delineation of the logical alternatives involved in the acceptance or rejection of the apostolic doctrine of biblical inspiration. In a chapter on "The Real Problem of Inspiration," Warfield emphasized that if one restricts the divine authority of biblical teaching, he not only rejects the biblical testimony to the plenary inspiration of Scripture, but also undermines the trustworthiness of the apostles.[56] The consequence is that no persuasive case can then be made for any preferred segment of the content of Scripture.

Warfield analyzes the four main formulas on which critics have relied to expound a broken or partial authority for NT teaching: (1) Christ's teaching versus apostolic teaching, (2) apostolic accommodation or ignorance versus apostolic beliefs, (3) apostolic opinion versus apostolic teaching, and (4) Scriptural phenomena versus apostolic doctrine.

The emphasis on the superior reliability of Christ's teaching over that of the apostles must come to terms with the facts that we do not have Christ's teaching except in apostolically attested writings and that the Christ of the Bible is committed to the trustworthiness of the apostles as teachers. If the apostles are untrustworthy as teachers of doctrine, their portrait of Jesus cannot be salvaged.

If apostolic teaching on inspiration is viewed as an accommodation to the then-prevailing Jewish culture and is contrasted with the actual personal beliefs of the apostles, the difficulties are no less staggering. On one hand it cannot be shown that the apostles held their doctrine of inspiration merely as a cultural accommodation. If it is implied, moreover, that wherever the apostles agreed with what their Jewish contempo-

---

[55] Karl Barth, *Church Dogmatics*, I, 1 (Edinburgh, T & T Clark, 1936), p. 719.
[56] Warfield, *Inspiration and Authority of the Bible*, pp. 169ff.

raries believed they are not to be considered trustworthy, then their writings could be authoritative only where they teach novelties. Worse yet, the veracity of the apostles is impugned if they imputed a divine quality to their own writings simply to project divine reinforcement for their own ideas. An appeal to apostolic ignorance as an alternative to an accommodation to culture is of little help, even if it seeks to preserve moral integrity by denying that the apostles intentionally claimed divine authority for what they knew to be untrue. A separation of apostolic teaching into two parts, true and false, on the basis of supposed apostolic ignorance, cannot anywhere escape the consequences of undermining their trustworthiness.

The contrast of apostolic opinion with apostolic teaching likewise creates insuperable problems if it is intended to shed light on their promulgation of the concept of inspiration. It has been argued that the apostles personally believed the high view of inspiration, but did not teach it as doctrine. But the inclusion in the apostolic writings of didactic passages expounding the full authority of Scripture (e.g., 2 Tim 3:16), contradicts this. On the basis of what accessible sources are we to discriminate apostolic opinions from express teaching in the apostolic writings? That the apostles were personally fallible and as ordinary men wrote letters unrelated to their apostolic office is unquestionable. But that is another matter from the letters the apostles addressed to the churches as divinely authoritative through the special revelational and inspirational work of the Spirit. If in 1 Corinthians 7:6, 12 the apostle Paul distinguishes personal opinion from inspired teaching—which is not the only possible view of the passage—he differentiates rather than merges the two. But even here the emphasis indicates that, in distinction from any specific commandment directly attributable to Jesus' teaching (7:10), Paul is conveying inspired apostolic teaching, which he places on the same level of authority as the teaching of Jesus and adduces as apostolically given in his name. If the apostles held certain opinions that some critics have even labeled blasphemous (e.g., that their writings are God's Word), how can the apostles be considered authoritative religious teachers? Quite apart from this, if we are to regard as untrustworthy their underlying assumptions and fundamental conceptions, how can their doctrinal teaching be isolated and exalted as trustworthy?

The emphasis that certain biblical phenomena contravene the apostolic doctrine of inspiration, and hence are decisive for our understanding of that doctrine, is one that we have discussed earlier. The doctrine of the apostles is to be decided not by inferences from the character of the text as a matter of coequal determination, but by responsible exegesis of the apostolic teaching itself. For the character of the text can be variously contemplated according to the assumptions with which scholars approach it. The insistence that the textual data contradict the apostles' teaching on Scripture destroys not only their doctrine of inspiration, but their reliability as teachers of doctrine.

Mediating evangelical thinkers have sought, in view of concessions to criticism, to limit the infallibility of Scripture to doctrinal matters, while forfeiting any claim to their infallibility in respect to historical or scientific matters. But this ploy—which professes to champion infallibility while in fact compromising it—is wholly implausible. Scripture does not make this contrast in its comprehensive claim to divine inspiration, and the God of truth (Isa 65:16) could not have inspired error. The church father Tertullian properly asked why men should trust Scripture concerning invisible realities if it is declared to be unreliable concerning testable data (history and nature). Although not a few details in the Bible are indeed of an incidental nature, Scripture nevertheless contains some central affirmations about history and the cosmos that are integral to the doctrines of sin and redemption.

Whether one speaks of older liberals or of neoliberals, there is, as Runia notes, "hardly any place left for inspiration" in their views. As neo-Protestants have weakened this doctrine, their theology has become chaotic confusion. If it retains vitality, it lacks stability. "They are willing to allow for some kind of illumination, but ... of the same nature as that which all believers receive. It may be a little 'higher' or 'stronger', but ... [it is] only a difference of degree. Of the Bible itself one can only say that it is inspired because it inspires ... a subjective concept."[57] Neoorthodox theologians seek to rise above these limitations, yet also reject the historic view that the biblical writings *are* the Word of God; rather, it is held, they "become" the Word of God when and as and if the reader hears and submits to the divine Spirit speaking through them. "While the liberal subjectivizes and relativizes inspiration, the neoorthodox actualizes it. It is something that happens again and again."[58]

But, as Bromiley insists, the inspiration—that is, the "inspiredness"—of Scripture "is part of the essence of Christianity. To confess it is part of being a Christian. ... Scripture proclaims its own inspiration as part of what it says about God the Holy Spirit."[59] To maintain silence about the doctrine of inspiration is therefore in effect to minimize the ministry of the Spirit. Bromiley emphasizes that "any work of the Spirit is a breathing, a 'spiration,' and the Spirit's ongoing work must not be denied as a vital aspect of a divine ministry." But "in an important sense inspiration, like Christ's atonement, is a finished work. The breathing took place in history, on the authors."[60]

In the Roman Catholic Church's *Dogmatical Constitution on Revelation,* Vatican II declared, "The divinely revealed realities, which are contained and present in the text of sacred Scripture, have been written down under the inspiration of the Holy Spirit." The Roman Church, "relying on the faith of the apostolic age, accepts as sacred and canonical the books of the Old and New Testaments, whole and entire, with all their parts, on the grounds that, written under the inspiration of the Holy Spirit (cf. John 20:31; 2 Tim 3:16; 2 Peter 1:19–21; 3:15, 16), they have God as their author, and have been handed on as such to the Church herself." To be sure, Rome greatly restricts and even nullifies the authority of Scripture by correlating it with oral tradition and with that church's teaching function as the seat of infallible interpretation. Also its inclusion of apocryphal books in the canon remains unacceptable to evangelical Protestants. Rome thus provided a precedent for liberal theology, which set other factors alongside Scripture in formulating the doctrine of authority. In the case of liberalism, not merely tradition and the church hierarchy in its teaching office, but culture, experience, and philosophical reasoning were considered sources of revelation.

If one interprets Scripture according to its own nature, standards, and purpose, there is no need whatever to hesitate in affirming its infallibility both in respect to dynamic efficacy and factual truth. The word of man is fallible, carrying no absolute assurance of fulfillment of what man says and deriving its truth from a reason higher than that man himself says this or that is so. With the Word of God it is otherwise. God is himself the Truth, and his Word never falters. One cannot, to be sure, demonstrate the inspiration of the Bible by a running appeal to its infallibility, since historical and scientific verification are never absolute and do not go beyond probability. One can refute the charge of pervasive unreliability, but in the nature of the case cannot provide a comprehensive

---

[57]Klaas Runia, "What Do Evangelicals Say About the Bible?" *Christianity Today* (December 4, 1970), p. 6.
[58] Ibid.
[59]Bromiley, "Inspiration and Authority of Scripture," p. 12.
[60]Ibid., p. 14.

demonstration of infallibility. The logical dependence is the other way around: divine inspiration assures the inerrancy of what God inspires.

Assuredly, the inspired accounts exhibit a variety of literary genres—poetry, prophecy, parable, history, Gospels, letters, and so on—though there is no evidence that myth is an ancient form that the biblical writers employed to convey what assertedly cannot be rationally conceived or sensually experienced, or to effect an existential encounter. Certainly one cannot turn poetry or parable into objective history and insist on its factual reliability. Likewise, one cannot impose on an earlier era the requirements of mathematical exactitude common to our day. Nor is the Bible to be declared unscientific because it speaks of the sun "rising," using the language of ordinary sense experience as even learned men do in our times. But whoever approaches Scripture on its own terms and in view of its own claims will avoid that arbitrary reduction of the factual so characteristic of the modern mind now widely and uncritically given over to empirical scientism and historical positivism.

IV. Bibliography

Beegle, Dewey M. *Scripture, Tradition and Infallibility.* Grand Rapids: Eerdmans, 1973.

Bender, Harold S. *Biblical Revelation and Inspiration.* Scottsdale, Penn.: Mennonite, 1959.

Berkouwer, G.C. *Modern Uncertainty and Christian Faith.* Grand Rapids: Eerdmans, 1953.

Clark, Gordon H. *Religion, Reason and Revelation.* Philadelphia: Presbyterian and Reformed, 1961.

Dodd, C.H. *The Authority of the Bible.* London: Nisbet, 1952.

Harris, R. Laird. *The Inspiration and Canonicity of the Bible.* Grand Rapids: Zondervan, 1957.

Henry, Carl F.H., ed. *Revelation and the Bible.* Grand Rapids: Baker, 1958.

Johnson, Robert C. *Authority in Protestant Theology.* Philadelphia: Westminster, 1959.

Packer, James I. *Fundamentalism and the Word of God.* London: Inter-Varsity, 1958.

Preuss, Robert. *The Inspiration of Scripture.* Edinburgh: Oliver and Boyd, 1955.

Ramm, Bernard. *The Pattern of Authority.* Grand Rapids: Eerdmans, 1957.

Robinson, H. Wheeler. *Inspiration and Revelation in the Old Testament.* Oxford: Clarendon, 1946.

Runia, Klaas. *Karl Barth's Doctrine of Holy Scripture.* Grand Rapids: Eerdmans, 1962.

Tenney, Merrill C. *The Bible—The Living Word of Revelation.* Grand Rapids: Zondervan, 1968.

Van Til, Cornelius. *In Defense of the Faith.* Vol. 1, *The Doctrine of Scripture.* Den Dulk Christian Foundation, 1967.

Walvoord, John F. *Inspiration and Interpretation.* Grand Rapids: Zondervan, 1957.

Warfield, B.B. *The Inspiration and Authority of the Bible.* Philadelphia: Presbyterian and Reformed, 1948.

Young, E.J. *Thy Word Is Truth.* Grand Rapids: Eerdmans, 1957.

TRANSMISSION AND TRANSLATION OF THE BIBLE

F.F. Bruce

F.F. Bruce

M.A., Universities of Aberdeen, Cambridge, Manchester; D.D., University of Aberdeen
F.B.A. (Fellow of the British Academy)

Rylands Professor of Biblical Criticism and Exegesis (Emeritus), The University of Manchester

TRANSMISSION AND TRANSLATION OF THE BIBLE

F.F. Bruce

I. Old Testament

A. *Transmission*

1. *Early period.* We are scantily informed on the transmission of the preexilic parts of the OT. The direction in Deuteronomy 31:9ff., 26, that "the book of the law" was to be put by the side of the ark of the covenant and read publicly every seventh year at the Feast of Tabernacles indicates one form of preservation and transmission; the discovery of "the book of the law in the house of the LORD" in 621 B.C. (2 Kings 22:8) is relevant here. The oracles of at least some of the prophets were preserved by their disciples. Isaiah's earlier oracles, for example, were committed to writing and entrusted to his disciples for safekeeping until they should be fulfilled and the prophet vindicated (Isa 8:16). We are given exceptionally full details of the first two editions of the oracles of

39

Jeremiah: when in 605 B.C. Baruch wrote down at the prophet's dictation the oracles delivered during the first twenty-two years of his ministry, and read them aloud next year at a public gathering, King Jehoiakim cut up the scroll and burned it (Jer 36:1–26). But a second and enlarged edition, similarly written by Baruch at Jeremiah's dictation, quickly followed (Jer 36:27–32). Even that was not the last edition of the oracles of Jeremiah, for he continued to prophesy for some seventeen years more, and the edition reproduced in our common versions of the OT includes many of his later oracles, with further biographical data supplied by Baruch. This is not the only edition including his later oracles that has come down to our day; we also have a rather shorter one in a Hebrew MS from Qumran Cave 4 and in the LXX.

It is something of a miracle that so much earlier material survived the Babylonian exile. Those psalms, for example, that had figured in preexilic worship remained unsung for two generations while the temple lay in ruins. Yet, even if the exiles could not "sing the LORD's song in a foreign land" (Ps 137:4), they did not forget the familiar words, and in due course they were reincorporated into the postexilic psalter and sung in the second temple.

Critical moments in the transmission of the sacred writings in the postexilic period are Ezra's mission to Jerusalem with the law of his God in his hand (Ezra 7:14) and the public reading of "the book of the law of Moses" in Jerusalem during the Feast of Tabernacles in (apparently) the first year of Nehemiah's governorship (Neh 8:1–18). References to "the former prophets" (Zech 1:4 et al.) may imply a written corpus of preexilic prophetic oracles soon after the return from exile.

A later threat to the transmission of the sacred writings came with the persecution under Antiochus IV (c. 167 B.C.), when his officials tore up and burned "the books of the law" that they found and executed those Jews who were caught with such books in their possession (1 Macc 1:56f.). Fortunately, the persecution lasted only three years, and when it was over, copies of the Scriptures could be procured from Jewish communities outside Judaea.

2. *Evidence from Qumran.* The earliest biblical MSS now available to us are those from the Qumran caves, which came to light in 1947 and the following years (cf. article on THE DEAD SEA SCROLLS by William S. LaSor). They belong for the most part to the period between the end of the persecution under Antiochus IV and c. A.D. 70. They represent three main types of Hebrew text: (1) the ancestor of the later Masoretic text, perhaps emanating from the Jewish community in Babylonia; (2) that from which the LXX was translated, having therefore Egyptian associations; (3) so far as the Pentateuch is concerned, a text of Samaritan type, without the sectarian readings of the Samar. Bible, probably a popular Palestinian text. In addition to MSS that exhibit one or another of these text types, we have others that exhibit a mixed text, or a form of text not otherwise identifiable. It is particularly interesting to find Hebrew MSS containing readings previously known only from the LXX version, like the two Isaiah MSS from Cave 1 that have the noun *light* as the object to the verb *see* in Isaiah 53:11. Plainly there was a greater variety of Heb. texts current in Palestine before A.D. 70 than afterwards. The biblical texts from Murabba'āt, to be dated a couple of generations after A.D. 70, are exclusively of "proto-Masoretic" type.

3. *Masoretic Text.* The reason for this uniformity was the establishment of one standard form of Hebrew text by Rabbi Aqiba and his colleagues, c. A.D. 100. Henceforth (apart from the Samaritan Pentateuch) no other text of the Hebrew Bible is attested. This is

the text quoted in the Mishnah, the Talmud, and other rabbinical compilations; this is the text underlying the Targums, the Peshitta, and the Vulgate. This is the text that the Masoretes, from the sixth century A.D. onwards, equipped with an apparatus of points, accents, and marginal notes, recording the tradition (*masorah*) of the vocalization, punctuation, and interpretation of the consonantal script.

Samples of the work of the earliest Masoretes were preserved in the *genizah* or store-room of the ancient "Ezra Synagogue" in Fustat (Old Cairo), the contents of which came to light late in the nineteenth century. There were schools of Masoretes at work in both Babylonia and Palestine; the school whose method was ultimately adopted was that of Tiberias in Palestine. The *genizah* samples are fragmentary; apart from them our oldest Masoretic MSS belong to the end of the ninth century and the following decades. A codex of the Prophets in the Qaraite synagogue of Cairo was completed in 895; a codex of the Pentateuch in the British Museum is only a few years younger. Until 1948 the synagogue at Aleppo contained an early tenth-century codex of the whole Hebrew Bible. In the troubles of that and ensuing years, it suffered some damage, but it is now in Israel, where it is being used as a basis of the Hebrew University Bible Project. The Leningrad collection of Hebrew MSS includes a codex of the Latter Prophets of date 916 and a codex of the complete OT dated 1008, which has been used as the basis for Kittel's *Biblia Hebraica* from the third edition (1937) onwards. Only a few years younger is an almost complete codex of the Hebrew Bible in the Bodleian Library, Oxford.

Most of these codices represent the text edited by the Ben Asher family of Tiberias. The Ben Asher edition is reproduced also in a group of British Museum MSS used by Norman H. Snaith for the British and Foreign Bible Society's new edition of the Hebrew Bible (1958).

4. Samaritan Bible. A distinct ed. of the Hebrew Pentateuch has been preserved by the Samaritans. As has been said, this is essentially a popular Palestinian text, with several additions and alterations designed to vindicate the Samaritans' claim to be the true Israel, with Gerizim, not Zion, as the place chosen by the LORD to be a dwelling for his name (Deut 12:5).

The earliest MSS of the Samaritan Bible proper are some centuries younger than the earliest Masoretic MSS. The oldest known cod. of the Samaritan Bible (that is, a MS of folios and pages, as distinct from a scroll) bears a note indicating that it was in existence by A.D. 1149–50. The most famous Samaritan MS is the Abisha scroll, so called because it reproduces a colophon claiming to be the work of Abisha, great-grandson of Aaron (cf. 1 Chron 6:4f.); actually it comprises two MSS: an older one from Numbers 35 to Deuteronomy 34 and a later one (fourteenth century) from Genesis 1 to Numbers 34.

B. *Translation*

1. Septuagint. Most important of all the translations of the OT is the pre-Christian Greek version called the Septuagint (LXX) because of the legend that it was produced by seventy (or seventy-two) Jewish elders at the behest of Ptolemy II, king of Egypt (285–246 B.C.). This legend is told in the *Letter of Aristeas,* a work probably written c. 100 B.C. to enhance the prestige of the already-existing Greek version of the Pentateuch. This version of the Pentateuch was made at the instance of the Jewish leaders in Alexandria, Egypt, for the benefit of the Greek-speaking Jewish community in that city. A Greek version of the Pentateuch was particularly necessary for synagogue use; the translation of the remaining books of the OT seems to have been carried through more informally. The oldest known MS of the LXX is a fragmentary papyrus of Deuteronomy 25–28 in the John Rylands University Library, Manchester, of date c. 150 B.C. From the same century comes another papyrus fragment of the Gr. Deuteronomy in Cairo. The Qumran and neighboring caves have also yielded several LXX fragments. With these exceptions, all the LXX MSS that have come down to us were copied and preserved by Christians, not Jews. When the Hebrew text of Scripture was standardized c. A.D. 100, a version based on another type of text was no longer acceptable; moreover, the LXX seemed to lend itself too readily to Christian interpretation. A new Gr. version by Aquila was therefore approved for Jewish use early in the second century A.D. It was an extremely literal translation. Later in the same century a more idiomatic translation was produced by Theodotion. Later still, a Jewish Christian of the Ebionite party, named Symmachus, produced yet another Greek version of the OT; and further Greek versions of some books were in circulation.

The LXX translation is of unequal competence. As might be expected, the Pentateuch was treated with special care. Much of the translation is an attempt at a word-for-word rendering, but in parts we are presented with an interpretative paraphrase, bringing the text into conformity with current religious and ethical attitudes.

The importance of the LXX lies partly in its being based on a pre-Christian Hebrew text of a different type from the Masoretic, and partly on its having been the Bible of Greek-speaking Christians from early apostolic days. This is the version in which the OT is most commonly quoted in the NT, and many of the theological terms in the NT bear the meaning they had in the LXX rather than in pagan Greek usage.

The Christian MSS of the LXX are mostly codices of the Greek Bible, in which the LXX and the Greek NT are bound together. The Chester Beatty biblical collection includes seven papyrus codices of various parts of the LXX (second and third centuries A.D.). The great uncial codices Vaticanus and Sinaiticus (later fourth century A.D.) included, when complete, the whole LXX, with the "apocryphal" books in addition to those appearing in the Hebrew Bible. The same is true of two famous fifth-century MSS: the Codex Alexandrinus (A) in London and the palimpsest Codex of Ephraem (C) in Paris. Over 2,000 MSS of the LXX have been cataloged. It remains to this day the officially approved version of the OT in the Greek Orthodox Church.

2. *Aramaic Targums.* When in Nehemiah 8:8 the Law is said to have been read "with an interpretation," the meaning may be that it was read in Hebrew and translated orally into Aramaic, the vernacular of many of the people. If so, we have here the first recorded instance of the provision of a *targum* ("translation")—a provision that was to become regular in the synagogues of Aramaic-speaking Jews in Palestine and Mesopotamia. While the *targum* was oral at first, it was not infrequently written down for use outside the synagogue. An Aramaic *targum* of Job has been identified among the scrolls from Cave 11 at Qumran; this could be the work of which another copy was built into the temple wall at the instance of Gamaliel. A Palestinian Targum on the Pentateuch has been preserved in its entirety in a Vatican MS (Neofiti 1); its language is Palestinian Aramaic of the first century A.D., such as Jesus might have spoken. The two official Targums are later: they are the Targum of Onqelos on the Pentateuch and the Targum of Jonathan on the Prophets. There are others also in addition to these.

These Targums are not literal translations but interpretative paraphrases; they include a good deal of traditional and homiletic material.

3. *Peshitta.* The Syriac version of the Bible is called the *Peshitta* or "simple" version.

Syriac is a form of Aramaic, and the Peshitta OT presents several of the features of the Aramaic Targums. It may have been produced in the latter part of the first century A.D.; although it is based on the standard Hebrew text, there is evidence that it has been influenced at some stage in its transmission by the LXX.

4. *Vulgate.* The older Latin versions of the OT were translations of the LXX. It was Jerome who, between 386 and his death in 405, first translated the OT direct from Hebrew into Latin. His version, together with the companion NT part of the work, is traditionally known as the Vulgate or "common" version. Like the Peshitta, the Vulgate is based on the standard Hebrew text, but reflects a stage in the history of that text considerably earlier than the Masoretic period. It has therefore some value for the textual criticism of the OT; for example, it goes along with the Samaritan text and the LXX and Peshitta versions in preserving Cain's words to Abel in Gen 4:8, "Let us go into the field" (or "Let us go outside"). Although Jerome translated the Hebrew Psalter with the rest of the OT, the Psalter that continued to be used by the Latin-speaking church was one based on the LXX. Otherwise, Jerome's work superseded the older Latin versions, and formed the basis for translations into all other Western European languages until the sixteenth century.

II. New Testament

A. *Transmission*

The NT documents were all written in Greek within the first century. Some transmission of individual documents took place before they began to be collected together. When, however, early in the second century the fourfold Gospel and the Pauline corpus began to circulate as two collections, it was mainly as collections that they were transmitted from then on. Somewhat later, Acts and the catholic Epistles were commonly collected in a single codex; Revelation occupied a slim codex by itself.

The earliest surviving MSS of the NT belong to the second century. The oldest is a fragment of a papyrus codex of John 18 (P^{52}) in the John Rylands University Library, Manchester, to be dated c. A.D. 130. It is too small to be used for textual criticism; its main value is its witness to an early date for John. More substantial are some NT papyri in the Bodmer Library, Geneva, from the late second and early third centuries: a codex of John (P^{66}), another containing the latter part of Luke and the first thirteen or fourteen chapters of John (P^{75}), and yet another that is our oldest witness to the Greek text of 1 and 2 Peter and Jude (P^{72}). The Chester Beatty biblical papyri in Dublin include three NT codices: the Gospels and Acts (P^{45}), ten Pauline letters and Hebrews (P^{46}), and Revelation (P^{47}), also from the late second and third centuries.

Mention was made above of the great codices containing the complete Greek Bible. Some of them are of special importance in the history of the NT text—outstandingly so the Vatican codex in Rome (B; 03) and the Sinaitic codex in the British Museum (א; 01). These are written on parchment and in the capital letters called uncials (in the numerical list of NT MSS uncials are given numbers beginning with 0). The two MSS named are the chief representatives of the Alexandrian type of text. From the fourth century onwards we can distinguish types of NT text associated with various geographical centers or areas: Alexandria, Caesarea, Antioch, and the West. These text types cannot be traced back to the beginning of our MS tradition; most of the second-century papyri cannot be assigned to one or another of them, although shortly after the discovery of P[45] the text of Mark that it contains was found to be Caesarean in type. The Alexandrian type is the result of a careful and scholarly revision of the text and, although it cannot be equated without more ado with the text of the first century, as B.F. Westcott and F.J.A. Hort were disposed to do,[1] yet it probably approaches it more closely than any other early text type. It is represented by a number of other MSS and by the Coptic versions.

The Caesarean text type is represented not only by Mark in P[45] and in the uncials Theta (038) and W (032), but by NT citations in some of Origen's works and in the writings of Cyril of Jerusalem and also by certain early versions, notably the Old Georgian. The Antiochian text type has not been identified in any Greek MS, but it is the name given to the Greek text from which the Old Syriac (pre-Peshitta) versions of the Gospels were translated.

The Western text type was widely spread and in modern textual criticism it has been the most serious rival of the Alexandrian text as a witness to the first-century text. In the Gospels and Acts it is most signally attested by the bilingual (Graeco-Latin) codex of Beza (D; 05), dating from the fifth or sixth century and housed in Cambridge University Library. This codex is one of a group containing the text of the Gospels and Acts; there is a similar group of Graeco-Latin MSS exhibiting the Western text of the Pauline Epistles. The Western text is marked by additions and amplifications, which are almost certainly editorial, even if some are based on sound tradition or local knowledge. In the Gospels it omits, however, some few passages present in the other text types; these omitted passages were called by WH "Western non-interpolations" and regarded as unauthentic—but on inadequate grounds. The OL (pre-Vulgate) versions of the NT, particularly that circulating in the Roman province of Africa, attested both in a number of MSS and in citations in the works of Latin fathers, are also Western in textual character.

The witnesses to the Greek NT text are commonly classified as MSS in Greek, early versions in other languages, and citations in early Christian writers. The MSS run to well over 5,000 in all, containing either part or the whole of the NT. Even after the invention of printing in Western Europe in the middle of the fifteenth century, the production of NT MSS continued into the next century. The great majority of the MSS are medieval, and exhibit what is commonly called the Byzantine type of text. This is based on a fourth-century revision of the Greek text, incorporating features from most of the already existing text types. The revision aimed at producing a smoother and more lucid text, at combining variants from two or more text types, and at harmonizing parallel passages. It was probably produced in Syria, but from the late fourth century onward it was disseminated from Constantinople or Byzantium, the new eastern capital of the Roman Empire, whence it has come to be known as the Byzantine text. Since it appears in most of the later MSS, it is reproduced also in the earliest printed editions of the Gr. NT, and so is the parent of the Textus Receptus ("Received Text" [TR]). This expression was used by the Leiden printing house of Elzevir in 1633, to commend the second edition of its Greek NT, and has come to be used of the text of the early printed editions in general.

---

[1] *The New Testament in the Original Greek* (Cambridge and London, 1881-2).

B. Translation: Early Versions

As has been said, the versions in various Coptic dialects were based on Greek MSS exhibiting the Alexandrian type of text, while the surviving OS texts reflected a hypothetical Greek text tentatively associated with Antioch. There are two important MSS of the OS Gospels: the fifth-century Curetonian MS (so called after William Cureton, who discovered it in Egypt in 1847) and the fourth-century Sinaitic Syriac palimpsest, discovered in 1892 by Agnes Smith Lewis in the library of St. Catharine's Monastery on Sinai (where the Greek Codex Sinaiticus [ℵ] was discovered by Constantine von Tischendorf in 1844). Another form in which the Gospels were available in Syriac in the early centuries A.D. was the *Diatessaron*, a rearrangement of the material in the four Gospels so as to form one continuous narrative, compiled by Tatian (c. 170). So popular was this compilation among Syriac Christians that it was with great difficulty that Rabbula, bishop of Edessa 411–435, replaced it by a revised Syriac NT in which the Gospels were restored to their separated form. This revision, the NT part of the Peshitta, was based on the Byzantine Greek text.

The OL version of the NT first appeared in the province of Africa (modern Tunisia and Algeria) before A.D. 200, and some decades later in Western Europe. While the African OL version was of the Western text type, the European OL shows the influence of Greek MSS of Alexandrian type. It was on the basis of good European OL MSS, corrected with the aid of Greek MSS, that the Vulgate NT was produced. The Vulgate Gospels were revised by Jerome in 384, as the first part of the task of producing a standard Lat. text of the Bible, imposed on him by Damasus, bishop of Rome, whose secretary he was. As for the rest of the Vulgate NT, it is usually believed that this also was the work of Jerome, but that here his revision was carried out with a lighter touch. It is maintained, however, by Dom Bonifatius Fischer and his colleagues at the Abbey of Beuron, Germany, who are engaged on a new and magnificent edition of the OL Bible, that the revision of the Vulgate NT apart from the Gospels was done by someone other than Jerome.

III. The Bible

A. The Manuscript Period

The replacement of the scroll form of book by the codex, at the beginning of the Christian era, made it possible to include a much larger body of literature within one volume. Whereas one of the longer NT books, such as Luke or Acts, represents about as much writing as could be accommodated in a scroll of normal length in the first century, a codex could quite conveniently contain all four Gospels, or even the whole NT, or (later still) both Testaments together. We have seen that the great uncial codices contained the complete Greek Bible. The first complete codex of the Latin Bible of which we hear was in the library of Cassiodorus in the sixth century.

The most reliable surviving MS of the whole Vulgate Bible is the Codex Amiatinus, so called because it was housed at one time in the monastery library of Monte Amiata, Italy, whence it made its way to the Laurentian Library in Florence, where it still is. In origin it was one of three complete copies of the Vulgate Bible made in the north of England by command of Ceolfrid, abbot of the twin monasteries of Jarrow and Wearmouth, at the beginning of the eighth century. This copy was taken from England to

Rome and presented to Pope Gregory II in 716. It was based on a master copy brought to England from South Italy.

In its earlier days, the Vulgate text was copied so frequently by men who had been brought up on the OL version that its wording became quite contaminated with OL readings. Successive revisions were therefore undertaken to remove these OL readings. One such revision was the work of Cassiodorus; the Codex Amiatinus reflects its influence. Other revisions were undertaken about A.D. 800 by Alcuin of York, a scholar attached to the court of Charlemagne at Aachen, and by Theodulf of Orleans. A later revision carried out in the thirteenth century by scholars of the University of Paris formed the basis of the earliest printed editions of the Vulgate.

The first Bible translation into a language of the Germanic family (the family to which English belongs) was the Gothic Bible, translated from Greek into the language of the Ostrogoths on the lower Danube in the second half of the fourth century. The translater was Ulfilas, bishop of the Goths, member of a Christian family of Cappadocia that had been taken captive by the Goths in the previous century. The NT part of the Gothic Bible was of Byzantine type. So was the NT part of the Slavonic Bible, translated from Greek in the ninth century by Cyril, one of two missionaries from Thessalonica who were invited by Rostislav, founder of the Moravian Empire in East-Central Europe, to direct the Christian life of his realm.

During the Middle Ages a number of Bible versions based on the Latin Vulgate appeared in Western and Central Europe. Some of these were produced as part of the widespread activity of the Waldensians. There are two Provençal versions (one in French Provençal and one in Piedmontese), and associated in some way with these is a Catalan version. A German version of the NT was made from Provençal in the fourteenth century, and had a considerable circulation until it was superseded by Luther's version in 1522. The same century saw a translation of the NT in the Czech language. All these medieval versions reflect a form of the Latin text current in Southeast France, which included several OL readings of Western type.

B. *The English Bible in the Manuscript Period*

When the Germanic people (Jutes, Saxons, Angles) first came to Britain in the fifth century, they were pagans. They brought with them their dialects, of which West Saxon became the Standard Old English. The Romano-Britons whom they dispossessed were Christians, using the Latin Bible. The evangelization of the English began at the end of the sixth century; the beginnings of Bible translation into English date from the seventh century. These beginnings took the form of verse paraphrases of the Bible story, the work of Caedmon of Whitby and others. An Old English translation of the Psalter is said to have been made by Aldhelm, bishop of Sherborne, soon after 700. Bede, the learned monk of Jarrow, translated at least part of the Gospels into Old English; he is said to have been engaged in this task when he died on Ascension Eve, 735.

When Alfred, king of Wessex (871–901), had subjugated the Danish invaders of his kingdom, he energetically fostered religion and learning, including Bible translation, in which he may even have taken a hand personally. He had some experience of translating from Latin into Old English—doing it, as he said himself, "sometimes word for word, and sometimes meaning for meaning." His law-code was introduced by an Old English translation of the Ten Commandments with other extracts from Exodus and the apostolic decree of Acts 15:23–29.

Some of the earliest continuous biblical texts in Old English take the form of interlinear glosses in Latin MSS. For example, the British Museum possesses a beautifully illuminated MS of the Gospels in Latin, called the Lindisfarne Gospels, written towards the end of the seventh century. About the middle of the tenth century a priest named Aldred wrote a literal translation into the Northumbrian dialect of Old English between the lines of the Latin text. The Rushworth Gospels, copied from the Lindisfarne MS and now in the Bodleian Library, Oxford, are similarly glossed. An eighth-century Latin Psalter in the British Museum exhibits an interlinear Old English gloss executed in the following century.

Apart from such glosses, we have the Wessex Gospels, an independent Old English version of the Gospels, from the mid-tenth century; a decade or two later is the Old English Heptateuch, a translation of the first seven books of the OT made by Abbot Aelfric of Eynsham, Oxfordshire.

These Old English versions, whatever form they took, were based on the Latin Vulgate. Old English culture received a heavy blow from the Norman Conquest of 1066 and its aftermath, and when English versions of the Bible next appear, the form of the language is Middle English, in which the powerful influence of the conquerors' French had wrought radical changes. About 1200 an Augustinian monk named Orm or Ormin produced the *Ormulum,* a poetical version of the Gospels and Acts, accompanied by a commentary. In the middle of the thirteenth century appeared a translation of Genesis and Exodus in rhyming English verse, and a little later a metrical version of the Psalms. Two prose translations of the Psalms in Middle English have survived from the earlier part of the fourteenth century; from the later part of the same century we have a version of the NT Epistles made by a member of a religious order for others in that walk of life; it was later augmented by translation of Acts and the early sections of Matthew, and introduced by a prologue summarizing OT history from Adam to Moses.

It is also from the last decades of the fourteenth century that we have the two English versions associated with the name of John Wycliffe. It was part of Wycliffe's political philosophy that the Bible—the codification of God's law, as he saw it—should be widely available in the vernacular, since every man was, in his view, God's tenant-in-chief, directly responsible to God. How far he himself took part in the work of translation is uncertain, but it is certain that under his influence two English versions of the complete Bible were produced. The earlier of these, completed shortly before Wycliffe's death in 1384, was translated by his supporter Nicholas of Hereford from Gen 1:1 to Baruch 3:20. When Nicholas was prevented from completing the work, it was taken up by others, among whom Wycliffe may have been one. This earlier Wycliffite version was a painstakingly literal rendering of the Latin, as befitted a law-code, designed to replace existing canon law.

But after Wycliffe's death his secretary, John Purvey, undertook a thorough revision of the earlier version and produced a really idiomatic English Bible. In a tract called the *General Prologue* Purvey tells us something of his technique, which involved four stages: (a) the establishment of a sound Latin text to be the basis of the translation; (b) the study of this Latin text with the aid of commentaries to ascertain its meaning; (c) the consultation of grammarians and theologians for help with problems of language and doctrine; (d) the actual translation, done in such a way as to make the sense plain and submitted to competent critics for correction. Purvey's translation won instant popularity, despite official disapproval (because the Lollard movement, to which he and his late master belonged, was condemned as politically and religiously subversive), and for more than a century, it enjoyed a remarkably wide circulation when one considers that each copy had to be written out separately by hand. Even when William Caxton set up his printing press in Westminster in 1476 and launched a voluminous output of printed works, the English Bible remained unprinted. No one could obtain a copy without the permission of the bishop of his particular diocese, and Caxton probably realized the impossibility of securing such permission for such wholesale production and circulation as the printing press facilitated.

C. From 1450 to 1650

1. *Before Tyndale.* The decades that followed the mid-point of the fifteenth century witnessed a revolution in Western European thinking. The invention of printing, the capture of Constantinople by the Turks (1453), and the European discovery of the New World (1492) were independent events, but they coincided with a general shift in popular outlook and indeed made their distinctive contributions to it.

The invention of printing meant that, whereas previously each copy of a book had to be written separately by hand, now an edition of several hundred or thousand copies could be produced in one process. The first substantial work ever to come off a printing press was the Latin Bible of 1456, known from the printer's name as the Gutenberg Bible. (It had been preceded two years previously by a printed Latin Psalter.) The Hebrew Pentateuch was printed at Bologna in 1482; the first complete printed Hebrew Bible appeared at Soncino in 1488. In those years Bibles were printed also in the principal vernaculars of Western Europe—with the single exception of English. The complete Greek Bible was printed as part of the six-volume Complutensian Polyglot, at Alcalà in Spain, between 1514 and 1517. Publication of the Polyglot was deferred until 1522; thus, although the NT volume had been printed in 1514, the first printed Greek NT to be published was the first edition of Erasmus, at Basel in March 1516. Erasmus (or his printer) was in such a hurry to get the work out, in advance of the Complutensian edition, that where (as at the end of Revelation) the Greek MS from which he worked was defective, he could not wait to procure another but translated the missing verses from Latin into his own Greek. Although in successive printed editions a good deal of the genuine Greek text was restored, two words in Revelation 22:18, 19, supplied by Erasmus and not attested in any MS, have survived in the TR to the present day. Five editions of Erasmus's Greek NT were issued between 1516 and 1536. The third of these (1522) contained the spurious text about the three heavenly witnesses (1 John 5:7), which Erasmus had not included in his first two editions because it was absent from his Greek MSS. Its omission was fiercely criticized, and he incautiously agreed to include it if he could be shown it in any Greek MS. A Greek MS on which the ink was scarcely dry (it was written about 1520) was produced in which the text was present (manifestly translated back into Greek from Latin) and, while Erasmus was morally certain that it had been hastily copied out with the express purpose of putting him on the spot, he yielded to pressure and included the words in his next edition. From that edition the words were taken over into Luther's German NT and Tyndale's English NT, and were retained in subsequent English versions of the sixteenth and seventeenth centuries, including KJV.

The relative lateness in the printing of any part of the Greek Bible was due to a variety of causes. Fonts of Greek type suitable for the printing of a book of any size were difficult and expensive to produce. Jewish communities were quick to exploit the printing press for the production of Hebrew books, but there were no comparable communities in the West to foster Greek printing. Indeed, throughout the Middle Ages the study of Hebrew had been pursued in the West by Christian scholars as well as Jews; opportunities for Greek study were not so readily available. The migration of Greek scholars and Greek

MSS to the West after the fall of Constantinople changed this situation, and the Revival of Learning in the second half of the fifteenth century created a new interest in Greek learning and the Greek way of thinking, which notably helped forward the Christian humanist movement. When John Colet (later Dean of St. Paul's, London) returned from an academic visit to the European continent in 1496, he delivered at Oxford a course of lectures on the letters of Paul, which made a deep impression because of his break with the scholastic tradition and his exposition of the text in accordance with the plain meaning of the words viewed in their historical setting. Colet exercised a great influence on Erasmus and Sir Thomas More. The time had come for a fresh, unprejudiced look at what the Scriptures, and especially the NT writings, really had to say.

The Reformation gave rise to a succession of new vernacular Bible translations— translations that differed from those of the Middle Ages in that they circulated in print and not in MS, but also in that they were made directly from the original languages and not from Latin. The first of these was Luther's: his German NT was published in 1522, followed by the Pentateuch in 1523 and the complete Bible in 1534.

2. *The work of Tyndale.* William Tyndale (1494/5–1536) started a tradition in English Bible translation that is still alive and vigorous; its latest manifestation is the RSV of 1946/52. After graduating at Oxford and Cambridge, Tyndale was disappointed to find that the bishop of London, reputed to be a patron of the new learning, would not sponsor his projected work of Bible translation. Deciding that he could prosecute it more easily outside of England, he departed for the continent in 1524, and by August 1525 his NT translation was complete. A Cologne printer, Peter Quentel, had printed ten sheets of it (80 quarto pages) when he was forbidden to proceed; the work of printing had to be started again at Worms. There Peter Schoeffer printed an octavo edition of 6,000 copies, which was selling in England by April 1526. In 1530 Tyndale issued the Pentateuch; in 1531, the book of Jonah; in 1534, a revision of Genesis; and later in the same year, a revision of his NT. Although he published yet another revision of the NT in 1535, it is the 1534 revision that is commonly recognized as the definitive edition of Tyndale's English NT. B.F. Westcott called it "altogether Tyndale's noblest monument"; the whole of the 1526 edition was gone over in scrupulous detail, and almost all the changes were improvements, reflecting mature judgment and feeling. The influence of the 1534 edition on later revisions may be gauged from the fact that nine-tenths of the NT in KJV is Tyndale's. Moreover, in several places where KJV departed from Tyndale's wording, the RV of 1881 went back to it. For example, the erroneous rendering "one fold" in John 10:16, KJV, is not Tyndale's. Tyndale correctly had "one flock," which is reproduced in RV and later versions.

In an appendix to the NT of 1534 Tyndale translated from the original texts forty OT lessons prescribed to be read at the communion service in the Church of England on certain days of the year. Many of these are from the poetical and prophetic books, and the felicity of rendering makes us regret that Tyndale did not live to complete the translation of the OT. He was arrested on May 21, 1535, and after an imprisonment of seventeen months was condemned and executed for heresy at Vilvorde, Belgium, on October 6, 1536. At the time of his death he left in MS a translation of the historical books from Joshua to 2 Chronicles, which was published in 1537.

3. *Coverdale and others.* A year before Tyndale's death the whole Bible in English was circulating in England without hindrance (though he probably heard nothing of it). This was the edition of Miles Coverdale, later bishop of Exeter, a friend and helper of

Tyndale. Coverdale was no expert in the original tongues; his edition was based on Tyndale in the Pentateuch and the NT, and, for the rest, was translated from Latin and German editions. It was equipped with a complimentary dedication to King Henry VIII. This was the first Bible to separate the apocryphal books and print them in an appendix to the OT. A second edition of Coverdale's Bible (1537) bore on the title page the words "Set forth with the king's most gracious licence." So did another version of the English Bible published at the same time—a version produced under the pen name Thomas Matthew, but actually edited by John Rogers, also a former associate of Tyndale. Rogers probably used a pen name because the version was not his own, and it was still impolitic to name the man who was really responsible for it—William Tyndale. It was in this version that Tyndale's translation of the OT historical books was first published. Those parts of the Bible that Tyndale had not translated were taken over from Coverdale's Bible. There was then no copyright law to prevent this; in any case, neither Coverdale nor Rogers stood to make any material profit from their editions, but both worked for the good of a common cause.

Coverdale's work on the English Bible was not ended with his second edition of 1537. The following year he was entrusted with the editing of an official version of the English Bible that was to be installed and read in every parish church in England. In April 1539 this version, the "Great Bible," was published; one edition succeeded another in rapid sequence, the seventh appearing in December 1541. From the second edition onwards, the Great Bible carried a prologue by Archbishop Thomas Cranmer. It was called the Great Bible because of its size; so far as its text went, it was essentially Coverdale's revision of the Thomas Matthew Bible, which means that it was basically Tyndale's translation so far as that had gone.

One part of the Great Bible remains in use today: the Psalter printed in the English Book of Common Prayer is the Psalter of the Great Bible. It is from this, and not from the KJV, that some of the commonest of quotations from the Psalms in English literature are taken, such as "the iron entered into his soul" (Ps 105:18). A revision of the Prayer Book Psalter (*The Revised Psalter*) was published in 1963—the work of a commission under the chairmanship of Dr. F.D. Coggan, then Archbishop of York.

4. *The Elizabethan Bible*. England's return to Papal allegiance under Mary Tudor (1553 –58) meant that many adherents of the Reforming party sought refuge on the continent, especially at Frankfurt and Geneva. During their exile, they gave themselves to the work of Bible translation. An early product of this activity was a revision of the Thomas Matthew NT by William Whittingham, formerly Fellow of All Souls, Oxford, brother-in-law to John Calvin and successor to John Knox as pastor of the English congregation in Geneva. This octavo volume of 1557 was set in roman type, with the words that were added in English to make the sense plain set in italics; the text was divided into verses (an arrangement taken over from the fourth ed. of the Gr. NT printed by Robert Estienne at Geneva in 1551).

But Whittingham's NT was an interim edition; he and his associates were preparing something more ambitious, which was produced in 1560. This was the Geneva Bible, so called from the city of its first printing and publication. It carried a dedicatory epistle to Elizabeth I of England, described as a new Zerubbabel, a rebuilder of the temple of God. It had the same typographical features as Whittingham's NT, but more importantly, it was the first English Bible translated throughout from the original languages. It was the best English translation of the whole Bible ever to have appeared, and it retained that distinction until the publication of KJV in 1611.

The Geneva Bible instantly won widespread acceptance. Its publication coincided with the establishment of the Reformed religion in Scotland, and it became the undisputed Bible version in Scotland. In England, too, it quickly became the household version for Protestants. It was, for example, the Bible of Shakespeare. Some seventy editions of the whole Geneva Bible and thirty of the NT alone were published during the reign of Elizabeth (1558–1603). Most of these were published in England, although it was not until 1575 that it was first printed in England. In 1579 an edition was published in Scotland—the first Bible ever to be printed in Scotland. In both kingdoms it remained in use long after the appearance of the KJV in 1611. It was the Geneva Bible that the Pilgrim Fathers took with them when they crossed the Atlantic in 1620; to them the KJV was "a fond thing vainly invented" and they reckoned that "the old was better." The selection of biblical extracts issued in 1643 for Cromwell's army, entitled *The Soldier's Pocket Bible*, was taken from the Geneva Bible. The last edition of the Geneva Bible was printed in 1644 (if we exclude a modern reprint of the first edition). But in some places it continued in use for a generation and more after that.

Different people appreciated different features of the Geneva version. Some liked the radically Reformed sentiments that found expression in its marginal notes and elsewhere. Others were impressed by its scholarly accuracy. In this regard it was far ahead of any of its predecessors. It drew attention to a number of textual variants found in available MSS. Geneva was the home at that time of Theodore Beza, the greatest textual scholar of the Reformation, and the translators were naturally influenced by his studies.

For all its merits, it did not win complete approval from the leaders of church and state in England, mainly because its introduction and annotations were out of step with the Elizabethan settlement. Yet its virtues were so patent that it was impossible to go on using in church such an obviously inferior version as the Great Bible. Accordingly, Matthew Parker, Archbishop of Canterbury, initiated a revision of the Great Bible, which was completed in 1568 and was known as the "Bishops' Bible"—because the translators were either bishops at the time or became bishops in due course. Had the Geneva Bible never been published, the Bishops' Bible would have been the best English version to have appeared thus far. One admirable feature of it was the translators' refusal to add any bitter or controversial notes. But it started off with the insuperable disadvantage that there was a far better version in the field. Nineteen editions of the whole Bible and eleven of the NT were printed between 1568 and 1606. It immediately superseded the Great Bible as the version read in churches throughout England, but the queen gave it no formal recognition or preferential status. She was scholar enough to know that the Geneva Bible was a better work, whatever she thought of its accessories.

When Elizabeth died in 1603, then, English Protestantism had two competing versions of the Bible, and it depended mainly on one's churchmanship which version he preferred to use. To bring this state of affairs to an end and replace the competing versions by one that was better than either was the achievement of the following reign.

5. *The King James Version*. Some months after James VI of Scotland became king of England as James I (1603), he convened a conference at Hampton Court to deal with various controversial issues in the church. The one positive result of this conference was the execution of a project first proposed by John Reynolds, President of Corpus Christi College, Oxford, and then warmly approved by James, to produce a new translation of the Bible in English that should be used in church services to the exclusion of all others. The "new translation" was formally a revision of the 1602 ed. of the Bishops' Bible, but

many other versions and helps were used by the translators, who paid attention throughout their work to the original texts. Forty-seven scholars were appointed to carry through the enterprise; these were divided into six panels, three of which were responsible for the OT, two for the NT and one for the Apocrypha. The draft tr. produced by the six panels was finally reviewed by a committee of twelve. Miles Smith (later bishop of Gloucester), who helped to see the work through the press, also contributed the informative preface entitled "The Translators to the Reader." The work was published in 1611, seven years after it was initiated.

In Britain it has commonly been called the Authorized Version, and this raises the question of when and by whom it was authorized. The answer almost certainly is that it was authorized by Order in Council; unfortunately no record of this is extant because all the books and registers of the Privy Council from 1600 to 1613 were destroyed in a fire at the beginning of 1619. Because of the sponsorship and active interest of King James, it has also come to be known as the King James Version (KJV).

The KJV did not meet with instant acceptance; like some recent versions it was vehemently denounced on grounds of scholarship and sound doctrine. But it triumphed over its critics and for 300 years retained an unrivalled place as "The Bible" throughout the English-speaking world. The absence of controversial notes meant that it was acceptable to all sections of theological and ecclesiastical opinion in the churches of the Reformation. It was, moreover, a literary masterpiece; its prose rhythms and avoidance of harsh combinations of sound made it an eminently suitable version for reading aloud in public. But when tribute is paid to its literary excellence, it is essentially to Tyndale that tribute is paid. It was he who set the stylistic pattern followed in the KJV.

6. *The Douai-Rheims Version.* A number of Roman Catholic scholars from England who sought refuge on the Continent after the Elizabethan settlement of 1558 and the following years established an English College in Northern France. From 1568 to 1578 the College was situated at Douai, from 1578 to 1593 at Rheims, and in the latter year it returned to Douai. One of the professors of the College, Gregory Martin, translated the Bible into English for the benefit of adherents of the old religion: the NT was published at Rheims in 1582 and the OT (although it had been translated before the NT) was published at Douai in 1609 and 1610.

This version differed from other English versions of the same period in being a translation from the Latin Vulgate. In 1546 the Council of Trent ruled that the Latin Vulgate should be treated as the one authoritative edition of the Bible, and a standard text of the Vulgate (the Clementine Vulgate) was published in 1592 in the papacy of Clement VIII. Henceforth, until our own generation, all approved Bible translations from Roman Catholics had to be based on this text. But Gregory Martin's Douai-Rheims version antedated the Clementine Vulgate.

The Douai-Rheims version was a scholarly work. Although it was based on the Vulgate, the translator consulted the Greek NT, which guided him particularly in the use of the definite article (a part of speech that is lacking in Latin). The use of the definite article, indeed, is more accurate in Douai-Rheims than in KJV. In general, the language of Douai-Rheims is highly latinate—to a point where it could be understood only by educated readers. Gregory Martin's colleagues equipped his work with an apparatus of notes, calculated to interpret the text in conformity with the decrees of the Council of Trent and to rebut Protestant arguments, and constituting a substantial body of controversial divinity.

What commonly passes as the Douai-Rheims (or more simply the Douai) Bible today is not the version as produced by Gregory Martin, but a revision carried through in the mid-eighteenth century by Richard Challoner, Vicar-Apostolic of the London District. Bishop Challoner was a convert from Protestantism, brought up on the KJV, and his revision of Douai-Rheims brought it into considerable conformity with the diction of the KJV.

D. *From 1650 to 1870*

The two centuries following the appearance of the KJV were marked not so much by intensive Bible translation as by progess in the study and recovery of the original text, especially of the NT. The KJV was, in the NT, essentially a translation of the TR, which was based in turn on late and inferior copies of the Byzantine text. Codex Alexandrinus (A; 02), a fifth-century MS of the Greek Bible, which provides the earliest example of the Byzantine text in the Gospels and exhibits the Alexandrian type of text in the rest of the NT, and would thus have supplied a far better basis than anything available to King James's translators, did not come to England until 1627. James Ussher (1581–1656) interested himself in the text of both Testaments; he procured from the East, for example, several MSS of the Samaritan Bible, and compiled a critical apparatus to the NT, which was included in 1657 in volume 6 of Brian Walton's Polyglot Bible. In 1675 John Fell (later bishop of Oxford) published at Oxford a pocket edition of the Greek NT with a critical apparatus quoting variant readings from MSS and early versions. A much more elaborate edition, with prolegomena and an apparatus listing about 30,000 variants, was published by John Mill in 1707. The TR continued to form the basis for these editions. Richard Bentley (1662–1742) planned to construct a critical text, for which he collected copious materials, but the plan, first promulgated in 1720, remained unexecuted.

Johann Albrecht Bengel published at Tübingen in 1734 a quarto edition of the Greek NT in the apparatus of which he classified variant readings in five categories according to their relative probability or improbability. It is to him that textual critics owe the formulation of the canon that "the more difficult reading is to be preferred." Johann Jakob Wettstein published in 1751 and 1752 a more elaborate edition in two folio volumes, in which the TR was printed, but his own preferred readings were indicated in the margin. William Bowyer, a London printer, produced a critical text of the Greek NT in 1763, which incorporated most of Wettstein's preferred readings and (in an appendix) a list of conjectural emendations. Among these emendations was the insertion of "Enoch" in 1 Peter 3:20 (familiar to readers of Moffatt's and Goodspeed's translations).

The first German edition of the Greek NT to print a critical text was that of Johann Jakob Griesbach (Halle, 1774–77). Griesbach formulated principles of critical procedure and distinguished what we know as the Alexandrian, Western, and Byzantine recensions. The increase of evidence and improvement of critical method led to further editions in the nineteenth century, notably those of Karl Lachmann (Berlin, 1831), Constantine von Tischendorf (who produced eight successive editions between 1841 and 1872), and Samuel Prideaux Tregelles (London, 1857–72).

The necessity for revising the KJV became increasingly apparent: not only was its diction "dated" (in itself no serious matter for those who spoke Shakespeare's tongue) but the textual basis of its NT section was far from satisfactory. Accordingly, a series of private enterprises in KJV revision appeared during those decades, one of the most distinguished of which was Henry Alford's edition of the English NT (1869), in which he insisted that all other considerations must yield to "truth of testimony, or truth of rendering." These paved the way for the major revision of 1881–1901.

E. *The Revised Version and After*

The RV was initiated by the Anglican Convocation of Canterbury in 1870. Two companies of revisers were set up, one for the OT and one for the NT, on which representatives of other British churches than the Church of England sat. The OT company retained the Masoretic Text as its basis, but because of the advance of Heb. scholarship since 1611 was able greatly to improve the KJV, sometimes making sense of formerly meaningless passages. The NT company included a predominant number of scholars whose zeal for the precise rendering of Greek tenses and the like was greater than their literary appreciation; in consequence, the NT in the RV is stylistically much inferior to the KJV, whereas textually it is far superior. On the textual side, the NT company was dominated by the scholarship of B.F. Westcott and F.J.A. Hort, whose magisterial edition of the Greek NT was published five days before the NT in the RV. Westcott and Hort were convinced (not unreasonably, in the light of the textual knowledge then available) that the Alexandrian text came as close to the first-century text of the NT as to make no difference. The rule that changes in the text required a two-thirds majority gave a conservative bias to the company's decisions; even so, the RV of the NT is as recognizably a translation of the Alexandrian text as the KJV is of the TR.

The NT appeared in 1881, the complete Bible in 1885, the Apocrypha in 1894. Modernization of the KJV idiom was minimal, partly because the revisers adopted the principle of using no expression that was not current in 1611. This archaizing policy was modified in the American counterpart to the RV. Shortly after the inauguration of the revision in Britain, parallel companies of revisers were set up in the United States of America. It was hoped at one time that an agreed revision might be produced for both sides of the Atlantic. This hope was unrealized, and the American revision—the American Standard Version—was published in 1901. The ASV did not include the Apocrypha. The tradition of including the Apocrypha in the English Bible was weaker in the U.S. than in Britain; the first English Bible to be printed in the U.S. (1782–83) lacked these books. A revision of the ASV, undertaken with the aim of promoting its usefulness, has been completed in recent years, the New American Standard Bible (NASB); the NT appeared in 1963, the whole Bible in 1972.

F. *The Twentieth Century*

1. *The first seventy years.* The twentieth century had barely opened when a series of new translations, especially of the NT, appeared in quick succession. Some of these were designed to render the Bible in a simpler idiom than the rather stilted archaisms of the RV and ASV. Some aimed at making use of the advances in linguistic and textual knowledge that marked the years following the appearance of the RV. At the end of the nineteenth century new light was cast on the nature of NT Greek by the study of vernacular papyri from Egypt, and fresh discoveries in ancient MSS and versions showed that the claims of WH for the primacy of the Alexandrian text could not go undisputed.

The Twentieth Century New Testament, an admirable production (1898–1904), was followed by R.F. Weymouth's New Testament in Modern Speech (1903), which in some respects was more accurate even than the RV. Less accurate and more colloquial was James Moffatt's translation (NT, 1913; OT, 1924), which attained wide popularity in spite of its Scotticisms and cavalier treatment of the text. The Bible: An American

Translation, by Edgar J. Goodspeed and others (NT, 1923; whole Bible, 1927, 1935; Apocrypha, 1938), was designed to exclude British expressions that might be strange in American ears and achieved a dignity of diction beyond that of Moffatt's version. The Bible in Basic English (NT, 1940; whole Bible, 1949) was subject to the vocabulary limitations of Basic English (850 words, specially augmented to 1,000) but is nevertheless a serious translation made from the original texts by S.H. Hooke. At the opposite extreme are such productions as Kenneth S. Wuest's Expanded Translation of the New Testament (1956–59) and The Amplified Bible (1958–65), which attempt to give verbatim expression to all the grammatical and lexical nuances discerned by the translators as implicit in the text. The chief place among paraphrases must be given to J.B. Phillips' New Testament in Modern English (1947–58, revised 1972). The Authentic New Testament (1955), by Hugh J. Schonfield, approaches the NT documents "as if they had recently been recovered from a cave in Palestine or from beneath the sands of Egypt, and had never previously been given to the public." The Berkeley Version of the Bible (NT, 1945; whole Bible, 1959, 1969) is a masterpiece of evangelical scholarship that can hold its head high and unashamed among modern translations of the Bible. The Living Bible, by Kenneth N. Taylor (1962–71), is a paraphrase notable for its readability, with a special appeal to younger people.

Recent Roman Catholic versions include that of Ronald A. Knox (NT, 1945; OT, 1949; whole Bible, revised 1955), a translation from the Vulgate noteworthy for its elegant English style, and the Confraternity Version, begun in 1941 on the basis of the Vulgate but continued on the basis of the Hebrew and Greek texts, and published in 1970 in a thoroughly revised form under the new title The New American Bible. The Jerusalem Bible (1966) is a scholarly production based on the French edition by members of the École Biblique in Jerusalem.

2. *The present situation.* In the English-speaking world today, as in the reign of Elizabeth I, we have two competing versions of the Bible. The Revised Standard Version (NT, 1946; whole Bible, 1952, revised 1962 and 1972) is a revision of the KJV, RV, and ASV, and is thus in the Tyndale succession. It was produced by American and Canadian scholars, and is copyrighted by the Division of Christian Education of the National Council of the Churches in the U.S.A., but its circulation and acceptance are international, and have been stimulated by the latest revision (1972), which has resulted in a "Common Bible" approved by Roman Catholic and Eastern Orthodox as well as by Protestant Christians. Of all modern versions, the RSV comes nearest to fulfilling the all-purpose role once filled by the KJV.

The New English Bible (NT, 1961; whole Bible, 1970) was produced by panels of scholars and literary advisers responsible to a joint committee of the principal non-Roman churches of Great Britain and Ireland. It has broken away from the Tyndale tradition and, instead of being a revision of earlier translations, aims at being a completely new translation from the original texts into "timeless English." While it is the product of teamwork, one can discern in the OT the influence of one outstanding scholar. This is specially evident in the way in which other Semitic languages are drawn upon to provide new meanings for Hebrew roots, sometimes convincingly and sometimes not. Thus, while there is less conjectural emendation in this version than in some of its twentieth-century predecessors, a comparable impression of novelty is made on the reader who is familiar with the older versions.

In the NT, the NEB, like the RSV, represents an eclectic text. In the words of C.H. Dodd, General Director of the NEB:

The problem of restoring a form of text as near as possible to the vanished autographs now appears less simple than it did to our predecessors. There is not at the present time any critical text which would command the same degree of general acceptance as the Revisers' text did in its day. Nor has the time come, in the judgment of most scholars, to construct such a text, since new material constantly comes to light, and the debate continues. The present translators therefore could do no other than consider variant readings on their merits, and, having weighed the evidence for themselves, select for translation in each passage the reading which to the best of their judgement seemed most likely to represent what the author wrote."[2]

In our survey of translations, considerations of space have limited us almost completely to the English language. In most of the national languages of Christendom, however, the situation today is much the same: there is an older version, venerated because of literary worth and hallowed associations, but contemporary needs are giving rise to a variety of modern versions. Outside of the English-speaking world also there is a proliferation of versions, so that practically every age-bracket and every cultural (or subcultural) group is provided with the Scriptures, in whole or in part, in a form specially adapted to its requirements, in addition to those versions whose appeal transcends such divisions.

The American Bible Society's publication, Today's English Version (TEV) is the work of men specially equipped in tr. technique and is designed to serve as a basis or model for translations into other languages. The translators have sought to achieve the goal of equivalent effect, in the conviction that a tr. should as far as possible produce the same effect in readers today as the original text produced in those for whom it was first intended. The TEV NT appeared in 1966 and counterparts have appeared in other languages; the OT was published in 1976. The British and Foreign Bible Society's Translators' New Testament (1973) is similarly designed as a basis for other translations. Alongside these, honorable mention must be made of the New York International Bible Society's New International Version (NT, 1973; OT, 1978), a transdenominational work made by about one hundred evangelical scholars. It is a cooperative production the quality of which is evident throughout the present work, since it supplies the text on which *The Expositor's Bible Commentary* is based.

There has never been a time when the work of Bible translation has been so closely tied to the study of the text and transmission of the Bible as today; Bible translation is all the more effectively executed on this account.

IV. Bibliography

Birdsall, J.N. et al. "Text and Versions." *The New Bible Dictionary.* Edited by J.D. Douglas. Grand Rapids: Eerdmans, 1962.

Bruce, F.F. *The Books and the Parchments.* London: Pickering & Inglis, [3]1963.

———. *The English Bible.* New York: Oxford University Press, [2]1970.

Cambridge History of the Bible. Cambridge University Press. vol. 1, 1970; vol. 2, 1969; vol. 3, 1963.

Kenyon, F.G. *Our Bible and the Ancient Manuscript.* Revised by A.W. Adams with an introduction by G.R. Driver. London: Eyre and Spottiswoode, 1958.

Macgregor, G. *The Bible in the Making.* London: John Murray, 1961.

Metzger, B.M. *The Text of the New Testament.* New York: Oxford University Press, [2]1968.

Reumann, J.H.P. *Four Centuries of the English Bible.* Philadelphia: Muhlenberg, 1961.

---

[2]Introduction to the New Testament, NEB.

_____. *The Romance of Bible Scripts and Scholars.* Englewood Cliffs, N.J.: Prentice-Hall, 1965.

Roberts, B.J. *The Old Testament Text and Versions.* Cardiff: University of Wales Press, 1951.

Robinson, H.W., ed. *The Bible in Its Ancient and English Versions.* Oxford University Press, [2]1954.

THE INTERPRETATION OF THE BIBLE

Geoffrey W. Bromiley

Geoffrey W. Bromiley

M.A., Cambridge University; Ph.D., D.Litt., D.D., University of Edinburgh (New College)

Professor of Church History and Historical Theology, Fuller Theological Seminary

THE INTERPRETATION OF THE BIBLE

I. Introduction—The Significance of Interpretation
II. The Problem of Interpretation

    A. General Hermeneutical Difficulties
    B. Special Hermeneutical Difficulties
    C. Personal Hermeneutical Difficulties

III. The History of Interpretation

    A. The Patristic Age
    B. The Medieval Period
    C. The Renaissance and Reformation
    D. Liberal Protestantism

IV. The Principles of Interpretation

    A. General Principles
    B. Technical Principles
    C. Theological Principles

V. Conclusion—Residual Problems
VI. Bibliography

I. Introduction—The Significance of Interpretation

Christians and Christian groups have generally affirmed the unique authority of Holy Scripture. They have construed it differently, introduced qualifications, imposed restrictions, and worked out divergent implications. But whatever they have done, they have seldom ignored or denied its reality.

What in fact does this authority tell us to believe and do? What is the Bible actually saying? What is the meaning of this venerable text of the Old and New Testaments?

This is the question of interpretation. It is a crucial one. To bind oneself to the word of Scripture is good and necessary. But it is not enough. If Scripture is to function as an effective norm, one has also to know precisely what it is saying and asking. Fixing as accurately as possible the general and also the detailed meaning of Scripture is the vital and inescapable task of interpretation. Interpretation, or hermeneutics, is the discipline that tries to establish the principles used in exegesis and exposition.

It is crucial for four reasons. First, the authority of Scripture is nullified if its real meaning is missed. Second, understanding Scripture is not so easy as it might seem, for while the Bible means what it says and generally speaks in simple terms, it does not escape the difficulties that beset all communication. Third, even in important matters of faith and conduct, Christians differ about what Scripture is teaching; commitment to its authority is no safeguard against disagreement. Fourth, there is real danger of confusing authorities—that of Scripture and that of individual interpretation of it—if the hermeneutical question is disregarded.

In fact, all Christians interpret. The sad thing is that many do so without self-awareness, reading Scripture on the assumption that whatever the words suggest is right and not studying to get the true sense. The need is not just for readers but for informed readers who see interpretation as indispensable and tackle it seriously in order that Scripture may exercise real authority in Christian life and mission. The starting point for doing this is to consider the three most important aspects of the problem of interpretation.

II. The Problem of Interpretation

A. General Hermeneutical Difficulties

1. *Meaning.* Interpretation of any text carries with it certain difficulties as to the precise intent of what is said. The initial problem is that of the specific meaning of the words employed. Most short, factual, detached sayings raise no difficulties for normal adults. But once statements become longer and more complex, we soon realize that words are not exact tools. They can have various senses. They can be handled differently—in a literal, a transferred, or a metaphorical sense. They can carry possibly obscure or esoteric allusions that may or may not apply in a given saying. If the general drift of most passages is clear enough, establishing the detailed sense can be a very different matter.

2. *Context.* In an extended passage the component clauses do not stand alone and hence are not to be interpreted alone. This is already true of the words in the single clause. On a larger scale, it is true of the clause in the relation to the surrounding statements that make up the passage. Indeed, in a more extended work the passage too is part of a broader context. Here the context can be hermeneutically helpful. The general throws light on the particular. Thus when Paul speaks of olive trees (Rom 11:16-25), the context shows that we are given an illustration, not information on horticulture. Possible word meanings are narrowed down considerably by the context. Yet context also raises new problems. First, extension can also broaden the range of meaning. Second, fixing the context, e.g., where a train of thought begins and ends, and how it relates to other ideas or arguments, can be harder than it looks. Third, the manner and degree to which a statement in context qualifies or is qualified by the other statements in it can be very arguable. Interpretation in context is demanded, but it is no hermeneutical panacea.

3. *Relation.* The relation of a work must also be considered. One might call this the external context, i.e., the setting or occasion, whether broadly as background or immediately as situation. Fixing this is a delicate business, especially when information is incomplete, e.g., as in the case of the historical setting of many prophecies or the

doctrinal error refuted in a work like Colossians. Often the relation or reference is clear enough, and the text itself may provide adequate inner information. But one cannot count on this, especially in matters of detail. Abstract or arbitrary meanings may result if the relation is insufficiently considered or knowledge is overconfidently presupposed.

4. *Application.* Finally, there is the bearing or application of a statement or passage. This issue does not arise in all cases. Thus when information is passed on, either there is no application or it is very simple. Sometimes, however, even information implies a call to belief or action. Deciding whether this is so is part of the problem. In other instances, as in ethical injunctions, estimating the application is an important expository task. When Jesus issues the Great Commission, does he speak only to the disciples or to all Christians? When Paul tells women to pray with covered heads, is his request local or universal? If the former is general but not the latter, why the distinction? Again, when good acts are performed, e.g., Peter speaking boldly or Barnabas donating his land, are these normative? Or is the one normative and not the other? Or are both normative for some but not all, and if so, for whom? Or is neither normative? Application is particularly vital in relation to a norm, such as, e.g., legal enactment in secular life. This is why cumbersome legal jargon has developed in an effort to show the precise reference. But the jargon itself then demands training for a correct understanding. In its own way, Scripture poses something of the same problem.

B. *Special Hermeneutical Difficulties*

1. *Distinctiveness of Scripture.* With the difficulties it shares with other written statements, Scripture has some special hermeneutical difficulties of its own. The first is posed by the distinctiveness of Scripture as compared with other human literature. For all the parallels of form and content between it and other religious writings, there are obvious dissimilarities that demand special hermeneutical treatment.

Thus Scripture makes use of unique literary genres, or at any rate makes a unique use of genres. The creation stories are an example. The whole phenomenon of Hebrew prophecy also claims our attention here. So, too, do the parables of Jesus. If parables are not peculiar to the Bible, those of Jesus raise special questions. Are they simple illustrations or do they work obliquely? Is there a single point in each parable or are the details important too? What does it mean that they are parables of the kingdom? Do they carry with them an element of realized eschatology?

Scripture also contains distinctive material elements that pose a problem of interpretation. Most important here are the "miracles." Accounts of the miraculous abound in other religious works, but in contrast to these the biblical miracles offer several intriguing features. The Hebrew and Greek terms themselves form a significant study. The relation of these mighty works of God to his general activity is also to be noted. The function ascribed to miracles, e.g., in the Gospels, constitutes a problem of its own, as does the relation of these signs to the proclamation of the kingdom of God by Jesus and the apostles. Above all, the God of these mighty acts is himself a point of decisive differentiation.

2. *Scripture as God's Word.* Mention of God leads on to the second and even more important hermeneutical difficulty that Scripture poses. The distinctive features in the form and content of the Bible are a pointer to a deeper and more fundamental difference between these writings and all others. Scripture poses a special set of hermeneutical

problems, not merely because of the uniqueness of its form and content, but because it is God's Word as well. The divine Word is given through human words. Is then a divine message to be abstracted from what is concretely said? Are we so to identify God's Word with the human statement that in the upshot there is no difference? The problem is rather like that of trying to understand Jesus. One is not to isolate the deity and the humanity, nor to let the one be swallowed up in the other, but to find the one in the other. This is by no means easy.

3. *The unity of Scripture.* A third special difficulty in biblical interpretation is that of expounding Scripture in its unity. Scripture seems to be a collection of writings, or detached pieces within writings, bound together loosely and contingently, or as part of a common tradition, literature, or religious development. Here again the crux is whether these writings are seen as God's Word. The divine origin is the real bond of unity. Yet even granting this, understanding the unity between individual books, the Testaments, and all the books, is still a question to which different answers are given. Nor is this merely an academic question, for important beliefs and practices, e.g., the covenant or infant baptism, depend on the interpretation of scriptural unity.

4. *The hermeneutical key.* Given the unity of Scripture, so large and varied a collection can be expounded as a unity only if a unifying key or center be adopted. But what is this key and how is it to be discerned and demonstrated? Is it to be sought in a doctrine? Does it lie in a book or group of books? May we simply find it in the NT? Do we look for it in history or in a dispensational scheme? Are we to think eschatologically of end, *telos?* Or should we think in personal terms—Israel, the church, Christ, God? Can we conjoin some of these, and, if so, which, and in what combinations or permutations? The variety of possibilities is itself sufficient indication of the difficulty.

5. *Particularity.* God's Word, as noted, comes through the human word. This means that it is historically set and grounded. Hence the problem of relation is particularly severe in the Bible. God has selected a specific background in the form of a people, its changing milieu, its history, customs, tradition, language(s). Interpretation has to reckon with this particularity. It must begin with the notoriously difficult procedure of translation. It has then to immerse itself in the alien background with the urgency imposed by the fact that here and thus God speaks. Finally, it has to decide continually whether, or how far, the particularity is contingent or essential, or at different levels or both. In other words, is interpretation simple exposition or is it also reinterpretation? Must we all become Hebrews? Must we transpose Hebrew modes of expression into European, American, Asiatic, or African ones? Is there a delicate balance between the two? Can we wrap the gospel in other packages? Or is the package integral to the content? Or is some part integral, and, if so, which, and by what criteria?

C. *Personal Hermeneutical Difficulties*

1. *The personal relation.* A new dimension opens up with the personal equation. Interpretation is not just a matter of a machinelike reader studying a lifeless text. The reading subject brings something with him—his own background, education, presuppositions, culture, character, needs, and desires. Again, the text also has independent reality. It is not just clay to be molded. It is what it is, not what the reader or hearer makes of it. It is a datum no less than the data of nature or history. It has been given indeed by another

subject, the author, who through it does not just provide a starting point for the hearer's thoughts but conveys what is in his own mind. Scripture is the text that communicates to the first subject, the reader or hearer, what is meant by the second subject, the author. But, to adapt a proverb, there is many a slip between the lip and the ear, partly through difficulties in the text, as discussed above, but not least through the predisposition of the hearer. Overcoming the problem of predisposition is a big part of the hermeneutical task.

2. *The hearing subject.* The predisposition of the hearer or reader, including also the interpreter, is in fact one of the greatest single hermeneutical difficulties. It arises in all communication. We hear or read what we want to hear or read or are conditioned to hear or read. Every debate makes this plain. Arguments may be distorted or ignored rather than pondered. What is brought affects what is there. Nothing is harder to achieve than a true objectivity of listening. If this is a general hermeneutical problem, it is especially acute in relation to Scripture. Historically the biblical world seems so alien in its particularity that one instinctively tries to view it through the lens of the familiar world. At the divine level the world of God is even stranger, for his thoughts and ways are not ours, and, as Paul says in 1 Corinthians 2:11, only the Spirit of God can know divine things. At our own human level, we are all sinners, with alienated hearts and darkened minds. The special tendency of the sinner to see things out of focus notably affects the reading of the divine message in Holy Scripture. Sinful man is himself a primary problem when it comes to interpreting God's Word.

3. *The speaking subject.* Communication naturally has at least two sides. If one could approach a text with the sincerest possible objectivity, there would still be the problem of discovering, not just what is said, but what the author or speaker means. As noted earlier, words, however carefully used, are not precision tools. To cross the personal bridge one must cross a linguistic and literary bridge. In the case of Scripture the situation is complicated by the fact that God communicates through human speakers and writers. Hence, there are two speaking subjects—first, the specific author and then God himself. If the first difficulty is to know precisely what, e.g., Jeremiah or Peter is saying, the second is to know what God is saying through Jeremiah or Peter. From one standpoint it might seem that the second difficulty is less serious than the first, for after all God, unlike Jeremiah or Peter, is still alive and at work. This truth will certainly have to be taken into account, as it has been both in the NT and also in the history of interpretation. Nevertheless, God has elected to speak mediately through the human authors rather than immediately, so that to hear him we must hear them. This shows God's wisdom, for immediacy in his speaking to sinners would obliterate the personal element in reception, apprehension, and response. Yet the mode of God's communication means that hermeneutics operates at a twofold if related level in terms of the speaking subject. To know what the speakers mean, and hence to know what God means, is both the ultimate goal and the ultimate difficulty of hermeneutics.

III. The History of Interpretation

A. *The Patristic Age*

1. *The continuity of the Testaments.* Some basic principles of interpretation came to be generally recognized in the patristic age. The first of these is the belief that the NT

fulfills the OT, so that neither can be properly understood without the other. This belief is integral to the NT itself. Jesus saw himself as the Messiah bringing salvation by his life, death, and resurrection and coming again to consummate his promised lordship. The apostles preached him as the fulfillment of the OT prophecies. Paul proclaimed him as the seed of the covenanted promise. Hebrews offered a christological interpretation of sacral law and Revelation took up again the themes of Genesis in the closing eschatological visions.

This NT understanding found clear expression in the apostolic fathers and apologists. OT precedents were adduced for Christian conduct (1 Clement) and fulfilled prophecy formed an important argument to both Jews and Gentiles (Justin). The OT Scriptures, for Justin, were really the Christian's, since he alone saw their true meaning (Dial., 29). The Epistle of Barnabas made the same point in a polemical and extravagant reinterpretation of law, temple, and sabbath.

The principle met with opposition, especially from Marcion. While the Gnostics were ready to retain parts of the OT in spiritualized form, Marcion advanced a hermeneutic that set the judicial God of the OT over against the gracious God of the NT and consequently decanonized all the OT and such of the NT as supported it. A peculiar reading of Paul underlay this drastic procedure. Irenaeus and Tertullian refuted Marcion. The creeds equated Father and Creator. Canonical discussion never even considered demoting what had been Scripture from the beginning. Conciliar rulings increasingly assimilated the church to OT concepts and practices. In a decision no less momentous because largely tacit and self-evident, patristic thought "Christianized" the OT. In this regard later writers like Origen, Theophilus, and Jerome simply developed the established thesis. Augustine summed it up in his famous aphorism that the NT is latent in the OT and the OT is patent in the NT.

2. *The centrality of Christ.* Related and indeed basic to the continuity of the Testaments is the centrality of Christ in all Scripture. Even before the NT canon existed, Christ in his person, word, and work constituted the fulfillment of OT promise and prophecy. This understanding, too, is from the very first the essence of Christianity. Christ expounded the things concerning himself in all three parts of the OT. The apostles preached Christ as the theme and goal of the OT. Stephen offered a christological interpretation of OT history. Philip answered the question of the Ethiopian eunuch by pointing to Christ. Paul set Christ at the heart of salvation, the "from whom," the "by whom," and the "to whom."

Early Christian writings adopt the same christological focus. OT interpretations all have Christ as theme or center. Justin in his *Dialogue with Trypho* seeks to induce acceptance of Christ as Emmanuel, Suffering Servant, and Messiah. Barnabas finds the true reality of the temple or sabbath in Christ; indeed, he even descries Christ and the Cross in the 318 servants of Abraham (300 = T = cross, 18 = IS = Jesus). Irenaeus sees in Christ the second Adam reversing the fatal disobedience of the first. For Origen, the sin offering points to the once-for-all sacrifice on Golgotha. Augustine applies the principle to the NT even in points of detail; the Good Samaritan represents Christ. Theodore of Mopsuestia, advocate of historical exegesis, still finds a secondary application to Christ, especially in many psalms. Jerome advances Christ more boldly as the subject of all Scripture typified in Joshua or the Branch of Jeremiah. If Christ is related to the Bible in different ways, his hermeneutical centrality is everywhere advocated.

3. *The ministry of the Spirit.* Because the Holy Spirit is the true author of Scripture, he

is essential to its proper understanding. In the NT the disciples show an obtuseness that only God's work can penetrate. Paul explains in 1 Corinthians 2:14 that the natural man can understand divine things only if he has the mind of God, i.e., the Spirit. The Jews read the OT with a veil, having only the letter (cf. 2 Cor 3). The Lord, the Spirit, alone can pierce the veil so that the proper sense is discerned. What applies to the OT also applies to the gospel and hence by ready extension to the NT too.

The fathers universally endorse this principle that there can be real understanding only in and with the Holy Spirit. What precisely the Spirit does is hard to define. Sometimes the stress seems to be more academic, but then a volitional element also enters in, the accepting of that which is perceived as well as its perception. In general one may say that the Spirit's work is to give the understanding in which things plain in themselves fall into place and hence are almost necessarily accepted.

The two main exegetical schools from the third century on, the allegorical at Alexandria and the historical at Antioch, both emphasized this essential ministry of the Spirit. The one naturally tended to relate it to the deeper senses of the text, whether christological or practical. The other, while rejecting allegorical insights, especially when strained or fanciful, and pleading for consistent contextual exposition, still sought a unified interpretation for which *theoria* or insight was required as well as ordinary intellectual apprehension. *Theoria* entails a connected understanding of all Scripture, and it is in this area that the interpretative ministry of the Spirit proves indispensable.

The Holy Spirit does not give intelligibility to what is otherwise incomprehensible. Scripture is in general plain in and of itself. What the Spirit does is to grant understanding of the spiritual reality in and behind the historical material. This understanding involves both realization of what it is all about and also conviction of its truth. Naturally, if Scripture does not have this "divine" dimension, the idea of the Spirit's ministry is illusory. But the fathers believed it does; hence the reality and necessity of that ministry.

4. *The problem of allegory.* While agreeing on the Spirit's ministry, the fathers differed about the validity of allegorizing as a hermeneutical device. Philo of Alexandria was already allegorizing the OT in his apologetic presentation to Hellenism. Barnabas moved from typology to allegory in his Christian interpretation of the OT. The Christian Gnostics, whose Hellenizing ruled out a literal interpretation, took the significant step of allegorizing the NT as well as the OT. So the five foolish virgins could be the five senses, or the unforgiving servant the demiurge. Orthodoxy seems to have taken up the same method largely in self-defense. In the OT field, allegorizing met many of Marcion's drastic conclusions, while in the NT alternative allegorizings countered the Gnostic interpretation.

Two important considerations inclined Origen to adopt the allegorical system. First, he followed the Platonic principle of his predecessor Clement that the lower symbolizes the higher. Second, he found in Scripture things so implausible in a literal sense that a higher meaning had to be sought. The ontic presupposition and the apologetic concern combined to produce the full-scale allegorizing of Alexandria.

Origen abandoned the literal sense only in a few instances where the surface meaning seemed impossible. Normally he added to it two other senses to achieve correspondence to man's tripartite being. We thus have the literal, the moral, and the spiritual senses suitable for the simple stage, the more mature, and the fully mature. Application is made to the will in the second stage and to Christ and the church (typology) in the third, though in practice Origen often reverses the two. Thus Noah's ark refers historically to the Flood, then typologically to Christ's provision of an ark of salvation (the church), and finally, devotionally, to the individual preparation of an ark of conversion. For Origen and his school, Scripture thus became a vast ocean or forest full of hidden depths to be explored.

The Antioch school, championed by Theodore and Theodoret, found here a dangerous, if exciting, method. Allegory too quickly divorced itself from the real meaning. Pursuing byways, it hampered connected exposition. It also allowed the easy intrusion of alien matter. In contrast, the historical school, while permitting typology, insisted on the stringent rules that the natural sense be retained and that the connection between it and the typological meaning be demonstrated. If greater flexibility could be allowed homiletically, as in Chrysostom, this hermeneutic meant the restriction of allegorizing, not its proliferation.

Allegorization established itself in the later patristic age. Yet under Antiochene influence, and indeed the scholarly work of Origen himself, extravagance was largely avoided. Even Augustine with his principle of nonbiblical signs and his orientation to a spiritual goal came increasingly under the historical element in Scripture and moved generally from earlier strained exegesis (e.g., the water pots of Cana as the six ages of the world) to a more sober typology not unlike that of the scholarly Jerome, whose primary focus, even in allegorizing, was on a Christian understanding of the OT.

5. *Alien intrusion.* As noted, allegorizing provided easy access for ideas alien to Scripture itself. An early critic, Porphyry, noted this, being credited with the remark that Origen "introduced Greek ideas into foreign fables." Yet if allegory almost invites this intrusion, adoption of another hermeneutical scheme does not exclude it. Origen, in fact, was more careful than most to insure that his interpretation would be true to the text, language, and background of Scripture. The danger of seeing the Bible through alien spectacles, perhaps under the illusion that they have been fitted by the Holy Spirit, is one against which all interpreters have to be on guard.

Ironically, the fact that most of the fathers were Greek-speaking compounded the problem rather than resolved it. Since the OT was available in Greek, few took the trouble to check it by the Hebrew. Inevitably then, apart from the checks of tradition, the Greek was often interpreted in terms of the familiar Hellenic or Hellenistic world rather than the Hebraic or Judaic background. This happens in any language, but the danger is, if anything, more subtle when the language is either the same, as in the NT, or has virtually replaced the original, as in the OT.

The training many fathers received made matters worse, for, while valuable in itself, it furnished them with constructs different from those of Scripture. Deceptively simple words like "truth" or "hope," as well as difficult ones like "hypostasis," could undergo a shift in content. Indeed, the whole approach changed, as one may see from the nature and form of early theological problems and debates. The fathers were immersed in the task of presenting biblical material in alien forms and with an intellectual and cultural equipment only partially derived from Scripture itself. An unhappy result was the increasing use of texts to establish positions which, even if orthodox, were hardly the real concern of the passages themselves, as one may see from the complicated debates between Athanasius and the Arians. Where the intrusion is only of form and issue, not of basic content, the hermeneutical distortion is, of course, less severe. But even the dogmatic exegesis of orthodoxy demonstrates the distortion.

B. *The Medieval Period*

1. *Language.* A difficulty seen already among the fathers increased seriously in the Middle Ages. This was the loss of the original language, Greek as well as Hebrew in the West, and dependence on translation. Now the Eastern church still had Greek, Jerome's Vulgate was a good rendering, and Hebrew (and Greek) scholarship did not die out, staging indeed a strong recovery in the later Middle Ages. Nevertheless, inadequate linguistic study had a harmful effect on medieval hermeneutics.

This may be summed up as the loss of the effective control that only the original can maintain. Positively, this control means knowledge of the precise meaning in a given context. Negatively, it means exclusion of impermissible meanings that might seem plausible in translation. Furthermore, it carries with it the ability to compensate for historical development in the language of translation. When this control is forfeited or impaired, as in the Middle Ages or indeed at any time when translations are no longer checked against the original, poor interpretation inevitably flourishes.

2. *Allegory.* The virtual canonizing of allegorization made matters worse. The school of natural interpretation did, of course, persist. It found some notable representatives in the early Middle Ages and came back in full force in the fifteenth century. Generally speaking, however, allegorizing dominated medieval hermeneutics.

Gregory the Great had given it a solid start with his remarks on the sense of Scripture in the preface to Job. Origen's threefold sense quickly developed into the fourfold sense (literal, allegorical, moral, and spiritual) as classically stated and illustrated by Guibert of Nogent, for whom Jerusalem in the Bible was literally the earthly city, allegorically the church, morally the individual Christian, and spiritually the new Jerusalem. In true interpretation, all these senses had to be understood with each mention of the name.

Of the innumerable instances of allegorizing, two of the most striking are in pretentious papal statements. Innocent III based papal supremacy on the two great lights of Genesis 1, the sun representing the spiritual power, the smaller one, the moon, which takes its light from the sun, representing the temporal power. Boniface VIII found his biblical support in the NT. The two swords of Luke 22, which again stand for the two kingdoms, are both in the hands of the disciples (i.e., the church), of whom Peter is head; hence the one is to be used *by* the church and the other *for* it.

These crass examples show clearly how allegorizing distorts exegesis. It can produce little agreement, for the popes did not go unchallenged. Even at best, it becomes strained and fanciful, bearing only a remote relation to the text. It lends itself to manipulation in various interests—theological, ethical, and devotional as well as ecclesiastical. Its complexity makes interpretation an esoteric pursuit from which ordinary readers are debarred. Attention is shifted away from the real meaning, so that understanding is in fact hampered and the Bible cannot function properly as a theological and practical norm.

3. *Secondary authority.* The complexity of allegorical exposition also combined with other factors to enhance the role of secondary authority. The rule of faith had been advanced as a hermeneutical criterion in the early church, not altogether without cause in the conflict with Gnostic hermeneutics. With every conciliar decision, especially in doctrine, Scripture came under the increasing restriction of permissible interpretation. Much of this was beneficial, since developing orthodoxy was demonstrably biblical. The Middle Ages soon showed how dangerous the principle was. Expansion of the sphere

of orthodoxy meant limitation of the freedom of exposition and indeed of the freedom of Scripture to speak for itself, especially when "orthodoxy" came to be dubious from a biblical standpoint. Secondary authority, whether in the guise of creed, oral tradition, fathers, councils, or teaching office, came more and more to impose an obligatory sense on Scripture, to the detriment both of good hermeneutics and also of the Bible's own authority.

Exegesis of the eucharistic sayings offers a notable example. Originally these seem to have caused little trouble, but from the ninth century the literal school of Radbert collided with the figurative school of Ratramn in the same western convent of Corbie in France. Eleventh-century synods then ruled that in their natural sense the sayings are literal, and the foisting of the dogma of transubstantiation on the church quickly followed. Hermeneutically important here is not the dogma as such but the replacement of authoritative Scripture by an authoritative interpretation (backed by force) against which no further appeal could be made even on exegetical grounds.

If the primary mischief lay in the sphere of authority, the effect on interpretation was hardly less detrimental. In an ever-expanding sphere, interpretation was brought under tight control. Wild views were checked, but so too was ongoing study along sober and constructive lines. The task of the interpreter changed. Instead of trying to get at the true sense, he now had to substantiate the imposed interpretation, or, indeed, to provide the texts that might seem to support what was agreed in advance to be the authentic dogmatic meaning.

4. *External orientation.* Medieval interpretation suffered also from external rather than internal orientation. Scripture's own concerns were not studied. Scripture was subjugated to extraneous needs. Thus, interpretation became very largely application, the wrong type in which imposed ends are served, not the right type in which Scripture can fulfill its own ends.

One may see this devotionally, not merely in the extravagancies of the mystics, but also in the evangelical expositions of Bernard of Clairvaux. Bernard made Canticles religiously exciting and rewarding, but only by an application that transgresses the bounds of hermeneutical sobriety.

In philosophical theology the situation was far worse. Anselm, it is true, had not tried to thrust an alien philosophical role on Scripture; he had shown by philosophy the inner rationality of Scripture's teaching. Scholastic theology, however, attempted a synthesis in which theology became academic syllogisms and Scripture was allotted the artificial task of supporting the positions adopted. Even when the synthesis broke down, the method largely remained. No biblical theology arose under the impulse of authentic contextual study. Orientation to extraneous goals excluded proper expository work. In a specious display of relevance—the relating of Scripture to current interest—a basic hermeneutical irrelevance resulted.

C. The Renaissance and Reformation

1. *Language and history.* If wrong hermeneutical choices and procedures characterized the medieval period, better principles always found advocates. In an astonishing reversal, these finally triumphed in the Renaissance, of which the reformers were, hermeneutically, a part.

The Renaissance restored linguistic and historical study to its proper place. It did so, first, by going back to the originals. Textual and lexical investigation under men like

Linacre, Erasmus, and Reuchlin became the foundation on which a Luther or Calvin could build.

It did so, in the second place, by insistence on the natural or historical sense. This did not exclude figurative usage, for what the original intended as a symbol or metaphor should obviously be construed as such. What it did exclude was an additional allegorical sense where the original had none such in view. Adoption of this principle revolutionized both interpretation and the derived teaching and practice.

It did so, in the third place, by a first approach to the consideration of background as well as text. This was rudimentary enough. The biblical world was still largely seen as self-contained. Yet a beginning was made. Since God had rooted Scripture in world history, its full understanding could be attained only against the divinely given background. Broader historical study had necessarily to be initiated.

2. *Christology and soteriology.* The reorientation begun by the Renaissance was carried a stage farther by the Reformation with the restoring of the primitive christological and soteriological emphasis. If Luther's problems contributed in part to this, the main impulse came from the new study started by the hermeneutical revolution. Luther did not just read Scripture in the light of his own situation; he learned to know his own situation by reading Scripture.

Fundamental to the Reformation interpretation is the realization that Scripture's real theme is God's word and work of salvation in Christ. Different aspects might be stressed by individual reformers: justification by Luther, God's sovereign grace by Zwingli and Calvin, doctrines like election or the covenant by later dogmaticians. Nevertheless, the underlying theme in each case was not an abstract concept, but Christ and the grace of God in him. This provided the unifying core for detailed interpretation.

The christological and soteriological core explains three Reformation rules: 1) Books that best present the gospel, like Romans or John, form the starting point of exposition. This was Luther's view and, while other reformers did not follow him exactly, they agreed that one should work from the center to the periphery in the analogy of faith (and love). Paul's Epistles always played an important role here.

2) Difficult passages are to be explained in the light of the more perspicuous ones. What is clear, essential, and unequivocal (like the rule of faith of Irenaeus and Tertullian) is the key to the obscure, peripheral, and ambivalent. The implication is that Scripture, self-consistent as the divine Word, should not be so construed as to make it at odds with itself.

3) Typological exposition is valid. The reformers trod warily here. Realizing the dangers of unchecked allegory, they strongly advocated the linguistic study and natural exegesis that had freed them for evangelical understanding. Nevertheless, they saw that the Bible's christological unity grants material validation of typology, and NT practice adds formal validation. NT practice, however, constituted a norm as well as a model. Only types found in Scripture may be admitted in strict exegesis. Thus the Red Sea and the Flood are true types of baptism, but not Naaman's cleansing. This rule curbed the ill-advised exercise of typologizing ingenuity.

3. *Testimony of the Spirit.* While endorsing linguistic and historical study, the Reformation did not reduce Scripture to a book of human religion. Focus on the christological and soteriological center involved a perspective which, if demonstrably that of Scripture, still demands a decision of faith. At this level the Spirit's ministry found a place in Reformation hermeneutics.

The Reformation perspective is that Scripture is God's Book, so that the divine authorship, theme, and purpose have also to be understood in proper interpretation. Granting realization of the divine authorship, assurance of its truth, and perception of its message is the work of the Holy Spirit, described in the Reformation phrase as the inner testimony.

Three points should be noted in relation to the Spirit's testimony. Primarily, it confers persuasion that Scripture is what it purports to be, that its word is truth. Second, this implies not mere cognition, but believing insight into what Scripture says as personal entry into its meaning. Third, this in turn, while not replacing ordinary study or postulating an esoteric sense beyond the natural, opens the door to understanding of Scripture from its own standpoint and not in terms of alien presupposition.

For reformers like Luther, Zwingli, and Calvin, the Spirit's testimony was no mystical experience. It accompanied hard study of the Greek and Hebrew text. To the intellectual apprehension thus afforded it added the assurance of truth, entry into biblical reality, and the hermeneutical understanding that human study alone cannot achieve. Word and Spirit work together in true interpretation.

4. *Biblical unity.* Recognizing the divine authorship and truth of Scripture, the reformers naturally viewed it as a unity despite all its variety. Here, however, important differences also developed. The Anabaptists, after the fiasco of apocalyptic biblicism, retreated into an early dispensationalism that focused on the NT and largely spiritualized the OT. The main reformers, while appreciating the distinction of the Testaments, laid greater stress on their unity, as illustrated by the one covenant with circumcision/baptism as its sign.

Yet tension also existed between the Lutherans and the Reformed. The former made more of the antithesis between law and gospel while the latter set law within the general work of grace, adding to Luther's two uses of the law a third use in which it would give direction for the Christian life. Yet distinction could still be made within the law, for, as the Anglican article (7) points out, only the moral law is now binding. The ceremonial law was fulfilled in Christ's work (cf. Hebrews) and the political and economic law applied only to God's people as a nation-state. If a tendency still persisted—in Geneva, New England, and the English Commonwealth—to transfer the status of Israel to Christian nations, strict insistence on all the details of OT legislation found little advocacy.

Fundamentally, it is clear that neither Luther nor the Anabaptists had any real quarrel with the permanent validity of the moral law as a guide to Christian conduct. The Lutherans in particular stressed also the role of the OT as witness to the coming Christ in harmony and comparison with the NT as witness to Christ already come. The Anabaptists made a more serious hermeneutical breach between the Testaments with their sharper dispensationalism and their spiritualizing absorption of the OT into the NT. Even here, however, the differentiation is only hermeneutical; the material unity of Scripture remains intact.

D. *Liberal Protestantism*

1. *Achievements.* The post-Reformation era saw a decline from the hermeneutical insights of the reformers. This came not from basic reorientation but from dogmatic concentration that tended to impose a new yoke on Scripture. Pietist and apologetic concerns had a similar effect. A new epoch of biblical study then began, however, with

liberal Protestantism, and this brought not only serious losses but also outstanding achievements.

a. The first achievement was a new attention to the humanity of Scripture and the consequent expansion of literary, historical, and cultural investigation. As the eighteenth-century scholar J.G. Herder put it, the Bible was to be studied as a book written by men, about men, and for men. The relentless research that followed opened up a wealth of hermeneutical material that no age, not even that of the rabbis or the fathers, had ever before had at its command.

b. As a second achievement, one may refer, more specifically, to the detailed fields of expansion. Textual study was set on a scientific basis. Lexical knowledge made vast improvement to fix the precise meanings of words and phrases. Historical, geographical, and archaeological information was amassed to give new vividness and pertinence to many passages and incidents. Literary criticism, if often destructive, offered a new appreciation of the form, style, character, and patterns of the component writings of Scripture, their relation to similar works, and their function as the vessel of divine self-revelation.

c. Third, historical study naturally carried with it a focus on the religious aspect of Scripture, which, if one-sided, is still of value. Comparative religion has been of service here. Even more so has been the concern to use Scripture in the nurture of pure religious life. This was part of the liberal Protestant tradition from the outset; indeed, it dated back to the Renaissance. It did much to counteract more sterile factors.

d. Finally, if incidentally, liberal Protestant studies helped to give new meaning to the concept of the historical particularity of God's Word and work. Hitherto not enough had been known about the details for a proper grasp of this. If historicity was important, the tendency to generalize, whether allegorically or philosophically, had blunted the sharp contours of historical singularity. Even the reformers could not get far enough here. Only as the human element in Scripture came to light could the distinctiveness of the divine work be perceived.

2. *Losses.* Unfortunately the achievements, though real, were accompanied by serious losses. This is why the liberal orientation, if it is not to do more harm than good in hermeneutics, must be firmly handled as a servant rather than foolishly accepted as a master.

a. Failure to interpret Scripture as God-given is the first loss. While study of the human aspect is good, justice is not done to the reality of Scripture if it is viewed only as a human work. Thus as human literature it could be seen as the record of a religious quest. Its concepts of God, though reviewed sympathetically, could be assessed simply as human ideas or gropings. This is good hermeneutics, however, only if the Bible is not divine revelation and the concepts do not correspond to authentic realities. The open or tacit assumption that this is so has plagued liberal exegesis and put it completely out of focus if, as the Bible believes about itself, the assumption is wrong. Barth had this in view when he described the historical objectivity of liberal Protestantism as supremely "comical"; it does not accept the object for what it is and claims to be.

b. Related to this is the effort to make a new Scripture out of the existing one. Liberal study has never been satisfied with the Bible as it is. Textually it has wanted emendations or excisions. At the literary level it has had an urge to break up, to rearrange, to find redactional strata. Historically it has constantly attempted reconstruction. If not all of this has been bad or unjustified, the plain fact is that there can be no solid interpretation of a conjectural Scripture. Until hard facts support the re- or de-redaction, exegesis based on it is itself conjectural. Hermeneutics can deal only with an objectively real document.

c. Liberal study has also been vitiated by a persistent distinction between husk and kernel. Herder and Schleiermacher differentiated religion from religions. Harnack plucked out verities like the divine fatherhood as the kernel. Bultmann sought the existential reality behind the mythological garb. Common here is interpretation at two levels, the one essential and permanent, the other peripheral and disposable. The first hermeneutical task is to distinguish between them. But serious problems arise. By what criteria can one distinguish between them? How can these criteria be other than subjective? Does not this invite reading "in" rather than "out"? What guarantee is there for the truth of the proposed differentiation? Unless Scripture itself plainly supports the procedure, hermeneutics is in fact brought into disarray by this dualistic principle.

d. The relativizing that is integral to the husk/kernel distinction is hermeneutically destructive in other ways too. Historically, the discovery of new materials, Persian in Herder's day or Gnostic in our own, has produced excited efforts to interpret Scripture, or part of it, one-sidedly in this new relation. More generally, the search for relevance has caused trouble. False questions have been put to Scripture, artificial answers squeezed out of it, and its content arbitrarily discarded or refashioned. The broader cultural aspect of relativism should also be noted. Historical study has emphasized that Scripture speaks in specific cultural forms. If, however, its message is for men of all cultures, how important is the cultural particularity to the message? Can the message be abstracted from the setting as in the husk/kernel procedure? Can it be put in other settings? Is this after all the real task of interpretation? A question of delicacy arises here. The Bible's cultural relativity is undeniable and yet, as translation shows, the element of cultural particularity is not to be treated as mere contingency. The problem with liberal Protestant interpretation is that, concentrating on Scripture's humanity and stressing comparative study, it has initiated excessive relativizing and therewith the dissolution of biblical and Christian uniqueness.

e. Reference should be made finally to the liberal bias towards specialization. Exposition of Scripture has again become a matter for experts, and ordinary readers can even be discouraged. By a different route the same hermeneutical constriction is thus reached as that of the Middle Ages. A scholars' veil is drawn over perspicuous Scripture. Reading may continue freely, but the constitution of biblical experts as a modern teaching office imposes a new authoritarianism whose destructiveness is enhanced by the fact that it is so confusing and self-contradictory. For all its achievements, then, liberal Protestantism has also contributed heavily to hermeneutical obfuscation and disintegration.

3. *The issue.* The underlying issue raised by liberalism has been brought into sharp focus by recent work in hermeneutics. On the basis of linguistic and epistemological analysis, theologians like Bultmann and Tillich have expanded the field to cover the whole relationship of God and man in communication. How do human words convey God's truth in such a way that it can be understood? How can man appropriate what is spoken to him?

The primary contention in the new hermeneutics is that if meaning is to be grasped, there must be a preunderstanding in the recipient or a correlativity between man's word and God's. The preunderstanding has naturally to be enlarged and corrected but without it communication is impossible. Thus the fatherhood of God means something to us only because of a prior knowledge and experience of fatherhood. The divine message is correlative to the prior concept. The preunderstanding forms the indispensable starting point of appropriation.

Now at one level this is an incontestable truism. God has not chosen to speak in an ineffable mode surpassing all human experience. As the Creator who made man in his image, he condescends to speak in intelligible forms and to act in understandable history. The higher dimension of his words and works does not cancel the fact that he uses speech and action that man can formally understand.

Unfortunately, however, the new hermeneutics overemphasizes the preunderstanding and draws exaggerated and invalid inferences from it. It seems to be saying that man cannot learn what is not yet within the grasp of his experience and knowledge. It allows the need to explain to become a need to replace when we come up against statements in Scripture that do not fit in with modern thought-forms or concepts, so that the whole message can call for reconstruction. It minimizes the possibility that words and concepts can and do acquire a new meaning or dimension when they are used by God. The ministry of the Holy Spirit is thus eliminated or restricted. The prejudgment can become a preconceived notion that hampers proper interpretation, shutting out the God whose thoughts and ways are not ours, but who is himself seeking to communicate with us in his Word.

The issue is brought to light here because the new hermeneutics reduces theology to anthropology. This is not just a question of method. Hermeneutics from the standpoint of the recipient is not inherently illegitimate. What is illegitimate is to allow the possibilities (or limitations) of the recipient to dominate interpretation to such a degree that the object cannot do its own work, that the particularity of God's Word and work is relativized, and that the possibilities of the Holy Spirit, of God as speaking subject, are restricted or ignored. The basic fault of liberalism is the reduction of God to the measure of man instead of bringing man under the measure of God. The renewing and regenerating ministry of the Holy Spirit comes under the yoke of the self upon which it works and is no longer an authentic reality in the understanding and appropriation of Holy Scripture. Hermeneutics is thus brought into the anthropological bondage that is in fact the essence of the liberal deviation.

IV. The Principles of Interpretation

A. General Principles

1. *Objectivity.* Surveying the problems and history of interpretation might induce a pessimistic mood. Attempts to apply the biblical norm seem to be beset by insuperable difficulties. In fact, however, certain principles emerge that, if observed, offer the possibility of authentic and constructive understanding. To begin with general principles, we see first the need for an objectivity that expounds the Bible as it is, as an entity in its own right, a datum that is not to be ignored, replaced, reconstructed, or oriented to something else.

Objectivity, while simple and self-evident, proves hard to achieve in practice. There is pressure to find a text behind the text, to read out or in what is not there, to read what is there in the light of something else. Yet once we accept the difficulty, we can achieve a degree of objectivity in biblical science as in natural science. The student cannot come to Scripture in a vacuum. Yet he can come recognizing the independent validity of the object of study and trying to learn what it is from itself, not from his preconceptions or reinterpretations. This recognition furthers good hermeneutics.

2. *Receptivity.* Overlapping objectivity, yet surpassing and supplementing it, is receptivity. This is not just seeing what the object is from itself but also openness to learn from it, to accept correction by it. It is humility before Scripture, the teachability of the learner. Obviously one does not have to be predisposed toward the message of Scripture to attain any understanding of it. But one does have to let Scripture say its own piece without criticizing, answering back, or readjusting. The time will come for decision. Some may arrogantly or regretfully reject what they hear, just as others will gladly or hesitantly believe it. But to get even an inkling of what it is all about, and thus to make significant assessment possible, receptivity is an indispensable prerequisite.

3. *Heterocentricity.* Objectivity and receptivity imply heterocentricity, i.e., finding a center outside the self. Where they are absent, and misinterpretation results, one may ascribe this mainly to egocentricity. The subject holds the stage, setting his own goals, imposing his own ideas and criteria, exploiting for his own purposes, relating to his own needs or situation, demanding relevance to his individual or collective self. The scholar has his theory, the churchman is concerned about his ecclesiology, the dogmatician wants confirmation of his teaching, the philosopher tests by his system, the man with a problem requires an answer to his own question. A basic egocentricity gets in the way of real understanding and usually defeats the end in view. A true dialogue with Scripture is replaced with a monologue using biblical materials in various ways. The principles of objectivity and receptivity cannot operate properly because the center is not shifted away from the self to the object, to Scripture. To function, they must be accompanied by the closely related principle of heterocentricity.

B. *Technical Principles*

1. *Natural exegesis.* General principles must be supported, of course, by technical principles. These, too, may be stated with some degree of certainty. The first is obviously that of natural exegesis. Scripture is to be read and understood, not as an esoteric work, but in its plain sense. The plain sense does not exclude transferred or metaphorical meanings where these are intended. It does not rule out the use of parable, illustration, symbol, or even, on occasion, allegory. It leaves room for typology insofar as the NT itself presents a typological understanding of the OT. It recognizes the presence of different literary genres. Nevertheless it cannot tolerate the arbitrary introduction of any or all of these things where the Bible does not intend them. Granted that the natural sense may sometimes be debatable, in most cases discerning the true purport presents little serious difficulty. What the Bible says, and means to say, is the factual reality to which the student's objectivity, receptivity, and reorientation relate. The natural sense alone constitutes this factuality.

2. *Scientific aids.* In arriving at the natural sense, certain scientific aids are indispensable and their employment is thus a second technical principle. Since the autographa of Scripture no longer exist, textual study must be pursued to establish the correct wording. Words, however, do not have fixed or single meanings, and hence the help of lexical investigation must be enlisted to find the right sense in given cases. Texts do not exist in a historical or cultural vacuum; the narrower and broader background has to be studied for the light it sheds on what is said or recorded. The aim of these researches is not, of course, to overturn the factuality of Scripture, to master Scripture, to subordinate it to external factors, to make it other than it is. They are in the strict sense aids.

They are to be used as such. When they are so used, the insights won from them make an invaluable contribution to a proper interpretation of Scripture in the natural sense of what it says and is meant to say.

3. *Historical study.* Expounding Scripture in the natural sense and with textual, linguistic, and contextual aids still leaves a basic question unanswered, namely, that of the enduring message of Scripture in and through its historical form. In the face of this question a third and final technical principle emerges. A twofold investigation has to be conducted (1) with reference to the Bible itself and (2) with reference to its intellectual or cultural transplantation in the postbiblical period. As regards (1), the point is to establish what elements in Scripture are merely relative to the existing situation and what elements, even though culturally conditioned, have been given the stamp of divine particularity and are thus to be accepted as integral, constitutive, and normative. As regards (2), the point is to supplement (1) by examining concepts and practices that have been historically adopted in different cultures as expressions of biblical theology and ethics with a view to distinguishing between the legitimate and the illegitimate. Along these lines, misinterpretation can be avoided both by not ascribing normativeness to what is contingent and by learning to see what is invalid in one's own or other cultural expressions of biblical teaching. Carrying out the principle of historical study is more difficult than carrying out the first two and yet its importance is no less decisive. Even the natural sense attained with the best available aids is defenseless against ultimate subjectivity if the reader chooses arbitrarily, or wrongly, between what is contingent and what is absolute, or if he equates the absolute with this or that in his own or another intellectual, spiritual, philosophical, or cultural background. Part of attaining the sense intended and of making proper use of scientific aids is the fixing of an objective differentiation between the essential and the contingent. A study of this in Scripture and a survey of its outworking in Christian history—successful, disastrous, or ambivalent—form an illuminating part of hermeneutics that no reader of Scripture can afford to ignore.

C. *Theological Principles*

1. *Divine authorship.* Coming to Scripture objectively and seeking its essential content by study of the natural sense with scientific aids, one quickly sees that many theological principles followed by past exegetes can claim validity and ought to be endorsed and practiced in sound hermeneutics. Primary here is the divine authorship of Scripture. This is a doctrine plainly taught by Scripture, and neither arbitrarily imported into it nor fancifully extracted from it. Scripture understands itself, not as an essay in human religion but as divine self-revelation.

Now the student may believe Scripture is wrong. He may prefer a human factuality to that which Scripture itself asserts. If so, he is making a historical judgment rather than engaging in interpretation. Even if the judgment attempts an explanation of the Bible's self-understanding, what is interpreted is the presumed reality rather than the reality as it is. Good interpretation demands that Scripture be expounded in its factuality, including its self-understanding as divine revelation. There remains the alternative of viewing this self-understanding as merely a contingent and conditioned factor but this has little cogency in view of the centrality of divine initiative in biblical theology. Good hermeneutics must proceed on the principle that Scripture views itself and its substance as God-given and that exposition can be sound only according to this perspective, whether or not the interpreter is finally persuaded of its truth.

2. *Christology.* When the OT and NT are seen and interpreted in relation to each other, the principle of christological exposition needs little demonstration. The whole point of the NT, and indeed of Christianity, as the Fathers and the Reformers recognized, is that God's Word and work are brought to fulfillment in Christ. The truth of this NT insight may be contested, as in Judaism. Historical factors may be adduced to explain the notion as a construct of human thought, as in liberal Protestantism. Nevertheless, sound interpretation deals with what is there, not with its supposed falsity or the alleged reason for its being there. Nor can there be any question here of treating Christology as simply an impermanent expression of a different enduring truth. If Christology can be carried too far, as in wilder allegorical and even typological flights, Christianity by its very nature, accepting the NT as well as the OT as Scripture, is committed by the object itself to the christological principle.

3. *The role of the Spirit.* The Bible, viewing itself as God-breathed, seems to state plainly that proper interpretation has to be in the Holy Spirit. This gives us a third theological principle. The student can certainly give an objective account of what the Bible says if he follows the general and technical principles already noted. But he cannot by himself come to full understanding of what is read and expounded. It is the Holy Spirit who grants this ultimate apprehension, as he alone can do so in view of the divine nature of the factuality at issue. The Spirit's role is not to be seen, of course, in mystical terms nor in terms of the esoteric. Normal hermeneutical procedures are not superseded. The general and technical principles still apply. But another principle is added. As Scripture is God-given, and Christ, the Son of God, is its theme, so God the Spirit must be invoked for the grasping of its truth in full understanding.

4. *Scriptural unity.* As the Bible is the Book of God—Father, Son, and Holy Spirit—it is one book, for all its diversity. A final theological principle, then, is that one must interpret it in its unity. Nor does this unity exist merely at the human or historical level. If characteristics of unity may be found a this level, e.g., religious thrust or Hebraic derivation, the unity that counts depends on the divine relation. In human terms, differences may also be perceived. Only as all Scripture, NT as well as OT, is seen according to its self-understanding does its essential unity emerge. Unity does not mean uniformity. Thus different aspects of the OT stand in different relations to the fulfillment in Christ. For this reason variety arises when exegetes or exegetical schools offer their unified interpretation.

The fact remains, however, that to achieve good interpretation that is true to the reality itself, the principle of biblical unity has to be practiced in spite of variation in outworking. Judaism agrees, except that it denies NT canonicity and treats the OT as a self-contained whole. Liberalism questions the NT understanding of Scripture as "mere" interpretation, so that unity is either set aside or established from another angle. Christian hermeneutics, in contrast, finds the true object in the one Bible of OT and NT, so that any breach of scriptural unity on any ground necessarily entails misinterpretation.

V. Conclusion—Residual Problems

The principles listed can go a long way toward insuring good interpretation and consequently a beneficial use of the biblical norm. At the same time certain problems remain and a brief account of these may be given in conclusion.

First, the student's textual, lexical, and historical knowledge, while vast and increasing, inevitably falls short of completeness. Interpretation is always reformable.

Second, sometimes the knowledge available suggests different but equally valid possibilities of understanding. Decisions will thus have to be made that are tenable but not regarded as definitive.

Third, differences of opinion are unavoidable. All readers will accept a difference between the superseded or indifferent on the one hand and that which has enduring validity on the other. Nevertheless, different interpreters will draw the boundary at different points and in different ways. Nor is it easy to see any basis for agreed or irrefutable ruling on the matter. Even when applicability is accepted, the nature, degree, and range are still debatable, as when issues not directly handled in Scripture are brought under biblical scrutiny, or when it is asked whether biblical functions or standards apply to all or only to some Christians.

Fourth, the debate about cultural transplantation still continues in spite of historical investigation. At root, this is another form of the distinction between the essential and the temporary or indifferent. At the center, every Christian has to learn to think and speak in the terms God himself has selected. At the periphery, translation into the cultures is both legitimate and necessary. The problem is fixing the distinction between center and periphery.

Fifth, another form of the same problem remains in relation to biblical unity, which can be viewed very differently even though commonly accepted. Thus dispensationalism, or a concept of progressive revelation, will undoubtedly stress a unity grounded in divine plan and governance, but in practice the result may be widely varied applicability. This does not arise to the same degree, however, when what is stressed is the divine constancy in words and way and will and work.

Finally, the persistent personal problem should also be noted. In dealings with God and his self-revelation, sinfulness constantly militates against a true objectivity, receptivity, and reorientation. It inclines the reader to prejudice, arrogance, self-assertion, and a combativeness often expressed even at points of valid disagreement in understanding. The Holy Spirit can, of course, break through man's sinfulness, so that good interpretation is still a possibility and indeed often a reality. Yet the Holy Spirit is not to be taken for granted as though he were a tool automatically guaranteeing the correctness of any Christian's interpretation. Prayer for the guidance of the Spirit is demanded that he may dispel harmful preconceptions, counteract the damaging effects of sin, and impart the evenness of mind and temper that makes it possible for exposition to be done by the community of believers and not just by individualists. In the last resort, then, prayer is by no means the last or least requirement for good biblical interpretation.

VI. Bibliography

Barth, K. *Church Dogmatics*, vol. 1, part 2. Edited by G.W. Bromiley and T.F. Torrance. Edinburgh: T & T Clark, 1956.

Bartsch, H.W. *Kerygma and Myth*. Translated by R.H. Fuller. London: SPCK, 1953.

Bruce, F.F. *The Christian Approach to the Old Testament*. London: IVF, 1955.

_____. "Interpretation," in *Baker's Dictionary of Theology*. Edited by E.F. Harrison. Grand Rapids: Baker, 1960.

_____. *The New Testament Development of Old Testament Themes*. Grand Rapids: Eerdmans, 1968.

Bultmann, R. *Faith and Understanding,* vol. 1. Translated by L.P. Smith. London: SCM, 1969.

Cambridge History of the Bible, vols. 1–3. Cambridge: Cambridge University Press, 1963–70.

Dodd, C.H. *According to the Scriptures.* London: Nisbet, 1954.

Dugmore, C.W., ed. *The Interpretation of the Bible.* London: SPCK, 1946.

Ebeling, G. "Hermeneutik," in *Religion in Geschichte und Gegenwart.* Edited by K. Galling. Tübingen: Mohr, 1956–65.

Farrar, F.W. *History of Interpretation.* New York: Dutton, 1886.

Grant, R.M. *The Bible in the Church.* New York: Macmillan, 1948.

_____. *The Letter and the Spirit.* London: SPCK, 1957.

Hanson, A.T. *Jesus Christ in the Old Testament.* London: SPCK, 1965.

Hanson, R.P,C. *Allegory and Event.* Richmond: John Knox, 1959.

Kelly, J.N.D. *Early Christian Doctrines.* New York: Harper and Row, 1959.

Lampe, G.W. and Woollcombe, K.J. *Essays in Typology.* Naperville: Allenson, 1957.

Ramm, Bernard. *Protestant Biblical Interpretation.* 1950. Reprint, 3rd. rev. ed. Grand Rapids: Baker, 1970.

Rowley, H.H. *The Unity of the Bible.* Philadelphia: Westminster, 1953.

Smalley, B. *The Study of the Bible in the Middle Ages.* Oxford: Oxford University Press, 1952.

Smart, J.D. *The Interpretation of Scripture.* Philadelphia: Westminster, 1961.

Thielicke, H. *The Evangelical Faith,* vol. 1. 1968. Translated by Geoffrey W. Bromiley. Grand Rapids: Eerdmans, 1974.

Vischer, W. *The Witness of the Old Testament to Christ,* vol. 1. Translated by A.B. Crabtree. London: Lutterworth, 1949.

Walvoord, J.F. *Inspiration and Interpretation.* Grand Rapids: Eerdmans, 1957.

Wood, J.D. *The Interpretation of the Bible.* London: Duckworth, 1958.

THE GEOGRAPHICAL
SETTING OF THE BIBLE

James M. Houston

James M. Houston

M.A., University of Edinburgh; M.A., B.Sc., D.Phil., Oxford University

Principal of Regent College; Honorary Lecturer in the Department of Geography, University of British Columbia

THE GEOGRAPHICAL
SETTING OF THE BIBLE

I. Introduction

People live more comfortably with universals than with particular, concrete realities. The geography of the Bible is relevant to biblical study because the acts of God with men are dealt with in a particular geographical setting and a specific historical context. This article deals with the world of the Bible first within the broad setting of the Near East and then within the local setting of Palestine itself. It describes the major geographical and ecological features of climate, relief, vegetation zones, and the economics of the traditional modes of life. Then it gives more detailed attention to the geographical features of Jerusalem in relation to its location, site, and urban evolution.

Geography shares with history a concern for the particular—for places as well as events. The Bible takes both geography and history seriously in order to narrate events accurately in a real and particular environment. It was not, however, intended to be used either as a mere chronicle of events or as a topographic manual. The reader interested in such events is reminded time and again that he will find such data in *The Book of the Wars of the Lord* (Num 21:14), *The Chronicles of the Kings of Israel* (1 Kings 14:19), and *The Chronicles of the Kings of Judah* (2 Kings 23:28). If, as Lord Acton once said, history is about problems, not periods, then the biblical historiosophy is basically concerned with moral issues. It is primarily the historical revelation of a particular people, embarked on possessing an enduring way of life under God; as such it also has universal appeal and validity. This merger of the particular and the universal creates a tension that many find difficult to accept.

For example, Arnold Toynbee in his *Study of History* has asked, "How can the presence of a hypothetically infinite and eternal God be suffered to make itself felt more palpably in Palestine than in Alberta?" To him and to others also, this religious parochialism in time and place seems a "sacrilegious chauvinism."[1] And yet the biblical assertion that in Palestine in the first century A.D. God was incarnate in Jesus Christ and that his advent was preceded by a sequence of other specific events in definite places by the obedience of certain individuals is logical to the Christian faith. Those who find it impossible to believe that the Incarnation could occur in a particular time and place should logically find it impossible to accept the Incarnation at all. For it is surely illogical to accept the idea of "incarnation" as an emotional idea in a generalized or abstract sense, unless it is tied down to history and geography. And if the Incarnation as a concrete event in space and time is rejected, then clearly Christianity is rejected and the claims of the Bible are rejected too. Unless God was present in Palestine first through his "mighty acts" for his people Israel and then in the life–death–resurrection of his Son, Jesus Christ, then the whole of Christianity is false. That is why Christians take the geography of the Bible as seriously as they take its historical truth.

II. The World of the Bible

Because the world of the Bible is a real world, the study of its material life, the ecology of its peoples, and the spatial issues of its geopolitical setting are all essential to its study. Shaped as a vast trapezoid, the area is popularly known as the Near East; it lies between Egypt and Asia Minor in the west, the Gulf of Suez and the Persian Gulf in the south, the Kurdistan and Zagros mountains in the east, and the Black Sea in the north. It is the hinge area that unites in one great mass the lands of Asia, Europe, and Africa. No wonder it has been the meeting place and the melting pot of numerous peoples and cultures. In antiquity it was at the very center of the civilized world, proudly associated with a number of major human achievements. As the history of plant and animal domestication unfolds, it is becoming clear that this area was the primary home of some of the most significant early stages of agriculture. In the hills to the north of the Fertile Crescent, the first appearance of agricultural villages occurred as early as the eighth and seventh millennia B.C. Irrigation is probably as old as the sixth or seventh millennium B.C. Urbanism first began in this area, three or four millennia later. The first great civilizations of Mesopotamia and Egypt also began here, and their subsequent influences dominated the world of the OT. Archaeologists have given most attention to the human occupancy on land. Yet it may eventually be shown that the early navigators of the eastern Mediterranean, Red Sea, and Indian Ocean may also go back to remote times and that they were influential in the transference of plants and animals and in cultural achievements. Further discoveries will therefore only enhance the central importance of the Near East as man's oldest cradle of civilization.

The geographical characteristics of the Near East may be summarized by the uniformity of climatic conditions, the diversity of its land forms, and the contrast of its two major hydrographic systems, the Nile and the Tigris-Euphrates.

---

[1] Arnold Toynbee, *A Study of History*, 7:430, 431.

A. *Climate*

Throughout the Near East, the climate is an extreme variety of the Mediterranean regime. Winters are mild to fairly cold, depending on altitude, with Jericho having the mildest winters at 820 feet below sea level and Nakl in Sinai having the coldest weather at a 2,500-foot elevation. Summers are hot to extreme, altitudinal differences being less marked than in winter. But local topography may exaggerate the summer heat, as at Elath at the head of the Gulf of Aqaba, which has high mountains east and west of it, and where air waves already hot are further heated by forced descent into the bay. Heat waves can reach 45°–48° C (113°–118° F) in the Jordan Valley, compared with 35°–38° C (95°–100° F) on the coastal plain of Palestine. The absence of barometric lows in the Near East in summer and the general decrease of isobars from west to east explain the persistent westerly winds that blow for successive weeks and months. These strong, steady "etesian" or seasonal winds of summer played a vital role in the development of Phoenician and Greek navigation between Greece, Egypt, and the Levant. With the disappearance of this pressure pattern in winter, depressions from the Mediterranean reach into the Near East, providing a variability of wind direction familiar to the writer of Ecclesiastes: "The wind goeth toward the south, and turneth about unto the north; it turneth about continually in its circuits" (Eccl 1:6).

In three-quarters of the area of the Near East the annual rainfall is below 8 inches. But in the zone first described by Breasted as "The Fertile Crescent"—the ridge of high land from Palestine through Syria into the hills of the upper and middle courses of the Tigris and Euphrates—the rainfall exceeds 8 inches annually. The deserts have less than 2 inches and the indeterminate broad zone of "steppe" has between 8 and 2 inches. For its modest elevation, Palestine is among the most favored areas of the Near East for its rainfall, because of its position on the coast of the eastern Mediterranean. As in the Near East generally, precipitation decreases from north to south and from west to east. In Mount Hermon there are 50–70 inches, the mountains of Galilee have 38–42 inches, southern Judea 20 inches, and the southern Negev 2–4 inches. Interior depressions like the Dead Sea have 3.2 to 1.6 inches from north to south, while the shores of the Red Sea have only about 0.4 inches.

Rainfall is typically seasonal, occurring in the winter months between October and April, with a maximum in midwinter. The biblical description of "the former and the latter rains" (Deut 11:14; Hos 6:3; Joel 2:23) refers to the onset and termination of the rainy season. But the rain is usually concentrated into heavy, sharp falls with torrential storms of short duration, so that brief periods of precipitation characterize much of the Near East. On the coasts of the Levant, rainfall comes from cyclonic storms but towards the east in the Mesopotamian area and in the north in central Anatolia convectional rains are the main source of precipitation. In the Zagros mountains, a combination of cyclonic and convectional storms explain the late spring storms, during which severe floods may occur, combined with winter snow melt. Disastrous floods may then occur in the river flood plains.

The barometric differences of summer and winter also affect the nature of cloudiness. In summer, clouds are absent or rare between June and September, conspicuous in the period of October to April, especially in the mountains. The length of day and especially the low amount of annual cloudiness explains the intense radiation that reaches a global maximum in the summer months. The intense effect of light was recognized in the building of Solomon's temple, which had windows transparent within and opaque without (1 Kings 6:4).

Dew is abundant in Palestine, notably in the western Negev, the coastal plain, the plain of Jezreel and the summit of the Carmel range. In the central Hula valley and the lower Beth Shean valley dew is also important. However, the foothills of these districts, as in other foothills of the entire ranges of western Palestine, have little dewfall because of descending mountain currents of warm air that flow down at night. These are warmed in their descent and prevent condensation of dew. Most dew falls in August and September. It is of great agricultural significance, since it enables some crops to be grown without irrigation and enables cultivation to advance into otherwise barren areas (Ecclus 18:16; 43:22). The absence of dew reinforced the conditions of drought in several biblical allusions to famine (2 Sam 1:21; 1 Kings 17:1; Hag 1:10; Zech 8:12).

B. *Land Forms*

At first sight, the relief and geological structure of the Near East appear simple. The region is an ancient continental block long exhumed above the sea. Only its edges have oscillated above and below sea level and have had a varied geological history with a sequence of sedimentary rock cover. The continental block consists of very ancient, crystalline rocks, shattered here and there by intense coastal movements that have shaped the interior depressions, the coasts, and faulted mountain blocks. Rift valleys and block mountains characterize the Red Sea area, the Arabian peninsula, and the Gulf of Aden. The rift valley system then continues from the Gulf of Aqaba, the Dead Sea, and the Jordan Valley northward through Lebanon and Syria to the borders of Turkey. The other end of the system extends through the East African lakes. Between Egypt and the ranges of Palestine and Syria, thence into upper Mesopotamia, the more recent sediments are moderately folded, though the rigid platform of ancient rocks below them inhibit the development of deep folds. Faulting, rather than folding, is still determinative. It is only in southern and northern Anatolia and in the Zagros mountains that alpine areas of young folded mountains occur, linking up with the mountains of Baluchistan and central Asia. Recent volcanic rocks outcrop in eastern Anatolia, the Hauran (in Palestine), in western Arabia and Ethiopia. The remaining areas are continental blocks broadly covered with recent or older sediments, comprising most of the Arabian and Syrian deserts.

The coasts tend to be rocky, with limited wave-built benches and narrow discontinuous coastal plains. The limited fetch of the waves in enclosed seas and the absence of tides with low rates of tidal scour help to explain the structural features of concordant coasts shaped by the folds and fractures, with the occurrence of deltas at the river mouths. Depositional coastal plains occur in only two areas, because of the significance of the Nile and Mesopotamian sediments, associated with the only two major river systems of the Near East. Because these areas are exceptional, the coasts are usually isolated, both from their hinterland and from each other by stretches where the mountains plunge steeply to the sea.

As in most of the Mediterranean area, earthquake incidence has been a common feature. But in Palestine the Jordan rift valley is an aggravating factor, since the whole of this line of tectonic weakness, from northern Syria to East Africa, is still unstable. The most active and severe earthquake epicenter is in the area of Alexandretta-Antakia (ancient Antioch) in north Syria, where the northern end of the rift valley hinges into the geologically young mountains of Southern Anatolia. In Palestine there are two major epicenters of earthquake activity, Safed and Nablus, with others at Ramle-Lydda, Tel-Aviv, and Joppa, another near Nazareth, and still another in the Jordan valley, especially at Jericho. They may all be associated with structural intersection of the NNE-SSW folds and intersecting faults. Picard has suggested the NNE-SSW folds are mid-to-late Tertiary in age, while the faults of the rift valley and other associated movements are geologically recent (Quarternary) and still an active cause of earthquake movements.

Biblical allusions to earthquakes are frequent. Earthquakes occurred at the giving of the Law (Exod 19:18); in the incident of Korah (Num 16:31); and in the days of Saul (1 Sam 14:15), Elijah (1 Kings 19:11), Uzziah (Amos 1:1; Zech 14:5), and Paul and Silas (Acts 16:26). There was also the earthquake at Christ's crucifixion (Matt 27:51). Prophetic allusions to events such as the cleavage of Mount Carmel, suggest that the writers were familiar with the effects of such coastal movements.

C. Major River Systems

In this arid area of the earth, major perennial rivers are few and these, therefore, have been of fundamental importance to its civilization. In Palestine, for example, all water courses, apart from the Jordan and a few of its major tributaries, are episodic, carrying flood water a few times each winter and seldom having more than thirty days of annual flow. Palestine, however, is favored with many springs, compared with vast areas such as the deserts of Arabia, eastern Egypt, Sinai, and the high plateaus of Persia that are riverless and dependent on underground supplies in widely scattered oases. The major rivers of Mesopotamia and Egypt have, therefore, dominated the whole region since prehistoric times.

Mesopotamia, "the land between two rivers," is nurtured by the Euphrates and the Tigris. The Euphrates, the largest river of southwest Asia, referred to in the Bible as "the river" (Deut 11:24), rises in eastern Turkey within a hundred miles of the Mediterranean. It then curves southeastward to flow into the Persian Gulf, joined by only one significant tributary in its 1,200-mile course. It has functioned as a broad channel of communication between the Mediterranean and the Indian Ocean. From low water at the end of the summer, it reaches floodwater in its lower course in May, fed by snow melt and winter rains in its upper course. The Tigris is the other major river of Mesopotamia, rising in the Armenian mountains and flowing 1,146 miles along the foot of the Zagros mountains, to join the Euphrates 40 miles from the Persian Gulf. It meanders widely in Babylon (Dan 10:4), fed by major tributaries from the Persian mountains, the Greater and Lesser Zab, Adhem, and Diyala rivers. With steep, mountainous gradients, rapid run-off and snow melt, the floods on the Tigris and its main tributaries are severe and exaggerate the irregular flow of the lower Tigris with its peak in April–May.

The Mesopotamian civilization, based on the lower sector of these rivers, stretched 400 miles from Samarra to the Persian Gulf and some 125 miles across the basin of the two rivers. The first towns developed at the head of the Persian Gulf, in the Sumerian period, during the fourth and third millennia B.C. By about 3200 B.C., the Early Dynastic period had begun in this area of the delta. But salinization of the soil began about 2400 B.C. and spread over the area in the course of the next millennium, perhaps explaining the shift of civilization upstream. Cumulative sedimentation of the delta has led also to the down-warping and progressive subsidence of the head of the Persian Gulf, so that many early settlement sites may lie buried beneath the waters of the gulf. Another factor of change has been the westward shift of the river Euphrates, so that early Mesopotamian towns once on its banks now lie several miles east of the river.

In Upper Mesopotamia, the rainfall is greater, permitting dry farming, and the risk of salinization of soil is much less. Centered on the middle basin of the Tigris, there arose the greater Assyrian empire in an area of some 5,000 square miles. Easy communications astride the great trade routes, with no natural frontiers except to the northeast, encouraged Assyria to establish here the first "world empire," succeeded later by the Persians. It is dangerous to generalize about the effects of environment on civilizations, but the Mesopotamian area was an open land, with strategic lines of communication, where diverse ethnic groups mingled and fought for possession of its resources—irrigation works and towns along the rivers, minerals in the eastern mountains, and vital trade routes. The turbulent conditions of its rivers challenged its people, while the subsidence of the delta, the problems of salinization, and other physical problems, all tended to promote dynamic qualities in its civilizations.

Egypt, in comparison, has had a more secure environment, more isolated, and with more predictable hydrological conditions on its life-line, the river Nile. It has tended to breed a monolithic civilization, totalitarian, and eventually static. Its immense military power is sensed throughout the OT and its religious conditions were the antithesis of the life of Israel, so that freedom from Egypt is a significant motif of the biblical narrative.

Almost completely rainless, the land of Egypt depends on the irrigation water of the Nile. Then, as now, Egypt was divided into Lower Egypt, based on the delta, a triangle 155 miles long and 135 miles at its widest extent. Marshy, it was only gradually reclaimed, with the small port of Rhacotis founded about 1500 B.C. and later expanded by Alexander the Great as Alexandria in 332 B.C. Upper Egypt commenced at Memphis and extended to Syene (Aswan) at the first cataract, a narrow ribbon of alluvial valley land extending uninterruptedly for 600 miles, and from 1 to 24 miles wide. Six transverse zones of hard sandstone comprise the sequence of cataracts that have formed natural frontiers for the history of Egypt. Between the first and third cataracts was Nubia, which the First Dynasty of Egypt, about 3000 B.C., first began to conquer. South of that lay Cush, and at the time of the Israelite monarchy, Cush arose to be a world power. In 720 B.C. the Nubians actually conquered Egypt for a short-lived period, during the Assyrian invasion of Judah (Isa 18:1–6; 19:1–15).

In contrast to Mesopotamia, the floodwaters of the lower Nile are much more regular, predictable, and agriculturally more effective. For the monsoonal region of Ethiopia, where the Blue Nile has its source, provides the summer maximum flow of the Nile between mid-July and mid-November, when the grain can be sown. The regularity of the Nile's flow, the effective planning of agricultural production measured by inundation basins and their survey from year to year, enhanced the totalitarian power and deification of the ruling Pharaohs. In this effective technological enterprise, the Israelites were only too well aware that their land was not "as the land of Egypt, where thou waterest the land with thy foot" (i.e., the shaduf irrigation bucket) but was dependent on their God who provided the rain from heaven (Deut 11:10, 11). It was a wholly contrasting environment, and in a negative way resentment against Egypt, deliverance from its power, and a denial of its gods, constituted a major binding force to form the Hebrew people.

III. Modes of Life in Biblical Times

Palestine is at the junction of three great phytogeographical regions (regions distinguished by their plants): the Mediterranean, the Irano-Turanean, and the Saharo-Sindian. The coastal plain of Palestine and the western mountains of Palestine and Syria have

Mediterranean flora, with some 2,250 species of flowering plants, chiefly annual or perennial herbs. With a mild climate and an annual rainfall of over 14 inches, this area once sustained forests on the mountains and a stable agriculture in the valleys and plains. A dry scrub forest occupied the highlands east of the main watershed and only in southern Judea was the land naturally scrub or grassland. The Lebanese forests were especially coveted by the neighboring countries, notably Egypt and Mesopotamia, both devoid of timber. Today, it is a wild karstic area in the Sannin mountains. In biblical times, though reference to deforestation is made at the time of Joshua's settlement of the land (Josh 17:18), good timber was so scarce that even then it had to be imported from Lebanon (Deut 20:19). Mount Hermon and Golan were the only other areas of dense forest in biblical times, with cedars, firs, oaks, and pines. But the sycamore yielded the common building timber that was grown in special forests (1 Chron 27:28). Other timber, such as the cedar of Lebanon, had to be imported (1 Kings 5:2–18; Ezra 3:7). Many forests referred to in the Bible have disappeared—e.g., at Bethel (2 Kings 2:24) and Ephraim (Josh 17:15–18; 2 Sam 18:8). The biblical description of "a land flowing with milk and honey" (Exod 3:8) aptly describes the mellifluent flora of scrub and shrubs so typical of degraded plant cover in the Mediterranean area today (Deut 8:7–9).

The beginnings of agriculture in the Near East have been traced to the Natufian era of the seventh to sixth millennium B.C. Wild wheat and wild barley have been found on the slopes of Mount Hermon and in the Jordan Valley.

In the caves of Nahal Mishmar, in addition to these grain crops, remains of lentils, broad beans, olives, dates, walnuts, carobs, pomegranates, almonds, onions, garlic, and other wild bulbs have been found, dating from this Natufian period. In the Neolithic (6000–5000 B.C.) and Chalcolithic (4000–3000 B.C.) periods, the beginnings of town life and irrigation practices developed in Palestine. By the fourth and third millennia, wheat, barley, millet, olives, figs, grapes, sesame, flax, dates, onions, garlic, lettuce, vegetable marrows, melons, horse beans, and chick peas were being cultivated throughout the Near East, though concentrated especially in the riverine lands of Mesopotamia and Egypt (Num 11:5). By the nineteenth and eighteenth centuries B.C., agricultural villages and towns that practiced irrigation were scattered throughout the Fertile Crescent. The famous Code of Hammurabi, the Amorite king who developed the Babylonian empire, reveals the important incentives given to land reclamation for irrigation, which was to be rent-free for its first three years of colonization.

The patriarchs of the Bible were not nomads like the Bedouins today who have evolved a specialized economy based on camel raising in the desert. This nomadic mode of life has developed relatively recently, compared with the seminomads who domesticated the ass and engaged partly in agriculture and partly in irrigated agriculture, such as is accurately described in Genesis 13:10. When the descendants of Abraham moved into Palestine in the Middle Bronze Age, agriculture was already well developed there west of the Jordan. During the succeeding Iron Age the Israelites conquered the land and colonized the hill lands with the aid of a new invention: limestone cisterns lined with clay to store water in the winter rainy season. (The earliest cisterns date from 1500 B.C., and the Covenant Code regulates that cisterns should be kept covered [Exod 21:33]. The ideal was to have "every one . . . drink the water of his own cistern" [2 Kings 18:31; Isa 36:16]). Since that time, agricultural village life in Palestine has had remarkable continuity and importance, especially in Galilee where spring water, isolated pockets of agricultural land, and more moisture made possible a greater variety of crops than could be grown farther south. Stability of climate since the biblical period can be demonstrated by the importance of barley over wheat in Judea, the fame of Carmel for its vines, the olives of Galilee and Ephraim, the specific correlation between biblical locations for date palms, and the comparable agricultural rhythm of life since biblical times.

The other two phytogeographic regions of the Near East and constituting the west extensive areas are the Irano-Turanian and the Saharo-Sindrian. The former stretches across the Near East from Ammon to north of Baghdad and eastward. It has a more continental climate than the Mediterranean area, with a steppe flora with 8 to 14 inches of annual rainfall. Its soils are poor, arid, incapable of supporting forests or scrub forest. Its agriculture is unstable, though it was the home of many of the plant domesticates of the area. The southern half of the Near East comprises the Saharo-Sindrian region, true deserts that stretch from the Sahara to Arabia and east to the Sind. With a rainfall that fluctuates from less than 1 to some 8 inches annually, it has never sustained dry farming, and its vegetation consists of a sparse cover of dwarf-shrubs and herbs. Annuals that complete their life cycle within a few weeks of the annual incidence of rains are common. Despite their apparent monotony, the deserts are varied in character, largely because of their different soil conditions and their associated plants. Wormwood communities (*Artemisia herba alba*) are common in the grey-soil steppes on the eastern and southern borders of the Mediterranean region. The loess steppes of the northern Negev in Transjordan have special weeds associated with cultivation in the sagebrush steppe.

The gravel deserts of the *Hammadas* have very little plant cover except along the wadi floors. The sand deserts have bunched grasses. The saline desert soils have many species of tamarisk, except where the salt concentrations are too strong for any plants to grow.

Man has made use of a variety of wild plants, and few areas of the Near East, even in the deserts, have not at some time or other been utilized by him. Ass nomads first traversed the deserts and it was not until c. 1500 B.C. that the Arabian camel was domesticated. Game was extensive in the deserts, and it is probable that sheep and goats were pastured much farther into these areas than they are now. But they inhibited true nomadism, since sheep are less mobile and die if overdriven in the heat (Gen 33:13). Anthropological evidence now suggests that seminomadism was very ancient in the Near East, involving both altitudinal movements in the mountains and horizontal displacements. But true nomadism developed only with the domestication of the camel. The first biblical reference to camel nomads concerns the invasion of the Midianite camel-riding Bedouins into the plain of Jezreel (Judg 6:5; 7:12). Although molars of domesticated horses have been found in the Chalcolithic, the hypothesis of the horse being introduced by the Hyksos into Palestine has long been accepted. Certainly the invention of the war chariot in the Iron Age revolutionized military strategy in the Near East, as the chariot fortress towns of Israel attest—e.g., Megiddo.

IV. The Trade Routes

Commerce, with agriculture and nomadism, have been the traditional occupations of the Near East. As the land bridge of three continents, the area has been constantly enriched by the trade that passed through. A picture of Palestine's role in world trade occurs in Ezekiel 27:12–25. At least as early as the second millennium B.C., international highways ran through Palestine; echoes of these are heard in Genesis 37 where Ishmaelite caravans carried merchandise from Canaan to Egypt. Trade routes crossed the deserts or followed along the foot of mountain barriers or along the coasts. Others were sea routes through the Red Sea and in the eastern Mediterranean.

Two great international highways linked Egypt and Mesopotamia via Palestine. "The way of the sea" (*Via Maris* to the Romans) is traceable back to the fourth millennium B.C. It began at Qantara, crossed the Sinai desert, and thence passed along the coast of the Negev and Judaea, crossed the Sharon, turned inland via Megiddo in the plain of Esdraelon to pass through the plain of Beth Shean. There it bifurcated, one branch proceeding along the west shore of the lake of Galilee to Dan and Damascus, the other moving east to Golan in Bashan to Damascus. There it continued into Babylon, to join the Euphrates valley, and proceeded thence to Ur. This great highway was used both for commerce and military conquest, with ancient fortresses built along it, such as Aphek, Dan, Hazor, Beth Shean, Megiddo, Lydda, Ashdod, Ashkelon, and Gaza. The armies of Egypt, Babylon, Assyria, Persia, Greece, and Rome marched along it in the annals of biblical history.

The second great highway, "The way of the kings," is traceable to the Early Bronze Age at the beginning of the fourth millennium B.C. It also connected Babylon with Egypt, passing through the Sinai desert to Kadesh Barnea, thence across the Negev via the Mount of Haar to Edom. From there it followed the western edge of the plateaus of Transjordan across Moab, Ammon, and Gilead to Damascus and thence to Mesopotamia. The southern half of the highway is described as the "way of the wilderness of Edom" (2 Kings 3:8). Secondary branches diverged from the highway. From Kadesh-barnea an inland route led to the Gulf of Eilat, probably the "way of the Red Sea," along which the Israelites were commanded to go to avoid the Amalekites and Canaanites (Num 14:25). Another branch of the kings' way divided south of the Dead Sea, going from Bostra to Eilat, referred to in Genesis in the battle between the kings of Sodom and Gomorrah against Chedorlaomer and his allies (Gen 14:5, 6). The Israelites later begged permission of the king of Edom and the Amorite King Sichan to have passage along this highway but were refused (Num 20:17; 21:22).

Eilat was a main junction for other routes that parted for Mesopotamia and Arabia. The route from Eilat to Babylon crossed the Arabian desert, with caravan stations at Dumah and Tema en route for Ur. At Dumah another route moved north via the Wadi Sirhan to Damascus.

The broken terrain of Palestine made it difficult to develop new routes or to modify the pattern of the old ones, so the network remained more or less fixed for all its history. Key points and junctions were recognized in the location of fortress towns, whose fate was bounded by the commercial and military importance of these routes. Professor Aharoni has identified, in addition to the two international highways described above, another twenty-three regional or local routes that traversed Palestine in biblical times, many of which were transverse routes that ran W-E between the "way of the sea" and the "kings' way." But longitudinal N-S roads ran through the hills of Judea and Samaria (Judg 21:19), along the Jordan rift from Jericho to Beth Shean (2 Sam 18:23), and from the Gulf of Aqaba to Tamar, Zoar, and the Dead Sea (Exod 13:18; Num 14:25; 21:4; Deut 1:40; 2:1). The latitudinal or transverse routes often fixed the sites of key towns along the N-S highways, such as Kadesh Barnea, Hebron, Bethlehem, Jerusalem, Samaria, Shechem, and Bethel.

The trade of Palestine in OT times was mostly in agricultural products. Phoenicia was supplied by Israel with grain, oil, and wine. Egypt, with a surplus of grain, had to import oil and wine. Figs, dried fruits, and herbs also were traded with surrounding peoples. In the time of Solomon, the shipment of copper smelted in the Gulf of Aqaba was traded with Arabia and Africa for spices, perfumes, gold, and incense. Wool was another surplus export of Palestine, and flax was possibly exported to Phoenicia. Grain in great quantities from Hauran was exported along the desert routes. Biblical allusions to the export of agricultural surpluses are notable—e.g., grain, oil, wine, and honey (1 Kings 6:11; Ezek 27:17). The balm was extracted from certain trees in Gilead (Jer 8:22). Lumber and fish were imported from Phoenicia (Neh 13:16), and luxury garments and wares from Egypt (Ezek 27:7).

Navigation was never important in Israelite times and sea trade was largely in the hands of the Philistines and the Phoenicians. There were a few harbor towns in Palestine such as Accor, Dor, Joppa and Ashkelon, but for most of Israel's history these were not under the control of the Israelites. Acco, for example, was in the hands of David (Josh 19:29; 2 Sam 24:7) but it was restored to Tyre's jurisdiction in Solomon's reign (1 Kings 9:11). Dor was perhaps the most prominently under Israelite control. Israel was never a sea power, and even when Solomon built the port of Ezion Geber close to Elath for the copper trade of the Red Sea, he inaugurated shipping with the help of Phoenician sailors (1 Kings 9:26; 2 Chron 8:17).

V. The Land of Palestine

The position of Israel in the Land of Promise was a delicate one—that of seeking liberation from Egypt and independence of Mesopotamia. The totalitarian oppression of Egypt was rejected in the Exodus, and only God was able to effect it. On the other hand, there was much that might influence a liberal Israelite in Mesopotamia. There no single god or ruler had the ultimate source of power, and authority and human society were only a replica of the heavenly economy. Democracy was further enhanced by the reverence for law and covenant. Much, then, of the patriarchs' background was Mesopotamian, and their basic struggles were with Egypt. And yet the patriarchal faith was no syncretism with Mesopotamia, but a personal affirmation based on experience of the one God whose covenant with one man, Abraham, was to be the cornerstone of Hebrew faith. Likewise, it was the personal struggle of one man, Moses, who was to lead out his people from the bondage of Egypt. Henceforth, covenant and liberation were the motive force of Israelite identity.

Even in the land of Palestine, however, the Israelites did not easily achieve their identity and independence. For its strategic position had long made it a whirlpool of conflicting cultures, varied political and economic interests, and ethnic diversities. To the Akkadians, it was *Mat Amaru*, the land of the Amorites. Later, to the Egyptians, it was *Haru*, land of the Hurrians, who settled there in the seventeenth century B.C. Then in the fifteenth century it was first called *Canaan*. With the advent of the sea people who invaded the coast possibly from the Aegean, it became known as *Philistia* by the thirteenth century. Much later, the Greeks translated this as "Palestine."

One of the most interesting geographical documents of the Bible is Numbers 34:1–12, which defines the boundaries of the land of Israel. The delineation of the land begins at the southeastern border of the Dead Sea and Zoar in the northeastern portion of Arabah. It was important for its copper mines. Then it proceeded westward to Kadesh Barnea, the richest and most centrally located springs of the southern edge of Negev, and continued to the Mediterranean coast at the "Brook of Egypt," the Wadi-el-Arish that naturally divides Egypt from Palestine. The western border is the "great sea" or Mediterranean. The northern boundary of Israel is at Lebweh (Lebo-hamath on the watershed between the Orontes and the Litani and at Sadad Zedad) on the edge of the desert. Mount Hor, to the west, is probably to be identified with one of the northern summits of Lebanon, north of Byblos. The eastern boundary of the land is not clear, as the places are not all identifiable. But it seems clear that the northeastern border passed the edge of the desert to include Bashan and at least part of Hauran, to descent south-westward to the Sea of Galilee, the Yarmuk valley, and the Jordan. This territory was never fully Israel's, however, for even in the time of David, "the land of Canaan" never passed north of Sidon, and included Gilead that was excluded in the conquest period. From other Egyptian evidence, however, it appears clear that this description of Israel fits accurately into the context of the thirteenth century B.C.

The biblical land of Israel was considered both a "holy land" and "the Promised Land." Here the patriarchs first erected their altars where they worshiped God: at Shechem (Gen 12:6, 7), at Bethel (Gen 12:8; 35:1–7), at Mamre (Gen 13:18), and at Beer-sheba (Gen 22:31–33; 26:23–25). These sanctuaries are all situated along the central watershed of the Palestine mountains that carried a longitudinal highway and that had good cultivated lands. It was also "the land of promise," because there Abraham believed in the covenant of God concerning the future destiny of his seed. The land was not "promised" in some imperialistic way; rather, it was the environment in which his people could respond and relate to the promises of God, both spiritual and material. Indeed, there is no Hebrew word for "promise" as such. Rather, it was the sphere in which God demonstrated his grace and loyalty to his people. The Promised Land was, likewise, that geographical sphere in which the people of Israel were to be loyal in their covenant with God and as "holy" people were to be set apart from the idolatrous practices of their pagan neighbors (Lev 26).

This was no easy task, as the biblical story shows. Some twenty ethnic groups are referred to Palestine in the Bible. Sometimes original ethnic groups are conceived of as cultural areas that coincided with natural regions, such as Philistia, Ammon, Moab, Edom, Gilead, Galilee, Samaria, etc. For, despite the small size of the country, its fragmentation into hills, valleys, coastlands, wilderness, and desert, has produced considerable differences of economy, of settlement patterns, and distinctive landscapes. For example, Joshua 12 refers to some thirty-one "kings," each of whom ruled over one town and its satellite villages. Thus it was the Israelite kingdom that first successfully overcame the natural fragmentation of the country, merging various ethnic elements and creating an independent culture that, though much influenced by the two great civilizations of Mesopotamia and Egypt, remained apart in its faith, morality, and political character.

A. The Regions of Palestine

In the historical geography of Israel, four parallel belts of terrain have been recognizable, running from south to north: the coastal plain, the western mountains, the Jordan valley, and the Transjordan plateaus.

1. *The coastal plain.* The coastal plain was never extensively occupied by the Israelites, since it remained occupied to some degree by the more powerful Iron-Age Philistines who arrived just prior to the Israelite conquest. The southern border at the Wadi-el-Arish, was a phyto-climatic rather than physiographic boundary, for beyond it the climate deteriorates into the desert, "the wilderness of Paran." It was the home of the Amalekites, camel nomads with whom the Israelites contended before they settled in Palestine proper.

A series of zig-zag faults separate the coastal plain from the interior hills that once represented a broken shoreline. This has now been filled in by sea and land sediments.

Continental sandy deposits are from 30 to 300 feet deep in the plain, overlain by sand dunes blown in from the shoreline. It is a landscape of quick changes, associated with shifting sand dunes, and changing wadi beds that intersect the plain from the interior hills. Thus, even within historic times the distribution and extent of swamps, shorelines, settlements, and even the extent of the plain, have altered significantly.[2]

Sand dunes have choked the river mouths, diverting the lower courses of the streams into swamps. These were barriers to communication, so the main route ran inland along the border of the foothills, marked by the sites of fortresses such as Gerar, Gath, Gezer, and Lydda. The main plain of Philistia, 47 miles in length and some 13 miles wide, was least swampy, and here between the Wadi Ghazza and the borders of Sharon was the heartland of Philistia, in an area of c. 600 square miles (Exod 13:17).

To the north is the smaller plain of Sharon, some 400 square miles, that is wide in the Tel-Aviv area (c. 13 miles) and narrowing north to 9 miles, in the Caesarea area. It was swampy in the past, with extensive oak forests, as the Septuagint translation of the word "Sharon" suggests in Isaiah 65:10. It also contained good cattle pasture (1 Chron 27:29). Near Caesarea, the inland limestone mountains approach the coast, narrowing the Carmel plain to a strip along the sea, backed by the Carmel ridge, and terminating south of Haifa. The plain opens again north of that port, to die out again at Rosh ha-Niqra. Then for some seven miles northward are "the Ladders of Tyre," mountains that plunge steeply into the sea.

2. *The western mountains.* The backbone of Palestine consists of folded anticlinal ranges that are of varying geological age, though chiefly Jurassic and Cretaceous limestones and chalk. They were folded in mid-Tertiary times, and subsequently faulted in recent times. In the south, the folds run SW-NE, in the center and north SSW-NNE. The oldest rocks outcrop along the axes of the anticlines, often with steeper slopes and craggy appearance. Toward the north in Samaria and Galilee, the rocks have been heavily cross-faulted to break up the folded ridges into transverse valleys and basins, so that the maritime winds and rainfall penetrate more easily into the interior and favor a more prosperous agriculture.

Altogether, the mountain chains run for some 250 miles from the vicinity of the Gulf of Elath to the Litani in the north. The maximum width is about 50 miles in the Negev, while in the extreme north it narrows to some 22 miles. The ranges are traditionally subdivided into those of the Negev (3,320 sq. miles), Judaea (1,740 sq. miles), Samaria (1,200 sq. miles), and Galilee (1,100 sq. miles).

3. *The Negev highlands.* The Negev highlands in the south differ in three respects from the rest of the mountainous backbone. First, in the north, the plain of Beersheba (c. 100 sq. miles) is an upland that slopes gently toward the surrounding mountains that form the watershed between the Mediterranean and the Dead Sea at c. 1,800 feet below sea level. South of the Beersheba plateau, the mountains of the high Negev run NE-SW, in a sequence of five ridges parallel to each other. They have a marked asymmetry, the abrupt escarpments on the southeast flanks contrasting with the gradual ascent to the northwest. These ridges—Rekhme, Kumub, Ma'ale Aqrabim, Ramon, and Arief—make

---

[2]For the contrast between the stability of village life in the mountains and the more unstable conditions of settlement on the coast, see D.H.K. Amiran, "The Pattern of Settlement in Palestine," *Israel Explor. Journal,* 3 (1953): 192–209.

E-W communications across the Negev difficult. But the crests of these pitched anticlines are eroded into depressions, called *maksteshim,* often 1,300 feet below the crests,
and dictate the alignment of seasonal wadis, lines of communication, and the settlement
pattern. South of these ridges is the ancient mountain system of Sinai, that rises to over
2,300 feet, separated from the Negev proper by a wide syncline from the mountains of
Elath. In the central and southern Negev and Sinai there has never been permanent
settlement apart from caravan stations and military posts, but in the northern Negev,
sedentary settlement reached a high stage of development with irrigation by the second
half of the third millennium B.C. (Gen 14:6, 7). Later, for some 700 years preceding the
Arab conquest under the Pax Romana, the Nabateans practiced a scale of agriculture
that is the envy of modern Israel. In those periods Beer-sheba was the primary center,
owing its unique advantage to a local high water table.

4. *The central mountains.* The central mountains, north of Beersheba have steep flanks,
especially to the east, explaining the relative isolation of Judea. These hills may be
divided into three groups: those of Hebron, Jerusalem, and Bethel. Hebron has the
highest range, rising to 3,370 feet in Mount Halhul. Then northward toward Jerusalem
there is a gradual descent, though Jerusalem itself is ringed by summits that reach 2,730
feet. The major watershed veers west of the city, so that Jerusalem is already within the
catchment area of the Dead Sea. Broad shoulders of the hard Cennomanian limestone,
on the western flanks of the Judean hills, are more extensively cultivated than the softer,
porous Senonian chalk to the east, which has less surface runoff. Its rain-shadow position
also explains the more intense aridity of this area, called "the wilderness of Judea" that
plunges steeply in escarpments, overlooking the trough of the Dead Sea. Farther north,
the hills of Bethel rise several hundred feet above those of Jerusalem, with almost a flat
plateau along the major watershed, with its villages of Ramah, home of Samuel, and
another Ramah, home of Deborah (Judg 4:5).

The western slope of the central mountains is flanked by the strategic Shephelah, or
foothills that run some forty miles N-S, and up to 8 miles wide, from under 300 to over
1,300 feet. A series of W-E valleys dissect the area to give a series of strategic routes from
the coast, notably the valley of Aijalon, where the Israelites struggled against the Philistines for mastery of the area. The Elah valley is the site of David's epic fight against
Goliath.

Northwards into *Samaria,* the mountain dorsal is more broken by erosional or tectonic
valleys that open up the country to maritime winds and more precipitation. Unlike Judea,
the compression of folds in Samaria has caused distortion by horizontal movements along
faults, both running NW-SE. These faulted rift valleys—Zebulun, Kishon, Jezreel, Beth
Shean, Beth-netophah—offer transverse route ways. Unlike Judea, Samaria and Galilee
have also been more exposed to outside cultural influences.

The southern hills of Samaria are dominated by Mount Gerizim (2,840 feet) sacred to
the Samaritans as the Mount of Blessings (Deut 11:29). Shechem, a central meeting place,
lacks natural protection, so the capital, Samaria, was sited 6 miles to the north on an
isolated hill. On one occasion, it withstood an Assyrian siege for three years (2 Kings
17:5). Mount Ebal (3,080 feet) is the highest peak in this mountainous district. It is
succeeded by the rift valley of Dothan that connects with the plain of Jezreel. Two
triangular-shaped horsts split off in the north: Carmel (1,810 feet) and Gilboa (1,648 feet)
composed of hard dolomite limestone (Cennomanian). Through the southern part of
Carmel runs the Iron Valley (Wadi Ara) offering the shortest route from the plains of
Sharon to the crossings of the Jordan; it is first mentioned in a document of the time of
Thutmose III (1479 B.C.).

5. *Galilee.* Galilee is divided traditionally into Lower and Upper Galilee. Lower Galilee commences with the plain of Jezreel or Esdraelon, the largest rift valley in Palestine (155 sq. miles) and the only one to transect the mountains. Its Hebrew name Jezreel, "sown by God," suggests its fertility, but it was readily converted into a malarial swamp in times of desolation, as occurred in the long periods of Arab and Turkish rule. For thousands of years its strategic character has been reinforced by its trade, its military campaigns, and its ancient fortress towns, such as Megiddo and Beth Shean. To the north, the low rolling hills of Lower Galilee rise to 1,800 feet in Hazan and Nazareth, with extensive outcrops of lava.

North of the Acre-Safad road, Parod and in a straight line to the Lake of Galilee, rise the mountains of Upper Galilee, consisting of limestone outcrops. Here relief is more dissected and higher, with rugged ridges that reach 3,960 feet in Mount Meron. Structurally, it is an appendage of Hermon, which dominates it to the northeast at 9,232 feet. Over a rough terrain, 16 miles N-S and 25 miles E-W, it is ideal guerrilla country, which has given it its name of "the district of the nations" (Isa 8:23). Autonomous village groups of various ethnic groups have long persisted here, and even under Arab rule, there were still villages of Jewish rule until the fourteenth century A.D.

6. *The Jordan valley.* East of these mountains chains, the inland depressions (of which the Jordan was the most important) were formed in Miocene times or later, as a consequence of fracture and subsidence along the faults that run N-S or NNE-SSW. Fed by springs at the foot of Mount Hermon, three rivulets carry the headstreams of the Jordan into the Hula swamps. Obstructed by recent lava flows that the Jordan has not yet entrenched, the Hula lake and swamp have formed behind this barrier. In ancient times, the basin floor was extensively irrigated, and Caesarea Philippi was a prosperous agricultural district. South of the Hula, the Jordan drops some 885 feet in 10 miles, flowing in a narrow valley before it debouches into the Sea of Galilee at 650 feet below sea level. The lake covers 66 square miles, some 13 miles long and 7 miles at its widest. It is rich in fish, and the lake shore was densely populated in antiquity. The mountains descend steeply to the lake shore and accentuate the treacherous downdraft of air currents that stir up the lake into sudden storms.

At its outflow on the south side of the lake, the Jordan continues its descent for 66 miles to the Dead Sea in deeply entrenched meanders, so that the actual length of the river is about 150 miles, some 50-100 feet below the general level of the rift valley. The flood plain floor is still covered with dense vegetation, which has been the hiding place of wild animals, including lions (Jer 49:19; 50:44; Zech 11:3). This is "the pride of Jordan" as mentioned in the OT (Zech 11:3). Five miles south of Galilee, the major tributary—the Yarmuk—joins the river on its left bank and contributes wildly to the seasonal run-off—28,000 gallons a second in flood; 1,200 gallons a second at the end of the summer. At the confluence with the Harod brook, the Jordan valley, which is normally 5 to 6 miles wide, is enlarged by the eastern plain of Jezreel, here called the Beth Shan or Beisan plain, and favored by perennial streams and springs. It was a little Egypt in antiquity with more evidence found here of Egyptian relics than anywhere else in Palestine. At Jericho, the valley widens again, in "the steppes of Jericho" west of the river, and "the plains of Moab" to the east. Soft deposits have been dissected into badlands, and, except for the underground spring of Aines-Sultan, the oasis of Jericho could not exist in this desert.

West of the Dead Sea, the rift valley rises steeply in "the wilderness of Judaea," with vertical slopes of over 1,000 feet. Traces of lake terraces on the lower flanks suggest four or five stages in the high evolution of the lake floor. The landscape is dissected in the form of badlands with little or no vegetation cover. The Dead Sea, 30 percent of whose water consists of salts, lies 1,300 feet below sea level, with a maximum depth of 1,320 feet and a total area of c. 400 square miles. There is a widespread view that the towns of Sodom and Gomorrah were submerged at the southern end of the Dead Sea, but this has yet to be proved. (The name *Sodom* has been preserved in the Arabic Jebel Usdum, a hill of table salt near the southwestern shore of the Dead Sea.) Only in the southern end of the Dead Sea is the coast flat and low-lying, washed by sweet water from the Zered River and springs in the Valley of Zoar. South of Zoar the land rises rapidly toward Arabah, which is 720 feet above sea level. The Arabah valley is 100 miles long, extending as far as the Gulf of Arabah. A desolate region, its inhabitants were formerly active in the smelting of copper, or engaged in caravan trade between the oases.

7. *Transjordan.* In its wide sense, Transjordan includes all the plateaus east of the Jordan rift valley. It may be divided into three main plateaus: the Seir mountains, from the Gulf of Elath to the Zered river; Moab and Gilead, from the Zered to the Yarmuk river; and Bashan, from the Yarmuk to the northern border of Palestine.

The mountains in the south, in Seir, are much higher than those in the north, reaching 5,690 feet in Ash-Shira, where there is still a relict pine forest. Here in the remote valleys the Nabateans built their capital at Petra, which served as a storehouse for goods brought from as far afield as China, the islands of the Indian Ocean and Arabia. Moab slopes northward from 4,160 feet near the Jered brook to 2,980 feet on the border of Gilead. Although the plateau characterizes the relief, deep ravines on the edge of the Jordan valley have dictated the alignment of the "king's highway" (Num 21:22). In Gilead, the outcrops of sandstone and basalt weather into deeper, moister soils, which have accounted for the greater agricultural wealth of this region. Forest remnants are still to be found in the area. To the north is the most fertile and largest part of the Transjordan—Bashan (4,380 sq. miles). Its western border, the Golan, has numerous volcanic summits at 3,600–3,900 feet. The Bashan plain to the east is covered by rich volcanic soils, well known for their cattle pasture (Ps 22:12). In the east, the Hauran mountains rise in two stages of lava outcrops at 4,900 and 5,900 feet. Because of their altitude they receive adequate rainfall for agriculture. Their remoteness from Jerusalem was such that the psalmist likened them to "the depth of the sea," as the extremities of the Hebrew world (Ps 68:22).

B. *Jerusalem*

Palestine shares with Mesopotamia and Egypt some of the oldest villages and towns of the Near East. Jericho is one of the most remarkable, with a continuous occupancy that goes back to the fifth or sixth millennium B.C. Jerusalem is later, possibly first occupied at the beginning of the third millennium B.C. and its first written record is found in the Execration Texts of the nineteenth century B.C., when the settlement was a vassal of Egypt and called *Urushamem.* Later the biblical record speaks of Melchizedek, king of Salem, as "the priest of the most high God" (Gen 14:18); this may suggest that Jerusalem was then known as a religious center. But it was probably as a garrison town on the only direct route from Jericho to the coast via Higher and Lower Beth-horon in the Shephelah, that it developed under the Canaanites. The El Amarna Letters of the fourteenth century B.C. include reference to the threatened capture of the city by nomadic Habiru: "Now they are trying to take Jerusalem. . . . Are we to let Jerusalem fall?" The Bible narrates how Joshua fought with the king of Jerusalem, but adds that "the children of Benjamin did not drive out the Jebusites that inhabited Jerusalem" (Judg 1:18, 21). Only three hundred years later did David capture the city and make it the royal capital of his kingdom.

Two, and possibly three, factors were influential in the site and location of Jerusalem as a small fortress. Where the E-W route from Jericho to the sea intersected the N-S highway of the mountains that linked Beer-sheba, Hebron, Shechem, and Jennin in Galilee, a town was likely to develop. But the site itself was probably fixed by the perennial spring of En Gihon on the northeast flank of the site of Jebusite Jerusalem. It has a flow of 227 cubic meters per day even in the dry season. It is probable that a water gate with out-thrust towers to defend and give access to this vital water supply was built in Canaanite times, with an underground channel leading within the city wall. The walled town occupied about 10.5 acres, naturally defended except on the north side where a high wall was built on the narrowest part of the ridge, with the small embayment of the Kidron acting as a natural force outside the wall. A third element in the site and location of Jerusalem was the borderland character of vegetation. The geological out-crops of the area run N-S, in a sequence of older to younger rocks. Cennomanian limestone is found west of the city, which carried a good forest cover especially in the pockets of *terra rossa* soils. Then a narrow band of Turonian limestone, softer and forming excellent building stone, occurs on the site of the city. A maze of underground quarries in the Old City, called "Solomon's quarries," testifies to the important use made of this stone in the successive building of the city. To the east, there is an outcrop of the soft, infertile Senonian chalk, which, because of its porosity and thin soils, marked the border between the original Mediterranean forest and scrub of the "Judean wilderness."

A further factor, this time historical and cultural, has influenced the importance of Jerusalem. When David captured the city c. 1000 B.C., he deliberately did not maintain the royal residence at Hebron, because it was too far south and too closely associated with the southern tribes if he wished to integrate all the tribes of Israel. Likewise, he could not choose a northern capital. Jerusalem lay at the border between Benjamin and Judea, and this neutrality gave it political value. David did not add significantly to the Jebusite town plan. Recent archaeological discoveries show that the northern wall was some 650 feet south of today's southern wall, and its southern boundary was close to the pool of Siloam. It is possible that the "Millo" often referred to (2 Sam 5:9; 1 Kings 9:15; 11:27; 2 Chron 22:5) was a system of terraces outside the city walls that David built to reinforce the stability of the hill slopes.

Under the reign of Solomon, Jerusalem was expanded northward to enclose the Dome of the Rock, and also slightly to the west. The site of the temple was selected at the highest point of the city (2 Sam 24), and below this Solomon built his palace. After the division of Israel and Judah, Jerusalem was more than big enough for several subsequent centuries. Its active kings—Joash, Uzziah, and Hezekiah—concentrated their efforts in the rebuilding or strengthening of the city walls. Hezekiah also cut a 600-yard tunnel to lead the Gihon spring into the pool of Siloam (2 Kings 20:20; 2 Chron 32:30). Eventually in 587 B.C. Nebuchadnezzar destroyed the city, and its inhabitants were exiled. For nearly a century and a half the city lay derelict, until the walls of Jerusalem were rebuilt by Nehemiah (Neh 2:12–15; 3:1–32) on a narrower *enceinte*. Then in 168 B.C. Antiochus pillaged the city and set fire to it. Pillaging and burning were repeated several times in the Maccabean period.

Eventually, in the Hasmonean period, a vigorous development took place.[3] Josephus describes a new wall built around an extensive new city west of the Tyropoeon and the western valley, linked to the old city by a bridge. It is possible that this extension was first defended in the reign of Hyrcanus. Herod the Great further enlarged the city's defenses with a new, walled area south of the bridge and as far north as the fortress of the Antonia to include the northern part of the central valley. He also rebuilt the Antonia, which had been first constructed by Hyrcanus. Jerusalem then reached its greatest extent in the years immediately preceding the revolt of A.D. 60. During Herod's reign (A.D. 40–44), a new south wall was added, together with a major expansion in the northwest, "the third wall" described by Josephus. Only after A.D. 135 did the Emperor Hadrian rebuild the city as a Roman colony, after the ruin of the city in the two revolts of A.D. 70 and 132–135.

VI. Bibliography

Bible Atlases:

Aharoni, Y. and Avi-Yonah, M. *The Macmillan Bible Atlas.* New York: Macmillan, 1968.
Baly, Denis and Tushingham, A.D. *Atlas of the Biblical World.* New York: World, 1971.
Blaiklock, E.M. (ed.) *The Zondervan Pictorial Bible Atlas.* Grand Rapids: Zondervan, 1969.
Negenman, Jan H. *New Atlas of the Bible.* Edited by H.H. Rowley. New York: Doubleday, 1969.

Geography:

Baly, Denis. *The Geography of the Bible.* London: Lutterworth, 1957.
Raoul, Blanchard, and Du Buit, M. *The Promised Land.* Translated by Robert Hunt. New York: Harper and Row, 1966.

Historical Geography:

Aharoni, Yohanan. *The Land of the Bible, a Historical Geography.* Translated by A.F. Rainey. Philadelphia: Westminster, 1967.
Anati, Emmanuel. *Palestine Before the Hebrews.* New York: Alfred A. Knopf, 1963.
Jeremias, Joachim. *Jerusalem in the Time of Jesus.* London: SCM, 1969.

Archaeological Studies:

Albright, W.F. *The Archaeology of Palestine.* 5th edition. Baltimore: Pelican, 1960.
Kenyon, Kathleen M. *Archaeology in the Holy Land.* London: Benn, 1970.
Negev, Avraham, ed. *Archaeological Encyclopedia of the Holy Land.*
Thompson, J.A. *The Bible and Archaeology.* London: Paternoster, 1962.

Topographical Studies:

Blaiklock, E.M. *Cities of the New Testament.* London: Paternoster, 1965.
Kopp, Clemens. *The Holy Places of the Gospels.* Edinburgh: Nelson, 1963.
Simons, J. *The Geographical and Topographical Texts of the Old Testament.* Leiden: E.J. Brill, 1959.

---

[3]Cf. Tushingham's article "Jerusalem" in Denis Baly and A.D. Tushingham, *Atlas of the Biblical World.* New York, 1971, pp. 155–176.

THE ESCHATOLOGY OF THE BIBLE

Robert L. Saucy

Robert L. Saucy

A.B., Westmont College; Th.M., Th.D., Dallas Theological Seminary

Professor of Theology, Talbot Theological Seminary

THE ESCHATOLOGY OF THE BIBLE

I. Introduction

Eschatology, a term derived from the Greek *eschata,* "last things," designates the doctrines of the final consummation of all things. Some variation, however, has arisen among scholars concerning its specific application. In the narrow sense it has been confined to the absolute end of this world's history and the initiation of the eternal state through the catastrophic in-breaking of a transcendent order. More generally, however, it is used to refer to the events of the final consummation of God's redemptive activity that involves a climactic visitation of God within the framework of history. The latter sense more accurately conveys the biblical concept.

The importance of eschatology to the whole of the biblical faith is difficult to exaggerate. From its beginning, the Bible looks forward, with predictive prophecy occupying a large portion of its total message. As the goal and consummation, eschatology determines and influences the meaning of the entire biblical program. Every doctrine of biblical faith stands in the shadow of eschatology.

The peculiar nature of the eschatology of the Bible arises out of the biblical belief in God as the God of history. In contrast to the systems of eschatology prevailing in the surrounding ancient Semitic peoples and founded on a cyclical view of eternally recurring ages similar to nature's own rhythm of life and death, the Hebrew faith included a sense of ongoing history. In it, God, who continually influenced the course of history, is expected to intervene even more directly in the future to accomplish his will and final goal.

This relationship of history and eschatology provides an important element in understanding the nature of biblical eschatology and its interpretation. The hope of the biblical writers was not simply in the end events, but in God who would come to bring the final transformation and who in the meantime acts in the near future to further his redemptive purpose. Since these near interventions of God's visitation for judgment or salvation are inherently related to the final events, the prophetic writers often wrote of the near event in juxtaposition with the ultimate eschatological event of the same content with no differentiation of time. Sometimes the historical "day of the LORD" is set before the backdrop of the great eschatological day, as in Amos, where, after describing an impending visitation of God for judgment upon Judah and Israel (Amos 2:5; 3:9–11) as the "day of the LORD" (5:18–20), the prophet looks forward to the final day of judgment and restoration of his people (9:7–15). At other times, the historical and eschatological are so interwoven that it is difficult if not impossible to separate them clearly. The description of the day of the historical judgment of Babylon is also the day of the eschatological disruption of earth and heaven and universal judgment (Isa 13:1–16). Likewise Joel's description of the plague of locusts and drought (1:2–20) blends in with the picture of a universal eschatological judgment (cf. 2:1–10; 3:11–15). This same prophetic perspective occurs in the Olivet Discourse on eschatology, which concerns both the impending destruction of Jerusalem by the Romans and the final Great Tribulation without any clear differentiation or chronological separation (cf. Mark 13). The problem, however, is somewhat compounded for the interpreter when similar language depicts both the historical and the eschatological. Not only is the "day of the LORD" applied to both, but futuristic expressions such as the "days are coming" or "in that day" are used for the near as well as remote future (e.g., Isa 5:30; Jer 7:32; Amos 4:2).

In general, the biblical prophets were not concerned primarily with the time and chronological arrangement of future events. For them the spiritual state of their contemporaries was the point of importance and the great eschatological visitation of God for the judgment of unrighteousness and the blessing of the pious was interjected for its ethical impact in the present. The people were dealing with a God who not only would intervene in the near future, but would someday visit the earth in the final eschatological event to render justice and fill the earth with his glory.

The frequent note of imminence in relation to eschatological events must be understood within this prophetic perspective. The nearness of the day of the LORD in both the OT and the NT does not denote fundamentally a chronological brevity, but the always-impending intervention of God with its strong ethical exhortation for life.

Biblical eschatology encompasses the entire scope of God's creation, including the destinies of individuals, world history, and creation itself. The primary focus, however, is on the consummation of God's great redemptive program of history. Especially in the OT, individual eschatology is subordinated to the historical purpose and goal of the corporate people of God. This priority again highlights the historical perspective of the Bible. Time is not a static dimension from which individuals are plucked into eternity; it is history moving toward God's intended goal. This same priority continues in the NT with its new emphasis on the necessity of a personal relationship to Christ. But this relationship only determines a share in the great eschatological redemption for all of history that God accomplishes through Christ.

II. The Eschatology of History

A. *The Hope of the World*

The goal toward which all history moves is the coming of God to manifest his glory and establish his holiness among his people and throughout the whole world. All phases and programs, including God's dealings with Israel, the church, and the nations, culminate in this end, which, according to the Scriptures, will affect even the heavenly universe.

This world destiny is expressed in a variety of themes that provide the fundamental structures of biblical eschatology. The most prominent of these is the coming of God's rule or kingdom. Concepts of "the age to come" and "the day of the LORD" also play a vital part in the biblical understanding of eschatology. Basic to the fulfillment of these themes is the return of Christ.

1. *The coming of the kingdom.* There is general agreement among biblical scholars that the overriding theme of all Scripture is the kingdom of God, by which is meant the dynamic rule of God. The term involves both the abstract sovereignty of a king and the concrete realm over which this rulership is exercised.[1] According to Bright, it "involves, in a real sense, the total message of the Bible. Not only does it loom large in the teachings of Jesus; it is to be found, in one form or another, through the length and breadth of the Bible."[2]

According to the Scriptures, there is a sense in which God has always ruled and is even now the King over all creation (1 Chron 29:11, 12; Ps 103:19; 145:13). But there is another thread of truth that views the kingdom as yet to come (Zech 14:9; Matt 6:10). It is this last theme that dominates the eschatological hope of Scripture. God is King over all his creative works, but his kingdom is not established on the earth in human history. While he rules over the affairs of earth with nothing occurring apart from his permissive will, he has allowed sin and rebellion to enter history and Satan to have a certain dominance as the "god of this age" (2 Cor 4:4). God's rule might be said therefore to be *over* the earth, but not directly *on* the earth. It is the coming of God to establish this latter condition, to bring his kingdom to earth in the vindication of his sovereign holiness, that has constituted the hope of God's people throughout all time. Although the phrase "kingdom of God" is not found in the OT, the nearest expression being perhaps Daniel's declaration that "the God of heaven will set up a kingdom" (Dan 2:44; cf. 7:13, 14), the idea permeates the prophets. God was presently King over Israel and the whole earth, but he was yet coming to rule in their midst (Isa 24:23; 52:7; Obad 21; Zeph 3:15; Zech 14:9ff.). Beginning with the proclamation of both John and Jesus, "Repent, for the kingdom of heaven is near" (Matt 3:2; 4:17), the NT takes up this theme and carries it to completion in the second coming of Christ (Rev 19:11ff.; cf. 11:15) and the final new heavens and new earth (Rev 21:3–5).

2. *The age to come.* The expression of the biblical hope is also found in the doctrine of the two ages, "this age" and "the age to come."[3] Although the terminology does not occur in the Scriptures until the NT, the concept is much earlier, having its roots in the

---

[1]Karl Ludwig Schmidt, "Βασιλεία [*Basileia*]," TDNT 1:579.
[2]John Bright, *The Kingdom of God* (New York: Abingdon, 1953), p. 7.
[3]Cf. Sasse, "αἰών" (*aiōn*), TDNT 1:204–207.

OT prophets. The coming of the kingdom of God will bring a radical transformation that can only be expressed as a new order or age. Isaiah reflects this concept in his prophecy of "a new heavens and a new earth" (65:17; 66:22). The doctrine gradually developed in the later Jewish writings. Implied in the language of 1 Enoch, the terminology becomes explicit in later pseudepigraphical writings of the last of the first century A.D. (4 Ezra, 2 Baruch, and Pirke Aboth) and in the NT.

The fundamental import of the two ages is a temporal dualism, though at times it is also interfused with the spatial distinction between the visible and invisible worlds. The two ages are radically distinct in their character. Sin and wickedness dominate this age, which is ruled over by Satan and his angels. It is a time of rebellion against God, resulting in suffering and grief especially for the people of God. But this age is temporary; it will give way to an eternal order of righteousness when God breaks in with his kingdom to judge the wicked and rule in glory with his people.

Explicit NT references to the two ages are found in the synoptic Gospels, the writings of Paul, and the Book of Hebrews. Jesus promised his followers multiplied blessing for their sacrifice "in this present age . . . and in the age to come, eternal life" (Mark 10:30). Blasphemy "against the Holy Spirit will not be forgiven, either in this age or in the age to come" (Matt 12:32). The ethical connotation of the present time is emphasized when Jesus contrasts the "sons of this age" with "the sons of light" (Luke 16:8, NASB). The majority of Pauline uses refer to the present age and identify it as "evil" (Gal 1:4; cf. Rom 12:2; 2 Tim 4:10) and ruled by those who do not know God's purposes (1 Cor 2:6; 2 Cor 4:4). But he too looks forward to the age to come (Eph 1:21; 2:7). For the writer of Hebrews, the coming age is characterized by power that may already be "tasted" in the present (Heb 6:5). While the terminology is not used by John, the same eschatological structure is maintained in his use of "world" for this age and "eternal life" for the one to come: "The man who loves his life will lose it, while the man who hates his life in this world will keep it for eternal life" (John 12:25).

Through the doctrine of the two ages, the believer is reminded that the present will not continue as it is forever. Human history, which grows worse and worse as it records the deeds of a world impregnated with evil, will someday give place to a new world, an age of righteousness and peace in harmony with its Creator and Redeemer.

3. *The day of the* LORD. The most popular expression used in the OT to describe God's eschatological intervention is "the day of the LORD." First found in the prophet Amos (5:18–20), the phrase was used by most of the OT prophets (Isa 2:12; 13:6, 9; Ezek 13:5; 30:2, 3; Joel 1:15; 2:1, 11, 31; 3:14; Obad 15; Zeph 1:7, 14; Zech 14:1; Mal 4:5). In addition to these specific references, many other passages by their very nature must be associated with this concept. In the NT the phrase occurs less frequently (Acts 2:20, citing Joel 2:31; 1 Thess 5:2; 2 Thess 2:2; 2 Peter 3:10), but when the related phrase, "the day of Christ" (e.g., Phil 1:6) and its variations are considered, it is evident that the concept dominated the NT eschatological hope as well.

The day of the LORD speaks of God's final intervention in history to overthrow his enemies and establish his rule. The name is perhaps best accounted for by the language of Isaiah: "The arrogance of man will be brought low and the pride of men humbled; the LORD alone will be exalted in that day" (2:17). God had manifested his power again and again throughout history in acts of judgment or salvation, but these historical "days" were but precursors of the final "day."

The note of judgment is always prominent in the descriptions of the day. It is a day of darkness and gloom, of wrath and destruction (cf. Isa 13:9–13; Zeph 1:14–18). Beginning with his people, God judges all wickedness in its opposition to his kingdom. The self-righteous Israelites in the time of Amos longed for the day as the bearer of blessing for them and the downfall of their enemies. But the prophet predicted it as a time of doom. "Alas, you who are longing for the day of the LORD, for what purpose will the day of the LORD be to you? It will be darkness and not light" (Amos 5:18, NASB; cf. 1 Peter 4:17). But judgment will also fall on the nations of the world who have resisted God and persecuted his people. Obadiah declares, "For the day of the LORD draws near on all the nations. As you have done, it will be done to you. Your dealings will return on your head" (v.15, NASB). Even nature will be convulsed with cataclysmic events as God unleashes his fury on his enemies (Joel 2:30, 31).

But the day that begins in the darkness of wrath breaks forth into the glory of divine blessing (cf. Isa 60:2). God's judgment of wickedness is for the purpose of delivering the righteous and establishing his rule in which his glory is manifest for the blessedness of all creation. Israel and the nations will experience peace and prosperity (Amos 9:11–15; Isa 2:2, 4). Even nature will be freed from the bondage of the curse (Isa 11). The day of the LORD thus represents the whole series of events beginning with the outpouring of God's judgment during the Great Tribulation and continuing until the final transformation with the new heavens and new earth (2 Peter 3:10).

4. *The return of Christ.* The preceding expressions of the biblical eschatological hope center on the great event of the coming of Christ. The kingdom, the new age, and the day of the LORD, were all associated in the prophetic writings with the coming Messiah who would execute God's rule, bringing salvation to his people and judgment on his enemies. His humiliation and glory were both predicted in the OT (cf. Isa 53, Zech 9:9, 10), but it awaited the NT revelation to explain their relation in the two distinct advents of Christ. And although they are separated by many centuries, both comings must be seen together in the fulfillment of God's eschatological plan. Christ's entrance into the world to suffer and die was the initial eschatological event that laid the basis for all to follow. The Cross was the work of salvation for his people and judgment on the world and its prince. Nevertheless, the final realization of these themes awaits the future coming of Christ. Thus the NT writers who have entered into the initial fulfillment of the eschatological promise eagerly await the return of Christ to usher in the consummation.

B. *The Present Realized Eschatology*

The relation of Christ to the eschatological drama of the Scriptures has evoked considerable discussion and a variety of interpretations. The center of focus is the teaching of Jesus, but the whole of NT eschatology is involved.[4]

Prior to the turn of the century the "old liberal" school exemplified by Ritschl[5] and Harnack[6] had essentially abandoned any eschatological proclamation in favor of a present inner, ethical kingdom, which they held to be the genuine teaching of Jesus. The eschatological passages of the Gospels were said to be written back into the life of Jesus by the later Jewish apocalyptic church.

Eschatology again gained prominence with the work of Johannes Weiss and especially

---

[4]George E. Ladd, *Jesus and the Kingdom* (Waco, Texas: Word Books, 1964), pp. 3–38.
[5]A. Ritschl, *The Christian Doctrine of Justification and Reconciliation* (Edinburgh: T & T Clark, 1902).
[6]Adolph von Harnack, *What Is Christianity?* (New York: G.P. Putnam, 1901).

that of Albert Schweitzer. In 1901, Schweitzer published a small book entitled *The Mystery of the Kingdom of God* and later his famous *Quest of the Historical Jesus* (1906). In these he proposed the belief that has become known as "consistent eschatology." Contrary to the earlier liberal position, Schweitzer saw eschatology, including the apocalyptic element, as central to Jesus' teaching of the kingdom. Jesus believed, according to Schweitzer, that the kingdom was in no sense a present reality. Instead, it was an imminent apocalyptic age that he as the Son of man would bring in during his lifetime. He died attempting to bring it to pass. Although Schweitzer's view did not gain wide acceptance, he had demonstrated that the eschatological teaching of Jesus was too significant to be ignored.

The position of "realized eschatology" associated with the name of C.H. Dodd has accepted the significance of eschatology in the NT. But instead of conceiving it as future, Dodd and his followers have emphasized the teachings that view the kingdom as a present reality (e.g., Matt 12:28).[7] With the coming of Jesus and the subsequent gift of the Spirit, all OT prophecies concerning the kingdom were considered fulfilled. To come to this conclusion, Dodd understood Jesus as seeing his death, resurrection, exaltation, and second advent all as aspects of one event, which the church later separated. Dodd did recognize a fuller experience of the kingdom after death in the eternal order, but did not derive this from the futuristic apocalyptic pictures of the NT. According to him, these must all be interpreted to indicate the "other-worldly" character of the kingdom, which is a present reality.

While realized eschatology correctly points to the eschatological reality in the presence and ministry of Jesus at his first coming and in the subsequent life of the Spirit, it fails to do justice to the vast NT future-oriented eschatological teaching.

It is Bultmann and his followers[8] who have provided an existential interpretation of the eschatology of the NT. Agreeing with the advocates of consistent eschatology that the NT portrays Jesus as teaching an imminent apocalyptic kingdom, Bultmann reinterprets this to find a present existential meaning in it. The apocalyptic language is simply the mythical form of the true meaning. The kingdom is not a future event as the goal of history but rather represents the suprahistorical, transcendent realm of God. The proclamation of the imminent kingdom is the demand of God for faith on the part of each individual to be open to his own future with God and thus live eschatologically now. Thus, although through different means, existential eschatology, like realized eschatology, is reduced by Bultmann and his followers to the history of the individual as opposed to the history of the world.

The most prominent interpretation of eschatology, and that which best represents the NT data, sees the beginning of eschatological fulfillment as inaugurated by the coming of Christ, but with its consummation awaiting his second advent. The following sections will outline the events related to the end. But before going on to this, we must consider the biblical teaching that portrays the present as already within eschatological times.

In accord with the OT prophecies, Jesus saw his presence as related to the promised kingdom. He announced it as imminent (Matt 4:17; Mark 1:15). But he was more than the prophet John; in him a new era dawned in which "the good news of the kingdom of God" was being preached and men were entering it (Luke 16:16; cf. Matt 11:12; 21:31).

---

[7]C.H. Dodd, *The Parables of the Kingdom* (New York: Scribner, 1961).

[8]Rudolf Bultmann, *Theology of the New Testament*, 2 vols. (New York: Scribner, 1951–55).

The kingdom was present not only in word but also in power. The eschatological hope envisioned a battle between God and the demonic powers. God's kingdom rule would destroy the kingdom of Satan. With the first coming of Christ, the decisive victory was won. Already in his ministry he declared the kingdom present in the power of the Holy Spirit as he bound "the strong man" (Mark 3:27) and cast out demons (Matt 12:28). Through this same power the demons were compelled to submit to the disciples, as they invoked the name of Jesus (Luke 10:17). But the final defeat of the demonic powers came through the Cross. Satan, who schemed to destroy Christ, was himself defeated and finally condemned (John 16:11; cf. 12:31).

The evidence of victory according to the apostolic proclamation was the resurrection of Christ. As part of the eschatological hope, the resurrection of the dead signaled the beginning of the new age and the new creation. Thus the new era has been inaugurated. Christ is but the firstfruits of a whole procession to follow (cf. 1 Cor 15:20–23).

The mysteries of the kingdom of heaven likewise indicate the presence of the kingdom. Spoken in response to his rejection by Israel as a nation, Jesus gave instructions to his disciples concerning the operation of the kingdom during this period before he returns to establish the prophesied kingdom. The kingdom is to be here and working in an inward, spiritual way (Matt 13:33). The "message about the kingdom" is to be sown (13:19) and "sons of the kingdom" planted in the world (13:37, 38).

While agreeing that the mysteries of the kingdom have reference to the kingdom in this present age, some premillennialists, on the basis of the dominant use of leaven as symbolic of evil throughout Scriptures, interpret the parable of leaven (Matt 13:33) as portraying the corrupting influence of false doctrine that would pollute the manifestation of the kingdom during this time.[9] Leaven in the Bible, however, does not exclusively signify evil.[10] The context must finally be the deciding factor, and in this parable it would appear to relate to something good, placing emphasis only on the permeating quality of leaven. It thus signifies the spreading of the message of the kingdom throughout all nations before the close of the age (Matt 24:14; Mark 13:10; Luke 24:47; Acts 1:8).

The NT writers proclaimed the same concept of inaugurated eschatology. The "latter days" foretold by the OT prophets had dawned. Christ had appeared "at the end of the age" (Heb 9:26); they were in the "last hour" (1 John 2:18; cf. 1 Tim 4:1); "the fulfillment of the ages has come . . ." (1 Cor 10:11).

But more significant than the time was their experience of the salvation of God, which according to the prophets was ultimately an eschatological act (Gen 49:18; Isa 12:3; 46:13; 49:6; cf. Luke 1:67ff.). In that great future day, God would enact a new covenant (Jer 31:31ff.), and pour out his Spirit (Joel 2:28ff.). This salvation was now the experience of the NT saints. They were enjoying the new covenant blessing and the promised life of the Spirit (Heb 8:8ff.; 10:15ff.; Acts 2). The judgment was past, and eternal life was their present possession (John 5:24). To be sure, there will be a final manifestation of these realities, but they are already determined by one's relationship to God's eschatological Word, his own beloved Son (Heb 1:2).

The eschatological intervention of God has thus begun with the coming of Christ and while the Parousia is separated in time from his death, resurrection, and exaltation, they are all part of one great eschatological drama. The new age to come had entered this old age without displacing the old as the prophets had predicted. This was the message

---

[9] New Scofield Reference Bible, note *in situ*.

[10] Cf. O.T. Allis, "The Parable of the Leaven," EQ 19 (1947): 254ff.

of the mysteries of the kingdom brought by Jesus. But if the new had begun, it was not here in its consummated form. Despite the evidence for present eschatological fulfillment, the bulk of the NT eschatological teaching still looks foward. There is a day yet to come, according to the teaching of Jesus, when the world will behold him in power and glory (Matt 24:30; 26:64; Mark 13:32), and the kingdom in its consummated form will come (Matt 13:43; 19:28). People must take care to be ready for that day, which will involve the judgment of all (Matt 24:36ff.; 25:31ff.; Luke 10:13–15; Mark 8:38).

The Epistles likewise view the kingdom primarily as future; it is an inheritance yet to be entered (e.g., Acts 14:22; Eph 5:5; James 2:5; 2 Peter 1:11). The Book of Revelation makes it clear that the complete fulfillment of the kingdom awaits the climactic act of Christ's return in relation to which all the remaining events are enacted.

C. The Coming of Christ

As we have seen, biblical eschatology rests on faith in the God who comes. So it is not surprising to find the anticipation of his final coming a major theme of biblical prophecy. The OT writers used a variety of expressions for this hope. On the one hand, they simply longed for the glorious appearance of the LORD, who would effect final deliverance. In that day, the prophet declares, the people will say, "Surely this is our God; we trusted in him and he saved us. This is the LORD, we trusted in him; let us rejoice and be glad in his salvation" (Isa 25:9). The glory of the LORD would appear not only to Israel (24:23), but "all mankind together will see it" (40:5).

On the other hand, the deliverance was to be effected through the Messiah. As early as Genesis 3:15, victory over the powers of evil was promised through the seed of the woman. As revelation progressed, his characteristics were further delineated. He would be of royal lineage destined to fulfill the promise to David of an everlasting kingdom (2 Sam 7:12–16; Jer 23:5, 6; Isa 11:1–5). But he was to be more than human, for the prophet Micah saw "his goings forth" as "from long ago, from the days of eternity" (5:2). He was none other than the "Mighty God" (Isa 9:6). The eschatological coming of the LORD was therefore to be effected through the coming one who would be God in flesh (Isa 7:14).

The coming of the Messiah was described in the OT prophecies along two apparently conflicting lines that were cleared up only with the NT revelation of the separate advents of Christ. He was to be both a suffering servant (Isa 53; Psa 22; Zech 13:7) and the reigning King (Isa 9:6, 7; Jer 23:5–8). Of special significance in the latter category is the prediction of the heavenly "Son of Man," the favorite self-designation of Jesus, who receives an everlasting dominion from the Ancient of Days (Dan 7:13, 14). At least half of the OT predictions refer to Christ's coming in glory.

The NT is replete with the idea of Christ's glorious coming. It has been calculated that over three hundred verses refer to this event, or one out of every twenty-five. Beginning in the Gospels with Christ's own prediction, it is included in all but four books (Gal, Philem, 2 and 3 John) with the climax in John's apocalyptic description of the rider on the white horse emerging from heaven to wage war on his enemies (Rev 19:11ff.).

Various terms are used to set forth the full import of this event.[11] In relation to his absence, the return of Christ is his *parousia* (coming). This word is built from two Greek terms, the preposition *para* meaning "with" and *ousia*, the participial form of the verb

---

[11]Cf. George Milligan, *St. Paul's Epistles to the Thessalonians,* (Grand Rapids: Eerdmans, 1953), pp. 145–151; also TDNT, in. loc.

"to be." *Parousia* thus signifies a coming with the resultant active presence of the one arriving. In addition to its common use, *parousia* was used as a technical term during NT times for the arrival of a ruler or higher official. Special coins were struck in various places commemorating the *parousia* of an emperor. The word was also used for the coming of the gods with their consequent help for men. Eager anticipation preceded the *parousia* of a dignitary, and his arrival was a momentous event marked by celebration and on occasion even the erection of monuments. The NT writers thus found a fitting term in *parousia* ready at hand to describe the coming and consequent presence of their Lord (e.g., Matt 24:3, 27; 1 Cor 15:23; 1 Thess 4:15).

Another term closely related to *parousia* is *epiphaneia*. Like *parousia*, this word was used in the Greek world for the visitations of kings and emperors, and especially for the manifestation of deities to help men. Related to the verb, appear or shine forth, *epiphaneia* emphasizes the striking appearance of the Lord from heaven in splendor to intervene in the affairs of this earth (2 Thess 2:8; 1 Tim 6:14; 2 Tim 4:1; 4:8; Titus 2:13).

The second coming is also the *apokalypsis* or revelation of Jesus Christ (1 Cor 1:7; 2 Thess 1:7; 1 Peter 1:7, 13). Signifying an uncovering or unveiling of that which was covered or hidden, *apokalypsis* looks at the second advent as the unveiling of him who since his earthly days has been hidden. At the same time his revelation in glory is also the consummation of the unveiling of God's salvation history, which was prepared in the OT and actualized in the incarnation, death, and resurrection of Christ (TDNT, 3:591).

Even as his first advent, the second coming of Christ is a complex series of related events that take place over a period of time. Two primary phases involve the descent of Christ in the air to catch the church up to himself (1 Thess 4:13–18) and the later coming to earth in radiant glory to establish his reign (Zech 12:10; 14:3–4; Matt 24:30). The resurrection of the righteous dead and their final judgment, along with the judgment of living Israel and the nations are also associated in Scripture with his return.

Attempts to establish the date of the second advent throughout church history have inevitably ended with failure and will continue to do so. Jesus plainly told his disciples, "It is not for you to know the times or the dates the Father has set by his own authority" (Acts 1:7; cf. Matt 12:36; 1 Thess 5:1, 2). As we saw in OT eschatology, the concern of biblical eschatology is not chronological. Rather it is the significance of these events for the present age. Thus from the time of the ascension the second coming of Christ has been revealed as an imminent event (Mark 13:33–37; Luke 12:35–46), which will occur "soon" (Rev 22:7, 12, 20). The latter expression, however, may also be understood as "suddenly" or "unexpectedly." The concept of imminence pertains, no doubt, to the initial event of his coming with the succeeding events following in order. Nevertheless, the Scriptures do not clearly distinguish these events according to time and often simply refer to his coming as one climactic event for which all are to "watch."

Although the exact time is unknown, the Scriptures do reveal precursory signs and events that herald the approach of his coming. The OT looked forward to a period of darkness before the dawn of the coming age. The prophet Isaiah declared, "See, darkness covers the earth and thick darkness is over the peoples, but the LORD rises upon you and his glory appears over you" (60:2). While it would affect the whole world, it would particularly touch God's people Israel as "a time of trouble for Jacob" (Jer 30:4–8). Daniel also predicted "a time of distress such as has not happened from the beginning of nations until then" (12:1).

On the basis of the OT predictions, Judaism developed the concept of the woes of the Messiah. The new age would be born only through the travail of birth pangs at the close of the present age. This concept is carried into the NT and associated with the coming of Christ. Jesus spoke of the coming of false Christs, wars, famines, and earthquakes as "the beginning of birth pains" (Matt 24:4–8; Mark 13:8). Not only men, but the whole creation groans with "the pains of childbirth" anticipating the revelation of the sons of God at the revelation of the Son (Rom 8:18–22).

The last days will see an intensity of evil as the enemies of God rise to challenge his rule. Paul warned of "terrible times in the last days," characterized by lawlessness in all orders of society (2 Tim 3:1–5). Scoffers and deceiving false teachers will threaten the faith of many (1 Tim 4:1–3; 2 Peter 3:1–4; Jude 17–19). The early church, living as it already was in the latter days, felt the foretaste of these conditions, but they would intensify as the end approached (2 Tim 3:13). In particular, this intensification of evil would take the form of the Great Tribulation, a specific period of time just before the glorious appearing of Christ in which human and demonic madness are turned loose in rebellion against the coming King as they are led by the Antichrist (2 Thess 2:3–8; Rev 13). Thus, although the date of his return is not known, believers are challenged to be alert to the times (Matt 16:2, 3; Luke 21:25–36). As lightning does not strike out of a clear sky, so the people of God can watch the clouds gather from which he will suddenly appear in glory. Even if the rapture of the church is placed before the final tribulation period and some of these events occur following its departure, the church still can see the beginning of the fulfillment of these end times.

Christ's return will bring to consummation the work he accomplished on the cross. He died and rose again, bringing judgment on the world and its prince, Satan, and salvation from sin for his people. But his people yet suffer because of sin, and the world continues in rebellion. The great transactions of the Cross remain to be executed in the experience of this world. For this purpose, according to the Scripture, Christ is coming again to bring final deliverance for his people and judgment on the sinful world. These two main actions of salvation and judgment are the themes of eschatology encompassing the church, Israel, and the nations.

D. The Second Coming and the Church

The church, which already enjoys the foretaste of the eschatological fulfillment in the presence of the Spirit, lives its life in the eager expectation of the personal coming of its Lord (1 Cor 1:7; Phil 3:20). This is the "blessed hope" that conduces to Christian living during this age of suffering (Titus 2:13; cf. Rom 8:23, 24). Since NT times, it has been "near" (James 5:8) and has demanded constant alertness and a corresponding purification of life (Matt 24:36ff.; Mark 13:33ff.; Luke 21:36; 1 Thess 5:6; 1 John 3:2b, 3).

In the coming of Christ, the church looks not only for the Rapture to meet the Lord in the air (1 Thess 4:13ff.) but beyond that to the revelation of his glory in the world. Until Christ's enemies and the persecution of his people are put down, the Second Coming is not complete even for the church. For this reason, the hope of the church extends beyond the Rapture itself to the ultimate manifestation of the glory of Christ at his coming. Thus Paul describes "the blessed hope" as "the glorious appearing of our great God and Savior, Jesus Christ" (Titus 2:13). The believer longs for the Rapture because it means that the glory of the Lord is about to be manifest in all of creation. At this revelation the sons of God in the church are also revealed in their true identity (Rom 8:19–21).

The time of the Rapture in the complex of eschatological events is a matter of dispute, since the Scriptures nowhere set it in a strict temporal sequence. The discussion involves many exegetical details and even broad theological concepts of God's historical dealings with Israel, the church, and the nations.

Pretribulationists place the Rapture before the final period of tribulation, which is usually understood as the seven-year period of Daniel's seventieth week (Dan 9:27).[12] The advocates of this position rest their case on the complete lack of evidence for the church in this period. Nowhere in the Epistles are warning and instruction given for the church regarding the Tribulation; nor does the description of this period in the Book of Revelation make any mention of the "church." In addition, the promise to be kept "from the hour of trial that is going to come upon the whole world to test those who live on the earth" (Rev 3:10), though its meaning is disputed, may be cogently interpreted in support of a pretribulational Rapture. Besides the reference to the earth-dwellers or all nations (cf. Isa 24:21; 26:1), this time is also specifically related in Scripture to Israel (Jer 30:7; Dan 12:1; Matt 24:15ff.; Rev 7), which, according to this position, is distinct from the church.

Pretribulationalism also bases its teaching on the concept of imminency, which understands the various exhortations to readiness because of the unknown time of Christ's coming as indicating that the Rapture is the next great event, the first in the series of final events. If the Rapture were later, the church could look for previous happenings to occur that would clearly point to the Rapture to follow, which would thus no longer be imminent. Finally, the different descriptions of the happenings at the Rapture and the Second Coming proper appear to demand some separation in time, making the seven-year period a possible construct.

Midtribulationalists, using many of the same arguments, hold with the pretribulationalists that the church will be raptured before the Tribulation.[13] But they associate this period only with the last half of the seventieth week, which is clearly divided both in Daniel (9:27) and in Revelation (11:2, 3; 12:6; 13:5). Only this portion is specifically called the "great tribulation" (Matt 24:21, NASB); the first part of the seventieth week will, according to this view, be one of relative peace and safety (1 Thess 5:3). Midtribulationalism, therefore, sees the Rapture occurring near the midpoint of this last seven-year period and, considering its understanding of the Tribulation, may therefore be considered a form of pretribulationalism.

Posttribulationalists, on the other hand, maintain that the church will remain on earth during the time of tribulation. It will suffer the persecution of man and Satan, but not the wrath of God, which occurs only at the very end. Some interpreters see the church as divinely protected during the outpouring of wrath,[14] while others see it as raptured just prior to this brief time.[15] In either case, there is no appreciable time interval between the Rapture and the actual return of Christ to the earth. As the citizens of an ancient city went out to meet a visiting emperor and accompany him back to their city, so the church is caught up to meet its Lord in the air and to accompany him as he proceeds on to the earth.

Posttribulationalism rests primarily on the fact that the Scriptures do not specify a time interval between the Rapture and the coming of Christ to earth. Rather, in many instances, they appear to be involved in the one great event of Christ's return. The

---

[12]John F. Walvoord, *The Rapture Question* (Findlay, Ohio: Dunham, 1957); *The Blessed Hope and the Tribulation* (Grand Rapids: Zondervan, 1976).

[13]Norman B. Harrison, *The End: Rethinking the Revelation* (Minneapolis: The Harrison Service, 1941).

[14]George E. Ladd, *The Blessed Hope* (Grand Rapids: Eerdmans, 1956).

[15]Robert H. Gundry, *The Church and the Tribulation* (Grand Rapids: Zondervan, 1973).

believer's entrance into the kingdom and rest is placed alongside the judgment and destruction of the wicked (cf. Matt 13:40, 49; 24:29–44; 2 Thess 1:6–10). Moreover, the "first resurrection," which includes the church, occurs only after the tribulation, immediately before the kingdom reign (Rev 20:1–6).

In the light of these and other references, and the absence of any clear teaching to the contrary, posttribulationalists maintain that there is no biblical reason to posit a Rapture before the end. It is imminent only in the sense that the events leading up to it are imminent and take place in a short space of time (cf. 2 Thess 2:1–12).

It is obvious from this brief sketch of the various views that interpreters of biblical eschatology should avoid rigid dogmatism about the time of the Rapture. As in other areas of prophecy, the concern of the Scriptures is not with the chronological scheme, but with the significance of the event. The Rapture means the call of the church to her Head, her final judgment, and her entrance into the fulfillment of salvation.

Although believers have already passed from death to life and now stand justified in Christ, they must yet stand before the judgment seat of Christ to hear the final pronouncement of this verdict and receive rewards commensurate with their deeds (Rom 2:5–7, 17; 14:10–12; 2 Cor 5:9, 10). The Scriptures refer a number of times to the matter of rewards, holding forth the prospect of much blessing but also of "loss" (1 Cor 3:15). While the doctrine of rewards must never supplant grateful love for Christ as the motive for service, neither can it be ignored as a motive for service.

The coming of Christ for his church also means final salvation. Those on earth who are "in" Christ will be caught up to be "with the Lord forever" (1 Thess 4:17) and will be changed into his likeness (1 John 3:2). Those already in the Lord's presence will receive their resurrection bodies and together with the others will share in the glory of Christ's coming and future rule.

E. *The Second Coming and Israel*

The day of the LORD and the coming of the Messiah relate especially to the nation of Israel in OT prophecy. The day will first bring a purifying judgment, and will then issue in the fulfillment of the many prophecies of a glorious destiny for the nation. The nation of Israel plays a special role in God's program of history. God created Israel from the seed of Abraham through the twelve sons of Jacob; he established Israel as a unique nation among the other nations of the world (Deut 7:6–8; Num 23:9). To Abraham and his seed, God promised not only that he would establish a great nation but would provide them with a permanent land (Gen 12:2; 15:18–21; 17:7, 8). But God's elective purpose of Israel did not end with the nation; it included the entire world. He called Israel to be a "kingdom of priests" (Exod 19:5, 6) through which his saving revelation would flow to all peoples. To Israel he committed "the very words of God" (Rom 3:2; cf. 9:4, 5) and the coming of the Word incarnate. These were destined to flow through this nation to the blessing of all, as Jesus declared to the Samaritan woman, "Salvation is from the Jews" (John 4:22). God's very dealing with Israel in judgment and restoration is for the purpose of glorifying his name among all nations (Ps 102:14–16; Ezek 39:21–29).

In the light of the nation's rejection of Christ at his first coming and its subsequent judgment and dispersion, some have understood the church as the new Israel that fulfills spiritually the promises of the OT nation. But nowhere does the NT demand such an interpretation.[16] Israel continues as a nation among nations distinct from the church,

---

[16]Peter Richardson, *Israel in the Apostolic Church* (Cambridge: Cambridge University Press, 1969).

which is called from all peoples. During this time when the nation has been set aside, God has continued his program of salvation, grafting in the Gentiles to share in the blessings covenanted to Abraham and first enjoyed by Israel (Rom 11:17–24). The promised kingdom has begun according to the mysteries (Matt 13). But this in no way precludes the fulfillment of the specific promises to the nation. The covenant blessings to Abraham that lie at the root of God's total salvation history encompass the nation and all peoples (Gen 12:1–3). The church may therefore have a share as the "seed of Abraham" in Christ (Gal 3:29) without being Israel and fulfilling the specific promises to this nation.

Both testaments consistently teach that Israel has a future. The judgment of Israel's world-wide dispersion, a scattering that exceeded that of the Babylonian exile, was predicted by the prophets. "And the LORD will scatter you among the peoples, and you shall be left few in number among the nations where the LORD will drive you" (Deut 4:27, RSV; cf. 28:65–67). During the time of her dispersion, Israel is to be dominated by gentile powers (cf. Jer 27:5ff.; Dan 2:37–45) and Jerusalem trodden underfoot (Zech 14:1–5; Luke 21:24). This period will climax with a period of great persecution spoken of by Jeremiah as "the time of Jacob's distress" (Jer 30:7; cf. Dan 12:1; Rev 12:13ff.). The entire time comes as a judgment of the Lord, but the final climax is the eschatological judgment of purification in preparation for salvation. Referring to that final suffering when only a remnant is left, God declares, "And I will bring the third part through the fire, refine them as silver is refined, and test them as gold is tested..." (Zech 13:9, NASB; cf. Matt 3:1–5). Again he states, "I shall bring you into the wilderness of the peoples, and there I shall enter into judgment with you face to face" (Ezek 20:35, NASB).

This final judgment is in preparation for the eschatological restoration of Israel to fulfill its role in God's prophetic kingdom program. Throughout Israel's history, which has often seen the nation despise its God and turn away in disobedience, God has remained faithful even during the necessary judgments. In Leviticus, the promise was made that "when they are in the land of their enemies, I will not reject them, nor will I so abhor them as to destroy them, breaking My covenant with them; for I am the LORD their God" (26:44, NASB). Moses also looks forward to a restoration far surpassing anything that took place in the return from Babylon (Deut 30:1–8). Again, Isaiah speaks of a "second" recovery from the "four quarters of the earth" (11:10ff.). Ezekiel pictures this same restoration in his vision of the dry bones coming together and later receiving life by the Spirit (37:1–14). Finally, there is no clearer expression of this truth than the word of the LORD spoken through Amos: "For behold, I am commanding, and I will shake the house of Jacob among all nations as grain is shaken in a sieve, but not a kernel will fall to the ground.... In that day I will raise up the fallen booth of David, and wall up its breaches; I will also raise up its ruins, and rebuild it as in the days of old.... Also I will restore the captivity of My people Israel, and they will rebuild the ruined cities and live in them..." (9:9, 11, 14, NASB).

Although references to the restoration of Israel are not as frequent in the NT as in the OT, the same truth is revealed. Christ came to fulfill the promises to Israel, cast off the yoke of her enemies, and bring spiritual salvation (Luke 1:32–33, 67ff.). These prophecies were not completed at his first advent, but they were never withdrawn. The apostle affirms that the covenants and promises of Israel still stand even after the inauguration of the church (Rom 9:4). "God did not reject his people, whom he foreknew" (11:2; cf. vv. 28, 29). Jesus himself spoke of a future day when he would return in glory and the twelve disciples would "sit on twelve thrones, judging the twelve tribes of Israel" (Matt 19:28). The kingdom would certainly be restored to Israel, only the time was unknown (Acts 1:6; cf. 3:20, 21).

Furthermore, the NT speaks of Jerusalem as having a place in the eschatological drama. It would be "trampled on by the Gentiles until the times of the Gentiles are fulfilled" (Luke 21:24; cf. Rev 11:2). The city will also be the focus of the final revolt of Gog and Magog against the rule of Christ (Rev 20:9).

The Lord will restore Israel not only to the land, but to himself. In that day, the nation will experience the blessings of the new covenant promised by the OT prophets. God will forgive their sins and pour out his Spirit on them in times of refreshing. He will put a new heart within them and enable them to walk in his ways (Jer 31:31–34; Ezek 36:24–27; 39:28, 29; 37:1–14; Joel 2:28–32; Zech 12:10; Matt 23:39; Rom 11:23–27). Then the goal of God's covenant will be complete: "Then they will be My people, and I shall be their God" (Ezek 11:20, NASB; cf. Exod 19:5).

This final salvation will also bring release from tribulation and oppression, so that Israel will rejoice in freedom and security under the protection of her Messiah. The LORD will destroy the troubling nations and Jacob "shall be quiet and at ease, and no one shall make him afraid" (Jer 30:10, NASB; cf. Isa 14:3–8). Israel will then rejoice in the presence and love of the LORD (Isa 12:1–6; 35:10; Zeph 3:14–17).

F. The Second Coming and the Nations

Although in Scripture the nation of Israel is the focal point of the prophecy concerning the Messiah's coming, his coming has world-wide effects with judgment and salvation involving all nations. Throughout biblical history the nations (e.g., Egypt, Assyria, Babylon, Rome) are viewed primarily as the enemies of God's people. Under God's sovereignty, their evil intentions have been used to punish the sin of his people. But God has promised that one day he will judge them for their wickedness. According to prophecy, the forces of evil throughout history will culminate in the total world rule of the Antichrist (Rev 13, 17). The nations will give their allegiance to this one who will be empowered by Satan (Rev 13:4) and they will unleash an unprecedented attack on the people of God (Rev 13:7ff.). In their final assault, the nations of the entire world will be demonically gathered together at a place called Armageddon "for the battle on the great day of God Almighty" (Rev 16:13–16). The prophet Zechariah pictures these nations gathered "against Jerusalem." In the midst of the battle, the Lord from heaven will return to save his people and destroy the armies of the nations (Zech 14:1–5; Rev 19:11–21; cf. 2 Thess 1:6–10).

Those of the nations not killed in this onslaught will then be caused to stand before the Lord in judgment. The prophet Joel vividly describes this final assize, including the battle itself: "I will gather all the nations, and bring them down to the valley of Jehoshaphat. Then I will enter into judgment with them there on behalf of My people and My inheritance, Israel, whom they have scattered among the nations. . . . Let the nations be aroused and come up to the valley of Jehoshaphat, for there I will sit to judge all the surrounding nations. Put in the sickle, for the harvest is ripe. Come, tread, for the wine press is full; the vats overflow, for their wickedness is great. Multitudes, multitudes in the valley of decision!" (3:2, 12–14, NASB). The Lord also describes this judgment in the account of the separation of the sheep and goats (Matt 25:31–46). The outcome of the judgment, based on the actions of individuals toward God's people, which will be manifest evidence of faith in Christ, will be entrance into the kingdom of eternal life or everlasting punishment.

While many of the prophecies of the day of the LORD relate to the judgment of the nations as the enemies of God, judgment by no means exhausts God's purposes for the nations. His purpose to bless all peoples of the earth (Gen 12:3) finds its fulfillment through the coming of Christ. It must also be noted that this blessing is related to the restoration of Israel to the place of fellowship with the LORD. Referring to Israel, the apostle declares, "But if their transgression means riches for the world, and their loss means riches for the Gentiles, how much greater riches will their fullness bring! . . . If their rejection is the reconciliation of the world, what will their acceptance be, but life from the dead?" (Rom 11:12, 15). This word of the apostle is confirmed again and again in the prophetic Scriptures. Typical of the many statements of Gentile blessing are these words of Isaiah: "In the last days the mountain of the LORD's temple will be established as chief among the mountains; it will be raised above the hills, and all nations will stream to it. Many peoples will come and say, 'Come, let us go up to the mountain of the LORD, to the house of the God of Jacob. He will teach us his ways, so that we may walk in his paths' " (2:2, 3; cf. 42:4; Jer 16:19–21; Micah 4:1–5; Amos 9:11; Hab 2:14). The psalmist also views the universality of the salvation and rule of the LORD: "All the ends of the earth will remember and turn to the LORD, and all the families of the nations will worship before Thee. For the kingdom is the LORD's, and He rules over the nations" (22:27, 28, NASB; cf. 65:2, 5; 86:9). Some have charged that the interpretation of prophecy that holds to the restoration of the nation of Israel implies a retrogression from God's present universal work of salvation. But far from turning blessing away from the world, Scripture reveals that the restoration of Israel entails fullness of blessing for all peoples when God's elective purpose for Israel is accomplished.[17]

G. *The Millennial Reign of Christ*

A prominent theme of Scripture is the glorious reign of Christ, which, despite its frequent reference, has evoked different interpretations. The problem lies, on the one hand, in the occasional blending of Christ's glorious reign with the eternal new heavens and new earth (Isa 65:17) and with the apparent bringing in of the final state by the second coming of Christ (e.g., Matt 25:46; 1 Cor 15:50), while, on the other hand, other details, such as the presence of natural bodies, sin, and death during the glorious reign (Isa 65:20–23) point to less than ultimate perfection during Christ's kingdom rule.

There are three main interpretations of the messianic kingdom. Postmillennialists construe a thousand-year reign of Christ on earth that, instead of following, precedes the second coming.[18] According to this view, the OT prophecies concerning Israel and the kingdom are to be symbolically interpreted to refer to this era of the church age during which the gospel will gradually permeate society till all nations acknowledge Christ as Lord and peace prevails on earth (cf. Matt 13:33). The deterioration of world conditions and general loss of optimism since the World Wars have largely eroded this position. A natural interpretation of the Scriptures concerning the kingdom and especially references to the increase of lawlessness and rebellion during this age are difficult to harmonize with postmillennialism.

A second and more popular position is that known as amillennialism.[19] Among the adherents of this view, there are certain variations relating to the explanation of the kingdom prophecies, but the most dominant amillennial view sees the thousand-year period as representing the blessedness of believers during this present age. The

[17]Robert Martin-Achard, *A Light to the Nations* (Edinburgh: Oliver and Boyd, 1962).
[18]Loraine Boettner, *The Millennium* (Philadelphia: Presbyterian and Reformed Publishing Co., 1957).
[19]Oswald T. Allis, *Prophecy and the Church* (Philadelphia: Presbyterian & Reformed Pub. Co., 1945).

amillennarian view takes the thousand years as symbolical, including all the time between the first and second comings of Christ. It includes symbolically the heavenly position of the saints in Christ and the triumph over Satan through the word of Christ. Amillennialism finds its primary support in the Scriptures that appear to portray the coming of Christ as bringing in the final state. It must be remembered, however, that the biblical prophetic perspective frequently places in juxtaposition events that are in reality separated in time, and does so without indicating a temporal interval. Amillennialism also requires the symbolic interpretation of great portions of Scripture that, if accepted in their natural historical-grammatical meaning, look to a literal reign of Christ on the earth.

The premillennialist views the return of Christ as inaugurating a literal thousand-year messianic kingdom before the ushering in of the eternal state. The basis of this interpretation is the many covenant promises in the OT that predict a restoration of the Davidic throne from which the Messiah is to rule over his people Israel and the nations of the earth. (The majority of the later noncanonical Jewish apocalyptic writings also saw an intervening messianic kingdom before the fullness of the age to come.)[20] Revelation 20:1–7 provides the clearest NT reference to this time and also the only biblical indication of its duration (a thousand years), though such a kingdom reign is indicated in other passages (Matt 19:28; 1 Cor 15:23–28).

The millennium is characterized as the time of the greatest glory and prosperity the earth will ever have known. Satan, the deceiver of the nations, will be bound for the thousand years (Rev 20:3, 7) and Christ will reign in justice and righteousness bringing a golden era of peace (Isa 2:4; 11:3–5; Micah 4:3–5; Zech 9:10; Ps 72:3, 7). The curse brought on nature through sin (Gen 3:17–19) will be lifted and the earth will be unprecedentedly productive (Ps 72:16; Isa 11:6–9; 35:1–10; 65:25; Amos 9:13–15; Rom 8:19–22). Longevity and fullness of joy will be the portion of the people under their king (Isa 9:2, 3; 25:6–8; 65:20–23).

Although outward acts of sin will be judged and righteousness will prevail, not all who live during this period will accept Christ's rule. At the close of the millennium, Satan will be released to lead those whose hearts have not been changed (identified as Gog and Magog) in one final rebellion against "the camp of God's people, the city he loves" (Rev 20:7, 8; cf. Ezek 38–39). The final manifestation of sin on the earth will be crushed by supernatural fire from heaven and the devil will be consigned to his final destiny, the lake of fire, to be followed shortly by his followers' receiving the sentence of the "second death" at the great white throne judgment that takes place at the close of the millennium (Rev 20:10–15).

The messianic reign thus culminates God's historical kingdom purpose. Destined to rule the earth for God (Gen 1:26–28; Ps 8; Heb 2:6ff.), man failed through sin, but God will triumph over failure through his own Son, Christ the God-Man, who will bring his kingdom on earth as it is in heaven (Matt 6:10). When this is accomplished, the Son gives up the kingdom to the Father and this inaugurates the eternal state (1 Cor 15:24ff.).

A variation of the above premillennial view understands the messianic prophecies to be fulfilled through the church.[21] According to this position, the church supersedes Israel as the people of God. But instead of the complete fulfillment of the millennial promises during this age as in amillennialism, this type of premillennialism believes that

---

[20] D.S. Russell, *The Method and Message of Jewish Apocalyptic* (Philadelphia: Westminster, 1964), pp. 291ff.
[21] George E. Ladd, *Jesus and the Kingdom* (Waco, Texas: Word, 1964).

God will yet redeem the order of this world at the second coming of Christ and he will establish his rule of righteousness and peace on earth before the eternal state.

H. *The New Heavens and the New Earth*

"Behold, I am making all things new" (Rev 21:5). With these words, biblical eschatology attains its goal. The creation of new heavens and new earth completes the divine regeneration of all things spoiled through sin. Begun in the microcosmos of individual hearts during the present age, the process will not be complete until the macrocosmos of the universe is made new. From a regenerate heart to a glorified body at the first resurrection and the lifting of the curse of nature during the millennium, each phase of the eschatological drama is a step toward this final goal. In this final act, the very structure of the universe is transformed. The old will be disrupted to make room for the new. "The heavens will disappear with a roar; the elements will be destroyed by fire, and the earth and everything in it will be laid bare" (2 Peter 3:10; cf. Isa 34:4; 51:6). This must not be interpreted as an annihilation. Rather, as in all of God's regenerative acts, the old must die to be created anew, but continuity is retained.

The picture of this final state is one of sublime perfection. While it is frequently spoken of as heaven, in reality the heavenly comes down to earth. In the final vision of the Apocalypse John says, "I saw the Holy City, the new Jerusalem, coming down out of heaven from God, prepared as a bride beautifully dressed for her husband. And I heard a loud voice from the throne saying, 'Now the dwelling of God is with men, and he will live with them. They will be his people, and God himself will be with them and be their God'" (Rev 21:2, 3). There will yet be the new heavens above the earth and God will still be transcendent over the earth and will therefore be the God of heaven. But heaven is more than a place beyond the earth; it is the abode of God. Thus the heavenly realm comes to earth. What was formerly described as the "heavenly Jerusalem" (Heb 12:22) becomes the "new Jerusalem" of the new earth.

Three characteristics stand out in John's description of the eternal abode of God's people. While the apostle's description of the city as being made of pure gold, as pure as glass, with walls of jasper and gates made of single pearls (Rev 21:18–21) is probably symbolical, it is without question intended to reveal a place of exquisite beauty. "It shone with the glory of God, and its brilliance was like that of a very precious jewel, like a jasper, clear as crystal" (Rev 21:11).

It is also a place of fullness of life. With all sin and death forever banished (Rev 20:10ff., 21:8; 22:3), it is "Paradise regained." The "river of the water of life," with the "tree of life" on each side, flows in "the middle of the great street of the city" depicting the plenitude of eternal life enjoyed by all (Rev 22:1, 2; cf. Ps 46:4, Zech 14:8). It is the "Sabbath-rest" of God (Heb 4:9) with release from all burdensome toil (Rev 14:13), but filled with the joyful activity of loving worship and service (Rev 5:8, 9; 7:15; 22:3).

Above all, and at the foundation of all its beauty and perfection of life, the final abode brings perfect fellowship with God. In the first phase of the realized eschatology of this age, we enjoy the presence of the indwelling Holy Spirit. When Christ returns, we will be with him, but in the new creation, God's redemptive plan will be complete and we will be forever in the presence of the fullness of the revelation of the triune God. Of this day John writes, "The throne of God and of the Lamb will be in the city, and his servants will serve him. They will see his face, and his name will be on their foreheads" (Rev 22:3, 4). While biblical eschatology holds forth the new creation with all of its glories as the inheritance of the saints, it is ultimately the inheritance of God himself that brings perfection. Long ago, the heart of the psalmist was fixed on this hope: "The Lord is the portion of my inheritance and my cup. . . . Indeed, my heritage is beautiful to me" (Ps 16:5, 6, NASB).

III. The Eschatology of the Individual

The eschatology of human history and the universe most certainly includes that of individuals. It might, in fact, be argued that these broader aspects of eschatology are rooted in God's ultimate desire for relationships with individuals—his purpose to be the God of his people and dwell with them (Rev 21:3). For this reason, the Bible does not submerge the destiny of individuals in the solidarity of the corporate eschatology. On the contrary, general eschatology has its ultimate meaning in relation to the individuals who participate in it. The triumph of God and the defeat of evil involves those who throughout history have been loyal either to God or to evil. The revelation of the Scriptures concerning the future of individuals thus relates the details of personal involvement in God's final goal for history. This personal involvement includes continued existence after death, which issues in the resurrection, and the final judgment, which determines the individual's position in eternity.

A. The Existence of Life After Death

In the OT there is only a limited emphasis on life after death. The hope of the individual was closely tied to the national destiny in the land. A long, prosperous life on earth with numerous offspring to follow were significant aspects of the hope of the individual. Rewards for righteousness and penalties for sin were also chiefly temporal.

But with all its emphasis on the earthly and temporal, the OT contains clear indications that life does not cease with physical death. Despite its emphasis on the solidarity of the individual with the blessings of the nation, the OT also speaks of belief in a personal relationship with the Lord who is the source of life—a relationship death cannot break. The first scriptural intimation of life beyond this temporal existence is the reference to Enoch, who was taken directly to God without dying (Gen 5:29). Abraham also, according to the writer of Hebrews, had his hope set on a life based on something more permanent than the things of the present earthly existence (Heb 11:8–16). In his hope he stands as the prototype of the many OT saints who died not having received the promises but having believed that their existence did not end with death and that they would live to enjoy the fulfillment of the words of their God.

In the OT, existence after death is connected with the concept of Sheol and its NT equivalent, Hades. Sheol denotes the unseen world, the place or abode of the dead. In the OT, the righteous and unrighteous alike go to Sheol, where they are are said to be gathered to their people (Gen 25:8; 35:29; 49:33; 2 Sam 12:23; 1 Kings 2:10). The descriptions of Sheol are many and varied. Conceived of as situated in the depths of the earth (Ps 63:9; 86:13; Isa 14:9; cf. Num 16:30), Sheol is a place of feeble, shadowy existence compared with life on earth. It is a place of darkness (Job 10:21, 22) and silence (Ps 94:17), without remembrance or praise of God (Ps 6:5; 88:12; 115:17) or knowledge of what takes place on earth (Job 14:21). Its inhabitants, who are termed "shades" (Job 26:5; Prov 2:18; Isa 14:9), are but shadows of their former existence. It must be remembered that these descriptions are for the most part poetical and are not to be pressed literally. Primarily, they stand in contrast to the vitality of life on earth with all of its brightness and activity (cf. Job 10:22). Because of its gloomy oblivion and inactivity, the living anticipated Sheol with reluctance and dismay (cf. Isa 38:17–19), though to the troubled it was a welcome rest (Job 3:13–19).

Despite many references to inactivity in comparison with life on earth, Sheol is yet a place of consciousness. The dead meet and greet each other there (Isa 14:9, 10; Ezek 32:21–31), and Jesus uses God's declaration to Moses that he is the God of Abraham, Isaac, and Jacob (Exod 3:6) to show that these patriarchs had not ceased to exist even though they had long been absent from the earth (Matt 22:31, 32).

The general state of shadowy enfeebled existence in the OT picture of Sheol did not permit any strong distinctions between the state of the righteous and that of wicked. Nevertheless, the OT does not portray their condition as identical in Sheol. The righteous "enter into peace" and are at "rest" (Isa 57:1, 2). There is the desire to "die the death of the upright," apparently implying a difference between the outcome of such a death and that of the wicked. As God's anger burns against the wicked on earth, it extends to the "lowest part of Sheol" (Deut 32:22). The proud and haughty are thrust down to Sheol, "to the depths of the pit" (Isa 14:15; cf. Ezek 32:23). Perhaps these latter references indicate some separation between the just and the unjust, the latter being consigned to the lowest part of Sheol.

The hope of the righteous, however, did not rest on their position in Sheol. Sheol, like death, was an unnatural state caused by sin. Ultimate hope looked forward to deliverance from Sheol into life and fellowship with God as a whole man in the body. This hope rested on two main foundations. First, there was the belief that true life consisted in fellowship with God, the source of all life (Ps 16:11; 30:5; 63:3). The life that was begun for the pious in this world could not be ultimately cut off by death. Between the righteous and their God there was an indissoluble tie. Second, the distinction between the righteous and the wicked, which was evident on this earth, was not always manifest in the earthly destinies of each class. That distinction called for a final state in which each class was requited according to its nature.

Although this ultimate hope for the righteous is only briefly mentioned in the OT revelation, there are indications that it includes the resurrection of the body. The psalmist declares, "My flesh also will dwell securely. For Thou wilt not abandon my soul to Sheol. . . . Thou wilt make known to me the path of life" (Ps 16:9–11, NASB). Again, after mention of the prosperity of the wicked, he expresses his own hope: "As for me, I shall behold Thy face in righteousness; I will be satisfied with Thy likeness when I awake" (Ps 17:15, NASB). Even more explicit is the faith that God would receive him: "But God will redeem my soul from the power of Sheol; for He will receive Me" (Ps 49:15, NASB; cf. Ps 73:24). The concept of being "received" by God has its parallels in the taking of Enoch and Elijah out of the world, with this difference, that for the psalmist, it must refer to resurrection following death.[22]

The Book of Job has two passages that most probably can be interpreted as positing faith in a bodily resurrection. After voicing a pessimistic view of the possibility of man living again after death, Job's faith dares to claim the opposite: "If a man dies, will he live again? All the days of my struggle I will wait, until my change comes. Thou wilt call, and I will answer Thee; Thou wilt long for the work of Thy hands" (Job 14:14, 15, NASB). Although the precise rendering of Job 19:25–27 is problematic (cf. KJV, NASB), this passage likewise expresses the hope, if not for the resurrection of the flesh, most cer-

---

[22]Cf. Delitzsch, *Biblical Commentary on the Psalms*, 2:118, 119.

tainly for a continued existence in the presence of God. As the sense of individuality grew stronger in the prophets, so did the clarity of the resurrection. Isaiah proclaims, "Your dead will live, their bodies will rise" (26:19). Finally, we find for the first time in Scripture the prediction of the resurrection of the wicked as well as the righteous. "Multitudes who sleep in the dust of the earth will awake, some to everlasting life, others to shame and everlasting contempt" (Dan 12:2).

The concept of the afterlife underwent certain development in the intertestamental period. The literature from this period, known as the Apocrypha and pseudepigrapha,[23] reveals a varied and often conflicting eschatology influenced as it was by Babylonian, Persian, and Greek concepts as well as by the OT. Nevertheless, these writings give us a glimpse into the popular Jewish faith of that period and provide background for some of the concepts of the future life in the NT.

Among the various teachings of the Apocrypha and pseudepigrapha, certain conceptual links with the NT are significant. The individualism begun in the OT prophets developed along with an increasing concern for reward and retribution in the future life. Thus Sheol, though still pictured much as in the OT, more and more came to be regarded as an intermediate state with a separation between the righteous and the wicked, who are suffering punishment. But the concern for the individual led to the resurrection. In many instances it was only the righteous who would be raised to share in the glory and joys of God's reign or the messianic kingdom (e.g., 1 Enoch 5:8; 61:5; 90:33; 91:10; Wisd Sol 3:16). In other places, however it is both the just and the unjust who are resurrected (e.g., Baruch 50:2; 1 Enoch 51:1; 2 Esd 5:45; 7:32).

Individual eschatology reaches its climax in NT revelation. Although the emphasis is still on the end events of history, one's participation in these depends on a personal relationship with Christ. The same themes of the future life that were initiated in the OT and developed in intertestamental times are taken up in the NT and brought to completion.

In the NT, Hades is the immediate abode of the dead. This is especially true of the wicked, though many interpreters see in the Lord's story of Lazarus and the rich man a reference to the two-compartment view of Sheol/Hades found in earlier Jewish literature.[24] Also, however, the righteous are clearly viewed as being in the presence of their Lord and not in Hades. Jesus gave the dying thief assurance that he would immediately be with him in paradise (Luke 23:43). Stephen saw his Lord in heaven waiting to receive his spirit (Acts 7:56). Paul hoped "to be at home with the Lord" (2 Cor 5:8), to "be with Christ" (Phil 1:23), immediately after departing this life. The "spirits of righteous men" are presently among inhabitants of the heavenly Jerusalem (Heb 12:23; cf. Rev 6:9; 7:9).

The explanation of the change in the location of the righteous dead is usually associated with Christ's accomplishment of redemption. Basing its teachings on the references to his triumph over Hades (Acts 2:27, 31; Rev 1:8) and his proclamation to the spirits in prison following his death (1 Peter 3:18ff.), the church early developed the doctrine of Christ's descent into Hades to proclaim victory and triumphantly lead out the righteous to the heavenly glory. Paul's reference to the Lord's leading of "captives in his train" at his ascension (Eph 4:8) is sometimes interpreted to mean the removal of the righteous from Hades to heaven. Whether or not the latter two passages, which are much disputed

---

[23]Cf. B.M. Metzger, "The Apocrypha and Pseudepigrapha," EBC 1:161–175.
[24]Cf. Jeremias, "ᾅδης [hadēs]," TDNT 1:147.

among interpreters, teach such a descent and removal of the righteous, they are clearly in heaven, and the finished work of Christ on the cross and his subsequent exaltation in triumph without doubt explain the change.

The doctrine of the resurrection, though only partially revealed in the OT, becomes a major theme in the NT. While the NT emphasizes the resurrection as the glorious goal for believers, it also affirms the resurrection of unbelievers. Jesus declares that "a time is coming when all who are in their graves will hear his voice and come out—those who have done good will rise to live, and those who have done evil will rise to be condemned" (John 5:28, 29). In the Apocalypse, John speaks explicitly of the resurrection of the just and unjust. After mentioning the "first resurrection," which involves believers (Rev 20:4–6), he speaks of another resurrection that includes those whose names were not written in the book of life (20:12–15).

The new emphasis on the hope of personal resurrection rests on the resurrection of Christ. No longer is it simply a hope based on prophecy. There is the historical fact of the risen Christ. For the believer, this resurrection of Christ is the assurance of his own resurrection, because he has come into a living union with him. In salvation, the believer not only shares in Christ's death on the cross but also in his resurrection—a spiritual sharing now that results in the renewal of the inner man and an ultimate sharing in which one is completely and forever renewed (Rom 6:4, 5). The believer lives by the resurrection life of the risen Lord (Col 3:1–3), which is made effective in him through the presence of the indwelling Spirit. As a sharer in this new life in the Spirit, the believer already participates in the eschatological life. Through the outpouring of the Spirit, those who belong to Christ participate in the "powers of the coming age" (Heb 6:5).

The resurrection of the body is only the culminating act of personal redemption that includes the entire person—a redemption the believer longingly awaits (Rom 8:23). So certain is this final act that it can already be spoken of as an accomplished fact (Eph 2:5, 6).

Only in a limited way does Scripture describe the nature of the resurrection body. This is in keeping with the way Scripture deals with all eschatological phenomena, which in our present state we cannot truly comprehend. Nevertheless, the limited description of the future body portrays it as one of power and glory. Contrasting it with our present body, Paul writes in the great resurrection chapter: "The body that is sown is perishable, it is raised imperishable; it is sown in dishonor, it is raised in glory; it is sown in weakness, it is raised in power; it is sown a natural body, it is raised a spiritual body" (1 Cor 15:42–44). Its "spiritual" nature does not imply a body made of nonmaterial spirit, but rather a body formed and adapted to the principle of life that is spirit as opposed to the present body, which is adapted to the natural, soulish life of this earth. In this life, the spirit is hampered by the weaknesses and limitations of the body; in the future life the spirit will have perfect freedom and control in the resurrection body. Though the description in 1 Corinthians 15 is detailed, the most succinct and yet comprehensive statement is Paul's word in Philippians that Christ at his return "will transform our lowly bodies so that they will be like his glorious body" (Phil 3:21; cf. 1 Cor 15:49).

The only clue to the manner of the resurrection is the analogy of the sowing and sprouting of natural seed (1 Cor 15:35ff.). Even as what is sown springs up into something radically different, yet continuous with it, so through the power of God the body that is sown even in decay is raised a body that is gloriously different but maintains its continuity. The processes of the resurrection remain a mystery.

The time of the resurrection of the body remains a point of dispute among scholars. The problem is inextricably linked to the question of the millennium. Those who view

Christ's present heavenly session as the fulfillment of his kingly mediatorial reign see one general resurrection of the just and the unjust occurring at the second coming of Christ. Scriptures that are used to support a general resurrection are, e.g., Daniel 12:2, 3 and John 5:28, 29, where there is no time distinction between the raising of the just and the unjust. Moreover, advocates of a general resurrection view Paul's description of the order of the resurrection as identifying the "end" with the resurrection of those who at Christ's coming belong to him (1 Cor 15:23, 24).

On the other hand, those who understand that the Scriptures teach an earthly reign of Christ following his parousia view the resurrection as occurring in two general phases. Those who belong to Christ are raised in connection with his coming so that they may share in his kingdom reign (Rev 20:4–6), while the rest of humanity awaits the termination of this period before being resurrected (vv. 12–15). This passage in Revelation, along with the general biblical support of Christ's millennial reign, favors the latter interpretation. Christ's mention of the repayment "at the resurrection of the righteous" for good deeds done on earth (Luke 14:14) and the expression of the resurrection of believers as "out from the dead" (cf. Phil 3:11) also suggest two resurrections.

The passages that teach the resurrection of both the just and the unjust without distinction in time neither affirm nor deny a distinction in time (see commentaries). Nor does 1 Corinthians 15:23, 24 deny an interval between the resurrection of believers at Christ's coming and the final consummation. The Greek word *eita*, translated "then" at the beginning of v. 24, is simply an adverb denoting sequence (compare its use in vv. 5, 7). There is nothing to preclude the "end" (v. 24) from being separated from Christ's parousia by the millennial reign and thus being interpreted in harmony with the resurrection sequence of Revelation 20.

B. *The Final Judgment and Final Destiny*

The numerous judgments of God upon men individually and collectively, which have occurred during this life, and even the separate condition of the just and the unjust at death are but preliminary to the final judgment of every person. That God will execute judgment is clearly foreseen by the psalmist: "But the LORD abides forever; He has established His throne for judgment, and He will judge the world in righteousness; He will execute judgment for the peoples with equity" (Ps 9:7, 8, NASB; cf. 96:13; 98:9). Whether this judgment extends to the individual in the future life or refers to the judgment of this world at the close of history is not explicit. A personal judgment after death does appear to be the thought of the writer of Ecclesiastes, who, after discussing certain actions during this life, concludes, "Yet know that God will bring you to judgment for all these things" (11:9, NASB; cf. 12:13.)[25] Daniel 12:2, however, provides the first clear reference to a final judgment for the just and the unjust: "Multitudes who sleep in the dust of the earth will awake: some to everlasting life, others to shame and everlasting contempt." The final judgment necessitates the resurrection, as the retribution of the wicked and reward of the righteous cannot be complete in the intermediate state, for retribution and reward regard man in his completeness.

With the progression of revelation in the NT, the outlines of the final judgment become more distinct. All must stand before "the judgment seat of God" (Rom 14:10; cf. 2:5, 6). Such judgment extends to the "living and the dead" (1 Tim 4:1). The executor

---

[25]See Salmond, *The Christian Doctrine of Immortality*, pp. 216, 117.

of this final judgment of God is none other than Christ (John 5:22; Acts 17:31; 2 Cor 5:10), who is especially suited for the task "because he is the Son of Man" (John 5:27).

The time of the judgment is related to the coming of Christ and the resurrection. Those of amillennialist persuasion, who view the general resurrection of the just and the unjust at the return of Christ, see a general judgment of both groups at this time issuing in their final destiny in the eternal state. But as we have previously pointed out, the NT appears to view the resurrection in separate phases. So likewise the judgment occurs in two phases. The final assize of believers is clearly linked to the return of Christ, at which time they will be resurrected to stand before him along with the living who have received their glorified bodies (1 Cor 4:5; 3:10–15; 1 Peter 5:4). Christ appears to speak of this separate phase when he promises the recompense of blessing "at the resurrection of the righteous" (Luke 14:14). The judgment of unbelievers follows the millennium, at which time they are resurrected to stand before the "great white throne" to receive the execution of their final state (Rev 20:11–15). Although Scripture is not explicit on the problem of the death and resurrection of the righteous during the kingdom reign, presumably they also have part in this final resurrection and judgment.

Scripture passages related to the final judgment everywhere reveal the criterion of judgment as the works done in this life (Rom 2:5–8; 2 Cor 5:10; Rev 20:12). On the other hand, the manifest teaching of Scripture is salvation by grace through faith (Eph 2:8, 9) and a personal faith relationship to Christ (John 3:16, 18; Matt 7:23; 19:28). This seeming paradox between grace and works as a basis of final salvation is, however, only apparent. For in the case of the believer, it is "work produced by faith" (1 Thess 1:3; 2 Thess 1:11; James 2:18–25). Works are never the cause of one's final salvation but the evidence of saving faith (cf. Gal 5:6). And, as evidence, they provide a good basis of judgment (cf. Matt 7:16–20). The unbeliever's works likewise stem from and evidence a heart of sinful autonomy and unbelief. It is, therefore, one and the same thing whether we speak of condemnation because of unbelief (John 3:18) or final judgment based on the works issuing from unbelief.

The final judgment determines the destiny of every individual either in a state of blessedness or of punishment. While both states admit of some degrees, based on gracious rewards for the saved (Rev 22:12) and the extent of guilt in relation to the knowledge of the divine will for the lost (Luke 10:12–15; 12:47–48), there is ultimately no alternative position. The bliss of the saved—described variously as a situation of "eternal life" (Rom 2:7), "glory" (Rom 2:10; 2 Cor 4:17), "rest" (Heb 4:11), "happiness" (Matt 25:21), etc.—finds its ultimate reality in direct and intimate communion with God and Christ (Rev 21:3; 22:3, 4). The most complete description of that final state is given in John's portrayal of the new Jerusalem where, often in symbolic language due to its transcendent character, the eternal abode is pictured as one of perfect beauty and fellowship both with God and fellow saints (Rev 21–22).

The final state of the wicked is described in equally vivid but terrifying expressions. It is "the lake of fire" (Rev 20:15), "eternal" and unquenchable fire (Matt 25:41; Mark 9:43, 48; Isa 23:14), a place where there is "weeping and grinding of teeth" (Matt 13:42, 50; 22:13) and "eternal punishment" (Matt 25:46) where the inhabitants "will be tormented day and night for ever and ever" (Rev 20:10; cf. 14:11). As opposed to eternal life and glory, it is "the second death" (Rev 20:14), "darkness" (Matt 22:13; 2 Peter 2:7; Jude 13), "everlasting destruction" (2 Thess 1:9; cf. Phil 3:19), and "shame" (Dan 12:2). As in the description of the state of the blessed, transcendent otherness rules out a simple literalistic understanding of these vivid expressions. The ultimate nature of the state of the wicked is rather to be thought of as the opposite of the life that is known through fellowship with him who is the source of life. Such life is at least partially expressed in the list of personal qualities, headed by love, that are termed "the fruit of the Spirit" in Gal 5:22, 23. The "second death" is thus the personal experience of the total lack of love and its concomitant qualities forever. Since believers and unbelievers while on earth are all to some extent surrounded by the manifestation of God's love in his gracious goodness, the despair and agonies of existence forever in the total absence of God, except for his wrath, defies our comprehension.

Various groups throughout the history of the church have attempted to evade the fearful reality of such an eternal condemnation. Some, including many in modern times, have adopted the doctrine of universalism, basing it primarily on the misinterpretation of certain Scriptures that appear to describe the scope of Christ's work in universal terms. Others, relying on passages that describe the destiny of the unsaved as eternal destruction, have believed in the concept of the final annihilation of the lost. But the evangelical church, supported by many explicit references such as those mentioned above and especially by the passages that parallel eternal punishment with eternal life (cf. for example, Matt 25:46; Rev 20:10; 22:5), has consistently resisted any tendency to avoid the manifest teaching of Scripture on this dark and awesome subject.

IV. Bibliography

Allis, O.T. *Prophecy and the Church.* Philadelphia: Presbyterian and Reformed, 1945.

Beasley-Murray, G.R. *Jesus and the Future.* London: Macmillan, 1954.

Berkhof, L. *The Kingdom of God.* Grand Rapids: Eerdmans, 1951.

Berkouwer, G.C. *The Return of Christ.* Grand Rapids: Eerdmans, 1972.

Charles, R.H. *A Critical History of the Doctrine of a Future Life,* 2nd ed. London: Adam and Black, 1913.

Fison, J.E. *The Christian Hope: The Presence and the Parousia.* London: Longmans, 1954.

Glasson, T. Francis. *The Second Advent.* London: Epworth, 1963.

Gundry, Robert H. *The Church and the Tribulation.* Grand Rapids: Zondervan, 1973.

Ladd, G.E. *Jesus and the Kingdom.* Waco, Texas: Word, 1964.

_____. *The Blessed Hope.* Grand Rapids: Eerdmans, 1956.

McClain, Alva J. *The Greatness of the Kingdom.* Grand Rapids: Zondervan, 1959.

Moltmann, Jurgen. *Theology of Hope.* New York: Harper, 1967.

Moore, A.L. *The Parousia in the New Testament.* Leiden: Brill, 1966.

Pache, Rene. *The Return of Jesus Christ.* Chicago: Moody, 1955.

Peters, George N.H. *The Theocratic Kingdom of Our Lord Jesus Christ,* 3 vols. Grand Rapids: Kregel, 1957.

Salmond, Stewart D.F. *The Christian Doctrine of Immortality.* Edinburgh: T. & T. Clark, 1901.

Shedd, W.G.T. *The Doctrine of Endless Punishment.* New York: Scribner, 1886.

Smith, Wilbur M. *The Biblical Doctrine of Heaven.* Chicago: Moody, 1968.

Vos, Geerhardus. *The Pauline Eschatology.* Grand Rapids: Eerdmans, 1952.

Walvoord, J.F. *The Millennial Kingdom.* Findlay, Ohio: Dunham, 1959.

THE BIBLE AS LITERATURE
Calvin D. Linton

Calvin D. Linton

A.B., George Washington University; A.M., Ph.D., Johns Hopkins University

Dean of Columbian College of Arts and Sciences and Professor of English Literature, George Washington University

THE BIBLE AS LITERATURE

I. Introduction

There is only one Bible, theologically speaking, but we have it in two main categories: the Bible in the original languages and the Bible as it exists in hundreds of translations into the languages of the world, including the scores of translations into English. Because literary style is significantly, though not exclusively, the product of the arrangement of certain words in a certain order, an examination of specific stylistic traits requires recognizing differences between the literary effects of various translations. Such stylistic features as word sound, connotation, and rhythm are peculiar to a certain set of words placed in a certain order—peculiar, that is, to a particular translation. Sometimes such traits are hard to reproduce in any other language. When Keats speaks of the song of the nightingale as that which "hath/ Charm'd magic casements, opening on the foam/ Of perilous seas, in faery lands forlorn," he exhibits elements of style almost untranslatable, for his effects are dependent on the sounds, meanings, and rhythms of a certain set of English words.

To discuss the Bible as literature with chief attention to stylistic effects generated by word choice and order, therefore, would require limiting ourselves either to the original languages or to a particular translation. If the latter were our purpose, the choice of a translation would be comparatively easy, for the King James Version is universally conceded to be the finest writing in the English language.

There are, however, elements of literary excellence that do not depend on peculiarities inherent in any particular language. They include such formal elements as prose and poetry, narrative, drama, allegory, and biography; and such stylistic elements as parallelism, imagery, symbolism, and the like. It is with such literary elements as these that this article will deal.

In further clarification of purpose, several questions may be asked. Is it our intent to judge or "criticize" the Book? Or, even more bluntly, to evaluate the literary style of the Holy Spirit, who inspired Scripture? This last question is not so fanciful as it may seem. The great seventeenth-century writer and clergyman John Donne undertook to do so. "The Holy Ghost is an eloquent author," he said, "a vehement and an abundant author, but yet not luxuriant" (Donne's 79th *Sermon*).

Our purpose, however, is neither to judge the value of God's Word nor to assess the literary style of the Holy Spirit. Nor does this disavowal evade the issue. A high view of the infallibility of the Scriptures in the original languages need not embrace any "dictation theory" of inspiration. The consequence of being filled by the Holy Spirit is not a diminishment of human individuality, freedom, and personality, but a realization of all that being human means. The various writers of the books of the Bible wrote in their own styles, reflecting their temperaments, degrees of learning, and differences of aesthetic sensibility, as indeed do all authors. Amos's style is not like Ezekiel's, nor John's like Paul's. This does not suggest that God the Holy Spirit did not breathe upon each of them his will, nor that he failed to preserve them from all error. It only means that he used his servants by fulfilling their capabilities as his creatures in a special way for a special purpose, not that he anesthetized their individuality and merely used their fingers to indite his dictation. Had he done so, the literary style of the Bible would not vary from writer to writer, and Donne's attempt to measure the literary competence of the Holy Spirit would be valid.

This article, then, is written in the belief that the Bible is without error of any kind in the original manuscripts or autographa, preserved from any error by the Holy Spirit; that the spoken words recorded are truly reported; that the events as described actually occurred, all being fashioned by the will of God into a divine, organic unit, revealing God's will to man; and that in accomplishing his purpose, God used his servants in the full power and exercise of their individual capabilities, including literary skill. That he was, indeed, concerned with the beauty and grandeur of his Book is evident to all who read it.

As to method, we shall select some of the major dimensions of literary quality as derived from and normally applied to other works of literature, to see how they reveal themselves in the Bible. In doing so, we recognize the cogency of this statement by C.S. Lewis:

> No translation can preserve the qualities of its original unchanged. On the other hand, except where lyrical poetry is in question, the literary effect of any good translation must be more indebted to the original than anything else. This is especially true of narrative or moral instruction. Where the originals are Hebrew it holds in an unusual degree even for lyrical poetry because the parallelism of form is a translatable quality. Except in a few passages where the translation is bad, the Authorized Version owes to the original its matter, its images, and its figures.[1]

His conclusion with regard to the Authorized Version (KJV) applies to any accurate translation.

II. The Nature and Purpose of Literature

Great literature is that kind of writing which, in addition to whatever other purposes it may serve, is characterized by aesthetic and artistic qualities. It differs, for example, from expository prose, not in that it does not communicate, but in that it communicates in a way rendered more moving and memorable than writing designed merely to transfer an idea from one mind to another with a minimum of loss. It is writing that, whether it

---

[1]C.S. Lewis, "The Literary Impact of the Authorized Version," *Selected Literary Essays* (Cambridge: Cambridge University Press, 1969), p. 126.

be chiefly aimed at informing, exhorting, narrating, dramatizing, or whatever, is additionally concerned with its aesthetic quality. It is peculiarly fitting, therefore, that so much of God's Word to us should be beautiful as well as true—reminding us that God created man with the wonderful and mysterious capability of responding with delight to beauty of many kinds.

Literary quality is not merely decoration. Because man is deeply moved by beauty, literature informs and teaches more effectively than does unadorned verbal communication. Nor need the term *adornment* suggest anything elaborate or calculatedly artificial. There is, for example, abiding beauty in truth, as one may feel when he reads any translation of the first few verses of John's Gospel, where the writing is of the simplest expository kind.

Elaborate decoration, on the other hand, need not be viewed with suspicion when the adornment is appropriate to the truth being expressed. God, who is the source of all beauty, shows his concern for beauty on many pages of the Bible, as he shows it in the design of the flowers, the birds, the snowflakes, and the outflung heavens, and even in his instructions concerning the adornment of the temple and the garments of the priests. In the Bible the reader gets at least a glimpse of the beauty of God, rather like the hint Moses had when he was hid in the cleft of the rock, or like the glory the shepherds saw in the brightness of the heavenly host.

III. Some Basic Elements of Literary Form

Literary beauty, like all beauty, results from the harmonious blending of many elements, and the complexity begins at the simplest level, that of the words themselves. For almost every object, the biblical languages—Hebrew and Greek (and in a few OT passages, Aramaic)—present us with multiple choices. E.g., whether one writes "girl," "maiden," or "young woman" depends on the connotation one wishes to convey. Some words, indeed, come so richly robed in an aura of feeling that the connotative dress may say more than the denotative "thing" within. The Bible is rich and subtle in its use of precisely the right word, ranging from the multiple implications of a common word like *shepherd* to the rich suggestiveness of such words as *lamb, candlestick,* and *vine.*

From at least the time of the Greeks, it has been recognized—i.e., discovered, not decided—that there are certain essential characteristics of all great literature. Terminology relating to these characteristics, and even in some cases their identity, varies in the history of literary criticism. But almost all would agree that included are *unity, harmony,* and *radiance.* (Or, in Thomist terms, *integritas, consonantia,* and *claritas.*) By the first is required singleness (not simplicity) of purpose; by the second, internal congruence, absence of contradictoriness; and by the third, the effusion of light, figuratively taken to be the revelation of the beauty that shines from truth.

It is scarcely necessary to argue the Bible's claim to supremacy in each of these categories. In all of them the Bible is incomparable, the measure by which all else is measured. Its unity is the unity of God himself, showing forth at its center the oneness of the Godhead—Father, Son, and Holy Spirit—dramatically concentrated in the Word made flesh, Jesus Christ himself. Its internal harmony is the delight of believers and the despair of skeptics, for on what other grounds than the controlling power of the Holy Spirit is one to explain the intricate, ever-unfolding marvel of its harmony, written as it was over many centuries by many authors? And its radiance is the light of Christ himself, who declared that he is the light of the world as well as the truth. If Keats had had Christ in mind (as, sadly, he did not) when he declared that "Beauty is truth, truth beauty," he would have succinctly defined the radiance of the Bible.

Other qualities broadly held to be essential to literary greatness include *magnitude* (that is, the work must be of a certain dimension; a cherry stone, be it never so cleverly carved, is not comparable to Michelangelo's "David," nor any couplet to Milton's *Paradise Lost*); *universality* (that is to say, the broader the spectrum of human experience the work encompasses, the greater the work); and *sublimity* (that is, the appeal should be to the elevated, ennobling capabilities of humankind). It is apparent that here again the Bible not only illustrates the terms in this triad, but also sets the measure of them.

IV. Literary Genres in the Bible

The rather grand terms used thus far in describing the literary greatness of the Bible cannot exist in a vacuum. It is not enough to have a grand concept; there must be the skill to actualize it. One may imagine a superb violin and in general terms describe one's conception of it in terms of sonority, brilliance, and the like; but making the violin itself is another matter, requiring the artifice of a disciplined craftsman.

So we must examine some of the principles of the craft of fashioning great literature as they are found in the Bible. And we may be sure that if such principles are found, they are there because of the conscious artistic purpose of gifted writers, not by accident. Not that all the writers of the books of the Bible were equally gifted with literary skill, nor that every part of each of the books is of equal literary value, for God has blended the talents of a great variety of writers and has used the beauty of many genres (or forms) to produce his written Word.

We have mentioned, with regard to stylistic devices, the felicitous congruence between the Hebrew and Greek on the one hand and English on the other. Similarly, one finds that the major genres represented in the Bible are familiar to all students of English and other world literatures. Prose and poetry, narrative, history, drama, parable, symbolism, allegory (used comparatively rarely in the Bible), aphorism, epic, debate (in the literary sense of *débat*—Job may be said to have initiated the form in world literature), and exposition—all of these, plus a few others, are found in distinguished form in the Bible. It is, indeed, essential to a proper interpretation of a particular portion of Scripture to be aware of the form used at that point. It is as important to take passages of exposition literally as to read symbolic passages symbolically. Nor does this principle open up any Pandora's box of subjective exegesis. Honest disagreement may, of course, occur in the interpretation of particular passages, but it is usually apparent in what genre a book or passage is cast.

Of some of the literary forms appearing in the Bible it is more accurate to say that the Bible inaugurates them than that it reflects them, so far as their later employment in secular literature is concerned. If an early date for Job is accepted, for example, one may see in that book the seeds not only of later drama but of the "short epic" as well. A lesser example is the exemplum, or short tale designed to teach a moral, which from medieval days to the present is such a staple of preaching. An exquisite biblical example is the story told King David by Nathan the prophet about the rich man who stole the "one little ewe lamb" of the poor man, and heartlessly killed it. One can see the wrath rising in the face of the great king as he demanded to know who had done such a thing. "You are the man!" said Nathan, and brought home to David the heinousness of his adultery and his murder of Uriah (2 Sam 12:1–7).

While it is not possible in the scope of this article to comment in any detail on each of the literary forms of the Bible, a brief overview of one or two is in order with (cf. section VI) a final consideration of certain NT genres.

Narration, a major form and one of the four types of prose composition (the others being argumentation, description, and exposition), occupies a central place in the Bible, ranging from the long historical passages in the OT to the Book of Acts and such superbly shaped "short stories" as those of the Prodigal Son and the Good Samaritan in the NT. Whether the narrative recounts history or fiction, the literary requisites are the same: vividness of characterization; selective and revealing dialogue; straightforward story line; suggestiveness rather than discursiveness; sensuously depicted setting; and, above all, economy. In all these traits biblical narrative excels. Consider, as one example, Moses' telling of the story of Joseph, a narrative that occupies most of the last thirteen chapters of Genesis. Characters ranging from the aging believer Jacob to the sensual pagan wife of Potiphar; positions running from demeaning slavery to the glorious rulership of the mightiest nation then on earth; vivid and telling touches like those of the hidden cup and the many-colored coat—everything catches our attention and stirs our imagination.

Or consider the unforgettable vividness of numberless narrative vignettes in the other historical books—the chariot driving of Jehu, who "drove furiously"; the surreptitious entry of David into the cave where Saul lay; Esther standing in the oriental splendor of the court of Ahasuerus (Xerxes); the death of Jezebel; the annihilation of the hosts of Sennacherib; the contest between Elijah and the priests of Baal—the list is almost endless. In the narratives of the Bible we have supreme examples of how a story should be told.

When we turn from narrative to drama, we see an equally vast panorama. Not that the Bible is in any of its parts illustrative of specific dramatic form (except perhaps for Job or the Song of Solomon). Yet its dramatic power is unmistakable. Indeed, *drama* in its general sense is the term that best hints at the literary majesty of the entire Book. What could be imagined more overwhelming than the drama of man's creation and fall, the intervention of God in redemption, the glory of an incomparable "hero," the culmination of the age-long conflict between good and evil, and, finally, a new heaven and a new earth? Taken as a whole, the Bible is the mightiest drama ever conceived or conceivable. Nor does the immense scope of the drama diminish the internal harmony or vitality of its innumerable characters, blur the story line, or diffuse the theme. The fusion of such complexity and multiplicity into organic unity is unique in the literature of the world and is only hinted at in Milton's epic-drama, *Paradise Lost,* a work modeled on the Bible.

Thinking of drama as primarily a quality of effect and not necessarily as a form comprised of acts and scenes exhibited in a theater, we recognize the significance of such elements as dramatic conflict, dialogue, theme, action, foreshadowing, culmination, and tone. Illustrations of each crowd the mind as episode after episode from the Bible crosses our memory: Adam and Eve, expelled from the garden, looking back at their once blissful home that is now guarded by the blazing swords and terrible faces of God's messengers; the confusion of tongues at Babel; Israel crossing the Red Sea; Solomon dedicating the temple; the mob before Pilate when he brings Jesus out to them, having himself found no fault in him but asking them whether they want to crucify their king, and the people of Jerusalem, heirs of the promise, daring to cry out, "We have no king but Caesar!"; the dark hours of the crucifixion; the glorious power of the resurrection; and the coming of the Holy Spirit at Pentecost.

Moreover, to speak of the Bible as drama in the larger sense is to realize that the play is not over. A climax transcending human imagination awaits fulfillment, for all is "scripted," the plot determined, and the roles cast.

V. Literary Devices

Whatever the form of literature, its aesthetic impact and its stylistic effect depend on the use of appropriate literary devices. By its nature, poetry makes more elaborate use of stylistic devices than prose. And in an age that tends to see man as moving from primitive crudity to modern sophistication, we need to be reminded that poetry is not only an earlier and more natural way of expressing ideas and feelings than prose, but that extensive portions of the OT were originally cast in verse forms—and very elaborate ones, too. Poetry differs from prose chiefly in that the poet seeks, through the artful use of diction, rhythm, and imagery, to stir the imagination and to communicate more than the writer of prose can do. When prose presents the possibility of more than one meaning, it is said to be ambiguous, which is quite a different thing from poetry and its simultaneous communication on several levels. Poetry is rather analogous to striking a consonant chord on the piano, each separate note blending with others to form a complex but organically unified sound.

Of the several devices so far mentioned, diction is of course to be fully savored only by those competent in the original languages. But the Bible, as we have noted, is eminently translatable, and one reason for this is that its diction is pervasively direct, objective, and closely tied to familiar objects. Consider the vivid questions put to Job: "Can you pull in the leviathan with a fishhook or tie down his tongue with a rope? Can you put a cord through his nose?" (Job 41:1-2). The emphasis is on the physical "things" of an account, as when one verse is used to dispose of the mighty Sisera: "Then Jael Heber's wife took a nail of the tent, and took a hammer in her hand, and went softly unto him, and smote the nail into his temples, and fastened it into the ground: for he was fast asleep and weary. So he died" (Judg 4:21, KJV).

The rhythm of Hebrew poetry is readily recaptured in translation because the original tends to follow exact patterns in a parallelism of thought. The chief forms of this parallelism are synonymous, antithetic, and synthetic, and may readily be reproduced in translation. "The LORD watches over you—the LORD is your shade at your right hand" (Ps 121:5); "Who has believed our message and to whom has the arm of the LORD been revealed?" (Isa 53:1). These are instances of synonymous parallelism. Almost equally frequent (particularly in Proverbs) are instances of antithetic parallelism, in which a truth is stated first in its positive form and then in the obverse form, as in "Fear of man will prove to be a snare, but whoever trusts in the LORD is kept safe" (Prov 29:25) and "He who conceals his sins does not prosper, but whoever confesses and renounces them finds mercy" (Prov 28:13). In synthetic parallelism, the thought is added to and enriched as in Job 11:18, "And you will be secure, because there is hope; you will look about you and take your rest in safety." Such parallelisms are to be distinguished from simple repetition, which is an effective device in itself for heightening feeling, as in the reiteration of "Utterly meaningless! Everything is meaningless." in Ecclesiastes, or in the moving repetitions in David's lament over Absalom: "O my son Absalom! My son, my son Absalom! If only I had died instead of you—O Absalom, my son, my son!" (2 Sam 18:33).

In addition to their function in enhancing literary beauty, parallelism and repetition are often used as mnemonic devices. In an age when writing was hard to achieve and hard to preserve, entire cultural heritages, including wisdom literature, were preserved orally, including laws, genealogies, and history, from generation to generation, with astonishing faithfulness.

But the literary device most effective in the style of the Bible, as in all literature, is figurative language, or imagery, chiefly simile and metaphor. Its power derives from that mysterious capability called "imagination," which permits us to find enriching three-dimensional correspondences among a number of images clustered around a single idea. The memorableness of the twenty-third Psalm is almost entirely due in the literary sense to one metaphor: "The Lord is my shepherd," for from that simple declarative sentence there move out resonating rings of meaning and implication. Superficially and literally, of course, the statement is not "true"—we are not literally sheep and the Lord is not literally a shepherd; but we are like sheep and he is like a shepherd, and in the correspondence we see into the heart of the Lord's care for his own. (Remember that a simile is a stated comparison: "The kingdom of heaven is like a mustard seed" [Matt 13:31] and a metaphor is an implied comparison: "Why does your anger smolder against the sheep of your pasture?" [Ps 74:1].)

The major purpose of imagery is to enliven an abstract concept by investing it with sensuousness (the quality of physical experience) so that one may feel a thought in his pulses as well as comprehend it in his mind. The result is that one is moved as well as informed. Another purpose is to say much with few words. The single figure comparing the church to a bride, the bride of Christ, communicates more than many pages of abstract prose could do. When Luther observed that "Paul's words are alive; they have hands and feet; if you cut them they bleed," he was describing a quality that is characteristic of the entire Bible, and one that comes from its intensive use of figurative language.

The power of figurative language lies also in its philosophical validity; namely, its capacity for showing the interrelatedness of all things, the unity and orderliness of God's universe, the interconnected purposefulness of his cosmic pattern. It implies that God's nature, law, and purposes harmoniously permeate all things, the microcosm and the macrocosm congruently intertwined. A familiar metaphor of the seventeenth century presented God's creation as a great dance, or a mighty orchestration, each element (save as sin has marred the harmony) moving in rhythm and melody as the divine Artificer has determined. One thinks of the time when "the morning stars sang together, and all the angels shouted for joy" (Job 38:7).

Almost without exception, the imagery of the Bible relates to basic, natural, universally understood things—the passing of the seasons, the heat of the sun, the beauty of the moon, the healing and fructifying influence of the rain, the loneliness of the wanderer, the drought of the desert and the upgushing of a spring, the security of the sheepfold, the fragility of pottery vessels, the majesty of mountains, the strength of the horse (which "in frenzied excitement . . . eats up the ground" and "at the blast of the trumpet . . . snorts, 'Aha!' " [Job 39:24, 25]), the defenselessness of the lamb and the power of the lion. To open the Old Testament at random is to find a dozen images, and from the Book as a whole there are scores that have imbedded themselves in everyday speech, such as "by the skin of his teeth," "apple of the eye," "light under a bushel," "treasures in heaven," and "a house divided against itself." Even the parable, so characteristic of Jesus' teaching, may be thought of as an extended metaphor.

Only a very cursory comment is possible on several types of figurative language other than simile and metaphor. Among them is synecdoche, a figure in which a part represents a whole, as in "your rod and your staff, they comfort me," or in "the sweat of your face." Metonymy is similar, involving the use of a term closely related to a concept instead of the name of the concept (or object) itself, as in the use of "horn" to denote power, rule, and kingdom. Litotes, or the making of a statement outwardly opposite to its intended effect, the tone sometimes being ironic, is occasionally found, as in Job's satiric comment on his friends: "Doubtless you are the people, and wisdom will die with you!" (12:2). Hyperbole, exaggeration to press home a truth, is not common, but one sees it in God's promise to Jacob: "I will truly . . . make your descendants like the sand of the sea" (Gen 32:12) and in some of Jesus' sayings—e.g., the beam in one's eye, the camel going through the eye of a needle.

Symbolism is not technically a figure of speech, but its importance as a literary device can hardly be overstated. Through suggestiveness and multiple implications, it has the power of expressing unseen reality, as is so dramatically seen in such books as Ezekiel and Revelation. After all, much of our knowing is by comparison, known things compared to unknown, and such symbols as the wheels within wheels, the four living creatures, the sea of glass, the great white throne, the gates of pearl, and the river of the water of life transcend expository instruction both quantatively and qualitatively. The imponderable glory of the heavenly realm is so foreign to our experience that only by symbols can it be hinted at.

VI. Certain New Testament Genres

Each of the major literary forms of the NT—Gospels, history (Acts) letters, and apocalyptic writing—has ancient models of varying relevance. The Gospels, however, which to the casual reader might seem to be simply "biographies" of Jesus, differ so markedly from the many biographies known in the classical world that they constitute a new and vital form. (Setting them apart as a different form from Acts should not be taken as impugning their historicity.) Trying to explain what literary form they were most like, Justin Martyr compared them to reminiscences or *memorabilia,* a form with which contemporary readers were familiar. There is also a dim similarity to the essays called "characters," as notably written in the fourth century B.C. by Theophrastus, pupil and successor in the Peripatetic school in Athens of Aristotle and teacher of Menander. Such essays, however, totally lack the brilliant vividness with which the Gospels depict the personality of Jesus, being, rather, abstract treatments of types of personality, not individuals.

The differences between the Gospels and, say, Philostratus's biographies of the leading Sophists three hundred years before the Christian era, or those of Plutarch, almost contemporary with the Gospels themselves, are major ones of both purpose and technique. The purpose of the Gospel writers was, of course, to present Jesus of Nazareth as the Messiah, the culmination of OT prophecies, Maker and Redeemer of the world. The technique, accordingly, permits nothing irrelevant to this theme and purpose, no piling up of details of personal appearance or of contemporary events or personages save as they bear on the work and teachings of the Christ. No curiosity-satisfying details are given of the long silent years of Jesus' boyhood or young manhood, for they are not essential to the heraldic announcement of the King. And because the heart of Jesus' fulfillment of prophecy and of his redemptive work lies in those few days clustered about the betrayal, trial, crucifixion, and resurrection, an inordinate amount of space (in terms of a standard biography) is given to that brief period. (See the article JESUS IN THE GOSPELS, pp. 515–541.)

Most strange, though, and most amazing is the presentation, in such small compass, of the most real, dramatic, and overwhelming personality world literature records, the One whose coming became the hinge of time, so that we date all history in terms of its occurring before or after his birth. How is it that these four relatively short documents, only one of which, that by Luke, displays professional literary skill, have so permeated the world's consciousness with this Man that no one who has ever read the Gospels ever forgets him?

There can be no adequate answer in purely natural terms, but a few aspects of the writers' techniques may be mentioned. High on the list are selectivity, objectivity, and economy—and a matter-of-fact style, lacking almost all adjectives of feeling, a style that dramatizes the greatness of the events by contrast to the simplicity of the tone. As John hyperbolically says, the world could not hold the books that might have been written about him (John 21:25); yet in these few pages we see him as really and as vividly as if we had been Peter, or John, or Thomas. Not a word is wasted; not an episode lacks organic unity; not a gesture is without force. How vividly we see the way his enemies gazed at him as he hung on the cross, but about all we are told is that they passed by, "shaking their heads" at him, a detail that helps us feel the pain of their contemptuous scorn. We see and hear the pushing, elbowing mob crowding around him when the sick woman timidly touched his garment; we sense the mingled bewilderment, awe, and antagonism when he silently stooped and wrote in the dust; we experience the awesomeness of the silent figure standing before the arrogance of Pilate; we hear the trumpet call of his command to Lazarus to come forth, and the gentleness of his words to the dead daughter of Jairus, words that sounded through the long arcades of his universe and brought back to the child's body the soul he had created her to be.

What these Gospel writers put down was brought to their minds by the Holy Spirit, whose knowledge of what moves the heart and illuminates the mind surpasses that of the greatest writers of the ages. This is most transcendently true of the words Jesus spoke. It is a literary truism that no writer can depict a better man than he is himself, for only a good man has some awareness of how it feels to be good. But "no one ever spoke the way this man does" (John 7:46), and no combination of human resources could have invented his words that have been recorded for us.

We have noted that among the Gospel writers only Luke, who was almost certainly not a Jew, exhibits familiarity with the intricate literary principles and devices of the Greek rhetoricians, a familiarity he displays exquisitely in both of his books. Alliteration, balanced syntax, patterns of organization, elegant turns of phrase—these and other literary devices remind us of the beauty and elegance of formal literary style in the first century A.D.

Literary differences equally as great as those among the Gospels distinguish the Epistles, those of the brilliant, learned, and passionate Paul taking the preeminence. (For polish, easy cadence, and familiar use of sophisticated refinements of language, however, the anonymous Epistle to the Hebrews must take first place.) It is quite likely that Paul was familiar with the traditions of the schools as well as with Hebraic literary practices. If he had not been, he could not have held his own while disputing daily in such schools as that of Tyrannus in Ephesus. But, except for two or three quotations from Greek authors (quotations that might have been in common use at the time), he does not exhibit any great interest in classical writers or literary rules. His book of studies was the Old Testament, and his quickness of mind, flashes of verbal brilliance, impetuosity, and subtlety of reasoning pour out as the picture of the man himself, not as a reflection of conscious artistry. Yet no man has ever been so able as he to clothe his feelings with exact words, and to express his passion while retaining a firm grasp on logical continuity, sometimes at the cost of orderly syntax, but never at the cost of clarity. When deeply moved, as in the magnificent hymn about love in 1 Corinthians 13 or in the soaring close of Romans 8 where he writes with the kind of controlled power that is possible only when one has complete mastery over his medium.

As to the form of the epistolary writing of the NT, it does not seem that anyone in the first centuries after Christ had to have it explained to him as Justin Martyr explained the Gospels. The classical models were numerous and familiar, including those that combined personal and public purposes, as the NT Epistles do. Such writing made it possible to join the ease of personal conversation with the reasoned presentation of a general theme, sometimes (as one sees in the Epistle to the Romans) using the argument-versus-counterargument (*diatribe*) form traditionally used to teach in the Greek academies. The method of composition was customarily dictation to an amanuensis (as Paul's usual practice seems to have been). Horace, Seneca, or Pliny, through careful revision, would seek the kind of sophisticated urbanity and conformity to the literary rules that would display their erudition. It seems likely that Paul had little time for revision; so his achievement is the greater. (For a fuller discussion of NT epistolary writing, see THE EPISTOLARY LITERATURE, pp. 543–554.)

The grandeur of the apocalyptic Book of Revelation stems from the majesty of its content, the brilliant and haunting suggestiveness of its symbolism (derived in part from the OT), the rich sensuousness of its imagery (which is auditory as well as visual) and the direct, unadorned style that uses such powerful and simple devices as balanced repetition and structured climax. Ancient models apart from the OT provided little real precedent for Revelation, though Chaldean, Egyptian, and Greek literature, and the apocrypha and pseudepigrapha all include works on "last things," though on a lower level. Mostly they describe only an imagined life in the shadowy realm of the dead. But Revelation has its own unique authenticity. Passages of exquisite beauty and matchless power so abound that it is difficult to make a typical selection; but one cannot without wonder read of the sun-dimming majesty of the risen Christ in chapter 1, the sublime chorus of praises to the Lamb in chapter 5, the haunting cadences that conclude chapter 7 ("Never again will they hunger; never again will they thirst. The sun will not beat upon them, nor any scorching heat. For the Lamb at the center of the throne will be their shepherd; he will lead them to springs of living water. And God will wipe away every tear from their eyes," vv.16, 17), the threnody on the fall of Babylon (symbolic of the entire system of this rebellious world) in chapter 18 ("Fallen! Fallen is Babylon the Great! She has become a home for demons. . . ," v.2), or the glorious portrayal of the new heavens and the new earth in chapters 21 and 22, culminating in the sublime love and beauty of the quiet words " 'Yes, I am coming soon.' Amen. Come, Lord Jesus" (22:20). Even if this work is considered simply as literature, no other writing can equal the power of it, written as it was under the inspiration of the Holy Spirit by the aged John, once the "son of thunder" but now the deep-eyed seer of God-given visions.

VII. Bibliography

Bruce, F.F. *The English Bible: A History of Translation*, new rev. ed. Oxford: Oxford University Press, 1970.

Butterworth, C.C. *The Literary Lineage of the King James Version, 1340–1611*. New York: Octagon, 1970.

Buttrick, George A., ed. *The Interpreter's Bible*, Vol. 1. New York: Abingdon, 1952, and Vol. 7. New York, 1951 (appropriate introductory essays).

Chase, Mary Ellen. *Life and Language in the Old Testament.* New York: Norton, 1955.

Frye, Roland Mushat, ed. *The Bible: Selections From the King James Version for Study As Literature* (With introduction and notes by the Editor). Boston: Riverside Editions, Houghton Mifflin, 1965.

Gardner, J.H. *The Bible As English Literature.* New York: Charles Scribner's Sons, 1927.

Greenslade, S.L., ed. *The Cambridge History of the Bible.* Cambridge: Cambridge University Press, 1963.

Henn, Thomas R. *The Bible As Literature.* Oxford: Oxford University Press, 1970.

Lowes, John L. *Essays in Appreciation.* Boston: Houghton Mifflin, 1936.

Moulton, Richard G. *The Literary Study of the Bible.* New York: AMS, 1899.

Ryken, Leland. *The Literature of the Bible.* Grand Rapids: Zondervan, 1974.

Sands, Percy C. *Literary Genius of the New Testament.* Westford, Conn.: Greenwood, 1932.

Sprau, George. *Literature in the Bible.* New York: Macmillan, 1932.

Sypherd, Wilbur Owen. *The Literature of the English Bible.* New York: Oxford University Press, 1938.

CHRISTIANITY AND THE WORLD'S RELIGIONS

Sir Norman Anderson

Sir Norman Anderson, O.B.E., Q.C.

M.A., LL.D., Cambridge University; D.D., St. Andrews University; F.B.A. (Fellow of the British Academy)

Lately Director of the Institute of Advanced Legal Studies; Professor Emeritus of Oriental Laws, The University of London

CHRISTIANITY AND THE WORLD'S RELIGIONS

I. The World's Religions
II. Their Origins
III. Their Concepts of "Salvation"
IV. Their Understanding of Deity
V. The Christian's View of Other Religions
VI. The Eternal Destiny of Individuals
VII. Bibliography

I. The World's Religions

Books on comparative religion (or, to be more accurate, on the comparative study of different religions, or on the phenomenon of religion in general) proliferate today. This is scarcely surprising in an age of frequent and rapid travel, widespread emigration and immigration, and the coincidence of a marked decline in the authority of traditional religious belief with a continuing search for some spiritual antidote to the enervating influences of materialism. Not unnaturally, the reaction of Christians has often been to deny that Christianity should ever be regarded as "a species of the genus religion" or "a sub-division of the general human preoccupation with the divine,"[1] for the Christian is convinced that his faith cannot rightly be regarded as one form of human quest after God, but rather as an inadequate response to a unique divine revelation. But if religion is to be defined as "the service and adoration of God or a god as expressed in forms of worship," or indeed as one of the world's "systems of faith and worship,"[2] it is virtually impossible to maintain that the most widespread of all these systems should never be compared in any way with those other systems that claim the allegiance of so many millions of our fellowmen, just because its followers are convinced that it is uniquely authoritative.

Statistics about religious affiliation are notoriously unreliable. To begin with, census figures are in many cases suspect or nonexistent, and even those figures that are available can throw little light on the variety of beliefs and practices that prevail, the phenomenon of successive strata of elements from different religions that may inhere in a single individual, or the degree to which ancestral faiths have in reality been discarded. At a rough estimate, however, we have these figures: some nine hundred million persons who would claim some sort of allegiance to the "Judaeo-Christian tradition"; a similar number made up, in roughly equal proportions, of Muslims and Hindus; several hundred million

---

[1] W.A. Visser't Hooft, *No Other Name* (London: SCM, 1963) pp. 94f.
[2] *Webster's New Collegiate Dictionary.*

143

Buddhists, some of whom combine Hindu, Shintoist, Confucian, or other teachings with their Buddhism; the teeming millions of China, who may be classified as Communists, Confucianists, Taoists, Buddhists, or a mixture of two or more of these alternatives; and many thousands of persons who still follow tribal or "primitive" religions—to say nothing of Shintoists who have adopted little or no Buddhist teaching, and such "minority" religions as are represented by the Sikhs, Zoroastrians, Jains, Bahā'īs, and others.[3]

All that seems possible, in a single article, is to discuss some of these major world religions from the point of view of the nature of their origins, of their concept of "salvation," and of their understanding of the nature of ultimate reality or deity— together with the view a Christian should take of these religions as "systems" and of the spiritual possibilities open to their adherents. In all this, moreover, two opposite tendencies must be rigidly rejected: (1) the tendency to syncretism and a failure to perceive the sharp differences that distinguish one religion, or even one sect or school of thought, from another and (2) the tendency to caricature other religions and exaggerate some of the beliefs commonly attributed to them. There are, of course, certain features that most religions share: a belief in what may be termed the "transcendental," a fellowship of the faithful, a priesthood or ecclesiastical hierarchy of some sort, principles designed to govern moral behavior, etc. In an age marked by an ever greater tendency toward materialism, it is all too easy, therefore, to fall into the fatal mistake of saying, with John Haynes Holmes, that "religion has not many voices, but only one." Yet scarcely anything could, in fact, be further from the truth. But sympathy and understanding are essential to the study of any religion, however mistaken we may believe it to be, and the temptation to parody what others hold sacred must be resolutely shunned. First, then, the question of origins.

II. Their Origins

Syncretism, as A. Oepke asserts, is "based on the presupposition that all positive religions are only reflections of a universal original religion and show . . . only gradual differences."[4] But the most elementary study reveals that some religions can be traced back to a particular historical event—together, of course, with its interpretation and implications—while others are frankly mythological or philosophical in orgin. It is abundantly clear from the NT, for example, that the primitive Christian *kerygma* was not basically the proclamation of a theological or ethical system, but of the "Good News" that the God of Israel had intervened decisively in human history in the incarnation, death, and resurrection of a specific historical person—Jesus of Nazareth. The implications of these historical events in regard to the concept of "salvation," of the character of God, and of the way of life to which such a salvation leads and such a God calls are, of course, integral parts of that proclamation, but without the historical facts on which they rest these implications would be meaningless. It was indubitably the wonder of the Resurrection—as an objective, historical fact that had turned despair and disillusionment into wondering joy—that was the heart and soul of the apostolic *kerygma*.

---

[3]Here, and elsewhere in this article, cf. my book *Christianity and Comparative Religion* (London: Tyndale, 1970).

[4]Quoted by Visser't Hooft, *No Other Name*, from *Das neue Gottesvolk* (1950), p. 124.

There is all the difference in the world between this and the typical Hindu approach—or, as Lesslie Newbigin puts it:

> between a statement about the nature of God, and a report that God has, at a certain time and place, acted in a certain way. In the latter case the occurrence is the essence of the message. The care which is taken in the New Testament to place the events recorded in the continuum of secular history is in striking contrast to the indifference which is generally shown with regard to the historicity of the events which Hindu piety loves to remember in connection with the character of the gods. There is no serious attempt to relate them to events in secular history, nor is it felt that there would be any advantage to be gained from trying to do so—even if it could be done. Their value is that they illustrate truths about God which would remain true even if these particular events had not happened.[5]

Somewhat the same is true, in a modified form, of Buddhism. Here there is no need to question the historicity of Gautama, or of the "Enlightenment" that formed the basis of his message. But that does not materially alter the fact that the origin of the religion that goes by his name can be found in a subjective experience, however much the one who had that experience was himself a historical figure, and it is the view he reached of the suffering that characterizes human life, what causes this suffering and how it can be eliminated, that constitutes the heart and soul of Buddhism as originally propounded. In the NT, by contrast, the primary emphasis is not on what Jesus taught, vitally important though that is—and always has been—for the Christian. Instead, the Good News fundamentally consists in who Jesus was and what he has done, or what God himself has done in Jesus.

It is this same basic question of historicity, moreover, that sharply distinguishes Christianity from the mystery religions that flourished in the Middle East at much the same time and with which it has so often been compared. There are, of course, certain parallels and similarities between them, although these have been much exaggerated, as B.M. Metzger and others have shown.[6] Many of the supposed parallels, indeed, result from an arbitrary amalgamation of heterogeneous elements drawn from a number of different religions, out of which is built up, in Albert Schweitzer's words, "a kind of universal Mystery-religion which never really existed, least of all in Paul's day."[7] The NT, moreover, was written almost exclusively by Jews, whose "strict monotheism and traditional intolerance of syncretism" would have militated strongly against any wholesale borrowing from pagan cults. But the fundamental difference is the historical basis of the Christian faith over against the mythological character of the mystery religions. The deities they proclaimed were no more than "nebulous figures of an imaginary past," whereas the Jesus of the apostolic *kerygma* was a historical person who had lived and died only a very few years before the first NT documents were written. The mystery religions essentially celebrate a dying nature god who then, like the coming of spring, is revived or reborn. There is all the difference in the world between this and the resurrection "on the third day" of a historical figure to whose resurrection appearances many could testify from personal experience. It is significant, moreover, that the references to a three-day gap between death and revival that we find in regard

---

[5]Lesslie Newbigin, *The Finality of Christ* (London: SCM, 1969), pp. 52ff.

[6]Cf. "Mystery Religions and Early Christianity," in *Historical and Literary Studies* (Leiden: E.J. Brill, 1968), pp. 6ff; E.O. James, *In the Fulness of Time* (London: SPCK, 1935), pp. 87, 88; et al.

[7]A. Schweitzer, *Paul and His Interpreters* (New York: Macmillan, 1912), pp. 192, 193.

to Attis (possibly Adonis according to one account) and Osiris cannot be dated earlier than the second century A.D.,[8] while the tradition about the resurrection of Christ on the third day, as recorded in 1 Corinthians 15, can be traced back to well before the middle of the first century. So, if borrowings there were from one religion to another, it is tolerably clear which way they went.

This is not to suggest for a moment, of course, that Christianity is the only religion that has a historical origin. Far from it. It has already been remarked that, whatever may be said of much else in Buddhism, Gautama himself should certainly be accepted as a historical figure. Precisely the same applies, with even greater force, to Abraham, Moses, and Muhammad, for example. It is not only to the teaching of the Law and the Prophets, moreover, that Judaism looks back, but to an act of divine intervention in the Exodus, while Muslims accept the date of a historical event (the Hijra, or flight of Muhammad from Mecca to Medina) as the beginning of their era. But neither the Hijra in Islam nor even the divine intervention in the Exodus in Judaism can be compared in nature or importance with the decisive intervention of God himself in human history that the Christian finds in the incarnation, the cross, and the empty tomb, and it is precisely for this reason that he is compelled to reject the syncretistic view that "holds that there is no unique revelation in history, that there are many different ways to reach the divine reality, that all formulations of religious truth or experience are by their very nature inadequate expressions of that truth and that it is necessary to harmonize as much as possible all religious ideas and experiences so as to create one universal religion for mankind."[9] Over against any such attitude stands the "scandal of particularity" that is inherent in the Christian faith: the Jesus who said "I am the way—and the truth and the life. No one comes to the Father except through me" and the cross the apostles proclaimed as the only remedy for human sin.

III. Their Concepts of "Salvation"

Here we find, again, a vast difference between one religion—or even school of thought —and another. In the so-called "political religions," such as Communism, Nazism, and various forms of nationalism, salvation is understood exclusively in terms of this life.[10] Other religions concentrate almost entirely on the attainment of some distant goal that can never be reached here on earth, or on a view of life that regards the phenomenal world as mere illusion. Yet others—including Christianity—proclaim a doctrine of salvation embracing both this world and the hereafter, regard the eternal and the spiritual as of supreme importance without neglecting the temporal and the physical, and—in the case of Christianity, in particular—believe in an "eternal life" that begins here on earth and extends, in a far more perfect form, into the life beyond the grave.

But in what, precisely, does this salvation consist? The word *salvation* almost always has a double significance: both negative and positive. In its negative sense man is saved, delivered, or set free *from* something, while in its positive sense it means health, wholeness, and well-being. In its negative meaning salvation, in tribal religions, seems chiefly to signify deliverance from harm, calamity, magic, sorcery, and the malignity of the spirits of the dead or of other supernatural forces.

---

[8]Metzger, "Mystery Religions," pp. 6ff.

[9]Cf. Visser't Hooft, *No Other Name*, p. 11.

[10]Cf. H.J. Laski, *Reflections on the Revolution of Our Time* (London: Allen and Unwin, 1943), pp. 71ff.; S.C. Neill, *Christian Faith and Other Faiths* (London: Oxford University Press, 1961), pp. 154ff.; L. Lyall, *Red Sky at Night* (London: Hodder and Stoughton, 1969), pp. 69, 70.

In the many different schools of thought in Hinduism the common element is deliverance (*moksha*) from the seemingly endless sequence of successive reincarnations. In Buddhism, again, much the same concept is found, but united with a concentration on deliverance—whether in this life or some future incarnation—from passion or desire, which is the cause of the suffering that, as we have seen, the Buddha came to regard as the basic characteristic of human life.

In Judaism and Islam the concept becomes much more personal and concrete: deliverance from the wrath and judgment of a "personal" God. In Judaism, moreover, this is far more intimately connected with a sense of the sinfulness of men over against the holiness of God than it is in Islam. In Christianity this is basic, with an increased emphasis on moral rather than ceremonial defilement, and on the need for heart cleansing as well as forgiveness.

When we turn to the positive rather than the negative side of salvation, the differences between the various religions and sects become more abstruse, for they are inevitably bound up in the concept of ultimate reality that characterizes the school of thought concerned. In Hinduism, for example, the basic meaning of salvation seems to be a conditon of peace and rest conceived not in terms of liberation from moral guilt but from the human condition as such—from space and time and the felt experience of immortality.[11] But different schools of Hindu thought prescribe a wide variety of ways in which this can be achieved. The Advaita Vedānta school teaches, for example, that there is in fact only one Absolute Reality (Brahman) and that all else is illusion; so the union of the individual soul with this Absolute Reality is already a fact, and all that is needed is for man to come to a full realization of this. The Sāmkhya-Yoga system, on the other hand, does not regard *moksha* as "seeing all things in the self and the self in all things," but as the total isolation of the individual soul from the entire process of transmigration and from all other "selves" within its own eternal and timeless existence. But yet other leaders of Hindu thought, in the various *bhakti* schools, teach that release from the trammels of mortality is only a prelude to a positive experience of union and communion with God.[12]

One finds tolerably close parallels to much of this in Buddhist thought. This is not surprising, since Buddhism originally sprang from Hindu soil. The ultimate goal of all Buddhist aspiration is to attain *nirvāna*, and most schools of Buddhism teach that this can normally be reached only after an indefinite number of rebirths. It is virtually exclusive to Zen-Buddhism to insist that it can be reached here and now, in this life, by a discipline of concentrated contemplation. But the fundamental difficulty to the outsider, in regard to most forms of Buddhism, is to understand in what *nirvāna*, in its future sense, really consists. In the West it has sometimes been equated with annihilation, but this has been strongly challenged by Buddhists themselves. What is extinguished, they insist, is "not life itself but the craving and vain attachments which must be destroyed if nirvana . . . is to be attained." But it is difficult to reconcile this state of no-self (*anattā*) with the description of *nirvāna* as "the further shore, the harbour of refuge, the cool cave, the matchless island, the holy city. It is sheer bliss," since it is not altogether easy to understand how one who has reached a state of no-self could enjoy such bliss.[13]

---

[11]Cf. R.C. Zaehner, *Hinduism*, 2nd ed., (London: Oxford University Press, 1966), p. 138.

[12]Cf. Zaehner, *Hinduism*, pp. 70, 98, 128, 143, 144.

[13]Cf. H.D. Lewis and R.L. Slater, *World Religions* (C.A. Watts, 1966), p. 63; N. Smart, *World Religions: A Dialogue* (London: SCM, 1960), pp. 51, 52; Charles Eliot, *Hinduism and Buddhism* (London: Edward Arnold, 1921), 1:191ff.

There is also the basic problem of how *moksha* or *nirvāna* can be attained. As we have already seen in part, some schools of both Hindu and Buddhist thought place a primary emphasis on what man himself can do about it. In Hinduism, for instance, the Upanishads and Gītā teach that this release can be achieved in one of several different ways: by fulfilling not only the temporal *dharma*, or duty, of one's caste, but the eternal *dharma*, which is more fundamental; by practicing the rigorous discipline of the Yoga technique; by coming to realize that individuality and all "duality" is an illusion and that there is in fact only One without any second; or by attaining, after liberation, to a state of unification, but *not* identification, with a personal God. In other words, salvation is sometimes thought of as attained by righteousness, but much more often by asceticism, knowledge, or devotion.[14] And the same fundamental emphasis on man's working out his own "salvation" is found in the Theravāda doctrine of Buddhism, which teaches that the way of salvation is by knowledge of the Four Noble Truths and by practicing the eightfold discipline, moral and mental, of the "Middle Way."[15]

Yet in Hinduism we also get glimpses of the concept of a savior-god. This is particularly true of the picture of Krishna in the Gītā (which has come largely to dominate popular Hinduism). And the same basic idea can be found in the Mahāyāna form of Buddhism (which is today far more widespread than the classical Theravāda doctrine), for in Mahāyāna Buddhism we find a parallel to the Hindu concept of *avatārs*, or descents of celestial beings (or, indeed, of the One God) in human form.[16] Thus Gautama himself is widely regarded as the greatest of a series of eternal Buddhas who have appeared on earth to "spread the saving Dharma (i.e., sacred law or principle of existence) to suffering humanity." There is also a belief in mythical heroes or Bodhisattva, who have themselves attained perfect knowledge but, following the example of Gautama, have "refrained from entering on the state of nirvana in order to help mankind by propagating the Dharma of the middle way."[17] In Tibet, moreover, Mahāyāna Buddhism has fused with the Bon religion (itself, very probably, a mixture of primitive Tibetan religion with Taoism) to form Lamaism. This differs in many respects from Buddhism elsewhere, but it is especially noteworthy in this context that its devotees often seek salvation by endlessly turning a prayerwheel.[18] In China and Japan, on the other hand, Pure Land Buddhism largely prevails, and this looks back to a Bodhisattva—now a heavenly Buddha—named Amitabha, who "accumulated such a vast store of merit during his progress towards Buddhahood that he vowed to bestow on all who trusted in him with perfect faith and sincerity, an assured rebirth in his paradise far away in the western quarter of the universe."[19]

We have already referred to the mystery religions of Egypt, Western Asia, and the Mediterranean basin. In Syria there was Adonis; in Phrygia, Attis; and in Egypt, Osiris, whose sister-wife Isis "sought and reassembled thirteen of the fourteen pieces into which his body had been dismembered by his wicked brother." He then became "Lord of the Underworld and Ruler of the Dead," and was believed to "assign to the souls of the departed their proper reward for virtue or punishment for wrongdoing."[20]

---

[14]Cf. Zaehner, *Hinduism*, pp. 96, 124, 70ff., 75ff. and 78f. Cf. also K. Klostermaier, *Hindu and Christian in Vrindaban* (London: SCM, 1969), pp. 20, 21.

[15]Cf. Lewis and Slater, *World Religions*, pp. 61, 62; and Eliot, *Hinduism and Buddhism*, 1:213ff.

[16]Cf. Anderson, *Christianity and Comparative Religion*, pp. 43, 44.

[17]Cf. E.O. James, *Christianity and Other Religions* (London: Hodder and Stoughton, 1968), pp. 81, 82.

[18]Eliot, *Hinduism and Buddhism*, 3:394, 395.

[19]James, *Christianity and Other Religions*, p. 83. Cf. Eliot, *Hinduism and Buddhism*, 2:28ff.

[20]Metzger, "Mystery Religions," pp. 20, 21.

The great world religion of Islam differs from most of these religions in almost every respect. Unlike them, it had an unquestionably historical rather than mythological origin, as we have seen, and its central doctrine has always been a rigid and austere monotheism. Its articles of belief (*'aqā'id*) have never been enunciated with an authority that can claim any universal acceptance, but it is generally agreed that a Muslim must believe in God, his angels, his prophets, his divinely revealed books, his decrees, and his judgment on the Last Day. More important in practice, however, are the "Pillars of Religion" (*arkān al-dīn*): the recitation of the creed, the saying of the daily prayers, the observance of the Ramadān fast, the practice of almsgiving, and the performance, where possible, of the pilgrimage to Mecca (to which some Muslims would add, as a sixth "Pillar," response to a summons to the *jihād* or holy war). For Islam is preeminently a religion of law, in which there is far more emphasis on the Sharī'a, or the path of God's commandments, than there is on the nature and character of the One from whom the commands are believed to have come. It would only be natural, therefore, to conclude that "salvation" in Islam (that is, deliverance from the Fire and an entrance into Paradise) must depend exclusively on the quality of obedience to the sacred law shown by the individual concerned. But, as in so many other religions, there are fundamental divisions within the community of the prophet. In the view of the "heretical" Khawārij (represented today by the Ibādīs of Oman and parts of North Africa), anyone guilty of a major sin of which he has not repented ceases to be regarded as a believer at all. In the strict doctrine of many Shī'ī sects, on the other hand, the Muslim who dies without recognizing the lawful Imām, or leader of the community, "dies the death of an unbeliever"—and many of the Shī'a not only regard their Imāms as the sole media of divine blessing but attribute to the death of al-Husayn at Karbala something approaching an atoning significance. But it would probably be fair to say that among "orthodox" or Sunnī Muslims, who make up some ninety per cent of all those who profess Islam as their religion, the majority of ordinary people believe that if they say the *shahāda* (or Muslim creed) from their hearts and if they make some attempt to fulfill their obligations in regard to fasting in the month of Ramadān and performing the fivefold ritual of their daily prayers, though they may have to enter the fire of judgment for a time, they will eventually be "saved" and admitted to paradise by the timely intercession of their prophet. The practice of animal sacrifice is by no means absent, but it can scarcely be said to occupy any central position in the religion of Islam.

In the Judaism of the OT, on the other hand, the sacrificial system held a central place, and the national Day of Atonement became the most important day in the year. In the daily ritual of the temple there was a variety of offerings—trespass or guilt offerings, sin offerings, and others—but while these dealt with all matters of ceremonial defilement and comparatively minor moral offences, and must have inculcated a profound realization that sinful man can never saunter, as it were, into the presence of a holy God, they did not cover "sins with a high hand." James Atkinson insists, moreover, that the sacrificial system

did not mean that by sacrifice a Jew hoped to attain God's grace, but rather that in penitence and faith he sought to retain it and avert its withdrawal. He sought in penitence to recover a favor, a relationship he had once known and had now lost owing to his sin. . . . The whole sacrificial system was an evangelical sacrament of forgiveness and deliverance, and forgiveness and deliverance were entirely God's work, never man's. It was not that man was doing anything to please or propitiate an enigmatic and uncommitted God who had not so far shown his hand. On the contrary, the central element in all Israelite worship was the collective liturgical recollection of all that God had done in their history in visiting and redeeming his people.[21]

But the Old Testament prophets proclaim how often animal sacrifices and ritual observances were regarded as providing a substitute for real repentance and living faith, and the apostle Paul shows how the Jews as a whole, instead of using the ceremonial law and sacrificial system as the God-given means of expressing their penitence for their failure to live up to the moral law and their faith in God's mercy in pardoning his people's sins, tended to make the moral and ceremonial law together into a way in which they sought to establish a righteousness of their own (Rom 10:3, 4).

Any study of the Gospels seems to make it clear that Jesus himself saw his messianic mission largely in terms of the Suffering Servant passages in the later chapters of Isaiah. But his references to this in the days of his ministry were completely misunderstood by his disciples, and it was only when the risen Christ opened their eyes that they began to grasp what he had meant. Even in the early sermons recorded in Acts the primary emphasis is clearly on the resurrection, but the apostolic *kerygma* soon came to place an equal emphasis on the fact that the seeming shame of a criminal's death had in fact constituted the supreme moment of victory over Satan, sin, and death—and even over the divine Law itself when regarded as the accuser of those united with Christ in living faith. For it was on the cross that Christ had borne the guilt of their sin and had set them free from its bondage. And the Epistle to the Hebrews (the early date of which seems sufficiently evident from the fact that it could scarcely have been written after A.D. 70 without any reference to the fact that the temple and its ritual had then been brought to an abrupt end) shows how fully the early church came to realize that the manifold and ever-repeated sacrifices of the Old Covenant had been fulfilled, finally and forever, in the never-to-be-repeated sacrifice of the One who had died for sin once for all, and was now living in the "power of an endless life."

IV. Their Understanding of Deity

This brings us to our third point of comparison between the world's religions—their understanding of deity, or at least of the transcendental—which can, of necessity, be summarized here only in the most cursory fashion. In regard to tribal religions, recent studies have in one case after another confirmed that they acknowledge a supreme, creator God, although in practice they virtually ignore his existence and concentrate on appeasing a multitude of far more imminent and malignant spirits—in a way that provides a practical illustration (or vindication) of Romans 1:18–23. Nor is this true only of the "tribal" religions, for W. Schmidt and his collaborators have shown that a belief in some supreme being is almost universal. It can be found in ancient Egypt, Mesopotamia, Iran, and China, for example, but it has in each case been combined with, or overlaid by, various forms of polytheism.[22] Obviously enough, the possibility of cross-fertilization

---

[21]In *A Dictionary of Christian Theology* (London: SCM, 1969), p. 301.
[22]Cf. *The Origin and Growth of Religion*, trans. H.J. Rose (London: Methuen, 1931), pp. 88, 191, 192, 198, 251ff.; James, *Christianity and Other Religions*, pp. 51, 53f., 60ff.; Neill, *Christian Faith*, pp. 131, 132.

of ideas between one religion and another cannot be excluded, but the evidence for retrogression in religious beliefs and practices, in some cases at least, is quite as cogent and convincing as that which is cited to prove the progress or evolution of religion. If, moreover, the import of the Old Testament is not to be distorted beyond recognition, it seems clear that the history of Israel represents a unique record of a primitive monotheism that was repeatedly compromised by man's fatal tendency to lapse into superstition, idolatry, and syncretism—only to be recalled by yet another summons to return to the God he already knew but so easily forsook, and who continued to inspire one prophet after another with a message that represented an ever-deepening disclosure of himself.

It is also true, of course, that many traces of what used to be called animism have survived—whether openly or under the surface—in countries that have come to adopt a more sophisticated religion. Nor is this confined to a fundamentally "nature" religion (such as Shintoism, or even popular Hinduism), for S.M. Zwemer has shown how many former beliefs and practices may survive for decades or even centuries in the popular religion of those who have officially embraced the stern monotheism of the Muslim creed.[23] Much the same is also true of many who call themselves Christians. Those features of former beliefs and practices that are regarded as most objectionable by the new faith may, indeed, be discarded, but many of the former observances, places of pilgrimage, or supposedly supernatural beings are given new names and then incorporated, in whole or in part, in the new religion.

Beliefs and theories about the transcendental may, moreover, run almost the whole gamut of possible variations in such a religion—or umbrella for a variety of heterogeneous religions—as Hinduism. It can scarcely be denied that the popular Hinduism of many Indian villagers represents a crude form of polytheism (or, at best, a very qualified monotheism) to which expression is given by means of a variety of idolatrous practices; but the same religion is interpreted by more sophisticated persons sometimes in pantheistic, sometimes in monotheistic, and sometimes in monistic terms. A Hindu, in short, may be a polytheist, a pantheist, a monotheist, a monist, or even an atheist. Buddhism, likewise, takes a number of different and even contradictory forms and can be understood either as a theistic religion or as a variety of monism; or it can degenerate into something very near to polytheism; or it can represent a philosophy that puts its primary emphasis on man.

In a polytheistic religion the problem of evil can be explained, in part at least, by the existence of both good and evil gods and by the simple fact of which of them happens, in any given circumstance, to be in control. Much the same may be said of Zoroastrianism, although in this religion the explicit dualism of two equally powerful forces of good and evil locked in perpetual conflict is qualified, in the final analysis, by the belief that the good is destined ultimately to prevail.[24] In the more sophisticated schools of Hindu thought, on the other hand, no sharp distinction seems to be made between good and evil. To those who hold to a rigidly monistic philosophy, there is only one reality and all else is illusion. To those who interpret Hinduism in pantheistic terms, everything in the universe constitutes, and is essentially one with, the deity. And even to those who accept a monotheistic view, all that exists, whatever its moral character, proceeds

---

[23]S.M. Zwemer, *The Influence of Animism on Islam* (New York: Macmillan, 1920).
[24]Cf. James, *Christianity and Other Religions,* p. 62.

equally from the same God.[25] In Buddhism, as we have seen, there is a vivid apprehension of the suffering (which finds its origin in the self and its passions) inherent in human life. But there is all the difference in the world between "the serene and passionless Buddha," with his teaching that the self that suffers does not really exist, and the "tortured figure on a cross," who recognized the stark reality of sin and suffering, embraced them in himself, and died to set men free.[26]

In Islam—as in Judaism—there is a clear belief in a personal devil. Yet in the strictest school of Islamic orthodoxy *everything* flows directly from the will of God, who creates and recreates, moment by moment, the atoms of which all matter is composed—including, of course, the minds of those sentient creatures who believe that they are making decisions and putting them into effect. There are some exceedingly beautiful and uplifting passages in the Qur'ān and in the books of Muslim theology, law, and devotion that depict the majesty, preeminence, and omnipotence of the one true God. And there can be no doubt whatever that Muhammad himself was deeply moved by the tragedy of men and women giving the worship that belongs to God alone to a multitude of lesser beings, whether real or imagined. Yet the God of Islam is so utterly separate and different from his creatures that even the ninety-nine "beautiful names" by which he is described bear no necessary relation to their human meaning—so how can men aspire to know him? Again, he is so transcendant and utterly self-sufficient that he cannot in any way be affected by his creatures—neither saddened by their sin and rejection nor gladdened by their repentance and love. To orthodox Muslims it is sheer blasphemy to imagine that the Almighty could ever become man, and it is unthinkable that he would ever have allowed his chosen apostle 'Isā (Jesus), mere man though they believe him to have been, to be crucified by his traducers. Nor do they see any need for him to have died, for is it not God's absolute prerogative to forgive or retain sin as he pleases, quite regardless of any moral basis? The predominant emphasis in orthodox Islam is on the divine sovereignty, omnipotence, and mercy, rather than self-giving love.

Broadly speaking it is only among some of the Sūfīs, or mystics of Islam, that we find a primary emphasis on the place of love in religion, but the writings (and reported sayings) of some of the masters of the mystic path are burning in their fervor. Yet even in this context the Christian is conscious of something that is lacking—a cornerstone that is not there, and a facet of experience that remains, at best, unexplained. In Islam there is no adequate appreciation of the barrier sin must necessarily erect between a holy God and his fallen creatures; of the *only* way in which the God who is, at one and the same time, the source and origin of the moral order and the righteous judge before whom his creatures must one day stand, could himself remove this barrier; and of the perfect forgiveness he would thus make freely available to all who turn to him in repentance and faith.

Even in OT Judaism, moreover, these "mysteries" (as the apostle Paul terms them) were only dimly discerned. The prophets and psalmists, of course, gave marvelous expression to the utterly unearned and even inexplicable love of God for Israel and his tender longing for her repentance and restoration, to the joy men and women can experience in a realized forgiveness and an intimate fellowship with God, and to much else besides. And behind all this there was the repeated promise of something far more wonderful to come: a Savior who would be more than man and whose reign would be

---

[25]Cf. Klostermaier, *Hindu and Christian*, p. 46.
[26]Cf. Neill, *Christian Faith*, pp. 123, 124.

both universal and eternal, a Suffering Servant who would vicariously bear his people's sins, and a salvation that would extend to all nations and entail the writing of God's law on the hearts and minds of his people, rather than on tablets of stone that challenged an impossible—and, indeed, unwilling—obedience. But so much of this was depicted as future rather than present and was discerned only, as it were, "in a glass, darkly."

V. The Christian's View of Other Religions

The final question, for the Christian, must be the view he takes of the other world religions and their followers. First, how is he to regard the other religions as such? Whatever view he takes, it cannot involve either syncretism or caricature, as has been emphasized in section 1 of this article. But are these other religions ultimately derived from God, and do they represent stepping stones or stages on the road to his final revelation of himself in Christ? Or are they Satan-inspired, poor counterfeits of the truth as it is in Jesus, designed to keep people from the only Savior and the only gospel that can save and satisfy? Or again, do they represent man's varied attempts, sincere but mistaken, to reach out after the unknown God?

None of these alternatives can, by itself, be regarded as adequate. In every religion, for example, there is something of the truth, and all that is true ultimately comes from God; so it is possible to see some reflection of the "Light that lightens every man" everywhere displayed (e.g., in the recurrent idea of a savior-god and of the need for sacrifice). As William Temple put it: "By the word of God—that is to say by Jesus Christ—Isaiah and Plato, Zoroaster, Buddha and Confucius uttered and wrote such truths as they declared. There is only one Divine Light, and every man in his own measure is enlightened by it."[27] This was the view taken by Justin Martyr and the Christian philosophers of Alexandria in the second and third centuries, and it has been held by many others down the years. But we must remember that in non-Christian religions (other than the Judaism of the OT) there is also much falsehood, and no falsehood comes from God, but from the "father of lies."

It is this fact that has led some Christians to a diametrically opposite view: that the non-Christian religions as a whole are basically from Satan rather than God. Those who adopt this attitude give prominence to the darker side of the ethical teaching of these religions and the more regrettable elements in their theological concepts, and they explain those rays of truth undeniably present in the non-Christian religions in terms of the fact that even Satan himself can, and sometimes does appear as an angel of light. Above all, it is insisted, these religions inevitably deny—whether by explicit statement, as in Islam, or by implicit teaching, as in the great pre-Christian religions—the unique claims of the "Word make flesh" and deceive men into believing that there is a way to God that does not rest on the fundamental need for the redemption that God himself made available at the cross on which Jesus died.

Yet other Christians would put a primary emphasis on the human element in non-Christian religions (other than that of the OT). One and all, these religions—they would say—represent man's attempts to solve the insoluble: sincere yet inadequate reachings out after the God to whose existence man's heart bears witness. In this quest he is open, of course, to impressions and convictions that truly come from God. But he is equally

---

[27]William Temple, *Readings in St. John's Gospel*, vol. 1 (New York: Macmillan, 1943), p. 10.

open to impressions and influences that come from below. And it is clear from the Bible that when man rejects God's self-revelation, he inevitably seeks his own answer to life's problems, invents his own religion, and sets up his own "idols"—whether material or ideological (cf. Rom 1:18–23). It is equally clear, moreover, that Satan can and does use every substitute—whether morally good or bad in itself—to keep people from seeing the truth in Christ.

But what of the mystics who, coming from different religions, seem at times to speak in strangely similar terms? Sayings of this sort commonly emanate from those mystics who concentrate on their own consciousness and experience, believing that there, in their own hearts, lies the "image of God," ready for them to behold it, if only they can cleanse their hearts—and, indeed, the eyes with which they look—from the dross of false values and from absorption in the material and the finite. And this is, in some sense, perfectly true. Temple wrote, "Because man is made in the image of God, the attempt to find God through penetrating to the inmost recesses of the self leads in men of all times and all races to a similar experience." But the image of God in man has been defaced by sin, and the mind that seeks to reach that image is distorted by sin, and molded both for good and for evil by tradition. So the

> *via negativa* of the mystics cannot be perfectly followed. To rely on a supposedly direct communion with God, in detachment from all external aids, is to expose the soul to suggestions arising from its distortion as well as to those arising from the God whom it would apprehend. Mediation there must be; imagery there must be. If we do not deliberately avail ourselves of the true Mediator, the 'express image' (Hebrews 1:3) we shall be at the mercy of some unworthy medium and of a distorted image.[28]

And even so—even when we turn to the Christ of God—we need the quickening power of the Holy Spirit before we can see, know, and worship him as he is.

VI. The Eternal Destiny of Individuals

What can we say about the eternal destiny of those who follow these other religions? If we believe that all men, whatever their religious allegiance, are sinners; that no sinner can ever enter into the presence of a holy God; that all men, therefore, need forgiveness and need a Savior; and that there is in fact only one Savior—then does this mean that all those who, through no fault of their own, have never heard of this Savior are *necessarily* lost? That would be an agonizing doctrine (held though it was by many of our missionary ancestors—and by a number of evangelicals today). Yet what other view can one who believes in the revelation of the Bible, and the finality of Christ, legitimately hold?

Light on this pressing problem can, I think, be found in the experience of the Jews under the Old Covenant. There can be no doubt that Abraham, Moses, David, and John the Baptist, for example, died in a "state of grace," or that they were saved by the only Savior (to whom they had in fact borne their testimony). But what of the multitude of less-enlightened Jews who, truly convicted of sin, brought the prescribed sacrifices and threw themselves on God's mercy—or, in the case of sins such as David's, threw them-

---

[28]Temple, *Readings in St. John's Gospel*, p. 92. Cf. also G. Campell Morgan, *The Crises of the Christ* (London: Pickering and Inglis, 1945), pp. 29ff.

selves on that mercy, quite apart from any sacrifice, in repentance and faith? It would seem certain that they, too, were saved, not by an animal sacrifice, which can never atone for human sin, but by the Christ who was still to come and on the basis of the final atonement he was to make. For the apostle Paul states unequivocally that "by observing the law [including those sacrifices that were divinely ordained signposts, as it were, pointing on to the Lamb of God, whose advent and death the prophets dimly foresaw] no one will be justified" (Gal 2:16). It was not that all those Jews who took their part in the sacrificial system shared in this salvation (as the prophets made crystal clear), but only those who brought their sacrifices, or threw themselves on God's mercy, in repentance and faith. Nor could even this repentance and faith in any way "earn" their salvation; this could rest only on that redemption—still to come—which was to provide the essential basis on which alone a holy God can (and does) accept the repentant sinner. It is only through the atoning death of Christ that OT believers now enjoy the redemption that "set them free from the sins committed under the first covenant," and have received "the promised eternal inheritance" (Heb 9:15; cf. Rom 3:25).

What, then, can we say—or surmise—about the eternal destiny of those others who, through no fault of their own, have never heard of the only Savior? What is certain is that they can never earn salvation through their own religion, whatever that may be; but neither could a Jew through Judaism, nor can a Christian through the church to which he happens to belong. But surely there is a similarity as well as a difference, between a man like that and his Jewish counterpart, is there not? The difference is obvious: the Jew in OT days had a revelation that was both valid and trustworthy, even if partial and incomplete, while the non-Christian today may have a concept of God that is not only incomplete, but positively mistaken. But there is, I think, an essential similarity as well. Just as the Jew of the OT was utterly dependent for salvation on a Savior he did not know, so too are those today, from whatever religion, who have never heard the gospel. And just as the Jew of the OT was saved in and through Christ, not by his direct knowledge of the Savior but rather by a sense of sin, a repentance, and a casting of himself on the divine mercy prompted by God himself, may not this—in some cases—be the experience of others, too? Surely the Spirit of God can still speak directly to men and women in their need—whether through dreams, visions, conscience, or an inner voice. So if, and where, the Holy Spirit (who alone can do this) convicts individuals in other religions of their sin and enables them to throw themselves on the mercy of the God whom they seek in the twilight, will they not also be saved in Christ—on the basis, that is, of what God himself did in Christ on the cross for the sins of the whole world?

It is quite inadequate to say (as many do) that those who have never heard the gospel will be judged and justified by a different standard, according to the "light" or truth that was in fact available to them. This is true, no doubt, insofar as the standard by which they will be judged is concerned; for we have biblical authority for the statement that, whereas the Jew will be judged on the basis of the Law revealed on Sinai, non-Jews will be judged according to the criterion of the requirements of the law "inscribed on their hearts" (Rom 2:11–15) But the fact remains that, just as no Jew has ever succeeded in keeping the Mosaic Law or the injunctions of the prophets, so no one else has ever succeeded in living up to the standard of the moral and ethical principles according to which he knows that he ought to regulate his life. The verdict of God is explicit and unequivocal: "*All* have sinned and fall short of the glory of God" (Rom 3:23).

What, then, did the apostle Peter mean in the house of Cornelius when he said, "I now see how true it is that God has no favourites, but that in every nation the man who is godfearing and does what is right is acceptable to him" (Acts 10:34 NEB)? He *cannot* have meant that anyone can earn salvation by trying to be religious and moral, for that is contrary to the whole burden of biblical teaching. But may not his words mean that the man who realizes something of his sin and need and throws himself on the mercy of God with a sincerity that shows itself in his life (which would always, of course, be a sure sign of the inward prompting of God's Spirit), will find that mercy—although without understanding it—where it is always available, at the cross where Jesus made propitiation for "the sins of the whole world" (1 John 2:2)? Or, to put it another way, is it not possible that an omniscient God will judge such people, if they have never heard the gospel, on the basis of what he knows would have been their response if they had heard—a response manifested instead, in their ignorance, by that search after God and abandonment to his mercy that only the Holy Spirit could have inspired? After all, the Bible is full of promises that those who truly seek shall find (e.g., Jer 29:13).

If such persons subsequently hear the gospel adequately explained, may we not surmise that they will be among the company of those whom one does meet on occasion in a non-Christian land who accept it at once and say, "Why did you not come and tell me this before? It is what I have been waiting for all my life." And if they never hear it in this world, then may we not believe they will awaken, as it were, on the other side of the grave to worship the one in whom, without understanding it, they found forgiveness? But it is important to emphasize that this suggestion is in no sense a doctrine of a "second chance," since here the basis of salvation is firmly related to this life; and it is still further removed from any concept of "universalism" (i.e., that everyone will ultimately be saved)—for the few verses in the Bible that can be quoted in support of the universalist thesis must be set against the far more numerous and explicit verses to the contrary.

But, finally, might not the view expounded here weaken the urgency of our missionary incentive? Surely not. To begin with, the Christian is under an explicit command to go and tell the gospel. Then again, if we ask ourselves what enabled us to give up trying to save ourselves and to throw ourselves on God for salvation, the answer will almost certainly be the message of the gospel. So it is imperative that we should give others the same opportunity. Yet again, those who find forgiveness in this way may sadly lack assurance, and will almost certainly lack a message they can pass on to others or the joy and victory that a knowledge of the risen Christ alone can give. How, then, can we withhold from them the full truth as it is in Jesus?[29]

VII. Bibliography

Anderson, J.N.D. *Christianity and Comparative Religion.* London: Tyndale, 1970.

Eliot, Charles. *Hinduism and Buddhism.* London: Edward Arnold, 1921.

James, E. *Christianity and Other Religions.* London: Hodder and Stoughton, 1968.

Klostermaier, K. *Hindu and Christian in Vrindaban.* London: SCM, 1969.

Lewis, H.D., and Slater, R.L. *World Religions.* London: C.A. Watts, 1966.

Lyall, L. *Red Sky at Night.* London: Hodder and Stoughton, 1969.

Metzger, B.M. *Historical and Literary Studies.* Leiden: E.J. Brill, 1968. Chapter on "Mystery Religions and Early Christianity."

---

[29]For a fuller treatment of this subject, cf. Anderson, *Christianity and Comparative Religion,* pp. 91–111—on which these last two sections have been largely based.

Neill, S.C. *Christian Faith and Other Faiths*. London: Oxford University Press, 1961.

Newbigin, Lesslie. *The Finality of Christ*. London: SCM, 1969.

Schmidt, W. *The Origin and Growth of Religion*. Translated by H.J. Rose. London: Methuen, 1931.

Smart, N. *World Religions: A Dialogue*. London: SCM, 1960.

Visser't Hooft, W.A. *No Other Name*. London: SCM, 1963.

Zaehner, R.C. *Hinduism*. 2nd ed. London: Oxford University Press, 1966.

Zwemer, S.M. *The Influence of Animism on Islam*. New York: Macmillan, 1920.

THE APOCRYPHA AND PSEUDEPIGRAPHA

Bruce M. Metzger

Bruce M. Metzger

A.B., D.D., Lebanon Valley College; Th.B., Th.M., Princeton Theological Seminary; A.M., Ph.D., Princeton University; L.H.D., Findlay College; D.D., University of St. Andrews; D.Theol., University of Münster

George L. Collard Professor of New Testament Language and Literature, Princeton Theological Seminary

THE APOCRYPHA AND PSEUDEPIGRAPHA

I. Meaning and Use of the Terms *Apocrypha* and *Pseudepigrapha*
II. The Apocrypha
III. Representative Pseudepigrapha
IV. Influence of the Apocrypha and Pseudepigrapha
V. Bibliography

I. Meaning and Use of the Terms *Apocrypha* and *Pseudepigrapha*

The word *apocrypha* is used in a variety of ways. Etymologically, it is of Greek derivation and signifies books that are "hidden away." (Like the word *data*, it is plural in number; the singular is *apocryphon*.) From one point of view, certain books were "hidden" or withdrawn from common use because they were regarded as containing mysterious or esoteric lore, too profound to be communicated to any except the initiated (cf. 2 Esd 14:45, 46). From another point of view, however, it was held that such books deserved to be "hidden" because they were questionable or spurious or heretical. Thus, the term had either an honorable significance or a pejorative one, depending on the intent of those who made use of it.

A third usage of the word can be traced to Jerome, the Latin church father. He was familiar with the Scriptures in their Hebrew as well as in their Greek and Latin forms, and for him, apocryphal books were those outside the Hebrew canon. The generally accepted modern usage is based on that of Jerome. Thus "The Apocrypha" is the designation applied to a collection of fourteen or fifteen books (or parts of books) not included in the Masoretic Hebrew Bible, which were written during the last two centuries before Christ and the first century of the Christian era.[1] The following are the titles of these books as given in the RSV (1957):

1. The First Book of Esdras
2. The Second Book of Esdras
3. Tobit
4. Judith
5. The Additions to the Book of Esther
6. The Wisdom of Solomon
7. Ecclesiasticus, or the Wisdom of Jesus the Son of Sirach
8. Baruch
9. The Letter of Jeremiah

---

[1]The KJV (1611) contains fourteen books of the Apocrypha, for the Letter of Jeremiah is attached to the end of the book of Baruch, as chapter 6 of that book. In the RSV and other modern translations the Letter of Jeremiah stands as a separate book after Baruch.

10. The Prayer of Azariah and the Song of the Three Young Men
11. Susanna
12. Bel and the Dragon
13. The Prayer of Manasseh
14. The First Book of the Maccabees
15. The Second Book of the Maccabees

These works, being outside what is commonly regarded as the Palestinian canon, form no part of the Hebrew Scriptures, although the original language of some of them was Hebrew (at least Judith, Ecclesiasticus, Baruch 1:1–3:8, and 1 Maccabees). The Jewish synagogue considered them uninspired, and some of their authors disclaim inspiration (Prologue to Ecclus; 2 Macc 2:27; 15:38).

With the exception of 2 Esdras, all the Apocrypha are in the Greek version of the OT (the LXX), made for Greek-speaking Jews in Egypt. Although they are never directly quoted by Jesus or the apostles (but cf. Enoch below), in the early church they were read for edification and even sometimes recommended to catechumens for study. Several early church fathers quote them as Scripture, for their Bible was the LXX.

In Greek and Latin MSS of the OT the Apocrypha are dispersed throughout, generally in the places most in accord with their contents. Thus Tobit and Judith stand between Nehemiah and Esther; 1 and 2 Maccabees between Esther and Job; Wisdom and Ecclesiasticus between the Song of Songs and Isaiah; while items 10, 11, and 12 in the list above are parts of the Book of Daniel, and the sections of item 5 are distributed throughout the Book of Esther.

The term *pseudepigrapha*, a word of Greek etymology, means writings attributed to fictitious authors. Although this would appropriately characterize almost all the books of the Apocrypha (not, however, Ecclesiasticus), it is customarily applied to certain Jewish writings of the period from about 200 B.C. to A.D. 200. There is no standard or traditional order of such books, and in Section III below selected Pseudepigrapha are grouped in accordance with their original background, whether Palestinian (composed in Hebrew or Aramaic) or non-Palestinian (composed in Greek).

Yet another difficulty of definition arises when one compares Protestant usage with Catholic usage. Following Jerome, Protestant churches regard as authoritative Scriptures of the OT only those books that are present in the Hebrew canon. The Roman Catholic Church, in accord with a decree issued in 1546 by the Council of Trent, holds that the OT includes not only the thirty-nine books of the Hebrew canon but also Tobit, Judith, Wisdom, Ecclesiasticus, Baruch, 1 and 2 Maccabees, and certain supplementary parts of Esther and Daniel. Adopting a distinction introduced by Sixtus of Sienna in 1566, modern Catholic scholars are accustomed to refer to the books of the Hebrew canon as protocanonical and to the ones mentioned above as deuterocanonical, meaning "later added to the canon." Thus Catholics accept as inspired and authoritative those books and parts of books that Protestants call the Apocrypha, except 1 and 2 Esdras and the Prayer of Manasseh, which both groups regard as apocryphal.

Eastern Orthodox Churches have tended to regard the longer canon as authoritative, including in this case also the 151st Psalm and 3 Maccabees. These items, along with 4 Maccabees, are present in several of the oldest copies of the Greek OT.

In 1973 an ecumenical edition of the RSV was issued. It provides in one volume an arrangement of the disputed books that has been approved by both Protestants and Catholics. In this "Common Bible" the Apocrypha and the Deuterocanonical books are grouped together between the Testaments, with a blank page separating those that the Catholic Church holds as authoritative from 1 and 2 Esdras and the Prayer of Manasseh.

In 1977 an expanded edition of the New Oxford Annotated Bible with the Apocrypha (RSV) was published. It contains 3 and 4 Maccabees and Psalm 151 in addition to the customary Apocryphal and Deuterocanonical books. Thus, for the first time an edition of the English Bible provides *all* of the books regarded as authoritative by Eastern Orthodox, Roman Catholic, and Protestant Churches.

Finally, it should be mentioned also that in addition to the fifteen books described in section II., which are the traditional OT Apocrypha, there are other writings that are classified as NT Apocrypha. These include dozens of Gospels, Acts, Epistles, and Apocalypses produced during the early centuries of the Christian era in competition with those of the NT. No church today regards them as canonical.

II. The Apocrypha

The **First Book of Esdras** is called 3 Esdras in the Latin Vulgate Bible, where, since the Council of Trent, it is placed in an appendix after the NT. Beginning abruptly with a description of the great Passover celebration under King Josiah, the book relates Jewish history down to the reading of the Law in the time of Ezra, reproducing, with minor changes, 2 Chronicles 35:1–36:21, the book of Ezra, and Nehemiah 7:73–8:13a (leaving the last sentence unfinished).

The chief difference between the canonical accounts and 1 Esdras is the insertion at 3:1–5:6 of the story of three young guardsmen in the court of Darius. According to this story, a contest was held to determine what is the strongest thing in the world. Three young pages among the king's bodyguard expounded, successively, the views (a) that wine is the strongest, because it affects so deeply the minds of all who drink it, from slave to king (3:18–24); (b) that the king is strongest, being lord and master (4:1–12); and (c) that women, because they dominate over men, are strongest (4:13–32). The third speaker then concluded, "But truth is great, and stronger than all things" (4:35). This famous story, which in the Latin Vulgate provides the proverb *Magna est veritas, et praevalet* ("Great is truth, and it prevails" 4:41), is used by the unknown editor as the context in which King Darius rewards the third guardsman (who is identified as Zerubbabel) by authorizing him to rebuild the temple (4:47–63).

As to the date of the compiler, it is generally assumed that he lived in the first century B.C.; the most that can be said with certainty is that the book was used by Josephus in the first century of the Christian era.

The **Second Book of Esdras,** which in the Latin Vulgate is called 4 Esdras and, like 1 (3) Esdras, stands in an appendix after the NT, differs from the other fourteen books of the Apocrypha in being an apocalypse. The main part of 2 Esdras is a series of seven revelations (3:1–14:48) in which the seer is instructed by the angel Uriel concerning some of the great mysteries of the moral world. It was written, perhaps in Hebrew (or Aramaic), in the latter part of the first Christian century and reflects Jewish despair and bewilderment following the destruction of Jerusalem in A.D. 70. The purpose of the author was not only to denounce the wickedness of Rome (under the symbolism of "Babylon") and to bewail the sorrows that had befallen his people, but also to wrestle with the problem of theodicy, that is, the reconciliation of God's justice, wisdom, power, and goodness with the many evils that beset mankind. Although the book is essentially pessimistic in its overall perspective, the author's strong religious faith enabled him to rise above the fires of adversity to high spiritual levels.

The main part of the book (3:1–14:48) survives in a Latin version (made from Greek) and in several oriental versions (Syriac, Coptic, Ethiopic, Armenian, Georgian, and two independent Arabic versions). Subsequently, this section was enclosed within two Christian supplements (chs. 1, 2 and 15, 16), written in Greek about A.D. 150 and 250 respectively. Almost all of the Greek text of the book has been lost, except for three verses in chapter 15, which survive on a leaf of parchment dating from the fourth century (Papyrus Oxyrhynchus 1010). Most Latin MSS and all editions of the Vulgate (and therefore the KJV) lack seventy verses of chapter 7. The omission of this section is the result of the removal of one folio from the codex Sangermanensis (written A.D. 822, now in the Bibliothèque Nationale in Paris), the ancestor of most extant Latin MSS of the book. In 1874, however, Robert L. Bensly of Cambridge University discovered the missing Latin text (now numbered 7:36–104) in a ninth-century manuscript in the public library of Amiens, France. It is probable that the lost section was deliberately cut out of Sangermanensis for dogmatic reasons, for the passage contains an emphatic denial of the value of prayers for the dead (v.105).

The book of **Tobit,** written about the year 200 B.C., combines an entertaining story with kindly Jewish piety and sound moral teaching (including the negative Golden Rule, 4:15). Tobit of the tribe of Naphtali was exiled to Nineveh, where he continued to observe zealously the Law of Moses. Having become blind as an indirect result of burying the bodies of Jews executed by Sennacherib, he became so depressed that he prayed that God would take his life (3:1–6). At the same time in the distant city of Ecbatana in Media, Tobit's kinswoman Sarah also prayed that God would let her die, for she had been plagued by Asmodeus, a demon-lover that had murdered successively seven of her husbands before marriage could be consummated (3:7–15). God graciously heard the prayer of both and sent his angel Raphael to help them (3:16, 17). Tobit, having remembered that he had left ten talents of silver in trust with Gabael at Rages in Media, sent his son Tobias to collect the money. Accompanied by a guide, Azarias (who is Raphael in disguise), Tobias not only recovered the money but also married Sarah, having routed Asmodeus by burning the heart and liver of a fish that Azarias had previously bidden him to catch in the Tigris (chs. 4–9). Having returned to his home, at the angel's suggestion Tobias anointed his father's eyes with the gall of the fish, whereupon Tobit regained his sight (chs. 10, 11). Raphael, after giving good advice to the family, ascended to heaven (ch. 12), and Tobit, having written a prayer of thanksgiving (ch. 13), advised Tobias to leave Nineveh before it would be destroyed. So Tobias returned with his wife and sons to Ecbatana, where he heard of the destruction of Nineveh (ch. 14).

The book, which had great popularity and exercised a deep influence in molding Jewish piety, exists in three Greek recensions: (a) a longer recension in codex Sinaiticus, and two shorter recensions, (b) one in codices Vaticanus and Alexandrinus and most minuscule MSS, and (c) another, later than the others, in several minuscule MSS. Both KJV and RSV follow recension (b), while NEB and NAB are based on recension (a). In 1955, fragments of the book in Aramaic and in Hebrew were recovered from Cave IV at Qumran. These texts are in substantial agreement with Greek recension (a). There are also versions of recension (a) in Latin, Armenian, and late Hebrew and of recension (b) in Syriac, Coptic (Sahidic), Armenian, and Ethiopic.

The book of **Judith** is a vivid and stirring story, telling how, in a grave crisis, God delivered the Jewish people through the instrumentality of a woman. The heroine, Judith (whose name means simply "a Jewess"), combines the most scrupulous observance of the Law of Moses with a grim and cunning bravery in the face of great personal danger.

The first part of the book (chs. 1–7) describes, at somewhat wearisome length, the war of the Assyrians against the Jews. Holofernes, commander-in-chief of the armies of Nebuchadnezzar, laid siege to Bethulia, a town lying on the route to Jerusalem, and cut off its water supply. After thirty-four days the exhausted Jewish defenders began to lose heart, but reluctantly agreed to resist five more days before surrendering.

The second part of the book (chs. 8–16) introduces Judith, a beautiful and pious widow, who promised, with God's help, to defeat the Assyrians. After prayer for divine help (ch. 9), she put on her best clothes and, accompanied by her maid, went to the Assyrian camp (ch. 10). Here she convinced Holofernes that soon he would be able to conquer the Jews because they had provoked their God by proposing to eat the offerings set aside for the temple (ch. 11). On the fourth day Holofernes invited her to a private banquet in his tent (ch. 12). As he was lying in a drunken stupor, Judith prayed, took his own sword, and cut off his head, which she then put into a sack and carried back to the elders of Bethulia (ch. 13). The enemy, having discovered Holofernes's death, fled in panic and were slaughtered and despoiled by the Jews (chs. 14–15). The book closes with a psalm of thanksgiving to God in gratitude for the notable deliverance (ch. 16).

The story is fiction, but it reflects something of the patriotic mood and religious devotion of the Jews after the Maccabean rebellion. It was written in Hebrew about 150 B.C. and has been transmitted in three slightly different Greek versions, two Latin versions, and a Syriac version, as well as several later Hebrew recensions.

The **Additions to the Book of Esther.** When the Book of Esther was translated into Greek, six sections totalling 107 verses were added in order to provide references to God, prayer, and Judaism, all of which are lacking in the original Hebrew form of the book. According to the colophon (11:1), the Greek version, containing these additions, was made either in 114 or in 78 B.C., probably by Lysimachus, an Alexandrian Jew who lived at Jerusalem.

The present sequence of the Additions is the work of Jerome, who had been commissioned by Pope Damasus to prepare a standard Latin version of the Bible. After translating the Hebrew text of the Book of Esther, he gathered together at the close of the book the several additions current in Greek and Latin MSS, attaching notes to indicate where each addition belonged within the canonical book. Subsequent copyists carelessly omitted these explanatory notes, and the result was a meaningless amalgam of disparate portions. The final confusing step came in the Middle Ages when Stephen Langton, Archbishop of Canterbury (died 1228), having divided the Latin Bible into chapters to facilitate its citation, numbered the chapters of the canonical and the apocryphal material of Esther consecutively as though all of the latter material formed a direct continuation of the former.

The **Wisdom of Solomon** was composed in Greek by an Alexandrian Jew during the first century B.C. Impersonating King Solomon, reputed to have been the wisest ruler of Israel, the author directs his words to several kinds of readers, including both apostate Jews as well as Gentiles. He promises reward and immortality to the righteous and warns the wicked of judgment (chs. 1–5), praises wisdom and describes her nature and works (chs. 6–9), illustrates wisdom's guidance of God's people from Adam to Moses and recalls God's judgments on the Egyptians and the Canaanites (chs. 10–12), explains the origin and folly of idolatry (chs. 13–15), and contrasts God's plagues on the Egyptians and his acts of kindness to his people (chs. 16–19). The book ends quite abruptly, without reaching a culminating point or other natural conclusion.

The theological doctrines of the book are basically derived from the OT, yet modified and expanded at significant points by Platonic and Stoic teachings current in Alexandria at the time of its composition. Particularly in the domain of eschatology the author passes far beyond the OT. From Platonism he derives the view that man is inherently immortal. Though affliction, suffering, and the early death of the righteous may seem to be divine punishment, after death their souls are forever safe and at peace with God, enjoying sure immortality (3:1–9; 5:15, 16). Man's body is regarded as a weight and clog to the soul (9:15), a view that is foreign to the OT and the NT alike. Though God created man in his image to be immortal, the devil brought death into the world (2:24).

There is an OL version of the book, which Jerome took over unchanged for the Vulgate, as well as two versions in Syriac (the Peshitta Syriac is full of mistakes and paraphrases) and others in Coptic, Armenian, and Arabic.

Ecclesiasticus, or the Wisdom of Jesus the Son of Sirach, is not only the longest but also one of the most important and most highly esteemed of the apocryphal books. The author, a Jewish sage named Joshua (in Greek, Jesus), who conducted an academy for young men at Jerusalem, was thoroughly imbued with love for the OT laws, the priesthood, the temple, and divine worship. About 180 B.C. he turned his classroom lectures into Hebrew couplets and collected them in two books (chs. 1–23 and 24–50), each of which commences with an encomium on wisdom. Two-thirds of the Hebrew text, in a longer and a shorter recension, has been preserved in several eleventh- and twelfth-century MSS found in a synagogue storage-room in Old Cairo in 1896–1900. More recently, fragments of 6:20–31 have come to light in Cave II at Qumran, as well as chs. 39–43 (with lacunae) in a manuscript found at Masada. Soon after 132 B.C. the Hebrew book was translated into Greek by the author's grandson, who also wrote a prologue to the Greek version (this is the *second* prologue of KJV[2]). A Syriac translation was also made from a form of the Hebrew text that differed somewhat from the text lying behind the Greek. The Greek text itself circulated in two recensions, a shorter one (preserved in codices Vaticanus, Sinaiticus, Alexandrinus, and most minuscule MSS), and a longer one (preserved in minuscule MS 248). Secondary versions from the Greek text of the book are extant in Latin, Coptic, Syriac (made by Paul of Tella), Ethiopic, Armenian, Slavonic, and Arabic.

The book contains numerous maxims, formulated with care in about 1,600 couplets. Many of these are grouped by affinity of topic, such as marriage, poverty and wealth, merchants, physicians, the law, and various religious and social customs of the time. The book concludes with an appendix (ch. 51) in which the author expresses his gratitude to God and appeals to the unlearned to acquire true wisdom.

The book of **Baruch,** reputed to have been written in Babylon by the son of Neraiah, companion and amanuensis of Jeremiah (Jer 32:12; 36:4), is largely a mosaic of sentences drawn from canonical works such as Jeremiah, Daniel, Isaiah, and Job. Most scholars

---

[2]KJV also provides at the beginning "A Prologue made by an uncertain Author." This prologue, which treats of the origin and contents of Eclesiasticus, is taken from the Greek "Synopsis of Holy Scripture" wrongly attributed to Athanasius. The unknown author, who lived long after Athanasius, has misunderstood references in the book concerning the author and his grandson and so provides quite confused misinformation.

agree that it is a composite work, put together by two or more authors of uncertain date, the latest of whom may be of the first century B.C. or even (as some think) just after A.D. 70. It contains a prayer acknowledging guilt and imploring God's forgiveness (1:15–3:8); a poem praising wisdom, which God gave to Israel exclusively (3:9–4:4); and a poem of comfort and restoration (4:5–5:9), in which personified Jerusalem speaks to the exiles, promising salvation to Israel and ruin to Babylon. The three sections (at least 1:1–3:8) probably had a Hebrew origin, now lost. Today the book is extant in Greek, from which other ancient versions were made, including two in Latin, two in Syriac, and others in Coptic, Armenian, Ethiopic, and Arabic.

The **Letter of Jeremiah** purports to be a copy of a letter written by the prophet to the exiles of Judah at the time of their deportation to Babylon, warning them of a lengthy captivity (seven generations; cf. Jer 29:1, seventy years) and repeatedly exhorting them to beware of the folly of idolatry (vv.16, 23, 29, 40, 44, 52, 56, 65, 69). Patterned after the earlier letter of Jeremiah (Jer 29), the style of the tractate is florid and declamatory, with no logical connection in the sequence of its statements.

The Letter, which is of uncertain date, was written originally in Hebrew. Fragments of five or six MSS were found in Cave IV at Qumran. The oldest manuscript remains of the Letter is a tiny scrap of papyrus, thought to date from about 100 B.C., found in Cave VII at Qumran and preserving several words in Greek from vv.43, 44.

The Letter stands at different places in various MSS and versions. In codices Vaticanus and Alexandrinus (it is not included in codex Sinaiticus or codex Ephraemi), in the Syriac Hexaplar MS at Milan, and in the Arabic version, it stands as an independent piece between Lamentations and Ezekiel. In other Greek and Syriac MSS, as well as the Latin version, it is attached to the book of Baruch, and consequently it stands as the final chapter (6) of that book in many English versions, including KJV and RV (1894), as well as several Catholic Bibles (Douay-Rheims, JB, and NAB). In an early Coptic (Sahidic) MS, known as Bodmer Papyrus XXII, the Epistle stands between Lamentations and Baruch.

The ancient Greek and Latin versions of the Book of Daniel contain three major additions that are not in the original Hebrew and Aramaic text of that book. In the Apocrypha of RSV they bear the titles The Prayer of Azariah and the Song of the Three Young Men; Susanna; Bel and the Dragon. The textual transmission of the Additions is the same as that of the several ancient versions of the canonical book of Daniel. Thus the three Additions have come down to us in two Greek recensions: the LXX text (preserved in the ninth-century codex Chisianus alone), and Theodotion's revision of the LXX, which became standard in Christian Bibles, ancient and modern (Greek, Latin, Syriac, Coptic, Ethiopic, Arabic, Armenian; and English, German, etc.). The date when these Additions were composed is probably sometime in the second or first century B.C. Scholars have debated whether they were written originally in Hebrew, Aramaic, or Greek. Of the three Additions, the Prayer of Azariah and the Song of the Three Young Men has the best claim to have been composed in Hebrew.

The **Prayer of Azariah and the Song of the Three Young Men** is introduced into the narrative of Daniel after 3:23. At this point the Book of Daniel tells of the punishment decreed against three Jewish youths—Shadrach, Meshach, and Abednego—for refusing to worship the golden image that Nebuchadnezzar had set up. Then follows the interpolation in which Azariah (his Hebrew name; Abednego is his pagan name, see Daniel 1:7) prays to God, confessing Israel's sins and imploring national deliverance (vv.2–22). This is followed by details about the continued stoking of the fiery furnace and the descent of the angel of the Lord (vv.23–27). The Addition concludes with the Song of the Three Young Men (vv.28–69), which falls into two parts, one beginning, "Blessed art thou, O Lord, God of our fathers" (v.29), and the other, "Bless the Lord, all works of the Lord" (v.35). A certain solemnity is achieved by the regularly recurring refrain, "Sing praise to him and highly exalt him for ever," which occurs thirty-two times.

The story of **Susanna** has often been regarded as one of the best short detective stories in world literature. While inculcating lessons of morality and trust in God, the narrative also grips the reader's interest from the beginning. The virtuous and beautiful Susanna, whose name in Hebrew means "a lily," lived in Babylonia with her prosperous husband Joachim (vv.1–4). Two Jewish elders became inflamed with passion for her, and, surprising her as she prepared to bathe in her garden pool, threatened to accuse her of adultery if she did not submit to their unlawful desires (vv.5–21). When Susanna refused, they accused her of adultery with a young man, and brought her to trial, where she was condemned to death (vv.22–41). Protesting her innocence, Susanna prayed to God for help. At that moment Daniel came forward and demanded the right to interrogate the witnesses. Charging the two elders with bearing false testimony, Daniel proved it when they disagreed about the tree under which the adultery had allegedly been committed (vv.24–59). Thereupon the elders were executed in accordance with Deuteronomy 19:18, 19, all the assembly praised God that innocent blood had been saved, and "from that day onward Daniel had a great reputation among the people" (v.64).

The location of this Addition to the book of Daniel varies in the MSS and versions. In the Greek text of Theodotion, as well as the OL, Coptic, and Arabic versions, the account of Susanna forms the introduction to the book of Daniel, being prefixed to chapter 1. In LXX and the Latin Vulgate it follows the last chapter of Daniel (ch. 12 in Hebrew) and is numbered chapter 13.

The account of **Bel and the Dragon** comprises two popular tales, both designed to ridicule paganism. The first story (vv.1–22) tells of a great statue of Bel (the Babylonian god Marduk) before which great quantities of food and drink were placed daily. Since these offerings disappeared every night, the king tried to convince Daniel that Bel was a living god which should be worshiped. Daniel, however, by means of a clever trick proved that it was really the priests of Bel who were consuming the food and that Bel was inanimate. Thereupon the king put the priests to death and allowed Daniel to destroy Bel and its temple.

In the second story (vv.23–42) the king commanded Daniel to worship a great dragon. Refusing to do so, Daniel asked permission to slay it "without sword or club" (v.26). Granted permission, Daniel fed the beast lumps of indigestible pitch, fat, and hair, so that the dragon burst open (v.27). The people, angered by the death of their god, forced the king to throw Daniel into a den of lions. Though the lions were starved, they did not devour Daniel. An angel transported Habukkuk from Judea with food for Daniel. On the seventh day the king released Daniel and threw his enemies to the hungry lions.

In Greek MSS the account of Bel and the Dragon follows chapter 12 of Daniel. In the Latin Vulgate it forms chapter 14, the story of Susanna being chapter 13.

The **Prayer of Manasseh** is a short penitential psalm drawn up by someone who read in 2 Chronicles 33:11–19 that while Manasseh, the wicked king of Judah, was in exile, he composed a prayer beseeching divine forgiveness for his many sins. The idiomatic

Greek in which the prayer is expressed suggests it was written in that language rather than in Hebrew. Its date is problematic; most scholars prefer the first century B.C. or A.D. The earliest extant text is in the Syriac Didascalia (ii, 22), a church manual of the first half of the third century A.D. In LXX it is placed among the fourteen Odes (hymns and canticles from both Testaments) that follow the Psalms in some MSS. Though it was unknown to Jerome, in later manuscripts of the Latin Vulgate it follows 2 Chronicles (as it does also in the English Bible published at Geneva, 1560). In official printings of the Vulgate after the Council of Trent, the Prayer is placed in an appendix following the NT, whereas in the Catholic Douay Version of 1609–10 it stands in an appendix after the OT. It is not included in JB or NAB.

The **First Book of the Maccabees** is a generally reliable historical account of the fortunes of Jewish people between 175 and 134 B.C., relating particularly to their struggle with Antiochus IV Epiphanes and his successors. It was probably written shortly after the death of John Hyrcanus I, who was high priest from 134 to 104 B.C., since it refers to the chronicles of John's reign (16:23–24). The name of the author, a patriotic Jew at Jerusalem, is unknown. From the nature of his work, however, is evident that he was well-versed in the geography of the Palestinian countryside and quite conversant not only with ancient Hebrew historiography (particularly the books of Kings and Chronicles) but also with the history of the Seleucid dynasty. Though the name of God is never mentioned in the book, this fact is to be ascribed to the scrupulous reverence of contemporary Judaism for the Creator, for the author obviously saw the hand of God (referred to frequently as "Heaven") operative in the victories of Judas Maccabeus and his family.

According to the explicit testimony of Jerome, the book was originally composed in the Hebrew language, though no other evidence of that is known today. Several poetic sections (e.g., 1:25–28, 36–40; 2:7–13; 3:3–9; 14:4–15) imitate the style of classical Hebrew poetry. The extant Greek text, from which the later versions (OL, Vulgate, and two Syriac recensions) were made, is full of Hebrew idioms. On the basis of these, occasional corrections can be made by assuming an error in the reading or copying of the original Hebrew.

The **Second Book of the Maccabees**, unlike 2 Samuel, 2 Kings, and 2 Chronicles, is not the continuation of the first book, but is an independent work, partially covering the same period (175–161 B.C.). Prefixed to the book, but not belonging to it originally, are copies of two letters (1:1–10a and 1:10b–2:18) purporting to have been sent by the Jews of Jerusalem and Judea to their Jewish brethren in Egypt. The central theme of the two letters is the Feast of Dedication commemorating the reconsecration of the temple after its profanation by Antiochus IV Epiphanes. Then follows a prologue describing the author's condensation and embellishment of a five-volume history, now lost, written by a certain Jason of Cyrene (2:19–32). The abridgment itself falls into two main parts. First the epitomist sets forth aspects of pre-Maccabean history and the causes that provoked Jewish rebellion (3:1–7:42). The remainder of the book (chs. 8–15) corresponds broadly to 1 Maccabees 3–7 and describes the rise and progress of the Maccabean insurrection until the crushing defeat of the Syrian general Nicanor at the hands of Judas Maccabeus.

The purpose of the anonymous epitomizer is to give a theological interpretation to the history of the period. There is less interest, therefore, in the actual exploits of Judas Maccabeus than in God's miraculous interventions through celestial apparitions. Of significance in the history of Jewish theology is the teaching that the living may offer prayers and sacrifices for the dead (12:39–45) and that the saints in heaven intercede for people living on earth (15:11–16).

The date of Jason's history and of the work of the epitomizer is unknown. Most scholars, however, place the latter within the first century B.C. While both letters in the opening chapters would have been written originally in Hebrew, the rest of the book (2:9–15:40) was certainly composed in Greek. Today the book is extant only in Greek, from which several versions were made, including the OL (which Jerome took over unchanged into the Vulgate text), another Latin version, and a paraphrastic Syriac rendering.

III. Representative Pseudepigrapha

Many pseudepigraphic works of Jewish (and Jewish-Christian) origin were produced during the last two centuries B.C. and the first two centuries A.D.[3] Some have a polemic purpose against paganism both within and outside the Jewish fold, the key concept being separation from the Gentiles. On another side, the purpose of several books was the production of a strongly framed Jewish propaganda. The writings constitute a national theodicy, with the intent of strengthening believers in their faith and practice. Prophecy was supplanted by apocalyptic, and its grotesque imagery veiled the teaching from hostile overlords while at the same time conveying new wisdom to the initiated concerning heaven, hell, and the future of the world. The character of these books, therefore, makes them appeal to varied interests.

A. Palestinian Pseudepigrapha

The **Testaments of the Twelve Patriarchs** is a pseudepigraphic work modeled on the "testament of Jacob" in Genesis 49. It professes to relate in its twelve books the message that each of the twelve sons of Jacob gave to his descendants on his deathbed. The contents of each message are warnings and exhortations that fit the character of the patriarch speaking and are elaborated from the personal experiences of the speaker as told in the OT. The purpose is chiefly to give moral encouragement and spiritual consolation to its readers, whose confidence in its worth would have been stimulated and sustained by its revelations, which are prophetic *ex post facto* of the later history of the several Israelite tribes.

With curious unanimity, nearly all the patriarchs speak of the leadership of Judah and Levi. There is a reference to Christ as Savior (T. Levi 10:2), and one to Paul as the apostle to the Gentiles (T. Benj. 11:2). Numerous parallels in thought and diction to the NT occur throughout the book, e.g., exhortations to humility, brotherly love, and almsgiving, as well as the conjoining of the two great commands of love to God and love to one's neighbor (T. Dan 5:3). Several passages reflect a patripassian Christology. Consequently, it has been much debated whether the book was written by a Christian or whether it is essentially a Jewish composition (perhaps in Hebrew) with Christian glosses interpolated when it was translated into Greek. That the latter view is correct seems to be confirmed by the discovery at Qumran of fragments of an earlier recension of the

---

[3]The number of Jewish and Jewish-Christian pseudepigraphic writings must once have been great. Jewish legend ascribes to Enoch no fewer than 366 such works, and 2 Esdras (14:46) tells of 70 secret books that are discriminated from the 24 canonical ones. For the titles of more than 200 pseudepigrapha (some of them no longer extant), see the works by James and Denis in the bibliography at the close of the article.

Testaments of Levi and Naphtali in Aramaic and Hebrew. Besides the Greek version, the book survives in Armenian and in two Slavonic recensions.

The **Book of Jubilees** is a midrashic expansion of biblical history from creation to the institution of the Passover (Gen 1:1–Exod 12:47). In it the author reinterprets the narrative under a scheme of dating by years, weeks of years, and "jubilees" (Lev 25:11). The period from creation till the entrance into Canaan is arranged in fifty jubilee periods of forty-nine years each (2,450 years), and each event is located with reference to this chronological framework. In the interest of assisting Jews to keep the feasts on the proper day, the author advocates a 364-day year (instead of the traditional lunar calendar). Written in Hebrew probably during the first century B.C., the book seems to have been highly regarded by the sectaries at Qumran, where fragments of no fewer than nine different Hebrew MSS have thus far come to light. A Greek translation, which has disappeared except for brief quotations made by several church fathers, was the parent of a version in Latin (of which about one-fourth has been preserved) and in Ethiopic.

The **Psalms of Solomon,** eighteen in number, were composed, as is generally agreed, in Hebrew during the post-Maccabean period, probably about the middle of the first century B.C. (several Psalms seem to allude to Pompey's capture of Jerusalem in 63 B.C.). The writer advocates a righteousness of works done in accordance with the Law (14:1f.; cf. 9:9), declares the justice of God in punishment of his people on account of their sins, and looks forward to a resurrection when one's past deeds will determine whether it shall be to life (3:16) or to condemnation (13:9ff.; ch. 15). The Psalms depict the nation as divided into two classes: "the righteous" (comprising almost entirely the Pharisees, to which party the author undoubtedly belonged) and "the sinners" (the Saducees). On the basis of the messianic prophecies of the OT, the author pictures the coming age when God will send his Messiah, of the house of David, who will purge Jerusalem, punish sinners, subdue Gentile nations hostile to Israel, and rule in righteousness as a kind of deputy of God (14:2; 17:23–25; 18:5, 6).

The text of the Psalms of Solomon, lost until it was first edited in 1626, survives today in eight Greek MSS from the eleventh to the fifteenth century and in three not-quite-complete Syriac MSS.

B. *Non-Palestinian Pseudepigrapha*

The **Book of Enoch** (sometimes called 1 Enoch or Ethiopic Enoch), a passage of which (1:9) is cited in the Epistle of Jude (vv. 14–15), is the longest of the surviving Jewish pseudepigraphic writings. It is a composite work, written by various authors in Aramaic (or Hebrew) during the last two centuries B.C. Professing to embody a series of revelations granted to Enoch, the seventh from Adam, the anonymous authors discuss such matters as the origin of evil, the angels and their destinies, the nature of Gehenna and Paradise, and various astronomical and cosmological fancies. The section comprising chapters 72 to 82, sometimes called "The Book of Celestial Physics," is one of the curiosities of ancient pseudoscientific literature, for it sets forth a variety of contemporary speculations concerning such meteorological and astronomical phenomena as lightning, hail, snow, the twelve winds, the sun, the moon and its phases, and the stars that lead the seasons and the months. Of more specifically religious significance is the section comprising the so-called Similitudes of Enoch (chs. 37–71), which consists of three parables dealing mainly with the theme of the coming judgment on the wicked. After the resurrection, judgment will be meted out by the Messiah, the Elect One, also called the Son of Man, a pre-existent, heavenly being who possesses all dominion and pronounces judgment on all men and angels.

The Book of Enoch came to the attention of European scholars in the eighteenth century when the Scottish traveler James Bruce acquired three Ethiopic MSS of the work in Abyssinia. This version had been translated about A.D. 500 from a Greek text of the book, of which chapters 1 to 32 and 97 to 107 have turned up in a papyrus codex found in Egypt earlier this century. A few verses are preserved also in Latin and in Syriac. The controversy whether the book was composed originally in Hebrew or in Aramaic does not seem to be settled, despite the discovery at Qumran of fragments of ten Aramaic MSS of various sections of the book—but nothing from the Similitudes (chs. 37–71). (For the Book of the Secrets of Enoch, see p. 173.)

The **Letter of Aristeas** claims to have been written by a certain Aristeas, an official at the court of Ptolemy II Philadelphus (285–246 B.C.), to his brother Philocrates, purporting to give an eyewitness account of the translation of the OT Torah into Greek by seventy-two elders (six from each Hebrew tribe) sent by Eleazar the high priest at the request of the king. The apologetic interest of the unknown author is revealed in a section bearing on the vindication of the purpose and function of the Jewish laws (§§ 128–171) and in the lengthy account of the table-talk between Philadelphus and his guests, exemplifying the wisdom, moral insight, intellectual ability, and philosophical acumen of the leaders of the Jewish people (§§ 187–300). Scholars have debated the time of the composition of the Epistle; the dates proposed range from about 200 B.C. to just after A.D. 33.

The **Third Book of the Maccabees,** which has nothing to do with the Maccabees, professes to describe three stages of the conflict of Ptolemy IV Philopator and Judaism. The book was given its present name probably on the analogy of the events described with those of the Maccabean period. The narrative runs as follows: After Ptolemy's victory over Antiochus the Great at Raphia (217 B.C.), he visited Jerusalem and tried to enter the temple, despite the frantic opposition of priests and people. Stricken by God, Ptolemy fell senseless to the ground and later retired to Egypt. Here he resolved to take vengeance by slaughtering the entire Jewish population of the country, but his plans were all circumvented through circumstances that stretch the credulity of the reader.

Whatever historical reminiscences the story may preserve, the book as it stands today is full of impossibilities and exaggerations. The author was probably an Alexandrian Jew who wrote either shortly before or after the beginning of the Christian era. He had command of an exceptionally large vocabulary in Greek but used a bombastic and inflated style.

Third Maccabees seems to have been practically neglected by the Jews. On the other hand, it is listed in the biblical catalogue of the Apostolic Canons (c. 85) and it appears to have been highly esteemed in the early church. The book is found in the uncial codices Alexandrinus and Venetus, and in many minuscule MSS. It is not in the Latin Vulgate but is included in the Peshitta Syriac version in a free and expanded rendering. There is also an Armenian version.

The **Fourth Book of the Maccabees** is a Greek philosophical treatise addressed to Jews on the supremacy of devout reason over the passions. After a statement of the theme (1:1–12) and a careful definition of the philosophical terms (1:13–30a), the author illustrates his oft-reiterated thesis with examples drawn from the OT (1:30b–3:17) and from the Maccabean period (4:1–18:24). The section on the Maccabean martyrs is a greatly expanded version of 2 Maccabees 6:18–7:42. It can be summarized as follows: narrative of the trial and torture of the aged priest Eleazar (5:1–6:30), detailed and gruesome description of the torture of seven Jewish youths (8:1–12:19), comments on their fortitude (13:1–14:10), reflections on the sufferings and constancy of the mother (14:11–17:6), concluding comments on the character and significance of the martyrdoms just described (17:7–18:24).

Throughout, the author handles his subject with rhetorical power, moral earnestness, and a desire to edify his readers. The style is smooth, flowing, and vigorous, characterized by classically constructed sentences. Hebraisms are almost totally absent. The identity of the author is unknown. Jerome (*De viris illustr.* 13) attributes it to Flavius Josephus, but this is erroneous. It was probably written by a Hellenistic Jew of Alexandria sometime later than 2 Maccabees and before A.D. 70. The book is present in the three great uncial codices Sinaiticus, Alexandrinus, and Venetus, as well as in many minuscule manuscripts, and was early translated into Syriac.

The so-called **Slavonic Enoch** (also known as 2 Enoch or the Book of the Secrets of Enoch) is an apocalypse current today in two recensions, one longer and more recent in South Russian, and the other shorter and more ancient in Bulgarian. It appears to have been composed originally in Greek, the author utilizing Hebrew materials, but it is not dependent on 1 Enoch. The book relates Enoch's travels through the seven heavens and the divine revelations that he received concerning creation, the history of the world, hell, and paradise. Its composition is dated by most scholars in the first half of the first Christian century, but on the basis of astronomical data included in the book, Fotheringham argued that it is no older than the seventh century.[4] It is possible that an earlier form of the book was reworked in the seventh century.

The book known as the **Prayer of Asenath** (sometimes called Joseph and Asenath) is a legend of uncertain date, belonging to the midrashic propaganda against mixed marriages. It relates how the patriarch Joseph met Asenath, the daughter of Potiphera, priest of Heliopolis. She fell in love with him. Joseph, however, rejected her because she was a pagan, whereupon she withdrew to her chamber and spent seven days there in tears, penitence, and prayers. At the end of this time Michael appeared to her to tell her that God had heeded her prayer and that she would "eat the blessed bread of life and drink the cup filled with immortality and be anointed with the blessed chrism of incorruption." Subsequently, Joseph married Asenath, and the book concludes with a tale of intrigue, murder, and an attempt of Pharaoh's son to abduct Asenath.

It is much debated how far the Jewish romance shows traits derived from the ritual meals observed by Essene communities and/or from the celebration of the Christian Eucharist. The book is extant in Greek, Syriac, and Latin.

IV. Influence of the Apocrypha and Pseudepigrapha

The books commonly designated the Apocrypha and Pseudepigrapha are important in more than one respect. First, most of them provide information concerning the history

---

[4]J.K. Fotheringham, *Journal of Theological Studies*, XXIII, 1921–22, pp. 49–56.

of the Jews between the Old and New Testaments. The development of the sects of the Pharisees, the Sadducees, and the Essenes; the growth of interest in the coming of the Messiah; the extension of beliefs concerning angels and demons; the dissemination of the doctrine of the resurrection—in all these matters the Apocrypha and several of the Pseudepigrapha provide valuable information for tracing the growth of institutions and beliefs that are taken for granted in the NT but of which there is scarcely an allusion in the OT.

Second, these books are useful in interpreting and elucidating various aspects of Western culture. Besides inspiring homilies, meditations, and liturgical forms, the books of the Apocrypha have provided subject matter for poets, dramatists, composers, and artists in all ages. Even the discovery of the New World can be traced in part to the conclusion that Christopher Columbus drew from 2 Esdras—namely, that the distance he would need to sail westward before finding land must be of limited extent, for the proportion of land to water is said to be six to one (6:42).

It is not strange that the Apocrypha exerted such a pervasive influence. Until relatively modern times they were included in most of the vernacular Bibles of Europe. Even after the Reformation, when they were segregated between the Old and New Testaments, they continued to be included in the Bible, though printed in smaller type to indicate that they were not to be regarded as on a par with the canonical books. In fact, one of the translators of KJV, George Abbot, as Archbishop of Canterbury, issued a decree in 1615 that if any printer should dare to bind up and sell a copy of the Scriptures without the Apocrypha, he would be liable to a whole year's imprisonment.

In English literature, Chaucer, Shakespeare, Milton, Ruskin, Longfellow, and many others borrowed, more or less freely, themes and expressions from the Apocrypha. In art, many of the old masters, as well as several modern painters, have chosen subjects from this body of literature. Almost every large gallery in Europe and America has one or more works of the old masters depicting Judith, Tobit, or Susanna. In music, such hymns as "Now Thank We All Our God," "O Come, O Come, Emmanuel," "It Came Upon a Midnight Clear," and dozens of Charles Wesley's compositions incorporate ideas, phrases, and even whole sections from the Apocrypha. Anthems, oratorios, and more than one opera embody extensive material from these books. (Since there is not room here to document these and other examples of the pervasive influence of the Apocrypha, the reader who is interested is referred to Metzger's *Introduction to the Apocrypha*, where all these and many other examples are discussed.)

Third, despite the presence of obviously erroneous, frivolous, and superstitious statements in many of the intertestamental books, it cannot be denied that they also contain more than one passage of great inspirational and devotional value. The saintly Bishop Lancelot Andrewes, one of the translators of the KJV, incorporated the greater part of the apocryphal Prayer of Manasseh in his book of *Private Devotions*. In conducting a funeral service, many a clergyman who reads the words of a modern hymn of comfort also makes use of the exalted passage in the Wisdom of Solomon beginning, "The souls of the righteous are in the hands of God, and no torment will ever touch them" (3:1–5).

V. Bibliography

Charles, R.H., ed. *The Apocrypha and Pseudepigrapha in English, with Introductions and Critical and Explanatory Notes to the Several Books.* 2 vols. Oxford: Clarendon, 1913.

Charlesworth, James H. *The Pseudepigrapha and Modern Research.* Missoula Montana: Scholars, 1976.

Denis, Albert-Marie. *Introduction aux pseudépigraphes grecs d'Ancien Testament.* Leiden: E.J. Brill, 1970.

James, Montague Rhodes. *The Lost Apocrypha of the Old Testament, Their Titles and Fragments.* London: S.P.C.K., 1920.

Metzger, Bruce M. *An Introduction to the Apocrypha.* New York: Oxford University Press, 1957.

Metzger, Bruce M., ed. *The Oxford Annotated Apocrypha,* expanded edition [Contains 3 and 4 Maccabees and Psalm 151]. New York: Oxford University Press, 1977.

Pfeiffer, Robert H. *History of New Testament Times, with an Introduction to the Apocrypha.* New York: Harper and Brothers, 1949.

Rost, Leonhard. *Judaism Outside the Hebrew Canon.* Trans. by David E. Green. Nashville: Abingdon, 1976.

Torrey, Charles C. *The Apocrypha: A Brief Introduction.* New Haven: Yale University Press, 1945.

Periodicals

Metzger, Bruce M. "Literary Forgeries and Canonical Pseudepigrapha" in *JBL* 91 (1972): 3–24.

_____. "Right and Wrong Uses of the Apocrypha" in *Christianity Today,* (September 30, 1957), pp. 3–5.

BETWEEN THE TESTAMENTS
Harold W. Hoehner

Harold W. Hoehner

B.A., Barrington College; Th.M., Th.D., Dallas Theological Seminary; Ph.D., Cambridge University

Associate Professor of New Testament Literature and Exegesis, Director of Doctoral Studies, Dallas Theological Seminary

BETWEEN THE TESTAMENTS

I. **Historical Development**

    A. **Persian Rule, 539–331 B.C.**
    B. **Grecian Rule, 331–143 B.C.**
    C. **Hasmonean Rule, 142–63 B.C.**
    D. **Roman Rule, 63–4 B.C.**

II. **Internal Developments**

    A. **Literary Activity**
    B. **Spiritual Conditions**
    C. **Parties**
    D. **Preparation for the New Testament**

III. **Bibliography**

I. Historical Development

A. *Persian Rule*, 539–331 B.C.

1. *Period of Persian strength, 539–423* B.C. In 539 B.C. Cyrus of Persia defeated the Babylonians and allowed the dispersed nations, including the Jews, to return to their homeland (2 Chron 36:21–23; Ezra 1; 6:3–5). The Jews returned under Zerubbabel in 538/39 B.C. (Ezra 2–6) and under Ezra in 457 (Ezra 7–10). Nehemiah came to rebuild the walls of Jerusalem in 444 and remained in Jerusalem until 433/32 (Neh 13:6), when he returned to Persia. He returned to Judah (Neh 13:6–31) sometime before the death of Artaxerxes I in 423 B.C.

2. *Period of Persian decline, 423–331* B.C. This was an uneventful period for both Persians and Jews. Darius II (423–404 B.C.), son of Artaxerxes I, reoccupied Lydia (in 413) during the Peloponnesian War (431–404) when he helped Sparta financially in defeating Athens. However, there were revolts in Syria, in Lydia (before 413) and in Media in 410. In 410, after a massive revolt in Egypt, the Egyptians destroyed the Jewish

---

Note: Aside from the sources referred to in the text of this article and in the bibliography, the author consulted the following writers:

Appian	Justin	Strabo
Arrian	Livy	Tacitus
Curtius Rufus	Plutarch	Valleius Paterculus
Diodorus	Polybius	Xenophon

temple at Elephantine because of popular sentiment against animal sacrifices. The Elephantine Jews reported the destruction and need for assistance to the Persian governor Bagoas and to Johanan. This Johanan, or Jonathan, was high priest in Jerusalem during Darius II's reign (Neh 12:11, 22, 23). Not having received a reply, the Elephantine Jews in 407 B.C. addressed a second letter to Bagoas alone, seeking authorization to rebuild the temple of Yaho in the fortress of Elephantine. Permission was granted. In 419 Darius ordered Arsanes, satrap of Egypt, to allow the Jews to celebrate the Feast of Unleavened Bread in the Jewish garrison.

Darius II was succeeded by his son Artaxerxes II (404–358 B.C.). After crushing his brother Cyrus's rebellion and repelling the Spartans' intervention in Asia Minor (peace at Antalcidas, 386), he failed in two attempts to recover Egypt (385–383 and 374). Artaxerxes II occupied Jerusalem, defiled the temple, imposed a heavy fine on the people, and persecuted them for several years. The Samaritans were more pliable and escaped persecution.

Succeeding Artaxerxes II was his son, Artaxerxes III, who killed most of his relatives regardless of sex or age. In 351 B.C. his failure to drive Egypt back caused a general revolt in Palestine. In 345 he marched against Sidon and in 343 reconquered Egypt with the help of Mentor of Rhodes. In 338 Artaxerxes III was poisoned by his minister Bagoas ("eunuch kingmaker"), who placed Arses, son of Artaxerxes III on the throne. Striving for independence from Bagoas's control, Arses tried to poison him, but Bagoas killed him and all his children and appointed Darius III to the throne in 336 B.C. When Darius was becoming powerful, Bagoas attempted to poison him also, but Darius forced the eunuch himself to drink the fatal cup.

Shortly after Darius III's accession, Philip of Macedon was murdered while preparing to destroy the Persian empire. Darius reconquered Egypt and built a palace in Persepolis. In 334 B.C. Alexander the Great defeated the Persians at the Granicus River, pushed them westward and defeated them at Issus, Cilicia, in 333. Darius fled to the East to consolidate, but in 331 his army was decisively scattered at Gaugamela, and Darius fled to Ecbatana. Finally, in 330 the Bactrian Bessus stabbed Darius and left him to die. Alexander found his body and gave him a royal funeral at Persepolis.

B. *Grecian Rule,* 331–143 B.C.

1. *Alexander the Great,* 356–323 B.C. Philip of Macedon's son, Alexander III, the Great, was only twenty when he took the throne. Taught by Aristotle, he dreamed of continuing his father's conquest of the world in order to Hellenize it. He first consolidated the Hellenic League. In 334 B.C. he crossed the Hellespont and soundly defeated the Persian army at the foot of Mount Ida by the River Granicus. This opened Asia Minor to him, and soon he was at Issus. Darius was defeated at Issus in 333 and fled to the East.

Although this opened the East to Alexander, he adhered to his original plan to occupy Phoenicia, Palestine, and Egypt. Alexander moved southward and defeated the Phoenician cities and finally overcame Tyre in 332. Palestine went over to him, and he conquered Gaza after a two-month siege. Alexander apparently went to Jerusalem, offered sacrifices to God in the temple under the direction of the high priest Jaddua, and was shown from the Book of Daniel that he was predicted to destroy the Persian Empire (cf. Dan 8:5–7, 20, 21). He accepted this interpretation, granted the Jews' request that Jews in Palestine, Babylonia, and Media be allowed to live according to their ancestral laws and be exempt from tribute every sabbatical year. (Scholars question the historicity of this account.)

Alexander then proceeded to Egypt, which yielded to him with no trouble. In the spring of 331 B.C. he began his trek northward and, after a great battle, defeated Darius at Gaugamela and occupied the Persian capitals (Babylon, Susa, Persepolis, and Ecbatana). After Bessus killed Darius, Alexander was free to assume the title "King of Asia." He overran Bactria and Sogdiana (330–327 B.C.), and the Indian expedition extended his eastern frontiers to the Hyphasis and Lower Indus (327–325). In 323, at the age of thirty-two, he died as a world conqueror.

2. *Ptolemaic rule, 323–198 B.C.*

a. *Division of the empire, 323–301 B.C.* The generals asked Alexander on his deathbed to name his successor, but the response was ambivalent. He gave his ring to Perdiccas, one of Philip's generals. The generals met to choose between Alexander's half-sane brother Arrhidaeus and the unborn child (if a boy) of Alexander's Bactrian wife Roxane. A compromise was reached: Arrhidaeus, whose name was changed to Philip, and Roxane, would be corulers, with Perdiccas as regent. The empire was divided into more than twenty satrapies.

Perdiccas wanted to become the central figure of the empire, and the satraps regarded him with suspicion. When they brought the body of Alexander from Babylon to be placed at Macedonia, the satrap Ptolemy of Egypt met the retinue in Syria, seized the body, and took it to Egypt for burial. For this challenge to his authority, Perdiccas attacked Egypt but was killed (321 B.C.) by his generals, among whom was the cavalry commander Seleucus. Antipater was now elected regent, and the satrapies were redistributed. In 320, feeling temporarily safe from Babylonian attack, Ptolemy claimed Syrian Palestine as part of Egypt and deposed Laomedon. In 319 Antipater died, and Antigonus became leader and devoted himself to reuniting Alexander's empire under himself. He removed generals who were opposed to him. Hearing this, Seleucus of Babylonia, not powerful enough to defend himself against Antigonus' demands, fled to Ptolemy in 316.

Seleucus's warning Ptolemy against Antigonus resulted in the satraps Ptolemy, Lysimachus, Cassander, and Seleucus allying themselves against Antigonus. When Antigonus was in Syria in 315, Ptolemy stated that Syria and Palestine belonged to Ptolemy and Babylonia to Seleucus. Antigonus invaded Syria and Palestine and occupied all the country down to Gaza. In 312 Ptolemy and Seleucus attacked Demetrius, son of Antigonus who was in charge of Gaza, and defeated him. By 311 Seleucus was acknowledged as ruler of Babylonia—this being the commencement of the Seleucid dynasty. Ptolemy also seized Jerusalem with no resistance because it was the Sabbath. Finally, however, a peace treaty was signed in 311 by Cassander, Ptolemy, and Lysimachus with Antigonus; by it Ptolemy lost control over Syria and Palestine and Antigonus was to control Asia. Antigonus in 310–309 attempted to gain control of Babylonia but could not subdue Seleucus. Antigonus fortified himself in Syria and controlled Palestine.

In 301 B.C., however, Antigonus was killed in a decisive battle at Ipsus in Phrygia. An agreement had been made by Ptolemy, Seleucus, Lysimachus, and Cassander (in 303) that Coele-Syria Palestine should be given to Ptolemy. Ptolemy had not taken part in the battle; so it was decided to give it to Seleucus, but Ptolemy forestalled Seleucus and took possession of Lower Syria, Palestine, and Phoenicia south of the River Eleutherus. This caused lasting contention between the Seleucid and Ptolemaic houses. The empire was divided into four areas: Egypt and Palestine went to Ptolemy, Phrygia as far as the Indus (including Syria) to Seleucus, Thrace and Bithynia to Lysimachus, and Macedonia to Cassander. Thus, in twenty-two years Palestine changed hands six times. Also the four who would succeed Alexander, according to Daniel 11:4, are not identified until between 312 and 301.

b. *Domination of the Ptolemies,* 301–198 B.C. Egypt did not consider Judea strategically important, Ptolemy II and others fortified the cities Ptolemais and Gaza, as well as some Decapolis cities; these were all outside the Judean domain. Judea also remained under the leadership of the high priest as in the days of Ezra and Nehemiah. The annual payment of tax to the crown was made by the high priest from his own resources, not from the temple. Judea was treated as a sacerdotal province under the leadership of the high priest and was comparatively unmolested.

There was relative peace in the land under the leadership of Ptolemy I. Although Seleucus felt that Palestine should have been his, he did not contest it, remembering Ptolemy's past help. The years 282–281 B.C., however, marked a turning point in the friendship between Ptolemies and Seleucids. In 282 Ptolemy I died and Ptolemy II Philadelphus succeeded him. In 281 Seleucus took Phrygia, then marched into Europe, aiming to take his beloved birthplace Macedonia and become master of Alexander's empire, with the exception of Egypt and Palestine. Soon after crossing the Hellespont, he was assassinated by Ptolemy Ceraunus, who had accompanied him. He was succeeded by his son Antiochus I Soter, who had been coruler since 293/92.

In the ensuing confusion, Antigonus Gonatas (son of Demetrius) gained control of Macedonia. Three superpowers resulted: the house of Seleucus over Babylon, Upper Syria, and Asia Minor; the house of Ptolemy over Egypt and Coele-Syria (Lower Syria); and the house of Antigonus over Europe. That division remained until the Roman invasion.

Antiochus I and Ptolemy II disagreed, and the "Syrian wars" broke out between them for the domination of Coele-Syria. Ptolemy II conquered important districts of Upper Syria as far as Damascus and the Marsyas Valley and, later, parts of Asia Minor. Antiochus I planned to invade Egypt but was kept busy in Asia Minor because of Egypt's inroads there. By 273/272 B.C. Antiochus was forced to make peace. He lost parts of the Asia Minor Coast. Later he regained the Marsyas Valley but not Damascus. Ptolemy gained much of Asia Minor, all of Phoenicia, and Damascus.

Antiochus I of Syria, slain in battle against the Gauls in Asia Minor in 261 B.C., was succeeded by his son Antiochus II Theos, who planned revenge against Ptolemy II. Helped by Antigonus II Gonatas of Macedonia, Antiochus II regained the coasts of Asia Minor and all of Phoenicia north of Sidon. In 253 a brilliant political triumph was accomplished by Ptolemy when Antiochus (surprisingly) agreed to marry Ptolemy's daughter, Bernice, on the condition that he would get rid of his first wife, Laodice, and with the understanding that the kingdom should go to Bernice's son. The marriage was consummated in 252, but the ensuing peace was short-lived—both Antiochus and Ptolemy died in 246. Ptolemy II was succeeded by his son Ptolemy III Euergetes. After a struggle, Antiochus II's first wife Laodice succeeded in enthroning their oldest son, Seleucus II Callinicus.

The Third Syrian War (246–241 B.C.) started when Ptolemy III realized that his father's dream of a union had not been realized. He invaded Syria to rescue his sister Bernice (Antiochus's second wife) and her son (Dan 11:7, 8). When the latter were murdered at Laodice's instigation, the residents sided with Seleucus II and, considering Ptolemy III a foreign invader, drove him southward. Although Ptolemy III kept Phoenicia and southern Syria, Seleucus regained most of northern Syria and Damascus and captured southern Syria (Dan 11:9). A treaty was signed in 241, establishing peace between the houses for about two decades.

Seleucus II died in 225. His son Alexander, Seleucus III Soter, was assassinated in 223 and was succeeded by his brother as Antiochus III (The Great). In 222 Ptolemy III died and was succeeded by his dissolute son Ptolemy IV Philopator.

The Fourth Syrian War (219–217 B.C.) commenced when Antiochus III invaded Lebanon in an attempt to take Palestine from Ptolemy IV. He captured Seleucia, Tyre, Ptolemais, and inland cities between Philoteria and Philadelphia. By 217 he pushed southward as far as Raphia where he was utterly defeated, leaving Ptolemy in undisputed control of Coele-Syria and Phoenicia (Dan 11:11, 12).

However, when the seven-year-old Ptolemy V Epiphanes became ruler in 203, Antiochus III saw another opportunity to take Coele-Syria from Egypt. In 202 Antiochus agreed with Philip V of Macedon on a division of Egypt. In 201 he invaded Palestine and finally captured Gaza. He then invaded the dominions of the pro-Roman Attalus, king of Pergamos in 199/98. Scopas, an Egyptian general, hearing of Antiochus's absence, invaded Palestine and recovered the lost territories. Antiochus returned to oppose Scopas, and at Panias (NT Caesarea Philippi) Ptolemy V was decisively defeated (Dan 11:14–16). He released prisoners, granted the Jews freedom of worship, let them complete and maintain the temple, and exempted the council of temple officers from taxes. This exemption the citizens of Jerusalem enjoyed for the first three years; thereafter they were exempted one-third of their taxes. From 198 until Roman control in 63, the Jews were under the Seleucid dynasty, and soon experienced fierce persecution.

3. *Seleucid rule,* 198–143 B.C.

a. *Seleucid control,* 198–168 B.C. There was a brief period of tranquility while the Seleucids were concentrating their effort in the West. Rome had defeated Hannibal at Zama in 202 and the Macedonian monarchy in 197. Antiochus therefore discontinued his war with Egypt and made a treaty with Ptolemy V Epiphanes in which the latter married Antiochus' daughter, Cleopatra—Antiochus hoping that her son (his grandson) would be the next king of Egypt and would be partial to the Seleucids (Dan 11:17). Antiochus invaded Thrace in 196 and, helped by Hannibal, he invaded Greece in 194; but the Romans retaliated, defeating him at Thermopylae in 191 and at Magnesia in 190. A peace treaty was signed at Apamea in 189. In this treaty Antiochus gave up Asia Minor north and west of the Tarsus Mountains, much of his military force, and had to pay a heavy indemnity over a twelve-year period. As surety, he had to deliver twenty hostages (one of whom was his son Antiochus IV) to Rome (Dan 11:18–19; 1 Macc 1:10; 8:6–8).

Antiochus III was succeeded by his second son Seleucus IV Philopator in 187 B.C. He attempted unsuccessfully to rob the temple via his chief minister Heliodorus (2 Macc 3:7; cf. also Dan 11:20). In 175 Heliodorus assassinated Seleucus, but Antiochus III's third son, Antiochus IV Epiphanes, having been released from Rome as a hostage, went to Syria and, helped by Eumenes II, king of Pergamon, ousted Heliodorus and made himself king. Since that kingdom lacked political and financial stability, he attempted to unify it by a vigorous Hellenization program and by encouraging the people (c. 169) to worship himself in the form of the Olympian Zeus (Dan 11:21–24). His title "Theos Epiphanes," meaning "the manifest god," was changed by his enemies to "Epimanes," meaning "madman" or "insane". A dispute between the pro-Ptolemaic high priest Onias III and Onias's pro-Seleucid brother Jason ended in 174 when Jason secured the high priesthood by offering a larger payment of money to Antiochus and by pledging his whole-hearted support in the Hellenization of the Jerusalemites (1 Macc 1:10–15; 2 Macc 4:7–17). In 171 Jason's friend Menelaus offered Antiochus more money than Jason for the high priesthood. Antiochus accepted. Since Menelaus was outside the Aaronic line (cf. 2 Macc 4:23; 3:4), it would break a great unifying force among the Jews.

In 170 B.C. the amateur regents Eulaeus and Lenueus advised Ptolemy VI Philomater to avenge Panias and recover Coele-Syria. Antiochus heard of their plans and with a large army invaded Egypt in 170/169, defeating Ptolemy VI. He proclaimed himself king of Egypt and instigated a rivalry by making Ptolemy VI Philomater king of Memphis and his brother Ptolemy VIII Euergetes king of Alexandria (Dan 11:25–27). On returning from Egypt, Antiochus heard that the Jerusalemites with Jason's help had forced Menelaus to take refuge in the Acra. The Jews had revolted because Menelaus plundered the temple. With Menelaus, Antiochus also desecrated and plundered the temple, leaving the city under one of his commanders, Philip, a Phrygian (1 Macc 1:20–29; 2 Macc 5:18–22).

b. Maccabean revolt, 168–143 B.C.

1. *Antiochus's vengeance, 168–166* B.C. The next contact Jerusalem had with Antiochus IV was in 168 B.C. when his rival nephews united against him. Antiochus went to Egypt that same year. He subdued Memphis, and when he was nearing Alexandria, a Roman representative handed him an ultimatum from the Senate to leave Egypt at once (Dan 11:28–30). Knowing Rome's might, he quickly retreated to Palestine.

He determined to make Palestine a buffer state between himself and the Romans. He ordered a cultic Hellenization in Palestine and in 167 forbade the Jews to keep their ancestral laws and to observe the Sabbath, customary festivals, traditional sacrifices, and the circumcision of their children. He also ordered the destruction of the copies of the Torah. Idolatrous altars were set up, and the Jews were commanded to offer unclean sacrifices and to eat swine's flesh (2 Macc 6:18). On Chislev (= December) 25, 167 the temple of Jerusalem became the place of worship of the Olympian Zeus, with swine's flesh offered on the altar of Zeus erected on the altar of burnt offering (Dan 11:31–32; 1 Macc 1:41–64; 2 Macc 6:1–11). These were to be offered monthly and dedicated to Antiochus Epiphanes.

2. *Mattathias,* 166 B.C. Every village in Palestine was ordered to set up its heathen altar, and imperial delegates saw to it that the citizens offered the heathen sacrifices. In the village of Modein an aged priest named Mattathias refused to offer a heathen sacrifice when asked to do so by Antiochus IV's agent. When another Jew volunteered to offer the sacrifice, Mattathias killed him and the agent. He then tore down the altar and proclaimed, "Let everyone who is zealous for the law and supports the covenant come out with me" (1 Macc 2:15–27; Dan 11:32–35). Mattathias, his five sons (John, Simon, Judas, Eleazar, and Jonathan) and many followers fled to the mountains. This marked the beginning of the Maccabean revolt. The Hasidim, a religious group within Judaism with a great passion for the law of God, joined Mattathias in his struggle against Hellenization. They waged war against the Jews who complied with Antiochus, tore down heathen altars, circumcised children who had been left uncircumcised, and exhorted Jews everywhere to join their crusade. Mattathias died in 166 B.C., and his third son, Judas, became leader (1 Macc 2:42–70).

3. *Judas Maccabeus*, 166–160 B.C.

a. *Rededication of the temple*, 166–164 B.C. Judas proved to be the terror of his enemies and the pride of his nation. Under him the Maccabean struggle went from guerrilla warfare to well-planned battles. He won more volunteers to fight for freedom when he defeated the Syrian governors Apollonius and Seron (1 Macc 3:10–26). Antiochus, preoccupied in the East, ordered Lysias, regent of the western part of the empire, to end the rebellion and destroy the Jewish race (1 Macc 3:32–36). Judas, however, decisively defeated the Syrians at Emmaus (1 Macc 4:1–22). In 164 B.C. Lysias attacked Jerusalem from the south but was completely defeated at Beth-zur and withdrew to Antioch (1 Macc 4:28–35). Judas had regained the entire country. He marched on Jerusalem and occupied all of it except the Acra. He restored the temple, selected priests who had remained faithful, destroyed the altar of the Olympian Zeus, and built a new one. Exactly three years after its desecration (on Chislev 25), the temple with its altar was rededicated and the daily sacrifices began (1 Macc 4:36–59; 2 Macc 10:1–8). This marked the beginning of the Jewish Feast of Dedication or Lights (Hebrew Hanukkah). Judas fortified the Jerusalem walls and the city of Beth-zur on the border of Idumea.

b. *Religious freedom gained*, 163 B.C. Judah was now reasonably secure, but two things remained undone. First, all the Jews of Palestine must be independent from Antiochus's rule. After several campaigns this was accomplished.

Second, the Maccabees wanted to get rid of the Syrian control of the Acra in Jerusalem. In 163 Judas laid siege to it. Some Syrian soldiers and Hellenistic Jews escaped and went to Antioch for help (1 Macc 6:18–27). Antiochus IV had been succeeded by his nine-year-old son Antiochus V Eupator, whom Lysias crowned king (see 1 Macc 6:5–17). Immediately, Lysias and the boy-king went south where they defeated Judas at Beth-zechariah and laid siege to Jerusalem (1 Macc 6:28–54). Judas, in desperate straits for food, was saved when Lysias heard that Philip was marching from Persia to Syria to claim the kingdom for himself. Lysias was therefore anxious to make peace with Judas and guaranteed him religious freedom, but he did tear down the walls of Jerusalem (1 Macc 6:55–63). Although still under Syrian rule, the Jews had obtained religious freedom.

c. *Political freedom desired*, 162–160 B.C. Judas now wanted political freedom, but the Syrian government strengthened the Hellenistic elements among the Jews. Lysias apparently appointed the high priest Alcimus (Hebrew Jakim, or Jehoahim) who, although of Aaronic descent, was ideologically a Hellenist (cf. 1 Macc 7:14; 2 Macc 14:3–7). Meanwhile in Syria Demetrius I Soter, cousin of Antiochus V, escaped from Rome, killed both Lysias and Antiochus V, and assumed the throne. He confirmed Alcimus as high priest (162 B.C.) and sent him to Palestine, backed by an army. The Hasidim accepted Alcimus as high priest, and the Syrians guaranteed them freedom of worship. The Hasidim split from Judas's ranks but quickly returned when Alcimus broke a promise and killed sixty of them (1 Macc 7:15–20). Alcimus asked Demetrius for more military help against Judas and his followers (Hasideans) (2 Macc 14:6). Demetrius sent Nicanor, but sustained crushing defeats at Adasa (where Nicanor was killed) and at Gazara. Alcimus fled to Syria (1 Macc 7:26–50). Judas requested help from Rome, but first Demetrius sent Bacchides with Alcimus to avenge Nicanor's death. Fearful of the Syrian army, many deserted Judas, and in the Battle of Elasa Judas was slain in 160.

4. *Jonathan*, 160–143 B.C. Judas's death was a great blow to morale. The Hellenists

were temporarily in control while Jonathan and his followers were in the wilderness of Tekoa, only carrying on guerrilla warfare. Bacchides fortified Jerusalem and the Judean cities against possible Maccabean attacks. In 159 B.C. Alcimus died, and no successor was chosen. In 157 Bacchides returned to Jerusalem but was defeated at Beth-basi, made a peace treaty with Jonathan, and returned to Antioch.

Jonathan made Michmash his headquarters where he judged the people, punishing the Hellenizers (1 Macc 9:23–27). His power increased, further helped in 152 by internal struggles for power in Syria. Alexander Balas, who claimed to be the son of Antiochus Epiphanes, challenged Demetrius I. Jonathan sided with Alexander Balas. In 150 Demetrius was slain in a battle against Alexander. Alexander made Jonathan a general, governor, and high priest of Judah and was considered one of his chief friends (1 Macc 10:22–66).

New troubles came in Syria. Demetrius' son, the sixteen-year-old Demetrius II Nicator, challenged Alexander Balas in 147 B.C. and finally defeated him in 145. Jonathan unsuccessfully attacked the Acra in Jerusalem, still held by Hellenistic Jews. Demetrius II opposed this, but later conceded to Jonathan by confirming his high priesthood and granting Jonathan's request for three districts of southern Samaria.

In 143 Demetrius II's army rebelled, and Diodotus Tryphon (a general of Alexander Balas) claimed the Syrian throne for Alexander Balas' son, Antiochus VI. Jonathan sided with Tryphon and was made head of the civil and religious aspects of the Jewish community and his brother Simon head of the military. Fearful of Jonathan's success, however, Tryphon killed Jonathan.

C. Hasmonean Rule, 142–63 B.C.

The term *Hasmonean* is generally used in referring to the high priestly house from the time of Simon to 63 B.C., because the Maccabean dream had finally come true: the Israelites had become an independent nation. This independence endured until Rome's intervention in 63.

1. *Simon, 143–135 B.C.* Simon, second oldest son of Mattathias, succeeded his younger brother Jonathan. In Syria Tryphon killed Antiochus VI and reigned in his place (1 Macc 13:31–32) as a rival to Demetrius. Because Tryphon had killed Jonathan, Simon attached himself to Demetrius II on condition of Judea's complete independence. Since Demetrius no longer controlled the southern parts of the Syrian empire, he gave Simon complete exemption from past and future taxation (142 B.C.). The yoke of the Gentiles over Israel had then been removed for the first time since the Babylonian captivity, and Judea's political independence meant that they could write their own documents and treaties (1 Macc 13:33–42). Because of Tryphon's threat, Simon seized the fortress of Gazara, expelling Gentiles and replacing them with Jews and appointed his son John Hyrcanus as governor (1 Macc 13:43–48, 53; 16:1, 21). Shortly after, Simon captured the Acra in Jerusalem, which had been under Hellenistic control for more than forty years. Simon made a peace treaty with Rome and Sparta, who guaranteed freedom of worship.

Commemorating Simon's achievement, the Jews in 140 B.C. made him leader and high priest forever until there should arise a faithful prophet (1 Macc 14:25–49). The high priesthood formerly belonged to the house of Onias, but this ended in 174. Thereafter, the appointment was made by the Syrian king, but now the Jews had placed the priesthood in the hereditary line of the Hasmoneans.

In 139 Antiochus VII Sidetes took over the struggle of Demetrius (captured by the

Parthians) and enlisted Simon's cooperation. With Tryphon defeated, Simon refused to submit. Antiochus VII sent his general, Cendebeus, but he was defeated by Simon's two sons Judas and John Hyrcanus (1 Macc 15:1–14, 25–16:10).

In 135 Simon and his two sons were slain by his son-in-law, Ptolemy. He then sent men to capture Simon's second son, John Hyrcanus, at Gazara, but being forewarned, Hyrcanus captured and killed them.

2. *Hyrcanus I*, 135–104 B.C. John Hyrcanus succeeded his father as high priest and ruler of the people. Before long he had trouble because Antiochus VII asserted his claim over Judea and seized Joppa and Gazara, ravaging the land and besieging Jerusalem for more than a year. The resultant peace settlement stipulated that the Jews hand over their arms; pay heavy tribute for the return of Joppa and other cities bordering on Judea; and give hostages, one of them Hyrcanus's brother. The walls of Jerusalem also were to be destroyed, but the Syrians were not to establish a garrison in Jerusalem. Thus Israel lost her independence again.

In 129 B.C. Antiochus died after launching a campaign against the Parthians. Demetrius, released by the Parthians, again gained control of Syria (129–125), but internal troubles prevented him from bothering Hyrcanus. Hyrcanus renewed the alliance with Rome whereby Rome confirmed his independence and warned Syria against any intervention into Hyrcanus's territory. Hyrcanus promptly extended his borders, conquering Medeba in Transjordan, capturing Shechem and Mount Gerizim and destroying the Samaritan temple (128), and taking the Idumean cities of Adora and Marisa, forcing upon the Idumeans circumcision and the Jewish law. In 109 Hyrcanus and his sons conquered Samaria, enabling him to occupy the Esdraelon Valley all the way to Mount Carmel. Hyrcanus's independence was further demonstrated with the minting of coins bearing his own name, something no other Jewish king had ever done (110/109 B.C.).

With Hyrcanus's successes, there came a rift between him and the Pharisees. The Pharisees, descendants of the Hasidim, felt that the high priesthood had become worldly by Hellenization and secularization. They questioned whether Hyrcanus should be the high priest. The Sadducees, however, were antagonistic toward the Pharisees and sided with Hyrcanus.

After a thirty-one-year rule, Hyrcanus died peacefully in 104, leaving five sons.

3. *Aristobulus I*, 104–103 B.C. Hyrcanus I wanted his wife to head the civil government while his oldest son, Aristobulus I, would be high priest. Disagreeing, Aristobulus imprisoned his mother, who died of starvation, and imprisoned all his brothers except Antigonus, who shared his rule until Aristobulus had him killed. Aristobulus's rule lasted only a year, but he conquered Galilee and compelled its inhabitants to be circumcised.

4. *Alexander Janneus*, 103–76 B.C. When Aristobulus died, his widow, Salome Alexandra, released his three brothers from prison. One of them, Alexander Janneus, she appointed as king and high priest and subsequently married. He, too, had an eye for territorial expansion. He captured the coastal Greek cities from Carmel to Gaza (except Ascalon), forcing the Jewish law on the inhabitants. So successful were his conquests in Transjordan and the south that the size of the kingdom was equal to that of David and Solomon's day.

However, there were conflicts within his domain. The Hasmoneans were deviating more from their ideals, for Alexander Janneus was a drunkard who loved war and was allied with the Sadducees. Finally, at a Feast of Tabernacles celebration, Alexander

Janneus poured the water libation over his feet instead of on the altar as prescribed by the Pharisaic ritual. The people, enraged, shouted and pelted him with lemons. Alexander ordered his mercenary troops to attack, and six thousand Jews were massacred.

Revenge came in 94 when Alexander Janneus attacked Obedas, king of the Arabs, but suffered a severe defeat, barely escaping with his life. In Jerusalem, helped by foreign mercenaries, he fought six years against his people, slaying fifty thousand Jews. The Pharisees finally called on the Seleucid Demetrius III Eukairos to help them. Alexander Janneus was defeated at Shechem and fled to the mountains. However, six thousand Jews, realizing that their national existence was threatened, sided with Janneus choosing rather to side with him in a free Jewish state than be annexed to the Syrian empire. But when Alexander Janneus reestablished himself, he forced Demetrius to withdraw, and ordered eight hundred Pharisees to be crucified and to see their wives and children killed. Because of these atrocities, eight thousand Jews fled the country.

Upheavals in the Seleucid empire then affected Janneus. The Nabateans under King Aretas, opposed to Seleucid rule, invaded Judea (c. 85 B.C.). Janneus retreated to Adida, but Aretas withdrew after coming to terms with Janneus. Aretas conquered Pella, Dium, Gerasa, Gaulana, Seleucia, and Gamala (83–80 B.C.).

5. *Alexandra*, 76–67 B.C. On his deathbed (76 B.C.), Alexander Janneus appointed his wife Salome Alexandra as his successor. She selected their eldest son Hyrcanus II as high priest. Alexander Janneus advised Alexandra to make peace with the Pharisees, since they controlled the mass of the people. She did so (her brother Simeon Ben Shetah was the Pharisees' leader), and this marked the revival of the Pharisaic influence. Her younger son, Aristobulus, however, sided with the Sadducees. With Alexandra's permission, the Sadducees left Jerusalem and took control of several fortresses in other districts. Alexandra died in 67. Her reign was marked with peace both at home and abroad.

6. *Aristobulus II*, 67–63 B.C. Hyrcanus II then became king and high priest, but Aristobulus declared war on him. With many soldiers deserting him, Hyrcanus fled to Jerusalem's citadel, finally surrendered, and was forced to relinquish his positions as king and high priest (positions he had held for only three months) to Aristobulus and to retire from public life.

Hyrcanus was willing to accept this, but Antipater II, appointed governor of Idumea by Alexander Janneus, had other plans for him. He himself could not be high priest because he was an Idumean. Antipater convinced Hyrcanus that Aristobulus unlawfully took the throne that Hyrcanus was the legitimate king, and that Hyrcanus's life was in danger. Hyrcanus traveled by night from Jerusalem to Petra, the capital of Edom. Aretas offered to help Hyrcanus if he would give up the twelve cities of Moab taken by Alexander Janneus. Hyrcanus agreed, and Aretas therefore attacked Aristobulus, who was defeated and retreated to the temple mount at the time of the Passover, 65 B.C. Many people sided with Hyrcanus.

Meanwhile the Roman army under Pompey was moving through Asia Minor. Pompey sent Scaurus to Damascus where he heard of the dispute between the two brothers. Both sent emissaries asking for support. Aristobulus offered four hundred talents; Hyrcanus followed suit, but Scaurus accepted Aristobulus as being better able to pay. He commanded Aretas to withdraw or be declared an enemy of Rome. He pursued Aretas, inflicting a crushing defeat. Shortly after, Pompey arrived in Damascus, and envoys approached him from Hyrcanus, who complained that Aristobulus seized power unlawfully; from Aristobulus, who claimed his brother incompetent to rule; and from the

Pharisees, who asked for the abolition of Hasmonean rule and the restoration of high priestly rule. Pompey wanted to delay his decision until after the Nabatean campaign.

Aristobulus, displeased with this, stopped fighting for Pompey against the Nabateans. Pompey dropped the Nabatean expedition and went after Aristobulus. Aristobulus lost heart and Pompey asked for the surrender of Jerusalem in exchange for stopping hostilities. When Pompey's general, Gabinius, was barred from the city, Pompey was outraged and attacked it. Aristobulus's followers wanted to defend themselves, but Hyrcanus's followers, the majority, succeeded in opening the gates. Aristobulus's men held the temple mount for three months before Pompey entered and killed twelve thousand Jews (63 B.C.). Pompey entered the Holy of Holies, but did not disturb it; in fact, he ordered its cleansing. He also ordered the resumption of sacrifices. Hyrcanus was reinstated as high priest, and Aristobulus, his two daughters and two sons, Alexander and Antigonus, were taken to Rome as prisoners of war. Alexander escaped. In the triumphal parade in 61 Aristobulus was made to walk before Pompey's chariot.

This marked the end of the seventy-nine years of the Jewish nation's independence and the end of the Hasmonean house. Hyrcanus, the high priest, was merely a vassal of the Roman Empire.

D. Roman Rule, 63–4 B.C.

1. *Hyrcanus II, 63–40 B.C.* Although Hyrcanus was reappointed high priest, Antipater was the power behind the throne and responsible for Hyrcanus's honor. Antipater proved useful to the Romans in government and in operations against the Hasmoneans. Gabinius again defeated Alexander, Aristobulus's son (55 B.C.) and in Jerusalem he reorganized the government according to Antipater's wishes.

Antipater and his Arabian wife Cypros had four sons: Phasael, Herod, Joseph, Pheroras, and a daughter—Salome.

When Julius Caesar defeated Pompey in Egypt in 48 B.C., Hyrcanus and Antipater joined him. Caesar made Antipater a tax-exempt Roman citizen, appointed him procurator of Judea, and reconfirmed Hyrcanus's high priesthood with the title of Ethnarch of the Jews. Antipater then suppressed disorder in the country and appealed to the restless Judean population to be loyal to Hyrcanus. The real ruler was Antipater, who appointed his son Phasael governor of Jerusalem and his second son Herod governor of Galilee in 47. Herod rid Galilee of bandits.

After Julius Caesar's murder in 44, Cassius and others came to Syria. Antipater selected Herod, Phasael, and Malichus to raise the taxes demanded by Cassius. Herod was very successful in this, and Cassius appointed him governor of Coele-Syria. Since the Herods were gaining strength, Malichus bribed the butler to poison Antipater. Herod killed Malichus.

Herod, an Idumean, became betrothed to Mariamne, granddaughter of Hyrcanus II. This betrothal strengthened Herod's position, for he would become natural regent when Hyrcanus died.

In 42 B.C., when Antony defeated Cassius, the Jewish leaders accused Herod and Phasael of usurping power while leaving Hyrcanus with titular honors. Herod's defense nullified these charges. Antony asked Hyrcanus who would be the best qualified ruler, and Hyrcanus chose Herod and Phasael. Antony appointed them as tetrarchs of Judea.

2. *Antigonus, 40–37 B.C.* In 40 B.C. the Parthians appeared in Syria. They joined Antigonus in trying to remove Hyrcanus. After several skirmishes, the Parthians asked for

peace. Phasael and Hyrcanus went to Galilee to meet the Parthian king, who treacherously put Phasael and Hyrcanus in chains. Herod moved to Masada and then to Petra. Antigonus was made king. To prevent the possibility of Hyrcanus's restoration to high priesthood, Antigonus mutilated him. Phasael died and Hyrcanus was taken to Parthia.

Herod went to Rome where he was designated king of Judea. Late 40 or early 39 B.C. Herod returned to Palestine and, aided by Antony's legate Sossius, he recaptured Galilee, and finally Jerusalem fell in the summer of 37. At Herod's request, the Romans beheaded Antigonus so ending Hasmonean rule.

3. Herod the Great, 37–4 B.C.

a. *Consolidation, 37–25 B.C.* During this period Herod had to contend with four powerful forces. First, the people and the Pharisees. The Pharisees did not like Herod—he was Idumean, half-Jew, and a friend of the Romans. Judeans who opposed him were punished; those he won over received favors and honors.

The second hostile group was the aristocracy with Antigonus. Herod executed forty-five of the wealthiest and most prominent and appropriated their property.

The third adversary was the Hasmonean family. Alexandra, mother of Herod's wife, Mariamne, caused much of the trouble. This began when Herod appointed as high priest the Aaronic Ananel (Hananeel) to replace Hyrcanus, disqualified through mutilation. Alexandra considered this an offense to the Hasmonean line and pressed the claim of her son Aristobulus. Finally, Alexandra, with Cleopatra's pressure on Antony, unlawfully forced Herod to set aside Ananel (a high priest was to hold office for life) and made Aristobulus high priest at age seventeen. Because of Aristobulus's growing popularity, Herod contrived to have him "accidentally" drowned at a swimming pool at Jericho, and arranged an elaborate funeral. Although the people never questioned the official version, Alexandra believed Aristobulus was murdered. She reported this to Cleopatra who persuaded Antony to challenge Herod, but Herod persuaded Antony to free him of any charges. Returning to Judea, he put Alexandra in chains and under guard.

The fourth enemy was Cleopatra. In 34 B.C. she persuaded Antony to give her Phoenicia, part of Arabia, and the fertile district of Jericho. In 32, however, civil war broke out between Octavius and Antony, resulting in Octavius's victory in the Battle of Actium. Herod executed Hyrcanus II, the only remaining claimant to the throne, convinced Octavius of his loyalty, and was confirmed in his royal rank (30 B.C.).

Octavius gained control of Egypt when he defeated Antony, who with Cleopatra committed suicide in 30 B.C. Herod went to Egypt and Augustus not only gave him the title of king but returned to him Jericho, Gazara, Hippos, Samaria, Gaza, Anthedon, Joppa, and Straton's Tower.

Herod's domestic affairs, however, were far from peaceful. Having long doubted the loyalty of Mariamne he finally had her executed in 29 B.C. Herod never got over this. He fell ill, and because his recovery was doubtful, Alexandra plotted against him, but he had her executed in 28. A similar fate befell his brother-in-law Costobarus, governor of Idumea, who was again suspected of Hasmonean sympathies. Herod killed Costobarus and his followers who had remained loyal to Antigonus; no male relatives of Hyrcanus survived to dispute Herod's occupancy of the throne.

b. *Prosperity, 25–14 B.C.* Herod carefully trod the road between Roman and Jewish demands. He introduced quinquennial games in honor of Caesar and built theaters, amphitheaters, and race courses for both men and horses, all in violation of the Jewish law. About 24 B.C. Herod built a royal palace and built or rebuilt many fortresses and Gentile temples, including the rebuilding of Straton's Tower, renamed Caesarea. His greatest building was the temple in Jerusalem, begun c. 20 B.C., and perhaps his "atonement for having slain so many sages of Israel" (Midrash: Num 14:8).

In 23/22 B.C. Octavius, now named Augustus, gave Herod Trachonitis, Batanea, and Auranitis, and (in 20 B.C.) Zenodorus. Herod's brother Pheroras, was given Perea. Herod in return erected a beautiful temple for Augustus near Paneion in Zenodorus. At this time Herod remitted a third of the taxes to bring good will among those displeased with his emphasis on Graeco-Roman culture and religion. Later in 14 B.C., Herod once again reduced the taxes by one-fourth.

This period (25–14 B.C.) was the most brilliant in his reign, but its end marked the beginning of great trouble in the area.

c. *Domestic troubles, 14–4 B.C.* Herod had married ten wives and this led to domestic infighting. His first wife was Doris, mother of Antipater. Herod repudiated them in 37 B.C. when he married Mariamne I, granddaughter of Hyrcanus, who bore him five children. The older sons were Alexander and Aristobulus, who played an important part during this period of Herod's life. In late 24 Herod married Mariamne II, by whom he had Herod (Philip). His fourth wife was a Samaritan, Malthace, by whom he had Archelaus and Antipas. His fifth wife, Cleopatra of Jerusalem, was the mother of Philip (the Tetrarch). Of the other five wives, only Pallas, Phaedra, and Elpsis are known by name.

The main rivalry was between Mariamne I's two sons, Alexander and Aristobulus, and Doris's son Antipater. Herod's will in 22 B.C. would have made Alexander and Aristobulus his successors, but because they allegedly plotted against him, Herod made out a new will in 13 B.C. declaring Antipater to be the sole heir. A later will, however, named Antipater as first successor and after him were to be Alexander and Aristobulus.

Strife flared up again between Antipater, Herod's sister Salome, and Herod's brother Pheroras on one hand, and Alexander and Aristobulus on the other. Antipater played on Herod's morbid fears. The unhappy situation ended finally in 7 B.C. where, on Augustus's instructions, Alexander and Aristobulus were tried, found guilty, and executed by strangulation at Sebaste, the place where Herod had married their mother thirty years before.

Herod then drew up a fourth will, naming Antipater sole heir, and Herod (Philip, Mariamne II's son) successor in the event of Antipater's death. The death of Herod's brother Pheroras was found to have been caused by a poison Antipater had sent to Pheroras in order to kill Herod. This sealed the fate of Antipater. Herod made out a fifth will, which bypassed his eldest sons, Archelaus and Philip (the Tetrarch), and named Antipas as his sole successor.

Shortly before Herod's death, there occurred the well-known incident of the magi; the divine instruction that took Joseph, Mary, and Jesus to Egypt, and Herod's massacre of all the male children of Bethlehem who were two years and under (Matt 2:1–16).

Herod was now nearly seventy years old, and his sickness grew worse. Two rabbis stirred up the people to tear down the offensive eagle from the temple gate. Herod had those involved in the act executed. Antipater also was executed, permission having finally arrived from Rome. Herod altered his will by nominating Archelaus as king, his brother Antipas as Tetrarch of Galilee and Perea, and his brother Philip as Tetrarch of Gaulanitis, Trachonitis, Batanea, and Paneas. Five days later Herod died. Although the will was disputed, his last wishes remained intact except that Archelaus was designated ethnarch rather than king.

II. Internal Developments

A. Literary Activity

During the intertestamentary period, literary activity within Judaism centered around the Septuagint (see the article THE TRANSMISSION AND TRANSLATION OF THE BIBLE, pp. 39–57) and the Apocrypha and pseudepigrapha (see the article THE APOCRYPHA AND PSEUDEPIGRAPHA, pp. 161–75).

B. Spiritual Conditions

Returning from the Babylonian captivity, the Jews ceased their idolatrous worship. The restored temple was meager compared to Solomon's, and their interest in it waned. The increasing importance of the synagogue diminished the singular importance of the temple. With the synagogues came also the rabbis, who taught the Torah and its observance. Although the temple ritual was still observed, the teaching of the synagogue encouraged a deep personal religion. Hence, Judaism during the intertestamental times became a religion of the Torah.

Because of the persecution suffered, there was a rise of the messianic expectation as seen in the increase of apocalyptic literature. God would raise up a messianic leader or leaders to deliver them from the foreign oppressors and set up the promised messianic kingdom.

C. Parties

1. *The Pharisees.* The first mention of the Pharisees was at the time of Jonathan (160–143 B.C.), but the first time they appear during the Hasmonean period was in their conflict with John Hyrcanus (135–104). Their probable origin goes back to the Hasidim who fought with the Maccabees against the Seleucid Hellenism. The word *Pharisee* probably came from the word meaning "separated" (i.e., separated from the sinful or unclean). The Pharisees were primarily of the middle class and had the following of the people. They used the synagogue for teaching purposes, maintaining that the oral law was equal in authority with the written Torah. They believed in the immortality of the soul, reincarnation, and in the over-ruling of fate. They expected the Messiah to deliver them from the foreign oppressors.

2. *The Sadducees.* The Sadducees' origin has been debated; some trace it from Zadok, the high priest in Solomon's time. But the Sadducees never claimed that. In fact, they appeared when the Zadokite priesthood died out. They had more interest in the ceremonies of the temple than in some of the hairsplitting interpretations of the Torah. They believed in a literal interpretation of only the written Torah and not the oral law. Their interests were in the political and secular realm in order to continue the temple and the priesthood. Their influence was among the wealthy of the nation. They believed that fate is in one's own hand and denied both the resurrection of the dead and the existence of angels (Matt 22:23; Mark 12:18; Luke 20:27; Acts 23:8). They did not see any messianic deliverance.

3. *The Essenes and the Qumran.* The Essenes and the Qumran community probably had their origin in the Hasidim of the Maccabean times, who were zealous for the Torah

and resisted the advance of Hellenism. (see the article THE DEAD SEA SCROLLS, pp. 395–405, for the Qumran community and the DSS.)

D. Preparation for the New Testament

When the Persians defeated Babylon, the Jews went back to their homeland with no desire to worship idols, but unable to restore the temple to its former glory. With the importance of the synagogue increasing, Jewish life centered around the Torah rather than the temple. With the increasing influence of Hellenism, they saw the need to have their Scriptures translated into Greek; persecuted by the Seleucids, they became more engrossed with the hope of a messianic deliverance. Rome's capture of much of the Mediterranean world brought peace, although its power brought tyranny. At this point, Jesus Christ entered human history to bring man into an eternal communication with God, to bring peace to individuals as well as to the world, and to deliver people from the bondage of sin. He was rejected and crucified both by his people and by the pagan world, but the message of Christ's death and resurrection went out in Greek, the *lingua franca* of the day, into the world that was under the Pax Romana, bringing the hope of messianic deliverance both for the present and for the future, when Messiah will rule the world.

III. Bibliography

Aharoni, Yohanan, and Avi-Yonah, Michael. *The Macmillan Bible Atlas.* New York: Macmillan, 1968.

Bevan, Edwin R. *The House of Seleucus.* 2 vols. London: Edward Arnold, 1902.

_____. *Jerusalem under the High-Priests.* London: Edward Arnold, 1904.

_____. "Syria and the Jews." In *The Cambridge Ancient History.* Edited by S.A. Cook, F.E. Adcock, and M.P. Charlesworth. vol. 8, pp. 394–436. Cambridge: Cambridge University Press, 1932.

Bartlett, John R. *The First and Second Books of the Maccabees,* in *The Cambridge Bible Commentary.* Edited by P.R. Ackroyd, A.R.C. Leaney, and J.W. Packer. Cambridge: Cambridge University Press, 1973.

Bickerman, Elias. *From Ezra to the Last of the Maccabees.* New York: Schocken, 1961.

Cross, Frank Moore. *The Ancient Library of Qumran and Modern Biblical Studies.* Rev. ed. Garden City, N.Y.: Anchor Books, 1961.

Eddy, Samuel K. *The King Is Dead.* Lincoln, Neb.: University of Nebraska Press, 1961.

Farmer, William Reuben. *Maccabees, Zealots, and Josephus.* New York: Columbia University Press, 1956.

Grant, Michael. *The Jews in the Roman World.* New York: Scribner, 1973.

Hengel, Martin. *Judaism and Hellenism.* 2 vols. Translated by John Bowden. London: SCM, 1974.

Jeremias, Joachim. *Jerusalem in the Time of Jesus.* 3rd ed. Translated by F.H. and C.H. Cave. Philadelphia: Fortress, 1969.

Jones, A.H.M. *The Herods of Judaea.* Rev. ed. Oxford: Clarendon, 1967.

LaSor, William S. *The Dead Sea Scrolls and the New Testament.* Grand Rapids: Eerdmans, 1972.

Mansoor, Menahem. *The Dead Sea Scrolls.* Leiden: E.J. Brill, 1964.

Metzger, Bruce. *An Introduction of the Apocrypha.* New York: Oxford University Press, 1957.

Moore, George Foot. *Judaism in the First Centuries of the Christian Era: The Age of the Tannaim.* 3 vols. Cambridge, Mass.: Harvard University Press, 1927–30.

Neusner, Jacob. *The First Century Judaism in Crisis.* Nashville: Abingdon, 1975.

Olmstead, A.T. *History of the Persian Empire.* Chicago: University of Chicago Press, 1948.

Reicke, Bo. *The New Testament Era.* Translated by David E. Green. Philadelphia: Fortress, 1968.

Rostovtzeff, M. *The Social and Economic History of the Hellenistic World.* 3 vols. Oxford: Clarendon, 1941.

Russell, D.S. *Between the Testaments.* London: SCM, 1960.

————. *The Jews From Alexander to Herod.* vol. 5 of *The New Clarendon Bible.* London: Oxford University Press, 1967.

Safrai, S., and Stern, M., eds. *The Jewish People in the First Century.* 2 vols. Assen, Netherlands: Van Gorcum, 1974-75.

Schürer, Emil. *The History of the Jewish People in the Age of Jesus Christ (175 B.C.-A.D. 135).* Rev. ed. by Geza Vermes and Fergus Millar, vol. 1. Edinburgh: T. & T. Clark, 1973.

Snaith, Norman H. *The Jews From Cyrus to Herod.* Nashville: Abingdon, n.d.

Tarn, W.W. "The Struggle of Egypt against Syria and Macedonia." In *The Cambridge Ancient History.* Edited by S.A. Cook, F.E. Adcock, and M.P. Charlesworth. vol. 7, pp. 699-731. Cambridge: Cambridge University Press, 1928.

Tcherikover, Victor. *Hellenistic Civilization and the Jews.* Translated by S. Applebaum. Philadelphia: Jewish Publication Society of America, 1961.

Zeitlin, Solomon. *The Rise and Fall of the Judaean State.* 2 vols. Philadelphia: Jewish Publication Society of America, 1962-67.

THE LANGUAGE OF THE OLD TESTAMENT

G. Douglas Young

G. Douglas Young

B.Sc., Acadia University; B.D., S.T.M., Faith Theological Seminary; Ph.D., Dropsie University

President, Institute of Holy Land Studies (Jerusalem)

THE LANGUAGE OF THE OLD TESTAMENT

I. Introduction

The primary purpose of this article is to point out and describe those areas of the languages of the OT where variant interpretations of phenomena are possible. It is not intended to be a grammar of the languages themselves or to deal with matters comprehensible only to technical students. But those who cannot read the languages should know some of the problems the translator or interpreter faces. To put it in another way, one might say that the article deals with those aspects of the languages of the OT that are of importance for the translation and interpretation of the OT. It should, then, help the reader understand why the various English language versions differ and show him why Bible translation is a process that goes on from year to year as the knowledge of these and other Semitic languages progresses.

II. Relation to the Semitic Language Group

Two languages were employed in the writing of the OT. Aramaic occurs in Ezra 4:8–6:18; 7:12–26; Jeremiah 10:11; Daniel 2:46–7:28; and two words in Genesis 31:47. The rest of the text is in Hebrew. Apart from these two languages, only isolated loan words are used. They come from Egyptian, Greek, Persian, and other languages. They are found in their proper contexts, as, for example, Egyptian loan words in the Genesis account of the presence of the Israelites in Egypt, and Persian words in the exilic and postexilic writings.

Hebrew and Aramaic are both members of the Semitic language family (so named by modern scholars after Noah's eldest son, Gen 6:10). Both of them belong to the northwestern group of these languages, viz., those spoken in antiquity mainly by peoples of the Levant (modern Syria, Lebanon, and Israel). Within this grouping there were at least three main languages: Aramaic, Canaanite, and Ugaritic. Hebrew is evidently a descendant from Canaanite along with Phoenician and Moabite. Strong Aramaic influences were brought to bear on the language of the Israelites and are felt in the resultant biblical Hebrew. Though Canaan is reckoned as a descendant of Ham, the Canaanite language(s) is/are Semitic.

Abraham came to Palestine from the ancient Sumerian-Akkadian world in the southern part of Mesopotamia, the region between the Tigris and Euphrates rivers, but only after a sojourn of some seventy-five years in the north central part of the land between the rivers. He is called an Aramaean (Deut 26:5) and he married his son Isaac to Rebekah, the sister of Laban, both of whom were Arameans (Gen 25:20). That Hebrew grew up in Palestine itself is seen from the use of the words *yām* (sea) for the west, and *negeb* (dry, parched) for the south.

The OT itself refers to its language in two ways: the language of Canaan (Isa 19:18) and the language of Judah (2 Kings 18:26, 28; Neh 13:24; Isa 36:11). Not until 130 B.C. is it referred to as Hebrew—in the prologue of the apocryphal book Ecclesiasticus; later, in the NT (John 5:2; 19:13; Acts 21:40), it is also referred to as Hebrew.

One of the basic structural features of all of the Semitic languages is triconsonantalism. This means that a given concept is carried by three consonants. For an example, the consonants *m-l-k* carry the idea of ruling or reigning. With changes of vowels between the consonants, with the addition of prefixes and suffixes, or with both, various related ideas are expressed. In Hebrew, *melek* is "a king"; *melākîm*, "kings"; *malkêhem*, "their kings"; *yimlōk*, "he will rule"; *mālekāh*, "she ruled"; *himlîk*, "he caused to reign"; *mamlākāh*, "kingdom"; *malkût*, "royalty"; etc.

III. Phonetics

Prior to the middle of the first millennium A.D. the biblical texts were not written with vowels or diacritical marks. *Malkêhem*, "their kings," was written *mlkhm*, for example. While Phoenician remained consonantal in its spelling throughout the OT period, Hebrew and Aramaic (and Moabite) eventually developed the use of certain consonants as vowel indicators at the end of words. In the earlier stages, *h* was used for vowels of the a, e, and o classes, while *y* served for i vowels and *w* for u vowels (and later on for final o vowels). Within a word, heterophonous diphthongs, *ay* and *aw*, were represented by *y* and *w*, but in dialects where these diphthongs had been reduced to ê and ô respectively (e.g., Phoenician, Northern Israelite), no consonantal sign was written. In the Judean dialect, the reduction of internal diphthongs was not thoroughly carried out; we find *šôr*, "ox," (from **šawr*)[1] and *yôm*, "day," (from *yawm:* some scholars have posited an original **yam*) alongside *mâwet*, "death," and *ḥêq*, "breast, lap," (fr om **ḥayq*) alongside *bâyit*, "house." In inscriptions from the eighth century B.C. (Siloam tunnel) and the seventh century (Hashavyahw, Lachish, Arad), some of these differences are reflected in the spelling. Final diphthongs, usually arising from the loss of a short vowel after a *y* or *w* (or the ellision of *h* between two vowels in pronominal suffixes), were usually reduced to a vowel (though not always), which was then represented by a consonantal sign. Unaccented diphthongs were usually reduced, though just when this happened in the Judean dialect it is impossible to ascertain since the scribes continued to write them with consonantal signs. Toward the end of the Judean monarchy (the seventh to sixth centuries B.C.), scribes had already begun to use *y* for writing internal long *i* vowels but not uniformly. Their guiding principle seems to have been the need to avoid ambiguity. The recently discovered Arad letters provide several striking examples of this innovation and have led to reevaluation of the Lachish letters as well.

When vowels were finally added, two separate systems, the Babylonian and the Palestinian, were used. The former for the most part consisted of supralinear marks and the latter of sublinear ones. Since only the consonantal signs appeared in the autographs (the texts as they came from the pens of the authors), only the consonantal texts are considered inspired in the historic, theological sense of that word.

Vowel letters, and later a full vocalic system, were added to the consonantal texts because the ancients feared the loss of the ability to pronounce the words as the language became more and more classical and the texts were no longer those of a living spoken language. Earlier pronunciations of isolated words or phrases may be checked in various ways. This is true particularly, but not exclusively, of proper names found in the Greek and other early translations of the Bible, and also in the Assyrian historical texts.

The alphabets of both of the OT languages consist of twenty-two consonants (later twenty-three when *ś* [s] and *š* [sh] were distinguished). These languages are written and read from right to left. There are sounds not found in the English form of the Indo-European language group such as ', a glottal stop; *ḥ*, a fricative sound made in the throat by a strong aspiration or friction while the throat is not constricted; *ṭ*, an emphatic *t* distinguishable from the normal *t* sound but hard for a speaker of English to produce; ' a guttural or laryngeal sound made by a severe restriction of the throat and actually heard only by its effect on the following vowel; *ṣ* another emphatic sound, pronounced somewhat like English *ts* but with a mild explosive or emphatic addition; *q* a stop distinguished from *k*, made in the uvular area; and *r*, a trilled sound made in the uvular area (a fairly satisfactory substitute is a trill formed with the tongue on the roof of the mouth). The English *sh* sound is carried by the phoneme *š*.

The vowels are basically three—an *a*, an *i*, and a *u*. Under definable circumstances, depending on the origin of the vowel, the position of the accent in the word, the nature of the syllable, and the position of the syllable with relation to the accent, these basic three vowels are modified. They have longer and shorter variants, so that two *a*'s are possible, four types of *i*'s (*ĭ, ĕ, ē, î*) and four types of *u*'s (*u, û, ō, ŏ*). All three vowels under the proper circumstances may shorten to a "shewa," a sound like the *a* on the end of the English word "sofa" or the *o* in the verb "to convict."

---

[1]The asterisk indicates that the form is not actually found in the language but is a hypothetical suggestion of a possible original form.

IV. Parts of Speech

The parts of speech are best described in three categories by the manner in which they are inflected. Category one—nouns, adjectives, and "participles" (see further below)—consists of words inflected in one way. (While pronouns are not inflected and are nondeclinable, they are here listed with the nouns as independent words on the order of proper nouns rather than with the particles.) Verbs, the second category, are inflected in another manner. What are in English called prepositions, conjunctions, and adverbs are classed here as particles, noninflected. The infinitives, like the particles, are also noninflected but are usually included with the nouns.

A. Nouns, Adjectives, Participles, Infinitives

The first category is inflected for "state," gender, and number. The "states" are two, absolute or construct. The latter is used in genitival relationships. The genders are masculine and feminine only. There is no neuter. All things are categorized either as male or female. This creates certain problems for the translator and the interpreter. Besides singular and plural, these languages are inflected for a "dual," in both masculine and feminine genders. The "dual" endings indicate a pair, such as two eyes, two ears, two hands, etc. Possessive pronouns are suffixed to nouns and "participles."

The "participle" in form is a simple noun but of adjectival or descriptive character in function. At the same time, however, it has a verbal character in that it is in some way connected with an action or an activity. Thus the "participle" occupies a position between the adjective and the verb. (It is for this reason that the word is here placed in quotation marks.) In form it is a noun (adjectival) but it describes or expresses the state or condition of the activity of the person or thing being described. It is inflected like a noun, yet can take a direct object like a verb. Two "infinitives" are recognized by the grammarians. The infinitive absolute is called by Gesenius (*Hebrew Grammar*, Kautzsch, Cowley, paragraph 113a) "the name of an action." It speaks of an action without regard to the time or mood of that action. The infinitive construct, like a noun, may be the subject or object of a verb or the genitive after a noun, and thus it often functions as a gerund.

B. Verbs

1. *Morphology (stems and "tenses").* The Hebrew verb by internal modifications, vowel changes, and/or doubling of one or other of the three root consonants, is made to express various modifications of the basic idea of the three root consonants. The simple stem, called the Qal, carries the basic idea of the three consonants. The Niph'al is primarily reflexive but in many cases is passive. The Hiph'il and Hoph'al are frequently but not exclusively causative active and causative passive. The Pi'el is primarily factitive or causative. Its passive may be the Pu'al or the Hithpa'el, which expresses reflexive or reciprocal action, but may also be passive.

An example might help to clarify the system. The root *r'h* expresses the idea of seeing in the simple or Qal stem. In the Niph'al it is "to appear" or "to be seen." In the Hithpa'el the meaning is "to look at each other." In the Hiph'il it is "to cause (one) to see (something)" or "to show" and in the Hoph'al it is "be caused to see" or "be shown."

This system is by no means as simple or cut and dried as just outlined. For an example, "to study, to learn" is expressed by the Qal stem. "To teach," however, is not Hiph'il, causing someone to learn, but Pi'el. It is not learning intensively but urging someone to learn, perhaps. In the Qal stem the verb *ḥyh* signifies "to live." In both Hiph'il and Pi'el it can mean "to restore to life" or "to make to live" (after killing). The meaning is the same (2 Kings 8:5; Deut 32:39). The point is that the system is not an automatic one but the dictionary (which is a compendium of all usages) must in the last analysis supply the definition in most cases. This is another instance where the nuances may be known only by careful reference to the Hebrew or Aramaic. Here, therefore, is another area of significant difference between English and Hebrew usage, an area of great importance to the interpreter or translator of the Bible.

Verbs are inflected for person, gender, and number. They may be transitive and thus capable of taking a direct object, or intransitive, expressing a state and not taking direct objects. There is a suffixed "tense" often called by English grammarians the perfect, and a form with prefixes (sometimes suffixes also) called the imperfect. A modification of the imperfect, called the imperative, basically expresses commands. Another modification (sometimes seen as a shortened form of the second and third persons, yet sometimes also indistinguishable from the ordinary imperfect), is called jussive. It expresses a desire that something should or should not happen. The fact that the forms are often indistinguishable creates further problems for the interpreter and provides yet another reason why a knowledge of the original language is highly important for the translator or interpreter. The so-called cohortative (another modification of the imperfect) is used to express self-encouragement, a wish, a request for permission, and other nuances of the basic verbal idea. It is noted by an *āh* suffixed to the first person imperfect, singular or plural, or to the second person singular imperative.

2. Syntax (older view). One of the most complicated syntactic considerations in the Hebrew language is that of the "tenses." Of all the variables that tax the translator and interpreter, none is more complex or more important than the interpretation of the tenses. Such interpretation is further complicated when the particle *wa* or one of its derivatives is prefixed to the verbal form. For many years, following S.R. Driver's *Hebrew Tenses*, the "perfect" and the "imperfect" were interpreted as aspects of action and not as actual tenses in the sense of representing order of time whether past, present, or future. The "perfect" was thought to represent the aspect of completed action. The context had to determine the order of time, whether past, present, or future. The "imperfect" was said to express the idea of incomplete, continuing, inceptive, terminating, or frequentative action. Again, the order of time had to be inferred from the context.

The verbs preceded by some form of the particle *wa* were said to express other functions. Some called the *wa* a "*waw* conversive" while others called it "*waw* consecutive." The first conceived of the *wa* that was accompanied by a doubling of the verbal preformative in the "imperfect" as having the effect of converting that "imperfect" into a "narrative past tense" and the *wa* that did not double the preformative (called the simple *waw*) as causing the "imperfect" to serve a modal function in its clause, expressing an idea such as "that it may." Those who conceived of this *wa* with the "imperfect" as the "*waw* consecutive" felt that there was an idea of consecution of tenses in Hebrew. If a section of narration commenced with a "perfect," it would be followed by an "imperfect" with "*waw* consecutive" prefixed and so on until the sequence of perfect ideas was to be discontinued and some other aspect was to be introduced. In effect, this made this particular form into a narrative past tense.

The "*waw*" with the "perfect" was looked upon in a somewhat similar manner. It "converted" the "perfect" to conform to a preceding "imperfect" idea, or else it continued (consecution) a previous "imperfect" idea. Driver said of the simple "*waw*" with the "perfect" that "it is a rare and isolated occurrence." Thus, for Driver, the majority of the "*waws*" with the "perfect" were converting, or as others called them, consecutive, ones. This exception to the system should have raised questions for the descriptive grammarian as to the authenticity of the entire system. (Yet one must reckon with the fact that some of the "*waws*" with the first and second persons singular and first person plural of the "perfect" do shift the accents to the last syllable while others do not.)

Thus some have regarded the verbal system of Hebrew as an aspectual one where order of time or tenses (past, present, and future) is absent in general and kind of action (continuing, inceptive, frequentative, incomplete, complete, etc.) is the predominant feature. With that assumption, many have said that Hebrew cannot be an "exact" language and therefore is incapable of exactness of expression like Greek or Latin. The implication is that Hebrew is not a language that can express philosophical ideas and concepts as the others. The assumption that a tense system does not exist is now proved incorrect and there is no reason why, had Hebrew been their mother tongue, Plato or Aristotle could not have expressed themselves as precisely in Hebrew as they did in Greek.

3. *Syntax (contemporary view)*. While not all the data has yet been adequately analyzed and described—scholars too long wrongly assumed that Hebrew did not have a tense system—enough research now clearly indicates the presence of such a system. This basic fact established, scholars are at work analyzing such matters as the use of particles, sentence structure, word order, and other factors, in order to progress in describing the language system accurately.

As will be seen below, the various conjugation patterns may not have been intrinsically temporal in nature, but since they were adaptable to various nuances of tense, they came to be used in clearly understood syntactic patterns to express tenses.

The suffix conjugation usually called the "perfect" (*qātal*) arose from the nominal sentence, noun or adjective (including the participle) plus the pronominal subject. It was tenseless in origin, and not a past tense. In East Semitic the stative (intransitive) function predominates but does not completely eliminate the transitive function. In West Semitic it becomes predominantly the simple past tense for the transitive verbs and present general tense for the stative (e.g., "I" plus "love," "I" plus "know," "I" plus "(am) old," etc.). Words with the thematic vowels *i* and *u* in the basic form are usually statives and denote the state of the subject instead of describing an action. So are many of the words where, because of a guttural, an *a* appears in the place of the *i* or *u*. The thematic vowel *a*, except in the case of some of the words with gutturals as just noted, usually indicates words that are transitive (Barth's law). In some cases a thematic *a* is found in words whose meaning has shifted over the years from being purely stative to expressing definite action. Here, then, is another case of the importance of control not only of the Hebrew language itself but of its sources too.

The suffixed conjugation (noted immediately above) preceded by the particle *w* (*wᵊqātaltā*) is one way in which the future is expressed. The tense is clearly future when the sufformatives are *tā* or *tî* and the accent rests on them instead of on the next-to-the-last syllable. In all other cases (with other sufformatives), it is quite generally also future. Mere coordination of past tenses with this form is very rare. This in itself is evidence of the future tense of the form. The construction is ancient, for it is seen in Ugaritic and the El Amarna letters.

The form *yaqtulu* (the original form of the prefixed, or the "imperfect" tense) expresses continuousness, the present-future tense, the narrative historical present ("he reaches," "he leaves"), e.g., habitual or customary action, and even sometimes the past iterative or past continuative. One may wonder how a form can be present-future yet sometimes also past. A question and its answer will show us how this may be. Someone asks, "Are you going to town?" To this the reply is, "Yes, I'm going." Now, this may mean, "I will be going" (present-future). Or it may also mean, "I do go," meaning "I go and have gone from time to time in the past." So present-future and past continuative may be seen in one form. In Hebrew the final *u* is lost and the earlier forms ending in *ina* (2nd fem. sing.) and *una* (2nd and 3rd masc. pl.) lost the *na* in each case. (Occasionally archaizing forms with the *nun* are still found.)

Some are trying to demonstrate that there is a present-future form with the second radical doubled (e.g., *iparras*, to use the Akkadian paradigm word). H.L. Ginsberg long since has proved this form to be nonexistent in Ugaritic. The El Amarna scribes, who knew the Akkadian verbal system, did not normally use *iparras* forms to express present-future and past-continuous; instead, they put their own Canaanite sufformatives (for *yaqtul-u*, etc.) on Akkadian verbs!

The form *yaqtul* is the volitive or jussive. Due to the loss of final short vowels in Hebrew, the strong verbs usually do not distinguish *yaqtulu* from *yaqtul*. The two forms, however, may be separated from one another by noting changes of the thematic vowel when that vowel is essentially a long one and occurs in the final syllable. It may also be noted in the verbs *lamed-he* when the final *h* is cut off. The volitive, called jussive, expresses a wish or permission. The sense is modal and may be expressed by using "may, might, would, could, should," etc. In Hebrew this form is preserved mainly in the second and third persons.

The verb *yaqtula* is an emphatic volitive or jussive derived from the Arabic energic by older grammarians. In Hebrew this form is preserved in the first person, cohortative. That the *yaqtula* was a more emphatic volitive is seen by the occasional use of the *a* suffix on imperatives singular.

Besides its jussive functions, the *yaqtul* form could also serve as a past tense, usually for single occurrences—*yaqtul* preterite. This was certainly the case in pre-Hebraic dialects such as southern Canaanite and Ugaritic, though Phoenician tended to prefer the *qatal* in this function.

The *yaqtulu*, *yaqtul*, and *yaqtula* cannot be differentiated from one another by form in every case in Hebrew, for there the final vowels (*u* or *a*) were dropped and therefore all sometimes appeared as *yaqtul*. However, clear cases of the three are readily noticeable in the biblical text. That is sufficient evidence to indicate that the three forms did exist in Hebrew. Further research will doubtless show that context, syntax, word order, or other characteristics will make the finer differentiations clear. The translation value is not only dependent on the form, as noted. The kind of sentence or clause in which the verb is used is also a determining feature. One illustration of the contextual importance may serve to clarify this matter: An "imperfect" (volitive) *yaqtul* preceded by *wᵉ* and following an imperative, jussive, or cohortative has modal force: "Write [imperative] ... so that he may hear [*wᵉyišma'*]." This is to say that tense and mode differentiation is expressed both by a variation of the word order within the clause and by a variation of the verbal form used immediately after the *wᵉ*.

The word *yaqtul* is a preterite when preceded by *wa* with the doubling of the preformative. This form was formerly mistakenly called "the *waw* conversive" or "*waw* consecutive with the imperfect." It is the narrative past tense so common in Hebrew prose and is used when the past tense is required at the beginning of either a sentence or a clause. In Hebrew poetry, the *yaqtul* preterite is usually found without the *waw*.

Evidence from the El Amarna letters confirms that *yaqtul* could serve as a preterite (without the *wa*), thus suggesting that Hebrew poetry reflects an older usage while the prose shows a new differentiation by the addition of the tense particle *wa* with its concomitant accent and vowel changes.

In summary, then, one may see exactness in how the verbs are used in Hebrew. For just one example, if the past tense is needed at the beginning of a sentence or clause, the "*waw*" plus "imperfect" (with the preformative doubled) is used; but if the past tense is needed within a clause (not at its start) the "perfect" is used. Similarly, if the future is needed at the start of a clause or sentence, the "perfect" with *wa* is used; but if the future is needed inside a clause, the "imperfect" is used. These are but two illustrations of the "exactness" of the tense system. They illustrate, among other things, that the system is a matter of tenses and not aspects.

C. Particles

An important particle is the *wa*. Too frequently this particle is interpreted as the conjunction *and*. A quick glance at the following references will show some of the varied ways it is interpreted in KJV: "even of," Isaiah 57:11; "also," 1 Samuel 25:43; "nor," Exodus 20:10; "but," Genesis 2:17; "and" introducing a question, Jeremiah 25:29; "both," Numbers 9:14; "whose," Genesis 11:4; "when," Judges 16:15; "or," Jeremiah 32:43; and many others. It may also introduce the apodosis of a conditional sentence as with the word "then" (*wa*) in Exodus 19:5. This verse is especially instructive, since one of the "*waws*" (the first one) is rendered as the conjunction *and*. Thus we must conclude that the particle *wa* is merely a connective between clauses and the relationship of the clauses one to the other is to be determined only from the context. This is not a phenomenon strange to those who work closely with the Hamito-Semitic languages, however. There is much latitude, then, in the interpretation of clausal relationships so introduced in Hebrew and it is important in biblical interpretation to work from the Hebrew text in order to be able to see where interpretations other than those of a given version are possible and even preferable. The other particles ("conjunctions" and "prepositions") in Hebrew can be interpreted each in a number of ways when the context is made the vital consideration. Clausal relationships are the most crucial area for biblical interpreters and translators and yet the one least understood by many. Conservative biblical scholars need to devote intensive research to it.

V. Other Factors Affecting Translation and Interpretation

Although the understanding of the Hebrew verbal system, of clause and sentence relationships, and of the particles is vitally important, other aspects of the language of the OT are also important. Among these are the following: poetic and prose styles, figures of speech and literal interpretation, style in relation to dating and interpretation, loan words, related languages, cognates, etc. The interpreter or translator must take them all into consideration.

A. Poetic and Prose Styles

Biblical poetry does not have either rhyme or meter but it secures its poetic style by a parallelism or repetition of thoughts in successive clauses with the use of synonyms.

Other devices, such as transposition in word order, for one example, are also used. Both are illustrated in the following lines from Isaiah 2:3 (RSV):

> For out of Zion shall go forth the law,
> and the word of the Lord from Jerusalem.

Where repetition of ideas occurs in successive clauses, where ideas are antithetically presented in successive clauses, or where ideas are related but built up synthetically, there we have OT poetry.

The preceding quotation (Isa 2:3) illustrates synonymous parallelism; the following quotations from Proverbs 15:15, 16 (RSV) illustrate antithetic and synthetic parallelism respectively:

> All the days of the afflicted are evil,
> but a cheerful heart has a continual feast.

> Better is a little with the fear of the Lord
> than great treasures and trouble with it.

From even such a brief discussion of Hebrew poetry as this, it is evident that the frequent uses of synonyms raises problems for the translator and the interpreter of the OT. To cite just one example, are *nephes* (soul) and *rûah* (spirit) synonyms or are they two different ideas? Or in some verses are they synonyms and nothing more, while in other verses they express theologically different ideas? Only careful study of context and usage can decide such matters.

B. *Figures of Speech and Literal Interpretation*

The Bible makes extensive use of anthropomorphisms, allegory, figures of speech, and parables. Such elements contribute to the unique literary beauty of the OT. But is their interpretation to be reconciled with grammatico-historical Christian concepts of interpretation? Obviously it is essential to determine first of all what the words and sentence structure of a given passage meant to the original writer and to the people for whom he wrote the words *in his day*. When that is determined, God's message for them and us may be known. The translator and the interpreter must make use of more than grammar, syntax, and word meaning. They must know the ancient idioms, culture, and anthropology in order to achieve the proper understanding of figures and parables. But while metaphors and other figures need to be understood, this does not mean that they are to be reduced to prose.

C. *Style in Relation to Dating and Interpretation*

The interpretation of hortatory literature such as Deuteronomy differs from that of legal literature such as Leviticus. And both differ from the interpretation of straight historical material like Kings or Chronicles. The perspective of the writer also bears on interpretation. For example, some scholars say that Isaiah 40–66 was not written by the same person as Isaiah 1–35 because of stylistic differences. But differences of style may be accounted for on the basis of perspective. Isaiah 1–35 was written from the perspective of the Babylonian captivity as yet to come; on the other hand Isaiah 40–66 was written as if the captivity had already occurred, whereas actually it had not. The difference accounts for a marked change of style. Chapters 36–39, on the other hand present another style, since they are straight historical narration.

Again, the style of Ezra and Nehemiah differs from that of Moses in part because nearly one thousand years separate their writings.

D. Loan Words, Related Languages, Cognates, Textual Variants, Versions, Systematization

Non-Hebrew words borrowed from other languages need to be interpreted in the light of the language from which the word is borrowed. A case in point is the Egyptian loan word *'āḥû* (Gen 41:2). The Egyptian original means "the [green] reeds or rushes."

Usages in related languages sometimes point the way to the more exact interpretation of the meaning of the Hebrew word. Examples may be the use of the preposition *b* as "from," when it normally means "in" or "with." Witness the parallel of *min* and *b* in Ugaritic also found in Psalm 18:8. Another example is the use of the particle *kî* before a verb at the end of a clause to emphasize the verb. While this is a common phenomenon in Ugaritic, it is also seen in the Bible. "God will redeem my soul; from the power of the grave he surely (*kî*) will receive me" (Ps 49:15). Again, there is the use of the noun in the construct state before a finite verb—a usage now known to have the significance of a relative or temporal clause. "By the hand of you will send" (Exod 4:13) means "by whom you will send" and "all the days of it is shut up" (Lev 14:46) means "all the days when it is shut up."

Some words that are alike have different meanings in related languages, or cognates; this may indicate a new possibility for interpretation of the Hebrew. One example could be the Hebrew *kābēd* meaning "liver." In Arabic the related word can mean "[anything] *large, thick* in the middle." In Akkadian it may mean, figuratively, "temper" or "heart." In Aramaic it may mean "be angry." Therefore when *kābēd* occurs in the Bible, may it not also have one of these other meanings?

Variant readings of a text found in different Hebrew MSS, for example a Dead Sea Scroll variant, or a different meaning found in one or another of various early translations (Greek, Latin, Aramaic of the Targums, Syriac, etc.) are factors translators and interpreters must take into consideration, as are the footnotes (*kerê* and *ketîb*) found in the Masoretic text. These are all important considerations as they reflect a time earlier than that of our extant MSS.

Two more factors are relevant to the problem of the translator. One of these is created by homonyms, the falling together of certain phonemes, such as *ḥ* and *h* or ' and *g*. The words sound alike, but coming from different origins, they have different meanings. The other factor is the difficulty of interpreting *hapax legomena* (words found only once in a given document; e.g., the OT, the NT, or the entire Bible). In such a case, should the interpreter use content alone or should he follow the suggestions derived from cognate languages, from comparative Semitic grammar?

Finally, translators and interpreters must have a command of systematic theology and of comparative syntax and comparative textual knowledge.

VI. Influence on the New Testament

Aramaic and Hebrew expressions or loan words are sometimes found in the NT. Two illustrations must suffice. Jesus said on one occasion, "*Talitha cumi*," which is pure Aramaic for "Young lady, arise." The Greek behind the word *earnest* in Ephesians 1:14 is *arrabōn*, a pure transliteration of the Hebrew *'ērabōn* where the vowel *ē* before the r indicates the existence of a double r in the Hebrew word. The use of this word in Genesis 38:17, 18 casts light on its meaning in the passage in Ephesians.

VII. Modern Hebrew and the Interpretation of the Old Testament

The principal differences between modern and biblical Hebrew are the syntax of the verb, where in modern Hebrew there is a very simple tense system, and in the vocabulary where words have been created for modern things and ideas. The phonetics, morphology, and much of the syntax remain unchanged. One who is able to speak modern Hebrew will find his reading and understanding of the Hebrew Bible greatly simplified.

VIII. Aramaic

The Aramaic language is not one, but a group of Semitic dialects that are cognate to Hebrew. The extant portions of Aramaic available to us come from as early as post-Davidic times, those of the kings of Judah and Israel. In the early seventh century B.C. the Assyrian emissaries used Aramaic in speaking to the Judaeans (2 Kings 18:26). This dialect is often referred to as "official Aramaic." Inscriptions in Aramaic have come also from this period in Egypt, Cilicia, and even Arabia. The language continued in use through the Neo-Babylonian times from the end of the seventh century B.C. till the Persian conquest in 538. It is in the Persian period (538–331 B.C.), commencing with their defeat of the Neo-Babylonians till they in turn were defeated by the Greeks in 331 B.C. that this language had its widest use in the Middle East. Aramaic was the lingua franca of that period and continued to be widely used in Herodian times and so down to the times of Jesus and the NT writers.

Some have endeavored to prove that the Aramaic dialect of the Bible is a late one and thus those parts of the OT in which it is used, notably in Daniel and Ezra, are late documents and do not come from the times traditionally assigned them, namely, the mid-sixth and mid-fifth centuries B.C. It should be noted, however, that this dialect closely resembles that of the Aramaic papyri from Elephantine in Egypt, which are from the mid-fifth century B.C.

The form of writing of the biblical Aramaic is the same as that used for the Hebrew. As with all cognate languages, there are minor differences in phonology but more major ones in morphology. In words that are cognate, we find a z in the Hebrew word but often a d in its Aramaic cognate, a Hebrew š is sometimes a t in Aramaic, etc. The nouns are declined in the same way as the Hebrew nouns but the definite article, which is expressed in Hebrew with a prefixed ha (and a doubling of the first consonant of the noun), is expressed in Aramaic by a suffixed 'a.

The verb in Aramaic has basically only three stems and their passives, a much less complex system than its cognate Hebrew. Here also much that has been said of the usages of the Hebrew verb also applies syntactically. One development rarely found in Hebrew but found frequently in biblical Aramaic is the use of the verb "to be" as an auxiliary verb.

IX. Bibliography

Ben-Hayyim, Z. and Ornan, U. "Hebrew Grammar." *Encyclopedia Judaica.* Edited by C. Roth and G. Wigoder. Jerusalem: Keter, 1970–72.

Blake, F.R. *A Resurvey of Hebrew Tenses.* Roma: Pontificium Institutum Biblicum, 1951.

Cross, F.M. and Freedman, D.N. *Early Hebrew Orthography.* New Haven: American Oriental Society, 1952.

Dahood, M. "Ugaritic-Hebrew Parallel Pairs." *Ras Shamra Parallels* I. Edited by Loren Fisher. Roma: Pontificium Institutum Biblicum, 1972.

Driver, G.R. *Problems of the Hebrew Verbal System.* Edinburgh, 1936.

Driver, S.R. *A Treatise on the Use of the Tenses in Hebrew.* Oxford, 1892[3].

Gesenius, W. *Gesenius' Hebrew Grammar.* Translated by A.E. Cowley from corrected sheets of the second English edition. Oxford: Clarendon, 1910[28].

Moran, W. *A Syntactical Study of the Dialect of Byblos as Reflected in the Amarna Tablets.* Ann Arbor: University Microfilms, 1961.

Moscati, S.; Spitaler, A.; Ullendorff, E.; and Von Soden, W. *An Introduction to the Comparative Grammar of the Semitic Languages.* Porta Linguarum Orientalium, edited by S. Moscati. Neue Serie VI. Wiesbaden: Otto Harrassowitz, 1964.

Muraoka, T. "Notes on the Syntax of Biblical Aramaic." *Journal of Semitic Studies* 2 (Autumn 1966):151–167.

Rabin, C. Article in *Current Trends in Linguistics* 6 (1971):304–346.

Young, G.D. *Grammar of the Hebrew Language.* Grand Rapids: Zondervan, 1951.

―――. "Ugaritic Prosody." *Journal of Near Eastern Studies* 9 (July 1950):124–134.

THE TEXTUAL CRITICISM OF
THE OLD TESTAMENT

Bruce K. Waltke

Bruce K. Waltke

B.A., Houghton College; Th.M., Th.D., Dallas Theological Seminary; Ph.D., Harvard University; Post-doctoral Fellow, Hebrew Union College, Jerusalem

Professor of Old Testament, Regent College

THE TEXTUAL CRITICISM OF
THE OLD TESTAMENT

I. The Hebrew Manuscripts

    A. From the Time of composition to c. 400 B.C.
    B. From c. 400 B.C. to c. A.D. 70
    C. From c. A.D. 70 to A.D. 1000
    D. From c. A.D. 1000 to the Present

II. Ancient Versions

    A. The Septuagint
    B. The Aramaic Targums
    C. The Old Latin and Latin Vulgate
    D. The Syriac Peshitta

III. Canons of Textual Criticism
IV. Bibliography

To restore the original text of ancient documents, such as the OT Scriptures, is the task of textual criticism. The critic must know both the tendencies of scribes and the history and character of the sources bearing witness to the documents. No one source perfectly preserves the original text of the OT, and in cases of disagreement the critic must decide on the original reading in the light of all the sources and his knowledge about them. The two principal types of sources for the text of the OT are MSS directly descended from the original Hebrew text and ancient versions directly influenced by these MSS.

I. The Hebrew Manuscripts

Just as the great variety of English Bibles reflects the philosophies and abilities of the translators, so also the variants in the ancient MSS reflect the philosophies and abilities of the scribes who produced them. The scribes were further influenced in their attitudes toward the transmission of the text by their own time and place in history. Similar differences characterize the sources of information that are available to modern textual scholarship.

A. From the Time of Composition to c. 400 B.C.

No extant MS of the Hebrew Bible can be confidently dated before 400 B.C. by the disciplines of paleography, archaeology, or nuclear physics. Therefore, scribal practices before this time must be inferred from evidence within the Bible itself and from known scribal practices in the ancient Near East at the time the OT books were being written. These two sources suggest that scribes at this time sought both to preserve and to revise the text.

1. *Tendency to preserve the text.* The very fact that the Hebrew Scriptures persistently survived the most deleterious conditions throughout its long history demonstrates that indefatigable scribes insisted on its preservation. The OT books were copied by hand for generations on highly perishable papyrus and animal skins in the relatively damp, hostile climate of Palestine in contrast to the dry climate of Egypt, so favorable to the preservation of these materials. Moreover, the prospects for their survival were uncertain in a land that served as a bridge for armies in unceasing contention between the continents of Africa and Asia—a land whose people were the object of plunderers in their early history and of captors in their later history. That no other writings, such as the Book of Yashar or the Diaries of the Kings, survive from this period shows the determination of the scribes to preserve the OT books. But the worst foes of Hebrew Scripture were the very heirs of its treasures, because they sought to kill many of its authors (cf. Matt 23:35) and destroy their works (cf. Jer 36). One must assume, however, that from the first the OT Scriptures captured the hearts, minds, and loyalties of some in Israel who at risk to themselves kept them safe. Such people must have insisted on the accurate transmission of the text even as those of similar persuasion insist on it today.

In addition, both the Bible itself (cf. Deut 31:9ff.; Josh 24:25, 26; 1 Sam 10:25) and the literature of the ancient Near East show that at the time of its earliest composition a psychology of canonicity existed (see THE CANON OF THE OLD TESTAMENT). This psychology must have fostered a concern for the care and accuracy in the transmission of the sacred writings. For example, a treaty of the Hittite international suzerainty treaties parallel to Yahweh's covenant with Israel at Sinai contains this explicit threat: "Whoever changes but one word of this tablet, may the weather god ... and the thousand gods of this tablet root that man's descendants out of the land of Hatti." Likewise one of the Sefire Steles (c. 750 B.C.) reads, "Whoever ... says, 'I will efface some of its words,' ... may the gods throw over that man and his house and all in it." Again, at the conclusion of the famous Code of Hammurabi imprecations are hurled against those who would try to alter the Law. And Moses insisted that Israel "observe all these laws with care" (Deut 31:12). Undoubtedly this psychology coupled with a fear for God in the heart of the scribes who did their work in connection with the ark inhibited them from multiplying variants of the texts.

Moreover, scribal practices throughout the ancient Near East reflect a conservative attitude. As Albright noted, "The prolonged and intimate study of the many scores of thousands of pertinent documents from the ancient Near East proves that sacred and profane documents were copied with greater care than is true of scribal copying in Graeco-Roman times."[1] To verify this statement one need only consider the care with which the Pyramid texts, the Coffin Texts, and the Book of the Dead were copied, even though they were never intended to be seen by other human eyes. Kitchen has called attention to the colophon of one text dated c. 1400 B.C., in which a scribe boasted, "[The

---

[1]W.F. Albright, *From the Stone Age to Christianity* (Garden City, N.Y.: Doubleday, Anchor Books, 1957), pp. 78–79.

book] is completed from its beginning to its end, having been copied, revised, compared, and verified sign by sign."[2]

2. *Tendency to revise the text.* The statement, however, that the scribe quoted by Kitchen claimed to have "revised" the text indicates a contrary concept and practice on the part of some scribes. Apparently they also aimed to teach the people by disseminating an understandable text. They undoubtedly revised the script and orthography according to the literary conventions of the times. Then too, they apparently changed linguistic features of the text. By the science of comparative Semitic grammar we can with reasonable confidence reconstruct the form of Hebrew grammar before the Amarna Period (c. 1350 B.C.). If these reconstructions are correct, we must infer that the Masoretes preserved a form of Hebrew grammar from a later period—e.g., after final short vowels were dropped. On the other hand, Gerleman demonstrated that the Chronicler used a modernized text of the Pentateuch,[3] and Kropat demonstrated that the Chronicler's Hebrew is later than that of Samuel-Kings.[4]

Since, as will be argued below, the Masoretes were not innovators of Hebrew grammar, it seems plausible to assume that after 1350 B.C., probably in one major step, earlier linguistic forms were revised in conformity with the current grammar. But this change had little effect on the consonantal text. Such revisions are consistent with known practices. Albright said, "A principle which must never be lost sight of in dealing with documents of the ancient Near East is that instead of leaving obvious archaisms in spelling and grammar, the scribes generally revised ancient literary and other documents periodically. This practice was followed with particular regularity by cuneiform scribes."[5] Kitchen has produced evidence showing that also in Egypt texts were revised to conform to later forms of the language.[6] What influence inspired writers at the temple may have had on the revision of the text is difficult to decide. Moreover, as stated above, the Chronicler used a modernized form of the Pentateuch.

Finally, the many differences between synoptic portions of the OT strongly suggest that the priests entrusted with the responsibility of teaching the Bible felt free to revise the text (cf. 1 Sam 22 = Ps 18; 2 Kings 18:13–20:19 = Isa 36–39; 2 Kings 24:18–25:30 = Jer 52; Isa 2:2–4 = Micah 4:1–3; Ps 14 = 53; 40:14–18 = 70; 57:8–12 = 108:2–6; 60:7–14 = 108:7–14; 96 = 1 Chron 16:23–33; 16:34–36; and the parallels between Sam-Kings and Chron). Scribal errors such as dittography (unintentional repetition of a letter or syllable), haplography (omission of a letter or syllable that should be repeated, sometimes because of homoioteleuton and homoiarcton—similar ending and similar beginning respectively), confusion of letters, and the like occurred even in the best MSS in all stages of their transmission.

B. *From c. 400 B.C. to c. A.D. 70*

The same tensions happily labeled by Talmon as centrifugal and centripetal manifest themselves in the extant MSS and versions between the time of the completion of the canon (c. 400 B.C.) and the final standardization of the text (c. A.D. 70–100).

---

[2]K.A. Kitchen, *Ancient Orient and Old Testament* (Chicago: Inter-Varsity, 1966), p. 140.

[3]Gerleman, G., "Synoptic Studies in the Old Testament," *Lunds Universitets Arsskrift* (N.F. Avd. 1), 44 (1948).

[4]Kropat, A., "Die Syntax des Autors der chronik verglichen mit der seiner Quellen," Beihefte ZAW 16 (1909): 14f.

[5]*Stone Age to Christianity*, p. 79.

[6]K.A. Kitchen, "Egypt," in *The New Bible Dictionary* (Grand Rapids: Eerdmans, 1962), p. 350.

THE TEXTUAL CRITICISM OF THE OLD TESTAMENT

1. *Tendency to preserve the text.* The presence of a text type among the DSS (c. 200 B.C. to A.D. 100) identical with the one preserved by the Masoretes, whose earliest extant MS dates to c. A.D. 900, gives testimony to the unbelievable achievement of some scribes in faithfully preserving the text. Of course, this text must have been in existence before the time of the DSS, and its many archaic forms in contrast to other text types give strong reason to believe that it was transmitted in a circle of scribes dedicated to the preservation of the original text. Moreover, M. Martin's studies show that the DSS reveal a conservative scribal tendency to follow the exemplar both in text and in form. According to Rabbinic tradition, the scribes attempted to correct the text. Thus the Talmud (Ned. 37b–38a) informs us of five words of the Hebrew text at that time that were to be read without the *waw* conjunctive, of six words that are to be read but had been dropped from the text, and of five words written but that should be cancelled. Again, the following critical additions of the scribes preserved in the extant text handed down from the Masoretes evidence a desire to preserve an accurate text: (1) the fifteen extraordinary marks that either condemn the Hebrew letters so marked as spurious or else simply draw attention to some peculiar textual feature; (2) the suspended letters found in four passages may indicate intentional scribal change or scribal error due to a faulty distinction of laryngals; (3) the nine inverted *nuns* apparently marking verses thought to have been transposed, though Kahle suggested the *nun* is an abbreviation of "pointed."

2. *Tendency to revise the text.* On the other hand, the Sopherim, called by Ginsburg "the authorized revisers of the text,"[7] some time after the return of the Jews from the Babylonian captivity altered the script from its angular paleo-Hebrew form to the square Aramaic form, aided the division of words—a practice carefully observed in the Hebrew inscriptions from the first half of the first millennium—by distinguishing five final letter forms and aided the reading of a text by continually inserting consonantal vowels called *matres lectionis.*

More significantly, some liberal-minded scribes altered the text for both philological and theological reasons. Thus, they modernized the text by replacing archaic Hebrew forms and constructions with forms and constructions of a later Hebrew linguistic tradition. They also smoothed out the text by replacing rare constructions with more frequently occurring constructions and they supplemented and clarified the text by the insertion of additions and the interpolation of glosses from parallel passages. In addition, they substituted euphemisms for vulgarities, altered the names of false gods, removed the harsh phrase "curse God," and safe-guarded the sacred divine name by failing to pronounce the tetragrammaton (*YHWH* [*Yahweh*]) and occasionally by substituting other forms in the consonantal text.

As a result of this liberal tendency, three distinct recensions and one mixed text type emerged during this period (c. 400 B.C. to c. A.D. 70). The three text types already known from the LXX, the Samaritan Pentateuch, and the text preserved by the Masoretes—the *textus receptus*—were corroborated by the finds at Qumran. Here the Hebrew text lying behind the Greek translation, the Jewish text type adopted and adapted by the Samaritans for their sectarian purposes, and the *textus receptus* are all represented. Following the lead of Albright, who argued from the forms of place names and proper names in LXX and in the received text that these text types originated in Egypt and Babylon

[7]Christian D. Ginsburg, *Introduction to the Massoretico-Critico Edition of the Hebrew Bible,* with a Prolegomenon by Harry M. Orlinsky (New York: Ktav, 1966), p. 307.

respectively, Cross championed the theory of three local recensions.[8] The Samaritan recension, he reasoned, must belong to Palestine if for no other reason than that it exists exclusively in the paleo-Hebrew script. Goshen-Gottstein, et al., however, rejected the notion that we must assume that textual variation depends on geographical separation.

At the beginning of the nineteenth century Gesenius demonstrated that the numerous agreements between LXX and the Samaritan Pentateuch in secondary readings can be explained only by assuming that both texts had a common ancestor. His view has now been confirmed and clarified by two later independent studies. Cross demonstrated that 4QSam[a] preserves a text much closer to the text of Samuel used by the author of the book of Chronicles than to the traditional text of Samuel surviving in the Masorah.[9] In a separate study, Gerleman concluded, "It is a fact which has not received due attention that the latter [the genealogies and the lists of names in 1 Chron 1–9] show greater resemblance to the Samaritan Pentateuch than to the Massoretic."[10]

Since the Samaritan sectarian recension did not originate until 110 B.C., as Purvis has demonstrated, it seems reasonable to suppose that the common ancestor to which both LXX and Samar. go back existed in Palestine at the time of the Chronicler (c. 400 B.C.). Cross has labeled this text for the Pentateuch and Samuel "the Old Palestinian recension."[11] This Old Palestinian recension was brought to Egypt during the fifth century B.C., if we may trust the indications of its place names, and was further vulgarized in the course of transmission before it became the base of LXX (c. 200 B.C.). It survived in Palestine with lesser revision and became the basis for the Samaritan Pentateuch c. 110 B.C.

From this history of the text, one can conclude that when the Samar. and the LXX agree against the received text, they bear witness to this Old Palestinian recension. Normally, therefore, the Samaritan Pentateuch shares an original reading with LXX. But it must be borne in mind that the Old Palestinian recension from which both descended was itself revised by scholarly reworkings and modernizations.

The archaic and stable Babylonian text, possibly surviving in Babylon from the time of the Exile, was possibly reintroduced into Palestine at the time the Jews returned to Palestine after the autonomous Jewish State was achieved by the Maccabees. But the evidence for this is not conclusive.

The confusion of text types in Palestine at this time is reflected in the citations from the OT in the NT, the Apocrypha, and the rabbinic traditions. The NT shares readings with the received text, Samar., LXX, Targ. Onkelos, Sirach, Testimonia, Florilegium, and Theod.

In addition to rabbinic traditions about the textual emendations of the scribes cited above, other rabbinic tradition tells of the need for "book correctors" in Jerusalem attached to the temple and even of divergent readings in Pentateuchal scrolls kept in the temple archives. Moreover, collations made from the Codex Severus and preserved by medieval rabbis show variants from the *textus receptus* in the scroll taken to Rome by Titus in A.D. 70. Talmon concluded, "The latest manuscripts from Qumran which give evidence to the local history of the Bible text in the crucial period, the last decades

---

[8]F.M. Cross, Jr., *The Ancient Library of Qumran and Modern Biblical Studies* (Garden City, N.Y.: Doubleday, 1961), pp. 188–94.

[9]Ibid., p. 142.

[10]G. Gerleman, "Synoptic Studies in the Old Testament," *Lunds Universitets Arsskrift* (N.F. Avd. 1), 44 (1948): 9.

[11]Cross, *Ancient Library of Qumran*, p. 189.

before the destruction of the Temple, do not present the slightest indication that even an incipient *textus receptus* did emerge there, or that the very notion of a model recension even was conceived by the Covenanters."[12] Whether the identical conclusion is valid for the Jewish community centered in the temple is less certain.

C. From c. A.D. 70 to A.D. 1000

1. Standardization of the text. On the other hand, the rabbinic testimony reflects a movement away from a plurality of recensions toward a stabilization of the text. Indeed, the seven rules of biblical hermeneutics, compiled by Hillel the Elder at the time of Herod, demanded an inviolable, sacrosanct, authoritative text. Moreover, Justin's complaint against Trypho the Jew that the rabbis had altered the venerable LXX to remove an essential arm from the Christian propaganda also demonstrates that the rabbis desired an authoritative text.

A recension of the Greek OT (R) found at Nahal Hever dated by its editor, D. Barthélemy, from A.D. 70 to A.D. 100 confirms Justin's complaint. Barthélemy demonstrated that this is the rabbinic text Justin used for purposes of debate with the Jews. He showed the recensional character of the text by noting that all the modifications of the traditional Greek text are explained by a concern to model it more exactly after the Hebrew text that ultimately crystallized into what came to be known as Masoretic. He also noted that alongside hundreds of variants of this type, in a certain number of readings the recension departed from both LXX and the *textus receptus,* and suggested that in these instances the Hebrew text on which the recension is based differed from the received Hebrew text.

If C.H. Roberts is correct, however, in dating this scroll 50 B.C. to A.D. 50, we may have to view R as part of the fluid stage of the text.

In any case, rabbinic testimony, once again combined with other empirical data from the DSS, bears witness to the existence of an official text with binding authority from a time shortly after the destruction of the temple. With regard to Halakic discussions from this time, N. Sarna noted that exegetical comments and hermeneutical principles enunciated by Zechariah b. ha-Kazzav, Nahum of Gimzo, R. Akiva, and R. Ishmael all presuppose that in this period a single stabilized text attained unimpeachable authority and hegemony over all others. The dominance of the Masoretic-type text is amply attested by the Hebrew biblical scrolls and fragments discovered at Masada (A.D. 66–73), at Wadi Marabbaᶜat, and at Nahal Hever (c. A.D. 132-135), because all of those are practically identical with the received text. These scrolls, though exhibiting few substantial variants, to a large extent lack even the minor variants found in the great recensions of the Greek OT attributed to Aq. (c. A.D. 120), Symm. (c. A.D. 180) and Theod. (c. A.D. 180), which were attempts to bring the Greek translation of the Bible closer to the accepted text during the second century A.D. Their variants as well as those found in later rabbinic literature, in the Targums, and in Jerome do not represent a living tradition but are either survivals predating the official recension or secondary corruptions after its acceptance. In effect, the combined evidence essentially supports de Lagarde's study of the last century that all the Hebrew medieval MSS were descended from a single master scroll that could be dated no earlier than the first century of the Christian era.

---

[12]Shemaryahu Talmon, "Aspects of the Textual Transmission of the Bible in the Light of Qumran Manuscripts," *Textus* 4 (1964): 98.

By at least A.D. 100, then, the rabbis had settled on the conservative and superbly disciplined recension that possibly had its provenance in Babylonia. Its adoption as the official text in effect destroyed all variant lines of tradition in established Judaism. Probably the need to stabilize Judaism by strong adherence to the law after the fall of Jerusalem spurred these efforts.[13]

In the course, then, of the first century A.D., the scribal mentality changed from one of preserving and clarifying the text to one of preserving and standardizing the text. The text established was not, as Kahle theorized, the beginning of an attempt to standardize the text that finally became fixed only in the time of Maimonides (12th century A.D.) after a long and bitter struggle among the rabbinical schools.

It cannot be overemphasized that this official text is archaic. Numerous grammatical forms not attested in later Hebrew are now attested in the Ugaritic texts (c. 1400 B.C.). If the text is a later creation, we may well ask why the Alexandrian translators understood these same forms so imperfectly.

Because the scribal mentality from now on sought merely to conserve the text, no further developments of any significance occurred in the transmission of the biblical consonantal text.

2. *The activity of the Masoretes*

a. *In conserving the consonants.* Between c. A.D. 600 and 1000 schools consisting of families of Jewish scholars arose in Babylon, Palestine, and Tiberias to safeguard the consonantal text and to represent symbolically the vowels and liturgical cantillations, which until that time had only orally accompanied the text, by adding diacritical notations to the text. These scholars are known as Masoretes or Massoretes, possibly from the postbiblical root *msr* "to hand down." In their endeavor to conserve the consonantal text, they hedged it in by placing observations regarding the external form of the text in the margins. In the side margins they used abbreviations (*Masorah parvum*), in the top and bottom margins they gave more detailed and continuous explanations (*Masorah magnum*), and at the end provided alphabetical classification of the whole Masoretic material (*Masorah finalis*). In addition to these annotations made directly in the text, they compiled separate manuals called *Ochlah we-Ochlah*. When the MSS they inherited differed, they preserved the variants by inserting one reading in the text called *Kethib* and the other in the margin called *Qere*. Alternative readings may also be indicated in the margin by *sᵉbîr*, an Aramaic word meaning "supposed."

b. *In conserving the vocalization.* Owing largely to the work by Kahle on scrolls found in the Cairo Genizah, it is now clear that the medieval codices of the Hebrew Bible as well as the printed editions of it preserve the forms of the symbols invented by the Masoretes at Tiberias between c. A.D. 800 and 900, which in turn grew out of an earlier Palestinian system. The earlier simple supralinear and the later complex system of annotations developed in the Babylonian centers did not survive.

Ever since Maimonides supported the ben Asher tradition against Saadiah b. Joseph Gaon, who favored the b. Naphtali tradition, it has been agreed that a true Masoretic Bible must follow b. Asher.

Barr has brought together conclusive evidence that the Masoretes did not invent the

---

13Paul de Lagarde, *Anmerkungen zur grieschen Übersetzung der Prover bien* (Leipzig, 1863).

vowels but preserved a firm tradition of vocalization.[14] Allowing for peculiar interpretative techniques, Aq. supports this vocalization and can cite rare words in forms close to the MT. Similarly, Jerome supports the same tradition. Most impressive here is the contrast between Jerome's version of the Psalms based first on LXX and then on the Hebrew. In many instances LXX preserves the same consonantal text as MT, but differs in the matter of vocalization; e.g., Ps 102 (101): 24f. In these instances Jerome in his *Iuxta Hebraeos* reads with MT against LXX. (The erratic and intrinsically improbable vocalizations of the Hebrew in LXX show that it was the Alexandrian Jews who did not possess a fixed tradition of vocalization but proposed an interpretation for the consonants.)

The following Talmudic passage further proves Barr's contention that the Masoretes were preservers and not innovators: "It is written: for Joab and all Israel remained there until he had cut off every male in Edom" (1 Kings 11:16). "When Joab came before David, the latter said to him: Why have you acted thus? He replied: Because it is written: Thou shalt blot out the males [*zekar*] of Amalek (Deut 25:19). Said David: But WE read, the remembrance [*zēker*] of Amalek. He replied: I was taught to say *zekar*. He [Joab] then went to his teacher and asked: How did you teach me to read? He replied: *Zekar*. Thereupon Joab drew his sword and threatened to kill him. Why do you do this? asked the teacher. He replied: Because it is written: Cursed be he that does the work of the law negligently."[15] This makes clear that a reader of the ancient biblical text received his vocalization from a teacher.

Furthermore, philological considerations certify the thesis. The very fact that the Masoretic grammar admirably fits the framework of comparative Semitic grammar proves the credibility of the work of the Masoretes. Bergsträsser made this point when Kahle first announced his theory that the Masoretes were innovators. The innovators, Bergsträsser argued, must in that case have read Brockelmann's smaller comparative grammar (1903–13), for how else could they have come up with a grammar reconcilable with use in a comparative reconstruction!

Occasional anomalous forms sometimes supported in ancient cognate texts unknown to the Masoretes put the case beyond doubt. A case in point is *tormāh* "treachery," an anomaly whose pattern fits an Akkadian parallel according to Dossin. In this connection Morag demonstrated that many forms that look bizarre are genuine and reflect ancient phonological, morphonemic, and morphological features of Hebrew. Finally, the MT maintains dialectical differences such as those between Hosea, Job, and Ruth. On the other hand, the internal evidence suggests that some dialectical differences have been smoothed over, such as the leveling of the second masculine singular pronominal suffix and that corrections were made in the vocalization to adjust to errors in the consonantal text; cf. Psalm 18:11 and 2 Samuel 22:12. These changes in the vocalization probably occurred at a time when the text was more fluid than after it became established c. 70 A.D.

D. *From c. A.D. 1000 to the Present*

R. Salomon b. Isamel, c. A.D. 1330, adopted the Christian numeration of chapters and placed the numerals in the margin of the Hebrew Bible in order to facilitate reference

---

[14]James Barr, *Comparative Philology and the Text of the Old Testament* (Oxford: Clarendon Press, 1968), pp. 207–22.

[15]*Baba Bathra* 21ab, cited in Barr, *Comparative Philology*, p. 213.

to a passage in controversy. Although the chapter divisions largely correspond with the Masoretic divisions, they nevertheless contradict these divisions in others.

The story of the printing of the Hebrew Bible has been superbly summarized by Sarna,[16] whose account is closely followed here. The story begins with a poor edition of the Psalms produced in 1477 most probably in Bologna. The edition of the Bologna Pentateuch in 1482 set the pattern for many future editions culminating in the Bomberg rabbinic Bibles of the next century. A little later the great firm of Joshua Solomon Soncino was founded in a small town in the duchy of Milan. Attracting Abraham b. Hayyim from Bologna, they produced the first complete Bible, the Soncino Bible of 1488 with vowels and accents. Gershom Soncino in 1495 produced an improved and small pocket edition. It was this edition Martin Luther used to translate the Bible into German.

About 1511 Daniel Bomberg, a Christian merchant of Amsterdam, established a printing office in Venice and produced the first Great Rabbinic Bible in 1516–17. In connection with Jacob b. Hayyim ibn Adonijah, he produced the second Great Rabbinic Bible of 1524–25, which became the standard Masoretic text for the next 400 years and is frequently referred to as the ben Hayyim text.

Buxtorf in 1618–19 printed at Basel his four-volume rabbinic Bible in which the text was influenced by the traditions of the Sephardim (the occidental branch of European Jews early settling in Spain and Portugal), and not dominated by the Ashkenazai (the Eastern European Yiddish-speaking Jews), as were all previous editions printed under Jewish auspices. The text became the basis for J.H. Michaelis's critical edition in 1720.

S. Baer, supported by Franz Delitzsch, produced single volumes of the Hebrew Bible between 1869–95 in rigid conformity with rules established from the Masorah rather than on the basis of MSS. C.D. Ginsburg (in the British and Foreign Bible Society edition of 1911–26) notes that various Masorah traditions disagreed with the text and with each other, and so he paid more attention to the MSS than to the Masorah or ben Hayyim.

With the third edition of Kittel's *Biblia Hebraica* (1936), P. Kahle began the new approach of getting behind the ben Hayyim text to the Ben Asher text by basing the work on the Leningrad MSS B 19A (L), "the oldest dated MS of the complete Hebrew Bible" and related directly to the Ben Asher Codex. Unfortunately its critical apparatus swarms with errors of commission and omission, as Orlinsky put it. A new edition, *Biblia Hebraica Stuttgartensia*, also based on MS L is now appearing in fascicles. In addition to making minor changes, the editors, K. Elliger and W. Rudolph, inform the reader that the contributors "have exercised considerable restraint in conjectures." This welcome restraint, in marked contrast to the earlier editions of Kittel's Bible, shows that, as the result of the discovery of the DSS, scholars have learned a new appreciation for the credibility of the received text. Unfortunately the apparatus followed by *Biblia Hebraica Stuttgartensia* continues to swarm with errors of omission and commission and cannot be depended on.

In 1928 N.H. Snaith edited a text based on British Museum's Or. Ms 1616–18, a codex close to the tradition found in the 1720 Michaelis Bible. The text, though compiled from completely different sources, is very close to that of Kahle. This shows that the Ben Asher text is found in both the Leningrad MS and in the Sephardic MSS not corrected by a second hand to the ben Hayyim tradition. The same type of text will be used in the Hebrew University Bible Project based on the Aleppo Codex known to belong to the family of ben Asher and which has been hidden and so preserved from "correction."

---

[16]N.M. Sarna, "Bible Text," *Encyclopedia Judaica* 4 (1971): 831–35.

II. Ancient Versions

A. The Septuagint

1. *Name, origin, date.* The version most important for textual criticism is the Greek one, described in its most ancient MSS "according to the LXX" (written in full: *Interpretatio septuaginta vivorum* or *seniorum*—i.e., "translation of the seventy elders"). This version probably owes its name to the story recounted in the pseudonymous *Letter of Aristeas,* according to which seventy-two scholars summoned from Jerusalem by Ptolemy Philadelphus (295–47 B.C.) rendered in seventy-two days a perfect Greek translation of the Pentateuch. Christian writers credited the translation of the entire Hebrew Bible to these seventy-two interpreters.

Although many details of the story are fictitious, it is widely accepted that the translation of the Law was made in the time of Philadelphus. Contrary to the story, however, it is concluded that LXX arose out of the needs of the Alexandrian Jews and was done by various literary Greeks at Alexandria on a text type already present in Egypt. According to the general consensus, the Prophets were translated before the end of the third century B.C. and some, if not all, of the Hagiographa by 132 B.C., because the prologue to the Greek Ben-Sirach refers to an already-existing version of "the Law, Prophets, and the other writings." Scholars agree that a complete version of the Bible existed at least at the beginning of the first century A.D.

2. *The question of a proto-LXX.* Proceeding from his studies of the Samaritan Pentateuch Targums, P. Kahle brought a new model to the study of the history of textual transmission. Instead of thinking of a standard original from which variants developed, Kahle imposed a schema of many independent texts at the beginning that were later officially standardized for theological reasons. While his model is accurate in the case of the Targums and sometimes late in the history of a text's transmission, it has worked mischief when applied universally to the beginnings of other texts. According to Kahle, a great number of independent Greek translations existed for all the books, and LXX as we know it now was a creation of the church. The modern consensus, however, is returning to Lagarde's view that all Greek MSS go back to one text tradition. This return is due largely to the independent studies by Margolis on Joshua and Montgomery on Daniel, as well as to the new realization that recensional activity during the first two Christian centuries introduced many variants into the Greek tradition and that this gave an illusion that all these variants could not go back to the one original.

Lagarde argued that all extant MSS of the Old Greek translations, as well as all the MSS of translations made directly or indirectly from LXX, go back to the three recensions mentioned by Jerome; namely, the Egyptian, Palestinian, and Syrian produced by Hesychius, Origen, and Lucian respectively during the third and fourth centuries of the Christian era. These three recensions in turn go back to the original Greek translation. Furthermore, he argued, it is possible to identify the Septuagintal MSS as belonging to one or the other recensions with the aid of patristic citations and some of the daughter versions. It therefore follows that a critic of the Greek text must evaluate any given reading in the light of its recension and its properties and date.

Margolis supported Lagarde's theory by comparing MSS of the Greek text of Joshua with its hundreds of proper names. He gathered his MSS from all corners of the earth, together with the secondary versions (such as the Old Latin, Syriac, Sahidic, Bohairic, Ethiopic, Arabic, and Armenian) and all the earlier patristic writers (such as Justin,

Origen, Eusebius, and Theodoret). He concluded from his collation that the sum of the witnesses yields four principal recensions: the Palestinian (P)—i.e., the Eusebian edition of LXX column in Origen's Hexapla and Tetrapla; a recension used in Constantinople and Asia Minor (C); the Syrian or Antiochian (S); and the Egyptian (E).

Montgomery, working independently and on another type of book altogether, found the facts and interpretation in Joshua to hold true by and large in the case of Daniel also.

Then too, Barthélemy concluded that his recension of the Greek text found at Nahal Hever dated c. A.D. 70–100 had LXX as its base and therefore contradicted Kahle's thesis of an essentially Christian diffusion of LXX.

Orlinsky refuted in detail the works of Sperber, Kahle's pupil, who is the only one who tried to support Kahle's thesis with detailed evidence. He concluded, "All talk of an independent and equally original Greek translation is without foundation."[17]

Not surprisingly, then, the two great modern editions of LXX are based on Lagarde's model, but their approach in presenting the texts differs. The Cambridge LXX, containing the Pentateuch and the historical books, presents the text of Codex B or *Vaticanus* (fifth century A.D.) because it exhibits the relatively purest and most original Septuagintal text. Its gaps are filled in from A or *Alexandrinus* (fifth century A.D.) and ℵ or Sinaiticus (fourth century A.D.). It includes an immense critical apparatus based on the collations of the uncials and a large number of cursives and uses data from the daughter versions together with the quotations of Philo, Josephus, and the church fathers. The Göttingen LXX, which does not include the Pentateuch and historical books, provides a restored original text, though it generally comes back to B as the best source; it includes a vast critical apparatus in which the sources are grouped in accordance with Lagarde's principles for reconstructing the text as far as possible into families.

3. *Character of LXX.* Swete concluded that the majority of the translators learned Hebrew in Egypt from imperfectly instructed teachers[18] and Barr concluded that these translators invented vowels for the unpointed text.[19] Translations of individual books vary, however, with the background and skill of each translator. Except in passages such as Genesis 49 and Deuteronomy 32, 33, the Pentateuch is on the whole a close and serviceable translation of a smoothed Hebrew recension. The Psalter is tolerably well done, though Ervin concluded that the theology of Hellenistic Judaism left its mark on it. About Isaiah, Seeligman concluded, "The great majority of the inconsistencies here discussed must be imputed to the translator's unconstrained and carefree working method, and to a conscious preference for the introduction of variations." He added, "We shall not, however, do the translator any injustice by not rating his knowledge of grammar and syntax very highly."[20] Regarding Hosea, Nyberg found that "it is overly composed of gross misunderstandings, unfortunate readings and superficial lexical definitions which often are simply forced into conformity to similar Aramaic cognates. Helplessness and arbitrary choice are the characteristic traits of this interpretation."[21]

[17]Harry M. Orlinsky, "On the Present State of Proto-Septuagint Studies," *Journal of the American Oriental Society*, 61 (1941), copied in Studies in the Septuagint: Origins: Recensions, and Interpretations (New York: Ktav, 1974), p. 90.

[18]Henry B. Swete, *Introduction to the Old Testament in Greek*, rev. by Richard R. Ottley (New York: Ktav, 1968), p. 319.

[19]Barr, *Comparative Philology*, p. 209.

[20]I.L. Seeligman, *The Septuagint Version of Isaiah: A Discussion of Its Problem* (Leiden: Brill, 1948).

[21]H.S. Nyberg, "Studien zum Hoseabuche," in *Zugleich ein Beitraz zur Karung des Problems der alttestamentlichen Textkritik* (Uppsala: Uppsala Universitets Arsskrift, 1935), p. 116.

Albrektson said of Lamentations: "LXX, then, is not a good translation in this book. But this does not mean that it is not valuable for textual criticism. On the contrary, its literal character often allows us to establish with tolerable certainty the underlying Hebrew text. It is clearly based on a text which was in all essentials identical with the consonants of the MT; indeed the passages where it may have contained a variant are notably few."[22] Gerleman said of Job that the translator interprets the text as well as he can and, with the help of his imagination, attempts to give an intelligible meaning to the original, which he does not understand. He added that the many deviations between the Hebrew and the Greek translations of Job are not the result of an essential difference between the original of LXX and our Hebrew text. They have come about in the course of translation when the translator has not mastered the difficulties of the original. Swete concluded, "The reader of the Septuagint must expect to find a large number of actual blunders, due in part perhaps to a faulty archetype, but chiefly to the misreading or misunderstanding of the archetype by the translators. Letters or clauses have often been transposed; omissions occur which may be explained by homoioteleuton; still more frequently the translation has suffered through an insufficient knowledge of Hebrew or a failure to grasp the sense of the context."[23] In the case of Jeremiah, the text represented by LXX deviates so considerably from the MT as to assume the character of a separate edition. The LXX of Samuel, parts of Kings, and Ezekiel is of special value because the text preserved by the Masoretes of these books suffered more than usual from corrupting influences. Shenkel concluded that the Old Greek preserves the original chronology from Omri to Jehu.[24]

4. *Recensions of LXX.* From his studies in Samuel-Kings, Cross concluded that the original LXX was revised no later than the first century B.C. toward a Hebrew text found in the Chronicler, some Qumran MSS, quotations of Josephus, the Greek minuscles boc_2e_2, and in the sixth column of Origen's Hexapla, which is not Theodotionic but also Proto-Lucianic. This so-called Proto-Lucianic recension was then revised by a *kai ge* revision in favor of the Proto-Masoretic text. The third revision came in the second century A.D. by Aq. and Symm., who revised the *kai ge* recension toward the Rabbinic Masoretic text. Barthélemy, on the other hand, contended that this Proto-Lucianic text is the original LXX and thus envisions only two subsequent revisions. But G. Howard contended that both these lack definitive proof.

But the evidence in the Minor Prophets is more conclusive. Here R (= redactor = editor) shows a systematic revision of the Old Greek to the Proto-MT as explained above, and Barthélemy has given proof that his recension lies at the base of Justin's citations and the three great recensions of the second century. Aquila, the student of R. Aqiba, produced an extremely literal work necessary for the exegetical principles of Aqiba. Symm. sacrificed literalness for the sake of the Greek idiom. In the case of Daniel, Theodotion's version superseded the original translation in the ordinary MSS and editions of LXX.

In the third and fourth centuries the recensions of Hesychius, Origen, and Lucian

---

[22]Bertil Albrektson, *Studies in the Text and Theology of the Book of Lamentations* (Lund: Gleerup, 1963), p. 210.

[23]Swete, *Introduction*, pp. 329–30.

[24]James D. Shenkel, *Chronology and Recensional Development in the Greek Text of Kings* (Cambridge: Harvard University Press, 1968).

appeared. Of these, the most influential on later copies of LXX was Origen's fifth column of his Hexapla, a text consistently corrected to the Hebrew *textus receptus* and therefore most corrupt.

In the light of this history, Lagarde is perfectly correct in saying that, other things being equal, the Greek reading deviating from MT should be regarded as the original LXX.

The Lucianic recension is important because in its passion for fullness, which encouraged the accumulation of doublets, it embodies readings not found in other MSS of LXX. In the case of Samuel and Kings it presupposes a Hebrew original, self-evidently superior to the existing MT. Whether it is the original LXX or based on the MSS still remains undecided.

B. *The Aramaic Targums.*

Less serviceable than LXX for textual studies are the Aramaic Targums (derived from the Aramaic word *targum* meaning "translation") both because they were standardized only later in their history and because they contain aggadic (nonlegal or narrative) and paraphrastic material, obviate anthropomorphisms, explain figurative language, and modernize geographical names.

1. *Origin of the Targums.* During the Persian period the majority of the Jews began to use Aramaic in addition to Hebrew, and as a result it became the custom to interpret in the synagogue the reading of the Hebrew Bible with Targums after every verse of the Pentateuch and after every third verse of the prophets. The rabbis forbade the use of written Targums, at least for the Pentateuch, for the Sabbath worship service, but permitted the preparation and use of them by individuals for private study and school instruction. There are indications both in the rabbinic literature and in the Targums themselves that they were committed to writing at least by the first century A.D.

2. *Targums to the Pentateuch*

a. *Targum Onkelos.* Because the Babylonian Talmud (Meg. 3a) attributes the official Targum of the Pentateuch to Onkelos in a text obviously parallel to a related account in the Jerusalem Talmud attributing the Greek translation to Aq. (note the phonetic similarity in the two names), A.E. Silverstone, along with many others, arrived at the conclusion that Onkelos and Aquila are one and the same, but the Babylonian applied to the official Aramaic version the tradition in Palestine regarding Aquila's Greek translation. On the other hand, we should note that on the basis of the mixture of Western and Eastern Aramaic in Onkelos, some of the most competent Aramaists believe it originated in Palestine while its final redaction took place in Babylonia. Then too, its halakhic and aggadic content betray the Palestinian school of Aqiba of the second century A.D. Possibly, then, Aquila had a hand in its Palestinian base after which it was imported to Babylonia where it was revised in the third century A.D.

Like Aquila's Greek recension, the Hebrew text lying behind the Aramaic is the one that ousted all rival recensions. While it aims to conform the Targum as closely as possible to this base, it misses the mark through the paraphrastic influences on all Targums.

b. *Palestinian Pentateuch Targums.* After the destruction of the cultural centers of Judea in the first and second revolts against Rome, the centers of Jewish life shifted to

Galilee. Here Targums in the Galilean dialect evolved, but it is widely agreed that they contain much earlier material. The recently discovered *Codex Neofiti I* is the oldest complete MS of this tradition and according to its editor, Diez Macho, belongs to the first or second century A.D.

Targum Yerushalmi I, mistakenly ascribed to Jonathan and therefore known as Targum Jonathan (b. Uzziel) or pseudo-Jonathan but more correctly called Targum Erez Israel by earlier Jews, lacks only fifteen verses. It aggravates the distinctive traits of the paraphrastic translation. Its early base was revised not later than the seventh century.

Targum Yerushalmi II, also called Fragmentary Targum, contains c. 850 verses, preserving fragmentary portions of the Pentateuch. It is not clear how these fragments came together.

The Genizah Fragments edited by Kahle date from between the seventh and ninth centuries A.D., represent various recensions, and contain both older and younger materials.

3. Targums to the Prophets

a. *Targum Jonathan.* The history of this Targum is like that of Targum Onkelos: it originated early in Palestine, was later revised in Babylonia, and was then recognized as being of ancient authority. According to the Babylonian Talmud, it was written by Jonathan b. Uzziel who is named as Hillel's most prominent pupil in the first century B.C. A conspicuous affinity between Targum Jonathan and Targum Onkelos has led some to conclude that Targum Jonathan influenced Onkelos. The usual rules of Targumic interpretation are observed, but the renderings in the latter Prophets are more paraphrastic on the whole than in the former Prophets.

b. *Targum Yerushalmi to the Prophets.* This work is known mainly from citations in Rashi and David Kimchi. Codex Reuchlinianus, written in 1105 A.D., in the form of eighty extracts, belongs to a later period, when the Babylonian Talmud began to exert an influence on Palestinian literature.

4. Targums to the Hagiographa.

In general, though these contain older materials, they did not originate until a later period. Written at different times by different authors, they never enjoyed official recognition.

a. *Job and Psalms.* According to the Babylonian Talmud (Shab. 115a) a Targum of Job existed in the first century A.D., but it cannot be identified with the one now extant. Both it and the Psalms aim at giving a fairly faithful rendering of the Hebrew text and their brief aggadic additions can easily be separated. Moreover, each contains an unusually high number of variants in vowels and consonants from MT, and numbers of these also occur in the Pesh. and LXX. Both emphasize the law of God and its study, and the future life and its retribution. Both allude to situations in the Roman Empire after its division and before the fall of Rome.

b. *Proverbs.* This work is unique because about one third of its verses agree with the Pesh. against the Hebrew original. The relationship is not clear.

c. *Five Scrolls.* Zunz characterized these as "a Midrashic paraphrase, exceedingly loose and free in character; containing legends, fables, allusions to Jewish history, and many fanciful additions." The exception is the text of Targum Esther in the Antwerp Polyglot, which is a literal translation. The text of the London Polyglot is essentially the same but with many aggadic additions. Targum Shenei is yet a third Targum to Esther and is regarded as an amalgam from other Targums and Midrashim.

d. *Chronicles*. Its author made use of both the Palestinian Targum and Targum Jonathan.

C. *The Old Latin and Vulgate*

1. *The Old Latin*. The existence of early Latin translations called *Vetus Latina* or Old Latin (OL) is known not from any complete ancient MS, but from Latin Bible MSS exhibiting a pre-Vulgate text, from the lower texts of palimpsests, from quotations by Latin church fathers, and from marginal annotations on the Vulgate. Scholars dispute whether these reflect one original or several independent translations. Possibly it was a Jewish translation, because Jewish catacombs in Rome from the first century A.D. bear verses in Latin translated from the Hebrew Bible. In the main, however, it was based on LXX.

2. *The Latin Vulgate*. Recognizing the need for a uniform and reliable Latin Bible, Pope Damasus commissioned Jerome (A.D. 345–420) to produce such a work. At first Jerome revised the existing Latin texts of the NT and Psalms in the light of Hebrew and Greek originals. Some, however, deny that this *Psalterium Romanum* belongs to Jerome. Dissatisfied with this approach, he decided, they say, to prepare an entirely fresh Latin translation from the "original truth of the Hebrew text," the *Hebraica veritas*. After he settled down in Bethlehem, however, he apparently first produced a translation based on the Hexapla, which still serves as the text of Psalms in the Vulgate. In addition to this so-called *Gallican Psalter*, other extant books based on the Hexapla include Proverbs, Ecclesiastes, and Song of Songs. The other books of the Vulgate, however, were rendered directly from the Hebrew.

D. *The Syriac Peshitta*

The origin of the Pesh. (which means "simple, straightforward, direct") is uncertain. Some traditions assign the work to the time of Solomon, but Christian tradition ascribes it apparently to the king of Adiabene, who, having been converted to Judaism in the first century A.D., sent scholars to Palestine to translate the Bible into Syriac. Most scholars now agree that it originated in Edessa, that the Pentateuch was begun in the first century A.D., and that the entire Bible was completed by the end of the fourth century A.D. However, conflicting data suggest either that its authorship was Christian with Jewish help, or Jewish with later Christian revisions.

Although the Pesh. preserves a close conformity to the Hebrew text, it is currently believed to have been translated from LXX, especially from the Hexapla. In style, the translation of the Pentateuch, Isaiah, the Minor Prophets, and partly the Psalms, shows the influence of LXX; Ezekiel and Proverbs are in close agreement with the corresponding Jewish Targums; Job is literal, Ruth is midrashic, and Chronicles is partly midrashic and of a late period.

In the fifth century A.D., theological differences divided the Syrian Christians into the Nestorians and Jacobites. Each group then proceeded to formulate its own Pesh. text based on previous versions, with the result that today there are the Western and Eastern forms of the Pesh.

Important to the autonomous Septuagintal studies is the translation (in 617) by Paul, the bishop of Tella, based on Origen's Hexapla. It is important because, like the Armenian version, it preserved the signs of the fifth column of Origen's Hexapla and noted the works of Aquila, Theodotion, and Symmachus in the margin.

III. Canons of Textual Criticism

In the light of this varied history, it is not surprising that a strictly prescribed method of OT textual criticism has never been worked out. There are, however, basic rules that help place the criticism of the OT text on firm basis in order to avoid arbitrariness and subjectivity.

1. Where the Hebrew MSS and ancient versions agree, it may be assumed that the original reading has been preserved.

2. Where Hebrew MSS and ancient versions differ among themselves, one should choose either the more difficult reading (*lectio difficilior*) from the point of view of language and subject matter or the reading that most readily makes the development of the other reading(s) intelligible. To make this choice, one should be fully knowledgeable of the history and character of the recensions discussed above. Moreover, these criteria should be understood as complementing one another so that one may arrive at a reasonable and worthy text, for a "more difficult reading" does not mean a "meaningless and corrupt reading."

3. Where Hebrew MSS and ancient versions offer good and sensible readings and a superior reading cannot be demonstrated on the basis of the above two rules, one should, as a matter of first principle, allow MT to stand.

4. Where Hebrew MSS and ancient versions differ and none offers a passable sense, one may attempt a conjecture concerning the true reading—a conjecture that must be validated by demonstrating the process of the textual corruption from the original to the existing text-forms. Such conjectures, however, can never be used to validate the interpretation of the whole passage in that they will have been made on the basis of an expectation derived from the whole.

IV. Bibliography

Hebrew Manuscripts

(For extensive bibliography of handbooks, monographs, and articles on the text of the OT, see Hospers, J.H. *A Basic Bibliography for the study of the Semitic Languages,* vol. 1 Leiden: E.J. Brill, 1973, pp. 203–05.)

Albright, W.F. *From the Stone Age to Christianity.* Garden City, N.Y.: Doubleday, 1957, p. 79.
———. "New Light on Early Recensions of the Hebrew Bible." *Bulletin of the American Schools of Oriental Research* 140 (Dec. 1955): 29–30.
Barr, J. *Comparative Philology and the Text of the Old Testament.* Oxford: Clarendon Press, 1968, pp. 194ff.
Cross, F.M., Jr. *The Ancient Library of Qumran and Modern Biblical Studies.* New York: Doubleday, Anchor Books, 1961, pp. 169ff.

_____. "The Development of Jewish Scripts." In *The Bible and the Ancient Near East*. Edited by G.E. Wright. New York: Doubleday, 1961.

_____. "The History of the Biblical Text in the Light of Discoveries in the Judean Desert." *Harvard Theological Review* 57 (1964): 287ff.

Gesenius, G. *De Pentateuchi Samaritani origine, indole et auctoritate*. Halle: Renger, 1815.

Goshen-Gottstein, M. "The Authenticity of the Aleppo Codex." *Textus*, I (1960).

Kitchen, K.A. *Ancient Orient and Old Testament*. Chicago: Inter-Varsity, 1966, p. 140.

Kline, M. *The Structure of Biblical Authority*. Grand Rapids: Eerdmans, 1972.

Margolis, M.L. *Hebrew Scripture in the Making*. Philadelphia: Jewish Publication Society, 1922.

Martin, M. *Scribal Character of the DDS*. Luvain: Publication Universiataires, 1958, pp. 170ff.

Morag, S. "On the Historical Validity of the Vocalization of the Hebrew Bible," JAOS (1974), pp. 307–15.

Moran, W.J. "The Hebrew Language in Its Northwest Semitic Background." In *The Bible and the Ancient Near East*. Edited by G.E. Wright. New York: Doubleday, 1961, p. 59.

Sarna, N.M. "Bible." JE 4 (1971): 831–35.

Talmon, S. "Double Readings in the Massoretic Text," *Textus* 1 (1960): 144–84.

Waltke, B.K. "The Samaritan Pentateuch and the Text of the Old Testament." In *New Perspectives on the Old Testament*. Edited by J. Barton Payne. Waco, Texas: Word, 1970.

Ancient Versions

(For extensive bibliography up to 1951, see Roberts, B.J. *The Old Testament Text and Versions*. Cardiff: University of Wales, 1951, pp. 287–314.)

1. LXX

(For extensive bibliography on LXX from about 1860 to 1969, see Brook, Sebastian; Fritsch, Charles T.; and Jellicoe, Sidney. 'A Classified Bibliography of the Septuagint," in *Arbeiten zur Literatur und Geschichte des Hellinistischen Judentums*, VI. Leiden: Brill, 1973.)

Albrektson, B. *Studies in the Text and the Theology of the Book of Lamentations*. Lund: Gleerup, 1963.

Daniel, S. "Bible." JE 4 (1971): 851–55.

Driver, S.R. *Notes on the Hebrew Text ... of the Books of Samuel*. Oxford: Clarendon, 1913, pp. xxxiii–lxxxiii.

Gerleman, G. *Studies in the Septuagint I. Book of Job*. Lund: Gleerup, 1946.

Jellicoe, Sidney. *The Septuagint and Modern Studies*. Oxford: Clarendon, 1968.

_____. *Studies in the Septuagint: Origins, Recensions, and Interpretations*. New York: Ktav, 1974.

Klein, R.W. *Textual Criticism of the Old Testament*. Philadelphia: Fortress, 1974.

Ottley, R.R. *A Handbook to the Septuagint*. London: Methuen, 1920.

Shenkel, J.D. *Chronology and Recensional Development in the Greek Text of Kings*. Cambridge: Harvard University Press, 1968.

Swete, H.B. *An Introduction to the Old Testament in Greek*. Revised by R.R. Ottley. Cambridge: Cambridge University Press, 1914.

Walters, Peter. *The Text of the Septuagint*. Edited by D.W. Gooding. 2 vols. Cambridge: Cambridge University Press, 1973.

2. Targums

(For bibliography see Bowker, J. *The Targums and Rabbinic Literature*. Cambridge: Cambridge University Press, 1969; and McNamara, M. *Targum and Testament*. Grand Rapids: Eerdmans, 1972.)

Grossfeld, B. "Bible." JE 4 (1971): 842–51.

3. Latin

Kedar-Kopfstein. *The Vulgate As a Translation.* Jerusalem: Hebrew University Press, 1968.

4. Peshitta

Baars, W. "A Palestinian Syriac Text of the Book of Lamentations." VetTest 10 (1960): 224–27; 13 (1963): 260–68; 18 (1968): 548–54.

Goshen-Gottstein, M. "A List of Some Uncatalogued Syriac Manuscripts." BJRL 37 (1954/55): 429–45.

————. *Text and Language in Bible and Qumran.* Jerusalem: Orient, 1960.

Narkiss, Bezalel. "Bible." JE 4 (1971): 958–59.

Rowlands, E.R. "The Targum and the Peshitta Version of the Book of Isaiah." VetTest 9 (1959): 178–91.

Vööbus, A. *Discoveries of Very Important Manuscript Sources for the Syro-Hexapla.* Stockholm: Estonian Theological Society, 1970.

————. *The Hexapla and the Syro-Hexapla.* Stockholm: Estonian Theological Society, 1971.

————. *Peshitta und Targumim des Pentateuchs.* Stockholm: Estonian Theological Society, 1958.

Wernberg-Møller. "Prolegomena to a Re-examination of the Palestinian Targum Fragments of the Book of Genesis Published by P. Kahle and Their Relationship to the Peshitta." *Journal of Semitic Studies* 7 (1962): 253–66.

————. "Some Observations on the Relationship of the Peshitta Version of the Book of Genesis to the Palestinian Targum Fragments." *Studia Theologica* 15 (1961): 128–80.

HISTORICAL AND LITERARY CRITICISM OF THE OLD TESTAMENT

R.K. Harrison

R.K. Harrison

B.D., M.Th., Ph.D., University of London; D.D., University of Western Ontario

Professor of Old Testament, Wycliffe College, University of Toronto

HISTORICAL AND LITERARY CRITICISM OF THE OLD TESTAMENT

I. **Historical Criticism**

    A. **Purpose and Nature**
    B. **Place of Archaeology**
    C. **Middle Bronze Age**
    D. **Iron Age**
    E. **Babylonian Period**
    F. **Persian Period**
    G. **Greek Period**

II. **Literary Criticism**

    A. **Pentateucal Criticism**
    B. **Liturgical Tradition Criticism**
    C. **Isaiah**
    D. **Daniel**
    E. **Other Books**

III. **Conclusion**
IV. **Bibliography**

I. Historical Criticism

A. *Purpose and Nature*

Historical criticism of the OT may be defined as that branch of study which deals with the actual historical content of the scriptural text. It is concerned primarily with attempts to establish the historicity of such diverse events as the Noachian flood, the Exodus from Egypt, the campaigns of Joshua, the vicissitudes of the monarchy, the postexilic restoration, and other happenings of Hebrew history as recorded in the OT. It also seeks to root within the historical process the important personages mentioned in the narratives, whether Israelite or not. The primary purpose of this activity is to give the readers of Scripture as accredited an historical picture of ancient Hebrew life as possible.

This is important not merely because it may confirm or enhance the trustworthiness of the biblical record, but because it provides an assured basis for other kinds of investigation. Thus, in a study of the various aspects of Hebrew religion, the reader ought to know whether or not a characteristic institution such as the tabernacle was in fact as historical an entity as is indicated by the Pentateuch and other narrative sources. If historical criticism cannot help us do this, the validity of the institution is immediately thrown into serious doubt—a situation that has repercussions not merely for the primary objectives of the investigation but also for the authenticity of the narrative material and the means by which it has been transmitted and preserved.

For those who hold that the OT is replete with legend, particularly in the early canonical writings, there will be little point in trying to apply the principles of historical criticism. If, however, these same OT sources are regarded as early Semitic historiography, they appear in an entirely different light and so warrant investigation by all the means available to the modern scholar, of which historical criticism is one.

This latter discipline involves a number of related activities such as form criticism, a study that enables literary materials to be recognized and classified according to their genres. In addition, historical criticism demands a thorough knowledge of ancient Near Eastern historiography, so that methods of transmission and the significance of scribal techniques may be appreciated fully. Furthermore, it requires a wide understanding of the nature of Near Eastern culture in antiquity, since the Hebrews formed an integral part of that culture throughout the biblical period and therefore should not be in isolation from the rest of contemporary society.

Comparative historiographic studies have shown that, along with the Hittites, the ancient Hebrews were the most accurate, objective, and responsible recorders of Near Eastern history. Indeed, a realization of this is fundamental to any proper preliminary application of historical criticism. The contemporaneous nature of much Near Eastern historiography has now become apparent to modern scholars with the discovery that, in antiquity, events were written down at the time when they occurred, or shortly thereafter. This recording was frequently done in the form of annals, regardless of the existence of accompanying oral or sometimes pictorial tradition. Documents of this kind have survived the ravages of time and serve as important complementary material to the biblical record. Form-critical studies of books such as Genesis and Deuteronomy, based on specific types of tablets recovered from sites that include Mari, Nuzu, and Boghazköy, have shown that the canonical material has certain nonliterary counterparts in the cultures of some ancient Near Eastern peoples. As a result, it is possible to view with a new degree of confidence and respect those early traditions of the Hebrews that purport to be historiographic in nature.

Historical criticism is not without its problems, of course, one of which is the a priori notion that nothing in the OT should be accepted as historical fact until it can be demonstrated as such by extrabiblical evidence. Clearly this is both unacceptable as a theoretical position and impossible of attainment in specific instances. Many of the scriptural records have to do with people and situations that were of no interest whatever to non-Hebrews who might otherwise have provided confirmatory source material. Even where the latter may perhaps have existed, as with inscriptions dealing with Joseph or Moses, it has in most cases failed to survive the passage of time.

B. *Place of Archaeology*

While such problems might appear to be a serious obstacle to historical criticism, they have been offset to a great extent by archaeological discoveries that have brought into relief the larger Near Eastern background against which the Hebrews can be more accurately assessed. Even so, archaeology must not be regarded as the sole determining consideration in matters of historical criticism, since it, too, is beset with its own kind of problems. These include poor excavating techniques in earlier days, the varied interpretation of specific artifacts, and the difficulty of establishing an assured chronological framework into which events can be placed with confidence. Archaeology is in no sense an adequate "control" mechanism by which OT historic sequences stand or fall.

Nevertheless, archaeological discoveries have assisted enormously in demonstrating the historicity of certain OT events and personages, and in other areas have furnished an authentic social and cultural background against which many OT narratives can be set with assurance. Numerous cuneiform texts that have been unearthed show how the Mesopotamian writers of early historiographic material expressed themselves in terms of a world view, as is the case in the first few chapters of Genesis, thereby indicating that the latter should not be taken as myth, but as Mesopotamian historiography.

C. Middle Bronze Age

Excavations at sites such as Mari, Nuzu, and Alalakh have furnished a great deal of information about the Middle Bronze Age, in which it is now possible to set the Patriarchs, without, however, having recovered any actual personal remains of the individuals themselves. Some of their names were preserved in the designation of sites such as Serug, Peleg, and Terah, located in the Balikh valley south of Haran, while in the Mari texts Nahor was known as Nakhur and was the home of some of the Habiru. In the second millennium B.C. Jacob was occurring as a Palestinian place-name.[1]

The adoption-texts recovered from Nuzu show that Abraham was guided by contemporary customs in his choice of Eleazar as heir (Gen 15:2, 3) and Hagar as his concubine (Gen 16:2). Two generations later Rachel was to give Bilhah to Jacob in conformity with the same social traditions (Gen 30:3). The transfer of the birthright from Esau to Jacob (Gen 25:31ff.) has been explained satisfactorily by reference to the Nuzu tablets, as have the relations between Jacob and Laban (Gen 31) and the character of the patriarchal benedictions in Genesis (Gen 27:27ff.; 49:3ff.). Even the biblical traditions about the early domestication of the camel have at last been vindicated by archaeological dicoveries.[2] As noted above, no artifacts have been unearthed that can be identified unquestionably with any of the patriarchal figures. This is not to say that they do not exist, however, and if the excavation of the Cave of Machpelah ever becomes a possibility, there is little doubt that the historical criticism of the patriarchal narratives would be marked by immediate and significant advances.

Attempts to argue from archaeological discoveries to the historicity of the Noachian deluge have proved inconclusive to the present. Late Jemdet Nasr levels at Shuruppak revealed the presence of a large alluvial deposit, while at Kish an analogous stratum measured eighteen inches in depth. Langdon described this latter in terms of Noah's flood, and Woolley adopted a similar position regarding an eight-foot alluvial deposit from the middle Obeid period at Ur. Unfortunately for their interpretation, these two levels are not contemporary, and alluvial levels at Uruk and Lagash do not correspond with the dating of the Ur stratum. At Tell el-Obeid, about four miles from Ur, there were no traces of water-laid strata when Woolley excavated the mound. Similar problems of identification are connected with what may be thought to remain of Noah's ark.[3] The mountains of Ararat (Gen 8:4) where the vessel rested may possibly be identified with the district known in Assyrian inscriptions as *Urartu*, though this is still uncertain. For

---

[1]Cf. W.F. Albright, *The Biblical Period From Abraham to Ezra* (New York: Harper & Row, 1963), p. 2.
[2]Cf. A. Parrot, *Syria* (1955), 32:323.
[3]J. Warwick Montgomery, *The Quest for Noah's Ark* (Minneapolis: Bethany Fellowship, 1972), pp. 23ff.

some centuries reports have persisted of a mysterious shiplike object located under the ice at the 14,000-foot level of Mount Ararat, and although attempts have been made recently to initiate the excavation of the artifact, they have been unsuccessful at the time of writing. Wooden fragments allegedly taken from the site have been dated c. 2000 B.C. by radiocarbon assessment, but even if the object proved to be an ancient wooden vessel, problems of identification would still remain.

But should these problems be dispelled by the recovery of some object such as a clay tablet that would confirm the association of the artifact with Noah beyond any reasonable doubt, the historicity of the celebrated deluge would be established on a basis acceptable to even the most skeptical observer. Until corroborative evidence for particular situations is available, it is not possible for the scholar to do any more than argue from the Near Eastern background as currently known to the probability of consonant phenomena in Scripture's being actual historical occurrences. Interestingly enough, however, the current flow of archaeological discoveries tends to confirm, rather than repudiate, the claim of the OT to historicity. Hence, the main problem faced by historical criticism in this and other areas seems to be a lack of contemporary objective data associated with the specific biblical personages and events.

This situation is particularly acute in the case of Moses, for whom no secular corroborative information is extant. This is not to say that such never existed, but merely that it has not been recovered, and may never be. From the standpoint of external evidence, therefore, the historicity of Moses is very hard to demonstrate. Yet archaeological discoveries have furnished a rich background of information about the New Kingdom period against which the biblical Moses can be placed with great reliability. For example, papyrus documents relating to the royal *harîm* in the Fayyum described the varied activities of the women and children who lived there, and this may be taken as typical of other similar royal residences in the Delta area. Young princes in the *harems* were given tutors for their basic education (cf. Acts 7:22), and subsequently were trained in sports, athletic pursuits, and military activities. Semites and Asiatics occupied positions at every level of New Kingdom society. One of them, a Syrian named Ben-'Ozen, actually helped to oversee the work done on Meneptah's tomb in the Valley of the Kings. Another Syrian controlled Egypt for a short time at the end of the Nineteenth Dynasty.[4] Some Canaanite deities were well known to many New Kingdom Egyptians, having been assimilated into cultic worship at an earlier period, and even the language of Canaan was not unfamiliar to Egyptian scribes and government officials.

While none of this information proves conclusively that the biblical Moses actually underwent the sort of training in literary and administrative areas that the educated classes received, it does furnish an accredited historical and cultural background against which the recorded activities of such a person as Moses can be credibly set. It shows, furthermore, that there was nothing unusual about Semites being brought up in royal *harems* and trained for various levels of responsibility in the state during the New Kingdom period. Hence if the correctness of the tradition in Exodus 2:10, 11 is granted, it will immediately follow that Moses would have passed through the same kind of training as that accorded other *harem-princes*, though it should be noted that even the biblical narrative furnishes no details about this.

---

[4]According to Albright, the proto-Sinaitic inscriptions (c. 1500 B.C.) can be interpreted to indicate that the Semites still maintained their own language and culture while serving as slaves within the Egyptian empire (W.F. Albright, *Proto-Sinaitic Inscriptions and Their Decipherment* [Cambridge: Harvard University Press, 1969]).

However, even this latter is unexceptionable, since apart from a few individuals such as Samuel and the young Jesus, little interest is shown in Scripture about the boyhood or adolescence of its notable personages. As indicated above, an Egyptian New Kingdom milieu suits the narratives dealing with Moses better than any other historical period. The fact that the Exodus material needs to be linked with the Avaris era for this purpose shows something of the extent to which chronological considerations are involved with historical criticism.

Attempts to demonstrate the historicity of the Exodus from Egypt encounter similar problems through lack of specific external corroboration. A fifteenth- and thirteenth-century B.C. date have been postulated, both of which can claim some support from the OT and archaeology.[5] A chronological note in 1 Kings 6:1 would place the date of the Exodus at about 1441 B.C., assuming that Solomon reigned from c.971 to c.931 B.C. If, however, the reference is schematic rather than literal, it might indicate a cycle of twelve generations comprising forty years each, and thus may throw no real light on the problem.

Some scholars equated the activities of the marauding Habiru as mentioned in the Tell el-Amarna letters with a fifteenth-century B.C. Hebrew conquest of Canaan under Joshua, but more critical study of the tablets has dispelled that theory. Attempts by John Garstang to show from excavations at OT Jericho that the Exodus occurred under Amenhotep II (c.1436–1422 B.C.) have also proved abortive with the discovery by Kathleen Kenyon that the city level on which Garstang was relying for his dating sequence was about a millennium older than he had thought and thus not relevant either for Joshua's campaigns or the Exodus.

A date for the latter in the first half of the thirteenth century B.C. is based primarily on archaeological evidence, although it depends partly on the reference in Exodus 1:11, which implies that Israelites helped enlarge Pithom and Raamses. This would make Ramses II (c.1290–1224 B.C.) the pharaoh of the oppression and the ruler named on statues, stelae, and other artifacts recovered from excavations by Montet at Nineteenth Dynasty levels of Per-Re'emasese (House of Ramses), the contemporary name for Avaris, the former Hyksos capital. The stele of Meneptah precludes a date much beyond 1220 B.C. for the entry of Israel into Canaan, since the inscription, written in the fifth year of his reign (c.1219 B.C.) and recording his victories in east Asia, mentioned Israel as a people, thus implying sedentary occupation of Western Palestine.

But even this kind of information fails to say anything that would establish the time of the Exodus firmly. Excavations at thirteenth-century B.C. levels of sites such as Ai, Bethel, Lachish, Debir, and Hazor have shown clear evidence of the destruction that has been associated by many scholars with Joshua's campaigns. Even here, however, there are some difficulties, chiefly in the identification of Bethel, Ai, and Debir and the interpretation of the evidence from the cities burned on their tells, namely Ai, Jericho, and Hazor. This latter has been taken by scholars such as Rowton, Waltke, and others as indicating a fifteenth-century B.C. date rather than one occurring at the end of the Late Bronze Age. Unfortunately, it is possible to arrive at a date for the Exodus only on the basis of the cumulative evidence, since there are no surviving monuments or stelae to supply an exact chronology of events. However, such evidence as is available seems to the present writer to support a later rather than an earlier date for the Exodus, though certainty will be precluded until more conclusive evidence is obtained.

---

[5]Cf. L.T. Wood, in J.B. Payne, ed., *New Perspectives on the Old Testament* (Waco: Word, 1970), pp. 66ff.

D. Iron Age

Archaeology has thrown a good deal of light on the state of the early monarchy, with contemporary conditions amply reflected in artifacts recovered from the Late Canaanite stage at Beth-shemesh (Ain Shems) and from Gibeah (Tell el-Ful) in the time of Saul. The pagan Canaanite culture of Ugarit has been starkly illustrated by excavations at Ras Shamra, and it is now clear that the OT statements that related to this depraved people were not merely strictly factual but, if anything, rather moderate in tone. The Ras Shamra texts have added immensely to what was already known from the OT about preexilic religion in Canaan, and have confirmed all the strictures of the prophets.[6]

Explorations in the Wadi Arabah have uncovered evidence of metallurgical activity at Iron Age I and II levels. This evidently began in the time of Solomon and was developed under his successors. What was once thought to have been a smelter at Ezion Geber, however, is now interpreted by some scholars as a citadel or granary,[7] an interpretation in which Glueck, the discoverer of the evidence, concurred.

The invasion of Judah in 925 B.C. by Shishak I of Egypt, who carried off much of the treasure accumulated by Solomon over a lifetime, has been confirmed by Shishak's inscription on the temple walls at Karnak. A fragment of one of his steles was actually unearthed as far north as Megiddo, showing the extent of his Palestinian penetration.

From this period onward, historical confirmation of the OT narratives is a much simpler matter, due to the comparative availability of extrabiblical evidence. The inscribed stele of Benhadad I, found in 1940 at a north Syrian site,[8] has furnished general confirmation of the Syrian list in 1 Kings 15:18, without, however, identifying the Rezon who founded the Damascene dynasty or being specific about the number of Benhadads who ruled in Damascus. The discovery of the Moabite Stone in 1868 illustrated the vigor that Omri of Israel (c.880–873 B.C.) displayed toward neighboring nations, and not least toward the Moabites. At this time Israel was referred to in Assyrian records as *Bit-Humri* (House of Omri), a designation that was also applied to Samaria, the royal capital. Omri's successors were known as *mar-Humri* or "offspring of Omri." "Ahab the Israelite" was mentioned in the Monolith Inscription of Shalmaneser III (c.858–824 B.C.) as the leader of a powerful military group, while the Black Obelisk of Shalmaneser, found by Layard at Nimrud in 1846, depicted Jehu, or his representative, kneeling submissively before the Assyrian king and offering tribute.

A jasper seal found by Schumacher at Megiddo in 1904 and inscribed "Shema, servant of Jeroboam" almost certainly refers to Jeroboam II (c.781–743 B.C.). The Khorsabad annals of Sargon II (c.772–705) recorded the fall of the northern kingdom in 722, while two decades later the Assyrian invasion of Judah, which resulted in Hezekiah's becoming tributary, was described in the annals of Sennacherib. The discovery in 1880 of a tunnel leading from the pool of Siloam and containing an inscription written in eighth-century B.C. script (c.701) amply confirmed the activity mentioned in 2 Kings 20:20 and 2 Chronicles 32:30. The Canaanite characters of the Siloam Inscription are particularly valuable because of the scarcity of contemporary material written in Hebrew.

The discovery by D.J. Wiseman in 1956 of four additional tablets of the Babylonian Chronicle in the archives of the British Museum provided the first extrabiblical confir-

---

[6]Cf. C.F. Pfeiffer, *Ras Shamra and the Bible* (Grand Rapids: Baker, 1962).

[7]B. Rothenberg, PEQ (1962) pp. 5–71; K.M. Kenyon, *Archaeology in the Holy Land* (New York: Praeger, 1970), p. 346.

[8]Cf. W.F. Albright, *BASOR*, no. 87 (1942), pp. 23ff.; ibid. no. 90 (1943), pp. 30ff.

mation of the capture of Jerusalem in 597 B.C., dating it precisely on the second of Adar (March 15–16). In addition to mentioning the defeat of the Egyptian forces at Carchemish in 605, the tablets preserved an account of a previously unrecorded battle between Egypt and Babylon in 601, in which both sides suffered heavy losses. This material thus confirms the OT tradition that Jerusalem fell to Babylon in 597 and again in 587.[9]

The recovery between 1935 and 1938 from Lachish of twenty-one potsherds inscribed in the ancient Canaanite script illumined in an invaluable way the times of the prophet Jeremiah. The sherds were found in the ruins of a guardroom just outside the city gates and comprised correspondence and lists of names that can be dated quite accurately from the autumn of 589 B.C. The letters consisted of military dispatches written from an outpost north of Lachish to a person named Joash, who was one of the commanders of Lachish. One ostracon mentioned a "prophet" who had been relaying messages, but whether this was Jeremiah or some other (unknown) contemporary cannot be determined from the evidence. Another potsherd complained about the royal officials sending out demoralizing communications that were "weakening the hands" of the populace. Ironically enough, this was the identical charge the same officials had laid against Jeremiah in the time of Zedekiah (Jer 38:4). Small wonder, then, that the Lachish correspondence has been considered an important secular "supplement" to the book of Jeremiah.[10]

E. *Babylonian Period*

The historicity of the Babylonian captivity has been demonstrated by excavations near the Ishtar Gate. These uncovered several tablets listing rations of grain and oil given to captives living in Babylon between 595 and 570 B.C. The list of the royal princes included Jehoiachin, described as "Yaukin, king of the land of Yahud," who was mentioned in 2 Kings 25:29, 30 as a recipient of Babylonian royal bounty.[11] Even the general area occupied by the exiles in Babylonia can be identified with reasonable certainty as the result of excavations at Nippur. The "river Chebar" of Ezekiel's day was referred to on two tablets dated about 443 and 424 under the designation of *naru kabari* or *nehar kebar*. It was an irrigation canal that joined the Euphrates just north of Babylon and flowed through Nippur. The name "Tel Abib" (Ezek 3:15), the Hebrew form of the Babylonian *Til Adubi* ("mound of the flood") was commonly found in all phases of Babylonian history, and this makes it difficult to identify the actual site of the exilic occupation with complete confidence.

Another problem of identification within this general period concerns the identity of Darius the Mede. One of the Nabonidus texts discovered at Haran refered to the "king of the Medes" in 546 B.C., thereby inviting the suggestion that it might have been an alternative royal title used by Cyrus. Another solution, also based on cuneiform sources, has been proposed by J.C. Whitcomb, who emphasized that most translations of the Nabonidus Chronicle failed to distinguish between two separate persons mentioned in the narrative, namely Ugbaru and Gubaru.

Accordingly, he suggested that the former was the governor of Gutium who participated in the attack on Babylon and died shortly afterwards in 539 B.C. Thereupon Cyrus appointed Gubaru governor of Babylon, and he reigned for about fourteen years, being

9D.J. Wiseman, *Chronicles of Chaldean Kings* (London: Trustees of the British Museum, 1959), pp. 32ff.
10Cf. H. Torczyner, *Lachish I, The Lachish Letters* (New York: Oxford University Press, 1938).
11Cf. W.F. Albright, BA (1942) 4:49, 50.

known in the book of Daniel as Darius the Mede. Despite the lack of additional corroborative evidence, it is now clear that Darius the Mede can be regarded legitimately as an historical personage, whatever his true identity may prove to have been.[12]

F. Persian Period

The Hebrew version of the decree by which Cyrus permitted the exiles in Babylon to return to their homeland is preserved in the first chapter of Ezra. The official Persian record on the Cyrus Cylinder shows that peoples other than the Hebrews had also been enslaved by the Babylonians. The semiautonomous nature of the returned Judean community as indicated in Ezra and Nehemiah has been corroborated by the discovery of fifth- and fourth-century B.C. seal impressions of the province of Judah.

Geshem, the Arab who opposed Nehemiah, was mentioned in a late-fifth-century B.C. Aramaic inscription on a silver bowl found at Tell el-Maskhutah, and on another recovered from Hegra in Arabia. These sources show that Geshem controlled an Arab domain that included Sinai, North Arabia, Edom, part of the Nile delta, and possibly the southern area of Judah, where small altars similar to those recovered from south Arabia have been found. This large Arab kingdom enjoyed a good measure of autonomy within the Persian empire.

The authenticity of the Aramaic correspondence in Ezra was demonstrated with the discovery of the Elephantine papyri in 1903.[13] This material comprised Aramaic letters and other documents from Jews living in a military colony on the island of Elephantine near Aswan, and can be dated between 500 and 400 B.C. Legal contracts and deeds recovered were attested by witnesses, sealed, and identified as to their contents by means of a brief notation on the outside of the papyrus in the familiar Babylonian manner the Persians had adopted unchanged. The papyri are important for the historicity of Ezra, because they make it clear that the Aramaic used there was characteristic of contemporary language and style.

There is some difference between the biblical spelling of royal names and that current after the fifth century B.C., but it may be that Ezra preserved earlier Persian forms subsequently modified. The descendants of Tobiah, one of Nehemiah's opponents, can be traced as far as the second century B.C. by means of the ruined family dwelling in Transjordan, which was built by the last governor in the family between 200 and 175 B.C. On the rock face near the burial vaults the name Tobiah was carved in the Aramaic script of the third century B.C., confirming the identification.

G. Greek Period

The spread of Greek culture throughout the Near East after the collapse of the Persian empire is well attested historically, as is the reaction in the second century B.C. of the orthodox Jews to the attempted Hellenizing of Judea. This is important in furnishing information about a period that stands outside the lower historical limits of the OT canonical writings, but which is anticipated in works such as the Book of Daniel. Where points of contact occur, the secular historians confirm the accuracy of their biblical counterparts.

From the foregoing survey it will be evident that the principal obstacle to the appli-

---

[12]J.C. Whitcomb, *Darius the Mede*, (Grand Rapids: Eerdmans, 1959), pp. 5ff.
[13]Cf. A. Cowley, *Aramaic Papyri of the Fifth Century B.C.*, 1923; E.G. Kraeling, *The Brooklyn Museum Aramaic Papyri*, 1953.

cation of historical criticism to specific events and personages is the lack of adequate information. It is a commonplace among Near Eastern scholars that relevant modern archaeological discoveries support rather than refute the testimony of the biblical authors. When they are interpreted by means of an accredited Near Eastern methodology, they provide a proper background against which events may be understood. While there are periods on which historical criticism is as yet unable to throw much light, there are also many potential sources of information that await excavation. We might hope, therefore, that the limitations characterizing this approach in certain areas will be removed by discoveries that will furnish the factual information necessary for a clear understanding of what actually occurred. Should this take place, we can expect it to confirm the authenticity of the biblical record, as other discoveries have done, and increase the respect of the reader for the accuracy of OT historiography.

II. Literary Criticism

Literary criticism deals predominantly with such matters as underlying literary sources, types of literature, and questions relating to the authorship, unity, and date of the various OT materials. It reflects a lengthy period of growth, beginning with the attempts of second-century A.D. Gnostics to disparage certain OT writings, and continuing in the following century with the diatribes of the Neoplatonists, of whom Porphyry was a notable representative. The fact that these persons and others in later periods adopted a largely negative view of the traditional authorship and date of much of the OT should not be taken to imply that literary criticism is itself necessarily negative in character. It is a branch of study that investigates as impartially and objectively as possible the matters mentioned above that lie within its scope. That it has at times been captious and overly negative in attacking the authenticity of specific materials and the historicity of certain events and persons is an unfortunate outcome of the way literary criticism began. But it does not invalidate the value of this kind of criticism when responsibly used.

A. Pentateuchal Criticism

The negativism of earlier literary studies continued during the medieval period, and by the eleventh century a number of difficulties had been raised in connection with the Pentateuch, which seemed to present the most pressing problems, and also with the Book of Daniel. Bodenstein, a contemporary of Luther, rejected the Mosaic authorship of the Pentateuch, a position that was adopted with some modifications by Thomas Hobbes, Spinoza, and Richard Simon. The latter, a Roman Catholic priest, used literary criticism to show that the Pentateuch could not have come from Moses himself and that the historical books resulted from a prolonged redactional activity by generations of scribes.

By the eighteenth century the Pentateuch was becoming the focal point of literary-critical attention. Astruc (1684–1766) introduced the fact of the divergent use of divine names in Genesis and Exodus as a "criterion" for literary-critical analysis of the Pentateuch. He did not deny Mosaic authorship, but felt that Genesis had been compiled by Moses on the basis of the sources supposedly indicated by the variant divine names. But even Astruc realized that his new-found "criterion" was inadequate and needed to be supplemented by textual manipulations.

The process of fragmenting the Pentateuch into supposedly underlying sources had now begun, and the essential subjectivity of the approach led to widely differing conclusions as to "documents," dates of materials, authorship, and the like. J.G. Eichhorn (1752–1827), a moderate rationalist, extended Astruc's "criterion" to include literary peculiarities and stylistic diversities, while J.S. Vater suggested about forty different fragments as sources for the Pentateuch and assigned the finished form to the exilic period. W.M.L. de Wette dated the earliest parts of the Pentateuch much later than other scholars and was the first to suggest that the legal nucleus of Deuteronomy was in fact the law scroll discovered in King Josiah's reign.

These views ran into vigorous opposition from those convinced of the essential Mosaic authorship of the Pentateuch, including H. Ewald, who advanced arguments for the literary unity of Genesis and roundly condemned fragmentation. E.W. Hengstenberg was an even more vigorous opponent of the various documentary hypotheses, and published many books denouncing the new critical approaches.

The classical liberal position regarding Pentateuchal source-analysis was established by K.H. Graf and J. Wellhausen. Building on the evolutionary philosophy of Hegel, Wellhausen adapted earlier speculations to isolate four allegedly underlying "documents" in the Pentateuch, as expounded in his book *Die Komposition des Hexateuchs*, published in the *Jahrbücher für Deutsche Theologie* in 1877. These were the Jehovistic (J), Elohistic (E), Deuteronomic (D), and Priestly (P) sources respectively. The first was dated in the ninth century B.C., not long after writing was supposed to have been invented; the second about a century later; the third about the time of Josiah (640–609); the fourth from perhaps the fifth century B.C. Wellhausen also rewrote Hebrew history to conform to the evolutionary notions of the day, with the result that the Mosaic legislation became the basic code of postexilic Judaism rather than the point from which Israelite religious institutions began.

So attractive was the evolutionary concept in literary criticism, as also in contemporary biological science, that the source theory of Pentateuchal origins began to prevail over all opposition, however notable or vocal, and was soon entrenched as the only respectable view of the composition of the Pentateuch. However, this turn of events did not entirely deter those who thought differently. A mediating view of some aspects of the theory was expressed by C.F.A. Dillmann, R. Kittel, W.H. Baudissin, A. Klostermann, and others, while Franz Delitzsch rejected the hypothesis outright in his commentary on Genesis, E.C. Bissell and James Orr also stood in this same general tradition of opposition to developmental theories of origins.

A new approach to the criticism of Wellhausenian theorizing came with the application of the developing discipline of archaeology to OT study. It focused attention on vulnerable areas of literary-critical speculation, for Wellhausen and his followers had ignored the increasing corpus of archaeological material that was demonstrating the antiquity of Near Eastern religious and cultural institutions. In the hands of A.H. Sayce this type of study began to erode the liberal position, and not long before his death, S.R. Driver, who had modified European literary criticism to suit the less-radical British tastes, was himself constrained to write a book showing how modern archaeological research was "illustrating the Bible."

Out of an increasing stream of objections to the arbitrary nature and essential subjectivity of the new method of study arose a type of investigation known as form-criticism. Associated with Hermann Gunkel, it was an attempt to trace the fundamental religious ideas of the OT back to their oral form. The method assumed that the Genesis narratives had originally been transmitted orally, and reduced to written form at some period before the eighth century B.C. to form the basis of the alleged "documents" underlying the Pentateuch. Gunkel was endeavoring to recover the spiritual values the Graf-Wellhausen theory had obscured, but at the same time he made it clear that for him the Genesis material was folklore. He extended his method to the Psalter with somewhat greater success,[14] and though his approach was subsequently criticized, it constituted an important challenge to the validity of earlier literary-critical speculation.

Other scholars also found themselves increasingly at variance with previous liberal interpretations, though often in the direction of greater fragmentation. Thus R. Smend and W. Eichrodt attempted to prove that there were two Jehovistic authors, not one, but this trend was reversed partially by P. Volz and W. Rudolph, who rejected the four-document hypothesis of Pentateuchal compilation in favor of authorship by the Jehovistic narrator with perhaps some editorial assistance. The postulated unity of the Genesis priestly material was opposed by G. von Rad, who in 1934 attempted to show that it had consisted originally of two independent parallel strands placed side by side. Although von Rad hinted at a comparatively early date for the priestly narratives, his suggestions met with little enthusiasm among scholars generally.

Meanwhile, interest was shifting to Deuteronomy, and to an examination of the view that had linked it with Josiah's religious reforms. In 1911 J.B. Griffiths argued on archaeological and philological grounds that Deuteronomy could not possibly have originated in the time of Josiah, and eight years later Kegel also urged acceptance of the antiquity and genuineness of the work. In 1920, however, R.H. Kennett went further than previous scholars in placing Deuteronomy in the exilic age, but was outmatched two years later by G. Hölscher, who assigned the finished book to the postexilic period. A return to an earlier date occurred in 1923, when Oestreicher placed Deuteronomy prior to the age of Josiah and was followed in this by W. Staerk, Adam Welch, Edward Robinson, R. Brinker and others. The researches of von Rad, who used form-critical principles to associate Deuteronomy with Shechem and priestly authorship, did little to dispel the subjectivity that had long been a mark of Pentateuchal critical study.

B. Liturgical Tradition Criticism

A group of Scandinavian scholars headed by S. Mowinckel established a "liturgical tradition" in which literary origins were related to preexilic sanctuary rituals and sociological phenomena. Using Babylonian analogies, Mowinckel argued for the existence in ancient Israel of an annual "enthronement-ceremony" in which God was enthroned ceremonially as king during an autumn New Year festival.[15] The necessary textual evidence was lacking, but this did not deter Mowinckel from manipulating the Hebrew and making unsubstantiated assumptions about a supposed "New Year festival" in preexilic Israel.

An offshoot of this liturgical approach occurred in the "myth and ritual" school led by S.H. Hooke, which attempted to show that a distinctive set of rituals and myths had been common to all Near Eastern peoples, including the Hebrews. Hooke, like Mowinckel, tried to adduce evidence for a Hebrew enthronement feast based on Babylonian *akîtu* or New Year festival.

These and other views constituted at best only modest variations on the classical literary-critical theme. Apart from the positive affirmations of conservative scholars,

---

[14]H. Gunkel, *Einleitung in die Psalmen* (Gottingen: Vandenhoeck and Ruprecht, 1928–1933) Parts I, II.

[15]S. Mowinckel, *Psalmenstudien* (Kristiania: Dybwad, 1922) 2:204.

little realistic Near Eastern evidence was forthcoming until E. Naville broke new ground by suggesting that the early Pentateuchal genealogies were copied out by Moses from tablets of patriarchal origin that Abraham and his offspring had preserved. This view was ignored, however, until P.J. Wiseman developed it in 1936, using the somewhat enigmatic KJV phrase "these are the generations of " to show the presence of a Babylonian-type colophon in the text at that point.[16] Using this criterion, he was able to isolate eleven sections that correspond remarkably to the form of tablets recovered from various Mesopotamian sites, and for the first time he adduced accredited Near Eastern compositional methods as a means of throwing light on the literary origins of Genesis.

As the discipline of archaeology matured, it became used increasingly as a method of external validation of biblical data. Due largely to the work of men such as C.L. Woolley, W.F. Albright, A. Parrot, Petrie, Breasted, E. Chiera, and C.F.A. Schaeffer, the broad outlines of biblical chronology have been established and detailed information furnished about specific eras within that chronology. Such discoveries as the early usage of portable shrines of the tabernacle variety struck hard at Graf-Wellhausenian speculations, while the flood of information relating to the Middle Bronze Age (c.1950–1550 B.C.) provided an authentic background against which the patriarchal narratives could be evaluated properly for the first time.

The unexpected discovery of the Dead Sea Scrolls in 1947 cast further doubt on the validity of the Graf-Wellhausen theory of "documents" by showing that, in the time of Christ, there were at least three different Pentateuchal textual types in circulation, not one fixed form, as Wellhausen had imagined.[17] The effect of this and other Near Eastern material has been to bring under grave suspicion the classical liberal theory of Pentateuchal composition, and to make its adherents much more cautious in their pronouncements to the point where some of them are thinking less in terms of "documents" and more about "streams of tradition." With the tentative application of redaction criticism to the OT, certain scholars are examining the theological motives and presuppositions of those thought responsible for assembling the various canonical writings. But this may be an exercise in futility unless speculations and unproved hypotheses are abandoned in favor of a properly accredited Near Eastern method of study. In the same way the "tradition criticism" of the OT will need to understand the concept of the continuity of tradition and the significance of alleged or actual gaps in the tradition, from the standpoint of ancient Near Eastern usage rather than that of occidental hypothesis if it is to be at all valid as a method of criticism.

Critical investigation of the classical theory of Pentateuchal criticism, once so confidently heralded as "scientific," has shown that it actually employed the a priori method, instead of the a posteriori approach used by modern science.[18] This presupposition was combined with a complete ignorance of Near Eastern methods of scribal transmission, a deliberate and calculated rejection of archaeological data in favor of a few late Arabic parallels, and the arbitrary selection of evidence to the point where facts that militated against the analytical theory were suppressed, distorted, or blandly ignored to produce a concept of literary origins that has never had anything in common with what is known of the composition and dissemination of any other item in the entire ancient Near

---

[16]P.J. Wiseman, *New Discoveries in Babylonia About Genesis* (London: Marshall, Morgan, and Scott, 1958 ed.), pp. 46ff.

[17]Cf. J.M. Allegro, *The Dead Sea Scrolls* (New York: Penguin, 1956), pp. 57ff.

[18]Cf. R.K. Harrison in D.F. Wells and C.H. Pinnock, eds., *Toward a Theology for the Future* (Carol Stream, Ill.: Creation House, 1972), pp. 11ff.

Eastern literary corpus. The "criteria" for documentary analysis suggested by Astruc were subjected to critical examination by R.D. Wilson as far back as 1929 and applied to the Koran, where precisely the same "criteria" can be discovered. Though the Koran is much later than the Pentateuch, the transmission of the latter must have been analagous to that of the Tradition in Islam. Wilson found no basis whatever for a "documentary" theory of compilation for the Koran based on variant designations of God, and succeeding Islamic scholars have supported this position. Much earlier rock inscriptions from the ancient Near East can also be interpreted in the light of Astruc's "criteria," and yet it is known that they exhibit no literary prehistory whatever.[19]

Literary criticism based on an accredited Near Eastern methodology will recognize the existence of literary sources underlying certain of the OT writings, but these sources will be authentic in nature, not the wholly hypothetical and entirely undemonstrated ones of the Graf-Wellhausen theory. Form-critical studies of Genesis make it possible to isolate eleven "tablets" that, with the Joseph narratives, comprised the true literary sources. The "tablets" exhibit the same form as many excavated in Mesopotamia, including typical genealogical material, and in the light of what is now known about such sources they constitute by far the most realistic underlying documents suggested to date. The literary holism of Deuteronomy has been illustrated abundantly by international treaties recovered from Boghazköy, the ancient Hittite capital, making it possible to place the book with confidence in the period from which it purports to have come, namely the second millennium B.C. rather than the age of Josiah.[20]

In all other Near Eastern cultures, priestly material is early rather than late, so that if the appropriate sections of Exodus, Leviticus, and Numbers followed the contemporary priestly patterns, they too would have originated in the second millennium B.C. The antiquity of the Proto-Samaritan Pentateuchal text, which has been illumined by the manuscript discoveries at Qumran,[21] makes it clear on both linguistic and historical grounds that the entire Pentateuch was in existence as canonical literature long before some of the material assigned by liberal critics to the "P document" had supposedly been written.

C. *Isaiah*

Concurrent with the literary criticism of the Pentateuch came an investigation of the authorship of Isaiah. In about 1780, Koppe suggested that chapter 50 might perhaps have been written during the Exile, perhaps by Ezekiel, while J.G. Eichhorn held that chapters 40–66 were the work of another person than Isaiah, who came to be styled "Second Isaiah" or "Deutero-Isaiah." By 1888 it was becoming increasingly common for scholars to assert that chapters 56–59 had been written by an individual different from "Deutero-Isaiah," and this supposed author was dubbed "Third Isaiah" or "Trito-Isaiah" by K. Budde, K. Marti, and others. After the time of B. Duhm this explanation of the compilation of Isaiah quickly became the standard liberal view of the authorship of the book, though it was opposed in a variety of ways by some liberals as well as by conservatives.[22]

19Cf. K.A. Kitchen, *Ancient Orient and Old Testament* (Downer's Grove, Ill.: InterVarsity, 1966), pp. 117, 121ff.

20Cf. Kitchen, *Ancient Orient*, pp. 90ff. and accompanying bibliography.

21Cf. B. Waltke in Payne, ed., *New Perspectives*, pp. 212–239.

22For bibliography, see R.K. Harrison, *Introduction to the Old Testament* (Grand Rapids: Eerdmans, 1969), pp. 765ff.

The theory of multiple authorship was advanced on three grounds: first, that internal evidence was held to indicate that chapters 40–66 were written towards the end of the exile in Babylon; second, that these chapters differed on stylistic grounds from the rest of the prophecy; third, that the theological emphases of chapters 40–66 differs quite markedly that of from chapters 1–39. Involved with these considerations was the view of many critics that Isaiah could not possibly have projected and maintained the prolonged futuristic standpoint that parts of the prophecy appear to necessitate, so that multiple authorship is for them the only logical alternative. It is an interesting commentary on the liberal scholarship of the day that it was never thought necessary to prove these assertions, but merely to maintain them. A vast welter of conflicting opinions soon arose about the authorship of Isaiah, and the essential subjectivity of the method involved found scholars disagreeing vigorously among themselves and with their more conservative opponents.

One of the most notable of the latter was J.A. Alexander, whose brilliant studies anticipated most of the later objections to the unity of the prophecy. During this same period Rudolf Stier also wrote a voluminous commentary on Isaiah in which he maintained the unity of the prophecy. In 1866 Franz Delitzsch produced an outstanding treatise on Isaiah, which as the editions progressed became increasingly accommodated to current literary-critical views regarding the authorship of chapters 40–66, without, however, giving unqualified approval to the concept of a "Deutero-Isaiah." Subsequent writers who defended the conservative position included C.P. Caspari, L.D. Jeffreys, D.S. Margoliouth, N.H. Ridderbos, A. Kaminka, C. Wordsworth, O.T. Allis, and E.J. Young.

The first signs of dissension within liberal ranks came with the work of Sidney Smith in 1944, in which he applied form-critical principles to Isaiah in an attempt to connect chapters 40–55 with the historical events of 547–538 B.C. He saw the material of these chapters as "pamphlets" composed and apparently delivered by the prophet Isaiah during the decade in question. Though some of his historical identifications were open to doubt, his researches marked a significant degree of diversion from liberal norms of criticism. A commentary by J. Mauchline in 1962 recognized that parts of the prophecy assigned to a postexilic period might well have belonged to the time of Isaiah himself, and that the prophet most probably wrote most of chapters 13–18, a section that many critics had held to be of multiple authorship.

As with Pentateuchal criticism, the division of Isaiah into several hands rested on numerous unproved assumptions. When pressed, scholars advocating it found it impossible to adduce anything other than a Palestinian milieu for chapters 40–66. Indeed, C.C. Torrey, a radical critic, dismissed all allusions to Babylon in that section and opted for a Palestinian locale and a writer composing the material about a century following the restoration. However, this type of approach found little favor among other liberal scholars, who, following Duhm, preferred to speculate, beg the question, and go far in excess of the available facts in postulating theories of multiple authorship. Only when the large Isaiah manuscript (1QIsaᵃ) was discovered accidentally in 1949 among the Dead Sea Scrolls was sufficient objective evidence available for a new assessment of the situation. This scroll has definitely eliminated a "Trito-Isaiah" because the autograph is now known to have come from a time several centuries earlier than the Maccabean copy found at Qumran. Since some so-called "Maccabean psalms" have now been advanced by scholars to the Persian period on the basis of certain manuscript material recovered from Cave 4 (4QPsaᵃ), it would seem that similar treatment should be accorded Isaiah.

The supposed authorship of material beyond chapter 40 by "an unknown prophet of the exile" came into further question when photocopies of 1QIsaᵃ revealed no textual break at the end of chapter 39, but instead, a space of three lines coming before chapter 34. This phenomenon suggested to W.H. Brownlee and others that Isaiah was actually written in two parts as a bifid composition, (i.e., a book written in two parts), a practice employed in antiquity for dealing with lengthy works and alluded to by Josephus,[23] who spoke of Ezekiel, Isaiah, and Daniel as having left "books" behind. By comparing literary themes, W.H. Brownlee showed that specific topics in part one (chapters 1–33) were paralleled remarkably in part two (chapters 34–66), and held that this was a way of viewing the completed work from the standpoint of the ancient editors.

While in the mind of some scholars this development has not entirely eradicated the gratuitous figure of "Deutero-Isaiah," it has made possible for the first time a view of the authorship of Isaiah, that is grounded in objective data and reflects the authentic scribal customs of the ancient Hebrews. Speculations and hypotheses are now giving place increasingly to an estimate of Isaiah that sees it as a two-volume prophetic anthology written and produced either within the lifetime of Isaiah, or else not more than half a century after his death. An attempt was made recently by Y.T. Radday of the Hebrew University of Jerusalem to demonstrate the presence of two different authors in Isaiah by means of a computer. Computers, however, reflect the presuppositions of those who program them, and the essential subjectivity of the latter exercise inevitably lends little credibility to the result in the field of literary criticism.

D. *Daniel*

Another favorite topic for literary criticism since the days of Porphyry has been the Book of Daniel.[24] Like Isaiah, it too is a bifid composition, the first half (chapters 1–6) consisting of narrative against a historical background and the second half (chapters 7–12) consisting of Daniel's visions. At a time when ancient bifid writing was unknown in the western world, it was assumed that Daniel was a composite work—a view held by Spinoza (1670), Isaac Newton (1773), Eichhorn (1803), J.D. Michaelis (1771), and many others. However, the literary unity of Daniel was defended by F. Bleek (1882) and his followers, along with Von Gall, Cornill, and other liberal writers. C.C. Torrey, O. Eissfeldt, Th. Vriezen, and G. Hölscher were the principal adherents of a view that suggested that the first section had been compiled in the third century B.C. and the latter in the Maccabean period. Welch, B.D. Eerdmans, and A. Weiser developed Hölscher's position by regarding the first seven chapters as a unit, with the remainder coming from the Maccabean era.

Most Roman Catholic scholars adhered to the traditional view of authorship and date, but some, including M.J. Lagrange, L. Bigot, and H. Junker, placed the entire work in Maccabean times. Upholding the unity of Daniel were numerous distinguished liberal and conservative scholars including E.B. Pusey, S.R. Driver, J.A. Bewer, R.D. Wilson, H.H. Rowley, C.F. Pfeiffer, and E.J. Young. This great difference of opinion about integrity, authorship, and date is unfortunately self-defeating by calling the whole matter of critical method into question.

A theory of diverse authorship based on the use of two languages in the book can now be abandoned in the light of Near Eastern evidence. This latter shows that the device of encompassing the nucleus of a composition in a literary or linguistic framework of a

---

[23]Jos. Antiq. X, 5, 1; X, 11, 7.
[24]For bibliography see Harrison, *Introduction to the Old Testament*, pp. 1107ff.

contrasting pattern so as to increase the overall effectiveness of a unified work was employed in such notable instances as the Code of Hammurapi. In this corpus, a poetic prologue and epilogue enclose the principal prose section, the reverse of which occurs in the book of Job.[25] Daniel thus comprises an integrated composition in which Hebrew and Aramaic elements combine to make a consciously constructed literary unit.

Questions of authorship of Daniel turn largely on the date assigned the book. Traditional Jewish and early Christian views were opposed by the Neoplatonist Porphyry (third century A.D.), who denied the possibility of predictive elements in prophecy and assigned the work to the Maccabean period, maintaining that its purpose had been to sustain persecuted Jews in their adversities. This general position was adopted by European rationalists, and became "one of the most assured results" of the literary-critical movement, even though it was consistently challenged by conservative scholars and was entirely lacking in objective proof.

Aside from the whole matter of prediction in prophecy, liberal writers alleged the presence of several historical inaccuracies in the text itself. One of these regarded Daniel 1:1 as anachronistic when compared with Jeremiah 25:1, 9; 46:2, where a difference of a year occurs. This has now been resolved by more recent research. This research shows that Daniel reckoned according to the Babylonian calendar, which included an "accession year" for the new king, whereas Jeremiah followed Palestinian patterns, which during certain periods ignored accession years. Another objection, the use of "Chaldean" in a ethnic sense to designate a group of wise men in a manner not found elsewhere in the OT or on inscriptions, has been resolved by the discovery that Herodotus (c.450 B.C.) spoke of them in exactly the same manner, as did Assyrian annals from the tenth century B.C.

The apparent inability of historians to record the madness of Nebuchadnezzar was also adduced as evidence of an error on the part of the supposed Maccabean author that would never have occurred had the work been written in the sixth century B.C., as traditionally claimed. However, Berossus, a third century B.C. Babylonian priest, actually preserved a tradition that Nebuchadnezzar was taken ill just before the end of his reign, while a century later Abydenus recorded that Nebuchadnezzar was "possessed by some god or other," whereupon after a startling prophetic outburst he disappeared from Babylon. The account in Daniel 4 actually preserves a striking clinical description of a rare mental disease known as boanthropy, a form of monomania in which the sufferer imagines himself to be a bull or cow. The presence of this objective record of insanity stands in stark contrast to the garbled traditions of Babylonia, where mental disorders were regarded as the evil product of possession by the underworld deities, and those who were afflicted were sedulously avoided for fear of contagion.

The discovery at Qumran of a manuscript fragment called the "Prayer of Nabonidus"[26] led some scholars to think that the illness of Daniel 4 had been ascribed wrongly to Nebuchadnezzar, and should actually have been attributed to Nabonidus. One writer even suggested that the author of Daniel used the "Prayer" as his source for the fourth chapter, but altered names and places. Nabonidus, however, was already well known in Palestine for his brutality in slaughtering the inhabitants of Teima in Arabia when he settled there about 555 B.C. Examination of the "Prayer" shows that, unlike Daniel 4, it contains elements totally unfamiliar to medicine, and elsewhere deals with

---

[25]Cf. C.H. Gordon, *Introduction to Old Testament Times* (Ventnor, N.J.: Ventnor, 1953) pp. 72, 73.
[26]Cf. J.T. Milik, *Revue Biblique* (1956), 63:407ff.

tissue inflammation, not insanity. The "Prayer" can thus throw no light on the content, composition, or date of Daniel, and must consequently be assigned to the realm of myth and folklore.

Another objection to the historicity of the book relates to the personage of Darius the Mede, who is not mentioned outside the OT and who was widely regarded by liberal critics as the product of conflation of confused traditions. J.C. Whitcomb helped clarify the consequent misunderstandings by showing that the Nabonidus Chronicle mentioned two distinct individuals, Gubaru and Ugbaru, who helped Cyrus overthrow Babylon in 539 B.C. Ugbaru died about three weeks later, perhaps from wounds, and Gubaru was appointed governor of Babylon by Cyrus. Whitcomb suggested that Gubaru was the person mentioned in Daniel as "Darius the Mede." One of the Nabonidus texts discovered at Haran referred to the "King of the Medes" in the tenth year of Nabonidus (546 B.C.). Whether this title referred to Cyrus the Persian, as suggested by D.J. Wiseman, to Gubaru, or to some other individual as yet unidentified, it is at least clear that "Darius the Mede" was an accredited historic individual, regardless of who he might turn out to be.

The presence of three supposedly Greek names for the musical instruments in Daniel 3 translated in the KJV as harp (RSV, "lyre"), sackbut (RSV, "trigon") and psaltery (RSV, "harp") was also adduced by nineteenth-century critics as evidence of a Maccabean rather than a sixth-century B.C. date of composition. Subsequent archaeological discoveries have shown that Greek culture had penetrated the Near East from at least the mid-seventh century B.C. in the form of Greek mercenary troops and small colonies.[27]

Excavations in Babylonia and Assyria have made it clear that the three instruments specified were all Mesopotamian in origin, and only the terms for harp and psaltery corresponded at all closely to the Greek forms. There is little doubt that the names of the instruments in Daniel were Old Persian in character, and were assimilated by the Greeks into their own culture with some orthographic modifications. Consequently this particular argument is no longer important for the literary criticism of Daniel.

The alleged linguistic evidence of the book advanced to support a Maccabean date has also been subjected to severe modification since 1891 when S.R. Driver wrote that the Greek demanded, the Hebrew supported, and the Aramaic permitted a date later than 332 B.C. Modern linguistic research has indicated that the term *Aramaic* actually designates four principal groups, namely Old Aramaic, Official Aramaic, Levantine Aramaic, and Eastern Aramaic. The second of these was already in use among government officials in the Assyrian period (c.1100–605 B.C.), and in the succeeding Persian empire it was the accredited language of diplomacy. The antiquity of Aramaic as a spoken language is reflected in its use by Laban (Gen 31:47), while specific Aramaisms, including some occurring in Daniel, have been found in the Amarna-Age texts from Ras Shamra (Ugarit).

The Aramaic of Daniel was the kind used in government circles from the seventh century B.C. onwards, and thus akin to that of the Elephantine papyri of the fifth century B.C. and the book of Ezra. The Hebrew with which the book begins and closes, thereby establishing a framework mentioned above in relation to Job and the Code of Hammurapi, resembles that of Ezekiel, Haggai, Ezra, and Chronicles. The evidence is therefore much more in favor of a sixth-century B.C. date than a Maccabean one, and not least if the first seven chapters were written by Daniel in neo-Babylonian, as seems probable.

27Cf. E.M. Yamauchi in Payne, ed., *New Perspectives*, pp. 174ff.

Persian loan words in Daniel point also to an earlier rather than a later date of composition. All the words involved are specifically Old Persian, including the term *satrap,* which was once thought to be Greek but is now known to have been derived from the Old Persian form *kshathrapān,* the Greek being a modification of the cuneiform rendering *shatarpānu.* No Persian term in use later than 300 B.C. is found in Daniel, thus indicating the pre-Hellenistic nature of the Aramaic in that particular respect.[28]

The literary criticism of Daniel must now be reassessed against the manuscript discoveries at Qumran, where several copies of the work were found. In addition, two fragments located in Cave 1 have proved on examination to be related palaeographically to the large Isaiah scroll (1QIsaa), dated by Millar Burrows about 100 B.C. All these documents, of course, are copies from the Maccabean age or later, making it necessary to remark, as Burrows has observed, that the originals came from a period several centuries in advance of the earliest date to which these manuscripts and fragments can be assigned on any basis of reckoning.[29] Part of the reason for this is that the ancient Hebrews generally allowed an interval of time to elapse between the autograph and its recognition as canonical Scripture by its readers. This process had the effect of ensuring the consonance of the particular work with the ethos of the Torah, which constituted the standard of revelation and spirituality.

It would thus appear that, whatever may be thought about the place of prediction in prophecy, the manuscript evidence from Qumran absolutely precludes a date of composition in the Maccabean period, but does indicate one in the Neo-Babylonian era (626–539 B.C.). In support of this position, as noted above, is the fragmentary copy of the Psalter from Qumran (4QPsaa), which shows quite clearly on the same grounds that the collection of canonical psalms had already been fixed by the Maccabean period.[30] As a result, scholars have advanced those compositions formerly regarded as "Maccabean psalms" to the Persian period. All future literary-critical studies of Daniel will have to take proper account of this objective evidence.

A curious ambivalence among liberal scholars regarding the date of Daniel permits them to allow the validity of evidence from Josephus, which states that Jaddua was high priest in Jerusalem in the time of Alexander the Great (Jos. Antiq. VI, 7, 2; XI, 8, 5), and on this basis to date the Chronicler between 350 and 250 B.C., yet from the very same literary source to either deny or ignore the fact that the scroll of Daniel was in its completed form by 330 B.C. (Jos. Antiq. XI, 8, 5). To the present, no liberal writer has offered an explanation of just how this dilemma can be resolved. But in the light of the foregoing discussion, it would appear that the fewest difficulties are raised by regarding Daniel as a product of the Persian period rather than of the age of the Maccabees.

E. *Other Books*

Although the literary criticism of certain other OT books is inconclusive in some areas, it is now evident from the findings at Qumran that no canonical writing can be dated later than the end of the Persian period, i.e., much beyond 350 B.C. Compilations of material such as the Psalter must also be governed by this principle, as noted above, even though individual compositions may come from widely separated periods.

---

[28]Cf. K.A. Kitchen, *Notes on Some Problems in the Book of Daniel* (London: Tyndale, 1965), pp. 31ff.
[29]M. Burrows, *The Dead Sea Scrolls* (New York: Viking, 1955), p. 118.
[30]Cf. F.M. Cross, *The Ancient Library of Qumran and Modern Biblical Study* (Garden City, N.Y.: Doubleday, 1961), p. 165.

The book of Job can no longer be assigned to a date later than the middle of the fourth century B.C., as a result of the Qumran discoveries, but aside from this consideration, questions of authorship and date are still far from being resolved for this work. The literary unity of Job is now clear, however, since it follows compositional patterns analagous to the Code of Hammurapi and the book of Daniel, but estimates of the date of the composition go all the way back to about 2100 B.C. The anonymity of this magnificent piece of writing, coupled with its objective of narrating familiar traditions about a famous individual, only make the problems more difficult, and even to date the work at the end of the fifth century B.C. at the latest, as the present writer does, is fraught with uncertainty.

Literary criticism has been equally unfruitful in dealing with the unity, authorship, and date of Joel. Nothing is known about the attributive author, and no archaeological discoveries to date have added to what is already evident about his prophetic activities. The juxtaposition of historical and apocalyptic sections in the prophecy has led to suggestions of duality of authorship, but the stylistic smoothness and integrity of the work appear to preclude this possibility. A total lack of internal evidence for an assured date has made it possible for different scholars to place it in either the pre- or postexilic period with considerable confidence, a situation that is clearly undesirable.

Research into the historical literature has not been successful in determining the authorship of anonymous works such as Samuel, Kings, and Chronicles, and even questions of dating cannot be settled with anything like precision. As many as five underlying literary sources have been suggested by some scholars for the book of Samuel, while others have seen its compilation in terms of independent cycles of sagas. Kings, by contrast, exhibits clear traces of several basic sources that were unified by means of certain literary formulae to describe the significance of the covenant in theocentric terms. Chronicles, too, was carefully constructed from historical source material no longer extant, and, like Kings, it expounded specific metaphysical themes. Some scholars have followed rabbinic tradition in ascribing the compilation of Chronicles to Ezra, but there is no factual evidence for this view.

The historical, social, and religious background of the Minor Prophets has received much attention from scholars of all schools. As noted above, literary criticism has failed to elicit any information about the authorship and date of Joel, and in liberal circles it has been the tendency to regard Malachi as the work of an anonymous postexilic writer who can be called Malachi for convenience. Jonah has been explained by liberal writers less as a historical narrative and more as either an allegory or a parable, and as coming from a period as late as 200 B.C., according to some scholars. However, dates of this order are precluded by the Qumran evidence, and more probably Jonah emerged from a time between the eighth and seventh centuries B.C.

III. Conclusion

It will have become apparent from the foregoing discussion that literary criticism has far too long been characterized by purely subjective considerations, and this is one of the grave weaknesses of the method. Part of the problem lies in the fact that its earliest practitioners knew little or nothing about ancient Near Eastern life other than what was implied by biblical or classical traditions. By the time modern archaeological discoveries had begun to unlock the past, the theoretical postulates were so well established that any modification in the light of factual evidence would have been devastating.

With the passing of the heyday of liberal criticism, many of its advocates are experiencing considerable difficulty in accommodating themselves to the demands of the objective evidence, and in certain instances can only maintain nineteenth-century critical positions at the cost of ignoring modern archaeological and other information. Therefore, if literary criticism is to retain credibility and serve as a useful tool for studying the OT, it must abandon the speculative a priori approach that characterized its origins and pursue further researches according to a proper a posteriori method, as in modern science.

This will involve, first, the selection of a problem, and second, the assembling of all the relevant factual material to see if the objective data give any indication of providing a tentative explanation of the problem. If they do, the suggested answer will have to be submitted to still more rigorous testing by additional data before it can be regarded as a working hypothesis. Only if it survives this process unscathed can the explanation begin to be elevated to the level of a hypothesis. If observed facts militate against or refute the hypothesis, it can either be modified to accommodate the new information, be replaced by a different and more satisfactory explanation, or be retained tentatively till a more comprehensive hypothesis can be formulated.

Clearly this kind of inductive generalization precludes such nineteenth- and, in some cases, twentieth-century literary-critical activities as the rewriting of Hebrew history to make it conform to an evolutionary schema, the arbitrary emendation of the Hebrew text, and the ignoring of relevant archaeological and other external data. Scholars must now engage in a proper inductive investigation of problems, using all the appropriate information, instead of merely adopting a less-extreme position regarding classical literary criticism. Only by this means will the exercise of the discipline produce realistic, responsible, and beneficial results.

IV. Bibliography

Archer, G.L. A Survey of Old Testament Introduction. Chicago; Moody, 1964.

Brownlee, W.H. The Meaning of the Qumrân Scrolls for the Bible. New York: Oxford University Press, 1964.

Burrows, M. The Dead Sea Scrolls. New York: Viking, 1951.

Harrison, R.K. The Dead Sea Scrolls. London: Hodder and Stoughton, 1961.

Rast, W.E. Tradition History and the Old Testament. Philadelphia: Fortress, 1972.

Smith, S. Isaiah, Chapters XL–LV: Literary Criticism and History. Oxford: The University Press, 1944.

Thomas, D.W., ed. Archaeology and Old Testament Study. Oxford: Clarendon, 1967.

Torrey, C.C. The Second Isaiah: A New Interpretation. New York: Scribner, 1928.

Weiser, A. The Old Testament: Its Formation and Development. New York: Association, 1961.

Whitcomb, J.C. Darius the Mede. Grand Rapids: Eerdmans, 1959.

Wiseman, D.J. Chronicles of Chaldaean Kings (626–556 B.C.) in the British Museum. London: The Trustees of the British Museum, 1956.

Wiseman, P.J. New Discoveries in Babylonia. Grand Rapids, Zondervan, 1956.

Woolley, C.L. Ur of the Chaldees. London: Ernest Benn, 1950 ed.

Young, E.J. An Introduction to the Old Testament. Grand Rapids: Eerdmans, 1960 ed.

OLD TESTAMENT HISTORY

J.A. MOTYER

J.A. Motyer

A.B., M.A., B.D., Trinity College (University of Dublin)

Principal and Dean, Trinity College, Bristol

OLD TESTAMENT HISTORY

I. History in Its Biblical Setting

How does the OT understand its own historical record? How, in the light of this understanding, are those who stand within the biblical testimony to interpret the larger canvas of world affairs? To answer these questions and their implications is the purpose of this article.

The OT is a book much occupied with history—in some senses even preoccupied with it. It has its own witness to bear concerning the nature of history and the purpose of making a historical record at all. To grasp what this witness is must be our first concern; otherwise we may fall into the error of subjecting the OT record to wrong principles of interpretation and then complaining that biblical historiography cannot be animated by the same concern for veracity and chronological accuracy as its modern counterpart.

A. The Place of History in the Bible

History is the loom on which the OT is woven. Not only is a considerable proportion of the OT devoted to historical records, but throughout, say, the prophetic literature the reader is ever aware of the ebb and flow of history. Nothing is further removed from ivory-tower speculation than the writings of the OT prophets. While they never forgot the throne of God, they were deeply involved in the life and problems of their times.

1. *History and prophecy.* Bible history is the product of prophetic (and not simply historical) inspiration. It was a correct and deep perception that entitled the corpus of literature from Joshua to Kings "The Former Prophets." Like prophecy, history in the OT is a declaration from God about God. P. Ellis characteristically remarks that the Yahwist's saga has no "hero" in the accepted literary sense—not Abraham, Jacob, Joseph, or even Moses—"because the protagonist . . . is the Lord God."[1]

2. *History and theology.* The point, however, of using history as the vehicle for declaring truth about God is that in this way theology is rescued from relativism; it ceases to belong to the departments of opinion and speculation and becomes objective and verified.

Surely this is what lies behind Isaiah's use of the Rahab myth in 51:9, 10. There is more here than an illustrative reference to Marduk's precreation victory; Isaiah's unmistakeable identification of the overthrow of Rahab with the Red Sea crossing implies that whereas Marduk did all his mighty deeds before the world was, before there were spectators who could witness them, Yahweh's mighty acts belong in history, involve people and places, and invite inquiry and testimony. "He is a God," says Westerman, "who evinces himself as lord through the continuity of his word and his act."[2]

Other voices than Isaiah's make the same point. Jephthah may have been reflecting the customary scorn of other gods when he invited the Ammonites to be content to possess what Chemosh had given them (Judg 11:24), but doubtless Chemosh's devotees would have taken his words at face value. The Ancient East did see the work of its deities in this event or that, "but it never occurred to them to identify the nerve of the historical process as the purposeful activity of God."[3] Thus it was Isaiah and not the Marduk priests who could make history the undergirding of theology and past history the guarantee of history yet to come and even of eschatology. The OT is historical because it is theological. That it takes theology seriously guarantees its sober realism in dealing with historiography, for unless there is veracity in OT history, there can be no authenticity to OT theology.

3. *Selectivity and veracity.* Historical veracity need not be imperilled when history is being related selectively in order to elucidate a message. Like every attempt to write history, the OT is selective. Very little is committed to writing out of those forty years in the time of Moses. The eighteen verses allotted to Manasseh (in 2 Kings 21) dismiss to oblivion the contents of fifty-five busy regnal years. But the nature of much of the material that was not "selected out"—especially certain flagrant sins of some of the OT's

---

[1]P. Ellis, *The Yahwist* (London, 1968), p. 158.
[2]C. Westerman, *Isaiah 40–66* (London, 1969), p. 17.
[3]W. Eichrodt, *Theology of the Old Testament* (London, 1961) 1:41.

greatest people—shows that it was not tendentiousness but a clearly formulated purpose that dominated the writers.

B. *History and Teleology*

The purpose mentioned above is intimately linked with the clear onward flow apparent in OT history. It was the genius of the OT historians to see this while they themselves were involved in the events. There are four aspects of their teleology.

1. *The Day of Yahweh.* The OT came to use the idea of the "day of Yahweh" as shorthand for the belief that history is heading toward a goal. From our perspective it resembles a mountaineer making for a great peak but compelled by the terrain to climb other summits en route. Yet the interim climbs are not without purpose: each is a further guarantee that presently the final peak will be reached. So OT history proceeds in a series of promises and fulfillments. But as OT history progressed in this way, hope was mingled with disappointment as covenant institutions failed and covenant persons fell short of the promised ideal. But it was a theocentric hope so that well before the time of Amos it had been crystallized into the expectation of a climactic "day of Yahweh" in and by which all would be consummated.

2. *The Deuteronomic view of history.* Amos purged from the "day of Yahweh" the element of moral complacency that had eroded the true heart of biblical history. OT history is animated by a moral purpose which, often called the "deuteronomic view," holds that righteousness exalts nation, whereas sin brings disgrace and ruin (cf. Deut 28, 29; Judg 2:11–23). This view is worked out at length in the postconquest history books and accepted as axiomatic by the prophets. When a history is written on this presupposition, it is idle to complain, for example, that Manasseh's sins receive more attention than his policies. Far from rejecting such a view of history in favor of a supposedly more "factual" approach, we should be ready to learn from the Bible. For in reality it was Manasseh's sin that constituted the hinge of Jerusalem's history (2 Kings 24:3), effecting a downfall that good policies could not avert nor bad ones so fully accomplish. To the OT, then, history is the arena of moral decisions, moral conflicts, and moral consequences.

3. *All the families of the earth.* This moral spirit animates the whole OT record, not least the opening eleven chapters of the Bible. Selective like all other Bible history, the story of mankind between the creation and the call of Abraham is succinctly summarized in three incidents: the fall, the flood, and the scattering. Over them all, God presides in sovereign control and sovereign mercy. He enters the sphere of rebellious man in Genesis 3 with exactly the same air of unquestioned sovereignty with which he has acted in the two preceding chapters, yet with this difference—that the sovereign benevolence of chapter 2 has become a sovereign imposition of mercy upon sinners in chapter 3. Equally, in a world that merits death (6:5–7) and that God devotes to destruction, mercy finds and sets forth one man (6:8), marked out by God for salvation. So history is a handmaid to theology: There is one God over all the earth; the turn of events is the outworking of his edict; his will is not to be gainsaid, whether it is to save or to destroy.

The third selected story focuses on another side of man's character and brilliantly shows yet another aspect of God's determination of the flow of history. To man who is the rebel of Genesis 3 and man who is the totally depraved in Genesis 6 is added man the self-assured in Genesis 11:3, 4. To this human aspiration to be self-sufficient the Lord says his decisive no and brings upon the race the peril it dreaded (Gen 11:4, 9). But abruptly the historian turns. Another genealogy (Gen 11:10ff.) intervenes. It reaches back to the time of the new beginning but terminates at another new beginning of even greater significance—the gap between Noah and Abraham, the man in whom all the families of the earth will be blessed (Gen 12:3). It is spanned by an imperceptible, patient work of God who thus declares that, whereas man left to himself can only accomplish and merit universal destruction, the Creator-Redeemer God would and will not have it so. His mind is set on universal blessing.

4. *Creative redemption.* Bible history belongs in the setting of Creation. To speak of God as Creator means three distinct things: that he initiated all things, that he controls them in their operation, and that he guides them to a predetermined conclusion. The OT has no room for historical evolution as the controlling (or even the explanatory) principle of world history. In OT history a double line manifests itself: on the one hand, there is man who at best is intractably sinful; and on the other, the Creator God, who uses the events of history to unfold to us more of his inner being. When man became man the sinner, therefore, it is as though that very circumstance had "turned" God into a Savior of sinners. But he remains the Creator, and his endless creative capacity turns to redemptive ends. Thus Isaiah foresaw the climactic day of Yahweh, when sin's power of self-destruction will have reached the end and when the Creator's power (Isa. 4:5) will achieve the glory God had intended from the first.

C. History and Providence

In the arena of history, therefore, two forces are at work: the human will and the divine will. Does the historical narrative do more than set these in opposition to each other? Does it explain their relationship?

The problem runs throughout, from the heart of Pharaoh (Exod 4:21; 7:22) to the heart of Sennacherib (Isa 10:7, 12). Isaiah's own metaphor is as near as the OT ever brings us to the solution of the problem: Sennacherib is the tempestuous horse; Yahweh is the all-directing rider (Isa 37:29). All the sinful impulse—and its concomitant blameworthiness and condemnation—belong in the "horse"; all the direction of these impulses, so that they serve the interests of a pure moral providence, belong to the "rider." In his assault on Jerusalem, Sennacherib was giving a wholly free expression to his sinful pride, his corrupt ambition, and his insensate imperialism. In his overarching, sovereign providence, God directed all this sinfully motivated energy to punish the errors of Jerusalem, and then, because the assault on Jerusalem was in itself the fruit of a freely chosen path of godless pride, God, in the same sovereign providence, dealt punitively with Sennacherib.

All OT history shares this character. It is holy history; by the grace of God it is salvation history. It is moral, judgmental history, and by the sovereign working of a merciful Creator, it looks forward to the coincidence of the climax of wrath and the triumph of grace. Apart from these categories, OT history is a sealed book.

II. The People of the Covenant

Biblical historiography tends to introduce its leading ideas unobtrusively. From Abraham onward, the notion of the divine covenant dominates all God's dealings with his people, but its introduction might almost be described as off-hand. At the time of the Flood, viewing a world astray from himself, God determined to save one chosen sinner, Noah (Gen. 6:8), to provide a means of salvation (6:13, 14), to incorporate the immediate family of the chosen man (6:18), and to extend through him a universal blessing (9:12). This divine determination is, as an oath or promise of God, called the "covenant" (Gen 6:18). And it was at that time that the word "covenant" first had its distinctive meaning. We must now trace the outcome as God developed his covenant mercies into their normative OT expression. The Bible story from Abraham and the patriarchs to Moses and Joshua shows us how God did this.

A. The Period of Promise: Abraham to Joseph

1. *The covenant idea.* The patriarchal narratives are presented to us in the Bible as history written pointedly and selectively within a declared frame of reference. Until we know the standpoint, we cannot appreciate the flow of the story.

The idea of a divine covenant did not originate with Abraham but with Noah. Both the deliberate interlocking of Abraham with Noah by means of the genealogy of Gen 11: 10ff. and the identity of principle involved declare to us that the OT presents here a single, developing work of God. In the case of Noah, the covenant idea consisted of the selection of one man out of a world of sinners, the divine promise to him of salvation, the provision of the means of salvation, and the extension of the benefits through him to his family and in a broader sense to the whole world.

The abrupt account of Abram's call (Gen 12:1), the promise of greatness, and the extension of blessing to the world (Gen 12:2, 3) clearly continue the same kind of divine action. The pledge has a twofold significance: first, the covenant promises of God are sealed by an unexplained sacrifice in which God alone goes on oath, accepting for himself all the responsibilities of maintaining the covenant and all the consequences of a broken covenant (see Gen 15:9–21; cf. also 1 Sam 11:7; Jer 34:18). Second, in regard to Noah, the covenant sign is a public element belonging in the constitution of the world (Gen 9:11–17), whereas for Abraham and his descendants it is a secret mark carried in the person's own body (Gen 17:10ff.): that which God expressed verbally in terms of promises (Gen 17:1–8) he next expressed visibly in a sign, so that in each successive generation each individual would see himself as recipient of divine promises and therefore under obligation to walk conformably to the will of God (Gen 17:1, 2). Here is the relationship between grace and law that remains unchanged throughout the Bible.

The covenant people were therefore conscious of their distinctiveness among all people on the earth. Religiously this difference showed in the total absence of idolatry in their devotions, but even where they resembled the people of their day, the points of difference emerge. For example, Abraham's nomadic migrations followed the trade and pilgrim routes of his day. He is found at the ancient shrine of Bethel, but builds his own altar there (Gen 12:8). Again, Abraham knew God by the common generic title *El*, but the special revelations granted him by God filled out this title with unique significance (cf. Gen 14:18, 16:13; 17:1; 21:33).[4] Notice specially that when Abram received new theological light from Melchizedek, he was careful at once to integrate it into the theology he had already received (Gen 14:19, 22) thus indicating awareness of the distinctiveness of his beliefs. More specialists are now concluding that the patriarchs

---

[4]See also J.A. Motyer, *The Revelation of the Divine Name* (London, 1959).

were monotheists.[5] Furthermore, though the patriarchs received no detailed law code from God (cf. Gen 17:1), they had clear awareness of moral distinctiveness; so the alleged rape of Dinah is "folly in Israel" (Gen 34:7), and Joseph knows that to yield to Potiphar's wife would be to sin against God (39:9).

2. *The fathers.* When we turn from the covenant idea itself to those who received its promises, the story reveals an extreme disparity between privilege and performance. The historian has clearly purposed to expose the failure of man within the covenant and show the determined faithfulness of God to his promises. The Hebrew historian was not concerned about dating the patriarchs by reference to the events and personages in the world around them. He does not even give us enough information to enable us to date the kings so freely named in Genesis 14! The most important thing about these men is evidently their covenant status, and the most significant question is whether they lived up to the grace that had been given them.

How the call of God was made clear to Abram in Ur we are not told. It is gratuitous, therefore, to picture a lofty-souled man fretting against the surrounding polytheism. In obedience, Abram took the caravan route to Haran and thence to Canaan, though in disobedience he accepted Lot into his company (cf. Gen 12:1). He set up his first altar at Bethel (Gen 12:8) apparently in recognition of having reached the land to which he had been called, but at once he deserted it for the seemingly more fruitful prospects of Egypt. He was bold enough to live among the alien Canaanites, yet cowardly enough to shelter behind a conscious half-truth about his wife (Gen 12:10ff.; cf. 20:13). His treatment of Lot was generous (Gen 13:7ff.), self-endangering (14:1ff.), and concerned (18:16ff.). Abram paid dearly for his early compromise in not separating from his family, yet the Lord did not withdraw the richness of the promise to him (13:14ff.). Abram could rise to the faith expressed in 15:5, 6, and at once fall to the impatient compromise of Hagar and Ishmael, once more sowing by faithlessness the seed of a bitter harvest. But when human hope was past (Gen 17:1ff.), the promise was renewed and Isaac was born. Even though Abraham was involved in a further deceitful episode with Sarah (20:1ff.) and a shameful desertion of Hagar (21:1ff.), he was still strong in faith when the crisis came, and God honored the man who held nothing back (22:12ff.). In the same faith by which he believed that the promise of inheritance would be kept, he buried Sarah in Canaan (23:1ff.) and sternly forbade the removal of Isaac back to Mesopotamia (24:6–8).

The story of Isaac is the same blend of faith and defection. His quiet walk with God is well exemplified in his prayer concerning his wife's inability to conceive (25:21), but at once we encounter that human determination to grasp by effort what had been promised by grace. Jacob, the promised inheritor, schemes to realize God's will before its time (25:23–34). Isaac tarries obediently and peaceably in the land (26:1ff.), but in his old age, human schemes of self-salvation again invade the household of faith. Rebekah aims by trickery to achieve for Jacob what God had promised to him but what Isaac in his dotage would forgetfully and disobediently give to Esau. The family of Isaac falls into disunity, and Jacob leaves home, never again to lay eyes on his fond mother.

Jacob's story is one of ceaseless human wiliness. When God meets him with grace, Jacob replies with a bargain (28:13–15, 20–22). He reaches Padan-Aram in Mesopotamia where two great opportunists of the ancient world pit their wits against each other. If

---

[5]Cf. M.H. Segal, *The Pentateuch* (Jerusalem, 1967).

Laban removes all speckled cattle so that none such will be begotten, Jacob can match this with a trick of his own, laying stripped rods in the watering troughs. But it was the Lord who gave the increase, not the craft of man (30:34–39; 31:10–13). Returning to the land of promise, Jacob thinks to enter it in safety by a mixture of prayer (32:9–12) and bribery (32:13–20). Small wonder, then, that the supernatural man wrestled with him, for God allows inheritance of the promise only on the basis of faith. Therefore when Jacob, maimed and defeated in the contest (32:25), protests that he will not let the "man" go until he has bestowed a blessing, he is talking the language of faith and he knows that he is pleading with one who blesses the helpless. From this moment Jacob begins, but how slowly, to change from the self-reliant opportunist to the man who recognizes that all is of God (e.g., 48:16, 21).

The remarkable story of Joseph is set in Jacob's latter years. As a pampered and somewhat priggish youth, Joseph was cruelly sold into slavery (Gen 37). In Egypt, Joseph shows sterner mettle. He survives the assault of Potiphar's wife and the testing years of imprisonment (39:1ff.). His release was as unexpected and his exaltation as dramatic as his imprisonment and slavery were unjust. Presently he is face to face with his now suppliant brothers (42:1ff.). His seemingly teasing and unfeeling treatment of them may have been intended to bring them to repentance. Dramatically, it is the revelation of the humbled, transformed Judah (44:18) that breaks Joseph's heart. The family is reunited under Joseph's quasi-royal patronage, and the patriarchal faith rises to one of its climaxes in his great affirmation that whatever of ill man has perpetrated, "God meant it" for good and for salvation (50:20).

So the patriarchal story begins with the covenant pledge of God and ends with a testimony that God has done all things well, caring for a people who invariably failed to deserve the privilege grace had given them.

B. The Period of Fulfillment: Moses to Joshua

1. *Egypt and Canaan.* The patriarchal period ended with the people of the covenant as resident aliens in Egypt. Why did the Lord of history so plan the course of his people? The OT provides two answers—one directly and the other by a clear implication of its theology. The direct answer is given in Genesis 15:16: The Promised Land must not be taken from its Amorite inhabitants till their iniquity has forfeited their right to its tenure. The Judge of all the earth always does right (Gen 18:25), and when Joshua's armies invade, they do so with a just mandate from the Most High. The implied reason for the Egyptian sojourn—visible only by hindsight—is that inheritance must be by the redemptive act of God and that the covenant people must be taught that all their privileges are blood-bought. Divine sovereignty appointed that this lesson should come through Egyptian bondage and divine deliverance.

2. *Moses.* Once again we revert to the frame of reference in which the biblical history is written—and find that the key name in this whole epoch of Scripture is that of Moses.

Even if the narrative of the infancy and upbringing of Moses did not possess a clear ring of truth, we should now be bound to give it credence. R.K. Harrison writes, "There is nothing particularly unusual about ... a west Semite being brought up in court circles in ancient Egypt. ... [Moses] would become familiar with the religious beliefs and practices of . . . Canaan . . . and the wide range of priestcraft that would be included in the education of one who came from the royal household."[6]

The narrative in Exodus plainly suggests that Moses was fully aware of his Hebrew origin and affiliation (Exod 2:11) and we may assume that he had acquainted himself with his own patriarchal forebears and their traditions. Certainly the terms of the theophany in Midian are consonant with this supposition; it is a fresh revelation of the God of Abraham, Isaac, and Jacob (Exod 3:6) and presently and inevitably the revelation is expounded in covenantal terms (6:5; cf. 2:23ff.).

Three features distinguish the Mosaic development of the covenant and bring the concept into its normative biblical form. First, there is the revelation of the divine name (Exod 3:13ff.; 6:2, 3). Patriarchal and earlier traditions insist that the name had been known and used long before the time of Moses (Gen 4:26 et al.). Prior to Moses the name had never been developed into a revelation of the divine nature.[7] But now, with Moses as the chosen prophet, this central revelation is to take place. The relation of the name YHWH (Yahweh) to the Hebrew verb "to be" suggests that he is the God who makes himself known by his active presence among his people, for it is central to the meaning of the verb that it expresses not simply "existence" but "active reality." So, for example, the well-known phrase "The word of the Lord came . . ." is literally "The word of the Lord was . . . ," i.e., it "became an active reality in the experience of the recipient." The developing narrative from Exodus 3:13 onwards reveals that God purposes to be present as the Redeemer of his people and the Destroyer of his foes. This revelation reached its climax at the Passover when God's people were sheltered from his destructive wrath by the blood of the lamb, while their unprotected adversaries suffered a token but terrible judgment.

This is in fact the second special strand in Mosaic thinking. The Abrahamic covenant was sealed by an unexplained sacrifice (Gen 15); the Mosaic covenant has as its center the sacrifice of the Passover, spelled out in redemptive and substitutionary terms: the exact equation between the lamb and the people of God (Exod 12:3, 4), the protective efficacy of its death as betokened by the sprinkled blood, and the propitiation of a wrathful God on seeing that the blood had been shed (Exod 12:13).

The third feature of the Mosaic economy is the elaboration of the law into a complete code, providing a pattern for the life and conduct of the redeemed people. Grace redeems, and the holiness of the gracious God demands. As divine holiness is the bracket within which the whole Exodus movement takes place (cf. Exod 3:5; 19:1ff.), only the blood of the lamb can bring the people safely into that holy presence and only a life exhibiting a holiness like his (cf. Lev 19:2) can walk in his company. So Moses lays the foundation of OT and biblical religion upon the twin rocks of grace and law.

3. Exodus and wilderness

a. *The date of the Exodus.* The historicity of the Exodus cannot be seriously questioned. "The Bible's own witness is itself so impressive as to leave little doubt that some such remarkable deliverance took place."[8] Its date, however, is by no means clear, and students have interpreted the evidence differently. The Egyptians were not in the habit of recording defeats, and in any case the loss of a slave people was not necessarily as

---

[6] *Old Testament Times* (London, 1970), p. 124.

[7] Cf. Motyer, *Revelation of the Divine Name.*

[8] J. Bright, *History of Israel* (London, 1960), p. 111.

significant to them as was the gaining of liberty to Israel. We must therefore set side by side the two possible views.

If Solomon came to the throne about 970 B.C., 1 Kings 6:1ff. places the Exodus 480 years before the fourth year of Solomon, i.e., 1446 B.C. Thus Joseph and Jacob would have entered Egypt in the reigns of Sesostris II and III respectively. Two centuries of peace followed until Egypt was conquered by Ahmosis I, known in the Bible as the pharaoh who "knew not Joseph" (Exod 1:8), where antisemitic policies were continued by Amenhotep I, perhaps in the genocidal action of Exod 1:15ff. If Moses was eighty years old in 1446 (Exod 7:7), he would have been born in this reign. Amenhotep II becomes the Pharaoh of the Exodus. The Amarna letters of fifty years later, complaining about attacks on the Canaanite cities and the absence of Egyptian defending forces, point to the period of the invasion and its aftermath. About 1100 B.C., Jephthah (Judg 11:27) indicates that the Israelite residence has by then lasted 300 years, and this too would mean an entrance to Canaan at about 1400 B.C.

No view of the date of the Exodus is free from difficulties, but the evidence for the early date is not now generally considered at its real strength in specialist study. Additional to an impressive statement of the case by Merrill,[9] B.K. Waltke demonstrates that even the supposedly contrary evidence of Jericho has been wrongly appraised and that Jericho may well support the early date but contradict the late date. His article on this is a foundational study.[10]

The other view supposes the Exodus to have occurred in the thirteenth century. It is known that Ramses II (1290-1224) was involved in building works, and this fact may be best linked with the Pithom and Raamses of Exod 1:11. We know that Ramses II employed Apiru slaves for his public works. He or his father Seti I (1303-1290) would be the pharaoh of the oppression. Some hold that the stele left by Ramses' successor, Marniptah, implies that Israel was present but not yet settled in Canaan, but the point is in dispute. If we then date the Exodus (with Albright) in 1282 B.C., the desert march took place when Edom and Moab were established kingdoms and the diplomatic activity outlined in Numbers 20:14ff. and elsewhere makes sense, as does the evidence for wholesale destruction of Canaanite cities in the latter part of the thirteenth century.

This dating does not concur with the plainest meaning (to us) of the 480 years of 1 Kings 6:1, but can we be certain of the method of computation of such periods? If the date of the Exodus must be placed later rather than earlier, an "important consideration is that the number in question looks like a round figure of twelve 'generations' of forty years each, the usual conventional length.... Therefore it is not unreasonable to see the 480 years as a reference to the twelve generations known to have elapsed between exodus and Temple"[11] —a most judicious assessment.

b. *The route of the Exodus.* The biblical account is well documented with place names, but we cannot now trace the route, since most sites cannot be identified. The precise location of Sinai itself adds to our problems. Exodus 13:17, 18 points to a deliberate turning south along the line of the Red Sea, and 14:2 indicates a retracing of steps northward. The phrase "entangled in the land" (14:3) suggests that Israel had apparently strayed from main roads and could be assumed "lost"—and as Cole well remarks "so are

---

[9]E.H. Merrill, *An Historical Survey of the Old Testament,* (Craig Press, 1966), pp. 99ff.

[10]BS, January 1972.

[11]R.A. Cole, *Exodus* (London, 1973), p. 42.

we!"[12] The abandonment of the Philistine road coupled with the remark about Israel being "lost" tells against too northerly a crossing; the return to Pi-hahiroth forbids too southerly a crossing. It cannot have been a shallow marsh, as some have assumed from the suggested alternate translation 'Reed Sea,' for this would not allow the returning waters to drown the Egyptian forces. The motivation here has sometimes been to minimize the miraculous element in the crossing. The facts demand otherwise, but in the present state of knowledge certainty of location is impossible.

c. *The wilderness.* The same uncertainty besets the attempt to retrace Israel's steps through the wilderness. In this desolate area, with no settled life, many of the places recorded in the biblical itineraries were named after events private to Israel, other names perhaps were coined by the travelers at brief stopovers.

The forty years of wilderness life were divided into two unequal parts by the rebellious refusal of the people to enter the land, following the report of the spies (Num 13, 14; Deut 1:22ff.). The focus of the earlier period was Mount Sinai, usually located in the southern Sinai Peninsula, and of the later period, Kadesh Barnea (Deut 1:46). The experiences on the way to Sinai (Exod 15:22–17:16) show how the people ought to have learned to trust the foreordering providence of the Creator since he had gone before them to plant a tree (15:25), plot the course of migratory birds (16:13), and set the rock on the hill (17:6). The events from Sinai onward show that far from learning this trustfulness, complaint turned into rebellion against the Lord's designated gift of the land (Num 13, 14), against his appointed leaders (Num 16), and against his moral and religious purity (Num 25).

In the biblical insistence that history is prophecy, i.e., declarative of the divine nature and will, the message here is the same as in the patriarchal narrative: The maintenance of the covenant and the fulfillment of the covenant promises are both utterly dependent on the determination of the covenant God to have his way. The Sinai events themselves reveal this. Sinai placed the capstone on the work of grace begun at the Passover. The covenant scheme was completed by the giving of an itemized law whereby the redeemed became aware of how to live so as to please their God (Exod 19ff.), and the Passover sacrifice was elaborated and its efficacy continued in Israel by the full levitical system. Thus the biblical balance and emphasis were made clear—the primary call to the people of God is to obey him whose grace has saved them, but that same grace makes a provision (the blood of the sacrifices) by which those who lapse from obedience may yet live and continue in his fellowship.

The second great Sinai event, the making of the tabernacle according to divine specification, symbolized this arrangement. Here was made plain the whole objective of the deliverance from Egypt, which was that the Lord might dwell among his people (Exod 29:44–46). But sadly, the climax was marred by the "sin of the golden calf" (Exod 32). Alike impatient and puzzled by Moses' long stay on the mount, the people pressed Aaron to provide an alternative god. The law was broken before it was received (32:19), dire punishment followed and, since the people had not fulfilled the condition on which they could become a kingdom of priests (Exod 19:4–6), the faithful Levites were given office (Deut 33:8ff.). But it should be noted that this narration falls between the detailed plan of the tabernacle (Exod 25–31) and the detailed carrying out of the plan (Exod 34–40).

---

[12]Ibid., p. 45.

The deliberate repetition, detail for detail, has its prophetic message; it is neither otiose nor misplaced. Rebellion or not, what the Lord purposed, the Lord will do.

The post-Sinai wanderings climax in the story of Balaam (Num 22–24). Once more the narrative is significantly placed. The selected events narrated in Numbers designate the entire period as one of rebellion. But there was a threat—of which the rebellious people were unaware—a threat that struck at the heart of their distinctiveness, for Balaam was presented as a direct challenge to the Abrahamic promise (Gen 12:3; Num 22:6) and therefore to the special function of Israel on earth as the keepers of that promise. The Lord, in spontaneous grace and in order to stand by his word, interposed and turned the threat into a blessing. Thus the covenant rests upon the covenant-maker. The symbolism of Genesis 15:17 was no empty form.

4. The conquest. Moses was barred from the Promised Land for his open act of disobedience (Num 20:1–13) and the divine motivation was described by Moses as "for your sakes" (Deut 1:37; 4:21). Rebellion had cost a whole generation their inheritance (Num 14:26–37). Knowing therefore his exclusion, Moses selflessly sought the welfare of the people of God in the matter of leadership, and Joshua was appointed (Num 27:12–23).

At first sight, the books of Joshua and Judges give very diverse views of the occupation of Canaan. In Joshua there are sweeping campaigns, involving destruction and conquest, yet the early stories in Judges tell of actions initiated by tribes meeting with indifferent success.

The problem of interpretation thus raised has been given varying answers. The first of these is espoused by Noth.[13] Starting from the apparent contradiction between the narratives in Joshua and Judges, from differences in the order and naming of the tribes in the various lists (e.g., Gen 30, 49) and in the relationships between the tribes as shown in the allocation of the land in Joshua 13ff., and from his belief that tribal names existed prior to the conquest as place names within Palestine, Noth proposed that there was a peaceful infiltration of Canaan as seminomad tribes settled in various parts of the land, adopted the name of the area as their own name, and formed links with racially related settlers. In the process of forming these links, the tribes set up an "amphictyony"—a twelve-unit religious grouping around a central shrine. They cemented their relationship by contributing individual tribal traditions and memories to the common pool. Somehow, there emerged a corporate story of how the amphictyonic group came into possession of their land. From rewritings, reeditings, and additions evolved the present set of narratives.

Noth has been criticized for an inadequate account of the wholesale destruction of the Canaanite cities in the late thirteenth century, since he attributes it to intercity strife. Bright[14] and Rowley[15] find the evidence suggests a piecemeal conquest. Rowley holds that the Joseph tribes with Levitical elements attacked the center under Joshua; that a Judah-confederation that included Kenites and Kenizzites moved in from south to north through the Negev, the opposite direction to that given in the editorially rewritten account in Joshua 10; and that units that later came to be called after the names of Jacob's concubines (in order to integrate them into "Israel") infiltrated the north.

These views hold that no such entity as a twelve-tribe "Israel" existed before the

---

[13]Martin Noth, *The History of Israel* (London: Black, 1959).

[14]Bright, *History of Israel,* pp. 126–139.

[15]H.H. Rowley, *From Josephus to Joshua* (London, 1950), pp. 109–163.

amalgamation of immigrants in the land of Canaan.[16] But this is all far from the unbroken testimony of the Bible that twelve tribes descended from Abraham through his grandson Jacob, that these twelve tribes came into Egyptian bondage and were led out by Moses, that under Joshua they invaded Canaan from the east and swept the whole land into their possession from a unified military headquarters at Gilgal near Jericho. Their first campaign covered the central area, and the historian records in particular the taking of Jericho, Ai and Bethel (see Josh 6–8). The terrified Gibeonites made peace with Joshua (Josh 9) and this defection from their ranks alerted the kings of the southern area who advanced as a confederacy against Gibeon. Joshua hastened to its aid and the initial victory was followed up by his second campaign, an advance into the south that subdued it and crushed all resistance (Josh 10). This Israelite victory mobilized the forces of the north, Jabin of Hazor realizing that he must now overthrow Joshua or suffer the fate of the rest of the land. But neither was his great alliance able to withstand the people of God in their third campaign of conquest (Josh 11), and thus "Joshua took the whole land, according to all that the Lord spake unto Moses" (Josh 11:23).

The Book of Joshua tells also of much land still unoccupied (13:1), of cities left undestroyed even though their armies had been defeated (11:13); of possession coming through individual tribal enterprise and of the slowness of some tribes to win their inheritance (15:13ff.; 15:63; 17:14ff.; 18:3, 4). Joshua's task was a war of occupation followed by the allocation of the land to the tribes. But this had to be implemented by wars of possession that individual tribes or partnerships of tribes undertook on their own responsibility with only partial fidelity and success. Harmonistic and interpretative problems remain, but they remain within the admitted testimony of the Bible and await fuller knowledge to supply the full answer.

III. Theocracy and Monarchy

With the work of Moses and Joshua finished, God had fulfilled one great part of his promise to Abram. For the children of the covenant possessed the land. But now they must exchange their mobile, desert life for settled, rural life. They must secure their possession against those who would dispossess them. But at last they will experience bitterly the curse of the covenant (Lev 26:25; Deut 28:15; et al.) and go into captivity all over again. Only by the grace of God are covenanted promises possessed; further work of God is necessary to guarantee that possession against human willfulness and weakness.

A. The Days When the Judges Judged

1. *Canaan.* The land into which Joshua's troops marched was incredibly mixed in population, possessing all the seven components mentioned in Joshua 3:10 (cf. 9:1; 11:3; 12:8; 24:11) plus the Philistines (13:2). The Canaanites were a Sem. people in the land before available historical records. They were mainly along the coastline (cf. Deut 1:7). The hill country was mainly populated by Amorites who came in the early second millennium, in the same migratory wave as Abram. The Hittites were the fringe of the great Hitt. empire that extended from Asia Minor well into northern Palestine. The name was

---

[16]E.g., H.H.Rowley, *Worship in Ancient Israel* (London, 1967), pp. 58ff.

widely used for the non-Sem. elements in the population. Perizzites and Hivites were remnants of the Old Hurrian immigration that climaxed between 1700 and 1500 B.C. and that may have included Girgashites and Jebusites. The Philistines, the "peoples of the sea," surface about 1220 B.C. trying to secure a foothold on the Egyp. coast. In the records of Pharaoh Marniptah (1224ff.) they include Achaeans, Lysians, and others who were set on a migratory course by the break-up of the Greek Mycenaean empire after the Trojan War. The "sea peoples" finally established themselves on the Palestine coast, which was to be their home throughout the OT period. The migration of the tribe of Dan (Judg 18) was probably caused in part by Philistine pressure, though in other ways they did Israel a service by diverting Egyp. attention from Palestine during the time of the settlement.

Palestine was probably as mixed religiously as it was racially.[17] One point will help explain the later religious tensions and temptations of the people of God. The religion of Canaan and that of Israel had one common factor: fertility, or prosperity. All-important in an agrarian community is how to guarantee the fertility of man, animals, and land. For Canaan, the religion of Baal was the answer. He was lord of the land and bestower of fertility. But Baal was an impersonal force, not a moral agency. He was under no obligation; no entreaty could be relied on to move him. In this context, the religious practice of "sympathetic" or "imitative" magic was developed—let man do on earth, openly and visibly, what he wished his god to do in heaven and the god would see and be stimulated into action. Since the object of the exercise was fertility, it was obvious what man must do: human acts of generation. So the religion of Baal was based fundamentally on "sacred" prostitution.

The Bible, however, does not merely forbid this (e.g., Deut 23:17); it has its positive and costly alternative—that just as righteousness exalts a nation politically, so obedience is the guarantee of its prosperity (cf. Deut 28, 29, et al.). The way of Canaan was to pressure God by techniques, the way of Israel was to acknowledge the sovereignty of God by obedience; the way of Canaan was unbridled self-indulgence, the way of Israel was self-mortification in obeying the law of holiness. The story of Israel is the story of the church: Will man submit to God or seek to mold him to the human will? Will man recognize his sinfulness or somehow attempt to bring sin within the sphere of the divine? This contemporary conflict emerged in the book of Judges.

2. *The Book of Judges and its message.* The period of the Judges is often considered the theocracy par excellence, for the Judges were charismatics raised by God alone to meet specific crises. This was their strength and their weakness.

Judges is a pro-monarchic tract produced either about the time of 1 Samuel 8:5, or, more probably, emanating from the honeymoon period of the early monarchy. Its object is twofold. In chapters 3–16 it offers portraits of typical judges under whom the land experienced a see-saw existence between victory and defeat but no stable continuance in welldoing. In chapters 17 to 21 the book shows how under cover of these great charismatic victories there was a deadly deterioration of national life religiously (chs. 17, 18), morally (ch. 19), and socially (chs. 20, 21), attributed to the absence of kingship (18:1; 19:1; 21:25).

According to the earlier date of the Exodus, the period of the Judges commenced

---

[17]John Gray, *Archaeology and the Old Testament World* (Santa Fe: Gannon, 1962), pp. 105–120; idem, *The Canaanites* (London, 1964), pp. 119–138.

about 1300 B.C. (Merrill[18] dates Cushan-rishathaim [Judg 3:8] 1380 B.C.). The later date of the Exodus moves the period of the judges forward to 1200 B.C. (Bright[19] dates Deborah at c. 1125 B.C.). We need doubt neither the existence of the men and women named nor the record itself. Yet it cannot at present be related with any certainty to world leaders or events. Samson would, of course, have to be dated after the establishment of the Philistines in strength along the southern sea coast. The dates suggested vary according to the preferred date of the Exodus. The period 1170–1070 B.C. must be considered for the commencement of Samson's judgeship; the strength of the Philistine opposition would point in the direction of the lower dating.[20]

Cushan-rishathaim of Mesopotamia (3:7ff.) threatened Israel from the north, marching around the fertile crescent. Since he was opposed by Othniel, a Calebite-Judahite (cf. Num 13:6), he presumably constituted a threat to the whole land and was met by a national federation of tribes. In contrast, Eglon (3:12ff.) pressing merely across Jordan against Benjamin, was countered by the local enterprise of Ehud of Benjamin. Shamgar (3:31), not even called a judge, should perhaps be linked with Ehud, translating "Among his [Ehud's] followers was . . . ," understanding that Ehud also faced pressure on his people from the Philistine West. Deborah and Barak (4:1ff.) faced the threat of the northern kingdom of Hazor, and the Song indicates (Judg 5:1ff.) that they considered themselves potentially leading a national coalition, or at least a coalition of the tribes of the center and north; Judah is not mentioned, but every tribe north of Judah is either praised or blamed. Gideon delivered his people from the southern and eastern threat of the Midianites and Amalekites (6:1ff.). His call went out to "all Manasseh," presumably including Manasseh in Transjordan, on the line of advance of the invaders. In addition, Gideon summoned the tribes of the north and center. The next judge mentioned was Jephthah, called from exile (11:1ff.) to meet the eastern threat of the Ammonites. This was apparently a local threat in the Transjordan area. The final judge about whom substantial records have survived is Samson (13:1ff.), who single-handedly took on the Philistine threat from the western seaboard.

So we are given a representative statement of the precarious situation of the people of God threatened with enemies on every side. The historian notes the faithfulness of God in raising up leaders to meet each threat, but he does not conceal the failure of these brilliant and gifted men to effect any lasting benefit for the people. On the contrary, he shows that their rule was followed by relapse, chastening, and defeat. The episode of the Shechmite monarchy of Abimelech (9:1ff.) revealed the danger of pseudo-charismatic charlatans stepping into the vacuum caused by the disappearance of the preceding leader and troubling the people of God. The sacrifice of Jephthah's daughter (11:34ff.) is left without comment, and is probably a reflection of substandard accommodations in matters of religion. This leads on naturally to the stories of Samson. That God serves his own cause by overruling the cruelties, vanities, and immoralities of his servants is one thing; but that his servants should think that he is to be served in this way is quite another. Therefore, the closing chapters (17–21) unsparingly unveil things as they are, showing that behind the curtain of charismatic brilliance, national life was in decay and disorder. Nothing but monarchy could mend it.

---

[18] *Historical Survey*, p. 170.
[19] *History of Israel*, p. 157.
[20] See Merrill, *Historical Survey*, p. 81, for list.

B. *The Monarchy: Hopes, Ideals, Tragedy*

1. *The Monarchist movement.* Many assert that the Bible gives two opposing views of the introduction of monarchy: The first (1 Sam 9:1–10:16) thinks in terms of the Lord's command and Samuel's wholehearted cooperation; the second (1 Sam 8 and 10:17–27) relates it to popular pressure, stoutly resisted by Samuel. The latter view is supposedly truly theocratic, later than the first, and historically dubious.[21]

The two "accounts" require each other at least in one major point: 1 Samuel 10:22 is inexplicable without 10:1. Also, to consider the monarchy antitheocratic is erroneous. The people of God are always and essentially a theocracy. The Lord did not define "theocracy" as "direct rule by God without human intermediary." The theocracy has always been mediated through an appointed human agent. The monarchy, therefore, is neither nontheocratic nor antitheocratic. A usurper among the judges, like Abimelech, violates the theocracy; so would a self-willed or apostate king. But monarchy itself no more violates the theocratic principle than judgeship.

Furthermore, once monarchy was established, it was evidently not disputed. Individual kings were opposed, even assassinated, but they were always freely replaced by others and the monarchy remained intact. Where, then, would originate notions opposed to the foundation of the monarchy? There is no other known source than Samuel. Remembering this, we can explain satisfactorily all allegedly double and contradictory narration. Naturally, as the last of the judges, Samuel defended the system; but he set himself to cooperate with the monarchy, once he knew the will of God.

Two motivations led to the establishment of the monarchy. First, the people longed for security. Though the Philistine threat had been reduced by the victory at Ebenezer (1 Sam 7:7ff.), other dangers threatened: the presence of Nahash the Ammonite (12:12) and the advanced age of Samuel himself, coupled with the unsatisfactory character of his sons. Thus the Lord declared that the call for a king was not a rejection of Samuel but of the Lord himself (8:7). Samuel returned to this point in his farewell address (12:6–12), saying that on every past occasion when the people prayed in the face of danger, their prayer had been heard. Why, then, must they now have the security of a self-perpetuating leadership?

But it was no contradiction of this divine exposure of a lack of faith when in 9:16 the Lord urged the appointment of a king because the cry of his distraught people had reached him. As the law was designed to lead people to Christ, so judgeship was designed to lead them to monarchy; as the groaning of a people to whom the law was a standard that they could not reach provided "a prompting" for the sending of the Messiah, so the prayer of those whose faith was not strong enough to face the human uncertainties of judgeship called on the Lord to bring in his perfect ideal of kingship.

Samuel's hesitation and defensiveness here sprang from a zeal for God coupled, perhaps, with a longing that the report about his sons might be mistaken. Samuel was a very great man. By birth a Kohathite Levite (1 Chron 6:22–28), he lived in the location that Joshua had given to the Kohathites (1 Sam 1:1 cf. Josh 21:20ff.). He early served in the house of the Lord at Shiloh, grew up to exercise the functions and perform the deeds of a judge (e.g., 1 Sam 7:7–12, 16, 17), and was by divine calling a prophet (3:1–4:1). He inherited a situation of national and religious decline. The aged and godly Eli relinquished control of the house of the Lord to his self-seeking and immoral sons (2:12–17,

---

21G. Fohrer, *Introduction to the Old Testament* (London, 1970), p. 217.

22–25; 3:13). Their religion was one of observance but not of devotion. They assumed typically that the religious presence of the ark could save them (4:3ff.). They died in the service of a religion they had created for their own pleasure; their father died in grief for the truth he had let slip from the people of God and from his own family (4:18). Fitting was the epitaph of Phinehas's wife when she said that the glory had gone into captivity (4:21). In this religious vacuum, the house of the Lord at Shiloh presumably destroyed by the Philistines (cf. Jer 7:12–14) and the ark itself moved from the center of national life (1 Sam 7:1), Samuel provided a national and spiritual focus, keeping the flame of faith alight and preparing the people for the time, twenty years later, when they would seek God (7:2–4). His contest with an established Philistine power and his proximity to the reigns of Saul and David give us a date for the judgeship of Samuel of about 1050 B.C.

2. *The interim monarchy: Saul (c. 1020–1000).* Answering the plea for a king, the Lord gave his people Saul, a man of royal stature (10:23). Saul was chosen and anointed secretly, and given an inner sense of divine enabling (10:1, 9). Publicly elected to office (10:17–24), he took his royal position with a modesty (10:21, 22) that later degenerated into insecurity and desperate depression in the face of supposed persecutions. He proved himself in the Ammonite war (11:1ff.), wherein his ties to the old system of the judges are apparent. Equipped with the Lord's Spirit for the Lord's battles (11:6), Saul had that magnetic quality of leadership found also in Deborah, Barak, and David. This early test of Saul's monarchy was followed by public acclaim and consolidated his hold on the kingdom (7:14, 15). The ceremony with the young king at Gilgal, the place from which Joshua had once led his troops to victory, was a moving experience.

While a later hint (28:3b, 9) indicates that Saul was a reforming king, purging the land religiously, the historian moves his narrative forward to David without amplifying this point. Yet the reference is an attractive glimpse into the godly ideals of Israel's first king, just as passages like 23:19; 26:1 reveal the hold he had on his people's loyalty. Abner later held the allegiance of the majority to the house of Saul, who seemingly appealed to the northern tribes in a way David never quite equaled.

Saul's kingship, however, was marred by mistakes accounted small by the world but seen by Bible history as the hinges on which turn the fate of men and nations. On his coronation day, his wish to retire from public gaze can pass as commendable humility. Yet as Saul's story develops, it reveals first the nervous discomposure that would not allow him to wait the allotted time for Samuel (13:8ff.), then the religious scrupulosity that eroded a potentially crucial defeat of the Philistines (14:24ff.), next the weakness that put the people's will before God's command (15:9, 15), and finally the paranoiac suspicion of David (18:9ff.) that bedeviled the latter part of his reign. In turn, Saul lost dynasty (13:13, 14), throne (15:23), sanity (18:10), and life itself (31:4).

3. *The normative monarchy: David (c. 1000–960).* David's personal career not only holds our interest as a story; it is a crowning example of covenantal and Deuteronomic history writing. It begins as a supreme triumph of the promises of God. Samuel was roused by God from the lethargy of sorrow into which the failure of Saul had cast him (1 Sam 16:1) and was sent to anoint one of the sons of Jesse. The divine choice fell on David, who was forthwith anointed and filled with the Holy Spirit (16:13). At once we see matters set in train to secure David's imminent elevation to the throne. He enters Saul's court (16:14ff.) and, by slaying Goliath, becomes the darling of the people (18:30), and a member of the royal family (18:27, 28). But Saul's insane jealousy leads to David's flight (19:10, 18; 20:1; 22:1). David has lost more than the king's favor; people turn against him

(23:11, 12, 19; 26:1) till he faithlessly abandons the land promised him (27:1). More dereliction follows and he is dismissed by the Philistines (29:9–11). He returns home to Ziklag, only to find that it has been burned to the ground in an Amalekite reprisal raid and his wives and children taken captive. David's own men speak of stoning him (30:1–6). But when hope is gone, hope is fulfilled: God keeps his promise. David leaves the ashes of Ziklag to mount the throne of Judah (2 Sam 2:4; cf. Ps 113:7, 8). A long war of attrition with the remnants of Saul's kingdom follows until the violent deaths of Abner and Ish-Bosheth (3:30; 4:1ff.). David accepts the invitation to reign over Israel also.

But what God does by grace man despoils by sin. David's sin with Bathsheba (2 Sam 11:1ff.) is the turning point in his personal affairs; his family falls to pieces as the rape of Tamar by Amnon (13:1ff.) finds David too morally weakened by his own sin to exert discipline (13:21). Absalom takes the law into his own hands (13:23), and this taste of the rule of force tempts him to rebellion, revealing also how superficially David had knit the two sections of his kingdom into one (15:1–6).

The rest is soon told: Further rebellions threaten the kingdom (20:1) and David instigates tragedy in sinfully numbering the people. Finally, the enfeebled and bed-ridden king fails to implement his proclamation of Solomon as king (1 Chron 23:1) and Adonijah wins the support of Abiathar the priest and Joab in his aspirations to the throne. Nathan and Bathsheba alert David and take the coronation of Solomon in hand (1 Kings 1:1ff.). David dies with words of vengeance on his lips (1 Kings 2:1–9). The grace of God brought David to the throne; the sin of David exposed his weaknesses. The glory and tragedy of David were together to become the seed of messianic hope.

Yet David's solid achievements were great. His reputation as the king by whom to judge all later kings was not ill-deserved. Politically, he offered his people security, expansion, and unity. In three campaigns he dealt a death blow to the Philistine threat, which had long dogged Israel (2 Sam 5:17ff.; 8:1). Syria was forced to make peace after two punitive defeats (8:4–8; 10:8–19). Moab (8:2), Ammon (10:1–19; 11:1ff.; 12:26–31), and Edom (8:14) became his servants. David unified his kingdom by the strategically brilliant capture of Jerusalem and its nomination as capital city of the twin kingdom of Israel and Judah (5:6–10).

David's master stroke was not simply that he gave metropolitan status to a city that neither section of his people could view with jealousy, but that he united city, royalty, and worship by bringing in the long-neglected ark and so making Jerusalem the hoped-for central place of the people of God (6:1). In this, David saw himself as fulfilling the Deuteronomic expectation (cf. 7:1 with Deut 12:10), though it was left for Solomon to crown Zion's hill with a worthy house. Perhaps David found the Melchizedek priesthood still in Jerusalem when he captured it (note the continuance of the royal-priestly name, from Melchizedek [Gen 14:18] through to Adoni-zedek [Josh 10:1]. This would explain the priest-king in Psalm 110, and help foster the royal-priestly messianic hope associated with David's house in the Psalms and Prophets.

4. *Hope deferred: Solomon (c. 970–930)*. Solomon introduced a new type of kingship into Israel. Both Saul and David had a charismatic gift of leadership and also reigned by popular acclaim. Solomon came to the throne by a palace revolution. His brother Adonijah, relying on the supposed right of primogeniture made a potentially successful bid for the throne of his enfeebled father, and received powerful support from Joab and Abiathar, army and church linking hands to control the destiny of the state (1 Kings 1:7ff.). Solomon seemingly did not propose himself as king in any such way but was apparently nominated, unasked, by an alliance of Nathan and Bathsheba, that is, the

inner circle of court life (1 Kings 1:11ff.). More than successful intrigue contributed to Solomon's accession. Nathan's support was crucial. While Adonijah was backed by the priesthood and the army, Solomon enjoyed divine sanction expressed through the prophet. Here, indeed, was the central issue: Would God's kingdom be ruled by self-appointed men or by his nominee? The Davidic charisma was such that he had only to rouse himself sufficiently to set the coronation of Solomon in train for popular acclaim to be given the young regent and for Adonijah's cause to disappear without trace (vv.49ff.). Yet it was not an auspicious beginning for the reign of the first Davidic king. Moreover, the blood-bath whereby Solomon secured his throne (aided by David's death-bed testament, 1 Kings 2:1ff.) does no credit to him or to Benaiah, his not unwilling hatchet man (vv.24, 25, 28–34). Nevertheless, to this same Solomon there was opened the liberal fount of covenant blessings: "Ask what I shall give thee" (1 Kings 3:5). Here again is the inner mainspring of the covenant history of the OT: the undefeated mercy of the Lord, gleaming at its brightest where it is most strikingly seen to be mercy pure and simple.

Solomon inherited the military domination of the Near East secured by his father's prowess. Fighting no battles himself, he appeared to be a fit bridegroom for the Pharaoh's daughter (1 Kings 3:1). That Solomon left his kingdom as he found it—somewhat shaking but still intact—indicates his success as a national leader and an international politician. Internationally, his great influence is seen in the visit of the Queen of Sheba (1 Kings 10), but this colorful story must not blind us to the equally impressive achievements of Solomon at home: his mighty, regular army (4:26), the fortresses along the perimeter of Israel to provide defense against raids from Israel's neighbors (1 Kings 9:15–19). Nor should we forget his administrative ability (4:1ff.), his development of trade (9: 26–28; 10:22–29), the enormous wealth accumulated through this royal enterprise (10:14, 15), and the affluence enjoyed by the people (4:20, et al.).

Solomon's most notable achievements were in the realms of wisdom and religion. His shrewdest action was to ask God for wisdom (3:9). The historian doubtless delighted in the story about how fully God had answered that prayer (3:16ff.). The wisdom of Solomon had its fruit in practical discernment and in pithy, proverbial sayings, songs, and research into the world of nature (4:29ff.), all crystallized in the Book of Proverbs.

In the religious sphere, Solomon's genius for administration flowered in the masterly construction of the Temple, just as his own deep and genuine piety finds expression in the prayer by which it was dedicated (8:1ff.).

Yet God was subjecting His people to the discipline of the less than best. Solomon enjoyed an unparalleled international sway, but corrupted it by assembling an army of wives and concubines taken in token of successful alliances. He gave his people prosperity, then subjected them to hard labor to support his grandiose schemes (4:6; 9:15ff.). The nature of Israel showed marked deterioration as the religious confederation of twelve tribes became a bureaucratic organization of twelve administrative districts to support luxurious and expensive royalty (4:7ff.). Solomon built a magnificent house for the Lord, but presently turned the same skills to providing for the religious needs of his wives, not even scrupling to include the odious worship of Molech (11:1–8).

A divine principle insured that the prayer for wisdom was answered not with wisdom alone but also with wealth, power, and length of days. No blessing is enjoyed till exercised in the teeth of temptation to abuse it. Solomon received the gift but failed the test.

Monarchy in Israel was essentially messianic—born out of national longing for a savior. The birth of messianism—the actual hope of a son of David who would be Yahweh's Son—must have occurred when the brilliant hope set on Solomon faded. Was it not at this time that 2 Samuel 7 ceased to be merely dynastic and became prophetic of the everlasting kingdom of God's appointed king? For the people, in their ceaseless and divinely fostered hope for perfection, foresaw this perfect kingship with increasing clarity—a kingship that even the best (David, who henceforth was the standard of comparison) and the most promising (Solomon, the man of "peace") had failed to bring to realization.

5. *The great schism: Rehoboam and Jeroboam (c.922).* The story of the kingdom of David and Solomon does not conceal the fragility of the situation. Israel had only slowly been incorporated into David's rule after her own primary loyalty to Saul lapsed with the death of Ishbosheth and the absence of the strong, guiding hand of Abner behind another Saulite candidate. It had apparently been a comparatively easy task for the gifted Absalom to wean the northern tribes away to his own cause (2 Sam 15:1ff.). After Absalom's rebellion, David brilliantly continued to restore national unity and Solomon ably consolidated the situation. When, however, he was succeeded by one who lacked both charisma and genius, this ancient crack became a rift.

Solomon had four enemies (1 Kings 11:14ff.): Hadad of Edom; Rezon of the Aramean kingdom of Damascus; Jeroboam the son of Nebat, a native Israelite; and the prophetic movement with Ahijah as its mouthpiece. The prophet Nathan's initiative had brought Solomon to the throne, and it was the prophetic movement, alienated by Solomon's defection from pure prophetic Yahwism (v.33), that had promoted the punitive schism.

Things came to a head when Rehoboam went to Shechem, presumably to seek the acknowledgment of the northern tribes to his accession. Years earlier, David had become their king by covenant (2 Sam 5:3), unlike the apparently unconditional loyalty accorded him by Judah (cf. 2 Sam 2:5). Solomon's oppressiveness had obviously reanimated their memory and they sought to bind Rehoboam to 'a constitutional monarchy (1 Kings 12:1ff.). They were acting according to a preconceived plan, for they had already recalled Jeroboam from exile (v.3). Rehoboam's reactionary politics sealed his own doom, and the northern tribes became the separate kingdom of Israel.

This great schism as recounted by the sacred historian dramatically illustrates the Deuteronomic view of history. Three things, characteristic of the Deuteronomic schema, converge: the declension from Yahweh that brings ruin in its wake (1 Kings 11:31, 33); the undefeated purpose of Yahweh who keeps his promises (v.32); and his management of world history to establish what he wills. We see this not only in the action of Shemaiah (1 Kings 12:22), who forbade Rehoboam to go to war with Jeroboam, but more so in the attack Shishak of Egypt made against Jerusalem (1 Kings 14:25ff.). The Bible simply relates this attack to its moral causation. Secular records, however, reveal that Shishak was attempting to spearhead an Egyptian revival, shaking the country out of the national lethargy of the 21st dynasty, and that he penetrated north as far as Galilee, bringing both Judah and Israel to their knees. The Lord of history used sinful, imperialist ambitions to punish his own erring people, making it impossible for either side to contemplate the absorption of the other.

C. *Decline and Fall in the North*

The monarchy of Jeroboam was prophetically promoted as an act of divine chastisement on the house of David (1 Kings 11:29–39; cf. Isa 7:17) and was therefore according to God's will (cf. 1 Kings 12:24). But from the start it had a pervasive element of human willfulness. Jeroboam was promised dominion "over all that your soul desires" (1 Kings

11:37). Thus here again the Lord was ruling and directing essentially sinful impulses for His own holy purposes. But Jeroboam's kingship was granted to him conditionally (1 Kings 11:38) and he failed his probation dismally. So willfulness and human ambition prevailed. From Jeroboam to the end, these characteristics marked the northern dynasties; when the kingdom had run all but twenty of its two hundred years, God could say, "They have set up kings, but not by me; they have made princes and I knew it not" (Hosea 8:4). Five distinct royal houses ruled over Israel, and each ended its dynastic course by an assassination (1 Kings 15:27; 16:9, 10; 2 Kings 9:24; 15:10, 25). It was a wild, restless, willful kingdom both set on its course and doomed by the sin of its first king.

1. *The sin of Jeroboam (c. 930–910).* Apart from the incursion of Shishak, Jeroboam's twenty-two years apparently were free from foreign interference. Assyria was still nearly one hundred years from its time of imperial greatness, and the nearby Aramean states of northern Palestine were too newly liberated from Solomon's control to constitute a threat. Jeroboam could concentrate therefore on establishing his kingdom, partly by maintaining a running fight with Judah (1 Kings 14:30; 15:7; cf. 2 Chron 13:2–20), but chiefly by establishing religious and royal distinctness from Judah and the house of David. The Bible recounts this in three steps: the sin of Jeroboam (1 Kings 12:25–33); Jeroboam's rejection of the word of Yahweh concerning his sin, even though that word was confirmed by the death of the prophet (13:1–34, esp. vv.33, 34); and Jeroboam's forfeiture of the divine favor, announced by the same Ahijah whose prophecy had hastened Jeroboam to his throne (14:1–20).

The sin of Jeroboam was many-sided. Formally, it was the sin of religious schism, the setting up of an alternative worship system to that authorized by Yahweh. Basically, it was the sin of religious corruption: most probably the calves of gold were not intended as representations of Yahweh but as pedestals over which he was thought to be invisibly enthroned. Nonetheless, Yahweh was thus wedded to a symbol inseparable from Baalism and the gross sexuality of sympathetic magic. Personally, the sin of Jeroboam was pride and willfulness. So he made his own priests, fixed his own feasts, and officiated at his own altar. Most seriously, Jeroboam set out to use Yahweh as a mere prop for his own political ends. Thus, he became the measure by which the errors of the later kings were assessed.

2. *The prophetic revolt.* We must by-pass the troubled but insignificant time of Nadab (910–909, 1 Kings 15:25ff.); his assassin, Baasha (909–886, 1 Kings 15:33ff.); Elah (886–885); and his assassin, Zimri (885, 1 Kings 16:8ff.) till we come to the house of Omri (880–874, 1 Kings 16:21ff.). This was the first dynastic success in Israel, three kings of the same family following the founding father, but even so, the house lasted but a pitiful thirty-five years. It was during this period that Assyria began to stir into life and exert pressure on Syria, and Syria in turn began the career of militarism that was to augur ill for Israel.

The greatest king in the dynasty of Omri was Ahab (874–853, 1 Kings 16:29–22:40). It is wholly in keeping with biblical historiography that the sacred historian gives Ahab so much space, not because of his military or political powers, but because of the religious issues his reign produced and because of the towering figure of Elijah, who was raised up to oppose him.

The abruptness with which Elijah enters the royal presence (17:1), takes the welfare of the nation into his hands (17:1), gives orders to the king (18:19), and brings affairs to a climactic victory in the name of Yahweh (18:38, 40) well merits the title "prophetic revolt." Through his servant the Lord was saying no to Ahab and his Tyrian wife, Jezebel, and to their determination to replace Yahweh by Baal. This was no battle against syncretism. Decline in the north had gone far beyond the "Baalizing" trends of Jeroboam. Elijah captured the central issue crisply in his "either Yahweh or Baal" call to the people. Furthermore, the terms of the contest proposed and the language used by Elijah show that the fundamental issue was one of monotheism; Who is God? In this Elijah sets the tone for the whole subsequent prophetic movement, a Yahwistic, monotheistic movement brooking no interference with the Deuteronomic principle of one God, one people, one loyalty (cf. Deut 6:4ff.).[22]

3. *The light that failed: Jehu's house (841–752).* The word of Yahweh is always followed by his deed. Elijah returned home from Horeb (1 Kings 19:15–18) as a man who has heard the word and who was commissioned to guarantee its perpetuation in the ministry of Elisha, but also as one who was to provide for the chastisement of those who reject the word by his commissioning of Jehu and Hazael. These two men scourged the people of God. Each came into power by assassination (2 Kings 8:15; 9:24) and each acted with notorious cruelty (8:12; 9:33; 10:1ff., 25ff.). Hazael was imbued with Syrian nationalism; Jehu, with a mistaken form of zeal for Yahweh. Hazael contributed to the momentary glory of Syria; Jehu, to the gradual dissolution of Israel. Jehu delighted in the truth (9:22–26; 10:15, 16) but his life was deep in error and his influence became a disaster. Jehu glorified the concept of a kingdom saved by military action, so committing his son to a policy that could only fail before the rising power of Hazael (13:1–7) and that left no room for the exercise of visionary and imaginative faith (13:14–19).

Yet the Lord never deserts his people (13:22ff.). The death of Hazael in 801 B.C. brought his son Ben-hadad to the throne and was the signal for renewed Assyrian ventures against Syria. Jehoash enjoyed three victories over Syria, thus preparing the way for the last flowering of prosperity in the north, the reign of Jeroboam II (782–753, 2 Kings 14:23–29).

Scripture tells us only that this able king restored the northern kingdom virtually to Solomonic boundaries (14:25), yet continued in the disastrous course set by his namesake.

In the days of Jeroboam Israel heard the powerful voice of Amos, in whose book we learn the inside story of the last great king of Israel. It was in measure a time of extraordinary prosperity (cf. Amos 6:4–6) but of very uneven distribution of wealth. Commerce was booming (8:5), but so were the law courts, where processes of law were subverted to personal aggrandizement. Morality was turned upside down (5:7–15), and there could be no other alternatives than either repentance (4:6–5:8) or the full force of the curses of the covenant.

The voice of Amos, though apparently effective, (7:10), failed to alter either the national policies or the national character. The contrasting ministry of Hosea likewise could not save the kingdom from destruction. The assassination of Jeroboam's son Zechariah (2 Kings 15:8ff.) opened the floodgates of disaster.

4. *The tide goes out (753–722).* In the last twenty-four years of the northern kingdom, five kings reigned. Only one was succeeded by his son, two were murdered, and the last perished at the hands of the Assyrians.

---

[22]See Leah Bronner, *The Stories of Elijah and Elisha as Polemics Against Baal Worship* (Leiden, 1968).

In 745 B.C. the determined and able Tiglath-Pileser III mounted the throne of Assyria. He turned his gaze westward to include Palestine in his empire. Syria under Rezin (c.740–732) and Israel under Pekah (740–732) formed a defensive coalition; but when they attempted to coerce Ahaz of Judah to join them, he undercut their position by summoning the Assyrian to his aid. Damascus fell in 732, and its people suffered deportation. Hoshea of Israel incurred the wrath of the next king of Assyria, Shalmaneser V (727–722), by heeding Egyp. blandishments and refusing tribute to Assyria (2 Kings 17:4). After a three-year siege, Samaria fell in 722 B.C. to Sargon II, and the story of the northern kingdom ended in deportation. The voices of Amos and Hosea might well speak of a hope yet to dawn (e.g., Amos 9:9–15; Hos 3:1ff.; 14:4ff.), but the bitterness of their experience must have exercised a more compelling lesson: that human willfulness, pride, and self-devised religion can never bring salvation.

D. The Felled Oak

1. *A tale of two monarchies.* Bible historiography is always purposeful; it insists that the recital of facts must serve some proclamation of truth. Thus, we must ask what purpose is served by the interwoven histories of the monarchies of Israel and Judah. From its beginning, the Ephraimite monarchy was the product of human willfulness. Many of its kings were truly great men; full of political, military and commercial skills, they were richly gifted as strong, natural leaders. But they achieved only an unrelieved disaster. The northern monarchy, therefore, proves the inadequacy of man to solve his own problems. In the end, the most perceptive voices in the north could only look beyond the catastrophe to the advent of the Lord's own David, the fully adequate leader (Hos 3:5; Amos 9:11).

In the southern monarchy however, all the kings were of David's line, reigning in the chosen place and within covenant norms. But still they failed! Following out the pattern of Deuteronomic history, covenant kings, disloyal to the covenant, inherited covenant curses, and again the perceptive, prophetic voices called for the true David (e.g., Isa 9:7; 11:1; 55:3; Jer 23:5)

The whole of the OT is "torah" or "law" and the purpose of law is to lead to Christ. So the sacred historian swings his spotlight on men of ability operating without grace, or rebelling within the sphere of grace that we may learn to long for the true David, the King whom the Lord, in his zeal, will enthrone and uphold.

2. *The world around Judah.* No external pressure can be blamed for the failure of the Davidic monarchy, only the inadequacy of the kings themselves. Following the Shishak invasion of 917 B.C (1 Kings 14:25), Judah was unmolested by any major power for nearly two hundred years. Asa (911–870) experienced a Cushite (2 Chron 14:9) and an Ephraimite (1 Kings 15:17) invasion; there were Edomite and Philistine wars for Jehoram to fight (848–841, 2 Kings 8:20; 2 Chron 21:16); Joash fought with Syria (835–796, 2 Kings 17:17; 2 Chron 24:23) and Amaziah (769–767) fought with Edom successfully (2 Kings 14:7; 2 Chron 25:5) and with Israel unsuccessfully (2 Kings 14:8; 2 Chron 25:14). Uzziah subdued the Philistines and Arabians (2 Chron 26:7). Only the war with Syria and the gratuitous challenge to Israel caused severe national disruption.

But in 745 B.C. Assyria awoke and initiated events that culminated in the fall of Jerusalem. The Mesopotamian power aimed at the conquest of Palestine. Syria, under immediate Assyrian threat, reversed its traditional role as an inveterate foe of Israel, and the two formed a defensive alliance. In Jotham's reign (740–732) they began to exert pressure on Judah to join them (cf. 2 Kings 15:37), intensifying the demand during the reign of Ahaz (732–715). Even though Jerusalem itself did not fall, Ahaz suffered calamitous losses (2 Kings 16:5, 6; 2 Chron 28:5–8), and must have been forced to take seriously the Syro-Ephraimite threat to end the dynasty of David (Isa 7:6). Under this pressure, Ahaz rejected the way of faith (Isa 7:4–9, 10–17) for political astuteness. He formed with Assyria an alliance that was really a capitulation. The Gentile domination of Jerusalem had begun.

Assyria rid Judah of the Syro-Ephraimite threat. Damascus fell in 732 B.C. Samaria followed suit in 722, but Judah became a vassal state. Disaffection under Assyrian rule was constantly fomented by Egypt, never herself strong enough to challenge Assyrian supremacy. Hezekiah was tempted by specious promises of an Egyp. alliance (Isa 28–32) and joined an anti-Assyrian rebellion. In 711 B.C. heavy reprisals fell on the Philistine states. Hezekiah might have escaped with a fine had he been able to resist further temptations to rebel. As it was, Judah was invaded by Sennacherib in 701 B.C., only to be delivered by an eleventh-hour act of God (2 Kings 19).

Assyria, however, had troubles of her own. The threat from the powerful Merodach-Baladan of Babylon (cf. 2 Kings 20:12) created a balance of power in the east. At the time of Hezekiah's sickness (c.711?) the possibility of a Babylonian captivity (2 Kings 20:17) was certainly a live issue.[23] But Assyria triumphed and Babylon was overthrown with the usual Assyrian savagery—the last throw of a dying cause. The Assyrian empire was over and Nineveh fell to a revived Babylon in 612 B.C.

Egypt's policy now changed. Clearly if she could help to create an Assyrian-Babylonian impasse in the east, she herself might recover her own long-lost Palestinian empire in the west. Pharaoh Necho consequently began annual incursions in the Assyrian cause, and in 609 B.C. in somewhat mysterious circumstances (2 Kings 23:29, 30; 2 Chron 35:20–24) the good Josiah interfered and lost his life. Although Egypt thus became the technical overlord of Judah (2 Kings 23:33–35), dominion really rested with Babylon, a situation confirmed after the Battle of Carchemish in 605 B.C. (2 Kings 24:7). Again, however, the restless kings of Judah chafed under their subject role. Jehoiakim (609–597) rebelled (2 Kings 24:1) and was defeated (2 Chron 36:6), but died before he could accompany his people into captivity. His wretched son, Jehoiachin, went to Babylon with the first captivity of the elite (2 Kings 24:12–16) and endured thirty-seven years' imprisonment (2 Kings 25:27). Zedekiah, his successor, was like putty in the hands of the politicians. But they characteristically blundered: they manipulated a weak king into revolt, but failed to see that such a king can never lead his people to victory! Jerusalem fell for the second time in 587, and a more sweeping captivity left the land to enjoy its mournful sabbaths.

3. *The inadequacy of reform.* From Rehoboam (930 B.C.) to Zedekiah (597 B.C.) twenty rulers sat on David's throne. Apart from the usurpation of Athaliah (2 Kings 11), the Davidic line was unbroken. Monarchy within the covenant was given time and opportunity to prove itself. It was also visited with four gracious reformations.

a. *Royal reform: Rehoboam to Athaliah (930–840).* Rehoboam (930–913 B.C.) consolidated his diminished kingdom militarily and administratively (2 Chron 11:5ff., 23) and aided by religious refugees from the north (2 Chron 11:13ff.) continued in the best

---

23Cf. S. Erlandsson, *The Burden of Babylon* (Lund, 1970).

ways of David and Solomon. Security, however, beguiled him (2 Chron 12:1) to desert Yahweh. It needed the invasion of Shishak (2 Chron 12:2ff.) to recall him to repentance. His successor Abijah/Abijam (913–911) was the first king to be compared adversely with David (1 Kings 15:3). But the next king, Asa (911–870) was a man of genuine godliness who reversed the religious decline of the day, banishing the so-called "holy men," practitioners of Baalistic sexual rites, and purging even the royal family (1 Kings 15:12ff.). He earned the accolade of one who "commanded Judah to seek the Lord" (2 Chron 14:4). Yet there were two defects: The reform itself was incomplete (1 Kings 15:14) and Asa himself did not pursue faith and godliness (2 Chron 16:2ff., 10–12).

Jehoshaphat (870–848) continued the royal reforms, holding two teaching missions throughout Judah (2 Chron 17:7ff.; 19:4). But here also personal weakness marred his record; as was manifest by his alliance with Ahab of Israel (2 Chron 19:2). He paid dearly, for his son married Ahab's daughter, the notorious Athaliah, and the period of the royal reformers fizzled out into a kingdom dominated by Baal and ruled by a foreign woman. Jehoram (848–841) walked in the ways of the kings of Israel and only God's faithfulness to the Davidic ancestry preserved Jerusalem from destruction (2 Kings 8:18, 19). Ahaziah (841) soon perished through involvement in Israelite politics (2 Kings 9:27), and Athaliah seized power (2 Kings 11, 841–835).

b. *Priestly reform: Joash to Uzziah (835–740).* When Athaliah butchered the royal family, the dynasty of David was preserved, humanly speaking, by the bravery of Jehoiada the priest and his wife (2 Kings 11:2). Six years later the priest incited rebellion, Athaliah was murdered, and young Joash reigned as the covenant monarch (2 Kings 11:17). A typical priestly reform, centered on the house of the Lord, followed (2 Kings 12:4ff.), but it lasted only for Jehoiada's lifetime (2 Chron 24:17ff.) and had sadly left the ruling classes untouched. Their defection merited a punitive and damaging Syrian onslaught (2 Chron 24:22, 23ff.) and the bright hopes of Joash, the renewer of the covenant, ended with assassination (2 Kings 12:20).

The good but impetuous Amaziah followed (796–767, 2 Kings 14:1–16), but he marred his record by worshiping captured gods (2 Chron 25:14). His son, Uzziah, in a long reign (767–740) brought his kingdom prosperity and security (2 Chron 26), but he wrote the epitaph of the priestly reformation by usurping the priestly prerogative (2 Kings 15:5; 2 Chron 26:16ff.) and spending his remaining years as a leper, unclean and excluded, in consequence. Once more, the unfitness of the monarch undid the hope of the reformer.

c. *Prophetic reform: Jotham to Manasseh (740–642).* Coterminous with the uprising of the Assyrian threat, the Lord in mercy gave to his people the majestic comfort of the prophet Isaiah. Jotham ordered his ways before God and was made strong (2 Chron 27:6), but the threat was mounting from the north (2 Kings 15:37) as he bequeathed the kingdom to his weak and religiously corrupt son, Ahaz (732–715). While Isaiah's call for faith went unheeded by Ahaz (Isa 7:1–17), and history grew darker, hope grew brighter, for the remarkable prophet saw the coming David more clearly and gloriously (cf. Isa 8:21–9:7). Unlike his father, Hezekiah (715–687) listened to the prophet, and we can safely assume that Hezekiah's reforming zeal had an Isaianic stimulus. This is poignant, for the heart of Isaiah's message was a call for faith (cf. 7:9), and the heart of Hezekiah's failure was to desert the way of faith for the way of worldly security (2 Kings 20:12ff.). At the center of the reform for which Isaiah called was the specific failure in the monarch himself. Having failed at the point of faith in the divine promises, he handed the kingdom to Manasseh (687–642)—a son who did not believe at all and who became the king whose sins made the doom of Judah certain (2 Kings 21; 24:3). The chronicler records that Manasseh endured his own taste of captivity and was brought to repentance (2 Chron 33:11–13), but he had nonetheless set in motion events that could not be averted. The prophetic voice had not stayed the decline of the kingdom of Judah.

d. *Law-book reform: Amon-Zedekiah (642–587)*. The brief and evil reign of Amon ended in the third and last assassination of David's dynasty. The great and good Josiah mounted the throne (639–609) and set out early on a reforming career (2 Kings 22:2; 2 Chron 34:3). The course his reformation took was determined by the discovery of the book of the Law in the temple. Details are obscure. Whether the book was Deuteronomy in whole or in part, or some other section of the Pentateuch, or the whole Pentateuch, and how it came to be lost, we simply do not know. But it was recognized as the Word of God, and caused the king to bring the people into a covenant with the Lord (2 Kings 23:3). There followed a widespread purge of Judah and the former territory of Israel and something of a national revival that apparently deteriorated into a revival of nationalism. How else are we to explain Josiah's uncharacteristic and gratuitous interference with Pharaoh-Necho? Moreover, this same insensate pride in nationality bred in Jehoiakim (609–597) and Zedekiah (597–587) the incredible stupidity of rebellion.

4. *Postscript*. This, then, is the tragic record of the house of David. We could not concern ourselves above with the puzzling problem of harmonizing the dates given for individual kings.[24] Primogeniture never carried an inevitable right of inheritance. David himself guaranteed Solomon's succession by having him crowned before his own death (1 Kings 1:32ff.). Very likely many of the Davidic kings adopted the same procedure.

The essential question raised by the sacred historian's account is not one of harmonization but rather this: Where is David to be found? Covenant blessings can be fully secured only by the perfect covenant king. Five hundred years of Davidic history failed to produce him. History is the handmaid of expectation, exposing the need and creating the longing for the one who is yet to come. The oak of David's house, though felled, is the stock from which he will yet spring (Isa 6:13).

IV. The Long Night of Hope

A. *The Period of the Captivity*

Deportation was an Assyrian technique first applied, according to C.F. Pfeiffer, by Tiglath-Pileser III, the architect of the Assyrian revival of 745 B.C. It fell in full severity on the Northern Kingdom; not only were its inhabitants transported to Mesopotamia (2 Kings 17:6) but Ashurbanapal (the "Osnappar" of Ezra 4:10) completed the process in 669 B.C. by settling foreigners in Israel's lands (2 Kings 17:24). Northern Israel thus disappeared, never to be reconstituted as a kingdom. This, of course, is very different from the theory of the "ten lost tribes." Paul spoke of "our twelve tribes" (Acts 26:7) as an existing reality. The OT constantly assumes that, whereas the nation went into captivity in its two sundered parts, it would return as one. While, then, we know nothing

---

[24] Cf. E.R. Thiele, *The Chronology of the Hebrew Kings* (Grand Rapids: Zondervan, 1977).

of the condition of the northern exiles in their captivity, we are right in assuming that when Judah went captive to Babylon, the same conditions would prevail for all and that in an alien environment the ancient tribal affiliations would prevail over more recent divisions.

1. *The remainder in Judah.* The depopulated Judah was organized as a Babylonian province, with Mizpah as the provincial capital. The Babylonian authorities evidently looked favorably on this tiny community until a surviving member of the royal family, the otherwise unknown Ishmael, assassinated Gedaliah the governor. Nevertheless, Jeremiah advised the scared remnant to continue in the province. Terror prevailed, however, and a pitiful exodus-in-reverse brought them, with the unwilling Jeremiah, back to Egypt (2 Kings 25:23-26; Jer 40-43). Some Judahites remained in the land of their fathers, but in the following years Edomites apparently pressed in from the south and foreign settlers from the north, to be a thorn in the side of the remaining community.

2. *The exiles in Babylonia.* There is no biblical evidence that Babylon followed any policy of deliberate severity against the exiles. According to Jeremiah's letter (Jer 29), they were at liberty to settle down in the land, to build, marry, and found families. Ezekiel (8:1, et al.) reveals a community organized under its own elders. It was seemingly prosperous enough to contribute handsomely to the material needs of those who chose to make the homeward march (Ezra 1:4). The Bible also encourages us to see the hand of God in this. Just as the patriarchs descending to Egypt found that God had gone before them in the person of Joseph (cf. Gen 50:20; Ps 105:17ff.), so the exiles found they had a "friend at court" named Daniel (Dan 1:19-21) who continued in authority as long as they needed him.

Their hands would also have been strengthened by the ministry of Jeremiah and Ezekiel, who not only spoke of a sure hope to be fulfilled, but also enabled men of faith to endure the protracted years of chastisement. Jeremiah's emphasis on individual religion prepared the people for a situation in which the great communal aspects of religion were impossible and in which each person had to walk with God. Ezekiel's teaching that in the exile the Lord would himself be the sanctuary of his people (11:16; cf. John 4:21, 23) obviously continued this emphasis. More particularly, however, Ezekiel's theology of a transcendent God, a God as powerful and as present in Babylon as in Judah, undergirded faith and held hope high, as the exiles waited for the appointed hour of their return.

B. Return Without Revival

The return was as unexpected as it had been long awaited. It came through one reputedly even more powerful than their conqueror. It is typical of the God who is sovereign over all human rulers that such a one should send his people home.

1. *Cyrus.* Nebuchadnezzar died in 562 B.C. and was succeeded by Amel-Marduk (the "Evil-merodach" of 2 Kings 25:27). Babylonian power was already on the wane. Both Amel-Marduk and his successor died by assassination, and one of the assassins, Nabonidus, ascended the throne, reigning 556-539. From 553 B.C. he shared his throne with his son, Belshazzar. Indeed, at times Belshazzar was sole ruler of Babylon, as the book of Daniel states.

Vacuums are not left unfilled, and as Babylon declined, Cyrus of Anshan was rising to establish the Persian Empire in its place. He acceded in 559 B.C., by 549 was undisputed ruler of Medo-Persia, and in 546 overthrew Croesus of Lydian and added Asia Minor to his empire. In 538 the great city of Babylon fell without a blow struck. Overnight (cf. Dan 5:30) the Persian Empire in its definitive form was born.

The "Cyrus Cylinder" (now widely accepted as authentic, as is the parallel "dikrona" or official memorandum in Ezra 6:1–5) records his policy—namely, returning captive people and gods to their localities. The conqueror was truly concerned about the welfare of the people of God. That the "Cyrus Cylinder" attributes the success and policy of Cyrus to Marduk and the book of Ezra applauds Yahweh need not surprise or alarm us. Neither need reflect the religious conviction of Cyrus; many a soldier turned politician has discovered that he has exchanged the sword in the hand for the tongue in the cheek. Certainly the OT insists that Cyrus had, in the predictions of Isaiah, a clear indication regarding which of the many gods was the living and true God. But Isaiah 45:4 shows that he did not trouble to pursue the matter. Diplomacy dictated that he would speak to each as each would want to hear, and so to Babylon he spoke of Marduk and to Israel of Yahweh.

Cyrus's policy was one of clemency and conciliation. The people of God thankfully, though in smaller numbers than one might have expected, entered into its benefits.

2. *Opposition and encouragement.* The fortunes of the first group of returned exiles are recorded in Ezra 1–6. (In this passage, 4:7–23 belongs to a later stage in the history and is obviously filed here because of identity of subject.) Haggai and Zechariah also speak of this first group of exiles.

The people returned under the leadership of Sheshbazzar (Ezra 1:11), but effective leadership seemingly passed at once to Zerubbabel, the civil governor, and Joshua, the high priest, one of the most notable partnerships in biblical history. Their first communal act (Ezra 3:2, 3) was to set forward the restoration of the temple by building the altar of the Lord. Then (Ezra 3:8–13) the foundations of the temple were laid. But the enthusiasm of the people was eroded by bitter opposition and trailed off into dispirited inactivity.

The immediate cause was the approach of the existing population of imported settlers, who professed Yahwistic faith and desired to participate in temple-building. Abrupt rejection of their advances (Ezra 4:3) turned their hearts to enmity. We should not think the Jerusalem leaders wrong in the intention of their reply or that they were deliberately rejecting the supposed "universalism" of hope expressed in Isaiah. Isaiah's hope could never be fulfilled by sinking the identity of Israel into the world; it was rather the hope that the world would come to be identified with Israel. A church indistinguishable from the world has no ground for evangelism. The question of purity and separation thus forced on Zerubbabel remained a critical problem throughout the recorded postexilic history. But it was vital for God's purposes that it should have been answered in the terms if not in the manner of Ezra 4:3.

Nevertheless, enmity had been created, influence against the returned community was exercised in high places (Ezra 4:4, 5). For sixteen years the work on the temple flagged and then ceased altogether.

But not only on the temple site was progress slow and hope at a low ebb. Haggai, in 520 B.C., reveals a community turned in on itself, barely making ends meet and feeling that nothing could be less opportune than a call to rebuild the temple. Haggai, however, knew that, though the economy was inflated (1:6), affluence and comfort were considerable (1:4). Politically, Haggai's ministry may have come at a time when the central authority of the new king Darius the Great (522–486) was occupied with revolts in the east, so that building activity in the west would pass unheeded or be allowed as a conciliatory move. In any event, under the encouragement of Haggai and Zechariah the second temple was completed in the four years between 520 and 516.

C. The People of the Book

At this point recorded biblical history lapses for almost a century until the work of Ezra (Ezra 7–10) and Nehemiah.

1. *The historical problem.* One of the thorniest problems of historical interpretation in the Scriptures has centered on Ezra and Nehemiah. Its complexity forbids extensive discussion.[25] Traditionally, it has been accepted that the order of the books in the Bible is chronological, that Ezra came to Jerusalem in 458 B.C. in the reign of Artaxerxes I (Ahasuerus, 465–424) and that Nehemiah followed twelve years later (Ezra 7:7; Neh 1:1). Among others, H.H. Rowley[26] considers that the facts will be satisfied only if Ezra is dated in the seventh year of Artaxerxes II, i.e., 398 B.C., long after the end of Nehemiah's work. What is involved is a straightforward issue of interpretation aimed at understanding what the facts in the two books assert. They offer a general chronological framework within which the stories of these two very great men can be set satisfactorily.

Ezra came to Jerusalem in 458 B.C., charged with a spiritual and civil task: to bring certain offerings to the temple (7:14ff.) and to appoint magistrates who would administer the affairs of the province according to God's law (vv.25ff.). It came to light that, contrary to the law, both religious and civil authorities had indulged in marriages outside the bounds of the people of God. Ezra led the people in repentance over this and brought them into a covenant with God to preserve their separated status (Ezra 9:1ff.; 9:6ff.; 10:3ff.).

Coming to Nehemiah, who dates himself in 445 B.C., we find him concerned for Jerusalem because its wall was broken down. The implication is of a recent calamity. Ezra 9:9 could be a forward reference to the building of such a wall—i.e., that when he came to Jerusalem, Ezra began to feel that he ought to look to the security of the city. The letter to Artaxerxes in Ezra 4:7 arose from renewed building operations at that date and may have ended (4:23) in the tearing down of what had been accomplished. If Ezra had thus gone beyond his commission, it would account for the period of eclipse in which we hear nothing further of him till the great reading of Scripture in the time of Nehemiah (8:1).

Nehemiah's work was in two parts: he sought and gained permission to rebuild the city and, despite relentless opposition, completed the task (Neh 1–6). Second, he took it upon himself (suitably seeking the help of Ezra) to people his city with a qualified and holy citizenry (Neh 7–12), stressing their birthright (7:5) and focusing consecration on the three cardinal points of marital separation (10:28–30), sabbath-keeping (10:31), and the maintenance of God's house and its ministers (10:32ff.). Nehemiah concludes by recording that he returned to the king after twelve years in Jerusalem and that on his coming back to Jerusalem "after certain days" (13:6), he found all these matters of consecration had been forgotten (13:11, 15, 23) and needed to be restored.

---

[25]Those who want to acquaint themselves with the details may consult special studies, especially the definitive work by J.S. Wright, *The Date of Ezra's Coming to Jerusalem* (London: Tyndale, 1947).
[26]"The Chronological Order of Ezra and Nehemiah" in *The Servant of the Lord and other Essays* (London, 1952), pp. 131ff.

2. *Tensions: revelation and response.* If we follow the work of Ezra and Nehemiah into the prophecy of Malachi, we find that the same issues are being fought over (e.g., 2:10ff.; 3:8ff.). The people of God are waiting for the fulfillment of all the good their God has promised and finding the night long and the life of holiness and separateness a demanding discipline in which they often fail. This is the situation to which Ezra and Nehemiah, considered to be books within the OT Torah, are addressed. The central emphasis of both books is the insistence that the people of God are the people of the book. Ezra was sent precisely because he had the law of God in his hand and had made it his purpose to teach this law in Israel (Ezra 7:6, 10, 11, 12, 14, 21, 25). The first public act in Nehemiah's city is that the people gather to hear the great reading of Scripture (8:1). Thenceforward the book is the center of all that is done. The night of waiting has yet many hours to run but the will and wish of God is one—that till his day dawn his people will read, love, and obey what he was written for their learning.

Thus, the OT gives us our last glimpse of its saints before the coming of the Lord. Can we have any greater aspiration for ourselves as we await his coming again?

V. Bibliography

Ackroyd, P.R. *Exile and Restoration.* London: SCM, 1968.

Albright, W.F. History, *Archaeology and Christian Humanism.* New York: McGraw-Hill, 1959.

Bright, J. *History of Israel.* London: SCM, 1960.

_____. *The Kingdom of God.* New York: Abingdon, 1953.

_____. *Early Israel in Recent History Writing.* London: SCM, 1956.

Foster, R.S. *The Restoration of Israel.* London: Darton, Longman and Todd, 1970.

Goldingay, J. "A Study in the Relationship Between Theology and Historical Truth in the Old Testament." In *Tyndale Bulletin,* vol. 23, 1972.

Guthrie, H. *God and History in the Old Testament.* Greenwich: Seabury, 1961.

Harrison, R.K. *Old Testament Times.* London: Inter-Varsity, 1970.

Kitchen, K. "Old Testament Chronology" (with T.C. Mitchell) and "Moses." In *The New Bible Dictionary.* Edited by J.D. Douglas. Grand Rapids: Eerdmans, 1962.

McKay, J. *Religion in Judah Under the Assyrians.* London: SCM, 1973.

Merrill, E.H. *An Historical Survey of the Old Testament.* Nutley: Craig, 1969.

Motyer, J.A. *The Revelation of the Divine Name.* London: Tyndale, 1959.

Noth, M. "History and Word of God in the Old Testament." In *Laws in the Pentateuch and Other Essays,* p. 79; " 'David' and 'Israel' in II Samuel VII," idem., p. 250; "The Jerusalem Catastrophe of 587 B.C. and Its Significance for Israel," idem., pp. 260ff.

_____. *The History of Israel.* London: Black, 1959.

Pfeiffer, C.F. *Old Testament History.* Grand Rapids: Baker, 1973.

Robertson, E. "The Disruption of Israel's Monarchy—Before and After." In *Bulletin of the John Rylands Library,* vol. 20, no. 1, 1936; "Old Testament Stories, their Purpose and their Art," *BJRL* vol. 28, no. 2, 1944; "Samuel and Saul," *BJRL,* vol. 28, no. 1, 1944.

Robinson, D. *Josiah's Reformation and the Book of the Law.* London: Tyndale, 1951.

Rowley, H.H. "Nehemiah's Mission and Its Background." In *Men of God.* London: Nelson, 1963.

Von Rad, G. "The Deuteronomic Theology of History in I & II Kings." In *The Problem of the Hexateuch and Other Essays.* London: Oliver & Boyd, 1966, pp. 205ff.

Weippert, M. *The Settlement of the Israelite Tribes in Palestine.* London: SCM, 1971.

Wenham, J.W. "Large Numbers in the Old Testament." In *Tyndale Bulletin,* vol. 23, London: Tyndale, 1967, pp. 19ff.

Wright, J.S. *The Date of Ezra's Coming to Jerusalem.* London: Tyndale, 1947.

THE THEOLOGY OF THE OLD TESTAMENT

Walter C. Kaiser, Jr.

Walter C. Kaiser, Jr.

A.B., Wheaton College; B.D., Wheaton College Graduate School; M.A., Ph.D., Brandeis University

Professor and Chairman of the Department of Semitic Languages and Old Testament, Trinity Evangelical Divinity School

THE THEOLOGY OF THE OLD TESTAMENT

I. Introduction

   A. The History of Old Testament Theology
   B. The Definition of Old Testament Theology

II. The Content of Old Testament Theology

   A. Prolegomena to the Promise: Prepatriarchal Period
   B. Provisions in the Promise: Patriarchal Period
   C. The People of the Promise: Mosaic Period
   D. The Place of the Promise: Premonarchical Period
   E. The King of the Promise: Monarchical Period
   F. Life in the Promise: Wisdom Period
   G. The Prophets and the Promise: Divided Kingdom Period

III. Bibliography

I. Introduction

Somewhere between 1960 and 1970 the "Golden Age"[1] of OT biblical theology, which had opened in 1933 with the publication of Walther Eichrodt's first volume of his monumental work,[2] ended with the collapse of at least the existential variety of that discipline known as "the biblical theology movement." To use Brevard S. Childs's apt description, "the cracking of the walls"[3] of this new movement came with Langdon B. Gilkey's now-famous 1961 article[4] and James Barr's inaugural address in 1962.[5]

Nevertheless, in spite of the recognized bankruptcy of the biblical theology movement, the need for the discipline of biblical theology has increased rather than decreased. The criticisms leveled in recent days against the biblical theology movement

---

[1]The term comes from Robert C. Dentan, *Preface to Old Testament Theology*, rev. ed. (New York: Seabury, 1963), pp. 72ff., although he dates the turning point to 1949 with the appearance of Otto J. Baab's work.

[2]Walther Eichrodt, *Theology of the Old Testament*, 1933, trans. J. Baker (Philadelphia: Westminster, 1961).

[3]Brevard S. Childs, *Biblical Theology in Crisis* (Philadelphia: Westminster, 1970), ch. 4 pp. 61ff.

[4]Langdon B. Gilkey, "Cosmology, Ontology, and the Travail of Biblical Language," *Journal of Religion* 41 (1961): 194–205. (Also published in *Concordia Theological Monthly*, 33 (1962): 143–54).

[5]James Barr, "Revelation Through History in the Old Testament and Modern Thought," *Interpretation* 17 (1963): 193–205. (Also published in *Princeton Seminary Bulletin*, 56 [1963]), and James Barr, *Old and New in Interpretation* (London, SCM, 1966).

were the same as the criticisms against neoorthodoxy; viz., its failure to define the nature of history[6] and its equivocal use of biblical words.[7]

In its usage in this article, OT biblical theology is that twin discipline to exegetical theology that searches for the rudiments of the plan of God in its earliest divine disclosure to men and then collects and organizes the subsequent additions and responses strictly in accordance with the historical process of God's self-revelation set forth in the OT.

A. *The History of Old Testament Theology*

Both the word *theology* as a designation for teaching about the Christian faith and its epithet *biblical* are of comparatively recent origins; the former appeared for the first time in the twelfth century (*Dictionaire de theologié catholique* xv, Paris: 1946, "Theologie") and the latter in the sixteenth century as a pietistic protest against the current scholastic forms of theology.

But in the eighteenth century, "biblical theology" became a programmatic term announcing a new and independent method of approaching the Bible in theological research. This new development was attributed to Johann Philipp Gabler, who, in his inaugural address at the University of Altdorff in March 30 1787, announced that "Biblical Theology is historical in character."[8]

Unfortunately, Gabler was also heavily influenced by his rationalism and critical approach. Consequently, this young discipline was marked for the next half century with the imprint of rationalism.

The first half of the nineteenth century carried the philosophy-of-religion influence of a Hegel and a Schleiermacher into biblical theology. This movement was sporadically interrupted in the middle of that century by such conservative scholars as E.W. Hengstenberg (*Christology of the O.T.*) G.L. Oehler, H.A.C. Hävernick, J.L.S. Lutz, Heinrich Ewald, with assistance from the conservative biblical exegetes J.C.K. Hofmann, M. Baumgarten, Franz Delitzsch, and C.F. Keil.

With the death of these giants and the advent of Julius Wellhausen's *Prolegomena zur Geschichte Israels* in 1878, OT theology became a history-of-religion discipline as source criticism and *Religionsgeschichte* dominated the field of OT studies.

After World War I the discipline began to emerge from the domination of the current philosophical fads only to be captured by existentialism and neoorthodoxy. The renaissance of the discipline can be fixed at 1933 with the publication of Walther Eichrodt's first volume of his *Theology of the Old Testament.* To be sure, it had been preceded by E. König's (1922) and J. Hänel's (1931) monographs and two important journal articles by C. Steuernagel (1925) and Otto Eissfeldt (1926), but it was Eichrodt who set the pace and captured the attention of scholars in 1933.

If Eichrodt began the "golden age" of OT biblical theology, then Gerhard von Rad's *Old Testament Theology* (2 vols. 1957, 1962; Eng. tr.: New York: Harper & Row, 1962, 1965) marked its climax and its reversion to a history-of-religion type of study. Between these two giants, who still tower above all others, came E. Sellin (1933), L. Köhler (1936),

---

[6]See Barr, "Revelation Through History." Already in 1951 Paul Minear had pointed to the same problem in "Between Two Worlds," *Interpretation*, 5 (1951): 35f.

[7]See Gilkey, "Ontology."

[8]"*Oratio de iusto discrimine theologiae biblicae et dogmaticae regundisque recte utriusque finibus*" in his *Opuseula Academica.* 2, Ulm: 1831, pp. 183ff.

M. Burrows (1946), Th. C. Vriezen (1949), O. Procksch (1950), G.E. Wright (1952), E. Jacob (1955), and G.A.F. Knight (1959). Among this galaxy of writers were the Roman Catholics Paul Heinisch (1940) and P. Imschoot (1954, 1956) and the evangelicals E.J. Young (1958) and J. Barton Payne (1962).

Now in this post–von Rad era, with its tendency to self-analysis, the following volumes have been added: Hans-Joachin Kraus, *Die Biblische Theologie: Ihre Geschichte und Problematik* (1970); Brevard S. Childs, *Biblical Theology in Crisis* (1970); R.B. Laurin, ed., *Contemporary O.T. Theologians* (1970); Chester K. Lehman, *Biblical Theology: O.T.*, 1 (1971); Walter Zimmerli, *Grundriss der alttestamentlichen Theologie* (1972); Georg Fohrer, *Theologische Grundstrukturen des Alten Testaments* (1972); W.J. Harrington, *The Path of Biblical Theology* (1973) and John L. McKenzie, *A Theology of the Old Testament* (1974).

History has underscored the need for a solution to unresolved issues of the definition, method, and focus of OT theology. The resolution of these tensions, which have dogged the steps of biblical theologians from its inception, would do more than anything else to free the discipline from periodic enslavement to reigning fads and its imminent capture by a new historicism.

B. *The Definition of Old Testament Theology*

1. *The nature of OT theology.* Eichrodt began this "golden age" by rightfully bemoaning the fact that under the pressure of historicism, the OT had been reduced to a collection of detached periods with little or no unity left to the OT text (1:30–31). After a quarter century, von Rad has come almost full circle and adopted the very position that had originally prompted Eichrodt's rebuke. Accordingly, von Rad rejected Eichrodt's "structural type" of theology with the observation that he had failed to carry the "covenant" theme into the whole canon. Furthermore, Eichrodt's organizing categories were derived mainly from systematic theology. Instead, von Rad emphasized a "diachronic type" of OT theology that treated the variegated, conflicting, and separate theologies of each successive historical period in the canon with the unity and center placed outside the books themselves in a movement he trusted would lead to Jesus Christ.

But the debate did not revolve merely around the issues of a systematic versus a chronological treatment of the topics of theology or an internal theological center or unity versus an external center found in a movement. It also involved the debate over the separation between "what the Bible meant" (descriptive theology, *Historie*) and "what the Bible means to us" (so-called normative theology, *Geschichte*).[9] That in turn raised other issues: What remains of historical value in the OT text? What relationship does biblical theology have to systematic theology, exegetical theology, the history of religion, or homiletics? Each of these questions insists that the nature and task of the discipline of biblical theology be defined before we turn to its practice.

As a contribution to that definition, we submit that all future biblical theology must take a "diachronic" form—i.e., it must choose primarily a longitudinal approach that pays attention to the chronological sequence of the books and their messages rather than an arrangement dictated by a series of theological, philosophical, or even lexicographical themes, topics, or words. Biblical theology has had from its inception the basic mission

---

[9]For a fuller description and defense of this distinction, see Krister Stendahl, "Biblical Theology," *IDB* 1 (1962): 418–32.

of showing the historical progressiveness of revelation in the Bible. In contradistinction to the other theological disciplines, it is charged with the task of recognizing that revelation basically came in historical events, even though it was more often than not preceded by a declarative word or a pronouncement and followed by interpretation.

This assemblage of data has more than a problem-solving value; it is needed not so much by systematic theology as by every valid exegesis or exposition of any selected part of Scripture. The interpreter and listener must know what backlog of events, teachings, and terms originally "informed" or went into the initial hearing and thus into all valid subsequent listening to that part of Scripture. Only the historic progress of revelation can provide that knowledge. Hence the independent mission of the discipline of biblical theology can be firmly fixed.

But to work out a diachronic framework is not the sole task of OT theology. It must also identify and discuss the organic nature of this historic process. The question of a center, an internal unity, and a normativeness to the OT did not suddenly occur to the wise men of the last three centuries! It had long since occurred to the original participants in the historic process of revelation. Therefore their witness or record of all interconnections and ways in which the activity and its corresponding message were passed from one key figure, generation, country, and crisis to another is essential to establishing the focus of our study. From an inductively derived center the direction of the progress of OT theology should come.

Such progress need not exclude organic relationships, for the record of the OT words and events will itself often point to such relationships in its movement from one event to another. Many will quarrel with the factuality and originality of these textual connections by insisting that the assured results of source criticism have deleted most of them or exposed their artificiality.[10] Others will try to overcome this prejudice by taking the literature as it comes, as they believe, from the hands of its most recent editors.[11] But ultimately, the text will have to be dealt with on its own terms, and not on the basis of some new impositions.[12]

Neither must belief in progress in revelation exclude the possibility of recognizing a full maturation of one or more points of the divine revelation along the route of growth and development. Revelation, like history, does not proceed at a uniform rate or according to any prescriptive set of maturation dates from its recipients. Rather, it is epochal in its timing and often seemingly erratic in its comparative development of all component parts. Once in a while a truth of revelation appears in its final form at once, but more frequently its development is a long process.

2. *The method of OT theology.* Rather than using the abstract categories of Western philosophy, biblical theology should draw its very principles of systematization from the biblical text itself. In this respect, it is radically different from systematic theology. This, however, must not be interpreted as a vote for an objective, nonnormative approach to the Scriptures. A splitting of the Bible into descriptive versus normative theology ulti-

---

[10]Gerhard Maier, *Das Ende der historisch-kritischen Methode* (Verlag Rolf Brockhaus, 1974). See an English review article by Eugene F. Klug, "The End of the Historical-Critical Method," *Springfielder* 38: 289–302.

[11]We cannot treat these objections in any detail here, but see the critique by Pieter A. Verhoef. "Some Thoughts on the Present-Day Situation in Biblical Theology," *WTJ* 33 (1970): 1–19. On the last option, see James Barr, *The Bible in the Modern World* (London: SCM, 1973), p. 64, n.8.

[12]James Orr dealt with this problem already in his Lake Forest University lectures: "The Progressiveness of Revelation," in *The Problem of the Old Testament* (London: Nisbet, 1909), pp. 433–78.

mately ends up either in devising a new canon within the canon of Scripture or in dividing history arbitrarily into "true" history and "kerygmatic" history and limiting the scholar and theologian to the former, while giving the preacher and believer free reign in the latter.

Can such a procedure be a credible methodology? As Roland de Vaux argued,[13] even the so-called "kerygmatic interpretations of history" must at once "be true" and "originate from God" himself; otherwise Israel's faith and ours are misplaced, since the very foundation of our faith—the truthfulness of God—has been destroyed. The God who is the Lord of all history is the Lord of its interpretation!

But where does Scripture state its principle of organization? Was the principle consciously formulated and carefully carried out over the long haul of history? Did it have a single center or plan? Or were there competing lines of thought in the successive eras? What is the alleged biblical answer to this methodological problem, and is it a uniform and consistent witness?

It is our contention that, amid all the multiplicity and variety of materials, events, and issues, there is an eye in this storm of activity. Such a "focal point" is textually supplied as a given and textually confirmed in that it is the central hope of the canon, its ever-present concern, and its measure of what was theologically significant or normative!

Such was what the NT eventually referred to as the "promise" (epangelia)[14], but what the OT knew under a constellation of words[15] and a network of interlocking and developing features that were organically united.

The focus of the record fell on the content of God's covenant, which remained epigenetically constant (i.e., there was, as time went on, a growth of materials around a fixed core that contributed life to all that was to follow). This content was a divine "blessing," a "given word," a "declaration," a "pledge" or "oath" that God himself would freely do or be something to a certain person or to certain persons there and then and in the future, so that he might thereby do or be something for all men, nations, and for nature generally.

While the revelatory event or declaration was often an immediate "blessing" from God to men, most frequently it was a promissory "word" or "pledge" that God would work in some future great moment or moments of redemptive history so as to give meaning to their present history and to future generations. It had unity in that it was God's everlasting plan. But in its composition, it contained such variegated elements as to promise (1) a proliferation of man and beast, (2) a special human offspring, (3) a land, (4) a gift to all the nations, (5) a national deliverance from bondage, (6) an enduring dynasty and kingdom, (7) a Messiah, (8) a forgiveness of sin, and (9) a renewed heavens and earth—all this with the appropriate human responses of the fear and praise of God.

No "abstract divining-rod" can be formulated that will yield such theological wealth; but textual claims and repeated emphases of Scripture can direct our attention to such a constellation of terms and interconnected contents of the promise. That promise was given to Eve, Shem, and Abraham. Through them it was directed to the whole human race as the history of Israel became the temporal unfolding of the promise. It led

---

[13]Roland de Vaux, "Is It Possible to Write a 'Theology of the Old Testament,'?" in *The Bible and the Ancient Near East,* trans. Damian McHugh (London: Darton, Longman, & Todd, 1971), pp. 56ff.

[14]Willis J. Beecher, *The Prophets and the Promise* (1905; reprint ed., Grand Rapids: Baker, 1963), pp. 175–94.

[15]Foster R. McCurley, Jr., "The Christian and the Old Testament Promise." *Lutheran Quarterly* 22 (1970): 402, n.2.

climactically to the two advents of Jesus Christ and it has never ceased in its process of fulfillment. Its boundaries are eternity itself!

3. *The scope of OT theology.* With the question of the unity of the OT and its correlation with the NT at stake, OT theology is properly limited to the canonical literature. All attempts to include extrabiblical works seriously weaken any purpose to do biblical theology as a whole within a stream of revelation in which the writers were consciously contributing under divine command to an existing record of divine revelation. Above all, there stands the judgment of Christ himself, for he decisively pointed to the Jewish collection of books and affirmed that these were the ones that spoke of him (Luke 24:27; John 5:39, 40). His judgment ought to settle the question for believers and at least caution other students of OT theology to restrict the scope of their studies to the canon. (Of course, a history-of-religion approach will need to enlarge its area of study to include all of the intertestamental literature.)

Likewise excluded are all historiographic, cultic, institutional, or archaeological discussions. The goal of a theology is not to deal laboriously with every piece of information bearing on religion or the history of religion. Rather, key words, central issues for the text, and large teaching blocks where the text itself begins the process of grouping its theological precepts must set the pace and govern selectivity.

This should not rule out the separation of OT theology from NT theology. While the connecting links must be discussed in both theologies so as to show the continuity of the message, the sheer enormity of the task and the usefulness of each theology as an exegetical aid make it better to write separate OT and NT theologies rather than a single biblical theology.

4. *The motivation for OT theology.* Ultimately OT theology seeks to identify the center or core of the canon and thereby aid the exegete, interpreter, preacher, and hearer of the individual pieces of text to perceive God's normative word. Thus the discipline, rather than having a primary reference to systematic theology, is a twin tool with exegesis.

There is a distinctive pattern, a family resemblance within the OT that can be detected no matter what part or historical period in the OT is explored. Furthermore, the OT writers explicitly or implicitly claim such a center of interest. In our judgment, "the quest for a centre was too easily given up."[16] Moreover, such a center, if demonstrated to be at the core of each OT writer's interest, will provide verification and justification for all theological or normative judgments made about individual texts. In biblical theology the documents of Scripture must themselves be allowed to pass on any and all alleged statements about dominant currents or "canonical theologies."

Also, biblical theology must demonstrate the progress of growth in these "centrally accredited" norms, if the interpreter is to be aided. This growth of teaching and normative response may be called the "analogy of [antecedent] Scripture" in contrast to the method used by systematic theology called the "analogy of faith." The former is strictly inductive and groups its materials according to historic periods as an aid to exegesis. Depending on where the exegete is working in the canon, he will use the theology of the periods that preceded his text as they introduce analogous or identical topics, key

---

[16]James Barr, "Trends and Prospects in Biblical Theology," *Journal of Theological Studies* 25 (1974): 271; R. Smend agrees; "Die Mitte des Attentestaments," *Theologische Studien* 101 (1970), 54; see also Walter C. Kaiser, Jr., "The Centre of Old Testament Theology: The Promise;" *Themelios*, 10 (1974): 1–10.

words, or theological interests. The "analogy of faith," however, is deductive and collects all materials bearing on any doctrine, topic, or issue, regardless of its relative dating, or often even in such an abusive method as that which disregards the material's own contextual setting—viz., the so-called "proof-texting" method. Only by separating these aims and methodologies will the discipline of biblical theology make a separate contribution to theological studies. Only then may its results become valuable for tracing OT-NT relationships. Only then will systematic theology have another valid contribution to make alongside historical theology, exegetical theology, and philosophic theology. Only then will the pulpit be rescued from the tedium of moralizing, spiritualizing, psychologizing, historicizing, and allegorizing a text. The way to get from the "then" of the "B.C." grammatical-historical interpretation to the "now" of the "A.D." needs of a congregation is to ask OT theology to locate in all the historically antecedent theology (an "analogy of Scripture") the explicit normative theology behind a given text and to point to the repetition or new contribution to that stream of revelation in this new context under exegetical examination.

II. The Content of Old Testament Theology

A. Prolegomena to the Promise: Prepatriarchal Period

1. *A blessing.* There are four distinctive moments in the progress of revelation in the prepatriarchal narratives of Genesis 1–11. Each receives its importance from the free but surprisingly gracious divine word to man.

The first, at creation, was a unique and unrepeatable event. There the original "promise" was given initially to the sea creatures and birds (Gen 1:22) as a gift or blessing:[17] "Be fruitful and multiply." Likewise, the Creator climaxed his work by investing man with an even greater blessing: "Be fruitful and multiply, and fill the earth and subdue it; and have dominion over [it] . . ." (Gen 1:28 RSV). Note that ASV, NEB, NAB and JB correctly join the blessing with its content, whereas AV, RSV, and NASB separate the blessing with a command to the creatures. However, the subsequent usage of the writer of Genesis supports the former and not the latter construction. This blessing continued to reverberate in early history—viz., in the prepatriarchal times of Noah (Gen 8:17; 9:1, 7); the patriarchal times of Abraham (Gen 17:2, 20–21), Jacob (Gen 28:3–4; 35:11), and Joseph (Gen 47:27; 48:3–4); and in the days of Moses (Exod 1:1–7).

From an absolute beginning of this world ("In the beginning God created. . ."),[18] Scripture makes a clear distinction between the finite creatures and the infinite God. The method of creation, insisted on by the repeated "And God said," drew attention to a gap and difference between the being of the Creator and that of the creature. It was creation by divine word—a word that not only preceded the existence of the finite things and beings and called them into being, but one that went on to appoint their specific purpose. In each case, God assessed his work with the approbation: "And it was good"—i.e., perfect in its form and function as it came from his hands.

A special endowment, however, made it possible for man to transcend his finiteness.

17Gerhard Wehemeier, "Deliverance and Blessing in the Old and New Testament," *Indian Journal of Theology,* 20 (1971): 30–42.

18Gerhard F. Hasel, "Recent Translations of Genesis 1:1: A Critical Look," *Bible Translator* 22 (1971): 154–67.

For he was also made in "the image of God." Thus man shared his creatureliness with all finite things and his vitality with all living things, but his image he shared with God.

2. *A Seed.* This continuous action of God in sustaining, multiplying, nourishing, prospering, and communing with his people was interrupted by three tragic events in the remaining chapters of this prepatriarchal narrative: the Fall (ch. 3), the Flood (chs. 6–8) and the building of the Tower of Babel (ch. 11). In spite of each failure, a new word of blessing and promise surmounted each new obstacle.

For man and woman, the transgressors, and for "the serpent," their tempter, God gave his word of curse and blessing in Genesis 3:14–19. Especially significant was the divinely implanted personal "hostility" (*'êbāh*) that began with the serpent pitted against the woman and continued between his "seed" and her "seed." But, surprisingly, we read of a male descendant who was to issue from the woman and deliver a mortal blow to the serpent's head while the serpent would merely strike this descendant's heel.

3. *A race.* Not until the second great failure of the human race (Gen 6:5) with its accompanying judgment of the Flood did this gracious blessing and word of promise in Genesis 3:15 receive amplification (cf. Gen 9:25–27). Here, in a seven-part pronouncement that is divisible into three parts corresponding to the verse numbers, we again meet a mixture of curses and blessing. The ancient word of blessing was renewed and fell this time on Shem, progenitor of the Semitic peoples (9:26). Now the identity of the male heir was narrowed to Semitic origins. Furthermore, if the unstated subject of verse 27b was, as expected, the same as that of 27a, then not only was the Lord God of Shem singled out, but so was Shem. God would now "tabernacle" in the tents of Shem! In a distinctive way, God could be expected to take up his residence and abide with Shem. (Thus, "his" in 27c also refers to God in that the people of Canaan, insofar as they were spared, became "hewers of wood and drawers of water" in perpetuity for God's people; cf. the Nethinim in the postexilic period.)

4. *A gospel.* The division and separation of the seventy families and nations of the earth (Gen 10) happened when man, the arrogant, set out to institute in the tower of Babel a permanent unity of his own devising (Gen 11). No doubt such a tower provided a pagan synthesis of state and religion as observed in the recovered Ziggurats of the Mesopotamian valley. Hence the resulting judgment of God and the dispersement of all nations. The dreaded division happened.

Yet once again, what men sought on their own terms was now made possible by a triple blessing of God—the Abrahamic promise of Genesis 12:1–3. In this new word, all the nations (cf. Gen 10) of the earth could be blessed. For what had been the promise of a conquering male descendant (Gen 3:15) residing in the tents of Shem (Gen 9:27) now became nothing less than a world-wide divine plan to extend this happy word and good news to every nation on earth.

B. *Provisions in the Promise: Patriarchal Period*

1. *An Heir.* The first three clauses of Genesis 12:2 contained promises made to Abraham alone. God would make him a great nation, bless him, and make him famous. But the significance of this special treatment eludes us until we notice the attached result or purpose clause: "So that you [or "it" = the nation] will be a blessing." God planned to make this man into a great nation with great blessing and a great name so that he and

the nation might become a divine means of benefiting all others. This blessing was to be conferred on the believing, for through the material instrumentality of this one man, all the nations of the earth would be "blessed."[19]

This single promise was repeated to Abraham, and enlarged initially in four chapters: Genesis 12:1–3; 13:14–16; 15; 17. God reaffirmed his ancient word about the "seed'" that was to be born to the woman and repeatedly assured Abraham and Sarah that they, in spite of their advanced age, were to be the instruments for this divine blessing. They would receive the promised progeny as a divine gift. In a very real sense, Abraham received Isaac, and he in turn received Jacob. Each birth was both an immediate "blessing" of that promise and an earnest of that one Heir par excellence who was to come. Here the one "seed" represented the many offspring and their historical appearance pointed to a partial historic fulfillment ("blessing") and a climactic fulfillment in the One who was to come ("promise"). Thus the historical series of fresh births of sons in this promised line was both the embodiment of a fulfillment in that immediate historical situation (by virtue of the office and promise each son represented) and a pointer to God's final Heir who would come in that same historic line. To Abraham he had often pledged such a son (Gen 12:7; 13:15–16; 15:4–5, 13, 18; 17:7–10, 16–17, 19; 21:1, 12; 22:17–18; and to Isaac and Jacob he had repeated the same pledge (26:4, 24; 27:28–29; 28:14 and 35:12).

2. *An inheritance.* The second feature of the promise was a material or temporal feature: the inheritance of the land of Canaan. While Albrecht Alt had argued that this feature was later added to the original promise, Martin Noth insisted that both land and seed were part of patriarchal religion (see *TDOT*, 1:401–405 for a summary). Genesis 15:18 clearly marked the boundaries: They extended from the "little" river of Egypt to the Euphrates. These statements, expressing the gift of the land, were identical to legal formulae for the conveyance of property in the Ancient Near East—even the claim to be valid in perpetuity (Gen 13:15; 17:7–8) was matched by similar donation formulae found in Susa, Alalah, Ugarit, Elephantine, Assyria, and Babylon.[20] Again, the record repeated this word numerous times (Gen 12:1, 7; 13:15, 17; 15:7–8, 18; 17:8; 24:7; 26:3–4; 28:13–15). God's promise, then, involved more than a mere spiritual or redemptive plan; it included a philosophy of history and also an accomplishing on earth what he intented to do in the hearts of men. Already there was a hint of a kingdom of God and the promise of dynasty, for God also declared to Abraham that kings would come from him (17:6, 16; 35:11). Even the promise to make Abraham's name great (12:2) became a royal word later repeated to David: "David will have a name like the great ones of the earth"—a stipulation that also carried political overtones in ancient Near-Eastern literature.

3. *A heritage.* But there was a third element added to the promise of an heir and an inheritance: the heritage of the gospel. Five times, always in the climactic position, the text pointedly asserts: that all the nations of the earth would be blessed in Abraham (Gen 12:3; 18:18; 22:18; 26:4; 28:14). Thus a universal address was given to this new word of

---

[19]After five Hebrew imperfect cohortatives, a consecutive perfect is reserved for the surprise ending. On the grammatical necessity of translating this phrase as a passive, see O.T. Allis, "The Blessing of Abraham," *Princeton Theological Review,* 25 (1927): 263–98.

[20]M. Weinfeld, "The Covenant of Grant in the Old Testament and in the Ancient Near East," *Journal of American Oriental Society,* 90 (1970): 199.

blessing. This built a "counterhistory" to the world-wide curse already noticed in Genesis 3–11. Both promise and blessing were joined (especially in 12:1–3) even though the actual fulfillments were realized both in their own day and later.[21]

At all three levels the promise continued to receive ever-widening horizons. It moved from a son to many descendants; from a land given to patriarchs to a country given to a nation (cf. Gen 15:13–21), to a future "rest" made possible by God; from personal blessing to blessing conveyed to every terrestrial nation. Hence the promise was not limited to one generation, for God constantly renewed and enlarged his blessing and promise combination in new acts and words. Yet it did not thereby possess double or multiple meanings. The very fact that it was given in collective terms, though as one single plan, clearly argued against successive generations attaching different or divergent interpretations to it. The lineal "fulfillments" had to be generically connected links and divinely appointed means joining the prediction with its one grand climactic object.

Behind this joining of God's gracious word of blessing with his promise was the norm of divine self-revelation. Whether it was by vision and dream (15:1; 28:10–15), the angel of the Lord (22:11, 15), appearances of this messenger or of God (12:7; 17:1; 18:1; 26:2, 24; 35:1), or spoken communication (12:1; 13:14; 22:1; 31:3, 11; 35:1), behind the promise with its focus on the future stood the divine communication.

C. *The People of the Promise: Mosaic Period*

1. *A divine presence.* Even more striking were the formulae that accompanied the promise. In Genesis 15:7, the formula was "I am Yahweh who brought you out of Ur of the Chaldeans." In Exodus 20:2, he announced himself as "I am Yahweh your God who brought you out of the land of Egypt. . ." (about 125 times in the OT). In Genesis 17:7, 8, God promised in the first part of what eventually became a tripartite formula "to be a God to you" (cf. 28:21b). During Mosaic times, the formula received its complete form. In Exodus 6:7, the second part was added: "I will be a God to you and to your descendants after you, you shall be my people (cf. "My son," "My firstborn," [Exod 4:22]; my "distinctive [or moveable] treasure," [Exod 19:5–6]). The final part came in Exodus 29:45–46: "I will dwell in the midst of you" (Lev 11:45; 22:33; 25:38; 26:12, 44, 45; Num 15:41, et al.).

This declaration was matched with the manifestation of God's active presence. Isaac and Jacob and Joseph were told fourteen times that God would be "with" them. Thus the promises were guaranteed (*TDOT*, 1:450–63). Such an assurance, of course, was also the connecting point between the patriarchal promise and its continuation in Mosaic times. That Yahweh was indeed with Abraham's descendants was emphasized in Exodus 1:7 with the use of seven terms that echoed the blessing of Genesis 1:28 and the promises of Genesis 15:5; 17:6. The Israelites had become so numerous that the Egyptians felt obligated to deal with the alleged threat they posed (Exod 1:7–11). Nevertheless, every strategem to control this rapid and divinely accelerated growth failed.

Furthermore, when Israel appealed for divine relief from their afflictions, God "remembered his covenant with Abraham, with Isaac, and with Jacob" (Exod 2:24), for he "heard their groaning," "saw," and "knew their condition."

Meanwhile, the promise concerning Canaan had not as yet been realized. Accord-

---

[21]Contrast and cf. Islwyn Blythin, "The Patriarchs and the Promise," *Scottish Journal of Theology*, 21 (1968): 56–73; P.V. Premsagar, "Theology of Promise in the Patriarchal Narratives," *Indian Journal of Theology*, 23 (1974): 112–22.

ingly, Yahweh pledged to bring the numerous progeny of Abraham, Isaac, and Jacob out of Egypt into Canaan as he had promised four to six hundred years previously (Exod 3:16–17; 32:11ff.; 33:1; Lev 26:42, 45). That promise of the land was singled out as the basis for God's new act of redemption in the Exodus—an act that would highlight a previously unrecognized aspect of his character as Yahweh (the *beth essentiae* of "by my name the LORD"), the God who would be powerfully present to fulfill his word (Exod 6:2–8). In addition, the conquest and expulsion of the enemies occupying Canaan (Exod 23:22ff.; 33:2; 34:11–12) was mentioned for the first time. This was also to be God's great act of judgment as well as salvation.

In the OT the fullest expression of the presence of God came in the theology of the "name," "face," "glory," and "angel" of the Lord. God's "name" was "in" the angel who went before Israel (Exod 23:21) and his "glory," i.e., the splendor of his actual presence, was seen in the pillar of fire and the cloud. The tabernacle and ark also became the visible symbols of the dwelling of Yahweh among his people (Exod 25:8, 45) and so the promise of God to be with his people, to be their God and to take them to be his people received its grandest provision when God began to dwell in the midst of Israel. The pillar of fire by night and the cloud by day reminded all that God's "face" (Exod 33:14; cf. Deut 4:37) was personally and powerfully present.

2. *A holy nation.* No longer were the descendants of the patriarchs regarded solely as a family. They took on a distinctive national identity, but one of an unusual sort. Collectively they were divinely designated as "my son," God's "firstborn" (Exod 4:11, cf. Jer 31:8). This idea of divine sonship of the whole nation was an extension of the idea of election. It also implied a familial relationship in which this group shared in the benefits purchased for them by their *go'ēl* ("kinsman redeemer") at the Exodus. Their status of "firstborn" meant they were selected for preeminence in rank and position (not necessarily in chronological order) in order that they might mediate the blessing of God to all the nations.

As such, they were to be a "kingdom of priests," a "holy nation" (Exod 19:6), and God's "treasured possession," *segûllāh* (Exod 19:5). They were set aside as God's movable possession among all the other nations to carry out the special purpose of election noted in Genesis 12:3.

Holiness, then, was not an optional feature. Since Yahweh had separated and called this people from all the other nations to be his own possession, they were to be holy, *qādôš*—i.e., to be uniquely set apart to God and separate from evil (Lev 20:26; 22:31b–33; 25:55). Not only were they his, but he was theirs; for he brought them out of Egypt "in order to become [their] God" (Num 15:40–41).

Holiness applied to two main areas: ethical or moral and ritual holiness.[22] Thus divine ownership implied personal obedience to the commandments of a holy God. The Decalogue, let it be carefully noted, was rooted in the atmosphere of grace and redemption. The formula no longer was "I am Yahweh who brought you out of Ur of the Chaldeans," but "I am the Lord your God who brought you up out of the land of Egypt" (Exod 20:2 et al.—125 times in OT).

The moral commands of the Decalogue were based on the moral character of an

---

[22]For a separation of aspects in God's one law, see Walter C. Kaiser, Jr., "The Weightier and Lighter Matters of the Law: Moses, Jesus and Paul," in *Current Issues in Biblical and Patristic Interpretation: Studies in Honor of Merrill C. Tenney* ... , ed. Gerald F. Hawthorne (Grand Rapids: Eerdmans, 1975), pp. 176–92.

unchangeably holy God. Consequently, those who by faith had put their personal trust in their Redeemer and had personally become part of the family of Yahweh were graciously aided in recognizing the sanctity of the internal and external worship of God, the name of God, and God's authority over time, family, life, marriage, property, truth, motives, and desires.

Similarly, ritual holiness, with its ceremonial notations on the tabernacle service, sacrifices, and laws about cleanness, focused on "fitness" for the worship of God. Cleanness was not cleanliness; it was moral preparedness to enter into God's praise or service. The measure of that preparation was again centered in the eternal character of a holy God. Hence in the totality of their life Israel was called to be a holy nation indeed.

3. *A royal priesthood.* Israel, this unique and treasured possession of God was destined to be a royal priesthood of believers ministering on behalf of themselves and the nations (Exod 19:6; cf. Isa 61:6). But so awesome and terrible was the magnificence of Yahweh's presence that the people immediately declined the privilege of being a nation of priests in preference to representation under Moses and Aaron (Exod 19:16ff.; 20:18ff.) and so they delayed this original purpose of God till NT times (1 Peter 2:9; Rev 1:6; 5:10). Moses, then, became the first Levite to represent the people.

The representative nature of the Levitical—Aaronic—priesthood was evident from the fact that each Levite was consecrated to God in lieu of the death of the firstborn son of each Israelite family (Num 3:12, 13) and from the fact that the high priest bore the names of all the tribes of Israel on his breastplate when he went into the sanctuary (Exod 28:29). Furthermore, the priesthood was to be a "perpetual statute" (Exod 28:29). (It was renewed to Phinehas in Num 25:13.) Observe, however, that this secured an eternal priesthood. Therefore it was not abrogated by the temporary transfer of the high priesthood from Phinehas's line to Ithamar's descendants. Once again, the promise remained, while the blessing depended on the individual's spiritual condition.

Through this representative priesthood, provision was made, in the same law that held high God's ethical norm, for failure to keep this law. The sacrifices of Leviticus 1–7 offered an opportunity for fellowship, but also for divine forgiveness. Since God would by no means clear the guilty (Num 14:18), the offender could only plead the mercy of God (Exod 34:6–9) and in true contrition, turn from his sin (Lev 16:29, 31—"afflict yourselves"), and look for God's forgiveness based on God's specified "substitute." The offender was promised not only forgiveness (Lev 1:4; 4:20, 26, 31, 35; 5:10, 16; 16:20–22), but also the removal of guilt and of the remembrance of the sin as depicted in the sending away of the second goat on the Day of Atonement (Lev 16:21ff.).

The efficacy of the guilt and sin offerings included all types of sins with the single exception of spiteful and deliberate blasphemy against the Lord (Num 15:30, sin "with a high hand"). Moreover, the atonement was not a mere "covering" of sins till Christ should die, but a deliverance or ransoming on the basis of a divinely authorized substitute. The Hebrew word *koper* ("atonement"), when contextually determined rather than etymologically ventured, signifies the use of a substitute (cf. Exod 21:28ff.; 30:12; Num 35:31; 16:41–50, et al.) Therefore, the principle of Leviticus 17:11 meant that God provided this substitutionary way of dealing with sin to show humanity that they owed their lives as a forfeit for their sins against God. Hence the animal substitutes. Ultimately, animals would never effect a permanent reconciliation, so the need still remained for the perfect God-man to sacrifice his life. In the meantime, subjectively real efficacy was authoritatively provided, based on God's plan to eventually provide objective efficacy in the death of his Son.

D. *The Place of the Promise: Premonarchial Period*

1. *A theology of rest: Deuteronomy.* One of the great ideas dominating the theology of Deuteronomy is the inheritance of the land of Canaan. Sixty-nine times the writer repeated the pledge that Israel would one day possess and inherit this land. Sporadically he linked this pledge with the word that had been promised to Abraham, Isaac, and Jacob (Deut 1:8; 6:10, 18; 7:8; 34:4).

Canaan was to be Israel's "inheritance" because it was "the inheritance of the Lord" (Exod 15:17; Lev 25:23; and later Josh 22:19; 1 Sam 26:19; 2 Sam 21:3; 1 Kings 8:36). There God would grant them "rest." The central teaching passage is Deuteronomy 12, especially v.9: "You have not yet come to the rest and to the inheritance which the Lord your God gives you."

Rest was "the place" where Yahweh would "plant" his people. But it had more than a geographic, material, and spatial reference to Canaan; it had spiritual associations also. Rest was where the presence of God took up residence in the wilderness journeys (Num 10:33). It was a condition of soul and mind denied to a disobedient Israel (Deut 28:65), but it assured a blessing-bringing presence to his people (Exod 33:34).

2. *An earnest of the rest: Joshua.* If the connecting link between the preceding blessings and promise made to Israel and the generation of the conquest was the word about a future inheritance of Canaan (God's new rest), one must not hastily conclude that Joshua 21:44–45 recorded the complete fulfillment of that pledge (cf. Heb 4:8, 9). Indeed, Joshua had emphasized that "not one of all the good promises" had failed (Josh 23:14). Yet the later OT writers held that the offer to enter into this rest was still open; for example, the psalmist stressed "today" in Psalm 95:11.

How was it possible to have this "rest" under Joshua (1:13, 15; 11:23; 21:44; 22:4; 23:1) and yet not have it—because the Lord "swore in [his] anger that they should not enter [his] rest"? (Ps 95:11; cf. Heb 4:3).

The solution is identical to the case of the patriarchs who, though they lived in "the land of their sojourning" (Gen 17:8; 28:4; 36:7; 37:1; 47:1; Exod 6:4), did not yet have it as their "possession." That is how Stephen also evaluated the situation in his speech in Acts 7:4–5: "God sent him [Abraham] to this land.... He gave him no inheritance here, not even a foot of ground. But God promised him that he and his descendants after him would possess the land...." The reasons for this are many. For one thing, the task of driving out the Canaanites was never finished and the consequences of this failure are made painfully obvious in Judges. Furthermore, Joshua's boundaries did not correspond with those given the patriarchs, because his was only a partial settlement. Consequently the emphasis in Joshua 21:43–45 must rest on the promised word, which had not failed. But total "peace" and "tranquility" of body and soul would not come until the day of "the man of peace and rest" (1 Chron 22:9), when God would extend his hand a "second" time to recover Israel from the four corners of the earth (Isa 11:11). Then the Lord would again choose Jerusalem and dwell there personally (Ps 132:14). Meanwhile, even NT believers are urged to enter into this offer of rest that remains open to all who will come by faith (Heb 3:15–4:11).

3. *A failure to obtain rest: Judges.* The closing editorial remarks of Joshua 24:28–31 were reiterated in Judges 2:6–7—viz., the people went each to his inheritance and served the Lord all the days of Joshua. That state of affairs, however, ceased after Joshua's death. Still the grace of God would ultimately triumph and Yahweh would raise up "deliver-

ers" or "judges" (*šôpēṭîm*) to rescue them from their difficulties (2:16). But the real "Judge" was Yahweh (11:27). It was he who sent the oppressors and raised up the "deliverers." These leaders of the people were equipped for their tasks by a special work of Holy Spirit, who "came upon" them when they "judged Israel" (3:10; 11:29; 14:6, 19; 15:14; also 6:34; 13:25).

But the sad refrain of the Book of Judges is this: "There was no king in Israel in those days; every man did what was right in his own eyes" (17:6; 18:1; 19:1; 21:25). At one point the writer was so distressed over the conditions he was describing that he appealed to the listener and reader "to consider" them and "speak out" on the issues (19:30). Surely such could not be the conclusion to the promise of God!

E. The King of the Promise: Monarchical Period

1. *A promised king.* It had been part of the promise-tradition that kings would come from the promised line (Gen 17:6, 35:11; 36:31). The Mosaic comment on this promise had added that a king would be established and chosen by none other than God subsequent to Israel's settlement in Canaan (Deut 17:14–20).

The offers the people made to Gideon to "rule over" (*māšal*) Israel were presumptuous in that they preceded any notice of a divine choice. So Gideon justly rebuked them: "I will not rule over you, and my son will not rule over you; Yahweh will rule over you" (Judg 8:22).

Neither was Samuel's generation any wiser when they also prematurely demanded a king (1 Sam 8:4–6) on the grounds that Samuel was old and his sons were corrupt and on the apparent assumption that God was powerless to help them. This was a rejection of Yahweh's kingship over them (1 Sam 10:19). Yet once again God graciously gave Israel better than her sins deserved and chose Saul, a Benjamite, to be her first national king.

Saul accomplished the divinely appointed task of delivering Israel from the enemy's oppression (1 Sam 11:6), as did the previous judges, from Othniel to Samuel. Consequently he was at first a totally effective and Spirit-empowered leader. But when Saul departed from the Lord, the Spirit of God was removed from him and he became a total failure. The kingdom, which theoretically could have been his (1 Sam 13:13–14; 15:26–28), was then given to David, whom God called "a man after my own heart" (Acts 13:22).

2. *A kingdom.* At first, nothing extraordinary appeared in the anointing of David as king. The Spirit also came on him as he had come on Saul and the judges (1 Sam 16:13). But when God made a covenant with him (2 Sam 7; 1 Chron 17), it became obvious that a deliberate connection was being made with the promise God had made with Abraham and had renewed at the Exodus. There were references to an "offspring" (2 Sam 7:12), a "place" (7:10), a "rest" (7:1, 11), a "a great name" (7:9), an adopted "son" (7:14), and a formula that said, in effect, "I will be your God and you shall be my people" (7:23, 24). Even the odd Hebrew grammar in 2 Samuel 7:23—literally, "who are like your people, like Israel, one nation in the earth whom Yahweh have gone [*sic*] to redeem . . ." clearly shows that it is a deliberate quotation from Deuteronomy 4:7–8, which exhibited the same grammatical peculiarity.[23] Even the exceptional use of the name Adonai Yahweh (2 Sam 7:10, 19, 22, 28, 29) does not appear again in Samuel or Chronicles. This divine

---

[23]See a list of twenty-four so-called "deuteronomistic" similarities to 2 Samuel 7 in Frank M. Cross, *Canaanite Myth and Hebrew Epic* (Cambridge: University Press, 1973), pp. 252–54.

address had, however, been used by Abraham in Genesis 15:2, 8, when God spoke to him about the promise. Its presence here is too striking to be accidental.

To be sure, more than a renewal of God's ancient promise was intended. David's descendants will compose a perpetual dynasty ("house") (2 Sam 7:11, 19, 25, 26, 27, 29) of kings who will sit on the "throne" of an everlasting "kingdom" (7:12, 13, 16). Again, the promise was to abide "forever" (7:13, 16, 24, 25, 26, 29), but the enjoyment of these blessings was conditioned by the response of each Davidic descendant. The individual descendants could forfeit their personal share in the promise, but they could neither cancel nor block the transmission of the promise to their Davidic successors (1 Chron 28:7; Ps 89:30–33; 132:11–12).

The kingship of David was in partial fulfillment of the patriarchal and Mosaic promise of a king (Gen 17:6, 16; 35:11; Num 24:7; Deut 17:14ff.) and so was his adoption as God's son (Exod 4:22–23; Deut 1:31; 32:6; 2 Sam 7:14; Ps 89:26–27, and v.7 in the "Royal Psalm"[2]).

Suddenly David realized the scope of the promise and blessing and cried out in uncontrollable joy that God had not only blessed him and promised to extend his line forever, but that "this [new addition to the promise doctrine] is the charter for all mankind, O Lord God!" (2 Sam 7:19).[24] A number of the Psalms elaborate on this new growth of doctrine. This kingdom is to triumph over every other kingdom (Pss 2; 18). It is to extend from east to west (Ps 72) and hold sway over all of nature, men, and nations (Pss 47; 93–100). Its king would be a conquering king and a mediating priest (Ps 110).

No wonder Yahweh held the exclusive right of wholehearted allegiance to himself and to his law in the theology of the Book of Kings (1 Kings 2:1–4; 18:21ff.; 2 Kings 5:15; 18:5; 19:15). Yahweh's government, based on righteousness and morality, controlled the destiny of men and nations (1 Kings 11:9, 14, 23; 21:17ff.; 2 Kings 23:25ff.) and extended to Israel and the Gentiles alike (1 Kings 17:8–24; 2 Kings 5:1–9; 6:21–23). Thus obedience was owed him, and the consequences of rebellion were catastrophic.

F. Life in the Promise: The Wisdom Period

1. *The fear of the Lord.* As the link connecting the prepatriarchal "blessing" and the "law" was the patriarchal "promise" and that connecting the Mosaic "law" and David's "charter for humanity" was Joshua and Deuteronomy's "rest" doctrine, so the link that bridged the Davidic era and the Solomonic age of wisdom literature was the emphasis on a proper response to the sovereignty of God in one's total life. What some writers have referred to as the work of the so-called "deuteronomist" (views common to the books of Kings and Deuteronomy—viz., "Keep his statutes, commandments and judgments"; "to walk in the ways of Yahweh"; "to do that which is right in the eyes of Yahweh"; "with all your heart and with all your soul")[25] is actually the theological key that ties together the kingdom of God, the law of God, and the broad areas of life now laid out in the wisdom books.

Beginning with Abraham in Genesis 22:12 and building to a central concept in the wisdom literature of the Solomonic era, "The fear of the LORD" became the symbol of

---

24For a vindication of this translation, see W.C. Kaiser, Jr., "The Blessing of David: The Charter for Humanity," in *The Prophets and the Promise*, ed. John Skilton (Philadelphia: Presbyterian and Reformed, 1974), pp. 298–318.

25S.R. Driver isolated forty-eight such parallel phrases in his *Introduction to the Literature of the Old Testament*, pp. 200ff. See Kenneth Kitchen's long review article on John Gray's *1 Kings* commentary in *Theological Students Fellowship* 41 (1965): 10–22 for a scorching attack on this arbitrary labeling of the "deuteronomist."

a believer's wholehearted response to his Lord. This reverential attitude of life had been that of Joseph (Gen 42:18), Job (1:1, 8, 9; 2:3), and the Hebrew midwives (Exod 1:15–21). Thus it took on the meaning closely akin to that of total "commitment to" or "trust in" the God he loved. The expression continued to appear more frequently with this meaning (Exod 14:31; 20:20; Lev 19:14, 32; 25:17) and already became a focal point of interest in the Mosaic writing of Deuteronomy (4:10; 5:26; 6:2, 13, 24; 8:6; 10:12, 20; 13:4; 14:23; 17:19; 28:58; 31:12, 13).

Not only does the "fear of Yahweh" serve as the motto for Proverbs 1:7, but it dominates with thirteen additional texts (1:29; 2:5; 8:13; 9:10; 10:27; 14:26, 27; 15:16, 33; 16:6; 19:23; 22:4; 23:17) and four more verbal examples (3:7; 14:2; 24:21; 31:30). Similarly, the "fear of Yahweh" was the conclusion to the argument in Ecclesiastes (12:8ff.), which was already anticipated in Ecclesiastes 3:14; 5:7; and 8:12 and a focal point in Pss 19:9; 34:11; 111:10; 119:38. The theme is both pervasive and strategically located in the wisdom literature.

2. *The fear of the Lord and life.* Wisdom commended all who would respond in the "fear of the Lord" to what Mosaic *torah* ("law") had commanded. However, unlike the Apocryphal wisdom books such as Ben Sirach, where "to fear the Lord" meant "to keep the law" (Sirach 2:16; 19:20; 23:27; 24:23), canonical wisdom did not totally equate *ḥokmāh* ("wisdom") with *tôrāh* ("law"). Nevertheless, the law of Moses did have a large part in teaching man the "way" or "path" he should travel. This "way" (*derek*) of wisdom (Prov 4:11) seems to be the same as the older "way of Yahweh" (Gen 18:19) and the way frequently referred to in Deuteronomy. Such obedience and "fear of the LORD" was the "path [or way] of life" (Prov 2:19; 5:6; 10:17; 15:24).

With the introduction of the concept of "life," the scope of wisdom is enlarged to a veritable creation theology. Many of the "blessings" connected with the work and word of creation are reintroduced and enlarged under the rubric of "life." That is not to say that such life was purely materialistic; neither was it the promise of (eternal) life in the future.

Life, whether as seen in Leviticus 18:5 ("Do this and you shall live") or in its close association with the "fear of the LORD" in Proverbs 10:27; 14:27; 19:23; 24:4, was simultaneously the rejection of all pride, arrogance, perverted speech, and devious behavior (Prov 3:7; 8:13; 14:2; 16:6; 23:17) and adherence to the way commended and commanded by God. The "fountain of life" (Prov 13:14; 14:27 was to be found in righteousness, gentleness of speech, and wisdom; each of these was a "tree of life" (Prov 3:18; 11:30; 13:12; 15:4). In Deuteronomy it is said that man does not live on bread alone, but on every word that comes from the mouth of God (Deut 8:3). With such a life-and-death choice before them, Israel was urged to choose life (Deut 30:15, 19). It was wise to love the Lord, obeying his voice and cleaving to him, "for he [was their] life" (Deut 30:20). Life, then was the enjoyment of the fruits of a relationship derived from faith—a relationship that led to the happy result of really living in the temporal process. The "obedience of faith," to use Paul's apt phrase, opened up the wholeness and fullness of time in a measure originally intended in the creation "blessings".

3. *The fear of the Lord and the unity of knowledge.* Life could also make sense, if the quest to know began with the fear of the Lord. So argued the writer of Ecclesiastes in his stirring conclusion. To "fear God and keep his commandments—that is the whole duty [the totality, *kol hā 'ādām*] of man" (Eccl 12:13).

Now this is true simply because of one very important feature of creation theology:

man was made in the image of God. God "has made everything [*hakkol*] beautiful in its time," but "he has also set eternity [*hā'ôlām*] in the hearts of men; yet they cannot fathom what God has done from beginning to end" (Eccl 3:11). Man, therefore, while hungering, as a creature made in the image of God, to know how all the pieces of life and truth fitted together in their "wholeness," was continually unable to come to any satisfying synthesis till he discovered the "fear of God" and the joy of keeping his commandments.

The "vanity" or "futility" of life was simply that life in and of itself could not supply the key to its meaning. Only in the fear of God did one begin to apprehend the unification of truth, learning, and living (Eccl 7:14; 8:14). Consequently, instead of Ecclesiastes yielding a negative or naturalistic judgment on life, it affirms eating, drinking, marriage (cf. S. of Sol), and earning one's pay check as gifts of God that could be integrated into a total world-and life view if the proper key—the fear of God—was found.

4. *The fear of the Lord and wisdom.* The fear of the Lord is likewise explicitly associated with wisdom in five passages in Proverbs (1:7, 29; 2:5; 8:13; 15:33). Rather than interpreting the fear of the Lord as a "prophetic reinterpretation of wisdom . . . imposed by some ancient sage to give a more Yahwistic flavor to an otherwise universal creation theology,"[26] the connection follows the same pattern observed with the themes of the way, life, and unity of knowledge.[27]

The central teaching passage on wisdom is Proverbs 8. The key portion, 8:22–31, an expansion of 3:19, contends that "by wisdom the LORD laid the earth's foundations, by understanding he set the heavens in place." Thus wisdom was present at creation as one of the means by which Yahweh created the world.

But all of this does not amount to a hypostatization; it is a poetical personification of an attribute of Yahweh that clearly argues for the divine source of any and all wisdom. Wisdom is a reflection of the character of God. Therefore, in its fullest sense, it cannot be had by men apart from a personal relationship to the owner of wisdom. Just as God's attribute of "holiness" supplied the yardstick or norm for Mosaic theology, so God's attribute of "wisdom" provided the norm for the biblical wisdom literature when men received it in "the fear of Yahweh."

G. *The Prophets and the Promise: Divided Kingdom Period*

With the establishment of the Davidic kingdom and the Solomonic temple, the subject of the previous promises had reached a provisional plateau in its development. God's future monarch was typified by David's ruling house. Furthermore, the temple had pointed dramatically to God's presence in the midst of his people. One might now expect an optimistic prophetic program for the world-wide prosperity of the people of God.

On the contrary, however, the prophets were obliged first of all to rebuke Israel for her apostasy from God and to foretell the coming dissolution of the kingdom of God in its present form. Yet even with the grim prospect of the destruction of the divinely sanctioned monarchy, especially in the division of the kingdom into two rivaling nations,

---

26So William McKane, *Proverbs· A New Approach* (Philadelphia: Westminster, 1970), p. 348; idem. *Prophets and Wise Men* (London: SCM, 1965), pp. 48ff.

27For a special refutation of this line of argumentation, see W.C. Kaiser, Jr., "Wisdom Theology and the Center of Old Testament Theology" EQ (forthcoming issue), footnote 41.

there was always the bright fringe of the promise of eventual salvation on the judgment cloud hanging over Israel and Judah.

The focus of prophecy continued to be the ancient promise of God—especially the rule of Yahweh as King of Kings. The inception of this perfected rule was designated temporally as the "day of the Lord" and locally as the "coming of the Lord."

1. *The day of the promise: the earliest writing prophets.* Without pretending to claim finality, one may argue with a reasonable degree of assurance that Obadiah and Joel were the first of the writing prophets, appearing in the ninth century B.C. And a great theological theme that claimed much of their attention was the day of the Lord. In fact no other prophet treated this theme so extensively or systematically as did Joel.

In both prophets, a future day in the end time was signaled by a foreshadowing of that day in the devastation of the locust plague and drought described in Joel and in Edom's malicious joy over Jerusalem's humiliation by an invader as described by Obadiah. To be sure, that day was not all judgment; it was also a day of salvation. For wherever genuine repentance was the outcome of the tragic course of events, men could expect as dramatic a change as was evidenced in the transition noted in Joel 2:18. In every case, however, the concept of the day was single: the near and the far were generically and corporately locked into one idea in the eye of the prophet, so that the near events were token reminders of God's future awful day.

In that day, Yahweh is to gather all the Gentile nations to Israel (Joel 3:2, 12; Obad 15) for judgment, but he will also establish his righteous reign on the earth (Joel 3:17ff.; Obad 17–21). Then Israel will recognize him as the Lord their God, dwelling in the midst of them, and see themselves as his people (Joel 2:27; 3:17, 21). The prophetic vision of the future remains part and parcel of the ancient plan of God.

2. *The servant of the promise: the Isaianic prophets.* The eighth century was graciously gifted with the services of Amos, Hosea, Micah, Jonah, and the greatest of them all— Isaiah. While warning of the imminent danger of national tragedy (especially for Samaria, Damascus, and Nineveh) if there was no real repentance before God for accumulated rebellion and sin, they held high the doctrine of the promise.

They regarded the promise both as a standing prediction already being fulfilled, with a climactic fulfillment yet to come in the messianic era, and as a doctrine that laid ethical and spiritual obligations on their contemporaries. For them the promise embraced not only the announcement of the successive series of historical persons and events divinely used to reach that promised result but also the climactic fulfillment itself. It saw all this as a single totality, not fragmented in a multiplicity of meanings!

The most prominent feature of the promise during the prophetic era was Isaiah's teaching about "the Servant of the Lord." While Isaiah relates the "servant" to the earlier teaching about the "seed" (Isa 41:8; 43:5; 44:3; 45:19, 25; 48:19; 53:10; 54:3; 59:21; 61:9; 65:9, 23; 66:22) and to the "covenant" already given (42:6; 49:8; 54:10; 55:3; 56:4, 6; 59:21; 61:8), not to mention "Abraham" (41:8; 51:2; 63:16) or "Jacob" (41:21; 44:6; 49:26; 60:16) or "David" and the "everlasting covenant" (55:3; 61:8), the "servant" added a new dimension to the promise. For as with the "seed" of the earlier promises, the "servant" was a generic or collective term to be equated with every Israelite who had received the promise. Notice the plural form ("servants")—all coming after Isaiah 53, viz., 54:17; 56:6; 63:17; 65:8–9, 13 (*ter*), 14–15; 66:14—and the corporate "servant" in the singular collective form in Isaiah 41:8–9; 42:19; 43:9; 44:1–2, 21; 45:4; 48:20; and 49:3. All of them refer to this same group of promise-doctrine themes.

This "servant," however, is also an individual who was distinguished from national Israel in that he had a mission to Israel. (See Isa 42:1–7; 49:1–9; 50:4–10; 52:13–53:12. The same usage will appear later in Jer 33:21; Ezek 34:23, 24; 37:24, 25; Hag 2:23; and Zech 3:8.) This individual shared the same qualities as the King-Messiah (e.g., "I will put my Spirit on him," Isa 42:1; cf. Isa 11:2) and the same mission (e.g., "a light for the Gentiles," Isa 42:6; 49:6; cf. Isa 9:2). He was the Davidic King—the very One who had been promised to Eve and Abraham.

As "servant" he would suffer death for the sins of the people, but he would triumph and have such "success" that the kings of the earth would be silenced in his presence (Isa 52:13–15). He would live to see his "offspring" and to receive the victor's spoils (Isa 53:10–12). Then from the throne of David he would rule over his kingdom with justice and righteousness forevermore (Isa 9:7) as the Immanuel of all believing Gentiles and Jews. Then David's "fallen booth" would be totally rebuilt and restored as in the former days (Amos 9:11–15). "The house of the God of Jacob" would be exalted in the estimation of the nations with the cessation of all international and petty hostilities (Mic 4:1–5). By then Israel would have served many days without a king, prince, or sacrifice, but would finally turn to the Lord and to David their king (Hos 3:4–5) and be welcomed home again to their land as "sons of the living God" with the ancient blessing of a population explosion in their race as a fulfilled blessing (Hos 1:10–11).

3. *The renewal of the promise: the Jeremian prophets.* The seventh century posed a new set of national calamities—the permanent fall of Nineveh and Jerusalem. Once again there was an advance guard of divinely commissioned prophets—Habakkuk, Zephaniah, Nahum and Jeremiah.

At the heart of their teaching, and indeed of all of biblical theology, was the "new covenant" (Jer 31:31–34). Set in the context of "The Book of Comfort" (Jer 30–33), a restoration of Jacob out of his great time of trouble (30:7) was promised when Yahweh would gather Ephraim his "firstborn son" (31:9) and soothe weeping Rachel (31:15ff.).

This new covenant stressed inwardness ("I will put my law in their minds and write it on their hearts"), fellowship ("I will be their God, and they will be my people"—two parts of the ancient tripartite formula of the promise), personal relationship ("They will all know me, from the least of them to the greatest"), and forgiveness ("I will forgive their wickedness and will remember their sins no more").

These features, of course, had already been announced in the earlier development of the promise—i.e., inwardness ("These commandments I give you today are to be upon your hearts," Deut 6:6–7; "The law of his God is in his heart," Ps 37:31), fellowship ("I will be God to you and your descendants after you," Gen 17:7; "I will take you to me for a people, and I will be a God to you" Exod 6:7), personal relationship ("They shall know that I am the Lord their God ... that I dwell among them," Exod 29:45–46), and forgiveness ("The Lord, a God merciful and gracious, slow to anger, abounding in loyal love ... forgiving iniquity and transgressions and sin," Exod 34:6, 7; Num 14:18; Deut 5:9, 10; Neh 9:7; Ps 86:15; Jer 34:18; Joel 2:13; Jonah 4:1; "As far as the east is from the west, so far has he removed our transgressions from us," Ps 103:8–12).

What, then, was the point of the designation "new covenant"? Basically it meant a renewal of God's ancient promise. But when the other names for the new covenant are introduced—viz., "everlasting covenant" (Isa 24:5; 55:3; 61:8; Jer 32:40; 50:5; Ezek 16:60; 37:26), "covenant of peace" (Isa 54:10; Ezek 34:25; 37:26), "new heart" or "new spirit" (Jer 32:39 [LXX]; Ezek 11:19; 18:31; 36:26) or just "covenant" or "my covenant" (Isa 42:6; 49:8; 59:21; Hos 2:18–20), there are new items to be considered along with the continuing features. These new items are a universal knowledge of God (Jer 31:34), universal peace in nations and nature (Isa 2:4; Ezek 34:25; 37:26; Hos 2:18), universal material prosperity (Isa 61:8; Jer 32:41; Ezek 34:26–27; Hos 2:22), and the age of the Spirit and the sanctuary of God as the focus of the nations (Ezek 37:26, 28).

Rather than warranting a radical break with the unfolding promise, Jeremiah's teaching renewed the central core of God's ancient word and added the emphasis that a divine capability could be expected in the eschatological day of God's judgment and salvation (Jer 30:3; 31:27, 31, 38, "The days are coming").

Those days are described with all their judgment and deliverance in Zephaniah as they were by the earliest prophets. They will, however, finally conclude gloriously for the believing remnant, with the Lord their God in their midst (Zeph 3:17) and Israel restored to her land (Zeph 3:18–20). But amid all the destruction, "the just shall live by faith" (Hab 2:4) and rejoice in the Lord (Hab 3:18) who is Lord over all of history (Hab 2:20).

4. *The kingdom of promise: the exilic prophets.* The "seed of Satan" (Gen 3:15) will come to full fruition in its representative person called "one who causes desolation" (Dan 9:27; cf. 11:31; 12:11). While he too was preceded by a number of historical personages (antichrists; cf. 1 John 2:18) who served as historical embodiments in a series of contemporary downpayments on that final person who was to come (e.g., Antiochus IV, Epiphanes), this "little horn" of Daniel 7:8ff. is *the* Antichrist who will attempt to destroy God's reign and realm by attacking his people Israel in the final "day of the Lord."

Just as the last of the kingdoms of men emerges from the sea of the nations, the "Ancient of Days" will arrive from the clouds of the heavens (Dan 7:13–14) and rightfully and finally receive his everlasting dominion over all peoples, nations, and languages—a dominion indestructable and secure forever. He is that "rock cut out, but not by human hands" (Dan 2:34, 44–45) that will instantly destroy the successive kingdoms of men and in that coming day establish an unconquerable kingdom over all.

He is that "good shepherd," "God's servant David" (Ezek 34:11–31, esp. 23), who will establish his "covenant of peace" with Israel, nature, and the nations (Ezek 34:25–30). In that day, the "whole house of Israel" will be reformed nationally and will then be revived by the Spirit and life-giving power of God (Ezek 37:7–14). Then Israel will once again be united as one nation (Ezek 37:15–19) and will have one king, one God, and even one shepherd (Ezek 37:22–24), as they are reestablished in their land again forever in accordance with the ancient patriarchal and Mosaic promise (Ezek 20:5–6; 37:25. Notice the joining of the patriarchal promise and the Mosaic law as two aspects of the one oath or covenant of God; cf. Jer 11:3–5). God will be their God, they will be his people, and Yahweh will personally dwell among them (Ezek 37:26–28). Consequently, all the nations will know that this God, who made a promise to Israel and so blessed all of them too, is the only true God (Ezek 37:28).

5. *Triumph of the promise: the postexilic prophets.* Three postexilic prophets—Haggai, Zechariah, and Malachi—with the three contemporaneous historical books of Ezra-Nehemiah, Chronicles, and Esther, depict in glowing terms the establishment of the new Davidic and messianic king on his throne in the postexilic and eschatological era.

In accordance with the promise made at the time of the Exodus, Yahweh will be with this newly returned remnant of Jews as surely as he will complete his triumph in the future (Hag 2:5). In that coming day, he will shake the heavens, the earth, and nations with such a seismic and cosmic rattling that the nations will yield up the wealth of their countries and bring it to enhance the splendor of Yahweh's sanctuary in Jerusalem—a lineal descendant of that reduced second temple (Hag 2:7–9, 21–22). Then Yahweh will dwell personally among his people as he had promised in the Mosaic symbols of the tabernacle and the promise formula (Hag 1:8; Zech 1:16; 2:10–11; 8:3). At this second advent, the fullness of the divine presence will have arrived on earth. Indeed, then the "messenger of the covenant" will have arrived at his temple, even the God for whom some had in the past pretended to have been looking (Mal 2:17–3:1).

The "signet ring" (represented by Zerubbabel, Hag 2:23) and the "Branch" who will have suffered by then (Zech 3:8), will now be the final "priest on his throne" (Zech 6:12–13) in a long series of priests and kings—one person with the twofold office of priest and king. God's true Messiah will rule "from sea to sea and from the Euphrates to the ends of the earth" (Zech 9:10), as David and Solomon had been promised (cf. 12:8–9). With the overthrow of the nations (Hag 2:21–22), a cleansing fountain from sin will be opened (Zech 13:1) and the great epiphany and battle of the day of the Lord will commence (Zech 14). When the Lord returns with his "holy ones" (Zech 14:5), the nations will be defeated and the survivors will ascribe worship and praise to him (Zech 14:16–21).

What these three postexilic prophets predicted is likewise argued in Chronicles. Standing at the end of Israel's long historical journey up to nationhood and thence into destruction followed by the postexilic period, the chronicler selected the historical events and words from the Davidic and Solomonic kingdom that would foster the hope of the anticipated eschatological David with his awaited reign that was promised of old.[28] As "all Israel" (a favorite theme of the chronicler) had enthusiastically embraced the Davidic house of old, so will a restored Israel anticipate their new David, who will come in even greater splendor than that of Israel's former golden age.

The garment was all of one piece. From start to finish it was God's single plan to bless a chosen nation and reveal his pledge to them, so that through them all the nations and individuals on the face of the earth might be blessed. This was and is God's everlasting promise.

III. Bibliography

Barr, James. *Old and New in Interpretation*. London: SCM, 1966.

Beecher, Willis J. *The Prophets and the Promise*, 1905. Reprint. Grand Rapids: Baker, 1963.

Childs, Brevard S. *Biblical Theology in Crises*. Philadelphia: Westminster, 1961.

Dentan, Robert C. *Preface to Old Testament Theology*. Rev. ed. New York: Seabury Press, 1963. (Note especially pp. 127–44 for the most extensive bibliographies on biblical theology from before 1787 to about 1960.)

Eichrodt, Walther. *Theology of the Old Testament*, 1933. Translated by J. Baker. Philadelphia: Westminster, 1961.

Harrington, Wilfrid J. *The Path of Biblical Theology*. London: Gill and Macmillan, 1973. (Note his more recent bibliography on pp. 405–17.)

Hasel, Gerhard. *Old Testament Theology: Basic Issues in the Current Debate*. Grand Rapids: Eerdmans, 1972.

Laurin, Robert B., ed. *Contemporary Old Testament Theologians*. Valley Forge: Judson, 1970.

28Phil Roberts, "An Evaluation of the Chronicler's Theology of Eschatology Based on Synoptic Studies Between Samuel-Kings and Chronicles" (M.A. thesis at Trinity Evangelical Divinity School, 1974), pp. 24–37.

ARCHAEOLOGY AND THE OLD TESTAMENT

D.J. Wiseman

Donald J. Wiseman, O.B.E.

B.A., D.Litt., University of London; M.A., Oxford University; F.B.A. (Fellow of the British Academy)

Professor of Assyriology, University of London; Chairman, British School of Archaeology in Iraq

ARCHAEOLOGY AND THE OLD TESTAMENT

I. Introduction

    A. Limitations
    B. Dating Evidence
    C. Methods
    D. Classification of Archaeological Periods

II. Archaeology and the Old Testament Periods

    A. Prehistory
    B. Nomadic Incursions
    C. The Patriarchal Age
    D. The Late Bronze Age
    E. The Monarchy (Iron Age)

III. Bibliography

I. Introduction

Archaeology—"the study of antiquity"—today uses all modern scientific methods to recover the material remains and meaning of the past, of ancient man and his environment. The finds include all *realia*, not merely artifacts and objects, ornaments, tools, weapons, and vessels, but also stone, metal, clay, papyri, and parchment that may have been used in building and decoration or as writing material. Archaeology usually involves the recovery by excavation of ancient places and their contents, including written documents, and provides essential data for the study of ancient history of which it is the handmaid.

Applied to the OT, biblical archaeology is the selection of the evidence for those regions, places, and periods in which the peoples of OT times lived. Critical evaluation of the results of archaeological research in the ancient Near East has contributed much to our understanding of these peoples and their manner of life. The abundant documentary evidence discovered has provided the means for us to enter at least partially into their contemporary thought. Such studies must not be expected to elucidate all problems, especially those of a nonmaterial nature. Yet they have given us illustrations and explanations of many biblical narratives, have provided extrabiblical confirmation of many details of the biblical history and have acted as a corrective to numerous erroneous interpretations

A. *Limitations*

Archaeology is not an exact science. Therefore its results may undergo subjective selection and interpretation, though the methodology and excavation techniques are basically agreed upon among scholars of various nationalities. However, the factual evidence produced may be limited in that only a fraction of antiquity has survived or been recovered. In Palestine alone, of more than six thousand sites surveyed, fewer than two hundred have been excavated, and of these only twenty-eight to any major extent. Roughly the same proportion applies to Syria, Jordon, Iraq, and Iran but not to Egypt. Some sites are still occupied (e.g., Damascus, Jerusalem, Erbil) and can therefore be only partially examined. The precise location of some prominent OT places (e.g., OT Jericho and Ai) is still questioned. Only a fraction of the objects retrieved from some sites has been adequately published. In Palestine, the high water table may have caused its principal writing materials (papyrus and parchment) to perish. Yet, of the estimated half a million documents from OT times—mostly those on clay and sherds from outside Palestine—fewer than ten percent have as yet been published.

B. *Dating Evidence*

Only in recent decades have refined and accurate archaeological methods of stratification and typology related to local conditions and places of origin of wares enabled reliable comparisons to be made between sites and objects. The value of archaeological evidence is greatly enhanced when it can be correlated with a definite time scale. The most reliable evidence, therefore, is found in the historical periods when dateable or dated inscriptions are discovered. The most common basis of dating other finds is that of the types of pottery shapes and fabrication. For Palestine between the twelfth and sixth centuries B.C. this ceramic index is remarkably close-knit, though it may yet be proved that similar types may have been introduced by custom or as imports at varying stages. The detailed correlation of certain types of objects (e.g., lamps, seals, or weapons) or architectural features (such as houses, palaces, or gateways) with other evidence enables the history of the development of the object and its use to be read. The association of certain types of pottery or architecture with specific peoples or periods enables the archaeologist to trace transitions and crosscultural influences. Pollen analysis and Carbon 14 dating methods have proved of particular and increasing use for assessing prehistoric periods, though the latter method still raises problems of close definition.

Inscriptions or documents may be tentatively and relatively dated according to the stage of the development of the script employed, whether it is monumental or cursive. Internal references to a known historical event or person also aid in dating. Many Sumerian and Akkadian texts are dated by year formulae (c. 2400–1600 B.C.); in Assyria, by the name of an eponym (*limmu*) official (c. 1900–620 B.C.) or in Babylonia by the regnal year of a king (c. 600–312 B.C.). Thereafter dating was by eras (e.g., Seleucid).

C. *Methods*

1. *Exploration.* Interest in the Holy Land early led travelers to record the topography and to try to identify biblical sites mainly on the basis of their location and correspondence with surviving Arabic place-names. The publications of the Americans Edward Robinson and Eli Smith after 1838 and the Swiss Tobler in 1867 were followed by the more systematic surveys made on behalf of the Palestine Exploration Fund (founded in 1865) by C.R. Condor and H.H. (later Lord) Kitchener. In the period from 1872 to 1878

this British expedition drew a map to the scale of one inch to a mile of their survey of western Palestine. In 1884/85 G. Schumacher did similar work on behalf of the American Palestine Exploration Society in northern Transjordan. In 1865 the PEF sent Charles Warren to excavate Jerusalem.

Farther afield, the Frenchman P.E. Botta had started digging in the ruins of Nineveh in 1842, to be followed there and at Calah (Nimrud) by the young Englishman A.H. Layard. W.K. Loftus worked from 1851 in the Babylonian plain at Nippur, Warka (Erech), and Ur; the French, at Susa (1854); and the Germans, at Babylon (1897–) and Asshur (1903–). So began a century of work in Mesopotamia that gave much new information about the major opponent of Israel and was of value to OT research, especially through the many cuneiform texts discovered there.

2. *Excavation.* In Palestine, the surface explorers lacked the means of dating the masonry, pottery, and other objects they discovered until Flinders Petrie, "the father of Palestinian archaeology," and P.J. Bliss, his assistant, adapted the experience they had gained in Egypt to show how the various levels of remains made by successive occupants at Tell el-Hesi in southwest Palestine in 1890 were associated with characteristic pottery types, some of which compared with dated Egyptian finds. Bliss adopted this technique when he later worked with A.C. Dickie at Jerusalem (1894–97) and with R.A.S. Macalister at Gezer (1902–09). These initial attempts, with those of G.H. Reisner at Samaria (1908–10), led to a developed method of stratigraphy that has been subject to relatively little modification since it was placed on a firm basis by the pottery chronology worked out by H. Vincent by 1918. Before World War I, excavation had also begun at Ta'anach, Megiddo, and Jericho.

Between the wars, W.F. Albright worked at Tell Beit Mirsim, once thought to be the biblical Debir or Kirjath-Sephir (1926–32). The Americans at Megiddo (1929–38) planned to excavate the site completely, but because it covered thirteen acres, the task was impossible. Garstang's work at Jericho (1930–36) has in part to be reappraised following the continuation of work there by K. Kenyon (1952–58), who used more-developed techniques. Other noteworthy work was carried out at Tell el-Husn (Beth Shan), Sebastiyeh (Samaria), Tell Duweir (Lachish), Et-Tell (Ai?), Tell el-Fûl (Gibeah), Beitin (Bethel), Balatah (Shechem), Tell Seilun (Shiloh), Tell el-Kheleifeh (Ezion Geber), and Jerusalem. Work at many of these same sites resumed after World War II, with the important addition of Tell el-Far'ah (Tirzah), Tell Qasileh, Dibhan (Dibon), Tell Dotha (Dothan), Tell el-Qedar (Hazor), Tell el-Jîb (Gibeon), Tell Sheikh el-Areini (Gath), Qumrān, and Masada. A list of over two hundred Palestinian sites, with the dates they were excavated and primary publication references, is given in Eleanor K. Vogel, *Bibliography of Holy Land Sites* (Cincinnati: Hebrew Union College, 1972).

In Syria the excavations at Ras Shamra (Ugarit), Atshanah (Alalah), and Tell Hariri (Mari) have done much to increase our knowledge of OT times. The same applies to the continued work in the major cities of Mesopotamia at Nineveh, Nimrud (Calah of Gen 10:11–12), Asshur, Nuzi, Nippur, Warka, and Ur, among others, and at Ammān (Jordan) and Buseirah in Edom.

D. *Classification of Archaeological Periods*

The various levels or periods of occupation are commonly designated by archaeologists in the manner indicated in the following table, which also notes some of the alternative nomenclature sometimes used:

ARCHAEOLOGY AND OLD TESTAMENT TIMES

Approx. Date B.C.	Palestine/Syria/Jordan	Also called	Assyria/Babylonia	Egypt
I. Prehistoric				
–8000	Paleolithic	(Old) Stone Age		
8000–6000	Mesolithic	Middle Stone Age, Natufian, Tahunian/Jerichoan		
6000–4000	Neolithic	Prepottery N., Pottery N. (5000–)	'Ubaid	Prehistoric
4000–3200	Chalcolithic		Uruk	Tasian, Badarian, Naqada I–II
3200–3000	Esdraelon	Chassulian (end)	Proto-Literate	
II. Bronze Age				
3000–2800	Early Bronze (Age) I (= EB)	Early Canaanite (= EC)	Early Dynastic (= ED) I	Pre-Dynastic I
2800–2600	EB II		ED II	Archaic Period, Dyn. I–II
2600–2300	EB III		ED III	Old Kingdom, Dyn. III–IV
2300–2200	EB IV	EB IIIb, EB–MB	Sargonid	Dyn. V–VI
2200–1950	Intermediate Bronze (= IB)	MB I/MCI	Ur III	First Intermediate Period, Dyn. VII–XI
1950–1750	Middle Bronze (= MB) I	Middle Canaanite (= MC) IIa	Early Old Babylonian	Middle Kingdom (XII)
1750–1600	MB IIa	MB/MC IIb	Late Old Babylonian	Second Intermediate, Dyn. XIII–XVII
1600–1550	MB IIb	MB/MC IIc	Kassite	
1550–1400	Late Bronze (= LB) I	Late Canaanite (= LC) I	Middle Assyrian, Middle Babylonian	New Kingdom (XVIII–)
1400–1300	LB IIa	LC IIa		
1300–1200	LB IIc	LC IIc		Dyn. XIX

ARCHAEOLOGY AND OLD TESTAMENT TIMES

III. *Iron Age*

Date	Iron (Age) Ia (= I)	(Early) Israelite Early Iron (= EI) I		Egypt
1200–1150		(Early) Israelite Early Iron (= EI) I		Dyn. XX / Late Period / Dyn. XXI / Dyn. XXII (Libyan)
1150–1025	Ib			
1025–950	Ic	EI II	Neo-Assyrian	
950–900	Id			
900–800	IIa	Middle Iron Middle Israelite (= MI) I / Israelite II (970-840)		Dyn. XXIII–XXV
800–700	IIb	MI II / Israelite III (840-580)		Dyn. XXVI (Saite)
700–600	IIc			
600–330	III	Late Iron Late Israelite (= LI) / Israelite IV / Persian	Neo-Babylonian (Chaldean)	Dyn. XXVII–

IV. *Hellenistic Age*

Date				
330–165	Hellenistic I		Hellenistic	Hellenistic Egypt Dyn. XXVIII–XXX
165–63	Hellenistic II	Hellenistic- Herodian Maccabean		
63–A.D.70	Hellenistic-Roman			Roman

II. Archaeology and the OT periods

A. Prehistory

A sequence of Palaeolithic remains from the Carmel caves (Wadi al-Mughârah), 'Eron and 'Oren, with a gap in the Upper Palaeolithic-Mesolithic stages, gives evidence of food gathering and an early association with prehistoric Europe rather than with Africa. This is supported by the Middle Palaeolithic inhabitants' close relationship physically to the European Neanderthal race. A flint industry is associated with the Natufians when in Mesolithic times there is evidence for the beginning of settlement, agriculture, and domestication of animals. Neolithic sites are found in Yarmuk and Sha'ar Haggolan (Galilee) about the same time as those in the Nile, Cyprus (Khirokitia), and the Tigris Valley (Jarmo). At Jericho a prepottery people (c. 7500 B.C.) made massive defenses as well as remarkable plastered skulls and figurines, the purpose of which is as yet unknown.

In the Chalcolithic period, painted pottery, polychrome wall paintings, and simple copper axeheads are traced in the Jordan Valley, Telulat Ghassul, Esdraelon, northern Negeb, and near Gaza. Metal appears to have been in widespread use. Clay models show that curved vaulted roofs were being incorporated into houses and underground stores (Abu Matar), and rock cisterns for water supply are now found for the first time. The transition from the fourth millennium agricultural communities at Ghassul in the Jordan valley and at other Palestinian sites to the early Bronze Age is still ill-defined.

In 1974 to 1976 excavations at Tell Mardikh (ancient Ebla, south of Aleppo in northern Syria) uncovered about 15,000 clay tablets inscribed in the cuneiform script with an early N.W. Semitic dialect of c. 2300 B.C.—the time of the Babylonian king Naram-Sin (equated by some with Nimrod of Gen 10:9) who campaigned in the area. The texts include parts of the Epic of Gilgamesh, which includes the Babylonian account of the Flood, the epic of creation, the Babylonian "Job," literary, historical, administrative, and school texts of a type well known in later Syria (Ugarit). They thus attest an early literary tradition as already previously well known from Babylonia. New light is now thrown on the kingdom of Ebrum (cf. Eber of Gen 10:21) who had Duddiya as his vassal in Assyria (Ashur). The latter, as Tudia, is mentioned in the early genealogy heading the Assyrian King List as one of their ancestors "who lived in tents." He had been assumed to be a "fictitious" eponymous ancestor.

The texts mention Cyprus, Mesopotamia (Erbil), Palestine, and Canaan, as well as Hazor, Lachish, Gezer, Dor, Megiddo, and possibly Urusalem (Jerusalem) and Sinai. The naming of such individuals as Abarama and Isma'el, names that occur elsewhere in the ancient Near East, is not a direct reference to the later biblical characters of the name. At this time Syro-Palestine seems to have been the home of many nomadic groups. Further research on these texts will undoubtedly show much more of the history and culture of a period and place hitherto little known but adjacent to Amorite homelands. It should, moreover, counter the prevalent tendency of some scholars to belittle the reliability of the patriarchal narratives.

Early Bronze Age (EB I) settlements develop into towns at a number of sites. At first they were unwalled, as Megiddo (excavation level XIX), Beth Shan (XVII–XVI), Tell Shuneh (II–III), and Arad (IV), but later towns are walled, with gateways (Tell el-Far'ah, Gath), the mud-brick sometimes reinforced with stone. There is therefore a marked continuity from fully occupied open village to large walled town. The building of walls may be due to influence from Egypt and Sumer or to a growing intercity rivalry, though the latter is denied by some archaeologists.[1] At this time the pottery in the north (Beth Yerah II, Beth Shan XI) differs from the contemporary wares in the south at Jerusalem (Ophel), Gezer, Ai, Jericho (VI–VII), and Tell en-Nasbeh where a strong Egyptian influence can be traced (e.g., Jericho IV). The northern towns flourished and new pottery techniques (Khirbet Kerak) and architectural developments show a flourishing community. The developments include town walls and citadel and temple layout in which the holy of holies is approached directly via an outer court (Ai, EB III). The earliest towns often contained well-built rectangular houses, sometimes with roofs supported by rows of pillars (Tell el-Far'ah) and with well-constructed silos for grain storage (Jericho). These developments are not surprising and can be matched at the even larger complexes already long-established in southern Babylonia at Erech (Warka), Nippur, Ur, Lagash, and Eridu and reflected in Genesis 5 and 10. There, from a period long before the Early Bronze Age in Palestine, the first written documents have been found. Written in this period (c. 2700 B.C.), texts with a wide range of Semitic literature already showing a lengthy literary development have been discovered at Abu Salabikh, Fara, and other early Babylonian sites.

B. Nomadic Incursions

The break with the Early Bronze Age is marked by violent destruction of the towns (e.g., Jericho). Kenyon and others have associated this with the incursions of the Amorite nomads. But these peoples, only seminomads, had moved much earlier into Syria and Babylonia according to Liverani.[2] There is as yet little justification for identifying the population of the Early Bronze–Middle Bronze Age, with their distinctive pottery and weapon styles and lack of substantial buildings, exclusively with Amorite tribesmen. Certainly the rich tomb groups from Jericho, Tell el-'Ajjûl, and Megiddo, showing individual or double burials with personal possessions in rock-hewn tombs, are in marked contrast with the communal burials of the earlier period. The median chronology for these is given by objects from the Megiddo tombs that compare with similar types found at Ras Shamra and Mesopotamia and dated c. 2200–2000 B.C.

Just before 1900 B.C., a new civilization emerged that was to dominate Palestine without any apparent break for seven hundred years. These peoples, coming mainly from Syria and Phoenicia, brought with them a new type of wheel-made pottery. Once more the incursions appear to have been gradual and can be traced at Megiddo, Tell Beit Mirsim, and Tell el-'Ajjûl. Egyptian execration texts show that Palestine and Transjordan were still occupied by seminomads who controlled the areas between the Canaanite cities that were once more expanding on their earlier sites.

C. The Patriarchal Age (c. 1950–1750 B.C.)

The Patriarchs fit best into the early Middle Bronze Age (MBA I), though their association with the Amorites or other folk-movements (including early Hapiru) known from contemporary texts cannot be proved. The Genesis narrative accords well with the archaeologically known occupation of the city-states that were then a dominant feature of Palestine. The occupation of Bethel, Shechem, Hebron (Kiriath Arba), and the Dead Sea region of Sodom and Gomorrah is confirmed, as is that of the Negeb in southwest

---

[1]P. Lapp in *Near Eastern Archaeology in the Twentieth Century*, ed. James A. Sanders (Garden City, N.Y.: Doubleday and Co., Inc., 1970), pp. 111ff.; cf. R. Amiran (ibid.), pp. 83ff.

[2]D.J. Wiseman, ed., *Peoples of Old Testament Times* (Oxford: Clarendon Press, 1973), p. 109.

Palestine where flocks and herds (cf. Gen. 18:7; 20:1; 24:62) and grain crops (Gen 26:12; 37:7) are traced in MBA I. There is valuable evidence of the verisimilitude of the patriarchal personal and place names at this time. Thus, the name "Abram" occurs in a text from Dilbat (*Aba[m]rama*) and Aburahana (Abraham) and Zabilan (Zebulon) in Egyptian execration texts. Turahi (Terah), Nahur (Nahor), Sarugi (Serug), Laban, and Mar(Ben)-Yamin (Benjamin) are in eighteenth-century texts from Mari with reference to the Harran area and Ya'qub-il (Jacob) from nearby Chagar-Bazar. Other texts from these towns and from Alalah (from the eighteenth to the fifteenth century), Ur, Ras Shamra (fourteenth century), and Nuzi in Assyria (fifteenth century) throw considerable light on the patriarchal social customs. It can be seen that it was usual for a childless couple to adopt an heir and then displace him in the event of the birth of a real son (Gen 15:4). According to her marriage contract, a barren woman was to provide her husband with a slave-girl to bear a son. Marriages were arranged for public purposes by the rulers of Ugarit and Qatna, as well as by Egyptian kings, and this may be reflected in the adventures of Sarah (Gen 20) and Rebekah (Gen 26). The special position of the first-born son (cf. Gen 21:10ff.; 48:14ff.), the bridegroom "asking" for a daughter as bride, the use of betrothal and bride-gifts (Gen 34:12), and the stipulation of marriage-contracts that a man might take a third wife only if the first two were barren or take a second wife only if the first failed to give birth within seven years explain incidents in Genesis (e.g., 29:18,27: Jacob's possible need to wait seven years for Rachel). Nuzi texts refer to a man's transferring his inheritance for three sheep and uphold the validity of an oral blessing as a deathbed will. The type of sale contract involved in the purchase of the cave of Machpelah (Gen 23) is similar to both Old Babylonian and Hittite legal texts of this period.

From a study of the Mari texts, it is evident that an incident like that related in Genesis 14, in which Amraphel (not the same name as Hammurapi), Arioch (Arriwuk occurs only at this time), and Tidal (Tudhalia) were opposed by Abraham and his armed retainers (*hanîkîm*, a word otherwise found only in Egyptian texts of the nineteenth to eighteenth centuries B.C.) could likely have taken place only in this period, which, according to the Mari letters, was one in which such coalitions were formed.

Camel bones from Mari c. 2500; representations on seals, plaques, and figurines from Byblos, Babylonia, and Egypt; and references in Sumerian and Babylonian texts show that the citing of camels in Abraham's time is no anachronism. At that time camels were ridden behind the hump and, with donkeys, were used as slow-moving beasts of burden, though their major domestication and use in war did not occur until c. 1500–1250 B.C.

D. *The Late Bronze Age*

About 1700 B.C. a strengthening and enlargement of the massive defenses of walled cities can be seen in the addition of a steep slope of stone or beaten earth with a smooth plastered face held at its base by a retaining wall (glacis). This can be traced in Syria (Carchemish and Qatna), Palestine (Hazor), Dan (Laish), Shechem, Tirzah, Old Gaza, Tell el-Far'ah (Sharuhen), Tell el-Ajjûl, Ashkelon, Tell Beit Mirsim, Tell Jerisheh, and in Egypt at Tell el-Yahudiyeh. The construction of these is generally attributed to the Hyksos who seem to combine non-Semitic elements (Horites-Hurrians) with Semites (Amorites). These people, pressed southwest by the rising Hittite and Kassite powers, overthrew the native rulers of Egypt c. 1720. Their success was in part due to the use of chariots and horses (skeletons of which were found at Tell el-'Ajjûl) and to their organizational ability that led to the rise of strong local rulers, each major city having its own monarch. The nobility lived in well-built mansions that contrasted with the much humbler dwellings around them. Middle Bronze IIC tombs bear witness to the wealth of this period and numerous scarabs to the many sealed documents current within a domain stretching from the Euphrates to the Nile. This was an important period and later Hebrews were to marvel at the massive defenses (Num 13:28), meet the feudal type of monarchy in Palestine (1 Sam 27:6), and themselves desire a similar system (1 Sam 8:11–18).

In Egypt the Joseph history (Gen 37–50) fits well into the late Middle Kingdom (Dynasty XIII) and Hyksos period. The Wilbur papyri (c. 1740 B.C.) shows in a list of one hundred slaves that more than half were "Asiatics," i.e., Semites from Palestine, among them 'š-ra (Asher) and šp-ra (cf. Shiphra, Exod 1:15). Some of these rose to higher positions and some were domestic servants. The twenty silver shekels paid for Joseph (Gen 37:28) was the average slave price for the eighteenth century, whereas later the price rose until by the fifteenth to fourteenth centuries it was from forty to fifty shekels. A Ras Shamra text (RS 20.21) tells of a man in southern Syria who was sold by his companion to passing Egyptians, who, however, abandoned him, taking only his goods. The use of contemporarily attested technical terms (e.g., "butler," "baker" as courtiers [saris]), the prison procedure, and proper names, parallels with the Egyptian Tale of Two Brothers, the court etiquette (Gen 41:14), the investiture, and economic milieu all bear witness to the validity of the Joseph narratives. The fact that some Egyptian names (Potiphar, Asenath, Zaphenath-Paneah) are not attested in texts till the twelfth to tenth centuries B.C. could be due to the sparsity of earlier documentary evidence rather than to the proposal that modern subsitutes were inserted during the transmission of the text.[3]

The Hyksos empire seems to have broken up quickly following their expulsion from Egypt in the third quarter of the sixteenth century. The Egyptians harried them into Canaan, as illustrated by their local tomb paintings of the siege of Sharuhen and by the destruction levels at Tell Beit Mirsim, Beth-zur, Jericho, and Megiddo. The subsequent Late Bronze Age is well illustrated by the correspondence between the city-rulers and their allies and their overlords in the fourteenth to thirteenth centuries (The Amarna letters and cuneiform texts from Ugarit). Now, as in the earlier Middle Bronze Age, seminomads including (H)apiru moved in between the towns amid the uncertain situation caused by the growing weakness of Egyptian control. Despite some evidence of trade with Egypt, Cyprus, and Mesopotamia in the jewelry hoards from Tell-el-'Ajjūl tombs near Gaza and Megiddo, the hill towns were poorer than their coastal counterparts in Phoenicia and Syria. Art forms on cylinder seals, pots, and stelae show a mixed Egyptian and Mesopotamian (thus possibly local Canaanite) predominance with purely Egyptian stelae and statues set up in places where the Egyptians dominated (Beth Shan, Chinnereth).

1. *The Exodus.* The end of the Late Bronze Age in Palestine is marked by several destruction levels, some of which have been ascribed to the suppression of rebellion by the Egyptians. So Tell el-Hesi (Eglon?) was destroyed four times and Megiddo and Beth Shan twice by the end of the thirteenth century. The ruin of Tell Beit Mirsim and the contemporary occupation at Jericho is now ascribed to the fourteenth century, not the fifteenth as at one time supposed. The fallen walls at the latter city, taken by Garstang

---

3So J. Vergote, *Joseph en Egypte* (Louvain: Publications Un Universitaires, 1959-Orientalia et Biblica Louvaniensia 3), pp. 147, 148.

to be evidence of a destruction c. 1407 B.C., are now dated by Kenyon to the Early Bronze Age, though there is evidence of the abandonment of Jericho c. 1325. The now evident destruction of Lachish, Tell Beit Mirsim, and Ashdod (Judg 1:18) may relate to attacks by the incoming Hebrews, and the excavators attribute the burning of Hazor (XIII) to Joshua's attack (Josh 11). Those who argue for the earlier date of the conquest have to assign these thirteenth-century destructions to the Philistines, the Judges, or some other cause. They rightly point out that only Hazor, Ai, and Jericho are said in the Old Testament to have been burned and that there is possibly some archaeological evidence for this in the Late Bronze IIA levels there.[4] They also explain the reference to Ra'amses in Exod 1:11, as reference to an eighteenth-dynasty Ramesses,[5] or as a substitution of a later for an earlier name. Pithom and Ra'amses (probably Pi-Rammsē of Egyptian texts) were founded by Sethos I and mainly built by Ramesses II (1304–). The latter city is identified with Tanis or, more likely, Qantir.

Surveys by Glueck and others showed that Edom, Moab, and Ammon, which opposed Moses, were not settled to any great extent till the thirteenth century, though this may have to be modified by some recent findings in Jordan.[6] There is somewhat clearer evidence for the first mention of "Israel" in Palestine on the Merenptah stela at Lachish dated 1224 B.C., which names places and peoples that the Egyptian king claimed to have subdued. A stela of Seti I from Beth Shan dated 1313 names the "Apiru of the mountains of Yarmuth."

The main difference between proponents of the early (c. 1440 B.C.) and late date (c. 1270) for the Exodus lies in the interpretation of 1 Kings 6:1, which states that it was 480 years from the time the Israelites left Egypt to the founding of Solomon's temple in c. 960 B.C. Unger and Archer believe that this demands the earlier date.[7] On the other hand, Kitchen and other evangelicals argue that, since the archaeological evidence does not seem to support such a date, the 480 years may be the total of regnal years that may have in part been concurrent, as commonly occurs in Mesopotamian and Egyptian king lists (e.g., Turin Papyrus for Dynasties XIII to XVII; it gives a total of 450 years of reigns that are partly overlapping and known from other sources to have occupied a total of c. 240 years). The biblical account of the Judges does the same.

2. *The Sinai covenant.* The covenant made by God with his people at Sinai is at the heart of the OT and is unique. Nothing similar and no covenant direct from any god to man is found among ancient Near Eastern texts or any with purely moral subject matter. The literary form, however, may be compared with the international treaties of the fourteenth to thirteenth centuries known from Hittite sources but themselves based on a Mesopotamian style of text already attested and used in the fifteenth century (Alalah) and earlier. The scheme of these texts, which followed the oral deposition and oath at a solemn assembly, is as follows: (1) Preamble, or title, indicating the author (cf. Deut 1:1–5); (2) historical prologue, which may be stated (Deut 1:6–3:29), summarized (Exod 20:2), or assumed from the circumstances of the ceremony (as in the Esarhaddon Assyrian treaties of 627 B.C.); (3) detailed stipulations laying obligations on the vassal in the form "You shall (not) . . ." (cf. Exod 20–31); (4) ultimate deposition of the document (Deut

---

[4]Bruce K. Waltke, BS 129 (1972): 33–47.
[5]Gleason L. Archer, JETS 17 (1974): 49, 50.
[6]*Vetus Testamentum* 21 (1971): 119–123.
[7]Leon J. Wood, "The Date of the Exodus" in *New Perspectives on the OT*, ed. J.B. Payne (Waco: Word Books, 1970).

10:1–5; Exod 25:16) and arrangements for the periodic public reading of the terms and for their teaching to succeeding generations (Deut 31:10–13); (5) witnesses that are usually gods, but since the Lord swears only by himself, the only witnesses at Sinai are heaven and earth; and (6) curses and blessings on the vassal who breaks or keeps the terms of the treaty. Some of these were demonstrated. Note that Deuteronomy 28 has the reverse order of blessings before curses.

In these cuneiform and Aramaic texts (Bar-Ga'yah and Mati-el of the eighth century) the order of some sections may be varied or some omitted or recorded on a separate document. The discovery of these texts shows that such treaty/covenant law was the essential basis of all state, interstate, and interpersonal law and contract throughout the ancient Near East. It has recently given rise to a fresh study of covenant terminology both within and outside the OT.[8]

3. *Writing.* The cuneiform script used in Mesopotamia since c. 3500 B.C. was taught in scribal schools in Syria (Mari. c. 2400) and Anatolia also. At Alalah, an agricultural town in Syria, at least six scribes were at work at one time writing historiographic, legal, and economic texts in addition to the usual correspondence, administrative, recording, and school exercises. By the thirteenth century B.C. scribes at Ras Shamra (Ugarit) were using the Akkadian cuneiform script for all these same purposes alongside texts written in the local Semitic dialect, Hurrian, Hittite, Sumerian, and a simplified cuneiform alphabetic script used primarily for religious epics, according to extant texts in Ugaritic. The scribes wrote a number of literary compositions, including a Semitic version of the *Epic of Gilgamesh,* of which a fragment from the fifteenth century has also been found at Megiddo. Among other tablets was a local version of the "Babylonian Job," discussing the problem of suffering. The presence of this tablet indicates an earlier date for the origin of this type of literature and so of its biblical counterpart than some critics would normally allow. There are proverbs and other wisdom literature similar in genre to those in the OT. In the following century, tablets using the cuneiform script originate in Palestine (e.g., Amarna letters, Ta'anach, Megiddo, Jericho, Shechem, Gezer, Hazor, and Tell el-Hesi).

By the Late Middle Bronze Age the Semitic alphabet, perhaps developed under the use of the Egyptian hieroglyphs for writing foreign names, was already in use in Sinai (Serabit el-Khadem) and, in another form, soon thereafter in Byblos. By 1500 B.C. similar inscriptions, but now losing their original pictographic form, were found in Palestine at Gezer, Shechem (plaque), and Lachish (inscribed dagger). Well before the end of the second millennium the pressures of trade and need for communication led to the widespread use of this simple form of writing (e.g., in marking personal objects; cf. stone inscriptions of Ahiram). Thus, by the time of the entry of the Hebrews into Canaan in the Late Bronze Age they would be confronted, if not already familiar, with at least five different forms of writing systems used for eight or more languages: (1) Egyptian hieroglyphs (Beth Shan, Chinnereth); (2) the Byblos syllabic script; (3) "Proto-Hebrew" (Lachish, Hazor); (4) Akkadian (Mesopotamian) cuneiform; and (5) the Ugaritic alphabetic script (found also at Beth Shemesh). Since at this same time the Egyptian Wen-Amun writes of taking papyrus scrolls in quantity to Byblos, we must assume that the hazards of climate and survival have so far prevented the recovery of many texts from Palestine itself in any period.

---

[8]E.g., M. Weinfeld, "Covenant Terminology" in *Journal of the American Oriental Society* 93 (1973): 190–199.

One use of these scripts is commonly found in the manufacture of stamp seals, which may have the name of the owner and perhaps also the name of his father and the title of his profession. Vattioni has listed more than 260 Hebrew seals with inscriptions in the alphabetic script, or impressions from them dated mainly to the ninth to the sixth centuries.[9] Old Testament names on these seals include those of King Jotham (2 Kings 15:30ff.); Shema'ah, son of the king, probably a descendant of Jehoiakim (1 Chron 3:22); Shema', servant of Jeroboam; Jaazaniah, servant of the king (cf. 2 Kings 25:23); and Gedaliah "who is over the house" (cf. 2 Kings 18:18; NBD 1153–5).

4. *Religious architecture.* The Late Bronze Age has left remains of religious structures—temples and sanctuaries—several rebuilt on the same foundations over successive centuries as at Lachish (1500–1230 B.C.) and Megiddo. Most temples were small, but those at Beth Shan, Beersheba, and Tell el-Far'ah consisted of an anteroom and an inner room or covered niche, where the divine image or symbol rested. This was the traditional form of religious architecture throughout the ancient Near East. At Hazor a large temple had a porch added as in the later temple of Solomon. Massive walls surrounded a single room, the roof of which was supported by pillars and entered by the portico. It seems that some shrines at Middle Bronze Age Hazor, Megiddo, and Shechem had upper rooms similar to those depicted in the model temples used as incense burners. There is evidence here and at Megiddo and Shechem of the Middle Bronze Age, such as in the model temples used as incense burners, that there was an upper room in these "tower" shrines. This form was succeeded by the more conventional temple, as found at Ugarit and Alalah in Syria, where the antechamber is smaller than the holy place and was entered from the long side. Square temples of the Late Bronze Age are known from Shechem (Mount Gerizim) and Amman, but the former does not have evidence of cremated human beings as foundation deposits such as is found at the latter (cf. Josh 6:26).

The numerous small male and female metal and clay figurines (MBA-LBA), some skirted or holding weapons—figurines that have commonly been identified with Baals or Astarte—have not always been found in sacred buildings. So they may be amulets, charms, or votive objects, much like the many pottery plaques and figures of a naked female (the goddess Asherah?) found in this and earlier periods in Palestine as well as in Mesopotamia. The biblical account of Canaanite religious practices and of the actual deities in the pantheon can be checked from the bilingual lists from Ras Shamra. In these lists Ba'al Sapon, the Baal of the heights, is followed by "the god of the fathers" (*il abi*, sometimes wrongly interpreted as "god the spirit"). Then the god Dagan (*ilDagan*) is followed in the list by seven Baals. The banal antics of some of these deities portrayed in the thirteenth-century Ugaritic epics contrast with the high expressions of devotion found in some other contemporary texts.

At Gezer and other sites, standing stones (as later found also at Hazor) probably indicate a mortuary shrine. Hill shrines or "high places," common in the following centuries and known best from the Nabatean high place at Petra, can be traced only with difficulty, because most archaeological effort is directed to a town or its neighboring built-up areas. Such high places could be built of stones or earth to represent a mound, as at Megiddo in the Early Bronze Age, Naharayah near Haifa (Middle Bronze II), and Hazor in the Late Bronze Age. The earliest of such high places may show impregnation with the oil used in pouring libations on the site. Later Israelite high places included

---

[9] *Biblica* 50 (1969): 357–388; *Augustinianum* 11 (1971), pp.447–454.

open-air shrines approached by a flight of wide stone and brick steps, as at Tel Dan.[10]

E. *The Monarchy* (Iron Age)

1. *Philistia.* The Amarna correspondence and Ugarit texts of the fourteenth century already show that Ashdod and Ashkelon (under a non-Semitic ruler Widiya) were influential trade centers and that Gath, Gaza, and Joppa were independent towns. Raiders and settlers from Cyprus joined other sea peoples already settled on the Palestinian coast. There is therefore no reason to think of patriarchal relations with the "Philistines" as an anachronism. Aegean contacts continued into the thirteenth century, as shown by pottery finds at Ashkelon, Tell el-Hesi, Tell el-'Ajjûl, and Tell el-Far'ah and by Cretan seals found near Gaza. In the twelfth century, a new style of pottery, combining elements from Cyprus (Late Helladic III) with local Egyptian and Palestinian, appears. This is generally designated "Philistinian," since it is found at Gaza, Ashkelon, Ashdod, and in their rich hinterland—the area known to have been occupied by these people in the twelfth century. They mainly appear to have taken over older sites in Southwest Canaan by conquest, though some new foundations (Qasileh and Khirbet el Muqanna') are attributed to them.

The Philistines, possibly the Egyp(tian) *Prst*, and their associated Tjekker colonists depicted on the Egyptian wall paintings of the tomb of Ramesses III (1198–1166) at Medinet Habu, soon settled in southwest Palestine. Their arrival marks a destruction level that puts an end to the Late Bronze Age at cities in the coastal plain. Their characteristic feathered headdresses and weapons (some were found near Jaffa) associate them with peoples of a northern or Caucasian origin. While a number of clay anthropoid coffins found at Beth Shan and Lachish may be Philistinian, their presence there may be due to later trading. More certain evidence of Philistinian settlement is their painted pottery with its distinctive decorations and geometric and bird patterns found at Sharuhen, Gerar, as far north as Joppa, throughout the Shephelah, and from Debir to Gezer. Trade can account for these wares as far inland as Deir 'Alla in the Jordan valley, but only after an interval. Thus the biblical accent on the pentapolis centered on Gaza, Ashkelon, Gath (Tell el-'Areini or Tell en-Najila?), and Ekron is confirmed. But the extension and comparison of their form of rule under a lord (*seren*, Gk. "tyrant") to the Israelite amphyctyony is increasingly to be doubted.

A temple at Tell Qasile is the only Philistinian temple so far excavated (by Mazar in 1972). This had a structure basically different from Canaanite temples and Solomon's later construction. Two central pillars were the sole support for the roof, an architectural design that may throw light on Samson's action in pulling down the Gaza temple single-handedly (Judg 16:29, 30). The contrast between the well-drained foundations of the Canaanites and Philistines and the cruder Israelite habitations in the time of the Judges (e.g., at Bethel) is clear. Where the latter built on or occupied earlier property, they kept to the ground plan but used primarily only the ground floor. Few repairs were made and this may indicate that there was a lack of coordination with work in gangs at the larger sites.

The period of expansion brought the Philistines into contact with the Hebrews in c. 1100 B.C., first in the Southwest between Timnah and Ekron (Judg 3:31; 14:4), where they were a much-feared enemy (Judg 14:11, 12), and later at Shiloh. Their failure to

---

[10]*The Biblical Archaeologist* 37 (1974): 40–43.

penetrate farther against the united resistance of Judah under David is attested by the almost complete absence of evidence for any settlement, with some possible traces of trade at Gibeah, Jerusalem, Beth Zur, and Tell en-Nasbeh. The Philistines were not the first to develop the use of iron, which is found from the fourteenth century as a Hittite exploitation. A Tell el-Fara'ah tomb yields the earliest iron dagger and knife from Palestine, and the Israelites found it hard to break the Philistine monopoly in tempering iron and their consequent economic superiority (1 Sam 13:18–22). In the early monarchy, iron finally displaces copper and bronze for ploughshares and sickles.

2. *The united monarchy.* Israel gradually took over something of the technical ability of the Philistines who dominated the plains, while Saul and David consolidated their position in the hills. At Saul's hometown and capital, Gibeah (Tell el-Fûl), the earliest Israelite iron implements were already in use, and soon thereafter iron axes, mattocks, plow-points, hooks, and sickles led to improvement in agricultural methods and to an industrial revolution. Iron nails are now found in construction work (cf. 1 Chron 22:3). Whereas previously the Israelites had not been able to contain the Canaanite chariotry easily or to drive out their settled communities, now their own population increased and they were able to construct the vital wells and cisterns in places previously ill-watered.

The oldest dateable Israelite fortification is at Gibeah (IA I), three miles north of Jerusalem, excavated by W.F. Albright in 1923–33. A corner tower and adjacent massive casemate walls of a type traceable to the time of Abimelech at Tell Beit Mirsim and Beth Shemesh, formed a rudimentary palace-fortress. This building was soon destroyed by fire, perhaps after the battle of Michmash (1 Sam 13–14) and then rebuilt. Others interpret this as the place from which Saul and Jonathan drove out the Philistines (1 Sam 13:3). Shiloh (Khirbet Seilûn) reveals no direct evidence of the actual resting place of the ark of the covenant. Shiloh was certainly occupied in the early Iron Age (c. 1200–1000) and was destroyed soon thereafter by the Philistines (as Jer 7:12 recalls). The layout of a later Byzantine church there follows the pattern of the tabernacle. The cultural standard gradually improved, but little remains of the time of David unless the Jebusite glacis and part of the wall of Ophel, the new "city of David," can be attributed to him. The old Warren's shaft leading to Gihon ("Gusher") in the Kidron valley outside the city walls discovered in 1867 follows the line of an earlier Canaanite tunnel for bringing water into the city. This is generally considered to be the water course up which Joab and his men entered the city to capture it (2 Sam 5:6–8). Similar water shafts have been cleared at Gezer, Gibeon, and Hazor, and other tunnels for bringing water into a city from external springs have been found at Megiddo and elsewhere. The repair of the casemate walls at Beth-shemesh (and of the governor's residence there) and at Tell Beit Mirsim may represent action taken during David's reign to protect his territories against the Philistines.

David's organization of army leaders, personal bodyguard, priests, state archivist, and secretary, and his employment of twelve divisions taking turns at military duties, as well as of officials responsible for keeping accounts of the primary imports and exports of livestock, grain, oil, and wine, can be compared with similar arrangements revealed in texts from Ugarit and Alalah. From the latter and from Mari texts it can be shown that David's act of cutting off the hem of Saul's garment was tantamount to rebellion or freedom from a royal overlord, just as the act of seizing the hem of a king's robe denoted subordination. Although no copies of psalms from Judah have been found earlier than the Qumran texts, there are many parallels from the twelfth century and later Akkadian texts. These show that such compositions were easily and freely made, so that the attribution of psalms to David would be in keeping with this. All the musical instruments mentioned in the psalms are known from excavations or references before the eighth century. A vase from Megiddo dated c. 1000 B.C. depicts a man playing a lyre. Mazar thinks that an inscribed javelin head from El-Khadr, between Bethlehem and Hebron, may have belonged to a soldier following David into exile.

3. *The age of Solomon.* The second phase of the Iron Age shows an increase in the use of iron and improvements in building techniques. Yadin's discovery of a governor's palace and an administrative building of this period and of a monumental six-roomed gateway associated with casemate walls at Hazor is of importance. By a careful reinvestigation and redating of similar structures at Megiddo and Gezer, he has shown that all these were truly Solomon's work (1 Kings 9:15). At this same time the palace-fortress, defenses, and administrative quarters at Megiddo were enlarged, using the new solid bonded masonry techniques that began to displace the casemate type of constructions, perhaps under Phoenician influence. The so-called "stables" of Solomon found there (Level IV) have since been reinterpreted to be an administrative building of the days of Ahab. The Solomonic level may well remain unexcavated beneath. Similar storerooms have been unearthed at Tell el-Hesi and Ta'anach.

In Jerusalem, Solomon built his own central palace, as well as buildings elsewhere, apparently modeled on the lines of Syrian Late Bronze Age buildings already known from Alalah and Ugarit and popular in the Iron Age. Examples of these grandiose constructions with columned portico or entrance hall (Akkad. *bīt-hilāni*) are now known from Zincirli, Tell Halaf (biblical Gozan), Tainat, and Karatepe, and from the Assyrian bas-reliefs. The first temple used current architectural motifs and design technology. The construction of walls with layers of wood between the stone courses is known from Tainat and Alalah in Syria. Drawings on Syrian ivories illustrate cherubim (a pair of human-headed winged lions), palmettos, and lotus flowers. Lavers with pomegranate fringes have been found at Ras Shamra. The twin freestanding pillars in front of the temple have parallels elsewhere in the Near East. Solomon's work in the city may be marked by the casemate wall, blocks of stone worked by Phoenician craftsmen, and a proto-Ionic capital found in the north of Ophel. Kenyon considers the "Fill" (Millo) rebuilt by both David and Solomon to be the walled terraces on the slopes of Ophel, which needed, and show, frequent repair. The grand feast given on completion of the construction of the temple (1 Kings 8:65) is similar to that of King Ashurnasirpal II of Assyria, who describes in detail the provisions for his entertainment of 69,574 people for ten days to celebrate the opening of his new city and temple at Calah in 879 B.C.

The wealth needed for this activity was generated by the trading activity of the age. Evidence for the expeditions to Ophir (possibly [S]upara north of Bombay) is found in an inscribed potsherd from Tell Qasileh—"gold from Ophir for Beth Horon, thirty shekels." The buildings found by Glueck at the port of Tell el Kheleifeh (Ezion Geber or Elat) and once thought to be a foundry of Solomon are now interpreted as storehouse for the port. Zarethan, where Solomon cast his bronzes (1 Kings 7:45), may well be the recently excavated Tell es-Saidiyeh, east of the Jordan, since numerous open smelting pits have been found there and suitable ores have been found in the adjacent Arabah valley. It may have been to control this trade that David first subjugated Edom. At Hazor numerous bronze objects, weights, shovels, and a snake emblem for mounting on a pole (like Nehushtan?) have been found. Horned altars of the type used in the temple come from Arad and Beersheba and measure 157 cms (three large royal cubits high) as that of the tabernacle (Exod 27:1) and Solomon's temple (2 Chron 6:13). Supplies for Solomon's kingdom could have come from afar, for he controlled the overland trade routes from Cilicia (Que, so 1 Kings 10:28) to Egypt, and thus the import and export of horses.

Egyptian remains at the Aqabah mines and the destruction of Tel Mor (near Ashdod), Beth Shemesh, and Gezer may be attributed to raids by the Egyptian Siamun early in Solomon's reign. Solomon's ability to contract dynastic marriages with Egyptian and other princesses and to receive Gezer as a marriage gift attests to the power of Israel at that time. The authenticity of an inscribed South Arabian stamp seal from Bethel, dated to the ninth century and formerly thought to confirm Solomon's association with the Queen of Sheba, is now questioned. No native inscriptions of the reign have survived, unless the Gezer calendar (a farmer's almanac or a schoolboy's exercise) is from this reign. The list of Solomon's interests, however, closely parallels the texts studied in both Mesopotamia (HAR-*ra-hubullu*) and Egyptian schools. There, too, wisdom literature and proverbs of all kinds were collected and learned. Lyric poems, like the love songs of the Song of Solomon, survive from Egypt, Syria, and Mesopotamia from the thirteenth century onwards, as do descriptions of a woman by a son to his mother.

4. *The divided kingdom.* Israel was, however, economically exhausted by the wide-ranging policies undertaken by Solomon and his son Rehoboam, and this was to become a major factor in the defection of the northern kingdom. Rehoboam had to face an invasion by the Libyan usurper who now ruled Egypt. Shishak (Sheshonq I) in his fifth year (c. 928), instigated by the refugee Jeroboam, was only bought off from sacking Jerusalem by being given the temple treasures (1 Kings 14:25, 26). Shishak's triumphal reliefs and text in the Karnak temple of Amun in Thebes show him smiting Asiatic captives and list more than one hundred fifty towns in Phoenicia, Judah, the Esdraelon valley, Edom, and South Syria. A broken stela found at Megiddo attests part of this claim, as do destruction levels at Debir and Beth Shemesh. Egyptians reinforced the defenses at Sharuhen, and scarabs show their presence also at Gezer, Tell el-'Ajjûl, and Tell Jemmeh. Rehoboam's earlier strengthening of Lachish and Azekah is to be seen in work there.

Jeroboam I had now to find a new center for worship. The part of Bethel (Beitin) thought to be occupied at that time is so far unexcavated. At Dan, where the second golden bull-calf was worshiped as the throne of an invisible god, Biran has unearthed one of the largest city-gates yet found in Palestine. He believes the gates were built by Jeroboam. The ferocity of the internal war between Israel and Judah can be seen in Jeroboam's reconstruction work at Shechem and the refortification of Gibeah, of Bethel as the southernmost outpost of the northern capital, and of Tell en-Nasbeh (possibly Mizpah) with its twenty-foot thick walls and towers as the northern outpost of Judah at this time. Such work must have involved conscripted labor (1 Kings 15:15–22). The fortified gateway and courtyard were lined with benches where the elders sat during assemblies, local courts, and major trading transactions.

5. *The dynasty of Omri.* The unsettled northern kingdom found a strong leader in the usurper Omri (884–873 B.C.), who became the sixth king of Israel. The capital at this time was Shechem, where construction work may be assigned to this period (1 Kings 12:25), though it was not a site easily defended. Omri attacked Zimri at Tirzah, seven miles northeast of Shechem and probably to be identified with Tell el Far'a excavated by de Vaux in 1941–50. The first Iron-Age level there is marked by burning, which may represent Omri's capture of the town, where he lived for six years during the building

of his own new capital at Samaria. The site may have been bought so that Omri could be free to organize his own administration on crown property, as David had done at Jerusalem. The incomplete building at Tirzah may be Omri's unfinished palace, and occupation of the area may have continued, according to pottery finds similar to those in early Samaria, until Samaria itself was established when Tirzah was virtually abandoned.

Samaria, excavated carefully and primarily between 1908–1935, shows several occupation levels dating c. 875–721 B.C. Period I is ascribed to Omri and his son Ahab, who completed his work. The large palace and courtyard on the citadel was surrounded by defenses consisting of three walls, all of fine Phoenician-type bonded masonry. The city gate was approached through a colonnade lined with proto-Ionic (Phoenician) pillars and capitals. These and other finds show that the king was intent on luxury. Doubtless, Ahab was influenced by his alliance with Tyre (1 Kings 16:31), as he was by his wife Jezebel, and doubtless he sought separation from the body of the population. Many ninth- to eighth-century ivory fragments (with Phoenician markings on the reverse) from palace furnishings have been recovered. Ahab's palace could well have earned the reputation of being "a house of ivories" (1 Kings 22:39; Amos 6:4). At the northwest summit a large artificial pool or waterproofed cistern (33 x 17 feet) may well have been the "pool of Samaria" where Ahab's chariot was washed down after his dead body had been carried home in it (1 Kings 22:38).

1 Kings 16:21–28 puts most emphasis on the theological appraisal of Omri's life and his failure to put God's law into effective operation ("Omri did evil in the sight of the LORD"), as shown by contemporary Babylonian texts to be the requirement imposed. The OT hints at his greatness, and later Assyrian texts refer to Israel at Samaria as "the land or dynasty of Omri." Omri's widespread influence can be judged from the Mesha' stela (The Moabite Stone), found in 1868 and dated c. 830 B.C. On it the king of Moab tells of his father's defeat by Ahab during his thirty-year reign. This was attributed to the anger of the god Chemosh, who, it is said, allowed Omri to occupy the land of Madeba for forty years. The account tells how Moab regained its freedom, probably initially while Ahab was engaged in his war with Syria (2 Kings 1:1) and then finally in the abortive campaign led by Omri's grandson J(eh)oram (2 Kings 3:27). The construction of the Moabite town of Qrhh was by Israelite slave-labor. The stela tells how the Israelites had built and occupied the town of Ataroth for the tribe of Gad and Yahaz. It confirms the use of the "ban" (herem) and existence of the sanctuaries at high places during this time. Ahab also rebuilt Hazor (Level VIII) and may have been the king responsible for the excavation of the water system of Megiddo.

An Assyrian text of Shalmaneser III tells how he fought a massive battle at Qarqar on the Orontes north of Damascus in 853 B.C. This was against a coalition under Irhuleni of Hamath and Benhadad II of Aram-Damascus (called Adad-idri or Hadadezer by the Assyrian). This document is the first direct chronological point of reference between Israel and Assyria, for Shalmaneser lists "Ahab the Israelite" as providing "2,000 chariots and 10,000 men." His contribution in chariots was the largest. Musri (Egypt)—together with Cilicia, Arvad, Arabia, and Ammon—provided contingents. The discovery of a presentation vase of Osorkon II in the palace of Samaria may well indicate an Egyptian-Israelite alliance during Ahab's reign. The coalition was effective in halting the Assyrian advance. It is interesting to note the total numbers involved in the Qarqar battle. In addition to their precise numerical use, 10,000 is used to denote an army, 20,000 an army group, 1,000 a battle group, and 100 a company in both Assyrian annals and the OT. Of those who opposed him, Shalmaneser claims to have killed 14,000 out of the more than 73,000 men, 2,140 chariots, 19,000 cavalry and 1,000 camels.

6. *The last kings of Israel.* By 843 B.C. Hazael had displaced Benhadad II as king of Aram-Damascus and by 841 the usurper Jehu was on the throne of Israel. Hazael, "our lord Haza'el" (*mr'n hz'l*) according to an inscribed ivory fragment found in the plunder from Damascus, now led the Syro-Palestinian nations against Assyria and is so named in a text of Shalmaneser III. The same Assyrian king made Jehu his vassal, according to the Black Obelisk erected in his capital Calah (Nimrud) in 841 B.C. and now in the British Museum. This depicts the bearded "Jehu, son of Omri [i.e., in the ruling line or citizen of Beth Omri] bringing tribute of silver, gold, a gold bowl, a gold vase, gold cups, gold buckets, tin, a staff for the royal hand and . . . fruits." This may well be the only pictorial representation of any king of Israel to survive, if the kneeling figure who introduces the line of Israelite porters is the king himself and not his representative. This episode is not mentioned in the OT but could show that Jehu sought Assyrian aid against Hazael who was then hostile to Israel (2 Kings 10:32). In this he was unsuccessful, since other Assyrian documents show that Shalmaneser's successor Adad-nirari III, king of Assyria (810–783), was engaged elsewhere and did not venture west until after Jehu's death.

Hazael, "a son of a nobody" (i.e., usurper or illegitimate son) according to the Assyrian annals, attacked and destroyed Megiddo (Level IVA) where the administrative buildings had been rebuilt after Shishak's invasion and a new town (Level III) constructed on the same site but on a different plan. At Samaria (Period III) there was a reconstruction of the palace and fortification by Jehu and his successors when these had been burned down, perhaps by Hazael. The splendor of Omri's Samaria declined, however, and the mediocre buildings (Period III) common to provincial Israel and Judah are now found at that site and elsewhere.

Assyrian attacks on Damascus weakened that kingdom and the pressure on Israel under Joash (801–786) was accordingly relieved (2 Kings 13:24, 25; cf. v.14–19). An Aramaic stela records the triumph of Zakir, king of Hamath and Lu'ash, over Hazael's successor Benhadad III and, though a stone stele of Adad-nirari III from Rimah (west of Mosul) lists Ya'usu (Joash) of Samaria as paying him tribute, together with Mari' of Damascus, there is no evidence that Samaria itself had yet been attacked by the Assyrians. Jeroboam II, the contemporary of Amos (Amos 8:11), appears to have gained great influence during his long and prosperous reign (770–755 B.C.), which coincided with Assyrian weakness. The form of palace administration already developed by Solomon continued, so far as can be judged from sixty-three inscribed potsherds from Samaria usually dated to Jeroboam's reign (but to Menahem by others). These record imports of wine and oil from neighboring crown-estates and seem to be tax payments made in kind and dated to regnal years. Yadin thinks these may have been the additional taxes imposed by Menahem to cover the Assyrian impost of 738. His theory may be supported by the many biblical names on the ostraca, names that correspond with the names of Manasseh's descendants (cf. Num 26:29–33; 1 Chron 7:14–19). A large number of Baal names are included. A seal with the design of a roaring lion and inscribed "Belonging to Shema', servant of Jeroboam" shows that this Shema' was a royal official not named in the OT. That it was Jeroboam II can be judged from the form of the inscription and its letters.

Azariah (Uzziah) succeeded Jeroboam and seems, at least initially, to have maintained a wide-ranging influence, since references to *Azriau* of Yaudi (identified with Judah) in Assyrian texts show him as the active leader of the anti-Assyria coalition from Judah itself to the Middle Euphrates.[11] A fine but small royal construction outside Jerusalem at Ramat Rachel is thought by Aharoni, its excavator, to be the separate house to which Uzziah was consigned as a leper later in his reign (2 Kings 15:5). Similar buildings also made of stone are known from earlier periods at Samaria and Megiddo. The Aramaic inscription recording the removal of Uzziah's bones at Jerusalem is to be dated some seven hundred years after his reign.

Menahem (menuhimme) of Samaria is named by Tiglath-Pileser, king of Assyria 745–727 B.C., together with sixteen other kings, including Rezin of Damascus, the king mentioned in 2 Kings 15:37; 16:5–9; Isaiah 7:1ff.; 9:11, as bringing tribute to him about 739 B.C. This action may have been inspired by the defeat suffered by Arpad and an attempt to buy time, or by a demand by Assyria for an assurance of goodwill following their conquest of the area north of Damascus. Menahem had to pay one thousand talents of silver by levying fifty shekels from every wealthy Israelite citizen (2 Kings 15:19ff.). This was the equivalent of the value of a slave according to contemporary Assyrian contracts for the sale of slaves and represents a total of 70,000 men. The use of the native name of Pul(u) for Tiglath-Pileser in 2 Kings 15:19 is confirmed by the occurrence of this name for him in the Babylonian King List. According to a tablet found at Nimrud (Calah), Tiglath-Pileser in 734 attacked the coastal cities of Phoenicia and marched south to Nahalmuṣur ("The River of Egypt"), where he had a stela erected depicting himself as victor. He thus effectively cut off Egypt and Hanun of Gaza, who had fled there, from helping Israel and Judah. Among the towns listed as captured en route was Mahalab (the Meheleb or Ahlab of Judg 1:31) near Sidon.

Two years later the Assyrian relates how he invaded Damascus, which he calls in a broken text "the land of the house of Hazael" (once wrongly read as a reference to the "land of Naphtali") and instigated the murder of Pekah (Paqaha), who had foolishly allied himself with Resin of Damascus. He states that he put an Assyrian nominee, Hoshea (Ausi'), on the throne of Israel. Towns in the northwest borders of Israel (called "the house of Omri") are named by Tiglath-Pileser. They include Abilakku and Gal'za (Galilee or Gilead). Excavations show that the fortified citadel of Hazor was now sacked, though following this campaign the town was the seat of two Assyrian governors, according to texts. In the remains of the city a pot inscribed "Belonging to Pekah" was found. This invasion of Samaria and northern Israel seems to have been in response to the appeal by (Jeho)ahaz of Judah who had refused to join the anti-Assyrian league. According to the Assyrian annals dating from 731 B.C., Jehoahaz (Yauhazi) was named with the rulers of Moab, Ashkelon, Edom, and Gaza as paying tribute to Assyria (cf. 2 Kings 16:8). Such aid was given only on condition that the vassal submitted to the treaty terms imposed. These included political and religious supervision, marked by the installation of cult symbols, such as the altar erected by Ahaz in Jerusalem (2 Kings 16:10–16). Despite the warnings of Isaiah (7:9), Ahaz's dependence on Assyria so weakened the state that territory was lost to the coastal city-states and Edom became independent. In this way Judah was cut off from her coastal port of Ezion-geber, which was destroyed by a fierce fire and succeeded by a new Edomite industrial village (Level IV). The unchanged administrative system under Ahaz is perhaps attested by the discovery of a fine carnelian seal inscribed with the name of "Ushnu, official (servant) of Ahaz." A text from Nimrud in Assyria listing tribute from Judah may well date from this reign.

Hoshea of Israel rebelled c. 725, and this brought the inevitable punitive raid predic-

---

[11]H. Tadmor, "Azriyau of Yaudi," in *Scripta Hierosolymtana* 8 (1961): 232–271.

ted in the vassal treaty he had signed with his Assyrian overlord. After Tiglath-Pileser's death, his successor Shalmaneser V, according to the Assyrian eponym canon, besieged the city of Samaria for three years (cf. 2 Kings 17:3–6) and the city fell to "the king of Assyria" in 722/1 B.C. The latter could well have been Shalmaneser V himself, as the OT may imply, or his successor as king, Sargon II (722–705 B.C.), who may have taken over in the last stages of the attack or acted jointly with Shalmaneser before his death (note the plural in 2 Kings 18:10). The Babylonian Chronicle records that Shalmaneser "broke [the resistance of] the city of Shamarain," usually taken to be Samaria rather than the little-known Sibraim (Ezek 47:16). Sargon himself, in annals written in his fourth year at Khorsabad, claims to have been "the conqueror of Samaria," but he does not repeat this in later editions from Nineveh, Calah, or Asshur.

Sargon (who is depicted on his palace wall reliefs at Khorsabad) claims to have taken 27,270 or 27,290 men of Samaria as prisoners. (The number varies according to the date and edition of his annals.) Included in the booty he took were "the gods in whom they trusted," a clear allusion to the polytheism of Israel at this time, though polytheism was so strongly condemned by the prophets. The same text, found at Nimrud in 1952, in words strikingly parallel to Isaiah 13, also describes Sargon's destruction of Babylon. Sargon deported the prisoners from Samaria to Gozan (Guzan, Tell Halaf), where excavation has produced texts bearing names of apparent Jewish exiles. Others were taken to Halah, which, if it is the same as Calah (Nimrud), might account for the list of West Semitic names (Menahem, 'Uzza, Elisha, Hananel, Haza'el, Haggai, etc.) found on an ostracon written by a local scribe. The same Assyrian capital was the place of manufacture of a series of wax-covered ivory and wood writing boards dated 715 B.C. and capable of containing extended literary works equivalent in length to the speeches of Isaiah.

The resettlement of Samaria (now incorporated as an Assyrian province) by groups brought in from Babylonia and elsewhere accords with Sargon's known policy and conquests at this time (2 Kings 17:24). Fragments of pottery from Samaria imply occupation by persons from other parts of Assyria and the ancient Near East.

Hoshea's appeal to Egypt for help against the Assyrians was to "So king of Egypt" (2 Kings 17:4), almost certainly Osorkon IV, the senior pharaoh in the eastern Delta,[12] rather than to an otherwise unknown Egyptian commander, Sib'e, as has been suggested. But no help came from the broken reed of Egypt. By 715–712 it was too late and impossible for help to come, since Sargon marched to Palestine to suppress a revolt by Yamani of Ashdod, where fragments of his victory stela erected there were found in 1963. Destruction levels at Megiddo (III), Hazor, and at Tirzah (II may be 723 B.C.) show the stern action taken. Because the OT is silent as to any incursion into Judah by the Assyrians, it must be assumed that Sargon's claim to be "the subjugator of the land of Judah" (Nimrud building inscription) means that he received tribute from that land. This might have been given when he defeated an alliance of Ashdod and Gath, when they tried to include all Palestine in their opposition, in battle on the Egyptian border near Rapihu in 712. Since the Eponym list states that Sargon himself "stayed in the land" (i.e., Assyria), Isaiah's claim that he sent his commander-in-chief (*turtan*) for these campaigns is correct.

7. *Judah under Assyria.* Judah now had to be prepared to face Assyria alone. On Sar-

---

[12]K.A. Kitchen, *The Third Intermediate Period in Egypt* (1972), pp.372–373.

gon's death in 705 B.C., Hezekiah decided to break with Assyria, perhaps encouraged by the action taken by the rebel Marduk-apla-iddina II (Merodach-baladan) of Babylon whose activities can be followed in Assyrian state records and correspondence. In wise anticipation of the Assyrian reaction, Hezekiah repaired the fortifications of Jerusalem and dug a tunnel to bring water into the city in time of siege (2 Kings 20:20; 2 Chron 32:30). The American explorer Robinson mentions this tunnel in 1838, but it was not cleared until 1880, when an inscription was discovered at the point where the miners working from one end met those excavating from the other 300 feet underneath the surface. Though only six lines remain, this is the second longest monumental text in early Hebrew (now in the Istanbul Museum). It records the work done on this 1,749-foot-long water course:

> ... This is the account of the mining work. While [the men were swinging their] axes, each toward his fellow and while there was still three cubits [4-1/2 feet] to be cut through, the voice of one man calling to the other was heard showing that he was deviating to the right. When the tunnel was driven through, the excavators met man to man, axe against axe, and the water flowed for 1,200 cubits from the spring to the reservoir. The height of the rock above the heads of the excavators was 100 cubits.

In 701 B.C. Sennacherib, son of Sargon and now king of Assyria (705–681 B.C.), sent his army commander (*rab-šarēs*) and chief chamberlain (*rab-šaqeh*) to Jerusalem to parley. There is an interesting parallel to Hezekiah's officials' request that they speak Aramaic rather than the local Hebrew dialect, which would have been readily understood by the bystanders just as it was understood in a letter found at Nimrud. In it the Assyrian generals report their negotiations at Babylon with a Chaldean chief who requested similar action when he opposed entry, despite promises made to the Babylonians as was done to the men of Jerusalem.

Assyrian records provide a commentary on OT history. Sennacherib claims to have "shut up Hezekiah [*Hazaqiau*] the Jew in his royal city Jerusalem like a bird in a cage," but makes no claim to any capture. The Assyrian king himself moved to cut off any possible aid to Jerusalem by defeating the Egyptian army at Eltekeh and by laying siege to Lachish. The dating of these events to a single campaign in 701 B.C. has been questioned, primarily on the assumption that Tirharka (Taharqa) king of Ethiopia (2 Kings 19:9; Isa 37:9) would have been too young to lead an army. However, revised texts published in 1952 show him to have been about twenty-one in 701 and able to act on behalf of his brother Shebitku. His designation as "king," to which he became entitled as pharaoh of Egypt a few years later, would be in accordance with his responsibilities as ruler of Nubia. The theory that there must have been a conflation of the accounts of two expeditions, the second of which (c. 686) resulted in a defeat for the Assyrians, who omitted it from their records, can no longer be considered likely. The Old Testament account we now have is of one event written from a Judean standpoint.

Hezekiah's tribute of thirty talents of gold is given in both Assyrian and OT sources, but the Assyrians list eight hundred talents of silver as opposed to the three hundred of the Hebrew text. This divergence could be due to a textual corruption in Assyrian or Hebrew records based on a numerical notation, to deviation in the silver measures used, or to different items being included in the reckoning.

Although Sennacherib failed to take Jerusalem, he claims to have laid waste forty-six towns or villages in or surrounding Judah as he did to Lachish (Tell ed-Duweir). Excavations conducted there by J. Starkey for the Wellcome-Marston expedition in 1932–38 show that Level III was destroyed by fire. This is usually attributed to the siege of 701, though others (Albright, Wright, and Kenyon) think it marks the later destruction by the Babylonians in 597 B.C. The walls by the main gate at the southwest show signs of repairs where a breach had been made. In this area were found part of a ramp up which the siege-engines were pushed, and also slingstones, arrowheads, and the crest of a helmet, such as those worn by Assyrian lancers. Since all these are depicted on the bas-reliefs decorating the walls of Sennacherib's (northwest) palace at Nineveh, which bears the caption "Sennacherib, king of Assyria, sitting on his throne while spoil from the city of Lachish passed before him," there can be no question about Lachish having fallen to the Assyrians. A mass grave of more than 1,500 bodies on the northwest slope of the mound and associated with pig bones may show a later (Babylonian?) attempt to desecrate those who had died in the siege. Tell Beit Mirsim, another fortified town in Judah eight miles to the southeast of Lachish, shows partial destruction at this same time.

The Lachish reliefs are important also in that they provide the earliest portrayal of Jewish families being led as prisoners into exile. Barnett has argued that, according to the reliefs at Nineveh, some Jews were later shown to be serving in the Assyrian royal bodyguard, and others were shown maneuvering massive stone bull-colossi into position while work was going on at Sennacherib's new palace.

Sennacherib's death as recorded in 2 Kings 19:37 (and Isa 37:38) need not be interpreted as following immediately on his return from Palestine in 701 B.C. The OT says that the murderers were his two sons, Adrammelech (*Arad-maliki*[?]) and Sharezer (*Šar-uṣur*). The Babylonian Chronicle refers to only one son, though other texts tell of family intrigue and the death of an elder brother whom Esarhaddon succeeded as crown-prince, of opposition from his brothers, and of reference by King Ashurbanipal of Assyria thirty-two years later to Sennacherib's murder in a temple at Nineveh.

Esarhaddon of Assyria (681–669) continued to receive tribute from Judah and the Palestinian cities till Tirhakah incited Ba'al of Tyre to rebel. The Assyrian annals detail Esarhaddon's success in Egypt and list his vassals, who included "Manasseh (*Minse*), King of Judah" between Ba'al of Tyre and Qaush(Chemosh)-gabri of Edom. The kings of Moab, Gaza, Ashkelon, Ekron, Gebal, Arvad, Ashdod, and Beth-Ammon are also named by the Assyrian king. It may be that an undated Assyrian text listing payments belongs to this time. Ammon contributed two minas of gold, Moab one mina, and Judah, as probably Edom also, sent two minas of silver.

In May 672 B.C. Esarhaddon summoned Manasseh and his other vassals to Calah where he imposed on them new obligations to ensure continued loyalty to Assyria and to his successors. The texts containing the "covenant" requirements have survived and show the unchanged legal form known from the second millennium B.C. (see D.2 above). These required the vassals to take the god of Assyria as their god and threatened destruction of their cities and exiles for their citizens, should they break any of the terms.

The fiscal organization of Judah can be followed in the taxes paid in kind to the king (*lmlk*) in jars with stamped handles showing the collection centers—Hebron, Sokoh, Ziph, and *mmšt*—and bearing a symbol of a four-winged scarab-beetle for the reign of Hezekiah, a more stylized form with inscription in a later style for the reign of Manasseh, and a winged flying scroll for the period of Josiah and his successors (640–587 B.C.). About six hundred of these jar handles are known, a large number coming from Tell en-Nasbeh(Mizpah) and Lachish.

The aging Ashurbanipal handed over power or died in c. 627 B.C. and the outlying vassal states, including Babylonia and Judah, soon rebelled. Josiah proclaimed his independence from Assyrian domination by instigating religious and social reforms. In 609 he lost his life attacking Megiddo, once an Assyrian fortified outpost but by now taken over by the Egyptians (2 Kings 23:29). His hostility to the Egyptians, whom he sought to prevent from going to reinforce the beleaguered Assyrian government at Harran (to which it had withdrawn on the fall of Nineveh to the Medes in 612), can be seen in the destruction level (II) there. Megiddo ceased thereafter to be of major importance. The expedition by Necho II of Egypt to aid the Assyrians is recounted in the Babylonian Chronicle, which proves to be an objective, reliable, and unique historical source for many events between 626 and 595, and between 556 and 539 B.C.

8. *The Babylonian domination.* The same Chronicle describes the Babylonian attacks against towns in the Middle Euphrates area that culminated in the sack of Carchemish in the early summer of 605 B.C. Excavations there show that there was fierce fighting within the city, which was stubbornly defended until it was ravaged by fire. Objects found there show that the Egyptian garrison included Greek mercenaries. The Chronicle says that the survivors fled to Hamath, which was taken by the Babylonians. In the following years (604–603 B.C.), the Babylonians marched unopposed through Palestine ("Hatti-land"). Heavy tribute was brought to them by all the kings and with it many prisoners (including Daniel) were sent back to Babylon. Jehoiakim of Judah, who was to be a faithful vassal for three years, no doubt submitted during these incursions. The primary named target of these Babylonian campaigns was Ashkelon, which was sacked, and this led to the fast proclaimed by Jeremiah (36:1–9). An Aramaic letter from a Palestinian ruler to a king of Egypt appealing for help against the king of Babylon, whose army had advanced as far as Aphek (Ras el 'Ain, northeast of Joppa), may be connected with this event. Others, however, argue that the letter was a request for aid by Gaza or Ashdod when Nebuchadnezzar attacked in 589–587. This papyrus letter from Saqqara incidentally shows that Aramaic was the international diplomatic language of the day. According to the Chronicle, in 601 B.C. the Babylonians met the Egyptians in a fierce clash that resulted in such heavy casualties that the Babylonians spent the next year re-equipping. This would explain the swing in Jehoiakim's allegiance to Egypt despite Jeremiah's warnings (Jer 27:9–11). Pressure was gradually brought to bear on Judah and her neighbors, especially the Arabian tribes whose deities had been taken from them. The anxiety of the time is reflected by Jeremiah (49:28–33). The Babylonian Chronicle continues:

> In his [Nebuchadnezzar's] seventh year he called up his army and marched to Palestine. He besieged the city of Judah [i.e., Jerusalem], and on the second day of the month of Adar he siezed the city and captured its king. He appointed there a king of his own choice, received its heavy tribute, and sent [them] off to Babylon. (Cf. 2 Kings 24:10–17.)

This external evidence for the first capture of Jerusalem, now dated to 16 March, 597 B.C., is of primary importance. It provides a further firm point in both biblical and Babylonian chronology for this event and for the beginning of the exile. The captured king is the young Jehoiachin, who three months earlier had succeeded the dead Jehoiakim. He is named (*Yaukin*) in economic texts from Babylon dated between 595–570 B.C. These texts detail the issue of rations of oil and barley from the royal stores in Babylon. They also name eight other Judeans together with other royalty and craftsmen from Egypt, Philistia (Ashkelon), Phoenicia, Syria, Cilicia, Lydia, Elam, Media, and Persia who were held in Babylon. Some of these places are the specific objects of prophecy in

Jeremiah. Jehoiachin, though a hostage, is still called "King of Judah"; his estates there continued to be managed till 587 B.C. by "Eliakim, steward of Jehoiachin." Impressions of Eliakim's seal were found at Debir and Beth Shemesh.

The king chosen by Nebuchadnezzar as substitute for Jehoiachin was his uncle Mattaniah-Zedekiah (2 Kings 24:17). The heavy tribute included the sacred temple vessels that were dispatched to Babylon "at the turn of the year" (i.e., May/June, 2 Chron 36:10) with the captives.

The last days of Judah are also graphically illustrated by inscribed ostraca from Lachish. Most are written by Hoshaiah, a watchpost commander near Azekah north of Lachish, to Yaosh the commander of that city. They reflect the state of the country as it awaited the advance of the Babylonian army in 589–587, or soon thereafter to avenge Zedekiah's defection and reliance on Egypt. Communication between the forts was by fire signal (Jer 6:1; 34:7). The end of Judah as a state is marked by the large number of towns destroyed at this time and never occupied again: Lachish, Azekah (2 Kings 24:7), Tell Beit Mirsim, Beth Shemesh (II), and Ramat Rachel. Although there is little direct archaeological evidence for the destruction of Jerusalem in 587, there can be no question that the city was so severely raped that it would be difficult to trace the material remains of the humble existence endured by the survivors. Vincent attributes the mass grave in the Kidron valley to this destruction. The end of Tell Arad (Level VI) seems to indicate the deliberate policy of eliminating all the Iron Age III rectangular fortresses along the southern frontier, including Kadesh-Barnea.

9. *The period of the Exile.* If Tell en-Nasbeh in Palestine, rather than Nebi Samwil, is to be identified with Mizpah, then its continued occupation after the fall of Jerusalem shows it to have been the new capital of Judah and the center of the administration. Jar handles and containers for tax payments do still have "Judah" (*yhd*) or, more rarely, "Jerusalem" inscribed on them, and a few bear personal names. The majority are inscribed "Mizpah" (*mṣp*) and those with *mṣh*, if not also a reference to Mizpah, which continued an important center into the late Persian period, are to Mosah (cf. Josh 21:26), northwest of Jerusalem. Gezer also seems to have remained of importance until c. 100 B.C., and a Babylonian tablet has been found there. A clay sealing with the name of the pro-Babylonian governor—"Belonging to Gedaliah who is over the house"—was found at Lachish. This implies that at this time that city fell within Gedaliah's jurisdiction (Jer 34:7; 40:5). The presence at Mizpah of a bronze circlet inscribed "king of the world" in cuneiform, dated between 800 and 650 B.C., might imply that Nebuchadnezzar went there on his way to Egypt. Other objects from the site include a fine seal with the representation of a fighting cock inscribed "Belonging to Jaazaniah, the minister [servant] of the king"; perhaps he was one of the persons who murdered Gedaliah at Mizpah (2 Kings 25:23–25; Jer 40:8). In contrast, the towns of Megiddo, Bethel, and Samaria in the northern Assyrian province were left untouched, though probably occupied by garrisons since objects of the late Babylonian period have been found there.

In Babylonia itself in the time of the exile the splendor of Nebuchadnezzar's capital can be reconstructed from the results of the German excavations there. The northern citadel incorporated a museum, the southern was entered by the Ishtar Gate, one of eight named city gates. It incorporated a royal palace with a large throne room that might have been the one later used by Belshazzar, and the storeroom in which the ration tablets naming Jehoiachin were discovered. A sacred procession way ran from the Ishtar Gate for almost a mile to Esagila, the temple of Marduk, and its seven-staged temple tower (ziggurat). This road, named "The Enemy Shall Not Prevail," was forty feet wide and led to a bridge with seven piers that spanned the River Euphrates to give access to the new city. Texts list more than fifty temples in this city of which Nebuchadnezzar was so proud (Dan 4:30). Fifteen of these had been built by the king himself and the city was conspicuous for its many statues (Jer 50:38). There were 180 open-air shrines dedicated to the goddess Ishtar alone. The massive defense walls and flood defenses were to prove useless. Cyrus captured the city without a battle. The Persian army gained entry by diverting the river upstream at Opis and then marching down the dried-up riverbed under the walls. The Babylonian Chronicle records this strategy and the fall of Babylon, which occurred in October 539 B.C. It tells also of the disappearance of the Babylonian king Nabonidus, whose son Belshazzar, named in a Babylonian royal inscription as coregent, had acted as king for ten years while his father was absent in Tema' in central Arabia at a Babylonian-Jewish colony centered in Yathrib (Medina). This might in some way reflect the exile of the mad Nabonidus, who, like Nebuchadnezzar, was called Labynetus by Herodotus (I.188). Nabonidus, according to his Harran inscription, had returned to Babylon c. 546 on receiving assurances from the king of Egypt and the "king of the Medes," who at this time must have been Cyrus. This writer has suggested that since there is no record in any Babylonian historical text of any king ruling between Nabonidus/Belshazzar and Cyrus, or Cyrus and Cambyses, "Darius the Mede" may be a throne-name for Cyrus. Thus Daniel 6:28 could be translated "Daniel prospered in the reign of Darius even [i.e.,] the reign of Cyrus the Persian"[13] Whitcomb, however, rejects this, identifying Darius with the little-known Gubaru/Gobryas, a provincial governor of Babylon and Transpotamia.[14]

Cyrus in a Persian Verse Account shows his hostility to the defeated Nabonidus. In another document he records his proclamation by which he sent back from Babylon to their respective temples all the gods that had been brought to Babylon. This edict included the Jews who, having no gods to take back, were given a contribution toward the rebuilding of their temple (cf. Ezra 1:2–4). Thus, the arrival of the Persians in Babylon seems to have been peaceful and resulted in few innovations.

The return of the Jews to Judah can be seen in the sparse traces of resettlement found at Gezer, Lachish, Bethel, Beth-zur (north of Hebron), and Tell el-Far'ah. It was a slow process, and the country does not seem to have recovered until the third century B.C. The Phoenicians—to judge by settlements at Athlit, Dor, the site of the later Caesarea, and near Jaffa—seized the chance to expand their territory. Elsewhere (e.g., Tel Abu Hawam) the houses show a clear continuation in style from the early Iron Age.

Judah now formed part of the fifth satrapy of the Persian (Achaemenid) empire called "Beyond the River." This meant that it was dominated by the subgovernor at Samaria, who worked under the direction of Damascus. Sanballat (Sin-uballit) is named in papyri from Elephantine (Yeb), which include letters to his sons as well as to Johanan the high-priest of the Jerusalem temple (Neh 12:22, 23). The same group of exiles appealed in 407 B.C. to Bagoas, governor of Arabia, to whom is attributed the fine villa at Lachish with its distinctive columned and vaulted rooms (perhaps a Persian or Babylonian innovation). This building was protected by walls rebuilt by the fifth century on top of those destroyed by Nebuchadnezzar. Geshem is named in an inscription from Hegra in Arabia and on a silver vessel from Tell el Maskuteh (Succoth) in Egypt inscribed in Aramaic "Qainu, son of Geshem, King of Kedar." The third adversary named by Nehemiah (6:1),

---

13D.J. Wiseman, *Notes on Some Problems of the Book of Daniel* (London: Inter-Varsity Press, 1965).
14J.C. Whitcomb, *Darius the Mede* (Grand Rapids: Eerdmans, 1959).

Tobiah of Ammon, the founder of the ruling dynasty in Jordan, may well be the ancestor of the Ammonite Tobiah who sent a letter to Zeno, an official of Ptolemy Philadelphus (285–246 B.C.) and of the Tobiah whose name is inscribed in a rock-hewn tomb at 'Araq el-Emir in Jordan built by the last governor in the family c. 200–175 B.C.

Texts from the reign of Darius I dated between 21 March, 520, and 31 October, 519 B.C., show that Ushtannu (the Hystanes of Herodotus VII,177) was "Governor of Babylon and Beyond the River [*Eber nāri*]" and subordinate to him as the local governor of "Beyond the River" was one Tattanu (Tattenai of Ezra 5:3, 6; 6:6, 13) according to his own texts, one of them dating to 5 June, 502 B.C.[15]

The economy of the period of the exile can be judged from the many economic and administrative texts from Babylonia for which the cuneiform script was still used. Many Hebrew (and Aramaic) personal names are found in transactions by the Egibi family and by the house of Murashu and sons, whose records span several decades and show a vigorous community. Judah was allowed to strike its own coinage, inscribed *Yhd* (once mistakenly read as *Yh* = Yahweh).

10. *The Hellenistic age.* (331–63 B.C.). When Alexander took over the Persian empire in 333. Hellenization grew apace. From his death (323) to c. 198, Palestine was controlled by the Ptolemies (Lagides) of Egypt and lay on their frontier with the Seleucids in Syria. Trade with Greece had begun earlier and its development had been encouraged by mercenaries who followed earlier intruders like Necho and Nebuchadnezzar and by the local autonomy allowed under Persian rule. The progress can be seen in the imports of Greek Ionian and Attic black-figured and other wares from the sixth century onwards at coastal ports, including the Greek fort at Ashdod and at Hazor(I) and by the introduction of coinage when imitations of Attic coins were minted in the late fifth century. Similar numismatic influences from Arabia are found in the south.

Lachish was deserted and the newly planned Greek city of Marisa shows a combination of Greek, Phoenician, and Edomite influences, painted tombs, and pottery. Ptolemy II rebuilt Amman (Philadelphia) and Jarash (Antioch), but Nabatean culture thrived alongside these Hellenistic strongholds.

The Seleucid period has left the mausoleum of the Tobiad family at 'Araq el-Emir in early Hellenistic style with Corinthian capitals. At Samaria the old Israelite walls were strengthened by a series of Hellenistic round towers (c. 323–1). This was superseded by a fortress with four-meter-thick walls as part of the defenses in the war between the Seleucids and the Maccabees. The presence of a Greek garrison is inferred from the 2,000 or more Rhodian wine-jar handles found here and by ostraca at Arad. Shechem, rebuilt between 330–100 B.C., also appears to have been occupied by a Greek garrison, perhaps there to control a resurgent Samaritan religious community. The town was destroyed by John Hyrcanus in 107 B.C., by which time coins on the site cease. Beth-zur, on the boundary with Idumea, had an extensive Hellenistic-type citadel-fortress, rebuilt by Judas Maccabeus on the site used by the Macedonian general Bacchides for his fortifications (c. 161 B.C., 1 Macc 9:52). Coins date the periods of occupation to the time of Antiochus IV (Epiphanes, 175–164 B.C.) and his son Antiochus Eupator (164–162). The attempt of Antiochus Epiphanes to suppress Judaism and its temple led to the Maccabean revolt. Houses, shops, and water cisterns show a lively economy; and the jar handles inscribed with the name of the potter, magistrate, or tax collector over a number

---

[15] A. F. Rainey, "The Satrapy 'Beyond the River,'" in *Australian Journal of Biblical Archaeology* 1 (1969):53.

of years attest the presence of a Greek garrison and the maintenance of order. Gezer was fortified by the Maccabees c. 140, and outside the town an inscription in the rocks marks the boundary of a sabbath day's walk. Gezer, like Beth Zur and Marisa, was abandoned c. 100 B.C., probably when Alexander Janneus removed the garrison when Palestine was under his firm and peaceful rule. At this time Qumrān was occupied (see DEAD SEA SCROLLS) and the pre-Herodian buildings and cisterns at Masada were also his work. By 37 B.C. the Herodian dynasty replaced the Maccabees, and under Herod the Great Hellenistic architecture and culture flourished.

III. Bibliography

Books

Albright, W.F. *The Archaeology of Palestine*. Harmondsworth: Penguin Books, 1960.

Anati, E. *Palestine Before the Hebrews*. London: Jonathan Cape, 1963.

Burrows, M. *What Mean These Stones?* London: Thames and Hudson, 1957.

Franken, H.J. and Franken-Battershill, C.A. *A Primer of Old Testament Archaeology*. Leiden: Brill, 1963.

Freedman, D.N. and Wright, G.E. *The Biblical Archaeologist Reader* 1. Garden City, New York: Doubleday, 1969.

Harding, G.L. *The Antiquities of Jordan*. London: Lutterworth, 1959.

Kenyon, K.M. *Archaeology in the Holy Land*. London: Ernest Benn, 1960.

Kitchen, K.A. *Ancient Orient and Old Testament*. London: Tyndale, 1966.

Oppenheim, A.L. *Ancient Mesopotamia*. Chicago: University of Chicago Press, 1964.

Sanders, J.A. *Near Eastern Archaeology in the Twentieth Century*. Garden City, New York: Doubleday, 1970.

Thomas, D.W., ed. *Archaeology and Old Testament Study*. London: Oxford University Press, 1967.

Unger, M.F. *Archaeology and the Old Testament*. Grand Rapids: Zondervan, 1962.

Wiseman, D.J. *Chronicles of Chaldaean Kings (626–556 B.C.) in the British Museum*. London: British Museum, 1956.

_____, ed. *Peoples of Old Testament Times*. Oxford: Clarendon, 1973.

Wright, G.E. "The Archaeology of Palestine." In *The Bible and the Ancient Near East*, edited by G.E. Wright. London: Routledge and Kegan Paul, 1961.

_____. *Biblical Archaeology*. Philadelphia: Westminster, 1962.

Yamauchi, E. *The Stones and the Scriptures*. London: Inter-Varsity, 1973; Philadelphia and New York: Lippincott, 1972.

Periodicals

The Biblical Archaeologist (American School for Oriental Research).

Israel Exploration Journal (Jerusalem).

Levant (London: British School of Archaeology in Jerusalem).

Palestine Exploration Quarterly (London: Palestine Exploration Fund).

THE RELATION OF
THE OLD TESTAMENT
TO ANCIENT CULTURES

G. Herbert Livingston

G. Herbert Livingston

A.B., Wessington Springs College; A.B., Kletzing College; B.D., Asbury Theological Seminary; Ph.D., Drew Theological Seminary

Professor of Old Testament, Asbury Theological Seminary

THE RELATION OF THE OLD TESTAMENT TO ANCIENT CULTURES

I. Introduction
II. The Early Bronze Age (3200–2200 B.C.)

   A. The Sumerians
   B. The Akkadians
   C. The Eblaites
   D. The Egyptians

III. The Middle Bronze Age (2200–1550 B.C.)

   A. The Babylonians
   B. The Amorites
   C. The Canaanites
   D. The Egyptians

IV. The Late Bronze Age (1500–1200 B.C.)

   A. The Egyptians
   B. The Hittites
   C. The Canaanites

V. The Iron Age I (1200–900 B.C.)

   A. The Canaanites
   B. The Philistines
   C. The Egyptians
   D. The Syrians
   E. The Arabians

VI. The Iron Age II (900–600 B.C.)

   A. The Egyptians
   B. The Syrians
   C. The Moabites
   D. The Phoenicians

I. Introduction

As recently as 150 years ago, Bible students had very limited information about cultural conditions in the ancient Near East. The men and women of the OT were as unreal as silhouettes acting out their lives against a vacant backdrop.

The flood of data about ancient cultures that was produced during the nineteenth and twentieth centuries has changed the silhouettes into people living in sophisticated nations. The backgrounds of Bible times have come more sharply into focus.

To cover adequately all aspects of cultures in the ancient Near East is impracticable. Technically, the term *culture* refers to a composite of human expressions and inventions. Since this article is brief, it will deal with only a limited number of features of ancient cultures—viz., those aspects reflected in the culture of the Hebrew people. It will focus on the major components of the cultures that existed from 3000 to 400 B.C. in the Mesopotamian valley, in the Levant, in the Nile Valley, and in a few neighboring areas. The major components touched upon will be literature (involving both language and script), religious ideas and practices, and the arts and crafts.

This discussion will combine the geographical locale of what Breasted happily called the "Fertile Cresent" (i.e., from the tip of the Persian Gulf through the Mesopotamian Valley, the Levant, and into the Nile Valley) with a chronological set of divisions. These divisions will be presented according to archaeological nomenclature. Culture necessarily implies people, so the major peoples of these areas—the Sumerian, Eblaite, Akkadian, Babylonian, Egyptian, Canaanite, Hittite, Assyrian, Phoenician, Syrian, Arabian, and Persian—will be subjects of analysis and comparison with the dominant people of the OT, the Hebrews.

II. The Early Bronze Age (3200–2200 B.C.)

A. *The Sumerians*

In general, the geography of Genesis 1–11 is the Mesopotamian valley with its two major rivers, the Euphrates and the Tigris. To this land and its people, we turn first.

About 3500 B.C., the coming of the Sumerians was a major event. The Sumerians are not mentioned in the OT, except obliquely as "the land of Shinar" (Gen 11:2). Nevertheless, they established a civilization that became the foundation and model for a series of empires. Abraham came from Ur, the major city of the Third Dynasty toward the end of which period there was a brief revival of Sumerian power.

The Sumerians were a highly intelligent and inventive people, who may have come from the region of the Caspian Sea. Building upon the family as their basic social unit, they perfected the city-state as a governmental model. Outside of Egypt, this model was followed by Semitic peoples through several millennia, even when successive empires were in full power.

One of the Sumerians' most valuable contributions to civilization was the art of writing, which developed from pictograph to a sophisticated cuneiform script basically syllabic in character. This system could be adapted to any language and was employed by a variety of nations till after the time of Christ. With it, the Sumerians produced an extensive literature during this era and into the Middle Bronze Age. They valued writing so highly that they recorded an array of information on clay tablets that were first identified as Sumerian by Jules Oppert in A.D. 1869.

During the past century, archaeologists have excavated tens of thousands of Sumerian tablets. Linguists have struggled to translate and publish their contents. Gradually it has become apparent that the Sumerian tablets contain various literary forms—prose, poetry, law, and letters—that were to become the models for centuries of Semitic literature.[1] The biblical writers were influenced by these Semitic conquerors and their imitators.

The high regard of the Sumerians for writing as an effective means of communication and of preserving ideas for future generations, inevitably filtered through to the Hebrews. Those who insist on a lengthy period of oral transmission of biblical literature before it was written down overlook this heritage that during many centuries spread so pervasively from Sumer through many peoples over a large territory. In this atmosphere the Hebrews grew up and traveled among and traded with many of the peoples so influenced.

Religious literature was early put in written form. The best tablets bearing this literature come from the end of the Sumerian culture—namely, in the eighteenth century B.C.—but fragments date back to the Early Bronze Age. The literature touches on the origin of the world and of man. In some respects, such references resemble the biblical creation stories and contain material similar to the biblical flood story. The polytheistic concepts and immorality of the gods prevalent in these stories, however, are vastly different from the monotheism of the biblical accounts.

The legal records of the Sumerians show that law and order established by courts and preserved on clay tablets were of primary concern to them. Deeds, contracts, covenants, invoices, and law codes were inscribed on clay and treasured, for the written word carried the authority of officials and made oaths binding. The Hebrew people show this same high regard for the written word—only more so, however, because they believed their Scriptures possessed the authority of God.

The Sumerians were the earliest known practitioners of arts and crafts that continued to be useful to many peoples, including the Hebrews. They were workers in metal and their skills are reflected in the Hebrew love of decorating their sanctuary with gold, silver, and bronze. Also the potter's wheel, the wheeled vehicle, the arch, the dome, and the vault were all legacies eventually passed on to and utilized by the Hebrews.

B. The Akkadians

In the middle of the Early Bronze Age, Semitic nomads from the desert infiltrated the rich, irrigated valley of the Sumerians and took control of the land about 2350 B.C. The

---

[1]Samuel Noah Kramer, *The Sumerians* (Chicago: University of Chicago Press, 1963), pp. 165–228.

Sumerians threw off the Semitic yoke from c.2100 to c.2000 B.C., then yielded again to the overwhelming power of a people known as Akkadians, whose main city was Agade (Akkad), and, at a later period, Babylon.

The Akkadians absorbed the Sumerian culture completely and added adaptations of their own. They reduced their language to written form—the cuneiform script of the Sumerians. In so doing, the Akkadians inherited the same high respect for the written word and produced inscribed clay tablets and stone slabs by the thousands.

Since the Akkadians were empire-minded, they moved up the Mesopotamian valley to the northeast tip of the Mediterranean Sea to unify the territory under a single power. As a result, they spread the fruits of the Sumerian culture far and wide. With the rise of the Third Dynasty of Ur, the Akkadians suffered a setback but soon regained supremacy. It was within the context of a network of trade routes dominated by the power of the Akkadians that the patriarchs were to travel to Canaan.

The Akkadians took the literature of the Sumerians and expanded it imaginatively. The scattered thoughts on creation found in various Sumerian tablets became the "Epic of Creation," and the earlier brief flood story became the complex "Epic of Gilgamesh." Both of these epics have scattered items that parallel words, phrases, and some ideas of the biblical accounts. Yet the stories of the Bible have structural features much different from these epics and marked by a thoroughgoing monotheism.[2]

Abraham and his ancestors were Semites, like the Akkadians. But Abraham grew up in Ur, an important city of the surviving Sumerian culture. He probably knew of, and possessed, some of the skills of both these cultures. Thus he doubtless knew their literature and shared their respect for the written word. His language would have been Akkadian, or a dialect of it.

C. The Eblaites

Between 1974 and 1976, news of a spectacular discovery filtered out from an excavation at Tell Mardikh, Syria. One of the excavators, Giovanni Pettinato, states that more than 16,000 clay tablets have been discovered.[3] They date from 2400 to 2250 B.C. and come from ruins of a community known in ancient times as Ebla. (See the article ARCHAEOLOGY AND THE OLD TESTAMENT, pp. 307–335.)

No one had suspected that Ebla was the capital of a Semitic empire, basically commercial, that stretched from the mountains east of the Mesopotamian valley to the center of the area now called Turkey, and on south to the Sinai Peninsula.

About 80 percent of the tablets were written in the Sumerian language with the cuneiform script. The remainder were written in a Western Semitic dialect, also in cuneiform, and much like Canaanite and Hebrew.

Literature of many kinds—including trade invoices, deeds, contracts, treaties, letters, poems, and laws—is in these archives. There are also myths of the creation and flood, as well as liturgies and incantations.

The tablets especially interesting to scholars are those written in a "proto-Canaanite" dialect. These are the earliest specimens of this dialect and come from the area to which Abraham and his family migrated a century or so later. A number of names known in the OT—e.g., Eber, Abram, Ishmael, Israel, Micah, and David—appear on these tablets.

---

[2]George Herbert Livingston, *The Pentateuch in Its Cultural Environment* (Grand Rapids: Baker, 1974), pp. 241–243.

[3]Giovanni Pettinato, "The Royal Archives of Tell-Mardikh-Ebla," *Biblical Archeologist* 39 (1976): 44–52.

There are also names of cities, such as Salim, Sodom, Gomorrah, Hazor, Lachish, Megiddo, Gaza, and Joppa.

The scribes of Ebla were trained by Sumerian scribes during the time of the Akkadian dominance of those people by Sargon I and his successors. So in the Ebla finds we may have literature that for the first time will demonstrate how the Mesopotamian culture influenced Semitic people, including the Hebrews, who settled in the Levant. (See ARCHAEOLOGY AND THE OLD TESTAMENT, pp. 309-335.)

D. *The Egyptians*

The Sumerians and the Akkadians had trade contacts with the Egyptians during the Early Bronze Age; but the culture of the Nile Valley did not directly touch the Hebrews till the patriarchs migrated to Canaan. When Abraham and his descendants did make contacts with Egypt, they found it a sophisticated nation.

The Egyptians became a united people about 3200 B.C. and proceeded to build up the power of the Old Kingdom, in what is sometimes known as the "Pyramid Age" (c.2650-2200 B.C.). A gifted people, they early invented a calendar, a system of geometry, and a kind of writing called hieroglyphics. They became excellent craftsmen in stone, ivory, wood, and decorated earthenware. They developed a paper called papyrus, which, though not durable like clay tablets, was so light that it was easily and cheaply distributed and became a favored material for inscriptions and letters.

The all-powerful Pharaoh headed a priestly caste that developed a theological outlook destined to undergird Egyptian ideas and practices for centuries. In spite of a pervasive polytheism, there was a unifying concept of deity identified with the sun—variously called Atum, Ra, Amon, Horus, Aten, et al.—and a profound belief in life after death. This view led to the construction of huge pyramids and the mummification of the dead. Splendid temples, excellent statuary, expertly carved scenes from daily life, and brilliantly colored paintings vividly expressed creative ideas.

III. The Middle Bronze Age (2200–1550 B.C.)

All through the ancient Near East, the early centuries of this era were times of rebuilding. The powerful governments of the previous period had been reduced to chaos. There were migrations in and out of the Mesopotamian valley. The Sumerian culture was sinking into oblivion and a revived Semitic culture was struggling for identity. Abraham and his descendants were on the move from the lower valley to Haran and then on to Canaan.

A. *The Babylonians*

The rising Semitic culture was marked by literary activity, mostly of a preservative and adaptive nature. The older Sumerian mythology was cataloged and copied. Since the Semites borrowed heavily from the Sumerians, their creativity consisted mostly in embellishing the older myths. The results were the "Epic of Creation," the "Epic of Adapa," and the "Epic of Gilgamesh." Though fairly complete copies of these stories date from the seventh century B.C., enough fragments come from the Middle Bronze Age to show this period to be the time of their origin. The exact relationship of these myths to the creation and flood stories of Genesis has been hotly debated for a century, and the debate persists. Conservative scholars generally hold that the accounts in Genesis were not borrowed from the Babylonians, who became powerful under Hammurabi's leadership in the eighteenth century B.C. but that the Hebrews preserved the accounts from a different source.[4]

An extensive collection of clay tablets comes from the reign of Hammurabi, the sixth king of the Old Babylonian Empire. The contents of these tablets are mostly administrative and commercial, but they throw a great deal of light on the world from which Abraham migrated.

The most significant legal production is known as the Code of Hammurabi—a collection of 282 case laws dealing with civil, agricultural, and domestic matters. These laws are engraved on an eight-foot-high stone pillar. They have their roots in older Sumerian laws but contain many of Hammurabi's own legal decisions. A number of them resemble some of the civil laws of the Pentateuch.

Earlier in our own century, some scholars thought that the Amraphel mentioned in Genesis 14:1ff. was Hammurabi, but more recently the reading *Amud-pi-el* has been favored.[5] He was from Mari in southeast Syria.

B. *The Amorites*

On an important junction of caravan routes on the upper Euphrates River, a city called Mari had been powerful since 3000 B.C. Between 1933 and 1960 these ruins yielded over 20,000 clay tablets to the digger's spade. Most of the tablets were inscribed with a northwest Semitic language in cuneiform script. About one-fourth of the tablets are royal letters, the rest are contracts and treaties. Some are commercial records. The greater part of these tablets date from the nineteenth and the eighteenth centuries B.C. Hence they reflect the cultural environment of the patriarchs, who lived for a time just north of Mari.

Personal names occur in the Mari letters. These are similar to patriarchal names; e.g., Abraham, Jacob, Haran, Nahor, Terah, Serug (see Gen 11). A group of seminomads called Habiru (Hebrews?) was well-known, and a tribe of Ben-Yamini (Benjaminites?) was feared. Several names like *Yawi-el* and *Yawi-addu* suggest that the divine name Yahweh was known. Many biblical scholars have resisted this idea, but the presence of the same or similar form of Yahweh names in the recently discovered Ebla tablets (see above) makes the occurrence of Yahweh names at Mari quite likely.

Several patriarchal family customs are illustrated or referred to in the Mari tablets. Examples are the sister-wife marriage, the substitute wife to ensure a male heir, the sale of birthrights, and the adoption of "sons" by childless couples.[6]

The covenants, both religious and secular, made by the patriarchs are paralleled by a few contracts in the Mari letters. Tablets from another site, Nuzu, illustrate these same customs.

C. *The Canaanites*

Trade routes through Canaan carried heavy traffic of large donkey caravans. The patriarchs followed these routes in their travels and perhaps engaged in some of the trading themselves. Most of the significant religious experiences of the patriarchs oc-

---

[4]See, e.g., P. J. Wiseman, *New Discoveries in Babylonia About Genesis*, 6th ed. (London: Marshall, Morgan, and Scott, 1953).

[5]K. A. Kitchen, *Ancient Orient and Old Testament* (Chicago: Inter-Varsity Press, 1966), p. 44.

[6]R. K. Harrison, *Old Testament Times* (Grand Rapids: Eerdmans, 1970), pp. 50–67.

curred in Canaan; and according to scriptural accounts issued in a radical rejection of the polytheism of their Babylonian heritage and of their new homeland (cf. Gen 35:4; Josh 24:2, 14–20).

Excavated caves from this period neatly explain the recurring phrase "gathered to his people" (Gen 25:8; 35:29; 49:33), because these caves served generations of a family group who were buried together over a period of time. Such a custom was not limited to Canaan, for half a millennium earlier at Ur Sumerian families were burying their dead in common vaults, or in the basements of their homes.

Circumcision was practiced widely by Semites in the Levant and by the Egyptians. Beginning with the event recorded in Genesis 17:10–26, this rite had a special covenant meaning for the Hebrews.

Did the patriarchs become acquainted with the Canaanite's most significant invention, the skill of alphabetic writing? This question cannot yet be answered with confidence. Nevertheless, enough alphabetic inscriptions have been found in the Sinai Peninsula and in Canaan to demonstrate that the Canaanites were the inventors of this remarkable system of writing and preserved it as their unique method of communication. If the patriarchs themselves did not learn the alphabet, at least their descendants did so with great profit.

D. The Egyptians

During the Middle Bronze Age the Egyptians were mistrusted by the patriarchs, perhaps because of the unpleasantness of Abraham's visit to that land; yet Jacob and his family settled there during a time of famine.

During the patriarchal era, the Egyptians had recovered from several centuries of political weakness. The Twelfth Dynasty of their Pharaohs was vigorous and powerful, with a military and commercial outreach that extended into Canaan and along the southern coastline of the Mediterranean Sea.

When Joseph and Jacob died, both were embalmed after the manner of the Egyptians, but the Hebrew families were segregated in an area of the Nile delta, perhaps to reduce the possibility of intermarriage with Egyptians. The relationship of the Hebrews to the Egyptian culture was strained, for the Egyptians had contempt for the Hebrews' shepherd ways, and the Hebrews as a whole shunned Egyptian polytheism.

IV. The Late Bronze Age (1550–1200 B.C.)

A. The Egyptians

The descendants of Jacob lived in Egypt for several hundred years, and one would expect from this a certain measure of cultural interchange. The Pentateuch implies that the relationship was both negative and positive.

After the expulsion of the Hyksos, the Egyptians placed tight controls on the Semites and then enslaved them. The religious heritage of the Israelites was drastically different from the Egyptian polytheism, so the Israelites completely rejected the religious doctrines of Egypt. The Egyptians' forcing the Hebrews into hard labor, their attempt to destroy the male infants of the Hebrews, and their refusal to let them go into the desert created bitter antagonisms.

On the other hand, in working for the Egyptians, the Israelites learned many skills.

Moses himself was trained in the royal schools. In such an environment, he doubtless acquired knowledge of several kinds of writing, acquaintance with an extensive literature, leadership skills in government and warfare, and a knowledge of priestly functions. Moses' name was basically Egyptian (some scholars disagree), as were the names of Miriam, Phinehas, possibly Aaron, and others of the Levites.

The confrontation between the Israelites and the Egyptians became critical when Moses asked Pharaoh for permission for Israel to leave the land. The ten plagues were manifestations of a series of conflicts between the God of Israel and the deities of Egypt, of which the Pharaoh was chief. The victory came during the tenth plague when the first-born of Egypt were destroyed. Israel was told to go and was then pursued, but Israel's God, Yahweh, delivered his people in the never-to-be forgotten passage through the Red Sea (the Sea of Reeds).

Some scholars have held that Israel's monotheistic beliefs had their roots in the tendency of the Egyptians to concentrate the attributes of many deities into a mighty sun-god. However, the sophisticated concepts of Egypt were, rather, a naturalistic monism, whereas Israel was dedicated to a purely spiritual sovereign creator not identified with any aspect of nature or with any essence of nature. In this sense, Israel challenged the validity of the religion of Egypt and won, because Israel believed in God who acts mightily in human affairs and in natural events.

In other areas of culture, however, Egyptologists see a positive interaction between Egypt and Israel. Not only were some Levite names Egyptian in origin, but also many Semitic words entered the Egyptian language. The Israelites learned agricultural skills and in the desert yearned for the vegetables of Egypt (Num 11:5). They learned techniques for producing cloth, especially fine linen, and for tanning leather. Egyptian technology included excellent carpentry and metal working. All these skills were needed by the Israelites to build the tabernacle. Though God gave the floor plan of the tabernacle to Moses (Exod 26:30), it was similar to that of the Egyptian temples, which possessed an inner sanctuary having no source of light, a larger room, and an outer court.[7] These features were common to some Semitic temples also.

The Egyptian priests were anointed and had to be physically without defect and ceremonially clean. The office was passed from father to son.

Poetry with parallelism and vocal music with harps, horns, drums, and cymbals were common in Egypt and also among Semitic tribes. Both Egyptians and some Semitic tribes had portable shrines, similar to the ark of Israel, carried by poles on the shoulders of priests.

The Egyptians had no prohibitions comparable to the first and second commandments, nor did they have a Sabbath. Their literature, however, contained observations and exhortations about moral behavior similar to some of the Ten Commandments but not couched as strong prohibitions.

In brief, the relationship between Egypt and Israel was religiously antagonistic but technologically positive.

B. The Hittites

Only in recent years have biblical scholars realized that the covenants of God with the patriarchs, with Israel at Sinai, and with David had a firm rootage in ancient Near East cultures.

---

[7]Pierre Montet, *Egypt and the Bible* (Philadelphia: Fortress, 1968), pp. 16–34.

The old Sumerian "Vulture Stele" was a treaty sealed by an oath, and so were several treaties from the third millennium B.C. Excavators of the recently found Ebla tablets report treaties in their list of contents. The Mari tablets of the eighteenth century B.C. have treaties that possess covenant formats and terminology. One tablet comes from Alalakh in northern Syria, with a treaty written on it.

Perhaps the most extensive collection of treaties comes from the Hittite Empire of the fifteenth to the thirteenth centuries B.C. That empire was centered in the land now called Turkey. There is evidence that the Hittites and the Egyptians had military conflicts and made treaties during the Late Bronze Age. Whether the Israelites and the Hittites had cultural interchanges is not known and is probably unlikely. Nevertheless, the Hittite treaties, in format and vocabulary, have many parallels to the biblical accounts of covenant-making.

Since George Mendenhall alerted American scholars to the bearing of the Hittite treaties on biblical studies, various articles and books have appeared on the subject.[8] Apparently, God led some of the OT writers to use a basically secular treaty form, blot out its polytheistic features, and fill it full of his message to the covenant people.

Several features are common to the nonbiblical and the biblical treaties or covenants. Both have these components: (1) identification of the covenant-maker, (2) a résumé of previous and present relationships, (3) stipulations or laws, (4) provisions for deposit of treaty in a sanctuary and public reading of the treaty, (5) a list of curses and blessings. The nonbiblical treaties usually had lists of deities, but this list was eliminated from biblical covenants. Thus the theology of the biblical covenants was distinctive and the laws morally and spiritually superior.

Israel's relationship with the Hittites was distant and indirect, though in their treaty forms they had a common heritage.

C. The Canaanites

When the Israelites moved out of Egypt into the desert, into the Transjordan, and then into Canaan proper, they had contacts with a variety of tribes, small kingdoms, and city states. Some of these people were their relatives—viz., the Edomites, Moabites, and Ammonites; but most of the others were known as Canaanites, a term that came to cover a broad category.

Militarily, Israel's relationship to these groups was antagonistic, resulting in battle after battle. Tribes and kingdoms tried to stop the movement of Israel to their Promised Land but were defeated. The Israelites themselves were motivated by the divine promise of the land and the command to drive out the Canaanites and reject their deities and immoral practices.

Since only fragments of Canaanite inscriptions come from the Late Bronze Age, we must turn to the archives of Ras Shamra (Ugarit) for Canaanite literature. Although these clay tablets were produced many miles north of the land of Canaan, they remain the only source for an understanding of Canaanite concepts and practices.

The Ugaritic tablets mention Canaanite deities such as Baal, Asherah, Anath, Dagon, and Resheph—deities whose names occur also in the OT. The name of the Canaanite high god *El* is equivalent to the Hebrew *Elohim*, though the theology and understanding of El's character and activity were vastly different in Israel.

8George Mendenhall, "Covenant Forms in Israelite Tradition," *The Biblical Archaeologist, Reader 3*. ed. Edward F. Campbell, et al. (Garden City, N.Y.: Doubleday, 1970), pp. 25–53.

One of the priestly groups in Ugarit was designated by a word much like the Hebrew word for priest, and the Hebrews knew and used the Canaanite high place (an elevation used as a temple or altar).

The closest relationship between the Canaanites of Ugarit and the Israelites lies in similarities of grammar, syntax, and poetic parallelism. This similarity has greatly helped scholars in understanding difficult OT words and phrases and in realizing that poems in the Pentateuch and that certain of the Psalms are truly ancient.

V. The Iron Age I (1200–900 B.C.)

A. The Canaanites

In the course of settling in Canaan, the Israelites failed to carry out strictly the divine command to drive the Canaanites out and totally reject their religious views and practices. Moreover, antagonism toward the Canaanites repeatedly softened to acceptance and assimilation of Canaanite ways.

Each time his people turned away from him, God punished them, then raised up judges to deliver them from the oppressive rule of their neighbors. So each time God brought his people back to devotion and obedience.

How much the Israelites absorbed from the Canaanite culture before the establishment of the kingdom has been a matter of dispute among scholars. Some have held that the Israelites were rather primitive nomads when they entered Canaan and hence borrowed a great deal from the Canaanites. This approach, however, clearly exaggerates the situation. The Israelites were well versed in the ancient Semitic cultures; though vacillating in their loyalty to Yahweh, they were not simply a cultural sponge.

Whatever the Hebrews learned from the Canaanites they changed and adapted to their own needs. Albright has demonstrated that a number of names for Canaanite deities were stripped of theological meaning and employed by the Hebrews in a purely secular sense.[9] Something like this happened to agricultural festivals that coincided in the spring and fall. The faithful in Israel refused to associate sex worship with these festivals. Instead, they based their festivals on the Exodus and permeated them with dedication and thanksgiving to God.

When Israel desired a king such as other nations had, the nearest examples were Canaanite kings. The revered Samuel resisted the idea, but God showed him how to adapt this form of government to divine requirements (1 Sam 8 and 12). Not only was an Israelite to rule according to God's laws, but he was also to ban idols from the land. Those who deviated from this limitation were rebuked and punished. Likewise the priests were enjoined not to use Canaanite magical practices or domineer over God's people. They were to be servants only.

With Samuel, a new religious group entered into Hebrew society. Some scholars have insisted that this group was made up of prophets who were mere copies of ecstatic prophets known among the Canaanites. This view has been modified, however, for we now know that prophets were functioning at Mari in the eighteenth century B.C., and prophets are mentioned in the Ebla tablets, which are dated 500 years earlier. True, the same word *prophet* (*nabi'*) designates this kind of religious person, both among

---

[9]W.F. Albright, *Yahweh and the Gods of Canaan* (Garden City, N.Y.: Doubleday, 1968), pp. 183–193.

the Hebrews and among her neighbors, but their character and functions were different.

During the reigns of David and Solomon, Israel established a close alliance with the Canaanites at Tyre. This gave Israel access to the wealth and expertise of the seagoing Canaanites, usually called Phoenicians from 1000 B.C. on. In return, the port of Tyre provided an outlet for the rich cargoes transported over the caravan routes controlled by the Hebrew kings.

Solomon endeavored to build a navy of his own manned by Phoenician sailors. He employed Phoenician miners and smelters to exploit the copper and iron deposits in the Negev. He also hired Phoenician architects and artisans to construct his palace and the temple. Some Egyptologists, such as Sugden, have maintained that the temple in Jerusalem had Egyptian traits, but more recent data seem to suggest architectural detail of Phoenician origin.

When the Hebrews acquired the art of alphabetic writing is not yet clear. It seems well established, however, that the Canaanites used this script for several centuries before the Conquest. The Hebrews could have adopted it during the Late Bronze Age. At any rate, the earliest Hebrew literary production extant, the Gezer Calendar, dates from the reign of Solomon. The OT refers to the United Kingdom period as a busy literary time in which government annals, psalms, and wisdom literature were produced, most likely in the Canaanite alphabetic script.

B. The Philistines

Though they seem to have had colonies in Canaan during the patriarchal period, the Philistines, in large numbers, entered the southeastern coastal area of the Mediterranean Sea about 1200 B.C. from the Aegean area. They learned how to use iron for weapons and tools and maintained a monopoly of the metal (1 Sam 13:19-22). They also fitted their chariots with iron. Thus they had a military advantage over Israel during the life of Samuel and the reign of Saul. For the most part, the Israelites and the Philistines fought each other, and the latter introduced the Israelites to a new form of warfare, the duel of champions (1 Sam 17). David found refuge among the Philistines for a time while he was fleeing from Saul. But when he became king, he subjected them to his power. Later on the Philistines joined David's military units (2 Sam 8:18). One legacy the Philistines left behind was the name of the country, Palestine.

C. The Egyptians

Recent studies in ancient Near Eastern customs indicate that the Egyptian matriarchal system of inheritance influenced the early Hebrew monarchy. The marriage situations that troubled the relationship between David and Saul could have been due to a matriarchate concept. The man who married a high-ranking woman of the royal family would be heir apparent to the throne (1 Sam 25:42; 2 Sam 3:3, 16).

When David became king over all Israel, he evidently organized his kingdom somewhat along Egyptian patterns. David had no prime minister, but he had military heads of the regular army, the militia, and the mercenaries. He also had a royal herald, a secretary, and two chief priests. David's organization of temple choirs and instrumental groups probably followed Egyptian practices, though Phoenician contributions to it were not small.

Solomon was more closely associated with Egyptian ways, for his queen was a daughter of the Pharaoh who gave Gezer to his daughter as a dowry. Solomon was famous for his wisdom and in his use of proverbs he might have been influenced by Egypt's ancient maxims. Here again the Phoenicians and Arabs would share in influencing literary form and style. In his latter years, Solomon experienced difficulty with Egypt, because that land became the place where the troublesome labor leader Jeroboam found refuge (1 Kings 11:40).

D. The Syrians

Known in biblical times as Aramaeans, the Syrians had slowly gained power northeast of Israel and by the time of David had made Damascus their chief city. They joined with the Ammonites in battle with David's army (2 Sam 10:8–14), but were soundly defeated. They were then subject to David and Solomon against whom they rebelled toward the end of Solomon's reign.

E. The Arabians

The Israelites had few contacts with the Arabians who lived to the south till the reign of Solomon. His fame as a wise man led the Queen of Sheba to visit Jerusalem. Trade routes were also developed and controlled, for the Arabs operated camel caravans over a large area, and Solomon was a competitor. Apparently a commercial agreement was reached, for added wealth flowed into Solomon's treasury (1 Kings 10:14, 15).

VI. The Iron Age II (900–600 B.C.)

A. The Egyptians

The Egyptians were intimately involved in protecting Jeroboam during the last years of Solomon's reign. They had doubtless supported Jeroboam when he revolted against Rehoboam at Shechem. The Libyans had just taken control of Egypt, and their leader, Shishak, sought to establish Egypt's ancient claims of suzerainty over Palestine. Perhaps the fact that Shishak's sister-in-law was Solomon's queen contributed to this imperialistic desire. Shishak's expedition probed throughout Palestine (about 920 B.C.) and devastated the land, stripping it of its wealth (2 Kings 14:25–28). Because of internal problems in Egypt, Shishak had to return home.

A few years later, another Egyptian, Zerah, penetrated Judah but was defeated at Mareshah (2 Chron 14:9ff.). Thus the period of the divided kingdom began with an unpleasant relationship with Egypt. Not until Hezekiah's reign were efforts made to gain Egypt's help against the Assyrians. But Egypt was then too weak to help. The prophet Isaiah had nothing but contempt for Egypt (Isa 19).

Toward the end of the seventh century B.C., Israel's relationship with Egypt again became hostile. King Josiah tried to stop the aggressive Pharaoh Necho II at Megiddo and was killed. Josiah's son, Jehoahaz, was taken prisoner and another son of Josiah was installed as king and named Jehoiakim. Four years later (605 B.C.), the Babylonians forced Jehoiakim to switch his loyalty to Babylon. Thereafter, Egypt was a source of trouble for Israel. Conspiracies to throw off the Babylonian yoke resulted in disaster, for Egypt was no match for Babylon and her promises to help Judah were worthless.

Like Isaiah, Jeremiah did not trust Egypt, yet his lot was to spend his latter years in Egypt, much against his will. Other refugees settled there and were influenced by her customs, as shown by the Elephantine letters.

B. *The Syrians*

The breakup of Israel into two kingdoms gave the Syrians of Damascus an opportunity to build up their own power by playing off Israel and Judah against each other. The Syrians supported one side and then the other, but always to their own advantage.

Other than militarily and commercially, contact between Syria and the Israelites was apparently limited. The Lord told Elijah to anoint Hazael king of Syria (1 Kings 19:15). Later Naaman, a top military general, came to Elisha to be healed (2 Kings 5). Another Syrian king, Benhadad, requested Elisha to cure him of his sickness (2 Kings 8:8).

The Syrians and Israelites engaged in a prolonged and bitter contest for control of the Transjordan trade routes, for the Syrians were hard-fisted merchants. Syria often controlled these routes. The immediate commercial and military contacts of the Syrians with the Israelites slowed to a halt as the Assyrians pressed down from the north during the eighth century B.C. Finally, in 732 B.C. Syria lost its independence to Assyria, and the former's cultural impact on Israel was delayed because of diversion through Assyria and Babylon.

C. *The Moabites*

According to Genesis 19:30–38, the Moabites were related to the Hebrews through Lot. They inhabited the highlands east of the Dead Sea, between the Wadi Arnon and the Wadi Zered.

During Israel's conquest of Canaan, their relations with Moab were tense. The Moabites forbade their passing through Moab and then Moabite women seduced Hebrew men in the Plains of Moab (Num 22:1; Josh 3:1). Yet, Ruth (Naomi's daughter-in-law) converted to Israel's faith and married Boaz. King David was a descendant of this union and found occasion to take his parents to Moab to protect them from Saul.

For many years Israel and Moab fought each other. One such occasion is described on the so-called Mesha Stone, which dates from the middle of the ninth century B.C. The inscription on this stone has a dialect close to Hebrew and, until the recent Ebla discovery, was one of the earliest nonbiblical witnesses to the divine name Yahweh.

D. *The Phoenicians*

From a commercial and political perspective, Israel's relationship with the kings of Tyre was both peaceful and profitable. This alliance issued in a marriage between King Ahab of North Israel and the Phoenician princess Jezebel. She brought Phoenician culture and religion with her and infused them into the life of Israel. The prophet Elijah opposed this foreign, polytheistic culture. After the contest with the prophets of Baal on Mt. Carmel, Jezebel angrily sought Elijah's life. The outcome was her ignominious death. Her daughter, Athaliah, however, married Jehoram of Judah and succeeded in usurping the throne at Jerusalem, introducing Phoenician Baal worship and persecuting the devotees of Yahweh. After five years, her rule was overthrown and Athaliah was killed outside the temple. From that time on, Phoenicia ceased to have a direct influence in Palestine.

E. *The Assyrians*

During the ninth century B.C., Assyria slowly grew into a military power in the upper Tigris Valley. In the middle of the eighth century, her armies became a serious threat to the small nations located on the eastern coastal lands of the Mediterranean Sea. Israel joined Syria to stop the Assyrians and desired Ahaz of Judah to do the same. Ahaz refused and carried out his own scheme, which involved a bribe to the Assyrian king, Tiglath-pileser, to cause trouble on the northern borders of Syria. Going beyond the agreement, Assyria destroyed Syria as a nation.

Isaiah had warned Ahaz against this course of action and the king was soon to learn the folly of his scheme. Not only was Syria humiliated, but within a decade Israel was torn apart. Israel soon realized the full force of the ruthless policies of the Assyrians. Thousands of Israelites were deported to the Mesopotamian valley. Defeated people from elsewhere were settled among the Israelites who remained. Over the centuries the mixture developed into the Samaritans, a complex mixture of Hebrew and pagan culture.

Ahaz was reduced to a vassal and his nation forced to recognize Assyrian gods along-side Yahweh. An Assyrian bronze altar replaced the ancient altar in the temple court. A disobedient follower of Yahweh, Ahaz did little to resist an influx of pagan practices among his people and even sacrificed his son in accordance with pagan beliefs (2 Kings 16:3).

Hezekiah, the successor of Ahaz, opposed the influence of Assyrian culture on Judah. This opposition was tantamount to rebellion, so Assyrian soldiers besieged Jerusalem, which was saved by divine intervention (2 Kings 18; Isa 36, 37). The next king, Manas-seh, cooperated with the Assyrians, and during his long reign Judah was flooded with polytheistic views and activities. Faithful followers of Yahweh were suppressed and the people were led to believe that the worship of Baal and the worship of Yahweh were essentially the same.

Ashurbanipal, whose reign over the Assyrians began in 672 B.C., is famous for his library, in which he gathered more than 6,000 texts, mostly copies, of ancient Babylonian literature. These texts included the "Epic of Creation" and the "Epic of Gilgamish." The latter relates a flood story much like that of the flood of Noah's day.

When Manasseh died, his son Amon became king, but he was killed in a revolt of Yahwist priests who put Josiah on the throne. In effect, this coup was a move against Assyria, but that nation's power was fast disappearing and was utterly destroyed in 612 B.C.

F. The Classical Prophets

The general culture of the ancient Near East was not without influence on the way Israel's prophets functioned as men of God. Since 1950 extensive research has clarified how the prophets were related to their cultural milieu.

The covenant, the lawsuit, and the messenger system were the threefold means by which the divine Word was understood and proclaimed. The dynamics of relationship between God, prophet, and the nation also functioned within these frames.[10]

For the general Semitic background of the covenant, see above, under Hittites (IV.B). Though the word *covenant* does not occur frequently in the writings of the classical prophets, the concept is certainly present in much that the prophets wrote. The identification of Yahweh is frequent, and charges of breaking the covenant are based on the Ten Commandments. The statement "You are my people, I am your God" appears in both the major and minor prophets. The acts of God in the Exodus are often referred to, and covenant words like *loving-kindness, mercy, justice,* and *righteousness* are common.

---

[10]George Herbert Livingston, "Structural Aspects in the Old Testament Prophets' Work and Message," *The Seminarian* 32 (1977): 15–30.

More obvious in the prophetic books is the second framework, which is judicial, and basically Canaanite in origin. Israel and Judah had broken the covenant, so they must be brought to trial. Lawsuits and court procedures go back to the third millennium B.C. and were well known among all Semitic peoples, as well as Egypt. For the prophets, the judge was God. The prosecutor was the prophet himself. The charges were publicly declared against the defendants, the rebellious Hebrews. Sentence was passed and carried out, though the possibility of rehabilitation was proffered too. The contents of most of the books of Hosea, Amos, and Micah are set up as a series of lawsuits. Many lawsuit formulations can be found in Isaiah and Jeremiah, as well as in other books. Pronouncements of judgment contain many curses, which are much like those common to Semitic literature.

Closely akin to both the covenant pact and the lawsuit was the messenger system, which was as ancient as any of the cultures of the ancient Near East. One of the high officials of any ancient royal court was the messenger who supervised the correspondence between the king and foreign leaders, satellite kings, or royal officials. Many clay tablets from all the periods so far discussed reveal how the messages were composed and delivered. Recent studies have shown that the formulations of these letters have many similarities with the work of Moses and the prophets of the kingdom period from Samuel onward. Such formulations are often found in the prophets, particularly in Isaiah, Jeremiah, and Ezekiel.

In the OT all three structures—covenant, lawsuit, and messenger communication—were used to convey to the Israelites the authority of God, the seriousness of their rebellion, and the great benefits of obeying their God. An understanding of the presence and function of these structures in the messages of the prophet helps the Bible student gain a better grasp of that message.

VII. The Iron Age III (600–300 B.C.)

A. The Babylonians

The Babylonians rose to new power as Assyria sank into oblivion. Led by the young, brilliant Nebuchadnezzar, this nation swept up the Mesopotamian valley and down the eastern coast of the Mediterranean Sea into Palestine. They captured Jehoiakim and forced him to repudiate Egypt and accept Babylonian suzerainty. Jehoiakim did not make the switch with grace nor with constant loyalty. Rebellions broke out, leading to disaster. Jerusalem was captured in 597 B.C. and was utterly destroyed eleven years later.

The Babylonians followed the Assyrian policy of sending into exile the skilled, the educated, and the leaders of a captured land. In three deportations the Judaeans were taken to the Mesopotamian valley as exiles. According to Daniel, he and others were taken to Babylon as early as 605 B.C.

Jeremiah sought to convince King Zedekiah and the people that they ought to submit to Babylon, but his plea was not heeded. It is significant that, beginning with Babylon's capture of Judah, Jeremiah made chronological notations in his writings according to the Babylonian system of reckoning time. In fact, during the Exile, the Jews in Babylon adopted Babylonian names for the months of the year.

Ezekiel, too, sought to convince the exiles to submit to the Babylonians and as a prophet managed to lead his people in the beginnings of a spiritual renewal with the cleansing of the people from idolatry. But the shock of being destroyed as a national entity shattered the Jewish spirit, as the Book of Lamentations shows. The initial relationship of the Israelites with Babylonian culture was bitter indeed.

Many of the people, taking Jeremiah with them, moved to Egypt, and many remained in Palestine, but the future of the Hebrews lay with the exiles in Babylon. The Babylonians gave the exiles homes and jobs, and some like Daniel rose to high positions in the government and commerce of the land. Some also became wealthy.

From the limited biblical material about the exile, it is evident that the Jews were grouped in small villages and could grow their own food. They had opportunity for their own community life—something that served as one of the foundations for rebuilding a people of God.

The exiles finally recognized their lot in Babylon as a divine punishment for past apostasy and turned to their sacred writings for guidance. The Mosaic laws took on new importance for them, and the Psalms, wisdom books, and writings of the prophets became shining lights in the darkness. Histories of the kingdom period were composed and valued.

The temple, the priesthood, and the sacrificial system no longer existed as the familiar, prescribed way to worship God. Although the exiles could have followed Babylonian ways of worship, most of them repudiated such ways and gradually devised a unique worship form of their own. Open-air meetings and home gatherings sprang up (Ezek 8:1; 14:1; 20:1). The sacred writings were read, prayer offered, and the Psalms sung. The Sabbath took on a new importance as the day of worship. Thus the synagogue began.

The new form of worship appears to have been little influenced by Babylonian culture. The exiles, however, did become acquainted with the Aramaic language, which they adopted in their daily speech. Slowly the older Phoenician script was replaced with the Aramaic "square letters" of the scrolls. Even the Scriptures were transliterated into this new script. Ezra 4:8–6:18; 7:12–26; Jeremiah 10:11; and Daniel 2:4–7:28 were written in Aramaic. This was the delayed gift of the Syrians.

B. *The Persians*

The Babylonian Empire declined rapidly and in 538 B.C. fell before the onslaughts of Cyrus, king of Persia. Almost overnight the Jewish exiles found themselves in a new cultural world. For one thing, the Persians repudiated the concept of keeping conquered people in exile and their lands in poverty. Decrees were published and funds provided for displaced people to be returned home and rebuild their temples (see 2 Chron 36:23; Ezra 1:2ff.). Some of the Jews had been so acclimated to life in the Mesopotamian valley that they refused to leave it, but others dared to make the long journey home.

Though the Persians did not invent the technique of producing metal coins as a medium of exchange, they saw its advantages and quickly adopted it. So did the Jews, and from the sixth century B.C. on, coins were common property among them.

In 538 B.C. Cyrus ordered that the Jerusalem temple be rebuilt (Ezra 6:3–5), and by his permission the exiles began to return (Ezra 1:2–4). The Samaritans (not to be confused with those of the NT) resisted the rebuilding of the temple. Nevertheless, under the prodding of Haggai and Zechariah, as well as with assistance from Persia, the task was completed. This assistance continued into the fifth century B.C., during which the Persians appointed Ezra and Nehemiah to reorganize the Jewish community and rebuild the walls of Jerusalem. The book of Esther narrates how a Hebrew girl became a Persian queen and providentially saved the lives of many of her people from massacre.

C. The Greeks

Greek influence in the ancient Near East can be traced back to a time before the conquests of Alexander the Great. Accumulated data, archaeological and literary, show that contacts of Greek culture with Semitic and Egyptian nations go back to the third millennium B.C., mostly through trade.

Yamauchi has detailed the evidence for interchange of loan words, script, and trade items throughout these earlier years.[11] Mycenaean pottery is a key to dating Late Bronze Age strata in Palestinian ruins. The Greek term for "ship" (*naus*) appears to be reflected in the Amarna letters written in Palestine and sent to Egypt. The Hebrew language has a similar word ('*oniyah*). In Genesis 10:2, Japheth is much like the Greek name Iapetos and Javan is much like the Greek name Iafones.

Gordon has noted comparisons between Homeric society and narrative styles and those found in Judges and 1 Samuel.[12] The Hebrews also had contacts with the Greeks through the Philistines.

The proto-Aeolic column and capital techniques of decorating royal buildings found in Palestine during the kingdom period seem to have reached Greece via the Phoenicians. The same is true of the alphabet.

In the eighth and seventh centuries B.C., Greeks set up trading posts on the eastern coast of the Mediterranean and diffused their wares throughout the Assyrian Empire. Coins came to Hebrew society from the Persians, but the origin of coinage is credited to Gyges of Lydia (687–52 B.C.), a Greek. Many Greeks became mercenary soldiers in Egyptian, Assyrian, and Babylonian armies. A fort in Palestine, *Meṣad Hashavyahu*, located just south of modern Tel Aviv, had Greeks as some of its garrison. Black-figured and red-figured Greek pottery sherds from the sixth century B.C. have been found in several places in Palestine.

Ionian craftsmen were employed by Nebuchadnezzar in the sixth century B.C. and later by the Persians. Hebrews in those lands had contacts with these craftsmen. It is not necessary to insist that the names of three Greek musical instruments in Daniel 3:5 could not have been known before Alexander the Great and his armies swept across the Near East in 336 B.C. From 450 B.C. on, the Jews in Palestine imitated Attic coins and produced coins that bear the name Yahud, a variant of Judah.

VIII. Summary

The build-up of data from the ancient Near East provides a needed cultural background for the OT. Comparing the material in the OT with the broader cultural scene, one notes that the Hebrew people were much like their neighbors in regard to housing, food, dress, trade, farming, crafts, implements, weapons, language, script, and many other skills.

Where theology and morals were important, the Hebrews were vastly different from their neighbors. It was not easy for the Hebrews to maintain their distinctiveness, for the pressures of idolatry were both alluring and powerful. Many of them succumbed to polytheism, but there remained a faithful core or remnant. And it was this core that God built up as his "beachhead" in the world.

---

[11]Edwin Yamauchi, *Greece and Babylon* (Grand Rapids: Baker, 1967), pp. 61–84.
[12]Cyrus H. Gordon, *The Ancient Near East* (New York: W.W. Norton, 1965), pp. 101–112.

God used selected aspects of ancient cultures as means of communicating with his people and knitting them together. When legal, societal, or religious structures were taken from the surrounding cultures, they were cleansed of their polytheistic elements— e.g., the treaty (covenant) was cleansed of its deity list, the place of worship had no idols, the priests and prophets were prohibited from engaging in sorcery, the sacrifices were divorced from magic, and the king was not to be identified with deity.

In place of the polytheistic world view and practices, God instilled in these structures the truth about himself as the one true God, the Sovereign, Judge, Savior, and Creator. To tokens and symbols he gave a teaching function, so that his people could learn from generation to generation what sin is and how redemption could transform them into a new people.

The history of how God acted on behalf of his people was highlighted in the festivals, poems, narratives, maxims, and the rationale of law and ritual. Prohibitions designed to mark out the boundary lines between behavior acceptable to God and behavior that displeased him were proclaimed clearly.

The totality of the adaptations and innovations recorded in the OT were meant to expose the follies and the bankruptcy of idolatry and to lay solid foundations for the building up of a chosen and redeemed people. The goal was to prepare a holy people for the coming of the Messiah.

IX. Bibliography

Bright, John. *The History of Israel.* Philadelphia: Westminster, 1972.

Clay, A.T. *The Empire of the Amorites.* New Haven: Yale University Press, 1959.

Davis, John J. *Moses and the Gods of Egypt.* Grand Rapids: Baker, 1971.

Gurney, O. *The Hittites.* Baltimore: Penguin Books, 1952.

Hillers, Delbert R. *Covenant: The History of a Biblical Idea.* Baltimore: Johns Hopkins, 1969.

Livingston, George Herbert. *The Pentateuch in Its Cultural Environment.* Grand Rapids: Baker, 1974.

McCarthy, D.J. *Old Testament Covenant.* Richmond: John Knox, 1972.

Meilsheim, D. *The World of Ancient Israel.* New York: Tudor Publishing Co., 1973.

Mellaart, James. *Earliest Civilizations of the Near East.* London: Thames and Hudson, 1965.

Parrot, Andre. *Abraham and His Times.* Philadelphia: Fortress, 1962.

Pfeiffer, Charles F. *Ras Shamra and the Bible.* Grand Rapids: Baker, 1962.

Saggs, H.W.F. *The Greatness That Was Babylon.* New York: New American Library, 1962.

Van Seters, J. *The Hyksos.* New Haven: Yale University Press, 1966.

Wiseman, D.J. *Peoples of Old Testament Times.* London: Clarendon, 1973.

THE CHRONOLOGY AND METROLOGY OF THE OLD TESTAMENT

Gleason L. Archer

Gleason L. Archer, Jr.

A.B., A.M., Ph.D., Harvard University; LL.B., Suffolk Law School; B.D., Princeton Theological Seminary

Professor of Old Testament and Semitics, Trinity Evangelical Divinity School

THE CHRONOLOGY OF THE
OLD TESTAMENT

I. Introduction

A. *The Sources of Old Testament Chronology*

1. *Biblical sources.* The primary source for knowledge of biblical events is the Bible itself. The frequent references to individual age spans and to the regnal years of kings make it possible to arrive at fairly reliable dates for Hebrew history. There are also a few "long dates," such as the interval between the Exodus and the building of the temple of Solomon (1 Kings 6:1) and the length of the Egyptian sojourn (Exod 12:40), that serve to establish major milestones in OT history.

2. *Archaeological sources.* Important data for establishing the time period of successive layers of occupation at ancient Near Eastern sites derive from the styles of pottery or other artifacts (e.g., cylinder seals and scarabs) discovered by archaeologists. But for the most part, these furnish only relative dating and show which occupational levels were contemporaneous with comparable strata in other tells (mounds in which ancient settlements are found). Absolute dating for the third millennium B.C. is difficult to come by, since at that period regnal years were not usually employed to indicate the time of recorded events. The earlier practice was to describe each year by its most notable event. Thus, in the sixth dynasty of Egypt the thirty-seventh (?) year of Pepi II is referred to as "the beginning of time 14 when the oxen and all the small cattle were numbered."[1] Not till the Middle Kingdom (c. 2000–1780) was it usual to date events by the years of

---

[1] A.H. Gardiner, *Egyptian Grammar,* 3rd ed. (New York: Oxford University Press, 1957), p. 204.

the reigns of kings currently on the throne. In Mesopotamia the Sumerians also described each year by its most notable event. Thus a receipt tablet from the forty-sixth year of King Shulgi of Ur (c. 1977 B.C.) indicates the date by "the year in which Kimash and Numurti were destroyed." The Babylonians followed the same practice as the Sumerians till the Cassite dynasty took over their government and began to date events by the year of the current king's reign. The Assyrians dated by the name of an official known as the *limmu,* who normally held office for only one year. A new king usually served as limmu in the second full year of his reign,[2] but ordinarily never did so again. Incomplete *limmu* lists go back prior to 1200 B.C., but a complete collection has been assembled from cuneiform records dating from 911 to 649 B.C. (This method of dating resembles the later Roman system of dating by the names of the consuls in office during each successive year. Many of the Greek city-states, such as Athens, also dated by the names of their archons.)

Astronomical notices in Egyptian or Mesopotamian records furnish additional evidence for absolute dating. In Egypt the civil year was reckoned as 365 days (even though the solar year was known to be six hours longer), and the Egyptians never resorted to the insertion of an extra day during leap year, as the Romans did. Over a period of 1,460 years this meant the loss of an entire year from the Egyptian civil calendar and the gradual shifting of the four seasons around the calendar, so that the three months of "winter" (Egyp. *prt*) would occur during the hot summer season, and the season of "inundation" (*ȝḫt*) would fall during the dry period. This period of 1,460 years became known as a Sothic cycle, because the Dog-star, Sothis, had by that time risen on each different day of the civil year, till it had come back to its original date of July 19 (according to the Julian calendar). References to the date of the rising of Sothis on the horizon occur from time to time in the Egyptian records. Thus it is possible to establish, e.g., that the ninth year of Amenhotep I was 1545 and the seventh year of Senwosret III was 1877.[3] Still another helpful feature in the Egyptian system was the occasional reference to the celebration of the so-called *ḥb-sd* ("jubilee") festival, which apparently was celebrated every thirty years, regardless of whose reign it fell in. Van der Meer computes the *ḥb-sd* of the thirtieth year of Rameses II as 1260 and therefore dates his accession year as 1289[4] —a conclusion differing from Albright's date of 1299 and Jack Finegan's date of 1304.[5] There may have been some variables, therefore, in the *ḥb-sd* system that Van der Meer is unaware of, but in general the thirty-year intervals serve as a fairly reliable guide.

3. *Geological Sources.* Geochronologists, using such evidence as the rate of decay of Uranium 238, estimate the age of the earth as several billion years. Paleontologists, reasoning on a uniformitarian basis, conclude that the fossil-bearing strata of the earth represent vast periods of time. But these questions are beyond the scope of this article. The writer, while committed to the profoundly beautiful and truthful cosmogony of

---

[2]P. Van der Meer, *The Chronology of Ancient Western Asia and Egypt,* 2nd ed. (Leiden: Brill, 1963), p. 3.

[3]Gardiner, *Egyptian Grammar,* p. 205. Parker in CAHB (p.12) states that on the basis of the Lahun Temple inscription the date of Senwosret's seventh year "can be pinpointed with great probability at 1872 B.C." Palermo Stone gives the names of predynastic kings of Lower Egypt and then lists all of the regnal years of Dynasty I through V. (J. Finegan, *Handbook of Biblical Chronology* [Princeton: Princeton University Press, 1964], pp. 17–70).

[4]Van der Meer, *Chronology,* p. 84.

[5]Jack Finegan, *Handbook of Biblical Chronology* (Princeton: Princeton University Press, 1964), p. 28.

Genesis 1 and the authenticity of the Genesis record of the antedeluvian period, takes the life span of Abraham as the starting point for a firm Old Testament chronology.

B. *Problems in Regard to Precision*

Genesis 5 names the ten ancestors between Adam and Noah and gives the age of each father before his first (or most prominent) son was born and then his age of death. If the ages of the progenitors at the birth of their sons are totaled, they come to only 1,656 years, according to the Hebrew text; the Septuagint gives larger figures, totaling 2,242 years. The genealogy between Shem and Abraham in Genesis 11:10–32 totals only 353 years from the Flood to the birth of Abraham, which occurred c. 2166 B.C. This would mean that Noah had died just three years previously (cf. Gen 9:28) and that Shem was still alive. The problems attending this method of computation are compounded by the quite conclusive archaeological evidence that Egyptian Dynasty I went back to 3100 B.C., with a long period of divided kingdoms in the Nile valley before that. These could hardly have arisen until long after the Flood had occurred and the human race had multiplied considerably (cf. Gen 10). It therefore seems necessary to interpret the figures of Genesis 5 and 11 differently, especially in view of the gaps in other biblical genealogical tables.

For example, Luke 3:36 states that Cainan was the father of Shelach—a name missing from the list in the MT of Genesis 11:12–13. (The LXX text of these verses includes Kainan four times.) This shows that Arphachsad was actually the ancestor of Shelah, rather than his immediate father. See 1 Chronicles 7:13, where the grandsons of Bilhah (a secondary wife of Jacob) are referred to as her "sons" (Heb. *bānîm*). Thus the term *son* could be used of remoter descendants whom we would call "grandsons" or "great-grandsons." Moreover, Matthew 1:8 states that Jehoram son of Jehoshaphat "begat" Uzziah. The OT tells us that Jehoram was actually the father of Ahaziah (who reigned in 841) and the grandfather of Joash (who reigned forty-one years after the six years of Athaliah's usurpation). Joash was the father of Amaziah, who reigned six or seven years before associating his son, Uzziah, with him on the throne. So Jehoram was actually the great-great-grandfather of Uzziah, and seventy-four years intervened between his death and the beginning of Uzziah's sole reign in 767. Quite plainly, then, the purpose of these genealogical records, both in the OT and the NT, was to list the more important members of the line, without necessarily naming each generation. (Cf. Ezra 7:1–5, which omits six of the names given in the same genealogy as listed in 1 Chronicles 6:3–14.)

Therefore, by analogy we can understand "B" in the formula "A begat B" to mean either B himself or some unnamed ancestor of B. There is no good reason to doubt the literal accuracy of the total life-span assigned the patriarchs from Adam on; the milder conditions of life and the relative absence of disease might well account for their longevity before the Flood. (Henry Morris suggests that an ice canopy enveloped the earth prior to the Flood; this would have reduced the impact of cosmic rays and of ozone from the outer atmosphere.) But there is a possibility of adding their ages end to end, rather than postulating such extensive overlaps as Ussher's chronology implied. (He arrived at 4175 B.C. for the creation of Adam.) The grouping into two sets of ten (Gen 5 and 11) suggests a simplified genealogical chain for ease in memorizing, somewhat like the three groups of fourteen in the Matthew 1 genealogy of Christ. Thus we may postulate a span of at least five to eight thousand years between Adam and Abraham, depending on the number of overlaps involved.

Insuperable difficulties beset Ussher's chronology in regard to the interval of 353 years between the Flood and the birth of Abraham. If Abraham was born c. 2166 B.C. (as will be shown below), then the Flood must have occurred c. 2519. Yet there is conclusive evidence from archaeology and written documents that Egyptian Dynasty I began c. 3100 B.C. Inscriptions—all written in the same language with the same hieroglyphic writing—become increasingly plentiful from then on, especially in the pyramid-building Dynasty IV (2723–2563).[6] This evidence is impossible to reconcile with a 2519 B.C. date for the Flood, which would then have occurred in the midst of the fourth Dynasty and which reduced the entire human population to eight, all of whom spoke the same language and all of whose numerous descendants, engaging in the building of the Tower of Babel, were still speaking that same language (Gen 11:6). This evidence for an earlier flood was not Egyptian alone, for Sumerian inscriptions go back to as early as 3000 B.C. or earlier, and they attest a language basically the same as the Sumerian spoken in Ur by Abraham's time. Also Genesis 11:7 states that God confounded the speech of the tower-builders so that they could not understand each other. Hence there could have been no continuity between the language of Noah and his family and the languages (with the possible exception of one) that resulted from the confusion of tongues at Babel. This biblical testimony totally rules out the possibility of a 2519 B.C. Flood. It also destroys the validity of Ussher's chronology. Obviously the confusion of tongues at Babel must have preceded 3100 B.C. by a long period of time, since by that time there were already extremely diverse languages.

As for the chronological notices in Genesis regarding the patriarchs Abraham, Isaac, and Jacob, the data seem clear, though Abraham's longevity is quite unusual. He was 86 when Ishmael was born (Gen 16:16) and 100 when Isaac was born (Gen 21:5); he did not die till he was 175 (Gen 25:7). As for Isaac, despite his illness at the age of 137, he outlived Abraham, dying at the age of 180. Jacob was apparently already 77 when he left home to live with Laban, there to acquire his wives and most of his children. (A comparison of Genesis 47:9 with 41:46, 47, 54 and 45:11 substantiates this.) The entire time span between Abraham's first migration to Canaan and Jacob's migration to Egypt was apparently 215 years. Now, since the LXX text of Exodus 12:40 inserts "and in the land of Canaan" when stating that the Israelite sojourn in Egypt lasted a total of 430 years, some scholars have conjectured that only 215 years elapsed between Jacob's migration and the Exodus. But since the LXX consistently tends to tamper with numerals concerning the patriarchs (adding 100 years to the father's age whenever the MT states his age at less than 150 when his son was born), it affords a poor base for rejecting the reading of the MT. Furthermore, the trustworthiness of the MT record that 430 years elapsed between Jacob's migration and the Exodus is underscored by the prophecy given Abraham in Genesis 15:13: ".... your descendants will be strangers in a foreign country, and they will be enslaved and mistreated four hundred years." If the sojourn in Egypt lasted only 215 years, then God's prediction must have been erroneous. But a 430-year sojourn would allow not only for four centuries of oppression, but also for the ten generations between Ephraim and Joshua, his descendant, as listed in 1 Chronicles 6:1–3. As for Galatians 3:17 ("The law, introduced 430 years later, does not set aside the covenant previously established by God"), this should be understood of the entire period of the Abrahamic covenant, renewed to Isaac and Jacob, rather than of its initial promul-

---

[6]K.A. Kitchen so dates Dynasty IV in ZPEB 2:231; Encyclopaedia Britannica (1969 ed.) 8:38 dates it as 2613–2494. Earlier authorities, such as J.B. Payne (OHH, 1954), assign to Dynasties III-VI 2600–2250; C. Pfeiffer and H. Vos give the reign of Khefren in Dynasty IV as 2525 (HGBL, 69).

gation (Gen 12:1–3). Paul is simply referring to the well-known period of the Egyptian sojourn, which separated the patriarchal age from the lawgiving at Mount Sinai.

As for the period of the judges, extending from Joshua's time to the coronation of Saul, the figures in Judges clearly involve several overlappings. As will be shown below, the Exodus took place c. 1445, and Saul's coronation in c. 1043, or an interval of 402 years. The period from soon after the death of Joshua and his contemporaries (Judg 3:8–11), which was marked by the career of Othniel (c. 1374) and his victory over Cushan-Rishathaim, to the close of Samuel's term of service as judge totals 415 years (Othniel, 40; Moabite oppression, 18; Ehud, 80; Canaanite oppression, 20; Deborah and Barak, 40; Midianite oppression, 7; Gideon, 40; Abimelech, 3; Tola and Jair, 23; Philistine oppression, 40; Ammonite oppression, 18; Jephthah, 6; Eli, 40; Samson, 20; Samuel, 20). Yet the true interval between 1382 (the beginning of Cushan-Rishathaim's dominance) or the rise of Othniel eight years later (in 1374) and the crowning of Saul at the close of Samuel's regime (1043) could not have exceeded 331 years—the difference between 1374 and 1043. We must therefore understand several of these careers as running somewhat concurrently. For example, if Eli's service as high priest and judge began in 1120, right after Tola and Jair finished their careers in 1121, then Eli's ministry at Shiloh must have been contemporaneous with the Ammonite dominance in the East (1103–1085), the Philistine oppression in the West (1103–1063), and the career of Samson in the West (1090–1070).

One surprising feature of the record in Judges is the lack of any direct reference to the clash between the Hittites and the Egyptians in the region of Syria-Palestine during the Egyptian dynasties XVIII (Amenhotep III and IV) and XIX (Seti I and Rameses II). Nor is there any acknowledgment of continuing Egyptian power in the reign of Rameses III of Dynasty XX (1195–1164). Yet Hittite and Egyptian monuments show that the important trade routes and level sections adapted to chariot warfare were occasionally under the control of one or the other of the major powers from about 1380 to 1170. (Rameses III refers to a campaign in the Edomite territory of Mount Seir[7] and his temple in Beth Shan is well known.)[8] It is possible, however, to work out a satisfactory synchronism between Egyptian chronology and the record in Judges, provided the various periods of "rest" are understood as coinciding with Egyptian control of the coastal trade routes and the Valley of Jezreel (at the eastern end of which lies Beth Shan). J.B. Payne summarizes this synchronism (as worked out by John Garstang).[9]

Concerning the Hebrew monarchy, chronological difficulties arise particularly during the latter half of the eighth century, the age of Ahaz and Hezekiah. Here there are two competing chronological systems, each of which has advocates today. (This specific problem will be discussed later on, but suffice it to say here that the reigns of the kings of Judah occasionally overlapped.) The record in 2 Kings in such cases includes the earlier years of an enthroned crown prince, prior to his father's decease, in computing the total reign of each king of Judah. For the sake of avoiding the outbreak of a revolution upon his death (a frequent occurrence in the northern kingdom), the monarchs of the southern kingdom often had their oldest son officially crowned and installed as secod king in the latter part of their own reign. (Failure to understand this principle led to serious miscalculations in the biblical chronologies of a century ago.) Building on the fine

[7]Cf. Papyrus Harris I.
[8]ANET[3], p. 262, n. 21.
[9]ZPEB, 1:836.

work of his predecessors,[10] Thiele worked out these overlapping regnal years with real precision.[11] Regrettably, however, his espousal of a mutually conflicting two-source theory for the Hezekiah period has led (in the opinion of this writer) to a major dislocation of dates for that reign. This problem will be handled a little later.

II. From the Prehistoric Period to Abraham

As explained above, no firm, absolute dates are possible for this period, owing to the possibility of gaps in the genealogical series. The table below simply includes the age of each patriarch at the birth of his first son, and his age at the time of his death. The name of the "son" may actually have been that of a later descendant, as illustrated by examples from other genealogical lists in Scripture. The creation of Adam cannot be specifically dated. We can only say, assuming that the theory of gaps in the genealogies is sound, that it occurred thousands of years before the Flood.[12]

Genealogical Chart

Name of patriarch	Age at birth of first son		Age at death	Reference in Genesis
Adam	130	(Seth)	930	5:5
Seth	105		912	5:8
Enosh	90		905	5:11
Kenan	70		910	5:14
Mahalalel	65		895	5:17
Jared	162		962	5:20
Enoch	65		365	5:23
Methuselah	187		969	5:27
Lamech	182		777	5:31
Noah	500		950	5:32; 9:29
Shem	100		600	11:10-11
Arpachshad	35		438	11:12-13
Kainan	(130?)		(460?)	11:13b (LXX)
Shelah	30		433	11:14-15
Eber	34		464	11:16-17
Peleg	30		239	11:18-19
Reu	32		239	11:20-21
Serug	30		230	11:22-23
Nahor	29		148	11:24-25
Terah	70		205	11:26, 32

---

[10]Cf. John D. Davis, *Dictionary of the Bible*, 4th ed. (New York: Revell, 1965).

[11]Cf. his *Mysterious Numbers of the Hebrew Kings*, Grand Rapids: Eerdmans, 1951, rev. ed. 1965.

[12]For a discussion of the relation of such "cave men" as the Neanderthal man to the time span indicated by the genealogical lists of Genesis 5 and 10 and of these and earlier hominids being descendants of Adam, see G.L. Archer, *A Survey of Old Testament Introduction*, 2nd ed. (SOTI²) (Chicago: Moody, 1964), pp. 195-97.

If the ages at the birth of the first son are added up consecutively (including the age of Kainan, given only in LXX), the total number of years between the age of Shem at the time of the Flood (98 according to Gen 11:10) and the birth of Terah's oldest son come to only 420 years. Abraham could not have been Terah's oldest son, incidentally, because he was 75 at the time his father died (Gen 12:4), and Terah was 205 at his death. Therefore Abraham must have been born when Terah was 130. With this correction, then, the interval between the Flood and the birth of Abraham would come out to 480 years, at the very least.

Now since the biblical data indicate quite clearly that Abraham was born in 2166 or thereabouts, this would place the Flood at 2646 B.C., right in the midst of the Egyptian Old Kingdom, probably at the height of the pyramid-building activity of Dynasty IV. Since there is no archaeological trace of a world-wide inundation in Egypt at that time, but only a continuous production of temples and inscriptions throughout that entire century, the 2646 date cannot be correct. There is no indication whatever that the population of Egypt was completely wiped out at that period, a disaster the Flood would have brought about. On the contrary, we must allow for a sufficient lapse of time from the Flood to permit the growth of a large population somewhere in the Near East before they moved eastward to the Plain of Shinar and there began to build the enormous Tower of Babel (Gen 11:1–4). This would have required several centuries at least. Then, at the confusion of languages that God caused, they began speaking in different tongues and could no longer understand each other. Thus, considerable time was needed for language groups to build up into the great nations of the early third millennium B.C. It is difficult to imagine how this process could have taken place without the passing of a number of millennia. In view of these factors, a date quite remote, certainly much before 5000 B.C., would be reasonable for the occurrence of the Flood. If such was the case, of course, this woud involve a certain number of gaps in the genealogical series of Genesis 11:10–32. (As we shall see, gaps of this sort are demonstrable as the usual procedure in Exodus wherever the genealogy between the generation of Joseph and the generation of Moses is given.)

Abraham: his life span	2166-1991	(Gen 21:5; 25:7)
His migration to Canaan	2091	(Gen 12:4)
Birth of Ishmael	2080	(Gen 16:16)
Death of Sarah	2029	(Gen 23:1; cf. 17:17)
Isaac: his life span	2066-1886	(Gen 21:5;35:28)
His marriage to Rebekah	2026	(Gen 25:20)
Jacob: his life span	2006-1859	(Gen 47:9;47:28)
His sojourn in Haran	1929-1909	(Gen 31:41)
His migration to Egypt	1876	(Exod 12:40)
Joseph: his life span	2015-1805	(Gen 30:22-24;50:26)
His abduction to Egypt	1898	(Gen 37:2)
His appointment as vizier	1885	(Gen 41:46)
Sojourn of Israelites in Egypt	1876-1446	(Exod 12:40; 1 Kings 6:1)

III. From Abraham to Joseph and the Egyptian Sojourn

The date of Abraham's birth is computed by adding 290 to the 1876-B.C. date that marked the coming of Jacob and his family to the land of Goshen. The 215 years are computed from the age of Jacob at the time he moved to Egypt—130 (Gen 47:9), the age of Isaac when Jacob was born—60 (Gen 25:20, 26), and the age of Abraham at the time of Isaac's birth—100 (Gen 21:5). As for the commencement of the Israelite sojourn in Egypt at 1876 B.C., we find this by adding the 430-year period of the sojourn (Exod 12:40) to the 480-year interval between the Exodus and the founding of Solomon's temple in 966 B.C. (as specified in 1 Kings 6:1).

IV. From the Exodus to the United Monarchy

The 1446 date for the Israelite departure from Egypt falls within the reign of Pharaoh Amenhotep II (1450–1423), who was apparently the Pharaoh of the Exodus, having recently succeeded his father, Thutmose III, the long-lived king. Thutmose III reigned from 1483 after a long minority under his stepmother Hatshepsut, the rightful heir to the throne from 1504, when Thutmose II died. (This point is important, since it was only during the long reign of Thutmose III that Moses could have taken refuge in Midian for forty years [Acts 7:30] and then have been told at the burning bush that "all the men who wanted to kill you are dead" [Exod 4:19]—a statement to be coupled with Exodus 2:23: "During that long period, the king of Egypt died.") Removed from all knowledge of Egyptian affairs, Moses would in 1447 still need to be informed that Thutmose had died (in 1450).[13]

Advocates of a later date for the Exodus rely on an archaeologically deduced 1230 date for the fall of Lachish, and a nearly contemporaneous destruction of Debir and of Bethel, as well (which allegedly was confused with Ai in the account of Joshua 7) as indicating the probable time of Joshua's invasion of Canaan. This would push back the time of the Exodus to some interval between 1290 and 1260 (allowing for the forty years of wilderness wandering). But this evidence is most inconclusive, since Joshua 10:32 says nothing about the physical destruction of Lachish itself (only the slaughter of its inhabitants). Nor does Joshua 10:38 say anything about burning Debir. As for Jericho, no archaeological data have been discovered by K. Kenyon or any other excavator of Tell es-Sultan to overturn the finding of J. Garstang that the cemetery connected with the late Bronze City IV contained any scarabs later than those of the reign of Amenhotep III (1412–1376) or any pottery dating beyond 1400 (out of 150,000 pottery fragments, only one sherd was found that was of a definitely Mycenaean type).[14] Actually the archaeological evidence against the late-date theory is altogether decisive. Rameses II carried on extensive building in the Wadi Tumilat (Goshen) area, indicating that the Egyptians occupied this region in full force. Yet the record of the plague of flies, of hail, and of darkness (Exod 8:22; 9:25–26; 10:23) makes it abundantly clear that Goshen was occupied almost exclusively by Hebrews alone until the Exodus. The occasional occupation of palaces in the delta by Thutmose III is amply confirmed by a Dynasty XVIII scarab referring to the birth of his son Amenhotep II in Memphis and by an inscription of the latter[15] referring to his riding from the palace stables in Memphis to

---

13The dating of this period may need to be revised. Kitchen now offers the following for Dynasty XVIII: Thutmose I, 1505–1493; Thutmose II, 1493–1490; Hapshetsut, 1490–1468; Thutmose III, 1490–1436; Amenhotep III, 1402–1364 (ZPEB, 2:237–238).

14John Garstang, *The Story of Jericho* (London: Marshall, Morgan and Scott, 1948), p. 122.

15Translated in ANET[3], p. 244.

enjoy archery practice by the pyramids of Gizeh. These documents effectively overturn the usual contention that Thutmose III confined himself to Thebes and would therefore have had no use for Hebrew slaves living in Goshen. On the contrary, the fourteen campaigns he conducted against Syria-Palestine during his long reign made it imperative for him to build up his fortresses and supply depots and barracks in the eastern delta. A large reservoir of slaves in Goshen would be most useful for this.[16]

It should also be noted that the reference by Jephthah in Judges 11:26 to the three-hundred-year Israelite occupation of the Transjordanian territory contested by the Ammonite invaders strongly suggests a 1400 B.C. date for Joshua's invasion of Canaan. Most authorities agree that Jephthah's victory over the Ammonites occurred around 1100 B.C.

If the invasions of Joshua, then, began around 1405, when he was around 80, his death at 110 (Josh 24:29) occurred around 1375. As for the successive administrations of the judges between his death and the crowning of Saul (c. 1050), the relevant data have already been discussed above. As for the 1050 date, this assumes that Saul's reign of forty years (Acts 13:21) did not include the seven years of rule by his son Ish-bosheth before David became king of all the twelve tribes. If these seven years are included, then Saul must have been anointed king in 1043, and his oldest son Jonathan would have been no more than twenty years older than David (who must have been around thirty in 1010 B.C.).

Chronological Chart: From Moses to the United Monarchy

Birth of Moses	1527	(Exod 2:2; Deut 34:7)
Moses' flight to Midian	1486	(Acts 7:23)
Date of the Exodus	1446 (April)	(1 Kings 6:1)
Death of Moses	1406	(Deut 34:7)
Conquest of Canaan	1406-1385(?)	
Division among the tribes	from 1400 (Caleb's capture of Hebron) to 1385	(Josh 14:7-10)
Death of Joshua	c. 1375	(Josh 24:29)
Mesopotamian oppression	1382-1374	(Judg 3:8)
Othniel's term of service	1374-1334	(Judg 3:11)
Moabite oppression (Eglon)	1334-1316	(Judg 3:14)
Ehud's career and subsequent period of rest	1316-1235	(Judg 3:30)
Oppression by Jabin and Sisera	1235-1216	(Judg 4:3)
Victory of Barak and Deborah	1216	(Judg 4:23-24)
Subsequent period of rest	1216-1176	(Judg 5:31)
Midianite oppression	1176-1169	(Judg 6:1)
Gideon's victory and career	1169-1129	(Judg 8:28)
Tyranny of Abimelech	1129-1126	(Judg 9:22)
Tola and Jair	1120-1097	(Judg 10:2-3)

---

[16]For a fuller discussion of the evidence establishing a 1446 date for the Exodus cf. SOTI[2], pp. 223–34.

Chronological Chart: From Moses to the United Monarchy (cont.)

First Philistine oppression	1103-1063	(Judg 10:7;13:1)
Ammonite oppression	1103-1085	(Judg 10:8)
Jephthah's victory and career	1085-1079	(Judg 12:7)
Eli's term of service	c. 1120-1080	(1 Sam 4:18)
Samson's career	c. 1095-1075	(Judg 15:20;16:31)
Battle of Shiloh (Ebenezer)	1080	(1 Sam 4:1)
Samuel and his sons in office	1063-1043	(1 Sam 7:2)
Reign of Saul and Ishbosheth	1043-1003	(Acts 13:21)
Birth of David	1040	(2 Sam 5:4)
Amalekite war; David anointed	c. 1025	(2 Sam 5:3)
Battle of Mount Gilboa; death of Saul and Jonathan	1010	(Acts 13:21)
David king of Judah in Hebron	1010-1003	(2 Sam 5:5)
David king of all Israel	1003	(2 Sam 5:1-5)
Jerusalem captured, made the capital	1002	(? 2 Sam 5:5)
	(or possibly 995—cf. Acts 13:19-20)	
Revolt of Absalom	c. 979	(assuming 990 for Solomon's birth; 2 Sam 13:23, 38; 14:28; 15:7)[17]
Death of David	970	(2 Sam 5:5)
Reign of Solomon	970-930	(1 Kings 11:42)
Temple begun	966	(1 Kings 6:1)
Temple completed	959	(1 Kings 6:38)

Note: As for the date of the capture of Jerusalem, 2 Samuel 5:5 indicates that David actually ruled in Jerusalem for thirty-three years, which would place its capture within a year of his coronation as king of the entire nation. But this may mean no more than that during his thirty-three-year rule of the united kingdom he made Jerusalem his capital and its actual capture may have come a few years after his coronation. In Acts 13:19–20 Paul says, "After this [after the division of Canaan to the tribes] God gave them judges until the time of Samuel the prophet." In 1446 Israel left Egypt to take possession of the Promised Land (Exod 20:12). Samuel died c. 1020, but his ministry came to its fullest fruition when David, whom he had anointed, captured the chosen city predicted in Deuteronomy 12:11 and dedicated it as a holy place for God's name to dwell there. The interval between 1446 and 995 is 450 years. The number 450 may, however, have been intended only approximately; a 1003 date of capture would come out to 443 years.

In connection with the military success and broadened dimensions of the Davidic-Solomonic empire (stretching from the Wadi el-'Arish or "River of Egypt" to Tiphsah on the Euphrates), it is worth noting that the fortunes of the great kingdoms of both the Nile Valley and of Mesopotamia were at a low ebb early in the tenth century. By Solomon's time Dynasty XXI had virtually separated into two realms, and King Siamun (978–959) had capitals at Tanis in the northeast of the delta and at Memphis at its base.[18]

17Cf. J.B. Payne, *An Outline of Hebrew History* (Grand Rapids: Baker, 1954), p. 108.
18K.A. Kitchen, *The Third Intermediate Period in Egypt* (Warminster: Aris & Phillips, 1973), p. 267.

It was doubtless he who destroyed Gezer during a campaign against the Philistines (1 Kings 9:16) and then added it to the dowry of his daughter, who married Solomon between 966 and 960.[19] To the east, the lower Mesopotamian valley was controlled by the later Kassite (or Pashe) dynasty in Babylon (Mar-biti-apla-usur reigned 983–978, according to P. Van der Meer, and Nabu-mukin-apli, 977–942). The upper valley was under an Assyrian dynasty (Asshur-reshishi II 971–967; Tiglath-pileser II 966–935). The Hittite power had collapsed by 1200 B.C., and the Aramaean powers of Damascus and northern Syria were divided against each other (cf. the hostility between the king of Hamath and the king of Zobah, an ally of Damascus—2 Sam 8:5–10). The time was ripe for a united Israel under the gifted generalship of David and Joab to reduce their neighbors to vassalage.

V. The Divided Monarchy to the Fall of Jerusalem

The absolute dating for this period is firmly established by the data of the Assyrian eponym (*limmu*) lists and the Canon of Ptolemy (A.D. 70–161), correlated by recorded eclipses of the sun (e.g., June 15, 763 B.C.). On this basis we know that the Battle of Qarqar (not mentioned in the Bible) brought Shalmaneser III into conflict with Ahab of Israel and Benhadad II of Damascus in 853. He attacked once more in 841, when he compelled Jehu of Israel and Hazael of Damascus to pay him tribute.[20] The chronological notices and regnal years of 1 and 2 Kings can be accurately correlated with this information.

The one period beset with difficulties is the second half of the eighth century, the era of Ahaz and Hezekiah, as shown by the following points. (1) Second Kings 17:1–6 indicates that Hoshea of Israel began his reign in the twelfth year of Ahaz of Judah and that he ruled nine years before Samaria fell to the Assyrians in 722/721. This means that Hoshea came to the throne in 731/730 and Ahaz began his reign (as coregent with his father, Jotham) in 743/742. (2) Second Kings 18:1–2 (and 2 Chron 29:1) states that Hezekiah began his rule (as coregent with his father, Ahaz) in the third year of Hoshea, therefore 728/727. (3) Second Kings 18:9–10 records that Shalmaneser V of Assyria began his siege of Samaria in the fourth year of Hezekiah (the seventh year of Hoshea) and finally captured it at the end of three years (stated to be the ninth year of Hoshea). Since Samaria fell in 722/721, the siege began in 725/724, the fourth year of Hezekiah. All three passages unite in pointing to 728 as the commencement of Hezekiah's reign. But a problem arises with (4) 2 Kings 18:13, which in the MT declares that in the fourteenth year of Hezekiah Sennacherib of Assyria (705–681 B.C.) invaded Judah and threatened to capture Jerusalem. In the Taylor Prism inscription Sennacherib dates this campaign as his third. This means that the invasion occurred in 701, and if this was the fourteenth year of Hezekiah, then Hezekiah came to the throne in 715.

Thiele concluded that the original compiler of Kings had attempted to combine two incompatible sources and that it was necessary to adopt 715 as the beginning of Hezekiah's reign, despite the clear evidence of 2 Kings 15:30; 16:1–2; 17:1; 18:1, 9 that his reign began in 728. The 715 theory involves extending Hezekiah's reign to 687/686, or ten years after his depraved, idol-worshiping son, Manasseh had come to the throne in

---

[19]Ibid., p. 280.
[20]ANET[3], p. 281.

797/796. The 715 theory also involves the great improbability that the author of 2 Kings would have affirmed the 728 accession year for Hezekiah up through v.10 of chapter 18, and then suddenly changed his mind three verses later, and decided for a 715 date.

The solution to this apparent discrepancy lies in a simple correction of an obvious error in textual transmission. That is, the original wording must have been '-r-b-' '-s-r-m (the yod before mem was hardly used in eighth century Hebrew spelling) rather than the '-r-b-' '-s-r-h of the MT. In other words, the number as originally written was twenty-four rather than fourteen—a confusion arising from the miscopying of only one letter (he instead of mem).[21] If Hezekiah began his sole reign in 725, this would certainly work out to a twenty-fourth-year date for the Assyrian invasion of 701. This obviates the problem of charging the author of Kings with a factual error (as the 715 theory requires) and upsetting the otherwise well-established limits for the reign of Ahaz.

Connected with the Assyrian invasion of 701 is the theory of a second invasion, which allegedly took place (also under Sennacherib and against Hezekiah) in 687/686. This two-invasion theory was largely based on what proved to be a misinterpretation of the Egyptian Kawa Stela IV by M.F.L. Macadam. He took the wrong antecedent for certain verbs in a key passage, with the result that Tirhaqa (the leader of the unsuccessful Egyptian relief army in 701, according to 2 Kings 19:9) could have been only nine years old by that time. But by 687 he would have been old enough to command an army. The support for this entire theory collapsed when Leclant and Yoyette in 1952 published a more careful study of Kawa Stela IV showing that the inscription actually stated that Piankhy, the father of Tirhaqa, died in 717/716 or 713 at the latest. Hence Tirhaqa would have been at least fourteen, but more probably seventeen or older by 701. Macadam erred in assigning to 690/689 the Stela's statement that Tirhaqa was twenty; rightly interpreted, it stated that Tirhaqa was twenty shortly after Shebitku's accession in 702. He was probably twenty, then, when his older brother, Shebitku, gave him command over the Ethiopian-Egyptian expeditionary force against Sennacherib. The Stela states (IV:7–8) of Tirhaqa just before this appointment: "His Majesty was in Nubia, as a goodly youth . . . amidst the goodly youths whom His Majesty King Shebitku had summoned from Nubia."[22]

In the table below, overlaps begin with Jehoshaphat (Judah, no. 4), who reigned as viceroy from 872 to 869 before he took over as sole monarch. Similarly Uzziah served as viceroy under Amaziah from 790 to 767. When he became leprous in 751, Uzziah turned over most of the reins of government to Jotham, but he did not die till 740/739. Jotham ruled with his son Ahaz from 742 to 736. Hezekiah became junior king under Ahaz from 728 to 725; apparently Ahaz was deposed or deprived of any real power during those last three years. In each case there may have been some illness or danger that impelled the king to crown his heir apparent to preclude revolution or civil war after his death. In the northern kingdom there was only one overlap: Jeroboam II was viceroy under Jehoash 793–782. As for Pekah, he seems to have been acknowledged as king in the Transjordan part of Israel 752–740 before he attained to the throne of the entire realm of Israel; hence the maximum length of his reign was reckoned as twenty years (2 Kings 15:27), even though he controlled the west side of the Jordan for only eight or nine years. Hoshea may have been deposed during the final siege of Samaria, and so his reign may have ended a year or two before the city fell to the Assyrians.

---

[21]Cf. E.J. Young in NIC *Isaiah* 2:540–542 for a detailed verification of this textual correction.
[22]Cf. Kitchen, *Third Intermediate Period*, pp. 82–84.

Chronological Chart: The Divided Monarchy to the Fall of Jerusalem

Kings of Judah		Kings of Israel		Kings of Assyria	
1. Rehoboam	931-913	1. Jeroboam I	930-910		
2. Abijam	913-910	2. Nadab	910-909		
3. Asa	910-869	3. Baasha	909-886		
4. Jehoshaphat	872-848	4. Elah	886-885		
5. Jehoram	848-841	5. Zimri	885		
6. Ahaziah	841	6. Omri	885-874	1. Shalmaneser III	858-824
7. Athaliah	841-835	7. Ahab	874-853		
8. Joash	835-796	8. Ahaziah	853-852		
9. Amaziah	796-767	9. Jehoram	852-841	2. Adad-Nirari III	810-783
10. Azariah/Uzziah	790-739	10. Jehu	841-814		
11. Jotham	751-736	11. Jehoahaz	814-798	3. Tiglath Pileser III	744-727
12. Ahaz	742-728-725	12. Jehoash	798-782	4. Shalmaneser V	727-722
13. Hezekiah	728-725-697	13. Jeroboam II	793-753	5. Sargon II	722-705
14. Manasseh	697-642	14. Zechariah	753-752	6. Sennacherib	705-681
15. Amon	642-640	15. Shallum	752	7. Essarhaddon	680-669
16. Josiah	640-609	16. Menahem	752-742	8. Fall of Nineveh	612
17. Jehoahaz	609-608	17. Pekahiah	742-740	9. Battle of Megiddo	609
18. Jehoiakim	608-597	18. Pekah	752-740-732	10. Battle of Carchemish	605
19. Jehoiachin	597	19. Hoshea	732-723	11. Nebuchadnezzar II	605-562
20. Zedekiah	597-587	20. Fall of Samaria	722/721	(King of Babylon)	
21. Fall of Jerusalem	587				

VI. The Prophets

As for the great prophets, Elijah served during the reigns of Ahab and Ahaziah (Israel, nos. 7, 8), and Elisha under Jehoram, Jehu, Jehoahaz, and Jehoash (Israel, nos. 9–12). Obadiah probably wrote in the reign of Jehoram of Israel (no. 9), Joel in the time of Joash of Judah (no. 8) during the boy-king's minority.[23] Amos prophesied from 760 to 755 (or possibly as late as 746) under Jeroboam II of Israel (no. 13). Hosea's career was from 746 to 724, in the reigns of Menahem, Pekahiah, Pekah, and possibly Hoshea (Israel, nos. 16–19). Isaiah prophesied from 740 to 680, in the time of Jotham, Ahaz, Hezekiah, and Manasseh (Judah nos. 11–14). Micah was his contemporary, serving from 735 to 690 (or perhaps ten years less than that) under Ahaz, Hezekiah, and (probably) Manasseh. Nahum may have prophesied around 640, though some would place him ten years earlier or later than that. Zephaniah must have delivered his messages from 640 to 630. Jeremiah's ministry was from 626 to c. 585. Habakkuk prophesied from 608 to 597; Ezekiel, from 592 to 570. Daniel's ministry as a government official began c. 600 and continued until c. 532 or 530 a few years after his retirement, c. 537.

VII. The Exile and the Restoration

This last phase of OT history has few disputed areas. There is no question as to the regnal dates of the Chaldean and Persian kings. Some scholars, however, placed Ezra's ministry in the thirty-seventh year of Artaxerxes I rather than in the seventh year (as stated in the MT of Ezra 7:8) because of the allegedly depopulated condition of Jerusalem implied in Nehemiah 2, but not reflected in Ezra 8 (when Ezra first arrived at Jerusalem). It is also argued that if Ezra had already carried through in the 450s the

---

[23]Cf. SOTI[2], pp. 300–307.

reforms recorded in Ezra 9–10, there would have been no necessity for Nehemiah to have enforced the reforms recorded in Nehemiah 13 which were put through during his second term as governor in the 430s. A more likely time for Ezra's reforms would therefore be in 428 and the years immediately following. But actually this proposed emendation of "seventh" to "thirty-seventh" in Ezra 7:8 raises far more problems and improbabilities than it seeks to solve,[24] and the MT reading should be trusted as both original and accurate. (Cf. Frank Cross, "A Reconstruction of the Judean Restoration" in JBL 94 [1975]: 4–18. He argues for 458 as the right date for Ezra, and 445 for Nehemiah.)

Chronological Chart: Period of the Exile and the Restoration

Reign of Nebuchadnezzer	605–562
His years of insanity	c. 582–575
His second (?) invasion of Egypt	567
Reign of Nabonidus	555–539
Belshazzar as viceroy	550(?)–539
Cyrus the Great	558–529
His subjugation of the Medes	550
His conquest of the Lydian Empire	547
Fall of Babylon	539
Reign of Darius the Mede as viceroy	539–538
Cyrus assumes the crown of Babylon	538/537
Foundations of the temple at Jerusalem	536
Death of Daniel	c. 530
Reign of Cambyses	529–523
His conquest of Egypt	526–524
Usurpation by Bardiya (Smerdis)	523–522
Reign of Darius the Great	522–485
Ministry of Haggai	520/519
Ministry of Zechariah	520–475
Jerusalem Second Temple dedicated	516
The Ionian Revolt	500–493
Battle of Marathon	490
Reign of Xerxes (Ahashuerus)	485–464
Invasion of Greece	
(Battles of Salamis and Plataea)	480–479
Queen Esther	c. 478/477
Reign of Artaxerxes I Longimanus	464–424
Ezra sent to Jerusalem	457
Nehemiah's first term as governor	446/445
Ministry of Malachi	c. 435
Nehemiah's second term as governor	433–430
Darius II	423–406
Artaxerxes II Mnemon	404–359
Battle of Cunaxa (death of Cyrus II)	401
(March of the 10,000 Greeks)	

---

[24]SOTI[2], pp. 412–413.

After the fall of Babylon to Cyrus's troops under General Ugbaru of Gutium, Cyrus himself was compelled by pressing government business, or possibly by a military challenge on his northeastern frontier, to leave Babylon. He therefore entrusted the consolidating of Persian power over Babylonia to a trusted lieutenant named Gubaru (not the same as Ugbaru, who died a few weeks after capturing the city), who apparently assumed for the first time the title Darayawush (or Darius)—although it may have been an inherited family name. As Cyrus's representative, he assumed kingship over the newly conquered domains until a year to two later, when Cyrus returned to Babylon and was invested with the royal regalia in an elaborate Babylonian ritual. Thus the reign of Gubaru-Darius lasted only a year or two. Yet he remained governor of Babylonia, even after Cyrus had taken over his royal title.[25]

As for the Egyptian campaigns of Nebuchadnezzar, Josephus (Antiq. 10.9:5–7) dates his first invasion in the fifth year after the destruction of Jerusalem c. 581 B.C. and states that he rounded up all the Jewish refugees in Egypt (after the murder of Gedaliah) and dragged them off into captivity. Though some authorities question Josephus's reliability in this account, there can be no doubt about Nebuchadnezzar's later Egyptian campaign in 567. A fragment of the Babylonian Chronicle published by Pinches[26] states that in the thirty-seventh year of his reign Nebuchadnezzar invaded the Nile Valley. Whether or not this was the true date of his main campaign against Egypt, the depth of his penetration southward is attested by the inscription of the Egyptian governor Nes-hor now in the Louvre, which indicates that this army of "Asiatics" made a bid for the conquest of Ethiopa, averted only by the "favor of the gods." As for the dating of Nebuchadnezzar's years of madness (boanthropy), the seven-year segment of 582–575 was unmarked by any kind of activity so far as surviving records show. Thus it is reasonable to assign his dementia to that period.

It was during the post-Caldean period that Ezra returned—in 457. Apparently he came to Jerusalem with a royal decree permitting the rebuilding of the walls of Jerusalem (cf. Ezra 7:6–7 and especially 9:9 with its reference to "a wall in Judea and in Jerusalem"). This would seem to be the *terminus a quo* for the promise given Daniel in Daniel 9:25–26 that 69 heptads of years after the issuance of such a decree would witness the appearance of Messiah the Prince. Now, 483 years minus 457 leaves 26; but since a year is gained in passing from 1 B.C. to A.D. 1, it would really come out to A.D. 27, the year of the commencement of Christ's ministry (assuming the correctness of A.D. 30 as the year of his crucifixion). (See the article THE CHRONOLOGY OF THE NEW TESTAMENt, pp. 591–607).

It should be added that Harold W. Hoehner has put forth a well-reasoned argument in favor of a 444 B.C. terminus a quo for the 483-year interval (understanding these as lunar years rather than solar), and specifying A.D. 33 as the true date of the Crucifixion. Cf. his *Herod Antipas* Cambridge: Cambridge University Press, 1972.

Note: For the intertestamental period, see the article BETWEEN THE TESTAMENTS, pp. 177–194.

---

[25]Cf. the Nabonidus Chronicle, the Contenau Texts, the Pohl Texts, the Tremayne Texts, and several other sources, translated and discussed in J.C. Whitcomb, *Darius the Mede* (Nutley, N.J.: Presbyterian and Reformed, 1959), pp. 10–14.

[26]Cf. ANET[3], p. 308.

VIII. Bibliography

Archer, G.L. *A Survey of Old Testament Introduction*, 2nd ed. Chicago: Moody, 1974.

De Vries, S.J. "Chronology of the OT," in IDB, vol. 1. Nashville: Abingdon, 1962, pp. 580–99.

Finegan, J. *Handbook of Biblical Chronology*. Princeton: Princeton University Press, 1964.

Gardiner, A.H. *Egyptian Grammar*, 3rd ed. Oxford: Oxford University Press, 1957.

Hoehner, Harold W. *Chronological Aspects of the Life of Christ*. Grand Rapids: Zondervan, 1977.

Kitchen, K.A. *Ancient Orient and the Old Testament*. Chicago: InterVarsity, 1966.

————. *The Third Intermediate Period in Egypt*.

Payne, J.B. *An Outline of Hebrew History*. Grand Rapids: Baker, 1954.

————. "Chronology of the Old Testament," in ZPEB, vol. 1, ed. Merrill C. Tenney. Grand Rapids: Zondervan, 1975, pp. 829–45.

Pritchard, J.B., ed. *Ancient Near Eastern Texts Relating to the Old Testament*, 3rd ed. Princeton: Princeton University Press, 1969, 710 pp.

Thiele, E.R. *The Mysterious Numbers of the Hebrew Kings*, 2nd ed. Grand Rapids: Eerdmans, 1965.

Wood, L. *A Survey of Israel's History*. Grand Rapids: Zondervan, 1970 (excellent date charts on pp. 417–425).

THE METROLOGY OF THE OLD TESTAMENT

I. Introduction

    A. Common Characteristics of Ancient Near Eastern Metrology
    B. Factors Leading to Variation and Imprecision

II. Linear Measures
III. Measures of Volume
IV. Measures of Weight
V. Bibliography

I Introduction

A. Common Characteristics of Ancient Near Eastern Metrology

It is to be expected that the various nations, tribes, and city-states of the Fertile Crescent should have developed similar basic units of measurement of length, volume, and weight. For the primitive carpenter, for example, it was natural to use his finger or thumb to calculate the smallest width he needed to work with, just as the Romans derived their word for "inch" (*uncia*) from the width of a thumb. A larger distance could be calculated by the width of the hand at the base of the fingers, or else the broader stretch of the "span" (the distance between the tip of the thumb and the tip of the little finger when the hand is spread out). The basic unit for longer objects, however, was the "cubit" (from Lat. *cubitus*, "forearm"), the distance between the elbow and the tip of the longest finger. Although the foot was much used for measurements by the Greeks and Romans, it was scarcely used as such by the Egyptians or by the ancient Semites. As for measures of volume, the basic dry measure was the amount of grain that could be carried by a donkey (Heb. *ḥōmer*; cf. *ḥᵃmōr* "donkey," Akk *imēru*) or else a convenient-sized sack for flour (Egypt. *khar*). One tenth of the *ḥōmer* was called an *'ēphah*, an Egyptian word for "measuring unit" (*ip.t*, from *ip* "to count, reckon"). An Egyptian unit for liquid volume was the *hnw* (related to the Hebrew *hîn*, which was probably borrowed from it), which originally meant "jar"—presumably a jar of a specific size. The Hebrew *'ōmer* (one-tenth of an ephah) literally meant "sheaf," probably because that quantity of grain could be threshed from a single sheaf of wheat.

As for the various subdivisions, the general tendency towards decimalism (e.g., 10 baths to the *ḥōmer* or *kor*, 10 *seahs* to the *ephah*) came from Egyptian influence, since decimalism was followed quite consistently in Egypt. But the duodecimal tendency came largely from Mesopotamia, where twelve and its fractions or multiples played an important role. Thus, one cubit consisted of 6 handbreadths (*ṭephāḥîm*), the reed

375

(qāneh) was 6 cubits, the *bath* contained 6 *hīns*, the *hīn* consisted of 12 *lŏgs*, and the *seah* was composed of 3 *'ōmers*. There were two types of *mina* (or *maneh*), the one made up of 60 shekels, as in Babylonia (which correspondingly used a *biltu* or talent of 3,600 shekels), or the 50-shekel mina, used in Ugarit and in Syria-Palestine (in which regions, therefore, the 3,000-shekel talent—*kikkār*—prevailed). But it should be recognized that duodecimalism was by no means confined to Mesopotamia, for both in Italian culture (the Roman *libra* [pound] or *litra* [quart] was composed of twelve *unciae*, as was the *pēs* [foot]) and in Germanic cultures (possibly influenced originally by Roman example) the foot was subdivided into 12 inches and the pound into 12 ounces troy. Nor is it true that Mesopotamia was predominantly duodecimal, for the numerical notation system was for the most part decimal, both in Sumerian and in Babylonian circles.

B. *Factors Leading to Variation and Imprecision*

As has been suggested, some names for measurement units may have been derived from parts of the body or from the containers, such as sacks or jars, of substances measured or from tools used for measuring, such as rods or reeds. But since the dimensions of fingers and hands and forearms varied, as did the size of the sack or jar commonly used, the factor of variation was inherent in the measuring process from the beginning. As villages and cities or tribes traded with each other, some standards of uniformity became essential to meet the demands of fairness and justice.

Numerous ancient weights have been found, mostly fashioned from stone, but some from metal or glass. Some even have their weight-name or measure-unit inscribed on them. Quite a few containers made of pottery or stone have been recovered, labeled with the name of the measuring unit of their capacity. (Photographs of these appear in most recent Bible encyclopedias, such IDB, 4:832: the *neṣep* [possibly = shekel; cf. IDB 4:832a], the *beqah* [or half-shekel], and the *pīm*[1] [2/3 of a shekel]. There is a fine photograph of a stone *kikkār* or talent in ZEPB, 5:919. An Egyptian measuring rod from the reign of Amenhotep II is illustrated in IDB, 4:836, showing a *mḥ* or cubit carefully subdivided into fractions.)

These inscribed units of measurement show that very definite and official standards were imposed by mercantile custom or government sanction. Certainly the OT, with its solemn commands concerning weights and measures of *ṣedeq* ("justice" or "righteousness"), makes it clear that such was the case. It was of course especially abhorrent to the Lord and damaging to community welfare when a salesman defrauded his customers by using an overweight *'eben* (or weighing-stone) in his scales to calculate the amount of silver, bronze, or wheat the customer was to pay for his merchandise and then substituting an underweight stone in weighing the amount of goods he was selling his purchaser. This amounted to a double fraud. Only containers and weights and measuring tools standard for the entire community would be used by an honest tradesman, and he would use the *same* set of measurements throughout the transaction.

Nevertheless, in the absence of a strong central government concerned with maintaining uniform standards, it was entirely possible for one city or region to differ from another in the standard used. Even in the Greek world of the first millennium B.C. there

---

[1]Or *payim*; cf. R. De Vaux, *Ancient Israel* (New York: McGraw-Hill, 1961), p. 204.

were various standards of coin-weight in use for the drachma, such as the Phoenician, the Aeginetan, and the Attic. So also the Egyptian or Babylonian cubit or shekel might differ from those employed in Palestine. Even within smaller regions there were variations in the shekel or cubit employed, even though the same name might be used. Sometimes even in the excavation of a single ancient city, inscribed weights and measures are discovered that have such differences as to suggest that some were deceitful shekels or ephahs for cheating gullible customers. In view of such diversity it is futile to attempt any calculation of ancient Semitic weights to the precise gram or linear measure down to the exact millimeter. The ancients found less reason for such painstaking exactitude than modern society with its insistence on precision demands. Thus in computing the length of the galleries inside the pyramid of Khufu in Gizeh, or the dimensions of Noah's ark, there may be a considerable variation in trying to figure out modern equivalents of ancient measures, even where those measures are given precisely in the biblical text.

The following tables list the approximate or average value of the Hebrew units of measurement in the time of the monarchy, expressed in terms of English equivalents and according to the metric system. The Egyptian and Babylonian terms and values have also been subjoined, because of their relevance to the trade relations between Israel and the world powers on either side of her.

II. Linear Measures

Hebrew System

qāneh (reed) = 6 cubits = 8 feet 9 inches (2.67 meters)
'ammah (cubit) = 6 handbreadths = 17.5 inches (44.45 centimeters)
zeret (span) = 1/2 cubit = 8.75 inches (23.2 centimeters)
ṭōpaḥ or ṭepaḥ (handbreadth) = 1/6 cubit = 2.9 inches (7.4 centimeters)
'eṣba' (finger) = .73 inch (1.85 centimeters) (4 fingers = 1 handbreadth)

In Ezekiel 40–48

reed = 6 great cubits = 10 feet 3 inches (3.12 meters)
cubit = 7 handbreadths = 20.5 inches (50 centimeters)

Egyptian System

ḫt (rod) or ḫt n nwḥ (rod of cord) = 100 cubits
mḥ (cubit) short = 6 palms or handbreadths
    royal/long = 7 palms = 20.6 inches or 52.3 centimeters
šsp (palm or handbreadth) long = 3 inches or 7.5 centimeters
ḏb' (finger or digit) = .736 inch or 1.84 centimeters

Babylonian System

(Gudea of Lagash:) great cubit = 19.5 inches or 49.5 centimeters
    (Sumerian: kus; Akkadian: ammatu)
Sumerian finger (susi) (Akk. ubanu) 1/30 cubits = .66 inches or 1.67 centimeters
Sumerian span (ideogram ŠU.BAD) = 1/2 cubit = 8.8 inches or 25 centimeters

Mare points out that the Siloam tunnel cut through by Hezekiah in Jerusalem is stated to be 1,200 cubits long.[2] By measuring the tunnel itself, it was found that the cubit comes to 17.5 inches. Moreover the city gates of both Megiddo and Hazor were found to be 20.3 meters, which works out to 45 cubits of 17.7 inches (about the length of the Egyptian shorter or common cubit).

III. Measures of Volume

Liquid Volume

cōr or hōmer = 10 baths = 58.1 gallons or 220 liters
bath = 6 hins = 5.8 gallons or 2.2 liters
hīn = 12 lōgs = 3.5 quarts or 3.9 liters
lōg = .67 pint or .64 liter

Dry Measures

hōmer or cōr = 10 ēphahs or baths = 5.16 bushels (41.3 gallons)
letek = 1/2 homer or 5 ēphahs = 2.58 bushels
'ēphah = 10 seahs = 1/2 bushel or 4 gallons
seah (se'ah) = 3-1/3 omers = 2/3 peck (or 5-1/3 quarts)
'ōmer or 'issārōn ("tenth") = 2.09 quarts
qab = 1.16 quarts

It should be added, however, that the tendency to variation was especially marked in the category of volume measurement. Huey gives the hōmer as 7.25 bushels, or 58 gallons (220 liters), which is far in excess of the 41.3 gallons estimated by Sellers (in IDB). De Vaux suggests that the hōmer was originally 5 bushels, 6 gallons (or a total of 54 gallons). Correspondingly, the ēphah would be 5.8 gallons according to Huey,[3] rather than the half bushel (= four gallons) given by Sellers. Sellers makes the liquid hōmer or cōr equivalent to 55 gallons (6.875 bushels) or 208.2 liters, substantially more than the dry hōmer[4] —which seems most unlikely, since the OT text nowhere indicates any difference in volume between the two (whether liquid or solid). So far as the bath is concerned, Huey finds confirmation in some broken jars from Lachish and Tell en-Nasbeh that indicate a probable capacity of five gallons and bear the label bat lammelek (royal bath) or bath alone. The capacity of the "molten sea" in the court of Solomon's temple (the circumference of which is described as 30 cubits and its capacity as 2,000 baths [1 Kings 7:23–26]), though only approximate, points to the same five-gallon volume.[5]

Egyptian Measures of Volume

ipt (cf. Heb. 'ēphah) = 4 hḳit = 16 1/3 dry quarts or 19. 2 liquid quarts
hḳit = 4.086 dry quarts or 4.8 liquid quarts
ḫir ("sack") = 16 hḳit = 65.96 dry quarts, or 72.64 liters

---

[2]W.H. Mare, WBE 2:1796.
[3]ZPEB, 5:916b.
[4]IDB, 4:835b.
[5]ZPEB, 5:916b.

The Egyptians used no special names for subdivisions of the ḥeḳat, but simply indicated its fractions—1/2, 2/3, 1/3, 1/4, 1/16, etc.

Babylonian Measures of Volume

Assyrian imēru (cognate: ḥōmer) = 29 gallons 3 pints (= 134 liters)
Sumerian gur (Babylonian kurru, cognate: cōr) = 53 gallons 1 pint (241.2 liters)
šūtu = 1/30 of kurru (in Neo-Babylonian period) = 2 gallons 7 1/2 pints
qa (Neo-Babylonian) = 1/6 šūtu = 2.35 pints (cf. Heb. qab)

IV. Measures of Weight

Hebrew Measures of Weight

kikkār (talent) = 3000 shekels = 75.6 pounds, or 34.27 kilograms
māneh (mina) = 50 shekels = 1.26 pounds, or 571.2 grams
sheqel ("weight") = .403 ounce, or 11.4 grams
pim or payim = 2/3 shekel = .268 ounce, or 7.6 grams
beqa‘ or (Aram.) perēs = 1/2 shekel = .201 ounce, or 5.7 grams
gērah ("grain") = 1/20 shekel = 8.71 grains, or 0.57 gram

Just as in the English-speaking world there is the imperial gallon as well as the U.S. gallon, so there were royal cubits and royal (or heavy) shekels. In Babylonia the royal weights were exactly double the ordinary weights. The weights discovered at Ugarit show both heavy and light (or ordinary) shekels—the latter of which weighed .34 ounce (9.5 grams). At Gezer a bronze weight was discovered that was inscribed lammelek ("to the king" or "royal") and weighed out at .79 ounce (or 22.28 grams). Apparently it was intended as a two-shekel piece and therefore the shekel must have been .39 ounce (or 11.14 grams). Since this is .013 ounce less than the average weight listed in the table above, it could result in a substantial difference when multiplied 3,000 times in the form of a talent. The stone talent weights recovered from excavations vary between 75 and 80 pounds (34 to 36 kilograms). It would seem, therefore, that despite the establishment of a definitive standard at the beginning of Israel's career as a nation (in the form of "the shekel of the sanctuary"—Exodus 30:13, 24; 38:24–26), the lack of a national Bureau of Weights and Measures and the lack of machine precision in manufacturing the stone or metal weights themselves made this amount of variation almost inevitable.

In connection with the use of standard weights for the purpose of calculating quantities of merchandise, it ought to be pointed out that precision came to be of prime importance after the invention of coined money. Before the inauguration of government-certified coinage in the kingdom of Lydia in the late eighth century B.C., it was usual to evaluate payments in bullion (whether gold, silver, or bronze) by weighing them in the scales, like any other commodity. The Egyptians often used large metal rings of standard diameters as a convenient form in which to shape this bullion for tribute or for mercantile transactions. Presumably it was possible to calculate more conveniently the amount needed for payment because of the relative uniformity of these rings in weight. But it remained for the Lydians to initiate the use of uniform ovoid lumps of electrum stamped with the royal seal, thus ushering in a new level of convenience in trade. If the weight of the coin was known, the purchaser had only to count out the requisite number of them in order to cover his cost. The enterprising commercial port of Aegina in the

Aegean Sea was the first to mint somewhat larger coins in pure silver, calling them *staters* (or "weights"). The Asiatic Near East continued the use of bullion until the reign of Darius I of Persia, calculating by the *shekel* or *siglos* ("a weight") as their standard unit—although the size and weight of these shekels tended to vary from country to country and from age to age. But when the Persian imperial government finally adopted the example of the Lydians and the Greeks (especially the Athenians, whose tetradrachmas weighed a bit in excess of the heavy shekel), they adopted the term *siglos* or *shekel*, which was simply the name of the weight on which it was based. The Greeks, however, used not only the term *stater* (as mentioned above), but also a new unit called the *drachma* ("handful"), consisting of the value of six bronze spits (used for skewering meat). The drachma was a silver coin midway between a dime and a nickel in diameter and between two and three times the thickness of an American dime. Two or three of these drachmas were equivalent to a stater (although some staters—such as that referred to in Matt 17:27—were worth four drachmas). The tetradrachma (four-drachma piece) found the widest currency in international commerce, however, and by Hellenistic times (if not before) became equivalent to the Oriental shekel. Thus, the fee paid to Judas Iscariot for betraying Jesus, consisted of thirty shekels, or tetradrachmas (presumably the Melcart eagle coinage of Tyre). Of the higher monetary units, the mina was made up of coins or bullion weighing in at fifty shekels (among the Asiatics) or 100 drachmas (among the Greeks); the talent weighed 3,000 shekels or 6,000 drachmas (the Greek unit being considerably lighter in each case than the Oriental).

Egyptian Measures of Weight

dbn = 10 kdt = 3.2 ounces, or 91 grams (3.0 ounces troy)
kdt = .32 ounces or 9.1 grams
$s^{c}ty$ + 1/12 of a *deben*

We have no information from Egyptian documents regarding heavier amounts of weight, though the Egyptians undoubtedly employed some equivalent to the talent, just as their trading partners in Mesopotamia and Palestine did. But the surviving records seem content to record heavier weights in terms of the *deben*, even though hundreds or thousands of such units were involved in the calculation of weight.

Babylonian Measures of Weight

kikkaru, gaggaru, but usually *biltu* = 3600 *šiqlu* (60 *manû*)
= 66 pounds (light) (30 kilograms) = 132 pounds (heavy) (60 kilograms)
manû = 60 *šiqlu* = 1.1 pounds (light) (500 grams) = 2.2 pounds (heavy) (1 kilogram)
šiqlu = 0.295 ounce (light) (8.33 grams) = 0.6 ounce (heavy) (16.67 grams)

In addition to the light standard and the heavy standard used for ordinary purposes in Babylonia, there was also a royal weight that likewise appeared in both light and heavy standards. These were all approximately 5 percent heavier than the ordinary units. They may have been used to compute tax or tribute payments intended for the royal treasury. The inscribed Babylonian stone weights discovered in excavations show some variation. Sellers mentions one Babylonian oval stone inscribed "one half mina, true weight" that weighs out at 244.8 grams;[6] this comes out to 489.6 grams for the *mina* itself (= 1.08 pounds avdp.). An example of the heavy *mina* occurs in a cone-shaped stone marked "one *mina*, true weight"; it weighs 979.5 grams or 2.16 pounds.

So far as measurement of area is concerned, neither the Babylonians nor the Hebrews seem to have used any such technical terms as did the Egyptians (whose *sṯt* or *aroura* measured 2,735 square meters, or about 2/3 acre; they had a *rmn* or half-*sṯt* as well, and a *ḥsb*, or 1/4 *sṯt*). In Mesopotamia land was measured by its productive capacity, e.g., an *imeru* of land—or else this referred to the amount of seed needed to sow the tract properly.

In Israel the only comparable term was the *ṣemed* ("yoke"), which referred to the amount of land a yoke of oxen might plow in a single day (cf. 1 Sam 14:14). Apart from this, all statements of area were expressed by the linear measurement of the two sides that met at an angle. This was similar to the practice followed in Mesopotamia as well.

V. Bibliography

Gardiner, A.H. *Egyptian Grammar*, 3rd ed. Oxford: Oxford University Press, 1957, pp. 197–200.
Huey, F.B. "Weights and Measures" in ZPEB, vol. 5. Grand Rapids: Zondervan, 1975, pp. 913–22.
Mare, W.H. "Weights, Measures, and Coins" in *Wycliffe Bible Encyclopedia*, vol. 2. Chicago: Moody, 1975, pp. 1791–98.
Sellers, O.R. "Weights and Measures" in IDB, vol. 4. Nashville: Abingdon, 1962, pp. 828–39.

---

[6]IDB, 4:830b.

THE CANON OF THE OLD TESTAMENT

Milton C. Fisher

Milton C. Fisher

B.A., M.A., Johns Hopkins University; B.D., D.D., Theological Seminary of the Reformed Episcopal Church; Th.M., Pittsburgh-Xenia Theological Seminary; Ph.D. Brandeis University

President, Professor of Old Testament, Theological Seminary of the Reformed Episcopal Church

THE CANON OF THE OLD TESTAMENT

I. Preliminary Considerations

"Few realize," said George Adam Smith, "that the Church of Christ possesses a higher warrant for her Canon of the Old Testament than she does for her Canon of the New."[1] He was referring to NT certification of the scope and authority of the Hebrew Scriptures, especially in statements made by Christ himself.

Acceptance of the Bible as the infallible written Word of God entails prior historical conclusions as to which books constitute Scripture. Some branches of the Christian church—e.g., Roman Catholic, Eastern Orthodox—include more than sixty-six books in the canon. Some modern sects—e.g., Mormonism, Christian Science—claim extrabiblical revelation. Muslims believe that God revealed the *Qur'an* to Muhammad from heaven, word for word. So the question of canonization (how we inherited the precise contents of our Bible) becomes a vital one for Christian faith and practice.

Consideration of the OT canon (Gr. *kanōn* through Heb. from Sumer., "reed": "rule, standard") involves historical investigation rather than theological disputation. It has to do with facts. This does not mean, however, that it is a simple inquiry. History is no mere listing of bald facts. The study of the events and products of a former age calls for evaluation of the available data, and individuals or "schools of thought" differ as to how they handle the historical material.

Concerning the canonization of Hebrew Scripture, then, there are two opposing views. One of them is contained, at least by implication, in the statements of the OT that bear on the subject of the canon. What is found there is clear enough, though admittedly limited. The other view is the prevailing stance of modern critical scholarship. It assumes that the several books or collections of books that make up the canonical OT gradually

---

[1] G.A. Smith, *Modern Criticism and the Preaching of the Old Testament* (New York: Armstrong, 1901), p. 5.

acquired an "attributed" sacredness that was not originally theirs. One meets with such statements as "Every sentence in the OT was profane literature before it became canonical sacred scripture"[2] and "[the Hebrew Scriptures are] a body of writings which had been brought together by a process of selection, given authority not possessed by their other religious literature, and invested with a sanctity which set it apart...."[3] The former approach will be pursued here, since it deals with the evidence, both internal and external, as we find it rather than as theoretically reconstructed on naturalistic presuppositions that are both foreign to and diametrically opposed to the evidence within Scripture itself.

An early eighteenth-century German theologian, Loescher, said, "The canon itself was produced, not by one act of men, so to speak, but gradually by God, who controls minds and seasons."[4] This has been misleadingly quoted in isolation in support of the view that Scripture achieved canonicity only through a long process of selection. Loescher goes on, however, to make his position clear. "There existed," he held, "from the age of Moses canonical books, from their internal light and dignity esteemed as divine from their first appearance.... To these others, recognized as divine from the time that they were written and publicly read, were gradually added, not by the judgment of Ezra or the Synagogue, or by decrees of Council or Synod (Sanhedrin), but by the universal acceptance and usage of the whole Church, until by the Book of Malachi the canon was closed."[5]

II. Definition

By way of defining canonization, a necessary distinction must be drawn between that term and the activity of selection. The church, in both Jewish and Christian eras, has served as custodian of and witness to the contents of the inspired Scriptures, but the latter do not derive their authority from any ecclesiastical body. Canonization was not a matter of the closing of a list of entries, partial or final, but a recognition of the inherent canonical quality and qualification of each portion as it became available. Thus canonicity, an innate authenticity by virtue of divine inspiration, may be viewed as antecedent to canonization, the acknowledgement of the authenticity and authority of the writings by the community of believers. It was not, as Loescher says, a matter of decree by council. Our task today, then, is to recognize by careful research what has been accomplished historically, not to agonize anew over the acceptability of each component part of the Bible. By the time the last book was written, there no longer remained a procedure of selection, of choosing which books to put in and which to leave out. Even the later debates over books such as Ecclesiastes and Esther arose among religious leaders against the background of prior acceptance by the covenant people.

III. Three Guiding Principles of Canonization

Investigators admit that there is little direct extrabiblical witness to the origin of the OT books or the actual manner of their recognition and accumulation into a fixed body

---

[2]R.H. Pfeiffer, IDB, 1:499.
[3]A. Jeffery, IB, 1:32.
[4]W.H. Green, *General Introduction to the Old Testament: The Canon* (New York: Scribner, 1898), p.111.
[5]Ibid, pp. 110–111.

of writings, or canon. Thus we can do no more than draw inferences from the sizable amount of data available both inside and outside the Bible.

A. *Canonicity an Early Concept*

Many critical scholars try to reassure us concerning the "pious fraud" involved in their view of late-date pseudonymity of Daniel and half of Isaiah. They insist that there was no concept of canonicity or even private authorship in the centuries prior to Christ's birth. Nonetheless, there is now abundant evidence from the ancient Near East of a "psychology of canonicity"—viz., a sensitivity to the inviolability of authoritative documents as far back as early second millennium B.C. This will not surprise the careful reader of the Bible. He finds no difficulty in statements that Moses (Deut 31:9ff.), Joshua (Josh 24:25, 26), and Samuel (1 Sam 10:25) placed written covenant documents in the sanctuary, for this paralleled the common practice among surrounding peoples of that day.[6]

1. *Evidence of biblical statements.* As the biblical record progresses from Sinai onward, one observes the strongly obligatory terminology appended to reports of the writing down and careful preservation of the words God spoke to his covenant people and the instructions for public recital of these words (see Deut 31:10, 11). Then, at v.26, Moses receives orders to put his book by the side of the ark of the covenant "that it may be there for a witness against thee." Joshua, Moses' successor, was to be guided by the words of this book of the law (Josh 1:8). The future king was to possess a copy of the law for constant reference (Deut 17:18, 19). We find throughout the historical books references to its use, or lack of use, by various kings: Saul, Solomon, Jeroboam, Asa, Jehoshaphat, Joash, Amaziah, Hezekiah, Manasseh.

The events of Josiah's reign merit special attention. 2 Kings 22, 23 describes the finding of the law in the temple during its restoration and Josiah's subsequent reformation activities. The assumption that this was the full Pentateuch is more suitable than the claim that it was only one book—Deuteronomy. It could be that Josiah's grandfather, Manasseh, sealed up the accusing law during his long rebellious reign of fifty-five years and died even though he did repent, without recovering it. Most important, the respect paid the law at this instance, as well as upon the return from Babylon (Ezra 7:23–26, et al.), recognizes a longstanding sanction of the authoritative written law of God. Within the increasingly verified framework of OT history, this assertion is not a matter of theological speculation so much as a necessary historical deduction, as Green rightly observed at the end of the last century.[7]

An interesting parallel in the ancient world shows how reasonable this view is. On the "human side" of the recording and preserving of divine revelation there was the impelling, even compulsive factor of the fear of God. This element suffices to eliminate any likelihood of deception, falsification, or willful tampering with ("editing" of) the sacred Scriptures. Even outside the Israelite community a similar mentality assured historical accuracy, since Akkadian omen texts, products of superstitious yet meticulous priests of divination, turn out to be more dependable records than contemporary royal annals.[8] If

---

[6]Jeffery, IB, 1:34.

[7]Green, *Canon*, p. 35.

[8]See W.J. Lambert, "Ancestors, Authors, and Canonicity" in *Journal of Cuneiform Studies*, 99 (1957), and W.W. Hallo, "New Viewpoints on Cuneiform Literature" *Israel Exploration Journal*, 92 (1962).

respect for unknown forces motivated such care among pagans, much greater caution can be expected from God's servants the prophets.

The law of the covenant determined the message and ministry of the prophets of Israel. The poetical books of Psalms and Proverbs also reflect how highly venerated was God's Word by the faithful of Israel. The last two OT prophets, moreover, sensed that they themselves stood at the close of an era of special revelation (see Zech 13:2–5; Mal 4:5).

2. *Parallel external documentation.* Of the recent discoveries relevant to biblical canon, far more significant than even the Dead Sea Scrolls are the studies of Near Eastern treaty and covenant documents. These investigations by D.J. Wiseman, G.E. Mendenhall, D.R. Hillers, M.G. Kline, and others provide helpful insight into the conceptual patterns and literary structure of Israel's covenant document, received from her sovereign king, Jehovah, God of Hosts. The fact that strictures against additions or alterations to an official decree date back to the pre-Mosaic time of Hammurabi has been acknowledged by Aage Bentzen, and other modern critics, but he fails to pursue the issue. The most directly parallel type is the suzerainty treaty, of which the best examples come from fifteenth- and fourteenth-century B.C. Hittite documents, but countless other formal inscriptions from elsewhere, spread down through OT history, can be adduced.

A simple listing of the six basic features or sections of a typical treaty prepared for a vassal by a "great king" will call to mind the structural outline of portions of Exodus, or of the whole of Deuteronomy, the Pentateuch, or, in an expanded form, the entire OT Scriptures. These are (1) preamble; (2) historical prologue; (3) stipulations, both those demanded of the vassal and those pledged by the sovereign; (4) provisions for "sacred deposit" of the text and its mandatory public reading; (5) a list of divine witnesses; and (6) promise of blessings for keeping and curses for breaking or altering the agreement. For the purposes of this essay, the most pertinent points here are the obvious equation of the agreement ("covenant") with its written form and the inviolability of the same. Thus the covenant document itself became legally binding, and it is in just such terms that Israel's prophets spoke when pressing the Lord Jehovah's case against his covenant-breaking subjects.

Critical scholars insist that "by definition" the canon has to be at a late stage in the development and formal acceptance of religious literature. But the knowledge thus gained about the behavioral patterns of ancient peoples in relation to authoritative writings should silence the argument that each book of the Bible was open to additions and changes until "officially canonized." Canonicity is demonstrably inherent in the nature of the material from the time of its first appearance.

B. *The Bible Defines Its Contents*

The Bible itself claims to be a divine word to man, channeled through a select people. Only a view of the canon that takes into account all the facts, including this self-declared uniqueness and the attitude of the people historically involved in receiving and preserving the Scriptures, will prove adequate. We must comprehend what the Bible was to them if we are to get at the manner of canonization. To recognize the OT as a covenant document moves us close to the definition of the canon.

1. *Structural clues to development.* The Pentateuch and Joshua make many explicit references to an encoded body of law. The other historical books also strongly reinforce the concept that the authority of the covenant law given by the hand of Moses was the

constant, conscious, and necessary basis for the establishment of the Hebrew theocratic nation.

The prophets not only voice God's legal complaint against the apostate nation by reference to this covenantal constitution, but refer to one another's words as authorized supplements to it. "Thus saith Jehovah" was the keynote of most of the OT prophets. Daniel "understood from the Scriptures," (9:2) how the prediction of seventy years of captivity had come to Jeremiah. Indeed there is good evidence that the Book of Daniel was originally found among the prophetic books and only later, apparently for liturgical reasons, became grouped with the "Writings."[9] Furthermore, while such passages as 2 Kings 22:3ff.; Ezra 7:14, 25; and Nehemiah 8–10 cannot, because of their chronological context, substantiate a completed canon, they are adequate witnesses to the existence of the canonicity concept in Israel.

Structural clues involve more than the dominant centrality of the Torah heralded by scholars. For if the Law itself partakes of the nature of a suzerainty treaty, other parts of the canon also reflect specific elements of that literary type: the Psalter expresses a vassal's "ratification response," the wisdom literature (Job, Prov, Eccl) develops the superior "way of the covenant" (cf. Deut 4:6–8). All this indicates a formal unity among the component writings of the OT that many fail to discern.

2. *Jewish recognition of the canon.* Even many who are not committed to the orthodox view of inspiration grant that those directly responsible for collection and canonization of the Hebrew Scriptures obviously believed that every word in them was inspired by God. It is just such faith on the part of the Israelites that is decisive. They needed only to certify the writings of accredited prophets, from Moses onward, to ascertain the expanding contents of their canon. So conscientious were they that success in the preservation of the Hebrew Scriptures is unique among ancient literatures. As Paul observes, "They have been entrusted with the very words of God" (Rom 3:2).

Flavius Josephus, Jewish historian and apologist (A.D. 37–c.100), lends valuable witness to the consensus of Jewish tradition of that time. He mentions the preservation of Scriptures in the second temple and possession by individuals of copies of the sacred books during the persecution under Antiochus Epiphanes (Jos. Antiq., Jos. War) and he elaborates the extent and format of the Hebrew Bible in *Contra Apionem*, i,8. The 22 books to which he refers correspond to the modern 39, since "the Twelve" (minor prophets) were on one scroll and others were combined by twos (e.g. Sam, Kings, Chron). Especially informative is his insistence that all the inspired books were completed between the time of Moses and Artaxerxes, successor to Esther's husband Xerxes, at which time the prophetic succession ceased, no one daring to add, take away, or alter the contents of those writings ever after.

The reader may consult the OT canon entry in a standard reference work for a list of attestations from Jewish and Christian sources, ranging from the second century B.C. to the fifth A.D. This essay is concerned only to deal generally with the evidence for completion of the canon prior to the above testimonials.

Jeffery, for example, lists fifteen external witnesses to the extent of the OT canon.[10] But each of these must be evaluated, allowing for certain biases and limitations on the part of their authors, and in appraising them, we must respect the biblical guidelines as

---

[9]See R.D. Wilson, *Studies in the Book of Daniel, Second Series* (New York: Revell, 1938), chapter 1.
[10]Jeffery, IB, 1:32.

historically sound as well as authoritative. For instance, that the Samaritans limited themselves to the Pentateuch plus Joshua and that the LXX, as preserved for us in late copies, incorporated apocryphal books in no sense establishes that the canon was flexible in the periods they represent. Adequate reason exists for their variance: narrow sectarian bias in the one case and religious attitudes broadened by hellenization in the other. And the words of Ben Sirach "I will again pour out teaching like prophecy" (Ecclus 24:33) do not necessarily claim continuation of prophetic revelation, as some judge. Furthermore, the fact that the accounts in 2 Maccabees and 4 Esdras of the roles of Ezra and Nehemiah in collecting and rewriting the OT books are legendary and undependable does not thereby rule out some significant contribution by these leaders. Nor does it discredit recognition of a firm consciousness among God's people of a complete canon of the OT about that time.

The pivotal assumption involved in the three-stage canonization theory is not so clearly attested in the NT, which speaks mainly of "the law and the prophets" (the probable meaning of "psalms" in Luke 24:44), as some suggest. While the Baba Bathra tractate of the Talmud establishes the fact that three divisions $(5+8+11=24)$ were recognized by rabbinical Judaism in the early Christian centuries, this by no means confirms critical dating of those parts (Law c. 400 B.C., Prophets c. 200 B.C., Writings fluid until A.D. 100), as Josephus' earlier list is $5+13+4=22$. Philo's witness to the canon is of particular interest because, though an Alexandrian Jew, he refers to the Palestinian tripartite arrangement and also acknowledges the same number of books as Josephus. Yet his philosophical exaltation of the Law as possessing a higher order of inspiration than the rest exemplifies the breakdown of the canon concept that took place in Hellenized Judaism. This confused the picture for Christians for many centuries. The exclusion of the apocrypha and pseudepigrapha (see APOCRYPHA AND PSEUDEPIGRAPHA) was an accomplished fact well before the time of NT references to a recognized body of Scriptures. Subsequent debates about the proper contents of that canon raised questions of the possible exclusion of certain books (rabbinical discussions as to which books "defile the hands" by their sacredness). Inclusion of additional books, however, is never argued. This pertains also to the much-heralded Council of Jamnia (actually an academy of scholars), since it reflected rather than established the firm tradition of an already-existent Hebrew OT.

C. Christ the Final Authority

It is not historically accurate to speak of Christ's having himself canonized the OT. Yet his own affirmations, by statement and use, of its unqualified divine authority do certify to us its canonicity (Matt 4:4, 7, 10; 5:17, 18; 11:10; 19:4, 5; 21:13, 42; 22:29, 31, 32; 26:31, 56; Mark 12:10, 11, 24; Luke 24:25, 44; John 10:35). Unquestionably, Christ's constant quotation from the OT Scriptures and his utter reliance on them have a crucial relationship to the canon. Therefore, the NT references (many of them recorded in Matthew but paralleled in other Gospels) that establish the content of the previous Scriptures, conclusively define for the Christian a closed canon that concurs with that attested by Josephus, Philo, and the Talmud.

1. *New Testament evidence.* Summarizing NT quotations from the OT, Westcott finds direct quotations from 28 of the 39 books (64 from the Law, 69 from the Prophets, 45 from the Hagiographa—but over 700 if all the allusions are counted), three of the

omissions being from the one Book of the Twelve.[11] Green sees all but five (Ezra, Neh, Esth, Eccl, S of Sol) as quoted, dropping to four when the first two are counted as one scroll.[12] Moreover, it is significant that while questions have been raised about the apparent use of Jewish pseudepigraphal writings in Jude (vv.14, 15), there are in the NT no direct quotations from the Apocrypha.

Phrases like "it is written" and "that it might be fulfilled which was spoken by the Lord through the prophet" show the authority attributed to the OT Scriptures by Jesus and his apostles. Indeed there are instances where Jesus and Paul based an argument on one word alone (Matt 22:42–45; Gal 3:16). That they had a publicly recognized collection or body of scripture in view is evident from such expressions of Jesus as "the Law of Moses, the Prophets, and the Psalms" (Luke 24:44) and in the Abel-to-Zechariah allusion (Luke 11:51). Both of these imply the familiar Hebrew Bible format, with Chronicles as the last book, for the references are to events recorded in early Genesis (ch. 4) and late Chronicles (2 Chron 24:20, 21). But the NT also shows familiarity not only with the tripartite canon of Josephus but with the twofold canon of "Law and Prophets," named in the Dead Sea Scrolls.

2. *Christian recognition.* The early church fathers, excepting Origen and Jerome, were probably unfamiliar with both the Hebrew language and the Palestinian Jewish canon. Unlike the subject of Christology, the question of the limits of the content of the Bible was evidently not debated in the early centuries. The oldest Christian catalog of the OT books is that of Melito, Bishop of Sardis (after A.D. 170), and he found it necessary to travel to Judea to secure information. Even Melito's list, preserved for us in Eusebius's *Ecclesiastical History*, IV, 26, raises issues by reason of some missing names (we assume these are combined with those of other books). Moreover, because of Melito's deliberate omission of Esther, Athanasius and even Luther questioned the canonicity of that book.

Nevertheless, since sufficient evidence of the Palestinian Jewish canon is available, these minor disputes become matters of historical curiosity rather than serious problems. The debate about the Apocrypha at the time of the Reformation was an unwarranted reopening of an issue long closed. Such would-be uncertainties should reassure us that the church never was the ultimate establisher of the OT canon of our Bible. We can with confidence return to that fixed body of Scripture certified by Christ and the apostles.

IV. Conclusion

God's people of all eras have accepted the Scriptures as of divine origin through supernatural inspiration. So Christians today recognize their intrinsic authority, an un-derived authority, that does not depend on anything outside themselves. This means that any view of the canon or method of explaining its formation that confuses public recogni-tion of the canon with the inherent canonicity appertaining to every portion of the Word of God from the moment of its writing is inadequate.

On the other hand, the principles developed in this article show there is only one consistent explanation of how we got our OT—one that fully acknowledges all the data evident to any inquirer open to receive biblical and historical facts. Our treatment has

---

11B.F. Westcott, *The Bible in the Church.* (London: Macmillan, 1901), pp. 43–44.
12Green, *General Introduction,* p. 143.

indicated how recent discoveries throw light on the way God structured his revelation to his people, and how his people treasured this gift. When the findings are viewed against the biblical proclamation itself, they are seen to be completely adequate. They will reassure the Bible student that the Book he handles contains all the books (and only the books) divinely determined and that these will guide into truth and nurture in life and godliness.

V. Bibliography

Green, W.H. *General Introduction to the Old Testament: The Canon.* New York: Scribner, 1898.

Harris, R.L. *Inspiration and Canonicity of the Bible.* Grand Rapids: Zondervan, 1957.

_____."Was the Law and the Prophets Two-Thirds of the Old Testament Canon?" BETS vol. 9, no. 4 (Fall, 1966).

_____."Factors Promoting the Formation of the Old Testament Canon" BETS vol. 10, no. 1 (Winter, 1967).

Jeffery, A. "The Canon of the Old Testament." IB, vol. 1. Nashville: Abingdon, 1952.

Kline, M.G. *The Structure of Biblical Authority.* Grand Rapids: Eerdmans, 1972.

Lewis, J. "What Do We Mean by Jabneh?" *Journal of Bible and Religion* 32 (1964): 125–132.

Margolis, M.L. *The Hebrew Scriptures in the Making.* Philadelphia: Jewish Publication Society, 1922.

Pfeiffer, R.H. "Canon of the Old Testament." IDB, vol. 1. Nashville: Abingdon, 1962.

Ridderbos, N.H. "Canon of the Old Testament." NBD. Grand Rapids: Eerdmans, 1962.

Ryle, H.E. *The Canon of the Old Testament: An Essay on the Growth and Formation of the Hebrew Canon of Scripture.* London: Macmillan, 1892.

Sundberg, A.C., Jr. *The Old Testament of the Early Church.* Cambridge: Harvard University Press, 1964.

Wenham, J.W. *Christ and the Bible.* London: Tyndale, 1972.

Young, E.J. "The Canon of the Old Testament." *Revelation and the Bible.* Edited by Carl F.H. Henry. Grand Rapids: Baker, 1958.

THE DEAD SEA SCROLLS

William Sanford LaSor

William Sanford LaSor

A.B., University of Pennsylvania; Th.B., Th.M., Princeton Theological Seminary; A.M., Princeton University; Ph.D., Dropsie College; Th.D. University of Southern California

Professor of Old Testament, Fuller Theological Seminary

THE DEAD SEA SCROLLS

I. Definition

Dead Sea Scrolls: the name given to an amazing find of ancient MSS discovered in caves near the northwestern end of the Dead Sea between 1947 and 1956. Some scholars have suggested other names, such as the Scrolls from the Judean Desert, the Ain Feshkha Scrolls, and, probably the best, the Qumran Library. The name Dead Sea Scrolls, however, has become firmly fixed. According to many experts, the Dead Sea Scrolls (DSS) are the most remarkable MS discovery in modern archaeology.

II. The Finds

In late 1947 and early 1948, the scholarly world was informed of the discovery of ancient MSS resulting from a chance find by Bedouin goatherds who were chasing a straying goat. The original discovery was probably made in the summer of 1947, though it has been suggested that it was actually made several years earlier. On November 29, 1947, Eliezer Sukenik of Hebrew University purchased some scrolls from an Arab antiquities dealer. This was not publicized at the time. In February 1948, Father Butros Sowmy, of St. Mark's Convent, told the American School of Oriental Research in Jerusalem about some MSS he had and shortly after took the MSS to the school, where J.C. Trever examined them. Trever, who had some expertise in paleography, decided that the MSS were indeed ancient and arranged to photograph the scrolls. He also sent a negative off to W.F. Albright in America. Albright promptly called it "the greatest

395

manuscript discovery in modern times" and estimated the date of the scroll to be about 150 B.C.

The scrolls brought to the American School of Oriental Research included the following:[1]

The St. Mark's Monastery Isaiah Scroll (1QIsaᵃ)

The Habakkuk Commentary (1QpHab)

The Manual of Discipline (1QS)

The "Lamech Scroll," later identified as the Genesis Apocryphon (1QApGen)

The scrolls purchased by Sukenik included the following:

The Hebrew University Isaiah Scroll (1QIsaᵇ)

The Order of Warfare (1QM), also known as The War of the Sons of Light against the Sons of Darkness

The Thanksgiving Hymns (1QH)

Almost certainly, the most significant scrolls were the St. Mark's Isaiah Scroll, a complete scroll of Isaiah estimated to be about 1,000 years older than any other known MS of Isaiah; and the Manual of Discipline, a handbook setting forth regulations for admission to the Qumran community and details of life in the Community. Also of great importance was the collection of hymns or psalms, which gave details of the devotional practices of a member or members of the Community.

Recognition of the value of these MSS and fragments led to some clandestine exploration of the caves, which in turn led to an official exploration that was launched in January 1949. As a result of extensive exploration, about two hundred caves were found in the general vicinity of the first cave. Twenty-five of these contained pottery similar to that found in the first cave, and eleven contained scrolls or fragments of scrolls. The most important caves were Cave One, Cave Four (where tens of thousands of fragments, pieced together, proved to be fragments of between three hundred and four hundred MSS, one hundred of which were biblical MSS including all the OT books except Esther), and Cave Eleven (where an Aramaic translation of Job, a MS of Psalms, and a copy of Leviticus in paleo-Hebrew script were found; the "Temple Scroll" may also have come from this cave).

The discovery of the scrolls at Qumran (the Arabic name of the location of Cave One and its vicinity) led to other explorations, both clandestine and official, and other finds were made at Wadi Murabba'at and Wadi Mird, and subsequently at Nahal Hever (near 'En Gedi), at Wadi Daliyeh (northwest of Jericho), and at Masada. None of these has any connection with the Qumran discoveries, other than a few fragments at Masada that suggest that one or more refugees from Qumran may have found sanctuary at Masada. This article, therefore, will not deal with these other finds.

Not far from Cave One—south of it and on a plateau below the cave—are ruins known by the Arabic name of Khirbet Qumran ("the ruins of Qumran"). This site was long known to archaeologists. Canon Clermont-Ganneau noticed and described it in 1873; Albert Vincent visited it in 1906, as did Gustav Dalman in 1914. Providentially, it had not been excavated; certainly any excavation done prior to the discovery of the Qumran scrolls would have had little significance, and the damage done in excavating the site would have prevented proper study in the light of the scrolls. The Director General of

---

[1]For a complete list of the Dead Sea Scrolls, see pages xiii–xiv.

the Department of Antiquities of Jordan, G. Lankester Harding, and Père Roland de Vaux of École Biblique, Jerusalem, visited the ruins in 1949, and in 1951 systematic excavation was begun by de Vaux. He conducted campaigns there also in 1953, 1954, 1955, and 1956.

The ruins, which came to be known as "the Monastery of Qumran"—although the presence of a few female skeletons in the Qumran cemetery and provision for the admission of women and children in the sectarian literature raise a question about the accuracy of the name—consisted of a main structure, about 100 by 122 feet, several other buildings on the north, west, and south of the main building, and a complex system of aqueducts and cisterns. The two lowest strata of the complex were with sound reason associated with the community described in the Manual of Discipline. The top level, on the other hand, was used by an entirely different group. Probably the most interesting feature of the ruins is the large room at the southern end, which was next to a pantry and a kitchen. From the size of the room and from information found in the Manual of Discipline, it was concluded that this was the common room, used for the common meals and for the assemblies of the members.

III. Dating the Finds.

Of the nearly one thousand scholars who have written on the scrolls, there are very few (almost certainly less than a score) who reject a date remarkably close to that first suggested by Albright. Those who reject this date generally argue for a later one, either at the end of the first century A.D. or as much as a thousand years later.

But how are dates for the scrolls determined? The first suggestion, in the case of the Qumran writings, came from paleographers, scholars who specialize in types of ancient handwriting. They dated the first finds around the first century B.C. Detailed study of all the materials from Qumran, plus later finds in Nahal Hever, Wadi Daliyeh, and Masada, have enabled scholars to give closer approximation to the dates of individual documents from Qumran. The Leviticus MS from Cave Eleven, for example, is dated in the third century B.C., and the latest writing is placed around A.D. 50. To the best of my knowledge, no paleographer has suggested a date later than the first century A.D. Those who reject the early date are skeptical of the ability of paleographers to date MSS.

A second basis for dating is the type of pottery found in the Qumran caves. At first this was simply identified as "Hellenistic" (i.e., 323–63 B.C.). As more pottery was found, this identification was refined to "late Hellenistic or early Roman." Pottery dating, as every person familiar with the subject knows, is somewhat relative. The identification, therefore, does not mean that the pottery was made in 63 B.C.—it simply means that we have an approximate date for the period when that kind of pottery was made.

A third method of dating is the radiocarbon method. A fragment of linen from one of the scroll coverings found in Cave One was subjected to a test for radiocarbon dating. The resulting date was A.D. 33 ± 200—in other words, a date between 167 B.C. and A.D. 233. The half-life of Carbon-14 has since been revised, and the date should accordingly be revised to 20 B.C. ± 200 (220 B.C.—A.D. 180). Samples of palmwood from the ruins yielded an average date of A.D. 8 ± 40 (i.e., 32 B.C. to A.D. 48). No one claims absolute precision for Carbon-14 dates; however, all the dates obtained by this method agree with the other lines of evidence.

A fourth basis for dating has to do with numismatics. In excavating the ruins, archeologists have found a large number of coins, either trampled into the earthen floor or buried in jars. When cleaned and studied by numismatists, the coins (excluding a few late intrusions) could all be dated between 140 B.C. and A.D. 68. This furnished strong evidence that Levels I and II of the building complex were in use between these dates.

A fifth basis for dating is linguistic. The Aramaic of the Qumran Aramaic documents has been assigned by scholars to a period in the last centuries B.C. or the first century A.D.

Skeptics pick these bits of evidence apart. The date of the pottery does not in itself date the MSS, nor does the date of the linen or that of the coins. But the total evidence must be considered. Scrolls, and the piece of linen, were found in jars. So were the coins. All the discoveries come from the same area—namely, a region within several hundred yards of the ruins of the "monastery." It seems highly reasonable to assume that the data relate to the same original—a community of people who copied and composed MS documents and conducted their common life in the "monastery," who later hid their precious MSS in caves and their money in jars when news of the approach of the Roman legion was received, and who were destroyed by the Romans in their advance on Jerusalem in A.D. 68.

IV. The Qumran Community

Evidence for the reconstruction of the Qumran community comes from two sources: the sectarian documents (i.e., those documents that apparently were produced by the Community itself, some of which describe the Community or include details of its religious and social structure) and the building complex and its surrounding area where the life of the Community was lived out. To this are generally added the descriptions of the Essenes found in Philo, Josephus, Pliny the Elder, and Hippolytus of Rome. But this evidence skips a logical link—namely, proof that in discussing the Essenes these writers were describing the Qumran community. In other words, what is to be proved is assumed. In my work *The Dead Sea Scrolls and the New Testament,* I have devoted a chapter (pp. 131–141) to comparing these non-Qumran sources with what we know about the Qumran community. The rest of section IV of the present article summarizes my conclusions.

The Qumran community was composed of Jews. Of this there can be no doubt, since their library consisted mainly of the OT writings and their sectarian documents make it clear that they were Jewish in faith and liturgy. But they were sectarian Jews, who had clearly repudiated the Jewish leadership at Jerusalem and had gone out to found a community of God. Sprinkled through their literature are pejorative terms for the Jerusalem leadership. They called themselves "sons of light," while the others were "sons of darkness." Other self-designations were "sons of truth," a "house of truth," "men of God's lot," and many similar terms. The others were "sons of perversion," "men of the pit," "men of Belial's lot," etc. In the development of Judaism there had been several schisms. We know this from other evidence. The Asideans (the Ḥasidim) revolted against Antiochus and his attempts to secularize the religion of the Jews. Their descendants, the Pharisees, resisted efforts that would lead to further deterioration of their religion. A further division separated Sadducees from Pharisees, and somewhere along the line there was a schism that produced a sect that came to be known as the Essenes. At least seven, and perhaps as many as twelve Jewish sects are mentioned in various writings of the period. The similarities between the Qumran group and the Essenes have led many scholars (including myself) to see some connection between them. The differences between the Qumran group as described in their own literature and the Essenes as described by the writers already mentioned have led me to the conclusion that there was a further division between Essenes and Qumranians.

The Qumran group, then, was sectarian. To enter it, a Jew had to undergo a period of rigorous testing, something like that of a novitiate. He was indoctrinated in the laws of the Community (1QS 6:15), described in the words "[brought] into the covenant." This was done by the "Supervisor." At the end of a year he was examined by the "Many" (probably the entire Community). If he was accepted, he turned over his wealth to the "custodian of the property of the Many" (1QS 6:20)—obviously the Community practiced community of goods. But the candidate still faced a second year of testing, during which he could not "touch the drink of the Many" (1QS 6:20–21)—a reference, it seems, to a sacred religious item, which some have compared to the Lord's Supper. Meanwhile, his property, which had been turned over to the custodian, could not be spent for the Many; in other words, it was held in trust. If at the end of the second year, the novice was approved by the Many, he was given a rank in the Community, and his property, counsel, and judgment belonged to the Community (1QS 6:22–23).

The Community lived in the wilderness of Judea. Hence we can assume that their life was rigorous. They not only practiced community of goods but had very little if any private life. They ate in common and apparently spent much of their time in spiritual practices, such as reading the Scriptures and examining their own and each other's spiritual progress. If we properly understand the statements in their literature, they had something like an annual test, at which time a member was advanced or set back in his rank. For sufficient reason, a member could be banished from the Community—a penalty that, under the conditions, seems almost like a living death.

The system of aqueducts and cisterns or collecting basins has already been mentioned. The Qumran community was early identified, therefore, as a "baptist" sect, and many scholars have connected John the Baptist with it. At this point an investigation of the Qumran concept of baptism if there was such, is in order. There are references in DSS to the "purity of the Many" (1QS 6:17) and the "water of impurity" (1QS 3:4, et al.) No one who was not in the "covenant" (probably meaning fully accepted into the Community) was permitted to "enter into the water to touch the purity of men of holiness" (1QS 5:13). This seems to indicate that the "baptism" was not an initiatory rite, but was reserved for those who had passed all other tests. From these and other references we are inclined to the view that Qumran baptism was a sacred ritual reserved for those who were "pure," or who had purified themselves (cf. 1QS 3:6–9; 5:13–14). It was not a rite by which a person was admitted to the Community.

A. Beliefs of the Community

In *The Dead Sea Scrolls and the New Testament,* I have devoted several chapters to the daily life of the Community, their doctrine of God, their doctrine of man, and their eschatological views. Here is a summary of these beliefs. The life of the Community was, as has already become apparent, highly legalistic. They were committed to study and to the Law. Their doctrine of God was markedly deterministic. Because of the place they gave to Satan or Belial, they have often been described as holding a dualistic view, but a correct definition of dualism militates against this, for God and Satan are nowhere presented as coeval or coequal. God is sovereign. Satan is his agent, permitted to control the evil impulses. Stress on the Spirit in Qumran has led some scholars to see here the foundation of the doctrine of the Spirit that is more fully developed in the NT. But there are many passages in the Qumran literature where "spirit" seems to be used more of man's spirit, his inclination to good or evil than of the Spirit of God. Still, the doctrine of "spirit," whether we define it as something outside man or as part of his nature, is emphasized in the Qumran writings. Careful study of the Qumran idea of the spirit and its possible relationship to or bearing on the development of the NT doctrine is called for.

The eschatological ideas of Qumran are particularly significant. The Qumranians believed that they were living in the end-time. The Order for the Congregation begins with the words "This is the order for all the Congregation of Israel in the last days" (1QSa 1:1–2). The Order of Warfare is concerned entirely with the final war between the sons of light and the sons of darkness. But whether it is to be understood literally or figuratively is not clear. The Qumran literature has numerous references to the judgment, some of them quite graphically portrayed. The term *Messiah* occurs a number of times; from my studies I conclude that it was the son-of-David messianic concept, whereas the apocalyptic Son of man is totally absent in Qumran literature. God promised to send a "teacher of righteousness" in connection with the end of the age. That teacher is nowhere identified with the Messiah; in fact, he has more the role of one preparing for the Messiah.

The beliefs of the Community, then, can be summarized as basically Jewish beliefs, with an uncommon emphasis on determinism, on the part played by Satan, and on the person of the Messiah. The Thanksgiving Hymns (also known as the *Hôdayôt,* from the Hebrew word for "thanksgivings") present us with evidence of a deep devotional life that springs from the OT.

B. *The Teacher of Righteousness*

A figure is mentioned (a relatively few times, we might note), called by the Hebrew name *môrè haṣṣédeq,* which can be translated as "the teacher of righteousness," meaning either that he teaches righteousness or that he is righteous. Accordingly, we find him mentioned as "the righteous teacher" as well as "the teacher of righteousness." In spite of the paucity of material in the DSS directly relating to this figure, volumes have been written about him. Indeed, extreme claims have been made for him, one claim going so far as to say that Jesus Christ was only an "astonishing reincarnation" of "the teacher of righteousness"![1] If we add together various conclusions of a number of scholars, we get a composite picture of the Teacher of Righteousness that includes a virgin birth, a messianic significance, crucifixion, resurrection, ascension, and a second coming. Yet in the DSS themselves there is not a single statement to support any one of these claims! (For a detailed study, see LaSor, *The Dead Sea Scrolls and the New Testament,* pp. 106–130, 206–224.)

If we limit our study to what is specifically stated about the Teacher of Righteousness in the DSS, we get the following information. He did not found the Community. Rather, it was twenty years later that God "raised up for them a teacher of righteousness" (CD 1:8–11). It should be noted that the term is indefinite here and may not refer to the one called "the teacher of righteousness." This teacher they heeded, for the Community believed that he received from God the ability to interpret the prophets concerning the end of the age (1QpHab 2:1–3, 6–9; 7:4–5). On the other hand, he was opposed and persecuted by the "Wicked Priest" (1QpHab 11:4–8; cf. 1QpHab 1:12), and the "house

---

[1]André Dupont-Sommer, *The Dead Sea Scrolls* (New York: Macmillan, n.d.), p. 99.

of Absalom" did not help the Teacher of Righteousness "against the Man of Falsehood" (1QpHab 5:9–12). The exact meaning is not clear, but obviously there was external pressure, which resulted in persecution, and (if we may so interpret the statement "swallow him up") death for the Teacher. A similar expression, "the gathering in of the one teaching the Community" is found in the Damascus Document (CD 20:13–15). Since the Community believed in the resurrection of the dead, it may be assumed that they believed that their Teacher would be raised up, and this may possibly be the meaning in the statement "they will not attain to the rising of the teacher of righteousness in the last days" (CD 6:10–11). This, however, certainly cannot be understood to teach that God had already raised him up!

It is possible, of course, to find other passages in the Qumran writings that either refer to the Teacher (unnamed) or were written or spoken by the Teacher. For example, some scholars are convinced that many of the Thankgiving Hymns were composed by the Teacher. Other scholars are inclined to attribute to him much of the sectarian literature, such as the Order of Warfare and the Commentaries.

Such suggestions are warranted, and we have no doubt that there is a measure of truth in them. The person who left an indelible mark on the Community must have been a man of great spiritual stature. But to attempt to reconstruct his life on the basis of words and phrases pulled from context is to build hypothesis upon hypothesis. Would any of these scholars agree that we could reconstruct the life of David from selected portions of the Psalms? On the other hand, the spiritual stature of Jesus is beyond question. But what writings shall we attribute to the Teacher of Righteousness? The entire hypothesis is shaky. The fact is simple: we know very little about him.

V. The Significance of the DSS

The importance of this great discovery can be treated under four main heads: (1) the contribution to the study of the text of the OT, (2) the contribution to the study of the development of Judaism in the intertestamental period, (3) the contribution to the study of the development of Hebrew and Aramaic in the intertestamental period, and (4) the contribution to the study of the origin and development of Christianity. The fourth head is the least satisfactory, in many respects, and yet it is the one that has had the most attention. For that reason, we shall consider it first.

A. The Origin and Development of Christianity

How, we may ask, could the Qumran community have had any influence on early Christianity? First, John the Baptist may have grown up as a member of the Community, derived his ideas from them, and passed these on to his disciples who in turn became the first disciples of Jesus. Or, going a bit further, Jesus himself may have grown up at Qumran—at least some scholars have suggested this.

The second suggestion is absurd. There is no place in the NT record, either historically or psychologically, for Jesus to have "grown up at Qumran." When he began his ministry at Nazareth, the people of the town were offended. They knew him and they knew his background. He was the "carpenter" and the "carpenter's son." Where did he get his amazing wisdom and power? No one ever gave the slightest hint that he had been absent for a long period studying at some schismatic or sectarian institution.

The other suggestion, that John the Baptist lived at Qumran, has much to commend it. The NT records that he was "in the wilderness of Judea" until he began his ministry of baptizing (Luke 1:80; 3:23). Anyone who has visited the wilderness of Judea (that portion eastward from a line drawn between Jerusalem and Hebron) knows that there are exceedingly few places where a child could survive. Qumran is one of the very few places, and we have no knowledge of any others in that area at that time. Moreover, there are several points of similarity between John's teaching and the Qumran beliefs. He believed as they did that the end of the age was upon them. He quoted from Isaiah 40 as they did. He practiced baptism. But we must look at the complete picture, not only at the similarities. John's parents, Zechariah and Elizabeth, were members of the "establishment"—Zechariah, indeed, was one of those priests at Jerusalem whom the Qumranians labeled "sons of Belial," "men of the pit," etc. Is it likely that these devout people would have entrusted their son to schismatics who would teach him to hate his parents along with all the other "sons of darkness"? Again, John's doctrine of baptism was not the Qumran doctrine. His baptism was a baptism of repentance. It was for sinners. It was an initiatory rite, by which repentant sinners could enter into the kingdom of God. There was no period of testing. Baptism was administered as soon as the sinner repented. This is totally unlike the Qumran doctrine, which admitted only the pure to the waters of purifying. And yet again, John's attitude toward the Jerusalem leadership was diametrically opposite to that of Qumran. As far as the Qumranians were concerned, the "sons of darkness" were doomed to the pit. A Qumranian was strictly forbidden to make known the truth to the "children of the lie." John the Baptist, on the other hand, looked on all men as salvable. He called on all to repent and be baptized. The kingdom of God was open to all who would come by repentance and baptism. I therefore find it difficult to believe that John was ever a member of the Qumran community. If he was, he must have broken with it totally and must have repudiated the very points that were supposed to have been basic to his ministry.

There are many other points at which the church is supposed to have received influence from Qumran. Some of them are trivial (such as the "twelve" and the "three"; in Qumran they added up to fifteen; in the Church, the three—Peter, James, and John— were part of the Twelve), and some are of considerable importance (such as the "church idea," the concept of community and commonality of all things, or the stress on the spirit). These are dealt with one by one in my book *The Dead Sea Scrolls and the New Testament*, pp. 142–205. Here I can only summarize my conclusions. In the first place, both Christianity and Qumran were Jewish "sects." They had a common origin in the OT and the religion that developed from it in the intertestamental period. Both looked to the grace of God for their salvation. Both recognized the importance of the Law, but Qumran tended to be more legalistic, whereas Jesus and Paul looked on the Law as principial. Both had the tradition of the Passover. The sacred meal at Qumran, like the Lord's Supper, can ultimately be traced to the Passover. But the distinctives of the Christian Supper are not found in the Qumran meal. Both Qumran and Christianity had a tradition of twelve tribes, of elders, of priests, of sacrifice. Qumran distinguished between priests and "Israel," the laity; in Christianity all believers were considered priests. Both groups found unusual spiritual nourishment in the prophecy of Isaiah. Isaiah's emphasis on the Spirit of God could account for the development of the doctrine at Qumran. Certainly the Qumran doctrine of the Spirit falls far below that presented by Jesus and developed by Paul. Both Qumran and Christianity developed from the period when messianic and eschatological hopes were strong in Judaism. It is not necessary to say that Christianity developed from Qumranism. Jesus, as the Son of God, was certainly sufficiently creative in his teaching to develop the fundamentals of Christian doctrine. Consider just two points where the originality of Jesus is incontrovertible: he certainly was the first to combine the royal messianic idea (the son of David on the throne of David) with the suffering-servant doctrine in a single person, and he clearly seems to be the first to unite the human son-of-David messianic idea with the heavenly Son-of-man apocalyptic figure.

B. *The Text of the Old Testament*

The significance of the DSS for textual studies is unquestioned. Yet a lot of detailed and hard work will have to be done before the results are clear. Prior to the finding of the scrolls, textual scholars, seeking to discover the earliest likely form of the OT text, had to work from a Hebrew text from the tenth century A.D., a Greek translation (the LXX) made probably between 250 and 100 B.C., a Latin translation (the Vulgate) made between A.D. 385 and 420, and other early versions. Now, however, for the portions of the OT recovered at Qumran, scholars have a Hebrew text from around 100 B.C. Early results in general confirm the accuracy of the existing Hebrew text (often called the Masoretic Text, though it is several centuries earlier than the Masoretes). But at several points we have evidence that a Hebrew text different from the NT lay behind the LXX. The evidence of NT quotations of the OT should have already suggested this possibility.

C. *The Development of Judaism*

The significance of the scrolls for the study of the development of Judaism does not, unfortunately, interest many Christian scholars. All too often the religious background of Jesus and the apostles is presented as though there were no intertestamental period and no development of the religion of the Jews beyond that found in the OT. As a result, many Christians fail to see the connection of the OT with the NT. For an attempt to make a study of the scrolls on this point, see my dissertation, "A Preliminary Reconstruction of Judaism in the Time of the Second Temple in the Light of the Published Qumran Materials," later popularized in *Amazing Dead Sea Scrolls and the Christian Faith* (1956). Much more has been done since then, and doubtless much remains to be done. All scholars admit that the DSS fill a gap that previously could be filled only by questionable statements in Josephus, by statements in the NT suspected of pro-Christian and therefore anti-Judaism bias, and by oral tradition preserved in the rabbinical literature suspected of having been colored by the Pharisaic heritage that alone had survived the destruction of Jerusalem by the Romans in A.D. 70 and 135.

D. *The Development of Hebrew and Aramaic*

As for linguistic studies, here the significance of the scrolls (though of primary interest to this author) lies beyond the scope of the present article. It should, however, be noted that Hebrew was still sufficiently alive at the turn of the era for the Qumran sect to write its Manual of Discipline in Hebrew. Therefore, we should not shrug off the statement that Paul spoke "in Hebrew" (Acts 21:40) as meaning that he spoke in Aramaic. Moreover, we must note that the Aramaic of Daniel, which, according to the almost-unanimous opinion of critical scholars, could not have been written before 167 B.C., is considerably different from the Aramaic of the Qumran texts that are written in that language. Daniel, as Montgomery long ago noted in his commentary on Daniel, is linguistically closer to the fifth or fourth century B.C. than to the second or first.

Without question, the DSS are one of the greatest MS discoveries of all time. Thirty years after their discovery, their importance is in no way diminished.

VI. Bibliography

Discovery

de Vaux, Roland. *L'Archeologie et les manuscripts de la mer Morte*. Schweich Lectures, 1959. London: Oxford University Press, 1961.
Samuel, Mar Athanasius Yeshue. *Treasure of Qumran: My Story of the Dead Sea Scrolls*. Philadelphia: Westminster, 1966.
Trever, John C. *The Untold Story of Qumran*. Westwood, N.J.: Revell, 1965.
Yadin, Yigael. *The Message of the Scrolls*. New York: Simon and Schuster, 1957.

Interpretation

Bruce, Frederick F. *Second Thoughts on the Dead Sea Scrolls*. Grand Rapids: Eerdmans, 1956.
Burrows, Millar. *The Dead Sea Scrolls*. New York: Viking, 1955.
———. *More Light on the Dead Sea Scrolls*. New York: Viking, 1958.
Cross, Frank M., Jr. *The Ancient Library of Qumran and Modern Biblical Studies*. Garden City, N.Y.: Doubleday, 1958; rev. ed. Anchor Books. 1961.
Jeremias, Gert. *Der Lehrer der Gerechtigkeit*. Göttingen: Vandenhoeck & Ruprecht, 1963.
LaSor, William S. *Amazing Dead Sea Scrolls and the Christian Faith*. Rev. ed. Chicago: Moody, 1959.
———. *The Dead Sea Scrolls and the New Testament*. Grand Rapids: Eerdmans, 1972.
Rowley, H.H. *The Dead Sea Scrolls and the New Testament*. London: SPCK, 1957.
———. "The Qumran Sect and Christian Origins." *Bulletin of the John Rylands Library*. 44 (1961–62):119–156.
———. "The Teacher of Righteousness and the Dead Sea Scrolls." *Bulletin of the John Rylands Library*. 40 (1957–58): 114–146.

Texts

Barthélemy, D. and Milik, J.T., eds. *Discoveries in the Judaean Desert* (later volumes add *of Jordan*). Oxford: Clarendon, 1955ff.
Habermann, A.M. *mᵉgillôt midbar yᵉhûdā* (*The Scrolls of the Wilderness of Judah*). Tel Aviv: Machbaroth Lesifrut, 1959. (This work includes 1QpHab, 1QS, 1QM, 1QH, and most of the important fragments to the time of publication, with vowel-pointing and concordance.)
Lohse, Eduard. *Die Texte aus Qumran, Hebräisch und Deutsch, mit Masoretischer Punkation, Übersetzung, Einführung und Anmerkungen*. München: Kösel, 1964.

Periodicals

Revue de Qumrân (entirely devoted to the Scrolls, each issue giving the current bibliography on the subject).
Revue Biblique, The Biblical Archaeologist, Bulletin of the American Schools of Oriental Research (the major finds promptly and accurately reported in these).

Bibliographies

Burchard, Christoph. *Bibliographie zu den Handschriften vom Toten Meer*. Berlin: Töpelmann, vol. 1, 1957; vol. 2, 1965. (including practically all works to 1962).
Jongeling, B. *A Classified Bibliography of the Finds in the Desert of Judah 1958–1969*. Leiden: Brill, 1971.

LaSor, William S. *Bibliography of the Dead Sea Scrolls, 1948–1957.* Pasadena, Calif.: Fuller Theological Seminary, 1958 (listing works by subject with cross-reference and author indices).
Revue de Qumrân (each issue adding all known works on the Scrolls).

THE LANGUAGE OF THE NEW TESTAMENT

J. Harold Greenlee

J. Harold Greenlee

A.B., Asbury College; B.D., Asbury Theological Seminary; M.A., University of Kentucky; Ph.D., Harvard University; Senior Fulbright Fellow, Oxford University.

Missionary of OMS International and International Translation Consultant for Wycliffe Bible Translators

THE LANGUAGE OF THE NEW TESTAMENT

I. Periods of Greek Language Development

   A. Ancient dialects
   B. Rise of the Koinē

II. The Greek of the New Testament

   A. Knowledge of Greek in First-Century Palestine
   B. Bilingualism in the New Testament World
   C. Characteristics of the Koinē
   D. Importance of the Papyri
   E. Influence of the Old Testament on the Greek New Testament
   F. Styles of New Testament Authors

III. Bibliography

I. Periods of Greek Language Development

The Greek language has the longest and most fully recorded history of all European languages. It has been spoken for nearly 3,500 years and has a continuous written history since the Homeric literature of the seventh century B.C.

A. Ancient Dialects

The Greek language did not break up into distinct languages as did Latin, and ancient Greek is not a "foreign language" to a modern citizen of Greece as Anglo-Saxon is to a speaker of English. There has, of course, been constant development and modification of the language through the course of the centuries, with a general trend toward simplification of forms and with expansion, contraction, and change of areas of meaning of words. Five periods of language may be identified, though the following dates must be regarded as only approximations: (1) Prehistoric—prior to the eighth century B.C.; (2) Classical—to 300 B.C.; (3) Hellenistic—to A.D. 500; (4) Byzantine—to A.D. 1450; and (5) Modern.

During the early centuries of written Greek, the language had developed into several dialects of varying degrees of mutual intelligibility. At the same time, it became customary for educated writers to use different dialects for different types of literature. Homer, for example, wrote in the Epic dialect, which survived as the vehicle for epic poetry down to the Byzantine period. Lyric poetry was written in a modified Doric, while the

409

poet Sappho wrote in Aeolic. Attic was the dialect of drama and rhetoric, and prose literature was written in Ionic, with some in Doric. With the rise of the Athenian Empire under Pericles in the fifth century B.C., however, the Attic dialect began to spread its influence; and by the fourth century, beginning with Plato, most writers were using Attic, though the local dialects continued in use as well for everyday language.

B. Rise of the Koinē

About the middle of the fourth century B.C., Philip II of Macedon adopted the Attic dialect for his kingdom in place of the local Macedonian. When Philip's son, Alexander the Great, spread his empire around the Mediterranean world and as far as the borders of India to the east, his armies carried the Greek language with them and planted it in the conquered lands. The Greek they spread, however, was no longer pure Attic. Alexander's soldiers came from all parts of Greece and spoke various dialects. This, plus the factors of travel and commerce, helped produce a Greek that was Attic at its base but was modified by other dialects, especially Ionic. By the first Christian century, this Hellenistic—that is, "Greek-istic" rather than local—dialect had become the common language of international discourse throughout the Roman Empire; hence its designation koinē ("common"). It was both widespread and the language of the common people.

Paul speaks of the time for Christ's advent having "fully come" (Gal 4:4). In the first Christian century the Roman Empire had united vast areas and many peoples under her control and had established political tranquillity, the "Pax Romana." Thus, travel throughout the empire was relatively easy and safe when Christian missionaries set out to fulfill the Great Commission. Yet another factor of the greatest significance in the "fullness of time" was the common knowledge of Greek throughout these vast regions, making it possible to proclaim the Christian message without learning a new language at each frontier.

II. The Greek of the New Testament

A. Knowledge of Greek in First-Century Palestine

Evidence for the widespread use of Greek is not lacking in the NT. The mother tongue of Jesus and his disciples, and the language they doubtless used ordinarily in conversation and in teaching, was Aramaic (a Semitic language used in everyday speech in Syria, Mesopotamia, and Palestine from c.300 B.C. to A.D. 650). Yet when some visiting Greeks desired to see Jesus (John 12:20–23), there is no indication that Philip had any problem of communication with them or that Jesus would have had. The conclusion is much more likely that Jesus and the disciples knew Greek than that the Greeks spoke Aramaic. The very presence of Greeks "among those who had come up to worship at the feast," moreover, argues for some degree of bilingualism either by these Greeks or by some of the people of Jerusalem; and it is much more probable that Greek was known in Jerusalem than that the non-Jewish Greeks would know Aramaic. In the trial of Jesus there is no evidence that an interpreter was needed between Pilate and either the Jews or Jesus. It is unlikely that the Roman governor was conversant with Aramaic and even less likely that the Jews knew Latin. The logical assumption is that the entire discussion was carried on in Greek. Paul wrote his Epistle to the church at Rome in Greek, not in Latin or Aramaic. Even the Epistle "to the Hebrews" was written in Greek—indeed, in the most literary Greek of any book of the NT. It was in Greek that the Roman tribune and Paul conversed after the apostle had been rescued from the Jewish mob at the temple (Acts 21:37). Peter's communication with the Roman centurion Cornelius and his friends (Acts 10) must have been in Greek, and likewise his sermon on the day of Pentecost. It is noteworthy that Greece is not included in the list of lands in whose (foreign) languages the disciples' praises of God were being heard (Acts 2:5–11).

B. *Bilingualism in the New Testament World*

At the same time, local languages were maintained alongside the use of Greek, just as scores of tribal languages are maintained today alongside Spanish, French, and other trade languages. This was clearly the case with the Jews and their use of Aramaic. The fact that certain Aramaic expressions are found in the Gospels—as Jesus' words *"Talitha koum,"* spoken to the daughter of Jairus (Mark 5:41); *abba;* and *rabboni*—should not therefore be taken to mean that Jesus normally spoke in another language and interjected this Aramaic phrase for some special effect (though it could be thus interpreted if other evidence supported the hypothesis). It appears, rather, that they were words from expressions the NT writers chose to preserve in their original form because of their special significance or the significance of the events in connection with which they are used. In the same way a missionary, relating a story of his work in a foreign land, will occasionally quote a word or phrase from the language as originally spoken and then translate it into English.

It was bilingualism at Lystra that brought Paul and Barnabas into a rather difficult situation (Acts 14:8–20). The populace evidently had no difficulty in understanding the two Christian messengers, who certainly spoke in Greek. Yet in speaking among themselves about this matter of deep emotional overtones, they used their own Lycaonian language. Paul and Barnabas, not understanding what was being said, did not realize what the people were planning to do until the preparations for a sacrifice to them were well under way.

The references to Hebrew and Aramaic in the NT warrant a further word. The use of Hebrew, as written in the OT and spoken by the people of Israel in earlier centuries, had given way prior to the Christian era to Aramaic, a similar yet distinct Semitic language, as the spoken language of the Jews. By the time of Christ and earlier, therefore, though the rabbis and scholars knew Hebrew, when the Hebrew Scriptures were read in the synagogue, it was customary to give a translation into Aramaic for the benefit of the common people. At the same time, there is some uncertainty concerning the possible occasional use of Aramaic or Hebrew in certain incidents recorded in the Gospels and Acts. The fourth Gospel states that the inscription on the cross of Jesus was written in "Aramaic, Latin, and Greek" (John 19:20). Since the inscription was ordered by Pilate, "Aramaic" is probably correct, rather than archaic biblical "Hebrew." Jesus' cry from the cross "My God, my God, why hast thou forsaken me?" is given in slightly differing Greek transliteration by Matthew (27:46) and Mark (15:34), possibly representing Hebrew and Aramaic respectively. Paul, telling King Agrippa of his conversion, says that Jesus spoke to him on the road to Damascus in Aramaic (Acts 26:14). This could be either biblical Hebrew, which Paul knew well, or Aramaic, which he certainly ordinarily spoke. When Paul, after being rescued by the Roman soldiers from the mob at the temple, addressed the Jews, he spoke to them "in Aramaic" (Acts 21:40); and "when they heard him speak in Aramaic, they became very quiet" (22:2). It has been suggested that they were "very quiet" because Paul was speaking to them in the archaic language of the OT and they would need to give close attention in order to understand it; or because they at first had expected Paul to address them in Greek, which they realized they would not be able to understand; or, what is more likely, because they now realized that Paul was one of themselves, using the Aramaic a non-Jew was not likely to know. The term *Hebrew* ('Εβραϊστί, *Hebraisti*) as it appears in the Greek NT may simply mean "the language spoken by the Hebrew people," just as John 19:20 uses the term *Roman* ('Ρωμαϊστί, *Hrōmaisti*) rather than "Latin."

C. Characteristics of the Koinē

As has been mentioned, koinē Greek was somewhat of a mixture of dialects. For example, where Attic had the spelling *-tt-* (as in *thalatta*, "sea") and *-rr-* (e.g., *arrēn*, "male"), koinē Greek generally adopted the Ionic spelling *-ss-* and *-rs-* (*thalassa, arsēn*). Pronunciations of various vowels and diphthongs were merged, resulting in only about seven distinctions in pronunciation for twice that number of written forms. A prominent characteristic of koinē, however, was simplification of forms and style. The optative mood, a common feature of the classical dialect, was gradually lost, its functions taken over by the indicative or the subjunctive mood, much as the English subjunctive mood has largely been replaced by the indicative or by forms using "may," "should," etc. As a result, the NT contains relatively few instances of the optative, the most common being Paul's phrase *mē genoito* ("may it not be"; KJV, "God forbid"). The middle voice of the verb, by which Greek could say in one word, for example, "I-wash-myself" or "I-wash-(something)-for-myself," was giving way to the active voice plus pronoun, as in English. Irregular forms of verbs and declension endings tended to be modified to fit the pattern of regular forms. The future tense of the infinitives and participles were becoming rare and occur hardly at all in the NT. On the other hand, koinē tended to use prepositional phrases to replace pure cases (e.g., *ek* with the genitive case instead of the genitive case alone, and *en* with the dative case instead of the dative case alone). Prepositions—sometimes more than one—much more frequently than in classical Greek were prefixed to verbs and derived words to add a meaning or to give emphasis. At times the resulting compound form came to be no more emphatic than the simple form, as *erōtaō* and *eperōtaō* ("ask"), which are used synonymously in the NT. In other instances the compound form simply replaced the simple form. For example, the NT always uses the compound verb *apollymi* ("destroy"), never the simple form *ollymi*; and the simple verb *thnēskō* ("die") occurs in the NT only in the perfect tense, the other tenses using the compound form *apothnēskō*, which is synonymous in meaning.

At the same time, it must not be assumed that koinē Greek was a uniform entity. There is even some confusion concerning the term "Hellenistic Greek." All through the history of Greek there were naturally various literary levels of the language, depending on the writer or speaker, and there were differences between the written and the spoken style even of an educated person. About the first Christian century, moreover, a movement arose to turn back the linguistic clock by advocating the old classical form of Greek as the only proper form, decrying the koinē as debased and corrupt, somewhat as if present-day American authors would insist on writing in the style of the KJV. Unfortunately, this point of view won out, and authors began attempting to use a supposedly elegant style and archaic vocabulary that was divorced from the language of everyday life and was not really their own language; and this situation continues even to the present day. The term "Hellenistic," therefore, is sometimes restricted to this artificial or "Atticistic" style in contrast with the koinē dialect of everyday life and of unsophisticated writings including the NT.

The koinē dialect on its literary level is found in pagan Greek writers from about the third century B.C., including the historian Diodorus, the geographer Polybius, and the essays of Epictetus. Some light on koinē forms and words is to be derived from the works of the Atticistic grammarians, where they cite these koinē forms in order to warn against their use. Notes written on ostraca, or broken pieces of pottery, lie at the other end of the literary scale. Inscriptions on tombs and official inscriptions show examples of the koinē in a formalized style.

D. *Importance of the Papyri*

One of the greatest contributions to the understanding of koinē Greek has been made only during the past eighty years. Since the Revival of Learning, the Greek of scholarly study was classical Greek, and the norms and rules of classical Greek were applied to any Greek writing, including the NT. When the grammar, style, or vocabulary of the NT failed to agree with the classical form, one of three conclusions was usually drawn. Some scholars condemned the NT forms as "bad Greek." Others insisted that, since the NT was a divine revelation, it was proper that it should be in a form distinct from other literature, and consequently they called the Greek of the NT a special "language of the Holy Spirit." Still others referred to it as "Jewish Greek," to be accounted for by the influence of Hebrew and Aramaic on the writers.

In the meantime, during the nineteenth century, scholars and archaeologists were giving their attention to a wealth of documents from the koinē period, written on papyrus, that were being found in increasing numbers in Egypt. Many of them had been dumped onto ancient rubbish heaps and covered by the drifting sands of the desert. These MSS included samples of virtually the entire range of written Greek documents—from copies of works of the classical writers to legal matters, from personal letters and schoolboys' exercises to receipts and business inventories. In the 1890s, soon after some of these texts had been published, a German pastor, Adolf Deissmann, happened to be reading one such volume. He was struck by the similarities of these texts to the style, form, and vocabulary of the NT. Dedicating himself to this investigation, he published two books known in English as *Bible Studies* (1895) and *Light From the Ancient East* (1908). He concluded that the NT was neither bad Greek nor a special divine language, but rather that it represented the language of everyday life of the first century, Greek as it was spoken by people of the educational and cultural level of the writers of the NT. Meanwhile, many other scholars have studied the papyri. Today Deissmann's general thesis is universally accepted. Some 50,000 papyrus texts have been published, including some MSS of the NT itself that are older than any NT MSS previously known. Deissmann's contribution has been called "the greatest single discovery of an interpretative principle ever made in NT archaeology."[1]

Another result of the study of the papyri has been the finding of many Greek words that occur in the NT but were unknown in classical literature. As a result, instead of scores of words once thought to be unique to the NT, now all but a few have been accounted for outside the NT. Even words found in classical Greek as well as the NT have become better understood from the study of the papyri. Words are subject to change of meaning with the passage of time, and the papyri have repeatedly illuminated a meaning of a NT word that differed from its classical meaning to a greater or lesser degree. Moulton and Milligan's lexicon, *The Vocabulary of the Greek Testament Illus-*

---

[1] Cobern, *The New Archaeological Discoveries*, p. 30, quoted by Minn, p. 11.

trated From the Papyri and Other Non-Literary Sources (1930), is a valuable volume dedicated entirely to this class of material.

E. *Influence of the Old Testament on the Greek New Testament*

There is still another significant factor in the Greek of the NT. All the NT writers, with the possible exception of Luke (whom, however, W.F. Albright believed was a converted Jew),[2] were Jews. Their sacred Scriptures were the books of the OT. Although most of the OT references and quotations in the NT were from the Septuagint rather than from the Hebrew original, even the Septuagint is a book of Hebrew ideas and thoughts. Just as the expressions of the KJV have permeated the English language, so the concepts and expressions of the OT give an undercurrent to the Greek NT. At the same time, there are relatively few strictly Jewish-biblical words in the NT. The extensive lists of such words that are found in older works have now been reduced to a handful by discoveries in the papyri.

F. *Styles of the New Testament Authors*

The NT, then, is a monument of the Greek language as it was spoken in the first century A.D., not of the artificial and sophisticated style of the Atticists. Its heritage includes classical Greek, the OT in Hebrew and in Greek translation, and the speech of the common people. The NT, moreover, originated new classes of literature, which actually are not "literature" in any formal sense. The Gospels, for example, were a new type of work; they are not biography, for they do not give personal descriptions, nor an analysis of the principal characters, nor a full life-story even of Jesus. Neither the Gospels nor Acts are primarily "history." Paul's Epistles, while more than mere personal letters, are not literary oratory. The motivation throughout the NT was not to produce literature or promote its authors, but to proclaim the message of salvation through faith in Christ.

There are, of course, several levels of language and style in the books of the NT. At one extreme, the Epistle to the Hebrews, with its careful progression of argument and arrangement of words, is a model of the koinē in good written, as opposed to spoken, form. Luke and Acts, too (both books certainly the work of one author), reveal Luke's knowledge of good literary Greek. Luke is able to vary his style, making it more colloquial, more Jewish, or more elegant. There are interesting contrasts between the speech of Peter at the Council of Jerusalem (Acts 15:7–11), Paul's speech in Athens (Acts 17:22–31),[3] and the rhetorical formalities of the speeches of both Tertullus and Paul in the judicial hearing before Felix (Acts 24:2–9, 10–21). Yet Luke himself is not free from using colloquial irregularities, as in Acts 8:7; "for many of those who had unclean spirits, crying [i.e., the unclean spirits] with a loud voice, were coming out" (literal tr.).

Certain scholars have had a "field day" pointing out instances that they maintain show that John's Gospel is filled with Semitic expressions and with Greek "mistranslations" of an underlying Aramaic original. Yet one of the most remarkable features of these investigations is the almost total disagreement of such scholars with one another con-

---

[2]W.F. Albright, *History, Archeology, and Christian Humanism* (New York: McGraw, 1964), p. 296: "All the authors of the New Testament were certainly or probably Jews—even Luke, with his Aramaized Roman freedman's name and his use of Hebrew sources." Cf. also Albright, *New Horizons in Biblical Research* (London: Oxford University Press, 1966), p. 49: "In my opinion Luke himself was a converted Jew."

[3]In this speech Paul even refers to God as *to theion* (the pagan Greek neuter concept of "the deity"), which is the sole NT instance of this phrase.

cerning the specific examples of these "Semitisms." John's style, rather, is the style of a person of some education using a conversational form. His irregularities are generally colloquialisms, not Semitisms, which often find parallels even in the present-day English of educated people who would never use the same expressions in their formal written work. For example, the statement in John 15:5, "He who abides in me and I in him . . ." (RSV), is perfectly clear but "and I in him" cannot be construed grammatically. Similar expressions occur in John 1:15, "This is he whom I said . . ." (literal tr.) for " . . . concerning whom . . ."; the redundant possessive in John 1:27, ". . . *of whom* I am not worthy to loose the thong of *his* sandals" (literal tr.; cf. colloquial English, "He is the one *that* I am not worthy to loose the thong of *his* sandals"); and John 12:23, "The hour is come that the Son of man should be glorified" (KJV; instead of " . . . has come in which . . ."). John's frequent use of *kai* ("and"), not uncommon in the other Gospels, is a well-known feature of spoken English. With all of John's simplicity of style, however, his profundity of thought at times is unequalled.

The Epistles of John were certainly written by the author of the Gospel. But the question of the authorship of Revelation is not so simple. The grammar of Revelation is so inferior that most scholars have concluded that it is impossible for the author of the fourth Gospel and of the Epistles of John to have written Revelation, though W.F. Albright disagreed. "It is not impossible," he said, "that it [Revelation] was written by the author of the Gospel and the Epistles of John, the author using an amanuensis in these, but writing his own uncorrected Greek in Revelation." (Dr. Albright offered this possibility in a lecture at Asbury Theological Seminary, October 18, 1962.) Revelation has been said to be the work of a Semitic-speaking person who was just learning Greek, as evidenced by its poor grammar. It is true that Revelation is full of ideas and imagery of the OT. Yet its grammatical "blunders" are not Semitic idioms translated into Greek; they have parallels in colloquial Greek papyrus texts, many of which are grammatically inferior to Revelation.

Mark is the least literary of the Gospels, but has a simple and vivid style. The author uses the word *euthys*, "immediately," about forty times.

The style of Paul stands in contrast, in various ways, to those of John, Mark, Hebrews, and Revelation. Paul is thoroughly steeped in the OT, but he speaks the Greek of an educated man. In contrast with Hebrews, Paul's style exhibits the irregularities and broken constructions to be expected in letters that were more personal than formal presentations, that were often written in response to other letters, dictated without later revision, and sometimes written out of deep feelings. More than once Paul begins an argument, digresses to a different matter, and either never returns to his original point or returns by a different grammatical route. In Romans 8:3, for example, the subject "God" never receives its verb (which should be "did" or "accomplished"), though the point is clear enough. In 1 Thessalonians 4:14, what Paul clearly means but does not precisely say is that "if we believe that Jesus died and rose again, then *we also believe that* God . . . ."

Paul's Greek vocabulary, moreover, is permeated by the OT and by Christian concepts. Though this is evident in all the NT books, it is probably more extensive in Paul's writings. To cite but one example, *dikaios* and its family of words ("righteous," "justification," etc.) had an ethical significance in secular Greek that Paul sometimes uses. He also uses these words, however, especially in Romans and Galatians, in the sense of "forgiven" and "salvation." So in Romans 4:5, "who justifies the ungodly" means "who saves the ungodly," whereas in nonbiblical Greek it would mean to condemn or punish (i.e., "to give justice").

The style of the Greek NT has implications for translations into other languages. If the original was written in the language of common speech, then a translation into English or any other language should likewise be in the language of common speech. Part of the genius of the Greek NT (and OT) is that it was not written in the archaic and artificial style that many secular writers, and even later Christian writers, affected. Through the influence of the KJV, there has come down to our age something of a "religious" style of speech, sprinkled with such archaisms as "thou," "givest" (often used incorrectly), "forth," and "unto," in a manner quite foreign to the common style of speech of the original NT. Without failing to appreciate the beauty of the KJV and other literary versions of the Bible, it is well to note that translations into the language of everyday life, whether English or the language of an Indian tribe in the jungle, stand strictly within the tradition of those who wrote the original NT under inspiration of the Holy Spirit.

III. Bibliography

Browning, Robert. *Mediaeval and Modern Greek*. London: Hutchinson University Library, 1969.

Colwell, Ernest Cadman. "The Greek Language." *Interpreter's Dictionary of the Bible*, vol. 2, pp. 479–487. New York: Abingdon, 1962.

————. *The Greek of the Fourth Gospel*. Chicago: University of Chicago Press, 1931.

Metzger, Bruce M. "The Language of the New Testament." *Interpreter's Bible*, vol. 7, pp. 43–59. New York: Abingdon, 1951–57.

Minn, H.R. *Living Yesterdays*. Dunedin and Wellington, New Zealand: A.H. and A.W. Reed, 1939.

Moulton, James Hope. *A Grammar of New Testament Greek*. Vol. I, *Prolegomena*, 3rd ed. Edinburgh: T. & T. Clark, 1908.

Thomson, George. *The Greek Language*. Cambridge: W. Heffer, 1960.

Wilder, Amos N. *The Language of the Gospel*. New York: Harper and Row, 1964.

THE TEXTUAL CRITICISM OF THE NEW TESTAMENT

Gordon D. Fee

Gordon D. Fee

B.A., M.A., Seattle Pacific College; Ph.D., University of Southern California

Associate Professor of New Testament, Gordon-Conwell Theological Seminary

THE TEXTUAL CRITICISM OF THE NEW TESTAMENT

I. Introduction

Textual criticism, commonly known in the past as "lower" criticism in contrast to the so-called "higher" (historical and literary) criticism, is the science that compares all known manuscripts of a given work in an effort to trace the history of variations within the text so as to discover its original form. Textual criticism is, therefore, of special significance to the interpreter in at least three ways: (1) It helps to determine the authentic words of an author. The first question the exegete asks is, What does the text say? before he asks, What does it mean? (2) The majority of Christians have access to the NT only in translation, and the basic consideration in choosing a translation is its accuracy in representing the original text of the author. A translator's first concern must be that he is translating the actual words of the author before he decides what those words mean. (3) A knowledge of the history of textual variation will also help the interpreter to see how a passage was understood during the early history of the church. In many instances variant readings are a reflection of a scribe's or a church's theological interests, and sometimes such changes put one in direct contact with historical exegesis.

II. The Need

The need for NT textual criticism results from a combination of three factors: (1) The originals, probably written on papyrus scrolls, have all perished. (2) For over 1,400 years the NT was copied by hand, and the copyists (scribes) made every conceivable error, as well as at times intentionally altering (probably with the idea of "correcting") the text. Such errors and alterations survived in various ways, with a basic tendency to accumulate (scribes seldom left anything out, lest they omit something inspired). (3) There are now extant, in whole or in part, 5,338 Greek MSS, as well as hundreds of copies of ancient translations (not counting over 8,000 copies of the Latin Vulgate), plus the evidence from the citations of the NT in the writings of the early church fathers. Moreover, no two MSS anywhere in existence are exactly alike.

The task of the textual critic, therefore, is (1) to sift through all this material, carefully collating (comparing) each MS with all the others, in order (2) to detect the errors and changes in the text, and thus (3) to decide which variant reading at any given point is more likely to be the original.

III. The Sources

The sources for finding the original text are the Greek MSS, the ancient versions, and the citations by the early fathers. Although many of the extant MSS (both Greek and versional) are fragmentary and the majority do not contain the whole NT, there is such a quantity of material that even the most poorly attested NT book, the Book of Revelation, has been preserved in over three hundred Greek MSS, while the Gospels are extant in thousands of copies.

A. *The Greek Manuscripts*

Primacy of position in the quest for the original text belongs to the Greek MSS, partly because they are copies of copies in the original language of the biblical authors, and partly because the oldest ones are generally earlier than the other evidence (though age is no guarantee of better quality). The MSS are of four kinds: papyri, uncials, minuscules, and lectionaries.

The original documents of the NT were probably written on papyrus scrolls. The scroll, however, was cumbersome both for reading and for finding specific passages. As a result, Christians very early began to use the codex, or leaf-form of book, to copy their sacred writings. All extant fragments and copies of the NT, therefore, are codices; no copies on scrolls have ever been discovered.[1]

---

[1]Father Jose O'Callaghan recently suggested that some Greek fragments of scrolls in Qumran Cave 7 should be identified as parts of the NT (*Biblica*, 53 [1972]: 91–100; trans. by W.L. Holladay and published as a

The book form also allowed Christians to include more than one document in a single codex, though it was not until the development of the canon and the emergence of large parchment codices (4th century A.D.) that copies of the entire NT were made.

1. *The Papyri.* The earliest codices were written on papyrus leaves in uncial (capital letter) script, with no separation of words and little or no punctuation. Because papyrus is naturally perishable, few of the early copies have survived except in the dry sands of Egypt. So far, fragments or larger sections of eighty-five different papyrus MSS have been discovered. These range in date from approximately A.D. 125 (P[52], a single small fragment of John 18:31–34, 37–38) to the eighth century (P[41], P[61]), though the majority belong to the third and fourth centuries. Every NT book except 2 Timothy is represented in these MSS. Several of the papyri are well preserved and present the earliest significant witness to the NT text. For example, P[45] (c. A.D. 250) has substantial sections of the synoptic Gospels, P[75] (c. A.D. 200) contains more than half of Luke and John, P[66] (c. A.D. 200) about two-thirds of John, P[46] (c. A.D. 225) substantial portions of Paul's letters, P[72] (c. A.D. 275?) large sections of Jude and 1 and 2 Peter, and P[47] (c. A.D. 280) about one-half of Revelation.

2. *The Uncials.* About the beginning of the fourth century, vellum (or parchment) began to replace papyrus as the primary writing material. These prepared animal skins had the advantage both of greater durability and larger size, so that from the sixth century to the fourteenth almost all literary efforts of all kinds were written on parchment.

The scribes of the earlier of these codices (from the fourth to the ninth century) continued to use the uncial script. There are currently 268 known uncials, many of them preserved without blemish. Only one, however, Codex Sinaiticus (ℵ, c. A.D. 350), preserves the entire NT. (It also contains the Epistle of Barnabas and the Shepherd of Hermas.) The great Codex Vaticanus (B, c. A.D. 325) includes everything except Hebrews 9:14–13:25 and Revelation, while the majority contain NT sections, such as the Gospels or the Pauline letters. These MSS are designated in two ways: by capital letter and by Arabic numeral with a zero prefixed. The earlier known MSS have two designations (D-05), while the later ones simply have the number (0268).

3. *The Minuscules.* At the beginning of the ninth century a script of small letters in a running hand (called "minuscule" or "cursive"), which stands in contrast with the uncial (capital letter) script, was created. The advantages of minuscule texts both in speed and economy were quickly recognized, so that by the end of the tenth century, uncial texts were no longer produced. The vast majority—2,792 to date—of extant MSS are these late minuscules. They are designated by Arabic numerals from 1 to 2,792.

4. *Lectionaries.* The second largest group of MSS of the NT are the lectionaries. These are texts written, not in regular sequence, but in accordance with the designated daily and weekly lessons from the Gospels and Epistles—lessons that had been developed in very early times.

There are presently 2,193 known lectionary MSS, the earliest fragments dating from the sixth century and complete MSS from the eighth. They are, therefore, both uncial

supplement to the *JBL*, 91 [June, 1972]); however, his "find" has not held up under careful scrutiny (see, e.g., G.D. Fee, "Some Dissenting Notes on 7Q5 = Mark 6:52–53," *JBL*, 92 [1973]: 109–112).

and minuscule and contain either the Gospels or Epistles, or sometimes both. The lectionaries are designated by Arabic numerals prefixed with an italicized or cursive *l*(*l*2193).

B. *The Versions*

Because of the broad missionary outreach of the early church, copies of most of the NT documents had been translated by the end of the second century into Latin, Syriac and Coptic. In the following centuries other translations followed: Gothic, Armenian, Georgian, Ethiopic, Slavonic, and Arabic.

Because the Old Latin, Old Syriac, and Coptic versions were made very early and because their geographical location is fairly well fixed, they are particularly important in the recovery of the original NT text. Their use, however, is complicated by several factors. In the first place, certain features of Greek syntax and vocabulary are difficult or impossible to convey in translation. One can never be certain, therefore, what their Greek text looked like. For example, Latin has no definite article and the Syriac cannot distinguish between the Greek aorist and perfect tenses. Furthermore, it is highly probable that more than one translation was made in each of these languages by different persons, in different places, using different Greek texts. Finally, the earliest extant MSS of these versions are copies nearly two hundred years later than the original translation. Consequently they have very likely suffered their own fate of textual corruption.

In spite of these complications, however, the ancient versions are a valuable source not only in the quest for the original text itself, but also in the attempt to trace the history of textual transmission and corruption. These older versions are variously designated: some are identified by small Latin letters (a, b, c, or it^a, it^b, etc.) for the OL, while the others are identified by a superscript designation after an abbreviated form of the version (syr^c syr^{pal} cop^{bo}).

The later versions and the "authorized revisions" of the older versions, viz., the Vul. and the Syriac Peshitta, are of more limited significance. Scholars, of course, make use of all evidence. But the bewilderingly complicated history of the Vul., which makes it a textual study in its own right, tends to give it a place of secondary importance even among the versions.

C. *Patristic Citations*

The final source of data for the textual critic is from the citations and allusions to the NT found in the writings of the early church fathers. As with the versions, their usefulness is complicated by several mitigating factors.

Most often the fathers cited the NT from memory, so one can never be sure that their memory reflects the actual wording of their Greek text. Moreover, a father may have used several—and differing—copies of the NT. Finally, the available texts of the patristic writings also are copies, usually very late ones, and in some cases have suffered extensive corruption.

Yet when the painstaking work of reconstructing the NT text cited by one of the fathers is done, it is of great value. For it gives us a datable and geographically identifiable witness to the NT available to that particular father. Although such a witness is generally tertiary to the Greek MSS and the versions in the recovery of the original text, it is of primary importance in tracing the history of textual transmission.

D. Manuscript Relationships

The immense amount of material available to the NT textual critic, exceeding all other ancient documents by hundreds of times, is both his good fortune and his problem. It is his good fortune because with such an abundance of material he can be reasonably certain that the original text is to be found somewhere in it. Quite in contrast to those searching for other original texts (including the OT), he scarcely ever needs to resort to textual emendation, though the possibility must always be kept open that the very first copy of the original MS, from which all others derived, had some uncorrected errors.

However, the abundance of material is likewise the textual critic's problem, because no two copies are exactly alike, and the greater the number of copies, the greater the number of variants among them. Even in this day of computer technology, sifting through such an immense amount of material is a formidable task. This is especially so in light of the ideal that each piece of evidence must be used in order to identify the original by detecting possible corruption of the NT text.

The task, however, is not quite so formidable as it might at first appear. Although it is true that no two MSS are identical, it is equally true that many are so much alike that they tend to group themselves into three (some textual critics think four) major families of texts (text-types). Such text-types are identifiable on the basis of (1) the percentage of agreement certain MSS have with one another over a total area of variation and (2) the amount of agreement these MSS have in variant readings peculiar to them.

There is, first of all, a group of MSS that have all the appearances of being "local" texts, since they derive basically from Alexandria in Egypt. It is headed by P75 and P66 (c. A.D 200) in the Gospels, P46 (c. 225) in Paul, P72 (c. 275?) in Peter and Jude, Codex B (c. 325), and the citations of Origen (225–250). It is also supported to a lesser degree by several other MSS (e.g., ℵ C L W 33) and the later Alexandrian Fathers (Didymus, Athanasius, Cyril).

For many years textual critics have considered this text-type to be a carefully edited recension of the third century, created by the best Alexandrian scholarship on the basis of good ancient MSS. But the combined evidence of P75, P72, P46, and Origen has placed this text in all of its particulars squarely in the second century, or, so it seems, as early as Christianity was known in that city.

Although this text-type has occasional "sophisticated" variants, it commonly contains readings that are terse, somewhat rough, less harmonized, and generally "more difficult" than those of other text-types, though on closer study they regularly commend themselves as original. Furthermore, it is consistently so across all the NT books, with a minimal tendency to harmonize an author's idiosyncrasies with more common Greek patterns. All these facts give the impression that this text-type is the product of a carefully preserved transmission.

A second group, equally as early as the Alexandrian, is commonly called "Western," because variants peculiar to it are firmly established in texts found in North Africa (Tertullian, Cyprian, some OL), Italy (Novatian, some OL), and southern France (Irenaeus). "Western," however, is something of a misnomer, for many of the peculiar variants of this text-type are also found in the East (Tatian and the Old Syriac) and occasionally in Alexandria (some quotations in Clement, in John 6–7 in P66, in John 1–8 in ℵ, and in Mark 1–5 in W).

In spite of this early and wide attestation to such a text, these various witnesses lack the homogeneity found in the Alexandrian and later Byzantine witnesses. The textual relationships are not consistently sustained over large portions of text. On the contrary,

"Western" describes a group of MSS headed by Codex D, obviously related by hundreds of unusual readings, sometimes found in one or several, sometimes in others, but apparently reflecting an uncontrolled, sometimes "wild," tradition of copying and translating. This text-type is particularly marked by some long paraphrases and long additions, as well as by harmonistic tendencies and substitutions of synonyms. In fact, the Western text of Acts is about 10 percent longer than other texts and almost certainly reflects an early revision.

One must be careful, however, not to dismiss a variant reading out of hand simply because it is Western. There are several instances, especially in some striking "omissions" but in other places as well, where scholars have cogently argued that the Western text preserves the original NT text. Moreover, the very antiquity of this text, and its wide distribution, should always gain for it a full hearing.

The third text-type, the "Byzantine" or "majority" text, is made up of over 80 percent of all the MSS. As a text-type it does not appear in history until about A.D. 350, but even then its origins are shrouded in mystery. Readings peculiar to this text first appear in a group of writers associated with the church of Antioch: the Cappadocians, Chrysostom, and Theodoret of Cyrus. These fathers had a NT about 90 percent along the way to the full Byzantine text of the Middle Ages. The earliest MS to reflect this text is from Alexandria (Codex A; c. 475—in the Gospels only), while the earliest full witnesses to it are MSS from the eighth century (E and Ω).

Does this text, therefore, represent a revision effected in Antioch in the fourth century? Most textual critics think so, but they do so on the basis of the secondary nature of its peculiar readings, not because of firm data. There are no early MSS from Asia Minor or Palestine. The earliest writers from these parts reflect a Western text, but there was no Origen or Tertullian in Antioch in the early third century to give us a large amount of data to study. Later in the century the scanty evidence from Methodius of Lycia and Tyre and, still later, from the text of Eusebius of Caesarea and Cyril of Jerusalem seldom reflects the peculiarities of this text-type. Thus the nature of the text in Antioch over many years is virtually unknown.

What is known is that such a text was available by A.D. 350, that it had partially begun to influence the text of Alexandria and Rome (Jerome), that it was carried by Chrysostom from Antioch to Constantinople, and that probably through his influence it became the dominant text in the Eastern church.

Most of the readings peculiar to this text are generally recognized to be of a secondary nature. A great number of them smooth out grammar; remove ambiguity in word order; add nouns, pronouns, and prepositional phrases; and harmonize one passage with another. Its many conflate readings (e.g., Mark 9:49), where the Byzantine text-type combines the alternative variants of the Alexandrian and Western texts, also reflect this secondary process.

Some scholars also find a "Caesarean" text-type in the Gospels, supported sometimes by P45, W, Θ, family 1, family 13 and the citations of Origen (in Mark), Eusebius, and Cyril of Jerusalem. There is indeed some obvious textual relatedness among these witnesses (especially in Mark), but whether they constitute a separate text-type, rather than some unusual mixtures of the other three, remains doubtful.

Although there is general agreement that making such groupings is both a possible and a necessary task, the significance of such groupings remains contested. It is surely dubious procedure to accept or reject a reading solely because it is found in a certain text-type; on the other hand, such groupings, especially of the later (Byzantine) MSS, greatly reduce the work of sifting a multiplicity of MSS.

IV. The Text in History

In order to understand the "how" of NT textual criticism, it is necessary to understand something of the history of the transmission of the text, as well as to have some knowledge of the history of textual criticism itself.

A. Period of Confusion (to A.D. 400)

The vast majority of the errors in the NT MSS occurred during the period that is also the most difficult to reconstruct—the first four Christian centuries.

Much of the difficulty stems from the work of the earliest Christian copyists. In a time when the majority of people were illiterate and when Christianity periodically underwent severe persecution, there were probably few professionally trained scribes in the service of the church. Moreover, seldom were the scribes possessed by the spirit of the scribes of later times who worked according to the instructions of the Lord given in Deuteronomy 12:32: "Thou shalt not add thereto, nor diminish therefrom." In fact, the opposite seems to have been true of the scribes in the first two centuries. They introduced thousands of changes into the text. To be sure, the majority of their errors were unintentional and are easily discernible slips of the eye, ear, or mind. Hundreds of changes in the text were, however, made intentionally. Yet we should not think of these scribes as having acted from evil motives. If they often took many liberties in copying their texts, apparently they did so in most cases in an attempt to "help out." They were more interested in making the message of the sacred text clear than in transmitting errorless MSS.

Thus, early scribes (and sometimes later ones) often "smoothed out" the Greek of the biblical writer by adding conjunctions, changing tenses of verbs, and changing word order. They also tended to clarify ambiguous passages by adding nouns or pronouns, by substituting common synonyms for uncommon words, and sometimes even by rewriting difficult phrases. One of the most common causes of error was the tendency to conform one passage to another. This harmonizing tendency is particularly frequent in the Gospels. It also occurs in parallel passages in Paul and Acts. There are also some instances—and these are usually very important ones—where scribes have added (or less often, subtracted) whole sentences or narratives in the interest of doctrine or completeness.

During the second century in particular, when each NT book was being transmitted independently of the others and when there was wide geographical distribution of these documents with little or no "controls," such scribal errors proliferated. Once an error was introduced into the text, it was then copied by the next scribe as his "received" text. Quite often a scribe "corrected" what he thought to be errors and in doing so created errors of his own. If, as did the scribe of P66, he had a chance to check his copy against another, he may then have "corrected" his text by adding still other variants from that copy. So errors were created and compounded and so they tended to accumulate.

B. Period of Transmission (400–1516)

Two significant events affected the history of the NT after A.D. 400. The Alexandrian text, which by 450 was already greatly influenced by the Byzantine, generally disappeared from use. The major causes for this was the demise of the patriarchate in Alexandria and the subsequent rise and spread of Islam.

On the other hand, Latin had meanwhile become the predominant language in the West, so that production of Greek texts ceased there. The great number of discrepancies found in the OL MSS had finally resulted in an "authorized" translation, the Latin Vulgate, made by Jerome c. 384. But it took about two hundred years before it superseded the more popular older translations. Meanwhile, as it was being copied and carried from one part of the West to another, the Vul. was variously conformed to the OL and developed local textual histories. Several attempts were made throughout the Middle Ages to purify Jerome's text, but each of these recensions eventually resulted in further corruption. As a result, the over 8,000 extant Vul. MSS reflect an enormous cross-contamination of text-types.

The result of these two factors was that the transmission of the Greek NT was generally limited to the Eastern church, where the majority of copies reflected the standardized text used at the capital, Constantinople. Thus the history of the Greek text during this period, with a few notable exceptions, is simply the history of a thousand years of copying MSS of the Byzantine text-type.

C. *Establishment of the Textus Receptus (1516–1633)*

Johannes Gutenberg's invention of printing by use of movable type was the next major factor in the history of the NT text. For now many copies of a book, all identical, could be produced. Although the first Greek NT actually to be printed was edited by Cardinal Ximenes in 1514, the first text to be published appeared in 1516 and was edited by the great Dutch humanist, Erasmus.

Unfortunately, these first editions, which were to serve as a base for all subsequent editions until 1831, were themselves based on late medieval MSS of inferior quality. In fact, Erasmus's only MS of Revelation lacked the final leaf, which had contained the last six verses. For these verses Erasmus used the Vul., translating its text into Greek, with the result that his Greek text has readings that have never been found in any Greek MS.

Of the subsequent editions, three have special significance for the history of the NT text: (1) Robert Stephanus's third edition (1550), which was based on Erasmus's third edition, became the standard text in England and served as the base for the KJV of 1611. His fourth edition (1551) is also noteworthy in that it is the first text to be divided into numbered chapters and verses—the system still in use today.

(2) Theodore Beza, John Calvin's successor in Geneva, published nine editions between 1565 and 1604, and this tended to stamp an imprimatur on the text of Erasmus. His editions of 1588–9 and 1598 were also used by the King James translators.

(3) A Greek text very much like those of Erasmus, Stephanus, and Beza, edited by Bonaventure and Abraham Elzevir (1633), became the standard text used on the continent. The term *Textus Receptus* (TR = "received text") derives from the preface of this edition, in which the editors declared, "You therefore have the text which is now received by all, in which we give nothing altered or corrupted." This boast was to hold good for over two hundred more years.

D. *Period of Discovery and Research (1633–1831)*

The next period in the history of the NT text was one in which scholars made great efforts to amass new information from Greek MSS, the versions, and the fathers. Yet the texts published during this period continued to print the time-honored TR; the new evidence, especially that from much earlier MSS, was relegated to variant readings in the apparatus (i.e., the critical notes). Among the large number of scholars who made contributions during this period, especially noteworthy are J.A. Bengel (1734), who was the first to suggest a classification of MSS into text-types and to devise a system of evaluating variants according to merit; J.J. Wetstein (1751–2), who set forth extensive principles of textual criticism and began the device of designating MSS by symbols; and J.J. Griesbach, whose editions from 1774 to 1807 laid the foundation for all subsequent textual criticism. Griesbach modified Bengel's classifications of textual groups into the basic three, which are still recognized. He elaborated and carefully defined the principles of textual criticism and showed great skill in evaluating the evidence for variant readings. Although his own text was not so divergent from the TR as those that would follow, his pioneer efforts paved the way for what was to come.

E. *Period of Constructive Criticism (1831–1881)*

The period that followed Griesbach was to see the overthrow of the TR and the rise of new critical editions based on the more significant MS finds and the principles of criticism pioneered by Wetstein and Griesbach.

The first important break from the TR came in 1831 with the Greek text published by the German classicist Karl Lachmann. His was the first systematic attempt to produce a text using a scientific method rather than the mere reproduction of the text of the Middle Ages.

More significant still was the voluminous and monumental work of Constantine von Tischendorf. Besides bringing to light many hitherto unknown MSS, he published eight critical editions of the Greek NT, the last of which (1872) contained a critical apparatus giving all the variant readings of the known uncials as well as reading for many cursives, the versions, and the church fathers. This volume is still an indispensable tool for NT textual criticism.

Although many others made contributions during this period (especially S.P. Tregelles), the Greek text edited by B.F. Westcott and F.J.A. Hort (WH 1881) was to supersede all others in significance. So thoroughly and well did they do their work that almost all subsequent textual criticism is defined in relationship to it. Their forte was the refinement and rigorous application of a scientific methodology to the NT text. The result was issued in two volumes as *The New Testament in the Original Greek*. Volume 1 contained their resultant Greek text; volume 2 comprised a lengthy Introduction, written by Hort, and an Appendix, in which certain problem passages were discussed.

In the Introduction Hort set out in full detail what has become a classic statement of the methodology of textual criticism. Especially significant are his careful analyses and evaluations of the relative merits of the various text-types and their leading representatives. Above everything else, Hort forever laid to rest the TR. He offered three main arguments against the Byzantine text-type (he called it Syrian), which subsequent discoveries and researches have generally validated: (1) The Syrian text-type is filled with conflate readings, i.e., readings that combine the elements found in the earlier two text-types; (2) the readings peculiar to the Syrian text-type are never found in the ante-Nicene Fathers, neither East nor West; and (3) when the readings peculiar to this text-type are compared with rival readings on the principles of internal evidence, "their claim to be regarded as the original readings is found gradually to diminish, and at last to disappear" (Introduction, p. 116).

Westcott and Hort were thus left with a choice between the two earlier text-types. At this point internal considerations became the final arbiter, and they felt that a careful analysis of variants over many pages of text revealed the text of Egypt, or Alexandria, (which they presumed to call "Neutral") to be far superior in almost every case. Thus their resultant text was an edition of the Neutral text-type, except in those instances where internal evidence was clearly against it.

F. *Since Westcott and Hort (1881 to the present).*

As one might expect, such a radical departure from the "received text" was not immediately accepted by all. This is particularly true of the English-speaking world, where the TR had long been in the hands of the majority of Christians through the KJV. The reaction to WH was led especially by J.W. Burgon, Edward Miller, and H.C. Hoskier. Unfortunately, much of the reaction, especially that of Burgon, took the form of rhetoric rather than argument; and what argument one does find is basically theological and speculative, but seldom supported by the actual textual data.

This is not to suggest that all subsequent scholarship has followed WH. Most scholars found their affirmation of the Alexandrian MSS as neutral to be too ambitious. In spite of such disavowals, however, all subsequent critical texts look far more like WH than like the TR or the Western MSS. Therefore, it is fair to say that, whether intentionally or not, the mainstream of NT textual criticism since WH has moved toward modifying and advancing their work. In this brief survey it is possible to sketch only some of the more important advances.

1. *New Discoveries.* Probably the most important advance since WH is the discovery of large quantities of new textual data of all kinds. Among these, the most significant are the papyri, because for the most part they represent evidence earlier than that available to Westcott and Hort.

Many of the first discoveries of earlier evidence showed such a textual mixture that Westcott and Hort's theories of text-types were seriously called into question. But later discoveries, especially P46, P72, and P75, have tended to verify the basic positions of Westcott and Hort. Furthermore, the papyri have generally confirmed their opinion as to the late character of the Byzantine text-type. One does find an occasional variant in the early papyri that supports the later text-type, but none of the early papyri is even remotely related to the Byzantine MSS.

2. *Other Researches.* Besides the discovery of new MSS, other researches of various kinds have also greatly advanced the science of textual criticism since WH.

Especially noteworthy has been the work done that sheds more light on the versions and on Tatian's Diatessaron (an arrangement of the four Gospels to form a single narrative) and the collecting and editing of the citations of the early fathers. The usefulness of this work is now far greater than in 1881.

In recent years, methodology in establishing textual relationships has also been greatly improved, not only for text-types in general but also for clearer definition of relationships within the great mass of Byzantine MSS. Such refinements of method have greatly increased the ability of textual critics to group MSS into their proper families and text-types.

Of particular interest to the exegete has been the work of such scholars as C.S.C. Williams and E.J. Epp, who have studied the theological tendencies of certain groups of variants. Such studies have made clear that not all textual variation is accidental or theologically unbiased. They further aid the exegete by throwing light on how certain passages were understood, or misunderstood, in the early church.

Two projects of large dimensions involving broad international cooperation are also of interest both to the scholar and to the interpreter: (1) The International Greek New Testament Project, composed of a team of American and British scholars, is preparing a critical apparatus of the Gospels that will include all known papyri and uncials, extensively representative cursives and lectionaries, all early versions, and citations of all church fathers to A.D. 500. (2) A team of German and French scholars, under the auspices of the Institut fur Neutestamentliche Textforschung in Münster, is at work on a new major critical edition, including a full critical apparatus. The general Epistles are the first scheduled for publication.

3. *Critical editions.* These discoveries and researches have resulted in a spate of critical texts since WH. A few should be noted because of their broad significance.

In 1913 H. von Soden published a long-awaited and massive work that included a critical text, a large and complicated apparatus, lengthy descriptions of MSS, and his own textual theory. This work, however, turned out to be a great disappointment. His textual theory never gained acceptance, his classifications of MSS have often proved to be wrong, and some of his collations are completely untrustworthy. Nevertheless, his accumulation of evidence goes beyond that of Tischendorf and is helpful to the expert when used with care.

More important to most exegetes are the smaller "pocket" editions. The most common of these is a series of editions begun by Eberhard Nestle in 1898. A twenty-fifth edition of this text was published in 1963, now under the supervision of Kurt Aland. This text was not a new critical text, but was rather based on the majority reading of the critical texts of Tischendorf, Westcott and Hort, and B. Weiss. The great usefulness of this edition has been its extensive, but abbreviated, textual apparatus.

In 1966 the United Bible Societies published a new "handbook" edition, edited by K. Aland, M. Black, B.M. Metzger, and A. Wikgren (C. Martini was added to the editorial board for the second edition [1968]). This text has been prepared especially for Bible translators and therefore has the following distinctives: (1) The critical apparatus is restricted primarily to meaningful variants, i.e., variants that may make a difference in the translation of the text; (2) each variant adopted in the text is given a notation as to the degree of certainty the editors felt it had; (3) each variant has a full citation of carefully selected representative evidence; and (4) there is a second apparatus giving meaningful alternatives in punctuation. A commentary on each variant, written by Metzger, was published in 1973.

A comparison of this text with WH and TR shows where a significant consensus of modern scholarship stands. For example, in Luke 10 the UBS edition varies from WH only eight times (plus six spelling differences), while it differs from the TR fifty-six times (plus twenty spelling differences). The reason for the differences between WH and the UBS, or among any of the modern critical texts, is fundamentally a matter of emphasis in methodology.

V. The Method

For a full discussion of the method and practice of NT textual criticism one should consult the manuals by Greenlee or Metzger. Certain basic considerations may be noted here.

One criterion above all others superintends the scholar's choice at any point of textual variation: the variant that best explains the origin of all the others is most likely to be original. In order to "best explain the origin of the others," there are two factors that scholars must consider: external evidence (the MSS themselves) and internal evidence (having to do with the authors or scribes).

A. External Evidence

The first thing one must do at any point of variation is to weigh the MS evidence supporting each variant. Thus one usually asks the following questions: How old are the witnesses supporting each variant or how old is their text? How good is the general quality of the MSS? How wide is the geographical distribution of the witnesses? This latter question is especially important, because early and widespread geographical distribution of a reading points to an original parent much further back before the document in question was widely scattered throughout the early church. With few exceptions, however, scholars are agreed that knowing the age or the geographical distribution of early witnesses in no way guarantees finding the original text.

B. Internal Evidence

Internal evidence is of two kinds: transcriptional probability (what kind of error or change the scribe probably made) and intrinsic probability (what the author was most likely to have written).

1. Transcriptional probability has to do with scribal errors and is based on certain inductively derived criteria. For example, it is usually true that the more difficult reading is probably the original one, because it was the tendency of scribes to make the text easier to read. Again, the shorter reading is often the original one, because the scribes tended to add to the text. This criterion must, however, be used with great caution because scribes sometimes made omissions in the text either for smoothness or to remove what might be objectionable. Finally, a textual variant differing from quoted or parallel material is almost always original, since the tendency of scribes was to harmonize.

2. Intrinsic probability is the most subjective element in the methodology of textual criticism. It has to do with the style and vocabulary of the author, his ideas as they are elsewhere known, and the probabilities based on the immediate context.

Not all the criteria mentioned above are equally applicable in every case; in fact, in some instances they oppose one another. For example, the longer reading may be the more difficult one, or the reading most in accord with author's style may be a harmonization with that style. In such stalemates the textual critic is usually forced back to the external evidence as final arbiter.

It is noteworthy that for most scholars over 90 percent of all the variations to the NT text are resolved, because in most instances the variant that best explains the origin of the others is also supported by the earliest and best witnesses.

C. The Debate Over Method

With the rejection of Hort's genealogical method, by which the reading of the Alexandrian witnesses was adopted except where internal evidence proved it secondary, there has emerged a method that may properly be called "eclectic." Essentially, this means that the "original" text of the NT is to be chosen variant by variant, using all the principles of critical judgment without regarding one MS or text-type as necessarily preserving that "original."

Despite a few notable exceptions, most of the differences that remain among critical texts result from a varying degree of weight given the external evidence.

On the one hand, there is a kind of eclecticism that, when all other criteria are equal, tends to follow Hort and to adopt the readings of the Alexandrian witnesses. This may be observed to a greater degree in the UBS edition and to a somewhat lesser degree in the Greek texts behind RSV and NEB, where early Western witnesses are given a little more consideration.

Another kind of textual theory was advocated by M-E. Boismard and was used in D. Mollat's translation of John in the Jerusalem Bible. This is a kind of "eclectic Western" method in which great emphasis is placed on preference for the shorter readings as they are found in various Western witnesses, especially early versions and citations from certain fathers. The difficulty with this method seems to lie in the preference for the versions and fathers over against the whole Greek tradition, especially since many shorter readings may be shown to be translational paraphrase or untrustworthy citations apparently made from memory.

On the opposite side is the method of "rigorous eclecticism" practiced by G.D. Kilpatrick and his student J.K. Elliott. They advocate placing no weight on the MSS at all, but making every choice solely on the basis of internal principles. The difficulty with this method is that the results depend on the scholar's preference of internal criteria, which in the case of Kilpatrick and Elliott seems to be for variants in an author's style as over against the questions of transcriptional probability.

While, as has already been said, we may grant that not all of the principles of textual criticism are applicable to each variant, contemporary critics generally agree that questions of internal evidence should usually be asked first and that the weight of the MS evidence should be applied secondarily. What becomes obvious, however, is that on the grounds of internal evidence certain MSS tend to support the "original" text more often than others and that those MSS are the early Alexandrian. Therefore, when internal evidence cannot decide, the safest guide is to go with the "best" MSS.

VI. The Significance

What difference does all of this make to the expositor? Much in every way. On the one hand, it provides him with confidence that for the most part the text he is interpreting, whether it be from a modern Greek text or a contemporary translation, truly represents what the biblical author actually wrote.

Nevertheless, and more significantly, there are places where the original text is not so certain. At such points textual criticism becomes an integral part of exegesis. In some instances, such as in John 7:1, whether the original text says that Jesus "did not wish" to go about in Galilee or "did not have the authority" to do so, or as in v.8, whether Jesus said he was not, or was not yet, going up to the feast, the textual choice will affect the interpretation of the passage.

In other instances, exegesis and textual choice go hand in hand. In John 1:34, did John the Baptist say, "This is the Son of God" (KJV, RSV) or "This is God's Chosen One" (NEB, JB)? The MS evidence is divided, even among the early text-types. "Son" is found in the key Alexandrian witnesses (P[66] P[75] B C L cop[bo]) as well as in several OL (aur c f l g) and the later Syriac witnesses, while "Chosen One" is supported by the Alexandrians P[5] ℵ cop[sa] as well as the OL MSS a b e ff[2] and the Old Syriac.

The question must finally be decided on internal grounds. As to transcriptional probability, one thing is clear: the variant is intentional, not accidental. But did a second century scribe alter the text to support a kind of adoptionist Christology, or did an orthodox scribe sense the possibility that the designation "Chosen One" might be used to support adoptionism, and so alter it for orthodox reasons? In terms of probabilities, the latter seems far more likely, especially since "the Son" is not changed elsewhere in the Gospel to fit adoptionist views.

But the final decision must involve exegesis. Since what John the Baptist said was almost certainly intended to be messianic and not a statement of Christian theology, the question is whether it reflects the messianism of such a passage as Psalm 2:7 or that of Isaiah 42:1. In light of the suffering, or paschal, lamb motif of John 1:29, it is surely arguable that "Chosen One" fits the context of the Gospel.

What finally points to "Chosen One" as original is the use the evangelist makes of the many confessions in the Gospel. All of them pick up different messianic motifs (1:29, 41, 49; 4:42; 6:14; 6:69; 11:27) and all of them "fit" their specific context (e.g., the "true Israelite" confesses him as "King of the Jews"; in the bread [manna] from heaven context he is called the Mosaic "prophet who is coming into the world"). Since "Chosen One" fits the context and gives the evangelist yet another Messianic confession of Jesus, it seems to be preferred as the original. But in either case, the interpreter must also do textual criticism.

Thus textual criticism, rather than being simply an exercise for the expert preceding exegesis, is also an integral part of the interpretation of the Word of God.

VII. Bibliography

Books

Aland, K. *Kurzegefasste Liste der Griechischen Handschriften des Neuen Testaments.* Berlin: Walter de Gruyter, 1963.

Burgon, J.W. *The Traditional Text of the Holy Gospels Vindicated and Established.* Edited by E.F. Miller. London: 1896.

Colwell, E.C. *Studies in Methodology in the Textual Criticism of the New Testament.* Grand Rapids: Eerdmans, 1970.

_____. *What is the Best New Testament?* Chicago: University of Chicago Press, 1952.

Elliott, J.K. *The Greek Text of the Epistles to Timothy and Titus.* Salt Lake City: University of Utah Press, 1968.

Epp, E.J. *The Theological Tendency of Codex Bezae Cantabrigiensis.* Cambridge: Cambridge University Press, 1966.

Fee, G.D. *Papyrus Bodmer II (P66): Its Textual Relationships and Scribal Characteristics.* Salt Lake City: University of Utah Press, 1968.

Greenlee, J.H. *Introduction to New Testament Textual Criticism.* Grand Rapids: Eerdmans, 1964.

Hatch, W.H.P. *Facsimiles and Descriptions of Minuscule Manuscripts of the New Testament.* Cambridge: Harvard University Press, 1951.

_____. *The Principal Uncial Manuscripts of the New Testament.* Chicago: University of Chicago Press, 1939.

Kenyon, F.G. *The Text of the Greek Bible.* New ed. London: Duckworth, 1949.

Lake, Kirsopp. *The Text of the New Testament.* Rev. ed. London: 1928.

Metzger, B.M. *The Early Versions of the New Testament: Their Origin, Transmission and Limitations.* Oxford: Clarendon Press, 1977.

_____. *The Text of the New Testament, Its Transmission, Corruption, and Restoration.* Rev. ed. New York: Oxford University Press, 1968.

_____. *A Textual Commentary on the Greek New Testament: A Companion Volume to the United Bible Societies' Greek New Testament (third edition).* London/New York: United Bible Societies, 1971.

Streeter, B.H. *The Four Gospels: A Study of Origins.* Rev. ed. London: Macmillan, 1936.

Westcott, B.F. and Hort, F.J.A. *The New Testament in the Original Greek,* with *Introduction* and *Appendix.* 2 vols. London: MacMillan, 1881–82.

Williams, C.S.C. *Alterations to the Text of the Synoptic Gospels and Acts.* Oxford: Basil Blackwell, 1951.

Zuntz, G. *The Text of the Epistles.* London: The British Academy, 1953.

Articles

Birdsall, J.N. "The New Testament Text." *The Cambridge History of the Bible,* vol. 1. Edited by P.R. Ackroyd and C.F. Evans. Cambridge: Cambridge University Press, 1970, pp. 308–77.

Fee, G.D. "P75, P66, and Origen: The Myth of Early Textual Recension in Alexandria," *New Dimensions in New Testament Study.* Edited by R.N. Longenecker and M.C. Tenney. Grand Rapids: Zondervan, 1974, pp. 19–45.

_____. "Rigorous or Reasoned Eclecticism—Which?" *Studies in New Testament Language and Text.* Edited by J.K. Elliot. Leiden: Brill, 1976 pp. 174–197.

_____. "The Text of John in Origen and Cyril of Alexandria: A Contribution to Methodology in the Recovery and Analysis of Patristic Citations." *Biblica* 52 (1971): 357–94.

Hodges, Z.C. "The Greek Text of the King James Version." *BS* 125 (1968): 334–45.

Kilpatrick, G.D. "An Eclectic Study of the Text of Acts." *Biblical and Patristic Studies in Memory of R.P. Casey.* Edited by J.N. Birdsall and R.W. Thomson. Freiburg: 1963, pp. 64–77.

_____. "The Greek New Testament Text of Today and the Textus Receptus." *The New Testament in Historical and Contemporary Perspective: Essays in Memory of G.H.C. Macgregor.* Edited by H. Anderson and W. Barclay. Oxford: 1965. pp. 189–208.

THE HISTORICAL AND LITERARY CRITICISM OF THE NEW TESTAMENT

Donald Guthrie

Donald Guthrie

B.D., M.Th., Ph.D., University of London

Senior Lecturer in New Testament Language and Literature; Registrar for Advanced Studies, London Bible College

THE HISTORICAL AND LITERARY CRITICISM OF THE NEW TESTAMENT

I. The Background and Basic Characteristics of Criticism
II. Main Trends in Modern Criticism

    A. Debt to Rationalism
    B. Tübingen School
    C. Mythological Approach
    D. Liberal Movement
    E. Bultmann, Barth, and More Recent Developments
    F. Conservative Criticism

III. Historical Criticism

    A. Its Relevance and Dangers
    B. The Denial of Need for Historical Veracity
    C. History-of-Religion Approach
    D. Conservative View of History

IV. Literary Criticism

    A. The Oral Theory
    B. Source Theories
    C. Form Criticism
    D. The New Quest
    E. Redaction Criticism
    F. Literary Problems in the Epistles

V. Methods of Criticism

    A. Stylistic Criteria
    B. Linguistic Tests
    C. Criticism by Doctrine
    D. Arguments From Silence
    E. Critical Use of Tradition
    F. Laws of Tradition
    G. Dissimilarity and Coherence

VII. Criticism and Authority

A. Opposing Approaches
B. Criticism and Inspiration
C. Criticism and the Canon

VIII. Bibliography

I. The Background and Basic Characteristics of Criticism

Critical inquiry into the origins of the NT is comparatively modern, belonging to the nineteenth and twentieth centuries. This does not mean that there was no criticism of the NT prior to 1800. Critical opinions were expressed in the patristic period.[1] These, however, were only isolated comments and should be distinguished from the period of scientific criticism. In the times of the Reformers, certain NT books came under critical comment, but this tendency was almost wholly subjective.[2] The age of reason gave rise to modern criticism, for it was then assumed that criticism was not only a legitimate but even a necessary process for subjecting the biblical text to the scrutiny of human reason.[3] Rationalism set man firmly on the throne and all else, revelation included, was expected to bow to him. It is important to recognize this background of rationalism in approaching NT criticism. Many of the problems that have arisen in its wake are unintelligible unless its origins are appreciated.

The rise of criticism out of such a background draws attention to its essentially anthropological character, and this in turn raises problems. There was no doubt in the minds of the earliest critical scholars that human reason should be allowed to pronounce on the authenticity of the text. It was this tendency for criticism to exalt itself above the clear statements of the NT that led to the development both of skeptical schools of thought and of strong reactions from those committed to the absolute trustworthiness of the Bible.[4] These latter concluded that all criticism was negative and destructive and that it was somehow wrong to engage in any form of it. Undoubtedly much NT criticism has been destructive. Yet this does not mean that a true criticism is inadmissible. The fundamental notion of criticism is, in fact, a careful examination of relevant data. A critic is one who passes judgment and, provided his criticism is based on right presuppositions, there is nothing wrong with such criticism. But have men the right to examine critically the medium of God's revelation? If not, the idea of a genuine criticism of the NT is impossible.[5] Yet there is a decided difference between a scholar who accepts the divine origin of Scripture and inquires into its historical and literary origins and a scholar who

---

[1]Dionysius of Alexandria discussed the authorship of the Book of Revelation.

[2]Martin Luther made forthright statements about some NT books, mainly on the grounds of their unsuitability for directly supporting the doctrine of justification by faith. Although Calvin also made subjective judgments on NT books, he recognized the unifying influence of the Spirit within the canon.

[3]One of the earliest scholars of the critical school was F.E. Schleiermacher, who was strongly influenced by current philosophical trends. Hegel made a deep impression on early biblical scholarship.

[4]Cf. G.E. Ladd's discussion in his book *The New Testament and Criticism* (Grand Rapids: Eerdmans, 1966), pp. 7ff.

[5]Ladd points out that "a proper biblical criticism . . . does not mean criticizing the Word of God, but trying to understand the Word of God and how it has been given to man" (ibid., p. 217).

begins his critical inquiries with the assumption that there is nothing unique about the text and who claims the right to examine it as he would any other book. The former is not simply submitting the text to the bar of his own reason to establish its validity, but assumes that the text will authenticate itself when subject to reverent examination.

II. Main Trends in Modern Criticism

The development of the historical and literary criticism of the NT is too complicated to allow any more than the broad trends to be described in the context of this article.[6] A brief outline of these trends is necessary for understanding the principles on which NT criticism has proceeded.

A. Debt to rationalism

At the beginning of the nineteenth century the first signs of a serious invasion of the rationalistic spirit into the field of NT scholarship came from Germany. Scholars like Herder had earlier raised problems about NT interpretation.[7] It was Schleiermacher, however, who applied critical principles in a systematic way.[8] He was followed by Eichhorn, who had already done the same with the OT.[9] Both men denied the authenticity of certain NT books (e.g., the pastoral Epistles) on the grounds that the apostle Paul was not their author.

B. Tübingen School

Even more radical was the criticism of Baur at Tübingen, who reduced the number of authentic Pauline Epistles to four (Rom, 1 and 2 Cor, and Gal) and denied the genuineness of most other NT books.[10] The basis of his criticism was his reconstruction of early Christian history, by which he concluded that many of the NT writings had been written from a later point of view. This approach came to be known as "tendency criticism" (German *tendenz*). An extensive superstructure of negative views about NT books was built on the tenuous foundation of Baur's own theory of a fundamental clash between the Pauline and the Petrine parties, which the NT writers had supposedly sought to reconcile. But Baur's critical opinions fell into disrepute because of the rejection of his historical reconstruction and presuppositions.[11]

C. Mythological Approach

Other scholars began from equally tenuous presuppositions. Strauss, for instance, approached the Gospel narratives in the belief that much of the material was mythical,[12] though his radical theories were not acclaimed by his contemporaries. Most negatively

---

[6]For a detailed account, consult S. Neill, *The Interpretation of the New Testament* (New York: Oxford University Press, 1964).

[7]Cf. J.G. Herder, *Von der Regel der Zustimmung unserer Evangelien*, 1797.

[8]F.E. Schleiermacher, *Über den sogennanten ersten Brief des Paulus an den Timotheus*, 1807.

[9]J.G. Eichhorn, *Historische-kritische Einleitung in das Neue Testament*, 1814.

[10]Cf. F.C. Baur, *Paulus der Apostle Jesus Christi*, 1845.

[11]Some of Baur's ideas have recently been resuscitated, e.g., by S.F.D. Brandon, *The Fall of Jerusalem and the Christian Church* (London: SPCK, 1957).

[12]D. Strauss, *The Life of Jesus*, 1835.

critical of all were the nineteenth-century radical Dutch critics, who denied the authenticity of all the Pauline Epistles and ended in complete skepticism.[13]

D. Liberal Movement

During the past century many critical scholars concentrated on the quest for literary sources, and this movement found its most effective outlet in the liberal school that dominated the theological scene at the turn of the century. Holtzmann,[14] Harnack,[15] and others defined Christianity as belief in the fatherhood of God and the brotherhood of man; the result was that the historical Jesus was seen as man's perfect example. Of paramount importance, therefore, was the discovery of the Jesus of history. Source criticism and a multiplicity of interpolation theories[16] helped prune from the Gospel accounts whatever was impossible to emulate or whatever was beyond man's normal experience. The liberal Jesus did no miracles, claimed no divine nature, and did not aim to redeem man from sin. Literary and historical criticism joined forces to present a thoroughly human Jesus. The aftermath of this movement has, however, shown the wholly unsatisfactory character of such a picture.

As for developments in NT criticism in the twentieth century, these have been devoted to offering some alternative approaches, not all of which have avoided the pitfalls of the liberal movement.

E. Bultmann, Barth, and More Recent Developments

The two most dominating figures in NT studies during the first half of the twentieth century have been Bultmann[17] and Barth.[18] Both were reared within the liberal movement. Both reacted against it. Bultmann opposed the quest for the historical Jesus on the grounds that Christian faith cannot depend on historical research, which in his view was wholly inconclusive. Influenced as he was by the existential philosophy of Heidegger, he maintained that decision was more important than historical proof. He consequently stressed the Christ of faith as the antithesis to Harnack's Jesus of history. Bultmann had always accepted the older source theories and built upon them.[19] Analyzing the so-called laws of tradition, he claimed to have discovered ways of determining the authenticity of the words and events in the life of Jesus. The result is that he regarded very little of the material in the Gospels as genuine. Bultmann was not worried about his skeptical conclusions, since for him faith does not depend on them.

Barth dealt with critical problems in a different way. He regarded revelation as being contained within the NT but in no sense integrally identified with it. His views allow either a liberal or a conservative approach to critical problems. Unlike Bultmann, he produced no major work of a critical kind, but concentrated on dogmatics. More recent studies, especially in Germany, have followed Bultmann more closely than Barth, though there has been some reaction against the position of the former.

---

[13]W.C. van Manen, *Paulus*, 1890–1896; P.W. Schmiedel, *Encyclopaedia Biblica* (1914) s.v. "John."

[14]H.J. Holtzmann, *Einleitung in das Neue Testament*, 1885.

[15]A. Harnack, *What Is Christianity?* trans. T.B. Saunders, 5th ed. (London: Benn, 1958).

[16]Cf. J. Moffatt's survey of critical theories on the Synoptic problem, *Introduction to the Literature of the New Testament*, 3rd ed. (Edinburgh: T & T Clark, 1918) pp. 177ff.

[17]R. Bultmann, *The History of the Synoptic Tradition*, trans., J. Marsh (New York: Harper and Row, 1963); idem, *Theology of the New Testament*, trans. K. Grobel (London: SCM, 1952–55).

[18]K. Barth, *The Epistle to the Romans*, English trans. (New York: Oxford University Press, 1933); idem, *Church Dogmatics* (Naperville: Allenson, 1936–69).

[19]Cf. his *History of the Synoptic Tradition*, pp. 1ff.

Two newer movements, the "new quest"[20] and redaction criticism,[21] while linked to Bultmann, are moving away from his historical skepticism. The new quest exists among his own supporters who are not prepared to endorse his skepticism and who place more credence on the historical Jesus. Closely linked with the new quest is redaction criticism. It concentrates on individual writers as theologians in their own right rather than on problems of sources and origins. This increased interest in theology has developed without granting credence to the historical traditions.

F. *Conservative Criticism*

Against the background of all these critical movements, conservative scholars have consistently upheld the authenticity of the text, while making a careful examination of the problems posed by more critical scholarship.

III. Historical Criticism

As the foregoing historical survey has shown, there have been numerous approaches to the critical study of the NT. These need to be classified according to the way they affect historical and literary problems relating to the Bible. Such problems are all concerned with higher criticism as distinct from lower criticism. The latter concentrates on textual criticism (see THE TEXTUAL CRITICISM OF THE NEW TESTAMENT, pp. 419–433) and aims to establish as far as possible the basic text of the original autographs. In no case does textual criticism lend support to the variety of theories that challenge the authenticity of the text.[22]

A. *Its Relevance and Dangers*

Although historical and literary criticism overlap in some cases, the problems each raises are best considered separately. As has already been shown, among the earlier NT critics the principle of historical reconstruction played a major part. But are such reconstructions ever valid and, if so, to what extent are they valid?

Most scholars would agree that to put the NT into its historical setting is not only legitimate but essential for a right understanding of the text. It is not sufficient to maintain that as the Word of God the NT is applicable to any age irrespective of the original purpose of its parts. A true application of the NT text depends on a right understanding of its original aim. The Corinthian correspondence, for instance, is intelligible only against the first-century situation to which it is addressed, but it has universal application because it enunciates abiding principles in dealing with local needs. The scholar is dependent to a large extent on inferences from the NT text itself in reconstructing the historical background. This presents no difficulty so long as the NT writers are taken at their face value. But a real problem arises when scholars like Baur[23] in the

---

[20]For further details see note 65.

[21]Redaction criticism focuses on the theological perspectives of the evangelists. For a survey, cf. J. Rohde, *Rediscovering the Teaching of the Evangelists*, trans. D.M. Barton (London: SCM, 1968).

[22]E.g., in many of the instances where interpolations have been proposed for the Pauline Epistles, no textual evidence supports them.

[23]See note 10.

nineteenth century and John Knox[24] and Haenchen[25] in the twentieth century suggest that a writer like Luke has superimposed his own view of early Christian developments on the facts. The exegete must then unravel the original events. If this view of Luke's intention is accepted, the quest is laudable. But there is no reason to accept this estimate of Luke's work, since it lacks independent support.

B. *Denial of the Need for Historical Veracity*

A more radical approach to historical criticism is that which virtually denies its feasibility. This is essentially Bultmann's view.[26] He challenges the possibility of finding genuine history in the Gospels on the ground that the authors looked at events through the eyes of faith. The only historicity accessible under this view is the account of what the early Christians believed about Jesus. Such a view makes the highly dubious assumption that the major part of the Gospel material was the creation of the community. But Bultmann does not produce parallels to this process of communities' creating narratives to bolster their own tenets of belief. Moreover, in common with all who adopt an extreme form-critical view, Bultmann makes the assumption that the traditions were not controlled by eyewitnesses of the events. Again, this is an assumption difficult to justify from a historical point of view. There is no credible explanation of the disappearance of the eyewitnesses.

A more serious question—the relationship of history to faith—arises from the virtual denial of the historical. Since Christianity is a historical religion, faith cannot be divorced from history.[27] If the historical records of the NT are called into question, the nature of Christianity itself is affected. Bultmann's maintaining that faith is independent of history is inadequate, because then faith becomes wholly subjective and need not be centered in Christ at all. While the trend away from this historical skepticism on the part of some of Bultmann's followers is salutary, the continuing basis of form criticism underlying their views renders a true historical approach dubious.

C. *History-of-Religions Approach*

Another tendency in the field of historical criticism is the movement known as *Religionsgeschichte*, which traces the influence of contemporary religious ideas on early Christian texts. Under this movement may be grouped the Hellenistic school, the Gnostic school, and the Mysteries school, all of which appeal to parallels to show that the NT in many of its parts has been influenced by these pagan streams of thought. Such books as the Gospel of John and the Epistle to the Hebrews have been seen as products of a Hellenizing of Christianity.[28] Some scholars consider Gnosticism to have been part of the background of Paul's Epistles,[29] while the mystery religions are supposed to have

---

[24]J. Knox, *Chapters in a Life of Paul* (Nashville: Abingdon, 1954).

[25]E. Haenchen, *The Acts of the Apostles*, trans. B. Noble and G. Shinn, revised by R.McL. Wilson (Philadelphia: Westminster, 1971).

[26]Bultmann distinguishes between *Historie* (bare events) and *Geschichte* (history plus interpretation). He denies the possibility of establishing the former, but not the latter in relation to the life of Jesus.

[27]Cf. H.E.W. Turner, *Historicity and the Gospels* (Naperville: Allenson, 1963); F.F. Bruce, "History and the Gospel," *Jesus of Nazareth*. Edited by C.F.H. Henry. (Grand Rapids: Eerdmans, 1966).

[28]Cf. C.H. Dodd, *The Interpretation of the Fourth Gospel* (Cambridge: Cambridge University Press, 1953); E. Ménégoz, *La Théologie de l'Epître aux Hébreux*, 1894. For a general survey of Hellenistic influences, cf. W.L. Knox, *Some Hellenistic Elements in Primitive Christianity* (Oxford: Oxford University Press, 1944).

[29]Cf. W. Schmithals, *Gnosticism in Corinth* (Nashville: Abingdon, 1971). For a different view, cf. R.M. Wilson, *Gnosis and the New Testament* (Philadelphia: Fortress, 1968).

contributed some of the ideas of early Christian thought.[30] Nevertheless, this *Religionsgeschichte* movement is not based on reliable evidence, for much of it is culled from a much later period than the apostolic age. Dodd, for instance, strongly emphasizes parallels between John and the *Hermetica*,[31] Egyptian philosophical tracts from the end of the second century onwards, which he nevertheless believes preserve much earlier tradition. It is, however, unsatisfactory to attempt to place the NT in a historical religious setting that cannot be historically substantiated. In the same way, all attempts to find Gnostic influences within the NT are doomed because of the lack of any definite evidence of developed Gnosticism within the first century. At most we can speak of Gnosis or pre-Gnosticism during the apostolic period. Theories that have dated parts of the NT during the second century to avoid this difficulty (e.g., second-century dates for Colossians or the Pastorals[32]) are on no sounder footing historically, for the parallels between NT heresies and Gnosticism are markedly tenuous and unconvincing.[33]

D. *Conservative View of History*

Over against these movements, which in various degrees have called into question the historical validity of much of the NT, must be set those movements that have approached NT history from a more conservative point of view. Many scholars who belong to the form-critical school deny that the forms in which the traditions have been preserved can give any indication of the historical validity of those traditions.[34] In these cases, there is a sharp distinction between historical and literary criticism, and consequently a realistic approach to the history. The acceptance of the view that the early Christian traditions were based on eyewitnesses, however those traditions came into the hands of the Gospel writers, is highly credible and gives validity to those traditions. The view that eyewitnesses controlled the traditions would be expected; the burden of proof rests on those who deny this.[35]

There have been two main schools of thought among conservative evangelicals toward historical inquiry. The dogmatic approach has maintained that historical investigation is of small account because the Bible in itself is God's medium of revelation to any age.[36] But this view tends to cut itself off from scholarship altogether. Of greater relevance is the historical approach adopted by those who regard critical inquiry as valid, because they contend that a true revelation of God must be soundly based in history.

The real crux is the point of departure in the critical quest. Destructive criticism begins with the assumption that nothing is valid until proved true, which a priori rules out the possibility of treating such a basic Christian event as the resurrection of Jesus as historical. Constructive criticism takes the opposite view and regards as valid the claims of the NT until they can be proved false. That this view is more justifiable than

---

30Bultmann was particularly influenced in this direction by R. Reitzenstein, *Das hellenischen Mysterienreligionen* (Stuttgart: Teubner, 1927).

31C.H. Dodd, *The Bible and the Greeks* (London: Hodder and Stoughton, 1935).

32Cf. F.C. Baur's theory for Colossians (*Paul, the Apostle of Jesus Christ*, trans. E. Zeller, 1876) and B.S. Easton's for the Pastorals (*The Pastoral Epistles* (London: SCM, 1948).

33Wilson, *Gnosis and the New Testament*, pp. 31–59.

34E.g., V. Taylor, *The Formation of the Gospel Tradition* (London: Macmillan, 1935).

35Cf. D.E. Nineham's forced attempts to dispose of eyewitness influence in his articles on the subject in *Journal of Theological Studies*, new series 9 (1958): 13–25, 243–52; 11 (1960): 253–64.

36Most conservatives would accept some degree of historical inquiry.

the former is evident from its more realistic approach to early traditions regarding the NT. Destructive criticism has no alternative but to ignore early traditions, since these are regarded as biased toward a nonhistorical approach.[37] But constructive criticism sifts traditional opinions in order to reject only those that can be proved unreliable. This means that many early Christian comments on the NT that corroborate the self-claims of the text outweigh the speculative opinions of those who begin with a negative approach.[38] Much of the difference of opinion between conservative schools of thought and the more liberal ones arises from the presuppositions from which they assess historical validity.

IV. Literary Criticism

The effect of differing presuppositions on critical judgments comes clearly to light in the field of literary problems, particularly since the development of higher criticism. From the endeavor to place the NT writings in their historical setting, there developed the need to inquire into the origins of the literature that our knowledge of apostolic thought is based on. This inquiry branched out in two directions—interest in oral tradition and interest in written sources.

A. *The Oral Theory*

The view that the narratives in the Gospels and Acts were committed to writing from a fund of material that first existed in oral form has had few advocates. Nevertheless, it cannot be ignored.[39] It naturally goes hand in hand with the assumption that many reliable witnesses were available who could transmit authentic reports by word of mouth. Most scholars have rejected this assumption as an inadequate explanation of the origin of the Gospels, because of the great amount of material recorded in closely parallel words in more than one Gospel.[40] Though this objection may be valid, all too often insufficient attention has been given to the Jewish approach to oral tradition. Since oral transmission of authoritative tradition was not only practiced but also regarded as obligatory among the Jews, there is at least a possibility that some of their meticulous concern for the accuracy of the oral traditions would have influenced the early Christians. One cannot reason that oral preservation of NT materials involving both sequence of events and verbatim statements was impossible, for there is ample evidence of this from rabbinical sources.[41] Nevertheless, even those who place much credence in oral transmission do not necessarily rule out the parallel use the evangelists make of some written sources. The majority of source critics, however, have worked on the assumption that a high proportion of the material recorded in the Gospels (at least the synoptic

---

[37]E.g., Bultmann's approach to the resurrection is nonhistorical, because it cannot be established by the methods of scientific historical criticism.

[38]In *Acts of the Apostles*, Haenchen's approach to the early Christian testimony concerning Acts is a good example. He regards the witnesses to Lucan authorship as no more than a deduction from the book itself.

[39]Cf. B.F. Westcott, *An Introduction to the Study of the Gospels*, 7th ed. (London: Macmillan, 1888.)

[40]Cf. the various essays in *Oxford Studies in Synoptic Problem* (Oxford: Oxford University Press, 1911).

[41]Two scholars who have maintained this viewpoint are the Scandinavians H. Riesenfeld, "The Gospel Tradition and Its Beginnings," *Studia Evangelica* (Berlin, 1959, pp. 43–65), and B. Gerhardsson, *Memory and Manuscript* (Gleerup: Lund, 1961).

Gospels) must have come from literary sources. It is this basic assumption that has determined the history of source criticism and also led to its inadequacies.

B. *Source Theories*

During the nineteenth century, scholars poured much energy into attempting to solve the synoptic problem—i.e., the similarities and differences of material contained in the first three Gospels. After various theories of interdependence were suggested and then rejected,[42] it was proposed that the two basic sources were Mark[43] and an additional and hypothetical source Q (from the German word *Quelle*, "spring," "source"),[44] which were both used by Matthew and Luke in different ways. Among Continental scholars this solution to the problem has persisted. Many British and American scholars, however, have preferred a modification of this view—a four-source theory, because of the mixed character of the Q source. This modified view, introduced by Streeter,[45] restricted Q to material reproduced by both Matthew and Luke and postulated two other sources, M and L, for the material peculiar to each respectively. Under both these theories, Matthew and Luke are virtually reduced to editors who adapted existing materials to meet their respective needs. From this developed the inclination to attach more historical validity to the sources than to the finished Gospels, though no independent evidence for the hypothetical Q source has ever been produced.[46]

Though the Mark-Q hypothesis exercised a profound influence on the critical approach to the synoptic Gospels in the nineteenth and early twentieth centuries, more recently the Q hypothesis itself has come under increasing criticism.[47] Also the view that Luke used Matthew has gained support. This latter view goes a long way toward dispensing with Q.[48] Even the theory of Mark's priority has not gone unchallenged, though most NT scholars retain it for want of a better alternative. All in all, the changing fortunes of source criticism show that literary criticism has not achieved and cannot achieve conclusive results in the examination of the origins of the Gospels.

The critical approach to the Gospel of John has been altogether different. Because of its distinctive structure and content, this Gospel has always been placed in a class of its own in critical inquiry. For the most part, critics have regarded it as historically inferior to the synoptic Gospels in its presentation of Christ, in its chronology of events, and in its general accuracy. For a long time this view persisted and led earlier scholars to assign to it a date late into the second century.[49] This speculative dating, however, has had to be abandoned because of the discovery of the Rylands papyrus, which belongs to the early part of the second century and conclusively proves that the Gospel of John must

---

[42]E.g., J.J. Griesbach, *Commentatio qua Marci evangium totum e Matthaei et Lucae commentariis deceptum esse demonstratur*, 1789, and more recently H.G. Jameson, *The Origin of the Synoptic Gospels* (Oxford, 1922).

[43]The standard theory of Marcan priority was a development from the view of K. Lachmann, *Theologische Studien und Kritiken* 8 (1835): 570ff. An interdependence theory based on Markan priory but dispensing with Q is proposed by A. Farrer, in *Studies in the Gospels*, ed. D.E. Nineham (Naperville: Allenson, 1955), pp. 55ff.

[44]For a criticism of Q, cf. R.M. Grant, *A Historical Introduction to the New Testament* (New York: Harper and Row, 1963), p. 116; W.R. Farmer, *The Synoptic Problem: A Critical Analysis* (New York: Macmillan, 1964).

[45]B.H. Streeter, *The Four Gospels* (London: Macmillan, 1924).

[46]Cf. e.g., the arrangement in T.W. Manson, *The Teaching of Jesus*, 2nd ed. (Cambridge: Cambridge University Press, 1935).

[47]This is evident particularly where traditions unique to Matthew's Gospel are under consideration. Cf. V. Taylor, *The Gospels*, 5th ed. (London: Epworth, 1945), pp. 64ff.

[48]Cf. Farrer, *Studies in the Gospels*, and Farmer, *Synoptic Problem*.

[49]E.g., O. Holtzmann, van Manen, Baur (for details see Moffatt, *Literature of the New Testament*, pp. 580–81).

have been in circulation at least during the early part of the second century.[50] A further and more recent step towards the reinstatement of the historical respectability of John has been brought about by the discovery of the Dead Sea Scrolls.[51] One of the major arguments against the Johannine portrait of Jesus was the widespread use of abstract terms (e.g., logos, *logos*; light, *phōs*; life, *zōē*; truth, *alētheia*), which many scholars regarded as essentially Hellenistic and not Jewish. But this kind of abstract usage occurs in the Qumran literature, showing that such usage was not unknown in an exclusively Jewish milieu. With the return to a more historical approach to John there has been an attempt to locate his sources. Some scholars consider that he must have used Mark,[52] but others do not think he did so.[53] Indeed, John's Gospel is so highly individualistic when compared with the Synoptics that the literary problem of its sources is impossible to solve. While source criticism has been less relevant to John's Gospel than to the Synoptics, the question of the reliability of his basic traditions is equally important. For such a highly individualistic Gospel to have been accepted alongside the other Gospels certainly indicates belief in its authentic and authoritative basis. Although the portrait of Jesus differs in the Synoptics and John, those who accept the traditionally attested reliability of both see in the differences various aspects of Jesus and not irreconcilable narratives about him. Moreover, John clearly states his purpose (20:30, 31) as being theological. This has undoubtedly affected his portrayal of Jesus. There is no reason, however, to suppose that John has manipulated his history to achieve his purpose. A book aimed at the inculcation of faith would not attain its end if it were based on material of doubtful historicity.

Source criticism has not ignored the other NT books. There have been many theories regarding the sources used in Acts. Of these theoretical sources, the best known are the itinerary source and the Antiochene source.[54] But there is insufficient data to build a solid case for either one. All that can be reasonably assumed, although this is denied by some (e.g., Haenchen), is that the prologue to Luke applies to Acts. If this is so, the expressed method of the writer of the prologue was to investigate all available sources of information. It is evident that the latter part of Acts came from a "Pauline" source, which would be readily intelligible if the writer were a companion of Paul, such as Luke. There is a close interaction between historical and literary criticism over Acts and the critic's approach to this book often reflects his general approach to the rest of the NT and in some cases actually determines it.[55]

The literary criticism of the NT Epistles has been little affected by source criticism, though various partition theories have been proposed that challenge the unity of some of the books (e.g., 2 Cor, Phil, 1 Peter).[56] These theories have generally been based on the view that differences or difficulties within existing books can best be resolved by assigning different parts to different origins. Such criticism tends to be speculative, because it necessarily draws all its evidence from within the books themselves, and different scholars evaluate differences and difficulties in different ways. What strikes

---

[50]C.H. Roberts, *An Unpublished Fragment of the Fourth Gospel* (Manchester: University Press, 1935).

[51]Cf. F.M. Cross, Jr., *The Ancient Library of Qumran and Modern Biblical Studies* (New York: Doubleday, 1961), pp. 206ff.

[52]Most recently by C.K. Barrett, *The Gospel According to St. John* (London: SPCK, 1956), pp. 34ff.

[53]P. Gardner-Smith, *St. John and the Synoptic Gospels* (Cambridge: Cambridge University Press, 1938), strongly opposes the view that John used Mark as a source.

[54]For a concise summary, see D. Guthrie, *New Testament Introduction* (London: Tyndale, 1970), pp. 363ff.

[55]As, e.g., in the case of F.C. Baur and E. Haenchen.

[56]Cf. the relevant discussions in Guthrie, *New Testament Introduction.*

one as an insuperable contradiction, strikes another as a different facet of the same fact.[57]

Revelation is another book that has been subjected to a variety of source theories. These range from the view that the book was originally a Jewish apocalypse modified and enlarged to present a Christian viewpoint, to the idea that its author drew his imagery from various Jewish apocalypses.[58] The theories are unconvincing, because the overwhelming proportion of the imagery in Revelation may be traced back directly to the OT.

C. Form Criticism

Partly because of the multiplication of sources and partly because of doubts cast on the historical value of Mark[59] (the sheet anchor), source criticism developed into form criticism. Scholars recognized that source criticism had concentrated on the use of written material without paying sufficient attention to the origins of the sources. The natural question asked in considering the synoptic Gospels was how Mark and Q reached the form Matthew and Luke came to use. The focus, therefore, turned back to the period of oral tradition and scholars tried to show how the tradition was preserved. Working on the analogy of non-Christian traditional material, they suggested that a valuable method of doing this would be to analyze the shape or form of the various units of tradition and classify them accordingly.[60]

Though form criticism began as a strictly literary discipline,[61] it was tempting for some of its advocates to use forms to determine historical validity. A valuable feature of form criticism has been the attention given to the period of oral transmission, which had long been neglected by source critics. Unfortunately many of the value judgments made by form criticism are not only negative but are also the product of highly doubtful methods. Bultmann's historical skepticism exemplifies this kind of approach.[62]

According to form criticism, a variety of different forms exist in the synoptic Gospels, some consisting of narratives to illustrate an important statement of truth (like the episode of the coin with Caesar's image),[63] some consisting of sayings, some of miracles, and some of so-called mythical or legendary material. While no scholar would deny that a variety of forms exist, not all would accept such a classification as myths and legends, which presuppose a nonhistorical content.

There is no reason to reject the analysis of the literary material in the Gospels and classify it into differing forms. Careful attention must, however, be given to the methods used in the analysis. The more thoroughgoing form critics reject the miraculous because in their view miracle does not belong to the sphere of history.   This they adopt as a-priority, with the result that scholars who take this view cannot avoid regarding the miracle narratives as of secondary value.[64] As for myths, according to this school of form

---

[57]The wide variety of partition theories is sufficient witness to their subjective character.

[58]See the concise survey in Guthrie, *New Testament Introduction*, pp. 967f.

[59]Cf. W. Wrede, *Das Messiasgeheimnis in den Evangelien*, 1901, and K.L. Schmidt, *Der Rahmen der Geschichte Jesu*, 1919.

[60]Two works appeared independently but from the same point of view: M. Dibelius, *From Tradition to Gospel*, trans. B.L. Woolf, 2nd ed., from the German edition first published in 1919 (London: Nicholson and Watson, 1934); Bultmann, *History of the Synoptic Tradition*.

[61]Scholars like B.S. Easton and V. Taylor have mainly regarded it as a literary discipline.

[62]Bultmann maintains the historicity of little of the Gospel material, mainly certain of the sayings of Jesus.

[63]Dibelius called these "paradigms"; Bultmann, "apophthegms"; and Taylor, "pronouncement stories."

[64]It has been customary during the period of critical studies for those who reject miracles to do so on philosophical grounds.

critics, anything supernatural, such as the supernatural in the accounts of Jesus' temptation or transfiguration is also ruled out. Clearly scholars who approach the literary forms from different points of view will evaluate them differently. Acceptance of miracle does not depreciate study of the similarities in miracle stories; it does mean, however, that these stories will not be regarded a priori as the creation of the community. Because of the uniqueness of Jesus, miracles in the Gospels are to be expected rather than rejected.

D. The New Quest

The attempts of the movement known as the "new quest" to retain the basic assumptions of Bultmann's position without succumbing to his skepticism have resulted in a variety of modifications, each of which seeks to support some aspect of the historical as authentic, without in any way returning to the historical Jesus of the liberal school. Yet the different theories proposed by proponents of the new quest have little in common—a fact that does not inspire confidence in the method these critics use.[65]

E. Redaction Criticism

Another movement arising directly out of form criticism and based on it is redaction criticism. This method switches attention to the evangelists as writers. Redaction criticism has gained much support because it attempts a more positive approach. It regards the writers more as authors than as editors and in this respect is to be welcomed. Nevertheless, the main emphasis is on the evangelists as theologians with little attention paid them as historians. The German scholars Bornkamm, Marxsen, Conzelmann, and Haenchen[66] have devoted attention to Matthew, Mark, Luke, and Acts respectively. All see their authors as having used and manipulated their material to express their theological viewpoints. Thus Conzelmann invests Luke's geographical details with theological meaning.[67] Yet the average reader for whom Luke wrote would certainly have had difficulty in recognizing many of the allusions Conzelmann sees scattered throughout the book. Undoubtedly the evangelists and the writer of Acts did have a theological motive. They were interested parties in the movement they were describing. They had come to believe that Jesus was Lord and Savior and they could not regard him in any other way.

There is no reason, however, to suppose that theological interest must take precedence over historical validity. It is not a question, for example, of Luke's being a theologian or a historian but of his being a theologian as well as a historian.[68] It is difficult to think of the narration of bare facts without some interpretation. But there is no reason to suppose that the interpretation made by each evangelist was his own creation. On the contrary,

---

[65]E.g., E. Käsemann concentrates on the teaching of Jesus in his book *Essays on New Testament Themes*, trans. W.J. Montague (Naperville: Allenson, 1964); G. Bornkamm, on certain of the acts of Jesus in *Jesus of Nazareth*, trans. I. and T. Mchuskey with J.M. Robinson (New York: Harper and Row, 1960); and E. Fuchs, on the social concern of Jesus in *Studies of the Historical Jesus* (London: SCM, 1964).

[66]Cf. H. Conzelmann, *The Theology of Luke*, trans. G. Buswell (London: SCM, 1960); W. Marxsen, *Mark the Evangelist*, trans. R.A. Harrisville (Nashville: Abingdon, 1969); and G. Bornkamm, G. Barth, and H.J. Held, *Tradition and Interpretation in Matthew*, trans. P. Scott (London: SCM, 1963). It was Marxsen who coined the term *Redaktionsgeschichte*. For Acts, cf. Haenchen, *Acts of the Apostles*.

[67]E.g., the mention of the lake in Luke 7:22–39 is given a theological significance by Conzelmann, who calls it "a setting for the manifestation of power," *Theology of Luke*, p. 49.

[68]Cf. I.H. Marshall, *Luke, Historian and Theologian* (Grand Rapids: Zondervan, 1971).

there is sufficient agreement among them for us to regard the particular interpretation of each as a variation within a basic unity. There is only one gospel, not a plurality of gospels.

F. *Literary Problems in the Epistles*

So far, this article has dealt mainly with the Gospels. But literary criticism also has had much to say about the Epistles. In these books criticism has mainly concentrated on problems of authorship and composition. The problems concerning authorship fall into two main groups—those arising from writings in which an author is named and those arising from anonymous writings. The latter are less important than the former.

Yet the authorship of anonymous writings is not unimportant. Indeed, discussion of it can establish whether or not a work belongs to the apostolic age—a fact that has significant bearing on its canonicity. Certain writings, like the Epistle to the Hebrews and the Johannine Epistles, though anonymous in their texts, acquired an ascription to an author in their titles, and discussion has ranged around the validity of these ascriptions.

The group of Epistles that name their author within their text are of great importance, because in some instances criticism has declared these assertions of authorship to be unauthentic. In such cases criticism must come to terms with the dilemma of pseudonymous works within the NT.[69] Numerous attempts have been made to claim that such works conformed to current practice in the first century and for this reason cannot be classed as deceptive.[70] In many cases, however, these claims have been made without a thorough examination of first-century practice in relation to Christian literature. Such examination reveals remarkably little support for the practice of producing pseudonymous epistles during the period when the NT Epistles were written. Indeed it may be said that nothing comparable exists.[71] In spite of attempts to avoid the conclusion that pseudonymity applied to NT writings poses a moral problem, there has been no satisfactory explanation of the inclusion of pseudonymous Epistles in the canon. Therefore until such an explanation can be given, it is more credible to regard the claims of the texts as being correct—especially when, as in the majority of cases, traditional support is overwhelmingly in favor of these claims.[72]

Another line of approach to NT books that has been overemphasized is the confident appeal to parallels, whether linguistic or theological ("parallelomania").[73] It requires only a few common words in two Epistles for some scholars to assume a borrowing process, though who has borrowed from whom is not always clear. In many cases there is totally inadequate evidence of borrowing either way. For example, attempts to prove that Ephesians echoes language from all the other Pauline Epistles except the Pastorals, suffer from an excess of this tendency.[74] After all, parallels in thought may reasonably be expected in documents that all come from the milieu of early Christianity.

69The most notable examples are Ephesians, the pastoral Epistles, James, and the Petrine Epistles.

70Cf. Moffatt, *Literature of the New Testament*, pp. 40ff.; A. Jülicher, *Introduction to the New Testament* (English tr. 1904, pp. 52ff.

71Cf. the discussion on epistolary pseudepigraphy in Guthrie, *New Testament Introduction*, pp. 671ff.

72In the case of the Pastorals, there is no patristic evidence to suggest that anyone ever had doubts regarding their authenticity.

73This term was coined by the Jewish scholar S. Sandmel, *JBL* 81 (1962): 1ff.

74Cf. E.J. Goodspeed, *Key to Ephesians* (Chicago: University of Chicago Press, 1956).

V. Methods of Criticism

It is essential in any inquiry that purports to be "scientific" to define carefully the tests it applies. Where this has not been done, much literary criticism has fallen far short of scientific precision. It must always be recognized that the categories of scientific inquiry are not valid in many of the problems literary critics deal with.

The purpose of scholarly inquiry into the origins of NT literature is often to lead to critical conclusions. If scholars approach the NT from a purely anthropological viewpoint, their inquiry into its origins will assume greater importance than if they maintain a theological viewpoint in which the ultimate authorship of the NT is held to be the activity of the Holy Spirit working through the minds of men. In much NT criticism, the work of the Holy Spirit is not mentioned, because it does not belong to the normal categories of critical inquiry. Nevertheless, it is not irrelevant for scholars to focus on the personality of the human authors, since they were the agents used by the Spirit in communicating his revelation.[75]

A. Stylistic Criteria

In determining the authorship of the NT writings, stylistic and linguistic criteria are generally used. Such methods, however, are not without serious limitations. Stylistic criteria are notoriously difficult to establish. What appears to one scholar to be in harmony with a man's style does not appear so to another.[76] With the Pauline letters, before any of them can be considered non-Pauline on stylistic grounds, two things must be done: the authentic style of Paul must be defined and reliable methods of comparison with that style must be worked out. But neither of these requirements is possible. The definition of the authentic Pauline style is bound to be arbitrary, and stylistic comparisons are invariably subjective. For example, while Paul does show a tendency to digress in many of his Epistles, this provides no adequate test of style, because his digressions are so often caused by the subject matter. Therefore, the absence of digression is scarcely an indication of non-Pauline authorship. The same applies to other tests that have been proposed, such as the absence of characteristic Pauline particles, pronouns, and the like,[77] or the absence of unusual words that occur in the accepted letters, or the increase of complicated sentences (as in Eph 1).[78] All these depend on the assumption that an author will not vary his style beyond certain prescribed limits. But this assumption would rule out the individualists who refuse to conform to a pattern.

No more successful is the most recent attempt to evaluate style by means of statistical calculations.[79] This theory holds that every author has a certain fixed pattern in his use of incidental but frequently used words and in the length of his sentences. But such an assumption has not yet been demonstrated and till it has it cannot be used as an objective test of style.[80] Even if it could be shown to apply to all authors, its use within the Pauline Epistles would be severely curtailed by reason of their brevity. It may, then, confidently

---

[75]Ladd's *New Testament and Criticism* combines both the Godward and manward aspects.

[76]A.Q. Morton bases his statistics on the frequency of the most common words, but other scholars have judged style on the basis of unusual words.

[77]As in P.N. Harrison's approach to the Pastorals, *The Problem of the Pastorals* (Oxford: Oxford University Press, 1921).

[78]Cf. C.L. Mitton, *The Epistle to the Ephesians* (Oxford: Clarendon, 1951), pp. 9–10 for stylistic arguments.

[79]A.Q. Morton and J. McLeman, *Paul, the Man and the Myth* (London: Hodder and Stoughton, 1966).

[80]Several have challenged Morton's position; e.g., C. Dinwoodie, *Scottish Journal of Theology* 18 (1965): 204–18; J.J. O'Rourke, *JBL* 86 (1967): 110–12; H.K. McArthur, *New Testament Studies* 15 (1969): 339–349.

be stated that no objective tests of style have been devised that can prove the non-Pauline authorship of any of the writings attributed to him.

B. *Linguistic Tests*

The same may be said of arguments based on vocabulary. Today scholars place less reliance than formerly on the variation in the percentage of words used only once in the Pauline Epistles (such words are called *hapax legomena*). Emphasis on the "hapaxes" was long a feature of the attacks on the authenticity of the pastoral Epistles. Yet that kind of criticism rested on the assumption that each author had a kind of norm for using previously unused words and that marked deviations from this norm were evidences of another author. While the so-called "battle of the hapaxes" is not entirely finished, scholars now recognize that this method has to be used with caution.[81] Moreover, arguments based on vocabulary are bound to be limited because of the small amount of literature preserved from any author. The total vocabulary used in the Pauline Epistles undoubtedly represents only a portion of the apostle's repertoire of words. Therefore it is simply guesswork to suggest that any of the words in the Epistles cannot be Pauline.[82]

C. *Criticism by Doctrine*

The main principle of this critical method is that an author will reflect the same theological commitment throughout his works. Thus any deviations from it are taken as evidence that another author has been at work.[83] This principle is misleading, however, if it is assumed that an author must reflect all his theology in all his letters. Furthermore, during the apostolic period there were many facets of doctrine and no set way of stating a doctrine even within the writings of one author. Paul's approach to the second coming of Christ reflects several aspects of this truth. It is perhaps possible to attribute some change of emphasis to Paul's increasing conviction as he grew older that he would not live to see the Parousia. Such a consideration used with caution may indicate chronological order. Generally speaking, however, it is unsatisfactory to base chronology on supposed development of doctrine, because "development" is so often subjectively determined and thus no agreement is possible.[84]

D. *Arguments From Silence*

In relation to criticism by doctrine the argument from silence has been used. Sometimes scholars suppose that if a NT author has omitted some aspect of theology, he could not have held it. For example, the absence from the Pauline Epistles of any idea of Christ as high priest is for them evidence that he could not have held this idea.[85] Yet he may have had reason for not including it in any of the Epistles under his name in the NT.

81For a discussion of this approach with a critique, see D. Guthrie, *The Pastoral Epistles* (Grand Rapids: Eerdmans, 1957), appendix.

82According to P.N. Harrison's data, Paul's total vocabulary in his Epistles is 2, 177 words, *Problem of the Pastorals*, p. 160.

83Cf. Mitton's argument against the authenticity of Ephesians based on the difference between that Epistle and Colossians, *Epistle to the Ephesians*, pp. 61, 84.

84The idea of development of thought depends on the assumption that various emphases cannot coexist at the same time.

85Scholars are generally agreed that Paul did not write Hebrews, although it cannot be maintained that it was impossible for him to have done so because he did not elsewhere mention the high priestly theme.

Arguments from silence are clearly less conclusive than contradictory evidence would be. It is reasonable to assume that an author would not knowingly contradict himself. Yet it cannot be assumed that the totality of his doctrinal ideas is necessarily expressed in his extant writings.

E. *Critical Use of Tradition*

External evidence, or the testimony of early Christian tradition to the NT books, has its place in the criticism of the NT. It is a sound principle of criticism that where an ancient tradition comes from a reliable source, that tradition should be given weight until it can be proved wrong. In other words, the burden of proof rests with the challengers.[86] But many NT critics either explain away the external evidence or pay no attention to it. It is not convincing to claim that the early patristic authors were uncritical in their approach and therefore unreliable as witnesses. Although these men were not as well equipped as modern scholars to examine evidence in a scientific manner, they were writing at a time near the events and this fact must outweigh their supposed tendency to be naive.[87] Irenaeus's endeavor to demonstrate the fourfold character of the Gospels on the analogy of the four quarters of the earth does not qualify as scientific. But this does not invalidate all of his testimony.

Another aspect of tradition is the fragmentary nature of evidence from the early period. The gaps this leaves present special problems. Different scholars lay different stress on the lack of quotation from certain NT books in the patristic writings.[88] Some critics maintain that if a patristic writer does not quote from a certain NT book, this is evidence that he did not know that book. Others regard such lack of quotation as pointing to lack of use and not necessarily to lack of knowledge of the book. So in the case of James or 2 Peter the absence of any second-century citations would not necessarily be taken as evidence that these Epistles did not enjoy authoritative status during that century.[89] It is impossible to substantiate the view that the patristic authors must be expected to show acquaintance with every one of the NT books. The patristic writers whose works happen to be extant may not have had cause to appeal to certain NT books. Since lack of quotation can be interpreted in different ways, such evidence must be used with caution. Indeed, one of the major problems in any kind of NT criticism is the paucity of Christian or non-Christian evidence outside the NT itself for the historical and literary background of its writers.

F. *Laws of Tradition*

In their presentation of form-critical views for the Gospels, scholars like Bultmann and his followers have appealed to the laws of tradition,[90] a principle of criticism that has produced almost wholly negative results. How valid is it?

The so-called "laws" are in fact an attempt to reduce to systematic form what is

---

[86]This is frankly admitted by Mitton in his discussion of external evidence, *Epistle to the Ephesians*, p. 7.

[87]No serious historian would claim that all patristic traditions are correct, for some writers were notoriously inexact in their statements.

[88]E.g., J.N. Sanders, *The Fourth Gospel in the Early Church* (Cambridge: Cambridge University Press, 1943), attaches little importance to the early allusions to John's Gospel.

[89]Cf. R.V.G. Tasker, *The General Epistle of James* (Grand Rapids: Eerdmans, 1956).

[90]Cf. R. Bultmann and K. Kundsin, *Form Criticism*, trans. F.C. Grant, 2nd ed. (New York: Harper and Row, 1962).

observable from non-Christian traditions, the manner in which reports tend to be enhanced in the course of transmission, the tendency for heroes to become more heroic—in short, a tendency to a general crusting over of the facts through the imagination of the transmitters.

According to this principle, the critic's task is to strip off the accretions of transmission. But the process is valid only if the NT books can confidently be expected to conform to these so-called "laws of tradition," an assumption open to serious challenge. First, human thoughts cannot easily be reduced to laws. Second, there is no close link between secular traditions and Christian traditions. As for the latter, those who transmitted them were themselves committed to their contents. Therefore they would have had high regard for the veracity of their transmitted form. People do not normally invent traditions and then use them as their basis of faith, even to the extent of being prepared to die for them.[91] So powerful a movement as the Christian church cannot be placed alongside the conglomeration of traditions in the contemporary world. So once more, a principle of criticism widely accepted as valid is so open to challenge as to cast serious doubt on its serving as a reliable guide. After all, it is reasonable to suppose that events and especially teachings believed to be unique were handed on with special care. Moreover, there is the Christian conviction that the Holy Spirit guarded the traditions.

Another common assumption is that traditions when written down tend to be longer than in their spoken form. It is, however, by no means certain that this is an invariable rule, particularly where oral tradition overlaps written documents. Actually, in the synoptic tradition there are no observable "laws," for the tradition developed in different directions at the same time.[92]

G. *Dissimilarity and Coherence*

When form critics employ the method of "dissimilarity" and "coherence," their principles are most open to dispute. Under the former method they argue when examining the teaching of Jesus that only traditional material dissimilar from that which can be paralleled in Jewish tradition or in the faith and practice of the primitive church can be geniune.[93] By using this method, many form critics accept only a small number of the Gospel sayings as historically authentic.

This method, however, is invalid. While it can demonstrate what is distinctive in the teaching of Jesus, it can throw no light on what is authentic. We have no reason to suppose that Jesus would have rejected all the ideas of his contemporaries. A true picture of him cannot be arrived at in this way. The historical Jesus as presented by thoroughgoing form critics is not only one-sided; he is also divorced from the world he lived in.

Moreover, the principle of dissimilarity assumes that our present knowledge of first-century Judaism and of first-century Christianity is established beyond question. This assumption is far from being correct. In fact, it is difficult to establish just which Jewish traditions were contemporary with Jesus. What is more, the evidence for the Gospels compares favorably with the extant evidence for first-century Judaism. Much of the

---

[91]There are instances of people prepared to die for misguided opinions (as, e.g., in many of the sects embracing erroneous doctrines), but in these cases there is genuine belief in the authenticity of the doctrines held. Only a deluded person would come to believe in the divine authority of his own creations.

[92]E.P. Sanders, *The Tendencies of the Synoptic Tradition* (Cambridge: Cambridge University Press, 1969), considers that the tendencies to change in the tradition are insufficient to be called "laws."

[93]For some incisive comments on the use of this method, cf. the article by M.D. Hooker in *Theology* 75 (1972): 570ff.

evidence used in applying critical principles is drawn from a period much later than the first century.

Wherever comparisons are involved, it is difficult to establish objective criteria, for a scholar's decision about whether or not a teaching is dissimilar will inevitably be affected by his own presuppositions. A similar absence of objectivity applies when the principle of coherence is used.

This appeal to coherence assumes that what the principle of dissimilarity declares authentic, itself authenticates other teaching that is coherent to it, and does so in a way nothing else can. Here there is a real danger of circular reasoning. Obviously, little confidence can be placed in critical conclusions based on such methods. It is more logical to suppose that the traditions are preserved in an authentic form and that the teaching of Jesus had some real points of contact with contemporary teaching, while containing vital differences. Similarly it makes better sense to suppose that the subsequent teaching of the church was indebted to the teaching of Jesus rather than to maintain that the early Christians invented much of the teaching of Jesus as a basis for their own beliefs. Literary criticism is disingenuous when it proposes principles that allow scholars to arrive at any conclusions they want. When this happens, the critical method cannot be called scientific.

VII. Criticism and Authority

There remains the important question of the relation of critical inquiry to NT authority. Taking criticism in its basic sense of reasoned examination, it follows that the resultant approach to authority will vary according to the presuppositions accepted. For this reason, critical approach to authority has tended to fall into two opposing groups. Conservative critics had always maintained that a true criticism will be in harmony with the authority of the NT. In other words, they regard the self-claims of the NT as part of the data of criticism. This should, however, be distinguished from a purely dogmatic approach that, on the strength of the authority of the NT, denies the validity of any criticism at all. We cannot silence reason in the interests of faith. A more acceptable critical approach is to assume that, in its search for truth, reason needs at the outset to submit to the authority of God. In the field of criticism, this means that any conclusion reached in a historical or literary inquiry must be scrutinized with the utmost care whenever it impinges on the authority of the text.

A. *Opposing Approaches*

A very different approach is found among nonconservatives, though some of them would accept a higher degree of authority than others. Those whose methods of criticism are entirely subjective, as e.g., the more extreme form critics, dispense with the notion of authority altogether. When much of the material is confidently considered historically unauthentic, because it is believed to have been molded by the community, any authoritative approach is clearly impossible, except for those sections of the tradition that are thought to be genuine. In this latter case, the concept of authority is conditioned by the purely speculative nature of the approach. Since the critic has himself decided what is genuine and what is not, even the authority of the authentic texts is subjected to human decision; and this is bound to weaken the whole concept of authority.

Much that claims to be scientific criticism has rejected the idea of authority on the grounds that science deals only with objective facts and the notion of biblical authority cannot be historically demonstrated. But scientific criticism is not without its own presuppositions, which sometimes attain a wholly unwarranted authority.[94] Though it cannot be said that literary criticism has generally strengthened the appeal to the authority of the text, there is no valid reason why a true literary criticism cannot coexist with a high view of Scripture.

B. *Criticism and Inspiration*

The relationship between criticism and inspiration is of great importance. Literary critics have too often assumed that a critical approach must exclude all thought of the verbal inspiration of Scripture. Where critical principles lead to decimation of the text, either in pronouncing whole books nonauthentic or separate passages as additions to the original, the concept of verbal inspiration as distinct from general inspiration must clearly go. The literary critic who rejects verbal inspiration often does so on the ground that textual criticism has shown variations in transmission, but he overlooks the testimony to the importance of the words of Scripture seen in textual critics' careful examination of manuscripts. More damaging to verbal inspiration in the eyes of most literary critics are the problems surrounding the synoptic Gospels. Many critics maintain that a comparison between the first three Gospels leaves no doubt that the precise words of Jesus have not been preserved, for if they had been, there would be no disagreements. But literary criticism, which has no adequate tools to resolve the synoptic problem, has no right to pronounce upon this problem by suggesting that any approach aside from its own is invalid. To say this is not to deny the difficulties of the synoptic problem; it is rather to challenge the view that a true conservative criticism is untenable in the face of these difficulties. It is not, though it must be added that any adequate doctrine of inspiration must be flexible enough to take account of the synoptic problem.

C. *Criticism and the Canon*

Another problem arising from some scholars' rejection of the authority of the NT is the content of the canon. Can books that are considered nonauthentic in whole or in part retain their place in the accepted canon of the NT?[95] Most scholars would reply in the affirmative, though in doing so some of them would certainly not regard the canon as a collection of authoritative books. In other words, critics have often modified the idea of the canon in order to accommodate the conclusions of their own theories.

The issue is a crucial one. Can a pseudonymous letter carry the same weight as a genuine one? If not, are distinctions to be made within the canon, or is the canon to be adjusted to exclude the nongenuine letter? There are, of course, ways of getting over this difficulty by regarding pseudonymity as an established Christian literary device and therefore acceptable. Nevertheless, complete consistency would demand the exclusion of an unauthentic writing from the canon. Failure to do so would weaken the authority of the whole. It is difficult to see, for example, what actual authority the teaching of Jesus

---

94Cosmologists have sometimes pronounced on the origins of the universe only to find that in a few years their theories have been outdated.

95Cf. J.C. Fenton's article, "Pseudonymity in the New Testament," *Theology* (1955), pp. 49ff.; K. Aland's monograph on *The Problem of the New Testament Canon* (London: Mowbray, 1962); Aland's essay on "Pseudonymity" and D. Guthrie's essay on the same subject reproduced in SPCK Collections 4 *The Authorship and Integrity of the New Testament* (London, 1965).

can have for those who reduce his authentic sayings to a minimal core, especially since there can be no certainty that even those sayings would survive the next wave of negative criticism. Authority can become so tied up with one's own critical opinions that it becomes almost emptied of meaning. On the other hand, it is self-evident that a conservative criticism that maintains the authority of the NT and at the same time examines the problems relating to it is not faced with such difficulties over the canon. Authoritative books must be given full weight and their own claims respected. Critics who formulate principles of criticism that are in accord with the authority of the NT, stand in a stronger position than those who deny this possibility; authority does not for them depend solely on the results of human reason.

VIII. Bibliography

Fuller, R.H. *The New Testament in Current Study*. New York: Scribner, 1962.

Guthrie, D. *A Shorter Life of Christ*. Grand Rapids: Zondervan, 1970.

_____. *New Testament Introduction*. Chicago: Inter-Varsity, 1970.

Harrison, E.F. *Introduction to the New Testament*. Grand Rapids: Eerdmans, 1964.

Kümmel, W.G. *Introduction to the New Testament*. Translated by A.J. Mattill, Jr. London: SCM, 1965.

Ladd, G.E. *The New Testament and Criticism*. Grand Rapids: Eerdmans, 1967.

Rohde, J. *Rediscovering the Teaching of the Evangelists*. Translated by D.M. Barton. London: SCM, 1968.

Stonehouse, N.B. *Origins of the Synoptic Gospels*. Grand Rapids: Eerdmans, 1963.

THE THEOLOGY OF THE NEW TESTAMENT

Samuel J. Mikolaski

Samuel J. Mikolaski

B.A., M.A., University of Western Ontario; B.D., University of London; D.Phil., Oxford University

President, Columbia Bible Institute

THE THEOLOGY OF THE NEW TESTAMENT

I. Introduction

The NT presents a remarkably explicit unity to the reader. There also emerge from it perspectives so varied that they cause one to question whether they challenge this unity or reinforce its intensity.

For the vast majority of Christians, the unity of the NT stands upon confession of the Lordship of Jesus Christ. This is the heart of the gospel and the great mystery of faith: the eternal second person of the Trinity became incarnate in Jesus Christ, died upon the cross for our sins, rose from the dead, and ascended into heaven.

This common ground of belief—the lordship of Christ and the *kerygma* (the gospel message for the unsaved; cf. 1 Cor 15:3, 4)—comprise the major thread of NT unity. Paul's gospel, which he received, not invented (Gal 1:12), is claimed by him to be consistent with the message of the original Jewish apostles at Jerusalem: that the death of the incarnate Lord is the ground of the forgiveness of sins, whether preached to Jews or to Gentiles. Unity of message did not preclude varying motifs and neither do the various key concepts and modalities of teaching imperil the theological unity.

Resurgence of interest in biblical studies during the past half-century has given powerful impetus to the study of NT theology. Acceptance of the truth that in Jesus Christ God came to us commits Christians decisively to a historical revelation. It is in the attempt to answer the question "Whom do we encounter in Jesus Christ?" that the varieties of NT theology are formulated—from the standpoint of the writers as well as of the readers. Is Jesus Christ a historical figure or the product of sincere but imagining faith? What happens in our encounter with the fact of Christ?

The difficulty of assigning priorities in NT theology is compounded by the fact that there are many prominent NT themes. How does each Gospel present Jesus Christ? Which major concept, once isolated, is primary—e.g., the Logos and eternal life themes of John, the Son of Man and Man of the Spirit themes of Luke-Acts, the Servant of Yahweh of Mark, or the messianic thrust of Matthew?

Did the early Christian community unintentionally invent the messianic claim in the interval between the death of Jesus and the late writing of the Gospels (Strauss)?[1] Are we radically ignorant of the facts (Wrede)?[2] Do the differences between Jewish and Gentile Christianity make reconciliation impossible (Baur)?[3] Was Jesus the author and victim of a mistaken apocalyptic (Schweitzer)?[4] Are the Gospel accounts simply a key to a beautiful ethical casket of faith, hope, and love from which atonement is expurgated (Harnack)?[5] Must we demythologize the NT narrative into a contemporary non-supernatural model (Bultmann)?[6]

More positively, should we elevate the concept of the kingdom, the covenant, the church, or the second coming and triumph as the key feature of NT theology? Or, is NT theology a three-stage development involving the fact of Christ (Gospels), preachers of the fact (Acts), and interpreters of the fact (Paul, Peter, Hebrews, and John), as Hunter[7] has argued? Ladd[8] sees NT theology as a threefold pattern: the kingdom of God (the Synoptic Gospels), eternal life (the Johannine texts), justification and the life in the Spirit (Paul).

Others argue that in the NT we confront a history in which an eternal reality is present, which is known in the proclamation of the Easter faith, and which is not formed by historical interest (the New Quest theologians Käsemann[9] and Bornkamm[10]). Dodd[11] has compelled us to consider the *kerygma*, the gospel, as an essential component of NT theology. He urges us to rediscover and to maintain the integrity of the original apostolic missionary proclamation.

The gospel—that is, the gospel of Jesus Christ, the Son of God, the Savior, the Lord (Mark 1:1; Rom 1:16, 17)—is certainly at the heart of NT unity and theology. NT theology is concerned primarily with elucidating the mighty saving act of God in Christ. To be sure, the apostolic writings do inform, teach, and edify. But fundamentally they bring the Good News that binds the NT together and from which all else that is Christian follows.

There is an encouraging tendency in NT studies to see the Gospels and other NT

---

[1]D.F. Strauss, *The Life of Jesus Critically Examined* (1835–1836; reprint ed., Philadelphia: Fortress, 1972).
[2]W. Wrede, *The Messianic Secret* (1901; reprint ed., Cambridge: James Clarke, 1971).
[3]F.C. Baur, *Paul the Apostle of Jesus Christ* (1876).
[4]A. Schweitzer, *The Quest of the Historical Jesus* (1906; reprint ed., New York: Macmillan, 1960).
[5]A. Harnack, *What Is Christianity?* (1900; reprint ed., New York: Harper, 1957).
[6]R. Bultmann, *Jesus and Mythology* (New York: Scribner, 1958).
[7]A.M. Hunter, *Introducing New Testament Theology* (London: S.C.M., 1957).
[8]G.E. Ladd, *The Pattern of New Testament Truth* (Grand Rapids: Eerdmans, 1968).
[9]E. Kasemann, *Essays in New Testment Themes* (Naperville: A.R. Allenson, 1964).
[10]G. Bornkamm, *Jesus of Nazareth* (New York: Harper, 1960).
[11]C.H. Dodd, *The Apostolic Preaching and Its Development* (London: Hodder and Stoughton, 1936).

books less as fragments and more as wholes. The authors were not merely biographers and compilers, but theologians. They were not creators of fancy, but interpreters of the events associated with the actual history of Jesus Christ. They tell us what was going on in the things that were happening.

NT studies involve three critical elements: evidence, events, and meaning. Stated theologically these are: the text of the NT, the historical reconstruction and statement of what actually happened, and the theological significance that is attached to the events and teachings.

The task of NT theology is to elucidate the meaning of the NT. This cannot be done by simply preparing a statistical inventory of NT words, phrases, or ideas, nor by arranging NT passages according to a preestablished dogmatic framework. The *kerygma*, which stands at the heart of the NT, is not to be identified with any theology. NT theology has its genius in insight into, and interpretation of, the events that constitute the revelation of Jesus Christ and the personal experiences of the NT writers. Their thought has its foundation and content in their experience of Christ. The task before us is to expound this faith in its reference to the intrusion of God through Jesus Christ into human history and the resulting *kerygma*.

The goal of the NT writers is that the truth of this reality (which is to be believed), combined with the act of responding to and obeying Christ (which is to be experienced), should reach us through the sequential conditions of time (cf. John 20:30, 31).

In the following exposition, the plan is logical and theological. Special attention is paid to the frame of reference of NT teaching, to its basic categories, and to major doctrines, as these transformed the ancient world view and bear significantly upon ours. While the NT writers adopt many concepts in presenting Christ and the meaning of Christian discipleship, underlying all these concepts there is a solid conceptual and theological unity.

II. Revelation and Scripture

Throughout the NT, the source of all authority is God himself. The entire NT breathes the air of a monotheistic, creationist, and revelational basis for life. This is apparent as much in the record of our Lord's life as it is in the writers' perspectives. The structure of both thought and language substantiates this. The structure stems from the OT and is continuous with that revelation, with its promise climactically fulfilled in the life, death, resurrection, and ascension of Jesus Christ. The NT canon is more than biography or anthology, more than a collection of writings by the followers of Christ. The canon is a hermeneutic (a way of interpretation). Its essential criterion is a theology based on the teaching of Christ and the apostles in written form, identifying and preserving what was already accepted as relating to Christ as Lord and what was accepted as apostolic in the early church.

The NT writings orient the teachings of Christ in relation to the biblical authority of the OT. Christ accepted the OT as authoritative and subjected himself to it, as all four Gospel traditions clearly state and imply (Matt 5:17, 18; 9:13; 15:1–4; Mark 7:9; 9:13; Luke 4:16–21; 18:31; John 5:39; 10:33–38). Jesus declares the Scriptures to be authoritative, in contrast to religious traditions. His life and death are presented as the fulfillment of Scripture. His teachings are the very Word of God, brought from the Father, which truth is the foundation of apostolic faith (Mark 13:31; John 5:19, 38, 39; 6:63, 68; 12:48, 49; 17:8).

Of what, then, does the NT revelation consist? It is Jesus Christ and the truths that concern Jesus Christ. The apostles believed in him and proclaimed the salvation they experienced. As to mode of revelation, the NT parallels the OT as a historical revelation. The revelatory insights of the apostles follow upon their apprehension of Christ (e.g., Luke 24:25–27; Rom 16:25, 26; 2 Cor 5:14; Eph 3:1–7; 2 Peter 1:16–21). Undoubtedly, the apostles received the OT as the Word of God (Rom 15:4; 1 Cor 10:11), and they received our Lord as the Son of God and his teachings as the Word of God.

For the NT writers, revelation concerns truth. Truth is a function of language. In this way revelation and Scripture are inextricably joined in NT theology. Event and interpretation go together. The NT revelation as it concerns Jesus Christ involves not merely abstract and timeless ethical truths, or the subjective experiences of the disciples, but it has to do with events that are concrete, particular, and actual. The apostolic statement and interpretation of the events is the truth of the matter. The writers intend to convey to the reader what is actually the case—that is, to state what was going on in the things that were happening. Whatever charge may be made against the NT writers as to their religious beliefs, we must recognize that they claim to give us divine revelation expressed in human language (1 Cor 2:13).

This revelation was given under the inspiration of the Holy Spirit. The NT writers do not enlarge on the psychological processes that attended inspiration, but simply declare, as Paul does, that Scripture is given by God: "All Scripture is God-breathed and is useful" (2 Tim 3:16). Similarly, 2 Peter 1:19–21 states that Christian faith is not lodged in fables but in attested fact. Men spoke, as they were carried along by God's Spirit, about the things they had seen and experienced. This is consistent with Christ's recorded attitude to Scripture. For example, he states that what was written in the law cannot be broken (John 10:34, 35), the term "law" here having the status of Scripture.

It is in respect to the person of Christ and the gospel that NT language has a revelational function (Rom 10:8–11; 2 Cor 4:1–6; Heb 1:5; 1 Peter 1:22–25). Its goal is the personal meeting of the soul with God in Jesus Christ (John 3:16; Acts 2:36–38; 1 John 5:1, 9–11).

III. God

The truth that God is one, living, personal, and infinite is universally assumed in the NT. The NT makes no attempt to prove the existence of God, but only declares his reality, glory, and purposes. It does, however, present the reasonableness of belief in him: God is the adequate cause of creation and providence (Acts 14:17; Rom 1:19, 20; Heb 3:4); he is the purposeful Creator (Acts 17:24–28; Eph 1:11; Heb 11:3); his spiritual reality presses on the awareness of men (Acts 17:23, 24); the human spirit has an affinity with him (Acts 17:28, 29); he is the standard of righteousness and the judge of the world (Acts 17:31; Rom 1:32).

Because of man's sin and distortion of the truth of creation, God's nature and purposes are fully and authoritatively revealed only in Jesus Christ and the apostolic writings of the NT. In the NT, God is disclosed more fully than in his general revelation in nature, of which man is a part. The need for special divine revelation does not come from the absence of general revelation but rather from its distortion by sinful men (Rom 1:18–21). God is the Creator and Sustainer of all (Matt 6:32; 7:11; Luke 11:13; 12:30). He is adequately known, not merely by an act of intellectual assent, but only when he is acknowledged and obeyed. God in the NT is Yahweh of the OT, more fully revealed in the person, teaching, and work of Jesus Christ.

NT teaching on the doctrine of God is continuous with OT teaching. The same God who appeared to the patriarchs is made known in the NT (Mark 12:26; cf. Exod 3:6). The basis of biblical teaching about God, the truths that bind OT and NT together, is that God is Creator and Redeemer; he, the Lord of all, who delivered his people in the past, now comes in Christ to fulfill the promise of salvation (Matt 1:21, 22; Luke 1:31–33; 2:47–55, 67–79).

As to God's nature, a threefold emphasis epitomizes NT teaching: God is personal, God is love, and God is good.

That God is personal, neither impersonal nor suprapersonal, is unique to the Christian revelation. The truth of his divine fatherhood depends on this, as do his particular providential concerns and moral judgments. So also does the very possibility of trinitarian theism. In the NT, the highest level of reality is that of persons and personal relationships.

The names of God show that God is personal and self-disclosed. He is not arbitrarily named by men as one object among others. Thus, the petition in Lord's Prayer "Hallowed be your name" links the NT revelation to the historical self-disclosure of God in the OT as El, Adonai, El-Shaddai, Elohim, and Yahweh (Jehovah). Revelation in both testaments reaches its climax in the truth that God is Father: the personal, living, acting One who relates himself to us personally in holy and loving ways. The personal revelation culminates in Jesus Christ, who has made the Father known and is eternally one with him (John 14:9; 1 Cor 8:6; Heb 1:1–3).

The name "Father" is not unique to the NT. In the OT God is the Father of Israel and Israel is his son (Hos 11:1). There are occurrences in the OT where God is spoken of as being "thy father" (Deut 32:6), "a father" (Ps 103:13), "our father" (Isa 63:16; 64:8), "my father" (Jer 3:4, 19), "a father to Israel" (Jer 31:9), "a father" and "one father" (Mal 1:6; 2:10). But the disclosure of God the Father through Jesus is an advance on OT usage; Jesus employs the intimate Aramaic form Abba (the childlike term for "father") in contrast to general filial terminology. The frequent allusions to the divine fatherhood are so noteworthy as to be normative. Through Jesus, Christians are led into a new, intimate relationship with God as their heavenly Father (Matt 6:9; Luke 11:2; Rom 8:15; Gal 4:6).

God is the Father of all Christians. Jesus does not speak of God as the Father of all men, but only of his own—i.e., only by anticipation does he speak of the unregenerate as being potentially his children. Through the Good News all men are called to know God as Father through accepting the redeeming work of Christ.

Abstract theism is unknown in the NT. In it, God is not simply the Supreme Being, but the God and Father of our Lord Jesus Christ (John 1:14; Eph 1:3), fatherhood being one of the highest elements in the relations between God and man (Heb 12:9).

Second, God is love (1 John 4:8, 16). In the synoptic Gospels the term *love* (agape) occurs infrequently in the sayings of Jesus and the term grace (charis) not at all. This should be understood in the light of the personal presence of Christ, who is the personification of love and grace and should also be understood in the light of the stress laid on mercy, healing, forgiveness, self-sacrifice, raising the dead, feeding the hungry, and much more (Matt 9:36, 20:31, 32; Mark 1:41, 5:19; Luke 7:47, 15:7). God's goodness to men shows his love (Matt 5:45; 18:14; Luke 12:27, 28).

The Johannine writings use the language and develop the nature of the divine love. Christ is the gift of love (John 3:16; 1 John 4:9, 10). Love binds the Father and Son together (John 17:22, 23) and is the very nature of God (1 John 4:8, 16b). Paul parallels this teaching (Rom 8:39) with a strong emphasis on the atonement as the gift of love (Rom 5:8, 9). Peter expresses the love of God through his mercy (1 Peter 2:3, 10), which culminates in the sacrifice of Christ (2:24, 25).

Third, God is good. The holiness and righteousness of God are commonly referred to by the NT writers (Luke 1:49; John 17:11; Acts 17:24, 25; 1 Peter 2:9). God calls men to holiness. Within the terms of his own righteousness, he provides salvation (Rom 3:26). The pattern of NT teaching on the righteousness of God derives from the teaching of Jesus, who casts a new light on the ethical character of God in relation to the Law of the OT. The relation between judgment and grace, including the Cross, comprise a significant element of NT teaching.

God's goodness, expressed as righteousness, is more than justice (giving every man his due). Grace, the additional factor to which Jesus refers in Matthew 5:43–48, carries the meaning of divine righteousness beyond moral rectitude. It is the righteousness that, according to Paul, is "apart from law" (Rom 3:21), the righteousness that goes beyond "an eye for an eye and a tooth for a tooth." God is holy and just, yet in Christ he justifies the sinner. So the goodness and righteousness of Christ, as presented in the Gospels, transcend moral rectitude. Christ's whole life in its association with sinners, his teaching on forgiveness, and his sacrificial death for sin set forward God's loving concern for people and the truth about the nature of man.

The NT contains abundant detail regarding the attributes and perfections of God. Here the data are remarkably coherent and consistent, though care should be exercised in systematizing them; for one must bear in mind the theistic traditions and assumptions of the writers, their kerygmatic and didactic purposes, and their liberty in the variety of metaphors and images they employ.

God is spirit (John 4:24), infinite, invisible (John 1:18; Rom 11:33; Col 1:15; Heb 12:9; 1 John 4:12, 20), light (1 John 1:5). God is glorious, and his glory is disclosed in Christ (2 Cor 3:18; 4:6; Col 1:27; Titus 2:13; 2 Peter 1:16–18). God is the Lord, self-sufficient, the author of life (John 5:26; 1 Tim 6:16), free and sovereign in his works (Acts 18:21; Rom 15:32; Eph 1:11; James 4:15). God is holy (John 17:11), Jesus is holy (Acts 4:27, 30), and Christians are also to be holy (Rom 12:1; 1 Peter 1:15; 2:9). God is unchangeable (Rom 11:29; James 1:17). God is righteous. He judges justly (Acts 17:31; Rom 2:2, 6; 3:6; 1 Peter 1:17), yet is full of mercy and compassion (Luke 1:50; Rom 2:4; Eph 2:4; 2 Peter 3:15). God is all-powerful (Matt 11:25; Luke 1:37; Rom 4:17; Eph 1:11), and this prerogative of omnipotence belongs also to Christ (Matt 28:18; John 3:35; 13:3). God is patient and faithful in his dealings (Rom 2:4; 1 Thess 5:24; 2 Tim 2:13; 1 Peter 4:19). There is but one God (John 5:44; 17:3; 1 Cor 8:4–6; Eph 4:5, 6; 1 Tim 1:17; 2:5; James 2:19), who is omnipresent (Acts 17:24, 27, 28) and omniscient (Rom 11:33–36; Heb 4:13).

IV. Jesus Christ

The NT is supremely a Christ-centered book. Through its varieties of emphases and literary genre the writers affirm the truth that Jesus Christ is the eternal Second Person of the Holy Trinity, who took on human flesh at Bethlehem.

The data are comprehensive and unambiguous. These considerations tie the nature of Christ to his work, and significantly highlight the redemptive character of NT Christology: First of all, Jesus Christ is, at the inmost principle of his being, true God, from whom he came as the eternal, not temporal, Son (John 1:1; 17:5; Phil 2:6; Col 1:17; 2:9). Second, the eternal Son of God voluntarily emptied himself, took to himself flesh and became true man (John 1:14, 18; Phil 2:7, 8; Heb 2:14), so that in his nature he is true God and true man (John 3:13; Col 1:16, 17; Heb 1:3). Third, the purpose of the Incarnation is redemption, reconciliation, and Christ's triumph over the power of evil (Matt 20:28; Mark 10:45; John 3:16; 2 Cor 5:18, 21; Gal 4:4; 1 John 3:5).

The NT writers call Christ God (John 1:1, 18; 20:28; Col 2:9; Titus 2:13; Heb 1:8, 10). Without this confession, the faith of the apostles and of the first Christians would be without foundation. He is called the Son of God—the term in the NT that assigns him divine as well as messianic prerogatives (Matt 11:27; 16:16; 26:63–65; Mark 12:35–37; 14:61; Luke 1:35; 22:70, 71; John 1:34; 19:7). The words "Father" and "Son" are not used of him merely temporally, but in respect to an eternal relationship. "Son of God" is certainly a claim to deity, and "only begotten Son" refers as well to Christ's preincarnate dignity and privilege (Rom 8:29; Col 1:15–18; Heb 1:6). A clear distinction is drawn between Christ's eternal being and Abraham's finite becoming (John 8:58; cf. John 6:20; 8:24, 28; 18:6). The anarthrous construction (i.e., without the article) "the Word was God" (John 1:1) means that Christ, as the Word of God, is identified with the essential nature of God (cf. Rom 9:5).

Beyond the foregoing, the significance of Jesus Christ's titles is important in this respect, as contemporary NT scholars have shown (Vincent Taylor, T.W. Manson, O. Cullmann): the title "Messiah," or the Greek form "Christ," which means God's anointed or vicegerent, derives from the expectation of the Davidic Ruler who, anointed by the Holy Spirit, would establish the kingdom of God on earth (Matt 16:16, 20; 26:63; Mark 8:29; 14:61; Luke 2:11, 25, 26, 38; 9:20; 22:67; John 1:41; 4:25, 26, 29; 7:26–31; 9:22; Acts 2:36; 3:20; 18:28). The NT concept of Christ as the Messiah transcends its previous usage. It joins his divine nature and derivation to his passion as the Son of Man, the Suffering Servant of Isaiah.

A second important title is embedded in one of the earliest Christian confessions, namely, "Jesus is Lord" (Acts 10:36; Rom 10:9; 1 Cor 12:3; 2 Cor 4:5; Phil 2:11; 1 Peter 3:15). Christ's lordship is associated with the resurrection and the post-resurrection appearances (Luke 24:34; John 20:2, 13, 18, 25, 28; 21:7) and is central to apostolic preaching (Acts 2:36; Rom 10:9; Eph 4:5; Phil 2:11; Heb 7:14; James 1:1; 1 Peter 1:3; Rev 11:15). The title "Lord" in the earliest Christian proclamation attests to faith in Jesus Christ's divinity.

The third key title is "Savior" (Matt 1:21; Luke 2:11; John 4:42; Acts 5:31; 13:23; Phil 3:20), which conveys the purpose of Christ's coming. Apostolic and post-apostolic teaching concentrate on salvation as solely the prerogative of God to achieve and provide (2 Cor 5:19).

The integrity of Jesus Christ's humanity is common to all NT literature. This includes his birth at Bethlehem (Luke 1:35), boyhood at Nazareth (Luke 2:39–52), fasting and temptation, weariness (John 4:6), and death (John 19:28–30; Acts 2:23). NT Christology also vigorously emphasizes the ideal and normative character of Christ's humanity. The NT shows his uniqueness through his virgin birth (Luke 1:34, 35), his knowledge (Matt 11:27), his moral perfection (Luke 1:35; 2 Cor 5:21), his teaching (Matt 5–7), his works (Matt 11:20; 13:54; Mark 6:2), and his transfiguration and exaltation (2 Peter 1:16–18). He is the bearer of the promised Spirit (Mark 1:8, 10–11); the new Man for the new age (Acts 2:17, 18, 33; Rom 5:15–21).

The unity of the person of Jesus Christ is explicit in the NT writings, as the various combinations of his name show—Lord Jesus, Christ Jesus, Lord Jesus Christ, Jesus Christ. John's first Epistle was written to combat the heresy of those who sought to divide the historical Jesus from the eternal Christ and it strongly affirms the unity of his person in his incarnate life and redeeming death (1 John 4:3, 15; 5:1, 6). The fundamental theological premise of NT theology is that if Jesus Christ is not God incarnate, then, regardless of how great a being he might be, we have no contact with God through him. Christology must be adequate to the facts of redemptive experience. This is the point on which NT theology, proclamation, and experience converge.

V. The Holy Spirit

The NT data relating to the person and work of the Holy Spirit are given in a series of events primarily associated with the life of Jesus Christ. These are extended in the Epistles theologically to the life of the Christian and the church. The teaching on the Holy Spirit is consistent with OT revelation, especially in regard to fulfillment of the kingdom promise (Matt 12:18; Luke 4:16–21), but it incorporates the new revelation on the spiritual as well as the earthly nature of the kingdom (Acts 2:16–21, 29–33, 38, 39) and the corresponding understanding of the full personhood of the Spirit (John 16:7–14).

The primary sign of the new age of the Spirit in the NT is the person of Jesus Christ, while the consequent sign of the Spirit is Pentecost. The life of Christ is the historical instance and the promised fulfillment of life in the Spirit. He is the model of the new man. He was begotten by the Spirit (Matt 1:18), baptized in the Spirit (Matt 3:16), driven by the Spirit into the wilderness to be tempted (Mark 1:12), and he ministered by the Spirit (Mark 3:28). He is the permanent bearer of the Spirit and the giver of the Spirit (John 1:32–34). The synoptic and Johannine accounts fall into this pattern, which carries forward into the Acts and the Epistles.

The first significant NT reference to the Spirit is the proclamation of John the Baptist (Mark 1:8). Eight key passages sum up references to the Spirit in Jesus' sayings: blasphemy (Matt 12:31, 32; Mark 3:28–30; Luke 12:10), persecution (Matt 10:20; Mark 13:11; Luke 12:12), exorcism (Matt 12:28), inspiration (Matt 22:43; Mark 12:36), the gift of the Spirit (Luke 11:13), the Great Commission (Matt 28:19), the sermon at Nazareth (Luke 4:16–30), and the promise of Pentecost (Luke 24:49). In the synoptic Gospels the work of the Spirit pervades the life, teaching, and works of Jesus Christ as the canvas on which the whole painting appears.

The Johannine texts are strategic to the doctrine of the Spirit (7:39; 14:16–18, 26; 15:26; 16:7–16; 20:22, 23). Jesus names the Holy Spirit as the Paraclete (one who is helper or advocate) and also sets forth his ministries and his full personhood in language synonymous with that which relates to Christ's own personhood. Acts and the Epistles carry forward the Christ-centered and salvation-centered work of the Spirit.

The christological center of NT teaching and the new life in the body of Christ by the Spirit compel the majority of NT scholars to recognize that new revelational ideas control the meaning of Spirit in the NT and that this is a significant advance on the OT doctrine of the Spirit.

The NT teaching about the Holy Spirit entails the difficulty of dealing with two questions—namely, Is the Spirit personal? and Is the Spirit distinctly personal? No Christian scholar can be content to make of the Spirit as presented in the NT simply impersonal divine energy or invasive power. He must reckon with two strands of evidence. First, there are the passages where the personal pronoun is distinctly used of the Holy Spirit—i.e., the "he" passages (e.g., Mark 3:22–30; Luke 12:12; John 14:26; 15:26; 16:7–15; Acts 8:29; 10:19, 20; 13:2; 15:28; 16:6, 7; 20:28; Rom 5:5). Second, there are the other passages—i.e., the "it" passages, which may allow a personal reading but do not demand it (e.g., Matt 1:18; 4:1; 12:28; Luke 1:15; John 7:39; Acts 1:8; Rom 8:26, 27). The data compel us to think of the Spirit in fully personal terms. While it is possible to account for the "it" passages in terms of the "he" passages, it is impossible to account for the "he" passages in terms of the "it" passages.

Nor do the NT writers reduce the Spirit to the indwelling Christ. The NT never says that Christ is the Spirit of God (a single disputed passage, 2 Cor 3:17, should be taken to read "spirit of freedom" as against "spirit of bondage"). The point of the Gospels, with the consequent fulfillment in Acts, is that Christ will send the Spirit from the Father (John 15:26) and that for Christ's followers the Spirit would attest not to himself but to Christ (John 16:13, 14).

VI. The Trinity

Belief in the triune nature of God, in which each person of the triad is thought of as fully personal, pervades NT teaching. To argue that the doctrine of the Trinity is nowhere explicitly defined or discussed in the NT is to fail to recognize that other crucial doctrines are similarly implicit in Scripture and must be developed by careful study. The total NT presentation of salvation and all NT teaching rest on the trinitarian understanding of the nature of God. Not only is trinitarian teaching strongly evident in the NT proclamation of the gospel message, but the theological logic of trinitarian faith fits in with other important aspects of the biblical revelation. The NT Christians confess the two truths that God sent his Son into the world and that God was in Christ reconciling the world to himself (John 3:16; 2 Cor 5:19). It was the Son, not the Father, who died on the cross. The Father raised the Son from the dead, vindicating both. Other language concerning Christ's ascension, his session at the right hand of God, and his promised return means little apart from the trinitarian faith.

In the NT, trinitarian doctrine hinges on trinitarian redemptive experience, worship, and mission. It is a vital spiritual element in the apostolic writings. Trinitarian faith in the NT stems from the reality of the incarnation of the eternal Son at Bethlehem and from the descent of the Holy Spirit at Pentecost; from their distinctness; and from the fully personal language used of both Son and Spirit, and also of the Father.

Paul formulates statements concerning Christian experience and life in the body of Christ in trinitarian language (Rom 5:1, 5; 8:5; 1 Cor 12:4–6; Gal 4:4–6; Eph 2:18). In his Epistles, the benedictions (e.g., 2 Cor 13:14) and salutations should be recognized as religious high points erected on a pervasive trinitarian base. Of great significance is the use of the threefold name in the Great Commission (Matt 28:19), a usage that recurs in the NT confessionally and liturgically (John 14:26; Acts 2:32, 33, 37–40; Rom 1:1–4; 5:1–5; 8:1–4; Eph 1:17; 4:4–6; 2 Thess 2:13, 14; 1 Peter 1:2, 3). This ties the doctrine of the Trinity directly to the redemptive and baptismal experience of the first Christians. The NT language points to three distinct coequal persons yet one God, each person being the same God who works, says Paul (1 Cor 12:4–6). Christianity began as a sect of the Jews; it remained thoroughly monotheistic, yet the plethora of trinitarian language in the NT yields not a trace of embarrassment from Jewish attack through any charge of tritheism.

In the NT, trinitarian awareness and worship enrich Christian experience. Love is the bond of perfect union (Col 3:14) that joins Christians to God through the redeeming work of Father, Son, and Holy Spirit (Eph 4:2–6). Paul expounds a parallel between Christ's life and the believer's life (Rom 8:1–11): as the Spirit who came upon the Messiah is God's Spirit, so the Spirit who indwells Christians is God's Spirit, who raises them to a new quality of life in the fellowship of the triune God whom they now call "Father"

(8:14–17). Only in this way can we understand unity as the NT applies it to God. The prayer of Jesus in John 17 (especially vv. 20–23) point to a complex form of unity that is not abstractive but fully personal and interpersonal: "I in thee," "thou in me," "that they may be one in us."

VII. Creation, Providence, and Grace

The NT assumes and frequently affirms the creation of the world by God and its absolute dependence on him.

In the Gospels, the truth of creation is chiefly an inference from God's providential concern for and dealings with the world. In the Epistles the doctrine is explicit. Taken as a whole, NT teaching is consistent with the OT; indeed, the creation of the world by God and the corollaries of grace and freedom are axioms on which all biblical truth is erected.

In the Epistles of Peter and Paul, God is called the Creator (1 Peter 4:19; cf. Rom 1:25; Col 3:10); here the cognate terms point to the act of creating and to what is created. Other terms accord with this model: under God the world is a cosmos (an ordered reality, Acts 17:24), seen temporally as a series of interrelated ages (1 Cor 2:6–8; 2 Cor 4:4; Eph 6:12).

The NT expressly declares the absolute character of God's creation of the world. Paul says that God called into existence that which did not previously exist (Rom 1:20; 4:17; 2 Cor 4:6; Eph 1:4). Peter refers to the creation of the world by God (2 Peter 3:4), and Hebrews states that the world was created by the word of God (Heb 11:3; cf. 9:11). Luke's teaching is parallel (Acts 4:24; 14:15). Luke also quotes Paul who, in turn, speaks of the truth of creation as a common human heritage by citing the classical Greek poets Epimenides, Aratus, and Cleanthes (Acts 17:28). John states the doctrine in the Book of Revelation (10:6).

Such things as the time and duration of creation are not relevant to the main currents of NT teaching. These concern the central affirmation that the universe derives its existence from God the Creator, that God is ultimately responsible for everything in the world, that he is good, that he is personally active in the world and is our heavenly Father, and that man's chief end is God's fellowship and service.

While the OT states that creation is by the Word and Spirit of God, the NT shows the author of the creating word to be the living Word, the incarnate Lord, Jesus Christ (John 1:1, 14, 18; 2 Cor 5:17; Col 1:16, 17; Heb 1:1–4). Thus the foreshadowings of the OT are fulfilled in the trinitarian teaching of the NT.

In the NT the providence of God is directly related to the fatherhood of God and to the fact that the world is an orderly, not chaotic, reality. God's oversight of the world is personal and universal, encompassing both the spiritual and the material needs of people (Matt 5:45; 6:11, 25, 26; Luke 6:35; Acts 17:25; Rom 1:18). With regard to the kingdom and the church, God works cooperatively with persons, so that their dignity and responsibility are enhanced. They are co-workers or fellow laborers with him (Acts 15:4, 28; 1 Cor 3:6–9; 2 Cor 6:1).

It is of utmost importance to see that grace in the NT is the corollary of the divine providence and that grace is the key feature of Christian teaching in contrast to systems such as materialism and idealism. Grace is the way God deals with the world for the accomplishment of his beneficent purposes. The doctrines of creation, providence, and grace intertwine. They declare that God is neither too proud to create the world nor too remote to care for it. In NT teaching, as in the teaching of the OT, ultimate reality pertains to persons and personal life. Therefore, discrete, personal life with its prime characteristics of freedom and moral responsibility is not an intermediate step to a higher reality. For modern secular man the NT model of these things stands as the most challenging alternative to current secular models and the most effectual guardian of his personhood and freedom.

VIII. Man

In the NT, there is an important relationship between the doctrine of creation and human personhood. The NT does not view the personal life of God or the personal lives of individual human beings as transient modes in which a more real and enduring system of reality expresses itself. Nor does it view God and man as united in some more ultimate reality than Scripture presents.

That man is the creation of God is, in the NT, the heritage of the OT revelation, including the truth of a first historical pair (Matt 19:4; Mark 10:6; Luke 3:38; 1 Cor 15:45; 1 Tim 2:13). He is made aware of his uniqueness in relation to the revealing activity of God his Maker (Rom 1:19–23); he is also aware of his earthly origin from the dust of the ground. The duality of body and spirit pervade NT teaching about the nature of man.

Many scholars see NT terminology as significantly paralleling OT terms—viz., *pneuma* (spirit) and *psyche* (soul) in relation to *ruach* and *nephesh* in the OT, and *soma* and *sarx* in relation to *basar* for body and flesh, though the parallels are not exact. Some raise serious questions as to whether the Greek terminology introduces a dualism alien to Hebrew thought, though recently the congruence of NT with OT thought has been reaffirmed; indeed, that the root ideas of the NT are in the Hebrew rather than Greek world has been argued vigorously.

The distinctness of soul and spirit seems clear from Hebrews 4:12 and 1 Thessalonians 5:23. There are those who insist that a bipartite rather than tripartite view of man is demanded by the weight of NT teaching. But that man is tripartite (body, soul, spirit) appears to be more consistent with the data. The term *soul* designates man as a living being. The term *spirit* indicates that man is endowed with a personal spirit. Furthermore, the unique teaching of the NT is that the regenerated person, through the recreating work of the Holy Spirit, has communion with God as spirit with spirit.

Two questions are in the forefront of modern thinking about these things: first, the duality of body and spirit because in the NT human spiritual life in contrast to animal life apparently requires the distinctness of spirit; and second, the way the unity of man's life as a bodily life is to be thought of.

In the NT, the duality or "two-ness" of body and spirit is a fundamental premise, though the difference between this and non-Christian Greek teaching, especially in regard to the resurrection of the body, is important (Luke 24:37–39; Acts 23:8; 1 Tim 4:1; Heb 12:9, 23; 1 Peter 3:19, 20; 4:6). Nowhere does the NT denigrate the body (the "flesh" of the body in contrast to the "flesh" as carnal appetite). The NT sees man as an ensouled body and an embodied spirit. He is a psychosomatic unity. The NT data do demand that we think of man as one; nevertheless, in the NT the duality of his nature is everywhere apparent and may not be lightly dismissed. Redemption applies to the whole person (1 Thess 5:23).

What the biblical terms imply for a modern Christian psychology and theology of man has yet to be fully grasped. Three significant NT truths distinguish Christian teaching about man and carry important implications for the Christian understanding of man: (a) that God is personal, (b) that man as a person is a thing of value in himself, and (c) that there is a new order of love (*agape*) in human relationships and to God.

In the NT selfhood is a permanent spiritual reality and value. Selfhood is the peculiar constituting entity of individual humanity. Selfhood is further qualified in terms of intelligence, capacity of response to values, and capacity to act purposefully. At the heart of what it means to be human is the concept of the free, good person created in the image of God (John 8:31–36; Rom 8:14, 15; 1 Cor 3:16, 17; 2 Cor 3:17, 18; Heb 10:7).

This spiritualizing of the bodily life is unique to the NT. There is nothing like it in Greek philosophy. The bodily life is the material of which the spiritual life is to be built. The key to this is the Christian's daily self-offering of his whole being to God. Hence, the strategic significance of the incarnate life of Christ not only as the sinless One who comes to redeem, but as the pattern of the new man (Rom 5:14–21).

IX. Sin and Judgment

In regard to the problems of evil and sin, the NT is not reductionist. Evil and sin are present realities that God has overcome through the Cross (Col 2:14, 15) and that will finally be banished (Matt 25:33, 34; Rom 8:21–25; Rev 21:1–5). Evil and sin are not cured by thinking them away, but by God's redemptive intervention. Two correlatives dominate the moral realities of life—the universality of human sinfulness and the universality of human guilt.

Assumed and declared all through the NT is the fallen nature, sinful behavior, and moral culpability of man. Individually and universally, people are sinners. This fact is declared and its truth attested to in the experience of the biblical writers (Mark 10:45; Rom 3:10, 19, 23; Gal 3:22; 1 John 1:8–10). Associated with this is the concept of an evil-infected world system, significantly influenced by destructive satanic and demonic powers that oppose God, truth, and goodness (Luke 22:53; John 8:44; 2 Cor 4:3, 4; Gal 4:3; Eph 6:10–13; 2 Peter 2:19, 20).

As in the OT, a wide variety of terms identify sin in relation to the life situations and history that record its reality. Major terms are these: missing the mark (Rom 3:23), godlessness (Rom 1:18), disobedience (1 John 3:4), transgression (Heb 2:2), lapse (Acts 13:27), unrighteousness (Acts 1:18), and evil acts (Matt 6:13); but there are many other key terms and their cognates.

What is the essence of sin, in the light of NT thought? Interpreters concentrate chiefly on disobedience or rebellion, unrighteousness, pride, and independence from God. The origin of sin is the fall of the first man (John 8:44; Rom 5:12–21; 2 Cor 11:3; Rev 20:2). The NT ties the moral and spiritual import of the Fall to a historical event and thus rejects the views of both unmoral monism and ultimate dualism. The consequences of sin in the human personality are widespread, affecting the ego, spoiling relationships, distorting values, blunting the mind, and defeating the will (cf. Rom 6–7). The natural man is not able to perceive spiritual things properly, whereas the new man is characterized by a new mind, which is the mind of Christ (1 Cor 2:14–16).

This last is the essential question respecting original sin. In Romans 5:12–21 Paul refers to a condition and power of sin in human life that is other than actual sin. This is not an anachronistic idea peculiar to Romans 5, but comprises the backdrop of other NT teaching on the human condition, grace, and redemption. Nowhere does the NT assume or say that humanity is born into Adam's pre-fall state. Rather, fallen man has no capacity for the kingdom without rebirth (John 3:1–21); he is natural, not spiritual (1 Cor 2:14); his carnal mind is at enmity with God and cannot be subject to God (Rom 8:7, 8, 11); he is dead in sin (Eph 2:1, 5; 4:17–20). The NT model is supernatural renewal of fallen human nature, rebirth by the Holy Spirit through faith in Jesus Christ.

In the NT, law and judgment are not archaic ideas carried over from the concept of a wrathful deity in the OT, as some have said. The love of God is holy love. Law and punishment are functions and conditions of freedom. Judgment is neither purely reformative nor deterrent (which might make it immoral), but vindicates the righteousness of God and brings just retribution to bear on the wrongdoer. Punishment in the NT is the correlative of freedom (Rom 1:32). It thereby honors the moral integrity of human life.

X. The Kingdom of God

The kingdom or reign of God in the world is an important link between OT and NT theology. The promised messianic reign of the OT is fulfilled in Jesus Christ, in and through whom the kingdom is present (Matt 4:23; 9:35; 24:14; Mark 1:15; Luke 2:25, 38; 11:20; Col 1:13, 20; James 2:5). It also has a future fulfillment at Christ's coming and glory (1 Cor 15:24; 2 Tim 4:1, 18; 2 Peter 1:11).

While Scripture recognizes the reign of God as being eternal, it acknowledges that his sovereignty in the evil-infected world is only partial. Scripture declares that God's universal reign will be achieved at Christ's second advent. This reign, however, has already broken into history in the incarnation, death, resurrection, and ascension of Christ.

Important aspects of the kingdom include the revelation of the holy compassion of God, the reign of righteousness and love, triumph over the powers of evil, deliverance and healing for broken humanity, the forgiveness and restoration of people to God (Matt 6:10; Luke 4:16–21). There are also the final events of this age: the physical resurrection of the dead, the new spiritual bodies of the redeemed and their heavenly life, and the judgment and punishment of the wicked (Matt 13).

While the kingdom of God, present in Jesus Christ, includes the final reign of God in all human affairs, it is not a present political, economic, or social power. Rather, it is the spiritual rule of God in the hearts of those who have been freed from the sway of evil powers (Matt 5:3; 12:28; 21:31; Luke 7:17–23; 10:17–20; 17:21). To receive the kingdom, or to come under its sway, is to open the heart to God and acknowledge his presence in Jesus Christ and the power of Christ's life for one's own life. The most distinctive feature of the kingdom is the presence of the Holy Spirit. Jesus Christ comes as the Spirit-bearing Man, who promises the Spirit to his followers. They, as permanently transformed, Spirit-endued persons, are the signs of the new age, which is the kingdom of God (Acts 2:30, 33, 36, 38, 39).

XI. Redemption

The NT doctrine of redemption is complex, though it concentrates on a simple and direct idea: that "Christ died for our sins according to the Scriptures" (1 Cor 15:3). This complexity comes first from the many metaphors and other figures the NT writers use in presenting the significance of the work of Christ and second, from the trinitarian mystery of the Atonement. In respect to the latter, the rationale of NT thought converges on the twin truths that God sent his Son into the world to redeem us (John 3:16) and that God was in Christ reconciling the world to himself (2 Cor 5:19).

The redemption of the world and sinful people is inextricably bound up in the NT with the person and work of Jesus Christ. Though his work has been interpreted variously, the varieties in the biblical motifs regarding it are not contradictory; rather, they show the difficulty of encompassing Christ's work within a single category—or making the subject "stay put," so to speak.

Traditional NT patterns of redemption include the threefold office of Christ as Prophet (Matt 21:11, 46), Priest (Heb 3:1; 9:11–28; 10:1–14), and King (Matt 28:18; Phil 2:9–11). The concept of the covenant is undoubtedly crucially important. Christ comes to inaugurate a new and final covenant through his own blood, taking away the sin the first covenant could not remove (Matt 26:27, 28; Mark 14:24; Luke 22:20; 1 Cor 11:25–27; Heb 9:15–20; 10:29; 13:20, 21). Associated with this is the concept of final, vicarious sacrifice. The OT sacrifices are seen to prefigure the Cross. The Cross fulfills their meaning in that Christ makes the once-for-all sacrifice for sin. Another important theme is the Suffering Servant of the Lord. That the Suffering Servant of Isaiah 53 is the Son of Man of Mark 10:45, who comes to seek and save the lost, is a landmark of biblical redemptive theology.

The consistency of redemptive teaching in the NT is remarkable. Four important points bear emphasizing: First, the Cross originated in the eternal counsel of God and is his act for the salvation of the world. Second, the Cross relates directly to the world's evil and to human sin. Third, Christ's death was the judgment death for sin. Fourth, by that death people are saved.

All of the literary traditions of the NT declare these truths. For examples, see the Gospels (Mark 8:31; 9:31; 10:32–34, 45; 14:36, and parallel passages), Luke in Acts (2:23, 38; 3:17, 18; 4:27; 5:30, 31; 10:39, 43), Paul (Rom 3:25; 5:8; 8:3, 32; 1 Cor 15:3; 2 Cor 5:14, 15, 21; Gal 1:3, 4; 3:13), Peter (1 Peter 1:18–20; 2:24), Hebrews (1:3; 2:9; 5:1–5; 9:26, 28; 10:12), and John (John 1:29; 3:14–16; 10:17; 12:31; 1 John 1:7; 2:2; 4:10). (See James Denney, *The Death of Christ* [London: Tyndale Press. 1951].)

Careful examination of these and other NT data yields fascinating perspectives on the work of Christ, which are expressed through fundamental truths and supported by many terms. These include sacrifice (Lamb of God, forgiveness, vicarious suffering, purification, cleansing), atonement (propitiation, expiation, blood), redemption (ransom, substitution, representation), mediation (reconciliation, covenant), and triumph (victory over evil). (See Leon Morris, *The Apostolic Preaching of the Cross* [Grand Rapids: Eerdmans, 1955].)

The heart of the Atonement is the love of God. But this love is not seen as won, or simply disclosed, by the Cross; rather, as giving Christ to the Cross. The Cross is God's gracious and loving act of condescension in Christ by which sin is atoned for, evil is absorbed and overcome, men are reconciled to God, and the day of ultimate restoration of all things is assured (Rom 8:19–25; Eph 1:7–10; Col 1:20).

XII. The Gospel

No attempt to structure NT theology can avoid reference to the Gospel of Jesus Christ, the *kerygma*. The gospel concerns Jesus Christ (Mark 1:1). Its proclamation is the task of the church (Matt 28:19, 20). Frequent, substantial summaries of the gospel recur throughout the NT literature (Mark 10:45; John 1:10–14; 3:16; Acts 1:8; 2:38, 39; Rom 1:16, 17; 1 Cor 1:17, 18; 15:1–4; Gal 1:3, 4, 8–11; 1 Tim 3:16; Hebrews 1:1–3; 1 Peter 1:2, 3, 12, 18–25; 1 John 4:10).

Paul expresses the epitome of the gospel in the words "Christ died for our sins according to the Scriptures" (1 Cor 15:3). In this sentence, every word has profound Christian meaning. While the results of the gospel are apparent in the world in the amelioration of suffering and the social concerns of Christian people, these must be seen as the result of the gospel's proclamation. Good does necessarily issue from the gospel, but in itself the gospel is the Good News concerning Jesus Christ to which Christians attest.

Apostolic faith was not a casket of ethical virtues, important as these are; it was a testimony to God's salvation provided through Christ's Cross. Only the deity of Christ, the gratuitousness of forgiveness through the death of the Cross, and the appropriate human response of faith could overcome the deep-seated sociological barriers among the first Jewish Christians and extend the Christian faith from them to the entire Gentile world.

The earliest Christian preaching was to Jews. The original Jewish apostles preached the death of Christ as the atonement and basis for forgiveness in connection with witness to his messiahship. Paul's defense of his preaching to Gentiles (notably in Acts, Romans, and Galatians) is based on a summary of the gospel as common ground for all believers, including himself and the other apostles.

Fundamentally, therefore, the issue of the gospel is the issue of Jesus Christ, his incarnate life as true man and true God, his death and resurrection, and the forgiveness of sins through faith in him. The gospel is thus not only the starting point of the church; it is the point of meeting among the apostles, the hallmark of all that is truly Christian throughout the NT, and the point of meeting for faith and conduct of all Christians.

XIII. The Resurrection

The Resurrection is, along with the death of Christ for sin, the indispensible foundation of the NT faith and gospel, as seen in such confessions as Rom 10:9, 10; 1 Cor 15:3–5; 1 Peter 3:18, 21. In the NT the truth of the Resurrection is neither wishful thinking nor apostolic ingenuity bolstering up vain hope, but apostolic attestation to the risen Lord and a vital spiritual premise of every day experience (Rom 8:11; 1 Cor 6:14; 2 Cor 4:7–14). The Resurrection was totally unexpected by the disillusioned disciples (Luke 24; John 20:24–29). Its reality was reinforced in their minds by a coherent series of events and experiences, including the empty tomb, the appearances to them of the risen Lord, the Ascension, Pentecost, and Christ's continuing presence among them by the Holy Spirit (see Floyd V. Filson, *Jesus Christ the Risen Lord*, [New York: Abingdon, 1956]). Upon the Resurrection hang the significance of the Cross, the vitality of the gospel, one's union with Christ, the lordship of Christ, and the hope of the final resurrection from the dead (Acts 2:24, 31–33; 13:33; Rom 1:1–4; 1 Cor 15:12–20; 1 Peter 1:3).

XIV. Salvation

In the NT, the purpose of God in providing salvation and calling sinful men to himself is not a conundrum but a vital spiritual fact (Acts 2:39). Paul gives us the fullest exposition of the meaning of salvation, probably because of his missionary involvement and desire to protect the integrity of the gospel of grace (Rom 8:28–30; Gal 1:15, 16; Eph 1:1–12). The primary Pauline term with regard to election is "purpose" (Rom 8:28; 9:11; Eph 1:11; 3:11; 2 Tim 1:9), a purpose that is disclosed in Jesus Christ.

The application of salvation involves two groups of truths: first, repentance, faith, and forgiveness, as those realities that relate to the individual's response to the preaching of the gospel; and, second, regeneration, justification, and sanctification, as those that concern the new standing of the Christian and renewal of his nature.

As in the OT, repentance involves intellectual (2 Tim 2:25), volitional (Acts 8:22), and emotional aspects (Luke 15:11–24; 2 Cor 7:10). Faith involves belief, or assent to that which is true (Rom 10:9, 10; Heb 11:6; 1 John 4:3; 5:1, 10), acceptance of another's word in the sense of conviction as to its truth (John 4:21), and trust (John 10:9; 14:1). Faith is never associated with the ground of salvation but is always presented as the means or channel for receiving salvation. It is the only appropriate response to grace. Whether one reads the Gospels, in which trust (as in the case of blind Bartimaeus, Mark 10:46–52) is paramount, John's Gospel with his stress on faith (John 1:12; 3:16, 36), Peter's preaching at Pentecost (Acts 2:38–41), or Paul's extensive and frequent treatment of faith (Rom 1:16, 17; 3:24–28; 5:1), the NT uniformly emphasizes faith. Repentance and faith may be seen as two sides of the one reality of conversion (Acts 15:3).

Forgiveness is related in the NT directly to the vicarious death of Christ. Thereby it establishes for Christian experience a new principle—namely, vicariousness, which is the power of one to reach out and make the burden of another his own. This principle not only undergirds the divine forgiveness of sinful men, but is in the NT the basis of Christian social relationships (Luke 17:3, 4; 23:34; Acts 2:38; 5:31; 13:38; Gal 6:1, 2; Eph 1:7; 4:31; Col 1:14; Heb 9:26; 10:12).

Regeneration means quickening to new life from the deadness of sin (Eph 2:1, 5). Involved are the Holy Spirit (John 3:5) and the Word of God (1 Peter 1:23) as agents of the quickening. Regeneration is a "vertical" action; it is the supernatural work of God (James 1:18), in which men are channels for God's working (1 Cor 4:15; Gal 4:19).

While regeneration relates to human nature, justification relates to the sinner's standing before God. Hints of it in the OT come to full realization and revelation in the NT (Acts 13:38, 39; Rom 3–5; Gal 3). Justification deals with the restoration of sinful man's true relation with God through removal of condemnation by the gift of forgiveness, removal of guilt by reckoning Christ's righteousness to the sinner, and bridging the gap of alienation through reconciliation to God. The means of justification is faith alone. Its ground is the perfection and sacrifice of Christ. Its values are amplified by Paul in Romans 5 and 8.

The NT doctrine of sanctification, while closely allied to justification, is nevertheless distinct from it. As in the OT, sanctification points first to the separateness—the holy transcendence of God—and second, to a moral quality and relationship that is Godlike. Sanctification is the work of the Holy Spirit, who unites a person with Christ and renews his life spiritually. The NT language entails the baptism in the Spirit (1 Cor 12:13); the seal of the Spirit (Eph 1:13, 14; 4:30), the indwelling of the Spirit (John 14:17; Rom 5:4; 8:9–11; 1 Cor 3:16; 6:19; 2 Tim 1:14), instruction by the Spirit (John 14:26; 16:12–15), the filling of the Spirit (Eph 5:18), and the fruit of the Spirit (Gal 5:22, 23). Sanctification is related to justification, which is a standing before God (Heb 10:10), and may be thought of as development into a new ideal (10:14).

Underlying the entire ministry of the first Christians was their conviction of the pervasive work of the Holy Spirit in the world. In the NT, conviction of sinful men and the work of sustaining and vindicating good in the world is uniquely the task of the Holy Spirit. The promise of Christ in John 14, 15, 16 found ample fulfillment in the life of the witnessing church following Pentecost. As in the OT, God by his Spirit is Lord of creation. The boldness of the first Christians came from their belief that the Holy Spirit works in the world in the distinctions between good and evil, right and wrong, truth and error, freedom and bondage, beauty and distortion, fulfillment and frustration, life and death. Their witness was undergirded by the antecedent faith that the Holy Spirit is present and working in the world.

XV. Discipleship

The development of the Christian life, which begins with the commitment of faith to Jesus Christ, receives prominent attention in the NT. The nature of Christian discipleship constitutes an important, though often hidden, basis of difference among the ways the NT is read.

Christ's word of invitation "Follow me" stands at the heart of discipleship (Matt 4:19; 8:22; 9:9; 16:24; 19:21; John 10:27; 1 Peter 2:21, and other parallel passages). In the NT the exposition of, and instruction in, discipleship relate to the person of Christ: how to be like him in love for God, in moral perfection, and in loving concern for others. Expressions of the Christian ideal include the Sermon on the Mount, teaching on the virtuous life, activities and style of life to avoid, and the doctrine of the fruit of the Spirit. The hortatory sections of the NT are of great importance. They relate the response of faith to a life of good works, neither of which properly exists without the other (e.g., Rom 12–16; 1 and 2 Cor; Gal 5; Eph 4–6; 1 Peter; James).

The Christian life is a life of prayer, patterned after the devotional life of Christ (e.g., note the "withdrawal" passages of Mark 1:45; 3:7; 6:6, 30–32; 7:24; 8:27; 9:2; 11:11, 19; 14:1, 2, and John 17). But prayer and the saintly life in the NT are not simply contemplation of God, as they were in the Greek and Roman traditions, but vision issuing in fellowship and an interpretive message (the Word of God) that is both conceptual and verbal and that demands the response of obedience. Personal relationship to God and activity according to God's will and purpose are essential to prayer (cf. Acts 4:23–37).

Prayer, especially petitionary and intercessory prayer, does not conflict with the doctrine of creation and providence in the NT. The NT sees the world as stable and dependable. It is God's creation. He providentially cares for it and all creatures in it as an ordered, not disordered, world (Acts 17:24–26). Along with this, he exercises another mode of control over the world—i.e., through his conscious, intelligent purpose. It is God's purpose that his children grow in freedom and cooperative activity with him (1 Cor 12:6; 2 Cor 6:1; Phil 2:12, 13). In the NT, prayer assumes that God is able to control creation and to be involved in the lives of people, without either disorganizing the dependability of the world or inhibiting man's growth in freedom and responsibility. NT thought about prayer rests on the fact that God voluntarily waits upon our asking.

Good works, or doing good, are the logical results of discipleship. NT theology wholly denies good works any part in justification (Rom 3:27; 4:1–5). Nevertheless, good works are the essential and necessary outcome of faith (Rom 6:18–22; 8:4; James). Christian behavior involves the good in two senses: intrinsic or moral good (Rom 12:2; Eph 2:10; 4:28; Phil 1:6; 1 Tim 2:10) and works that grace or adorn the Christlike life (Matt 26:10; John 10:32, 33; 1 Tim 5:10, 25; Titus 2:7, 14; 3:8, 14; Heb 5:14). These last are closely related to the *charismata*, the gifts of grace, or virtues, that ought to grace Christian living.

Hope is a further significant element that Christianity injected into life and one that profoundly altered the outlook of the ancient world. So common is hope to the NT that its unique character *vis-à-vis* Greek and Roman culture is today often missed. In the NT, hope is associated with faith, as successful movement toward a goal. To live in hope entails not only looking toward Christ's return and the resurrection of believers, but also allowing hope to be a transforming and energizing element in purposeful living (Rom 12:12; 1 Cor 15:19; Eph 2:12; Col 1:27; 1 Thess 5:8; Heb 6:18, 19; 1 Peter 1:3). In the NT the final justification of the Christian faith to the world is the life of hope.

Another element in the theology of Christian experience in the NT is insight, which stimulates faith and hope. Ignorance, confusion, distortion, and contradiction characterize the natural man, whose outlook is not informed by the mind of Christ (Rom 10:2; 1 Cor 2:14; 2 Tim 3:7). Divine guidance, while it has its circumstantial side in the NT, operates, according to the NT, chiefly as spiritual insight into the will of God, because Christians are led by the Spirit of God in a way consistent with God's standards and purposes (1 Cor 2:16; Eph 1:17, 18; 4:13–24; Col 1:9). Such insight distinguishes a Christian world view from a secular one (Gal 4:3, 9; Col 2:8, 20).

Another theological element of Christian discipleship in the NT is priesthood. The doctrine of the universal priesthood of believers has its base in 1 Peter 2:5, 9 and Revelation 1:6; 5:10; 20:6. Rejection of a special class of priests by many Christians rests also upon the termination of the OT priesthood in the work of Christ, as expounded in Hebrews. While the NT sees the OT model of priesthood as mediation between God and the people that continues in the activities of ministry, teaching, and intercession, the NT mediatorial function includes the capacity to suffer vicariously and thereby to take upon oneself redemptively the burdens of others as well as one's own. But this is not to add to the work of Christ (which the NT sees as final and complete), but to implement a key feature of the Cross (Matt 20:22, 23; John 17:18, 22; Rom 8:17; 2 Cor 2:10; Phil 3:10; Col 1:24). Christian priesthood entails one's assuming the humility of Jesus.

The crowning characteristic of Christian discipleship in NT teaching is love. So pervasive is this theme that mere mention of it leads to an extensive interplay of NT facts and ideas. Love is the very nature of God, and this reinforces the doctrine of his personhood (1 John 4:8), in contrast to the abstract, nonpersonal Platonic conception. God's gift of his Son in the Incarnation and Christ's own life, teaching, and ministry exemplify it. The Cross is the gift of divine love (John 3:16; Rom 5:8; 1 John 4:10) and the very pattern of Christian love and altruism (John 15:13; Rom 12:1, 2; 1 Peter 1:22). Love sets an inestimable value on persons as being of the ultimate nature of reality, not as means to other ends but as ends in themselves. Love resists vengeance, cruelty, artifice. Paul beautifully expounded its nature in 1 Corinthians 13, and it is commanded of all Christians as the highest virtue and the greatest spiritual gift (1 Cor 12:31; 13:1; 14:1; 1 John 4:7–21).

A final NT theological motif in respect of Christian discipleship is the concept of the Spirit-bearing man. The promise of the Spirit for man, foreshadowed in the messianic promises of the OT, was fulfilled in Jesus Christ who came as the bearer of the Spirit and baptizer in the Spirit (John 1:32–34). He was the mark of the new age, and the progenitor of the new race (Luke 4:18; Rom 5:13–21). Through receiving him, one receives the Holy Spirit (Joel 2:28–32; John 14:16, 17; 16:13, 14; Acts 2:38, 39; Rom 8:11; 1 Cor 12:13; Titus 3:4–8). Through the Holy Spirit, Christ's way of life is being reproduced in his followers—the way that had been his on earth. For believers, this is expressed as the fruit of the Spirit (Gal 5:22, 23).

XVI. Ethics

In the NT, good and evil, right and wrong, stand for objective characteristics directly and inalienably attached to acts and their consequences. Thus, values in the NT are consistent with OT teaching: "Seek good, not evil" (Amos 5:14, 15) and "Hate what is evil; cling to what is good" (Rom 12:9) belong together. They ultimately relate the norm of the good to what God wills.

NT morality is not based on situation ethics; instead, it is based on human conduct as being subject to a standard of unconditional value—namely, the righteousness of God. The personification of this standard in human life is the incarnate Lord, who lived his life in the Spirit.

Christians are urged in the NT to obey the law and to be subservient to the civil power (Rom 13:1-7; 1 Tim 2:1, 2; 1 Peter 2:13-17). They are unavoidably part of a particular culture (Acts 6:1; 1 Cor 1:19-22), though no one culture or style of governmental authority is approved in the NT. Their ultimate obedience is directly to God rather than men (Matt 22:18-22; Acts 4:19; 5:28, 29). Obedience to God includes concern for social righteousness (Matt 25:31-46; James 5).

A theology of freedom pervades the NT. The distinction between master and slave is erased in Christ (1 Cor 7:21-24; Eph 6:5-9; Col 3:21-4:1; Philem), as are racial distinctions (Gal 3:26-29). This last passage from Paul emphasizes the equality of women in the gospel. Also, Christians are stewards of earthly possessions (Matt 25:14-30). Ultimately, God will redeem the natural order as well as humanity (Romans 8:21-23).

Many more matters may be mentioned. Suffice it to say that the NT turned a key aspect of personal morality in the ancient world upside down. In the place of arrogance (hybris), the gospel enthroned humility (Phil 2:1-16).

The ethics of the NT rest upon dedicating one's whole life to God daily, conforming all conduct to the standard of his righteousness, carrying altruism to the extent of self-sacrifice, and putting the interests of others before one's own.

XVII. The Church

Far from being a peripheral, optional doctrine and relationship, the reality of the church and the obligation of Christians to be part of it are essential NT teaching. God does not save an aggregate of individuals just as individuals and nothing more. The NT knows no such thing as particular individualism for Christians. The goal of the gospel and the work of the Spirit is a saved man in the church. How important this is may be seen from the price Christ paid for the church—the price of his own blood (Acts 20:28; Eph 5:25); the future purpose and glory of Christ in the church (Eph 1:22, 23; 5:26); and Christ's fulfillment of his present purposes in the world through the church (Matt 16:18; Acts 20:28).

The theological foundation of the church includes, first of all, its creation by the gospel through the giving and receiving of a revelation. The church is a kerygmatic creation. It is the community of forgiven sinners (Matt 28:19). Second, it was created through allegiance to Jesus Christ the Lord (Rom 10:9; Eph 1:22, 23; Phil 2:11) and involves the initiatory rite of baptism as the mark of forgiveness (Acts 2:38-41) and the Lord's Supper as the continuing pledge of faith and loyalty (1 Cor 11:26-29). Third, the life in the Spirit constituted the new body, the church (Luke 24:49; Acts 2:33, 38; 1 Cor 12:13; Eph 1:13). Fourth, the new man, born again of the Spirit, is the constituent element of the new community of reconciliation (2 Cor 5:17, 18; 1 Peter 1:22–25). Fifth, the mission of the church makes it a distinctive community; it is entrusted with a word, the word of Christ's gospel for the world (Luke 24:44–48; Acts 1:8; Rom 1:16, 17). Sixth, the church's view of history as being under God and as moving toward the climax of Christ's return and kingdom generated a new people with a new outlook on life and history (Rom 5:1–5; 8:23–26; 1 Thess 4:16–18; 5:23; Heb 12:1, 2; 13:20, 21; James 5:7, 8; 1 Pet 4:17–19).

As to the nature of the church, it is more than a collection, assembly, concourse, or gathering of Christian people. For NT theology, this is a crucial point. The church is not only an assembly of people called out (*ekklesia*) from the world by the Holy Spirit, but a particular kind of assembly. More than a body politic, social convention, or social compact, it is an assembly in the sense of being a body (*soma*), the body of Christ himself. The uniqueness of the church lies in its being the assembly of people called out of the world by the Holy Spirit and the proclamation of the gospel and constituted the body of Christ by that same Spirit and gospel (1 Cor 1:3, 13, 27).

In the NT the word *church* (*ekklesia*) is used flexibly. It applies to the Christian gatherings for worship (1 Cor 11:18; 14:19) and to local communities (Acts 8:3), some of which are named and spoken of as either single or plural (Acts 8:1; 15:41; Rom 16:1, 5, 16; 1 Cor 4:17). It also refers to the whole body of Christians (Matt 16:18; Acts 20:28; Eph 1:22; Phil 3:6; Heb 12:23). The metaphor of the body refers to the church as the body of Christ (Rom 12:5; 1 Cor 10:16, 17; Eph 4:4, 16; Col 1:18, 24), of which he is the Head. Each church is seen as a body under the lordship of Christ; nevertheless, the unity of all Christians in the body of Christ is affirmed.

The church is the context, the environment, in which Christian growth is nurtured through worship (*leiturgeia*), fellowship (*koinōnia*), teaching (*didachē*), witness (*martyria*), and service (*diakonia*). The grace and humility of Christ (Phil 2:1–13) is the model of selfless ministry in the body. The gifts of the Spirit in the church are for edifying others, not self-aggrandizement (1 Cor 12–14; Eph 4).

Initially, the church at Jerusalem consisted of the assembly of Christians under the leadership of the apostles. Their activities included witness, selection of Matthias to succeed Judas, local missionary activity (such as that of Philip in Samaria and on the road to Gaza), and the convening of a council in Acts 15 on the question of the gospel and the Gentiles.

The commissioning of Paul and Barnabas from Caesarea marks a turning point in the structure and ministry in the church. While the apostles are regarded as the pillars of the whole church, even by Paul (Gal 1:18–24; 2:9; 2 Tim 1:11), other ministries and offices developed through the extension and universalizing of the gospel. This includes not only ministries (1 Cor 12:8–10) but also offices of ministry as gifts of the Spirit (1 Cor 12:28–31) that are not universal.

Paul's list in Ephesians 4:11, 12 has been taken as a pattern by many evangelical churches that restrict the ministry of the apostles and prophets to the apostolic era but extend the ministry of evangelists, pastors, and teachers to the present. The correlation of the offices of elder and bishop by many (1 Tim 3:1–7; Titus 1:5–7) yields the rationale for most evangelical understanding of NT ministry; though extension of the concept of the bishop marks the point of departure for the episcopal claim. In the NT, commissioning for ministry appears to have been universal for all Christians by reason of baptism, whatever the additional force of the laying on of hands or ordination may have been.

Unity and diversity characterize the church in the NT, not only in the large number of varying offices, ministries, and gifts of its members, but also in the personal tensions, such as those between Paul and Barnabas, Paul and John Mark, Paul and the apostles at Jerusalem, and Paul and Peter. That the NT sees the church as one body is indisputable. That it is a complex rather than a monolithic, abstract, or undifferentiated unity is also apparent (John 17:21, 23). This unity is not organizational, though it powerfully unifies the church through commitment to the gospel, to the lordship of Jesus Christ, and to the fellowship of the saints locally. In the NT, distinctions of race, economic and social standing, sex, education, nationality, and language are erased in the body of Christ. The church is bound together by faith, love, hope, witness, and humble service.

XVIII. Last Things

NT teaching about the last things is bound up closely with the doctrine of creation (that God is the Creator and Lord of history) and the doctrine of redemption (that God will redeem the world as well as mankind and establish his reign upon earth). Concretely, NT eschatology concerns four major elements of teaching: hope, the resurrection of the body, the return of Christ, and judgment and the life everlasting. These are all aspects of the doctrine of the kingdom of God as the promise and realization of the reign of God in the world.

A large part of the NT is devoted to the return of Jesus Christ, which is seen to be personal and imminent. It is likely that some of the first Christians expected Christ's return in their own lifetime. The NT writers avoid specifying the time of his return, though they say much about the sequence of events once the end time is at hand (Matt 24–25; Mark 13; 1 and 2 Thess; 2 Peter; Jude; Rev). Some modern writers, through an extension of the concept that eschatology in the NT is already realized spiritually, have attempted to reinterpret the futurist emphasis on Christ's personal return, but this must be discounted if the words and faith of the apostolic community are taken seriously.

An important element of NT teaching is that of Christ's personal return in relation to the kingdom and the millennium, which is seen to be the thousand-year reign of Christ between his return and the final judgment. Some telescope the idea of the millennium into Christ's spiritual reign in the church (amillennialism), or make it a metaphor for the gradual ascendency of the gospel in the world through the Holy Spirit (postmillennialism). However, the promised kingdom of the OT is seen in the NT to be fulfilled not only through the spiritual transformation of believing people, but also in the glorious millennial kingdom, which anticipates the eternal state (Matt 24–25; Mark 13; Rev 20).

In the NT, the hope of Christ's return is a powerful current that bears Christians along through adversity, persecution, and injustice. It is full of comfort and joy (1 Thess 4:16–18). It is also a strong incentive to godly living (1 Thess 3:12).

The doctrine of the resurrection of the believer is the cornerstone of the gospel, says Paul (1 Cor 15). Christ's resurrection vindicates the gospel; it also authenticates the hope of redeemed individual's personal existence in bodily form in the life to come. NT teaching about the resurrection is based on the revelation of Jesus Christ and the miracle of his resurrection and also on the conviction of faith that by creation there is in human life an inward, spiritual reality that has the quality of being able to survive the temporal and the finite (Rom 3:24, 25; 2 Cor 5:1–11). The character and quality of the believer's life to come are disclosed in the resurrection and glory of Jesus Christ. The continuity between one identifiable personal existence now and in the life to come partly undergirds Christian ethics in the NT, because it does matter eternally what a person does here and now in this earthly bodily life. It is in our present bodily life that we are being fashioned into the kind of person we will be hereafter (Rev 22:11). While stressing the spiritual reality and uniqueness of man, NT teaching does not denigrate the body, or the earthly creation, but rather looks to the redemption of the whole person.

Recent studies see hope as integral to human spiritual well-being.[12] In this light, NT teaching about hope presents a body of doctrine that is remarkably relevant to the needs of modern man in the face of contemporary cosmic and existential hopelessness. In the NT, hope is based on the fact that sin has been atoned for (thus making peace possible) and the problem of evil has been dealt with by the triumph of Christ's Cross. Hope is related to the concept of creation and to the philosophy of history. The world process is not cyclical and meaningless, but purposeful, moving toward the goal of God's planning. In the NT, hope rests on the conviction that the whole world process and history declare the activity and glory of God. This secures the ground of its teleological interpretation. Sin will finally be judged and evil banished (James 5:1-11; Rev 20:10-15). The redeemed will be gathered into God's presence. In the NT, the greatest justification of the ways of God with man are the joy and hope of the saints (Rom 12:12; Col 1:27; Heb 6:19; 1 Peter 1:3).

XIX. Bibliography

Anderson, Hugh. *Jesus and Christian Origins*. New York: Oxford University Press, 1964.

Argyle, A.W. *God in the New Testament*. London: Hodder and Stoughton, 1965.

Barclay, William. *The Promise of the Spirit*. London: Epworth, 1964.

Beasley-Murray, G.R. *Baptism in the New Testament*. London: SCM, 1964.

————. *Jesus and the Future*. London: Macmillan, 1954.

Dodd, C.H. *The Apostolic Preaching and Its Developments*. London: Hodder and Stoughton, 1951.

Henry, Carl F.H. *Christian Personal Ethics*. Grand Rapids: Eerdmans, 1957.

Hunter, A.M. *Introducing New Testament Theology*. London: SCM, 1966.

————. *The Unity of the New Testament*. London: ACM, 1972.

Kevan, E.F. *Salvation*. Grand Rapids: Baker, 1963.

Ladd, George E. *Jesus and the Kingdom*. Waco: Word, 1964.

————. *The Pattern of New Testament Truth*. Grand Rapids: Eerdmans, 1968.

Longenecker, Richard N. *The Christology of Early Jewish Christianity*. London: SCM, 1970.

McDonald, H.D. *Jesus, Human and Divine*. Grand Rapids: Zondervan, 1970.

Mikolaski, Samuel J. *The Doctrine of Grace*. Grand Rapids: Eerdmans, 1966.

————. "The Triune God" in *Fundamentals of the Faith*. Edited by Carl F.H. Henry. Grand Rapids: Zondervan, 1969.

Morris, Leon. *Spirit of the Living God*. London: IVF, 1961.

Neill, Stephen. *The Christian Character*. London: Lutterworth, 1956.

Ramm, Bernard. *Special Revelation and the Word of God*. Grand Rapids: Eerdmans, 1961.

————. *Them He Glorified*. Grand Rapids: Eerdmans, 1963.

Richardson, A. *An Introduction to the Theology of the New Testament*. New York: Harper and Brothers, 1958.

Robinson, G.C., and Winward, S.F. *The Way*. Chicago: Moody, 1968.

Rust, E.C. *Nature and Man in Biblical Thought*. London: Lutterworth, 1957.

Schlatter, Adolf. *The Church in the New Testament Period*. London: SPCK, 1961.

Tasker, R.V.G. *The Biblical Doctrine of the Wrath of God*. London: Tyndale, 1951.

White, Reginald E.O. *Into the Same Image*. Nashville: Broadman, 1957.

---

[12]Viktor Frankl, *Man's Search for Meaning* (New York: Square Press, 1959). J. Moltmann, *Theology of Hope*. (New York: Harper, 1965). W.H. Capps, *The Future of Hope* (Philadelphia: Fortress, 1970). D.O. Woodyard, *Beyond Cynicism* (Philadelphia: Westminster, 1972). E.H. Cousins, ed., *Hope and the Future of Man* (Philadelphia: Fortress, 1972).

THE CULTURAL AND POLITICAL SETTING OF THE NEW TESTAMENT

Arthur A. Rupprecht

Arthur A. Rupprecht

B.A., Houghton College; A.M., University of Illinois; B.D., Faith Theological Seminary; Ph.D., University of Pennsylvania

Professor of Classical Languages, Wheaton College

THE CULTURAL AND POLITICAL SETTING OF THE NEW TESTAMENT

I. **Political Structure**

    A. The Emperor
    B. Provincial Administration
    C. Local Government
    D. Law
    E. Citizenship
    F. Communications

II. **Economic Conditions**

    A. Agrarian Economy
    B. Monetary Stability
    C. The Slave System
    D. Economic Structures

III. **Social Stratification**

    A. Rome
    B. Palestine

IV. **Religious Life**

    A. Traditional Religion
    B. The Mystery Cults
    C. Judaism of the Dispersion

V. **Bibliography**

New Testament times were almost as complicated as our own. The political, economic, social, and religious background of the period is as interesting as it is complex. To write about one aspect without involving the other three is impossible because of their almost total interdependence. Politically, the emperors were on the rise. The empire had settled down and was prosperous except for the distant frontiers and Palestine. Population decline had contributed considerably to a breakdown of the distinctions between the lower classes. Economic theory was nonexistent. The primitive, agrarian economy was remarkably stable because of the widespread use of slave labor in competition with free labor. In religion men sought for satisfying, personal religious experience. The old gods were dead everywhere but in Palestine.

I. Political Structure

A. *The Emperor*

The dominant force in the Roman political process was the emperor. In NT times the emperors began to assimilate all the power that formerly resided in the senate and popular assembly. They also made a small beginning in the process of winning popular support. By A.D. 100 the emperor had the power of an absolute monarch.

In the distant provinces imperial politics mattered little. It is imperative to keep in mind that throughout the last years of the civil war and the rise of the emperors the provinces were ruled with little change. There was a steady procession of able administrators who came annually to assume their duties in a generally conscientious way.

There were personal excesses on the part of many of the emperors; yet peace, commerce, and toleration continued with little interruption. Tiberius was a recluse. Caligula was horribly spoiled as a young man while on the German campaign and he overindulged himself while he was in power. Nero was so evil that he suffered *damnatio memoriae* at the hands of his successors. His elaborate palace was leveled and its lake used as the foundation of the Colosseum. Hadrian was a world traveler and a builder in the Pharaonic tradition. Despite the diversity of these rulers, the evidence suggests that the empire progressed socially and economically during their reigns. The archaeological evidence supports the conclusion that prosperity was very great in the first century A.D. Paul, the apostle, attests to the integrity of the Roman system of government and implores Christians to accept their government as ordained of God (Rom 13:1–7). It is no doubt true, as has been suggested repeatedly in the past, that our primary sources in Roman history were generally men of strong Republican sympathies who dwelt excessively on the failings of the emperors.

The change from a Republican form of government to a monarchy was a profound one for Rome. The reasons were certainly numerous, but one that has important implications for us is the radical change in the Roman constituency. Emperor worship, for instance, did not happen simply because the emperors sought deification as a new way to promote their public acceptance. It reflects the fact that increasingly Rome was the provinces, whose residents were not accustomed to democratic institutions. Italy prospered only because it was the political center. The real wealth of the Empire was overseas. Rome imported almost everything and exported little or nothing. In fact, when Ostia, the seaport of Rome, was enlarged to encourage imports in a port close to the city, this was precisely the complaint of the merchants. Their vessels left Ostia with empty holds. The great shift in the ethnic origins of the people of the Italian peninsula also contributed to the change. Orientals, whose numbers increased enormously, made up a large portion of the free populace by the first and second centuries of the Christian era. Their heritage was worship of their ruler and acceptance of political absolutism. The old Rome was dying along with the old Roman families. The rise of the Empire was more of a symptom than a cause of change.

B. *Provincial Administration*

The Romans devised a unique method for the administration of the provinces. After they had conquered a territory, they made it into a political entity ruled by ex-magistrates of the Senate. Each year at the end of their terms as praetors and consuls, elected officials were assigned provincial administrations by the Senate. In Republican times, politics played a large part in the appointments. Thus Julius Caesar was designated proconsul for 58 B.C. To his ignominy, his opponents gave him the supervision of the forests and cattle roads of Italy as his *provincia*. During the remainder of his year as consul he managed to reverse the sentiment of the Senate and acquired instead the command of the unsettled province of Gaul. Cicero was forced to serve as proconsul in Cilicia in 51 B.C. because his enemies wanted him out of the city of Rome.

During the time of the Empire, the provinces were divided into two categories, imperial and proconsular. The imperial provinces were the unruly ones or areas of extreme sensitivity, such as Egypt, the source of much of Rome's food. The emperors appointed legates or procurators of senatorial rank who served indefinite terms of office. They had legions directly under their command and they reported directly to the emperor. The senatorial provinces continued to be administered much as they had been. Generally, ex-consuls and ex-praetors held office for one year in the province by appointment of the Senate. In NT times, Paul spent long periods in the senatorial provinces of Asia, Achaia, and Macedonia.

While he was at Corinth, Paul confronted the proconsul of Achaia for the year 51–52 or 52–53, Lucius Junius Gallio. His biography gives us some interesting insights into Roman affairs of the period. He was born L. Annaeus Novatus at Cordova in Spain, the son of the rhetorician L. Annaeus Seneca, and elder brother of L. Annaeus Seneca, the philosopher. At Rome he was adopted by the rhetorician, L. Junius Gallio. Adoption was not an uncommon practice at the time among aristocratic Romans, who quite frequently were childless.

Gallio was a man of charming disposition, but poor health, at least in Greece, according to the sources. He was caught up in the unrest and maneuvering in the imperial court. As a result, he suffered banishment to Corsica with his brother. Both returned when Agrippina selected Seneca to tutor Nero. Gallio served as *consul suffectus* early in Nero's reign, but later he became involved in the conspiracy against him. He died in A.D. 65, either by execution under Nero or by suicide.

Gallio was one of the first provincials to attain senatorial rank. He was only one of many who served in the Senate because of their friendship with the emperor rather than because of family status. At this time the Senate had reserved for itself control over the peaceful provinces of the Empire, but the emperors were in the process of making the Senate into something of a private club for loyal friends.

As proconsul of Achaia, Gallio did not distinguish himself. The evidence suggests that he disliked Greece and provincial administration. However, he showed commendable impartiality towards Christianity in the encounter with Paul and the Jews of Corinth (Acts 18). He is known archaeologically from a lengthy inscription found at Delphi. Only small portions of the inscription survive. The date of it places Gallio's term in Achaia within one year, and is, therefore, pivotal in establishing the chronology of the Book of Acts and the Pauline Epistles.

Palestine was uniquely administered and always a problem for the Romans. They recognized Herod the Great, first as governor or tetrarch of Syria including Palestine, and, in 39 B.C., as King of Judea. He ruled by special treaty with the Romans during a long period of civil war at Rome and internal unrest in his kingdom. No petty king, he was called a "friend and confederate" by the emperors.

At Herod's death his empire was divided into three parts, each ruled by his sons who were demoted to the designation of ethnarchs and tetrarchs. Archelaus ruled only until A.D. 6 as ethnarch of Judea and Samaria. Upon his banishment to Gaul, his territory was made into an imperial province under a procurator. In 44, at the death of Herod Agrippa I, all Palestine came under direct Roman rule and was formed into a province ruled by a procurator, who answered to the emperor.

Throughout the last half of the century before Christ and until the middle of the first century A.D., internal affairs were left to the Herods. Roman intervention was necessary only during periods of extreme unrest. As these periods became more common and Herod the Great's descendants less capable of handling affairs, it became necessary for the Romans to assume direct command through the establishment of an imperial province.

C. Local Government

Local municipal government was very important in all areas of the Empire. It is too easy to overlook the large amount of autonomy granted to Roman citizens and provincials. Literary and archaeological sources make it apparent that local senates, councils, and assemblies attended to most of the affairs of the people. In the treaties that the Romans concluded with occupied territories, they took responsibility for external relations with other states, reserved for Roman authorities the right to administer the death penalty, and levied taxes. Other matters, such as land development, punishment for lesser crimes, and transfers of property, were handled by locally elected officials. Very often there were written into the agreements special conditions that took account of unusual circumstances of the people. Thus, the Jews were exempted from military service, and strangely, granted permission to erect synagogues by the seashore. In disputes with local magistrates or courts, an appeal could always be made to a Roman provincial administrator, who conducted assizes on a posted schedule throughout his province. Early in his term each new provincial administrator was expected to post notice stating which matters would be decided according to Roman law and ones according to local laws. In this manner Roman law was introduced to the provinces and gradually became the law for the entire Empire.

D. Law

Roman law made an immense contribution to the progress of civilization. It was the culmination of the efforts of men for centuries in Greece and the East to codify law for all to see and know it. Universal circulation and familiarity with the law made Romans and provincials aware of their rights and of the shortcomings of their society. These two factors caused them to strive earnestly to improve the laws and apply them with impartiality. Unlike our laws, the Roman laws were brief, clear, and, by the first century A.D., carefully collected and organized. Jurists and magistrates rarely interpreted them philosophically or neglected them. Paul clearly perceived that this type of government, with all its imperfections, was to be commended and certainly to be preferred to anarchy.

From his statements about adoption and bequest in Galatians it is clear that Paul knew Roman law. He no doubt studied it at some time during his training, probably as part of his advanced Jewish education or perhaps separately in a school specializing in Roman law. Tarsus was one of the three leading university centers of the Roman Empire. It was imperative for some of the leaders of the Jews to be familiar with the intricacies of Roman law. In the first century, however, the study of the law was much less involved than it is today. The *Commentaries* of Gaius, written in the middle of the second century A.D., are no longer than an average-size contemporary book, and they include both the text of existing law and a commentary on it. The laws were rationally organized, skillfully interpreted, and strongly supported by the emperors. It was the spread and acceptance of the law throughout the Empire that brought the Roman peace to the entire civilized world in the first four centuries of the Christian era.

Though we often ask, "Why did Rome fall?" we would do better to ask why she survived for so many centuries. Our own republic, after all, is only two hundred years old and is tragically threatened by a breakdown of law and domestic tranquility. We need to rediscover the precision with which the Romans wrote their laws and to learn from their impartiality in enforcing them.

E. *Citizenship*

Citizenship occupied the thinking of the best legal and political theorists for centuries before the Roman Republic. In his *Constitution of Athens*, Aristotle revealed the attitude of ancient Greece toward it. Citizenship was conferred on very few. The rest were those of mixed blood, resident aliens, and slaves. The Romans changed the prevailing attitude, but only after centuries of agonizing over the dilemmas that wider suffrage would bring. Generally speaking, Roman citizenship was sparingly conferred on provincials as late as the first century A.D. At the beginning of that century the Romans began to grant citizenship outside of peninsular Italy to those in colonies established for military veterans. Emperor Claudius did much to extend rights throughout the Empire. He increased the census roll of citizens by one million so that it included almost six million people. He also irritated many at Rome by enrolling some Gallic as senators, and by opening all public magistracies to all citizens in Gaul. This process continued until the *Constitutio Antoniniana* granted citizenship to all free inhabitants of the empire in A.D. 212.

Paul's claim to Roman citizenship is a bit perplexing. How could a Jew, born in Tarsus, who spent much of his life in Jerusalem, make such a claim? A suggestion can be made, but it is only that. Paul's rapid rise in Jewry suggests that he was the brilliant son of a wealthy family of the dispersion. He could reach high office only if he could claim pure lineage for four generations on both sides of his family. To do this, one usually had to be born in a wealthy family, for the social and political disorders of the period prevented ordinary folk from avoiding slavery or other loss of status. Further, to make the point, a succession of Roman generals granted Roman citizenship to wealthy supporters as their armies moved across Asia. In fact, Julius Caesar so benefited the members of the aristocracy of Tarsus that they applied the name Juliopolis to the city for a time. Therefore, it may be that Paul's father, a wealthy man and zealous Jew, had purchased his citizenship, which automatically passed on to Paul. In any event, Paul had the unique claims of religious purity and Roman citizenship, and these prepared him for his divinely appointed task.

F. *Communications*

The Romans did much to encourage travel and commerce. The motive for development in this field was originally political, because rapid communications did much to promote political stability in the far-reaching Empire. One of the greatest successes of the Romans was their system of roads. Intended initially for military conquest and consolidation, they made an immense contribution to the commerce, peace, and general stability of the Mediterranean world. By the beginning of the second century B.C., a magnificent network of roads connected all points in peninsular Italy with Rome. As Rome expanded, roads were built both east and west to connect with the provinces. The roadbeds were some four feet deep and consisted of five courses of cement and stone blocks. Their roads were much straighter than ours, presumably because the Romans had not mastered the steering mechanism necessary for a turnable front axle. A measure of the efficiency of the system may be found in the accounts of the travels of the emperor Hadrian. He used the post houses of the imperial communications system to travel as far as 180 miles a day, distances not surpassed till the last century.

The Romans also improved some aspects of sea travel as well. Fine ports were built throughout the Mediterranean. They provided all the necessities for active, prosperous commerce. Excellent breakwaters, lighthouses, wharves, storage sheds, customs buildings, banks, apartments, and shops were carefully laid out according to the best classical planning. However, as admirable as the roads and seaports of the Roman Empire were, sea travel itself remained in the Bronze age. Ships were made bigger and stronger, but even so, foreign commerce and travel were dangerous because of the inadequacies of ships and navigation. The Romans cleared the seas of pirates but did not exploit the opportunity by radically improving their own ships. Roman nobility left the export-import business in the hands of freedmen for good reason. To put it simply, it was hazardous to be out of sight of land anywhere in the Mediterranean. The best description of sea travel in antiquity and the best evidence for its attendant dangers is in Acts 27. Yet, despite their inadequacies, the seaports and ships were a necessary adjunct to the road system. Rapid communications and commerce did much to improve life in the Empire and helped spread the gospel quickly.

II. Economic Conditions

A. Agrarian Economy

The Mediterranean world from the beginning till well after the introduction of Christianity was essentially agrarian. Not only was this true in economic terms, but there was a spillover effect in the social structure of the entire region, and, to a lesser extent, in its religious outlook.

The agrarian economy led to labor surpluses throughout the NT era. Technology was virtually nonexistent. Small handicraft shops did exist, but they were limited to traditional methods of baking bread, building carts, fashioning jewelry, molding roof tiles, making wine, and producing armaments. The many who did not own land or were not employed in the shops were assimilated as underpaid free labor or as slaves of the wealthy.

Slavery was the result of the agrarian economy or conquest, and for many interpreters of the classical world, it was the cause of the failure to develop industry and technology. The cause and effect are not hard to understand. Wealthy landowners, who had a monopoly on land, were able to acquire slaves cheaply as a result of military conquests. At Rome, as new lands became available, the wealthy aristocracy seized them and developed them with slave labor. In the cities, "free labor," which had long existed, was forced to compete with cheap slave labor. The full effect of this can be felt when one realizes that slaves cost only two and one-half times the annual wages of the free laborer in classical Greece and about seven times the annual wages in Roman times. Generally it was easier and cheaper to use slave labor. Technology was effectively muffled by recourse to slave labor, and the wages of free labor were kept low because of the existence of slave competition. It was a vicious circle. Slave labor discouraged technology and depressed wages, and the absence of technology and its attendant higher skills discouraged demands for higher wages.

B. *Monetary Stability*

A significant result of the limited economic development was the monetary stability of the whole ancient world. The Roman silver denarius and the Greek drachma were of equal value in NT times and were in circulation everywhere. The denarius was by far the most common coin. It was minted at Rome and at Antioch and Caesarea in Cappadocia. In Palestine, coins from Tyre and Alexandria appear as well. The Tyrian shekel, a common coin of the NT, was approximately four times the value of the denarius and the drachma.

The stability in the coinage was paralleled by stability in prices and wages. From 100 B.C. to A.D. 150, at the least, the wages of unskilled and semiskilled labor was one denarius per day (cf. Matt 20:2). A reconstruction of life in the late Republic and early Empire is most instructive. It is probably correct to assume that the figures apply equally well to Palestine and the Near East, since the value of the coinage is the same. If we assume that free labor earned about 300 denarii per year, life was precarious indeed by contemporary standards. Food costs were about one-half denarius per day. The diet was limited to vegatables (such as cabbage, beets, turnips, peas, beans, and lentils), olive oil, fruit, and cheap wine. Slaves or free laborers could not expect to eat meat except on feast days. Usually this was provided by a wealthy patron, employer, or owner as part of a religious observance. A dwelling, usually a room or small apartment, cost about seven denarii per month. Of necessity, the worker spent only from five to ten denarii per year for clothing. In short, freeborn laborers and their slave counterparts worked hard and lived frugally, and the currency, as a result, remained very stable. The rich prospered.

C. *The Slave System*

Three interrelated factors were necessary for the development of the slave system of NT times: large tracts of arable land, greedy landowners, and a large surplus labor force. All three of these continued to exist in abundance in the eastern Mediterranean until the late Roman Empire. Their interplay produced and reinforced the agrarian economy of the time. Land was acquired by default of pressured small landowners. Men became slaves as a result of military conquest. In peninsular Italy this became a vicious circle. The peasants were drawn off their land to fight Rome's wars, which produced prisoners of war in enormous numbers, who became the slaves who worked the land that was taken from the peasants by the large landowners. The shock effect of the resulting economic and geographical dislocations affected the entire civilized world in the years before and after the birth of Christ.

It is clear from the foregoing that land was wealth, and it was the slave who made the land valuable. Is it any wonder, then, that the ancients considered the slave to be property? He was, as Aristotle said, a "human tool." Even for the small farmers who survived in Asia Minor and Palestine the slave was the difference between survival and ruin. He was as basic to the ancient world as land, silver, gold, and basic commodities. He was a possession rather than a human being.

D. *Economic Structures*

Economic conditions changed radically in the period from 150 B.C. to A.D. 50. At the beginning of the Roman conquest of the East, Sicily and southern Italy were self-sufficient. Asia, and Egypt (Egypt always going its separate way) were quite prosperous. As imperialism moved east and west, southern Gaul and Egypt supplied food. Greece and Asia Minor were systematically sacked. Their wealth, art treasures, and working populace were carted off to Rome. What the invading generals missed, the tax collectors harvested soon afterwards.

By the beginning of the Christian era, life had settled down remarkably. Political stability in most areas, the Pax Romana, and more equitable taxation led to a relative tranquility for the ancient world. Wealthy Romans, with the help of slave labor, developed vast tracts throughout the Empire, but free labor and small farmers, particularly the Roman veterans, who became colonists in such places as Philippi, prospered as well.

Earlier, civil war, brought on by conflicting groups in the wealthy aristocracy, plagued Rome and the provinces until the middle of the first century B.C. Peninsular Italy prospered for these few because of the vast wealth derived from land acquisitions, war, and trade. However, the dislocations of war had left them a vile legacy: a vast hoard of landless, poor citizens who were forced to compete with hundreds of thousands of slaves brought to Italy from all portions of the East. Much of the population of the Italian peninsula was made up of slaves or freedmen. Estimates run as high as eighty-five percent. Agricultural labor was almost entirely slave labor; even the superintendents of the farms were usually slaves or freedmen. In the cities, slaves did much of the work. Oftentimes slave and free labor worked side by side. Most of the commerce and handicraft manufacturing was carried on by freedmen. Their former owners were usually silent partners in the business, since a Roman nobleman could not openly engage in trade. The relationships in the shops and businesses are often difficult to sort out. The ostensible owner might be a freedman. Working with him could be slaves he himself owned and his own freedmen, or the slaves and freedmen of his patron. In addition, there was always the likelihood that there were also free laborers working alongside the rest.

During the years of the late Republic and early Empire, hundreds of thousands, no doubt even millions, of slaves were brought to Rome and Italy. They were usually of Eastern origin. The Romans had learned early that Teutonic slaves meant only trouble. Tens of thousands of slaves can be traced from Palestine, Syria, and Asia Minor. They made an immense contribution to the wealth of peninsular Italy. Most of them found freedom and personal fortune in a short time because of the unique social and economic conditions at Rome. The NT is witness to the wealth and nobility of a number of such Jews. The economic system was much the same throughout the provinces, which varied primarily in amount of wealth and the proportion of slave to free labor. For most of the provinces we have much less information than we have for Italy. In general it can be said with certainty that farming was on a smaller scale than the *latifundia* of the Roman aristocracy. Slaves and free laborers worked side by side in every capacity, but the proportion of slave to free seems to have been smaller.

About Palestine we know a great deal more. The more fertile areas of Galilee were developed on the Roman model. Absentee landowners, either Jewish or Roman, controlled large tracts that overseers managed for them. The parables of the wicked husbandman (Matt 21:33–44), the unjust steward (Luke 16:1–9), and the talents (Matt 25:14–30) described exactly this kind of situation. A number of rabbis and high priests were owners or the descendants of owners of vast tracts of land that they administered from Jerusalem. Among them were rabbis Eleazar ben Hyrkanos, Tarfon, Eleazar ben Harsom, ben Kalba, and Akiba.

This kind of wealth had a profound effect on the religion of the Jews in Greco-Roman times. One stipulation for high religious office was that a man be able to trace his lineage back four generations on both his father's side and his mother's to prove that he was a pure Jew. For a number of reasons it was easier for the wealthy to do this. Religious power was thus more accessible to them and with it went both political power and social status.

Numerous occupations that in the Roman world were usually assigned to slaves are noted as the work of free hired labor in Palestine. Among them were agricultural workers, building craftsmen, skilled vinedressers, teamsters, fishermen, and litter-bearers. The occupations of a number of rabbis, who are named in the Jewish sources as examples of poverty and dedication, were usually filled by slaves in Italy and Greece. For example, Rabbi Hilkia was a surveyor; R. Akiba, a woodcutter; R. Joseph, a burner of charcoal; R. Meir, a public writer; R. Saul, a grave digger; and R. Joachanan, a stove maker. The apostle Paul followed the humble occupation of tentmaking.

The usual wage for free labor mentioned in both Jewish and Christian sources is the same as that at Rome, a denarius a day (Tobit 5:15; Matt 20:2; Midrash on Genesis [Ber. R.] 61:7). It is said of Rabbi Hillel, a model for the devout poor, that he worked for one-half denarius a day, half of which he gave to the synagogue (b. Tal. Yoma 35b). A measure of the poverty of the widow (Mark 12:41–44) is the fact that her offering of two lepta represented an amount one seventy-second of a day's wages. Her poverty must have been intense indeed for Jesus to say of her that "she out of her poverty put in everything—all she had to live on" (v.44).

Household slavery is the kind of slavery most commonly depicted in the NT and Jewish sources contemporary with it. There are repeated references to slaves of the high priests. In the parable of the prodigal son, the household staff is made up of slaves, but the work in the fields was done by the father, his sons, and hired help.

Regulations in the Tannaitic sources regarding remuneration for hired labor are so involved that free labor must have been of considerable importance in the economy of Palestine. The absence of freedmen may likewise be explained by a provision of the law that forbade silent partners from receiving half of the profits of a business. This would make it almost impossible for combined businesses of freedmen and patrons to flourish in Palestine as they did elsewhere in the classical world (M. B. M. 5.5–7.7).

III. Social Stratification

A. Rome

The NT era was a period of profound social change at Rome. In fact, "social revolution" might be a more appropriate description. The old aristocracy was losing its place to the newly rich, because the old families were rapidly dying off and because they had picked the wrong side in the bloody revolution that ruined the Republic. There was a great upheaval in the lower classes as well because of a continuing decline in the birthrate. The old aristocracy and the free citizenry in general were dying off to be replaced, in numbers at least, by freed slaves who originated from the East. Every class was affected and even threatened by the sweeping changes in the orders.

1. *The aristocracy.* Traditionally, patricians, plebeians, and knights were the wealthy ruling class of ancient Rome. The patricians and plebeians had been rivals in early Republican times, but two centuries before Christianity they had settled their differences and had become the ruling aristocracy. Common interests, friendship, and intermarriage tied them closely together. They were the senators of the Republic. Their famous families included the Julii, Claudii, Sempronii, and Antonii. As Rome emerged politically and geographically, these families came into conflict with the emerging newly rich—the equestrians, or knights. By law, many aristocrats, because they were senators, could not engage in commerce. They maintained and expanded their wealth by ownership of productive land.

The Roman Republic, which had been ruled by senators of patrician or plebeian status, had only ceased to exist a quarter century before the birth of Christ. The NT era was a period of deep conflict as the Roman emperors established themselves, and, in the process, demoted the old aristocracy and transferred much of its power to the equestrians.

A man might qualify for knighthood by reason of free birth, blameless character, and a worth of 400,000 sesterces. The knights were the tax collectors, businessmen, and administrators of the Roman world. Always rivals of the Senate, they gained in power with the demotion of the Senate after the Augustan principate. That they were the commanders of the praetorian guard and the prefects of Egypt is an indication of their importance in later times.

2. *The lower classes.* Free citizens, freedmen (with some exceptions), and slaves lived very meagre lives, in stark contrast to the aristocrats and knights. The first three classes did the work in the Empire and competed, to their detriment, for wages.

Because of a decline in birthrate and the attrition of endless wars, Rome and Italy were continually faced with a decline in free population. As a result there was great upward mobility in the ranks of free people, freedmen, and slaves. Enormous numbers of slaves gained their freedom—some to their great economic gain, others to remain little better in their lot than a well-treated slave. Within a generation or two the freedmen lost the stigma attached to that designation and passed into the ranks of the free citizens. This is evident in both the pagan and Jewish catacombs of Rome. In family burials, the first generation retains a slave cognomen, but in the second or third generation this is invariably replaced by a traditional Roman name. If the burials had not been by families, it would be impossible to differentiate the Roman aristocrats from the immediate descendants of freed slaves.

There was less change in the upper ranks numerically, but the changes were of the utmost significance to freedmen. For some still unknown reason, despite the speculation and inquiry of many scholars and scientists, the patrician families declined rapidly in the late Republic and early Empire. There were originally fifty patrician families. By the beginning of the first century A.D. there were only fourteen, and by the end of the next century there was only one left. To some extent, they were replaced by the elevation of equestrians, but more generally there was simply a decline in influence in the upper classes. During imperial times many of the political offices and duties to which aristocrats and knights had aspired were assigned to imperial freedmen, sometimes men of enormous power.

Freedmen also gained in economic power. They began to compete aggressively with the knights in some types of business, particularly the precarious and the demeaning ones. Thousands of the freedmen of senators and the equestrians engaged in business, with their patrons as silent but wealthy partners. At times, there were even freedmen in business who had wealthy freedmen as their silent partners.

There was enormous pressure on the boundaries of the social classes. In 1934, Tenney Frank described the incorporation of vast numbers of Asians into the ranks of Roman citizens as "race pollution," to Benito Mussolini's great irritation. However, efforts by Il Duce's scholars to remove the stigma failed. The task was particularly difficult because Juvenal had expressed the same idea in a more colorful way nineteen centuries earlier. He lamented that the "Syrian Orontes was flowing into the Roman Tibur." There was an enormous amount of social change during the period, resulting in profound economic and political consequences throughout the Empire.

B. Palestine

The social order in Palestine was unique in two ways. First, we know a great deal more about it from the sources, and second, it is quite different from that of the rest of the Greco-Roman world. The same disparity between rich and poor existed. There were a few who were wealthy and a great many who lived always on the brink of poverty.

1. *The aristocracy.* The Roman hierarchy in Palestine belongs at the top or bottom of the orders, depending on the way in which they are measured. They were wealthy and possessed immense power, much of which they shared voluntarily with the Jewish religious and political authorities. Despite, or perhaps because of, their power and wealth the Romans were hated and considered *mamzerim*, "bastards," by most Jews. Clearly, the imperial administrative and officer class lived in comparative ease, which was interrupted only by the frequent outbursts of Jewish religious zeal and violence.

The Roman intervention in Palestine had done much to change Jewish social status. The OT legal codes indicate the manner in which slaves, both insiders and outsiders to Israel, were to be managed. What the law did not specify was how Jews enslaved to outsiders were to be considered. There were thousands, perhaps hundreds of thousands, of them and their descendants in NT times. The Tannaidic sources fill the void by specifying that one was not a pure Jew, eligible for high office in religious Israel, unless as has been stated before, he could prove his lineage pure four generations back on both his father's side and his mother's. The result was simple. The wealthy were able to preserve their status with their resources. Thus they alone could achieve leadership among the Jews. Rank, privilege, wealth, and power were carefully welded together by the stiff requirements of legal purity.

2. *The lower classes.* In Palestine, as in Italy, the work was done by a mixed group. There were agricultural slaves in competition with hired help, who were freeborn Jews. In the towns and cities freeborn men did most of the labor. Slaves were used only for domestic help. They were most conspicuous in the homes and palaces of the Jewish wealthy.

One must conclude from the NT evidence that the lower classes consisted largely of freeborn poor laboring folk, who nonetheless could claim a very clear Jewish lineage, as Mary and Joseph did. The rest were *mamzerim*, a mixture of Jewish poor whose lineage was unclear, Samaritans, Greeks, Syrians, Tyrians, Sidonians, and slaves of unknown origins.

It is no accident that Mary and Joseph were able to trace their lineage clearly. Origins were all-important in the Jewish social structure. There was some upward social mobility for those of pure lineage. One could, for instance, be poor and be a rabbi; in fact, it was almost expected that a rabbi be poor. But for those who could not claim to be purely Jewish, the door was shut and locked. They and their descendants were bastards forever. From this it becomes evident that questions and insinuations about Jesus' parentage were designed to destroy him as a leader of his people.

IV. Religious Life

A. Traditional Religion

The NT era was a period of religious instability throughout the Greco-Roman world. Most people had abandoned the traditional lower and rationalistic deities that had survived since prehistoric times. New religions and new deities were introduced from various places. While this was going on, efforts were made to bring together the best elements of the old religions in new syncretisms.

The catalyst for these changes was the growing dissatisfaction with traditional religion. The Roman conquest had a profound effect on religious thinking. Citizens had trusted in the gods of their city or state, but the deities had repeatedly failed to protect them from their enemies. In the realignment of ideas, men sought for a religion that was more personal, more eclectic, and more ecstatic, instead of a religion that represented national identity.

Early man had searched for reproductive power, physical strength, and ceremonial cleansing. He feared the gods. It never entered his mind that he should love the gods. He sought help in his adversity, and protection from disease and crop failure. The Greeks, as they first speculated about the nature of the physical universe and later about personal behavior and understanding of self, grew dissatisfied with traditional religious ideas of appeasement of otherwise hostile gods, of fertility of crops, and of human regeneration. For whatever reasons, they began to seek personal identification with the deity in a mystically satisfying way in this life and a claim on personal immortality. Deliverance or salvation was no longer equated with protection of the city and its cult from its enemies and victory in wars of aggression. By the fourth century B.C. there was an almost universal search for personal salvation and eternal deliverance. These the traditional religions could not supply.

Evidence that the classical world had abandoned the traditional religious systems is abundant. Plato had scoffed at Homer some four centuries before the introduction of Christianity. After Plato, the Greek religious experience profoundly changed. Drama, once a way of explaining the gods to men, became little more than comedies of manners. Dramas were staged in conjunction with the games at the old shrines, but the great sanctuaries of Apollo and Zeus became fairgrounds for the general amusement of the masses. In Hellenistic times, Asclepius (Roman Aesculapius), the new god of healing and formerly a mortal or hero, became the important deity because of the mystical healing he offered. But even the shrines of Asclepius soon became medical centers in the modern sense, and entertainment centers two centuries later.

Archaeological evidence of the decline of the old religions is most interesting. Pious fraud is evident at Corinth where a secret door hid access to a tunnel leading directly to the altar of a temple. It is obvious to the least discerning eye that there was no fissure in the earth under the temple of Apollo at Delphi, whence emanated sounds to be interpreted only by the priestesses of Apollo for the faithful. It is easy to imagine the divine response to the faithful from beneath the altar and the miraculous disappearance of the sacrificial offering from the altar.

Even more significant is the evidence for the later period from peninsular Italy. Of ten temples found by excavators at Pompeii, three were ruined by the earthquake of A.D. 62 and left unrepaired until the destruction of the city in 79. Another had been turned over to a private cult and two more were dedicated to emperor worship. The significance of the latter to the people may be evident in a *graffito* that reads, "Augustus Caesar's mother was a woman." Throughout Italy a succession of generals and emperors built momuments that were superficially religious but hardly of any practical sacerdotal use. It became the custom to build elaborate, terraced architectural masterpieces, which seem to include a small temple as something of an afterthought. On the whole, it may be useful to say that state or nationalistic religion was dead. Clearly, in Rome and the East wealth became the new state religion of the two centuries before and after the introduction of the Christian message. However, the search for satisfying religious experience was anything but over. Men sought something more personally fulfilling than identification with the state and its official religion.

Dissatisfaction with the traditional religions of Rome and the East is nowhere better expressed than in Vergil's *Aeneid*, that greatest piece of Augustan propaganda, which was officially commissioned to remind the Romans of the great piety and diligence of their forebears. Creusa, Aeneas's wife, dies in the withdrawal from fiery Troy. Aeneas enters the underworld to find her. However, she is but a shadow or shade in the darkness of Orcus.

> *Ter conatus ibi collo dare bracchis*
> *circum*
> *ter frustra comprensa manus effugit*
> *imago*
> *par levibus ventis volucrique simillima*
> *somno* (II 792–4).

> Three times then I attempted to put
> my arms around her.
> Three times, the phantom, grasped
> in vain, escaped from my hands.
> She was like a gentle breeze and most
> similar to winged sleep.

Is it any wonder that men shrank from the traditional classical religion and embraced Christianity? What a contrast between Vergil's view of the afterlife and the lively hope of the gospel!

Throughout the period of the Roman Republic and early Empire there was a small but influential group of wealthy men, well-born and well-educated, who espoused forms of religion quite different from that of the masses. Somewhat akin always to Unitarianism or Universalism in this country, they were eclectic and highly intellectual. Their influence was profound in the literature of the ancient world, but it is probably true that they affected the common people only indirectly, as it was the people of the ruling class who followed their precepts.

Stoicism emphasized the primacy of reason. Virtue, always an immediate concern, was based on knowledge. A Stoic expected to live in harmony with reason and with nature. "Resignation" is a bit too harsh a word to use to describe his basic tenet, but it is not wholly inaccurate. One must be brave and resolute in the face of pain or death. The Stoic belief that there would be a final world conflagration and then a final judgment parallels the New Testament closely and became the basis for Paul's argument in Romans 3:5, 6.

Roman worship of Fortuna was even more abstract. Originally a cult goddess of fertility (Lat. *Ferre*, "the bringer"), she became fate or destiny. Her will was written on the scrolls that were unrolled by the fates. The gods in turn carried out the will of the fates. The worship of Fortuna and the fates became associated with astrology. The stars revealed a fate so absolute that prayers and sacrifices were useless. The Christian apologists reacted to such an extreme fatalism by emphasizing the responsibility of men to act for their own good or ill (Min. Fel. *Oct.* 36.1).

A careful reading of Greek and Roman writers of the first centuries of the Christian era suggests that many intellectually oriented Romans had abandoned revealed religion and cult in favor of a form of religion more suited to the scientific speculations of Democritus and Leucippus, just as modern man has been profoundly affected in his religious beliefs by Darwin and his successors. In religious matters they were very close to modern man for many of the same reasons that we see today—the failure of traditional religion to satisfy, the rise of science, and disillusionment with politics and war as ways to meet people's needs.

B. *The Mystery Cults*

The mystery religions of the Eastern Mediterranean were always something of an alternative to the official religions. They emphasized feelings and personal nonrational identification with the god. By symbol, gesture, or words in the control of prophets, healers, and magicians, they attempted to supply a deeply felt sense of identity and personal gratification.

Orphism, Pythagoreanism, and the Eleusinian mysteries had introduced the Greeks to the basic aspects of the mystery cults, perhaps as early as the late Bronze Age in the case of the worship of Demeter and Kore, and certainly by the classical period. The Eleusinian mysteries, through identification with the dying and rising god of the crops, gave hope of human immortality. However, little is known of the secret rites of the initiates. Pythagoreanism and Orphism, like Gnosticism later on, emphasized the need for deliverance of the soul from the body, which was usually identified in some way with sin or finiteness. The Eleusinian mysteries flourished throughout ancient times, but they were overshadowed in Classical and Hellenistic periods by Greek preoccupation with philosophical speculation.

In Roman times, the Greeks in particular were responsible for the introduction of a number of new mystery religions, which they brought from faraway places and changed to suit the taste of the Greeks and Romans of NT times. Thus the worship of Isis and Serapis, Egyptian deities, spread throughout the Mediterranean, particularly in commercial centers. The worship of Mithras, a deity of Persia, was popular with the army, and as a result, reached as far away as the British Isles and northern Germany. The initiate, who presumably sought recovery or continuation of youthful vigor, participated through a sacrificial meal and a type of baptism in bull's blood. In the nineteenth century the ceremony was thought to be the basis of the Christian Eucharist and baptism. Today, it is clear from the archaeological evidence of the Empire that the worship of Mithras was later than the introduction of Christianity, and, if there is any relationship between them, Mithraism would have imitated Christianity.

The new mystery cults; the worship of Isis, Osiris, and Serapis; Mithraism; and the revivals of the older cults—Pythagoreanism, Orphism, and the Eleusinian mysteries—

attract a great number of worshipers. They all bear witness to the interest of people in finding an individual, ceremonial identification with a deity who would bring them deliverance from sin and finiteness and give them personal immortality.

C. Judaism of the Dispersion

Judaism was very much a religion of the Graeco-Roman world. It made contributions to the new syncretism as much as did any Hellenistic religion, and, in many ways, it was influenced by the other religions and philosophies in vogue.

Judaism in the Roman period was not a monolith. It was many different things. There was a common bond in the support of the temple by the temple tax and in the teaching of the Torah, but for many these bonds were more ethnic than religious. There were millions of Jews of the dispersion in Egypt, Babylon, Asia, Greece, and Italy. War and commerce had brought them to these places, which were all in religious, philosophical, and cultural crosscurrents. In general, wherever they were, their emphasis on monotheism, revelation, and high morality made the Jews attractive to many, won numerous converts (as the NT shows), and gained for Judaism the status of an approved religion throughout the Roman Empire.

The contrasts in the Judaism of the NT period are startling. Jewish sources describe the Pharisees as a progressive group open to new ideas. Jesus indicts them as whitened sepulchres full of dead men's bones. Saul of Tarsus was a strict Jewish literalist. In contrast, the Jews of Dura, Europas, elaborately decorated their temple with scenes from the OT despite the teaching of the Law. In similar accommodation to Gentile custom, the Jews at Sardis built their synagogue in the middle of the gymnasium. Those in the Black Sea region followed exactly the format of the Greeks in the manumission of slaves.

Philosophically, Judaism came under considerable Greek influence. Josephus indicates that the Pharisees had accepted the Stoic view of history and providence. Philo best represents Jewish eclecticism. He attempted to reconcile Greek logic and science with the OT. His ethics and theory of history were essentially Stoic. He followed the later Platonists in his view of God and matter. At every step along the way, he attempted to show that the OT had already provided a revelation of God to satisfy Gentile manifestation of God as *logos* and as a Person with whom one can achieve mystical union.

Saul of Tarsus and Philo represent the extremes of Jewish religious experience. In between, there were many of greater or lesser ethnic and religious commitment. They became a considerable moral force in the Empire. The destruction of the temple and the exile had directed them toward the law and away from the priesthood and ritual of the temple. This emphasis on OT revelation rather than ritual prepared the way for the rapid expansion of Christianity at its inception.

V. Bibliography

Charlesworth, M.P. *Roman Imperialism.* Oxford: Oxford University Press, 1914.
Frank, Tenney, ed. *An Economic Survey of Ancient Rome.* Baltimore: Johns Hopkins, 1933–40.
Grant, F.C. *Roman Hellenism and the New Testament.* New York: Scribner, 1962.
Guthrie, W.K.C. *The Greeks and Their Gods.* Boston: Beacon, 1950.
Heitland, W.E. *Agricola.* Cambridge: Cambridge University Press, 1921.
Jeremias, Joachim. *Jerusalem in the Time of Jesus.* Philadelphia: Fortress, 1969.
Machen, J.G. *The Origin of Paul's Religion.* Grand Rapids: Eerdmans, 1947.
MacKendrick, Paul. *The Mute Stones Speak.* New York: St. Martin's Press, 1960.

Rose, H.J. *Ancient Roman Religion*. London: Hutchinson's University Library, 1948.

Rostovtzeff, M.I. *The Social and Economic History of the Roman Empire*. Oxford: Oxford University Press, 1957.

Stevenson, G.H. *Roman Provincial Administration*. Oxford: Oxford University Press, 1939.

Westermann, W.L. *The Slave Systems of Greek and Roman Antiquity*. Philadelphia: American Philosophical Society, 1955.

THE SYNOPTIC GOSPELS

J. Julius Scott, Jr.

J. Julius Scott, Jr.

A.B., Wheaton College; B.D., Columbia Theological Seminary; Ph.D., University of Manchester

Professor of Bible, Graduate School, Wheaton College

THE SYNOPTIC GOSPELS

I. Definition

The term *synoptic* comes from two Greek words (*syn* and *optikos*) that mean "view together" or (from a) "common point-of-view." Matthew, Mark, and Luke are called "synoptic Gospels" because they view the life and ministry of Jesus from a common perspective different from that of John, the writer of fourth Gospel. In general, they follow the same outline and record similar material. They emphasize the Galilean setting of the initial part of Jesus' ministry, while John depicts considerable movement between Galilee and Judaea. The Synoptics give little information from which the length of Jesus' public ministry can be determined. John mentions at least three different Passover feasts (2:13; 6:4; 13:1 and possibly 5:1) and so suggests that this phase of Jesus' life lasted for at least two and a half to three years. The Synoptics emphasize Jesus' teaching in short sayings and parables centering on the theme of the kingdom of God. John relates long speeches by Jesus, frequently mentions eternal life, and emphasizes Jesus' teaching about himself. The Synoptics are primarily concerned with focusing attention on events and teachings that were typical and important in the earthly life of Jesus. John's purpose is more theological and he places more stress on the meaning and significance of Jesus and his work.

The word *gospel* means "evangel" or "good news." In the first-century Greek, "gospel" referred to a message from a king or a favorable report about a significant event. Various forms of the word were used by the Greek translators of the Old Testament (LXX) in such passages as Isaiah 40:9; 52:7; 61:1, which speak of a time of joy, peace, and salvation through the intervention of God. Jesus identified his own activities and teachings as "good news" (e.g., Matt 11:5; Mark 1:14, 15) and called men to make sacrifices for his sake and for that "of the good news" (Mark 8:35; 10:29). The later reports of the ministry of Jesus, in either oral or written form, were also called "the good news" (Mark 1:1; 13:10; 14:9; cf. 1 Cor. 15:1ff.).

The application of the term "good news" to the written records of the ministry of Jesus by both the original authors and by early Christians is an important clue toward understanding them. It suggests that they are not intended to be biographies in the formal sense of the word, but proclamations of the person and events that comprise the good news that God has intervened in history in order to bring salvation to his people (cf. Luke 1:68). Hence the Christian church has traditionally understood these documents as the work of God-inspired men who exercised their own investigative and critical abilities (cf. Luke 1:1–4) in order to inform their readers about the facts and implications of God's work in Jesus.

The motivating principle for determining material selection, organization, and emphasis stated in the fourth Gospel, by implication applies equally to the Synoptics. John claims knowledge of other facts concerning Jesus that he has not recorded. "But," he says, "these are written that you may believe that Jesus is the Christ [or Messiah], the Son of God, and that by believing you may have life in his name" (20:31).

II. The Common Synoptic Proclamation of Jesus

Through either a brief title (Mark 1:1) or accounts of his miraculous birth (Matt 1–2; Luke 1–2) the synoptic Gospels introduce Jesus of Nazareth as a unique person with a unique ministry to accomplish. They then proceed to proclaim the good news about him by recounting events and teachings organized around the four periods of Jesus' public ministry.

1. The Ministry of John the Baptist and the Baptism and Temptation of Jesus (Matt 3:1–4:11; Mark 1:2–13; Luke 3:1–4:13).
2. The Ministry in Galilee (Matt 4:12–18:35; Mark 1:14–9:50; Luke 4:14–9:50)
3. The Journey to and Ministry in and around Judaea (Matt 19:1–20:34; Mark 10: 1–52; Luke 9:51–19:27).
4. Jesus' Final Week in Jerusalem, His Death and Resurrection (Matt 21:1–28:20; Mark 11:1–16:8 [20]; Luke 19:28–24:53).

All of the Synoptics introduce the ministry of John the Baptist by quoting Isaiah 40:3, thus identifying him as the one to prepare the Lord's way. John's work of preparation involved both a denunciation of wrong and a call for positive response from his hearers. He exposed the emptiness of contemporary Jewish religious concepts and institutions that had become external ends in themselves. He called for a radical change involving an inner turning to God that would affect his hearers' daily life and attitude toward their neighbors. He insisted that his hearers, members of God's chosen people, humbly submit to a a water ceremony that cast them in the role of unacceptable, unclean persons or aliens. And John the Baptist also announced the near arrival of the kingdom of God and of "the Coming One," God's anointed agent who would judge, purify, and restore the community of God.

At his baptism Jesus identified himself with John's call for inner renewal and the arrival of a new order. He received the Spirit of God, the divine charismatic anointing, which commissioned and equipped him for ministry. The voice from heaven associated him with the dual role of Messiah-King, hailed as "Son" in Psalm 2:7, and the Servant of the Lord, the one in whom God "delights" (or is "well pleased") in Isaiah 42:1.

In the temptation Jesus confronted the enemy (Satan, or the devil), thus signifying that his ministry would be opposed by spiritual powers. Satan forced Jesus to face the question of how he would accomplish the primary goal of his ministry. Matthew and Luke show that he resisted suggestions to tailor his appeal to the popular, physical expectations of the people of his day. Instead, he overcame the enemy by depending and relying on the Word and will of God.

Each synoptic writer introduces the main portion of Jesus' ministry by recording his announcement of the arrival of the time of fulfillment predicted by the OT prophets. Their words for this phenomenon differ. Mark (1:14, 15) speaks of "the kingdom of God,"

Matthew (4:17) "the kingdom of heaven," and Luke (4:14–19) "the acceptable year of the Lord" foretold in Isaiah 61:1, 2. Nevertheless, in each case the writers clearly intend to proclaim that with the beginning of Jesus' ministry a new era in the relationship between God and man had begun.

The initial emphasis of the synoptic description of the Galilean phase of Jesus' ministry is on the question of his identity. The query "Who is he?" is either stated or implied in the records of the encounters of different groups with Jesus. The variety of answers shows his different responses. Through this emphasis, the synoptic writers, it seems, seek to confront their readers with the basic question "Who is Jesus?"

These gospels include short, selected narratives and sayings of Jesus that show him in action. They relate some of his travels, describe a number of his miracles, and give samples of his teachings. Thus, they give the reader data so that he, like the first-century Jews who saw and heard Jesus in person, can come to his own conclusion about the person and mission of Jesus.

The first part of the synoptic presentation of Jesus reaches its climax when Jesus himself asks the question that had been on the lips and in the minds of others. In a private interview with his chosen disciples, Jesus asked who they believed him to be. Peter, as spokesman, affirmed their faith that he was the long-expected Christ, the Anointed One or Messiah (Matt 16:13–16; Mark 8:27–29; Luke 9:18–22).

Jesus accepted this identification of himself as Messiah. At the same time he commanded secrecy (Matt 16:20; Mark 8:30; Luke 9:21) and predicted his rejection, suffering, and death at the hands of the Jewish leaders, to be followed by his resurrection (Matt 16:21; Mark 8:31; Luke 9:22). Furthermore, he insisted that those who would associate themselves with him and the kingdom of God he proclaimed must be willing to forsake all else and suffer the loss of even life itself in exchange for future acceptance and glory from the Father (Matt 16:24–27; Mark 8:34; Luke 9:23–26).

Peter's confession and Jesus' response to it marks the beginning of a second emphasis in the synoptic proclamation of Jesus. The Synoptics show that after he had convinced at least his own disciples that he was the Messiah, Jesus began to teach them the meaning of his messiahship for himself and for them.

This was necessary because of the vague and divergent ideas about the Messiah current in the first-century Jewish community. The majority expected the Messiah to be a divinely anointed king from David's family who would assume control in the political sphere, bring military deliverance from earthly oppressing powers such as the Roman Empire, and lead in a moral and spiritual renewal (cf. Luke 1:74, 75). The kingdom of God was anticipated as the rule of God through his Messiah, at least in part, on earth over the physical realms of men and nations. The Messiah's own people and especially his immediate followers would receive preferential treatment, places of prominence and power, and the honor and material wealth that goes with it.

Other versions of the messianic concept and of the kingdom of God, which the Messiah was expected to bring in, centered around one or another of the OT personalities. One or more of these, it was thought, would either reappear personally on earth or be represented in the person and work of another who would come in his "spirit and power" (cf. Luke 1:17). A messianic Moses or Prophet like Moses (cf. Deut. 18:15–19), for example, might be looked upon as the leader of a new Exodus to deliver God's people from spiritual and political bondage, as the founder of a new nation and the bearer of a new law or of a better understanding of the old law. A second Elijah, as either the Messiah or the forerunner of the Messiah (cf. Mal 4:4–6), might be expected sternly to denounce sinful social and religious conditions, call Israel back to the pure worship of

God as represented in the Mosaic legislation, and perform wonders in the natural order.

The title "Son of Man," a favorite self-designation of Jesus, might denote nothing more than a human being or one particular man. It appears over ninety times in the book of Ezekiel as the name by which God called the prophet to service. In Daniel 7:13ff., "one like a son of man" appears as a glorious, heavenly figure and receives a universal and eternal kingdom. Some of the noncanonical Jewish writings from the intertestamental period (especially the book of Enoch) show that in some first-century Jewish circles "the Son of Man" had come to represent a superhuman figure or even God himself. He would come with moral perfection in heavenly glory, would be accompanied by miraculous signs both in heaven and on earth, and would establish a divine kingdom that would be predominantly spiritual in nature.

Yet another OT concept concerning the Messiah relates to deliverance and salvation, not through political, military, or spiritual power, but through suffering. This idea is found in several Psalms (especially 22; cf. 2 and 16). Zechariah (chs. 9–14) describes a suffering leader, a smitten shepherd, who was rejected by men but was the instrument of God. Of special importance is the mysterious Servant, to whom allusion seems to have been made at the baptism of Jesus. He appears in differing contexts in Isaiah.[1] This Servant, it was said, would be the chosen and the delight of God, anointed by the Spirit of God, but he would be rejected, endure physical suffering, and be killed by men. Through the work of this Suffering One, the prophet says, God would reestablish his covenant with man and make righteousness or the forgiveness of sins available for "the many." Nevertheless, suffering does not appear to have been associated with the work and experience of the coming Messiah in the expectation of the majority of the Jews of Jesus' day.

Jesus knew well the popular conceptions of the nature of the Messiah and rejected them as inadequate. To prevent misunderstanding, he commanded secrecy till he could clarify what he meant by the term. In reply to Peter's confession Jesus began this process. In effect, he united in his own person several concepts usually considered separately. He also added to the messianic concept ideas that were foreign to the popular expectation of his day.

By combining the terms *Messiah* and *Son of Man*, he sought to free the messianic idea from any national, racial, political, or material associations. He affirmed that the Messiah's kingdom was to be the spiritual, eternal, universal dominion of the Son of Man. By implication, he renounced dependence on force and political manipulation in favor of spiritual means for bringing in the kingdom. Still more, he described the Messiah–Son of Man's purpose, work, and methods in terms of those of the Suffering Servant.

Jesus also showed that this new understanding of the Messiah's mission must be extended to a new understanding of what is demanded of and to be expected by the Messiah's followers. "It is enough for the student to be like his teacher" (Matt 10:25), he said. "Whoever wants to become great among you must be your servant. . . . For even the Son of Man did not come to be served, but to serve, and to give his life a ransom for many" (Mark 10:43, 45). The disciples of the Messiah must not seek the authority of an earthly government but spiritual power—not material rewards but the gifts of God from heaven, not personal prominence but the glory of God.

The latter portions of the synoptic accounts of the Galilean ministry and the entirety of what they present of the journey to and ministry in Judaea features this second

---

[1]Especially Isaiah 42:1–4; 49:1–9; 50:4–11; 52:13–53:12.

emphasis of Jesus' teaching. Such incidents as the Transfiguration (Matt 17:1–8; Mark 9:2–8; Luke 9:28–36), Jesus' miracles, and his claim to authority and power confirm the fact that Jesus is the Messiah. Yet these events and the major theme of the records of both the teachings and events of this period show that Jesus' primary concern was to clarify the spiritual nature and implications of messiahship and discipleship. In addition to his statement immediately following Peter's confession, all three Synoptics record that Jesus plainly predicted his death and resurrection in Jerusalem on at least two other occasions.[2] Time and again he stressed the spiritual, servant role of the disciple. In short, Jesus sought to impress upon his followers that his suffering and death and their implications for them were expected and necessary parts of the ministry of the Son of Man, who was also both Servant and Messiah. But, as the Gospels imply, these truths were fully understood by the disciples only after his death and resurrection.

Indeed, the synoptic writers view the events of Jesus' final week in Jerusalem and especially his death and resurrection as giving meaning to the rest of their story. These things are the grand climax toward which the proclamation has been building. They provide the only perspective for fully understanding Jesus' messiahship.

Jesus' entrance into Jerusalem during Passover season (Matt 21:1–9; Mark 11:1–10; Luke 19:28–38) marked a change in his method. Shedding the cloak of secrecy, he publicly cast himself into the unmistakable role of Messiah. The place, timing, and form of this dramatic entry implies a claim to be the conquering hero, King-Messiah of popular expectation. Yet Jesus' choice of a humble donkey to ride on, the palm branches instead of swords in the hands of his followers, his attacking religious abuse in the temple (Matt 21:10–17; Mark 11:11–19; Luke 19:45, 46) rather than directing attention to political affairs was alien to what the majority of the common people expected of the Messiah. These differences served as a tempering control on their messianic enthusiasm. Thus the dual motif of King-Messiah and Servant of God, first introduced at Jesus' baptism, the beginning of his public ministry (and implied throughout that ministry), and plainly enunciated after Peter's confession, again becomes a dominant theme as the curtain rises on the finale of his ministry.

In their accounts of the events after the triumphal entry and the cleansing of the temple, the Synoptics include a number of encounters between Jesus and the religious leadership of Jewry. Those initiated by Jesus' antagonists were related to the messianic implications of his actions and teachings. The priests asked by what authority he acted (Matt 21:23–27; Mark 11:27–33; Luke 20:1–8). The unlikely coalition of Pharisees and Herodians asked a question loaded with both political and religious implications—whether it was permissible to pay tax to Rome (Matt 22:15–22; Mark 12:13–17; Luke 20:20–26). The Sadducees confronted Jesus with a hypothetical situation growing out of his belief in the resurrection of the dead (Matt 22:34–40; Mark 12:18–27; cf. Luke 10:25–28). Jesus showed himself the master in each situation.

On a number of occasions Jesus instigated exchanges and conflicts with the leaders. The parable of the wicked tenants of the vineyard (Matt 21:33–46; Mark 12:1–12; Luke 20:9–19) is a thinly veiled denunciation of them (cf. Mark 12:12). His question about the Messiah and the Son of David (Matt 22:41–46; Mark 12:35–37a; Luke 20:41–44) exposed the inadequacy of much of the current thinking about the nature of the Messiah. Jesus' pronouncement of woes and warnings against the scribes, Pharisees, and lawyers (Matt

---

[2](1) Matthew 17:22, 23; Mark 9:31, 32. (2) Matthew 20:17–19; Mark 10:32–34; Luke 9:44. (3) Luke 18:31–34. Cf. Matthew 20:28; Mark 10:45.

23; Mark 12:37–40; Luke 20:45–47; cf. Luke 11:46ff.) attacked the failure of the most-respected religious groups of his day to live up to their own teachings. So in essence he rejected the legalism represented by these groups as an inadequate and improper understanding of the nature of God's requirements. The discourses in apocalyptic literary form describing "the end" and the relation of Jesus' followers to it (Matt 24–25; Mark 13; Luke 21:5–36)—whether these statements deal with the destruction of the Jewish state and temple by the Romans in A.D. 70, the consummation of history and the second coming of Jesus, or both—portray Jesus' rejection of the existing Jewish nation and religious institutions as the focal point of God's dealings with man.

In each Gospel these accounts culminate in the report of a coalition of several groups to plot the death of Jesus (Matt 26:1–5; Mark 14:1, 2; Luke 22:1, 2) and in the betrayal by Judas (Matt 26:14–16; Mark 14:10, 11; Luke 22:3–6). At the same time, it seems that Jesus continued to gain a hearing from the common people and to enjoy their favor (cf. Mark 12:12, 37b; 14:2; Luke 22:6).

At the Passover meal commemorating Israel's deliverance from slavery in Egypt (cf. Exod 12:1–13:10), Jesus reinterpreted the ceremonial foods to refer to himself and his death (Matt 26:17–29; Mark 14:12–25; Luke 22:7–38). In so doing he boldly made himself and especially his death, which he said was "for many for the forgiveness of sins" (Matt 26:28), the focal point of all redemptive history.

The agony of Jesus in the Garden of Gethsemane (Matt 26:36–46; Mark 14:32–42; Luke 22:40–46) again illustrates the interplay between the physical and spiritual, between heaven and earth, in the life of Jesus. It indicates the Messiah's consciousness of a special mission and destiny and the cost to himself involved in performing it.

Messiahship is also the major issue in both the Jewish and the Roman trials of Jesus. The Jewish leaders made use of the many-sided meaning of the term. The priests asked if he were the Christ, the Messiah, and clearly related the word to a religio-spiritual context (Matt 26:63; Mark 14:61; Luke 22:67). Jesus accepted the title and further defined it with reference to the heavenly Son of Man–King (Matt 26:64; Mark 14:62; Luke 22:67–69; cf. Dan 7:13; Ps 110:1). For this the Jews condemned him on the religious charge of blasphemy (Matt 26:65, 66; Mark 14:63, 64; Luke 22:70, 71).

Before the Roman governor the Jews used the politico-military side of messiahship. They sought to convince Pilate that Jesus' claim to be the Messiah was tantamount to rebellion against the Roman emperor.[3] In spite of the procurator's doubts, Jesus was eventually executed for treason. This is confirmed by the inscription "The King of the Jews" (Matt 27:37; Mark 15:26; Luke 23:38), written on the placard customarily affixed to the cross of condemned criminals and detailing the charges for which they were executed.

In the Synoptics the Crucifixion is depicted as a triumphant tragedy that is at the same time a study in contrasts. The Jewish leaders standing by derided Jesus for his claim of kingship, of a unique relationship to God, of being the savior of others, and of superseding the temple, the symbol of Jewish religious prestige and privilege (Matt 27:39–43; Mark 15:29–32; Luke 23:35). The two who were crucified with him did the same, though Luke says one sought mercy (Matt 27:44; Mark 15:32; Luke 23:39–43). On the other hand, the synoptic writers show Jesus himself as preoccupied with the conflict in which

---

[3]This is the obvious implication of Matthew 27:11; Mark 15:2; Luke 23:23. Note that in Matthew 27:22 Pilate uses the term "Christ" but in the parallel, Mark 15:12, he is said to have called Jesus "King of the Jews." John 19:12–15 clearly shows that the Jewish leaders were attempting to prove that Jesus was guilty of treason.

he was engaged. They record only those words from the cross that reflect this spiritual struggle. He assured the criminal of Paradise (Luke 23:43), in anguish he cried out because of being forsaken by God (Matt 27:46; Mark 15:34), and he committed his spirit into the hands of the Father (Luke 23:46). The Roman military officer in charge of the execution was so struck by the events surrounding Jesus' death and the way he died that he affirmed Jesus' innocence (Luke 23:47) and deity (Matt 27:54; Mark 15:39).

There were other teachers in the first century. There were others who claimed miraculous powers. There were even others who claimed to be the Messiah. The synoptic Gospels do not even bother to contest these claims or compare them with those of Jesus. For the synoptic proclamation of the Good News includes the affirmation that, if true, validates all else that is said about Jesus. After carefully recounting the fact of Jesus' death and burial, they confidently affirm that on the third day he was raised from the dead.

Their reports of the Resurrection are tantilizingly brief. There is no description of the emergence from the tomb. These Gospels are unanimous in the claim that God restored Jesus to life and that thereafter the tomb was empty (Matt 28:1–10; Mark 16:1–8; Luke 24:1–11). All traditions affirm that Jesus was seen alive by his followers. Luke also says that Jesus invited doubting disciples to prove to themselves that he was, in fact, alive by touching him (Luke 24:38–40; cf. John 20:24–29) and that he ate food in the presence of his friends (Luke 24:30, 41–43).

The synoptic proclamation ends with the notice that the resurrected Jesus explained his suffering in terms of the OT predictions about the Messiah (Luke 24:25–27, 44–47), claimed universal authority (Matt 28:18), commissioned his disciples to be witnesses to the facts and saving implications of his ministry (Matt 28:18–20; Luke 24:47, 48), and promised to send the Holy Spirit upon them (Luke 24:49). Luke, in both his Gospel and in Acts, says that the earthly ministry of Jesus ended by his being taken up into heaven (Luke 24:50, 51; Acts 1:9–11).

III. Distinctive Features of Each Synoptic Gospel

Although Matthew, Mark, and Luke present the ministry of Jesus within the same outline and generally from the same point of view, each gospel also contains distinctive features. Each has material not found in the others. The material within a particular synoptic Gospel found in one or both of the others is sometimes placed in different settings or contains different wording. As a result, each Synoptic has its unique character and emphasis and proclaims the Good News about Jesus in such a way as to make him most attractive to the audience each evangelist is addressing.

1. Matthew

The unique features of Matthew may be observed in material he alone records, in the structure of his composition, and in some of his distinct phraseology. His Gospel opens with a genealogy and birth narrative of Jesus differing from that of Luke in emphasizing Jesus' kingly heritage and mission.[4] Matthew's resurrection account is briefer than Luke's and focuses on appearance of the risen Christ to his disciples in Galilee rather than in Jerusalem (ch. 28, especially vv. 16–20).

---

[4]Matthew 1–2; cf. Luke 1:26–56; 2; 3:23–38. But observe that both Gospels affirm Jesus' virgin birth and physical descent from David.

A dominant feature of Matthew's structure is five collections of sayings[5] interspersed throughout the common synoptic outline. These, as has frequently been noted, are similar in general concern and in number to the first five books of the OT, the foundation of the Hebrew faith.

In addition, on thirty-three occasions Matthew mentions "the kingdom of heaven," a phrase found neither in Mark nor in Luke. In eleven of these occurrences, parallel passages in one or both of the other Synoptics read "kingdom of God." This latter phrase had politico-military connotations in first-century Jewish circles, and Matthew uses it only in contexts in which the other-worldly or spiritual character of that kingdom is evident.[6]

Matthew further demonstrates this sensitivity to Jewish interests and conditions by frequent quotations from the OT that are intended to show various facets of Jesus' life as either fulfillments of OT predictions or as recapitulations of OT themes. Matthew also displays more interest than the other Synoptics in matters related to the Jewish law and customs, Jewish national privilege, and the relation between Israel and faith in Jesus.

When the Gospel of Matthew is read with these clues in mind, it becomes obvious that it is addressed primarily to Jews. It is the Gospel that seeks to convince Jews that Jesus is indeed their long-awaited Messiah-King of David's line. Matthew suggests that in Jesus alone may Israel fulfill her God-given destiny and properly understand and observe God's will and law.

Although God maintains a special interest in, and purpose for, the nation Israel, Matthew implies that the real people of God are the people of the Messiah, the church, whose numbers include all who come to Jesus. The Messiah's kingdom transcends time, space, national, racial boundaries. For to Jesus, the crucified, risen Messiah, there has been given "all authority in heaven and on earth," his disciples come from "all nations" and are assured of his presence until "the very end of the age" (28:10–20).

2. Mark

Mark, the shortest of the Gospels, relates that basic proclamation common to all the Synoptics (over 90 percent of the material in Mark is recorded in one or both of the other Synoptics). An obvious feature of Mark is his fast-moving style and the way he frequently strings incidents together with "then," "and," or "immediately." Mark, though not neglecting the teachings of Jesus, is primarily concerned with relating his actions.

Mark's portrayal of Jesus often features extremes and the dramatic incidents. He reports popular acclaim alongside bitter opposition and struggle, divine power and authority alongside human fatigue and sorrow. Mark gives special attention to Jesus' miracles of healing and to his conflict with the spiritual world as demonstrated in his casting out demons. The theme of the suffering of the Son of Man and reflections of the imagery and wording of the Servant passages of Isaiah hold a conspicuous place. More clearly than the other Gospels, Mark shows Jesus' opposition to abuses associated with certain Jewish institutions and practices of his day, such as the Sabbath (2:23–3:6),

---

[5]The Sermon on the Mount, chs. 5–7; instructions to the Twelve when they were sent to preach, 9:37–11:1; parables of the kingdom, 13:1–53a; discourses on church discipline, 18:1–19:1a; and teachings concerning the Last Things, 24:1–26:1a.

[6]Matthew 12:28; 19:24; 21:31, 43 and in some texts of 6:33. Matthew 19:24; Mark 10:25; Luke 18:25 is the only place in which all three use "kingdom of God."

ceremonial laws concerning eating (2:15–17; 7:14–23), and the exclusive Jewish use of the temple (11:17).[7]

At least five times Mark uses Aramaic phrases, but indicates that he is not writing for Jewish readers by translating them (3:17; 5:41; 7:34; 14:36; 15:34). He gives Latin equivalents for terms and amounts (12:42; 15:16) and in so doing may provide a hint to the identity of his audience. This evidence, plus notice of Mark's style, when combined with ancient traditions seems to confirm that this Gospel was written to inform action-oriented Romans of "the gospel about Jesus Christ, the Son of God" (1:1), the Son of Man with authority to forgive sins (2:10), who came to serve and to suffer to redeem many (10:45).

3. Luke

The Gospel according to Luke exhibits the highest literary quality of any of the records of the ministry of Jesus. It is the longest book in the NT and, together with its sequel, the book of Acts, comprises the largest block of material by a single NT author. In the first four verses Luke reveals his purpose—to accurately inform the reader (originally, "most excellent Theophilus") regarding the Christian faith. His methodology, he says, is to write an "orderly [not necessarily chronological] account" based on careful research conducted among credible witnesses.

Some recent investigators,[8] seeking to emphasize Luke's theological motivation at the expense of his historical accuracy, have sought to find symbolic significance in such features as Luke's geography of the life of Jesus. For an example, Galilee, it is suggested, may represent Jesus' ministry to the Gentiles, the travel section Jesus' preparation for death, and Jerusalem the place of death, fulfillment, and final victory. These insights may prove helpful in understanding some of the factors that have influenced the author in organizing his "orderly account." But attention to Luke's overall sense of history and his general agreement with the other synoptics, including such matters as geography, should serve as a safeguard against pushing this approach too far.

Luke uses the same general framework as Matthew and Mark but introduces a number of variations in details from the structure of the others. His description of the Galilean ministry are shorter and organized differently from those of the other synoptics.

Luke's birth narrative includes information about the birth of John the Baptist, contains numerous details regarding the birth and early life of Jesus not found elsewhere, and features the visit of the shepherds (representatives of the common people) to see the baby. Luke's Gospel also contains the longer account of appearances of the resurrected Jesus to his disciples. Luke locates the above in Judaea. It is, however, within the

---

7Observe that the words "for all the nations" in Mark 11:17 are omitted in the parallel accounts in Matthew 21:13 and Luke 19:46.

8Hans Conzelmann, *The Theology of St. Luke* (German, 1953), trans. by Geoffry Boswell (London: Faber and Faber, 1960); Helmut Flender, *St. Luke, Theologian of Redemption* (German, 1965), trans. by Reginald H. and Ilse Fuller (London: SPCK, 1967).

Usually the investigation of Luke's method has initially centered upon Acts and then been applied to the Gospel. See Ernst Haenchen, *The Acts of the Apostles* (German, 1956), trans. by R. McL. Wilson (Philadelphia: Westminster, 1971); and Hans Conzelmann, *Die Apostelgeschichte* (Handbuch zum Neuen Testament) (Tübingen: J.C.B. Mohr, 1963); cf. also *Studies in Luke Acts*, ed. by Leander E. Keck and J. Louis Martyn (Nashville: Abingdon, 1966) and C.K. Barrett, *Luke the Historian in Recent Study* (London: Epworth, 1961).

For an evangelical appraisal of this approach see I. Howard Marshall, *Luke: Historian and Theologian* (Grand Rapids: Zondervan, 1971).

context of Jesus' journey to and ministry in and around Judaea just prior to his death that Luke's content and structure is most distinct.

Matthew and Mark devote relatively little space to this final journey. Luke makes it a section in which special emphasis is placed on the teachings of Jesus. Some material that Matthew locates in the Galilean ministry is included by Luke in this travel section (e.g., the Lord's Prayer, Luke 11:1-4 but Matt 6:9-13). Here also he introduces some material that shows a particular interest in presenting Jesus as a friend of outcasts, poor women, children—the disadvantaged in general. Such accounts as Jesus' encounters with the publican Zacchaeus (19:1-10) and with Mary and Martha (10:38-42), the healing of a woman with an infirmity (13:10-17), and the parables of the good Samaritan (10:29-37), the prodigal son (15:11-32), the rich man and Lazarus (16:19-31), the unjust judge (18:1-8), and the Pharisee and the publican (18:9-14) are examples.

Luke, evidently a cultured Greek addressing a Gentile of social rank, seeks to proclaim Jesus by weaving together material that will give an impression of his personality and a sample of a broad spectrum of his teachings. He emphasizes Jesus' humanitarian concern for the needs of despised and suffering individuals. More than any other NT writer, Luke seeks to show the interest of Jesus in all people, including non-Jews, and shows Jesus' relevance for everyone. However, these and other Lucan features illustrate distinctions in emphasis rather than any real differences from the other Gospels in understanding the essential content of the nature and ministry of Jesus.

Through the inspiration of God's Spirit Matthew, Mark, and Luke recorded the good news about Jesus from different points of view. Each Gospel stands by itself as a powerful proclamation of Jesus the Messiah, the Son of God. At the same time, theirs is a joint and basically united record of God's supreme act within history. As such, their similarities and differences, showing the integrity of each writer and the absence of an attempt to standardize reports about Jesus, tend to confirm and enhance their witness. As a three-fold cord is stronger than the total strength of the three strands taken individually, so the announcement of the Good News by the synoptic writers, complete with its unity in diversity and diversity in unity, is stronger than the sum of their three individual testimonies.

IV. The Synoptic Problem

Literary and historical critics of the Synoptics have raised a number of questions about their origin and character.[9] The more far-reaching of these concern "the synoptic problem"—the investigation of the relationships between these documents.

It has already been noted that there are both similarities and differences in the form and content of Matthew, Mark, and Luke. At times the use of identical words and grammatical constuctions, or the presence of subtle variations in vocabulary, verb tenses, word order, etc., is evident only in an examination of the Greek text of the parallel passages. Other similarities and differences can be seen in English translation.

Matthew, Mark, and Luke contain a common core of information, usually called "Mar-

---

[9]Descriptions of the rise, discussion, and alternative theories regarding these issues can be found in histories of NT studies and in standard introductions. See Stephen Neill, *The Interpretation of the New Testament 1861-1961* (New York: Oxford, 1964); Werner G. Kümmel, *Introduction to the New Testament.* Trans. Howard C. Kee. (Nashville: Abingdon, 1977); Donald Guthrie, *New Testament Introduction* (Downers Grove, Ill.: Inter-Varsity, 1970); and Werner G. Kümmel. *The New Testament: The History of the Investigation of Its Problems.* Trans. by S.M. Gilmour and H.C. Kee (Nashville: Abingdon, 1972).

can material." Marcan material is almost always presented in the same sequence and includes common use of even rare terms and unusual grammatical constructions. Matthew and Luke share an additional common core of material, designated as "Q," that is not found in Mark. The type of similarity between the Synoptics suggests literary dependence to most scholars. This may have involved writers using the same written sources or drawing upon one or both of the other Synoptics.

Within the Marcan material there are only minor variations from one Gospel to another. Between Matthew and Luke there is more variation in their Q sections than in their Marcan sections. This variation includes their sometimes recording Q material in different words, sequences, settings, or in different places in the synoptic outline of the ministry of Jesus. Each gospel also contains material not found in the others. In Mark there are fewer than fifty verses not found elsewhere but the distinctive material in Matthew exceeds 250 verses and in Luke 500 verses.

The synoptic problem received little attention until the modern period. During the eighteenth century, rationalism led some investigators to apply the same scholarly methods used in the study of other literature to the NT. Some of the earliest synoptic scholars attempted to show that our Gospels are different Greek translations or abridgments of older Aramaic documents. Others investigated the possibility that the writers drew from different collections of fragmentary written records about Jesus. Some nineteenth-century students turned attention to the possible use of various types of oral tradition. Recent scholarship has refined and built on earlier theories.

In the twentieth century, the study of the synoptic relationships has focused on stages through which it is assumed the information about Jesus has passed. Source (or literary) criticism is primarily concerned with identifying the written records used by the gospel writers. Form criticism attempts to determine the influences that acted on the gospel material while it was being passed on by word of mouth. Redaction (or editorial) criticism investigates the effects an author-editor's personal bias or objectives may have had on the way he recorded an incident or saying.

The majority of source critics now hold that Mark was written first.[10] Matthew and Luke then drew both outline and material from Mark, making editorial and stylistic changes. Matthew and Luke used another source, one primarily containing sayings of Jesus, from whence they derived their Q material. Opinions differ on whether the distinctive material in Matthew and Luke came from written documents (called "M" and "L" respectively) or from oral tradition.

Form criticism seeks to discover what happened to the information about Jesus while it was being transmitted orally.[11] The form critic believes that during this period the

---

[10]Until recent times it was assumed that Matthew was the first gospel. A number of scholars still question or reject the priority of Mark; see B.C. Butler, *The Originality of St. Matthew* (Cambridge: University Press, 1951), Ned B. Stonehouse, *Origins of the Synoptic Gospels* (Grand Rapids: Eerdmans, 1963), W.R. Farmer, *The Synoptic Problem: A Critical Analysis* (New York: Macmillan, 1964).

Among source critics who hold Mark's priority are the following: John C. Hawkins, *Horae Synopticae*, 2nd ed.; (Oxford: At the Clarendon Press, 1909); B.H. Streeter, *The Four Gospels* (New York: Macmillan, 1930); Vincent Taylor, *The Gospels* (London: Epworth, 1938); see discussion of the history of the attempts to solve the Synoptic Problem in Donald Guthrie, *New Testament Introduction* (Downers Grove, Ill.: Inter-Varsity Press, 1970); W.G. Kümmel, *Introduction to the New Testament*; rev. ed.; trans by Howard Clark Kee (Nashville: Abingdon, 1975).

[11]Some leading form critics are the following: Martin Dibelius, *From Tradition to Gospel* (German, 1919) (London: Ivar Nicholson and Watson, 1934); Rudolf Bultmann, *The History of the Synoptic Tradition* (German, 1928), trans. by John Marsh (Philadelphia: Westminster, 1963); Vincent Taylor, *The Formation of the Gospel Tradition* (New York: Macmillan, 1933); Edgar V. McKnight, *What Is Form Criticism?* (Philadelphia: Fortress, 1969).

gospel material circulated in short, independent units (pericopes) that were later collected, edited, and fitted into a setting and outline by the gospel writers. He further assumes that as they were transmitted, individuals and groups of the early church modified and gave literary form to the gospel units or pericopes. By identifying the form of a particular literary unit and by analyzing the history through which it has passed, the form critic seeks to uncover the conditions existing within that part of the church that preserved and transmitted it.

Precise categories for identifying and classifying the forms of the pericopes differ among form critics. The following terminology is representative: *Pronouncement stories* are short narratives that exist for a statement by Jesus and come to a climax in it. *Miracle stories* are those units in which the miracle itself is the main point. The standard form for miracle stories is (1) a description of the illness or condition, (2) a report of the miracle, and (3) a record of the reaction of those who witnessed the wonder. The *words of Jesus* is a major division. It may be subdivided to isolate those sayings that are patterned after Hebrew wisdom literature, prophetic sayings, legal sayings and church rules, sayings made in the first person (I-sayings), figures of speech, and parables. The longest and oldest form-unit is the *passion narrative*. Finally, *formless stories* (sometimes called *legend* or *myth*, but without necessarily implying historical judgment) is a catch-all category for material that does not fit elsewhere. Accounts involving the intervention of the supernatural world (such as the Transfiguration) and a number of descriptions of Jesus and his disciples (e.g., the calling of the Twelve and Peter's confession) are classified as formless stories.

The life setting of the early church (*Sitz im Leben*) revealed through a study of the form history of a pericope may involve the cultural setting, problems faced, and other points of major interest or concern within the group that transmitted it. In particular, the form critic seeks to determine if a pericope was used and developed within the context of the church's missionary preaching, instruction of converts, defense of its faith, relationship to the state, worship, or exercise of discipline.

The usefulness of some features of form criticism is recognized by a wide spectrum of NT scholars. Some of its adherents (e.g., Rudolf Bultmann) also seek to use it to pass historical judgments on a gospel unit, but more conservative scholars consider this a misapplication of the method. The radical form critic assumes that the church not only adapted and transmitted the gospel material but also created it when required by the situation in the church.

All form criticism proceeds on the assumption that principles that operate in the formation of oral tradition in general (principles isolated through a study of the development of folklore) also operated in the formation of the gospel tradition. The radical form critic also questions the historical authenticity of any piece of gospel material that in form, content, or emphasis displays a kinship with the Hellenistic (Greek) world or first-century Judaism. It often appears that in practice the more radical form critic automatically rejects as church creation any account that includes a supernatural element or hints of theological interpretation of the person and work of Jesus.

Since 1950 redaction criticism has played a growing role in the study of the Synoptics.[12] It is built on the presuppositions and conclusions of source and form

---

[12]Redaction criticism is explained and illustrated by Hans Conzelmann, *The Theology of Saint Luke* Trans. by Geoffrey Bushwell (London: Faber, 1960) and Willi Marxsen, *Mark the Evangelist* Trans. by Roy A. Harrisville (Nashville: Abingdon, 1969); Norman Perrin, *What Is Redaction Criticism?* (Philadelphia, Fortress, 1969).

criticism. But redaction criticism differs from the other disciplines by focusing attention on the author and his Gospel as a whole rather than on sources or individual units.

With the source and form critic, the redaction critic assumes that the Gospels were composed by bringing together units of previously existing, largely independent materials. He further postulates that the author's own purpose and theological stance affected his presentation of Jesus. Therefore, clarification of the factors that have shaped the gospel tradition must include an investigation of the theological motivation of each writer. This the redaction critic seeks to do by identifying and analyzing the original contribution of each author.

The redaction critic believes that the author's contribution consists in his collecting, editing, and modifying the written sources and oral units available to him. He also claims that the author reveals himself in his composition of settings for pericopes, transitional passages between sources, summary passages, and possibly even in creating an outline within which to present the ministry of Jesus.

Evangelical scholars in particular have strongly resisted the antisupernatural bias of the most prominent advocates of source, form, and redaction criticism. Also, though some evangelicals acknowledge that these critical tools may provide convenient categories for classifying the various types of material in the Synoptics, they reject the claim that these critical methods can indicate the origin of that material. Furthermore, it should be noted that a number of scholars of various theological viewpoints recognize that source, form, and redaction criticism simply have not succeeded in completely and conclusively explaining all the differences and similarities in the Synoptics. Consequently, the search for other critical tools to aid in understanding synoptic relationships continues.

In Scandinavia some scholars have suggested that a clarification of the teaching methods of Jesus may throw some light on the synoptic problem.[13] They believe that his didactic techniques were similar to those of the Jewish rabbis. The students of the rabbis were expected to memorize much of their masters' teachings. Consequently, it is reasonable to expect that Jesus' disciples committed his teachings to memory. The Scandinavian scholars claim that an investigation of the parallels between the gospel tradition and the transmission of oral and written tradition in rabbinic Judaism indicates that this is just what occurred.

Advocates of this "memory and manuscript" approach[14] have sometimes overstated their case. Yet they have called attention to elements in the historical background in the text of the NT that deserve further investigation.

Other possible explanations for the similarities and differences of the synoptic Gospels should also be considered. For an example, during the course of his ministry, Jesus probably repeated the same material at different times, places, and settings. This practice may explain some of the variations in reports of similar words and sayings. This and other suggestions may open the door to new lines of study that may provide positive contributions in the continuing effort to clarify synoptic relationships.

The scientific, critical study of the synoptic Gospels has produced both positive and negative results. Preoccupation with introductory issues and literary details has fre-

---

[13]The most important representative of this group is Birger Gerhardsson, *Memory and Manuscript* (Lund: Gleerup, 1961); see also Birger Gerhardsson, *Tradition and Transmission in Early Christianity* (Lund: Gleerup, 1964); Harald Riesenfeld, *The Gospel Tradition and Its Beginnings* (London: Mowbray, 1957).

[14]So called because of the name of the most complete exposition of this theory, Birger Gerhardsson's *Memory and Manuscript* (Lund: Gleerup, 1961).

quently given such undue emphasis to the vehicle that the cargo of the Gospels, the accounts of the ministry of Jesus, has been relegated to second place. When critical methods have been mixed with antisupernatural, rationalistic, idealistic, or existential presuppositions, they have obscured much of the uniqueness, authority, and significance of the words and work of Jesus.

But the synoptic Gospels are able to bear the weight of careful study using the most advanced critical tools when applied without bias. Recognition that writers used written and oral reports about Jesus and exercised their own abilities in composing their proclamations of the Good News underlines what Luke tells about his methods (1:1–4). A careful study of the history of the transmission of oral tradition confirms that in even its earliest forms it proclaimed Jesus as the divine Messiah, the conqueror of sin and death. Attention to distinctive elements in each Gospel clarifies the individuality of their witness to the life and ministry of Jesus.

But scientific, critical study has its limits. It has no equipment for recognizing, describing, or evaluating the presence of a more-than-human influence in the production of a body of literature. And it is the activity of just such an influence that is claimed for the NT as well as the OT Scriptures by a line of Christian tradition stretching unbroken from the apostolic age to the present. This tradition affirms that the Christian church has consistently held that the synoptic and all other writers of biblical literature were men who, as they wrote, "were carried along by the Holy Spirit" and thus "spoke from God" (cf. 2 Peter 1:20, 21).

V. Bibliography

Barclay, William. *The First Three Gospels.* London: SMC, 1966.
Beardslee, William A. *Literary Criticism of the New Testament.* Philadelphia: Fortress, 1970.
Briggs, R.C. *Interpreting the Gospels.* Nashville: Abingdon, 1969.
Bultmann, Rudolf. *The History of the Synoptic Tradition.* Translated by John Marsh. Oxford: Blackwells, 1963.
Dibelius, Martin. *From Tradition to Gospel.* Translated by Bertram Woolf. London: Nicholson and Watson, 1934.
McKnight, Edgar V. *What Is Form Criticism?* Philadelphia: Fortress, 1961.
Riesenfeld, Harald. *The Gospel Tradition and its Beginnings.* London: Mowbray, 1957.
Rohde, Joachim. *Rediscovering the Teaching of the Evangelists.* Translated by Dorothea M. Barton. Philadelphia: Westminster, 1961.
Stonehouse, Ned B. *Origins of the Synoptic Gospels.* Grand Rapids: Eerdmans, 1963.
Streeter, B.H. *The Four Gospels.* New York: Macmillan, 1930.
Tasker, R.V.G. *The Nature and Purpose of the Gospels.* Richmond: John Knox, 1962.
Taylor, Vincent. *The Formation of the Gospel Tradition.* New York: Macmillan, 1964.
_____. *The Gospels.* London: Epworth, 1962.
Tenney, Merrill C. *The Genius of the Gospels.* Grand Rapids: Eerdmans, 1951.

JESUS IN THE GOSPELS

I. Howard Marshall

I. Howard Marshall

B.A., Cambridge University; M.A., B.D., Ph.D., University of Aberdeen

Senior Lecturer in New Testament, University of Aberdeen

JESUS IN THE GOSPELS

I. The Nature of the Gospels

A. *The Gospel*

One of the most surprising features of the New Testament is that, with the exception of the evangelists, the writers pay so little attention to the historical life of Jesus in comparison with his death and resurrection. One of the oldest formulations of the early preaching of the church tells us "that Christ died for our sins according to the Scriptures, that he was buried, that he was raised on the third day according to the Scriptures, and that he appeared to Peter, and then to the Twelve . . ." (1 Cor 15:3–5). It is striking that this brief recital of facts is called "the gospel" and that it says nothing about the life of Christ but is concerned exclusively with his death and resurrection. This is the gospel message; by belief in it (that is, in the Person it presents) people are saved, and its concern is with a Christ who died for their sins and who did so in accordance with the Scriptures. When reduced to its essentials, the gospel is a statement about the death and resurrection of Jesus rather than about his earthly ministry.

This does not mean that the early Christians were ignorant of the facts about the life of Jesus. Paul himself and the writer to the Hebrews were clearly aware of various facts about the life and ministry of Jesus, and there are a number of echoes of his teaching in the writings of Paul. Both Peter and James were obviously familiar with the teaching of Jesus and allude to it in their Epistles. But for all of these writers the center of gravity lies in the Atonement and the Resurrection; the period from the Cross and exaltation of Jesus, through his heavenly ministry, and up to his second coming is more important than the details of his ministry.

Nevertheless, the early Christians were interested in what Jesus said and did, and this too formed part of the gospel message. This is clear from the sermons preserved in Acts and especially from Peter's address to Cornelius, which contains the fullest reference to the life of Jesus outside the Gospels themselves (Acts 10:37–43). Even here, however, it is notable that the ministry of Jesus is seen in the context of his death and resurrection. In other words, the NT implicitly insists that if we pay attention primarily to the earthly ministry of Jesus, we will misunderstand the purpose of his coming and end up with a merely human teacher and wonder-worker. The life of Jesus has to be seen in the light of its end and what lay beyond it. The Gospels themselves confirm this view of things. Of the sixteen chapters of the Gospel of Mark, a full six are devoted to the final visit by Jesus to Jerusalem—a visit that culminated in his death. In the Gospel of John the point is even stronger; ten of the twenty-one chapters are allotted to the last week of his life. Both the Gospel of Matthew and the Gospel of Luke also lay great stress on the last week of Jesus' life. It is no wonder that in a famous phrase M. Kähler described a Gospel as a passion narrative with an extended introduction.

B. *The Character of the Gospels*

1. *The good news of Jesus.* Although the word *gospel* refers primarily to the message about the saving significance of Jesus' death and resurrection, the early church was right in calling the narratives of his ministry by this name, using the word that originally designated the Christian message as "good news" to describe the documents that tell us about Jesus on earth. In this way the early church affirmed and underlined that what is done in "the Gospels" is the same as what is done in "the gospel." Both are testimonies to the acts of God that bring salvation to men and culminate in the death and resurrection of Jesus. The center of the Gospels is the event that forms their climax, his passion and resurrection. Thus the Gospels are essentially documents that preach the gospel. They tell the story of the One who was and is the Savior. This is their theme, this and nothing else. Their purpose is thus theological.

What, then, is the point of the remaining content—actually the bulk of the Gospels? It is to relate those things about Jesus that in one way or another were significant for understanding him as the Savior. Plainly this opened up the way for including a great variety of material—Jesus' own preaching of the good news of salvation, his instruction regarding the nature of discipleship, his own activity as Savior, the beginnings of the church among his group of disciples, the story of how he came to be rejected and crucified. All this was told because it was significant for the message of salvation. At the same time the Gospels were probably intended to stress the reality of the fact that "the Word became flesh and lived for a while among us" (John 1:14). It was essential to guard against the danger of thinking that the Christ of the apostolic message was merely a heavenly being who momentarily appeared on earth without truly being incarnate, or that the Christian faith is based on a timeless message rather than on a historical act of God interpreted in the message.

2. *The historical basis.* It follows from what has just been said that, though the purpose of the Gospels was primarily theological, their character is in no sense unhistorical. What they described was not invented but really happened. The writers did not make the story up out of their own heads in order to have a vehicle for conveying doctrinal propositions. The heart of the Christian message was that God had acted in history in Jesus. What they wrote, therefore, was historical, but their interest was not that of a historian concerned with the past merely for its own sake, but that of the Christian for whom the past is significant because of its character as salvation history. They wanted to acquaint their readers with what had actually happened so that they might know the certainty of the things they had been instructed about (Luke 1:4) and so come to faith in Jesus as the Christ and Son of God (John 20:30–31). The writing of history and the proclamation of a message are thus not two incompatible activities; on the contrary, the content of the message is a historical narrative about the action of God in a historical person.

This does not, however, make the Gospels into "lives" of Christ. There are no doubt many things we would like to know about Jesus that find little or no mention in the Gospels. They do not tell us what a more or less conventional "life," whether in the ancient world or in the modern world, would tell us. They give us no description of the physical characteristics of Jesus, except that his risen body contained the marks of the nails and the spear—the signs by which the identity of the risen Lord with the earthly Jesus could be seen. Nor do they speak explicitly of his mental and emotional character as such, though some details are mentioned casually (e.g., Mark 3:5; John 4:6; 11:35). We learn nothing about his early life beyond the events surrounding his birth and one brief glimpse into his boyhood; we can only surmise what the formative influences upon him were. We have no full account even of the period of his ministry, but simply a brief record of typical events and teaching that could have taken place in the space of a few months. We do not know for certain the dates of his birth and death. And so we might go on. The fact is that the ingredients of a modern biography are missing from the Gospel records. Nor is it likely that any fuller, historical accounts ever existed; the stories of some aspects of the life of Jesus, such as those about his boyhood found in second-century apocryphal gospels and infancy narratives are patently legendary and do not stem from the main stream of apostolic Christianity.

C. A Modern "Life of Christ"

1. *"The quest of the historical Jesus."* If the writers in the early church did not try to write "the life of Christ," the lesson for us is perhaps that we ought not to make the attempt and improve upon them. From the point of view of believing Christians, we

would be doing the wrong thing. Our duty is to abide by the form given us in the NT. That form is the new one created by the early church in order to meet the needs posed by the problem of communicating the Christian message. It is the unique literary genre of "gospel."

But it may be argued that even if there is a valid theological argument for presenting the story of Jesus in the form of a gospel, nevertheless there is no reason why a historian should not want to write a life of Jesus, whether out of sheer historical interest, or in order to see whether the actual facts of the life of Jesus correspond with the portrayal in the Gospels. For if the early Christians were writing in "gospel" form with a view to converting their readers (or to providing Christians with material for use in evangelism), it can be argued that they were presenting the facts in a particular, persuasive kind of way, and the reader has a right to ask whether the "real" historical Jesus corresponds with the picture that has been presented. A skeptic, for example, will want to question the accounts of the miraculous in the Gospels. These are fair questions to ask, and the historian is duty-bound to ask them, just as a Christian will feel it right and necessary to probe with equal skepticism into accounts of miracles attributed to pagan gods and semidivine men. The Christian is justified in asking whether the historicity of the Gospel narrative in general can be upheld. Was Jesus really like the picture of him painted in the Gospels? Have important facts been left out that might contribute to a different understanding of his character and career? Has the story been twisted, consciously or unconsciously, in the telling, so that it is not wholly reliable historically? In short, is the presentation biased?

These considerations invite us to undertake "the quest of the historical Jesus." But this very phrase reminds us of the existence of a series of attempts to get down to the "real facts" about Jesus by nineteenth-century authors, cataloged in A. Schweitzer's famous book by this title; nor has the twentieth century been less productive, for similar studies continue to flow from the presses. Schweitzer virtually concluded that the task was an impossible one. For all his striving after objectivity, the historian inevitably produces a picture of Jesus that is colored by his own presuppositions. G. Tyrrell aptly likened the process to that of a man peering down a deep well and seeing only the distorted reflection of his own face in the waters beneath. How can one distinguish the reflection from the reality? How can one see the real Jesus without personal bias?

Today we can see more clearly that much of this research was conducted by people who had some kind of rationalistic approach to religion and who therefore expected to find a nonsupernatural Jesus. Historical explanation was bound to produce a Jesus who was in essence an ordinary man. The cards were stacked from the beginning.

But could such rationalist ventures succeed? In a significant book that used the tools of modern historical criticism, Hoskyns and Davey concluded that the rationalist attempt is really impossible; no matter how far back we push our inquiries behind the Gospels in the hope of discovering an earlier picture of Jesus, we can never come to a stage when we reach a perfectly ordinary, human Jesus. Right from the start there is something different, something "messianic" about him.[1] Moreover, the verdict that can be passed on nineteenth-century Gospel research can also be passed on much of the research into the life of Jesus in the twentieth century,[2] except that now the bias is existentialist rather than rationalist.

---

[1]E.C. Hoskyns and F.N. Davey, *The Riddle of the New Testament* (London: Faber and Faber, 1931).
[2]Chronicled by J.M. Robinson, *A New Quest of the Historical Jesus* (London: SCM, 1959).

Although the search for the historical Jesus faces these difficulties, it cannot be ruled out as improper. But two things must be carefully distinguished. One is the attempt to explore the historical basis that lies behind the Gospels; the other is the attempt to write a biography of Jesus. The latter is impossible because, as we have seen, the Gospels do not provide us with the necessary evidence; and also because, as has just been argued, the historian is in danger of rewriting the story of Jesus in terms of his own presuppositions.

It is, however, both legitimate and possible to explore the historical basis of the Gospels. The theological legitimacy of the task is demonstrated by the writings of Luke who made it his purpose to give Theophilus, and all like him, certainty regarding the message of the church. He did this by presenting his Gospel in historical style, producing an orderly account that, he believed, would bring conviction to his readers. It is true that only Luke has voiced this specific aim, but though the other evangelists do not present a statement of their aims, they appear to have shared this purpose. John has recorded eyewitness testimony in order to lead his readers to belief; the comment on the evidence in John 19:35 is no doubt meant to apply more widely throughout the Gospel. To some extent the Gospel of Mark may be trying to deal with the historical question: "Why did the Jews not acknowledge Jesus as the Messiah?" and to answer it by showing that Jesus made no public claim to messiahship before his trial. Similarly, some of the material in Matthew's account of the resurrection appearances is meant to refute skeptical suggestions that the body of Jesus was stolen away from the tomb. We are entitled to continue to work in the same direction and to examine the historical grounds for the historical reliability of the account.

The modern reader will, however, demand more from the historian than has been provided by the evangelists. The Gospels must be subjected to patient historical analysis and the historical probability of the various episodes recorded must be carefully assessed. This is a task of great difficulty, and though it would be a proper concern of the present essay, it cannot be carried out satisfactorily within the brief space available.[3]

2. *The pattern to be followed.* In the NT we have four different presentations of Jesus. What is the modern Christian to do when faced by this variety of models to follow? Should he follow the example of Tatian who wove the four accounts into one in his *Diatessaron* (c. A.D. 150)? Or should he follow Marcion who chose one Gospel as being the right one for his particular situation (and for his highly unorthodox doctrinal standpoint) and consigned the rest to the trash basket? Neither course has ever commended itself to the Christian church as a whole. In the beginning it was certainly possible for a church to exist on one Gospel but in God's providence this was only a temporary stage that, as Marcion unwittingly demonstrated, could not be a final solution.

Marcion's course is certainly to be eschewed, since the church of today is bound by the existence of the canon. (See THE CANON OF THE NEW TESTAMENT, pp. 631 ff.) Indeed, it was dissatisfaction with the position of Marcion that led the church to delineate the canon with greater precision, and this historical response to Marcion is by no means to be set aside.

Such a procedure as that of Tatian, though much more plausible, is also of doubtful validity, since it inevitably submerges some of the distinctives of the four Gospels in the

---

[3]Cf. I.H. Marshall, *I Believe in the Historical Jesus* (London: Hodder and Stoughton, 1977; Grand Rapids: Eerdmans, 1977).

effort to combine them. It represents a compromise between four complementary pictures and forces a Figure who is too great to be bound within the confines of any one of the four Gospels to be in effect bound within the confines of a fifth. Nevertheless, something like this has to be attempted. For, after all, there is only one Jesus, though there are four portraits, and somehow the one Jesus must appear at the end of the operation. The Gospels do overlap to a considerable extent, and it is recognizably the same Jesus who appears in them all.

The course we will try to follow, therefore, is to put the various accounts together, so that their corporate and individual testimonies may stand together. This may not be entirely satisfactory, but it may be doubted whether we have any other choice in the matter.

3. *The Gospels and the modern world.* One further consideration enters in at this point to complicate the task and yet provide a further guideline for it. The writer of this article lives in Scotland in the twentieth century; he has had a particular education, inherited a particular culture, and looks out on life from his own particular times. He has to present the Gospel to a modern audience. His aim must be to write about Jesus in such a way that people of today will come to faith in him. It is impossible for him to escape from this time-conditioned environment. Any writer's picture of Jesus is inevitably slanted toward a particular audience and affected by the situation and outlook of the writer.

It was the same in the NT period itself. The various writers interpreted the tradition and re-presented it. On any view of Gospel origins and interrelationships, the evangelists recorded the same incidents and sayings in different ways, quite apart from discarding some of the things their predecessors thought important and adding other material that had seemed less important to them. There was fresh interpretation of Jesus in the early church, carried out under the guidance of the Spirit.[4]

We in our day must inevitably follow suit. Not that we are called to rewrite the Gospels in any way. They retain permanent validity as the inspired accounts of the life of Jesus and they continue to speak to people of every age and culture. But we have to do all we can to make their message plain to our generation. We can do this with a good conscience because the NT itself points us in this direction. We cannot claim the infallible guidance of the Spirit to direct our labors in the way he directed the evangelists. Yet we can in a more general way claim his help as we preach and teach Jesus. Our efforts will be imperfect; they will also be time-bound and will need to be discarded insofar as they prove to be inadequate. But even so, the task must be attempted. Few sermons reach the status of being written and preserved for the benefit of posterity, and some that have done so have hardly deserved it. But countless sermons have acted in their brief oral existence as vehicles of the Word of God and have communicated spiritual life to their hearers as the Spirit worked through them (cf. 1 Thess 2:13). What is true of the sermon can also be true of the written presentation of Jesus.

Although it is impossible to discuss here how this contemporizing of the story is to be carried out, we can at least point to the guidelines provided by the way in which the individual evangelists have worked in the NT. One of them (Mark) writes in a rather rough literary style, vivid and arresting, concealing theological profundity. There is room today for a simple presentation of Jesus in language and thought forms that will appeal to the humblest reader with no intellectual pretensions. Another (Luke) is written in the

---

[4]Cf. E. Schweizer, *Jesus* (London: SCM, 1971).

style of a history book to capture the more intellectual reader who wants to see Jesus as a historical person. Yet another (Matthew) is written for the members of the church who want a clear summary of the teaching of Jesus as their guide and source of direction. The fourth (John) is written by a man who begins philosophically and speaks a language full of theological depth and yet somehow manages at the same time to be simple and comprehensible to the uneducated and plainest of readers. The Gospels can speak to men and women of all kinds and in all situations and they point the way for our presentation: to be simple and yet to offer the fullness of the divine revelation in Jesus.

II. The Historical Framework

A. *The Environment of Jesus*

Elsewhere in this volume there is a description of the world in which Jesus lived (see THE CULTURAL AND POLITICAL SETTING OF THE NEW TESTAMENT pp. 483–498). There is also an assessment of the literary character of the four Gospels in which Jesus' ministry is recorded (see THE BIBLE AS LITERATURE, pp. 129–139). It is not necessary, therefore, in this article to describe the first-century background of the Gospels. Instead, the reader is referred to the articles just mentioned for essential information so that the message of Jesus may be appreciated against its own background and also that the presentation of the gospel in the setting of the twentieth century may take account of both the differences and the continuity between the past and present.[5]

Nor is it necessary to discuss here the character of the Gospels. The present writer accepts the hypothesis that Mark is the earliest Gospel, utilized by Matthew and Luke in the composition of their Gospels, and that, in addition to their own peculiar sources of information, Matthew and Luke shared access to a common tradition of sayings of Jesus ("Q"). The Gospel of John appears to be independent of the other three, but incorporates traditions related to those used by them. (See THE HISTORICAL AND LITERARY CRITICISM OF THE NEW TESTAMENT, pp. 437–456.)[6]

B. *Chronology*

The precise dates of Jesus' life are unknown, a feature he shares with many other famous men in the ancient world. Both Matthew and Luke place his birth before the death of Herod the Great (4 B.C.), and it was probably not long before it. What looks like a more precise date is implied by Luke's association of the birth of Jesus with a census conducted while Quirinius was governor of Syria (Luke 2:1), but Quirinius was governor *after* the death of Herod and made his census in A.D. 6. Luke appears to be referring to an earlier census that cannot be certainly dated and possibly to some earlier position Quirinius held in the Middle East.[7]

A better datum is given in Luke 3:1, 2, where the call of John the Baptist to commence his prophetic ministry is dated in the fifteenth year of the Emperor Tiberius. There is more than one possible way of reckoning the regnal years of an emperor, but the most

---

[5]Cf. J.D.M. Derrett, *Jesus' Audience* (London: Darton, Longman and Todd, 1973).

[6]Cf. also D. Guthrie, *New Testament Introduction*, 3rd ed. (London: Inter-Varsity Press, 1970); R.P. Martin, *New Testament Foundations*, vol. 1 (Exeter: Paternoster, 1975).

[7]F.F. Bruce, NBD, pp. 203, 1069.

usual modern estimate of the fifteenth year of Tiberius is A.D. 27–28. It may be presumed that the ministry of Jesus began not long after this, and that at this point he was "about thirty years old" (Luke 3:23), a round figure, which may reflect Luke's uncertainty about the exact date of Jesus' birth.

The date of the Crucifixion (and hence the duration of Jesus' ministry) is also controversial. A majority of modern scholars appear to favor A.D. 30, but the year 33 can also be defended.[8]

There is no internal evidence enabling us to fix with certainty the length of the ministry of Jesus, but John indicates that it contained more than one Passover (John 2:13; 6:4; 11:55), and this confirms the general impression that it lasted for two or three years, but hardly much longer. In any event, it was a short period to have such a world-shattering effect.

The difficulty of establishing a detailed chronology demonstrates the impossibility of trying to write a minute account of the life of Jesus. But this does not put the basic historicity of Jesus in doubt. Though works attempting to prove that Jesus never existed still appear—some of them by scholars highly competent in fields other than ancient history, the evidence is overwhelmingly against such theories. The rise of Christianity is historical and cannot be explained without some adequate cause. To suppose, therefore, that it started for some unknown reason and then created its own eponymous founder is to stretch credulity beyond the breaking point. If Jesus had never existed, we should have to postulate the existence of somebody remarkably like him, having the same name and living at the same time, in order to account for the rise of Christianity.

C. The Beginning

Mark begins his Gospel with the appearance of John the Baptist (Mark 1:1–11), and the other Gospels also regard this as the formal beginning of the events they record (see also Acts 1:22; 10:37), since the earlier material in them obviously has the form of a prologue.

But all four evangelists are eager to show that what they describe has its beginnings outside this world in eternity past. Mark does this by claiming at the outset that his book relates the beginning of the gospel of Jesus Christ, "the Son of God" (Mark 1:1; the omission of the phrase in some MSS is probably accidental). In this way he claims that his book is about One who is more than man. Then he announces that what happened took place in accordance with the prophecy in the OT of the coming of one who would prepare the way of the Lord. If John the Baptist appeared in fulfillment of this prophecy regarding the end time, it follows that the ministry of Jesus for which John made preparation must be seen as something that belonged to the age-old plan of God and as the supreme moment in the coming of God's final act in history. The story is thus to be seen *sub specie aeternitatis,* and Mark is warning his readers to be alert to the full significance of what he has to relate.

In a similar way John makes the same point by interweaving the story of John the Baptist and the account of the incarnation of the Word, the self-expression of God, who had been with God before time began. So his Gospel tells us of the earthly manifestation of One who came from God in order to reveal God and to bring humanity the opportunity of becoming the children of God (John 1:1–18).

---

[8]G. Ogg, NBD, pp. 223–225; H.W. Hoehner, *Chronological Aspects of the Life of Christ,* rev. ed. (Grand Rapids: Zondervan, 1978).

Luke also intertwines the stories of John and of Jesus, but in his Gospel the theme is the unusual birth of both of them, so that both may be seen as the special messengers of God—John as the prophet who prepares the way for the Messiah, and Jesus as the Son of God miraculously born to the virgin Mary. The story is replete with poetic imagery that brings out the significance of Jesus as the Savior, who was promised in the OT and who surpasses in glory and power the potentates of the world. The essential historicity of the account need not be doubted, even if some features of it are presented poetically and symbolically.[9]

In the prologue to Matthew (chs. 1 and 2) John the Baptist does not appear, and all the light falls on Jesus who bears the names of "Savior" and "Immanuel" ("God with us") (Matt 1:21, 23). He stands in the line of descent from David as the Messiah, and his coming arouses both homage and hostility on the part of the great men of the world (Matt 2; cf. Luke 2:34–35).

In every case, however, the real beginning of the story is the appearance of the herald who warns people to prepare for imminent judgment. John the Baptist preached repentance from sin to the people and told them to express their sincerity by submitting to a symbolic cleansing with water—something extremely hurtful to the pride of Jews, who insisted on baptizing non-Jews when they were converted to Judaism—lest they face one day a cleansing by fire. Those who were cleansed in this way were called to live a life befitting their repentance and were promised that they would receive the cleansing of the Holy Spirit from the coming One (Matt 3:1–12; Mark 1:1–8; Luke 3:1–18; John 1:1–34; John is less concerned with the Baptist's ritual of baptism and more with his self-effacing witness to the coming One than the other Gospels are).

The message of John the Baptist has often been thought of as a negative one, for it so strongly emphasizes judgment to come. But Luke calls it "good news" (Luke 3:18), and the force of this phrase should not be weakened. It was an announcement of God's promised intervention in history and thus deeply significant. John foretold the coming of Jesus. This was great good news indeed. And if John emphasized judgment, the sequel showed that he was justified in doing so, for Jesus also taught that God was offering his generation its last chance.

Admittedly, when Jesus did come on the scene, it was not in the way that might have been expected by a literal interpreter of John's words. There were no "fireworks" when he came from the obscure village of Nazareth where he had been brought up (Luke 2:39, 51) and where he began his work.

He came to where John was baptizing and sought baptism from him, just as many others had done. We should probably regard his submission to baptism by water as an act of identification with the people he came to save. If baptism represented the judgment of God upon sin, Jesus was later to identify his own death as a baptism so that his experience at the River Jordan could afterwards be seen to have been a foreshadowing of it (Mark 10:38–39; Luke 12:50). But for Jesus the event was also more than this. It became the occasion of a unique spiritual experience (symbolized by the voice from heaven and the descending "dove" [Matt 3:16–17; Mark 1:10–11, Luke 3:21–22]) in which God addressed him as his Son and poured out his Spirit on him; it was the divine acknowledgment of his mission and the empowering of him for it (Matt 3:13–17; John

---

[9]J.G. Machen, *The Virgin Birth of Christ* (Grand Rapids: Baker, 1967); J. McHugh, *The Mother of Jesus in the New Testament* (London: Darton, Longman and Todd, 1975); contra M. Dibelius, *Botschaft und Geschichte*, vol. 1 (Tübingen: Mohr, 1953), pp. 1–78.

1:32–34). The experience thus went far beyond anything that happened to the other people and showed that the new era of the Spirit had come (cf. Isa 11:1–3; 42:1; 61:1–3). Jesus was now anointed for his task (Acts 10:38) and in due course, but not till after his resurrection, he would fulfill John's prophecy by pouring out the Spirit on his disciples.

For Jesus, the activity of John was of immense significance. He regarded John as the greatest man who ever lived; he was a prophet, and yet more than a prophet, for he was the final messenger sent to prepare for the coming of God to his people (Luke 7:24–28). So John could be regarded as belonging with Moses and the prophets to the time of preparation and at the same time as marking the advent of the coming of the kingdom (Matt 11:12–13; Luke 16:16). He stood between the old age of promise and the new era of fulfillment. He was indeed a great man; yet it was more important for people to be members of the kingdom of God than to be the greatest of the prophets (Matt 11:11).

If the story of Jesus' baptism establishes his relation to God at the outset of his work, the immediately following story of the temptation in the wilderness (Matt 4:1–11; Mark 1:12–13; Luke 4:1–13) sets out his relationship to Satan and establishes the other super-natural dimension of his ministry. From the outset the work of Jesus took place against a background of Satanic opposition intended to deflect him from his course and to destroy him. But in the power of the Spirit he was able to overcome the opposition and commence his ministry. Jesus could speak of Satan in a figurative manner (Luke 10:18), and it may be that his very real experience of temptation by Satan has been to some extent presented in dramatic fashion; to say this is, of course, in no way to deny its objective reality.

D. *The Course of Jesus' Ministry*

According to the first three Gospels, Jesus commenced his work in Galilee after John the Baptist had been imprisoned by Herod Antipas. In the Gospel of Mark his ministry is basically located in the area around the Sea of Galilee, though there are accounts of travels to other places east of Galilee and northward toward Tyre. Mark evidently saw a turning point in the work of Jesus after a "retreat" with his disciples to Caesarea Philippi in the tetrarchy of Herod Philip: here came the recognition by Peter that Jesus was the Messiah and the first attempt by Jesus to forewarn the disciples of his suffering and death, followed by his transfiguration in which he appeared to three of his closest friends in heavenly glory and a heavenly voice confirmed his divine vocation (Mark 8:27–9:13). Soon after this, Jesus left Galilee and made his way south toward Jerusalem where he spent his last days. We are not given any detailed itinerary of his work in Galilee, and the precise order of events varies considerably within the same general pattern in Matthew and Luke. Matthew's account is closest to Mark's, but Luke lays more stress on the fact that Galilee saw the beginning of Jesus' work and states that Jesus worked in Judea as a whole (Luke 4:44; contra Mark 1:39). Luke also expands the story of Jesus' journey from Galilee to Jerusalem at considerable length.

In John, however, the picture is markedly different. Here Jesus began his work in the south, in the area where John baptized, and he did so before John's arrest (John 3:24). Then Jesus moved to Galilee (John 4:3; 4:43–54; 6:1–7:13; cf. earlier 1:43–2:12), but he appeared a number of times in Jerusalem before his last, fatal visit (John 5; 7:14–10:39; 11:1–53; 12:1–2), and there is also a report of his spending some time east of the Jordan before that last visit (John 10:40–42; 11:54–57; cf. Mark 10:1).

It is a puzzle to know how these two different representations are best to be reconciled with each other. The evidence of John is to be respected, and it is perfectly possible that

Jesus did work in Judea before the arrest of the Baptist, but the real beginning of his work was in Galilee when he was independent of John. The tradition that Jesus' main support came from Galilee guarantees that his chief area of work was in the north. Yet it is also probable that as a loyal Jew Jesus would have visited Jerusalem several times on the occasion of the annual festivals; the account of his final visit and various sayings (Luke 13:34) make better sense if Jesus was already acquainted with Jerusalem.

But it is difficult to be more certain than this, since the evangelists were not concerned to provide a detailed itinerary of the ministry of Jesus. What mattered—and still matters—is what Jesus said and did, not the order in which it all happened, or even where it all happened. Nevertheless, the evangelists do seem to have seen some significance in the rough outline of what Jesus did. There is something of a contrast between Galilee and Jerusalem, the former as the place that saw the light of the gospel (Matt 4:12–16) and the latter as the place that crowned its opposition to the prophets by murdering Jesus (Luke 13:34–35). Jesus himself, despite his birthplace, was regarded as a Galilean (John 7:52), more particularly as a native of Nazareth (Matt 2:23). While he found popular support among the people of Galilee and Jerusalem, it was the rulers who primarily instigated his death, and they were identified with Jerusalem. Nevertheless, we should not underestimate the degree of misunderstanding and opposition Jesus experienced in Galilee. It may be that his experience after feeding the multitude, when the people recognized him as prophet and wanted to make him king (John 6:14–15), hastened Jesus' departure from Galilee for fear that he might be associated with a nationalistic uprising. It was in this situation that he was particularly concerned that his disciples should come to realize who he really was.

III. The Message of the Kingdom of God

A. *Jesus and the People*

We can distinguish three main groups of people with whom Jesus came into contact, though the boundaries between them are somewhat fluid: the crowds, his disciples, and the people who were opposed to him. Although the different evangelists do not use identical terminology for each of these groups, it is usually quite clear which group is in mind. The first and most obvious aspect of Jesus' work was his activity among the people at large, for it was out of this that there arose the groups of people who sided for and against him. This activity had two aspects.

1. *Preaching and teaching.* On the one hand, there was the spoken word of Jesus. Sometimes this is referred to as preaching (*kērussō;* e.g., Mark 1:14, 38–39), at other times as teaching (*didaskō;* e.g., Mark 1:21–22; 2:13). Although it has sometimes been said that Jesus preached to the crowds and taught the disciples, in fact both words are used of both audiences. Rather, the two words bring out the point that Jesus' proclamation had a teaching content. When Jesus appealed to the people, it was on the basis of a presentation of facts. As a preacher, his task was to teach the people what God gave him to say. Luke uses a third word to describe this activity: "to preach the good news" (*euangelizō;* Luke 4:18, 43; cf. Matt 11:5).

Jesus could thus be regarded as a teacher (Mark 5:35; 9:17; 12:14) or, to use the Jewish word, a rabbi (Mark 9:5; 10:51; 11:21; 14:45), though he had not had the formal education of a rabbi (John 7:15). But the people recognized that he spoke with a confidence not shared by their own teachers (Mark 1:22). A more adequate designation for him might be that of prophet (Luke 7:16; 9:8, 19; John 4:19; 6:14), and this was how some of the people were prepared to characterize him (Mark 6:15; 8:28). He appeared like one of the OT prophets, and the parallel between his activity and that of Elijah did not escape the evangelists. This impression was confirmed by his activity.

2. *The mighty works.* On the other hand, there was the action of Jesus. He performed mighty works in healing the sick and casting demons out of those afflicted by them. Whatever modern medicine might have to say about the diagnosis and cure of those Jesus treated (and some of them at least appear to have been cases of psychosomatic disorders), to the people of his time he certainly appeared as a physician (Luke 4:23) able to cure by his word or touch. Although there are scholars who doubt the historicity of the miracles, usually because of a refusal to admit the possibility of the supernatural but also because of the nature of the historical attestation,[10] the case that Jesus actually wrought cures and exorcisms is strong.[11] Had he been unable to do so, he would not have been a serious rival to the many holy men and wonder-workers of his day. In a world that knew the reality of demonic possession, he brought sanity and peace (Mark 5:15). The Gospels claim that he had control over the forces of nature (Mark 4:35–41; 6:30–44, 45–52; 8:1–10) and that he could even raise the dead (Mark 5:35–43; Luke 7:11–17; John 11). These mighty works were an integral part of his ministry; his preaching and his healings belonged together (Matt 4:23; 11:5).

B. *The Era of Fulfillment*

What was the significance of Jesus' activity? It is continually presented in the Gospels as being the fulfillment of prophecy. This is especially clear in Matthew, where a series of quotations is given to show that Jesus fulfilled the promises made in the OT (Matt 1:22–23; 2:5–6, 15, 17–18, 23; 3:3; 4:15–16; 8:17; 11:10; 12:17–21; 13:14–15, 35; 21:4–5, 42; 26:31; 27:9–10). It is also evident in the other evangelists (e.g., John 12:37–41). In bringing out this point the evangelists were simply underlining the attitude of Jesus himself, who was conscious of following the path laid down for him by God (cf. the frequent use of "must" on his lips, e.g., Mark 8:31) and who saw his mighty works and teaching as a fulfillment of the promises of God concerning the coming of a new age (Matt 11:5; cf. Isa 35:5–6) and of God's messenger for that age (Luke 4:18–19; cf. Isa 61:1–3). The ministry of Jesus brought to an end the time of waiting for God to act (Mark 1:15) and signaled the arrival of the new era of fulfillment, the age of the kingdom of God (Matt 11:11–12; Luke 16:16).

Jesus, therefore, was to be seen as the final agent of God. As a prophet, he acted as God's messenger. But he was regarded as more than just another prophet. He was the final prophet, one like Moses who would usher in a new era of redemption (Acts 3:22; cf. John 6:14; 7:40). If John the Baptist could be regarded as fulfilling the role of the returning Elijah (Matt 17:10–13; but Jesus also showed traits of Elijah: Luke 4:25; 7:11–17; 9:51), it followed that Jesus was to be equated with the Lord himself (cf. Mal 3:1 with 4:5). It could truly be said that in the activity of Jesus God was coming to help his people (Luke 7:16). The course of Jesus' ministry was to show that he held a unique place as God's representative.

---

[10]E. and M.-L. Keller, *Miracles in Dispute* (London: SCM, 1969).

[11]H. van der Loos, *The Miracles of Jesus* (Leiden: Brill, 1965).

C. The Kingdom of God

1. *God's saving action.* But it was not primarily about himself or his own claims that Jesus came to preach, though the authority with which he spoke and the way he acted inevitably raised the question of his relationship to his own message and to the God who had sent him. If we want one phrase to sum up the message of Jesus, we cannot do better than follow the example of Mark who epitomizes it as the coming of the kingdom of God (Mark 1:15; cf. Luke 4:43); in Matthew (e.g., 4:17) the phrase "kingdom of God" is normally replaced by "kingdom of heaven," which has the same meaning. Jesus announced the rule of God—for "kingdom" is usually to be understood in an active sense—and told his disciples to pray for its coming (Matt 6:10).

Now of course God had been the ruler of the world from its creation, and the Jews spoke of him as the great king (Matt 5:34–35). But what Jesus had in mind was the promise that one day God would set up his rule in a new, powerful, and visible way, as promised by the prophets, and reign over men in person or through his appointed agent, the Messiah. This hope was associated with the end of time and the establishment of the eternal order when all that is evil and time-bound will pass away. Jesus announced that God's rule was near (Mark 1:15; Luke 10:9, 11) and that it had actually arrived (Luke 11:20). But however near Jesus may have portrayed the end of the present world-order and the establishment of the heavenly order as being, it seems plain that he was not thinking of this when he announced that the rule of God was near. He meant that after the long period of waiting since OT times, the rule of God was near in time to the people of his generation and that it was near in space to those who heard the message proclaimed by himself and his disciples. We should, therefore, distinguish between two (or possibly more) comings of the kingdom, which have been aptly described as "fulfillment" and "consummation." In the ministry of Jesus himself the OT promises regarding the kingdom were fulfilled, so that the kingdom can truly be said to have come at that time. But there is also a future consummation of the kingdom when the action of God fully begun in Jesus is brought to open completion. What God did in a veiled manner in Jesus must be openly manifested in due course.[12]

The rule of God means the establishment of his dominion over men and the world instead of the rule of Satan who holds men in his sway (cf. Luke 22:53; John 12:31). Thus the ministry of Jesus, so far from being "a peaceful pastoral wherein the serene wisdom of the Teacher accorded well with the flowers and birds of Galilee" turns out to be total war, with "the strong Son of God, armed with his Father's power, spear-heading the attack against the devil and all his works, and calling men to decide on whose side of the battle they will be."[13]

It is clear that something more than a message about God is involved here. Jesus' mighty works now fall into their proper place as the means of the restoration of God's rule in the world, removing pain and sickness and substituting health and well-being, curbing the unruly elements (Mark 4:39) and toppling Satan from his throne. Jesus regarded himself as setting men and women free from the power of Satan, both physical (Luke 13:16) and spiritual (Luke 8:2). And to those who had fallen under the sway of evil he announced divine forgiveness (Mark 2:5, 10; Luke 7:47–48). He called people to a new life in which they love God and one another (Mark 12:28–34; Luke 10:25–28). So

---

[12]G.E. Ladd, *Jesus and the Kingdom* (London: SPCK, 1966); R. Schnackenburg, *God's Rule and Kingdom* (Freiburg and London: Herder and Nelson, 1963).

[13]A.M. Hunter, *Introducing New Testament Theology* (London: SCM, 1957), pp. 17–18.

God's rule means his activity through Jesus as the Savior (Matt 1:21; Luke 1:77) and is effected through Jesus' work and words and also supremely through his death as a ransom for the people, because the kingdom of God could not come to its consummation except by the suffering and resurrection of Jesus (cf. Matt 26:28; John 1:29).

2. *The judgment of God.* What is fundamentally wrong with man is his sinfulness, expressed in rebellion against God.[14] But for the most part, people are blind to their true state, not because of an intellectual lack but because of a stubborn blindness of heart (Mark 3:5; 6:52; 8:17). It was thus inevitable that Jesus' message should contain an element of warning, telling his bearers that failure to accept the rule of God leads to bitter consequences in this life and to rejection by God in the end. Since Jesus' message was directed primarily to the Jews, his warnings were largely directed to the people who thought that as the descendants of Abraham they were free from the judgment of God, no matter how they behaved. But Jesus warned that cities that rejected his message and knowingly refused God's call would fare worse in the judgment than ignorant pagans; Gentiles would find their way to God's heavenly table, while unbelieving Jews would be cast out of his presence (Matt 8:11–12; 10:15; 11:20–24). And Jerusalem, which was to crown its murders of the prophets with the crucifixion of Jesus, would find itself deprived of the Messiah's presence (Luke 13:34–35) and laid waste. Rejection of the message of Jesus would lead to rejection by God on the day of judgment (cf. Luke 12:8–9), and people should pay due heed to the warning, for one day it would be too late to do anything about it (Matt 7:21–23; 25:1–13).

Men and women should therefore strive to come under the rule of God at any cost (Matt 6:33; Mark 9:43–48), and should do so despite the possibility of suffering persecution for their faith (Matt 5:10). Let them recognize their poverty and need (Matt 5:3; Luke 6:20) and respond to the message. To do this meant a fundamental reorientation in life, comparable with becoming a child all over again and even with being born afresh (Matt 18:3; John 3:3, 5). Negatively, it could be described as repentance, which is more than feeling sorry for sin and is rather a turning away from it to a new life (Matt 11:20–21; 12:41; Mark 1:15; 6:12; Luke 13:3, 5; 15:7, 10; 16:30). Positively, it can be described as faith, though the idea of trusting in Jesus himself as Savior belongs more to the thought of the early church (Mark 1:15; 9:42; Luke 8:12–15; John 1:12). The thought of faith in Jesus is especially characteristic of John's Gospel. But with this concept, as with others throughout the fourth Gospel, it is hard to be sure how far the wording represents what Jesus actually said and the way John has brought out the significance of Jesus' person and teaching for his readers. But if the actual wording "faith in Jesus" is rare, the *idea* is very much present, because the fundamental call of Jesus was that men should respond to his call "Follow me" (Matt 8:18–22; Mark 2:14; 8:34; 10:21) by becoming his disciples, accepting his teaching, and sharing his way of life.[15]

It was this that the rich young ruler was unwilling to do. His failure was not simply that, despite his endeavor to keep the commandments, he worshiped his wealth and could not give it up; ultimately he was unwilling to become a disciple (Mark 10:17–22). In so doing he failed to recognize the sheer joy that comes to those who discover the rule of God (Matt 13:44–46) and the rich blessings of spirit that come to those who accept that rule (Matt 5:3–12).

---

[14]W.G. Kümmel, *Man in the New Testament* (London: Epworth, 1963).
[15]TDNT 4:415–461.

3. *Discipleship.* We do not know how many people responded to the message of Jesus by becoming his disciples. But from a very early point in his ministry he was surrounded by a group of followers. Some of them had been followers of John the Baptist, who also had his circle of adherents and helpers (Mark 2:18; 6:29; Luke 11:1; John 1:35; 3:25). Out of a wider group of adherents Jesus chose twelve men to be his helpers in his ministry (Mark 3:13–19; 6:7–13). Yet the term *disciple* was not confined to this small number. Luke knows of a wider group of seventy-two (possibly seventy: Luke 10:1, 17 and mg.) who were also sent out on a mission by Jesus, and even this larger number did not exhaust the total. While, therefore, we can see most clearly what discipleship meant from the particular case of the Twelve who literally left all and followed Jesus, they were representative of a wider group for whom "following Jesus" was no less real but did not involve accompanying him on his travels (Mark 5:18–20). This is only what might have been expected. It would have been impossible for all who responded to the message of the kingdom to abandon their responsibilities and become part of an unmanageably large band of traveling evangelists.

The group who traveled with Jesus was probably not constant in composition; it included others than the twelve men—in particular a number of women who looked after the more domestic aspects of the mission (Mark 15:40–41; Luke 8:1–3). For women to receive religious recognition in this way was highly unusual. The typical rabbi of the time would have shunned having women as pupils, and hence it is not surprising that the first participation of women in the work of Jesus was confined to traditional women's tasks. To have taken the further step of employing them as evangelists at this point might have been so avant-garde as to scuttle the whole enterprise. Yet that step did follow later (Acts 18:26; 21:8–9; Rom 16:3–4). It is worth noting that, whatever other slanders were made against Jesus, he and his disciples were never, so far as we know, accused of improper relations with women. Indeed, Jesus was raising womanhood to a new status.

The list of names of the twelve disciples varies from Gospel to Gospel (Matt 10:2–4; Mark 3:16–19; Luke 6:14–16), possibly because some of the disciples, like Simon *alias* Peter or Cephas, had more than one name. Whether they were called "apostles" at this stage is a moot point (Luke 6:13), but the essence of apostleship—being sent out to preach and to bear witness to Jesus—was certainly present. The task of the Twelve was confined to preaching to the Jews, just as Jesus himself, despite some notable exceptions, directed his ministry to the Jews and did not go out of his way to make contact with Gentiles (Matt 10:5; 15:24; but see Matt 8:5–13; 15:21–28; possibly 8:28–34; Luke 9:52–56; John 4:1–42; 12:20–22). After his death it was different (Matt 28:19; Luke 24:47).

IV. Jesus' Teaching for His Disciples

It was to his disciples that Jesus gave much of his teaching—sometimes when they were alone, but often in the presence of the crowds so that the people might know what was involved in discipleship (cf. Matt 5:1 with 7:28; Mark 8:34). As a result, it is not possible to draw a clear line between what Jesus said to the crowds and what he said to the disciples, though we can allocate some of his teaching with the reasonable confidence that he reserved specific topics for particular audiences.[16] It was to his disciples

---

[16]Cf. T.W. Manson, *The Teaching of Jesus,* 2nd ed. (Cambridge: Cambridge University Press, 1935); J.A. Baird, *Audience Criticism and the Historical Jesus* (Philadelphia: Westminster, 1969).

that Jesus gave his more detailed teaching on the nature of discipleship, on his own person, and on the future of the kingdom of God (cf. Mark 4:11–12). It will be significant to see how the Gospels supplement one another on the first and third of these topics.

A. The Gospel of Mark

In Mark there is very little extended teaching by Jesus. Most of his sayings in this Gospel are brief statements, often in the form of answers to questions or comments on situations. But in three places in Mark we do have more extended accounts of what he taught.

1. *The parables of Jesus.* In Mark 4 we have a brief collection of parables used by Jesus. Mark states that Jesus regularly taught the crowds by means of parables, that the parables served to conceal the message, and that Jesus gave fuller explanations of their meaning to the disciples (Mark 4:10–12, 33–34). These statements are not easy to understand, for (1) it is obvious from the rest of the Gospels that not all Jesus' public teaching was in parables and (2) the meanings of some of the parables were so clear that the audience had no difficulty understanding them. (If we today do not always find the parables easy to understand, the reason may lie not in their basic obscurity but in our twentieth-century difficulty in understanding teaching given in a first-century oriental setting.) Mark's statement in 4:11 should probably be taken as applying to the whole of Jesus' ministry and not just to the parables, for it means that men needed to show faith if they were to understand the message. In other words, "understand" may mean more than intellectual apprehension. Therefore, though the message of the parable of the good Samaritan (Luke 10:30–37) is perfectly obvious on an intellectual level, it remains just a story to those who are not prepared to let it change their lives. This is probably the message of the parable of the sower (Mark 4:3–9) which deals with the way we ought to hear parables and describes the different responses people make to the teaching of Jesus. Similarly, the sayings about light (Mark 4:21–25) may refer to the need for hearers to understand the message if it is to be of any profit to them; if its point remains obscure, it is as useless as a lamp that is covered up. By teaching in parables and by refusing to reveal his own person openly, Jesus gave people the opportunity to make up their own minds whether they would respond to his message and see in him the One sent by God. His own work was perhaps ambiguous to the people, but to those with faith what appeared tiny and insignificant would grow and become great just as surely as a seed planted in the ground would grow and become great (Mark 4:26–32).

2. *The coming of the end.* Passing over the second main piece of teaching in Mark 7 about the true nature of defilement (discussed on p. 538), we come to Mark 13 where Jesus announces the imminent destruction of the temple in Jerusalem and then spells out to his disciples in greater detail what lay ahead. Here the teaching relates to the failure of the Jews to respond to Jesus' message and the consequent judgment of God on their place of worship, which was no longer fulfilling its appointed function (cf. Mark 11:11–18). In the background lies the prophecy in Daniel 9:27; 11:31; 12:11, partially fulfilled in 168 B.C. (1 Macc 1:54) and now to be fulfilled again. There would be intense suffering for the Jews and also suffering for the disciples in a time of persecution and breakdown of law and order. The rise of false prophets would be an especially insidious danger. But the period of tribulation would end with the revelation of the Son of man, the One sent by God to gather together God's people and establish his eternal kingdom

(cf. Dan 7:13, 14). In this situation the disciples would need to be continually prayerful and watchful so that they would not succumb to persecution or be misled by falsehood.

The problems of interpretation in this chapter are great and arise partly from the juxtaposition of the destruction of the temple with the coming of the Son of man. The imminence of the end is taught throughout the NT, possibly as a result of prophetic foreshortening and certainly because the end *is* imminent even if it appears to be delayed.[17]

B. The Gospel of Matthew

In the Gospels of Matthew and Luke there is much more of the teaching of Jesus, some of it drawn from a tradition known to both evangelists. In Matthew this material and other sayings of Jesus peculiar to this Gospel have been largely organized into a series of five discourses on the pattern of those in Mark. Probably, however, as the different order of the sayings in Luke indicates, they were handed down in smaller units, and it is Matthew who has gathered the teaching together thematically.

Thus Matthew 13 contains the parables in Mark 4 and more besides. There are the parables of the treasure hidden in the field and of the pearl—parables that stress the joy of discovering the kingdom and the need to make any sacrifice to gain it. Here too we have the parable of the leaven, apparently similar in meaning to that of the mustard seed. Like the parable of the sower, the parables of the tares and the dragnet reflect the mixed response of people to the gospel and warn of the judgment to come.

1) *The Sermon on the Mount.* The characteristic tone of Matthew is set by the Sermon on the Mount (Matt 5–7), a fuller version of the teaching of Jesus given in Luke 6:20–49. It describes the basic character of the people who long for the message of the kingdom and respond to it. We see that acceptance of the message leads to the promise of future blessings from God, the enjoyment of which can already be anticipated in this life. It also leads to a new moral and spiritual outlook (Matt 5:3–12) and to a readiness to bear witness to the world despite the threat of persecution (Matt 5:10–12, 13–16). Matthew gives in detail the teaching of Jesus about the OT law. He shows that Jesus was concerned with real obedience to the will of God, obedience going beyond that of the Pharisees. In a series of antitheses (Matt 5:17–48) Jesus heightens the OT law by applying it to the inward attitudes of men and so rendering parts of the external code redundant for those who obey God from their hearts. Ideally the members of the kingdom need no legal sanctions, because they will show real love for all people and so reflect the character of God their Father.

Their attitude to God, expressed in worship, will be both simple and modest, free from the pride that makes religious duties unspiritual because they are done for the prestige involved (Matt 6:1–18).

Embedded in this section is the prayer Jesus gave his disciples as a form of words to be repeated and a pattern to be followed in their own extempore prayers. It expresses the longing they should feel for the establishment of the rule of God and their dependence on God for the essentials of physical and spiritual life. This second part of the prayer is developed in Jesus' teaching about freedom from anxiety and trust in God to provide for daily needs (Matt 6:19–34)—teaching often misunderstood to mean that all people may expect God to care for their daily needs. Actually, however, it is the promise

---

17Cf. further G.R. Beasley-Murray, *Jesus and the Future* (London: Macmillan, 1954).

of God to provide in a fatherly way for the needs of the disciples. It is only the disciples who can know and address God as Father as they enter into a relationship with him similar to that which Jesus enjoyed (cf. John 20:17) and enjoy his fatherly care to the full.

So the Sermon becomes in effect a challenge to people to live according to the ethics of the kingdom, avoiding censoriousness and trusting in God. Let them not be led astray by false teaching, but let them respond to the teaching of Jesus, not merely hearing it but, above all, obeying it (Matt 7).

2) *Mission and the church.* Matthew also gives a fuller version of the teaching Jesus gave the disciples when they went out on mission (Matt 10; cf. Mark 6:7–13; Luke 10:1–16). This teaching says little about the message the disciples were to proclaim; it is much more concerned with how they were to conduct themselves, especially in the face of persecution and the rejection of their message. They are to do their work with the minimum of equipment, because disciples must trust in God to provide for them and are not in his service for material rewards. They are to be courteous and efficient in their work, not wasting time on those who will not respond. They must expect opposition and stand firm despite it, turning it into opportunities for witness. The Spirit of God will give them courage and the right words. But despite even betrayal by their own relatives, the outlook for the messengers is not uniformly gloomy; there will be those who welcome their message and show kindness to them.

In Matthew 18 we have further instructions for the disciples in their life together. Humility and forgiveness are the keynotes here, and there are strong warnings against attitudes and actions that can harm the lives of other people, particularly the young and helpless. Rather, the disciples are to imitate Jesus who is the good shepherd of the sheep (John 10) and care for those members of their group who go astray. Even when someone commits a fault against a fellow disciple, every effort is to be made to lead him to a better frame of mind, and only in an extremity is he to be debarred from the church. As God has forgiven the disciples their many great sins, so they must readily forgive one another their comparatively minor offences.

Matthew's final collection of sayings of Jesus is an enlarged version of Mark 13 to which he has added a number of Jesus' parables inculcating readiness and watchfulness during the period before the coming of the Son of man and the judgment day (Matt 24–25).

C. The Gospel of Luke

Much of the teaching of Jesus recorded in Matthew is also in Luke. Luke has used it and other teaching peculiar to his Gospel to bring out various aspects of Jesus' message he considered especially important. So Luke lays much stress on the way that Jesus justified his concern for the outcasts of society (Luke 15) and brings out clearly the nature of discipleship. He lays particular stress on the need for self-denial and readiness to face sacrifice (Luke 14:25–35; cf. Mark 8:34–38). Luke gives us the parable of the good Samaritan, a commentary on the meaning of the OT command to love one's neighbor (Luke 10:25–37; cf. Mark 12:28–34). If the emphasis here is on doing the will of God in active love (cf. Mark 3:31–35), it is striking that an incident strongly inculcating the importance of listening to Jesus as teacher follows it immediately (Luke 10:38–42). The gospel has two sides—a believing side and a behaving side—and neither can be ignored.

Luke stresses the importance of prayer. God will certainly answer prayer; he is not like a person who is unwilling to get out of bed to help a benighted traveler (Luke 11:1–13;

cf. Matt 7:7–11) or like a judge with no sense of justice; even if he seems slow to answer, the disciples must not lose heart (Luke 18:1–8). God will not hear hypocritical prayers in which people try to lay their own claims upon him. But when they say, "God have mercy on me, a sinner," it is music in his ears (Luke 18:9–14).

Finally, Luke lays stress on Jesus' warnings against being enamored of possessions (Mark 4:19; 10:17–31), for ultimately they are of no value compared with spiritual wealth (Luke 12:13–34; cf. Matt 6:19–34). The right thing to do with wealth is to use it for the benefit of the poor (Luke 11:41; 14:12–14; 16:1–15, 19–31)—a lesson modern Christians are strangely slow to apply to their own possessions. Yet there is no evidence that Jesus gave this counsel only to some of his disciples and not rather to all of them.

D. *The Gospel of John*

If the first three Gospels have to some extent systematized and rearranged the teaching of Jesus in order to adapt it to the needs of the churches—needs they specifically addressed—the fourth Gospel appears to have gone further in the same direction by interpreting Jesus' teaching to bring out its spiritual significance. If we cannot always be sure just how Jesus originally spoke to his audiences, we can be glad that the Spirit has inspired the evangelists to make his teaching relevant for their readers, not only in their time but throughout the years. But when all allowance is made for the element of interpretation in John, the main themes of the Gospel still faithfully reflect the mind of Jesus.

John reveals the sinful nature of people who live on a level lower than God intended them to and need to have their eyes opened to perceive spiritual truth (John 3:1–12). The Jews think that the OT contains the way to life, and so it does, but they refuse to come to the One to whom the OT bears witness (John 5:39–40). What they need is eternal life, "eternal life" being a phrase that in John largely replaces "the kingdom of God" (cf. Mark 10:17 with 24–25; John 3:3, 5 with 14–16). And this is received by faith in Jesus.

Much of the Gospel is concerned with the credentials of Jesus, and the nature of the witness borne to him by God and men is brought out in detail.[18] John expresses with great clarity how the mighty works done by Jesus are signs of the spiritual salvation he offers people, and he uses the great images of water, bread, light, and so on, that show Jesus as the supplier of human need.

This Gospel also emphasizes the importance of Jesus' new law of love for the disciples (John 13:34–35). Jesus anticipated the difficult time ahead after his departure and promised his disciples the help of the Holy Spirit as the Counselor (John 14:16).

It is not difficult to see that in this Gospel the significance of Jesus and his ministry is faithfully recorded. The basis of John's presentation is firmly anchored in what Jesus actually said and did, as this is confirmed independently by the other Gospels.[19]

V. Jesus' Teaching About Himself

As has already been pointed out, Jesus preached about the kingdom of God rather than chiefly about himself. Nevertheless, the question of how he thought of himself is an

---

[18]J.M. Boice, *Witness and Revelation in the Gospel of John* (Exeter: Paternoster, 1970).

[19]See, more fully, I.H. Marshall, NBD, pp. 645–652).

important one. He appears to have been remarkably reticent about himself in his public teaching. He made little use of the various titles his followers later applied to him. Consequently, many modern scholars doubt whether Jesus used any of these phrases to describe himself at all and suggest that these titles were used by the early church to bring out the claims implicit in Jesus' mission. Scholars of this persuasion point rightly to the unmistakable sense of authority to be detected behind the utterances of Jesus, to the way he acted as the One sent by God with the authority to declare the coming of his kingdom and to lay down the conditions on which men would be accepted into it, and to the way he placed his teaching alongside that of Moses. So Käsemann states: "The only category which does justice to his claim (quite independently of whether he used it himself and required it of others) is that in which his disciples themselves placed him—namely, that of the Messiah." At the same time Käsemann is quite convinced that Jesus did not understand himself to be the Messiah.[20]

We can agree with the positive side of these statements. The activity of Jesus *does* imply that he stood in a special relationship with God. But the suggestion that he himself was not conscious of being God's special emissary is wholly contrary to historical probability, and the denial that he used any titles to express this relationship does not do justice to the evidence. What is true is that Jesus did not parade who he was before the people at large. But we should distinguish between what he said to the crowds and what he taught his disciples, a distinction that is carefully preserved by Mark, who expresses what has come to be known as "the messianic secret." In the presence of the crowds Jesus deliberately veiled who he was (Mark 1:44; 3:11–12, 5:43; 9:9). And even to his disciples, to whom he spoke more fully and revealed the secret of the kingdom (Mark 4:11–12), he was an object of misunderstanding (Mark 8:14–21, 31–33), so that he could not fully reveal himself to them. It was only in the light of his death and resurrection that his full significance could become apparent.

Despite the consequent scantiness of the evidence, it is clear that Jesus knew God to be his Father in a unique way. He addressed him as "Father" (Aramaic, "Abba") with a familiarity previously unknown among Jews (Mark 14:36) and he initiated his disciples into a similar relationship (Luke 11:2). This relationship was expressed in Jesus' comment that only a father and son can truly know each other; hence only the Son can reveal the Father to men (Matt 11:25–30). Only rarely, however, did Jesus say anything to the people that might have indicated to them his claim to be God's Son (Mark 12:6; John 10:30–38), and it is unlikely that many of them grasped the point, although this charge did figure in his trial (Luke 22:70).

Nor did Jesus publicly claim to be the Messiah (i.e., the king appointed by God to rule on his behalf), though his ministry was of such a character that his disciples were able to discern that he was more than a prophet and should be regarded as the Messiah (Mark 8:29; cf. John 4:25–26). Moreover, in the presence of his disciples he emphatically accepted Peter's identification of him as the Messiah (Matt 16:13–20; Mark 8:30). When Jesus spoke about the Messiah to the people (Mark 12:35–37), however, he did not make any overt claim to be the Messiah. Some of those under the influence of demons recognized his supernatural origin (Mark 1:24; 3:11), but Jesus did not wish for testimony of that kind.

Sometimes Jesus was addressed as "Lord," but this possibly meant no more than "Sir," as a polite form of address. Nevertheless, Jesus was conscious that his relationship to his

---

[20]E. Käsemann, *Essays on New Testament Themes* (London: SCM, 1964), pp. 38, 43.

disciples went beyond that of a teacher (Matt 7:21; 21:3; John 13:14; 15:20), and the use of the title *Lord* in reference to him may suggest these deeper implications (cf. Mark 12:35-37; John 20:2). After the Resurrection it certainly took on a fuller meaning (Acts 2:36; cf. Luke 24:34; John 20:18, 25, 28).

The phrase that appears most frequently on the lips of Jesus to describe himself is "Son of man" (which simply means "the man" or "a man"). On occasion this may have been used merely as a self-designation with no theological significance (so possibly in Matt 8:20; 11:19). But often the phrase reflects the associations conjured up by memory of Daniel 7:13-14 and refers to God's agent who will be the leader of his people, who will be enthroned, and who will take part in the final judgment. Where the Messiah could be understood as an earthly man and his role could be seen in human political terms, the Son of man was a transcendent heavenly figure who took up into his own functions those ascribed to the Messiah. Apparently it was not a much-used term, and this fact, coupled with its appropriateness, made it eminently suitable as a self-description of Jesus. Therefore, Jesus used this term to refer to himself in reference to his future role at the consummation of the kingdom (Matt 16:27; 24:27, 30-31, 36-44; Luke 18:8). At the same time he made it clear to his disciples that the Son of man's authority would be rejected while he was on earth and that he must suffer and die before being raised and vindicated by God—a teaching that they found it impossible to comprehend (Mark 8:31-33; 9:31-32; 10:32-34).[21]

As stated earlier, behind Jesus' teaching about himself there lay his consciousness that God was his Father in a unique way and that he was his Son. This consciousness was confirmed for him by the heavenly voice at his baptism (Mark 1:11) and was tested in his experience of temptation by Satan (Matt 4:1-11). It received further confirmation at the transfiguration (Mark 9:7). Jesus revealed himself to his disciples as the Son (Matt 11:27; Mark 13:32), and, although he was reticent about revealing the deepest secret of his person to the crowds, the authority of the Son of God lay behind his teaching as a whole.

The question of Jesus' claims is especially difficult, and the above interpretation of the evidence[22] would be disputed by radical scholars.[23]

VI. Opposition and Conflict

A. *Jesus and His Opponents*

It is not surprising that the activity of Jesus aroused opposition from the Jews, particularly from their leaders, and that their reaction led to more direct teaching against them by Jesus. Although Jesus respected the OT law and the authority of Moses (Mark 1:44), he broke with the interpretation of that law in the oral teaching of the scribes who represented the Pharisaic point of view. According to Mark, this opposition emerged early in his ministry, as the scribes attacked his violation of their sabbath legislation by

---

[21]B.M. Metzger, *The New Testament: Its Background, Growth, and Content* (New York: Abingdon, 1965), pp. 151-154.

[22]For this see O. Cullmann, *The Christology of the New Testament* (London: SCM, 1959); I.H. Marshall, *The Origins of New Testament Christology* (Downer's Grove: InterVarsity, 1976).

[23]R.H. Fuller, *The Foundations of New Testament Christology* (London: Lutterworth, 1965).

his rejection of pettifogging regulations (Mark 2:23–28) and by his healings (Mark 3:1–6; Luke 13:10–17; 14:1–6; John 5:1–18; 9:1–16). Jesus justified his actions in terms of doing good on the sabbath.

Above all, they attacked Jesus for failing to follow their legalistic practices as to fasting and ritual hygiene (Mark 2:18–22; 7:1–5) and for consorting with people who were open sinners or did not maintain Pharisaic standards of behavior and were therefore a source of defilement (Mark 2:13–17; Luke 7:39; 15:1–2). They criticized him as "a friend of tax collectors and 'sinners'" (Luke 7:34) and cast aspersions on his own way of life. Jesus justified his conduct by an appeal to the love of God, who longs for the salvation of the outcasts (Luke 15). He saw his own mission as being primarily to such people and not to those who thought they were all right in the sight of God. In fact, the latter group really rejected God's message, and the way was clear for Jesus to summon the needy into the kingdom of God (Matt 22:1–14; Luke 14:15–24). The great reversal, prophesied in Luke 1:50–53, was taking place (Luke 7:29–30; cf. Matt 21:28–32).

In Mark 7 we have an example of Jesus' counterattack against the Pharisees. They could not see that their man-made traditions were a barrier between themselves and true religion. They made much of external ritual while neglecting the attitude of heart that alone is pleasing in the sight of God. Such an attitude was hypocritical. But the cleavage went deeper, because Jesus' attitude to ritual cleanliness and his insistence that defilement comes from a man's thoughts, not from what he touches (Mark 7:14–15, 20–23), had the effect of challenging the written law itself. It was one thing for Jesus to challenge the unwritten traditions (though these had the same authority for the Pharisees as the written law itself); it was another thing for him to appear to challenge the OT law. But how far Jesus openly did so is not clear. The statement that Jesus' principle made all foods clean (Mark 7:19) may represent the early church's interpretation of the debate, and it is not certain that Jesus expressed himself so bluntly. It was only in the light of his sacrificial death that the early church could understand the rationale of his attitude and realize that he was "the end of the law" (Rom 10:4).

Jesus' criticism of the Pharisees and scribes went further (Matt 23; Mark 12:38–40; Luke 11:37–54). He launched a burning attack against their type of religion that concentrated on nonessential, trivial practices and made them a burden for ordinary people instead of stressing the weighty matters of justice, mercy, and faith. Such a religion laid itself open to abuse, because it stressed what was outward and so made it possible for men to compete with one another in public show and indulge their spiritual pride. Such a religion left no room for humility and dependence on God and could be summed up as hypocrisy. It culminated in the attitude that refused to accept the prophets with their attacks on legalism and irreligion, and Jesus foresaw that the Jewish leaders would treat him no differently from the way they treated prophets in the past.

The attack made by Jesus on the Jewish establishment provoked the question of the nature of his authority, a question he was not prepared to answer directly (Mark 11:27–33). The fact of his claim to authority was apparent; he even claimed for himself God's right to forgive sins (Mark 2:1–11). But it is one thing to claim authority and another thing to have a basis for it. The authorities challenged Jesus to provide some accrediting sign for what he did, a clear and unmistakable guarantee of God's backing; after all, his mighty works could be attributed to the power of Satan. This, to be sure, was a foolish suggestion and Jesus quickly showed up its absurdity (Mark 3:22–27; Luke 11:14–23). But if men could not see for themselves that his authority was divine (Luke 11:20), Jesus would not give them the proof they desired. There would be no sign for them except the sign of his ministry, death, and resurrection (Mark 8:11–12; Luke 11:29–32).

B. *The Final Conflict and the Passion*

After this, events moved to a climax. The Gospels describe how when Jesus came to Jerusalem—to the accompaniment of yet another "sign" that should have made his claims clear (Matt 21:1–11)—the Jewish leaders from various parties gave him a final series of challenges. Their motives may have been various and it is probable that their intentions had taken some time to mature. We have seen that Jesus' teaching constituted a fundamental challenge to the religious outlook of the Pharisees. At the same time, they saw Jesus as a danger to the *status quo*. Especially did the Sadducean priestly party consider him a danger because they feared for their own positions if his activity led to any political disturbances. Earlier, on the occasion of the feeding of the multitude, there had been some attempt by the crowds to recognize Jesus as a king—no doubt in a nationalistic, political sense as a leader against Rome (John 6:15). Although Jesus had refused the honor, the possibility of an uprising by his supporters could not be written off. When Jesus finally launched his attack on the corruption in the temple, which the priests should have stopped themselves (Mark 11:15–19), it was time to act. The opportunity was provided by one of Jesus' disciples (Judas), who offered to furnish the leaders with an occasion on which Jesus could be arrested secretly without fear of a disturbance among the large crowds of Galileans who were in Jerusalem for the Passover festival.

Meanwhile Jesus, aware that events were moving toward a denouement, met his disciples for a last fellowship meal—whether the actual Passover meal or an earlier celebration of it, is not certain[24] —at which he declared his determination to go through the approaching ordeal. Only thereafter would he be able to share fellowship with his disciples in the kingdom of God (Luke 22:15–18). Then he proceeded to interpret his impending death in terms of a sacrifice by which the new covenant, prophesied by Jeremiah, would be inaugurated; as God's obedient servant, he would give his life as a ransom for mankind and secure forgiveness for them (Mark 14:22–24; cf. 10:45; Exod 24:8; Isa 53:10–12; Jer 31:31). Finally, Jesus gave warning and encouragement to his disciples. In Mark this is confined to warning Peter that he would betray his master (Mark 14:26–31). In Luke there is a fuller set of warnings and promises (Luke 22:21–38), and John has a lengthy discourse and prayer by Jesus in which the situation of the disciples after his departure is fully considered (John 14–17).

After leaving the upper room, Jesus sought a quiet place to pray, hoping even at that late hour that it might not be necessary for him to face the final agony involved in his death, but ready to obey God's will at whatever cost. A band led by Judas found him in a garden outside Jerusalem and arrested him. There followed a series of judicial inquiries whose precise legal status has not been certainly established.[25]

It is likely that there was an informal inquiry by the high priest, followed by some kind of decision on the part of the Sanhedrin. Various lines of evidence were pursued. Jesus' alleged threats against the temple were reported, but they apparently led to no firm conclusion. More important were the suspicions that Jesus claimed to be the Messiah or even thought of himself as the Son of God. But now, it seems, the time for voluntary concealment was over, and Jesus was prepared to make a guarded acknowledgment of his claims. His reply was regarded as blasphemous and provided the necessary basis for a sentence of death. But the Jews did not possess the authority to carry out such a

---

24Cf. J. Jeremias, *The Eucharistic Words of Jesus*, 2nd ed. (London: SCM, 1966).

25J. Blinzler, *Der Prozess Jesu*, 4th ed. (Regensburg: Verlag Friedrich Pustet, 1969); P. Winter, *On the Trial of Jesus*, 2nd ed. (Berlin and New York: Walter de Gruyter, 1974).

sentence except in certain, specified circumstances, of which this was not one. Therefore it was necessary to hand Jesus over to the Romans with suitable charges. Since Pilate, the governor, would be interested only in political matters, Jesus was charged with spreading sedition and claiming to be a king (Luke 23:2). But when Pilate heard the accusations and examined the prisoner, he realized that the charges were baseless. Jesus was worthy of contempt rather than crucifixion—a verdict echoed by Herod Antipas. In face of the pressure of the Jewish leaders, Pilate attempted to secure amnesty for Jesus, but the people favored Barabbas, a genuine revolutionary. So Pilate succumbed to the pressure—it may be that the Jews had some lever against him (cf. John 19:12)—and ordered crucifixion.

Crucifixion ranks among the most cruel forms of death in the ancient world. The process of dying was long, drawn-out, and agonizing, the victim being literally left to die of exposure, lack of nourishment, and the sheer physical strain and intense agony of his position, which was deliberately arranged to prolong the torture. In the case of Jesus, the period of agony was mercifully short, possibly as a result of earlier, physical exhaustion. John 10:18; 19:30 may suggest that Jesus himself chose the moment when he gave up his life.

The Gospels, however, do not dwell on the details of Jesus' suffering, but on the fact of his dying forsaken and despised in conformity with a pattern laid down in the OT (Pss 22; 69). He displayed a readiness to forgive his executioners, gave hope of eternal life to a penitent brigand crucified along with him, endured patiently the mockery of the bystanders, and impressed the leader of the execution squad by the manner of his dying. Two details stand out: first, the cry of dereliction recorded by Matthew and Mark (Matt 27:46; cf. Ps 22:1) and, second, the cry "It is finished," recorded by John (19:30). Latent in these two utterances are the spiritual significance of the death of Jesus as the triumphant bearing of the world's rejection by God that the world might be reconciled to him—a truth the Gospels are content to leave implicit in the narrative but which the Epistles expound with all desirable clarity (2 Cor 5:18–21).

C. The Resurrection of Jesus

The secular historian may be content to record merely that Jesus died and was buried, not in a common grave, but in the private grave of a wealthy man. But even the secular historian must add that after Jesus' death there were rumors that he had been seen alive by his friends and that some of them had claimed that his tomb was empty. To the Christian the content of these rumors is part of the historical story; in his judgment these rumors were true, and no other explanation than that Jesus rose from the dead by the power of God will fit the evidence.

Mark briefly recounts how some women found the empty tomb of Jesus and fled from it in confusion after an angelic vision (16:1–8). Then the story in Mark terminates abruptly without describing any appearances of the risen Lord. So it seems likely that the original ending of the Gospel has been lost. On the other hand, many scholars think the sudden ending is deliberate.

The gap is closed by Matthew who tells how Jesus appeared to the women as they departed from the tomb and then appeared to the disciples on a mountain in Galilee, where he charged them to continue his mission (Matt 28).

Luke and John have fuller accounts. To Luke we owe the account of how Jesus appeared to two of the disciples on Easter Sunday afternoon near Jerusalem and then to a larger group of disciples in Jerusalem itself before he led them out of the city and ascended to heaven. This Jerusalem appearance also figures in John's account (20:19–24), where it is followed by a later appearance for the benefit of Thomas (John 20:24–29). The closing chapter recounts yet another appearance of Jesus to the disciples by the Sea of Galilee. The implication of the accounts in Matthew and John is that some of the disciples returned to Galilee after the Passover. The various accounts of the appearances are incomplete—e.g., we lack details of the appearance of Jesus to Peter (cf. Luke 24:34), and it has not proved possible to achieve a completely satisfactory harmonization of them. Yet this does not affect the basic historical character of what lies behind them. Without the fact of the Resurrection, the transformation of the disciples into the church and the continued existence of the church would alike have been impossible. To Christians the Resurrection is God's seal on the life of Jesus Christ: "God has made this Jesus ... both Lord and Christ" (Acts 2:36).

VII. Bibliography

The following list is confined to works from 1950 onward.

Betz, O. *What Do We Know About Jesus?* London: SCM, 1968.
Bornkamm, G. *Jesus of Nazareth.* London: Hodder and Stoughton, 1960.
Dodd, C.H. *The Founder of Christianity.* London: Collins, 1971.
France, R.T. *The Man They Crucified.* London: Inter-Varsity, 1975.
Guthrie, D. *Jesus the Messiah.* Grand Rapids: Zondervan, 1972.
Harrison, E.F. *A Short Life of Christ.* Grand Rapids: Eerdmans, 1968.
Hoehner, H.W. *Chronological Aspects of the Life of Christ.* Grand Rapids: Zondervan, 1977.
Hunter, A.M. *The Work and Words of Jesus.* London: SCM, 1950, 1973.
Jeremias, J. *New Testament Theology I.* London: SCM, 1971.
Manson, T.W. *The Servant-Messiah.* Cambridge: Cambridge University Press, 1953.
Stauffer, E. *Jesus and His Story.* London: SCM, 1960.
Taylor, V. *The Life and Ministry of Jesus.* London: Macmillan, 1954.
Turner, H.E.W. *Jesus—Master and Lord.* London: Mowbrays, 1953.
Vermes, G. *Jesus the Jew.* London: Collins, 1973.

THE EPISTOLARY LITERATURE

E.M. Blaiklock

Edward M. Blaiklock, O.B.E.

M.A., Litt.D., University of Auckland (New Zealand)

Emeritus Professor of Classics, University of Auckland; Emeritus President, Bible College of New Zealand

THE EPISTOLARY LITERATURE

I. Introduction

The epistolary literature of the NT fits naturally into an age-old tradition of communication extending from the beginnings of Greek literature (*Iliad* 6.118ff.) to the papyri. It is a tradition that, next to satire (itself a not altogether different genre), made, in the Roman Empire, a distinctive Latin contribution to world literature. To achieve a firm and exclusive classification of epistolary literature is difficult. Nevertheless, the letter may be designed for wider attention than that of its addressee and by virtue of its style may indeed win a place in literature. Cicero's own classification (*Ad Fam.* 2.4) set down three heads: First came the newsletter, and in Cicero's surviving correspondence his letters to Atticus belong here as documents of supreme historical importance covering vital events during the years of the Republic's dissolution. The second type was the easy and friendly letter (*genus familiare et iocosum*); and the third, the serious and weighty letter (*genus severum et grave*). Both of the latter two occur in rich abundance in his collected correspondence. But Cicero's three types overlap, and the distinction between them might have been quite blurred had Cicero survived to edit his correspondence. Pliny's polished letters and Seneca's philosophic communications show what Cicero might have made of his letters had he survived to prepare them for wider publication.

The NT letters contain several types of epistolary literature. Moreover, the characteristics of more than one genre sometimes occur within the compass of a single letter. The following should therefore be regarded as a loose classifications of the letters in the NT.

II. Personal Letters

A. Letters of Commendation

1. *Philemon.* This small gem of epistolary literature raises the question discussed above. It is a personal letter. Its style makes it a piece of literature, and it is a letter of commendation. To illustrate its literary quality, set it beside a polished letter of Pliny, the Roman statesman and one-time governor of Bithynia, written perhaps forty years later. Sabinianus, a friend of Pliny, had a freedman, a man who had been his slave but who now, in return for legal manumission, was expected to remain his one-time master's henchman. The man had offended his patron and had fled to Pliny for help. Pliny sent him back with the letter quoted below. It is instructive to read it side by side with the letter to Philemon and compare Pliny's language of humane interest with Paul's language of brotherly affection. Pliny pleaded for forgiveness for the fugitive on humanitarian and philosophic grounds. Paul, on the other hand, based all he had to say on Christian fellowship. Here is the Latin letter:

> Your freedman, whom you lately mentioned as having displeased you, has been with me; he threw himself at my feet and clung there with as much submission as he could have done at yours. He earnestly requested me with many tears, and even with the eloquence of silent sorrow, to intercede for him; in short, he convinced me by his whole behavior that he sincerely repents of his fault. And I am persuaded he is thoroughly reformed, because he seems entirely sensible of his delinquency.
> I know you are angry with him, and I know, too, it is not without reason; but clemency can never exert itself with more applause than when there is the most just cause for resentment. You once had an affection for this man, and, I hope, will have again: in the meanwhile, let me only prevail upon you to pardon him. If he should incur your displeasure hereafter, you will have so much the stronger plea in excuse for your anger, as you show yourself more exorable to him now. Allow something to his youth, to his tears, and to your own natural mildness of temper: do not make him uneasy any longer, and I will add, too, do not make yourself so; for a man of your benevolence of heart cannot be angry without feeling great uneasiness.
> I am afraid that, were I to join my entreaties with his, I should seem rather to compel than request you to forgive him. Yet I will not scruple to do it—and so much the more fully and freely as I have very sharply and severely reproved him, positively threatening never to interpose again on his behalf. But though it was proper to say this to him in order to make him more fearful of offending, I do not say it to you. I may, perhaps, again have occasion to entreat you on his account and to obtain again your forgiveness —supposing, I mean, that his error should be such as would become me to intercede for and you to pardon. Farewell.

Paul's letter, like Pliny's, is also what the Romans called an *epistula commendaticia*, a letter of commendation. The practice of writing a letter to introduce its bearer, or secure his or her acceptance was an established one the NT frequently refers to (Acts 9:2; 22:5; Rom. 16:1; 1 Cor. 16:3; 2 Cor. 3:1, 3 John 11—and, as remarked above, Philemon). Cicero's correspondence contains many examples (e.g., *Ad Fam*.7.5, introducing Trebatius, Cicero's lawyer friend, to Julius Caesar). There is even an example, exquisitely tactful, among Horace's poetic epistles, that last development of Roman "satire." It introduces his friend Septimius to the future emperor Tiberius, in thirteen lines of elegant verse (*Ep*.1.11).

Papyrology has contributed numerous examples of letters of commendation. A papyrus from Oxyrhynchus (P.Oxy.1587) uses the very phrase of 2 Corinthians 3:1. Another Oxyrhynchus papyrus (P.Oxy.2.292), discovered by Grenfell and Hunt, and now in the Cambridge University Library, demonstrates the popular form. It runs:

> "Theon to his most esteemed Tyrannus, many greetings. Heraclides, the bearer of the letter to you, is my brother. Therefore I entreat you most earnestly to hold him as one recommended to you. I requested also Hermias your brother by letter to communicate with you concerning this. You will show me the greatest kindness if he [Heraclides] gains your attention. Above all, I pray that you may, without harm from the evil eye, be in good health and faring prosperously. Good-by.

The date is A.D. 25. A second example is a Latin letter to a military tribune of the second century. (Very few of the papyrus letters are in Latin; most of them are in Greek.) It runs:

> Greeting! Already I have recommended to you Theon my friend, and now also I pray, my Lord, that you may have him before your eyes as if he were myself [cf. Philem v.17]. For he is such a man that he may be loved by you. For he left his own people, his gods and business, and followed me. And through all things he has kept me in safety. And therefore I pray of you that he may have free access to you [cf. 1 Thess 1:9].

A Christian example of this kind of letter is one from the presbyter Leon commending a brother-Christian to the officers of a local church (P.Oxy.8.266.1162). It is from the fourth century.

2. *Third John*. This short letter, written to Gaius, is also a letter of commendation. It raises, however, such important matters of policy that, kept in the archives of the church, it found a place in the NT canon.

3. *Second John*. This letter was apparently written to a lady and her family. The mode of address, however, could be used to disguise a Christian community. (Cf. Introduction to 2 John, EBC, vol. 12.) If this is correct, 2 John approaches the style of the seven letters written to the churches of Asia from John's place of detention of Patmos during a time of imperial persecution.

B. *The Pastoral Epistles*

Paul's two letters to Timothy and his letter to Titus show a development of the personal communication. They are clearly (especially those to Timothy) addressed to an individual. Yet just as clearly they cover matters of congregational importance.

C. *The Other New Testament Epistles*

As the pastoral Epistles contained matters of a personal nature, so the other NT letters also contain certain personal elements. Paul observed with some care the forms of polite address common in his day. These included an opening salutation, followed by thanksgiving and prayer for the person or group addressed. Next came the special subject of communication, greetings to friends, and perhaps a closing word of prayer. Here is a second-century letter that shows the Pauline style in brief:

> Ammonous to her sweetest father, greeting. When I received your letter and recognized that by the will of the gods you were preserved, I rejoiced greatly. And as at the same time an opportunity here presented itself, I am writing you this letter, being anxious to pay my respects. Attend as quickly as possible to the matters that are pressing. Whatever the little one asks shall be done. If the bearer of this letter hands over a small basket to you, it is I who sent it. All your friends greet you by name. Celer greets you and all who are with him. I pray for your health.

Aside from the letters of commendation and the pastoral Epistles, the other NT letters may be broadly classified as follows:

1. *The general or catholic Epistles and Hebrews.* James to Jude, traditionally called the general or catholic Epistles, contain few or no personal matters. The same is true for the great Epistle to the Hebrews. They fall into the same category as Seneca's "moral epistles," the three long letters of Epicurus, the letters of Dionysius of Halicarnassus, and perhaps what Reginald Hackforth (*Oxford Classical Dictionary*, p. 497) calls the "hortatory" letters of Isocrates.

2. *Epistles for wider circulation*

a. *Colossians and Galatians.* A direction (Col 4:16) is attached to Colossians bidding the recipients to pass it on for private and public reading to the Laodicean congregation, a few miles west of them in the Lycus Valley. Likewise, they were to read a letter from Laodicea. This, however, does not make Colossians more of a "general Epistle" than the first letter to the Thessalonians, which was to be "read to all the brothers" (5:27).

The direction to Colossae was not without parallel. Oxyrhynchus Papyrus 10.1349 published in 1914 runs:

> To my lady mother, Germania, greetings. Since I came away from you yesterday without telling you about the pot, take and copy my letter and give it to my lady mother Apraxis for my sister Hagia. Well, do not forget. I pray that you are well.

As for the Letter to the Galatians, the problem it deals with involved a group of congregations. Therefore, it was undoubtedly copied and circulated.

b. *Romans and Ephesians.* These are profound and carefully considered statements that must have demanded wide circulation. But no specific directions regarding this survive. Among the notable features of Romans are the personal details at the end.

3. *Epistles of rescript or reply (1 and 2 Corinthians, Philippians).* Bearing in mind that the present classification of Paul's letters is by no means rigid, it may be proper to call

these two letters "rescripts" or replies. The final volume of Pliny's correspondence contains many replies of this sort from the pen of the Emperor Trajan, outlining in conversational rather than official style the ruler's will on some matter in question. One of these rescripts is famous for the first outline it gives of imperial policy regarding the rising Christian church. Also included in this volume of quite invaluable letters and replies, is one in which the governor of Bithynia makes inquiries about moving the remains of the dead, and another that contains the emperor's written judgment on these matters.

In writing to the church at Corinth and the church at Philippi, Paul seems to be answering a communication. The two letters to Corinth are so laced with comment on the existing situation—the sectarian situation, lapses in moral conduct and correct behavior, "baptism for the dead," Sadducean heresies about the resurrection—that it is impossible to avoid the impression that the letters are prompted by a written report. The tone of philosophic irony in the first four chapters of the first letter and the word play of the opening sections of the second letter look like a response. The criticisms of Paul's own standing and ministry could also have come by letter. Corinth was a week's sail away on a frequented shipping route. The impression pervades the text.

In the letter to Philippi especially, the reader almost feels that he can reconstruct the text, just as one-half of a telephone conversation will sometimes reveal the nature of the other. Look at 1:12: "What has happened to me has really served to advance the gospel." The Philippians must have expressed a fear that Paul's imprisonment would be a disaster for his work. At 1:26 Paul is surely accepting an invitation, in which the Philippian Christians said they rejoiced in him. At 2:19 he reminds them that he likes to hear all about them. In 2:26 he replies to a question about the good Epaphroditus's illness. The abrupt transition at 3:2 apparently answers a disconcerting piece of news. Too much must not, however, be inferred from such a transition. Its suddenness may indicate a resumption of dictation after a short or longer interval. We should remember that Paul's letters were usually taken down by their bearers. In fact, there may be some worth in the suggestion that A.S. Way made many years ago in the introduction to his translation (*The Letters of St. Paul and Hebrews* [London: 1935]). He contended that certain obscurities in Paul's text and some of his rapid transitions from theme to theme are at times the mark of a "brief." The amanuensis received certain instructions from Paul, and here and there jotted down in shortened form the outline of themes that were then conveyed by the bearer of the letter, who no doubt also read it to the congregation. At 4:10 Paul gracefully answers an apology for remissness. Perhaps 4:1 and 4:15 are hints that the Philippians should not, as they appear to do, doubt his pleasure in them.

III. Various Epistolary Details

A. *The Address*

This was always brief in papyrus letters because they were not sent by public post but carried by a responsible bearer. Tertius (Rom 16:22) was such a bearer and several others may be named in the NT (cf., e.g., 2 Cor 2:13; 7:6, 13; Eph 6:21, 22). There is a parallel to the Ephesians reference in a letter of 103 B.C., in which the writer enjoins the messenger to pass on his greetings with the letter. A letter of commendation in the Cairo Museum Collection is simply addressed: "To Philoxenos," another from Oxyrhynchus is addressed "To Tyrannos the Procurator" (P.Oxy., G. & H.2.p.292). Likewise the well-known letter from Hilarion to Alis, directing the exposure of an unwanted child, bears the address "Hilarion to Alis, deliver."

As for most of the Epistles, the original titles were similar—viz., "To the Corinthians," "To the Galatians," "To the Romans," "To the Hebrews," etc.

B. *The Signature*

The word of farewell at the end of a letter was often in the hand of the author, not of the amanuensis (e.g., 1 Cor 16:21; Gal 6:11). A. Deissmann quotes a papyrus (*Light From the Ancient East,* p. 170ff.) in which, without comment or preamble, "good-by" (cf. Acts 23:30—in Lysias's dispatch—in Rev.Gk., et al.) is added in what is quite clearly another hand. The letter, written by one Mystarion, is dated A.D. 50. Deissmann comments,

> Paul, we are told, has not in fact furnished all his letters with a salutation in his own hand, and that therefore the words "which is the token in every letter" cannot be genuine. . . . We must not say that Paul only finished off with his own hand those letters in which he expressly says that he did. Mystarion's letter . . . was written only a few years before Paul's second letter to the Christians of Thessalonica, and it proves that somebody at that date closed a letter in his own hand without expressly saying so.

The letter in question is as follows:

> Mystarion to his own Stotoetis, many greetings. I sent to you my Blastus on an errand concerning wooden forks for my olive-orchards. See now that you do not detain him. For you know how I need him every hour. Good-by.

Similarly, "I Heracleides have signed," a typical autograph, appears in a different hand (P.Oxy.G.&H.1, p.101ff.45.18). Cicero speaks of a letter of Pompey (*Ad Atticum* 8.1.1) in which the great man had made an autographic conclusion *ipsius manu*—"in his own hand." Paul's comment in Galatians 6:11 may be a whimsical reference to the contrast between his overbold signature and the neater, more practiced penmanship of his amanuensis.

C. *The Bearer*

Taking a hint from Colossians 4:7–9 ("Tychicus will tell you all the news about me . . . I am sending him for the express purpose . . . with Onesimus. . . . They will tell you everything that is happening here"), Way, as mentioned above, justifies a good deal of expansion in his rendering of Paul's letters (A.S. Way, *Letters of St. Paul and Hebrews* [London: 1935], pp. x-xiii).

A papyrus in the Loeb collection, edited by A.S. Hunt and C.C. Edgar (1932–1934—Loeb Classical Library), and dated 168 B.C., contains a bitter complaint addressed to a delinquent husband. It answers, apparently, an unsatisfactory letter from the man concerned, and the letter was evidently to be expanded by verbal communication by the bearer, for the concluding paragraph runs:

> As, moreover, Horus, who delivered the letter, has brought news of your having been released from prison, I am thoroughly displeased. Notwithstanding, as your mother also is annoyed, for her sake as well as mine, please return to the city, if nothing more

pressing holds you back. You will do me a favour by taking care of your bodily health. Good-by.

D. *Dictation*

In the ancient world, letters were commonly dictated. Writing on papyrus was an irksome process and demanded some expertise as well as good penmanship (e.g., Ps. 45:1). Illiteracy, complete or partial, was the common reason for dictation. Many surviving documents are marked by the amanuensis on behalf of such and such a person, "because he does not know letters" (e.g., P.Oxy.,G.H.2, p.262ff. 275.43—dated A.D. 66). In the same collection, 3.p.212ff.497.24, dated in the early second century, is a marriage contract marked: "I write on his behalf seeing that he writes slowly." A Tebtunis papyrus letter of a Nile fisherman named Ammonius, dated A.D. 99, was written by a friend for the same reason. Peter and John, the Galilean fishermen, may likewise have employed an amanuensis. First Peter 5:12 states that it was written "by Silvanus" (Tebtunis Papyri, Grenfell, Hunt, Goodspeed 2.p.118f.316). A medieval tradition names one Prochorus as the amanuensis of John. (For Paul's practice, see 2 Thess 3:17, 18, and also 1 Cor 16:12; Col 4:18; and especially Rom 16:22.) A parallel to Tertius's statement in Romans occurs in a third-century letter from one Helene's father Alexander: "And I, Alexander, your father send hearty greetings." There is no change of hand, so Alexander was clearly the scribe.

It is easy to see how the varied skill, responsibility, or understanding of the amanuensis might modify the sentence structure, grammar, and vocabulary of the letter in a manner in no way diminishing its authenticity and authority, for the finished message would be read back to the author and sanctioned. This, of course, damages recent computerized methods of determining authorship on the basis of grammatical and syntactical usage, vocabulary, and such details as might form data for "programming."

In the period from which the NT Epistles date, tachygraphy or shorthand was common. This is authenticated from Cicero (*Cato Minor* 23) on to the papyri and Pliny (*Epp.*3.5.14, p.36.2). A papyrus of 155 A.D. records a contract of a citizen of Oxyrhynchus apprenticing his slave to a tachygraphist for no less than two years (P.Oxy.G.&H., *sup.cit.*, 4.p.204f.724). "I have placed" (so he begins after the customary greeting) "with you my slave Chaerammon to be taught the signs which your son Dionysius knows," And then, after a reference to the salary already agreed upon between them, he proceeds, "You will receive the second installment, consisting of forty drachmae, when the boy has learnt the whole system, and the third you will receive at the end of the period when the boy writes fluently in every respect and reads faultlessly."

Some samples of such shorthand have survived—see, for example, one in a papyrus now in Leyden, dated A.D. 104. Such evidence, especially from Latin sources, could be multiplied.

E. *The Greeting*

As with Paul's letters, so with the papyri. The opportunity to send a kindly word to friends and acquaintances is not lost. Here is a simple and unaffected letter of A.D. 27:

Give my regards to Pausirion and Hermias and Heraclides and . . . your brothers' wives and the children and all those who love you. If you come upon any mustard relish, buy it and make pickle for us. If you are making anything good, make some extra for the brothers' house. And for the rest, good-by. The 13th year of Tiberius Caesar Augustus, Epeiph 12' (P.Oxy.17.2148).

[*Aspasasthe* ("greet" or "give my regards to") is Paul's frequent word (Rom 16:3, 5ff.; 1 Cor 16:19ff., and a score of similar contexts; cf. BAG, p.116, s.v. ἀσπάζομαι [aspazomai, "greet"]).

F. Ink and Pen

Third John 13 refers to ink and pen. Archaeological evidence shows that ink was soot and gum diluted with water—a compound of remarkable durability. On the other hand, such ink did not penetrate the fibers of the papyrus, and so was easily washed off. See Colossians 2:14 which may be translated "washed out the bond." So, too, Revelation 3:5, "I shall by no means wipe out his name from the book of life."

The pen was a papyrus reed. It was desirable to have the best surface for the pen and this led to the common practice of writing on the side on which the shorter fibers of the papyrus lay horizontally. This provided a smoother surface and gave the equivalent of ruled lines. It also facilitated proper rolling of the finished book. The need for economy when the manuscript contained many words sometimes led to writing on the other side (*in verso*). An example is a long papyrus concerning magic, now preserved in the British Museum (121 in the *Catalogue of Greek Papyri*). Revelation 5:1 is a biblical reference—a vivid metaphor from the rolled book.

IV. Value of the New Testament Epistles

A. Theological and Ethical

The letters of the NT form the corpus of Christianity's theology, its Christology, its evangel, the nature of the church, the state of man, the plan of salvation, the integration of the Testaments, and Christian eschatology.

The ethics that arise and take shape are similarly developed. They are concerned with Christian conduct, personal and social; the Christian's relations with the world; the nature of sin and temptation; the integration of faith and character; the idea of the community of the church; and the composition, functioning, government, and leadership of the church.

Exposition—doctrinal, ethical, philosophical—goes back in epistolary tradition to Plato, Isocrates, Epicurus, and others. Many of these collections are of established authenticity, and include such "open" letters as those of Paul to the Romans and others. Isocrates, for example, writes to Alexander, but refers to "readers" (OCD, s.v. "Isocrates," p. 460).

B. Historical

The Epistles of Paul, like some others, those of Plato and Cicero especially, are rich in biographical detail. They abundantly illustrate and fill out the Acts of the Apostles. A considerable list of persons from the early Christian communities could be drawn up from the Pauline Epistles, while other Epistles, especially those of Peter and John, reveal the molding of character by the Spirit of God and a vital faith that transformed men from the proletariat of Rome's most turbulent province into personalities of world history. The Epistles, like the Gospels and Acts, are documents of first-century history and afford a glimpse into common and provincial life not to be disregarded by the serious student of ancient history.

C. *Literary*

Certain passages in the Epistles touch the heights of literary power—e.g., Paul's self-analysis in Romans 7, his poem of triumph at the end of the next chapter, his great poem about love in 1 Corinthians 13, and the conclusion to the letters to the Ephesians and the Galatians.

Ramsay has a striking tribute in his *Teaching of Saint Paul in Terms of the Present Day* (pp. 412ff.). In a controversy with Adolf Deissmann, following the publication of the German scholar's misguided study of Paul in 1912, Ramsay published a cogent paper on the Epistles of Paul as literary documents. In the course of his argument he wrote:

> If one be required to select any one passage to serve as a specimen and proof of Paul's power in pure literature, it would probably be well to offer the first four chapters of First Corinthians. These four chapters form a special section of the whole letter; they were written or dictated in all probability at one effort, and are clearly divided from the next section. . . . I should take this passage, not as one of the most famous or the most exquisite pieces in his letters; it has not the continuous and lofty dignity and beauty of chapter xiii, or of chapter xv.12–49, or of Ephesians i–iv; but it is eminent in respect of the great variety of feeling and effect which it exhibits. Most of the devices for attaining literary effects are here brought into play, not with any purpose of ostentation, but simply because the alternations of feeling dictate or demand them. The dominant emotion changes backward and forward between thankfulness, hope, protective love, disappointment and the keenest irony or even sarcasm. The tone is sometimes one of affection, sometimes of congratulation, sometimes of sharp rebuke, sometimes of deep thankfulness. At one moment Paul writes in the elevated and remote spirit of the mystic, at others in the anxious spirit of the careful pastor.

Above all, as Ramsay proceeds to show, a subtle irony infuses Paul's style, and indeed the opening chapters of 1 Corinthians can scarcely be understood without realizing this tone. Paul is answering a letter from Corinth, and something in its content, some naive parade of philosophy, some inappropriate confidence in a local intellectualism, prompted alarm in the founder of the church there and led to the restrained irony, which pity and concern held back from scorn, of a man of supreme intelligence faced with the perilous assumptions of those who mistook sophistry for wisdom and words for understanding.

Nor is Paul the only contributor to the epistolary literature of the NT who can claim a worthy place as a writer. The letter of James, setting forth his truths and social observations in rapid pointed remarks, shows a fine command of common Greek. The latter half of the first chapter is a splended illustration of epigrammatical writing, full of familiar quotation that retains its flavor in translation.

The Epistles of Peter manifest a high standard of Greek. In fact, with a perversity not infrequent in NT studies, the language of the First Epistle of Peter is alleged as a ground of argument against its authenticity: "The Greek of the Epistle," says J.H.A. Hart (O.G.T.5.12), "is better than a Galilean peasant could compass." This fragile argument loses sight of the fact that the said peasant had had years of intercommunication with other Greek-speaking people. It also overlooks the amanuensis.

There remains the writer to the Hebrews—a superb weaver of words and one who is magnificently quotable.

D. *Linguistic*

The Epistles present the common dialect of Greek (koine) at its best, add a score of new words and meanings to the vocabulary of the Greek language, reveal semantic developments and novel applications of words familiar in classical literature, and show that the language, which became the second language of the world, was capable of exact communication and literary polish. Koine Greek became a vehicle of logical argument and exposition of the first order.

V. Bibliography

Alford, Henry. *Greek Testament,* vol. 2, 5th ed. London: Revingtons, 1865.

Field, Frederick. *Notes on the Translation of the New Testament.* Cambridge: Cambridge University Press, 1899.

Gundry, Robert H. *Survey of the New Testament.* Grand Rapids: Zondervan 1970, pp. 257ff.

Guthrie, Donald. *New Testament Introduction,* 3rd ed. revised, vols. 2 and 3. Downer's Grove, Ill.: Inter-Varsity, 1970.

Harrison, Everett F. *Introduction to the New Testament.* Grand Rapids: Eerdmans, 1964.

Hiebert, D. Edmond. *Introduction to the Pauline Epistles.* Chicago: Moody, 1954.

THE LIFE AND MINISTRY OF PAUL

PAUL

R. Alan Cole

R. Alan Cole

B.A., M.A., Ph.D., Trinity College (University of Dublin); B.D., M.Th., University of London

Master of Robert Menzies College, Macquarie University (Australia); Head of the Department of Old Testament Language and Literature, Board of Divinity Studies, University of Sydney

THE LIFE AND MINISTRY OF PAUL

I. Who Was Paul?

It is typical of our age, with its fondness for "debunking," that it sees Paul, not as the "prince of the apostles," but as an "ugly little Jew." Yet, although the second phrase may shock us, as it is meant to do, and though it may have been first coined in a pejorative sense, it may also contain some truth. Indeed, one of the benefits of our times is the ability to see clearly that there need be no conflict between this earthy description and the proud title of "prince of the apostles." For too long our forefathers had Paul on a pedestal, in spite of the evidence of his own letters. They ignored the wise advice given by Bishop Westcott against our habit of unconsciously clothing the early centuries with light. It mattered little whether he was seen as the ecclesiastical Saint Paul, bulwark of church order and liturgy, or the evangelical Paul, preacher and missionary; in either case, he was seen as superhuman, a colossus. Then came the leveling process of modern scholarship. First we learned to see the Christians of the first century as essentially the same as the Christians of our own day. Their problems were seen as our problems; they ceased to be supermen and became familiar contemporary figures, cut down to life size.

After the initial shock, the gain was immense. If God's word could come to ordinary people like them, and God's power could break out so mightily in their midst, then God could act in the same way for us today. The gospel, in its church setting, at once gained immediacy and relevance.

The next step was to see, not merely his converts, but Paul himself, in this new light of naturalness. The great apostle of the Gentiles was thoroughly humanized, and hence the description quoted above. Yet for all its crudity, it is not wholly incorrect, to judge from Paul's own admissions and the evidence of outsiders. Luke loved and respected his master too much to say anything derogatory, but Paul's Corinthian enemies had no such qualms. Unless their evidence is totally fabricated (and presumably it is only because it is a half-truth that it stings so much), "in person he is unimpressive" (2 Cor 10:10). The "Acts of Paul and Thecla" enlarges this brief description to "a man small of stature with

557

a bald head and crooked legs, in a good state of body, with eye-brows meeting, and nose somewhat hooked" (Hennecke, p.354). True, Schoeps sees this as a transferred portrait of Socrates: others, less polite, have seen it as a caricature of Silenus. But we may admit that there is nothing inherently unlikely in the details of this portrait of one who was Jew, Rabbinic scholar, and tentmaker (Acts 18:3; 22:3). True, the same second-century apocryphal "Acts" further describes Paul as "full of friendliness" and says that some-times his face looked like that of a man and sometimes like that of an angel; but all of us have ugly Christian friends of whom, by the grace of God, these things are equally true. Therefore, instead of rejecting the blunt description, we may well accept it. Our struggle to accept it shows how dominated we are by Greek thought and culture. We like to idealize our heroes as young demigods, but in the NT there is not a single physical description of any of God's heroes. "Man looks on the outward appearance, but God looks on the heart" (1 Sam 16:7).

There is, as usual, a complementary danger that comes with the advantages gained from the "humanizing of Paul." We may think of Paul as one who was just like us, but greater; and this may blind us to the exceptional use that God made of him. Though Paul of Tarsus may have been an "ugly little Jew," he was still God's chosen instrument (Acts 9:15), and the apostle to the Gentiles (Rom 11:13). The figure of Paul, "warts and all" (to quote Oliver Cromwell), still towers far above any of his later critics, as he undoubted-ly towered above his contemporaries, fully human though he was. We may not agree with those who claim that Paul was a great classical writer, but even his bitterest enemies admitted that "his letters are weighty and forceful" (2 Cor 10:10). Two thousand years of theologians have soberly agreed. Indeed, if this were not true, why should his letters have survived? To those who minimize the importance of Paul in God's plan for his church, the same objection may be made as to those who preach an attenuated "liberal Christ." Who would ever want to put to death such a nonentity? What danger could he possibly pose? No, the measure of the spiritual greatness of Paul is seen alike in the hatred of his enemies (Rom 15:31) and in the love of his friends and converts (Gal 4:15).

II. The Quest for the Historical Paul

In 1906 Schweitzer produced a brilliant book, the title of which (in the English translation) is *The Quest of the Historical Jesus.* In it, Schweitzer analyzed the various German views, past and present, as to the true meaning, significance, and nature of Christ. It would be beyond our purpose to trace the different views, some shallow and some oversubtle or perverse, but almost all assumed a sharp cleavage between a "Jesus of history" and a "Christ of faith." Few theologians today, of whatever school, would allow that this was a valid or total antithesis; yet we have witnessed virtually the same controversy over the past few generations in connection with Paul.

The basic question is whether we have in the NT an artificial "Paul of faith," as distinct from a real "Saul of Tarsus" of history. Can we depend on our material to give us a true picture of Paul as he was, or do we have at best an idealized portrait of him? The problem may be illustrated by contrasting the standard two-volume missionary biographies, cur-rent fifty years ago, with the paperback Christian biographies on sale today. The older "Victorian Age" missionary biographies are not misleading in the sense of fabricating or misreporting, but they are usually carefully selective, omitting all that is derogatory to their hero. The result is not so much inaccurate as one-sided. Do we face this same problem today in regard to Paul? If so, how can we know what the real Paul was like?

In general terms, while a conservative scholar would have difficulty in admitting such a lack of balance in the biblical evidence, he would agree at once that it is true of much of the extrabiblical material, whether it be pro-Pauline or anti-Pauline in tendency, As an example of biased pro-Pauline material, we may cite that second-century romance, "The Acts of Paul and Thecla" (Hennecke, p.353). The author was a presbyter of Asia Minor and a great admirer of Paul, but he was removed from office by the church simply because he composed this work. This shows clearly that the second-century church did distinguish clearly between the factual "Paul of history" (as in the canonical writings) and an imaginary "Paul of faith" fabricated by the presbyter and other partisans, and presented in this book. In other words, they were convinced of the historicity of the account of Paul given in the NT and on these grounds alone they ruled out this new "interpretation" as false and misleading. All thoughtful scholars would agree with them in their judgment, for this fabricated "Paul of faith" does not ring true to life.

Marcion could also be named as one who grossly misunderstood and misinterpreted the great apostle (in spite of his devotion to him) and who, because of this, was forced to reject much of the true "Paul of history." Was this perhaps the sort of bigoted partisanship that Paul had to face and discourage at Corinth (1 Cor 1:12)? We cannot tell. Paul rarely records false claims made on his behalf by overzealous supporters. He does, however, record false charges made against him by his enemies (2 Cor 10:10) and rebuts them by a simple, confident appeal to historic facts (Gal 1:11–2:10). Therefore, not only the early church, but even Paul himself, constantly appealed to the "Paul of history" against the "Paul of Faith."

So much for an imaginary "Paul of faith," as created by overzealous partisans of Paul in later years. But there was also an imaginary "Paul of faith" as painted by his detractors. For this, we have evidence in the Pseudo-Clementine literature (Hennecke, pp. 532ff.), where Paul, under the name of Simon Magus, is portrayed as being the archenemy of Simon Peter and of the truth. No doubt Paul's enemies sincerely believed this but the sober judgment of the church of the day (so much closer than we are to living oral tradition) was that this "Paul of faith" was likewise false, a distortion of the true "Paul of history," whom we know from the canonical books. So the Clementine material was rejected by the church as heretical and misleading, whether or not Simon Magus was really intended to be a picture of Paul. The tragedy of the Tübingen School was that they failed to accept this wise judgment of the primitive church and turned afresh to a blind alley in postulating a basic cleavage between Peter and Paul, which (they felt) had been carefully "cemented over" in Scripture for doctrinal reasons.

The church obviously rejected these other false interpretations, because they did not agree with the Scriptures. But what if the biblical evidence itself is one-sided? Well, whatever some have said about Acts' being 'second-hand evidence' (a questionable view at best), at least we have in Paul's letters first-hand contemporary source-material, written in a typical and distinctive Pauline style. If this is not the "Paul of history," it is hard to see who else it could be. If it be objected that the letters, even though Pauline, were collected by others at a later date and either selected or edited, the answer is that the first is certainly true and the second quite possibly so. Yet the strange thing is that no additional letters of Paul have survived. True, we do find references to two other letters in the New Testament: one was sent to the Laodiceans (Col 4:16), and one, a "stern letter," to the Corinthians (2 Cor 7:8). Most modern scholars believe, however, that both of these letters have in fact survived in Scripture, possibly in the form of our "Ephesians" and as part of the Corinthian correspondence respectively. The question, however, is not important here. (The existing Latin "Letter to the Laodiceans" is a late forgery.) The only possible conclusion would seem to be that the NT contains a collection of all the known Pauline letters that were extant. It cannot be a tendentious and selective collection for some trace would remain of the letters omitted, even if it were only a reference to them. This impression is heightened by the fact that some surviving letters are verbally very similar to one another in places (e.g., Colossians and Ephesians, Timothy and Titus). To publish one of the two would have been quite sufficient, had it not been that a pair of similar letters survived and were both firmly believed to be by Paul. Furthermore, these surviving letters contain much material that could be seen as derogatory to Paul (e.g., his admission of his weakness and humiliation in 2 Cor 11:30–33). These letters were not suppressed, even by his supporters, simply because they were believed to be Paul's own words, and thus part of the stubborn truth.

We have, therefore, absolutely no evidence for the view that the Paul of the NT is a nonhistorical "Paul of faith," created by later hero-worship. As we have seen, when any such attempts were made in post–NT days, they were ruled out by men who still remembered the peppery old bachelor missionary. Either the Paul of the NT is indeed the Paul of history or we have no knowledge whatever of the real Paul.

III. What Was Paul's Background?

If, then, there was in truth a "Paul of history," identical with the "Paul of faith," of whom we read in our documents, against what background are we to interpret him? There have been several answers, though not every interpretation falls neatly under the heading of one or the other. God will, of course, mold and use the raw material in his servant as he wills, but God's servant did not live in a vacuum. So we may legitimately see Paul's letters as being to some extent molded—at least in vocabulary, style, and expression, if not in thought-forms—by the milieu in which he grew up. Some would see the major background influence on Paul as the mystery religions or Gnosticism; others would see it as lying in the Hellenism of the Levantine world of his birth, though a Hellenism tinged by his Jewish faith. Others would see it in the Rabbinical background of the Palestinian learned schools; still others would explain it more simply in terms of a pious Jewish mind, steeped in the OT.

Paul might also conceivably be interpreted in terms of "sectarian Judaism," perhaps even in terms of an Essene outlook of the type known from the Dead Sea Scrolls. This would be on the basis of his known stay in "Arabia," and of his contacts with Damascus (Gal 1:17), both believed to be areas of Essene influence. John the Baptist has from time to time been so interpreted. But in the case of Paul, all we can detect is a polemic against some of the Essene views, so that any such influence seems strictly negative. Apocalyptic Judaism is another quarter from which influence has been suspected, but it could hardly be a major factor in view of the many non-Apocalyptic aspects of Paul's thought evident in his letters.

Paul's gospel cannot be accounted for as a mere reshuffling of the Mystery Religions, or as a Gnostic salvation-myth loosely tied to a historical personage. Indeed, with the exception of Bultmann and his followers, few modern scholars would be content with this view, whatever their theological position. But we may well agree that Gnostic terms are deliberately used against Gnostics by Paul in controversy (e.g., in Colossians), just as we may agree that Paul uses Essene terminology in quotation marks to refute Essene ideas (e.g., in Ephesians). A great deal here depends on the date of the emergence of Gnosticism as a coherent system. It is a fact that, while in the later strata of the NT certain tendencies and heresies that characterize developed Gnosticism at a later date are attacked, yet the earliest incontestably Gnostic literature is post-Christian, and indeed is parasitic upon Christianity.

With the mystery religions, the problem is simpler. We do not know what the nature of the mystery was. No uninitiated person did; so it is a priori unlikely that Paul the Jew would have known any more than we do. It is much more likely, both here and in the case of Gnosticism, that Paul used some of the technical vocabulary unconsciously. Similarly, many a person today, ignorant of philosophy, may yet use some of the vocabulary of existentialism, without necessarily in any way committing himself to a belief in it. Did Paul use such terminology deliberately, in order to establish rapport with his hearers or to preach the gospel to them in language familiar to them? The terms are used so naturally and unselfconsciously that even this seems unlikely. Besides, much that was once thought to be a reflection of the mystery religions is now seen as a reflection, if anything, of ideas found also in the DSS, though probably even then coming from a common source rather than from direct borrowing by Paul. Paul's use of *mystērion* ("mystery") is a good example. This is more likely to be a simple translation of the Semitic word *rāz*, found both in Daniel (2:28) and the DSS, than a direct borrowing from Greek, with the associated ideas of the Greek mystery religions adhering to it.

The relation of Paul to Hellenism is another complicated question: Glover considered Paul the greatest Greek writer of the first and second centuries A.D., but not many scholars would agree with him. Of course, Paul grew up in the wider world of Hellenism (if indeed his youth was spent at Tarsus and not in Jerusalem) but this Greek world filtered in through a Jewish window. His few quotations from the classics are such as might be picked up in ordinary conversation with educated men. (The unkind have called them "tags.") His apparent acquaintance with some aspects of Stoic and Cynic philosophy could come from the same general source. That this was the blunt opinion of an educated Athenian audience is plain from the scornful word *spermologos* (NIV has "babbler," but the meaning could be better conveyed by the word "parrot") by which they described him (Acts 17:18). Lest we think this a mere unkind gibe, we may compare Paul's deliberate rejection of "wisdom" as a means of winning men for Christ (1 Cor 1:17). His letters show few signs of a man steeped in Hellenism or the Hellenic spirit. Rather, they show a typical first-century "world citizen" with a Jewish background. Schoeps has an interesting section where he considers to what extent Paul's use of the Septuagint is in itself a sign of Hellenization. True, the LXX, in a hundred little ways, shows a deviation from truly Hebraic ways of thought by its method of translation and choice of words, let alone its many substitutions and omissions. Even this suggestion of "limited Hellenization," however, breaks down in view of our not really knowing how far Paul used the LXX, how far he used more "Judaic" Greek versions, and how far he made his own "amplified version" as he went along.

If the Gnostic "salvation myth" cannot be proved to be pre-Christian in date, and if the influence of Hellenism on Paul is doubtful, the matter is very different with Rabbinics. Here we stand on firmer ground as far as material is concerned. True, there is often a problem of dating of sources, for an indiscriminate reader may easily confuse the late with the early; but we do know the broad outlines of the Rabbinic tradition in the first century A.D. and its main teachings and typical viewpoints. No man would doubt that Rabbinism forms a major part of the background of Paul (see Davies). He is not a Hellenist with a smattering of Judaism, like some nonobservant Jew of the Western world today. Instead, he is a Jewish Rabbi with a smattering of Hellenism, more like the strictly Orthodox Rabbi of a big modern city.

But how far does this entitle us to say that Paul had made an intensive study of Rabbinics, its doctrine, and exegetical methods? Or how far was it merely a matter of the general mental background of a Pharisaic member of the "orthodox" synagogue of Tarsus? Probably those are right who say that we must not think of a unified "Hellenized Judaism" of the Dispersion of the first century any more than we may speak of a monochromatic worldwide Judaism today. Every shade of opinion doubtless existed side by side outside Palestine, if not within it, though perhaps not in equal strengths. Probably they also are right who say that any member of an orthodox Jewish family, whether at home or overseas, would have known as much of Rabbinics as Paul did (Phil 3:5). But since Acts makes it clear that Paul had studied under Gamaliel in Jerusalem (Act 22:3), this explanation is unnecessary. It is, however, important to note that there are certain areas where Paul's view diverges from what was certainly the later Rabbinical view. In such areas we may perhaps see a pious Pharisee, basing himself on the well-loved Torah, rather than a professional student of Rabbinics. Paul's letters smell of the marketplace, not of the study and lecture hall, so we may perhaps assume that this was as true of his early Jewish days as it was of his later Christian period.

IV. Paul: His "Cursus Vitae"

Critics often say today that Paul would never have been accepted by a modern missionary society, or appointed to the staff of a modern theological college, or designated as pastor of a modern church. To complete the picture, it only remains to add that his letters would not have been accepted by a modern Christian publishing house. While all this is somewhat cynical, it is worth further thought. True, Paul's psychological make-up was far from normal; so unusual was it, in fact, that some scholars have claimed he was an epileptic, judging this affliction to be the "thorn in the flesh" that irked him so (2 Cor 12:7). But, while admitting Paul's unusual temperament, we do not need to go to such lengths. For instance, he was a man who frequently received visions (Acts 22:17, 18), though his transforming experience near Damascus was not merely a vision but a real event, an actual meeting with the risen Christ (Acts 22:6ff.) But the unnamed individual of 2 Corinthians 12:2 who has mystic experiences of visits to heaven and of hearing unutterable words is almost certainly Paul himself. Also, he thanks God that he enjoys the ecstatic experience of "speaking with tongues" (whether or not this was similar to the modern phenomenon), far more than the most excitable Corinthian convert (1 Cor 14:18). He can be utterly prostrated by depression, so much so that he "felt the sentence of death" (2 Cor 1:8, 9). On the other hand, the extravagance of his joy knows no bounds (Phil 1:3, 4), and the "Christ-mysticism" of Paul (Gal 2:20), however understood, shows a tremendous depth of religious intensity. All was fortissimo and prestissimo in the life of this man. On the whole, "unusual" would be a better word than "abnormal," for characteristics mentioned above are combined with sober judgment and mental balance in dealing with the practical problems of the churches.

Paul's own life story cannot explain this temperament, though it can illustrate it. Of the hotheaded tribe of Benjamin, he appropriately bore the name of Saul, Israel's first king, who had himself been of this little tribe. Paul's father's name is unknown, possibly because he was not a Christian, and thus unfamilar to the members of the Christian community at Jerusalem. Perhaps, as tradition suggests, Paul's forefathers were from Gischala in Galilee, that home of fire-eating nationalists. As there is no reason why such a tradition should be invented (unless it was to give Paul a Galilean background, like that of the other apostles), it may well be true. But Paul's family were also settlers in Tarsus, the great cosmopolitan seaport of Cilicia, where they were both local citizens and Roman citizens, an unusual combination (Acts 21:39; 22:25). They may have been Jewish prisoners forcibly settled in Tarsus by some Syrian monarch or Roman general, or they may have fled there from Palestine as refugees. How Roman citizenship came to their family is unknown, except that it had been conferred at least in the generation before Paul, since he, unlike the tribune, was a Roman citizen by birth (Acts 22:28).

This mark of government favor normally was given either because of some service performed to the state or because of some local municipal office held, but our sources give no details. Perhaps as a Roman citizen Paul simply used the Roman name of "Paul" because of its assonance with his Hebrew name of "Saul." (Similarly, the Hebrew "Simeon" became the Greek "Simon.") Possibly, however, Paullus was an adopted Roman family name taken by his family. In the case of freed slaves, it was common to adopt the family name of the *patronus* who had freed them.

We know much about Tarsus; for instance, that it had a set of nature-mysteries of its own; that it had a "university"; that it had produced several philosophers; in fact, that it was a typical Hellenistic city. But we cannot allow all this to influence our picture of the background of Paul's youth, because we do not know the exact age at which he left Tarsus for Jerusalem. All we can say—unless, with critics like Knox, we dismiss the whole story of Paul's Jerusalem education as pure fabrication—is that Paul was "brought up" in Jerusalem (whatever that means) and was educated there under Gamaliel (Acts 22:3). Luke records Paul's mention of this latter fact in a speech, and Luke also emphasizes Gamaliel's conciliatory attitude to the Christians (Acts 5:34–39), which is probably his way of underlining the connection between the two men. Certainly it shows that he expected his Christian readers to be interested in Gamaliel. Of Gamaliel himself, we do know something. He was a recognized head of the Pharisaic group at Jerusalem and followed on the whole the milder interpretations of the Law favored by Hillel, rather than the stern rule of Shammai. This would again accord with Luke's account of Gamaliel's more tolerant attitude toward the Christian church. What his reactions were to the conversion of his brilliant disciple, we do not know. If, however, the various early Rabbinic references to an ungrateful Rabbinic pupil do indeed refer to Paul, then his reaction was not so gentle. (See Schoeps.) Paul, by his own account, was a brilliant student (Gal 1:14) and, when we read his letters, and see the agility of his mind, we can see how accurate this self-assessment was. It would be natural that such a vigorous young Pharisee would soon attain a position of importance and leadership in Jerusalem, though he must have been hated by the Sadducees from the start (Acts 23:6–7).

With his fiery temperament, Paul probably shared none of Gamaliel's fondness for Hillel, and certainly none of Gamaliel's tolerance of Christianity. We first meet him guarding the clothing of those who stoned Stephen (Acts 7:58), thus acting as an official witness and "giving approval to his death" (Acts 8:1). Whether this death was semijudicial, we do not know; early Christian tradition records Roman legal disapproval of other such irregular actions. This particular death made a great impression on Paul, as we can see from his later remorse (Acts 22:20). Indeed, there have been many attempts to see the genesis of Paul's theology in the theology of the speech of Stephen, as recorded in Acts 7. This agrees with the view that both Stephen and Paul were Hellenists, overseas Jews, rather than Hebrews, Jews of a narrower type. Yet even this interpretation of the two terms is uncertain. For what it is worth Paul describes himself as a Hebrew (Phil 3:5). Certainly Paul's preaching in later days was similar to that recorded of Stephen long before. Whether there was any conscious, direct connection between the two, or whether both were part of the one living tradition, it is hard to say. As noted above, we are not certain how far it is fair to call Paul a Hellenist, if we assume by using the word that he had been brought up in the Dispersion, surrounded by liberalizing Greek influences. If he had, in fact, spent his formative years in the "orthodox quarter" of "Hebrew" Jerusalem, nothing could be further from the truth. Paul's married sister seems to have lived in Jerusalem; his nephew was certainly a resident there, possibly as a student (Acts 23:16). Therefore, Paul may well have lived with members of his own family while in Jerusalem. If so, he would have been doubly insulated against Hellenism.

Whether Paul was a member of the Sanhedrin or not, has been debated. By later rulings, a member should have been married, which he clearly was not (1 Cor 7:7), and it is probable that as a "young man" (Acts 7:58) he was below the legal age of membership. However, the later rules may not have been strictly enforced in early days, or else Paul may have been present at meetings only as a legal assessor. He certainly knew well the constitution of the Sanhedrin, and used this knowledge to "split the house" (Acts 23:6). More puzzling, if Paul was a member of the Sanhedrin, is his failure at his trial to recognize Ananias the high priest, the chairman of the Sanhedrin (Acts 23:5). With the various rapid shifts of high priesthood over the years (and Paul had been absent from Jerusalem for several years), it is possible that the contemporary chairman of the Sanhedrin was either personally unknown to Paul or that his new position as high priest was unrecognized. Alternatively, Paul may have simply heard an illegal order to strike a prisoner, and shouted a heated response, without noticing the exact quarter in the chamber that the order came from.

Be that as it may, Luke records that Paul was actively engaged in the persecution of the church in Jerusalem immediately after the death of Stephen (Acts 8:1–3). The exact relation of this statement to Paul's later statement that he was personally unknown to the churches of Judaea (Gal 1:22) is not clear. He may simply have meant that at that time he had not yet returned to Judaea as a Christian, and therefore had not yet met the Christians face to face. They must surely have known him as a persecutor; otherwise, why were they so afraid of him when Barnabas tried, after Paul's conversion, to introduce him into the life of the Jerusalem church (Acts 9:26)?

This persecuting activity in Jerusalem was apparently within recognized legal limits, at least when it was short of the death sentence. Strictly speaking, the Jewish Sanhedrin did not have the legal power of life and death (John 18:31), which belonged to the Roman government alone. Stephen's stoning doubtless came near to mob lynching in Roman eyes, but we can be sure that it was not the only such death in those troubled years. Later on, only the intervention of the tribune saved Paul himself from sharing such a fate (Acts 22:22–24), but it is striking that the tribune felt it his duty to intervene and save him from it. Many critics, however, boggle over the possibility of Paul's Damascus persecuting mission. Some, like Knox, try to solve it by postulating that Saul had lived and worked in Damascus all the time, and that his previous persecution of the church had also been in Damascus, not in Jerusalem, so that no such journey was necessary. For a Damascus Pharisee to persecute Damascus Jewish Christians would seem easy and natural. This explanation, however, would make nonsense of the historical account given by Luke and is not necessary. True, we do not know much of the exact powers of the Jerusalem Sanhedrin over the Jewish community in Damascus, but we know of some relationship of Damascus with the Essenes, of Dead Sea Scroll fame. The "Damascus Rule" speaks of a retreat "to Damascus" at one stage (Vermes, p.59). This is probably to be taken as a literal migration from Palestine to escape persecution by Palestinian Jewry, to which there is reference in the Habakkuk Commentary (the "Wicked Priest" harries them, Vermes, p.60). If heterodox Jewish Essenes were already at Damascus and had reason to fear persecution from orthodox Jews, would not members of this other "heterodox" Jewish messianic sect equally have reason to fear? And where more likely than orthodox Jerusalem would be the source of a "commission of inquiry"? That the later orthodox Jewish-Christian church of Jerusalem followed this practice when confronted by "ecclesiastical irregularities" we can see from the Samaritan episode (Acts 8:14).

The story of Paul's conversion on the road near Damascus is too well known to need retelling, though its theological significance must not be bypassed. Its central importance for Paul's theology is shown by the three accounts of it in Acts (chapters 9, 22, 26) and one in Galatians (chapter 1). We know from Galatians 1:17 that immediately after his conversion at Damascus Paul went for a time to "Arabia," but no indication of purpose is given. Wherever the exact area was, whether near Damascus or not, he must have been there either for meditation or for evangelism. (We may dismiss the view of the Jerusalem Bible that he fled there to escape from Aretas; to go to "Arabia" to escape the Nabataeans would be "out of the frying pan, into the fire.") Since no early Christian churches are recorded from those parts (for the tradition about Philip's work in Arabia seems late) and since no references to such churches occur in the apostolic letters, the first view seems preferable. Because so many of Israel's earlier prophets and leaders, from Moses down to John the Baptist, had emerged from the desert, this stay in Arabia was doubly appropriate. On account of Essene links with both Damascus and the desert, some see a deeper significance in this sojourn. However, in view of Paul's opposition to Essene views, as shown in his letters, it is highly unlikely that he had any direct contact with them during this time in "Arabia." It would not have been a quick or easy task for the proud young man to readjust his thinking, now that his whole "house of thought" had suddenly come tumbling down.

After this initial readjustment, long or short, the fiery convert seems to have engaged in a whirlwind campaign of preaching in the synagogues of Damascus. Defeat in debate soon turned to hatred on the part of the Jews, and hatred turned to persecution. Perhaps it was influential Jews who persuaded the governor of King Harethath (Aretas) of the Nabataeans (died about A.D. 40) to watch the city gates to arrest Paul. But Paul escaped in a breadbasket, lowered over the walls at night (2 Cor 11:33). The ignominy of that escape still chafed (or amused) him years later. His total time in Arabia and Damascus was three years (or perhaps two, by Western reckoning) to judge from Galatians 1:18. On his arrival at Jerusalem, the Christians, not unnaturally, were terrified of him. Indeed, had it not been for Barnabas, he might never have met the members of the church. As it was, he says that, of all the apostles, he met only Peter and James (Gal 1:18, 19, if this refers to the same visit) and that his total stay was but a fortnight. Then violent Jewish opposition broke out, due once more to Paul's successful witness in the synagogues. As a result, he was rapidly spirited away—first to Caesarea (we do not know for how long a period) and thence to Tarsus, city of his birth (Acts 9:29, 30).

How long Paul remained at Tarsus is not clear. All we can say is that it was over a decade before he returned to Jerusalem (Gal 2:1). Nor do we know whether the time at Tarsus was another "silent period" of prayer and readjustment, like that assumed to have taken place in Arabia previously, or a time spent in evangelizing Cilicia and perhaps Syria as well. (There are no early references to churches in this area either.) Even in Galatians 1:21, Paul mentions only his going to "Syria and Cilicia" and says nothing of what he did there. At all events, Acts tells us that at some unspecified time later, Barnabas went to Tarsus, sought Paul out, and brought him to Antioch to minister to the new Gentile church. It was from Antioch that, at least a year after (Acts 11:26), Barnabas and Paul set out on an evangelizing tour that covered Cyprus (Barnabas's native island) and the southern part of the Roman province of Galatia.

After their return, apparently there was again a considerable period of ministry in Antioch (Acts 14:28), in the course of which contention arose with some Judaean Christians on the question of the rules for admission of Gentiles into the church (Acts 15:1). It is uncertain whether Paul's conflict with Peter (Gal 2:11) took place now or later. But that it was fundamentally a conflict on this same issue is clear. Acts 15 gives an account of how the matter was happily resolved, at least as far as the authorities at Jerusalem were concerned. Galatians 2:1–10 doubtless describes the same event from Paul's side. But extremist Jewish Christians apparently remained unconvinced and were still harrying Paul years later, even when he was in prison (Phil 1:15). The date of this conference at Jerusalem is uncertain, but if it was indeed the same occasion as that mentioned by Paul in Galatians 2, then it was at least fourteen years after his conversion. However, Paul still had a decade of active Christian ministry ahead of him, even at the latest dating of the conference.

Next followed the great sweep of missionary activity commonly called the "second missionary journey." This brought the gospel around in a circle through Asia Minor, Macedonia, and Achaia back to Roman Asia. (Acts 18:22 is usually taken as a reference to a further visit to the Jerusalem Church at the end of this period.) This journey was, however, undertaken without the cooperation of Barnabas. There had been a rift over the desertion of John Mark (Acts 15:38, 39) halfway through the first missionary journey, and henceforth Silas and others were to be Paul's traveling companions, not Barnabas.

After this follows the period traditionally called the "third missionary journey." Actually, it is better seen as a time of ministry now centered on Ephesus (Acts 19:10) rather than Antioch, with periodic visits to Macedonian and Achaian churches as needful. All through this period, short or long—if we follow the reconstructed chronology of Knox, only two or three years; if we follow the orthodox chronology, a decade or so—Paul had been pushing forward his great plan of an offering by the "Churches of All Nations" for the help of the poor of the Jerusalem church. This offering seems to have been one of the points advocated by the "Jerusalem Compromise" (not recorded in Acts 15, but cf. Gal 2). The response was gratifying enough to warrant not only the sending of several Gentile delegates (Acts 20:4) but also the presence of Paul himself (1 Cor 16:3, 4). Yet he went up to Jerusalem, under spiritual compulsion, with a strong foreboding of disaster (Acts 20:22), confirmed by the prophetic word in the churches of the cities through which he passed (Acts 21:11). It is significant that he was apparently convinced that this anticipated suffering was part of God's plan for him, and he would not be turned aside from it (Acts 21:13, 14).

The series of events leading to his arrest are recorded in Acts 21. It was ironical that the very gesture of reconciliation suggested by the Jerusalem church (Acts 21:20–24), and gladly accepted as such by Paul should have been the spark that ignited the powder keg. Arrest, interrogation, protective custody, judicial hearings—the weary tale dragged on for the prisoner, who had now of necessity to go to Rome since, as a Roman citizen, he had appealed to Caesar's imperial justice (Acts 25:11, 12). Two years of custody had already passed slowly at Roman Caesarea (Acts 24:27). Some have felt that Paul's prison Epistles were written during this imprisonment at Caesarea, not at Rome, but this seems unlikely. At last came shipboard, then shipwreck, and custody at Rome.

There Acts leaves us, and from tradition we can only surmise about Paul's martyrdom. No extant Pauline letters cover the actual arrest period, though Romans and Corinthians refer to a planned journey to Jerusalem, and the "Prison Epistles" take up Paul's story at a later stage—in Rome itself. But even these break off before Paul's actual trial and execution.

V. Founder of Christianity: Christ or Paul?

A question like this would have horrified Paul, who said, "to me, to live is Christ," and whose prayer was that "Christ will be exalted in my body" (Phil 1:20, 21). True, one party at Corinth seems to have called itself by the name of Christ, apparently in opposition to other parties called by the names of Paul and Apollos and Cephas (1 Cor 1:12). The question asked above would not be necessary were it not for the old bogey of a simple Galilean gospel of Jesus, as contrasted with an intellectualized gospel of Paul. Curiously enough, this view was shared at times both by those who held that this Pauline "development" was a good thing and by those who held it to be disastrous for Christianity. Alike they were agreed that the outlines of the developed "Pauline gospel" could not possibly have been laid down by Jesus of Nazareth.

Today, there is no need to argue this point. Exhaustive analysis of the Gospels over the past few decades has shown that, while scholars may still differ as to the exact aim and emphasis of the message of Jesus, at least all agree that there was never any such thing as a shallow "Galilean springtime" enshrining a simple ethical gospel taught by Jesus and affirming only the fatherhood of God, the brotherhood of man, and the natural goodness of human nature. It is hard now, on looking back, to see how anybody could have believed that such a superficial teaching could ever emerge from dour first-century Judaism, with its eschatological and apocalyptic overtones, its sense of impending doom, and its expectation of a coming "act of God." The first and second Jewish revolts never sprang from this sort of thin soil, nor were the DSS written against such a humanistic backdrop. This is not of course to say that the gospel as presented by Jesus is to be understood solely in eschatological or apocalyptic terms, but it is to draw attention to some of these features that make the charge of shallowness impossible. At whatever level the Gospels are studied, there still remain the depth and the urgency of the summons to a response. In other words, it is not a case of a shallow early gospel, later given more depth by Paul, but of a trenchant early gospel later explained and amplified by Paul in local situations.

But we can disprove any idea of a dichotomy between Paul's gospel and Christ's more simply. Paul himself continually asserted that the gospel he preached is Christ's gospel (Gal 1:11, 12). He claimed that it is the only gospel, since all other so-called gospels are false and thus perverted (Gal 1:7). He also appealed confidently to it as being the very gospel preached by the Jerusalem apostles (Gal 2:6). If there had ever been some simple Galilean gospel, unperverted by Paul and his supposed "Hellenism," surely it would have been preserved in the one church that owed nothing to Paul, the church where he had never ministered—indeed, the church from which Paul boasted that he had not received his gospel. Apparently not even Jerusalem knew another gospel. Although there were some Judaizers at Jerusalem, apparently Pharisaic Jewish-Christian circles around James, people who bitterly opposed Paul, their attack was not so much on his gospel in itself as on his failure to insist on circumcision and obedience to the Law of Moses as essential for gentile converts to this gospel. To them, Paul's gospel was too simple, not too complex, as some critics assume.

Some, however, may not be satisfied with the foregoing explanation. And they may ask whether this apparent agreement on the gospel might not be artificially constructed by those who, in the interests of orthodoxy, wish to show that, despite superficial troubles, no real or lasting rift existed between Jerusalem and Antioch. But close and rigorous analysis of the apostolic preaching in the early chapters of Acts has yielded exactly the same gospel as Paul's. To fabricate such evidence would be beyond human skill; the analysis of the situation has been so thorough that any internal inconsistency could not have escaped detection. In any case, while we may allow Luke some liberty in dealing with his speech material (if he was no Thucydides able to compose imaginary speeches, neither was he a tape recorder), a charge of complete fabrication would be utterly inconsistent with Luke's careful historical approach, amply demonstrated in other areas. Nevertheless, to those who are still not convinced by Acts there is another way to rebut this charge. If the incontestably Pauline writings are compared with the other apostolic writings of the NT, exactly the same Gospel will be found in them as in Paul when we make allowance for differences of temperament and circumstance. How could such a common apostolic gospel have arisen, except from a common source? And where should we seek the source but in Christ? This, after all, is exactly what Paul said in the letter to the Galatians. His gospel, he claimed, came to him by a revelation from Christ (Gal 1:12).

VI. Justification by Faith: Isolated Doctrine or Not?

Since the great days of the Reformation, it has been a truism to say that justification by faith is the message of Paul. No Reformer ever denied that the same doctrine was held by other NT writers (Luther's pungent remarks on James are an exception), but "justification by faith" was nevertheless held to be the peculiar glory of Paul. Progressively forgotten down the centuries and overlaid by institutional ideas of the church, it was held to have been rediscovered by the Reformers, largely through intensive study of the Pauline Epistles. Insensibly, Paul's battle with the Judaizers over this doctrine became identified in the mind of the Reformers with their own fight for spiritual freedom and thus the lines were drawn so hard that the Reformers and those who followed them may have been blinded to certain other equally important aspects of Paul's thought and theology.

Let us begin by gladly admitting that the Reformers were right: The reiteration by Paul of the theme of Habakkuk 2:4 is no accident (Rom 1:17, Gal 3:11). Paul does indeed fight the battle for acceptance of the sinner by God on the simple basis of faith in Christ alone (Gal 3:2). No thoughtful scholar would deny that today, especially at a time when some Catholic theologians see this truth more clearly than their Protestant counterparts. Also, the Reformers were right in seeing this principle as applicable wherever the church finds itself again in the same position as Paul was vis-à-vis Judaizers, those who insist, in addition to the gospel, also on outward forms as an equally essential condition of salvation. Nevertheless, justification by faith is not the whole of Paul's gospel, even if it is the basis, and we wrong him if we limit him in this way. There is nothing unusual in this unconscious preoccupation with a single principle. When men are fighting for their spiritual lives, it is natural that the truth vital to their survival temporarily blinds them to other truths, or at least looms so large that they slight other truths. What people sometimes fail to realize is that Paul himself was fighting for the very life of the gospel against the Judaizers. This is not to say that he was blinded to other aspects of the gospel (though we may be); he was too great a theologian for that. But, as when he wrote to the Galatians, the other aspects of the gospel did not loom so large at the moment because they were not at issue. None of Paul's letters (not even Romans) are theological treatises, though they are profoundly theological in content. They were called into being by the needs of particular situations; the balance and presentation of doctrine is therefore what was appropriate in the circumstances. Admittedly, each application by Paul to local circumstances was an application of timeless and eternal principles of God's revelation. These divine principles will always remain the same, and so they can be applied to our very different circumstances. Yet even the principles Paul chose varied according to the need of the local church at the time. This shows the fallacy of dividing Paul's Epistles into "doctrinal" and "practical" sections, and treating the first as all-important and in isolation from the other. The doctrinal sections *are* important because they arise from the problems of the practical sections (though the doctrinal sections usually precede the practical ones), not because they stand in isolation from them. This is clear in the letters to the church at Corinth and it is clear of the letter to the Romans, which was written to a church Paul had never actually visited himself.

We must be careful, therefore, not to assume that, had Paul written a "systematic theology," the balance of doctrines would have been exactly the same as they are, say, in Galatians. In point of fact, he was a missionary pastor, writing from the midst of pastoral situations. If we want to find out Paul's theological teaching in other areas, we must find it in his other letters, where different needs have called forth other great principles. To assert this in no sense minimizes the fundamental importance of the doctrine of justification by faith, but rather leads to its enrichment. Indeed, when we read Paul as a whole, the main impression we get is one of a remarkably broad balance and range of doctrine. Failure to realize this breadth has often meant the misunderstanding and misrepresentation of Paul as being legal, austere, and forbidding, so that persons who turn gladly to the gospel turn away from Paul. But this is a contradiction in terms; the gospel lies at the heart of Pauline theology, and the Paul who inspires such love in his converts was surely neither legalistic nor forbidding (Gal 4:15). Unfortunately, some of the classical commentaries on Romans, in their zeal to expand the theological niceties of the doctrine of justification by faith, have at times forgotten the human warmth and pastoral concern that underlay and motivated Paul's masterly presentation of justification.

What then are the other major aspects of the gospel that may be found in Paul and that in no way lessen the importance of justification by faith? They have been summed up succinctly as "union with Christ" and "salvation," to which we might add "life in the Spirit." While these are only alternative metaphors for the same spiritual state that is entered through justification by faith, they deserve brief examination.

The concept of "union with Christ" is clearly central to Paul's thought (Gal 2:20). Through the years it has been understood in various ways, ranging from mystical personal union to physical incorporation into the community of the church, the body of Christ. But Paul was no mystic in the classic sense of the word: he knew nothing of extinction of personality, nor of absorption into the absolute. All spiritual experience was for him firmly anchored in the historic events of the death and resurrection of Jesus the Messiah (Phil 3:10) and to the establishment of a personal relationship with God through the Messiah. Although he saw visions, to him every vision was rationally understandable and explicable to others. He was also no mystic in the sense that his meeting with Christ on the Damascus road was for him as real a meeting with the risen Christ as any that the other apostles had in Galilee and just as much a historical event. Moreover, while Paul's spiritual experience was intensely personal (Gal 2:20, "loved *me*"), yet it was never purely individualistic. To be "in Christ" was for Paul to be a "member" of Christ, a part of his body; and this involved a living organic connection with all other parts of his body (1 Cor 12:12). To that extent, those who see "union with Christ" as a "social" or "corporate" concept are right, though they may move into dangerous areas when they insist too strongly on the importance of outward rites of physical incorporation into this body. However, "salvation" is one of the widest and most inclusive of terms. Within it there is room, as often noted, for the "three tenses" of salvation—the past act of God, to which we have already responded in faith; the present experience of Christ within the community that is His body, where we build one another up in love; and the future hope of the redemption of the mortal body itself, and, with it, of all things. All this is thoroughly Pauline (Col 1:3–5).

We cannot isolate any of these Pauline teachings from the ongoing life of the Spirit within our hearts, for it is to the Spirit that we owe our new life in Christ. To Paul, all moral progress (for after justification, he looks for total moral change) is the result of the new relationship in which we have been placed. The motive for change is our deep sense of indebtedness to God, and the dynamic is God's Spirit at work deep within the transformed human personality. Sometimes Paul speaks of the indwelling Christ (Gal 2:20) sometimes of the indwelling Holy Spirit (Gal 3:2), sometimes of both (Rom 8:9, 10). There is no sense of contradiction in his mind, since it is by the Spirit that Christ lives in us. Life and light and strength are alike the Spirit's gifts, and the various facets of the transformed personality can therefore be called "the fruit of the Spirit" (Gal 5:22, 23).

Sanctification is another related area of which Paul speaks much, (e.g., 1 Thess 4:3), drawing on the rich imagery and language of the Old Testament and associating it too with the work of the Spirit. While theologians are right in warning us against the danger of confusing justification and sanctification, yet it is certain that Paul never considered either in isolation, but saw both as part of one and the same great spiritual activity. It is, however, typical of Paul's vivid thought that he regards sanctification as twofold—a past act by which we have been dedicated to God (1 Cor 1:2) and a present activity of continual service of God (Rom 12:1).

VII. What Was Paul's Secret?

What was Paul's own concept of his place and calling? Gone are the days when men could see Paul's secret as lying in his natural human qualities. But if it was not the result of his natural endowment, where did it come from? Did it come from his consciousness of being Paul, "the apostle to the Gentiles" (Rom. 11:13)? or Paul, "obligated" to all men (Rom 1:14)? Or does "a man in Christ" express his position best (2 Cor 12:2)? There is truth in all of these. But the heart of the secret lies in the phrases "Paul and Timothy, servants of Christ Jesus" (Phil 1:1) or "Paul, a servant of God" (Titus 1:1). Why should it lie peculiarly in Paul's consciousness of his servant relationship? That a servant is bound to obey his master is obvious; that God's will was the salvation of the Gentiles is clear; that Paul believed himself to be a "chosen instrument" to carry out that will is evident from Acts 9:15. Yet none of these is in itself a sufficient explanation. Rather, the true answer is that Paul sees his apostolic task in terms of the "suffering-Servant" theology of the second half of Isaiah. This theology reappears in the synoptic Gospels and forms one of the great strands of primitive Christian soteriology as seen especially in the apostolic preaching of the early chapters of Acts and also in 1 Peter. Though the servant concept is not a major strand in Pauline Christology, it is almost certainly present in the great passage in Philippians 2:6–11 which is apparently part of an early Christian hymn. The task of the Servant is, by definition, bound up with suffering and death; that is, in fact, his vocation, the very way in which he must accomplish God's purpose (Isa 53:10). So it had been with Christ (Matt 16:21); so it must also be with Paul (Acts 9:16). This accounts for his glad acceptance of persecution whenever it would come as the price of Christian service (Acts 20:23, 24) and also for his insistence that he must share the suffering and death of Christ (Phil 3:10), and indeed for his sense of thus filling up what was "still lacking in regard to Christ's afflictions" (Col. 1:24). While of course Paul's language refers primarily to spiritual experience, we do wrong to restrict, in our modern Western way, its interpretation to the spiritual. Often a spiritual experience has a physical counterpart. For example, Paul's three days of darkness at Damascus corresponded to the three days of Christ in the grave, not only spiritually but also in a physical sense. Paul's own words about his experiences at Ephesus (1 Cor 15:30–32) and of the time when he "felt the sentence of death" in his heart (2 Cor 1:9), as well as the list of physical sufferings in 2 Corinthians 11:21–29, illustrate this point. As clearly as Peter had done (1 Peter 2:21), Paul saw that suffering and death were the appointed path for the Christian to tread, just as they had been the appointed path for Christ. For a first-century Christian, "death to self" often meant also physical death (John 21:19). This explains Paul's attitude to his last journey to Jerusalem when he went under constraint of the Spirit, as surely as Christ had done when he "resolutely set out for Jerusalem" (Luke 9:51; cf. Isa 50:7). This too explains Paul's words to the Galatian disciples when he warned them that they too "must go through many hardships to enter the kingdom of God" (Acts 14:22). This last sacrifice of the Servant was the goal of his whole life; martyrdom was not to be an incident or accident, but the sign that he had "finished the race" (2 Tim 4:7, 8). We may reverently compare with this the cry of Christ on the cross "It is finished": death was the goal, even for Him (John 19:30), and the ultimate proof of obedience (Phil 2:8).

We may well ask, If this was really Paul's attitude, was it a true understanding of his calling or was he self-deceived? The answer comes in that last journey to Jerusalem, which was both a triumph and a tragedy. Paul, who was the servant of Christ, as Christ had been Servant of the Lord, did indeed suffer; he became, as he says, "the prisoner of Christ Jesus for the sake of you Gentiles" (Eph 3:1). Here the parallels with the suffering Servant of Isaiah are very close. Like the Servant, Paul was unjustly imprisoned; undoubtedly, the Judaizers would have considered him, like the Servant, "struck by God" (Isa 53:4). They would have seen Paul's imprisonment as God's just rebuke for his non-Jewish ways, as surely as the crowds at the Cross saw Christ's death as a similar sign of God's wrath (Matt 27:43). Paul's following, expressed by his words "I follow the example of Christ" (1 Cor 11:1), had become, involuntarily, an actual as well as a spiritual following. True, the prison years that followed were rich in letters that brought blessing to the gentile churches, and, like Christ, Paul saw "the fruit of the travail of his soul" (Isa 53:11, RSV). His very imprisonment encouraged and emboldened others in their witness (Phil 1:14); but what of his death at the end? Scripture makes plain that God's chosen plan (Isa 53:12) was that the Gentiles should finally be won through the suffering and death of his divine Servant. It was too little a thing that the Servant should be used thus for the salvation of Israel alone; through the Servant, God's salvation was to reach to the ends of the earth (Isa 49:6), that is, to the great gentile world. It is remarkable that this universal gentile mission had been precisely the vision God gave Paul at the beginning of his ministry (Acts 22:21). Furthermore, in the revelation of this purpose to Ananias (Acts 9:15, 16) it was associated with suffering from the start. This is not to say that Paul ever saw himself in any pseudo-messianic role, but that the pattern of the unique and perfect suffering Servant was to set the pattern for his humblest follower (1 Tim 1:16). It was quite enough for the servant to be like his Master (Matt 10:25). Paul was therefore conscious that in his case, suffering was not peripheral, but essential (Col 1:24), though not with the unique redemptive significance of the sufferings of Christ. So it was that the death under the headman's axe at Rome was to be to Paul the crown of his ministry, not an untimely end (2 Tim 4:6–8). The very fact that the gentile church survived and multiplied is proof that the promised fruitfulness had followed the servant's sacrifice (Isa 53:11, 12). Paul dead had achieved what Paul living could never have achieved; the grain of wheat had fallen into the ground and died, in order to bear fruit (John 12:24). Indeed, the very fact that Paul's letters were carefully preserved, painstakingly collected, and lovingly published by his gentile converts is proof of the success of his ministry. He had not been a servant of the Lord in vain, nor had he died in vain (Phil 2:16). To the end, he had been a faithful "servant of Jesus Christ" (Rom 1:1).

VIII. A Chronological Outline of Paul's Life

There is abundant internal evidence in Acts and the Epistles from which to construct a chronological outline of Paul's life, including many references to figures in Roman history—e.g., King Herod Agrippa (Acts 12), the proconsul Sergius Paulus (Acts 13:7), the proconsul Gallio (Acts 18:12), and the procurators Felix and Festus (Acts 24:27). There are also references to historical events—e.g., the famine under Claudius (Acts 11:28) and the expulsion of Jews from Rome (Acts 18:2). All these provide useful cross-references. Unfortunately, however, it is impossible to assign exact dates to most of these, in spite of their anchoring the biblical account firmly to contemporary history.

Of these references, the two most useful as fixed points are the procuratorship of Festus and the proconsulship of Gallio. Unfortunately Josephus and Tacitus are neither clear nor in agreement as to the exact date of the recall of Felix and the accession of Festus (though A.D. 59 seems likely, not the A.D. 55 of Eusebius). On the other hand, Gallio (to judge from the famous Delphi inscription) was almost certainly stationed in Achaia from A.D. 51 to 52; if Paul met him in A.D. 51, having already been in Corinth for a year and a half, then Paul must have arrived in Corinth in A.D. 49. As this date can hardly be more than a year in error at most, it provides the necessary fixed point, and a Pauline chronology can be constructed by working forward and backward from this date, using the evidence in Acts and the Epistles. Of course, scholars like Knox who completely reject the Acts account and use the Epistles alone as a basis will arrive at a very different result. But in view of the known historicity of Acts in other areas and the close correspondence between the general run of events in Acts and the Epistles, this seems wrong-headed as well as unnecessary.

Nevertheless, certain minor difficulties of chronology remain. These arise largely from the uncertainty of the interpretation of some of the terminology in Acts and the Epistles, an uncertainty that would not of course have existed for the original readers. For example, it is quite uncertain whether the "two years" of Acts 24:27 refers to the time Felix had been in office or the time Paul had been in jail (in which case it may have had the technical legal sense of the time a prisoner might be held without formal hearing). In other words, while the relative sequence of events is reasonably clear, their exact time lapse is not. This problem is increased by our uncertainty about the way years are counted—whether in the "inclusive" Eastern way (which counts for instance, Friday to

Sunday as three days) or the "exclusive" Western way (which counts Friday to Sunday as only two days).

Another example of possible ambiguity is the "fourteen years later" of Galatians 2:1. Does Paul mean fourteen years after his initial conversion or fourteen years after the last event described? But these at the most represent a possible marginal error of a few years, not wholesale reconstructions of the Pauline chronology (such as that favored by Knox) by which virtually all of Paul's missionary work was completed in the "fourteen years" before the Council of Jerusalem, leaving Paul little to do afterwards except to come to Rome and be martyred at an impossibly early date. Such extreme views are, however, untenable for those who regard the account given in Acts of Paul's missionary journeys as historical. The vexing question as to the exact relationship between the five visits to Jerusalem mentioned in Acts and the two mentioned in Galatians is too complicated to be discussed here, but there are several possible solutions that do no violence to the Bible (see EBC, the Introduction to Acts in vol. 9 and the Introduction to Galatians in vol. 10).

If we follow a more conservative reconstruction and work backward and forward from the date of A.D. 49 for Paul's arrival at Corinth, we should place the Council of Jerusalem in or about A.D. 38, with Paul's first missionary journey preceding it. If Paul's conversion was sixteen years before the Council, it must have taken place about A.D. 32, a year or two after the crucifixion (see THE CHRONOLOGY OF THE NEW TESTAMENT, pp. 591–607). We should then put his first visit to Jerusalem within a few years of Paul's conversion and place his long stay in Syria and Cilicia (whether a period of silence or of local missionary work) between this visit and the Council of Jerusalem. We must also fit in his various missionary journeys to Asia and Achaia into the years between A.D. 48 and 55 and place his arrival in Jerusalem not long after that date. After this, exact dating becomes more problematical because of the difficulty of dating Festus (mentioned above) and the uncertain duration of Paul's Caesarean imprisonment. It seems likely, however, that Festus entered on his procuratorship in 59, a date that would accord with the rest of the reconstruction and such evidence as we have. In this case, Paul would presumably have reached Rome in A.D. 60. Luke mentions "two whole years" of imprisonment at Rome (Acts 28:30), which should bring Paul to A.D. 62. From then on, there are only two points of evidence: the pastoral Epistles, which would seem to demand a release, and a further period of missionary work in the eastern Mediterranean region. Romans and early church tradition suggest a further period in the western Mediterranean as well. According to tradition, rearrest and death under Nero followed. This, however, is outside the range of ascertainable fact; all that can be said is that since this chronology does not conflict with known facts, a date of about A.D. 64 for the death of Paul would therefore seem reasonable.

IX. Bibliography

Bornkamm, G. *Paul.* London: Hodder and Stoughton, 1971.

Davies, W.D. *Paul and Rabbinic Judaism.* London: SPCK, 1948.

Deissmann, Adolf. *Paul: A Study in Social and Religious History.* Translated by W.W. Wilson. Gloucester, Mass.: Peter Smith, 1958.

Ellis, E.E. *Paul and His Recent Interpreters.* Grand Rapids: Eerdmans, 1961.

Hennecke, E. *New Testament Apocrypha.* London: Lutterworth, 1965.

Kasemann, E. *Perspectives on Paul.* London: SCM, 1971.

Knox, J. *Chapters in a Life of Paul.* London: Black, 1954.

Machen, J.G. *The Origin of Paul's Religion.* Grand Rapids: Eerdmans, 1965.

Munck, J. *Paul and the Salvation of Mankind.* London: SCM, 1959.

Ramsay, W.M. *Pauline and Other Studies in Early Christianity.* Grand Rapids: Baker, 1970.

Schoeps, H.J. *Paul: The Theology of the Apostle in the Light of Jewish Religious History.* London: Lutterworth, 1961.

Vermes, G. *The Dead Sea Scrolls in English.* London: Harmsworth, 1962.

THE APOSTOLIC CHURCH
A. Skevington Wood

A. Skevington Wood

B.A., University of London; Ph.D., University of Edinburgh

Principal, Cliff College, Derbyshire, England

THE APOSTOLIC CHURCH

I. Introduction

    A. Limits
    B. Sources
    C. Beginnings

II. The Church in Jerusalem

    A. Foundation and Growth
    B. Relation to Judaism
    C. Persecution
    D. Leadership
    E. Worship

III. The Church in Palestine

    A. Judea
    B. Samaria
    C. Galilee

IV. The Church in Antioch

    A. Position and Importance
    B. Foundation and Composition
    C. Relations With Jerusalem

V. The Church in Rome

    A. Origins
    B. Peter and Paul
    C. Membership and Importance

VI. Conclusion
VII. Bibliography

I. Introduction

No subsequent period has proved more critical for the survival and expansion of the Christian church than what is commonly called the apostolic age. From a purely human standpoint, the likelihood was that the infant society associated with the name of Jesus would disappear perhaps within a generation. The fact that by A.D. 64 the church had emerged from its obscurity as apparently a minor sect within Judaism and was regarded by the Roman authorities as a dangerous and potentially subversive force is an indication that this was not the work of unaided men, but of God himself. To the purely secular historian the astonishing vitality and growth of the apostolic church must remain an inexplicable enigma. The Christian, on the other hand, sees here the authentic operation of the Holy Spirit.

A. Limits

The apostolic age covers roughly the first generation after Jesus. Exact boundaries are not easy to determine. It is usual, however, to regard it as running from the ascension of Christ to the death of the last of the apostles, which takes us to the Neronian persecution of A.D. 64 and the presumed martyrdom of Peter and Paul in Rome. It is sometimes extended to include a second Christian generation during which the apostolic witness to Christ continued and the NT canon was completed. Eusebius of Caesarea, the acknowledged father of church history, referred to "the times of the apostles" ([περι...] τῶν ἀποστολικῶν χρόνων, [peri...] tōn apostolikōn chronōn) and significantly linked them with the establishment of "apostolic orthodoxy" (Historia Ecclesiastica III.31.6).

B. Sources

The documentary evidence for the period is found mainly, yet not exclusively, in the NT itself. Although far from exhaustive, what we know about the development of Christianity is much more detailed and specific than the surviving information about several other contemporary religions in the Roman Empire. As K.S. Latourette observes, this is what we should expect, since the records of a victor are more likely to be preserved than those of his defeated rivals.[1] Nevertheless, the records are far from complete. There are frustrating gaps in our knowledge of the apostolic church, for little or nothing is told us about the origin of some important Christian communities.

The letters of Paul constitute a primary source both in extent and quality. The apostle's first missionary journey was undertaken in or about A.D. 46 and it was after this that his correspondence began. He wrote to the local Christian communities he had founded. His purpose was to deal with their inquiries, to advise them on the issues confronting them, and to expound more fully the apostolic message that had already formed the substance of his preaching. Obviously this is an invaluable source of information.

The most direct evidence at our disposal is contained in Acts, which supplies an account of the expansion of the church from its inception in Jerusalem to its eventual establishment in Rome thirty years later. The plan of Acts is clearly stated in 1:8. The reliability of Luke as a historian has been substantially confirmed by recent research, although at the same time it is recognized that his aim was not simply to present a flatly objective report, but to vindicate the Gentile mission both to Christians who had their doubts about it and to pagans who were attracted by it. Acts, of course, is a continuation of Luke's Gospel, and that is a sufficient reminder that the Synoptics themselves answered to the condition of the church in the period of their composition. The seven remaining letters of the NT classified as catholic or general, complete the biblical sources for the apostolic church. The book of Revelation falls outside this immediate period.

---

[1]Kenneth S. Latourette, A History of the Expansion of Christianity (New York: Harper and Row, 1937), 1:69.

C. *Beginnings*

After the ascension the disciples were faced with an unprecedented situation. The great commission to go into all the world and make disciples in every nation had been entrusted to them (Matt 28:19, 20). But they had received no specifications as to how they were to live together as believers or what type of structure was to contain the community. All they had been told to do was to wait in Jerusalem until they were clothed with supernatural power (Luke 24:49).

The gift of the Holy Spirit at Pentecost marks the true birthday of the church. The apostles were driven out of their hiding places to proclaim the good news of what God had done in Christ. The first Christian church appeared in the holy city itself. It was the risen Lord who had reminded the disciples from the Scriptures that repentance and forgiveness of sins were to be proclaimed in his name to all nations starting from Jerusalem (Luke 24:47). It was in connection with the fulfillment of this promise that the apostles were ordered to wait for the bestowal of the Spirit (v.49). When he was given, the church began.

II. The Church in Jerusalem

A. *Foundation and Growth*

Paradoxically, the first Christian congregation was gathered in the very place where opposition to our Lord had been fiercest and where he was put to death as a criminal. Thenceforward, the Jerusalem Church became the mother of all subsequent Christian communities. The center of the old faith also became the center of the new, from which it would spread to the ends of the earth (Acts 1:8). Though Christianity was to be a universal religion, its initial focus was in the city where Jesus had not only died but risen again and ascended to his Father, and where the Holy Spirit was initially poured out. At the close of the age Christ will return to the Mount of Olives to consummate his kingdom (Zech 14:4; Acts 1:11, 12). Then the heavenly Jerusalem will come down to be the abode of those who belong to him. When the gospel began to win its way through the Mediterranean world and beyond, those who lived far from Jerusalem regarded themselves as branches of one body, which had its starting point in the holy city.

From its headquarters at Jerusalem, the tiny community that comprised the primitive church began to grow with remarkable rapidity. We read of three thousand who were added to the church on the day of Pentecost (Acts 2:41). Shortly afterwards the total had reached five thousand (Acts 4:4). The Sanhedrin felt compelled to restrain Peter and his colleagues because, as the high priests put it, they had "filled Jerusalem" with their teaching (Acts 5:28). Despite such opposition, the Word of God spread more widely and the number of disciples in Jerusalem went on increasing (Acts 6:7). Among the converts were Hellenistic Jews of the dispersion (v.1). Most remarkable of all, many of the priestly caste were won over to the Christian faith (v.7). Later in Acts we meet some of the party of the Pharisees who had become believers (Acts 15:5). In Acts 21:20 James and the elders of the Jerusalem church referred to Jewish Christians who could be counted in their thousands.

B. *Relation to Judaism*

Before long, the Jerusalem church was compelled to clarify its position *vis à vis* the Jewish authorities and the religion of Judaism. To the Jews the Christians at first represented a *hairesis* ("sect") or religious party like the Pharisees or the Essenes (Acts 24:5, 14; 28:22). The members of the Jerusalem church were careful to obey the law and to observe the worship of the temple (Acts 2:46). As Goppelt points out, they had not separated themselves publicly as much as had the Essenes.[2]

So the question arises as to whether the followers of Jesus in Jerusalem understood themselves as constituting a separate Jewish movement. Several of the designations by which they identified themselves were in fact similar to those adopted by the Essenes— "the holy ones" (Rom 15:25, 26, 31; 1 Cor 16:1), "God's chosen ones" (Mark 13:20, 22, 27), and "the congregation" (Matt 16:18). Some scholars wonder whether they even used the title "poor." "Brethren" was similar to the rabbinical use of *haber* ("associate"). It is possible that the Christians were looked on as a synagogue of Nazarenes.

Does this mean that the Christians claimed to be the true Israel as did the Pharisees and Essenes? It is clear that they intended something quite different by these designations. They considered themselves not so much the true Israel as the new Israel, in whom the promises were fulfilled. This conviction is apparent throughout the NT and stems from Jesus himself (John 15:1–8; Rom 9:6; Gal 6:16; Heb 12:22–24; 1 Peter 1:1). Our Lord's appointment of the Twelve and his inauguration of the New Covenant sufficiently indicated his purpose in this respect. The way in which Matthias was elected to make up the symbolic number suggests that the disciples had grasped what their Master had intended. When the Greek-speaking Christians later described themselves as belonging to an *ekklesia*, they made it plain that their community was more than a Jewish sect. They saw themselves as part of the new Israel, the messianic people of God. But this was not their own idea; they derived it from the Jerusalem Christians, though we do not know precisely what was the Aramaic equivalent of *ekklesia*.

If it is true, then, that the church in Jerusalem recognized the element of continuity between Judaism and Christianity, it also saw itself as a distinct community with a mission to fulfill—a mission that would eventually embrace both Jew and Gentile in the fellowship of Christ.

C. *Persecution*

It was this growing self-consciousness of the Jerusalem church that led directly to its first persecution at the hands of the Jewish leaders. One of the Hellenist Christians, Stephen by name, drew the fire of the authorities upon himself by his uncompromising accusations against those responsible for the judicial murder of Jesus. In the persecution that followed, Stephen himself was stoned to death and the Hellenists were expelled from the city (Acts 7:54–8:3). As Latourette observed, the proto-martyr of the church "appears to have paid with his life for the contention that Christianity was not just another school of Judaism, but was something new and would supersede the parent faith."[3]

A further attack was instigated by a zealous young Pharisee named Saul from Tarsus who had applauded Stephen's execution (Acts 7:58; 8:1). He set out to harass the Christians in Damascus as he had already done in Jerusalem and Judea (Acts 9:1; 26:10, 11). But soon the persecutor himself became a missionary and gave his life to propagating the gospel he had tried to hinder.

In A.D. 41 Herod Agrippa I succeeded to the jurisdiction formerly entrusted to the

---

[2]Leonhard Goppelt, *Apostolic and Post-Apostolic Times* (London: A. and C. Black, Eng. trans. 1970), p.26.
[3]Latourette, *Expansion of Christianity*, p.71.

procurators of Judea and started a fresh pogrom against the Christians. After securing the execution of James the son of Zebedee, he proceeded to arrest Peter, who miraculously escaped and left the city (Acts 12:1–17). It was only the sudden death of Agrippa that brought peace to the Jerusalem church (Acts 12:23, 24; Jos. *Antiq.* XIX 8). In the next decade, however, the Zealots exerted an increasing influence in Judaism, directing their campaign against those who deviated from the law by consorting with Greeks and Romans. Any Christians who appeared to default would arouse the antagonism of such fanatics. The determination of the Sicarii to assassinate Paul (Acts 23:12–15) shows the lengths to which they were prepared to go.

On the premature death of the governor Festus in A.D. 62, the high priest Annas II seized the opportunity presented by the interregnum to oppress the church again. James the brother of the Lord was charged with violating the law and was sentenced to death along with other believers. Even the Pharisees and the populace condemned this severity, since they knew how scrupulous James had been. Annas was removed from office by the new king, Agrippa II.

There was an uprising of Jews in the year A.D. 66 in protest against the repressive policy of Gessius Florus. Because of their neutral attitude many Christians were killed by the rebels as deserters and traitors. The rest fled for their lives. Most of them settled in Pella, though some joined the Gentile church (*Historia Ecclesiastica* III.5.2.).

With the destruction of Jerusalem in A.D. 70 the special preeminence of the mother church came to an end. Christians, like Jews, belonged to the dispersion. The future of Christianity lay with the pagan nations of the eastern Mediterranean. However, in one particular the virtual disappearance of the Jerusalem church left its mark on the developing communities beyond Palestine. The need to find a replacement for the authority it possessed led to the adoption of its structure and organization by the Christian congregations of the Middle East. Thus Jewish Christianity made a permanent contribution to the emergent universal church. It is to this that we must now turn.

D. *Leadership*

The primitive church did not regard itself primarily as an organized society. It was the New Israel whose members were chosen by God. It was the body of Christ holding within itself the fullness of the one who himself received the entire fullness of God (Eph 1:23). It was the temple not made with hands indwelt by the Holy Spirit. It was the people of God through whom he chose to act in history. Questions of order and oversight did not immediately arise.

Nevertheless, it is clear that from the first the apostles held a special place as guardians of the truth. Jesus had chosen the Twelve to be his representatives and their number indicates that they were to be regarded as the prince-rulers of the New Israel. Apostolic authority, however, was not restricted to the original disciples but included Paul, Barnabas, and others (Acts 14:14; 1 Cor 9:1). The theory that all power was vested exclusively in the original apostles and only delegated for practical reasons under the pressure of circumstances cannot be substantiated. The appointment of seven men to act as welfare officers or almoners in the Jerusalem church was not made by the Twelve alone. They consulted the whole body of believers and invited them to choose. It was only because the proposal commended itself to the entire congregation that the election proceeded. The apostles appointed them, but it was the people who voted for them. The imposition of hands was simply a commissioning and was not designed to impart the gift of the Spirit, for we are told that they were already full of the Spirit and of wisdom (Acts 6:3).

It is noteworthy that although the seven are traditionally regarded as deacons, Luke does not designate them as such in this passage. J.G. Davies thinks that it is arguable that he was deliberately drawing a parallel between this incident and the appointment of the seven elders by Moses (Num 11:16,17).[4] If this typology was calculated, then Luke was writing about the first elders or presbyters who eventually constituted a council in Jerusalem under the presidency of James (Acts 15:6ff.). Certainly we know that Paul and Barnabas appointed elders for each congregation as they pursued their missionary task (Acts 14:23) and it seems probable that such a practice stemmed from the Jerusalem church whether or not this is what is described in Acts 6.

If then James, Peter, and John were rightly regarded as "pillars" of the church, their authority was neither inherent nor exclusive (Gal 2:9). It was exercised in conjunction with elders and perhaps deacons (if they are to be distinguished) and always under the direction of the Spirit (Acts 15:28).

E. Worship

The worship of the Jerusalem church revolved around two centers—the temple and the home. Early in Acts we read how the first Christians met in the temple precincts in order to offer praise to God and teach the truths of the gospel (Acts 2:46; 5:42; cf. Luke 24:53). Jesus himself had regularly taught in the temple (Mark 14:49). The location appears to have been Solomon's Colonnade, which ran along the east side of the outer court (Acts 3:11; 5:12). There are obvious affinities with the voluntary Jewish societies known as ḥaburah, which featured a communal meal. In Acts 3:1 we are told that Peter and John went up to the temple at the ninth hour—the time of the service for public prayer that led up to the offering of the evening sacrifice. The implication is that the apostles continued to worship in the Jewish temple as well as to meet for distinctively Christian purposes. How long this persisted we do not know. We may assume that it ceased when persecution began.

At the same time the Christians also met in their own homes. One of these was in an upstairs room where the eleven lodged after the Ascension (Acts 1:13). This may well have been the same place where Jesus observed the Passover on the eve of his crucifixion, since the definite article appears to indicate a specific upper chamber. It may also have been the scene of the post-resurrection appearances described in Luke 24:33–36 and John 20:19, 26. The house of Mary the mother of John Mark is mentioned in Acts 12:12 as a meeting place for prayer and it is possible, though not demonstrable, that the traditional upper room was located here. Some incline to the view that the references in Acts 2:46 and 5:42—the one to breaking bread and the other to teaching and preaching—in private houses (κατ᾽ οἶκον, kat᾽ oikon) ought really to be translated by the plural "alternately in their houses," suggesting that several homes were made available in succession for this purpose. Others think that the expression simply means "at home," i.e., each family in their own house.

What was the form of worship in the Jerusalem church? It was based on the usage of the synagogue. The emphasis was on listening to the Word of God as it was read and expounded and on speaking to God in prayer and praise. It was natural that Christians should develop their own worship along similar lines. But our Lord himself added an important element to the synagogue ritual when he instituted the supper by which he

---

[4]J.G. Davies, *The Early Christian Church* (London: Weidenfeld and Nicholson 1965), p.47.

chose to be remembered. It is evident from the record in Acts that these two factors were combined in the worship of the Jerusalem church, which in turn set the pattern for other Christian congregations. We are informed that the believers met constantly to hear the apostolic teaching, to have fellowship, to break bread, and to pray (Acts 2:42). This fusion of the synagogue service and the sacrament of the upper room became the norm for all Christian worship.

III. The Church in Palestine

A. Judea

The first seven chapters of Acts concentrate attention on the activities of the church in Jerusalem. From chapter 8 onward the scope is widened to include Judea and Samaria. After the stoning of Stephen a time of violent persecution set in. The result was that all the Christians except the apostles themselves fled from the city and were dispersed throughout the rural areas. It was the Hellenists who were immediately involved, although it is perhaps an oversimplification to imagine that the Aramaic-speaking believers were altogether unmolested. Indeed, G.B. Caird contends that it was these latter who established the churches in Judea while the Hellenists went farther afield.[5] When Paul wrote to the Galatians, he explained to them that, though he visited Jerusalem, he remained unknown by sight to the congregations of Christ in Judea (Gal 1:22). Among the places where Christian congregations are known to have existed are Joppa (Acts 10:23), Lydda (9:32–38), and Caesarea (10:45).

B. Samaria

Like the churches in Judea, those in Samaria were founded by refugees from Jerusalem. The pioneer evangelist was Philip, one of the seven almoners. When driven from the capital, he went north to Samaria and preached the good news there (Acts 8:4, 5). It was a bold step on his part to go to those who were not of pure Jewish extraction. They did nevertheless share the messianic hope, and no doubt Philip regarded this as a starting point (John 4:25). It is not certain whether the city involved was actually Samaria itself, which had been renamed Sebaste. If the definite article is omitted, following some textual readings, then the allusion may be to Gitta, mentioned by Justin Martyr as the birthplace of Simon Magus (Apol I.26).

The work progressed so rapidly and grew so demanding that Peter and John were dispatched from Jerusalem to inspect it and to lend a hand. Afterwards a number of Samaritan villages were evangelized before Philip and the apostles returned to Jerusalem (Acts 8:25).

C. Galilee

How did the church in Galilee begin? Some of the resurrection appearances occurred here. Possibly the five hundred referred to in 1 Corinthians 15:6 belonged to this region, though it is more likely that they were from Jerusalem. Certainly we learn of Christians here at an early stage (Acts 9:31). Were the communities founded by refugees from

---

[5]George B. Caird, *The Apostolic Age*, (London: Duckworth, 1955), p.87.

Jerusalem like those in Judea and Samaria, or were groups of disciples there from the beginning?

The theory of an independent center of Christianity in Galilee has been invoked to clear up a number of unsolved problems raised by the NT. Saul of Tarsus was converted when he was on his way to harry the Christians in Damascus (Acts 9:21). How had the church there been founded? Was it the result of a mission from Galilee, which was nearer than Jerusalem? Where had Apollos been instructed in the way of the Lord (Acts 18:25)? The only baptism he knew was that of John. Had he been introduced to Christianity through a line of transmission that could be traced to Galilee? The same question might be asked about the twelve disciples at Ephesus who had not even heard about the Holy Spirit (Acts 19:2).

Fascinating as these speculations are, they have no firm basis in fact, and alternative answers can be provided for the questions they raise. It is safer to conclude with Caird that the Galilean churches, like those of Judea and Samaria, were founded by the missionary movement that followed the death of Stephen.[6]

IV. The Church in Antioch

A. Position and Importance

So far, we have considered only the apostolic church in Israel. We must now turn to the first largely Gentile church. It emerged at a remarkably early stage. While those who were compelled to leave Jerusalem after the martyrdom of Stephen went at first only to the Jews, it was not long before a Christian community was formed that included Gentiles as well. This was in Antioch, the capital of Syria.

Situated on a fertile plain fed by the river Orontes, this beautiful city was recognized as "the queen of the East." It was originally a Greek settlement founded by Seleucus I Nicator after his victory. By now it was the third largest metropolis in the Roman Empire, boasting a population of over 300,000, of whom one-tenth were Jews. It was an impressive place with its broad streets well-lit by lamps at night and its magnificent sculptured colonnades. Located at the junction of East and West both by land and sea, it was a cosmopolitan center of trade. Here the imperial legate had his residence. Antioch was renowned for its culture and was praised by Cicero in this respect. But it was also a byword for immorality: at nearby Daphne orgiastic rites were celebrated in sanctuaries dedicated to Artemis and Apollo. This was where the first Gentile church was planted.

B. Foundation and Composition

Antioch is mentioned in Acts 11:19 along with Phoenicia and Cyprus, as one of the places to which the persecuted Christians fled from Jerusalem. Initially they preached only to Jews, but soon some natives of Cyprus and Cyrene were more daring and actually announced the Good News of the Lord Jesus to pagans as well (Acts 11:19, 20). The power of God was displayed in the conversion of many and so the church was established (v.21). There is an obvious link with v.18. Soon Antioch was to become a missionary center and a mother church, like Jerusalem itself.

It was here that the name "Christian" was first applied to the followers of Jesus (Acts

---

[6] Ibid., p.89.

11:26). They were quite clearly differentiated from the Jewish community. Gentiles were freely received into their fellowship after being baptized. No attempt was made to enforce circumcision or any other requirement of the ceremonial law of Judaism (Acts 15:5; Gal 2:2–5, 11–13). Observers recognized that here was a community that, although in some way connected with Judaism, was obviously independent of it. A new name had to be coined to describe the members of this community. Perhaps around A.D. 40 they began to be known as Christians. "The event in Antioch was thus a second beginning in the setting of the stage for Church history," Goppelt claims.[7] Christianity was liberated from its Jewish swaddling-cloths and could now reach out into the Gentile world. Since the time of the Seleucid dynasty, Jews had enjoyed equal political rights with the Greeks (Jos. War VII 43–45). Now the Christian church recognized a similar parity. Greeks were accorded the full privileges of membership along with the Jews without the necessity of conforming to the ritual demands of the law.

C. Relations With Jerusalem

News of what had been happening at Antioch soon reached the apostles in Jerusalem. No doubt some were disturbed, though Peter had already realized the the need to reach out to the Gentiles. Barnabas was dispatched to make investigations and he was more than pleased with what he found. It appears that other members of the Jerusalem church followed later and some became recognized leaders. The names of those mentioned by Luke in Acts 13:1 reveal the fact that they came from Palestine. Manaen (the Greek form of the Hebrew Menahem) had been reared in the court of Herod the Great, where he was a close companion of Herod Antipas. Lucius was from Cyrene and evidently became a Christian in Jerusalem before going as a missionary to Antioch. Simeon, known as Niger (or "Black"), also came from Palestine, to judge by his names.

That these men from Jerusalem occupied such a prominent position in the Christian community at Antioch indicates that the essential unity of the primitive church was unbroken. Indeed, it was the Christians from Jerusalem who conveyed to the Gentiles their most precious treasure—the gospel tradition. "Thus the Christian portrait of Christ was protected from the dangers of mythology and gnostic speculation," A. Schlatter explained. "It might easily have happened, once the gospel was detached from its native Jewish soil, that Christianity should lose its roots in history."[8] It is significant that Luke, who in all likelihood became a Christian in Antioch, was one of the most careful historians of Jesus' ministry.

Before long, Barnabas realized that he needed a colleague to share the task of supervising the work at Antioch and the mission to the Gentiles that was to spring from it. He set off for Tarsus to enlist the help of Paul, who was evangelizing in his native city and its environs and had already seen a considerable number of converts among the Gentiles (Acts 11:25, 26). The arrival of Paul in Antioch marks the start of a new era in missionary outreach in which Paul himself was to be the key figure (see article on THE LIFE AND MINISTRY OF PAUL, pp. 557–574).

When Paul and Barnabas returned from their first missionary expedition, they reported to the church at Antioch, which had commissioned them (Acts 14:26, 27). It was at some point after this that a deputation arrived from Jerusalem, insisting that there could be no salvation apart from circumcision (Acts 15:1). It is not clear how official or repre-

---

[7]Goppelt, *Apostolic and Post-Apostolic Times.*, p.62.

[8]Adolf Schlatter, *The Church in the New Testament Period* (London: SPCK, Eng. trans. 1955), p.109.

sentative these visitors were; some texts add that they were Pharisees, and this is a probable conjecture. The way Luke described them does not seem to imply that they were either apostles themselves or delegated by the apostles. As a result of the controversy, however, it was agreed that Paul and Barnabas, together with other representatives of the Antioch church, should travel to Jerusalem to confer with the apostles and elders there (Acts 15:2). The future of Gentile Christianity was at stake. The Council of Jerusalem recognized a gospel free from the inhibitions of the law. That is apparent from the accounts both in Acts and Galatians (Acts 15:28; Gal 2:6). "In this matter the two branches of Christianity current at that time were brought together into an ecclesiological fellowship in spite of all the differences in their way of life," declares Goppelt.[9]

V. The Church in Rome

A. Origins

It is uncertain when or how the church in Rome was established. Probably Christianity arrived in the capital at a fairly early stage. By what means it was brought we are not told. Since, however, each Christian regarded himself as a witness responsible for propagating the faith, it may be concluded that it was through the rank-and-file believers that the gospel reached the hub of the empire. Since we do not read of any specific missionary enterprise that had Rome as its target, it is reasonable to suppose that it was in the course of normal social exchange—the movement of soldiers and merchants—that the saving news was conveyed. There were Jews from Rome in Jerusalem on the day of Pentecost (Acts 2:10). Converts among them could have been the pioneers in establishing the church within a year of the Crucifixion.

At first the authorities failed to distinguish Christianity from Judaism, as had been the case elsewhere. The church was undisturbed by persecution till the year A.D. 49 when, according to Suetonius, the Emperor Claudius banished the Jews from the city because they kept rioting at the instigation of "Chrestus" (*Vita Claudii* XXV.4). Evidently the formation of a Christian community in Rome had led to a split in the synagogues. Eight years later, so Tacitus records, Pomponia Graecina, wife of Aulus Plautus, conqueror of Britain, was brought before one of her husband's courts on a charge of embracing a foreign superstition. She was eventually discharged but thereafter "lived a long life of unbroken melancholy" (*Annales* XIII.32). This could be interpreted as meaning that she had become a Christian and had renounced worldly pleasures.

B. Peter and Paul

Much discussion has surrounded the connection between the apostle Peter and the church in Rome. Although it is evident that he was not the founder of the Christian society there, it is nevertheless likely that he did stay in the city after visiting Corinth (1 Cor 1:12; 9:5). The researches of O. Cullmann, among others, have established the probability of such a stay.[10] However, when Paul wrote to the Romans in A.D. 57, it can be assumed Peter was not there, for otherwise it would be incredible that no reference should be made to him. Cullmann thinks Peter may have gone to Rome after Paul had

---

[9]Goppelt, *Apostolic and Post-Apostolic Times* p.77.
[10]Cf. Oscar Cullmann, *Peter: Disciple, Apostle, Martyr* (London: SCM, Eng. trans. 1953).

written his letter.[11] When Paul speaks about his reluctance to build on the foundation laid by others (Rom 15:20), the reference would thus not be to Peter but to those who first preached the gospel in the capital.

As for Paul, he did not reach Rome until A.D. 60. He had been contemplating a visit for some time. He had met Aquila and Priscilla, who were evidently members of the original Roman congregation. In A.D. 57 Paul dictated a letter to his friend and amanuensis Tertius, designed to prepare the Christians in Rome for his coming to them and to set out the essence of the gospel as he interpreted and proclaimed it. Actually, he reached Rome as a prisoner to face his trial before the Emperor. He was met at the staging-post of Appii Forum by a group of Christians who escorted him into the city in a sort of triumphal procession (Acts 28:15, 16). For the next two years he was allowed to receive visitors in his private lodgings before his eventual martyrdom.

C. *Membership and Importance*

What kind of church existed in Rome when Paul arrived there in A.D. 60? Was it based exclusively on the concept of Jewish Christianity like that at Jerusalem, or was it a community in which Jews and Gentiles coexisted with equal rights like that at Antioch? We have to ask whether Paul would have invited a Jewish Christian church to accept one who was weak in his faith without attempting to insist on doubtful points (Rom 14:1) or whether he would have told its members that God is not God of the Jews alone but of the Gentiles also (Rom 3:29). On the other hand, if this was indeed a mixed church, it must have consisted mainly of proselytes and Hellenists, or at least of Gentiles who were familiar with the Jewish Scriptures and Jewish ideas. The Roman Church, then, was by no means predominantly Jewish. Indeed, it can be said to have been Gentile in general complexion. The list of names to whom greetings are sent in Chapter 16 (assuming that they are addressed to Rome) represents a cross section both of Jews and Gentiles.

The church in Rome must have grown to a considerable size by the time of Paul's arrival. Tacitus refers to "an immense multitude" of Christians who were arrested and punished during Nero's persecution in A.D. 64 (*Annales* XV.44). This is confirmed by Clement of Rome as he speaks about a "large body of the elect" who suffered indignities and torture (*Cor* 6:1). Unless the Christians had been convincingly numerous, it would hardly have been possible to accuse them of constituting a public menace. The remarkable progress of the church in Rome in succeeding decades, despite the heavy losses it sustained during the time of severe persecution and martyrdom, indicates its considerable strength.

The church in Rome undoubtedly attained a certain superiority in the Christian world. The reasons are not far to seek. It was the church of the imperial capital. Its centrality made it a rendezvous for Christians from many parts. Its association with both Peter and Paul gave it a special prominence. It was the first major Christian community to face persecution by the state and produce martyrs for the faith. The other churches looked increasingly to Rome for leadership as they formerly did to Jerusalem and Antioch.

---

[11] *Ibid.*, p.80.

VI. Conclusion

During the Pauline period the Hellenistic church displayed a remarkable homogeneity. This may be partly accounted for by the fact that the various Gentile Christian communities traced their origin to the missionary outreach from Antioch. Paul represented a coordinating factor of the first magnitude. At the close of the apostolic age the regional churches were beginning to assume their own distinctive characteristics within the recognized unity of the entire Christian body.

The expansion of the church took place in well-defined stages. Palestine was the first. Antioch and Syria constituted the second stage. Rome was to grow in prominence. Ephesus was the center for Asia Minor. There were notable Christian churches in Europe apart from Rome, especially in Greece. Paul talked about going to Spain, but we have no evidence that he ever got there or that Gaul was evangelized at that time. Egypt remains an enigma. Papyrus discoveries show that Christianity existed there at an early date, but there is no precise information about the foundation of the church in Alexandria. Apollos, who was an Alexandrian by birth, seems to have had some sort of acquaintance with Christian teaching prior to his arrival in Ephesus (Acts 18:25). Would Paul have failed to include Alexandria in his itinerary unless the church was already established there? By the end of the apostolic age the gospel was proving itself to be "the power of God for salvation" (Rom 1:16) over a considerable area.

Finally, a brief reference must be made to the condition of the church during the remainder of the first century. We have taken the view, held by recent historians, that the apostolic age proper terminated in A.D. 64. The following period is designated as subapostolic or postapostolic. Sometimes, however, it is described as Johannine in succession to the Petrine and Pauline era. It marks a transition from the apostolic to the early Catholic church.

Documentary sources for the second generation church are fewer than for the apostolic age. Once again, most of the information we possess comes from the NT itself, along with the accumulating traditions of the Christian communities. But the evidence is not comparable either in extent or detail with what the narrative in Acts and sundry allusions in the Pauline correspondence provide for the earlier period. F.V. Filson dubs these years after A.D. 64 "the obscure decade."[12]

With the migration to Pella and the fall of Jerusalem, Jewish Christianity was to exert little further influence. In Lietzmann's words, "It sank into oblivion in the lonely deserts of East Jordan."[13] A tiny minority returned to Palestine to restore the Christian presence both in Jerusalem itself and in Judea and Galilee. Some missionary impact was made on the population for we learn from rabbinic literature that about A.D. 90 a specific curse against the Nazarenes was interpolated into the Prayer of the Eighteen Petitions. Eusebius reported that Simeon, son of Clopas, succeeded James as the leader of the Jerusalem church and held office until his martyrdom in the second century (*Historia Ecclesiastica* III.11; 32 v. 1–4).

As for Gentile Christianity, rather more is known about the progress of the church in the province of Asia than elsewhere. The Apocalypse, probably written, as Irenaeus believed (*Adv. Haer.* 5.30.3), in the reign of Domitian (A.D. 81–96), is addressed to the seven churches faced with the threat of intensified persecution. A previous oppressive

---

[12]Floyd V. Filson, *A New Testament History* (London: SCM, 1965), p.295.

[13]Hans Lietzmann, *The Beginnings of the Christian Church* (London: Lutterworth Press, Eng. trans. 1937), p.183.

phase resulted in the martyrdom of Antipas from Pergamum (Rev 2:13; 6:9). But the writer anticipates a head-on collision between church and state, since Domitian was the first emperor to assume the divine title "Lord God" (Suetonius, *Domitian*. 13). The book of the Revelation was intended to encourage the Christians to stand firm in the impending crisis. Evidence of missionary expansion is afforded by the fact that five of the seven churches are not mentioned either in Acts or in the NT letters.

If the church was compelled to endure the pressures of external persecution, it was also troubled by heresy within. The Johannine letters roundly denounce "the spirit of antichrist" (1 John 4:3), which refuses to recognize the reality of the Incarnation. This incipient Docetism was one aspect of a primitive form of the Gnostic heresy that had already begun to assert its damaging influence. Antinomian tendencies are exposed by Jude. The church of the subapostolic age was concerned with defending the faith (Jude 3).

The question of ecclesiastical order and discipline assumed an increasing importance in this period. The passing of the apostles and the incidence of heresy and pseudo-charismatic excesses compelled the church to tackle this issue by the turn of the century. In A.D. 96 Clement of Rome wrote a lengthy letter reprimanding the Christians in Corinth who had deposed their elders. Since these leaders had been appointed on apostolic authority as well as by common consent, they were not to be regarded as dispensable.

The church moved into the second century conscious of the conflicts its mission involved, acknowledging the need for a considered *apologia* in view of deviations from orthodoxy, and ready to strengthen its structures so as to increase its effectiveness as the instrument of the gospel.

VII. Bibliography

Bartlet, J. Vernon. *The Apostolic Age: Its Life, Doctrine, Worship and Polity*. Edinburgh: T. and T. Clark, 1900.
Caird, George B. *The Apostolic Age*. London: Duckworth, 1955.
Goppelt, Leonhard. *Apostolic and Post-Apostolic Times*. London: A. and C. Black, Eng. trans. 1970.
Lietzmann, Hans. *The Beginnings of the Christian Church*. London: Lutterworth, Eng. trans. 1937.
Schaff, Philip. *History of the Apostolic Church*. New York: Scribner, 1869.
Schlatter, Adolf. *The Church in the New Testament Period*. London: SPCK, Eng. trans. 1955.

THE CHRONOLOGY AND METROLOGY OF THE NEW TESTAMENT

Lewis A. Foster

Lewis A. Foster

A.B., A.M., M.Div., Cincinnati Bible Seminary; A.B., University of Indiana; B.D., Yale University; S.T.M., Ph.D., Harvard University

Professor of New Testament, Cincinnati Christian Seminary

THE CHRONOLOGY OF THE NEW TESTAMENT

To bring into focus the chronology of the New Testament involves three steps: (1) determining the measurements of time and certain fixed dates contemporary with the NT writings, (2) examination of biblical data to be synchronized with secular events, and (3) review of variant suggestions, both ancient and modern, that point up difficulties and provide solutions leaving the fewest unresolved questions.

I. Contemporary Details

A. *Roman Records*

Just before the Christian era Julius Caesar had attempted to correct the confusion of former time records.[1] His Julian calendar divided the solar year into twelve months of

---

[1]E. Bickerman, *Chronology of the Ancient World* (Ithica, N.Y.: Cornell University Press, 1968).

thirty or thirty-one days with one month of twenty-eight days (twenty-nine days every fourth year). This reckoning, revised by Gregory XIII in 1582, has continued in use to the present. A week of eight days was common, but this was independent of the month and marked the time from one market day to the next. The seven-day week gradually prevailed, being introduced from the East and supported by the Christians.

The abbreviation A.U.C. stood for *ab urbe condita*, "from the foundation of the city," or *anno urbis conditae*, "in the year of the founded city." Varro[2] dated the founding in 01. 6, 3 (the first Olympiad [01.1] was supposed to have been held in 776 B.C., and the Olympiads occurred every four years: the numbers 6, 3 would be the third year of the sixth Olympiad). The later designation of the Christian era, 754 A.U.C. = A.D. 1, is commonly held to have been introduced by Dionysius Exiguus (d.c. 550), though some maintain that Hippolytus led to its adoption in the East at an earlier time.[3]

More common than the A.U.C. designation was the use of the names of rulers, especially the Roman consuls. Since consuls commonly served only one year, the reference to the two current consuls would suffice to define a year date. From the beginning of the Roman Empire in the time of Augustus, the year of the emperor's reign was also used to designate a specific time.

Another way of dating was by the citation of honors. Emperors received by special vote the consulship, tribunician power, and imperial acclamation (*imperator*). These were granted a number of times and reference to the honor plus the number of times it was received aided in determining the chronology of events. Also dates might be indicated by referring to local rulers in particular areas.

B. *Jewish Time*

The Jews used a lunar calendar with two New Year's days six months apart—one an ecclesiastical year for designating festivals and the beginning of Jewish reigns (Nisan 1), the other a civil year used for secular affairs and for the reigns of foreign kings (Tishri 1). To bring the lunar year back into harmony with the solar year, a thirteenth month was intercalated between Adar and Nisan when inopportune harvest time demanded it.

The first day of the month was determined by actual observation of the crescent of the new moon. A committee met in Jerusalem after the close of the twenty-ninth day and awaited the testimony of two witnesses that the new moon had been seen in the sky. The possibility of a cloudy night at the time of the new moon and the uncertainty of the year in which an intercalated month would be included, make unsure the absolute identification of any particular day in any particular year.

The Jews calculated the passage of days from sunset to sunset. Thus their day began at 6 o'clock in the evening, though they numbered their hours of the day from 6 A.M. This differed from the Roman method, which measured days from midnight to midnight. The difference is reflected in the Gospel narratives. Mark describes the time of Jesus' crucifixion as the "third hour" (15:25), but the Gospel of John notes the time of his earlier condemnation as the "sixth hour" (19:14). The difference is reasonably accounted for by recognizing that Mark uses the Jewish method (third hour = 9 A.M.) and John employs the Roman designation (sixth hour = 6 A.M.). John's use of hours in the rest of his Gospel

---

[2]See Plutarch, *Life of Romuluꞓ* 12.
[3]W.H. Hatch, *An Album of Dated Syriac Manuscripts.* (Cambridge: Harvard University Press, 1946), p. 19.

SYNCHRONIZED JEWISH CALENDAR			
Numbers		*Names of Months*	*Farm Seasons*
1	(7)	Nisan	(March-April)	Begin barley harvest
2	(8)	Iyyar	(April-May)	Barley Harvest
3	(9)	Sivan	(May-June)	Wheat harvest
4	(10)	Tammuz	(June-July)	
5	(11)	Ab	(July-Aug.)	Grape, fig, olive ripe
6	(12)	Elul	(Aug.-Sept.)	Vintage begins
7	(1)	Tishri	(Sept.-Oct.)	Early rains; plowing
8	(2)	Heshvan	(Oct.-Nov.)	Wheat, barley sowing
9	(3)	Kislev	(Nov.-Dec.)	
10	(4)	Tebeth	(Dec.-Jan.)	Rainy winter months
11	(5)	Shebat	(Jan.-Feb.)	New Year for trees
12	(6)	Adar	(Feb.-March)	Almonds blooming
13		Adar Sheni		Intercalary month

The first column indicates the numerical order of months in the sacred calendar; the numbers in parentheses show the civic year beginning with Tishri. After ZPEB, 1:688.

(1:39; 4:6; 5:52; 19:14), shows that the Roman method fits best for the whole of the book.[4] Elsewhere in the NT the Jewish method seems to be indicated.

C. Key Dates

Certain fixed dates assist in locating NT incidents in time. They serve as a knot in the end of the thread of biblical chronology.

1. *Death of Herod the Great.* One date that can be fixed with certainty is the death of Herod the Great. Josephus records the events accompanying Herod's end in such a way that the time is unmistakable. The week of the Passover was approaching, a lunar eclipse had just occurred, and the length of his reign is specified (Antiq. 17.6.4; 17.8.1; 17.9.3; 14.16.4). The year 4 B.C. is definite, and the day, April 4, is highly probable (cf. Matt 2:19).

2. *Death of Herod Agrippa I.* Evidence from Josephus makes fairly certain the date of Herod Agrippa I's death also (Antiq. 19.8.2; 18.6.10; 18.7.2; 19.5.1). He records that Herod had reigned seven years, four as Caligula was ruling the empire, and three under Claudius. Eusebius corroborates this in his *Chronicle.* The festival held at the time of the

---

[4]B.F. Westcott, *Gospel of St. John,* 3rd ed. 1903, p. 282; Norman Walker, "The Reckoning of Hours in the Fourth Gospel," NovTest 4 (Oct., 1960): 69–73.

king's death (see Acts 12:21; Jos. Antiq. 19.8.2) has been identified as the quadrennial games he instituted in 9 B.C. This has helped confirm Josephus and the establishment of A.D. 44 for the death of Herod Agrippa I.

3. *Gallio, proconsul of Achaia.* The date of Gallio's proconsulship in Achaia has been settled by a chain of notices. An inscription at Delphi records a letter from Emperor Claudius. His list of honors shows he had been voted *imperator* twenty-six times. It is likely that this vote came early in A.D. 52. The inscription also states that Junius Gallio was proconsul in Achaia. Although the time of his arrival or the length of his holding office is uncertain, it was either from the summer of 51 to the summer of 52 or from the summer of 52 to the summer of 53.

D. *Pivotal Points*

Certain other secular dates are equally important to NT chronology but cannot be settled with full assurance. Much depends on where these secular dates are placed as to how NT events are fixed in time.

1. *Aretas, authority in Damascus.* Aretas was a Nabataean king who reigned from Petra within the approximate limits of 9 B.C. to A.D. 40. He had authority in Damascus when the order for Paul's arrest was sent out early in Paul's Christian career (2 Cor 11:32). Aretas, however, had been out of favor with Tiberius, and Damascene coins struck in A.D. 33–34 and later in 62–63 bear the heads of the emperors Tiberius and Nero respectively, with no reference to a local prince. One is forced to conclude that Aretas did not have authority in Damascus till after 34 and more than likely not till after the death of Tiberius in 37.[5] The dating of Saul's conversion turns on this because he specified that he left Damascus, following the threat of arrest, three years after his conversion (Gal 1:17, 18; cf. Acts 9:19b–25; 2 Cor 11:32).

2. *The famine.* From Josephus[6] one learns of a famine in Judea. This must have occurred when Alexander was procurator in the land. The tenure of Fadus and his successor, Alexander, fell within the years of 44 to 48. The famine occurred in the winter of 45/46 or 46/47.

3. *Expulsion of the Jews.* Because of disorder aroused by the Jews, Claudius felt it necessary to expel them from Rome.[7] The explicit dating of this event comes from Orosius, a historian in the early fifth century.[8] He claims to be using Josephus as his authority, but no extant passage of Josephus confirms this. Orosius dates the expulsion in the ninth year of Claudius or A.D. 49.

4. *Festus succeeds Felix.* The most important pivot point in the chronology of Acts is the date of Festus's arrival in Caesarea to replace Felix. Upon this date turn all of the events in the life of Paul before and after his two years in the Caesarean imprisonment. One is forced to piece together bits of information in order to reach a conclusion. The

---

[5]C.H. Turner, "Chronology of New Testament," HDB, 1 (1901): 416.
[6]Antiq. 3.15.3; 3.32.1; 20.1.1, 2; 20.2.1–5; 20.5.1, 2.
[7]Suetonius, *Life of Claudius,* 25.
[8]7.6.15.

most puzzling statement to fit in is found in Josephus. He affirms that when Felix was recalled, he was forced to stand trial for his deeds but that "he was acquitted because of his brother Pallas, who was held in the highest esteem by Nero."[9] As a matter of fact, the record shows that Nero never did like Pallas.[10] He removed him from office in 55 and had him poisoned in 62. On the other hand, Pallas was a favorite of Claudius, Nero's predecessor, and it may be that Josephus has confused an observation that could have been made concerning Felix's prior court experience with Cumanus[11] and mistakenly applied it to Paul's second trial in the time of Nero.[12] The most likely date for the replacement of Felix is 60. This allows time for the many events of Felix's office recorded in Josephus and for the many years of rule cited by Paul in his speech delivered two years before Felix's recall (Acts 24:10). It also allows a reasonable length of time for the few events recorded of Festus before his death in June (?) of 62 and the arrival of Albinus three months later.[13]

II. Biblical Data

A. Dated Events

Luke follows most closely the practices of historians of his time. He stops on several occasions to date what he is speaking of. So he locates the beginning of John the Baptist's ministry by listing both Roman and local rulers (Luke 3:1–2). But even this leaves the specific year a maze of possibilities. Pontius Pilate was in power from A.D. 26 to 36; Herod Antipas was deposed in 39; Philip died in 34; nothing is known of Lysanius in this period; and Caiphas was deposed at a Passover, not later than 34. The one precise figure given is "the fifteenth year of Tiberius Caesar." Even this is open to various interpretations. If the fifteenth year is counted from the death of Augustus, this would be A.D. 29; but if the fifteenth year is counted from the Jewish system of beginning a foreign rule from the month of Tishri, this would designate the year 27 for the beginning of John's ministry; but Augustus gave Tiberius authority in the province in A.D. 11, and using this as a starting point, 26 would be the date in question. This narrows the possibilities, but still leaves necessary the use of other biblical data in order to find the exact point that best fits all the details.

Other NT notations of time show an awareness of chronology. The famine of Acts 11:28 is dated "in the days of Claudius Caesar." At other points at least the time of year is indicated: four months until the harvest (John 4:35), Passover (John 6:4), green grass in Galilee (Mark 6:39), the Feast of Unleavened Bread (Acts 20:6, 7), and winter storms (Acts 27:9ff.). It is necessary, however, to attempt to synchronize the historical allusions with secular notices before drawing final conclusions as to dates.

B. Birth of Jesus

The date of Jesus' birth is related to that of Herod the Great's death. When the wise men were on their way to honor Jesus, they stopped to make inquiry of Herod concern-

---

[9]Antiq. 20.8.9.
[10]Tacitus, *Annals* 13.2.
[11]Ibid., 12.54.
[12]See T. Zahn, *Introduction to the New Testament*, vol. 3 (New York: Charles Scribner's Sons, 1917), p. 473.
[13]Jos. Antiq. 20.9.1.

ing the birth of the new king. Obviously Herod was not yet dead, but by our system of denoting time, Herod died in 4 B.C., and this is a firm date (see above). Dionysius Exiguus made a mistake in calculating the division of time at Jesus' birth, and the calendar has continued in use, but Jesus' birth is known to have been at least before April of 4 B.C.

One might hope for further help from the dating of Augustus' first census when Quirinius was governor of Syria. But here also the secular records leave many blanks. That censuses were taken in the provinces is fully established. Later they were to be fourteen years apart, but when they were begun in Syria is not recorded.

One might observe that an early census based on the fourteen-year cycle should have taken place in Syria in 8/7 B.C. But since this is the first census in this province, it may well have been a year or two late. Under such circumstances the years 6–4 B.C. would be highly possible for the time of Jesus' birth.

That Saturninus is listed as governor of Syria 9–6 B.C. and Varus 6–4 B.C. does not rule out the possibility of Quirinius' being the next governor,[14] nor does it preclude the possibility of Quirinius's being a special imperial legate sent for the particular task of conducting the census while another official occupied the normal office of governor. The word used by Luke for "governed" (*hēgemoneuō*) is quite general and need not be restricted to one office.

After viewing the material Finegan can only affirm: "Perhaps a date for the birth of Jesus sometime in the winter of 5/4 B.C. best satisfies all the available evidence."[15]

C. *Ministry of Jesus*

Luke specifies that Jesus was about thirty years of age when he began his ministry (3:23). This might indicate a time anywhere from a year or two before age thirty to a year or two after.

When the Jews disputed with Jesus in the temple area early in his ministry, they specified that forty-six years had been spent in building the temple (John 2:20). Construction was still going on, and its completion was not reached till 64, just six years before its destruction. Josephus records that Herod started construction on the temple in the eighteenth year of his reign.[16] The date would be 19 B.C. This would indicate that Jesus was discoursing in the temple area in A.D. 27. In all probability Jesus' ministry began the year before. Since Jesus was about thirty years old at the time, the year 4 B.C. or a year or two earlier would be indicated for his birth.

The duration of Jesus' ministry is not specified in the Gospel narratives. But the Gospel of John records a number of annual feast days that necessitate the passage of several years. By counting the Passovers indicated (2:23; 6:4; 11:55 and numbering 5:1 as a Passover), the length of three and a half years is estimated as most likely for Jesus' ministry. Mark refers to seasons of ripe grain (2:23), green grass (6:39), and the final Passover (14:1). This might be used to reconstruct a two-year period, but it does not rule out the possibility of more.

D. *Date of the Crucifixion*

The four Gospels give the day of the week as a Friday. This day is called "Preparation"; it was the day before the Sabbath (Mark 15:42; Matt 28:1; Luke 23:56; John 19:31)

---

[14]Cf. W. Ramsay, *Was Christ Born at Bethlehem?* (New York: G.P. Putnam's Sons, 1898).
[15]Jack Finegan, *Handbook of Biblical Chronology* (Princeton: Princeton University Press, 1964), p. 392.
[16]Antiq. 25.11.1.

and the next day was the first day of the week (Mark 16:2; Matt 28:1; Luke 24:1; John 20:1). All four Gospels describe a meal eaten the evening before Jesus' death, and the Synoptics make clear that this was the Passover meal (Matt 26:17–19; Mark 14:12–16; Luke 22:15).

Some, however, feel that the terminology "three days and three nights" demands a period of a full seventy-two hours. This necessitates a date of the Crucifixion in mid-week and a reinterpretation of "Preparation" and "Sabbath" as referring to a Passover Sabbath and not necessarily the usual Friday and Saturday. On the other hand, Jews were accustomed to counting any part of a day as a full day and the question remains whether seventy-two hours is actually demanded or not. The Passover lamb was regular-ly slain on Nisan 14 and the meal was eaten that night. Since in the Jewish division of time a day began at 6 P.M., this means that the Passover was eaten on Thursday night, the beginning of Nisan 15, and that Jesus was crucified Friday morning, still Nisan 15.

Certain references in John have led some to maintain that Jesus was crucified on Nisan 14.[17] The day of Jesus' trial and execution is noted as "the day of Preparation of Passover Week" (John 19:14), the Jews refused to go into the judgment hall of Pilate because they did not want to become defiled and subsequently miss eating the Passover (John 18:28), and Jesus himself was the sacrificial "Passover lamb" (1 Cor 5:7). All this is interpreted by some to mean that despite the Synoptic description of the Last Supper, the Passover had not yet occurred. The word *Passover*, however, can mean three things: (1) the lamb, (2) the feast, and (3) the week (e.g., Ezek 45:21, ". . . the Passover, a feast of seven days"). If the concern of the Jews in their demand to Pilate refers to a feast later in the Passover Week, such as Chagiga,[18] and the day of Preparation means simply Friday of the Passover Week (*Preparation* is the usual word for Friday),[19] John can be understood as being in full agreement with the Synoptics. The Passover lamb was slain on Thursday afternoon and eaten that evening. There is no absolute requirement that Christ's death as the Passover lamb be restricted to one particular time, neither is it necessary to have Jesus' keeping the Passover a day ahead of time whether by Dispersion calculation or unofficial Jewish tactics[20] or keeping it on Tuesday according to the sect at Qumran.[21]

If Nisan 15 was on Friday in that year, astronomers should be able to designate the year this happened.[22] Unfortunately, the Jewish method of intercalating months and starting each month by the sighting of the new moon (see above), interject some uncertainty. Three possibilities are worthy of note: (1) "In A.D. 29 Friday, March 18, may have been Nisan 14 (if there was no intercalation); (2) In A.D. 30 Friday, April 7, was either Nisan 14 or 15; (3) In A.D. 33 Friday, April 3, may have been Nisan 14."[23]

The choices that seem most viable in dating the life of Jesus are a three-and-a-half-year ministry, with A.D. 30 as the date of Jesus' crucifixion and resurrection and sometime before April, 4 B.C. for his birth.

---

[17]Finegan, *Handbook of Biblical Chronology*, pp. 287–88.

[18]SBK 2(1956): 837–38.

[19]E.g., Jos. Antiq. 16.6.2.

[20]Finegan, *Handbook of Biblical Chronology*, pp. 289–90.

[21]A. Jaubert, *La date de la cene* (1957); Norman Walker, "Concerning the Jaubertian Chronology of the Passion," in NovTest, 3(1959): 317–20; cf. George Ogg, "Review of Jaubert, *La date de la cene*," in NovTest, 3(1959): 149–60.

[22]J.K. Fotheringham, "The Evidence of Astronomy and Technical Chronology for the Date of the Crucifixion," *Journal of Theological Studies* 35(1934): 146ff.

[23]G.B. Caird, "Chronology of the New Testament," IDB, 1 (1962): 603.

E. *Life of Paul*

Dates for the life of Paul are dependent on information drawn from the Book of Acts and Paul's Epistles. Some scholars attempt to discount Acts, claiming that it is not a reliable source for historical references to Paul (e.g., J. Knox; cf. III.B.4, below). Such denials fail to give Luke credit for the detailed accuracy proved in his writing and create unnecessary contradictions.

1. *Conversion of Paul.* By using the earliest possible dating, Paul's conversion may be placed at A.D. 34. Since Aretas evidently did not gain jurisdiction in Damascus until 37 (see D.1 above), and it had already been three years since Paul's conversion (Gal 1:17, 18), it would antedate Aretas's role in Damascus if Paul were converted before A.D. 34. Of course, his conversion could have come at a later time.

2. *First missionary journey.* The next point where secular events can be synchronized with biblical data is in the period between Herod's death and the major famine that moved the Antiochian Christians to send relief to the Christians in Jerusalem. The death of Herod was in A.D. 44 and sources external to the NT note a rather widespread famine in 45–47. This would fit in with the period of Paul's life described in Acts 11:27–12:25. Since the first missionary journey followed the return of Paul and Barnabas to Antioch and yet preceded the apostolic conference, this would include the years 47–49.

3. *Jerusalem conference.* In Galatians Paul explains his contact with the apostles at Jerusalem. He enumerates trips to Jerusalem as taking place three years after his conversion and then again fourteen years later (1:18–2:1). If the year 34 is used for the conversion of Paul, 37 is indicated for his first trip to Jerusalem, and by adding fourteen more years, one concludes that the Jerusalem conference occurred about the year 51.

The reason for Paul's not including the relief trip to Jerusalem (Acts 11:27ff.; 12:25) in his list in Galatians (1:18–2:10) is that it does not lie within the scope of his immediate purpose. He wanted to show how little contact he had with Peter and the other apostles. Paul was appointed by Christ, not by men—even those who were apostles and from Jerusalem. It is significant that in Luke's description of Paul's second visit to Jerusalem, no mention is made of the apostles. Gifts were delivered to the elders (Acts 11:30). This may indicate that the apostles were absent from the city at this time and that in Galatians where he is only recounting his relationship with the apostles, Paul simply omitted mention of the trip.

Some would identify the meeting with the apostles described in Galatians as occurring on Paul's second trip to Jerusalem (Acts 11:27–12:25). This allows a reconstruction that explains the differences between the reports of Galatians 2:1–10 and Acts 15:6–29, because they were different occasions. It also explains why Paul did not make mention of the decrees of the Jerusalem meeting in Galatians, because the meeting had not yet occurred.

Others, however, do not find the differences between the reports so great as to demand a different occasion and emphasize that Paul does not appeal to the apostolic decrees of Jerusalem because it would have been playing into the hands of the Judaizers who insisted Paul had to go to the first-line apostles in Jerusalem for his instructions.

To identify the meeting with the apostles described in Galatians (2:1–2) with the second trip to Jerusalem (Acts 11:27–12:25) creates more problems than it solves.

4. *Second missionary journey.* The account of Paul's second missionary journey introduces three passages in Acts of chronological significance: his length of stay in Corinth, his trial before Gallio, and his association with Jews expelled from Rome.

Paul stayed eighteen months in Corinth (Acts 18:11) and was dragged before the Roman proconsul Gallio on charges that were thrown out of court. It is not clear whether the attempted trial occurred early or late in the eighteen-month stay, and whether it was early or late in the period of Gallio's term of office in Corinth. Probably Gallio had but recently arrived and was being tried out by the Jews, and it was probably late in Paul's Corinthian ministry because he would have left soon after such notoriety. Had he remained, it might have brought hardship to the Christians in Corinth.

During Paul's stay there, he met and worked with Priscilla and Aquila—Jewish Christians who had been forced to leave Rome under the edict of Claudius. Whether this expulsion took place at an earlier date (A.D. 41) as some claim from Suetonius (Claudius 25; also Dio Cassius 60.6.6) or later (49) as affirmed by Orosius (7.16.5; see above), either date would be possible. The later date, however, would be preferred, since this would leave a reasonable length of time for the meeting of Priscilla and Aquila with Paul in the latter part of 51. Gallio was certainly in Corinth in 52 (see above).

5. *Third missionary journey.* Paul's third missionary trip included a two-year and three-month ministry at Ephesus (Acts 19:8, 22—three years in round numbers, Acts 20:31). This would include parts of the years 54–57.

6. *Arrest in Jerusalem and imprisonment in Caesarea and Rome.* Paul's trip to Jerusalem led to mob violence in the temple area, his arrest, and finally to his trial before Felix. This is a pivotal point in determining the chronology of Paul's life (see above). Felix was succeeded by Festus, probably about A.D. 60. Paul's appeal to Caesar must have been in the fall of that year. At least his subsequent voyage to Rome was extended into the period of dangerous winter storms and ended in shipwreck. Not till early spring of 61 did Paul enter Rome. Acts ends with a time-note that Paul spent two whole years in Rome awaiting trial.

If Paul was automatically released at the end of two years because his accusers did not appear,[24] he would have been free to leave Rome before the great fire broke out on July 18, A.D. 64 (Tacitus, *Annals* 15.38). This would allow time for Paul's travels to Philippi and Colossae (Phil 2:23 f.; Philem 22), and Ephesus, Corinth, Crete, Nicopolis, Miletus, and Troas—those places reflected in the Epistles to Timothy and Titus.

Whether Paul went to Spain or not,[25] it is significant that such a tradition arose. He had expressed his plan to go there, but if he had died in the persecution of 64, no time would have been left for the possibility of such a trip or for that matter such a tradition. So the tradition that Paul went to Spain, whether he did or not, can be used as an indication of Paul's release from his first Roman imprisonment.

Paul's later arrest and death in Rome probably came in 67/68, not long before Nero's own death in 68.

One's view about the date of Paul's death is an example of the importance of chronology in relation to other questions. If Paul were killed at the end of the first Roman

---

[24]See F.J. Foakes-Jackson and K. Lake, *The Beginnings of Christianity*, vol. 5 (Grand Rapids: Baker, 1933), p. 330.

[25]See I Clement 5 and the Canon of Muratori, but a silence in Eusebius, *Ecclesiastical History* 3.1 and the absence of local tradition.

imprisonment, there would be little likelihood that the happenings reflected in the Pastoral epistles ever occurred. Thus the authorship of the Pastorals becomes involved in the matter of chronology. One of Turner's major objections to Lightfoot's chronology was that "Lightfoot's year, and, to a less extent, Ramsay's year, for the release of St. Paul from the first Roman captivity, are difficult to reconcile with his martyrdom in A.D. 64–65" (HDB, 1:425). But how firm is his early date of Paul's death? Zahn concludes his chronological study of the NT with the observation: "Harnack's assertion, *Chronol. der altchristl. Lit.* S. 239, 240, that Paul was certainly executed in the year 64, is as incorrect as it is bold."[26]

F. *Apostolic Age*

Certain key events are used as milestones to mark the course of the first-century church. More is known of the life of Paul than of any of the other apostolic leaders, but through relating their lives to Paul and other datable events, one can determine approximate chronology. If the death and resurrection of Christ occurred in A.D. 30, this fixes the year of Pentecost and the beginnings of the church. If Saul's conversion took place in A.D. 34, this helps to determine the passage of time covered in Acts 1–8. The period to the death of Stephen may have occupied only about eighteen months.[27]

1. *Death of James the brother of John.* The order of Herod Agrippa I brought the death of James the apostle and brother of John (Acts 12:2). This may have occurred almost any time during Herod's reign, but since it was done to gain favor with the people, it probably should be dated earlier than just before the end of his life. The event described in Acts is placed between the note that Barnabas and Saul came to Jerusalem with alms (11:29, 30) and their return to Antioch (12:25). This passage concerning Herod includes also his death (A.D. 44, see above). It would seem that the famine that brought Barnabas and Saul to Jerusalem was felt in its worst way after the death of Herod.[28] But Luke need not be reflecting chronological order at this point. The death of James may have occurred just before Passover, 41.[29]

2. *Death of James the brother of the Lord.* Important to the life of the church in Jerusalem was the leadership of James the brother of the Lord (Gal 1:19, 2:9; Acts 15:13; 1 Cor 15:7). Josephus tells of his death[30] in the period of anarchy following the death of Festus (62) and prior to the arrival of his successor Albinus. This would probably be a matter of months, but Hegesippus seems to date James's death nearer the fall of Jerusalem.[31]

3. *Death of Peter.* The claim of some that Peter had a twenty-five-year episcopate in Rome is without historic grounds.[32] His presence at the conference in Jerusalem (A.D. 51), no mention of him in Paul's Epistle to the Romans (58), and no allusion to his association with Rome in the Book of Acts (63)—all this contradicts such a claim.

---

[26]Zahn, *Introduction to the New Testament*, vol. 3, p. 480; see below, III, B. 1, 2, 3.
[27]Cf. Irenaeus, *Against Heresies* 1.30.14.
[28]D. Plooij, *De Chronologie van het leven van Paulus*, 1918, pp. 10ff.
[29]Caird, "Chronology of the New Testament," p. 604.
[30]*Antiq.* 20.9.1.
[31]Eusebius, *Hist Eccl* 2.23.
[32]See J. Lebreton and J. Zeiller, *History of the Primitive Church*, vol. 1 (New York: Collier Books, Macmillan, 1942), pp. 293–94.

Cullmann concludes in his study of Peter that the apostle did come to Rome but only toward the end of his life.[33]

Clement of Rome gives the earliest extant notice of the deaths of Peter and Paul (I Clement 5) but does not specify how, when, or where these deaths occurred. Though it is unlikely that they were at the same time, they may well have been within a short interval of one another. It also is unlikely that they occurred at the time of the burning of Rome (64). Probably they occurred before the death of Nero (68). Peter was probably crucified, but only late sources insert the report that this was head downward.

4. *Fall of Jerusalem.* Persecution of the Christians in Jerusalem led to an early scattering of the church (Acts 8:1). They had also been warned to flee before encompassing armies (Luke 21:20, 21). From all indications, they did this and were not involved in the Jewish revolt of 66 and the fall of Jerusalem before the Roman army of Vespasian and Titus in 70. The Christians settled in Pella east of the Sea of Galilee, as their place of refuge.[34]

5. *Death of John.* It may have been the scattering associated with the fall of Jerusalem that took John as far as Ephesus. Nothing indicates he arrived there any sooner. Early sources testify to a long residence in Asia, broken by a period of exile on Patmos during the reign of Domitian (d. 96), and to his subsequent death in the time of Nerva (96–98) or Trajan (c. 100). Only a few late sources erroneously associate the death of John with his brother James at an earlier time (Georgios Hamartolus, 9th century; Philip of Side, 7th or 8th century; and a 5th-century Syriac calendar). Confusion with John the Elder seems to have been introduced by Eusebius's misinterpretation of Papias's statement.[35] From the prevailing evidence it seems clear that John was the last of the apostles to die, and with his passing the apostolic age came to a close.

III. Variant Chronologies

A. *Ancient*

There are certain reasons why we may expect variant chronologies: Antiquity had no uniform method of designating dates. No NT incident is so securely tied to a fixed date as to disallow some leeway. No one can approach the problem of chronology without being influenced by his own theological beliefs.

The ancient chronographers had major differences on the very points still debated today. Clement of Alexandria set the birth of Jesus in the 28th year of Augustus and 194 years, one month, 13 days from the death of Commodus. This would be November 18, 3 B.C. by Finegan's calculation.[36] A few years earlier, however, Irenaeus had affirmed, "Our Lord was born about the forty-first year of the reign of Augustus.[37] This would be 4 B.C., figuring not from the submission of Egypt, but from the death of Julius Caesar

---

[33]Oscar Cullmann, *Peter: Disciple, Apostle, Martyr*, 2nd rev. ed., trans. Floyd V. Filson (Philadelphia: Westminster, 1962).

[34]Eusebius, *Hist Eccl* 3.5.2–3.

[35]Ibid., 3.39.4ff.

[36]Finegan, *Handbook of Biblical Chronology*, p. 223.

[37]*Against Heresies* 3.21.3.

by the non-accession year system.[38] Eusebius dates the birth in the forty-second year of Augustus, which he equates with the thirty-second year of Herod the Great.[39] Both of these equations seem impossible but they agree in reflecting a time prior to Herod's death. Epiphanius adds the names of consuls, Octavian for the thirteenth time and Silvanus.[40] This indicates 2 B.C.

Later a difference over the day of Jesus' birth—January 6 or December 25—became another mark of separation between the Eastern and the Western churches.

The length of Jesus' ministry was a point of contention. Those who held to a one-year ministry were Clement of Alexandria, certain second- and third-century fathers, and the Valentinians. Irenaeus, on the other hand, held to a ten-year ministry. He felt that John 8:57 indicated that Jesus must have been more than forty years old at the time. Epiphanius and Eusebius represent the more conventional view of three years "plus" for the duration of Jesus' ministry.

As for the date of Jesus' death, Clement of Alexandria put it in the sixteenth year of Tiberius, forty-two and a half years before the destruction of Jerusalem. This dating is obviously associated with his position of a one-year ministry for Jesus. Tertullian interjects further complication by naming the consuls Rubellius Geminus and C. Fifius Geminus as in office in the year of Jesus' death.[41] This indicates the year 29. But he also specifies the eighth day before the Kalends of April and this does not satisfy Nisan 14 or Nisan 15 in the Jewish Calendar.[42]

The Quartodeciman controversy of the second century centered around the day of the week for the observance of the Resurrection, but it does not make clear the position of the Quartodecimans on the dating of the event.

In the life of Paul, data from Eusebius becomes essential in understanding variant modern theories. Eusebius puts the arrival of Felix in September A.D. 51-September 52.[43] He also puts the arrival of Festus in the fourteenth year of Claudius and the tenth year of Agrippa II. The first of these must be a mistake. Eusebius certainly was aware that Felix was recalled by Nero, not Claudius. One can see how Eusebius may have committed the error. Perhaps the source he was using (Africanus?) may have included only the reference about Agrippa, and Eusebius may have figured this from the death of Agrippa I—which would be the fourteenth year of Claudius. But there was an interval of six years between the time Agrippa I died and the day Agrippa II began his rule. Although Eusebius dates the coming of Festus in the last year of Claudius in his *Chronicle* (Armenian Version), the time is designated as the second year of Nero in Jerome's Version. Harnack uses this controverted testimony as a starting point for his chronology (see below).

B. *Modern*

Among first attempts to put biblical chronology on a sound basis was that of Ussher.[44] Unfortunately his findings have been included in editions of the Scripture in such a way that readers identify his opinions as final. His was only a beginning in the modern era,

---

[38]Finegan, *Handbook of Biblical Chronology*, p. 222.

[39]*Hist Eccl* 1.5.2.

[40]*Panarion haer.* 51.22.3.

[41]*adv. Jud.* 8.

[42]Finegan, *Handbook of Biblical Chronology*, p. 298.

[43]Turner, "Chronology of New Testament," p. 418.

[44]J. Ussher, *Annales Veteris et Novi Testamenti*, 2 parts, 1650-9.

for much remained to be done, both then and now. The ancients had the advantage of being closer to the events themselves. Modern scholars, however, have the help of a continuing progression of discoveries along with the testimony of the ancients.

There is general agreement on the birth of Jesus (6–4 B.C.). The vast majority of scholars hold to "three plus" years of Jesus' ministry. Von Soden defended a one-year ministry,[45] but this would have been dismissed even sooner had not the cautious and careful Hort advocated it as well.[46]

In the life of Paul, chronological differences hinge on the correlation of Acts and Galatians about Paul's trips to Jerusalem, and the date when Festus succeeded Felix. The results can be summed up in four general positions:

1. *The late date.* This has been given the designation the "received date." It is represented and ably presented by Lightfoot.[47] He dates the arrival of Festus in 60 because of Paul's reference to Felix's many years in office (Acts 24:10) and Josephus's account of the many events connected with his rule.[48] Ramsay's helpful work *St. Paul the Traveller and Roman Citizen* (1895) revised Lightfoot's dating somewhat but did not differ more than a year in fixing the various biblical events of Paul's life.

2. *The early date.* Harnack is the outstanding representative of this view.[49] He proposed that Felix was succeeded in 55 or 56 and this, of course, alters the time of Paul's earlier travels, limits extremely the extent of time covered by Paul's journeys, and also hastens his death. A ground for this is found in Eusebius's *Chronicle.* Eusebius dates Festus's arrival in the second year of Nero; but a date so early does not align with other details.[50] Turner suggests that Eusebius, finding himself at this point without a date, selected a time mid-way between the coming of Felix (51/52) and the coming of Albinus (62) for the coming of Festus.[51] Another ground for the early date is the association of Pallas as favorite of Nero and his influence on behalf of his brother, Felix (see above). Lake devised his chronology on the basis of this early appointment of Festus (55) as well.[52]

3. *The middle date.* Turner wrote the article that has become the classic presentation of NT chronological problems.[53] Whether one agrees with his conclusions or not, his treatment is comprehensive and helpful. He points up the impossibilities of Harnack's position and yet does not feel compelled to agree with Lightfoot. He maintains a middle ground of about 57/58 for the arrival of Festus.

4. *A new date.* Knox has introduced a radical method of determining Pauline chronology.[54] Since in his opinion the Book of Acts is historically untrustworthy, he dismisses chronological information gained from it and reconstructs a whole new pattern of events by putting together information from Paul's Epistles. He dates Paul's final visit

---

[45]EBi 1 (1899): 802–803.

[46]Westcott and Hort, *NT in Greek*, Int., 1882, App. pp. 77ff.

[47]J.B. Lightfoot, *Biblical Essays* (New York: Macmillan, 1893), pp. 213–33.

[48]Antiq. 20.8.1ff.; War 2.13.

[49]A. Harnack, *Geschichte der altchristlichen Literatur*, II, *die Chronologie*, I, 2nd ed. 1958, pp. 233–39.

[50]See above and also a detailed treatment in Zahn, *Introduction to the New Testament*, pp. 469ff.

[51]"Chronology of New Testament," p. 419.

[52]Foakes-Jackson and Lake, *Beginnings of Christianity*, pp. 445–74.

[53]C.H. Turner, HDB 1:403–25.

[54]J. Knox, *Chapters in a Life of Paul* (New York: Abingdon, 1950), esp. pp. 47–88.

to Jerusalem and his arrest as early as 53/54. Doing away with the three missionary journeys of Acts, he places Paul's activity in Asia and Achaia during the "silent years" between his conversion and the Jerusalem conference in 51. Thus Knox is even forced to deny that Gallio was proconsul in Achaia when Paul was there (cf. Luke's description of the attempted trial in Corinth, Acts 18:12–17). The difficulties that Knox feels necessitate his drastic rearrangement of Acts are more imaginary than real. His views have found favor with a few (e.g., F.R. Crownfield, M. Jack Suggs). Most scholars, however, have responded to Knox with caution rather than acceptance.[55] Knox's highhanded way of dismissing details in Acts in order to emphasize his own special interests leads to new but unfounded theories.

IV. Conclusion

The pieces of the puzzle of NT chronology can be put together. But this is made difficult by missing pieces of information; the distortion of some pieces of information, both ancient and modern; and the influence of the special interests of scholars that may sometimes help but often hinders their work.

The chart on p. 607 shows one way the information discussed in this article can be organized. Secular events appear on the left and biblical data on the right. This chronological scheme adopts the late date in the life of Paul (cf. III. B. 1, above).

V. Bibliography

Caird, G.B. "Chronology of the New Testament." *The Interpreter's Dictionary of the Bible,* vol. 1. Edited by George A. Buttrick. Nashville: Abingdon, 1962.

Finegan, Jack. *Handbook of Biblical Chronology.* Princeton, N.J.: Princeton University Press, 1964.

Grant, F.C. "Chronology of the New Testament." *Dictionary of the Bible.* Edited by James Hastings. New York: Scribner, 1963.

Harnack, Adolf. Die Chronologie. *Geschichte der altchristlichen Literatur bis Eusebius.* Teil 2, Band 1. Leipzig: J.C. Hinrichs, 1896.

Hoehner, Harold W. *Chronological Aspects of the Life of Christ.* Grand Rapids: Zondervan, 1977.

Knox, John. *Chapters in the Life of Paul.* Nashville: Abingdon, 1950.

Lake, Kirsopp. "The Chronology of Acts." *The Beginnings of Christianity,* vol. 5. Edited by F.J. Foakes-Jackson and Kirsopp Lake. London: Macmillan, 1933.

_____. *An Introduction to the New Testament.* London: Christophers, 1938, pp. 243–53.

Lightfoot, J.B. *Biblical Essays.* New York: Macmillan, 1893.

Ogg, G. "Chronology of the New Testament." *Peake's Commentary on the Bible.* Edited by Matthew Black and H.H. Rowley. London: Thomas Nelson and Sons, 1962.

_____. *The Chronology of the Public Ministry of Jesus.* Cambridge: Macmillan, 1940.

Ramsay, W.M. *St. Paul the Traveller and the Roman Citizen.* New York: Putnam, 1898.

_____. *Was Christ Born at Bethlehem?* New York: Putnam, 1898.

Turner, C.H. "Chronology of the New Testament." *A Dictionary of the Bible,* vol. 1. Edited by James Hastings. New York: Scribner, 1901.

Zahn, Theodore. *Introduction to the New Testament,* vol. 3. New York: Scribner, 1917, pp. 450–85.

---

[55]J.C. Hurd, "Pauline Chronology and Pauline Theology" in W.R. Farmer, et al., *Christian History and Interpretation: Studies Presented to John Knox,* (Cambridge: Cambridge University Press, 1967), pp. 225–48.

		Birth of Jesus
Death of Herod	4 B.C.	
Tiberius Caesar (authority in provinces)	A.D. 11	
15th year of Tiberius	26	Beginning of Jesus' ministry
	30	Crucifixion of Jesus Friday, Nisan 15
	34	Conversion of Saul
Aretas in Damascus	37	Paul's first visit to Jerusalem
Death of Agrippa I Famine	44 46	Paul's second visit to Jerusalem
	47-49	First missionary journey
	51	Apostolic conference
Gallio, proconsul of Achaia	52	Second missionary journey (Corinth)
	54-57	Third missionary journey (Ephesus)
	58	Paul's arrest in Jerusalem
Festus succeeds Felix in Judea	60	
	61	Paul, Prisoner in Rome
	62	Death of James, brother of the Lord
	63	Paul's release
Burning of Rome	64	
	67	Death of Peter and Paul
Fall of Jerusalem	70	
		John on Patmos
Death of Domitian	96	
	c. 98	Death of John

THE METROLOGY OF THE NEW TESTAMENT

I. Introduction
II. Measures
III. Length and Distance
IV. Weights
V. Money
VI. Bibliography

I. Introduction

Flux in standards of values was as much a problem in antiquity as it is today. Moreover, various units of measurement were used in different parts of the Mediterranean world. Frequently one country would employ two standards of its own, such as short and long, light and heavy, common and royal, plus a conglomeration of foreign standards. Added to this is the handicap of loss of information since those early centuries. Finally, there is in the study of measurements the difficult problem of translating the ancient values into current standards.

Metrological references are so few in the NT that each instance can be cited and the equivalent in current measurements noted. Conclusions in this field are based on notices in the Bible, plus extrabiblical works from antiquity, such as Herodotus, the Talmud, Josephus, and Epiphanius on weights and measures. Besides these sources, one can appeal to archaeological evidences from Palestine and surrounding nations. Modern treatments of the subject help point up both the problems and solutions.[1]

II. Measures

The *bath* was the standard Hebrew unit of liquid measure (equivalent to six U.S. gallons, 22.71 litres). The standard unit of dry measure in the OT was the *homer,* but it was also known as the *kor* (equivalent to ten to twelve bushels, 350 to 420 litres). Greek measures are found in the NT: *xestēs* (1 1/6 pints, .552 litres), *choinix* (1 quart, .946 litres), *metrētēs* (10.2 U.S. gallons, 38.607 litres). The Roman *modios* was 1/4 U.S. bushel, or 8.81 litres.

---

[1]E.g., R.B.Y. Scott, "Weights and Measures of the Bible," *Biblical Archaeologist* 22 (May 1959):22–39.

Hebrew measure	Greek word	Equivalent of a single unit in U.S. measurement and the metric system	Reference	Translation KJV	NIV
בת (bath)	βάτος (batos)	6 gallons (22.71 litres)	Luke 16:6	measures	gallons
כיר (kor)	κόρος (koros)	10–12 bushels (350–420 litres)	Luke 16:7	measures	bushels
סאה (seah)	σάτον (saton)	1 1/2 pecks (13.214 litres)	Matt 13:33	measures	large amount
			Luke 13:21	measures	large amount

Hellenistic and Roman

	μετρητής metrētēs	10.2 gallons 38.607 litres	John 2:6	firkins	gallons
	χοῖνιξ choinix	1 quart .946 litres	Rev 6:6	measure	quart
	ξέστης xestēs	1 1/6 pints .552 litres	Mark 7:4, [8]	pots	pitchers
	μόδιος modios	1 peck 8.81 litres	Matt 5:15	bushel	bowl
			Mark 4:21	bushel	bowl
			Luke 11:33	bushel	bowl

III. Length and Distance

The cubit was the basic unit of linear measurement in the Bible. Of the variant lengths used for this in different periods, the length in NT times appears to be 17.5 inches, or 44.45 centimeters. More common to mark distance between points were such designations as a "Sabbath day's walk" (Acts 1:12 [see Num 35:5; rabbinical rule, 972 yards, or 888.4 meters—a little over half a mile]), "a day's travel" (Luke 2:44), "a stone's throw" (Luke 22:41). Roman designations were employed as well: a fathom was the measurement from the tip of one middle finger across the chest to the tip of the other middle finger, one arm-stretch, about 6 feet, or 18.28 meters; a stadium was the length of the ancient Greek race course, 607 feet, or 184.85 meters.

Greek measure	Equivalent	Reference	Translation KJV	NIV
πῆχυς (pechys)	cubit 17.5 inches (44.45 centimeters)	John 21:8	two hundred cubits	hundred yards
		Matt 6:27	one cubit	single hour
		Luke 12:25	one cubit	single hour
		Rev 21:17	cubits	cubits
ὀργυιά (orgyia)	fathom about 6 feet (1.828 meters)	Acts 27:28	20 fathoms 15 fathoms	120 feet 90 feet

Greek measure	Equivalent	Reference	Translation KJV	NIV
στάδιον (stadion)	stadium about 1/8 mile (184.85 meters)	Matt 14:24	midst of sea (lit., many stadia from land)	considerable distance
		Luke 24:13	three score furlongs	7 miles
		John 6:19	25 or 30 furlongs	3 or 4 miles
		John 11:18	15 furlongs	less than 2 miles
		1 Cor 9:24	race	race
		Rev 14:20	1,600 furlongs	1,600 stadia (n. 200 miles)
		Rev 21:16	12,000 furlongs	12,000 stadia (n. about 1500 miles)
κάλαμος (kalamos)	measuring rod 6 cubits in length (2.705 meters)	Rev 11:1	rod	measuring rod
		Rev 21:15	reed	measuring rod
μίλιον (milion)	4,854 feet (8 stadia, Roman mile) (1.48 kilometers)	Matt 5:41	mile	mile

IV. Weights

The shekel, the mina, and the gerah were Hebrew weights that were apparently used by Jews in NT times. (See the article METROLOGY IN THE OLD TESTAMENT, pp. 375–381.) The shekel became the standard weight and later was designated for the coin and its comparable value. The thirty pieces of silver paid to Judas (Matt 26:15) may be a way of referring to the shekel. In the OT thirty shekels were given as the value of a slave (Exod 21:32). Words used to denote coins or sums of money could still be used to signify weight, and the NT shows this. The talent represents a large sum of money in Jesus' parable (Matt 18:24), but a heavy weight in describing extraordinary hailstones (Rev 16:21). The litra used in describing the precious ointment of Mary indicates the amount in weight, probably the Roman pound of 12 ounces.

Greek weight	Value[1]	Weight	Reference	Translation KJV	NIV
τάλαντον (talanton, talent)	$960.00	c. 75 pounds (c. 34 kilograms)	Matt 18:24	talents	talents
			Matt 25:15–28	talents	talents
			Rev 16:21	talent	100 pounds
μνᾶ (mna, mina)	$76.00	1 1/4 pounds (.566 kilograms)	Luke 19:13–25	pounds	minas
λίτρα (litra, pound)		12 ounces (.373 kilograms)	John 12:3	pound	a pint
			John 19:39	pound	pounds

---

[1]Since "talent" and "mina" refer to weight, when monetary usage is indicated their value depends on whether they are silver or gold.

V. Money

Whereas the Jewish standard coin was the shekel, the Greek was the drachma (1/4 of the shekel), and the Roman, the denarius. To attempt to specify what each of these was worth is misleading because of the constant change in purchase value, both in antiquity and today. The fact that both the Greek drachma and the Roman denarius, at one time or another, represented a day's wage gives us a better idea of their value than to attempt to translate these words into modern monetary equivalents.

Greek coin	Equivalent	Value	Reference	Translation KJV	Translation NIV
δραχμή (drachmē, drachma)	$.16	day's wage	Luke 15:8, 9	pieces of silver	silver coins
δίδραχμον (didrachmon, two drachmas)	$.32	2 days' wage	Matt 17:24	tribute	two drachmas
στατήρ (statēr, four drachmas)	$.64	4 days' wage	Matt 17:27	piece of money	four drachmas
Roman coin					
δημάριον (dēnarion, denarius)	$.20	day's wage	Matt 18:28	pence	denarius
			Matt 20:2, 9, 10, 13	penny	denarius
			Matt 22:19	penny	denarius
			Mark 12:15	penny	denarius
			Luke 20:24	penny	denarius
			Mark 6:37	penny ⎫	eight months wages (200 d.)
			John 6:7	pence ⎭	
			Mark 14:5	pence ⎫	more than a year's wages (300 d.)
			John 12:5	pence ⎭	
			Luke 7:41	pence	denarii
			Luke 10:35	pence	silver coins
			Rev 6:6	penny	day's wage
ἀσσάριον (assarion)	c. $.01	1/16 of a denarius or a drachma	Matt 10:29	farthing	penny
			Luke 12:6	farthing	pennies

Roman coin	Equivalent	Value	Reference	Translation KJV	NIV
κοδράντης (kodrantēs)	1/4 of $.01		Matt 5:26	farthing	penny
			Mark 12:42	farthing	penny
λεπτόν (lepton)	1/8 of $.01		Mark 12:42	mite	small copper coins
			Luke 21:2	mite	small copper coins
			Luke 12:59	mite	penny
ἀργύριον (argyrion, "silver")		Shekel (4 drachmas)	Matt 26:15	pieces of silver	silver coins
	day's wage	or	Matt 27:3, 9	pieces of silver	silver coins
		Attic silver (1 drachma)	Acts 19:19	pieces of silver	drachma
χρυσός (chrysos, "gold")	aureus (Roman coin)	25 denarii	Matt 10:9	gold	gold

VI. Bibliography

Barrois, A.G. "Chronology, Metrology, etc." *Interpreter's Bible*, vol. 1. Edited by George Buttrick. New York: Abingdon, 1952.

Goodenough, Erwin R. *Jewish Symbols in the Greco-Roman Period*, vol. 1. New York: Pantheon Books, 1953.

Hart, H.H. "Money." *Hasting's Dictionary of the Bible*. Edited by Grant and Rowley. New York: Scribner, 1963.

Kennedy, A.R.S. "Weights and Measures." *A Dictionary of the Bible*, vol. 4. Edited by James Hastings. New York: Scribner, 1901.

Petrie, W.M.F. *Ancient Weights and Measures*. London: Department of Egyptology, University College, 1926.

Scott, R.B.Y. "Weights, Measures, Money and Time." *Peake's Commentary on the Bible*. Edited by Matthew Black and H.H. Rowley. London: Thomas Nelson and Sons. 1962.

Segre, A. "A Documentary Analysis of Ancient Palestinian Units of Measure." *Journal of Biblical Literature* 64 (1945):357–75.

Sellers, O.R. "Weights and Measures." *The Interpreter's Dictionary of the Bible*, vol. 4. Edited by George Buttrick. New York: Abingdon, 1962.

Trinquet, J. "Metrologie Biblique." *Dict. de la Bible*. Supp. (ed. F. Pirat), farc. 28 (1955), pp. 1212–50.

THE OLD TESTAMENT IN THE NEW TESTAMENT

Roger Nicole

Roger Nicole

A.B., Gymnase Classique, Lausanne; M.A., Sorbonne; B.D., S.T.M., Th.D., Gordon Divinity School; Ph.D., Harvard University

Professor of Theology, Gordon-Conwell Theological Seminary

THE OLD TESTAMENT IN THE NEW TESTAMENT

One very notable feature of the NT is the extent to which it alludes to or quotes the OT. It appeals to the OT in order to provide proof of statements made, confirmation for positions espoused, illustration of principles advanced, and answers to questions raised. Frequently, even when no formal citation is given or perhaps even intended, the NT writers follow forms of thought or speech patterned after OT passages. It is apparent that the NT writers and our Lord himself were so steeped in the language and truths of OT revelation that they naturally expressed themselves in terms reminiscent of it.

Because of this strong affinity of the NT writers for the OT, it is not always easy to determine with precision when a quotation is intended, where it begins, where it ends, and what OT passage or passages are alluded to. Consequently, estimates of the number of OT quotations and passages quoted vary considerably.

A very conservative count lists 295 separate quotations: 224 direct citations prefixed by an introductory formula; 7 additional cases where "and" connects a second quotation to the one previously identified as such; 19 passages where a paraphrase or summary rather than a definite citation follows an introductory formula (e.g., Matt 2:23); and 45 quotations where the length (e.g., 1 Peter 3:10–12) or the specificity (e.g., Matt 27:46) makes it entirely clear that a reference to the OT is intended. Since many quotations are fairly extended, these 295 actually occupy some 352 verses of the NT. Two hundred and seventy-eight different verses of the OT are cited (some of them several times): 94 from the Law, 99 from the Prophets, and 85 from the Writings.[1]

As soon as allusions as well as direct quotations are included, the count rises sharply. Toy lists 613 instances; Shires, 1,604; Dittmar, 1,640, and Huehn yields a count of 4,105.[2] These figures are evidence of the very close relationship between the Testaments. In order to clarify this relationship, eight propositions will serve as the framework for this article.

---

[1]The Law (Gen, Exod, Lev, Num, Deut); the Prophets (Josh, Judg, Sam, Kings, Isa, Jer, Ezek, and the twelve minor prophets); the Writings (Pss, Job, Prov, S of Sol, Ruth, Lam, Eccl, Esth, Dan, Ezra-Neh, and Chron). This division of the Hebrew OT goes back to the period between 400 B.C. and the first century A.D.

[2]See the bibliography for the works these figures are drawn from.

I. Relevance of the Old Testament to New Testament Time

The NT writers assumed that the OT in its entirety was meaningful and relevant for their own time.

This principle was asserted in a sweeping manner by the apostle Paul in Romans 15:4, "Everything that was written in the past was written to teach us, so that through endurance and the encouragement of the Scriptures we might have hope." (Cf. Rom 4:23, 24; 1 Cor 9:10; 10:11.)

"All Scripture is God-breathed *and is useful*[3] ..." (2 Tim 3:16).
The NT use of the pronouns "you," "we," "us," in introducing quotations of the OT bears witness in the same direction, as these references show:
"Have you not read what God said *to you*... ?" (Matt 22:31). The statement quoted is addressed by Yahweh to Moses (Exod 3:6).
"Isaiah was right when he prophesied *about you*" (Matt 15:7; Mark 7:6). The reference is to Isaiah 29:13, where the prophet first of all describes a contemporaneous situation. (Cf. Acts 4:11; Heb 12:15.)
"The Holy Spirit also testifies *to us* ..." (Heb 10:15). Here a statement of Jeremiah is quoted. (Cf. Acts 13:47.)
The fairly common use of the present tense rather than the past of the verb that introduces the quotation is also significant. The author of this article has noted forty-one instances of this practice, including Hebrews 10:15, recorded immediately above.
This sense of the contemporaneity of Scripture was so keen on the part of the NT writers and our Lord himself that they perceived the applicability to their own times not only of passages expressing general principles but also of statements that appear at first sight to relate specifically only to incidents of past history.

II. Old Testament Prophecies Concerning Christ and the Church

The NT writers were convinced that many of the events of the life of our Lord and indeed of the beginnings of the Christian church had been prophesied in considerable detail by OT writers.

Here is a list of some of the more notable prophecies that were viewed as fulfilled in NT times. (Italicized references are to statements of Christ himself.)

Christ's divine sonship	Acts 13:33; Heb 1:5; 5:5
The Incarnation	Heb 10:5–9
Christ's Davidic descent	*Matt 22:43, 44; Mark 12:36; Luke 20:42, 43;* John 7:42
Christ's virginal conception	Matt 1:21–23
Christ's birth in Bethlehem	Matt 2:6; John 7:42
The flight to Egypt	Matt 2:15
The massacre of the innocents	Matt 2:17, 18
The return to Nazareth	Matt 2:23
John the Baptist's ministry in the wilderness	Matt 3:3; Mark 1:3; Luke 3:4–6; John 1:23

---

[3]Italics added here and in the references that follow.

John the Baptist as forerunner	Mark 1:2; Luke 1:76; 7:27
John the Baptist, the new Elijah	*Matt 11:14; 17:12; Mark 9:12, 13;* Luke 1:17
The cleansing of the temple	John 2:17
Christ's ministry in Capernaum	Matt 4:15, 16
Christ's prophetic ministry	Acts 3:22, 23; 7:37
Christ's ministry of compassion	*Luke 4:18–21;* Matt 12:17–21
Christ's ministry of healing	Matt 8:17
Christ's eternal priesthood	Heb 5:6; 7:17, 20
Christ's use of parables	Matt 13:35
The hardening of many who heard Christ	*Matt 13:14, 15; Mark 4:12; Luke 8:10;* John 12:37–41
Christ's triumphal entry on a young donkey	Matt 21:5; John 12:14, 15
Christ's rejection by the Jews	*Matt 21:42; Mark 12:10, 11; Luke 20:17;* Acts 4:11; 1 Peter 2:7, 8
The hatred of the Jews	*John 15:25*
Christ's suffering	*Matt 26:24; Mark 9:12; 14:21; Luke 18:32; 24:26, 46.*
The cowardice of the disciples	*Matt 26:31; Mark 14:27*
The betrayal by Judas	*John 13:18; 17:12*
The end of Judas	Matt 27:9, 10
Christ's arrest	*Matt 26:54, 56; Mark 14: 49*
Christ accounted a transgressor	*Luke 22:37*
Christ's trial before Gentiles	*Luke 18:32*
The conspiracy against Christ	Acts 4:25–27
The casting of lots over Christ's clothes	John 19:24
Christ's thirst on the cross	John 19:28
Christ's pierced side	John 19:36
Christ's death	*Luke 18:32;* Acts 8:32–35; 1 Cor 15:3; Gal 3:13
Christ's resurrection	*Luke 18:33; 24:46;* John 2:22; Acts 2:25–28, 31; 1 Cor 15:4
Christ's ascension	Acts 2:34, 35; 13:33–35; Eph 4:8
Christ's exaltation	*Matt 22:43, 44; Mark 12:36; Luke 20:42, 43;* Acts 2:34, 35; Heb 1:13; Rev 2:27
The replacement of Judas	Acts 1:20
The Pentecostal outpouring of the Spirit	Acts 2:17–21
The universal expansion of the gospel	*Luke 24:47;* Acts 13:47; 15:14–18; Rom 9:25, 26; 15:9–12; Gal 3:8; 4:27
The hardening of the Jews against the gospel	Acts 28:26, 27; Rom 9:27, 33; 11:8–10
The persecution of Christians	Rom 8:36
The blessings of the new covenant	2 Cor 6:16–18; Heb 8:8–12; 10:16, 17
Christ's viewing believers as his brothers	Heb 2:12, 13

This list—which could be considerably extended if passages relating to commandments, promises, or general principles were included—shows to what extent the NT writers viewed OT prophecy as describing in accurate detail the coming, career, and redemptive ministry of Christ. The correspondance is so striking that some critics have suggested that the NT authors invented incidents in order to make them fit certain prophecies.[4] While this insinuation is groundless, the fact that it is advanced at all bears impressive witness to the close correlation between prophecy and fulfillment. Whether or not we perceive how these are connected, it is indisputable that the apostles and our Lord himself did view them as most intimately related.

This relationship between the OT pronouncements and the NT event or representation occurs in the NT in four chief categories:

1. *Prophecy* or *commandment* and *fulfillment* (Matt 1:22; 2:15, 17, 23; 4:14; 5:17; 8:17; 12:17; 13:14, 35; 21:4; 26:54, 56; 27:9; Mark 14:49; [15:28]; Luke 4:21; 24:44; John 12:38; 13:18; 15:25; 17:12; 19:24, 36; Acts 1:16; 3:18; 13:27; Rom 13:8; Gal 5:14; James 2:23. See also, e.g. John 1:16 and Rom 13:10 where the noun *plērōma*—"fullness," "fulfillment"—appears). This form of language, perhaps the most common of all, indicates that something that remained incomplete is now brought to consummation. In some instances, there may be multiple fulfillments of one particular text. This is the case in relation to obedience to a commandment, but it may also apply to certain predictions that aptly relate to several situations. (Cf., e.g., Isa 6:10 and Matt 13:14, 15; John 12:40; Acts 28:26, 27.)

2. *Shadow.* That the OT needs to be supplemented by the NT is even more clearly attested by the term *skid*, "shadow" (Col 2:17; Heb 8:5; 10:1) commonly contrasted to "substance, reality, image." Both the preeminence of the NT revelation and the appropriateness of the OT are indicated by this language.

3. *Type* (Rom 5:14; 1 Cor 10:6) and *antitype* (Heb 9:24; 1 Peter 3:21). Gr. *typos* ("type"), *antitypos* ("antitype"), translated variously, e.g., "example," "pattern," "figure," "copy." These terms relate to the pattern of truth whose ultimate design (prototype) is in the mind of God and is revealed in a variety of concrete historical manifestations.

4. *Truth.* "True" (*alēthinos, alēthēs*) or "truth" (*alētheia*), especially as found in John's writings (John 1:9, 17; 6:32; 15:1; 1 John 2:8, et al.; cf. also Heb 8:2; 9:24; 1 Peter 5:12), may well be listed in this connection. The contrast implied is not between "true" and "false," but rather between "complete," "full-fledged" and "incomplete," "partial." The NT age is the time in which the blessings that were formerly present in seed-form have now come to full flowering and maturity.

III. The Old Testament—the Word of God

The ground of the NT writers' faith in the prophetic vision of the OT was their conviction, frequently and variously expressed, that the OT is the Word of God.

"All Scripture is God-breathed" (2 Tim 3:16).
"You nullify the word of God for the sake of your tradition" (Matt 15:6; cf. Mark 7:13).

---

[4]This is standard procedure for critics like D.F. Strauss and E. Renan, who assumed that all the supernatural elements in the life of Christ were inventions of the Gospel writers, but examples of this approach may be found also in more moderate critics, e.g., H.J. Holtzmann, *Handcommentar zum N.T.* 2d ed. (Freiburg i/B: Mohr, 1892), 1:230.

"They [the Jews] have been entrusted with the very words of God" (Rom 3:2).

The NT writers frequently introduce OT passages by formulae that ascribe their origin to God. This is the case even where what is quoted is not a saying of God recorded in the OT, but a portion of the narrative or even a statement addressed to God by the psalmist.

"Haven't you read ... that the Creator ... said, 'For this cause a man will leave his father and mother...?'" (Matt 19:4, 5). The context of Genesis 2:24 shows this to be part of the narrative of creation rather than a direct utterance of God.

Other instances of this type are in Acts 4:25; 13:35; Hebrews 1:5–8, 13; 3:7; 4:4.

Inversely, the NT writers sometimes attribute to Scripture statements made by God, thus personifying Scripture. Perhaps Romans 9:17 and Galatians 3:8 are the most striking examples of this phenomenon, because they ascribe to Scripture activities that are actually those of God himself.

"The Scripture says to Pharaoh: 'I raised you up for this purpose...'" (Rom 9:17). Here the pronoun "I" manifestly refers to God, not to Scripture *per se*. In any case, the Scripture was not in existence at the time of Pharaoh.

"The Scripture foresaw that God would justify the Gentiles by faith, and announced the gospel in advance to Abraham: 'All nations will be blessed in you'" (Gal 3:8). Obviously, the Scripture cannot "foresee"; this has to be the act of a rational agent. Furthermore, God's statement recorded here was made long before the Scripture was in existence.

These forms of language can be understood only on the ground that the NT authors had come to identify the Scripture with God's own Word to such an extent that formulae like "God says," "Scripture says," "It says," were to them practically equivalent, and they used them interchangeably, apparently without special regard to the nature of the material quoted.

The acknowledgment of the primary divine authorship of the OT did not eliminate due recognition of the function of the human authors. The names of Moses, David, Isaiah, Jeremiah, Daniel, Hosea, and Joel are specifically mentioned, and there are numerous references to "the prophet" or "the prophets," without specifying who is in view. Frequently in such cases what is actually quoted is not a personal statement made by these men, but rather a divine pronouncement they were commissioned to transmit and in which the pronoun "I" refers to God; e.g., "Isaiah was right when he prophesied about you: 'These people honor me with their lips ...'" (Matt 15:7, 8). Many more examples could be given.

Of special interest are some formulae in which the divine authorship and the human agency are placed side by side, as in the following:

"The Lord had said through the prophet ..." (Matt 1:22).

"David himself, speaking by the Holy Spirit, declared ..." (Mark 12:36; cf. Matt 22:43).

"The Scripture had to be fulfilled which the Holy Spirit spoke long ago through the mouth of David" (Acts 1:16; cf. 4:25).

"The Holy Spirit spoke the truth to your ancestors when he said through Isaiah the prophet ..." (Acts 28:25).

"He says in Hosea ..." (Rom 9:25).

Such language indicates that in the mind of NT writers the divine authorship and superintendence did not obliterate the responsible agency of the human authors. Rather, God used them in terms of their varied backgrounds, styles, spheres of interest, etc., so that what they wrote reflects the impact of their personalities. Yet the humanness of the product does not appear to have detracted, in the mind of NT authors, from the divine and incontestable authority vested in even the small details of their sacred writings.

The frequent use (more than sixty times) by our Lord and the apostles of "It is written" as a formula of introduction for quotations is also notable. It not only stresses that a reference to a written text is made, but it also implies an appeal to a final authority that brooks no argument. Of similar import is the reference to OT Scripture as "law," even in connection with passages from the Psalms or from Isaiah (John 10:34; 15:25; Rom 3:19; 1 Cor 14:21). These are not cases of clumsy, erroneous location of sources, but rather a testimony to the binding legal authority of the OT as a whole. One is reminded of the way the psalmist spoke of "law," "statutes," "commandments," and "ordinances" in Psalm 119, obviously with a broader point of reference than the Pentateuch. The use of the word *prophet* to introduce a passage from Psalms (Matt 13:35) similarly points to the view that the whole OT, rather than just certain portions of the canon, is prophetic, that is, it embodies God's message to his people mediated by his spokesmen.

IV. God's Meaning in Old Testament Prophecies

Because they viewed the OT as the Word of God, the NT writers did not hesitate to interpret its statements, not merely in terms of what the human authors could have thought, but in terms of what God himself meant in speaking through the prophets.

The principle that undergirds this thesis is perhaps most vigorously expressed, though not with reference to an OT quotation, in John's remark about Caiaphas's statement: "It is better for you that one man die for the people than that the whole nation perish." John comments, "He did not say this on his own, but as high priest that year he prophesied that Jesus would die for the Jewish nation, and not only for that nation but also for the scattered children of God" (John 11:51, 52).

The thought of Caiaphas was steeped, on the human level, in narrow and callous considerations of expediency. But God providentially guided Caiaphas to express himself in terms embodying the declaration of a principle elevated far above his own frame of reference. The fuller, divine sense is not unrelated to the fragmentary, earth-bound sense, but it rises above and beyond it, somewhat as the full plant rises above and beyond the place where the seed was planted (Matt 13:31, 32).

In Galatians 3:16 this principle is exemplified in relation to a quotation from the OT: "The promises were spoken to Abraham and to his seed. The Scripture does not say 'and to seeds,' meaning many people but 'and to your seed,' meaning one person, who is Christ." Here the original statement is an utterance of God himself recorded in Genesis. Obviously, it is God's own meaning that must be considered in interpreting the passage, not merely Abraham's or Moses' understanding of it. The point Paul is making is that the word "seed," though referring to a multiplicity of persons as a collective word, is nevertheless couched in the singular in both the Hebrew and the Greek texts. It is the presence of this word in the singular that Paul sees as indicative of God's purpose to accomplish his promised blessing supremely in one person descended from Abraham, namely Jesus Christ. That either Abraham or Moses understood this particular implication of the form of the promise seems unlikely. Yet Paul by inspiration declares that this was part of the divine intent.

I am aware that the position here espoused and further developed in propositions 5 and 6 differs from another view held by some evangelical scholars—viz., that any text of Scripture must be construed to have only a single meaning, and that this meaning must be determined strictly in terms of the historical context in which the text was originally written and of the natural grammatical construction and syntax of the original language. This single-meaning position may be bolstered by quotations from Luther and Calvin and by the advocacy of certain important scholars like Moses Stuart, Milton Terry, Frederic Gardiner, and others. Its advocates are, however, faced with the difficult task of showing how the meaning ascribed by NT writers to a number of OT quotations was already in the purview of the prophets who originally wrote the statements. I find it preferable to recognize a superintendence of God over the writing of the OT prophets by which he often gave their statements a meaning that went beyond what they had immediately in view.

The issue, however, is a difficult and debatable one. We need to avoid on the one hand the vagaries and subjectivities of an allegorical method that, by injecting fanciful interpretations into the Scripture, tends to undermine the substance of its authority (cf. Calvin's Commentary on Gal 4:21–26), and on the other hand such a strict adherence to a pedestrian system of interpretation that the nuances God may well have placed in the formulation of prophecy might be lost and the record reduced to a horizontal level of purely human conception.

V. Details of Prophecies Revealed in New Testament Light

In many cases the NT writers, being illumined by the Holy Spirit, perceived with greater clarity than the OT writers themselves God's intended meaning behind some prophecies. What the Prophets had seen only dimly and in terms of general principle, the NT writers saw in the glowing light of fulfillment in a perspective in which a wealth of details fall into place.

"The righteous will live by faith" (Hab 2:14) is quoted three times in the NT: Rom 1:17, Gal 3:11, and Heb 10:38. In those quotations the passage is variously related to justification and to perseverance, and some have suggested that these are not the topics envisioned by Habakkuk in his prophecy. Habakkuk does deal with the certainty of divine judgment and he emphasizes that it is in faith that the people of God can find assurance in the midst of universal calamity. The stress in the original prophecy, therefore, is on the attitude of trust in God as characteristic of the redeemed. It is this feature of trust that all three passages in the NT bring to the fore, although in a variety of contexts. One may not feel obliged to assert that Habakkuk envisioned the full range of implications present in his statement, but it is apparent that his formulation was divinely designed to embody a principle present in his day in the midst of the calamities of the Jewish people, but even more explicitly manifest in relation to the gospel of Jesus Christ, as Paul and the author of Hebrews have made it clear.

Matthew 1:22, 23 has been the center of much controversy and the relation of this text and of the virgin birth of Christ to Isaiah 7:14 has been hotly debated. There are two ways in which the appropriateness of the reference to Isaiah may be readily recognized:

1. One may hold that Isaiah was referring to the birth of a child who would be born in the house of Ahaz so that the prophecy had an immediate relevance to the contemporaneous situation and the war in which Ahaz was engaged. The language used by Isaiah, however, was so chosen that it applies with even greater adequacy to the Messiah's birth, so that Isaiah's prophecy would contemplate not merely one fulfillment but at least two. The key word *virgin*, which so explicitly describes the conception of Jesus Christ, would

have been chosen by God to foreshadow the coming of Christ, but would not necessarily imply that the child born in Ahaz's time was born of a virgin.

2. Another way of understanding the passage in Isaiah 7 is to view it as expressing a kind of chronological scale measured in terms of God's great promise of messianic deliverance. The supreme sign of God's blessing on Israel is the coming of Messiah. Ahaz in his unbelief was unwilling to ask God for a sign because he thought God would be incapable of providing one. Isaiah replies in substance: "If the Messiah were to be born now, before he would have reached the age of discretion (that is to say, before five years have elapsed) you would be delivered from your enemies." This is a poetic way to refer to the passing of time in terms of the anticipation of the coming of the Messiah. Naturally, when the Messiah did come, at the turn of our era, the prophecy was fulfilled and Matthew is precisely right in quoting this passage as being fulfilled in the virgin birth of Christ.

VI. The Deeper Insight of New Testament Writers

The NT writers had such a deep insight into the fullness of God's redemptive purpose that they could perceive foreshadowings and parallelisms where others might easily have missed them altogether. In many such cases it is not necessary to hold that the OT writers completely understood the way their pronouncements would relate to their fulfillment in the NT.

In Matthew 2:15 there is a quotation from Hosea 11:1, "I called my son out of Egypt." In the context of Hosea the reference is rather obviously to the nation of Israel, which was delivered out of Egypt at the time of the Exodus. Matthew, however, relates this to the flight of Mary, Joseph, and the Christ child to Egypt and their subsequent return to Palestine. Therefore, the quotation might appear to be based on a fundamental misapplication of the passage in Hosea. This impression, however, cannot be accepted. It is clear that Matthew understood Hosea very well, because there is no obscurity in the text of Hosea. Matthew did, however, recognize a certain pattern of divine intervention in the redemptive purpose of God. The Exodus was the great act of deliverance whereby God rescued his people Israel from the bondage of Egypt and moved the nation toward the Promised Land. In Jesus Christ we have the supreme divine intervention by which the great Liberator for all times has come to rescue God's people from the bondage of sin to establish them as a holy nation and lead them toward their heavenly destination. This parallelism, emphasizing the fundamental significance of the exodus motif, even has geographical correlations. This is what Matthew points to, and therefore his reference to the OT Scripture is wholly appropriate. It is unlikely, however, that Hosea could have discerned this kind of overtone in the prophecy he uttered. It remained for someone in possession of the facts of the Incarnation to point it out for us under the inspiration of the Holy Spirit.

VII. Unity in Diversity of Old Testament Passages

In a number of cases the NT authors saw a significant relationship between a diversity of OT passages. Sometimes they made this plain by a juxtaposition of quotations; in other cases, they appear to have united two or more passages in an illuminating combination.

One very apparent example of this type is Romans 3:10–18, where a series of quotations (from Pss 14:1–3; 5:9; 140:3; 10:7; Isa 59:7, 8; Ps 36:1) describe human wickedness. The effect is cumulative, and while the precise background of those various quotations may differ, all are notable expressions of the wickedness of fallen humanity.

Another significant example is Romans 15:9–12, where Paul uses four quotations (from 2 Sam 22:50; Deut 32:43; Ps 117:1; Isa 11:10) to show how the OT contained a promise giving hope even to the Gentiles.

In Mark 1:2, 3 there is a combination of quotations that may at first seem disconcerting. Mark says, "It is written in Isaiah the prophet" and then proceeds to quote a passage from Malachi 3:1, immediately followed by a quotation from Isaiah 40:3. We are not required to imagine that Mark was confused about the location of the passage of Malachi. What he appears to have done was simply to quote the passage of Isaiah and to introduce this quotation by a reference to Malachi, showing the unity of the messianic prophetic vision.

It is possible that Matthew 27:9, 10 may contain a similar procedure. This is a passage fraught with considerable difficulty, because the clearest point of reference in the OT is Zechariah 11:12, 13. Yet Matthew presents it as "what was spoken by Jeremiah the prophet." However, Jeremiah 32:6–9 (and possibly also 18:2 and 19:2) is a passage that may provide the background for Matthew's reference; so, rather than assert that there is a mistaken reference, we may well view the prophecy of Jeremiah as fundamental and the prophecy of Zechariah, including the precise reference to thirty silver coins, as subsidiary and complementary. This is one way among several in which this particular difficulty may be cleared.

Possibly the most notable example in this category is Matthew 2:23, where Matthew declares that the statement "He will be called a Nazarene" was said "through the prophets." No prophecy set forth in those terms is found anywhere in the OT. Yet we may well view this quotation as a statement condensing the OT foretelling of a life of humiliation for the Messiah. This seems to be a better understanding of the passage in relation to the OT than an appeal to the Nazarites, or to the word *nezer*, "branch" (Isa 11:1; 60:21. Cf. also Jer 23:5; 33:15, where a similar idea is found with another word for "branch.").

VIII. The Divine Authority of the Old Testament

While the NT writers draw attention mainly to the meaning of the OT passages, they do not hesitate to build an argument on one word of the original text. This method of quoting the OT manifests a supreme confidence in the divine authority of even the minutest details of Scripture.

Examples of this practice which should not be confused with rigid literalism, can be found in many places in the NT (Matt 2:15; 4:10; 13:35; 22:44; Mark 12:36; Luke 4:8; 20:42, 43; John 8:17; 10:34; 19:37; Acts 23:5; Rom 4:3, 9, 23; 15:9, 10, 11, 12; 1 Cor 6:16; Gal 3:8, 10, 13; Heb 1:7; 2:12; 3:13; 4:7; 12:26). In Galatians 3:16 the whole emphasis is on the use of the singular rather than the plural. In making such a use of the OT Scriptures, the NT writers are not suggesting that the language of the OT can be used as a kind of ciphered code. They are rather emphasizing that the divine meaning is incapsulated or embodied in the very words of the text, so that one word that might not at first appear particularly important may suddenly be recognized as pregnant with a fullness of meaning designed by God and made manifest by its inspired interpretation in the NT. Surely it is in this way that we can understand Christ's use of Psalm 82:6 in John 10:34, 35, or again, his use of Psalm 110 in Matthew 22:43–45 (cf. Mark 12:35–37; Luke 20:41–44).

In this article we have attempted to consider certain NT uses of the OT that have given expositors difficulty. It has not been our intention to suggest that the proposed solutions are final. Indeed, expositors will have to continue to wrestle with these passages. Yet such difficulties do not invalidate the remarkably uniform testimony of the NT writers to the authority of the OT. In fact, these very difficulties may be seen as added evidence of the regard the NT writers had for the OT, because no one would use a text as the NT writers used the OT, unless he held that everything in it was consigned by divine authority. Altogether, the NT approach to the interpretation of the OT commends itself to us very highly, even by the standards of modern exegetes. As Dodd states:

> It must be conceded that we have before us a considerable intellectual feat. The various Scriptures are acutely interpreted along lines already discernible within the Old Testament canon itself or in pre-Christian Judaism—in many cases, I believe, lines which start from their first, historical intention—and these lines are carried forward to fresh results. Very diverse Scriptures are brought together so that they interpret one another in hitherto unsuspected ways.... This is a piece of genuinely creative thinking.[5]

Such a clear statement, coming from a notable representative of biblical criticism like C.H. Dodd, is more impressive than anything a scholar committed to the conservative view of inspiration might say.

Our acceptance of the Bible doctrine of inspiration carries with it the assurance that the Holy Spirit enlightened and guided the writers of the NT in their understanding of the OT no less than he enlightened and guided the OT writers in whatever they wrote. Whether or not we understand the precise relation between a prophecy and its fulfillment, we remain confident of the full appropriateness of the NT handling of OT Scripture. Our assurance at this point is not dependent on our ability to resolve certain difficulties that we may occasionally encounter, although many such difficulties can be and have been resolved to a very satisfactory degree. Rather, our confidence rests in the emphatic statements of our Lord and the clear testimony of Scripture to itself, supported by a mass of objective evidence, confirming that the whole Bible is the Word of God written, truthful, and trustworthy in everything it asserts.

Bibliography

A great wealth of literature on this subject is available, written from many standpoints.

For an examination of the text, the best work is undoubtedly Wilhelm Dittmar's *Vetus Testamentum in Novo* (Göttingen: Vandenhoeck and Ruprecht, 1903). David M. Turpie's book *The Old Testament in the New* (London: Williams and Norgate, 1868), supple-

---

[5]C.H. Dodd, *According to the Scriptures* (London: Nisbet, 1952) p.209.

mented later by *The New Testament View of the Old* (London: Hodder and Stoughton, 1872), is still serviceable. In 1967 Robert G. Bratcher edited a pamphlet entitled *Old Testament Quotations in the New Testament* (New York: United Bible Societies), which conveniently places in parallel columns an English translation of the NT text and of the OT, both in the LXX and in the Masoretic text.

The form of the quotations of the OT in the NT is further discussed in the following:

Atkinson, B.F.C. "The Textual Background of the Use of Old Testament by the New" in *Journal of the Transactions of the Victoria Institute* (1947), 79:39–69.

Johnson, Franklin. *The Quotations of the New Testament From the Old considered in the Light of General Literature.* London: Baptist Book and Tract Society, 1896.

Nicole, Roger. "New Testament Use of the Old Testament" in *Revelation and the Bible.* Edited by Carl F.H. Henry. Grand Rapids: Baker, 1958, pages 135–151.

The following works may be consulted for a discussion of the interpretation of the OT by the NT writers:

Bruce, F.F. *The New Testament Development of Old Testament Themes.* Grand Rapids: Eerdmans, 1968.

Dodd, C.H. *According to the Scriptures.* London: Nisbet, 1952.

Fairbairn, Patrick. *Hermeneutical Manual.* Edinburgh: T. & T. Clark 1858. (The third part of the volume contains a very valuable discussion of OT quotations in the NT.)

Grogan, G.W. "The New Testament Interpretation of the Old Testament" in *Tyndale Bulletin* (1967), 18:54–76.

Hebert, A.G. *The Throne of David: A Study of the Fulfillment of the Old Testament in Jesus Christ and His Church.* New York: Morehouse-Gorham, 1941.

Lindars, Barnabas. *New Testament Apologetic: The Doctrinal Significance of Old Testament Quotations.* Philadelphia: Westminster, 1961.

Longenecker, Richard. *Biblical Exegesis in the Apostolic Period.* Grand Rapids: Eerdmans, 1975. (A valuable study by a conservative NT exegete. Important bibliography.)

McNamara, Martin. *Targum and Testament.* Grand Rapids: Eerdmans, 1972.

Oudersluys, Richard. "Old Testament Quotations in the New Testament" in *The Reformed Review.* XIV/3 (March, 1961), 1–12.

Shires, Henry M. *Finding the Old Testament in the New.* Philadelphia: Westminster, 1974. (Valuable indexes. Special attention given to quotations from the Psalms.)

Smith, D. Moody. "The Use of the Old Testament in the New" in *The Use of the Old Testament in the New and Other Essays: Studies in Honor of William Franklin Stinespring.* Edited by James M. Efird, pp. 3–75. Durham, N.C.: Duke University Press, 1972.

Tasker, R.V.G. *The Old Testament in the New Testament.* 1st ed. London: S.M.C., 1946. 2d rev. ed. Grand Rapids: Eerdmans, 1954.

Toy, C.H. *Quotations in the New Testament.* New York: Scribner's, 1884. (A radical critical work. Valuable bibliography of older works.)

Van Ruler, A.A. *The Christian Church and the Old Testament.* Grand Rapids: Eerdmans, 1971.

The following specialized studies should also be mentioned here:

Ellis, E. Earle. *Paul's Use of the Old Testament.* Grand Rapids: Eerdmans, 1957.

Gundry, Robert H. *The Use of the Old Testament in St. Matthew's Gospel.* Leiden: Brill, 1967. (*Supplements to Novum Testamentum XVIII*).

Kistemaker, Simon. *The Psalm Citations in the Epistle to the Hebrews.* Amsterdam: Van Zoest, 1961.
Prabhu, George M. Soares. *The Formula Quotations in the Infancy Narrative of Matthew.* Rome: Biblical Institute Press, 1976.
Stendahl, Krister. *The School of St. Matthew.* Uppsala: Gleerup, 1954.

THE CANON OF THE NEW TESTAMENT

Andrew F. Walls

Andrew F. Walls

M.A., B.Litt., Oxford University

Head of the Department of Religious Studies, University of Aberdeen

THE CANON OF THE NEW TESTAMENT

I. The Concept of the Canon

The Greek word *kanōn* means a "measuring rod." The canon of Scripture thus represents the yardstick by which the church's belief and practice is to be measured: its norms, the list of writings accepted as authoritative and binding.

Any concept of Scripture (i.e., a recognition of divine revelation in a written form) ultimately implies the concept of a canon that identifies and enumerates those writings. But it is equally clear from the history of the OT and NT canons alike that a considerable period may elapse between the two processes—the recognition of divine voice in revelation and the identification of the sacred writings—and that the former comes first.

II. The Early Church and the Jewish Canon

The earliest Christians were all Jews, "people of the Book," who took for granted the Law and the Prophets, which Jesus did not abolish but fulfilled (Matt 5:17). His own teaching assumed and was rooted in the Law and the Prophets[1] and he taught his disciples a way of reading the holy books that led the reader to him and his work.[2]

---

[1]Cf. R.T. France, *Jesus and the Old Testament* (London: Tyndale Press, 1971).
[2]Luke 24:27, 44–47; cf. C.H. Dodd, *According to the Scriptures* (London: Nisbet, 1952).

The first missionary preaching started from the demonstration that the OT Scriptures depicted a suffering, rising, and atoning Messiah (Acts 2:30ff.; 8:35; 9:22; 17:11). Fundamental to the whole activity was the conviction that the life and work of Jesus were "according to the [Jewish] Scriptures" (1 Cor 15:3ff.). That the Hebrew canon was "officially" delineated only at the Synod of Jamnia in A.D. 90 does not affect the fact that in the time of Jesus and his apostles—and well before that—the sacred books were recognized. As we have seen, recognition of the divine voice precedes the identification and enumeration of the holy books. Contemporaries might dispute the interpretation of Scripture with Jesus and his apostles, but no hint of controversy appears about its identification or extent. When early Christians, Jewish or Gentile, saw in the old books the path to "salvation through faith in Christ Jesus" and used them "for teaching, rebuking, correcting and training in righteousness," they were using what people like Timothy, brought up under devout Jewish influences, had known as "the holy Scriptures" from infancy (2 Tim 3:15, 16).

III. The Lord as Canon

The early Christians, therefore, had a "canon" (rule) of unquestioned authority before a single book of our NT was written. Unlike their Jewish brethren who did not believe in Christ, they could not, however, stop there, for the Lord, who had recognized and validated that Scripture, was himself unquestioned authority. At first sight he appeared to be a rabbi and was frequently so addressed (e.g., John 3:2). But contemporaries noticed that instead of building on a chain of traditional authorities in the usual rabbinical manner, he taught "as one who had authority" (Mark 1:22), even to the extent of declaring, "You have heard that it was said . . . but I tell you" (Matt 5:21, et al.). Believers recognized this as the authority of one who was "both Lord and Messiah" (Acts 2:36) and treasured his words. The disciples, as pupils of a rabbi, would have memorized his teaching; the ideal disciple, said a near-contemporary Jewish source, is "a plastered cistern that loses not a drop."[3] He also taught in a way that enabled his disciples more easily to remember the "holy word" he was transmitting.[4]

Paul's letters show the words of the Lord in use as an early Christian "canon," the authoritative measure of his people's actions. The existence of a "word of the Lord" is enough to settle a matter of, say, marriage and divorce (1 Cor 7:10–11). On subjects on which no such word exists—the case of a believing wife and a pagan husband, for instance, or unmarried people—the apostle legislates from first principles (1 Cor 7:12, 25). A word of the Lord about the institution of the Lord's Supper is enough to settle the conduct of Christian worship (1 Cor 11:23ff.); "from [or 'of '] the Lord" here probably refers to the possession of a saying of the Lord rather than to a private revelation.[5] The same passage refers to the formal passing on of these words to others; the same as is also said of the core of the Gospel itself (1 Cor 15:3).

These treasured normative "sayings of the Lord" mostly correspond with sayings in our Gospels: the Last Supper narrative of 1 Corinthians 11 with Mark 14:22–25; the word on marriage in 1 Corinthians 7:10 with Mark 10:9; the word in the support of missionaries 1 Corinthians 9:14 with Matthew 10:10; Luke 10:7. But Paul quotes at least one

---

[3] *Pirqe Aboth* 2:10.
[4] H. Riesenfeld, *The Gospel Tradition and Its Beginning* (Oxford: Mowbray 1957).
[5] Cf. A.M. Hunter, *Paul and His Predecessors* (London: SCM, 1961), pp. 18–22.

saying of the Lord that is not in our Gospels at all (Acts 20:35), and it is not impossible that other sources have preserved one or two other such "agrapha."

The origins of the four Gospels lie beyond the scope of this article. (See the article THE HISTORICAL AND LITERARY CRITICISM OF THE NEW TESTAMENT, pp. 435–456.) It is clear, however, that the "canonical" status of the words of the Lord produced a need for collections of these utterances and that such collections required careful regulation. Otherwise, what would happen if someone sought to justify some dubious doctrine or practice with a new "word of the Lord" which no one had heard of before? So need developed for accounts of the Lord's works and words that the churches could confidently receive as authentic. The four Gospels are a part of that process. Already by Luke's time "many" had undertaken the task of writing accounts (Luke 1:1), but the four Gospels soon left all the others behind. All four were certainly written within the first century, and now it is even argued that perhaps all existed before the fall of Jerusalem in A.D. 70. Some early second-century churches did not have all four Gospels, and many gospels (most of them with well-developed features showing they had a doctrinal axe to grind) appeared later. But there are few signs that early (i.e., first-century) gospels other than our four remained in use in the second century.

IV. The Apostles as Canon

One reason for this lack of other gospels is probably associated with the third branch of authority in the early church—that of the apostles.

The apostles were chosen by the Lord to "be with him" (Mark 3:14) and, on the basis of knowledge extending from John's baptism to the Ascension, to be witnesses of his resurrection (Acts 1:21–22). They thus provided a normative interpretation of the person and work of Christ and a normative repository of his teaching. The Holy Spirit was to remind them of the things Jesus had said to them (John 14:26) and guide them into all truth, making the things of Christ known to them (John 16:13–15). Their witness to Christ, based on intimate companionship with him from the beginning (John 15:27), does not, therefore, depend on their unaided memories and impressions. On several occasions, in fact, words or works of Jesus are mentioned as being remembered, or their significance not understood at the time (John 2:22; 12:16; cf. 7:39). Add to this the fact that, as we have seen, the Lord imparted his own method of reading the OT to the apostles, and the significance of the church as having been "built on the foundation of the apostles and prophets" (Eph 2:20) becomes clear.

V. Apostolic Tradition in the Subapostolic Church

In the nature of things, these apostolic functions could not be transmitted to others; in the full sense, the apostles could have no successors. Church leaders of the next generation, such as Ignatius, Bishop of Antioch (c. A.D. 115), acknowledge that the apostles belong to a clearly marked and now completed stage between the Lord and the contemporary church.[6]

Somewhat later (c. A.D. 130) another bishop, Papias of Hierapolis, was writing a book called *Expositions of the Oracles of the Lord.* He describes his method in these words:

---

[6]Magnesians 7:1; 13:1–2; Trallians 2:2; 3:1; 12:2; Philadelphians 5:1; Smyrneans 8:1.

633

> But I will not scruple also to give a place ... to everything that I learnt carefully and remembered carefully in time past from the elders, guaranteeing its truth. For, unlike the many, I did not take pleasure in those who have so very much to say, but in those who teach the truth; nor in those who relate foreign commandments but in those who record such as were given from the Lord.... And again, on any occasion when a person came who had been a follower of the Elders, I would enquire about the discourses of the elders—what was said by Andrew, or by Peter, or by Philip ... or any other of the Lord's disciples, and what Aristion and the Elder John, the disciples of the Lord say. For I did not think that I could get so much profit from the contents of books as from the utterances of a living and abiding voice.[7]

This passage shows a conscientious, if limited, second-century Christian leader facing the problem of knowing which traditions of the Lord were authentic. He is aware that on this subject there are works that are prolix but superficial (from people "who have so very much to say") and others that claim the Lord's authority for suspect doctrine ("those who relate foreign commandments"). How can one infallibly separate the wheat from the chaff? The answer is that if a saying or interpretation can be clearly traced to an apostle (including two people evidently still living at that time, Aristion and the elder John), its authenticity may be accepted. This is the clue to the meaning, often misunderstood, of Papias's remarks elsewhere about the Gospels of Matthew and Mark. However cryptic these passages,[8] it is clear that Papias associates those Gospels with Matthew and Peter respectively—that is, he has no doubts about their authenticity.

We do not know how successful Papias himself was in "screening" traditions by individual interview. But the important point is that his was the last generation that could even attempt it, because with the death of the last person to hear the last apostle it would be utterly extinct. What would then be left would be Papias's other source of confidence: the apostolic books.

VI. The Gnostic Teachers and Tradition

There was, however, another test of apostolic tradition, and it became increasingly necessary in view of what Papias called "those who relate foreign commandments." Tendentious teachers claimed that they derived their special teaching from a particular apostle and so had a source of information not available to other Christians. The Gnostic teacher Valentinus claimed the tradition of Paul via a disciple of Paul called Theudas. A follower of Valentinus offered inquirers "the apostolic tradition which we have received in a succession regulated [kanonisai] by the teaching of the Saviour."[9] Another major Gnostic group, the Basilidians, claimed a line of tradition via Matthias and another via one Glaukias who had worked with Peter. Apostolic names were attached to countless other works, some of them quite bizarre; the names of James the Lord's brother and Thomas—probably because his name Didymus ("the twin") was assumed to indicate

---

[7]Eusebius, *Eccl. Hist.* 3.39. J.B. Lightfoot's translation.

[8]Mark is described as the "interpreter" of Peter, who "wrote down accurately everything that he remembered, without however recording in order what was either said or done by Christ." Of Matthew he wrote simply, "So then Matthew composed the oracles (*Logia*) in the Hebrew tongue and each one interpreted them as he could." For the significance of these passages, cf. A.F. Walls, "Papias and Oral tradition," *Vigiliae Christianae* 21 (1967): 137–140.

[9]Ptolemy to Flora, in Epiphanius's *Panarion* 33.

that he was the twin of Jesus—were especially favored as having a unique relationship with the Savior.

VII. Catholicity and Canonicity

The answer to such claims did not lie in argument about whether there could or could not be a historical link between say, Matthias and Basilides. It was, rather, to stress a common apostolic tradition—viz., that, as Paul himself had argued (e.g., Gal 2:2, 6–9), all the apostles taught the same things. The natural place to look for this common tradition was in the agreement of the churches the apostles founded. In other words, apostolicity implies catholicity, universality.[10]

By the second half of the second century, with Christianity thoroughly transplanted from Jewish into Hellenistic soil, the threefold nature of authority—the Lord, the Scriptures of Israel, the apostles—was radically challenged from two directions. First, the authority of the Hebrew Scriptures, axiomatic for the first Christian generation, was being questioned by many who saw it as an alien Jewish imposition. Second, apostolic authority was in danger of being made private, treated as though it were secret and exclusive instead of a public and universal witness. Both tendencies were characteristic of Gnostic forms of Christianity, which in some respects represented the radical indigenization of Christianity, an attempt to cut it from its Jewish and thus its historical roots. In general, Christians held to the canon of the Jewish Scriptures and the universal witness of the apostles. The surest, indeed ultimately the only sure way, of identifying the latter was in the books universally accepted, or at least acceptable, as apostolic—that is, in an effective canon of Christian Scriptures parallel with the Law and the Prophets.

It is significant that all this took place not only long before the age of the general councils but also within the period of uncertainty and persecution, when a general council would have been unthinkable. As with Jewish attitudes to the Scriptures of Israel, recognition of the Scriptures long preceded conciliar action.

VIII. Marcion

In this process it is a matter of dispute how far the movement associated with Marcion was the catalyst. Marcion, who flourished about A.D. 140, was the most considerable—and successful—of the challengers to the structure of authority. He cut the Jewish links with Christianity completely, abandoning the OT as the work of the inferior god of the Jews. At the same time, he did not indulge in esoteric Gnostic speculations or claim a secret apostolic tradition; on the contrary, he claimed his position was based on open apostolic teaching and the outcome of Paul's assertion of the Christian's liberty from the Jewish Law. And the teaching of "the Apostle," as he called Paul, was to be found in the following letters: Galatians; 1 and 2 Corinthians; Romans; 1 and 2 Thessalonians; Laodiceans; Colossians; Philemon, Philippians (cf. Tertullian, *Against Marcion* 5). With these he associated "The Gospel"—that of Paul's companion Luke, with a text suitably altered ("restored," in Marcion's opinion) to remove accretions of OT origin.

This list poses several problems (apart from the relatively minor question of the order

---

[10]The best-known exposition of the argument is in Irenaeus, *Adversus Haereses* 3.3.4.

of the letters). First, of Paul's letters to churches only Ephesians is missing, a fact often noticed by those who postulate a post-Pauline authorship for this book. On the other hand, however, Marcion has a letter to the Laodiceans that no longer appears in our list of Pauline letters. What is this letter? The Muratorian Canon (see XIV below) speaks of letters to the Laodiceans and the Alexandrines as current then (c. A.D. 180) but "forged in Paul's name for the heresy of Marcion." There is indeed an Epistle to the Laodiceans that has survived—a forgery certainly, but with nothing Marcionite about it, a mere colorless transfer of phrases from Paul's other letters, and it is probably not the letter referred to here. Yet there is a more likely candidate than this. In Colossians, a letter that has much in common with Ephesians, Paul tells his readers to send his letter on to be read in the Laodicean church and to get the Laodiceans to send them their own letter (Col 4:16). Some important MSS of Ephesians omit the words "in Ephesus" in Ephesians 1:1. These facts, together with the unusual lack of specific personal reference in Ephesians, suggest that what we call "Ephesians" may have been written by Paul as a circular letter to several churches, including those at Ephesus and Laodicea, and that Marcion's canon was based on the Laodicean copy and our own on the Ephesian, while the MSS variants spring from an original with a "blank" to be filled by the name of the receiving church.

The absence of the pastoral Epistles from Marcion's list is less surprising. Their sharp attacks on the prohibition of marriage and other extreme ascetic practices (e.g., 1 Tim 4:3) and positions held by Marcion would have put them beyond the pale for him. We need draw no conclusions about the late origin of the Pastorals from their absence from Marcion's canon.

But the greatest problem of Marcion's list lies in its very existence. It is the earliest list of canonical books to have come down to us. Was he reacting against another wider canon—one that had four Gospels in it, perhaps? Or was he, as Harnack and many since him have held, in effect the pioneer of the canon, forcing the wider church to the assertion of its wider canon? Was it even, as others have suggested, Marcion who first collected the Pauline letters? In view of the huge gaps in our knowledge of the second-century church, the most it is safe to say is that Marcion (and the need to answer him) may have hastened and concentrated a process already begun—a process implied in the very concept of apostolicity.

IX. The Reading of the Scriptures in the Early Church

For the background of this we should look at the way early Christian communities worshiped. The first obvious model is the synagogue, to which so many early converts and almost all the early missionaries, were accustomed. Central to this worship was the reading of the Scriptures—the scrolls of the Law and the Prophets, the most precious possession of the synagogue. But in the Christian assemblies these Scriptures were not the only reading; as we have seen, Paul expressly planned for his letters be read in church and even arranged for letters between churches to be exchanged for public reading. The instruction to Timothy in 1 Timothy 4:13 is correctly translated in NIV: "Devote yourself to the public reading of Scripture." (The note to the reader in Mark 13:14 may be addressed to a public reader.) The practice continued well beyond the apostolic period. Justin Martyr, describing to pagans what goes on in a Christian service, speaks of the reading of "the memoirs of the apostles or the writings of the prophets for as long as time permits"[11] and elsewhere refers to "the memoirs of the apostles which are called Gospels."[12] So it is no surprise to find that the status of the authority of the books used in the Christian community in the second and third centuries depended on whether they were, or were not, read in church. Such reading was by implication to put them on a par with the OT prophets, as the former passage in Justin shows.

We do not know the literacy rate among Christians. But for a time it must have been lower than that of the Jews with their stress on education based on the Scriptures. In any case, books in antiquity were expensive, and the universal owning of books was out of the question. Public reading, therefore, played a part in worship far beyond what it does today, and the books read were an essential possession of Christian communities. When the little group of Christians tried and executed at Scilli in North Africa had been asked what were the contents of a suspicious-looking box they had, they had answered, "The Books, and the letters of Paul, a just man" (*Passio Sanctorum Scillitorum*). Later on, more systematic persecutors knew the importance of getting books "handed over."[13] It even looks as though the early Christians may have pioneered a change in book production; for while the standard format of solemn or holy books for Jew and non-Jew alike was traditionally the scroll, the Christians seem from very early times to have used the codex (flat papyrus leaves, like the modern book) for their church writings.[14]

Public, rather than private, reading must therefore have been the staple diet of many, perhaps most, early Christians, and the references and allusions to the books of our NT and early Christian literature must be understood in that light. Reading a book in church implied the use of it for the purposes described in 2 Timothy 3:16, just as the Jewish Scriptures had been similarly used from the earliest days of the church. So Paul's letters were first read and continued to be read. "Take up the epistle of the blessed Paul the apostle," writes Clement of Rome[15] to the Corinthian church at the end of the first century, revealing that both he and they had 1 Corinthians on hand for the purpose.

X. Apostolic Doctrine and Authorship

To be useful for teaching, no possible taint of false doctrine could appear in a book read in church. We have a letter of Serapion, Bishop of Antioch, c. A.D. 200, which, though obscure in parts, shows that he had acquiesced in the reading of the Gospel of Peter in the church at Rhossus till he learned more about its content and realized that harmless, indeed edifying, matter was mixed with the pestilential docetic teaching (i.e., denial of the reality of Christ's manhood).[16]

The standard for judging doctrine in such works was apostolicity. A work unquestionably by an apostle clearly fell into this category, but apostolic authorship was not—at least at first—an essential mark of apostolicity. No one ever suggested that Mark's or Luke's Gospels were the work of apostles, even though each author was associated with an apostle. The cryptic remark of Papias (see V above) suggests that Matthew was

---

[11] *Apology* 1.67.

[12] Ibid., 1.66.

[13] In the third-century persecutions it was an offense to be a *traditor*, one who "handed over" the Scriptures to the pagan authorities.

[14] Cf. C.H. Roberts, "The Codex," *Proceedings of the British Academy*, 1954, 169ff.

[15] *Epistle* 47.1.

[16] Eusebius *Eccl. Hist.* 6.12.3–6.

believed to be involved in only one stage of the production of the first Gospel. Later, however, under pressure from the Gnostic use of tradition, it was apostolic authorship that tended to determine whether a book was "read" or not. The history of the reception of the (anonymous) Epistle to the Hebrews illustrates this change. Its use in the church is widely attested at an early stage. Yet we find that by the late second century doubts were being expressed, especially by Western writers. These doubts were based on the conviction that the book was not written by Paul. Eastern writers maintained that it was, and they eventually carried the day; all accepted Hebrews when all accepted its apostolic authorship. But so distinguished an Eastern scholar as Origen, while believing Hebrews to be thoroughly apostolic in character and teaching, did not think it was Pauline and said, "In truth, God knows who wrote it."[17] In other words, Hebrews was received as authoritative in many churches independently of the question of its authorship, and the belief in its Pauline authorship simply clinched the matter for doubters.

Similarly, there were people in Rome, like the presbyter Gaius, who, though entirely orthodox in doctrine, would not accept either the fourth Gospel or the Apocalypse because they did not believe it to come from an apostolic source. Such people, clearly regarded as eccentric by most contemporaries, were nicknamed "Alogi" ("those without Logos"—in other words, without the Logos of John 1 *and* without reason). Gaius supported his case by stressing the difficulties of Johannine chronology in relation to that of the Synoptics. Eastern Christians, however, had long known and treasured the works associated with the beloved disciple at Ephesus.

Such controversies show that second-century Christians were neither credulous nor superficial in their approach to the holy books. They arose as a rule because churches in one part of the Roman Empire might have known certain works over a long period— works that had perhaps originated in their own area—whereas Christians from another area, with many of the sacred books in common, might have met these works only later and needed to be convinced before adding them to their working canon. In no church was this so critical, or so controversial, as in that at Rome, because in Rome there were Christians from every part of the empire, all with the traditions of their home churches. This gave Rome some of its claim to universality and also contributed greatly to the controversy within it.

XI. Pseudepigraphy

That forgery, even by the orthodox and for a worthy motive, was not tolerated, is made clear by a story Tertullian told about the author of the apocryphal "Acts of Paul and Thecla."[18] This presbyter, having been detected, was deposed, though he pleaded that he had written purely "for love of Paul" and, at least by the standards of the time, his work was quite orthodox. This suggests that deliberate pseudepigraphy was not, as is often stated, an established and acceptable convention. To this day, though hundreds of writings of a pseudepigraphic nature from the early Christian centuries have survived, the overwhelming majority of them are more or less affected by Gnostic or other tendentious influences, and many were clearly written to propagate such views. Most of the rest of them are works of what one might call "popular religion"—cheap

---

[17]Ibid., 6.25.14.
[18]*On Baptism* 17.

devotional literature, not intentionally deviant in theology but using expressions theologians would abhor and concentrating on the miraculous and the bizarre. The contrast with the works in the emergent canon is unmistakable.

XII. The Factor of Antiquity

The other striking aspect of the kind of pseudepigraphic literature referred to is its relatively late date. Second-century Christians wished to be assured of the antiquity of a work before it could be "read" as authoritative. The long work called *The Shepherd of Hermas*, which does not claim to be apostolic and seems to have been the work of a Christian prophet in Rome, was obviously greatly valued by many Christians and as savagely attacked by others, such as Tertullian. But for the author of the Muratorian Fragment (see XIV below), the status of the *Shepherd* is settled by one clear fact—its recent origin:

> The Shepherd was written very recently, in our own times in the city of Rome, when bishop Pius his brother was occupying the chair of the city of Rome; and therefore, while it is proper for it to be read, it cannot be publicly read in church to the people, to the end of time, either among the prophets, whose number is complete, or among the apostles.[19]

This passage introduces a nice distinction between books that could be "read" because they were profitable and instructive and those that could be "publicly read to the people" as apostolic and on a par with the sacred writings of the Jewish church. The existence of the former class may explain why Hermas and the First Epistle of Clement (a first-century work that no one seems to have proposed as canonical) are appended to some MSS of the NT.[20] But the latter class is the significant one: the books publicly read as Scripture are recognized as ancient, coming directly or indirectly from an apostolic source and maintaining the apostolic witness to Christ—"that which was from the beginning, which we have heard, which we have seen with our eyes, which we have looked at and our hands have touched ... concerning the Word of life" (1 John 1:1).

XIII. Christian Prophecy

The same passage from the Muratorian Fragment by implication raises the question of the works of Christian prophets. Of the works in the emergent canon, only the Revelation of John falls into this category and only the Apocalypse of Peter and *The Shepherd of Hermas* were seriously discussed. In fact, the age of Christian prophecy does not seem to have outlasted that of the apostles. There was indeed a revival of prophecy in the second century. Hermas reflects one aspect of this, but even more important was the Montanist movement, which we find above all in Phrygia, but also in Rome and North Africa from c. A.D. 157. The strenuous objections of Gaius and the

---

[19]R.M. Grant, trans. *Second-Century Christianity* (London: SPCK, 1946), pp. 118ff.

[20]Codex Sinaiticus (fourth century) includes Barnabas and Hermas; Codex Alexandrinus (fifth century) includes 1 and 2 Clement; but Codex Claromontanus interpolates a list of canonical writings that includes Barnabas (though it is possible that this means Hebrews), Hermas, the Acts of Paul, and the Apocalypse of Peter.

Alogi (see X above) to the fourth Gospel and the Apocalypse may reflect their antipathy to Montanist "new scriptures" and eschatology. It is worth noticing, however, that what we know of the "revelations" of the Montanist prophet and the prophetesses is either formal or peripheral (such as the ordering of supernumerary fasts) and that all the massive works of the great Tertullian, who became a Montanist, contain only some half-dozen oracles of the new prophecy. The effective canon, the source of apostolic doctrine, for the Montanists was the same as for most Christians.

XIV. The Muratorian Canon

Most second-century writers, going back to Ignatius and even the first-century Clement, quote or allude to words from the Lord or NT books, with or without a formula like "it is written," in such a way as to show that the texts are perfectly familiar to them and their readers and accepted by both as authoritative. Perhaps the most revealing work of all is the *Gospel of Truth* (ascribed to Valentinus) among the writings found at Nag Hammadi. Valentinus was a serious contender for the bishopric of Rome before developing a form of teaching that brought him excommunication. In the *Gospel of Truth* he is seeking to expound this teaching in a form acceptable as a whole to Christians (and doubtless especially Roman Christians), and his book presupposes acquaintance with the four Gospels, the Pauline Epistles, and the Revelation of John.[21] Van Unnik thinks it was written as early as 140–145 shortly before or after the expulsion of Valentinus.

The earliest formal list of received books (apart from what we know of Marcion's) is, however, the so-called Muratorian Fragment, which dates from about A.D. 180.[22] Unfortunately the text is corrupt (it is a translation from Greek into Latin) and the beginning is missing: the opening words are obviously concluding some observations about Mark. The author then says that "the third book of the Gospel is according to Luke," the physician and associate of Paul. Then comes a longer account of the fourth Gospel, with a story to indicate that John wrote this Gospel on behalf of all the apostles and that it was certified by all the apostles.

In other words, the position of the four Gospels is firm. Despite the overlapping material in the Synoptics and despite the differences between the Synoptics and John, the four stand together. The consensus has rejected both reduction to one (as Marcion attempted) and conflation of the four into a single harmony, like Tatian's *Diatessaron*, which was produced for some Syrian churches. The other sayings, collections, and early gospels disappear from sight, or are left among the more obscure Jewish Christian groups, to puzzle or interest those who identified them as the Gospel of the Nazarenes or the Gospel of the Hebrews.[23] The new, tendentious works, whether pure invention or reworked traditions,[24] have no chance of establishing themselves. The ancient four Gospels have driven every rival from the field. Irenaeus, who was Bishop of Lyons, was

---

[21]Cf. W.C. van Unnik, *The "Gospel of Truth" and the New Testament,* in F.L. Cross, ed. *The Jung Codex* (Oxford: Mowbray, 1955), pp. 79–129.

[22]There is a handy text and translation in H.M. Gwatkin, *Selections From Early Christian Writers,* 2nd ed. (London: Macmillan, 1897).

[23]On these, see E. Hennecke, W. Schneemelcher, and R.McL. Wilson, eds. *New Testament Apocrypha* I (London: Lutterworth, 1963), pp. 117–165.

[24]This class may include the *Gospel of Thomas,* discovered among the Nag Hammadi writings.

teaching about the same time (the late second century) that there must be four Gospels "as surely as there are four winds of heaven."[25]

Next in the Muratorian Fragment comes the Acts, ascribed by the writer to Luke. Oddly enough, considering its size, this is one of the least clearly attested books of our present NT before this period. But it clearly belongs with Luke's Gospel and can hardly be a second-century work. (The relationship that it portrays between Paul and Jerusalem is sufficient explanation of its neglect by Marcion.)

The writer then lists the Epistles of Paul in the order of Corinthians, Ephesians, Philippians, Colossians, Galatians, Thessalonians, Romans, with some thoughts on the number seven as expressing completion but acknowledging that there are two Corinthian and two Thessalonian letters. This, with Ephesians instead of Laodiceans, is in effect Marcion's list. Two letters, Laodiceans and Alexandrines, are described as Marcionite forgeries. Philemon, Titus, and the two letters to Timothy are then listed. Many theories, none provable, have been formulated about the publication of the Pauline corpus of letters. We have already mentioned the (unlikely) idea of Marcion as the first collector; E.J. Goodspeed and J. Knox suggested Onesimus, the author, on their theory, of Ephesians, the covering letter for the corpus.[26] More recently, Moule, pointing out the links between Luke and the pastoral Epistles, suggests that Luke, having completed the Acts, made the collection and first edition of the Pauline letters.[27]

The Muratorian writer does not mention Hebrews at all. In Rome at this period it was evidently not being "read" by anyone. It was Eastern Christians, whether they thought it Pauline or not, who knew it best and held it dear. Jude, however, is mentioned, and, somewhat oddly, *two* Epistles of John. There is another odd reference to "Wisdom written by the friends of Solomon in his honour": presumably the Book of Wisdom in the OT Apocrypha.[28]

The present text then reads, "We accept the apocalypses only of John and Peter, which some of us do not allow to be read in churches." Though Jude is mentioned, there is no reference to either *letter* of Peter. There may be some truth, therefore, in Zahn's suggestion that the original Greek had something like "We accept the Apocalypse only of John, and of Peter one epistle, which only we receive; there is also a second which some of us," etc. On this theory, a line or more dropped from the text. There follows the passage about Hermas already discussed (see XII above) and a hopelessly corrupt passage about rejected books, evidently those of contemporary deviant groups.

The Muratorian Fragment sets the outlines for the NT Canon that were to hold for some time to come. The four Gospels, the Acts, and the thirteen Pauline Epistles are universally accepted. First John and 1 Peter are also widely read in the churches, the two small Johannine letters usually, but not always, come in with 1 John. Hebrews and Revelation are widely known but occasion local difficulties; James (which is not mentioned in the Muratorian Fragment) and Jude (which is) are known in some areas but not in others. Among our present canonical books, 2 Peter occurs least often among those read.

25*Adversus Haereses* 3.11.11.

26See, e.g., C.L. Mitton, *The Formation of the Pauline Corpus of Letters* (London: Epworth, 1952).

27C.F.D. Moule, *The Birth of the New Testament*, 2nd ed. (London: Black, 1966), pp. 200–204, 220–221.

28Grant, *Second-Century Christianity.* Cf. Also Eusebius *Eccl. Hist.* 6.13.6.

XV. The Fourth-Century Consensus

By the time we reach the conciliar age, most Christians are reading the same books. Eusebius[29] lists the "Homologoumena," i.e., books acknowledged by all: the four Gospels, Acts, Paul,[30] 1 John, 1 Peter, and ("if it really seems right," says Eusebius) Revelation. Then he lists the "Antilogomena," i.e., disputed books "nevertheless familiar to the majority" (a revealing phrase): James, 2 Peter, 2 and 3 John. Then come the "Notha," or spurious works: the Acts of Paul, Hermas, the Apocalypse of Peter, Barnabas, the Didache—and some would add the Revelation of John and the Gospel According to the Hebrews. The "Notha" are "spurious" in the sense of being not from an apostolic source: they are "recognized by most churchmen" says Eusebius, but not as canonical. In a quite different class come the heretical works—"Gospels" or "Acts" put forth in the name of apostles. Such works are not even to be dignified with the appellation "Notha." They are altogether monstrous and impious.

The list of canonical writings in a *Festal Letter* of Athanasius (A.D. 367) is identical with that of our own canon.

One should perhaps note that the canon of the Syriac-speaking churches, whose development was to a large extent different from that of Greco-Roman Christianity, has a somewhat different history, but reaches the same conclusion. The main difference lies in the long period when the *Diatessaron*, a harmony of the four Gospels composed in the second century by Tatian, replaced the four. But it presupposed, of course, the earlier acceptance of the four. Second Peter, 2 and 3 John, Jude, and Revelation seem to have been known rather late by Syriac Christians. It is likely that in early days Syriac speakers used the Gospel according to the Hebrews: it dropped out as the Diatessaron became "the Gospel." Syriac Christians do not seem to have used as canonical any other books that were unrecognized by the Greco-Roman churches.

The whole story of the NT canon is the outworking of the implications of the situation well described by Wikenhauser:

> The primitive Church possesses three authoritative sources of revelation—the Old Testament, the Lord, and the Apostles—but the finally decisive authority is Christ the Lord, who speaks directly through his word and work and indirectly through the testimony of his chosen witnesses.[31]

XVI. Bibliography

Aland, K. "The Problem of Anonymity and Pseudonymity in Christian Literature of the First Two Centuries," *Journal of Theological Studies* NS 12 (1961): 1ff.

Bauer, W. *Orthodoxy and Heresy in Earliest Christianity*. Philadelphia: Fortress, 1971.

Birdsall, J.N. "Canon of the New Testament" in *NBD*.

Blackman, E.C. *Marcion and His Influence*. London: SPCK, 1948.

Gregory, C.R. *Canon and Text of the New Testament*. Edinburgh: T. & T. Clark, 1924.

Guthrie, D. *Introduction to the New Testament*. 3 vols. London: Tyndale Press, 3 vols., 1961. (See especially the essay on "Epistles, Pseudepigraphy," in vol. 1, *The Pauline Epistles*, pp. 282ff.)

Hennecke, E. and Schneemelcher, W. *New Testament Apocrypha*. 2 vols. London: Lutterworth,

---

[29] *Eccl. Hist.* 3.25.

[30] For Eusebius this includes Hebrews.

[31] Albert Wikenhauser, *New Testament Introduction* (New York: Herder and Herder; London: Darton, Longman and Todd, 1958), p. 4.

1963–1965. (An encyclopedic treatment, with texts, of uncanonical works attributed by their authors to apostolic sources.)

James, M.R. *The Apocryphal New Testament.* Oxford: Clarendon Press, 1924.

Knox, J. *Marcion and the New Testament.* Chicago: University of Chicago Press, 1942.

Metzger, B.M. *The New Testament: Its Background, Growth and Content.* New York: Abingdon 1965.

Mitton, C.L. *The Formation of the Pauline Corpus of Letters.* London: Epworth, 1952.

Moule, C.F.D. *The Birth of the New Testament.* London: Black, 1962, ch. 10.

Riesenfeld, H. *The Gospel Tradition and its Beginnings.* Oxford: Mowbray, 1957.

Sanders, J.N. *The Fourth Gospel in the Early Church:* Cambridge: Cambridge University Press, 1943.

Souter, A. and Williams C.S.C. *The Text and Canon of the New Testament.* London: Duckworth, 1954.

Walls, A.F. "The Montanist 'Catholic Epistle' and its New Testament prototype," in F.L. Cross, ed. *Studia Evangelica* 3, Berlin: Akademie Verlag, 1963, pp. 437ff.

Westcott, B.F. *A General Survey of the Canon of the New Testament,* 7th ed. London: Macmillan, 1896.

Wikenhauser, A. *New Testament Introduction.* London: Darton, Longman and Todd, 1958.

ARCHAEOLOGY AND THE NEW TESTAMENT

Edwin Yamauchi

Edwin M. Yamauchi

B.A., Shelton College; M.A., Ph.D., Brandeis University

Professor of History, Miami University (Ohio)

ARCHAEOLOGY AND THE NEW TESTAMENT

I. **Archaeology and the New Testament**

    A. **Ramsay and the Tübingen School**
    B. **Monuments, Materials, and Texts**

II. **Archaeology and the New Testament Periods**

    A. **Herod the Great**
    B. **Qumran**
    C. **John the Baptist**
    D. **Jesus of Nazareth**
    E. **The Apostle Paul**
    F. **The Apostle Peter**
    G. **The Apostle John and the Churches of Revelation**
    H. **The Jewish Revolt**

III. **Bibliography**

I. Archaeology and the New Testament

A. *Ramsay and the Tübingen School*

The radical skepticism of F.C. Baur and his Tübingen school of criticism (see the article THE HISTORICAL AND LITERARY CRITICISM OF THE NEW TESTAMENT pp. 435–456) was tempered by the development of NT archaeology in the late nineteenth and early twentieth centuries.

W.F. Albright rendered this verdict on radical NT criticism:

> In the same way, the form-critical school founded by M. Dibelius and R. Bultmann a generation before the discovery of the Dead Sea Scrolls has continued to flourish without the slightest regard for the Dead Sea Scrolls. In other words, all radical schools in New Testament criticism which have existed in the past or which exist today are prearchaeological, and are, therefore, since they were built *in der Luft* ("in the air"), quite antiquated today.[1]

The first to see that the archaeological data did not fit the theories of scholars but rather confirmed the NT itself, especially the writings of Luke, was the great archaeol-

---

[1] W.F. Albright in *The Teacher's Yoke*, ed. E.J. Vardaman (Waco: Baylor University Press, 1964), p. 29.

ogist of Asia Minor, Sir William Ramsay.[2] When he began his researches at the end of the nineteenth century, he had accepted the views of the Tübingen school about the late date and unreliability of Acts. The results of his own discoveries convinced him of the essential trustworthiness of the NT.[3] His researches and conclusions influenced scholars such as T. Zahn, A. Harnack, E. Meyer, and A.T. Olmstead to view the NT in a positive light. Ramsay's work has continued to influence such British NT scholars as F.F. Bruce and such classical historians as A.N. Sherwin-White.[4]

On the other hand, German commentators on Acts have virtually ignored the archaeological researches of Ramsay and have interpreted Luke's work primarily from a literary-theological perspective. Gasque explains the reason for the difference in approaches as follows:

> An important feature of early British criticism is that it was rooted firmly in historical study. Those who became the leading New Testament critics had received their preparation for this task by a careful and minute study of the classics and ancient history. This underlined for them the importance of the true environment of the New Testament writings, *viz*. The Hellenic world at large. It also prepared them to recognize the important contribution of archaeological research to the study of the New Testament as soon as this new science appeared on the scene.
>
> In contrast to criticism in Germany, British biblical scholarship was never the handmaid of philosophy.[5]

B. Monuments, Materials, and Texts

NT archaeology encompasses the areas of the eastern Mediterranean, following the course of the spread of the gospel as it radiated from the Holy Land especially through the missionary endeavors of Paul. The areas therefore of the greatest interest are, first of all, Palestine, Jordan, and Syria;[6] then Anatolia (Turkey), Greece, and Italy.[7]

In these areas many monuments have always remained visible, such as the temple platform in Jerusalem, the Parthenon in Athens, and the Colosseum in Rome. The vast bulk of monuments, inscriptions, and material remains have been recovered, however, in the course of archaeological excavations.

Archaeologists have uncovered remains of buildings, streets, siege works, mosaics, furniture, tombs, pottery, etc. In some cases these discoveries can be correlated with the NT or with Josephus, the Jewish historian who wrote at the end of the first century A.D.

Inscribed texts primarily in Hebrew, Aramaic, Greek, and Latin are of utmost interest for our understanding of the NT. The most sensational finds in this regard are the famed Dead Sea Scrolls from Qumran (see the article THE DEAD SEA SCROLLS, pp. 393–405).

The great mass of Greek inscriptions relating to the Jews are brief funerary inscriptions such as those found on ossuaries—limestone boxes for the redeposit of the bones of the dead. Of 683 published Jewish Greek inscriptions from the Diaspora, 65 are from

---

[2]W.W. Gasque, *Sir William M. Ramsay* (Grand Rapids: Baker, 1966).

[3]W.M. Ramsay, *The Bearing of Recent Discovery on the Trustworthiness of the New Testament* (Grand Rapids: Baker, 1953 repr. of the 1915 ed.); C.J. Hemer, *Tyndale Bulletin* 22 (1971): 119–124; idem, BJRL 60 (1977): 28–51.

[4]Cf. E. Yamauchi, *The Stones and the Scriptures* (Philadelphia: Lippincott, 1972), pp. 96–98.

[5]W.W. Gasque, *A History of the Criticism of the Acts of the Apostles* (Grand Rapids: Eerdmans, 1975), p. 108; idem, *Theologische Zeitschrift* 28 (1972): 177–96. Cf. F.F. Bruce, NTS 22 (1976): 229–42.

[6]M. Avi-Yonah, *The Holy Land* (Grand Rapids: Baker, 1966); E. Yamauchi, JAAR 42 (1974): 710–26.

[7]C.F. Pfeiffer and H.F. Vos, *The Wycliffe Historical Geography of Bible Lands* (Chicago: Moody, 1968).

a cemetery in Cyrenaica, 80 from Tell el-Yehudieh in Egypt, and 262 from catacombs in Rome.[8] The dominant position of Greek among the Jews of the Diaspora may be seen from a study of catacomb inscriptions from Rome, which shows that 74 percent were in Greek, 24 percent in Latin, and only 2 percent in Hebrew or Aramaic.[9]

Of the greatest value for dating purposes are coins (see the article THE METROLOGY OF THE NEW TESTAMENT, pp. 609–13), which are primarily of bronze but occasionally of silver. The coins of the various Herodian rulers and Roman procurators are quite revealing. Herod the Great's coins were mainly aniconic (without images) but in later years he introduced the eagle, symbol of Roman might. Herod Philip, who ruled in a largely Gentile region in the northeast, decorated his coins with the images of the emperor and of the god Pan (cf. Panias or Caesarea Philippi, which he founded). The Jewish zealots superimposed their own inscriptions on Roman coins, proudly proclaiming their mottos of independence.[10]

The coin most often mentioned in the NT is the silver denarius or "penny," which was the equivalent of a day's wage. The coin with Caesar's image shown to Jesus (Matt 22:19–21) probably bore the likeness of either Tiberius or Augustus. Other coins such as those mentioned in Luke 15: 8–9 were Tyrian shekels of silver, which were considered acceptable for the temple offering.[11]

II. Archaeology and the New Testament Periods

A. Herod the Great

When Jesus was born in Bethlehem, the king of Judaea was Herod the Great (37–4 B.C.). None of his coins bears his image. But at Seeia in the Hauran in Jordan there once stood a statue of Herod, of which only the base remains. H. Ingholt has suggested that a colossal head from Egypt acquired by the Boston Museum may well depict Herod.[12]

Herod was highly regarded by the Romans as a loyal client king and able military leader. An Athenian inscription calls him *philorōmaios*, "friend of the Romans." According to Josephus, Herod used his vast wealth in benefactions to many foreign cities and even provided funds for the Olympic Games.

Herod was the most prodigious builder in Israel since the days of Solomon. The beautiful buildings that adorned Jerusalem in the days of Jesus were erected by him.

1. *Jerusalem.* Herod's greatest undertaking was the complete rebuilding of the second temple of Zerubbabel. The rabbis said, "Whoever has not seen Herod's temple has never seen a beautiful building." Nearly twenty thousand workmen, including one thousand priests, labored on the task. Work was begun in the eighteenth year of Herod's reign, and the essential structures, including the massive platform, were completed by 9 B.C. Additional work continued, however, until about A.D. 64, only six years before the Romans razed the temple. When Jesus was challenged by his opponents, "It has taken

---

[8]G. Mussies in *The Jewish People in the First Century*, ed. S. Safrai and M. Stern (Philadelphia: Fortress, 1974), 1042–43.

[9]H.J. Leon, *The Jews of Rome* (Philadelphia: Jewish Publication Society, 1960).

[10]Y. Meshorer, *Jewish Coins* (Tel Aviv: Am Hassefer, 1967).

[11]A. Spijkerman, *Liber Annuus* 6 (1955–56): 279–98.

[12]*Journal of the American Research Center in Egypt* 2 (1964): 125–42.

forty-six years to build this temple, and you are going to raise it in three days?" (John 2:20), the date must have been about A.D. 27/28.

The excavations made by B. Mazar (1968–77) have brought into view additional courses of the finely drafted stones of the southwest section of the Herodian platform. These stones elicited the admiring comment of the disciples, "Look Teacher! What massive stones! What magnificent buildings!" (Mark 13:1). The limestone ashlars (hewn stones) average 3 to 4 feet in height and in some cases are almost 40 feet long. The larger stones weigh more than 100 tons.

At the southwest corner of the platform the springing of an arch, first identified by Robinson in the nineteenth century, has long been visible. In 1968 Mazar uncovered the lower pier of the arch. We now understand that the arch supported not a viaduct but a monumental staircase used by Herod and his family.

Wilson's Arch to the north is 10 feet below the modern street in front of the Gate of the Chain. It once supported a viaduct used by the priests to gain access to the temple.

A paved road ran along the western wall (the "Wailing Wall") and extended nearly a mile south. Under this street a water conduit led in the same direction.

The main entrances for the people were the two Huldah Gates on the southern side of the platform. The eastern gate is now a blocked triple gate; the blocked western gate is partially visible under the Al-Aksah Mosque. A recent examination of the interior shows that 85 percent of its construction goes back to the NT period. Jesus and his disciples must have entered by the eastern gate and exited by the western gate.

Before the western gate, Mazar uncovered a monumental stairway with thirty steps, over 200 feet wide. He also discovered the tunnels, called *mesibot*, designed for the quick exit of people and objects that had become defiled.

In the eastern section of the platform was the Susa Gate, probably where the Golden Gate is located today. The latter was blocked up by a Muslim ruler in 1530 to frustrate the prophecy of Ezekiel 44:1–2.[13] In 1969 an earlier gate, which may possibly have been the Herodian gate through which Jesus passed on Palm Sunday, was sighted about 8 feet below the bottom of the present Golden Gate.[14]

Above the southern edge of the platform was built the magnificent Royal Portico, a triple colonnade 800 feet long. Mazar found a block from the parapet of the southwestern corner with a Hebrew inscription, *le-beit hat-teqi'ah* "for the place of the blowing [of the trumpet]," which refers to the blowing of the ram's horn to announce the beginning and the end of the Sabbath. Other interesting objects found in the area include a fragment of a sundial, a limestone object inscribed *qorban* ("offering"; Mark 7:11), and Corinthian capitals of columns with gilded leaves.

The area on the platform was divided into a court open to the Gentiles and the smaller area around the temple proper. On a stone balustrade around this inner area warnings in Greek and in Latin were placed. In 1871 a Greek copy of the warning inscription was found; in 1935 a fragmentary Greek copy was found near St. Stephen's Gate. The text reads: "Let no Gentile enter within the balustrade and enclosure about the holy place; and whosoever is caught shall be responsible to himself because death follows."[15]

When Paul returned to Jerusalem for the last time, he precipitated a riot because the Jews believed that he had taken a Gentile into the inner area of the temple (Acts

[13]S. Steckoll, *The Gates of Jerusalem* (Tel Aviv: Am Hassefer, 1968), pp. 13–14.
[14]G. Giacumakis, *The Bulletin of the Near East Archaeological Society* 4 (1974): 23–26.
[15]J.H. Iliffe, *Quarterly of the Department of Antiquities in Palestine* 6 (1938): 1–3.

21:27–30). Paul was no doubt referring to this barrier when he wrote of the middle wall of partition between Jew and Gentile—the wall that had been broken down by Christ (Eph 2:14).

The gate separating the Court of the Women from the Court of Israel to the west was the ornate gate donated by Nicanor, a wealthy Alexandrian. At the beginning of this century an ossuary was discovered on Mount Scopus, bearing the name of Nicanor the Alexandrian. More recently an ossuary from Giv'at ha-Mivtar, Jerusalem, which bore the Aramaic inscription "Simon, builder of the temple," was recovered.

A. Muehsam has attempted a reconstruction of the facade of the temple building itself from the design on the coins of Bar Kochba.[16] M. Avi-Yonah has constructed this design on a model of Jerusalem in the scale of 1:50 on the grounds of the Holy Land Hotel in Jerusalem.[17]

In the Citadel area (Jaffa Gate) Herod had erected three great towers named Hippicus, Phasael, and Mariamne. Above the bases were added superstructures, including cisterns and living quarters, which made the towers about 100 feet high. The present "David's Tower" is built on the base of Phasael.

In the area south of the Citadel and extending to the Armenian Gardens, R. Amiran and A. Eitan have uncovered the foundations of Herod's palace over 1,000 feet long and 200 feet broad. Only a few rooms in the northwest corner have been preserved.[18] In 1977 M. Broshi uncovered sections of Herod's city wall near the Citadel.

2. *Sebaste.* Herod in 26 B.C. rebuilt the city of Samaria and renamed it *Sebaste* (the Greek equivalent of Augustus) in honor of the emperor. Herod settled six thousand of his veterans here. On the acropolis the broad staircase of the temple dedicated to Augustus survives; nearby the torso of a white marble statue of the emperor was discovered. One may also see the remains of the basilica, the great public building of the forum. On the plains below are the remains of a stadium that may possibly be Herodian in date. The theater and the colonnaded street are from later constructions of the second and third centuries.

3. *Caesarea.* One of the most significant projects of Herod was his construction of the artificial harbor at Caesarea, begun in 22 B.C. and dedicated to Augustus in 10 B.C. The enormous stone blocks, 50 by 18 feet, that Herod used to build the protective moles of the harbor have been located. In 1960 an underwater expedition recovered a coin that depicts the entrance to the harbor.[19]

Within the area of the Crusader city of Caesarea may be seen the podium of a building that has been identified as the temple dedicated to Augustus. Fragments of colossal statues, probably of Augustus and of Rome personified, have been recovered.

The city was supplied with water by two aqueducts: a low-level aqueduct 3 miles long and a high-level aqueduct 6 miles long.[20] The latter was built by Herod. Numerous Latin inscriptions of soldiers of the VIth, Xth, and XIIth legions record repairs made in

---

[16]A. Muehsam, *Coin and Temple* (Leeds: Leeds University Press, 1966).

[17]M. Avi-Yonah in *Studies in the History of Religions XIV*, ed. J. Neusner (Leiden: Brill, 1968), pp. 327–35.

[18]R. Amiran and A. Eitan, *Israel Exploration Journal* 22 (1972): 50–51.

[19]C.T. Fritsch, BA 24 (1961): 50–59.

[20]Y. Olam and Y. Peleg, *Israel Exploration Journal* 27 (1977): 127–37.

Hadrian's reign. It has been suggested that one of the soldiers mentioned in an inscription may have been a son of the historian Josephus.[21]

From 1959 to 1961 an Italian expedition excavated the 4,500-seat theater. The theater may have been the scene of Herod Agrippa I's fatal stroke (Acts 12:21–23). R. Bull, on the other hand, favors the site of the amphitheater, which appears to have been larger than the Colosseum in Rome. Soundings have been made in the second-century A.D. hippodrome, which was used for chariot races.

In one of the extensive warehouses on the sea front, R. Bull discovered in 1973 a third- or fourth-century A.D. mithraeum, which is the first ever to be discovered in Israel.[22]

4. *Jericho.* Herodian Jericho is located along both banks of the Wadi Qelt to the south of OT Jericho. Excavations by J.L. Kelso in 1950 and by J.B. Pritchard in 1951 have discovered some of the splendid buildings erected by Herod south of the wadi. They uncovered a great sunken garden, 360 feet long, adorned with statuary niches and flower pots. The use of concrete and special masonry reflects the use of Roman craftsmen.

Recent excavations by E. Netzer have uncovered a palatial area north of the wadi. The most interesting discovery was a swimming pool, 100 by 60 feet—no doubt the pool in which Herod had the high priest Aristobulus III drowned (Jos. Antiq. XV, 53–56).[23]

5. *Masada.* The most spectacular site in Israel is Masada, the plateau shaped like a battleship and located on the western shore of the Dead Sea. The site, developed by Herod between 37 and 31 B.C., became the last stronghold of the Jews against the Romans in A.D. 73 (see below under H. *The Jewish Revolt*). Excavations from 1963 to 1965 under the direction of Y. Yadin cleared almost all of the site.

One of the marvels of Herod's construction was the creation of huge cisterns to hold 1,400,000 cubic feet of water. Facilities using this water included a Roman bath house and a swimming pool. At the northern end of Masada Herod built a three-tiered palace with plastered walls painted to imitate marble. The mosaic designs were all aniconic in deference to Herod's Jewish subjects. A columbarium is believed to have held ashes of Herod's Gentile soldiers.

6. *Herodium.* Herod, who died at Jericho, was buried at Herodium, 3 miles south of Bethlehem. The steep hill, rising 400 feet above the plain, had been artificially heightened by Herod. From 1962 to 1967 V. Corbo uncovered the structures at the top of the hill, including a double concentric wall, four towers, and a bath house. In 1972 E. Netzer uncovered an impressive complex of buildings at the base of the hill, including a large pool, 230 x 150 feet. The actual tomb of Herod was not found, but an ostracon with his name was recovered.

7. *Hebron.* Though it is not mentioned by Josephus, the finely drafted masonry of the building above Sarah's burial cave at Hebron is clearly a work of Herod's craftsmen. Two miles north of Hebron at Ramat el-Khalil, the site of Mamre, an unfinished Herodian enclosure was rebuilt by Hadrian.

---

[21]L.I. Levine, *Caesarea Under Roman Rule* (Leiden: Brill, 1975), p. 37.

[22]R. Bull, *Israel Exploration Journal* 24 (1974): 187–90.

[23]E. Netzer, *Israel Exploration Journal* 25 (1975): 89–100; E. Netzer and E.M. Meyers, BASOR 228 (1977): 1–27; S.F. Singer, *Biblical Archaeology Review* 3 (1977): 1–17.

B. Qumran

Khirbet Qumran, the ruins of the monastery, is located a half mile south of Cave I, where the first of the Dead Sea Scrolls were discovered. Excavations were conducted here from 1951 to 1956 under G.L. Harding and R. de Vaux.[24]

The major settlement that can be associated with the MSS from the caves began in the time of Hyrcanus I (134–104 B.C.). The site was abandoned after the earthquake of 31 B.C. and reoccupied at the time of Herod's death in 4 B.C. Although no texts were found, pottery similar to that in which MSS were stored in Cave I were found. One sherd was used by a budding scribe to practice writing the alphabet. Several hundred coins that were found helped date the occupation levels.

The main settlement covered an area about 260 feet square. Two hundred to four hundred persons may have lived at Qumran at one time. Most of them must have lived in huts or tents outside the buildings. A few lived in nearby caves, where signs of occupation have been found.

The most striking feature of the Khirbet is the number of cisterns and pools found there, some of which may have been used for the ritual immersions of members of the sect. A plastered aqueduct from a mountain to the west supplied the cisterns with water.[25]

Low plaster tables (or benches) and inkwells were found. These came from the scriptorium, the room used for copying MSS. The largest room, 72 feet long, served as the refectory for the communal meals of the sect.

Some 2 miles to the south of the Khirbet, farm buildings were uncovered by the spring of 'Ain Feshka.

Between the Khirbet and the Dead Sea there was a sizeable cemetery with over one thousand burials. R. de Vaux excavated forty-three of these and found skeletons of women and children as well as men. In 1966–67 S. Steckoll uncovered ten additional skeletons.

In 1969 P. Bar-Adon discovered a site of 'Ain Ghuweir, 9 miles south of Qumran, where he uncovered a banquet hall. He also uncovered twenty burials and found a jar with the same script as that used in the Dead Sea Scrolls.[26]

C. John the Baptist

Inasmuch as John the Baptist grew up in the same area of the wilderness of Judea, was an ascetic, and practiced immersion as the Qumranian sect did, not a few scholars have associated the Baptist with the Qumran community. There are, however, striking differences that make such an association problematic.[27]

Luke's reference (3:1) to "Lysanias tetrarch of Abilene" at the beginning of John's ministry in the fifteenth year of Tiberius was for a long time held to be a chronological error because the only ruler of that name known from ancient sources was a Lysanias executed in 36 B.C. Two Greek inscriptions from Abila, northwest of Damascus, now prove that there was a "Lysanias the tetrarch" between the years A.D. 14 and 29. Luke's

---

[24]R. de Vaux, *Archaeology and the Dead Sea Scrolls* (New York: Oxford University Press, 1973).

[25]For an interpretation of the occupation periods with a history of the Essenes, see J. Murphy-O'Connor, BA 40 (1977): 121–24. Most scholars identify the Qumranians as Essenes.

[26]*Revue Biblique* 77 (1970): 398–400.

[27]W.S. LaSor, *The Dead Sea Scrolls and the New Testament* (Grand Rapids: Eerdmans, 1972), pp. 142–53; C. Scobie, *John the Baptist* (Philadelphia: Fortress, 1964), pp. 135–39.

additional reference to "Philip tetrarch of Iturea and Trachonitis" is corroborated by an inscription from Seeia.

For denouncing the illicit union of Herod Antipas and Herodias, John the Baptist was imprisoned and ultimately beheaded. According to Josephus, the scene of his imprisonment was the Herodian fortress of Machaerus, 4 miles east of the Dead Sea. In 1968 J. Vardaman conducted a brief expedition to Machaerus. He noted Herodian bath installations and aqueducts.

D. *Jesus of Nazareth*

1. *The Christmas census.* One of the most controversial questions as to the accuracy of Luke concerns the Christmas census (Luke 2:2). It is quite certain that Jesus was born before 4 B.C., the date of the death of Herod the Great. Now a census under Quirinius as governor of Syria is well known for A.D. 6 but none is known for the period before 4 B.C.

W.M. Ramsay attempted to interpret a Latin inscription as a reference to an earlier service of Quirinius as an extraordinary legate for military purposes. The view that Quirinius served before A.D. 6 has been accepted by J. Finegan,[28] but has been rejected by other scholars.[29] The fact remains, however, that Luke was well aware of the famous later census under Quirinius in A.D. 6—a census that provoked the revolt of Judas of Galilee (Acts 5:37).

2. *Bethlehem.* When we examine the places associated with Jesus, we find that we are often dependent on late traditions. In A.D. 70 Jerusalem was destroyed by Titus, and again in 135 by Hadrian, who made the city the pagan Aelia Capitolina, which was forbidden territory for any Jews or Christians of Jewish origin. A Gentile Christian community did, however, live on in Jerusalem during this period.

The tradition that Jesus was born at Bethlehem in a cave goes back to Justin Martyr, who was born c. 100 in Neapolis in Samaria. Jerome, who translated the Vulgate, made his home in an adjacent cave in 385. He tells us that Hadrian had desecrated the cave of the nativity by consecrating it with a grove of Tammuz-Adonis and that Constantine's mother Helena had built a church over the site in 326. The present Church of the Holy Nativity is a basilica built by Justinian (sixth century). Investigations in 1934 and 1948–51 have revealed floor mosaics below the present floor that belong to the Constantinian church.

Just east of Bethlehem, V. Tzaferis discovered a well-preserved fourth-century A.D. church in 1972 at Beit Sahur, the Greek Orthodox site of the shepherds' fields (Luke 2:8–18). The earliest chapel was a natural cave paved with mosaics.

3. *Nazareth.* Nazareth, where Jesus spent his childhood, is not mentioned in the OT, the Talmud, or Josephus. Its name on an epigraphic source was first discovered by Avi-Yonah in 1962 on a fragment from Caesarea describing the twenty-four courses of the priestly rotation (cf. Luke 1:5).[30]

Of the holy sites at Nazareth, none seems to be of certain association except Mary's

---

[28]J. Finegan, *Handbook of Biblical Chronology* (Princeton: Princeton University Press, 1964), p. 238.

[29]E.g., A.N. Sherwin-White, *Roman Society and Roman Law in the New Testament* (Oxford: Clarendon, 1963), pp. 162–71.

[30]M. Avi-Yonah in Vardaman, *The Teacher's Yoke* (note 1), pp. 46–57.

well, which is fed by the only good spring in Nazareth. Excavations by Bagatti from 1955 to 1960 beneath the Church of the Annunciation revealed what the excavator interprets as a fourth-century synagogue-church of Jewish Christians. Graffiti include such phrases as "Rejoice Mary," and "On the holy place of M[ary] I have written there."

4. *Capernaum.* The identification of the site of Tell Hum on the northwest shore of the Sea of Galilee as Capernaum (Kfar Nahum, "Village of Nahum") is certain. In the first century A.D. the town extended 250 yards along the shore and 500 yards inland and had a population of about a thousand.

The famous synagogue was first identified in 1866. It was excavated in 1905 by H. Kohl and C. Watzinger. They dated the building to A.D. 200. G. Orfali, who worked at the site from 1921 to 1926, argued that it was the actual synagogue where Jesus taught (Mark 1:21; Luke 4:31–37). V. Corbo and S. Loffreda, who conducted investigations from 1968 to 1972, now date the extant building to the fourth century A.D. on the basis of thousands of coins found in sealed places.[31] In the southeast corner, below the limestone steps, are black basalt blocks that may possibly belong to the synagogue of Jesus' day.

The main building was originally two stories high with a staircase to the rear. Orfali's conjecture that the upper gallery was used by women has been refuted by Safrai, who notes that such segregated galleries date only from the Middle Ages.[32]

The institution of the synagogue is commonly derived from the experience of the exiled Jews in Mesopotamia. But the earliest actual epigraphic evidence for synagogues dates from c. 250 B.C. and comes from Egypt. Remains of about twenty synagogues have been uncovered in the Diaspora, most notably the richly decorated synagogue at Dura Europos (A.D. 245). In Palestine remains of more than one hundred synagogues have been identified, almost all of them from the Late Roman and the Byzantine eras (A.D. 300–600).

5. *Chorazin.* Just inland from Capernaum is the site of Chorazin, the town that was severely reproached by Jesus (Matt 11:20–21). There is a basalt synagogue here of the second to third century, with a "seat of Moses" (Matt 23:2) for the chief official of the synagogue.[33] Similar chairs have been found at the synagogues of Hammath-Tiberias and of Delos.

6. *Magdala.* Just south of Capernaum is the site of Magdala, the home of Mary Magdalene. Recent excavations have identified its harbor and uncovered two Roman streets and a small synagogue (first century A.D.) with five stone benches seating only thirty persons.

7. *Kursi.* Jesus' exorcism of the so-called Gadarene demoniac has been a problem because of the textual variants of the name of the site (Matt 8:28; Mark 5:1; Luke 8:26). Archaeology has now shed some light on this textual problem. Origen's comment that there was an old town on the eastern shore of the Sea of Galilee was confirmed in the course of road-building operations in 1970. D. Urman has excavated a first-century A.D.

---

[31]R. North, *Biblica* 58 (1977): 424–31.

[32]In Safrai, *The Jewish People* (note 8), p. 939.

[33]In the same passage (Matt 23:5) Jesus denounced the Pharisees for making their phylacteries (*tefillin*) broad. The actual phylacteries recovered from Qumran are quite small. See Y. Yadin, *Tefillin From Qumran* (Jerusalem: Israel Exploration Society, 1969).

fishing harbor called Kursi in Jewish sources, and a fourth-century church, which commemorated the site of the miracle.[34]

8. *Sychar.* Mid-way between Galilee and Judea in Samaria is a site authorities believe to be fully authentic. This is Jacob's Well at Sychar where Jesus spoke with the woman of Samaria. As John's narrative describes it, the well is deep—about 100 feet. Above the site loom the twin mountains of Ebal and Gerizim. It was the latter the woman pointed out as the sacred place of worship for the Samaritans (John 4:20). The remains of the Samaritan sanctuary were visible from Sychar.[35]

9. *Pools in Jerusalem.* In Jerusalem there are two pools of water that can with confidence be associated with Jesus' ministry. The first is the pool of Siloam (John 9:7) to which Jesus sent a blind man. This is located at the end of Hezekiah's famous tunnel.
The other pool is that of Bethesda, the pool with five porches (John 5:1–4). In 1888, as the White Fathers cleared some ruins of the Church of St. Anne north of the temple area, they found an old fresco representing the story of John 5. Below this a flight of steps led down to twin pools surrounded by a portico. The northern pool was found to be about 150 feet long. M. Avi-Yonah, however, believes that the original pool sanctuary was located in a cave to the east of these remains.[36]

10. *Bethany.* The village of Bethany, just to the east of Jerusalem, is today called El-Azariyeh in memory of Lazarus. The traditional tomb of Lazarus was mentioned by the Pilgrim of Bordeaux (A.D. 333). Excavations that were conducted under S.J. Saller from 1949 to 1953 showed that a church was first built near the tomb c. A.D. 390.

11. *The Cenacle.* The traditional site of the Last Supper, the second-story room of the Cenacle on "Mount Zion" is only a construction of the Franciscans in the fourteenth century. A stairway descending from Mount Zion to the Kidron Valley (John 18:1) has been uncovered on the grounds of the Church of St. Peter Gallicantu ("of the crowing cock"). This may possibly date to the reign of Herod Agrippa I (A.D. 40–44).

12. *Residences of the high priests.* The Assumptionist Fathers believe that their Church of St. Peter Gallicantu is the site of the residence of Caiaphas, the high priest who tried Jesus (Matt 26:57). Most scholars favor a site farther up Mount Zion near the Cenacle complex. The traditional site of the House of Annas, the high priest emeritus (John 18:13), is in the Armenian Quarter of the present walled city. This tradition goes back, however, only to the fourteenth century.
The Upper City of Jerusalem, where the wealthy Sadducean high priests lived, is in the Jewish Quarter of the walled city of Jerusalem. Excavations under N. Avigad since 1969 have uncovered evidence of "how the wealthy lived."[37] In one of the houses Avigad found a stone weight inscribed with the name Bar Kathros, one of the priestly families the Talmud accused of exploiting the people.

---

[34] *Christian News From Israel* 22 (1971): 72–76.

[35] R.J. Bull, NTS 23 (1977): 460–62.

[36] M. Avi-Yonah, ed., *Encyclopedia of Archaeological Excavations in the Holy Land* (London: Oxford University Press, 1976), II, p. 608.

[37] N. Avigad, *Biblical Archaeology Review* 2 (1976): 1, 22ff.; for common dwellings, see H.K. Beebe, BA 38 (1975): 89–104.

One well-preserved Herodian house covered 2,000 square feet and had a central courtyard with four ovens. Near a stairway leading down to a cistern was a depression for washing one's feet. Signs of wealth included imported terra sigillata ware, expensive glass vessels, stone tables, mosaic pavements, and multi-colored frescoes. One fresco depicted the lampstand of the temple.

On the traditional site of the House of Caiaphas, M. Broshi in 1971–72 uncovered remains of a house with frescoes depicting representations of birds. The frescoes are similar in style to the frescoes of Pompeii.[38]

Outside the present wall between the Zion Gate and the Dung Gate, M. Ben-Dov has cleared additional buildings that are equipped with ritual baths.

13. *The trial.* The governor of Judea who condemned Jesus to be crucified was Pontius Pilate (A.D. 26–36). In 1961 A. Frova discovered in the theater at Caesarea an inscription of Pilate referring to a building he had erected in honor of Tiberius.[39]

In 1856 Father Ratisbonne bought the area near the so-called *Ecce Homo* arch for the Sisters of Zion because this was believed to be the beginning of the Via Dolorosa where Pilate said, "Behold the Man!" Later investigations showed that the arch was part of Hadrian's triple arch dated to A.D. 135.

Excavations under the Convent of the Sisters of Zion by H. Vincent in the 1930s uncovered huge striated flagstones that the excavator ascribed to the Fortress Antonia, built by Herod and named in honor of Mark Antony. The stones marked with games carved out by Roman soldiers recall the *lithostroton* or "pavement" (John 19:13) where Jesus was tried by Pilate.[40]

P. Benoit, however, has argued from the literary references that the governor's residence where the trial was held should be located at Herod's palace in the Citadel area. He further contends that the remains under the Sisters of Zion Convent are Hadrianic rather than Herodian in date.[41]

14. *The Crucifixion.* Pilate had Jesus scourged (John 19:1) with a brutal whip embedded with bits of bone or lumps of lead. Excavators have found the head of such a whip at Heshban in Jordan.

In 1968 the first physical evidence of crucifixion was found in an ossuary from Giv'at at ha-Mivtar in northeastern Jerusalem. The ossuary, which dates between A.D. 6 and 66, contained the heel bones of a young man named Johanan still transfixed by a four-and-a-half-inch iron nail. A crease in the radial bone shows that the victim had been nailed in his forearms not in the palms as in traditional paintings of Christ's crucifixion (*cheir* in John 20:27 can mean "arm"). Johanan's leg bones had been shattered to hasten his death as had been done to the malefactors who were crucified with Jesus (John 19:31–32).[42]

15. *The tomb of Christ.* The traditional site of Calvary and the associated tomb of Christ

---

[38]M. Broshi, *Israel Exploration Journal* 26 (1976): 84–85.

[39]J. Vardaman, JBL 81 (1962): 70–71.

[40]Marie Aline de Sion, *La forteresse Antonia à Jérusalem et la question du prétoire* (Jerusalem: Franciscan Printing Press, 1955).

[41]P. Benoit, *Harvard Theological Review* 64 (1971): 135–67; idem, *Australian Journal of Biblical Archaeology* 1 (1973): 16–22.

[42]N. Haas, *Israel Exploration Journal* 20 (1970): 38–59; cf. M. Hengel, *Crucifixion* (London: SCM, 1977).

was desecrated by Hadrian in A.D. 135. In the fourth century, Helena, the mother of Constantine, was led to the site, where she then built the Church of the Holy Sepulchre. Excavations in and around the church have helped demonstrate that it lay outside the wall in Jesus' day. Shafts dug in the church show that the area was used as a quarry and was therefore extramural, a conclusion also supported by Kenyon's excavations in the adjoining Muristan area. Thus there is no reason to doubt the general authenticity of the site.

In the course of repairs since 1954 remains of the original Constantinian structure have been exposed.[43] In 1975 M. Broshi found near St. Helena's chapel in the church a red and black picture of a Roman sailing ship and a Latin phrase *Domine ivimus* "Lord, we went" (cf. Ps 122:1). These words and the drawing were placed there by a pilgrim c. A.D. 330.[44]

As for the actual tomb of Christ, quarrying operations may have obliterated the grave.[45] A bench *arcosolium* (flat surface under a recessed arch) must have been used for Jesus. But early Christian pilgrims seem to have seen a trough *arcosolium* (rock-cut sarcophagus); this raises the question of whether they saw the actual tomb.[46]

In 1842 Otto Thenius, a German pastor, was attracted to a hill 150 yards north of the present walled city because of two cavities that gave it a skull-like appearance. The hill was popularized among Protestants as an alternative site for Calvary by General Gordon in 1883. A seventeenth-century sketch of the hill demonstrates, however, that the cavities were not yet present then. The nearby "Garden Tomb" likewise has no claim to be the authentic tomb of Christ.

Tombs that were closed with disc-shaped stones rolling in a channel may be seen at the Herodian family tomb near the King David Hotel and at the so-called Tomb of the Kings, actually the richly decorated tomb of Queen Helen of Adiabene. Recently such tombs have also been discovered at Heshban in Jordan.

A long Aramaic inscription discovered at Giv'at ha-Mivtar describes how a man named Abba buried another man named Mattathiah in a tomb, reminding us of the good deed of Joseph of Arimathea, who buried Jesus in his tomb (Matt 27:57–60).[47] In 1930 a Greek inscription, purportedly from Nazareth, was published in which an emperor, probably Claudius, sternly warned against damaging tombs, exhuming the dead, and transporting the dead from one tomb to another (cf. Matt 28:12–13). Bruce tentatively suggests the possibility that Claudius, "antiquarian as he was," may have heard about the rumors of Jesus' empty tomb and have concluded that it was the result of tomb spoliation.[48]

16. *Ossuary inscriptions.* Prior to A.D. 70 it was often customary to rebury the bones of the dead in ossuaries. We now have about 250 ossuary inscriptions in Hebrew, Aramaic, and Greek.

The discovery in 1931 of an ossuary with the name in Aramaic "Jesus, son of Joseph" created a sensation, until Sukenik—the great Jewish authority—quickly denied that this had anything to do with Jesus of Nazareth. At least six ossuaries with the name Jesus are now known; Josephus mentions no less than twenty persons with the name Jesus.

[43]C. Coüasnon, *The Church of the Holy Sepulchre in Jerusalem* (London: Oxford University Press, 1974).

[44]M. Broshi, *Biblical Archaeology Review* 3 (1977): 42–44.

[45]K.J. Conant, *Proceedings of the American Philosophical Society* 102 (1958): 16.

[46]J.P. Kane, *Religion* 2 (1972): 60.

[47]E.S. Rosenthal, *Israel Exploration Journal* 23 (1973): 72–81.

[48]F.F. Bruce, *New Testament History* (Garden City, N.Y.: Doubleday, 1972), pp. 300–303.

In 1874 C. Clermont-Ganneau reported the discovery of burials that yielded the names Mary, Martha, and Eleazar (Lazarus). Between 1953 and 1955 B. Bagatti conducted excavations on the grounds of Dominus Flevit ("The Lord Wept") on the slopes of the Mount of Olives. He recovered forty-three inscriptions with many of the same names as are found in the NT. Many of these names, however, are quite common: Simon occurs thirty-two times, Joseph twenty-one times, Mary eighteen times, Martha eleven times, etc.

Though many of the ossuaries bear cross marks, this does not demonstrate that these are Christian burials, inasmuch as clearly Jewish ossuaries, e.g., that of Nicanor, also bear such marks. The cross on Jewish ossuaries may represent the letter Taw (cf. Ezek 9:4) as a mark of those faithful to the Lord.

But in one case from Dominus Flevit what is inscribed seems to be the Chi-Rho symbol (⳨) for "Christ" or "Christian." Inscribed on another is a monogram of the Greek letters Iota, Chi, and Beta, standing perhaps for *"Iēsous Christos Boēthia"* ("Help!").[49]

Two ossuary inscriptions discovered in Talpioth, a southern suburb of Jerusalem, were called the "earliest records of Christianity" by Sukenik.[50] A coin of Agrippa I and pottery indicate that the ossuaries belong to the period before A.D. 50. The two ossuaries bear the enigmatic inscriptions in Greek: *IĒSOU IOU* and *IĒSOU ALŌTH*. These were interpreted by Sukenik as cries of lamentation addressed to Jesus. Kane, on the other hand, interprets these as simple personal names.[51] He does concede the possibility that the ossuary of Alexander of Cyrene, son of Simon, may be that of the son of the man who carried Jesus' cross (Mark 15:21).[52]

E. *The Apostle Paul*

1. *The synagogue of the freedmen.* A Greek inscription that may have belonged to the synagogue of the "libertines"—i.e., freedmen or former slaves—mentioned in Acts 6:9 was found by R. Weill in 1914 on the Ophel hill in Jerusalem.[53] The text mentions a Theodotos and his family who had built a synagogue and lodgings for Jews from the Diaspora. His father's name indicates that he was at one time a Roman slave.

Although the Jews in the Diaspora were generally lax in their observance of their religion, this was not true of Diaspora Jews like Theodotus and Saul of Tarsus who were so zealous for their faith that they emigrated to Jerusalem.

2. *Damascus.* Following his dramatic conversion, Saul came to the city of Damascus. The course of "the Street called Straight" (Acts 9:11) is still preserved by Darb al-Mustaqim (Bab Sharqi) Street. In 1947 the Syrians discovered a Roman arch about 13 feet below the present level. The eastern triple gate at the end of the street also dates from the Roman period.

Saul escaped from Damascus and eluded the grasp of Aretas, who guarded the gate (2 Cor 11:32). This was Aretas IV (9 B.C.–A.D. 40), the king of the Nabataeans whose

[49]J. Finegan, *The Archaeology of the New Testament* (Princeton: Princeton University Press, 1969), pp. 248–49.

[50]E.L. Sukenik, AJA (1947): 351–65.

[51]J.P. Kane, *Palestine Exploration Quarterly* 103 (1971): 103–8.

[52]Kane, *Religion* 2 (1972): 68.

[53]A. Deissmann, *Light from the Ancient East* (Grand Rapids: Baker, 1965 reprint of 1922 ed.), p. 440.

capital was Petra. He was the father-in-law of Herod Antipas. Inscriptions of this king have been found in Avdat in Palestine, Sidon in Phoenicia, and Puteoli in Italy.

3. *Paul's first missionary journey.* On his first journey Paul landed at Salamis on Cyprus and proceeded to Paphos. Extensive Roman ruins—including a gymnasium, theater, and amphitheater—are visible in Salamis. Polish excavators since 1965 have cleared a magnificent Roman palace at Nea Paphos.[54] At least one inscription found on Cyprus may be attributed to Sergius Paulus (Acts 13:7), the governor who was converted after hearing the Word of the Lord from Paul.[55]

Paul and Barnabas then proceeded to the southern coast of Turkey, and went inland, preaching the gospel in a number of cities.

At Perga, 7 miles from the coast (Acts 13:13–14), excavations have been conducted since 1967. Paul would have seen the Hellenistic towers and the magnificent town wall. The central avenue leading to the acropolis is 90 feet wide. A large food market over 200 feet square has been uncovered.

After the missionaries healed a lame man, the populace of Lystra worshiped Barnabas as Zeus and Paul as Hermes (Acts 14:12). Inscriptions with dedications to Zeus and to Hermes have been found in the vicinity of Lystra.

The discovery of inscriptions by M. Ballance in 1956 and by B. Van Elderen in 1962 have made probable the location of Derbe (Acts 14:20) at the site of Kerti Hüyük, a 65-foot-high mound.[56]

4. *Paul's second missionary journey.* On the second journey, Paul, Silas, and Timothy were directed through the interior of Anatolia to the seaport city of Alexandria Troas, 10 miles south of the famed city of Troy. They were joined there by Luke. This important city, which once held thirty thousand inhabitants, is unexcavated. Because of looting and quarrying activities, even fewer remains are visible today than were to be seen in the eighteenth century.[57]

When Paul crossed over to Neapolis, he was not conscious of the implications of bringing the gospel to Europe. Some 8 miles from the coast was Philippi, famed for the battle between Antony and Octavian's forces and the assassins of Caesar in 42 B.C. Luke's use of the Greek word *meris* (Acts 16:12) to mean a "region" was held to be an error till papyri from Egypt demonstrated that colonists from Macedonia idiomatically used the word with this meaning.

One of Paul's converts was Lydia, a seller of purple cloth from Thyatira. In 1872 a text was found reading, "The city honored from among the purple-dyers, an outstanding citizen, Antiochus the son of Lykus, a native of Thyatira, as a benefactor." Excavations by the French since 1914 have uncovered Roman shops around the forum and a fourth-century basilica on the little river to the east, commemorating the site of the gathering in which Lydia participated (Acts 16:13). •

Paul, Silas, and Timothy traveled from Philippi 75 miles west to Thessalonica on the famous Via Egnatia, parts of which are still visible. Luke's accuracy is again attested when he speaks of the *politarchs* of Thessalonica (Acts 17:6). As this term was not found

---

[54]P. Villiers, *Archéologia* 107 (1977): 25–33.

[55]B. Van Elderen in *Apostolic History and the Gospel*, ed. W.W. Gasque and R.P. Martin (Grand Rapids: Eerdmans, 1970), pp. 151–56.

[56]Ibid., pp. 156–61.

[57]C.J. Hemer, *Tyndale Bulletin* 26 (1975): 79–112.

in any classical author, Luke's use of the word was suspect. But the term has been found in at least seventeen inscriptions from the area of Thessalonica. Recent excavations have cleared a large forum, 210 by 330 feet, with buildings of the first or early second century A.D.

Paul preached his famous sermon in Athens either on the Areopagus (Mars Hill), a low hill below the Acropolis, or to the Areopagus Court, which sometimes met in the Royal Stoa.[58] In 1969 excavations north of the Athens-Piraeus railroad uncovered a small building that has been identified as the Royal Stoa. Hemer has suggested that it was here that Paul spoke to the Areopagus Court, in the very same site where Socrates once confronted his accuser.[59] Paul's reference to an inscription "TO AN UNKNOWN GOD" (Acts 17:23) has been illustrated by an inscription found at Pergamum dedicated to the "Unknown Gods."

Paul's ministry at Corinth has been richly illuminated by excavations. In the agora may be seen the *bema* or "judgment seat" before which Paul was tried (Acts 18:12–17). Paul's judge was Gallio, the brother of Seneca. Fragments of a stone inscription of Claudius found at Delphi refer to Gallio as the "Proconsul of Achaea." As the text is dated to A.D. 52, it fixes the date of Paul's stay in Corinth.

Near the theater was found an inscription that refers to the donation of a pavement by an *aedile*, or commissioner of public works, named Erastus. It is probable that this is the same Erastus who was Paul's co-worker (Acts 19:22) and who is also called the "manager" of the city (Rom 16:23).

In 1898 excavators found a broken Greek inscription that can be restored to read: "(Syna)gogue of the (Hebr)ews." Its crude lettering may indicate either the low social level of the Jews of Corinth or a late date. A marble fragment with a menorah has also been found.

The congregation at Corinth was endangered by immorality and by disputes over meats offered in pagan rituals. High above the city on the Acrocorinth stood the temple of Aphrodite with more than a thousand sacred prostitutes.[60] A thorough investigation of the Acrocorinth by C. Blegen in 1926 revealed some finely worked poros blocks that may have come from Aphrodite's temple.

Inscriptions found at the base of the Acrocorinth and in the theater testify to a flourishing cult of the Egyptian gods Isis and Serapis in the first century A.D. Recent excavations of the sanctuary of Demeter on the Acrocorinth have uncovered small theaters for religious spectacles and rooms with stone couches for cultic meals. Such rooms have also been found in the area of the Asclepius sanctuary north of the forum.

About 6 miles east of Corinth was Isthmia, the site of pan-Hellenic games attended by Nero and probably by Paul. O. Broneer has excavated the sanctuary of Poseidon, which also featured caves with cultic dining rooms. Paul's reference to a "corruptible crown" (1 Cor 9:25) can be illustrated by a stone head carved with a crown of pine leaves from Isthmia and by a mosaic of an athlete with a crown of celery leaves from Corinth.

Corinth had harbors on either side of the isthmus. Paul no doubt used the eastern harbor at Cenchreae, which was Phoebe's home (Rom 16:1). Warehouses from the first century A.D. have recently been uncovered at this port.

---

[58]R.E. Wycherley, *The Stones of Athens* (Princeton: Princeton University Press, 1978), p. 31.

[59]C.J. Hemer, NTS 20 (1973–74): 341–50.

[60]Cf. E. Yamauchi in *Orient and Occident*, ed. H. Hoffner (Kevelaer: Butzon & Bercker, 1973), pp. 213–22.

5. *Paul's third missionary journey.* Paul's third mission was spent largely at Ephesus in western Asia Minor. The city's greatest claim to fame was the temple of Artemis (Roman Diana), one of the seven wonders of the world and the largest edifice of the Hellenistic world. The remains of the temple were found by a persistent English architect who searched for seven years. Very little remains to be seen of the temple at the site today; one of the pillars is on display at the British Museum. Some idea of the appearance of the temple may be obtained from its depiction on coins.[61] An even better idea may be gained by viewing the well-preserved temple of Apollo at Didyma; this was designed by the same architect and was only slightly smaller than the Artemision of Ephesus.

Ephesus has been excavated by Austrian archaeologists since 1896. In 1965 they discovered near the site of the temple a horseshoe-shaped altar that dates back to 700 B.C.[62]

The great theater (Acts 19:29-31) where the angry Ephesians met to protest Paul's preaching held as many as twenty-four thousand persons. On the Street of the Curetes not far from the theater excavations in 1967 uncovered a house that was decorated with theatrical scenes from Menander's comedies and Euripides' tragedies. Paul may not have attended the theater but he was able to quote from Menander's play *Thais* (1 Cor 15:33).

It was especially the silversmiths (Acts 19:24ff.) who saw in Paul a threat to their business of making silver statues of Artemis. A Demetrius who is mentioned in an inscription may be the same as the ringleader of the riot.[63] An inscription in Greek and Latin from the theater describes the dedication of silver images of Artemis by a Roman official. A recently discovered inscription sheds further light on the intense devotion given to Artemis of Ephesus. It records that forty-five inhabitants of Sardis who maltreated a sacred embassy from Ephesus bearing cloaks for Artemis were condemned to die.[64]

From about 150 B.C. the goddess is depicted with several rows of bulbous objects on her chest, usually interpreted as breasts. Other scholars have interpreted the round objects as ostrich eggs, which were symbols of fertility, or as astrological symbols.[65] Statues of the goddess have been found at Hierapolis, Laodicea, Colosse, and even at Caesarea in Palestine.

Evidence of the Jewish community may be seen in a menorah carved in the steps leading up to the second-century A.D. Library of Celsus. Several lamps with the menorah design were found in the Cemetery of the Seven Sleepers.

After revisiting the churches in Macedonia and in Achaia, Paul sailed back to Troas and then walked to Assos (Acts 20:13). This coastal city, where Aristotle once stayed, was excavated from 1881 to 1883. The walls, still standing nearly 50 feet high, are the best preserved fortifications of the Hellenistic world.

Paul next came to Miletus, a great Ionian city famed for its philosophers and its colonies. Excavations begun by Germans in 1899 were intensified after 1955, when an earthquake destroyed the village that rested over part of the site. The theater at Miletus could seat more than fifteen thousand people. Two of the columns that supported the

---

[61]B. Trell, *The Temple of Artemis at Ephesus* (New York: The American Numismatic Society, 1945).

[62]A. Bammer, *Archaeology* 27.3 (1974): 202-5.

[63]Sherwin-White, p. 91.

[64]F. Sokolowski, *Harvard Theological Review* 58 (1965): 427-31.

[65]R. Fleischer, *Artemis von Ephesos und verwandte Kultstatuen aus Anatolien und Syrien* (Leiden: Brill, 1973), pp. 74-97.

imperial baldachin, or canopy, are still standing. An inscription in the fifth row marks the seats reserved for the "Jews and the God-fearing" proselytes.[66]

Other remains unearthed at Miletus include the two lion statues that guarded the main harbor, extensive stoas (colonnaded porches), and a synagogue. The north gateway of the southern Agora has been restored in the East Berlin Museum.

On his return voyage Paul stopped at the Lycian port of Patara. Ruins that can still be seen there are the city wall, a triple gate, baths of Vespasian, and a granary erected by Hadrian. Outstanding is a theater that dates from the time of Tiberius and was refurbished in A.D. 147.

6. *Paul's voyage to Rome.* After being held in prison at Caesarea for two years under Felix and then Festus, Paul took advantage of his status as a Roman citizen to appeal to Caesar in Rome. Felix was a Greek freedman, whose brother Pallas was in charge of Nero's treasury. In 1966 the first epigraphical reference to Felix was found 10 miles north of Caesarea.[67]

As it left the southwestern coast of Anatolia, Paul's ship sailed by the narrow isthmus of Cnidus (Acts 27:7). Excavations by Iris Love since 1967 have uncovered the ancient harbor, warehouses, and the round temple of Aphrodite Euploia (of Good Sailing) where once stood Praxitiles' sensational nude statue of the goddess.

After Paul's ship was wrecked on the coast of Malta, the survivors were lodged in the house of Publius, "the chief man of the island" (Acts 28:7). His title has been confirmed by Greek and Latin inscriptions from the island.

7. *Paul's arrival in Italy.* Paul landed at Puteoli on the Bay of Naples (Acts 28:13).[68] There he saw Mount Vesuvius, the volcano that was to bury Herculaneum and Pompeii in 79. This disaster has preserved gladiatorial barracks, palatial villas with their paintings, and the contorted forms of men and animals. Bronze statues, medical instruments, furniture, and carbonized food have been recovered.

The trace of a cruciform object at Herculaneum has been interpreted as evidence of a Christian chapel.[69] Two copies of an anagram from Pompeii that can spell *Pater Noster* ("Our Father") have also been interpreted as possible evidence of Christianity. Either a Jew or a Christian scribbled "SODOMA, GOMORRA" at Pompeii.[70]

Among the remains of structures Paul saw when he arrived in Rome are those of the Basilica Julia and the temple of the Vestal Virgins, the Altar of Peace and the Mausoleum of Augustus, and the theater of Pompey, now used as an apartment building. The Curia or Senate building dates from a rebuilding by Diocletian (A.D. 303). It was only after Paul's first imprisonment and the disastrous fire that devastated Rome in 64 that Nero erected his fabulous Golden House, sections of which may still be seen.

Paul doubtless saw the great Circus Maximus, which held 250,000 spectators for the chariot races, but he could not have seen the Colosseum, which was not dedicated until 80 by Titus.

Remains of the Jewish community in Rome include references to at least thirteen

---

66H. Hommel, *Instanbuler Mitteilungen* 25 (1975): 167–93.

67According to the restoration of M. Avi-Yonah, *Israel Exploration Journal* 16 (1966): 258–64.

68The site of Ostia at the mouth of the Tiber River was developed as a major port by Claudius, Trajan, and Hadrian. The well-preserved ruins include remains of *insulae* (apartment buildings), warehouses, and numerous Mithraea.

69J. Deiss, *Herculaneum* (New York: Crowell, 1970), pp. 65, 69.

70P. MacKendrick, *The Mute Stones Speak* (New York: St. Martin's, 1960), pp. 218–19.

synagogues. The overwhelming number of the 550 epitaphs from six catacombs are in Greek.

8. *Paul's imprisonment and burial.* The traditional site of Paul's final imprisonment is the Tullianum or Carcer Mamertinus, the state prison located below the Capitoline Hill. Behind the closed doors are two chambers one on top of the other. Famous captives such as Jugurtha and Vercingetorix were killed in the lower cell and cast into the Cloaca Maxima, the great sewer. The dank dungeon is described by Sallust as a chamber with a vaulted roof of stone: "Neglect, darkness and stench make it hideous and fearsome to behold."[71]

Writing late in the second century, Proclus noted the monument to Paul's burial on the road from Rome to Ostia. The traditional site is marked by a white slab (fourth century) reading: "To Paul, Apostle and Martyr" within the Church of St. Paul's Outside-the-Walls.

F. *The Apostle Peter*

1. *Peter's home in Capernaum.* About 30 feet from the synagogue in Capernaum, Franciscan excavators dug under a fifth-century octagonal church. Beneath this level they found what they describe as a fourth-century synagogue church. This was built over an enlarged private house that was venerated as early as the first century A.D. On the plastered walls are some 130 graffiti in Aramaic, Greek, and Latin primarily from the third century, including references to "Peter" and "Rome." On the basis of reports by Egeria (A.D. 385) and by the Piacenza pilgrim (A.D. 570), the excavators conclude that they have found Peter's house, which was later transformed into a church.[72]

2. *Peter's ministry.* On the day of Pentecost Peter preached to Jewish pilgrims from many countries of the Diaspora (Acts 2:5–11; cf. 1 Peter 1:1). Unfortunately the archaeological evidence from the Diaspora, except for papyri from Egypt[73] and a few Hellenistic synagogues, is almost entirely dated to the third or the fourth century A.D.[74] The synagogues of Delos and Miletus are Hellenistic; that at Ostia rests on a building that may have been used as a synagogue in the early Roman Empire.

Inscriptions of the first century A.D. from Acmonia in Phrygia (Acts 2:10) in Turkey indicate that some of the wealthy Jews were citizens of the city. Evidence from the first century B.C. to the first century A.D. from the cemetery at Cyrene (Acts 2:10) shows that members of the Jewish aristocracy received a gymnasium education and served as magistrates.

Peter was privileged to be instrumental in the conversion of Cornelius, the centurion at Caesarea. Cornelius commanded one hundred soldiers in a cohort of six hundred men. The Italian cohort he belonged to (Acts 10:1) may have been either the Cohors II Italica Civium Romanorum, a corps of freedmen known to have been stationed in Syria, or the Cohors Augustian Auranitis that later served under Agrippa II.

---

[71]M. Grant, *The Roman Forum* (London: Spring, 1970), p. 128.

[72]V. Corbo, *The House of Saint Peter at Capharnaum* (Jerusalem: Franciscan Printing Press, 1969).

[73]Cf. V.A. Tcherikover and A. Fuks, eds., *Corpus Papyrorum Judaicarum* (Cambridge: Harvard University Press, 1957), I, pp. 25–44.

[74]M. Avi-Yonah in Safrai (note 8), I, p. 53.

3. *Peter's tomb.* Excavations were conducted by Catholic scholars under St. Peter's Church from 1939 to 1950 and from 1953 to 1957. A set of bones was produced in 1965; in 1968 Pope Paul VI announced that he was convinced these are the very bones of Peter.

What is certain is that the archaeologists uncovered an *aedicula* or memorial shrine that may be identified with the "trophy" of Peter mentioned by Gaius c. A.D. 200, which had been set up c. A.D. 160.

Pope Paul's conviction regarding the alleged bones of Peter rests on the work of Margherita Guarducci, professor of Greek epigraphy at Rome.[75] She interpreted third- and fourth-century graffiti as a crypto-language used by the faithful. Though other scholars believe that the Vatican was the area of Peter's martyrdom, they doubt that the very grave or the bones of Peter have been discovered.[76]

G. The Apostle John and the Churches of Revelation

The Aegean island of Patmos (Rev. 1:9) where John was exiled during the reign of Domitian contains two monasteries dedicated to the apostle but no remains from a very early period.[77] In Revelation 2–3 letters are addressed to these seven churches of western Asia Minor:

1. *Ephesus.* A number of buildings that can be ascribed to Domitian have been identified, including a huge temple dedicated to the emperor and standing on a terrace by the upper or state agora. The head and the forearm of a colossal statue of Domitian have been recovered.

In the second century a church was erected over the traditional site of John's grave on a hill outside Ephesus. Here in the sixth century Justinian built a magnificent church over 300 feet long and about 100 feet wide. Excavations at the site were conducted between 1927 and 1929, and recently considerable restoration has been done.[78]

By the fourth century a tradition developed that John had taken Jesus' mother Mary with him to Ephesus. Part of an enormous Roman building, perhaps the grain and money exchange, 850 feet long, was transformed into the Church of the Holy Virgin c. A.D. 350. The Third Ecumenical Council was held here in A.D. 431.

2. *Smyrna.* Ancient Smyrna (modern Izmir), 35 miles north of Ephesus, was an important seaport of about two hundred thousand people. Its Hellenistic-Roman agora was excavated between 1932 and 1941. It consists of a large courtyard, 400 by 260 feet, surrounded by a two-story colonnade with a basement level.

3. *Pergamum.* The great Hellenistic city of Pergamum controlled western Asia Minor till its last king ceded his territories to Rome in 133 B.C. The city was built on a steep hill 10 miles inland from the coast.

Its greatest artistic monument, the huge altar of Zeus, was discovered in the nineteenth century and reconstructed in the Pergamum Museum of East Berlin. Some com-

---

75M. Guarducci, *The Tomb of St. Peter* (London: Harrap, 1960).

76G.F. Snyder, BA 32 (1969): 11–14; W. O'Connor, *Peter in Rome* (New York: Columbia University Press, 1969), p. 209.

77O.F.A. Meinardus, *St. John of Patmos and the Seven Churches of the Apocalypse* (Athens: Lycabettus, 1974), pp. 15–19.

78H. Plommer, *Anatolian Studies* 12 (1962): 119–30.

mentators have taken the statement regarding "Satan's throne" (Rev 2:13) as a reference to this altar.

Between 1878 and 1886 archaeologists cleared the upper city, including the library, which was second only to that in Alexandria. Excavations between 1900 and 1913 cleared the series of three gymnasiums on the slopes of Pergamum. At the foot of the hill is a huge building of red brick, a temple to Serapis that was converted into a church.

At some distance in the plain is the famous healing sanctuary, the Asklepion, approached by a 900-yard-long colonnaded avenue. The German excavators have cleared the sacred pools, lavatories, and rooms where patients slept in the hope of having dreams to aid them in their healing.

4. *Thyatira.* The site of Thyatira, east of Pergamum, is covered by the modern city of Akhisar. Recent excavations have unearthed a second-century A.D. Roman road and stoa in the center of the town.[79]

5. *Sardis.* Sardis served as the capital of the kingdom of Lydia under the fabled Croesus till its capture by the Persians in 546 B.C. Excavations were conducted early in the twentieth century and have been resumed since 1958 under G.M.A. Hanfmann. Archaeologists have discovered evidence of gold cupellation works—a discovery that lends substance to the legend of Croesus's wealth.

The great temple of Artemis has two of its 58-foot-high columns still standing. It was built in the Hellenistic period.

Excavations have confirmed Josephus's reference to an early Jewish community at Sardis (Jos. Antiq. XIV, 259ff.) by the recovery of more than eighty Jewish inscriptions. The most spectacular discovery was an enormous synagogue, 330 feet long and 60 feet wide, which was part of a municipal gymnasium complex. The foundations for the hall go back to the second century A.D.; as restored, the synagogue dates to the fourth century. The prominence of the Jews, many of whom were goldsmiths, is shown by the fact that nine of them were members of the city council.[80] The size and prestige of the Jewish community at Sardis may help explain the vehemence of the anti-Jewish polemic of Melito, bishop of Sardis (late second century), whose sermon, *Peri Pascha*, was discovered in 1937.

6. *Philadelphia.* The ruins of Philadelphia are buried under the modern city of Alashehir. The theater and the stadium may have been located in the depression between the summits of the acropolis. We have inscriptional evidence for games and festivals. Marble fragments of early Byzantine churches have been found. The Church of St. John dates from a late Byzantine period.

7. *Laodicea.* Laodicea was one of the three NT cities in the Lycus valley, together with Hierapolis and Colosse (Col 4:13). Excavations between 1961 and 1963 by Laval University cleared a nymphaeum, a fountain installation.[81] Unexcavated but visible remains include a stadium dedicated in A.D. 79, two theaters, etc.

---

[79]Meinardus, pp. 92, 100.

[80]G.M.A. Hanfmann, *Letters from Sardis* (Cambridge: Harvard University Press, 1972); idem, *From Croesus to Constantine* (Ann Arbor: University of Michigan Press, 1975).

[81]J. de Gagniers, *Laodicée du Lycos* (Quebec: Université Laval, 1969); J. Maigret, M. Bobichon, P. Devambez, R. Leconte, *Bible et Terre Sainte* 81 (March, 1966): 2–16.

The rebuke to the church of Laodicea (Rev 3:18) refers ironically to: 1) its wealth as a banking city, 2) its famed black wool, and 3) the Phrygian eye powder of the medical school at Men Carou 30 miles away. Though the extant aqueduct was designed to bring water from the area of Denizli, 6 miles to the south, the accusation that the church was lukewarm (Rev 3:16) suggests a reference to the water of the hot springs of Hierapolis, which surely became tepid by the time it was channeled to Laodicea.[82]

The site of Hierapolis is today called Pamukkale or "Cotton Castle" because of its glistening white carbonate terraces. An Italian excavation team under Paolo Verzone has worked there since 1957. At the side of the temple of Apollo the excavators have discovered the famed Plutonium described by Strabo, the sulfurous-smelling entrance to the Underworld.[83]

The inhabitants of Hierapolis used an elaborate system of channels and terra-cotta pipes for the distribution of the waters of their hot springs. A colonnaded street leads to an arch of Domitian. An extensive necropolis of twelve hundred tombs with three hundred epitaphs sheds light on the Jewish and Christian communities. Jewish guilds of purple dyers (cf. Acts 16:14) and of carpet weavers are attested. An octagonal martyrium of the fifth century commemorates the martyrdom of Philip the Evangelist (Acts 21:8).

At nearby Colosse the outline of a theater and building fragments are visible, but the site itself has never been excavated.[84]

H. *The Jewish Revolt*

The dire prophecies of Jesus regarding the fate of the temple (Matt 24:1ff.; Mark 13:1ff.; Luke 21:5ff.) were fulfilled within a generation when the Jews rebelled against the Romans in A.D. 66 in the reign of Nero. The "zealot" movement, which had its beginnings in the revolt of Judas of Galilee in A.D. 6 (Acts 5:37) and had included Simon Zelotes (Luke 6:15) and Barabbas (Mark 15:7), became increasingly violent during the governorship of Felix with the rise of the *sicarii* "assassins" (Acts 21:38), who murdered Roman collaborators.

Excavations have confirmed Josephus's vivid descriptions of the horrifying events of the war in which various zealot factions fought each other as well as the Romans.

At the beginning of the war Josephus was given command of Galilee. He surrendered Jotapata to the Romans under suspicious circumstances. The double defense wall and the cave openings may still be seen at the site of Yodefat just as Josephus described them. The stronghold of Gamala east of the Sea of Galilee has yielded scores of stone missiles and arrowheads from Vespasian's siege.

By A.D. 68 Vespasian had captured most of the Jordan valley, destroying the monastery at Qumran. By 69 the Jews held only the areas of Jerusalem, Herodium, Masada, and Machaerus—all sites that had been fortified by Herod.

When Vespasian was proclaimed emperor in 69, he sent his son Titus to consult the oracle of Venus (Aphrodite) on Cyprus. Excavators at Nea Paphos in 1968 recovered from a cistern an oval gem with the inscription of the XVth Legion Apollinaris; it must have fallen from the ring of one of Titus's officers on this occasion.

In narrating the siege of Jerusalem by Titus in 70, Josephus describes three northern walls. The first ran from the Citadel to the temple area. The second must have run east

---

[82]M. Rudwick and E. Green, ExpT 69 (1957–58): 176–78.

[83]G.E. Bean, *Turkey Beyond the Maeander* (London: Bean, 1971), p. 233.

[84]W.H. Mare, *Near East Archaeological Society Bulletin* 7 (1976): 39–59.

of the Church of the Holy Sepulchre to the Fortress Antonia. The course of the third wall, built by Herod Agrippa I, has been highly controverted. British scholars favor the line of the present north wall on the basis of masonry found at the Damascus Gate.[85] Israeli scholars favor a line of walls some 440 yards farther north, first discovered by E.L. Sukenik and L.A. Mayer in 1925.[86]

Evidences of the Roman siege of Jerusalem include thick layers of ash found by Mazar and Avigad, Roman catapult balls from below the Convent of the Sisters of Zion, and the skeletal remains of a woman from a house in the Upper City. The huge ashlars that were toppled from the parapet of the Royal Stoa crashed with such force that they buckled the Herodian pavement of the road below the temple platform.

Excavators have recovered evidence of the Zealot occupation and the Roman attacks at both Herodium and Machaerus, which fell soon after the capture of Jerusalem.

The most extensive evidence comes from Masada, the last Jewish stronghold, which fell in 73. The zealots built a synagogue, installed ritual baths, and established a hall for religious study. Under the floor of the synagogue copies of disused Scriptures were found; fragments of Ben Sira, of Jubilees, and of a Qumran-type document were also found. The zealots set up crude living quarters on the luxurious mosaic floors of Herod's palace and also in the 4,250-foot-long casemate walls surrounding the plateau. That even the zealot women were conscious of their appearance is proved by their cosmetic equipment. Over four thousand coins were recovered, including silver shekels minted by the Jewish rebels themselves.

At the base of Masada one can still see traces of eight Roman camps of the Xth Legion and a circumvallation wall of 3,800 yards. Against the western slope is the siege ramp built by Jewish prisoners. On the plateau are some of the 100-pound stones used by the defenders and hundreds of Roman ballista, the size of grapefruit. Of the 960 zealots who committed suicide at Masada, twenty-five skeletons were found in a cave and remains of three other victims in the northern palace. Among the 700 ostraca found is a lot with the name of the leader, Ben Jair; it may be one of the very lots used to decide who would kill the last survivors.

After the war the Romans stationed the Xth Legion Fretensis in Jerusalem. Numerous tiles with the legion's stamp have been found. Recently an inscription of the legion's commander, Lucius Flavius Silva (A.D. 73 to 80), has been found inscribed on a pillar in Jerusalem.[87] Roman governors of Judea after this period are known from other Latin inscriptions.[88]

The Flavian emperors—Vespasian and his sons Titus and Domitian—proclaimed their victory over the Jews in a series of Judaea Capta coins that depict the forlorn figure of a woman under a palm tree representing the Jewish nation. An inscription announcing the Roman victory has been recovered from the theater at Jerash in Jordan. The so-called Arch of Titus, which was actually erected by Domitian, depicts soldiers carrying the trumpets, the table of the shewbread, and the seven-branched menorah of the temple in a triumphal procession.

According to Eusebius, the Christians were warned to flee from Jerusalem to Pella, across the Jordan and south of the Sea of Galilee. Excavations by R.H. Smith at the site

---

[85] E.W. Hamrick, BA 40 (1977): 18–23.

[86] M. Avi-Yonah, *Israel Exploration Journal* 18 (1968): 98–125; S. Ben-Arieh and E. Netzer, *Israel Exploration Journal* 24 (1974): 97–107.

[87] M. Gichon and B.H. Isaac, *Israel Exploration Journal* 24 (1974): 117–23.

[88] E.M. Smallwood, *The Jews Under Roman Rule* (Leiden: Brill, 1976), pp. 546–57.

were cut short by the outbreak of hostilities in 1967. Smith believes that a sarcophagus based on earlier Jewish prototypes may be indirect evidence to support the tradition of the flight to Pella.[89]

III. Bibliography

Books

Akurgal, E. *Ancient Civilizations and Ruins of Turkey.* Istanbul: Mobil Oil Türk A.S., 1970.

Avi-Yonah, M., ed. *The Herodian Period (World History of the Jewish People VII).* New Brunswick: Rutgers University Press, 1975.

Barrett, C.K. *The New Testament Background.* New York: Harper & Bros., 1961.

Blaiklock, E.M. *The Archaeology of the New Testament.* Grand Rapids: Zondervan, 1970.

Deissmann, A. *Light From the Ancient East.* Grand Rapids: Baker, 1965 reprint of 1922 ed.

Finegan, J. *The Archaeology of the New Testament.* Princeton: Princeton University Press, 1969.

Inscriptions Reveal. Jerusalem: Israel Museum, rev. ed., 1973.

Jeremias, J. *Jerusalem in the Time of Jesus.* Philadelphia: Fortress, 1969.

Jerusalem Revealed. Jerusalem: Israel Exploration Society, 1975.

Kenyon, K. *Jerusalem.* London: Thames and Hudson, 1967.

Kopp, C. *The Holy Places of the Gospels.* Freiburg: Herder, 1963.

Mazar, B. *The Mountain of the Lord.* Garden City, N.Y.: Doubleday, 1975.

Meinardus, O. *St. Paul in Greece.* Athens: Lycabettus, 1972.

Meshorer, Y. *Jewish Coins.* Tel Aviv: Am Hassefer, 1967.

Safrai, S. and Stern, M., eds. *The Jewish People in the First Century.* 2 vols. Philadelphia: Fortress, 1976.

Sherwin-White, A.N. *Roman Society and Roman Law in the New Testament.* Oxford: Clarendon, 1963.

Unger, M.F. *Archaeology and the New Testament.* Grand Rapids: Zondervan, 1962.

Yadin, Y. *Masada.* New York: Random, 1966.

Yamauchi, E. *The Stones and the Scriptures.* Philadelphia: Lippincott, 1972; London: Inter-Varsity, 1973.

Periodicals

Anatolian Studies (London: British Institute of Archaeology at Ankara).

Biblical Archaeologist (Cambridge: American Schools of Oriental Research).

Biblical Archaeology Review (Washington, D.C.).

Hesperia (Athens: American School of Classical Studies).

Israel Exploration Journal (Jerusalem: Israel Exploration Society).

Palestine Exploration Quarterly (London: Palestine Exploration Fund).

---

[89]R.H. Smith, *Archaeology* 26 (1973): 250–56, idem, *Palestine Exploration Quarterly* 105 (1973): 71–82.

INDEX OF PERSONS

INDEX OF PERSONS

Harrington, W.J., 287, 305
Harris, R. Laird, 35, 392
Harrison, Everett F., 10, 79, 456, 541, 554
Harrison, P.N., 450, 451
Harrison, Norman B., 113
Harrison, R.K., 229, 242, 243, 245, 250, 259–260, 281, 344
Harrisville, R.A., 448, 512
Hart, H.H., 613
Hart, J.Y.A., 553
Hasel, Gerhard, F., 291, 305
Hastings, James, 606, 613
Hatch, W.H.P., 432, 594
Hatshepsut, 366
Hävernick, H.A.C., 286
Hawkins, John C., 511
Hawthorne, Gerald, F., 295
Hazael, 273, 326, 351, 369
Hebert, A.G., 627
Hegel, Georg, 22, 240, 286
Heidegger, Martin, 25, 440
Hegesippus, 602
Heinisch, Paul, 287
Heitland, W.E., 497
Held, H.J., 448
Helena, 654, 658
Heliodorus, 183
Hemer, C.J., 648, 660, 661
Hengel, Martin, 193, 657
Hengstenberg, E.W., 240, 286
Henn, Thomas, R., 139
Hennecke, E., 558, 559, 573, 640, 642
Henry, Carl F.H., 1, 22, 35, 442, 480, 627
Henry VIII, 50
Herder, J.G., 73–74, 439
Herod the Great, 99, 189–191, 335, 485–486, 523, 585, 595, 597–598, 604, 649, 652
Herod, Phillip, 526, 649
Herodius, 654
Herodotus, 246, 333, 609
Hesychius, 220
Hezekiah, 275, 276, 328, 352, 363, 369, 370, 371, 387
Hiebert, D. Edmond, 554
Hilarion, 550
Hillel the Elder, 216
Hillel, Rabbi, 491, 563
Hillers, Delbert R., 356, 388
Hippolytus, 398, 594
Hodges, Z.C., 433
Hoehner, Harold W., 177, 373, 374, 524, 541, 606
Hoffner, H., 661
Hofmann, J.C.K., 286
Holmes, John Haynes, 144
Holtzmann, H.J., 440, 445, 620
Holscher, G., 241, 245
Homer, 409

Hommel, H., 662
Hooke, S.H., 55, 241
Hooker, M.D., 453
Horace, 138, 547
Hort, F.J.A., 44, 54, 427, 428, 429, 430, 431, 433, 605
Hosea, 273, 274, 302, 371
Hoshaiah, 332
Hoshea, 327, 328, 369, 370, 371
Hoskier, H.C., 428
Hoskyns, E.C., 520
Hospers, J.H., 226
Houston, James M., 81
Howard, G., 222
Huey, F.B., 378, 381
Hume, David, 23
Hunt, A.S., 550, 551
Hunt, Robert, 99
Hunter, A.M., 460, 480, 529, 541, 632
Hurd, J.C., 606
Hyrcanus, John, 99, 169, 186–187, 192, 334, 653
Hyrcanus II, 188–191

Ignatius, 633, 640
Iliffe, J.H., 650
Imschout, P., 287
Ingholt, H., 649
Innocent III, Pope, 69
Irenaeus, 66, 71, 588, 604, 640
Isaac, 362
Isaac, B.H., 668
Isaiah, 276, 279, 302, 328, 350, 352, 371
Ishboseth, 271, 367
Ishmael, 278, 362
Ishmael, R., 216
Isocrates, 548, 552

Jaazaniah, 320
Jacob, 361, 362
Jacob, E., 287
Jaddua, 248
Jair, 363
James I, 51–52
James, E.O., 145, 148, 150, 151, 156
James, Montague Rhodes, 175, 643
Jameson, H.G., 445
Janneus, Alexander, 335
Jason of Cyrene, 169–170, 183–184
Jaubert, A., 599
Jeffery, A., 386, 387, 389, 392
Jeffreys, L.D., 244
Jehoahaz, 327, 350, 371
Jehoiachin, 275, 331, 332
Jehoiada, 276
Jehoiakim, 275, 277, 320, 331, 350, 353
Jehoram, 274, 276, 325, 351, 361, 377

INDEX OF SUBJECTS

INDEX OF SUBJECTS

Battle of Actium, 190
Battle of Carchemish, 275
Battle of Elasa, 185
Bay of Naples, 663
Bedouins, 89, 90
Beersheba: altar at, 323; architecture at, 320; plain of, 94
Beit Sahur, site at, 654
Bel and the Dragon, description of book of, 168
Ben Asher text tradition, 41, 217, 219
Benhadad I stele, 236
Ben Naphtali text tradition, 217
Ben Sirach Greek text, 220
Ben-Yamini, tribe of, 344
Berkeley Version of the Bible, 55
Beth Shean, 314; architecture at, 320; coffins at, 321; destruction of, 317; plain, 91; pottery in, 315, stela at, 318; temple at, 363; valley, 86
Beth Shemesh (Ain Shems), 236; destruction of, 324, 332; fortification of, 322
Beth Yerah II, pottery in, 315
Beth-zur, as archaeological site, 317; rebuilt, 334, resettlement at, 333; trade at, 322
Bethany (El-Azaniyeh), excavations at, 656
Bethel (Beitin), 235; as archaeological site, 311; destruction of, 366; occupation of, 315; resettlement at, 333; seal from, 324
Bethesda, pool of, 656
Bethlehem, and Jesus' birth, 654
Between the Testaments, 179–194; Grecian rule, 180–186; Hasmonean rule, 186–189; historical development, 179–192; internal developments, 192–193; Persian rule, 179–180; Roman rule, 189–191
"Beyond the River," 333, 334
Bible: attributes of, 8; authority and inspiration of, 3–35; bearing of archaeology on, 31; centrality of Christ in, 66; claim to distinctive divine inspiration and, 4; contents defined, 388–390; continuity of Testaments and, 65–66; deliberately written, 11–13; dialectical view of, 24–25; dictated by God, 15; divinely inspired, 10, 77; as drama, 133; dynamically vital, 7–11; in early church, 636–637; eschatology of, 103–126; geographical setting of, 83–99; God speaking to man, 13–20, 63; God's gift to the church, 12; hermeneutical view of, 24–25; imagery and, 135; infallibility of, 130; interpretation of, 61–79; literary devices in, 134–136; literary genres in, 132–134; as literature, 129–139; manuscript period and, 45–46; as means of grace, 26; ministry of the Spirit and, 66–67; NT genres and, 136–138; place of history in, 254; plan of salvation and, 25–26; problem of allegory

and, 67–68; Protestant principle of, 8; sole judge of Christian doctrine and morals, 26; source of Christian faith, 26; supernatural basis of, 4; symbolism and, 136; transmission and translation of, 39–57; unity of, 64, 78; witness to divine inspiration, 20–22; world of, 84–88; *see also* Scriptures
Bible, the: An American Translation, 54–55
Bible in Basic English, 55
Bible Studies (Deissmann), 413
Biblia Hebraica (Kittel), 41, 219
"Biblical background movement," 285
Biblical criticism: authority and, 454–456; background and basic characteristics of, 438–439; the canon and, 455–456; historical criticism, 441–444; inspiration and, 455; literary criticism, 444–449; main trends in, 439–441; methods of, 450–454
Biblical theology, meaning of, 286
Biblical Theology in Crisis (Childs), 287
Biblical theology: OT, 287; progress of growth in, 290
Bibliography of the Holy Land Sites (Vogel), 311
Bilingualism, in the NT world, 411–412
"Bishops' Bible," 51
Black Obelisk of Shalmaneser, 236, 326
Black Sea, 84
"Blessed hope," 112
Blue Nile, 88
Boanthropy, Nebuchadnezzar's disease, 246
Bodmer: library, 43; Papyrus XXII, 167
Boghazkoy: tablets from, 232; treaties recovered from, 243
Bologna Pentateuch, 219
Bomberg rabbinic Bible, 219
"Book of Celestial Physics, The," 171
"Book of Comfort," 303
Book of the Dead, 212
Book of the law, discovery of, 277
Book of Mormon, 4
Book of the Secrets of Enoch, 173
Book of the Twelve, 391
Book of Wisdom, 641
Boston Museum, 649
"Branch, the," 305
British and Foreign Bible Society, 41, 219
British Museum, 552, 662
"Brook of Egypt," 92
Buddhism, 4; concept of "salvation," 146–150; eternal destiny and, 154–156; origin, 144–146; understanding of deity, 150–153; as viewed by Christianity, 153–154
Buseirah, as archaeological site, 311
Byblos syllabic script, 319

Habiru, 344
Haburah, 582
Hades: place of, 122; and Sheol, 122
Hagiographa, LXX translation of, 220, 224, 390
Hamath, 331
Hamito-Semitic languages, 204
Hammadas, deserts of, 90
Hammath-Tiberias, synagogue of, 655
Hammurabi, Code of, 89, 246, 344
Hapax legomena, 206, 451; *see also* literary criticism
Hapiru, 315, 317
Haplography, definition of, 213
Harran inscription, 333
Hasidim, 184–185, 192, 398
Hasmonean, name of, 186
Hauran, the, 86
Hazor (Tell el-Qedar), 235, 325; as archaeological site, 311, 316, 323; architecture at, 320; burning of, 318; city gates at, 378; destruction at, 328; Greek foot at, 334
Hebraica veritas, 225
Hebrew: canon, 162; measure of weight, 379
Hebrew Grammar (Kautzsch), 200
Hebrew language: development of, 403; in the OT, 198; influence on the NT and, 206–207; loan words and, 206; parts of speech of, 200; poetic and prose styles in, 204–205
Hebrew manuscripts, 211–219; foes of, 212; from A.D. 70 to A.D. 1000, 216–218; from A.D. 1000 to present, 218–219; from 400 B.C. to A.D. 70, 213–216; from time of composition to c. 400 B.C., 211–213; revised by priest, 213; scribal errors and, 213; tendency to preserve them, 212–213, 214; tendency to revise text, 213, 214, 216
Hebrew Tenses (Driver), 201
Hebrew University, 245
Hebrew University Bible Project, 219
Hebrew University Isaiah Scroll, 295, 396
Hebrews, Book of: as a moral Epistle, 548; question of authorship, 638
Hebron (Kiriath Arba); occupation of, 315; Sarah's burial at, 652
Hegra, Arabia, 238
Heilsgeschichte theory, 24
Hellenic League, 180
Hellenistic age, 334–335
Hellenistic church: condition of, 588; expansion of, 588; homogeneity of, 588
"Hellenistic Greek," meaning of, 412
Herculaneum, destruction of, 663
Hermetica, 443
Herod Antipas (Hoehner), 373

Herod the Great: builder in Israel, 649; death of, 653, 654; palace built by, 652; statue of, 649; towers built by, 651
Herodium: excavations at, 668; Herod buried at, 652
Heshban, archaeological discovery at, 657, 658
Heterocentricity, in interpretation, 76
Hexapla of Origen, 221, 222, 223, 225–226
Hezekiah's tunnel, 656
Higher criticism; *see* textual criticism
Hinduism: concepts of "salvation," 146–150; eternal destiny and, 154–156; origins, 144–146; understanding of deity, 150–153; as viewed by Christianity, 153–154
Hippicus, tower of, 651
Historia Ecclesiastica (Eusebius), 578, 581, 588
Historical criticism: Babylonian period and, 237–238; conservative view of history and, 443–444; definition of, 231; denial of the need for historical veracity, 442; Greek period and, 238–239; history-of-religions approach and, 442–443; Iron Age and, 236–237; main trends in, 439–441; Middle Bronze Age and, 233–235; of the NT, 437–456; of the OT, 231–250; Persian Period and, 238; place of archaeology in, 232–233; purpose and nature of, 231–232; relevance and dangers, 441–442; *Religiongeschichte,* 442
Historical positivism, 35
Historical study, in biblical interpretation, 77
History: the captivity and, 277–278; creative redemption and, 256; definition of 254; Deuteronomic view of, 255; eschatology of, 105–120; goal of, 105; guarantee of eschatology, 254; heading toward a goal, 255; of the OT, 253–281; of OT theology, 286–287; place of, in the Bible, 254–255; prophecy and, 254; providence and, 256; return from captivity and, 278–280; teleology and, 255–256; of textual criticism, 425–429; theocracy and monarchy and, 264–277; theology and, 254
History of the Old Testament, 253–281; in its biblical setting, 253–256; captivity and, 277–278; divided kingdom period, 301–305; monarchical period, 298–299; Mosaic period, 294–296; patriarchal period, 292–294; people of the covenant and, 256–264; premonarchical period, 297–298; prepatriarchal period, 291–292; return from captivity and, 278–280; a sealed book, 256; theocracy and monarchy and, 264–277
Hittite(s): clash with Egyptians, 363; documents, 388; during days of judges, 264;

INDEX OF SCRIPTURE
REFERENCES

INDEX OF SCRIPTURE
REFERENCES

We want to hear from you. Please send your comments about this
book to us in care of zreview@zondervan.com. Thank you.

GRAND RAPIDS, MICHIGAN 49530 USA

ZONDERVAN.COM/
AUTHORTRACKER